P9-CRG-201

John Willis
Theatre World
1985–1986 SEASON

VOLUME 42

CROWN PUBLISHERS, INC.

225 PARK AVENUE SOUTH • NEW YORK, NEW YORK 10003

COPYRIGHT © 1987 BY JOHN WILLIS. ALL RIGHTS RESERVED. MANUFACTURED IN THE U.S.A.
LIBRARY OF CONGRESS CATALOG CARD NO. 73-82953.
ISBN: 0-517-56530-7

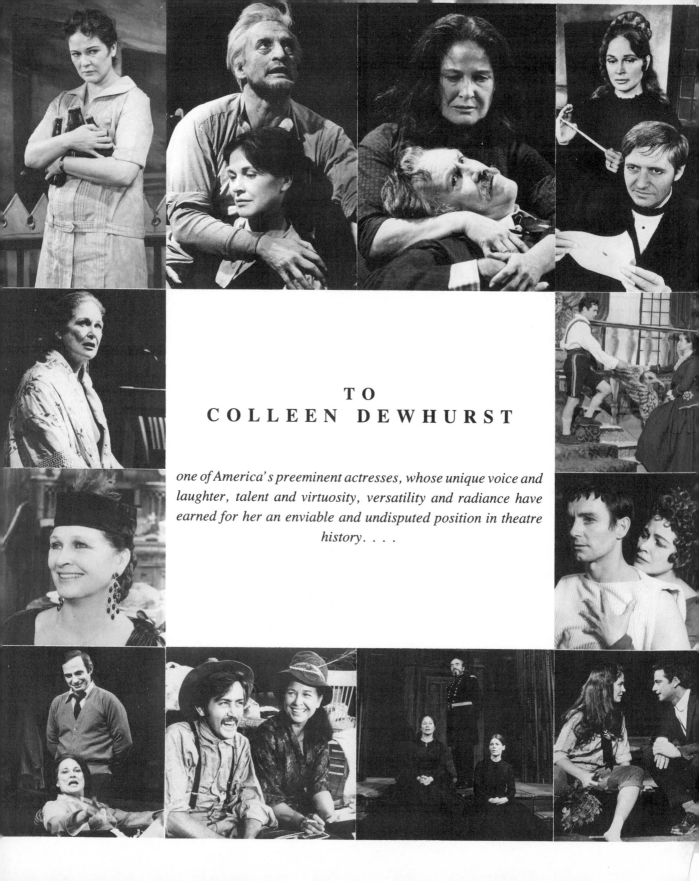

TO
COLLEEN DEWHURST

one of America's preeminent actresses, whose unique voice and laughter, talent and virtuosity, versatility and radiance have earned for her an enviable and undisputed position in theatre history. . . .

CONTENTS

Dedication: Collen Dewhurst 2

The Season in Review 5

Broadway Calendar:
    Productions that opened June 1, 1985 through May 31, 1986 6
    Productions from past seasons that played through this season 45
    Productions from past seasons that closed during this season 51

Off-Broadway Calendar:
    Productions from past seasons that played through this season 52
    Productions from past seasons that closed during this season 56
    Productions that opened June 1, 1985 through May 31, 1986 57
    Company Series 82

National Touring Companies 122

Professional Regional Companies 136

Annual Shakespeare Festivals 181

Award-winning Productions: Pulitzer, New York Drama Critics, "Tony" 187

Previous Theatre World Award Winners 188

Theatre World Awards of 1986 189

Biographical Data on This Season's Casts 194

Obituaries from June 1, 1985 through May 31, 1986 226

Index 233

EDITOR: JOHN WILLIS
Assistant Editor: Walter Willison
Assistants: Stanley Reeves, Giovanni Romero, John Sala
Staff Photographers: Bert Andrews, Evan Romero, Michael Viade, Van Williams
Designer: Peggy Goddard

Photos opposite page: (clockwise from top left) "Great Day in the Morning" (1962), with George C. Scott in "Desire under the Elms" (1963), with Jason Robards in "A Moon for the Misbegotten" (1973), with Arthur Hill in "More Stately Mansions" (1967), with Anthony Vorno in "The Eagle Has Two Heads" (1956), with Kenneth Haigh in "Caligula" (1960), with Lou Antonio in "The Ballad of the Sad Cafe" (1963), with Donald Davis, Pamela Payton-Wright in "Mourning Becomes Electra" (1972), with Martin Sheen in "Hello and Goodbye" (1976), with Ben Gazzara in "Who's Afraid of Virginia Woolf?" (1976), in "You Can't Take It with You" (1983), in "My Gene" (1987) *Photos by Freidman-Abeles, Ed Rooney, Martha Swope, Avery Willard*

Liann Pattison, Judd Hirsch, Cleavon Little
in "I'm Not Rappaport"
1986 Tony Award for Best Play *(Martha Swope Photo)*

4

THE SEASON IN REVIEW
(June 1, 1985–May 31, 1986)

For the second consecutive dismal season, Broadway has experienced, financially and artistically, the worst two years of this century. There were only 32 opening nights on Broadway and 2 at Lincoln Center's theatre. On May 31st only 4 more productions were playing than were on the boards at the end of the previous disastrous season. Several theatres were dark for the entire season. The Pulitzer committee agreed to award no prize this year for a theatrical production. The necessary playwrights were producing for films and television where the renumeration is greater and quicker. Again, the dearth of good plays and musicals, the high cost of labor, materials, rentals, fees, and tv advertising have made a weekly S.R.O. almost necessary to meet operating expenses. Boxoffice and attendance dropped for the fifth consecutive year, and was the lowest since the 1957–58 season. Serious plays on Broadway, even with stars and critical plaudits, do not find an audience. There have been no irrefutable smash-hit musicals since "La Cage aux Folles" in 1983. The League of American Theatres and Producers (formerly New York League) released a study made through 1980 reporting that Broadway ticket prices have risen less than the cost of the operations, and less than purchasing power of the consumer. Musicals have a $47.50 top ticket and plays, a $40 ticket. Attendance continues to decline in spite of the fact that the report says theatre is "more affordable" than it was 50 years ago. Previews may influence the first few weeks attendance but it is word-of-mouth after that, and many months before the initial investment is repaid and profits begin.

The season opened with Neil Simon's feminine re-write of his successful play, "The Odd Couple" with Sally Struthers and Rita Moreno (succeeded by Brenda Vaccaro) and was one of only 5 hits during the year. At the end of the season there were only 20 productions playing (6 were holdovers from previous seasons) and 8 closed shortly thereafter. The "Tony" (Antoinette Perry/American National Theatre Association Award) committee had difficulty finding enough eligible productions to fill its ballot. On the other hand, there was a plethora of excellent performers, one of the season's few compensations. Of the 10 revivals, "Sweet Charity" received a "Tony" for Outstanding Reproduction, Costumes, Featured Actress (Bebe Neuwirth) and Actor (Michael Rupert) in a Musical. Its choreographer, Bob Fosse, received another to add to his collection for his dances in "Big Deal." The winner for Outstanding New Musical was "The Mystery of Edwin Drood" that was also voted Best Book, Score, Direction, and Outstanding Actor in a Musical (George Rose). Bernadette Peters in "Song and Dance" was well-deserving of her "Tony" for Outstanding Actress in a Musical. The Best Play, Best Lighting, and Outstanding Actor in a Play (Judd Hirsch) went to Herb Gardner's "I'm Not Rappaport." Outstanding Actress was Lily Tomlin in "The Search for Signs of Intelligent Life in the Universe," a solo performance. Best Direction, and Best Scenery awards went to the revival of John Guare's "House of Blue Leaves," as did "Tonys" for Outstanding Featured Actress (Swoosie Kurtz) and Featured Actor (John Mahoney). Again this year, as they have been since first televised in 1967, presentation ceremonies were produced by Alexander H., Cohen and written by Hildy Parks for their last time. Both have contributed more than yeoman service to these exemplary productions, and their successors will find it difficult to equal their achievements. A new 7 year contract was made between the Theatre League and ANTA for the continuance of the awards, but no producer had been announced at presstime.

Noteworthy among revivals not already cited were "The Iceman Cometh" (4½ hours) with Jason Robards repeating the role that made him a star almost 30 years ago; "Hay Fever" with the consummate actress Rosemary Harris giving one of her most enchanting performances; "Blood Knot" with the playwright (Athol Fugard) acting with Zakes Mokae; "Loot" with the versatile John Maher and Zoe Wanamaker giving excellent performances; a fast-paced 3½ hour "Long Day's Journey into Night" with Jack Lemmon as James Tyrone. Last Season's "Tango Argentino" broke City Center records and returned this year for another successful run at the Mark Hellinger Theatre.

Plays above the average in quality were the British imports "Benefactors" with Glenn Close, Mary Beth Hurt, Simon Jones and Sam Water-

ston, and "The Petition" with Jessica Tandy and Hume Cronyn. Other productions of note were "Social Security" with Marlo Thomas and Ron Silver; "Boys in Autumn" with George C. Scott and John Cullum as the aging Huckleberry Finn and Tom Sawyer; "Precious Sons" with Ed Harris and Judith Ivey in superior characterizations. In December the Vivian Beaumont (a Broadway-rated house) and the Mitzi Newhouse theatres in Lincoln Center were re-opened with productions by the new Lincoln Center Theater Company under the guidance of Gregory Mosher (Director) and Bernard Gersten (Executive Producer). They had great success with their revival of "House of Blue Leaves," and it is sincerely hoped their good fortune will continue.

Among the most highly applauded Broadway performers during the season, in addition to those already mentioned, were Debbie Allen, Alec Baldwin, Gerry Bamman, Keith Baxter, Betty Buckley, Gregg Burge, Zoe Caldwell, Stockard Channing, Wayne Cilento, Patti Cohenour, Don Correia, Mary D'Arcy, Cleavant Derricks, Peter Gallagher, Nancy Giles, Joanna Gleason, Faye Grant, James Greene, Alisa Gyse, Julie Hagerty, Anthony Heald, Maurice Hines, Barnard Hughes, Earle Hyman, Zeljko Ivanek, Ken Jenkins, Charles Keating, Cleo Laine, Cleavon Little, Dorothy Loudon, Mary Elizabeth Mastrantonio, Kathryn McAteer, Howard McGillin, Donald Moffat, Bill Moor, Jenny O'Hara, Milo O'Shea, John Pankow, Chita Rivera, Barbara Rush, Jana Schneider, Kevin Spacey, Lewis J. Stadlen, Brian Tarantina, Jeffrey V. Thompson, Elisabeth Welch, and Lenny Wolpe.

Pulitzer Prize-winning playwright Sam Shepard, who has never had a play produced on Broadway, had another Off-Broadway success with a stellar cast in his four hour "A Lie of the Mind." In addition, his "Curse of the Starving Class" was successfully revived. Other impressive productions were "The Lisbon Traviata," "Season's Greetings," "The Importance of Being Earnest," "Gertrude Stein and Company," "Another Paradise," "Bosoms and Neglect," "Daughters," "So Long on Lonely Street," "Alice and Fred," Jane Connell as Dorothy Parker, "The Mad Woman of Chaillot," "A Map of the World," "Mrs. Warren's Profession" with Uta Hagen (in one of her infrequent performances), Eric Bogasian's solo "Drinking in America," "Aunt Dan and Lemon," and "Cuba and His Teddy Bear" with film star Robert DeNiro. The beautiful film ingenue Brooke Shields made her New York stage debut in an unworthy vehicle "The Eden Cinema." In addition to the company series, there were 139 opening nights Off Broadway. Among the best performances were those given by Ernest Abuba, Mason Adams, Joan Allen, Seth Allen, Trini Alvarado, Suzy Amis, Brian Backer, Lisa Banes, Kathy Bates, Elizabeth Berridge, Michael Kelly Boone, Julie Budd, Meg Bussert, Joanne Camp, Len Cariou, Carleton Carpenter, Steven Culp, Brenda Currin, Aled Davies, Laura Dean, Christine Estabrook, Lillian Evans, Tovah Feldshuh, Dann Florek, Boyd Gaines, James Gammon, Stephen Geoffreys, Anita Gillette, George Grizzard, Mark Hamill, Benjamin Hendrickson, Laura Innes, Zeljko Ivanek, Ernestine Jackson, Page Johnson, Eddie Jones, Donna Kane, Werner Klemperer, Kevin Kline, Michael Learned, Calvin Levels, Tom Ligon, Charles Ludlam, Peter MacNicol, W. H. Macy, Elizabeth McGovern, Lonette McKee, Anne Meara, Dina Merrill, Jan Miner, Lizan Mitchell, Cass Morgan, Ann Morrison, Cynthia Nixon, Geraldine Page, Will Patton, Amanda Plummer, Kathryn Pogson, Lonny Price, Aidan Quinn, Keith Reddin, Pamela Reed, Arleigh Richards, Marcia Rodd, Jo Anna Rush, Marian Seldes, Roshan Seth, April Shawhan, Alan Shearman, Victor Slezak, Derek David Smith, J. Smith-Cameron, Marianne Tatum, Marisa Tomei, Anne Wedgeworth, Walter Willison, and the entire casts of "The Golden Land," "Personals," "Professionally Speaking," "Nunsense," and "Mummenschanz."

Seemingly, it is becoming customary for the intimate Off-Broadway musicals to be more entertaining than the multi-million dollar productions mid-town. Among the superior ones, not already mentioned above, were "Olympus on My Mind," "Yours, Anne," "The Gifts of the Magi," "Sweet Will," Elisabeth Welch's "Time to Start Living," "Charley's Tale," "Options," and the revivals of "Dames at Sea" and "El Grande de Coca Cola."

BROADWAY PRODUCTIONS

(June 1, 1985 through May 31, 1986)

THE ODD COUPLE

Neil Simon's new version of his play; Director, Gene Saks; Scenery, David Mitchell; Costumes, Ann Roth, Lighting, Tharon Musser; Presented by Emanuel Azenburg, Wayne M. Rogers, The Shubert Organization (Gerald Schoenfeld, Chairman; Bernard B. Jacobs, President); Assistant Director, Philip Cusack; Casting, Meg Simon/ Fran Kumin; General Manager, Robert Kamlot; Technical Supervision, Theatrical Services (Arthur Siccardi, Peter Feller); Company Manager, Noel Gilmore; Wardrobe, Penny Davis; Assistant to the Director, Bill Molloy; Production Assistant, Marie McKeon; Props, Jan Marasek; Assistant Company Manager, Brian Dunbar; Stage Managers, Martin Gold, Bonnie Panson; Press, Bill Evans, Sandra Manley, Jim Baldassare, Leslie Anderson. Opened at the Broadhurst Theatre on Tuesday, June 11, 1985*

CAST

Sylvie	Jenny O'Hara[†1]
Mickey	Mary Louise Wilson[†2]
Renee	Kathleen Doyle
Vera	Marilyn Cooper
Olive Madison	Rita Moreno[†3]
Florence Unger	Sally Struthers
Manolo Costazuela	Lewis J. Stadlen
Jesus Costazuela	Tony Shalhoub

STANDBYS: Jenny O'Hara (Olive), Marilyn Pasekoff (Florence/Vera/Sylvie), Annette Miller (Sylvie/Renee/Mickey), David Ardao (Manolo/Jesus)

A comedy in 2 acts and 4 scenes. The action takes place at the present time in Olive Madison's apartment on Riverside Drive in Manhattan, NYC.

*Closed Feb. 23, 1986 after 295 performances and 9 previews.
†Succeeded by: 1. Annette Miller during vacation, 2. Debra Mooney, 3. Brenda Vaccaro

Martha Swope Photos

Right: Sally Struthers, Tony Shalhoub, Lewis J. Stadlen, Rita Moreno Top: Rita Moreno, Sally Struthers

Sally Struthers, Brenda Vaccaro

Marilyn Cooper, Rita Moreno, Jenny O'Hara, Mary Louise Wilson, Kathleen Doyle

SINGIN' IN THE RAIN

Based on the MGM film; Screenplay and Adaptation by Betty Comden and Adolph Green; Songs, Nacio Herb Brown and Arthur Freed; Directed and Choreographed by Twyla Tharp; With some original choreography by Gene Kelly and Stanley Donen; Scenery, Santo Loquasto; Costumes, Ann Roth; Lighting, Jennifer Tipton; Sound, Sound Associates; Film Sequences, Gordon Willis; Music Supervision-Arrangements, Stanley Lebowsky; Music Director, Robert Billig; Orchestrations, Larry Wilcox; Associate Producer, Eugene V. Wolsk; Casting, Slater/MCL; Presented by Maurice Rosenfeld, Lois F. Rosenfield and Cindy Pritzker; Music published by CBS Songs; Hairstylist, Paul Huntley; Wardrobe, Chip Mulberger, Sue Ann Beusman; Associate Conductor, Michael Dansicker; Production Assistant, James R. Suskin; Company Manager, Steven Suskin; Stage Managers, Steven Zweigbaum, Arturo E. Porazzi, Amy Pell; Props, Val Medina; Press, Shirley Herz, Peter Cromarty, Pete Sanders, Gary Lawrence. Opened Tuesday, July 2, 1985 at the Gershwin Theatre*

CAST

Dora Bailey	Melinda Gilb
Cosmo Brown	Peter Slutsker
Lina Lamont	Faye Grant
Don Lockwood	Don Correia
R. F. Simpson	Hansford Rowe
Roscoe Dexter	Richard Fancy
Rod	Robert Radford
Kathy Selden	Mary D'Arcy
Sid Phillips	Martin Van Treuren
Phoebe Dinsmore	Jacque Dean
Diction Coach	Austin Colyer
Sound Engineer	John Spalla
Ticket Taker	Martin Van Treuren
A Warner Brother	Austin Colyer
Zelda Zanders	Mary Ann Kellogg

ENSEMBLE: Ray Benson, John Carrafa, Richard Colton, Austin Colyer, Jacque Dean, Diane Duncan, Yvonne Dutton, Craig Frawley, Melinda Gilb, Katie Glasner, Barbara Hoon, David-Michael Johnson, Mary Ann Kellogg, Raymond Kurshals, Alison Mann, Barbara Moroz, Kevin O'Day, Robert Radford, Tom Gene Sager, John Spalla, Amy Spencer, Cynthia Thole, Martin Van Treuren, Shelley Washington, Laurie Williamson, Swings: Cheri Butcher, Brad Moranz, David Askler

UNDERSTUDIES: Donn Simione (Don), Cynthia Thole (Kathy), Brad Moranz (Cosmo), Barbara Moroz (Lina), Austin Colyer (Simpson), John Spalla (Roscoe)

MUSICAL NUMBERS: Fit as a Fiddle, Beautiful Girl, I've Got a Feelin' You're Foolin', Make 'Em Laugh, Hub Bub, You Are My Lucky Star, Moses Supposes, Good Mornin', Singin' in the Rain, Wedding of the Painted Doll, Rag Doll, Temptation, Takin' Miss Mary to the Ball, Love Is Where You Find It, Would You?, Broadway Rhythm, Blue Prelude, Finale.

A musical in 2 acts and 17 scenes. The action takes place in Hollywood in the 1920's.

*Closed May 18, 1986 after 367 performances and 38 previews.

Richard Avedon, Kenn Duncan Photos

Right: Faye Grant, Peter Slutsker, Mary D'Arcy, Don Correia Top: Mary D'Arcy, Don Correia

Peter Slutsker, Mary D'Arcy, Don Correia

"Doll Dance"

THE GRAND KABUKI

Artistic Director, Onoe Shoroku II; Associate Artistic Director, Onoe Kuroemon II; General Manager, Chikashi Mogi; Assistant General Managers, Tadashi Abiko, Haruhiko Akamat Su, Jiro Otani; Technical Directors, Shunichiro Kanai, Shigeo Shimada; Lighting, Kiyotsune Soma; Stage Managers, Thomas Connell, Takeshiba Ryoji, Takeshiba Joji; Company Manager, John H. Wilson; Simultaneous Translator, Faubion Bowers; Press, Mark Goldstaub, Kevin P. McAnarney, Philip Butler, Daniel Kellachan. Opened at the Metropolitan Opera House on Monday, July 8, 1985*

PRINCIPAL ACTORS

Onoe Shoroku II, Ichikawa Danjuro XII, Kataoka Takao, Bando Yasosuke V, Ichikawa Ginnosuke, Onoe Shokaku II, Kataoka Kamezo IV, Onoe Sakon, Onoe Tatsunosuke, Bando Tamasaburo V, Ichikawa Sadanji IV, Nakamura Shibajaku VII, Ichikawa Unosuke III, Kataoka Juzo VI, Kataoka Takataro

REPERTOIRE: The Scarlet Princess of Edo, The Earth Spider, Shibaraku, The Sword Thief, Name-Taking Ceremony, Kasane

*Closed July 20, 1985 after limited engagement of 16 performances.

Shochiku Photos

Left: Tamasaburo in "Sakura-Hime Azuma Bunsho"

Shoroku in "Tsuchigumo"

Danjuro XII in "Shibaraku"
Above: Shoroku in "Tsuchigumo"

THE SEARCH FOR SIGNS OF INTELLIGENT LIFE IN THE UNIVERSE

By Jane Wagner; Director, Miss Wagner; Production Supervisor, Charles Bowden; Lighting and Set, Neil Peter Jampolis; Sound, Otts Munderloh; Associate Producer, Cheryl Swannack; Hairstylist, Phyllis Della; General Management, Veronica Claypool; Wardrobe, Madeline Wing; Press, PMK Public Relations, Cheryl Dolby/ Domino Media, Elizabeth Rogers, Valerie Weinstein; Stage Managers, Janet Beroza, Pamela Young. Opened at the Plymouth Theatre on Thursday, Sept. 26, 1985*

CAST
Lily Tomlin

A solo performance in two acts. The action takes place in New York City, Los Angeles, Chicago, Indianapolis, and Greenwood, Indiana.

*Closed Oct. 4, 1986 after 398 performances to tour. Lily Tomlin received a 1986 Tony for Best Actress in a Play. She and Jane Wagner received a Special Citation from the NY Drama Critics Circle.

Norman Seeff Photos

Top: Lily Tomlin

Lily Tomlin (also top)

Bernadette Peters in "Song and Dance"
1986 Tony Award for Best Actress in a Musical

SONG AND DANCE

Music, Andrew Lloyd Webber; Lyrics, Don Black; American Adaptation, Additional Lyrics, and Direction, Richard Maltby, Jr.; Choreography, Peter Martins; Entire production supervised by Richard Maltby, Jr. and Peter Martins; Orchestrations, Andrew Lloyd Webber, David Cullen; Musical Adviser, David Caddick; Musical Supervision and Direction, John Mauceri; Associate Tap Choreographer, Gregg Burge; Casting, Johnson-Liff; Sound Martin Levan; Setting, Robin Wagner; Costumes, Willa Kim; Lighting, Jules Fisher; Executive Producers, R. Tyler Gatchell, Jr., Peter Neufeld; Presented by Cameron Mackintosh, The Shubert Organization, F. W. M. Producing Group by arrangement with The Really Useful Co.; General Management, Gatchell & Neufeld; Company Managers, Roger Gindi; J. Anthony Magner; Production Assistant, Marc Einsele; Technical Supervisors, Theatre Services; Props, George Green, Jr., Abe Einhorn; Wardrobe, Adelaide Laurino; Hairstylist, Leon Gagliardi; Stage Managers, Sam Stickler, Mitchell Lemsky; Press, Fred Nathan, Anne Abrams, Bert Fink, Glenna Freedman, Marc Thibodeau, Philip Rinaldi, Dennis Crowley. Opened at the Royale Theatre on Wednesday, Sept. 18, 1985*

CAST

Emma	Bernadette Peters[†1]
Joe	Christopher d'Amboise[†2]
The Women	Charlotte d'Amboise, Denise Faye, Cynthia Onrubia, Mary Ellen Stuart
The Men	Gregg Burge, Gen Horiuchi,[†3] Gregory Mitchell, Scott Wise[3]
Man from the streets	Gregg Burge
Woman in gold	Mary Ellen Stuart
Her Escorts	Scott Wise, Gregory Mitchell
Woman in blue	Charlotte d'Amboise
Customer	Gen Horiuchi[†3]
Two Singles	Cynthia Onrubia, Denise Faye
Woman in grey flannel	Cynthia Onrubia

STANDBYS & UNDERSTUDIES: Maureen Moore (Emma), Bruce Falco/Scott Wise (Joe), Valerie Wright/Mary Ann Lamb (Mary Ellen Stuart/Denise Faye/Charlotte d'Amboise), Mary Ann Lamb/Valerie Wright/Denise Faye (Cynthia Onrubia), Bruce Anthony Davis (Gregg Burge), Kenneth Ard (Scott Wise/Gregory Mitchell), Ramon Galindo (Gen Horiuchi)

MUSICAL NUMBERS: Take That Look off Your Face, Let Me Finish, So Much to Do in New York, First Letter Home, English Girls, Capped Teeth and Caesar Salad, You Made Me Think You Were in Love, Second Letter Home, Unexpected Song, Come Back with the Same Look in Your Eyes, Tell Me on a Sunday, I Love New York, Married Man, Third Letter Home, What Have I Done?, Finale.

A musical in two acts. The action takes place at the present time in New York and Los Angeles.

*Closed Nov. 8, 1986 after 474 performances and 15 previews. Bernadette Peters received a 1986 Tony for Best Actress in a Musical.
†Succeeded by: 1. Betty Buckley, 2. Victor Barbee, John Meehan, 3. Buddy Balou'

Kenn Duncan, Michael LePoer Trench Photos

Right: Christopher d'Amboise (top), Gregg Burge (also at top)

Christopher d'Amboise,
Bernadette Peters

Bernadette Peters,
Victor Barbee

11

THE ICEMAN COMETH

By Eugene O'Neill; Director, Jose Quintero; Scenery, Ben Edwards; Costumes, Jane Greenwood; Lighting, Thomas R. Skelton; Casting, Meg Simon/Fran Kumin; Presented by Lewis Allen, James Nederlander, Stephen Graham, Ben Edwards; The American National Theater Production; General Management, Joseph Harris Associates; Associate Manager, Thomas P. Santopietro; Assistant Manager, Russ Lori Rosensweig; Props, Liam Herbert; Wardrobe, Nancy Schaefer; Hairstylist, Andrew Reiss; Stage Managers, Mitchell Erickson, John Handy; Press, David Powers, Leo Stern. Opened at the Lunt-Fontanne Theatre on Sunday, Sept. 29, 1985*

CAST

Rocky Pioggi	John Pankow
Larry Slade	Donald Moffat
Hugo Kalmar	Leonardo Cimino
Willie Oban	John Christopher Jones
Harry Hope	Barnard Hughes
Joe Mott	Roger Robinson
Don Parritt	Paul McCrane
Cecil Lewis (The Captain)	Bill Moor
Piet Wetjoen (The General)	Frederick Neumann
James Cameron (Jimmy Tomorrow)	James Greene
Pat McGloin	Pat McNamara
Ed Mosher	Allen Swift
Margie	Natalia Nogulich
Pearl	Kristine Nielsen
Cora	Caroline Aaron
Chuck Morello	Harris Laskawy
Theodore Hickman (Hickey)	Jason Robards
Moran	Paul Austin
Lieb	Walter Flanagan

UNDERSTUDIES: James Greene (Harry Hope), Walter Flanagan (Mosher/McGloin/Wetjoen), Christopher McHale (Oban/Morello/Moran), Thomas Martell Brimm (Mott/Lieb), Paul Austin (Lewis/Cameron/Kalmar/Slade), Stanley Tucci (Pioggi/Parritt), Maggie Baird (Pearl/Cora/Margie)

A drama in four acts. The action takes place in Harry Hope's Bar in the summer of 1912.

*Closed Dec. 1, 1985 after 55 performances and 7 previews.

Martha Swope Photos
Right: Natalia Nogulich, John Pankow, Paul McCrane, Caroline Aaron, Harris Laskawy, Donald Moffat Top: Jason Robards (top), Barnard Hughes

Frederick Neumann, Roger Robinson, Bill Moor, Jason Robards

Natalia Nogulich, Caroline Aaron, John Pankow, Kristine Nielsen, Jason Robards, Leonardo Cimino

TANGO ARGENTINO

Conceived and Directed by Claudio Segovia, Hector Orezzoli; Choreography, Juan Carlos Copes; Musical Directors, Jose Libertella, Luis Stazo, Osvaldo Berlingieri; Scenery and Costumes, Hector Orezzoli, Claudio Segovia; Originally commissioned by the Festival d'Automne in Paris; Presented by Mel Howard and Donald K. Donald; General Management, McCann & Nugent; Company Manager, Daniel Kearns; Wardrobe, Rosalie Lahm, Lida Curletto; Makeup and Hair, Jean-Luc Domvito; Props, Timothy Abel; Stage Manager, Otto von Breuning; Press, PR Partners, Marilynn LeVine, Meg Gordean, Merle Frimark. Opened at the Mark Hellinger Theatre Wednesday, Oct. 9, 1985*

CAST

SINGERS: Raul Lavie, Jovita Luna, Elba Beron, Alba Solis
DANCERS: Naanim Timoyko (soloist), Juna Carlos Copes, Maria Nieves, Nelida and Nelson, Gloria and Eduardo, Mayoral and Elsa Maria, Virulazo and Elvira, The Dinzels, Maria and Carlos Rivarola

PROGRAM

PART I: Quejas de Bandoneon, El Apache Argentino, El Esquinazo, Milonga del Tiempo Heroico, La Punalada, La Morocha, El Choclo, La Cumparsita, Mi Noche Triste, Orgullo Criollo, De Mi Barrio, Bandoneones, Milonguita, Nostalgias, Cuesta Abajo, El Entrerriano, Canaro en Paris, Taquito Militar
PART II: Milongueando en El 40, Uno, La Ultima Curda, La Yumba, Nunca Tuvo Novio, Jealousy, Desencuentro, Tanguera, Verano Porteno, Balada Para Mi Muerte, Adios Nonino, Danzarin

*Closed March 30, 1986 after 199 performances and 1 preview.

Alberto Rizzo Photos

Maria and Carlos Rivarola
Alberto Rizzo, Marion-Valentine Photos

Juan Carlos Copes and Maria Nieves

Virulazo and Elvira
Above: Naanim Timoyko and Nelida
Right: Gloria and Eduardo

13

THE MARRIAGE OF FIGARO

By Pierre Augustin Beaumarchais; Adaptation and Translation, Richard Nelson; Director, Andrei Serban; Designed by Beni Montresor; Music, Richard Peaslee; Musical Director, Donald York; Wigs, Paul Huntley; Assistant Director, Charles Otte; Presented by Circle in the Square (Theodore Mann, Artistic Director; Paul Libin, Managing Director); Company Manager, William Conn; Casting, Hughes Moss; Props, Frank Hauser; Wardrobe, Claire Libin; Stage Managers, Michael F. Ritchie, Carol Klein; Press, Merle Debuskey, William Schelble. Opened at Circle in the Square Theatre on Thursday, Oct. 10, 1985*

CAST

Figaro	Anthony Heald
Suzanne	Mary Elizabeth Mastrantonio
Dr. Bartholo	Louis Zorich
Marceline	Carol Teitel
Cherubino	Caitlin Clarke
Count Almaviva	Christopher Reeve
Bazile	James Cahill
Countess	Dana Ivey
Fanchette	Debbie Merrill
Antonio	William Duell
Pedrille	Daniel D. Scott, Scott Lindsay Johnson
Gripe-Soleil	Dan Nutu

PEASANTS: Robertson Carricart, Francine Forbes, David Giella, Paula Redinger, Connie Roderick, Luke Sickle
SHEPHERD CHILDREN: Edna Harris, Piper Lawrence, Carol-Ann Plante
UNDERSTUDIES: Dennis Bailey (Figaro), Paula Redinger (Countess), Robertson Carricart (Count), Luke Sickle (Antonio/Bartholo/Bazile), Francine Forbes (Cherubino/Fanchette), Connie Roderick (Marceline), David Giella (Gripe-Soleil)

A comedy in two acts.

*Closed Dec. 15, 1985 after 77 performances and 21 previews.

Martha Swope Photos

Left: Mary Elizabeth Mastrantonio, Christopher Reeve, Anthony Heald (kneeling), Dana Ivey

Caitlin Clarke, Dana Ivey

(center) Dana Ivey, Christopher Reeve, Mary Elizabeth Mastrantonio, Anthony Heald

14

MAYOR

Music and Lyrics, Charles Strouse; Book, Warren Leight; Based on book "Mayor" by Edward I. Koch; Director, Jeffrey B. Moss; Choreography, Barbara Siman; Sets and Costumes, Randy Barcelo; Lighting, Richard Winkler; Musical Director/Arranger, Michael Kosarin; Orchestrations, Christopher Bankey; Original Cast Album by the New York Music Co.; General Management, Maria Productions; Assistant Choreographer, Laurie Brongo; Production Assistant, Melissa Davis; Hairstylist, Lloyd Kindred; Wardrobe, Nancy Lawson; Sound, Lewis Mead; Presented by Martin Richards, Jerry Kravat, Mary Lea Johnson with the New York Music Company; Associate Producer, Sam Crothers; Stage Manager, Marc Schlackman; Press, Henry Luhrman, Terry M. Lilly, David Mayhew, Andrew P. Shearer. Opened at the Latin Quarter on Wednesday, Oct. 23, 1985*

CAST

Douglas Bernstein	Ilene Kristen
Marion J. Caffey	Kathryn McAteer
Nancy Giles	John Sloman
Ken Jennings†1	Lenny Wolpe as The Mayor†2

UNDERSTUDIES: Krista Neumann, Scott Robertson, John Sloman
MUSICAL NUMBERS AND SKETCHES: Mayor, You Can Be a New Yorker Too!, Board of Estimate, You're Not the Mayor, Critics, March of the Yuppies, The Ribbon Cutting, Hootspa, Alternate Side, Coalition, What You See Is What You Get, In the Park, On the Telephone, I Want to Be the Mayor, The Last I Love New York Song, Ballad, Testimonial Dinner, Good Times, We Are One, How'm I Doin'?, My City.

A musical revue in two acts. The action takes place at the present time in New York City.

*Closed Jan. 5, 1986 after 70 performances. It was moved from the Top of the Village Gate where it had played 198 performances and 15 previews.
†Succeeded by: 1. John Sloman during illness, 2. Scott Robertson

Martha Swope Photos

Top: Douglas Bernstein, Lenny Wolpe
Right: Marion J. Caffey, Kathryn
McAteer, Ken Jennings Right Center:
Nancy Giles, Lenny Wolpe

Lenny Wolpe, Kathryn McAteer

15

THE NEWS

Patrick Jude, Charles Pistone, Jeff Conaway, Frank Baier, Cheryl Alexander

Music and Lyrics, Paul Schierhorn; Story, Paul Schierhorn, David Rotenberg, R. Vincent Park; Director, David Rotenberg; Choreography, Wesley Fata; Scenery, Jane Musky; Costumes, Richard Hornung; Lighting, Norman Coates; Sound, Gary Scott Peck/ATI; Conductor, John Rinehimer; Arrangements, John Rinehimer, Paul Schierhorn; Supervisor Orchestrator, John Rinehimer; Casting, David Tochterman; Associate Producers, Patricia Bayer, Annette R. McDonald, Quentin H. McDonald; Presented by Zev Bufman, Kathleen Lindsey, Nicholas Neubauer, R. Vincent Park, Martin and Janice Barandes; General Manager, Dorothy Olim Associates, George Elmer; Wardrobe, Chris Sanders; Hair and Wig Styles, Franko; Stage Managers, Robert I. Cohen, K. R. Williams, Jay Adler; Press, Jeffrey Richards, C. George Willard, Ben Morse, Susan Lee, Bill Shuttleworth, Marie-Louise Silva. Opened at the Helen Hayes Theatre on Thursday, Nov. 7, 1985*

CAST

Reporter	Cheryl Alexander
Circulation Editor	Frank Baier
Executive Editor	Jeff Conaway
Killer	Anthony Crivello
City Editor	Michael Duff
Feature Editor	Jonathan S. Gerber
Talk Show Host	Anthony Hoylen
Reporter	Patrick Jude
Girl	Lisa Michaelis
Reporter	Charles Pistone
Sports Editor	John Rinehimer
Style Editor	Peter Valentine
Managing Editor	Billy Ward

UNDERSTUDIES: Patrick Jude (Mr. Crivello), Anthony Hoylen (Jude/Pistone), Julie Newdow (Ms. Michaelis/Ms. Alexander)
MUSICAL NUMBERS: I Am the News, They Write the News, Mirror Mirror, Front Page Expose, Hot Flashes, Dad, She's on File, Super Singo, Dear Felicia, Horoscope, Classifieds/Personals, Wonderman, Shooting Stars, What's the Angle, The Contest, Dear Editor, Editorial, Hot Flashes, Talk to Me, Pyramid Lead, Beautiful People, Open Letter, Ordinary Extraordinary Day, Violent Crime, What in the World, Acts of God.

A musical performed without intermission. The action takes place in the City Room of a large metropolitan newspaper, the bedroom of a 15 year old girl, a one room apartment, and a city street at the present time.

*Closed Nov. 9, 1985 after 4 performances and 20 previews.

Ray Fisher Photos

Peter Valentine, Jeff Conaway, Jonathan S. Gerber

THE BOYS OF WINTER

By John Pielmeier; Director, Michael Lindsay-Hogg; Set, David Mitchell; Costumes and Effects, Carrie Robbins; Lighting, Pat Collins; Fight Director, B. H. Barry; Sound, Jan Nebozenko; Casting, Howard Feuer & Marsha Kleinman; Marine Drill Instructors, Josh Cruze, J. Kenneth Campbell; Presented by Ivan Bloch, Alan Levin, Bernie Sofronski in association with Elle Shushan; General Managers, Jay Kingwill, Larry Goossen; Associate to the Production, Deborah D. Mathews; Props, Liam Herbert, Dan Mirro; Wardrobe, Peter J. Fitzgerald; Production Assistant, Larry Reitzer; Stage Managers, Herb Vogler, Jay B. Jacobson; Press, Judy Jacksina, Marcy Granata, Kevin Boyle, Ted Killmer, Jane Steinberg, Darrel Joseph. Opened in the Biltmore Theatre on Sunday, Dec. 1, 1985*

CAST

Bonney	D. W. Moffett
Ho	Thomas Ikeda
Sarge	Tony Plana
Prick	Brian Tarantina
Flem	Andrew McCarthy
L.B.	Wesley Snipes
Monsoon	Matt Dillon
Doc	Ving Rhames
Billy	Grant Rader
Henry	Doug Hara
Radio Voices	Wendell Pierce, Mariye Onouye

UNDERSTUDIES: Rob Morrow (Prick/Flem), Wendell Pierce (Doc/L. B.), Nestor Serrano (Bonney/Sarge), Grant Show (Monsoon), Alvin Lum (Ho)

A drama performed without intermission. The action takes place December 22–26, 1968, before and after. . . . on a hilltop in Quang Tri Province, South Vietnam, near the Laotian border and the DMZ.

*Closed Dec. 8, 1985 after 9 performances and 31 previews.

Stephen Lupino, Martha Swope Photos

Right: Brian Tarantina, Matt Dillon, Wesley Snipes

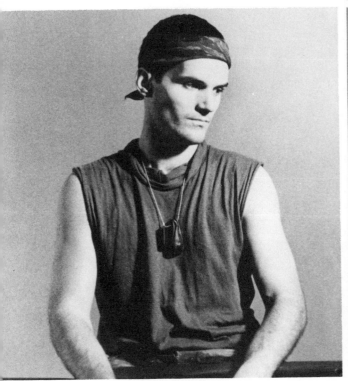

D. W. Moffett

Andrew McCarthy

I'M NOT RAPPAPORT

By Herb Gardner; Director, Daniel Sullivan; Set, Tony Walton; Costumes, Robert Morgan; Lighting, Pat Collins; Fight Staging, B. H. Barry; Presented by James Walsh, Lewis Allen, Martin Heinfling; General Manager, James Walsh; Company Manager, Stanley Silver; Casting, Pat McCorkle; Technical Coordinator, Robert Scales; Wardrobe, Lancey Clough; Stage Managers, Thomas A. Kelly, Charles Kindl; Press, Jeffrey Richards, C. George Willard, Ben Morse, Susan Lee, Marie Louise Silva, Ken Mandelbaum, L. Glenn Poppleton III. Opened at the Booth Theatre on Tuesday, Nov. 19, 1985*

CAST

Nat	Judd Hirsch[†1]
Midge	Cleavon Little[†2]
Danforth	Gregg Almquist
Laurie	Liann Pattison
Gilley	Jace Alexander[†3]
Clara	Cheryl Giannini[†4]
The Cowboy	Steve Ryan

UNDERSTUDIES: Salem Ludwig (Nat), William Hall, Jr. (Midge), Elaine Bromka (Clara/Laurie), Kevin M. Moccia (Gilley), Richard E. Council (Cowboy/Danforth)

A comedy in 2 acts and 4 scenes. The action takes place on a bench near a path at the edge of the lake in Central Park in New York City early in October of 1982.

*Still playing May 31, 1986. Winner of 1986 Tonys for Best Play, Leading Actor in a Play (Judd Hirsch), Best Lighting Design.
[†]Succeeded by: 1. Hal Linden, 2. Ossie Davis, 3. Josh Pais, 4. Mercedes Ruehl, Marcia Rodd

Martha Swope Photos

Judd Hirsch, Cheryl Giannini
Top Left: Judd Hirsch, Cleavon Little

Hal Linden, Marcia Rodd
Top: Judd Hirsch, Cleavon Little

Hal Linden, Ossie Davis

THE MYSTERY OF EDWIN DROOD

By Rupert Holmes; Suggested by the unfinished novel by Charles Dickens; Director, Wilford Leach; Choreography, Graciela Daniele; Scenery, Bob Shaw; Costumes, Lindsay W. Davis; Lighting, Paul Gallo; Sound, Tom Morse; Magic Lantern Projections, James Cochrane; Hair and Wigs, Paul Huntley; Musical Direction, Michael Starobin; Orchestrations, Rupert Holmes; Presented by Joseph Papp; Associate Producer, Jason Steven Cohen; A New York Shakespeare Festival Production; General Manager, Laurel Ann Wilson; Assistant Conductor, Edward Strauss; Company Manager, Bob MacDonald; Props, Walter Bullard; Wardrobe, Daniel Eaton; Hairstylists, David Lawrence, Sonia Rivera; Production Assistant, Connie Drew; Stage Managers, James Harker, Robin Herskowitz; Press, Merle Debuskey, Richard Kornberg, Bruce Campbell, Barbara Carroll, William Schelble, Don Anthony Summa. Opened at the Imperial Theatre on Monday, Dec. 2, 1985*

CAST

Mayor Thomas Sapsea/William Cartwright/ Your Chairman	George Rose
Stage Manager/Barkeep/James Throttle	Peter McRobbie
John Jasper/Clive Paget	Howard McGillin
Rev. Crisparkle/Cedric Moncrieffe	George N. Martin
Edwin Drood/Alice Nutting	Betty Buckley†1
Rosa Bud/Deirdre Peregrine	Patti Cohenour
Alice/Isabel Yearsley	Judy Kuhn
Beatrice/Florence Gill	Donna Murphy
Helena Landless/Janet Conover	Jana Schneider
Neville Landless/Victor Grinstead	John Herrera
Durdles/Nick Cricker	Jerome Dempsey
Deputy/Master Nick Cricker/Statue	Stephen Glavin
Princess Puffer/Angela Prysock	Cleo Laine†2
Shade of Jasper/Harry Sayle	Nicholas Gunn
Shade of Drood/Montague Pruitt	Brad Miskell
Clients of Princess Puffer/Alan Eliot	Herndon Lackey
Christopher Lyon	Rob Marshall
Succubae/Gwendolyn Pynn	Francine Landes
Sarah Cook	Karen Giombetti
Florence Gill	Donna Murphy
Isabel Yearsley	Judy Kuhn
Servants/Philip Bax	Joe Grifasi
Violet Balfour	Susan Goodman
Gwendolen Pynn	Francine Landes
Harold/James Throttle	Peter McRobbie
Julian/Alan Eliot	Herndon Lackey
Horace/Brian Pankhurst	Charles Goff
Bazzard/Phillip Bax	Joe Grifasi
Dick Datchery	???????????

CITIZENS OF CLOISTERHAM: Karen Giombetti, Charles Goff, Susan Goodman, Nicholas Gunn, Judy Kuhn, Herndon Lackey, Francine Landes, Rob Marshall, Peter McRobbie, Brad Miskell, Donna Murphy
UNDERSTUDIES: Judy Kuhn (Rosa Bud/Drood), Herndon Lackey (Jasper/Neville), Peter McRobbie (Chairman/Crisparkle), Brad Miskell (Deputy), Donna Murphy (Helena/Puffer), Swings: Laurent Giroux, Michele Pigliavento
MUSICAL NUMBERS: There You Are, A Man Could Go Quite Mad, Two Kinsmen, Moonfall, The Wages of Sin, Jasper's Vision, Ceylon, Both Sides of the Coin, Perfect Strangers, No Good Can Come from Bad, The Name of Love, Settling Up the Score, Off to the Races, Don't Quit While You're Ahead, The Garden Path to Hell, The Solution

A musical in two acts.

*Opened originally Sunday, Aug. 4, 1985 at the Delacorte Theater in Central Park where it played 27 performances before its transfer to Broadway. Still playing May 31, 1986. Winner of 1986 Tonys for Best Musical, Leading Actor in a Musical (George Rose), Best Book of a Musical, Best Original Score, Best Direction of a Musical.
†Succeeded by: 1. Donna Murphy, 2. Loretta Swit

Martha Swope Photos

Top Left: George Rose

George Rose (C)

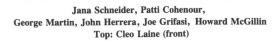

Jana Schneider, Patti Cohenour,
George Martin, John Herrera, Joe Grifasi, Howard McGillin
Top: Cleo Laine (front)

Joe Grifasi, Cleo Laine, Betty Buckley (also top), Jerome Dempsey,
George Rose

21

BLOOD KNOT

Written and Directed by Athol Fugard; Set, Rusty Smith; Costumes, Susan Hilferty; Lighting, William B. Warfel; A Yale Repertory Theatre Production; Presented by James B. Freydberg, Max Weitzenhoffer, Lucille Lortel, Estrin Rose Berman Productions in association with F. W. M. Producing Group; Executive Producer, Fremont Associates; Associate Producer, Christopher Hart; General Management, Fremont Associates, Maria Productions; Company Manager, Debbie Levy; Technical Supervision, Theatrical Services; Sound, Kieran Kelly; Wardrobe, Alan Eskolsky; Stage Managers, Neal Ann Stephens, Chan Chandler; Press, Bill Evans, Sandra Manley, Jim Baldassare, Marlene DeSavino. Opened in the Golden Theatre on Tuesday, Dec. 10, 1985*

CAST

Zachariah ....Zakes Mokae
Morris ....Athol Fugard

STANDBYS: Paul Benjamin (Zachariah), David Little (Morris)

A drama in two acts and seven scenes. The action takes place in a one-room shack in the non-white location of Korsten, near Port Elizabeth, South Africa.

*Closed March 2, 1986 after 96 performances and 13 previews.

Gerry Goodstein Photos

Top: Athol Fugard, Zakes Mokae
(also below)

Zakes Mokae, Athol Fugard
(also top)

HAY FEVER

By Noel Coward; Director, Brian Murray; Set, Michael H. Yeargan; Costumes, Jennifer von Mayrhauser; Lighting, Arden Fingerhut; Wigs, Paul Huntley; Casting, Meg Simon/Fran Kumin; Presented by Roger Peters in association with MBS Co.; Associate Producers/General Management, Robert Kamlot, Richard Berg; Company Manager, Richard Berg; Technical Supervision, Theatrical Services; Props, Jan Marasek; Assistant Company Manager, Sammy Ledbetter; Production Assistant, Robert Urbinati; Wardrobe, Robert Strong Miller; Hair & Wigs, Peg Scnierholz; Stage Managers, Martin Gold, John Vivian; Press, Bill Evans, Sandra Manley, Jim Baldassare. Opened in the Music Box on Thursday, Dec. 12, 1985*

CAST

Sorel Bliss	Mia Dillon
Simon Bliss	Robert Joy
Clara	Barbara Bryne
Judith Bliss	Rosemary Harris
David Bliss	Roy Dotrice
Sandy Tyrell	Campbell Scott
Myra Arundel	Carolyn Seymour
Richard Greatham	Charles Kimbrough
Jackie Coryton	Deborah Rush

UNDERSTUDIES: Angela Thornton (Judith), Richard Clarke (David/Richard), Ashley Gardner (Sorel/Jackie), Thomas Gibson (Simon/Sandy)

A comedy in two acts and three scenes. The action takes place at David Bliss' country house in Cookham, outside London in June of 1925.

*Closed March 29, 1986 after 124 performances and 16 previews. Original production opened Oct. 5, 1925 at the Maxine Elliott with Laura Hope Crews for 49 performances. Revived Dec. 29, 1931 at the Avon with Constance Collier for 95 performances, and at the Helen Hayes Theatre on Nov. 9, 1970 with Shirley Booth for 24 performances.

Martha Swope Photos

Right: Roy Dotrice, Rosemary Harris

Campbell Scott, Deborah Rush, Carolyn Seymour, Charles Kimbrough

JERRY'S GIRLS

Music and Lyrics, Jerry Herman. Staged and Directed by Larry Alford; Choreography, Wayne Cilento; Concepts, Larry Alford, Wayne Cilento, Jerry Herman; Scenery, Hal Tine; Costumes, Florence Klotz; Lighting, Tharon Musser; Sound, Peter Fitzgerald; Hairstylist, Phyllis Della, Robert DeNiro; Dance Arranger, Mark Hummel; Musical Supervisor, Donald Pippin; Orchestrations, Christopher Bankey, Joseph Gianono, Jim Tyler; Musical Director, Janet Glazener; Assistant Choreographer, Sarah Miles; Casting, Mark Reiner; General Management, Theatre Now; Presented by Zev Bufman, Kenneth-John Productions in association with Agnese/ Raibourn; Production Supervisor, Ethel R. Bayer; Company Manager, Sally Campbell; Props, Joe Harris, Jr.; Wardrobe, Max Hager; Associate Conductor, Maida Libkin; Stage Managers, Patrick Horrigan, Larry Bussard, Brenna Krupa Holden, Barbara Schneider; Press, Shirley Herz, Peter Cromarty, Pete Sanders, David Roggensack, Gary Lawrence. Opened in the St. James Theatre on Wednesday, Dec. 18, 1985*

CAST

Dorothy	Chita	Leslie
Loudon	Rivera	Uggams

Ellyn Arons   Terri Homberg
Kirsten Childs   Robin Kersey
Kim Crosby   Joni Masella
Anita Ehrler   Deborah Phelan

Swing: Jacquey Maltby
Onstage Pianist: Sue Anderson

MUSICAL NUMBERS: It Takes a Woman, Just Leave Everything to Me, Put on Your Sunday Clothes, It Only Takes a Moment, Wherever He Ain't, We Need a Little Christmas, Tap Your Troubles Away, I Won't Send Roses, Two-a-Day, Bosom Buddies, The Man in the Moon, So Long Dearie, Take It All Off, Shalom, Milk and Honey, Before the Parade Passes By, Have a Nice Day, Showtune, If He Walked into My Life, Hello, Dolly!, Just Go to the Movies, Movies Were Movies, Look What Happened to Mabel, Nelson, I Don't Want to Know, It's Today, Mame, Kiss Her Now, Dickie, Voices, Thoughts, Time Heals Everything, That's How Young I Feel, My Type, La Cage, Song on the Sand, I Am What I Am, The Best of Times

A "Musical Entertainment" in two acts.

*Closed April 20, 1986 after 139 performances and 14 previews.

Martha Swope Photos

**Top: Leslie Uggams, Chita
Rivera, Dorothy Loudon**

**Chita Rivera
Above: Leslie Uggams**

THE ROBERT KLEIN SHOW!

Written and conceived by Robert Klein; Musical Director, Bob Stein; Presented by Circle in the Square (Theodore Mann, Artistic Director; Paul Libin, Producing Director); Company Manager, William Conn; Props, Frank Hauser; Wardrobe, Claire Libin; Stage Managers, Michael F. Ritchie, Catherine Russell; Press, Merle Debuskey, William Schelble. Opened in the Circle in the Square Theatre Friday, December 20, 1985*

CAST

Robert Klein
Kenny Rankin

Singers: Betsy Bircher, Catherine Russell
Musicians: Zev Katz, Dave Rataczjak, Bob Rose

An entertainment in two parts.

*Closed Jan. 4, 1986 after 16 performances.

Dorothy Loudon
Top: Leslie Uggams

Kenny Rankin
Above: Robert Klein

25

WIND IN THE WILLOWS

Music, William Perry; Lyrics, Roger McGough, William Perry; Book, Jane Iredale; Adapted from the Kenneth Grahame classic; Staged by Tony Stevens; Choreography, Margery Beddow; Scenery, Sam Kirkpatrick; Costumes, Freddy Wittop; Lighting, Craig Miller; Sound, Jack Mann; Musical Supervision, Jonathan Tunick; Orchestrations, William D. Brohn; Dance and Incidental Music, David Krane; Musical Director and Vocal Arrangements, Robert Rogers; Production Supervisor, Steven Zweigbaum; Assistant Choreographer, James Brennan; Fights, Conal O'Brien; Casting, Johnson-Liff; General Management, Weiler/Miller; Presented by RLM Productions and Liniva Productions; Hairstylist, Angela Gari; Wigs, Paul Huntley; Makeup, J. Roy Helland; Stage Managers, Jim Woolley, Ellen Raphael, Scott Waara; Technical Coordinator, Arthur Siccardi; Props, Michael Durnin, Eric Durnin; Wardrobe, Nancy Schaefer; Production Assistant, Meryl S. Jacobs; Press, Fred Nathan, Glenna Freedman, Anne S. Abrams, Bert Fink, Marc P. Thibodeau, Dennis Crowley, Merle Frimark, Philip Renaldi. Opened at the Nederlander Theatre on Saturday, Dec. 21, 1985*

CAST

Mole	Vicki Lewis
Mother Rabbit	Nora Mae Lyng
Father Rabbit	John Jellison
Rat	David Carroll
Toad	Nathan Lane
Chief Stoat	Donna Drake
Badger	Irving Barnes
Chief Weasel	P. J. Benjamin
Wayfarer Rat	Jackie Lowe
Police Sergeant	Scott Waara
Court Clerk	Kenston Ames
Judge	John Jellison
Prosecutor	Michael Byers
Jailer's Daughter	Nora Mae Lyng
Jailer	Michael Byers

ENSEMBLE: Kenston Ames, Shell M. Benjamin, Michael Byers, Jackie Lowe, Marguerite Lowell, Nora Mae Lyng, Mary C. Robare, Jamie Rocco, Ray Roderick, Scott Waara, Swings: Teresa Payne-Rohan, Kevin Winkler

UNDERSTUDIES: Donna Drake (Mole), Scott Waara (Rat), Michael Byers (Toad), John Jellison (Badger), Shell M. Benjamin (Chief Stoat), Jamie Rocco (Chief Weasel)

MUSICAL NUMBERS: The World Is Waiting for Me, When Springtime Comes to My River, Messing about in Boats, Evil Weasel, That's What Friends Are For, Follow Your Instinct, The Gasoline Can-Can, You'll Love It in Jail, Mediterranean, The Day You Came into My Life, S-S-S-Something Comes Over Me, I'd Be Attracted, Moving Up in the World, Brief Encounter, Where Am I Now?, The Wind in the Willows, Come What May

A musical in 2 acts and 15 scenes.

*Closed Dec. 22, 1985 after 4 performances and 27 previews.

Martha Swope Photos

Irving Barnes, Ray Roderick, Shell M. Benjamin
Right Center: Vickie Lewis

BENEFACTORS

By Michael Frayn; Director, Michael Blakemore; Set, Michael Annals; Costumes, John Dunn; Lighting, Martin Aronstein; Casting, Howard Feuer; Presented by James M. Nederlander, Robert Fryer, Douglas Urbanski and Michael Codron in association with MTM Enterprises and CBS Productions; General Management, Joseph P. Harris Associates; Manager, Thomas P. Santopietro; Technical Supervision, Jeremiah J. Harris; Props, Paul Biega; Wardrobe, Karen Lloyd; Production Assistant, Larry Reitzer; Stage Manager, Laura deBuys; Press, Fred Nathan, Marc P. Thibodeau, Anne Abrams, Bert Fink, Glenna Freedman, Merle Frimark, Philip Rinaldi, Dennis Crowley. Opened in the Brooks Atkinson Theatre on Sunday, Dec. 22, 1985*

CAST

David	Sam Waterston†1
Jane	Glenn Close†2
Colin	Simon Jones
Sheila	Mary Beth Hurt

STANDBYS: Lewis Arlt, Dale Hodges

A drama in two acts. The action takes place in London over the course of several years.

*Closed June 29, 1986 after 217 performances and 12 previews. Received 1986 NY Drama Critics Circle citation for Best Foreign Play of the season.
†Succeeded by: 1. David Birney, 2. Maureen Anderman

Martha Swope Photos

**Right: Sam Waterston, Glenn Close
Below: Glenn Close, Mary Beth Hurt, Sam
Waterston, Simon Jones Right Center:
Mary Beth Hurt, Sam Waterston**

David Birney, Maureen Anderman

Simon Jones, Glenn Close

27

THE CARETAKER

By Harold Pinter; Director, John Malkovich; Set and Lighting, Kevin Rigdon; Costumes, John Malkovich; The Steppenwolf Theatre Company production presented by Circle in the Square Theatre (Theodore Mann, Artistic Director; Paul Libin, Producing Director); Company Manager, Susan Elrod; Production Manager, Michael F. Ritchie; Casting, Hughes Moss; Wardrobe, Claire Libin; Stage Managers, Teri McClure, Carol Klein; Press, Merle Debuskey, William Schelble. Opened in the Circle in the Square Theatre on Thursday, January 1, 1986*

CAST

Mick	Gary Sinise
Aston	Jeff Perry
Davies	Alan Wilder

STANDBYS: Stephen Daley, Tom Zanarini

A drama in three acts. The action takes place in a house in west London.

*Closed March 9, 1986 after 45 performances and 23 previews.

Brigitte Lacombe Photos

Left: Alan Wilder, Gary Sinise

Jeff Perry, Gary Sinise, Alan Wilder

CORPSE!

By Gerald Moon; Director, John Tillinger; Set, Alan Tagg; Costumes, Lowell Detweiler; Lighting, Richard Winkler; Presented by Martin Markinson, Gary Leaverton and Robert Fox; General Management, Brent Peek Productions; Production Associate, Scott Green; Company Manager, Marshall B. Purdy; Props, Val Medina; Wardrobe, Tina Ryan; Casting, Myers-Teschner; Hairstylist, Paul Huntley; Stage Managers, Franklin Keysar, R. Nelson Barbee. Press, Max Eisen, Maria Somma, Madelon Rosen, Barbara Glenn. Opened in the Helen Hayes Theatre on Thursday, January 9, 1986.*

CAST

Evelyn Farrant ....Keith Baxter
Mrs. McGee .... Pauline Flanagan
Major Walter Powell .... Milo O'Shea
Rupert Farrant ....Keith Baxter
Hawkins .... Scott LaFeber

STANDBYS: Paul Vincent (Farrant), Bernard Frawley (Powell/Hawkins), Paddy Croft (Mrs. McGee)

A "comedy thriller" in two acts. The action takes place in Evelyn Farrant's basement flat in Soho and in Rupert Farrant's house in Regent's Park, London, on December 11, 1936.

*Closed April 20, 1986 after 121 performances and 30 previews.

Top: Pauline Flanagan, Keith
Baxter, Milo O'Shea

Milo O'Shea, Keith Baxter

LILLIAN

By William Luce; Based on the autobiographical works of Lillian Hellman; Director, Robert Whitehead; Set, Ben Edwards; Costume, Jane Greenwood; Lighting, Thomas Skelton; Music and Sound Design, David Gooding; Presented by Ann Shanks, The Kennedy Center and Ronald S. Lee; Co-Producers, Bob Shanks, Kenneth Feld; General Management, Alan C. Wasser, Douglas C. Baker; Wardrobe, Karen Nowak; Wig, Paul Huntley; Stage Managers, Dianne Trulock, David Malvin; Press, David Powers, Leo Stern. Opened in the Ethel Barrymore Theatre on Thursday, January 16, 1986*

CAST

Zoe Caldwell
as
Lillian Hellman

Voices at HUAC Meeting: Committee Chairman Dudley Swetland, Committee Counsel Allen Leatherman, Reporter William Rhys, Joseph Rauh, John Buck, Jr.

The scene is a hospital in New York City on January 10, 1961, the day Dashiell Hammett died. Performed with one intermission.

*Closed Feb. 23, 1986 after a limited engagement of 45 performances and 5 previews.

Joan Marcus Photos

Zoe Caldwell as Lillian Hellman

JEROME KERN GOES TO HOLLYWOOD

Conceived by David Kernan; Written by Dick Vosburgh; Music, Jerome Kern; Director, David Kernan; Lyrics, Oscar Hammerstein II, Dorothy Fields, Ira Gershwin, Otto Harbach, Johnny Mercer, E. Y. Harburg, Jimmy McHugh, P. G. Wodehouse, Buddy DeSylva, Gus Kahn, Bernard Dougall, Herbert Reynolds; Lighting, Ken Billington; Musical Director, Peter Howard; Set, Colin Pigott; Costumes, Christine Robinson; Sound, Tony Meola; Musical Consultant, Clive Chaplin; Additional Staging, Irving Davies; Producing Associate, Eric Friedheim; Presented by Arthur Cantor, Bonnie Nelson Schwartz by arrangement with Peter Wilson and Showpeople; General/Company Manager, Harvey Elliott; Assistant Conductor, Arnold Gross; Wardrobe, Warren Morrill; Hairstylist, Gerry Leddy; Stage Managers, Robert Schear, Kenneth L. Peck; Press, Arthur Cantor, Ken Mandelbaum, Steve Cole. Opened in the Ritz Theatre on Thursday, January 23, 1986*

CAST

Elaine Delmar   Scott Holmes
Liz Robertson   Elisabeth Welch

Standbys: Jeanne Lehman, Michael Maguire

MUSICAL NUMBER: The Song Is You, I've Told Every Little Star, Let's Begin, I Won't Dance, Californ-i-ay, I'll Be Hard to Handle, Smoke Gets in Your Eyes, Yesterdays, Bojangles of Harlem, I'm Old Fashioned, Make Believe, Why Do I Love You?, I Have the Room above Her, It Still Suits Me, Day Dreaming, I Dream Too Much, Can I Forget You?, Pick Yourself Up, She Didn't Say Yes, The Folks Who Live on the Hill, Long Ago and Far Away, The Show Must Go On, Don't Ask Me Not to Sing, The Way You Look Tonight, A Fine Romance, Lovely to Look At, Just Let Me Look At You, Who?, Remind Me, The Last Time I Saw Paris, Ol' Man River, Why Was I Born?, Bill, Can't Help Lovin' Dat Man, All the Things You Are, I've Told Every Little Star, They Didn't Believe Me, Till the Clouds Roll By, Look for the Silver Lining, Make Way for Tomorrow

A musical revue in two acts.

*Closed Feb. 1, 1986 after 13 performances and 9 previews.

Martha Swope Photos

**Right: Liz Robertson, Scott Holmes, Elaine
Delmar Top: Scott Holmes, Liz Robertson,
Elaine Delmar, Elisabeth Welch**

Liz Robertson, Elisabeth Welch, Scott Holmes, Elaine Delmar

UPTOWN . . . IT'S HOT!

Conceived, Directed and Choreographed by Maurice Hines; Scenery, Tom McPhillips; Lighting, Marc B. Weiss; Costumes, Ellen Lee; Narrations written by Jeffery V. Thompson, Marion Ramsey; Musical Direction/Supervision, Frank Owens; Dance Arrangements, Frank Owens, Thom Bridwell; Production Supervisor, Beverley Randolph; Assistant Choreographer, Mercedes Ellington; Presented by Allen Spivak and Larry Magid; Associate Producer, Stanley Kay; General Manager, Roy A. Somlyo; Company Manager, Jodi Moss; Props, Tom Ciaccio; Wardrobe, Marianne L. Gutknecht; Technical Coordinator, David Reuss; Wigs, Cody Armstrong; Production Assistant, Craig Morton; Sound, Otts Munderloh; Stage Managers, Gwendolyn M. Gilliam, Jerry Cleveland; Press, Michael Alpert, Ruth Jaffe. Opened in the Lunt-Fontanne Theatre on Tuesday, January 28, 1986*

CAST

Maurice Hines	Alisa Gyse
Marion Ramsey	Jeffery V. Thompson
Lawrence Hamilton	Tommi Johnson

ENSEMBLE: Sheila D. Barker, Toni-Maria Chalmers, Leon Evans, Michael Franks, Robert H. Fowler, Lovette George, Ruthanna Graves, Yolanda Graves, Emera Hunt, Leslie Wiiliams-Jenkins, Lisa Ann Malloy, Delphine T. Mantz, Gerry McIntyre, Christopher T. Moore, Elise Neal, Leesa M. Osborn, Marishka Shanice Phillips, R. LaChanze Sapp, Cheryl Ann Scott, Darious Keith Wiliams
UNDERSTUDIES: Yolanda Graves (Marion Ramsey/Alisa Gyse), Gerry McIntyre (Jeffery V. Thompson), Robert Fowler/Michael Franks (Lawrence Hamilton), Leon Evans (Tommi Johnson)

A musical in two acts with an overture and a prologue. The scenes represent music from the 1930's through the 1980's.

*Closed Feb. 16, 1986 after 24 performances and 13 previews.

Right: Marion Ramsey (center)
Top: Maurice Hines

Alisa Gyse, Maurice Hines

Jeffery V. Thompson, Delphine T. Mantz

32

EXECUTION OF JUSTICE

Written and Directed by Emily Mann; Set, Ming Cho Lee; Costumes, Jennifer von Mayrhauser; Lighting, Pat Collins; Film sequences excerpted from "The Times of Harvey Milk" by Robert Epstein and Richard Schmiechen; Sound, Tom Morse; Casting, Johnson-Liff; General Manager, Allan Francis; Presented by Lester and Marjorie Osterman, Mortimer Caplin in association with Norton & Stark Inc.; Technical Supervisor, Arthur Siccardi; Assistant to Producers, Tara Jayne Rubin; Assistant Director, Molly Fowler; Props, Val Medina; Wardrobe, Kathleen Gallagher, Beverly Belletieri; Video Design, Dan Mirro; Stage Managers, Frank Marino, Fredric Hanson, Elise Warner; Press, Betty Lee Hunt, Maria Cristina Pucci. Opened in the Virginia Theatre on Thursday, March 13, 1986.*

CAST

Dan White	John Spencer
Mary Ann White	Mary McDonnell
Sister BoomBoom/Political Activist	Wesley Snipes
Jim Denman/White's Jailer	Christopher McHale
Young Mother	Lisabeth Bartlett
Milk's Friend	Adam Redfield
Gwenn Craig/Vice President of Harvey Milk Democratic Club	Isabell Monk
City Supervisor Harry Britt	Donal Donnelly
Joseph Freitas, D.A.	Nicholas Hormann
The Court	Nicholas Kepros
Court Clerk	Lisabeth Bartlett
Douglas Schmidt, D.A.	Peter Friedman
Thomas F. Norman, Prosecuting Attorney	Gerry Bamman
Joanna Lu, TV Reporter	Freda Foh Shen
Prospective Jurors	Josh Clark, Suzy Hunt
Jury Foreman	Gary Reineke
Bailiff	Jeremy O. Caplin
Coroner Stephens	Donal Donnelly
Rudy Notheberg, Deputy Mayor	Earle Hyman
Barbara Taylor, Reporter	Marcia Jean Kurtz
Officer Byrne	Isabell Monk
William Melia, Civil Engineer	Richard Riehle
Syr Copertini, Secretary to the Mayor	Suzy Hunt
Carl Henry Carlson, Aide to Milk	Nicholas Hormann
Richard Pabich, Assistant to Milk	Wesley Snipes
Inspector Frank Falzon, Homicide	Jon DeVries
Inspector Edward Erdelatz	Stanley Tucci
Denise Apcar, Aide to White	Lisabeth Bartlett
Fire Chief Sherratt	Gary Reineke
Psychiatrists	Earle Hyman (Jones), Marcia Jean Kurtz (Frediani), Donal Donnelly (Blinder), Gary Reineke (Lunde), Jon DeVries (Delman)
Carol Ruth Silver, City Supervisor	Marcia Jean Kurtz
Dr. Levy, Psychiatrist for the people	Gary Reineke
Action Cameraman	Richard Howard
Riot Police	Jeremy O. Caplin, Josh Clark, Jon DeVries, Richard Riehle, Stanley Tucci

UNDERSTUDIES: Elise Warner, Wesley Snipes, Christopher McHale, Carlotta Schoch, Josh Clark, Suzy Hunt, Gary Reineke, Jeremy O. Caplin, Richard Riehele, Richard Poe.

A drama in two acts. The words come from trial transcripts, reportage and interviews.

*Closed March 22, 1986 after 12 performances and 8 previews.

Gerry Goodstein Photos

Top Right: Peter Friedman, Nicholas Kepros, Gerry Bamman Below: John Spencer, Jon DeVries

Suzy Hunt, Gerry Bamman

PRECIOUS SONS

By George Furth; Director, Norman Rene; Set, Andrew Jackness; Costumes, Joseph G. Aulisi; Lighting, Richard Nelson; Sound, Tom Morse; Casting, Meg Simon/Fran Kumin; Presented by Roger Berlind, Marty Bell, Associate Producer, Michael Sanders; Company Manager, Susan Gustafson; Assistant Director, Diane Kamp; Props, George Green, Jr.; Wardrobe, Roberta Christy; Hairstylist-Makeup, Ron Abrams; General Management, Gatchell & Neufeld; Technical Supervisor, Theatre Services; Stage Managers, Steven Beckler, Phil DiMaggio; Production Assistants, Dana Baker, Richard Bly; Press, Solters/Roskin/Friedman, Joshua Ellis, Cindy Valk, Jim Sapp, Adrian Bryan-Brown. Opened in the Longacre Theatre on Thursday, March 20, 1986.*

CAST

Art	William O'Leary
Freddy	Anthony Rapp
Bea	Judith Ivey
Fred	Ed Harris
Sandra	Anne Marie Bobby

STANDBYS & UNDERSTUDIES: Kelly Bishop (Bea), George Bamford (Fred), Christopher Gartin (Art/Freddy), Mary B. Ward (Sandra)

A drama in 2 acts and 4 scenes. The action takes place in Fred and Bea's house on the South Side of Chicago, Illinois, on June 3, 1949.

*Closed May 11, 1986 after 60 performances and 28 previews.

Henry Grossman Photos

Left: Ed Harris, Judith Ivey

Ed Harris, Anthony Rapp, Judith Ivey

THE FLYING KARAMAZOV BROTHERS

Conceived, Written and Directed by The Flying Karamazov Brothers; Company Manager, Bridget Jennings; Lighting, Eben Sprinsock; Props, Doug Nelson; Wardrobe, A. Devora; Sets, Seiza de Tarr; Stage Manager, Peter Dansky; Presented by Lincoln Center Theater (Gregory Mosher, Director; Bernard Gersten, Executive Producer); Press, Merle Debuskey, Robert Larkin. Opened in the Vivian Beaumont Theater on Tuesday, April 1, 1986.*

CAST

Fyodor ....Timothy Daniel Furst
Dmitri ....Paul David Magid
Alyosha ....Randy Nelson
Ivan ....Howard Jay Patterson
Smerdyakov ....Sam Williams

"Juggling and Cheap Theatrics" performed with one intermission.

*Closed April 20, 1986 after 24 performances and 5 previews, and re-opened Wednesday, April 23, 1986 in the Mitzi Newhouse Theater for 16 performances, closing May 4, 1986.

LOOT

By Joe Orton; Director, John Tillinger; Sets, John Lee Beatty; Costumes, Bill Walker; Lighting, Richard Nelson; A Manhattan Theatre Club production; Presented by The David Merrick Arts Foundation, Charles P. Kopelman and Mark Simon; General Manager, Leo K. Cohen; Props, Leo Herbert; Hairstylist, Carole Morales; Casting, Johnson-Liff; Wardrobe, Jean Steinlein; Wig, Paul Huntley; Fight Coordinator, J. Allen Suddeth; Stage Managers, Peggy Peterson, Jon Nakagawa; Press, Solters/Roskin/Friedman, Cindy Valk, Joshua Ellis, Adrian Bryan-Brown, Jim Sapp, Jackie Green, Andrew Hirshfield. Opened in the Music Box on Monday, April 7, 1986.*

CAST

McLeavy	Charles Keating
Fay	Zoe Wanamaker
Hal	Zeljko Ivanek
Dennis	Alec Baldwin
Truscott	Joseph Maher
Meadows	Nick Ullett

STANDBYS: Nick Ullett (McLeavy/Truscott), Selena Carey-Jones (Fay), Steven Weber (Hal/Dennis/Meadows)

A black comedy in two acts. The action takes place at the present time in London in a room in McLeavy's house.

*Closed June 28, 1986 after 96 performances and 5 previews. Prior to Broadway, the production played 48 performances for the Manhattan Theatre Club in City Center.

Gerry Goodstein Photos

Zoe Wanamaker, Charles Keating
Top: Joseph Maher, Alec Baldwin, Zeljko Ivanek

BIG DEAL

Written, Directed and Choreographed by Bob Fosse; Based on film "Big Deal on Madonna Street"; Scenery, Peter Larkin; Costumes, Patricia Zipprodt; Lighting, Jules Fisher; Orchestrations, Ralph Burns; Sound, Abe Jacob; Hairstylist, Romaine Greene; Casting, Howard Feuer; Associate Choreographer, Christopher Chadman; Music Arranged and Conducted by Gordon Lowry Harrell; Presented by The Shubert Organization, Roger Berlind, Jerome Minskoff, in association with Jonathan Farkas; Executive Producer, Jules Fisher; General Management, Joseph Harris Associates; Technical Supervision, Jeremiah J. Harris; Company Manager, Steven H. David; Production Assistant, Catherine Nicholas; Assistant Manager, Kathleen Lowe; Props, Paul Biega, Joseph Harris, Jr.; Wardrobe, Jennifer Bryan; Stage Managers, Phil Friedman, Perry Cline, Barry Kearsley, Kenneth Hanson, Randall Whitescarver; Press, Fred Nathan, Bert Fink, Anne Abrams, Dennis Crowley, Merle Frimark, Philip Rinaldi, Marc P. Thibodeau, Larry Reitzer. Opened in the Broadway Theatre on Thursday, April 10, 1986.*

CAST

Lilly	Loretta Devine
First Narrator	Wayne Cilento
Second Narrator	Bruce Anthony Davis
Kokomo	Gary Chapman
Otis	Alde Lewis, Jr.
Charley	Cleavant Derricks
Pearl/Band Singer/Shadow	Valarie Pettiford
Slick	Larry Marshall
Sunnyboy	Mel Johnson, Jr.
Willie	Alan Weeks
Judge/Bandleader	Bernard J. Marsh
Phoebe	Desiree Coleman
Dancin' Dan	Gary Chapman
Second Shadow	Barbara Yeager
Little Willie	Roumel Reaux
Announcer	Candace Tovar

DANCERS: Ciscoe Bruton II, Lloyd Culbreath, Kim Darwin, Cady Huffman, Amelia Marshall, Frank Mastrocola, Stephanie Pope, Roumel Reaux, George Russell, Candace Tovar, Alternates: Bryant Baldwin, Diana Laurenson, Vince Cole.

STANDBYS & UNDERSTUDIES: Lloyd Culbreath (Willie), Frank Mastrocola (1st Narrator), Bryant Baldwin (2nd Narrator), Kenneth Hanson (Kokomo), Amelia Marshall (Phoebe), Roumel Reaux (Otis/Dancin' Dan), Ciscoe Bruton II (Dancin' Dan), Stephanie Pope (Lilly/Shadows), Kim Darwin (Shadows), Cady Huffman (Pearl), Vince Cole (Sunnyboy)

MUSICAL NUMBERS: Life Is Just a Bowl of Cherries, For No Good Reason at All, Charley My Boy, I've Got a Feelin' You're Foolin', Ain't We Got Fun, Chicago, Pick Yourself Up, I'm Just Wild about Harry, Beat Me Daddy Eight to the Bar, The Music Goes Round and Round, Now's the Time to Fall in Love, Ain't She Sweet, Everybody Loves My Baby, Me and My Shadow, Love Is Just Around the Corner, Just a Gigolo, Who's Your Little Who-Zis?, Yes Sir That's My Baby, Button Up Your Overcoat, Daddy You've Been a Mother to Me, Hold Tight, Happy Days Are Here Again, I'm Sitting on Top of the World

A musical in 2 acts and 23 scenes with a prologue. The action takes place in the 1930's on the South Side of Chicago, Illinois.

*Closed June 8, 1986 after 70 performances and 7 previews. Bob Fosse received a 1986 "Tony" for Outstanding Choreography of the year.

Martha Swope Photos

Top (Center): Alan Weeks, Cleavant Derricks, Loretta Devine, Wayne Cilento Below: Alde Lewis, Jr., Alan Weeks, Cleavant Derricks, Larry Marshall, Mel Johnson, Jr.

Valerie Pettiford, Gary Chapman, Barbara Yeager

SOCIAL SECURITY

By Andrew Bergman; Director, Mike Nichols; Set, Tony Walton; Costumes, Ann Roth; Lighting, Marilyn Rennagel; Sound, Otts Munderloh; Hairstylist/Makeup, J. Roy Helland; Presented by David Geffen and the Shubert Organization (Gerald Schoenfeld, Chairman; Bernard B. Jacobs, President); General Manager, Robert Kamlot; Casting, Ellen Lewis; Company Manager, Leonard Soloway; Technical Supervisors, Theatre Service; Props, Jan Marasek, Earl Kirby; Wardrobe, Chip Mulberger; Production Assistant, Nancy Simon; Stage Managers, Peter Lawrence, Jim Woolley; Press, Bill Evans, Sandra Manley, Jim Baldassare, Marlene DeSavino. Opened in the Ethel Barrymore Theatre on Thursday, April 17, 1986.*

CAST

David Kahn .... Ron Silver†1
Barbara Kahn .... Marlo Thomas†2
Trudy Heyman .... Joanna Gleason†3
Martin Heyman .... Kenneth Welsh†4
Sophie Greengrass ....Olympia Dukakis†5
Maurice Koenig ....Stefan Schnabel

STANDBYS: Caroline Aaron (Barbara/Trudy), John Rothman (David/Martin), Ruth Vool (Sophie), Joseph Leon (Maurice)

A comedy in 2 acts and 3 scenes. The action takes place at the present time in New York City in the Eastside apartment of Barbara and David Kahn.

*Still playing May 31, 1986.
†Succeeded vy: 1. Cliff Gorman, 2. Maureen Anderman, Marilu Henner, 3. Caroline Aaron, 4. Robert Dorfman, 5. Doris Belack

Martha Swope Photos

Left: Joanna Gleason, Marlo Thomas, Kenneth Walsh, Ron Silver Top: Stefan Schnabel, Ron Silver, Marlo Thomas, Olympia Dukakis

Ron Silver, Marlo Thomas

Cliff Gorman, Maureen Anderman

THE PETITION

By Brian Clark; Director, Peter Hall; Designed by John Bury; Presented by Robert Whitehead, Roger L. Stevens and the Shubert Organization, in association with Astramead Ltd. and Freeshooter Productions Ltd, Nathan Joseph, Executive Producer; General Manager, Max Allentuck; Props, David Gorel; Wardrobe, Elonzo Dann; Production Assistant, Catherine Zubo; Stage Managers, William Dodds, Amy Pell; Press, Fred Nathan, Merle Frimark, Anne Abrams, Dennis Crowley, Bert Fink, Philip Rinaldi, Marc P. Thibodeau, Larry Reitzer, Michelle Beck. Opened in the John Golden Theatre on Thursday, April 24, 1986.*

CAST

Lady Elizabeth Milne .... Jessica Tandy
General Sir Edmund Milne .... Hume Cronyn

A drama in two acts. The action takes place at the present time in an apartment in Belgravia, London, England, between 10 a.m. and 12 noon.

*Closed June 29, 1986 after 77 performances and 9 previews.

Joan Marcus Photos

Top: Jessica Tandy, Hume Cronyn

Jessica Tandy, Hume Cronyn

SWEET CHARITY

Book, Neil Simon; Music, Cy Coleman; Lyrics, Dorothy Fields; Directed and Choreographed by Bob Fosse; Based on "Nights of Cabiria" with screenplay by Federico Fellini, Tullio Pinelli, Ennio Flaiano; Scenery/Lighting, Robert Randolph; Costumes, Patricia Zipprodt; Musical Direction, Fred Werner; Orchestrations, Ralph Burns; Sound, Otts Munderloh; Presented by Jerome Minskoff, James M. Nederlander, Arthur Rubin, Joseph Harris; Hairstylist, Phyllis Della; Casting, Howard Feuer; Production Manager, Phil Friedman; General Management, Joseph Harris Associates; Assistant to Mr. Fosse, Gwen Verdon; Manager, Kathleen Lowe; Technical Supervision, Jeremiah J. Harris Associates; Assistant Conductor, Don Rebic; Props, Paul Biega, John Lofgren, Aarne Lofgren; Wardrobe, Nancy Schaefer; Hairpieces, Sergio Valente; Furs, Ben Kahn; Stage Managers, Craig Jacobs, Lani Ball, David Blackwell; Press, Jeffrey Richards, C. George Willard, Ben Morse, Susan Lee, Marie-Louise Silva, L. Glenn Poppleton III, Ken Mandelbaum. Opened in the Minskoff Theatre on Sunday April 27, 1986.*

CAST

Charity .... Debbie Allen†
Dark Glasses .... David Warren Gibson
Married Couple ....Quin Baird, Jan Horvath
First Young Man .... Jeff Shade
Woman with hat/Panhandler/Receptionist/
    Good Fairy .... Celia Tackaberry
Ice Cream Vendor .... Kelly Patterson
Young Spanish Man ....Adrian Rosario
Cop/Brother Harold ....Tanis Michaels
Helene .... Allison Williams
Nickie .... Bebe Neuwirth
Mimi .... Mimi Quillin
Herman .... Lee Wilkof
Doorman/Waiter .... Tom Wierney
Ursala .... Carrie Nygren
Vittorio Vidal .... Mark Jacoby
Manfred ....Fred C. Mann III
Old Maid .... Jan Horvath
Oscar .... Michael Rupert
Daddy Johann Sebastian Brubeck ....Irving Allen Lee
Brother Ray .... Stanley Wesley Perryman
Rosie ....Dana Moore

SINGERS AND DANCERS: Quinn Baird, Christine Colby, Alice Everett Cox, David Warren Gibson, Kim Morgan Greene, Ian Horvath, Jane Lanier, Fred C. Mann III, Allison Renee Manson, Tanis Michaels, Dana Moore, Michelle O'Steen, Kelly Patterson, Stanley Wesley Perryman, Mimi Quillin, Adrian Rosario, Jeff Shade, Tom Wierney, Alternates: Michelle O'Steen, Chet Walker
STANDBYS & UNDERSTUDIES: Bibi Neuwirth: (Charity), David Warren Gibsom (Oscar), Michael Licata (Oscar/Vittorio), Kelly Patterson (Vittorio); Dana Moore (Nickie), Kirsten Childs (Helene), Tom Wierney (Herman), Tanis Michaels (Daddy Brubeck), Christine Colby (Ursala), Jan Horvath (Ms. Tackaberry), Kim Morgan Greene (Charity)
MUSICAL NUMBERS: You Should See Yourself, The Rescue, Big Spender, Rich Man's Frug, If My Friends Could See Me Now, Too Many Tomorrows, There's Gotta Be Something Better Than This, I'm the Bravest Individual, Rhythm of Life, Baby Dream Your Dream, Sweet Charity, Where Am I Going, I'm a Brass Band, I Love to Cry at Weddings

A musical in 2 acts and 19 scenes with a prologue. The action takes place in New York City in the mid 1960's.

*Still playing May 31, 1986. 1986 Tonys were awarded Bebe Neuwirth and Michael Rupert for Best Featured Actress and Actor in a Musical, Best Costume Design, and Best Reproduction of a Play or Musical.
†Succeeded by Ann Reinking

Alan Pappé Photos

Alan Pappe, Martha Swope Photos
Top Left: Debbie Allen

Debbie Allen, Bebe Neuwirth, Allison Williams

Michael Rupert, Debbie Allen
Top: Dana Moore (right)

Ann Reinking

41

LONG DAY'S JOURNEY INTO NIGHT

By Eugene O'Neill; Director, Jonathan Miller; Set, Tony Straiges; Costumes, Willa Kim; Lighting, Richard Nelson; Presented by Emanuel Azenberg, The Shubert Organization, Roger Peters, Roger Berlind, Pace Theatrical Group; Associate Producer, Mona Schlachter; General Manager, Robert Kamlot; Technical Supervision, Theatrical Services; Props, Jan Marasek; Company Manager, Leslie Butler; Wardrobe, Penny Davis; Production Assistant, Katherine Feller; Casting, Meg Simon/Fran Kumin; Wigs, Paul Huntley; Stage Managers, Martin Herzer, Barbara-Mae Phillips, Laura MacDermott; Press, Bill Evans, Sandra Manley, Jim Baldassare, Marlene DeSavino. Opened in the Broadhurst Theatre on Monday, April 28, 1986.*

CAST

Mary Tyrone .... Bethel Leslie
James Tyrone .... Jack Lemmon
James Tyrone, Jr. .... Kevin Spacey
Edmund Tyrone .... Peter Gallagher
Cathleen ....Jodie Lynne McClintock

UNDERSTUDIES: Patricia Fraser (Mary), Michael Hammond (Edmund/James, Jr.), Laura McDermott (Cathleen)

A drama in 4 acts and 5 scenes, performed with one intermission. The action takes place in the livingroom of the Tyrone's summer home in August of 1912.

*Closed June 29, 1986 after 54 performances and 6 previews. Original production opened at the old Helen Hayes Theatre on Nov. 7, 1956 and ran for 390 performances. The cast consisted of Fredric March, Florence Eldridge, Jason Robards, Jr., Bradford Dillman and Katherine Ross.

Martha Swope Photos

Right: Kevin Spacey, Bethel Leslie, Peter Gallagher, Jack Lemmon

Peter Gallagher, Jack Lemmon
Above: Bethel Leslie, Jodie Lynne McClintock

Jack Lemmon

THE HOUSE OF BLUE LEAVES

By John Guare; Music and Lyrics, John Guare; Director, Jerry Zaks; Sets, Tony Walton; Costumes, Ann Roth; Lighting, Paul Gallo; Sound, Aural Fixation; Hairstylist, J. Roy Helland; Production Manager, Jeff Hamlin; General Manager, Steven C. Callahan; Presented by Lincoln Center Theater (Director, Gregory Mosher; Executive Producer, Bernard Gersten); Company Manager, Lynn Landis; Props, George T. Green; Wardrobe, Tony Karniewich; Piano music arranged and recorded by Rusty Magee; Stage Managers, Kate Stewart, Peter J. Downing; Press, Merle Debuskey, Robert Larkin. Opened in Lincoln Center's Vivian Beaumont Theater on Tuesday, April 29, 1986.*

CAST

Artie Shaughnessy	John Mahoney†1
El Dorado Bartenders	Ian Blackman, Peter J. Downing
Ronnie Shaughnessy	Ben Stiller
Bunny Flingus	Stockard Channing†2
Bananas Shaughnessy	Swoosie Kurtz
Corrinna Stroller	Julie Hagerty†3
Head Nun	Patricia Falkenhain
Second Nun	Jane Cecil
Little Nun	Ann Talman
M.P.	Ian Blackman
The White Man	Peter J. Downing
Billy Einhorn	Danny Aiello†4

UNDERSTUDIES: Ian Blackman (Ronnie), Peter J. Downing (M.P.), Brian Evers (Artie/Billy/White Man), Jane Cecil (Head Nun), Kathleen McKiernan (Bananas/2nd Nun/Little Nun), Melodie Somers (Bunny/Corrinna)

The action takes place in the El Dorado Bar and Grill and in an apartment in Sunnyside, Queens, New York, on October 4, 1965.

*Still playing May 31, 1986. 1986 Tonys were awarded for Best Featured Actor and Actress in a Play to John Mahoney and Swoosie Kurtz, Best Scenic Design, and Best Direction of a Play. It was first produced Off Broadway at the Truck and Warehouse Theatre on Feb. 10, 1971 and ran for 337 performances, and was revived Feb. 28, 1986 at the Off Broadway Newhouse Theater before moving to the Beaumont. †Succeeded by: 1. Jack Wallace, 2. Christine Baranski, 3. Patricia Clarkson, Faye Grant, 4. Mike Nussbaum

Brigitte Lacombe Photos

**Top Right: Swoosie Kurtz, Julie Hagerty,
John Mahoney, Stockard Channing
Below: Swoosie Kurtz, John Mahoney**

Julie Hagerty, John Mahoney

Stockard Channing, John Mahoney

THE BOYS IN AUTUMN

By Bernard Sabath; Director, Theodore Mann; Scenery, Michael Miller; Lighting, Richard Nelson; Costumes, Jennifer von Mayrhauser; Incidental Music, Bob Israel, Paul Epstein; Presented by Circle in the Square Theatre; Company Manager, William Conn; Props, Frank Hauser; Wardrobe, Claire Libin; Stage Managers, Michael F. Ritchie, Carol Klein; Press, Merle Debuskey, William Schelble. Opened in the Circle in the Square Theatre on Wednesday, April 30, 1986.*

CAST

Henry Finnegan, an older man .... George C. Scott
Thomas Gray, his friend of long ago .... John Cullum

UNDERSTUDIES: William Cain (Henry), William Hardy (Thomas)

A play in two acts. The action takes place on the front porch and in the yard of a house on a bluff overlooking the river outside the town of Hannibal, Missouri, on a sunny September afternoon in the early 1920's.

*Closed June 29, 1986 after 70 performances and 21 previews.

Martha Swope Photos

Left: John Cullum, George C. Scott

George C. Scott, John Cullum

BROADWAY PRODUCTIONS FROM PAST SEASONS
THAT PLAYED THROUGH THIS SEASON

A CHORUS LINE

Conceived, Choreographed and Directed by Michael Bennett; Book, James Kirkwood, Nicholas Dante; Music, Marvin Hamlisch; Lyrics, Edward Kleban; A New York Shakespeare Festival production presented by Joseph Papp in association with Plum Productions; Co-Choreographer, Bob Avian; Musical Direction/Vocal Arrangements, Don Pippin; Associate Producer, Bernard Gersten; Set, Robin Wagner; Costumes, Theoni V. Aldredge; Lighting, Tharon Musser; Sound, Abe Jacobs; Music Coordinator, Robert Thomas; Orchestrations, Bill Byers, Hershy Kay, Jonathan Tunick; Assistant to Choreographers, Baayork Lee; Musical Director, Robert Rogers; Wardrobe, Alyce Gilbert; Production Supervisor, Jason Steven Cohen; Original Cast Album by Columbia Records; General Manager, Laurel Ann Wilson; Company Manager, Bob MacDonald, Mitchell Weiss; Musical Conductor, Alphonse Stephenson; Stage Managers, Tom Porter, Morris Freed, Ronald Stafford, Robert Amirante; Press, Merle Debuskey, William Schelble, Richard Kornberg. Opened in the Shubert Theatre on Friday, July 25, 1975.*

CAST

Roy	Evan Pappas†1
Kristine	Kerry Casserly
Sheila	Susan Danielle
Mike	J. Richard Hart†2
Val	Mitzi Hamilton†3
Butch	Roscoe Gilliam†4
Larry	Jim Litten†5
Maggie	Pam Klinger
Richie	Gordon Owens
Tricia	Robin Lyon
Rom	Frank Kliegel
Zach	Eivind Harum†6
Mark	Chris Marshall†7
Cassie	Wanda Richert
Judy	Melissa Randel†8
Lois	Laurie Gamache†9
Don	Michael Danek
Bebe	Pamela Ann Wilson†10
Connie	Sachi Shimizu
Diana	Loida Santos†11
Al	Buddy Balou'†12
Frank	Fraser Ellis
Greg	Danny Weathers†13
Bobby	Ron Kurowski
Paul	Wayne Meledandri
Vicki	Cynthia Fleming†14
Ed	Morris Freed
Jarad	Troy Garza
Linda	Laureen Valuch Piper
Douglas	Tommy Re†15
Herman (formerly Ralph)	Bradley Jones†16
Hilary	Roxann Cabalero†17

UNDERSTUDIES: Robert Amirante (Greg/Zach), Roxann Cabalero (Connie), Gary Chryst (Paul/Larry), Karen Curlee (Maggie/Bebe/Diana/Kristine), Michael Danek (Zach), Michael-Pierre Dean (Richie), Fraser Ellis (Mark/Bobby/Don), Cynthia Fleming (Cassie/Sheila/Kristine/Judy), Morris Freed (Mark), Troy Garza (Mike/Greg/Paul/Larry/Al), J. Richard Hart (Zach/Mike), Angelique Ilo (Cassie), Frank Kleigel (Don/Zach/Bobby), Robin Lyon (Bebe/Diana/Val/Maggie), Laureen Valuch Piper (Sheila/Val), Trish Ramish (Kristine), Tommy Re (Greg/Al/Larry/Mike), Tracy Shayne (Diana/Maggie/Connie)

MUSICAL NUMBERS: I Hope I Get It, I Can Do That, And . . ., At the Ballet, Sing!, Hello 12 Hello 13 Hello Love, Nothing, Dance 10 Looks 3, The Music and the Mirror, One, The Tap Combination, What I Did for Love, Finale

A musical performed without intermission. The action takes place in 1975 during an audition in the theatre.
*Still playing May 31, 1986. Cited as Best 1975 Musical by NY Drama Critics Circle, winner of 1976 Pulitzer Prize, and 1976 Tonys for Best Musical, Best Book, Best Score, Best Direction, Best Lighting, Best Choreography, Best Musical Actress (Donna McKechnie), Beast Featured Actor and Actress in a Musical (Sammy Williams, Kelly Bishop), and a Special Theatre World Award was presented to each member of the creative staff and original cast. See Theatre World Vol. 31. On Thursday, Sept. 29, 1983 it became the longest running show in Broadway history.

†Succeeded by: 1. Tommy Re, 2. Danny Herman, Charles McGowan, Mark Bove, 3. DeLyse Lively-Mekka, 4. Michael-Pierre Dean, 5. Danny Herman, J. Richard Hart, 6. Robert LuPone, Eivind Harum, 7. Gib Jones, 8. Angelique Ilo, 9. Cynthia Fleming, 10. Tracy Shayne, 11. Roxann Cabalero, Gay Marshall, Roxann Cabalero, 12. Mark Bove, Kevin Neil McCready, 13. Bradley Jones, 14. Trish Ramish, 15. Evan Pappas, Gary Chryst, 16. Robert Amirante, 17. Tracy Shayne, Karen Curlee

**Gordon Owens Above: Wayne Meledandri
Top: Gay Marshall (center)**

Martha Swope Photos

45

BIG RIVER

Music and Lyrics, Roger Miller; Book, William Hauptman; Adapted from "The Adventures of Huckleberry Finn" by Mark Twain; Scenery, Heidi Landesman; Costumes, Patricia McGourty; Lighting, Richard Riddell; Sound, Otts Munderloh; Musical Supervision, Danny Troob; Orchestrations, Steven Margoshes, Danny Troob; Dance and Incidental Music, John Richard Lewis; Musical Direction/Vocal Arrangements, Linda Twine; Staged by Des McAnuff; Choreography, Janet Watson; Stage Movement/Fights, B. H. Barry; Casting, Stanley Sable/Jason LaPadura; General Management, David Strong Warner; Sound Effects, John Kilgore; Hairstylist, Angela Gari; Presented by Rocco Landesman, Heidi Landesman, Rick Steiner, M. Anthony Fisher, Dodger Productions; Associate Producers, Arthur Katz, Emily Landau, Fred Mayerson, TM Productions; Company Managers, Sandra Carlson, Jill Hurwitz; Assistant Conductor, Kenneth Kosek; Props, Richard Patria, Michael Fedigan; Wardrobe, Joseph Busheme; Production Assistant, Chris Fielder; Associate Scenic Designer, Bob Shaw. Stage Managers, Frank Hartenstein, Peter Glazer, Marianne Cane, Neal Jones; Press, Solters/Roskin/Friedman, Joshua Ellis, Adrian Bryan-Brown, Jim Sapp, Cindy Valk, Jackie Green, Bill Shuttleworth. Opened in the Eugene O'Neill Theatre on Thursday, April 25, 1985.*

CAST

Mark Twain	Gordon Connell
Huckleberry Finn	Daniel Jenkins†1
Widow Douglas/Sally Phelps	Susan Browning
Miss Watson/Harmonia Player	Evalyn Baron†2
Jim	Ron Richardson†3
Tom Sawyer	John Short†4
Ben Rogers/Hank/Young Fool	William Youmans†5
Jo Harper/Joanna Wilkes	Andi Henig
Simon	Aramis Estevez
Dick/Andy/Man in crowd/Hiredhand	Michael Brian
Pap Finn/Sheriff Bell	John Goodman†6
Judge Thatcher/Harvey Wilkes/Silas Phelps	Ralph Byers
The King	Bob Gunton
The Duke	Rene Auberjonois†7
Lafe/Counselor Robinson/Hiredhand	Reathel Bean†8
Mary Jane Wilkes	Patti Cohenour†9
Susan Wilkes	Peggy Harmon
Bill, a servant	Franz Jones
Alice, a slave	Carol Dennis†10
Alice's Daughter	Jennifer Leigh Warren

UNDERSTUDIES: Romain Fruge (Huck/Ensemble), Susan Glaze (Ensemble), Elmore James†11, Neal Jones (Huck/Ensemble), Linda Kerns (Ensemble), William McClary (King/Duke/Ensemble), George Merritt (Jim/Ensemble), Yvonne Over (Ensemble), Robert Sevra (King/Ensemble).

MUSICAL NUMBERS: Do Ya Wanna Go to Heaven?, The Boys, Waitin' for the Light to Shine, Guv'ment, Hand for the Hog, I Huckleberry Me, Muddy Water, The Crossing, River in the Rain, When the Sun Goes Down in the South, The Royal Nonesuch, Worlds Apart, Arkansas, How Blest We Are, You Oughta Be Here with Me, Leavin's Not the Only Way to Go, Free at Last, Finale

A musical in two acts. The action takes place along the Mississippi River Valley, sometime in the 1840's.

*Still playing May 31, 1986. Received 1985 Tony Awards for Best Musical, Book, Score, Director, Scenic Design, Lighting Design, and Featured Actor in a Musical (Ron Richardson).

†Succeeded by: 1. Martin Moran, 2. Karen Looze, 3. Larry Riley, 4. Clint Allen, 5. Patrick Breen, Russ Jolly, 6. Leo Murmester, John Connolly, 7. Brent Spiner, Ken Jenkins, 8. Gary Holcombe, 9. Karla DeVito, Patti Cohenour, Marin Mazzie, 10. Carol Woods, 11. Harry L. Burney III

Martha Swope Photos

Top Left: Larry Riley, Daniel Jenkins

Marin Mazzie, Larry Riley, Martin Moran

BILOXI BLUES

By Neil Simon; Director, Gene Saks; Presented by Emanuel Azenberg in association with Center Theatre Group/Ahmanson Theatre of Los Angeles; Setting, David Mitchell; Costumes, Ann Roth; Lighting, Tharon Musser; Sound, Tom Moore; Casting, Meg Simon/Fran Kumin; General Manager, Robert Kamlot; Technical Supervision, Arthur Siccardi, Peter Feller; Props, John Wright, Jan Marasek; Manager, Leslie Butler; Wardrobe, John Guiteras; Stage Managers, Charles Blackwell, Henry Velez, Joyce O'Brien; Press, Bill Evans, Sandra Manley, Jim Baldassare, Leslie Anderson. Opened in the Neil Simon Theatre on Thursday, March 28, 1985.*

CAST

Roy Selridge	Brian Tarantina†1
Joseph Wykowski	Matt Mulhern†2
Don Carney	Alan Ruck†3
Eugene Morris Jerome	Matthew Broderick†4
Arnold Epstein	Barry Miller†5
Sgt. Merwin J. Toomey	Bill Sadler
James Hennesey	Geoffrey Sharp
Rowena	Randall Edwards
Daisy Hannigan	Penelope Ann Miller†6

STANDBYS: Adam Silbar (Eugene), John Linton (Selridge/Wykowski), Jay Rubenstein (Epstein), Karen Sellon (Daisy), Jon Tenney (Eugene/Carney/Hennesy), Joan Goodfellow (Rowena)

A play in 2 acts and 14 scenes. The action takes place during 1943 in Biloxi and Gulfport, Ms.

*Closed June 29, 1986 after 524 performances and 12 previews. Recipient of 1985 Tonys for Best Play, Best Direction, and Barry Miller received a Tony for Best Featured Actor in a Play, a Drama Desk and Theatre World Awards.

†Succeeded by: 1. Mark McDermott, 2. James Shanta, 3. Jim Fyfe, 4. Geoffrey Sharp, Bruce Norris, William Radsdale, Zach Galligan, Jonathan Silverman, 5. Mark Nelson, 6. Lisa Waltz

Martha Swope Photos

Top: Matthew Broderick, Randall Edwards
Right: Zach Galligan

Jonathan Silverman

47

CATS

Based on "Old Possum's Book of Practical Cats" by T. S. Eliot; Additional Lyrics, Trevor Nunn, Richard Stilgoe; Music, Andrew Lloyd Webber; Director, Trevor Nunn; Associate Director/Choreographer, Gillian Lynne; Presented by Cameron Mackintosh, The Really Useful Company, David Geffen, The Shubert Organization; Executive Producers, R. Tyler Gatchell, Jr., Peter Neufeld; Design, John Napier; Lighting, David Hersey; Sound, Martin Levan; Musical Director, Rene Wiegert; Production Musical Director, Stanley Lebowsky; Casting, Johnson-Liff; Orchestrations, David Cullen, Andrew Lloyd Webber; Original Cast Album by Geffen Records; Company Manager, James G. Mennen; General Management, Gatchell & Neufeld; Associate Musical Directors, Keith Herrmann, Kevin Farrell, Bill Grossman; Production Assistant, Nancy Hall Bell; Wardrobe, Adelaide Laurino, Rachele Bussanich; Makeup, Candace Carell; Hairstylists, Leon Gagliardi, Frank Paul, Geordie Sheffer, Michael Wasula; Wigs, Paul Huntley; Production Supervisor, David Taylor; Dance Supervisor, T. Michael Reed; Assistant Choreographer, Jo-Anne Robinson; Stage Managers, Jeff Lee, Sally J. Jacobs; Assistant Conductor, Arthur M. Greene; Technical Supervisors, Theatre Services; Props, George Green, Jr., Merlyn Davis; Press, Fred Nathan, Marc P. Thibodeau, Anne Abrams, Merle Frimark, Dennis Crowley, Bert Fink, Philip Rinaldi, Larry Reitzer. Opened in the Winter Garden Theatre on Thursday, October 7, 1982.*

CAST

Alonzo	Brian Sutherland
Bustopher Jones/Asparagus/Growltiger	Timothy Jerome†1
Bombalurina	Marlene Danielle
Carbucketty	Steven Gelfer
Cassandra	Charlotte d'Amboise†2
Coricopat/Mungojerrie	Joe Antony Cavise
Demeter	Jane Bodle
Etcetera/Rumpleteazer	Paige Dana
Grizabella	Laurie Beechman
Jellylorum/Griddlebone	Bonnie Simmons
Jennyanydots	Anna McNeely
Mistoffolees	Herman W. Sebek†3
Munkustrap	Claude R. Tessier
Old Deuteronomy	Kevin Marcum†4
Plato/Macavity/Rumpus Cat	Brian Andrews†5
Pouncival	Ramon Galindo†6
Rum Tum Tugger	Terrence V. Mann†7
Sillabub	Denise DiRenzo
Skimbleshanks	Michael Scott Gregory†8
Tantomile	Sundy Leigh Leake
Tumblebrutus	Jay Poindexter
Victoria	Valerie C. Wright†9

CATS CHORUS: Susan Powers, Joel Robertson, Erick Devine†10, Colleen Fitzpatrick†11

STANDBYS & UNDERSTUDIES: Alonzo (Brian Andrews/Rene Clemente/Jack Magradey), Bustopher/Asparagus/Growltiger (Joel Robertson/Claude R. Tessier), Bombalurina (Nora Brennan/Roberta Stiehm), Carbucketty (Brian Andrews/Steven Hack/Marc Hunter/Jack Magradey), Cassandra (Nora Brennan/Roberta Stiehm/Lily-Lee Wong), Coricopat/Mungjerrie (Rene Clemente/Steven Hack/Marc Hunter/Jack Magradey), Demeter (Denise DiRenzo/Roberta Stiehm), Etcetera/Rumpleteazer (Jane Bodle/Denise DiRenzo/Dodie Pettit/Lily-Lee Wong), Grizabella (Denise DiRenzo/Brenda Pressley), Jellylorum/Griddlebone (Dodie Pettit/Susan Powers), Jennyanydots (Dodie Pettit/Susan Powers), Mistoffelees (Joe Antony Cavise/Rene Clemente, Robert Montano), Munkustrap (Steve Barton/Jack Magradey/Brian Sutherland), Old Deuteronomy (Bill Nolte), Plato/Macavity/Rumpus Cat (Brian Andrews/Brian Sutherland), Pouncival (Steven Hack/Brian Andrews), Rum Tum Tugger (Marc Hunter/Jack Magradey/Jamie Patterson/Claude R. Tessier), Sillabub (Jane Bodle/Dodie Pettit/Lily-Lee Wong), Skimbleshanks (Marc Hunter/Jack Magradey), Tantomile (Jane Bodle/Denise DiRenzo/Nora Brennan/Roberta Stiehm/Lily-Lee Wong), Tumblebrutus (Brian Andrews/Steven Hack), Victoria (Paige Dana/Dodie Pettit/Lily-Lee Wong)

MUSICAL NUMBERS: Jellicle Songs for Jellicle Cats, The Naming of the Cats, Invitation to the Jellicle Ball, The Old Gumbie Cat, Rum Tum Tugger, Grizabella the Glamour Cat, Bustopher Jones, Mungojerri and Rumpleteazer, Old Deuteronomy, The Awfull Battle of the Pekes and Pollicles, The Marching Songs of the Pollicle Dogs, The Jellicle Ball, Memory, Moments of Happiness, Gus the Theatre Cat, Growltiger's Last Stand, Skimbleshanks, Macavity, Mr. Mistoffelees, The Journey to the Heaviside Layer, Ad-dressing of Cats.

A musical in 2 acts and 21 scenes.

*Still playing May 31, 1986. Winner of 1983 Tonys for Best Musical, Best Book, Best Score, Best Direction, Best Supporting Musical Actress (Betty Buckley as Grizabella), Best Costumes, Best Lighting. For original production, see THEATRE WORLD Vol. 39.

†Succeeded by: 1. Gregg Edelman, 2. Jessica Northrop, 3. Herman W. Sebek, Jamie Torcellini, Herman W. Sebek, Michael Scott Gregory, Barry K. Bernal, 4. Clent Bowers, 5. Jamie Patterson, 6. Robert Montano, 7. Rick Sparks, 8. Robert Burnett, 9. Claudia Shell, 10. Bill Nolte, 11. Brenda Pressley

The Company Above: Laurie Beechman
Top: Rick Sparks

Martha Swope Photos

42nd STREET

Music, Harry Warren; Lyrics, Al Dubin; Book, Michael Stewart, Mark Bramble from novel by Bradford Ropes; Direction/Choreography, Gower Champion; Scenery, Robin Wagner; Costumes, Theoni V. Aldredge; Lighting, Tharon Musser; Presented by David Merrick; Musical Direction, Philip Fradkin, Eileen LaGrange; Orchestrations, Philip J. Lang; Dance Arrangements, Donald Johnston; Vocal Arrangements, John Lesko; Sound, Richard Fitzgerald; Hairstylist, Ted Azar; Casting, Feuer & Ritzer; Wardrobe, Elinor Harris, Gene Wilson; Props, Heather Herbert, Leo Herbert; Company Manager, Marcia Goldberg; General Manager, Leo K. Cohen; Assistant Musical Director, Bernie Leighton; Stage Managers, Jack Timmers, Harold Goldfaden, Janet Friedman, Dennis Angulo; Press, Solters/Roskin/Friedman, Cindy Valk, Joshua Ellis, Adrian Bryan-Brown, Jim Sapp, Jackie Green, Bill Shuttleworth. Opened in the Winter Garden Theatre on Monday, August 25, 1980, and moved to the Majestic Theatre on Monday, March 30, 1981.*

CAST

Andy Lee	Danny Carroll
Oscar	Robert Colston
Mac/Thug/Doctor	Stan Page
Annie	Beth Leavel
Maggie Jones	Peggy Cass†1
Bert Barry	Joseph Bova
Billy Lawlor	Lee Roy Reams
Peggy Sawyer	Clare Leach
Lorraine	Marla Singer†2
Phyllis	Jeri Kansas
Julian Marsh	Don Chastain†3
Dorothy Brock	Millicent Martin†4
Abner Dillon	Stan Page†5
Pat Denning	Steve Elmore
Thugs	Stan Page, Ron Schwinn
Doctor	Bill Nabel†6

ENSEMBLE: Diane Abrams, Dennis Angulo, Carole Banninger, Dennis Batutis, Jeffrey Cornell, Ronny DeVito, Rob Draper, Carla Earle, Brandt Edwards, Judy Ehrlich, Cathy Greco, Elisa Heinsohn, Suzie Jary, Jeri Kansas, Billye Kersey, Karen Klump, Neva Leigh, Mia Malm, Maureen Mellon, Gwendolyn Miller, Ken Mitchell, Bill Nabel, Don Percassi, Brenda Pipik, Rosemary Rado, Michael Ricardo, Lars Rosager, Linda Sabatelli, Ron Schwinn, Pamela S. Scott, Yveline Semeria, J. Thomas Smith, Karen Sorensen, Michael Steuber, Susanne Leslie Sullivan, Vickie Taylor, Mary Chris Wall

UNDERSTUDIES & STANDBYS: Connie Day (Dorothy/Maggie), Karen Sorensen (Dorothy), Beth Leavel (Maggie), Steve Elmore/Stan Page (Julian), Vickie Taylor/Debra Ann Draper (Peggy), Rob Draper/Dennis Angulo (Billy), Bill Nabel/Ron Schwinn (Mac), Bernie Leighton (Oscar), Lizzie Moran/Debra Ann Draper (Phyllis/Lorraine), Ensemble: Debra Ann Draper, Lizzie Moran, Brenda Pipik, Dennis Angulo, Doug Okersin

A musical in 2 acts and 16 scenes. The action takes place during 1933 in New York City and Philadelphia.

*Still playing May 31, 1986. Recipient of 1981 Tonys for Best Musical, Best Choreography. For original production see THEATRE WORLD Vol. 37.

†Succeeded by: 1. Marie Lillo, 2. Neva Leigh, 3. Jamie Ross, Barry Nelson, 4. Louise Troy, Dolores Gray, 5. Don Crabtree, 6. Stan Page

Martha Swope Photos

Top Left: Dolores Gray, Barry Nelson

Lee Roy Reams (C)

LA CAGE AUX FOLLES

Music and Lyrics, Jerry Herman; Book, Harvey Fierstein; Based on play of same title by Jean Poiret; Director, Arthur Laurents; Choreography, Scott Salmon; Presented by Allan Carr with Kenneth D. Greenblatt, Stewart F. Lane, James M. Nederlander, Martin Richards; Executive Producers, Barry Brown, Fritz Holt, Marvin A. Krauss; Scenery, David Mitchell; Costumes, Theoni V. Aldredge; Lighting, Jules Fisher; Musical Director/Vocal Arranger, Donald Pippin; Sound, Peter J. Fitzgerald; Hairstylist/Makeup, Ted Azar; Orchestrations, Jim Tyler; Dance Music Arrangements, G. Harrell; Assistant Choreographer, Richard Balestrino; Produced in association with Jonathan Farkas, John Pomerantz, Martin Heinfling; Casting, Stuart Howard; Original Cast Album by RCA; General Management, Marvin A. Krauss; Company Manager, Nina Skriloff; Props, Charles Zuckerman, Jack Cennamo, Tom Thomson; Wardrobe, Gayle Patton, Irene Bunis; Assistant Conductor, Rudolph Bennett; Stage Managers, James Pentecost, David Caine, Jay Adler; Press, Shirley Herz, Peter Cromarty, Pete Sanders, Glenna Freedman, David Roggensack. Opened in the Palace Theatre on Sunday, August 21, 1983.*

CAST

Georges	Van Johnson[1]
Les Cagelles:	
Chantal	Frank DiPasquale
Monique	Dennis Callahan
Dermah	K. Craig Innes[2]
Nicole	Eric Underwood[3]
Hanna	David Engel
Mercedes	David Evans
Bitelle	Linda Haberman[4]
Lo Singh	David Klatt[5]
Odette	Dan O'Grady
Angelique	Deborah Phelan[6]
Phaedra	David Scala
Clo-Clo	Sam Singhaus
Francis	Brian Kelly[7]
Jacob	Pi Douglass[8]
Albin	Walter Charles
Jean-Michel	John Weiner
Anne	Jennifer Smith[9]
Jacqueline	Elizabeth Parrish
Renaud	Jack Davison
Mme. Renaud	Sydney Anderson
Paulette	Betsy Craig
Hercule	Jack Neubeck
Etienne	Jay Pierce
Babette	Marie Santell
Colette	Pamela Cecil
Tabarro	Mark Waldrop
Pepe	Thom Sesma[10]
Edouard Dindon	Jay Garner
Mme. Dindon	Merle Louise

STANDBYS & UNDERSTUDIES: Jack Davison (Albin/Dindon), David Jackson (Jacob), Drew Geraci (Jean-Michel/Hercule/Photographer/Tabarro/Chantal/Hanna/Mercedes/Dermah), Jan Leigh Herndon (Anne/Mme. Renaud/Paulette/Babette/Colette/Angelique), Betsy Craig (Mme. Dindon), Sydney Anderson (Jacqueline), Frank DiPasquale (Francis), David Klatt (Etienne/Pepe/Phaedra)

MUSICAL NUMBERS: We Are What We Are, A Little More Mascara, With Anne on My Arm, The Promenade, Song on the Sand, La Cage aux Folles, I Am What I Am, Masculinity, Look over There, Cocktail Counterpoint, The Best of Times, Finale

A musical in two acts. The action takes place during summer in St. Tropez, France, at the present time.

*Still playing May 31, 1986 (1161 performances). Winner of 1984 Tonys for Best Musical, Musical Book, Musical Score, Outstanding Actor (George Hearn) in a Musical, Outstanding Direction, Costumes.

†Succeeded by: 1. Steeve Arlen, 2. Kyle White, 3. John Dolf, 4. Lynn Faro, 5. Eric Lamp. 6. Shannon Lee Jones, 7. Robert Brubach, 8. Darrell Carey, 9. Juliette Kurth, 10. David Jackson

Martha Swope Photos

Top Left: Les Cagelles
Below: Walter Charles

Les Cagelles

OH! CALCUTTA!

Devised by Kenneth Tynan; Conceived and Directed by Jacques Levy; Presented by Hillard Elkins, Norman Kean; Production Supervisor, Ron Nash; Authors and Composers, Robert Benton, David Newman, Jules Feiffer, Dan Greenburg, Lenore Kandel, John Lennon, Jacques Levy, Leonard Melfi, Sam Shepard, Clovis Trouille, Kenneth Tynan, Sherman Yellen; Music and Lyrics, Robert Dennis, Peter Schickle, Stanley Walden, Jacques Levy; Choreography, Margo Sappington; Musical Director, Stanley Walden; Music Conductor, Tim Weil; Scenery/Lighting, Harry Silverglat Darrow; Costumes, Kenneth M. Yount; Sound, Sander Hacker; Assistant to Director, Nancy Tribush; Projected Media Design, Gardner Compton; Live Action Film, Ron Merk; Company Manager, Doris J. Buberl; Producer, Norman Kean; Production Associates, Karen Nagle, Nancy Genuardi; Assistant General Manager, Tobias Beckwith; Assistant Musical Conductor, Dan Carter; Wardrobe, Mark Bridges; Stage Managers, Maria DiDia, Ron Nash; Press, Les Schecter. Opened at the Eden Theatre on Friday, June 17, 1969, and at the Edison Theatre on Friday, September 24, 1976.*

CAST

Deborah Robertson	Michael A. Clarke
Nannette Bevelander[1]	Charles E. Gerber[2]
Cheryl Hartley	David Heisey
Jodi Johnson	James E. Mosiej

Succeeded by: 1. Vivian Paxton, 2. Charles Klausmeyer

MUSICAL NUMBERS & SKITS: Taking Off the Robe, Will Answer All Sincere Replies, Playin', Jack and Jill, The Paintings of Clovis Trouille, Much Too Soon, Dance for George, Delicious Indignities, Was It Good for You Too?, Suite for Five Letters, One on One, Clarence, Rock Garden, Spread Your Love Around, Love Lust Poem, Four in Hand, Coming Together Going Together

An "erotic musical" in two acts.

*Still playing May 31, 1986. For original production, see THEATRE WORLD Vol. 33.

Top Left: Jodi Johnson, David Heisey,
Deborah Robertson, Charles Klausmeyer,
Nannette Bevelander Below: (back) Michael A. Clarke,
David Heisey, Charles Klausmeyer, (front)
Deborah Robertson, James E. Mosiej, Jodi Johnson, Cheryl
Hartley, Nannette Bevelander
Ron Nash, Martha Swope Photos

BROADWAY PRODUCTIONS FROM PAST SEASONS THAT CLOSED DURING THIS SEASON

Title	Opened	Closed	Performances
Arms and the Man	5/9/85	9/1/85	109
As Is	5/1/85	1/4/86	285
Brighton Beach Memoirs	3/27/83	5/11/86	1299
Doubles	5/8/85	1/4/86	277
Dreamgirls	12/20/81	8/4/85	1521
Sunday in the Park with George	5/2/84	10/13/85	604

OFF-BROADWAY PRODUCTIONS FROM PAST SEASONS THAT PLAYED THROUGH THIS SEASON

THE FANTASTICKS

Book and Lyrics, Tom Jones; Music, Harvey Schmidt; Suggested by Edmund Rostand's play "Les Romanesques"; Presented by Lore Noto; Director, Word Baker; Original Musical Direction/Arrangements, Julian Stein; Designed by Ed Wittstein; Associate Producers, Sheldon Baron, Dorothy Olim, Robert Alan Gold; Assistant Producers, Bill Mills, Thad Noto; Original Cast Album by MGM or Polydor Records; Production Assistant, John Krug; Stage Managers, Geoffrey Brown, James Cook, Jim Charles, Paul Blankenship; Press, Tony Noto. Opened in the Sullivan Street Playhouse on Tuesday, May 3, 1960.*

CAST

The Narrator .... Dennis Parlato[1]
The Girl .... Karen Culliver[2]
The Boy .... Bill Perlach
The Boy's Father .... Lore Noto[3]
The Girl's Father .... William Tost
The Old Actor .... Bryan Hull
The Man Who Dies/Indian .... Robert R. Oliver
The Mute .... Kim Moore[4]
At the piano .... Dorothy Martin
At the harp .... Elizabeth Etters
Understudies: Paul Blankenship (Narrator/Boy), Virginia Gregory (Girl), William Tost (Boy's Father)

MUSICAL NUMBERS: Overture, Try to Remember, Much More, Metaphor, Never Say No, It Depends on What You Pay, Soon It's Gonna Rain, Rape Ballet, Happy Ending, This Plum Is Too Ripe, I Can See It, Plant a Radish, Round and Round, They Were You

*The world's longest running musical was still playing May 31, 1986, after 10,864 performances.

[†]Succeeded by: 1. George Lee Andrews, 2. Jennifer Lee Andrews, 3. George Riddle, 4. Paul Blankenship

Lou Manna Photos

George Lee Andrews, Jennifer Lee Andrews
Top Right: Lore Noto

FORBIDDEN BROADWAY

Concept and Lyrics, Gerard Alessandrini; Director, Mr. Alessandrini; Presented by Playkill Productions (Sella Palsson, Executive Producer); Costumes, Chet Ferris; Music Supervisor, Fred Barton; General Manager, Elizabeth Hermann; Original Cast Album on drg records; Press, Becky Flora. Opened in Palsson's on Friday, January 15, 1982, and still playing May 31, 1986.

CAST

Roxie Lucas
Mark Martino
Mark Mitchell
Susan Terry
Craig Wells

A musical satire in two acts.

Henry Grossman Photos

Right: Mark Martino, Roxie Lucas, Craig Wells, Susan Terry

Roxie Lucas, Mark Martino, Susan Terry, Craig Wells (kneeling)

Roxie Lucas, Craig Wells, Mark Martino

THE FOREIGNER

By Larry Shue; Director, Jerry Zaks; Set, Karen Schulz; Costumes, Rita Ryack; Lighting, Paul Gallo; Sound, Aural Fixation; Casting, Deborah Brown; Assistant to Director, Dani Klein; Props, Karen McDuffee, Sara Gormley Plass; Wardrobe, Eileen Miller, Patricia White; Dialogue Coach, Arden Sampson; Stage Managers, George Darveris, Chet Leaming; Presented by John A. McQuiggan; Associate Producers, Douglas M. Lawson, Maxey R. Grossenbacher, Gina Rogak, Melanie Massey; Company Manager, Jean Spence; General Management, New Roads Productions; Props, Matthew Silver; Press, Henry Luhrman, Terry M. Lilly, Andrew P. Shearer, David Mayhew. Opened in the Astor Place Theatre on Thursday, November 1, 1984.*

CAST

"Froggy" LeSueur ....Larry Shue†1
Charlie Baker .... Anthony Heald†2
Betty Meeks .... Sudie Bond†3
Rev. David Marshall Lee ....Robert Schenkkan†4
Catherine Simms ....Patricia Kalember†5
Owen Musser ....Christopher Curry†6
Ellard Simms ....Kevin Geer†7

UNDERSTUDIES: Chet Leaming (Froggy/Owen), Rick Meyer (Rev./Simms), Anita Bayless (Betty), Cheryl Norris (Catherine Simms), Eric Tull (Charlie)

A comedy in 2 acts and 4 scenes. The action takes place in the recent past in Betty Meeks' Fishing Lodge Resort, Tilghman County, Georgia, U.S.A.

†Succeeded by: 1. Ian Trigger, Ian Stuart, 2. Larry Shue, Jack Gilpin, Eric Tull, Jeff Brooks, 3. Kathleen Claypool, 4. Alan Brooks, 5. Breon Gorman, Jacqueline Schultz, Deborah Coles, 6. Howard Sherman, Christopher Curry, Dave Florek, 7. Rick Lawless

*Closed June 8, 1986 after 686 performances and 16 previews. For original production, see *Theatre World* Vol. 41.

Bill Pierce, Van Williams Photos
Top: Anthony Heald, Kevin Geer
Below: Alan Brooks, Jacqueline Schultz

Howard Sherman, Jack Gilpin Top: Christopher Curry, Jack Gilpin, Alan Brooks

LITTLE SHOP OF HORRORS

Book and Lyrics, Howard Ashman; Music, Alan Menken; Based on film of same title by Roger Corman with Screenplay by Charles Griffith; Director, Howard Ashman; Musical Staging, Edie Cowan; Set, Edward T. Gianfrancesco; Lighting, Craig Evans; Costumes, Sally Lesser; Sound, Otts Munderloh; Puppets, Martin P. Robinson; Vocal Arrangements/Musical Supervision, Robert Billig; Orchestrations, Robby Merkin; Originally produced by WPA Theatre; General Manager, Albert Poland; Company Manager, Nancy Nagel Gibbs; Props, Van Farrier; Wardrobe, Craig Aspden, James Durso; Wigs/Makeup, Lenora Brown; Stage Managers, Kate Pollock, Donna A. Drake; Presented by the WPA Theatre, David Geffen, Cameron Mackintosh, and the Shubert Organization; Original Cast Album by Geffen Records; Press, Milly Schoenbaum, Kevin Patterson, Meg Bloom. Opened in the Orpheum Theatre, Tuesday, July 27, 1982.*

CAST

Chiffon	Suzzanne Douglas†1
Crystal	Tena Wilson
Ronnette	Louise Robinson†2
Mushnik	Fyvush Finkel
Audrey	Eydie Alyson†3
Seymour	Andrew Hill Newman
Derelict	Lynn Hippen†4
Orin/Bernstein/Snip/Luce	Ken Land
Audrey II: Manipulation	Lynn Hippen†4
Voice	Ron Taylor

STANDBYS: Katherine Meloche (Audrey), Michael Pace (Seymour/Orin/Snip/Luce/Everyone Else/Audrey II Voice), Arn Weiner (Mushnik), William Szymanski (Derelict/Audrey II Manipulation), Nicky Rene (Chiffon/Crystal/Ronnette)

MUSICAL NUMBERS: Prologue (Little Shop of Horrors), Skid Row (Downtown), Da-Doo, Grow for Me, Don't It Go to Show You Never Know, Somewhere That's Green, Closed for Renovation, Dentist!, Mushnik & Son, Feed Me (Git It), Now (It's Just the Gas), Call Back in the Morning, Suddenly Seymour, The Meek Shall Inherit, Finale (Don't Feed the Plants)

A musical in two acts.

*Still playing May 31, 1986. Recipient of 1983 citation from NY Drama Critics Circle as Best Musical.

†Succeeded by: 1. Melodee Savage, 2. Deborah Dotson, 3. Annie Golden, Marsha Skaggs, 4. William Szymanski

Peter Cunningham Photos

Top Right: Audrey II

Fyvush Finkel, Marsha Skaggs, Andrew Hill Newman

Andrew Hill Newman, Marsha Skaggs

PENN & TELLER

Presented by Richard Frankel and Ivy Properties, Ltd.; Set, John Lee Beatty; Lighting, Dennis Parichy; Sound Supervision, Chuck London Media/Stewart Werner; General Management, Richard Frankel Productions; Company Manager, Patricia Butterfield; Technical Director, Gordon Huff; Props, Walter Johnsen; Production Supervisor, Art Wolff; Stage Manager, Marc Garland; Press, Solters/Roskin/Friedman, Cindy Valk, Josh Ellis, Adrian Bryan-Brown, Keith Sherman. Opened in the Westside Arts Theatre/Downstairs on Thursday, April 18, 1985, and still playing May 31, 1986.

CAST

Penn Jillette
Teller

"Two eccentric guys who have learned to do a few cool things" with one intermission.

Gerry Goodstein Photos

**Below: Teller, Penn Jillette
(also right)**

OFF-BROADWAY PRODUCTIONS FROM PAST SEASONS THAT CLOSED
DURING THIS SEASON

Title	Opened	Closed	Performances
Curse of the Starving Class	7/30/85	2/16/86	287
Fool for Love	5/18/83	9/29/85	1000
Hannah Senesh	4/10/85	8/18/85	161
Isn't It Romantic?	12/15/83	9/1/85	733
The Marriage of Bette and Boo	5/16/85	7/28/85	86
Mayor	5/13/85	10/21/85	198
The Mystery of Irma Vep	10/2/84	5/31/86	331
The Normal Heart	4/21/85	1/5/86	294
Orphans	5/7/85	1/5/86	285
3 Guys Naked from the Waist Down	2/5/85	6/30/85	160

OFF-BROADWAY PRODUCTIONS

(Theatre Off Park) June 4,–July 13, 1985 (36 performances), Sherwin M. Goldman, Westport Productions, Inc., and Theatre Off Park (Producing Director, Bertha Lewis; Artistic Director, Albert Harris) present:
THE LISBON TRAVIATA by Terrence McNally; Director, John Tillinger; Set, Philipp Jung; Lighting, Michael Orris Watson; Costumes, C. L. Hundley; Sound, Gary Harris, David Paupaw; Stage Managers, John M. Atherlay, Charlie Eisenberg; Technical Director, E. F. Morrill; Production Assistants, Rene Bucciarelli, Gideon Grossman, Lisa Romano, Tom Yewell; Press, Howard Atlee. CAST: Benjamin Hendrickson (Stephen), Seth Allen (Mendy), Steven Culp (Paul), Stephen Schnetzer (Mike). A play in two acts. The action takes place in Mendy's apartment, and Stephen and Mike's apartment, in the recent past.

(Judith Anderson Theatre) Wednesday June 5–23, 1985 (8 performances and 13 previews). The Threshold Theater Company (Artistic Directors: Pamela Billig, Eugene Brogyanyi) presents:
THE COST OF LIVING by Yves Jamiaque; Adaptation, George Gonneau, Norman Rose; Director, Pamela Caren Billig; Set, Eugene Brogyanyi; Lighting, Ron Burns; Sound, Sam Agar, Gary Paul Hermus, Bob Goldberg; Costumes, Anita D. Ellis; Stage Managers, D. C. Rosenberg, Arlene Mantek, Mimi Choen; Production Assistants: Nina Pleasants, Florence Barrett, Dan Van Pelt; Technical Director: Alan Moyer, Stephen Edelstein; Business Manager, Richard Seader; Press, Jeffrey Richards Associates. CAST: Robert Lansing (Alexander), Lloyd Battista (Leon), Carole Mailman (Virginia), Lucy Martin (Eleanor), Jack Anthony Rose (Nicky), Lois Wheeler (Melie). A play in two acts. The action takes place in the present, in Paris.

(Playhouse 91) June 5–23, 1985 (16 performances and 7 previews). Beacon Street Productions in association with Jerry Goralnick presents:
FOR SALE by Jeffrey Gurkoff; Director, Andrew Cadiff; Set, John Culbert; Lighting, Arden Fingerhut; Costumes, Tom McKinley; Sound, Bruce Ellman; Stage Managers: Bill McComb, David Felder; General Manager, Leonard A. Mulhern: Paul Matwiow, James Hannah; Props, Larry Palazzo; Press, Shirley Herz Associates: Peter Cromarty, David Roggensack, Pete Sanders, Gary Lawrence. CAST: Katherine Cortez (Joy Price), Ron Parady (Edgar Adams), Craig Wasson (Michael Price), Innes-Fergus McDade (Beverly Adams/Perspective Buyer), Josh Blake (Paperboy), Richard Grusin (Frank Dill), Wayne Tippit (Buzz Hawthorne), Judith Barcroft (Edie Hawthorne), John P. Connolly (Lou Grebey), Stephen C. Prutting (Mr. Guerrero/Fiske), Dave Florek (Ted Lake), Jerry Mayer (Beazely). Understudies: Stephen C. Prutting (Michael/Ted), Innes-Fergus McDade (Edie), Jerry Mayer (Buzz/Edgar), David Felder (Lou/Frank). A comedy in two acts. The action takes place on the first floor of an expensive suburban home.

(Joyce Theatre) Thursday, June 6–15, 1985 (12 performances and 3 previews). The Joyce Theatre Foundation, Inc. and Yale Repertory Theatre (Artistic Director, Lloyd Richards; Managing Director, Benjamin Mordecai) present The Yale Repertory Theatre Production of:
FAULKNER'S BICYCLE by Heather McDonald; Director, Julian Webber; Costumes, Scott Bradley; Set, Pamela Peterson; Lighting, Mary Louise Geiger; Sound, Ken Lewis; Projections, William B. Warfel; Stage Managers, Patrice Thomas, Tamara K. Heeschen; Press, Ellen Jacobs Associates. CAST: Kim Hunter (Mama), Cara Duff-MacCormick (Claire), Tessie Hogan (Jett), Addison Powell (Faulkner). Performed without intermission. The action takes place in Oxford, Ms., during the last year (1962) of William Faulkner's life.

(American Place Theatre) Thursday, June 6,–November 10, 1985 (181 performances and 14 previews). James Walsh, Lewis Allen, Martin Heinfling present:
I'M NOT RAPPAPORT by Herb Gardner; Director, Daniel Sullivan; Set, Tony Walton; Costumes, Robert Morgan; Lighting, Pat Collins; Fight Staging, B. H. Barry; General Manager, James Walsh; Stage Managers, Thomas A. Kelly, Charles Kindl; Company Manager, Stanley D. Silver; Technical Director, Robert Scales; Wardrobe Supervisor, Jenna Krempel; Press, Jeffrey Richards Associates; CAST: Judd Hirsch (Nat), Cleavon Little (Midge), Michael Tucker (Danforth), Liann Pattison (Laurie), Jace Alexander (Gilley), Cheryl Giannini succeeded by Carolyn Hurlburt (Clara), Ray Baker (Cowboy). Understudies: Salem Ludwig (Nat), William Hall, Jr. (Midge), Carolyn Hurlbert Succeeded by Mercedes Ruehl (Clara/Laurie), Tim Ransom (Gilley). A comedy in two acts. The action takes place at a bench near a path at the edge of the lake in Central Park, in early October, 1982. The production was transferred to Broadway. See Broadway Calendar.

**Seth Allen (standing),
Benjamin Hendrickson
in "The Lisbon Traviata"**
(Martha Swope Photo)

(Harold Clurman Theatre) Sunday, June 9,–30, 1985 (22 performances and 6 previews). West Dobson presents:
LADIES AND GENTLEMEN, JEROME KERN; Conceived and Directed by William E. Hunt; Set, James Wolk; Lighting, Dan Kotlowitz; Costumes, David P. Pearson; Choreography, Valarie Pettiford; Musical Director, Hank Levy; Stage Managers: Donald Christy, Frank Torren; Assistant Choreographer, Wynona Smith; Assistant Lighting Designer, Dan Kelley; General Manager, David Musselman; Production Assistant, Felipe A. Benitez; Press, Henry Luhrman Associates; CAST: Delores Hall, Michael Howell Deane, Louise Edeiken, Audrey Lavine, Milton B. Grayson, Jr., Michele Pigliavento, John Scherer (succeeded by Edward Prostak) Toba Sherwood, Frank Torren, Juliette Koka (understudy). MUSICAL NUMBERS: How'd You Like To Spoon With Me?, They Didn't Believe Me, Till the Clouds Roll By, Go Little Boat, Who?, Sunny, Can't Help Lovin' That Man, Ol' Man River, Life Upon the Wicked Stage, Don't Ever Leave Me, Why Was I Born, She Didn't Say Yes, The Night Was Made for Love, I've Told Every Little Star, Let's Begin, Yesterdays, Smoke Gets in Your Eyes, All the Things You Are, I Won't Dance, Lovely to Look At, Pick Yourself Up, The Way You Look Tonight, This is a Fine Romance, The Folks Who Live on the Hill, Remind Me, The Last Time I Saw Paris, Sure Thing, Long Ago and Far Away, Can't Help Singing, In Love in Vain, All Through the Day, You Couldn't Be Cuter. An evening of Jerome Kern Songs: Act One: Music for the Stage; Act Two: Music for the Movies.

(South Street Theatre) Wednesday June 12–July 28, 1985 (38 performances and 8 previews). Willa Shalit and Robert Levithan present:
ONE MAN BAND with Book by James Lecesne; Music, Marc Elliot, Larry Hochman; Lyrics, Mark Elliot; Director, Jack Hofsiss; Choreographic Associate, Kay Cole; Set, Lawrence Miller; Costumes, William Ivey Long; Lighting, Natascha Katz; Musical Supervision, Debra Barsha; Orchestrations, Robby Merkin; Vocal Arrangements, Larry Hochman; Sound, Tony Meola, Brian Ronan; Stage Managers: Jacqueline Yancey, Yvette Freeman; Hair: Michael Gottfried, Ron Frederick; General Management, Marshall B. Purdy; Associate Producers: Edward P. Carroll, Dale Anderson, Lois Deutchman; Production Associate, Jeffrey Sanker; Production Assistant, Steven Fressola; Wardrobe, Annie Hickman; Technical Director, Travis De Castro; Press, The Jacksina Company, Inc. CAST: James Lecesne (Art), Kay Cole, Judy Gibson, Vanessa Williams (The Women), Debra Barsha (Piano Woman). Understudy: Yvette Freeman (The Women). MUSICAL NUMBERS: Overture, Hey Lady, Somewhere Out There, Moonlight, One Silk Shirt, Atlantic City, Singin' a Song, Female Animal, The Perfect Life, One Man Band, Atlantic City (Finale). A musical, performed without intermission. The action takes place during the present, in and around New York City.

**Addison Powell, Tessie Hogan, Kim Hunter,
Cara Duff-MacCormick in "Faulkner's Bicycle"**
(Martha Swope Photo)

(Lamb's Theatre) Wednesday, June 12, 1985–Feb. 9, 1986. (278 performances and 9 previews). Jordan Hott and Jack Millstein in association with The Asolo State Theatre of Florida and Lee Starr, Jack Tamen, Beverly Rich, Victoria Pierce present: DAMES AT SEA with Book and Lyrics by George Haimsohn and Robin Miller; Music, Jim Wise; Director/Choreographer, Neal Kenyon; Associate Choreographer/Tap Sequences, Dirk Lumbard; Musical Director, Janet Aycock; Stage Managers, Dan Carter, Gerald J. Quimby; General Manager, Jordan Hott; Company Manager, David Musselman; Production Supervisor, Mary T. Nealon; Technical Director, Victor Meyrich; Sound, Bert Taylor, Ted Wallas; Props, James Mayer; Wigs, Carl Wilson; Wardrobe, Lauro Castro; Scenic Artists: Kevin Lock, Richard E. Cannon; Press, G. Theodore Killmer. CAST: Susan Elizabeth Scott (Mona Kent), Richard Sabellico succeeded by Robert Fitch (Hennesey/Captain), Dorothy Stanley (Joan), Donna Kane (Ruby), George Dvorsky (Dick), Dirk Lumbard (Lucky). Understudies: Mana Allen, John Scherer. MUSICAL NUMBERS: Wall Street, It's You, Broadway Baby, That Mister Man of Mine, Choo-Choo Honeymoon, The Sailor of My Dreams, Singapore Sue, Good Times Are Here to Stay, Dames at Sea, The Beguine, Raining in My Heart, There's Something About You, The Echo Waltz, Star Tar, Let's Have a Simple Wedding. A musical comedy in two acts. The action takes place in any 42nd Street theatre, and on a battleship, in the early 1930's.

Right: Donna Kane, Dorothy Stanley, Susan Elizabeth Scott Below: Dirk Lumbard, Donna Kane, George Dvorsky in "Dames at Sea" *(Martha Swope Photos)*

(Circle Repertory Theatre) Tuesday, June 13–July 12, 1985 (19 performances). Jeffrey Betancourt Productions, Inc. and Marck Adrian Fedor present: OPTIONS with Book and Lyrics by Walter Willison; Music, Jefrey Silverman; Director/Choreographer, Michael Shawn; Tap Choreographer, Brenda Bufalino; Set, Ron Placzek; Costumes, Robert Turturice, Dona Granata; Lighting, Mal Sturchio; Tom Hennes; Sound, Rob Gorton, W. Scott Allison; Stage Manager, Nancy Harrington; Props/Production Assistants, Trish Kerle, Steven D. Twiss; Wardrobe, Mary Jestice; Hair, Michael Gottfried; General Management, David Lawlor, Thom Shovestull, Helen Nickerson; Press, Shirley Herz Associates/Pete Sanders, Gary Lawrence. CAST: Julie Budd, Jo Anna Rush, Jefrey Silverman, Walter Willison. Understudy: Amy Ryder. MUSICAL NUMBERS: Opening Numbers, Give a Girl a Break!, Life Don't Always Work Out, He's An Acrobat, Bareback Rider, Bubbles in the Bathtub, Perfect Strangers, Sex, Drugs, Musical Comedy!, Options, Diff'rent, The Kinda Girl I Am, The Front Page, The Man at the Piano, I Leave You with a Love Song, Finale. An evening of songs in two acts.

(Perry Street Theatre) Thursday, June 13,–August 25, 1985 (88 performances). The Rabboni Company presents: RABBONI with Book, Music, and Lyrics by Jeremiah Ginsberg; Director/Choreographer, Alan Weeks; Musical Director/Arranger/Conductor, Neal Tate; Set, Nancy Winters; Lighting, Curt Ostermann; Costumes, Phyllis Burgess, Lee Austin, Billie Taylor; Production Manager, Steven Koflanovich, Jr.; Stage Managers, Jerry Craig, David Shaw; Assistant Choreographer, Leah Bass; Production Assistants, Jerry Craig, Dan O'Mara; Wardrobe, Evelyn Smith, Mary Collins; Hair/Make-up, Freddie McDaniel; Dance Captain, Felicia Farone; Press, Howard Atlee, Barbara Atlee. CAST: Daryl Kroken (Simon Peter/Rabbi/Hawker/Pilate), Roumel Reaux succeeded by Steve Cupo (Guru Louie/Hawker/Pharisee), Lee Brock (Lust/Bride/Passer-by), Nick Corley (Andrew/Groom/Elder/Hawker), Diana Myron (Liar/Passer-by), Wilbur Archie (Fear/Leper/Hawker), Rende Rae Norman (Miriam of Magdala/Passer-by), Keith Tyrone succeeded by Kevin Ramsey (Hate/Thomas/Passer-by/Caiaphas), Dawn J. Lewis succeeded by Joan Henry (Pride/Dancing Girl), Scott Elliott (James/Hawker/Elder/Judas), Michele Scirpo (Mother Miriam), Stephen Hope succeeded by John D'Agnese (John/Joseph/Elder), David Young (Philip/Simeon/Yankel/Elder), Paul Clark (Yeshua), Ned York (Beelzebub/Pharisee). Understudies: Felicia Farone, Joseph Giuffre, Stephen Len White, Daryl Kroken, Lee Brock. MUSICAL NUMBERS: Bi-Dee Bi-Dee Bim Boom Boy, We the Children of Darkness, The Spirit of the Lord God is Upon Me, The Shepherd of Old, Where Would You Be Without Me, Blessed Be the Name of the Lord, I Found a Bright Shining Morning Star, A New Covenant, If I Have No Love, My Wedding Song, Who Put the Seeds Down and Brought the Rain?, I Am the Way, the Truth, and the Life, O Jerusalem Jerusalem, The Last Days of Rome, My God My God, Rabboni. A musical in two acts, based on the life of Christ from the Old and New Testaments.

Walter Willison, Jo Anna Rush in "Options" *(Kenn Duncan Photo)*

(The Women's Interart Center) Wednesday June 19–July 27, 1985 Interart Theatre (Artistic Director, Margot Lewitin; Managing Director, Jere Jacob) presents: DEPARTURES; Supervising Producer, Melody Brooks; Lighting, Jackie Manassee; Set, Seth Price; Stage Managers, James D'Asaro, Ruth E. Kramer; Production Manager, Joel Bassin; Press, Howard Atlee. . . . *About Anne* a selection from the works of Anne Sexton; Music, Charles Albertine; with Salome Jens. *Beatrice Roth's Trilogy:* Seventeen, At That Time I Was Studying Carole Lombard, The Father; Written and performed by Beatrice Roth; Special Direction, Valeria Wasilewski; Lighting, Rocky Greenberg; Sound, James Walsh. *Walking Through* by Bernett Belgraier; Director, Melody Brooks; Set, Daniel Kenney; Lighting, Paula Gordon; Sound, Jeff Sanders; Stage Manager, Ruth E. Kramer; Production Manager, Davida Amenta; Production Assistants: Byeager Blackwell, Kenya Johnson; Props, Rick Balian; with Connie Shulman, Maud Winchester, Kim Yancey

(Provincetown Playhouse) Wednesday, June 19, and still playing May 31, 1986. Theatre in Limbo (Artistic Director, Kenneth Elliott) and Gerald A. Davis present: **VAMPIRE LESBIANS OF SODOM and SLEEPING BEAUTY or Coma** by Charles Busch; Director, Kenneth Elliott; Choreographer, Jeff Veazey; Set, B. T. Whitehill; Costumes, John Glaser; Lighting, Vivien Leone; Stage Managers: Elizabeth Katherine Carr, Robert Carey; General Management: David Lawlor, Thom Shovestull, Helen Nickerson; Props, Joe Cote; Production Associate, Steve Wilkinson; Production Assistant, Mark Fite; Wardrobe, Donna Nelson; Wigs, Caracciolo; Press, Shirley Herz Associates, Pete Sanders. CAST: *Sleeping Beauty or Coma:* Andy Halliday (Miss Thick), Meghan Robinson succeeded by Becky London (Enid Whetwhistle), Kenneth Elliott succeeded by Ralph Buckley (Sebastian Lore), Charles Busch (Fauna Alexander), Tom Aulino (Ian McKenzie), Theresa Marlowe (Anthea Arlo), Robert Carey (Barry Posner), Arnie Kolodner (Craig Prince). *Vampire Lesbians of Sodom:* Robert Carey (Ali/P.J.), Arnie Kolodner (Hujar/Zack), Charles Busch (A Virgin Sacrifice/Madeleine Astarte), Meghan Robinson succeeded by Becky London (The Succubus/La Condesa), Kenneth Elliott succeeded by Ralph Buckley (King Carlisle), Andy Halliday (Etienne/Danny), Theresa Marlowe (Renee Vain/Tracy), Tom Aulino (Oatsie Carewe). Understudy: Michael Belanger succeeded by Randi Klein. Performed with one intermission. *Sleeping Beauty or Coma:* The action takes place in and around London in the 1960's. *Vampire Lesbians of Sodom* takes place in "Sodom, in days of old"; at the entrance to a forbidding cafe; Hollywood, 1920, at La Condesa's mansion; and Las Vegas today, in a rehearsal hall.

(Westbank Downstairs) Thursday July 9–11, 1985 (3 performances). Westbank Cafe Downstairs Theatre presents: **NEXT, PLEASE!** with Music and Lyrics by Dennis Andreopoulous, Faye Greenberg, Alison Hubbard, Michael Kessler, Rusty Magee, Suzy Mantell, Rocco Morabito, Michael Orland, Jerry Sternbach, Greer Suche, Danny Troob; Director, Sheryl A. Kaller; Musical Director, Michael Orland. CAST: Stuart Bloom, Michael Brian, Alison Fraser, Peter Herber, Mary Testa, Jennifer Leigh Warren. A musical revue. The action takes place on line in an unemployment office in New York City.

(Joyce Theatre) Thursday July 11–27, 1985 (12 performances and 3 previews). The Joyce Theatre Foundation, Inc. and Alley Theatre, Inc. (Artistic Director, Pat Brown; Managing Director, Tom Spray) present The Alley Theatre Production of: **SEASON'S GREETINGS** by Alan Ayckbourn; Director, Pat Brown; Costumes, Fotini Dimou; Set, Michael Holt; Lighting, Richard W. Jeter; Sound, Jan Cole, John Michener; Assistant to the Director, Beth Sanford; Stage Managers: Glenn Bruner, Robert S. Garber; Company Manager, Trent Jenkins; Production Manager, Bettye Fitzpatrick; Props, Megan McGavran; Dialect Coach, Cindia Huppeler; Press, Shirley Herz Associates. CAST: Robert Cornthwaite (Harvey Bunker), Dale Helward (Dr. Bernard Longstaff), Robin Moseley (Belinda), Cynthia Lammel (Pattie), Richard Poe (Neville), Charles Sanders (Eddie), Lawr Means (Rachel), Lillian Evans (Phyllis), Michael Alan Gregory (Clive). Understudies: Joe Barrett (Eddie/Clive), K. Lype O'Dell (male roles), Susan Pellegrino (female roles). A comedy in two acts. The action takes place in the home of Neville and Belinda Bunker; the time is the present, during the Christmas holiday.

(No Smoking Playhouse) July 15–21, 1985 (7 performances and 12 previews). Barton Wimble and Charles Jurrist in association with Norton Lyman present: **MAX'S MILLIONS** by Jerry Douglas and Raymond Wood; Director, Jerry Douglas; Sets, Ankers/Munier; Lighting, Edward R. F. Matthews; Technical Director, Tom Farrell: Stage Manager, Eve Sorel; Assistants: LouAnne Gilleland, Megan Svenson. CAST: Gerry McCarthy (Myrna Bangold), Raymond Wood (Max Van Der Platz), Matthew Kwiat (Behzad Mohammed), Michael Quevli (T. J. Watkins), Adrien Peyroux (Philip Thurston), Laurence Schwartz (Bognano Bongiovanni), Paul Malec (Peter Ray Purdy). A farce in two acts. The action takes place in a seedy theatrical office in midtown Manhattan.

(Riverwest Theatre) Thursday, July 25–Aug. 11, 1985 (16 performances and 4 previews). Jerry Tortoriello presents: **CARRIER and THE BOX** Written and Directed by Paul Benjamin; Set/Stage Manager, Ulric O'Flaherty; Lighting, Zebedee Collins; Music/Sound, David Lawson; Costumes/Production Manager, Aurelia Msimang-Lew; Stage Managers: Michael Sanders, Reggie Bennett; Press, Maya Associates/Penny M. Landau. CAST: *Carrier:* Cheryl Lynn Bruce (Tomeli), Moketsi Bodebe (Uta Moloi), Paul Benjamin (Cetumbu). *The Box:* Minnie Gentry (Mazwane), Themba Ntinga (Peter), Moketsi Bodibe (Kintu), Regina Taylor (Mbulai), Christopher Harvey (Henry), Paul Benjamin (Zulthe). Understudies: Pamela Reid (Tomeli/Mbulai), Michael Sanders (Cetumbu). Two One-Act South African Plays. The action takes place in the present.

**Becky London, Charles Busch
in "Vampire Lesbians of Sodom"
*(Marc Raboy Photo)***

(Parks Tour) Friday July 26–August 18, 1985 (20 performances). Joseph Papp presents The Riverside Shakespeare Company (Artistic Director, W. Stuart McDowell; Executive Director, Andrew B. Harris) production of: **THE TAMING OF THE SHREW** by William Shakespeare; Director, Maureen Clarke; Set, Richard Harmon; Costumes, Howard Behar; Music/Musical Direction, Frank Lindquist; Clown Master, David Carlyon; Stage Manager, Sheila Bam; Press, Lisa Salomon. CAST: Michael Preston (Lucentio/Joseph), Paul Hebron (Tranio/Phillip), Joseph Reed (Baptista), Vincent Niemann (Gremio), Sonja Lanzener (Kate), Gene Santarelli (Hortensio/Curtis), Laurine Towler (Bianca/Haberdasher/Nathaniel), Andy Alsup (Biondello/Walter), David Adamson (Petruchio), David Carlyon (Grumio/Vincentio), Norma Fire (Pedant/Tailor/Nicholas/Widow). A comedy in two acts. At intermission, members of the company performed a 10-minute travesty of *La Traviata,* entitled *Triviata.*

(Promenade) Tuesday, July 30–October 13, 1985. Moved to Theatre 890, October 16, 1985–February 16, 1986; (295 performances and 8 previews). Patricia Daily and Arthur Master Productions, Inc. present: **CURSE OF THE STARVING CLASS** by Sam Shepard; Director, Robin Lynn Smith; Set, Brian Martin; Costumes, Frances Nelson; Lighting, Mark W. Stanley; General Management, Brent Peek Productions; Stage Managers: Penny Marks, Bill McComb; Company Manager, Sally Campbell; Technical Director, Thomas Shilhanek; Wardrobe, Allison Campbell; Props, Lydia Hannibal; Production Assistant, Stuart Richardson; Press, Burnham-Callaghan Associates: Gary Murphy. CAST: Bradley Whitford (Wesley), Kathy Bates succeeded by Margo Martindale (Ella), Karen Tull (Emma), James Gleason (Taylor), Eddie Jones succeeded by Paul Austin (Weston), Jude Ciccolella (Ellis), Stephen Bradbury (Malcolm/Slater), Dan Patrick Brady (Emerson), Understudies: Jude Ciccolella (Weston), Dan Patrick Brady (Wesley), Stephen Bradbury (Taylor), Bill McComb (Ellis/Emerson/Slater/Malcolm), Carlotta Schoch (Emma/Ella). A drama in three acts. The action takes place at the present time in Southeast California.

**Karen Tull, Eddie Jones, Bradley Whitford,
Kathy Bates (seated) in "Curse of the
Starving Class"** *(Carol Rosegg Photo)*

59

**Raphael Sbarge, Josh Pais, David Breitbarth,
Lea Floden in "Short Change"**
(Ken Howard Photo)

(The Joyce Theatre) Thursday, August 8–31, 1985 (12 performances and 3 previews). The Joyce Theater Foundation, Inc. and the Center Theatre Group/Mark Taper Forum (Artistic Director/Producer, Gordon Davidson) present the Mark Taper Forum Production of:
IN THE BELLY OF THE BEAST by Jack Henry Abbott; Adaptation, Adrian Hall; Further Adaptation/Director, Robert Woodruff; Text from the book *In the Belly of the Beast: Letters from Prison* by Jack Henry Abbott, trial transcripts, and various interviews; Associate Producer, Madeline Puzo; Set, John Ivo Gilles; Costumes, Carol Brolaski; Lighting, Paulie Jenkins; Jayne Dutra; Music, Douglas Wieselman; Sound, Stephen Shaffer; Video: Chip Lord, Branda Miller; Company Manager, Lisa Baumgarten; Stage Manager, Al Franklin; Produced in association with Seymour Morgenstern; Executive Managing Director, William P. Wingate; General Manager, Stephen J. Albert; Technical Director, Robert Routolo; Press, Nancy Hereford. CAST: Andrew Robinson (Jack Henry Abbott), Andy Wood (Reader 1), William Allen Young (Reader 2). Understudies: Michael Tulin (Readers 1 and 2), Andy Wood (Jack Henry Abbott). Performed without intermission.

(Riverside Park Rotunda) Wednesday, August 14–September 8, 1985 (20 performances). Fleet Theatre Company (Artistic Director, Rosemary Camas; Managing Director, Barry Dunleavey) presents:
THE MERCHANT OF VENICE or Paper Promises: 1933 by William Shakespeare; Director, Rudy Caringi; Set/Lighting, Michael D. White; Costumes, Michelle Matland; Press: Lisa De Jager, Robert Burrichter. CAST: Rudy Caringi (Shylock), Rosemary Camas, Thomas DeCarlo, Robert Dixon, Barry Dunleavey, Harris Gruson, Peter Honchaurk, James Humphreys, Jacquelyn Mari Roberts, Roy Steinberg, Greta Turken. The action takes place in the New York underworld in the depression year of 1933.

(Federal Hall National Memorial) Thursday, August 22–29, 1985 (4 performances)
THE TRAGEDY OF JULIUS CAESAR by William Shakespeare; Director, Darryl Croxton; Presented by American Landmark Festivals, The Classic Theatre, and The King's Men Shakespeare Company. CAST: Ethel Ayler (Calpurnia), Henry Baker (Metellus Cimber), David Bloomquist (Lepidus), China Clark (Portia), Darryl Croxton (Caius Cassius), Charles Douglass (Soothsayer), Basil John Dufallo (Pindarus), Robert Graham (Dardanius), Robert Hull (Octavius Caesar), Mark Johannes (Decius Brutus), Peter Lang (Casca), Vance Mizelle (Julius Caesar), Stephan Morrow (Marcus Antonius), Esteban Fernandez Sanchez (Messala), Ronald Willoughby (Marcus Brutus)

(Judith Anderson Theatre) Wednesday, August 28–, 1985. The Lion Theatre Company (Artistic Director, Gene Nye) presents:
THE FLATBUSH FAITHFUL Written and Directed by Gene Nye; Set, Linda Skipper; Lighting, Terry Wuthrich; Costumes, Cordelia; Stage Manager, Dennis Cameron; Assistant to Director, Casey Korda; Wigs/Props, Candido Antonio; Electrician, Alan Sporing; Scenic Artist, Donna Lanai; Production Assistant, Eddie Rodas; Press, Shirley Herz Associates: Peter Cromarty, David Roggensack, Pete Sanders. CAST: Christopher McCann (Michael Brooks), Michael Guido (Vito Maggio), Jim Ricketts (Charlie Brewster), Alvin Alexis (Willie Allen), Sofia Landon (Mrs. Brewster/Nora/Jessica Anderson), Maria Cellario (Mrs. Brooks/Pam/Sherlock), Judith Granite (Grandma/Mrs. Maggio/Wendy/Marie/Psychiatrist), Robyn Hatcher (Mrs. Allen/Diane/Star), Alice King (Kathy/Marian), Chazz Palminteri (Mr. Connolly/Mr. Papp/Rodney/Mountain), Herbert Rubens (Mr. Brooks/Coach/Tony/Indian/Mortician), Jeremy Stuart (Billy/Ralph/Mr. Shore/Hal/Doctor). A play in two acts. The action takes place between 1945 and 1984, at various locations in Brooklyn and Manhattan.

(Second Stage Theatre) Tuesday, September 3–October 6, 1985 (17 performances and 22 previews). The William and Mary Greve Foundation, Tony Kiser, Producer, presents:
THE CUSTOM OF THE COUNTRY by Jane Stanton Hitchcock; From the novel by Edith Wharton; Director, Daniel Gerroll; Set, Kate Edmunds; Costumes, David Murin; Lighting, Ann G. Wrightson; Stage Managers: Buzz Cohen, Allison Sommers; General Management, Kingwill & Gossen, Inc.; Production Coordinator, Steven Katz; Assistants, Kate Amendola, Timothy Malloy; Props, Arthur Hansen; Press, Henry Luhrman Associates. CAST: Nesbitt Blaisdell (Abner Spragg), Michael Countryman (Ralph Marvell), Karen MacDonald (Indiana Rolliver), Valerie Mahaffey (Undine Spragg), Jane Murray (Clare Van Degan), Lenka Peterson (Leota Spragg), David Rasche (Raymond De Chelles), John C. Vennema (Peter Van Degen), Carl Wallnau (Claude Popple/Mr. Fleischauer), Trey Wilson (Elmer Moffatt). A play in two acts. The action takes place in 1913, particularly in Paris.

(Samuel Beckett Theatre) Wednesday September 4–October 20, 1985 (34 performances and 15 previews). Fred Kolo presents:
SHORT CHANGE by Geoffrey Gordon; Director, Fred Kolo; Set, Charles McClennahan; Costumes, Laura Drawbaugh; Lighting, Michael Moody; General Management, Brent Peek Productions; Stage Managers, Steve McCorkle, Carol Schneider; Company Manager, Claudette Sutton; Electrician, Cameron Jackson; Press, David Powers, Leo Stern. CAST: Raphael Sbarge (Benjamin), Lea Floden (Rayna), David Breitbarth (Fred), Josh Pais succeeded by Jeffrey Marcus (Daniel). A comedy in two acts. The action takes place in an off-campus apartment near an urban university.

(Colonnades Theatre) Friday, September 6–29, 1985 (16 performances). Illustrious Theatre presents:
THE FLYING DOCTOR by Moliere and **THE DISPUTE** by Marivaux; New Translations, Peter Basch; Director, Lee Bloomrosen; Stage Manager, Billy McMullen; Set, Marc D. Malamud; Costumes, Peter Basch; Sound, Jay Bloomrosen; Management Consultant, Craig S. Dorfman; Lighting, Noele Stollmach; Technical Director, Gerhard Brandmer. CAST: *The Flying Doctor:* Robert Boyd Newton (Valere), Ann Paffrath (Sabine), Spike Steingasser (Sganarelle), P. L. Carling (Gorgibus), Peter Basch (Gros-Rene), Wendy Makkena (Lucile), W. Allen Taylor (Lawyer). *The Dispute:* Mary Conklin (Hermione), Peter Basch (Prince), Karen Wilson (Carise), W. Allen Taylor (Mesrou), Wendy Makkena (Egle), Robert Boyd Newton (Azor), Ann Paffrath (Adine), Spike Steingasser (Mesrin). Two one-act plays with one intermission.

(Interart Theatre) Wednesday, September 11–Oct. 20, 1985 (42 performances) The Women's Interart Center (Artistic Director, Margot Lewitin) in association with the American National Theatre at the Kennedy Center, presents:
SOLO VOYAGES selected excerpts from the original plays of Adrienne Kennedy: *The Owl Answers, A Rat's Mass,* and *A Movie Star Has to Star in Black & White;* Director, Joseph Chaikin; Music, Skip LaPlante, Edwina Lee Tyler; Set, Jun Maeda; Lighting, Beverly Emmons; Costumes, Gwen Fabricant; Puppets/Masks, Ronnie Asbell; Supervising Producer, Melody Brooks; Assistant Director, David Willinger; Company Manager, Joel Bassin; Stage Manager, Dianne Houston; Press, Becky Flora. CAST: Robbie McCauley. An interpretation of three monologues.

Robbie McCauley in "Solo Voyages"
(Carol Rosegg/Martha Swope Photo)

**Larry Joshua, Randle Mell, Mary McDonnell
in "Savage in Limbo"** *(Adam Newman Photo)*

**Caris Corfman, Reed Birney
in "Filthy Rich"** *(Adam Newman Photo)*

(Double Image Theatre) Tuesday, Sept. 17,–Nov. 24, 1985 (35 performances for Savage in Limbo, and 36 for Filthy Rich) Double Image Repertory Company (*Premiere Season:* Founder/Executive Director, Helen Waren Mayer; Artistic Director, Max D. Mayer; Managing Director, Leslie Urdang) presents in revolving repertory:

SAVAGE IN LIMBO by John Patrick Shanley; Director, Mark Linn-Baker; Set, Adrianne Lobel; Costumes, Debra Tennenbaum; Lights, Stephen Strawbridge; Technical Director, John E. Jankowski; Props, Mark Allen Flesher; Wardrobe, Leslie Baker; Sound, Monroe Head; Stage Managers, Ruth Kreshka, William H. Lang; Press, Milly Schoenbaum, Mark Routh, Kevin Patterson. CAST: Randle Mell (Murk), Jayne Haynes (April White), Deborah Hedwall (Denise Savage), Mary McDonnell (Linda Rotunda), Larry Joshua (Tony Aronica). A "concert play" performed without intermission.

FILTHY RICH by George F. Walker; Director, Max D. Mayer; Set, Thomas Lynch; Costumes, Deborah Shaw; Lights, Susan Chute; Music, John Roby; Cinematographer, David Prittie; Stage Managers, Ruth Kreshka, William H. Lang. CAST: John P. Connolly (Tyrone Power), Reed Birney (Jamie McLean), Caris Corfman (Anne Scott/Susan Scott), Dan Moran (Detective Stackhouse), Joseph Siravo (Henry "The Pig" Duvall). A play in two acts.

(New Theatre) Tuesday, Sept. 17,–Oct. 12, 1985 (19 performances) Harriet D. Lucas in association with Kathryn Reimers presents:

THE SPARE SERAPHIM by Donald Yonker; Director, Sue Wolf; Set, Bill Bartlett; Lighting, Ferd Manning; Production Assistants, Hope Taylor, David J. Pfister; Stage Managers, Susan Selig, Laura Gewurz; Press, Harold Marmon. CAST: Archie Harrison (Tobias), Don Striano (Jacob Halliwell), Judy Del Giudice (Sara Goldsmith Halliwell), Hope Katcher (Miranda Sweet), Stephen Turner (Thomas Halliwell), Juan Valentin (Angel Torres), Annette Jones (Gloria Lord). A comedy in two acts. The action takes place at the present time on the terrace of Thomas and Sara's Long Island home.

(Playhouse 91) Saturday, Sept. 21, 1985–
YOURS, ANNE with Libretto by Enid Futterman; Music, Michael Cohen; Based on book Anne Frank: The Diary of a Young Girl, and the play by Frances Goodrich and Albert Hackett; Producer, John Flaxman; Director, Arthur Masella; Set, Franco Colavecchia; Costumes, Judith Dolan; Lighting, Beverly Emmons; Orchestrations, James Stenborg; Music Director, Dan Strickland; Movement, Helena Andreyko; Sound, Jack Mann; General Manager, John A. Caruso; Associate Producer, Arlene Caruso; Company Manager, John Caruso; Assistant Conductor, Mark Lipman; Hair/Makeup, Richard Allen; Props, Debra Alix Martin; Wardrobe, Suzanne Brashaw; Stage Managers, Beverley Randolph, Joseph Fuqua; Press, Becky Flora, Glen Gary. CAST: Betty Aberlin (Mrs. Van Daan), Trini Alvarado (Anne Frank), David Cady (Peter Van Daan), Merwin Goldsmith (Mr. Van Daan), George Guidall (Mr. Frank), Hal Robinson (Mr. Dussel), Ann Talman (Margot Frank), Dana Zeller-Alexis (Mrs. Frank), Standbys and Understudies: Joseph Fuqua (Peter), Hal Robinson (Mr. Frank), Edward Penn (Dussel/Van Daan), Chiara Peacock (Anne/Margot), Karen Gibson (Mrs. Frank/Mrs. Van Daan). A musical in two acts. The action takes place in Amsterdam, Holland, from June 12, 1942 to Aug. 4, 1944.

(Billie Holiday Theatre) Thursday, Oct. 3,–Dec. 22, 1985 (60 performances) Brooklyn Professional Resident Black Theatre Company (Marjorie Moon, Producer) presents:

MARK VIII: xxxvi by John H. Redwood; Director, Lillie Marie Redwood; Set/Costumes, Felix E. Cochren; Lighting, Tim Phillips; Wardrobe, Ardis Johnson; Stage Managers, Avan Littles, Sound, Roger Smiley; Press, Howard Atlee, Barbara Atlee. CAST: Joy Moss (Paige York), Dylan Ross (Rev. Morgan), Jack Aaron (Dr. Abel), Renetta Neal (Cora Drew), Barbara Christie (Mrs. Estelle Beale), Joseph V. Francis (Senator Hayward Beale), Thomas Hoyt Godfrey (Stewart Forbes), John Henry Redwood (Judge Horace Moore), Understudies: Joseph V. Francis (Dr. Abel), Thomas Hoyt Godfrey (Rev. Morgan), Doug Barron (Heantor/Forbes), Diane Ciesla (Estelle), Avan Littles (Judge). A drama in 2 acts and 11 scenes. The action takes place at the present time in the New York County Hospital, Rev. Morgan's office, and in Judge Horace Moore's court chambers.

(Judith Anderson Theatre) Friday, Oct. 4, 1985. Lion Theatre Company (Artistic Director, Gene Nye) presents:

THE CABBAGHEAD by Oliver Goldstick; Director, John Guerrasio; Set, Richard Jaris; Lighting, Terry Wuthrich; Costumes, Abigail Murray; Sound, Bill Kollar; Wardrobe/Props, Candido Antonio; Production Assistant, Joshua Roth; Stage Manager, Elsbeth M. Collins; Press, Shirley Herz Associates, Peter Cromarty, David Roggensack, Pete Sanders. CAST: Phyllis Somerville (Della Kohl), Art Kempf (Isaac Schakel), Jacob Harran (Max Braiker), William A. Lawrence (Deputy/Schwab/Judge), Jim Abele (Lucas Spangler), Patti McClenahan (Neva Spangler), Mathew Vipond (Travis), Jean Barker (Hattie Hagen), Carrie Garman (Katrina Spangler). A play in two acts. The action takes place Nov. 20, 1928 and Jan. 10, 1929 in Hollenbeck, and York, Pennsylvania.

(American Renaissance Theater) Thursday, Oct. 10–Nov. 3, 1985 (16 performances). The American Renaissance Theater presents:

THE AFFAIR AND BUBBE ADELSTEIN by Judith Present; Director, Janet Sarno; Set, Ernie Schenk; Sculptures and Props, Sheila Goloborotko; Lighting, David Shepherd; Stage Managers, Doug Ward, Max Arrow. CAST: Bill Britten (Artie), Claiborne Cary (Sylvia), Anita Keal (Lillian), Libby Lyman (Bubbe Adelstein), Paul Mantell (Waiter/Lawyer/MC), Richard Ross (Ted), Farnham Scott (Kenny). A comedy in two acts.

**David Cady, Betty Aberlin, Merwin Goldsmith,
Trini Alvarado, Ann Talman, George Guidall,
Dana Zeller-Alexis in "Yours, Anne"**
(Henry Grossman Photo)

61

**Edward Herrmann, Dylan Baker
in "Not About Heroes"** *(Bob Marshak Photo)*

**Victor Slezak, Laura Innes
in "Alice and Fred"** *(Martha Swope Photo)*

(Lucille Lortel Theatre) Thursday, Oct. 10,–Nov. 10, 1985 (24 performances and 12 previews) Luther Davis and Arthur W. Cohen by special arrangement with Lucille Lortel present:
NOT ABOUT HEROES by Stephen MacDonald; Director, Dianne Wiest; Set, Phillip Baldwin; Costumes, Linda Fisher; Lighting, Ronald Wallace; Sound, Robert Kerzman; Produced in association with Ray Larsen; General Management, Richard Horner Associates; Company Manager, Bruce Laffey; Technical Coordinator, Thomas Shilhanek; Production Assistant, Anthony Newfield; Sound, Heidi Brown; Wardrobe, Kate Amendola; Stage Managers, Trey Hunt, Patricia O'Halloran. CAST: Edward Herrmann (Siegfried Sassoon), Dyland Baker (Wilfred Owen), Standbys: John Jubak (Sassoon), Jack Koenig (Owen). A play in two acts.

(Douglas Fairbanks Theater) Thursday, Oct. 10,–Nov. 17, 1985 (25 performances and 19 previews) Eric Krebs presents:
TATTERDEMALION based on Israel Zangwill's novella "The King of the Schnorrers"; Book/Music/Lyrics, Judd Woldin; Director, Eric Krebs; Sets, Ed Wittstein; Costumes, Patricia Adshead; Lighting, Whitney Quesenbery; Music Supervision/Arrangements, Peter Howard; Musical Staging, Mary Jane Houdina; Orchestrations, Robert M. Freedman, Judd Woldin; Additional Lyrics, Susan Birkenhead; Musical Direction, Edward G. Robinson; Script Editor, Amy Seidman; General Management, Whitbell Productions; Wardrobe, Shirl Joshua; Props, Rachel S. Levine; Stage Managers, Patricia Flynn, Crystal Craft; Press, Bruce Cohen, Kathleen von Schmid, Naomi Cahn-Puiter. CAST: Annie McGreevey (Sadie/Mrs. Mendoza), Robert Blumenfeld (Isaac/Wilkinson/Cosmetician/Furtado), Ron Wisniski (Herschel/Belasco), Suzanne Briar (Rivka/Housekeeper), Stuart Zagnit (David), K. C. Wilson (Mendoza), Jack Sevier (DaCosta), Tia Speros (Deborah), Understudies: Ron Wisniski (DaCosta), Suzanne Briar (Deborah/Sadie/Mrs. Mendoza), John Barone (Isaac/Herschel/David/Wilkinson/Belasco/Cosmetician/Furtado). MUSICAL NUMBERS: Petticoat Lane, Ours, Chutzpah, Tell Me, Born to Schnorr, I Have Not Lived in Vain, A Man Is Meant to Reason, Blood Lines, Leave the Thinking to Men, It's Over, Murder, Dead, I'm Only a Woman, An Ordinary Man, Well Don DaCosta, Each of Us. A musical in 2 acts and 17 scenes. The action takes place in 1791.

(Apple Corps Theatre) Friday, Oct. 11,–Nov. 3, 1985 (20 performances) Sanmar Productions presents:
CRAZY ARNOLD by Alexander Marshall; Directed by Mr. Marshall; Set/Costumes, Elizabeth Jenkins; Associate Producer, Jon Mikel Zeigler; Lighting, Deborah Constantine; Assistant Director, John Mueller; Stage Manager, Angela Wright. CAST: Garson Stine (Arnold Kerek), Diana Georger (Alison Frasier), Catherine Cox (Millie Hyde), Mitchell Greenburg (Groucho), Peter Newman (Chico), Neal Arluck (Harpo), Peter Waldren (Seymour Waldren). A play in two acts. The action takes place at the present time in Arnold's New York apartment.

(Cherry Lane Theatre) Tuesday, Oct. 15,–Nov. 3, 1985 (14 performances) The Rolfe Company (Mickey Rolfe, Producer) and Joel Key Rice present:
ALICE AND FRED by Dan Ellentuck; Director, Gloria Muzio; Set/Lighting, Dale F. Jordan; Costumes, Lloyd K. Waiwaiole; Music/Sound, George Andoniadis; Produced in association with Billy Livingston; Casting, Stanley Soble/Jason LaPadura; Fight Choreography, Jack Fahey; Assistant to Producer, Penny Rolfe; Stage Managers, Kit Liset, Susan Greenlee, Barry Lee; Press, Howard Atlee, Barbara Atlee. CAST: J. Smith-Cameron (Alice Mitchell), Greg Germann (Frank Mitchell), Bruce Tracy (Harry Bilger), Victor Slezak (Ashley Roselle), Laura Innes (Freda Ward), Understudies: Susan Greenlee (Alice/Freda), Barry Lee (Ashley/Harry/Frank). A play in two acts. The action takes place in the summer of 1892 in Schofield, NY.

(Beckmann Theatre) Thursday, Oct. 17,–Nov. 10, 1985 (13 performances and 3 previews) Theta Theater and Mark McKenna present:
AMERICAN GOTHICS four short plays by Donald Kvares; Directors, Mark McKenna, Danny Ratigliano; Sets, Vera Stromsted; Costumes, Lyn Hoolahan; Sound, Frank Gallant; Lighting, Rob Chaskin; Stage Manager, Andy Andriuk; Press, Francine L. Trevens/FLT. CAST: *A Piece of Fog* with Christopher Jennings (Bobby), L. R. Hults (Father), Martha Lewin (Mother). A home in New Hampshire in the very near future. *Modern Statuary* with Patty Gliniewicz (Elena), Juanita Walsh (Hilda Gelb), Al Sperduto (Jacob Gelb), Billy Morrissette (Johnny), Kim Walker (Kitty), Vinnie Sassone (Freddy). The Gelb home on suburban Long Island at the present time. *Filling the Hole* with Mimi Sherwin (Mother), Leah Solo (Willa), Jay Reed (Will). A picnic area in Central Park on a sunny weekend in NYC. *Strangulation* with Marta Rose (Ruth), Mick Muldoon (Pa), Carol Billings (Ma), Mark McKenna (Strangler). An isolated farmhouse in the recent past.

(Eccentric Circles Theatre) Sunday, Oct. 20,–Nov. 13, 1985 (16 performances) **DANCE OF THE MAYFLY** by Judy Montague; Producer/Director, Paula Kay Pierce; Co-Producer, Gary Miller; Set, Al Ksen; Lighting, Richard Clausen; Stage Manager, Maryanne Mognoni; Producing Directors, Paula Kay Pierce, Rosemary Hopkins, Janet Bruders, Barbara Bunch. CAST: Doug Barron (Mack Macdonald), Michael Kuhn (Barney Picaro), Rosemary Hopkins (Mona Macdonald), Kathi Gati (Laurie Miller), Marie O'Donnell (Doreen Pate), Hal Blankenship (Ray Macdonald). A play in 2 acts, and 5 scenes. The action takes place at the present time in a small mid-western town.

**Mitchell Greenberg, Garson Stine, Peter Newman
Diana Georger, Neal Arluck in "Crazy Arnold"**

**Rosemary Hopkins, Michael Kuhn
in "Dance of the Mayfly"**
(Denise DeMirjian Photo)

**Susan Wands, Karen Kruger, Jean Richards
in "Whining and Dining"** *(S. Stava Photo)*

**Evan Thompson, Nancy C. Genuardi, John Graham,
Jeff Paul in "Macbett"** *(Robert Klein Photo)*

(13th Street Theatre) Thursday, Oct. 24,–Nov. 16, 1985 (20 performances). Stages of Community Enrichment presents:
BECOMING STRANGERS by George Freek; Director, Karen Gnat; Sets, Gordon A. Juel; Costumes, Kristina Katz; Lighting, Edward R. F. Matthews; Assistant Director, Kevin Kennison; Stage Managers, Dana J. Baker, Shannon Penrod; Press, Christine Stump. CAST: Connie Shulman (Betsy), Terrence Frawley (Pa), Douglas Treem (Duke), Ami Rothschild (Jane), Michael Gnat (Howard), Terrence Frawley (Man), Understudies: Karen Brubach (Jane/Betsy), Clay Dickinson (Howard/Duke).

(Perry Street Theatre) Sunday, Oct. 24,–27, 1985 (5 performances) Portia Productions and Robert K. O'Neill present:
WHINING AND DINING by Jeryl Turco; Director, Mitzi Metzl-Pazer; Set, Carla Lauren Messina; Lighting, Tracy Eck; Sound, Steve Elber; Executive Producer, Susan D. Atkinson; Stage Manager, Elisa Loprete. CAST: Jean Richards, (Catherine), Susan Wands (Jody), Karen Kruger (Simone), Cliff Weissman (John), Gerrianne Raphael (Mother), Dino Narizzano (Father), Vera Lockwood (Nonnie), Robert O'Neill (Robert), Elisa Loprete (Maid), Deloria Ruyle (Maid). A play in 2 acts and 14 scenes. The action takes place in the home of Mr. and Mrs. Mecca and in their daughter Jody's apartment.

(Symphony Space) Thursday, Oct. 24,–Nov. 10, 1985 (12 performances and 2 previews) Lincoln Center Institute (Director, Mark Schubart; Associate Directors, Robert J. Crane, June Dunbar; Assistant Director, Carol Sienkiewicz) presents:
THE WINTER'S TALE by William Shakespeare; Director, Andy Wolk; Set, Derek McLane; Costumes, Karen Gerson; Lighting, David Noling; Music Composed by Robert Dennis; Choreography, Randolyn Zinn; Producer, June Dunbar; Production Assistants, Jane Besthoff, Rosalind Goethals; Wardrobe, Leila Elias, Tamara Kirkman; Stage Managers, Johnna Murray, Liz Wright; Press, Joe McKaughan, Susanne Stevens, Lisa Batchelder. CAST: David Purdham (Leontes), Ellen Parker (Hermione), Bradley Kane (Mamillius), Peter Crombie (Camillo), Bill Schoppert (Cleomenes), Hewitt Brooks (Antigonus), Jean DeBaer (Paulina), Melody Combs (Emilia), Brian Smiar (The Jailor), Thomas Kopache (Polixenes), Steven Flynn (Florizel), Willie Reale (Autolycus), Brian Smiar (Old Shepherd), Hewitt Brooks (Young Shepherd), Ellen Parker (Perdita), Melody Combs (Mopsa), Bill Schoppert (Servant), Bradley Kane (Time). Performed with one intermission.

(Unitarian Church of All Souls) Friday, Oct. 25,–Nov. 10, 1985 (16 performances) The All Souls Players present:
MACBETT by Eugene Ionesco; Translated by Charles Marowitz from the French; Director, David McNitt; Costumes, Virginia Wood; Lighting, David Bean; Sound, Ira Stoller; Producers, Julia Parisi, Tran William Rhodes; Stage Managers, Marlene Greene, Linda Panzner, Terri Mintz, James Jacobus; Props, Sheila Mooney; Technical Director, David Bean; Press, Tran William Rhodes. CAST: Al D'Andrea (Macbett), Nancy C. Genuardi (Lady Duncan), Brian Carpenter (Banco), Evan Thompson (Duncan), Denise Dunayer (Lady in Waiting/Witch), Roy Steinberg (Candor), Tom Morrissey (Glamiss/Monk/Bishop), John Graham (Macol), Jeff Paul (Soldier/Officer/Sick Man), James Jacobus (Salesman/Orderly/Servant/Guest), Marie McMurrer (Maid/Orderly/Servant), Terri Mintz (Soldier/Sick Woman/Guest), J. Peter O'Connor (Soldier/Officer/Butterfly Hunter). A play in two acts.

(Folksbiene Playhouse) Saturday, Oct. 26, 1985–March 9, 1986
BROOME STREET, AMERICA by Sylvia Regan; Yiddish adaptation and lyrics by Miriam Kressyn; Director, Roger Sullivan; Music, Abraham Ellstein; Musical Arrangements/Direction, Andrea Goodzeit; Sets, James Wolk; Lighting, Arthur Resler; Costumes, Neil Cooper; Press, Bruce Cohen, Kathleen von Schmid. CAST: Betty Silberman (Fanny), Miriam Gordon (Esther), Zypora Spaisman (Becky Felderman), Jack Rechtzeit (Aaron Greenspan), James Harris (Hymie as a boy), I. W. Firestone (Harry Engel), Raquel Yossiffon (Sadie), Daniel Chiel (Irving Tashman), Jacques Brawer (Benjamin Brownstein), Menachem Bazian (Hymie as a young man), Jacob Mirer (Hymie Tashman). A play with music.

(The New Theater) Tuesday, Oct. 29,–Nov. 3, 1985 (6 performances)
AMONG THE FALLEN by Catherine Burns; Director, Adam Zahler; Costumes, Margot Avery; Lighting, Leon Hopkins; Stage Manager, Sarah Potok. CAST: Virginia Hoffmann (Heidi), Debra Neel (Lana), Liz Schuette (JJ), Frank Saracino (Jeff), Alan Altshuld (Corky), Betsy Howie (Scotti), Tony Cormier (Douglas), Debra Babcock (Mary), Leon Hopkins (Larry), James Reed (Michael), Margot Avery (Dorothy), Melissa Salmons (Suzanne), Lachlan Macleay (Neil), Henry J. Quinn (Dandy), Elizabeth Flynn-Jones (Elisabeth). A comedy in two acts. The action takes place in the converted garage-dressing room of the Valley Players in August 1975, the day of the tech-dress rehearsal of Gorky's The Lower Depths.

**Jean DeBaer, Hewitt Brooks, David Purdham
in "The Winter's Tale"** *(Susanne Faulkner Stevens Photo)*

**Jack Rechtzeit, Zypora Spaisman
in "Broome Street, America"**
(Carol Rosegg Photo)

63

(South Street Theatre) Tuesday, Oct. 29,–Nov. 16, 1985 (16 performances). Bruce Caro and Sherri Felt present:

ROCKBOUND with Book and Lyrics by C. J. Critt; Music, Roberta Baum; Director, Dennis Deal; Musical Direction, Jonny Bowden; Choreography, Michele Kadison; Set/Lighting, Marc D. Malamud, Julia Rubin; Costumes, Evadne Giannini; Special Visual Effects, Rusty Russell; Sound, Lia Vollack; Hair/Makeup, Jennifer Aspinall; Casting, Herman/Lipson; Production Coordinator, Melanie N. Dratfield; Assistant to Director, Mildred Lewis; Props, Bob D'Arinzo; Props/Wardrobe, Nickey Wiesner; Stage Managers, Pam Weinstein, Lisa Braden; Press, Becky Flora. CAST: Adinah Alexander (Mary Lou/Shira), David Cowles (Cliff/Roc I), Linda Dwyer (Pam/Leto/Others), David May (Blast/Roc II), Suzie Plaksin (Prof. Wilson/Clusterhead/Phyllis/Others), Ariel Powers (Zivia/Dormo/Others), Rob Rota (Jay Berd). MUSICAL NUMBERS: Rockbound Rap, Near Nuke Fluke, Here in My Hands, Time Travel, Miners Chant, After the Sadness, Glorion, Rock Release, Hugs and Kisses, What Does One Life Mean, Basic Love, Chain of Lies, Return to the Light, Gold, I Don't Want to Be in Love, Robot Bop, Lifetimes, Nu-Man, It Doesn't Stop Here. A new sci-fi musical in two acts. The action takes place on a university campus in Oregon in 1985. . . . and in the future.

(Town Hall) Wednesday, Oct. 30,–Dec. 29, 1985 (54 performances and 6 previews) Yiddish Musical Theatre of New York (Raymond Ariel, Stuart Rosenberg, Producers) presents:

A MATCH MADE IN HEAVEN with Book and Original Music, Jack Rechtzeit; Music Arrangements, Alexander Lustig; New Lyrics, I. Alper; Director, Yankele Alperin; Musical Staging, Derek Wolshonak; Sets Gary Grianti; Costumes, Clare Gosney; English translation, David Ellin; Lighting/Stage Manager, Bernard Sauer; Executive Manager, Ruth V. Ellin; General Production Manager, Sandy Levitt; Stage Managers, Stewart Figa, Shifee Lovitt; Technical Director, Wesley Sturgis; Dance Captain, Tara Tyrrell; Wardrobe, Thunder Marsh; Press, Max Eisen, Madelon Rosen, Maria Soma. CAST: Monica Tesler (Natasha), Eleanor Reissa (Tsipke), Yankele Alperin (Tzudik), Reizl Bozyk (Mintze), Stewart Figa (Berish), Leon Liebgold (Pesach), Shifee Lovitt (Lida), David Ellin (Smirnov), David Montefiore (The Rebbe), Ben Gotlieb (Grisha Smirnov), Ensemble: Nicole Flender, Carolyn Goor, Tara Tyrrell, Dean Badolato, Anthony Bova, Jay Tramel. A musical in two acts. The action takes place in the miller's yard in 1910.

(Circle in the Square Downtown) Thursday, Oct. 31,–Nov. 24, 1985 (46 performances)

HAMELIN presented by Craig Anderson; Book, Richard Jarboe, Harvey Shield, Matthew Wells; Music and Lyrics, Richard Jarboe, Harvey Shield; Choreography, Jerry Yoder; Director, Ron Nash; Set, Steven Rubin; Costumes, Mark Bridges, Steve C. Kleiser; Lighting, Rick Belzer; Sound, Charles Bugbee 3rd; Musical Supervisor/Routiner, Ronald Melrose; Synthesizer Programer/Designer, Steven Oirich; Associate Producers, Jan Jalenak, Golden Rose Productions; Company Manager, Robert W. Baldwin; Special Effects, Richard Desimone; Assistant Director, Michael Goldberg; Wardrobe, Charles Catanese; Production Assistants, Kay Pro, Mac Intosh; Stage Manager, Michael A. Clarke; Press, Becky Flora, Mary Bryant, Glen Gary. CAST: Scott Fless (Lech), Patrick Hamilton (The Piper), G. Wayne Hoffman (The Mayor), Steven Jacob (Rudolph), Andrew Kraus (Jigger/Otto), Liz Larsen (Gilda), Jodi Mitchel (Gertrude), Erica L. Paulson (Chigger/Utta), Stephen Terrell (Standby). MUSICAL NUMBERS: We're Rats, The Mayor Doesn't Care, Doing My Job, Rat Trap, Easy for Me, What a Day, Paradise, Charismatic, Better Keep Your Promise, Follow the Music Man, Feel the Beat, Serving the People, Mother, Gold, I'll Remember, You've Outstayed Your Welcome. A musical in two acts. The action takes place on a street in Hamelin on June 26, 1284.

Reizl Bozyk, Shifee Lovitt, David Montefiore, Eleanor Reissa, Monica Tesler in "A Match Made in Heaven" *(Martha Swope Photo)*

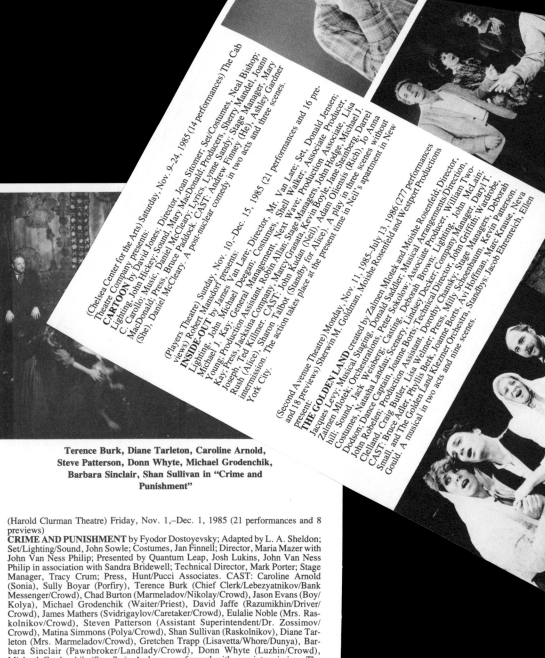

Terence Burk, Diane Tarleton, Caroline Arnold, Steve Patterson, Donn Whyte, Michael Grodenchik, Barbara Sinclair, Shan Sullivan in "Crime and Punishment"

(Harold Clurman Theatre) Friday, Nov. 1,–Dec. 1, 1985 (21 performances and 8 previews)

CRIME AND PUNISHMENT by Fyodor Dostoyevsky; Adapted by L. A. Sheldon; Set/Lighting/Sound, John Sowle; Costumes, Jan Finnell; Director, Maria Mazer with John Van Ness Philip; Presented by Quantum Leap, Josh Lukins, John Van Ness Philip in association with Sandra Bridewell; Technical Director, Mark Porter; Stage Manager, Tracy Crum; Press, Hunt/Pucci Associates. CAST: Caroline Arnold (Sonia), Sully Boyar (Porfiry), Terence Burk (Chief Clerk/Lebezyatnikov/Bank Messenger/Crowd), Chad Burton (Marmeladov/Nikolay/Crowd), Jason Evans (Boy/Kolya), Michael Grodenchik (Waiter/Priest), David Jaffe (Razumikhin/Driver/Crowd), James Mathers (Svidrigaylov/Caretaker/Crowd), Eulalie Noble (Mrs. Raskolnikov/Crowd), Steven Patterson (Assistant Superintendent/Dr. Zossimov/Crowd), Matina Simmons (Polya/Crowd), Shan Sullivan (Raskolnikov), Diane Tarleton (Mrs. Marmeladov/Crowd), Gretchen Trapp (Lisavetta/Whore/Dunya), Barbara Sinclair (Pawnbroker/Landlady/Crowd), Donn Whyte (Luzhin/Crowd), Michael Grodenchik (Standby). A drama performed with one intermission. The action takes place in St. Petersburg, Russia, in 1860.

(Hartley House) Thursday, Nov. 7,–30, 1985 (20 performances) Playwrights Preview Productions (Frances Hill, Artistic Director; Rick Porter, Producer) presents:

AN OUNCE OF PREVENTION by Hal Corley; Director, Susann Brinkley; Set, David Birn; Lighting, Richard Comfort; Costumes, Lauryn Axelrod; Hairstylist, Tony Thoman; Production Assistants, Deborah Hobart, Linda Shary, Stuart Laurence; Stage Managers, Elaine O'Donnell, Judy Cummings; Press, Ann Hollywood, Joel Spinetti. CAST: Tonya Pinkins (Mona), Carole Lockwood (Bobbie), Cindy Adkins (April), Angelini Fiordellisi (Hilda), Charles Keating (Ergun). Performed without intermission. The action takes place at the present time in a junior high school classroom in the suburbs.

(Jack Lawrence Theatre) Thursday, Nov. 7,–Dec. 8, 1985 (6 performances and 30 previews) Ivan Bloch, Joanne L. Zippel, New Day Productions and Mary Fisher Productions present:

JUST SO based on Rudyard Kipling's Just So Stories; Book, Mark St. Germain; Lyrics, David Zippel; Music, Doug Katsaros; Conceived and Directed by Julianne Boyd; Choreography, David Storey; Sets, Atkin Pace; Costumes, Ann Hould-Ward; Lighting, Craig Miller; Musical Supervision/Direction, David Friedman; Vocal and Dance Arrangements/Orchestrations, Doug Katsaros; Sound, Tom Gould; General Management, McCann & Nugent Productions; Technical Supervisor, Tom Shilhanek; Props, Katherine Conklin; Wardrobe, Laura Castro; Stage Managers, Renee Lutz, Richard Hester; Press, Jacksina Company, Kevin Boyle. CAST: Andre DeShields (Eldest Magician), Keith Curran (Giraffe), Teresa Burrell (Camel), Tom Robbins (Rhino), Tina Johnson (Elephant Child), Tico Wells (Leopard), Jason Graae (Man). MUSICAL NUMBERS: Just So, The Whole World Revolves around You, Arm in Arm in Harmony, Chill Out!, Camel's Blues, Eat Eat Eat, Dessert Dessert, Itch Itch Itch, Everything under the Sun, The Gospel according to the Leopard, My First Mistake, Shadowy Forest of Garadufi Dance, Giraffe's Reprise, The Answer Song, I've Got to Know, I Have Changed, Lullaby. A musical in two acts. The action takes place on the world's first day.

(Chelsea Center for the Arts) Saturday, Nov. 9-24, 1985 (14 performances) The Cab Theatre Company (Joan Sitomer, Director; Mary MacDonald, Producers; Sherry Mandel, Joann presents:

CARTOON by David Jones; Lyrics, Lynne Sandy; Stage Manager, Mary C. Carollo; Lighting, John Hickey; Sound, Daniel McCleary; Set/Costumes, Neal Bishop; MacDonald; Press, Bruce Paddock. CAST: Andrew Finney (He), Ashley Gardner (She), Daniel McCleary. A post-nuclear comedy in two acts and three scenes.

(Players Theatre) Sunday, Nov. 10,–Dec. 15, 1985 (21 performances and 16 previews) Robert Mansdorf presents:

INSIDE-OUT by James Van Lare; Director, Mr. Van Lare; Set, Donald Jensen; Lighting, John Michael Deegan; Costumes, Shell Walker; Associate Producer, Lisa Young; Production Assistant, Robin Allan; Stage Managers, Kevin Boyle, Jane Steinberg, Darrel Kay; Press, Jacksina Company. CAST: John Kudan (Neil), Adam Oliensis (Rich), Jo Anna Rush (Alice), Sharon Talbot (Standby for Alice). A play in three scenes without intermission. The action takes place at the present time in Neil's apartment in New York City.

(Second Avenue Theatre) Monday, Nov. 11, 1985–July 13, 1986 (277 performances and 18 previews) Sherwin M. Goldman, Moishe Rosenfeld and Westport Productions present:

THE GOLDEN LAND created by Zalmen Mlotek and Moishe Rosenfeld; Director, Jacques Levy; Musical Staging, Donald Saddler; Associate Producer, William Two-hill; Sound, Natasha Landau; Scenery, Lindey Decker; Lighting, John McLain; Costumes, Jack Weisberg; Orchestrations, Peter Sokolow; Musical Arrangements/Direction, Zalmen Mlotek; Casting, Lindey Decker; Technical Director, Dorothy Chansky; Stage Managers, Kevin Patterson, Deborah Dodson; Dance Captain, Joanne Borts; Production Assistant, Avi Hoffman, Marc Krause, Neva John Robelen; Production Assistant, Dorothy Chansky; Stage Managers, Kevin Patterson. CAST: Bruce Adler, Phyllis Berk, Joanne Borts, Milly Schoenbaum, Marc Ehrenreich, Ellen Cleland, Craig Butler, Lisa Welmer; Press, Avi Hoffman. Standbys: Jacob Ehrenreich, Ellen Gould. A musical in two acts and nine scenes.

Joanne Borts, Neva Small,
Krause, Neva Small, Land

**Susan Wands, Karen Kruger, Jean Richards
in "Whining and Dining"** *(S. Stava Photo)*

**Evan Thompson, Nancy C. Genuardi, John Graham,
Jeff Paul in "Macbett"** *(Robert Klein Photo)*

(13th Street Theatre) Thursday, Oct. 24,–Nov. 16, 1985 (20 performances). Stages of Community Enrichment presents:
BECOMING STRANGERS by George Freek; Director, Karen Gnat; Sets, Gordon A. Juel; Costumes, Kristina Katz; Lighting, Edward R. F. Matthews; Assistant Director, Kevin Kennison; Stage Managers, Dana J. Baker, Shannon Penrod; Press, Christine Stump. CAST: Connie Shulman (Betsy), Terrence Frawley (Pa), Douglas Treem (Duke), Ami Rothschild (Jane), Michael Gnat (Howard), Terrence Frawley (Man), Understudies: Karen Brubach (Jane/Betsy), Clay Dickinson (Howard/Duke).

(Perry Street Theatre) Sunday, Oct. 24,–27, 1985 (5 performances) Portia Productions and Robert K. O'Neill present:
WHINING AND DINING by Jeryl Turco; Director, Mitzi Metzl-Pazer; Set, Carla Lauren Messina; Lighting, Tracy Eck; Sound, Steve Elber; Executive Producer, Susan D. Atkinson; Stage Manager, Elisa Loprete. CAST: Jean Richards, (Catherine), Susan Wands (Jody), Karen Kruger (Simone), Cliff Weissman (John), Gerrianne Raphael (Mother), Dino Narizzano (Father), Vera Lockwood (Nonnie), Robert O'Neill (Robert), Elisa Loprete (Maid), Deloria Ruyle (Maid). A play in 2 acts and 14 scenes. The action takes place in the home of Mr. and Mrs. Mecca and in their daughter Jody's apartment.

(Symphony Space) Thursday, Oct. 24,–Nov. 10, 1985 (12 performances and 2 previews) Lincoln Center Institute (Director, Mark Schubart; Associate Directors, Robert J. Crane, June Dunbar; Assistant Director, Carol Sienkiewicz) presents:
THE WINTER'S TALE by William Shakespeare; Director, Andy Wolk; Set, Derek McLane; Costumes, Karen Gerson; Lighting, David Noling; Music Composed by Robert Dennis; Choreography, Randolyn Zinn; Producer, June Dunbar; Production Assistants, Jane Besthoff, Rosalind Goethals; Wardrobe, Leila Elias, Tamara Kirkman; Stage Managers, Johnna Murray, Liz Wright; Press, Joe McKaughan, Susanne Stevens, Lisa Batchelder. CAST: David Purdham (Leontes), Ellen Parker (Hermione), Bradley Kane (Mamillius), Peter Crombie (Camillo), Bill Schoppert (Cleomenes), Hewitt Brooks (Antigonus), Jean DeBaer (Paulina), Melody Combs (Emilia), Brian Smiar (The Jailor), Thomas Kopache (Polixenes), Steven Flynn (Florizel), Willie Reale (Autolycus), Brian Smiar (Old Shepherd), Hewitt Brooks (Young Shepherd), Ellen Parker (Perdita), Melody Combs (Mopsa), Bill Schoppert (Servant), Bradley Kane (Time). Performed with one intermission.

(Unitarian Church of All Souls) Friday, Oct. 25,–Nov. 10, 1985 (16 performances) The All Souls Players present:
MACBETT by Eugene Ionesco; Translated by Charles Marowitz from the French; Director, David McNitt; Costumes, Virginia Wood; Lighting, David Bean; Sound, Ira Stoller; Producers, Julia Parisi, Tran William Rhodes; Stage Managers, Marlene Greene, Linda Panzner, Terri Mintz, James Jacobus; Props, Sheila Mooney; Technical Director, David Bean; Press, Tran William Rhodes. CAST: Al D'Andrea (Macbett), Nancy C. Genuardi (Lady Duncan), Brian Carpenter (Banco), Evan Thompson (Duncan), Denise Dunayer (Lady in Waiting/Witch), Roy Steinberg (Candor), Tom Morrissey (Glamiss/Monk/Bishop), John Graham (Macol), Jeff Paul (Soldier/Officer/Sick Man), James Jacobus (Salesman/Orderly/Servant/Guest), Marie McMurrer (Maid/Orderly/Servant), Terri Mintz (Soldier/Sick Woman/Guest), J. Peter O'Connor (Soldier/Officer/Butterfly Hunter). A play in two acts.

(Folksbiene Playhouse) Saturday, Oct. 26, 1985–March 9, 1986
BROOME STREET, AMERICA by Sylvia Regan; Yiddish adaptation and lyrics by Miriam Kressyn; Director, Roger Sullivan; Music, Abraham Ellstein; Musical Arrangements/Direction, Andrea Goodzeit; Sets, James Wolk; Lighting, Arthur Resler; Costumes, Neil Cooper; Press, Bruce Cohen, Kathleen von Schmid. CAST: Betty Silberman (Fanny), Miriam Gordon (Esther), Zypora Spaisman (Becky Felderman), Jack Rechtzeit (Aaron Greenspan), James Harris (Hymie as a boy), I. W. Firestone (Harry Engel), Raquel Yossiffon (Sadie), Daniel Chiel (Irving Tashman), Jacques Brawer (Benjamin Brownstein), Menachem Bazian (Hymie as a young man), Jacob Mirer (Hymie Tashman). A play with music.

(The New Theater) Tuesday, Oct. 29,–Nov. 3, 1985 (6 performances)
AMONG THE FALLEN by Catherine Burns; Director, Adam Zahler; Costumes, Margot Avery; Lighting, Leon Hopkins; Stage Manager, Sarah Potok. CAST: Virginia Hoffmann (Heidi), Debra Neel (Lana), Liz Schuette (JJ), Frank Saracino (Jeff), Alan Altshuld (Corky), Betsy Howie (Scotti), Tony Cormier (Douglas), Debra Babcock (Mary), Leon Hopkins (Larry), James Reed (Michael), Margot Avery (Dorothy), Melissa Salmons (Suzanne), Lachlan Macleay (Neil), Henry J. Quinn (Dandy), Elizabeth Flynn-Jones (Elisabeth). A comedy in two acts. The action takes place in the converted garage-dressing room of the Valley Players in August 1975, the day of the tech-dress rehearsal of Gorky's The Lower Depths.

**Jean DeBaer, Hewitt Brooks, David Purdham
in "The Winter's Tale"** *(Susanne Faulkner Stevens Photo)*

**Jack Rechtzeit, Zypora Spaisman
in "Broome Street, America"**
(Carol Rosegg Photo)

63

(South Street Theatre) Tuesday, Oct. 29,–Nov. 16, 1985 (16 performances). Bruce Caro and Sherri Felt present:
ROCKBOUND with Book and Lyrics by C. J. Critt; Music, Roberta Baum; Director, Dennis Deal; Musical Direction, Jonny Bowden; Choreography, Michele Kadison; Set/Lighting, Marc D. Malamud, Julia Rubin; Costumes, Evadne Giannini; Special Visual Effects, Rusty Russell; Sound, Lia Vollack; Hair/Makeup, Jennifer Aspinall; Casting, Herman/Lipson; Production Coordinator, Melanie N. Dratfield; Assistant to Director, Mildred Lewis; Props, Bob D'Arinzo; Props/Wardrobe, Nickey Wiesner; Stage Managers, Pam Weinstein, Lisa Braden; Press, Becky Flora. CAST: Adinah Alexander (Mary Lou/Shira), David Cowles (Cliff/Roc I), Linda Dwyer (Pam/Leto/Others), David May (Blast/Roc II), Suzie Plaksin (Prof. Wilson/Clusterhead/Phyllis/Others), Ariel Powers (Zivia/Dormo/Others), Rob Rota (Jay Berd). MUSICAL NUMBERS: Rockbound Rap, Near Nuke Fluke, Here in My Hands, Time Travel, Miners Chant, After the Sadness, Glorion, Rock Release, Hugs and Kisses, What Does One Life Mean, Basic Love, Chain of Lies, Return to the Light, Gold, I Don't Want to Be in Love, Robot Bop, Lifetimes, Nu-Man, It Doesn't Stop Here. A new sci-fi musical in two acts. The action takes place on a university campus in Oregon in 1985. . . . and in the future.

(Town Hall) Wednesday, Oct. 30,–Dec. 29, 1985 (54 performances and 6 previews) Yiddish Musical Theatre of New York (Raymond Ariel, Stuart Rosenberg, Producers) presents:
A MATCH MADE IN HEAVEN with Book and Original Music, Jack Rechtzeit; Music Arrangements, Alexander Lustig; New Lyrics, I. Alper; Director, Yankele Alperin; Musical Staging, Derek Wolshonak; Sets Gary Grianti; Costumes, Clare Gosney; English translation, David Ellin; Lighting/Stage Manager, Bernard Sauer; Executive Manager, Ruth V. Ellin; General Production Manager, Sandy Levitt; Stage Managers, Stewart Figa, Shifee Lovitt; Technical Director, Wesley Sturgis; Dance Captain, Tara Tyrrell; Wardrobe, Thunder Marsh; Press, Max Eisen, Madelon Rosen, Maria Soma. CAST: Monica Tesler (Natasha), Eleanor Reissa (Tsipke), Yankele Alperin (Tzudik), Reizl Bozyk (Mintze), Stewart Figa (Berish), Leon Liebgold (Pesach), Shifee Lovitt (Lida), David Ellin (Smirnov), David Montefiore (The Rebbe), Ben Gotlieb (Grisha Smirnov), Ensemble: Nicole Flender, Carolyn Goor, Tara Tyrrell, Dean Badolato, Anthony Bova, Jay Tramel. A musical in two acts. The action takes place in the miller's yard in 1910.

(Circle in the Square Downtown) Thursday, Oct. 31,–Nov. 24, 1985 (46 performances)
HAMELIN presented by Craig Anderson; Book, Richard Jarboe, Harvey Shield, Matthew Wells; Music and Lyrics, Richard Jarboe, Harvey Shield; Choreography, Jerry Yoder; Director, Ron Nash; Set, Steven Rubin; Costumes, Mark Bridges, Steve C. Kleiser; Lighting, Rick Belzer; Sound, Charles Bugbee 3rd; Musical Supervisor/Routiner, Ronald Melrose; Synthesizer Programer/Designer, Steven Oirich; Associate Producers, Jan Jalenak, Golden Rose Productions; Company Manager, Robert W. Baldwin; Special Effects, Richard Desimone; Assistant Director, Michael Goldberg; Wardrobe, Charles Catanese; Production Assistants, Kay Pro, Mac Intosh; Stage Manager, Michael A. Clarke; Press, Becky Flora, Mary Bryant, Glen Gary. CAST: Scott Fless (Lech), Patrick Hamilton (The Piper), G. Wayne Hoffman (The Mayor), Steven Jacob (Rudolph), Andrew Kraus (Jigger/Otto), Liz Larsen (Gilda), Jodi Mitchel (Gertrude), Erica L. Paulson (Chigger/Utta), Stephen Terrell (Standby). MUSICAL NUMBERS: We're Rats, The Mayor Doesn't Care, Doing My Job, Rap Trap, Easy for Me, What a Day, Paradise, Charismatic, Better Keep Your Promise, Follow the Music Man, Feel the Beat, Serving the People, Mother, Gold, I'll Remember, You've Outstayed Your Welcome. A musical in two acts. The action takes place on a street in Hamelin on June 26, 1284.

Terence Burk, Diane Tarleton, Caroline Arnold, Steve Patterson, Donn Whyte, Michael Grodenchik, Barbara Sinclair, Shan Sullivan in "Crime and Punishment"

(Harold Clurman Theatre) Friday, Nov. 1,–Dec. 1, 1985 (21 performances and 8 previews)
CRIME AND PUNISHMENT by Fyodor Dostoyevsky; Adapted by L. A. Sheldon; Set/Lighting/Sound, John Sowle; Costumes, Jan Finnell; Director, Maria Mazer with John Van Ness Philip; Presented by Quantum Leap, Josh Lukins, John Van Ness Philip in association with Sandra Bridewell; Technical Director, Mark Porter; Stage Manager, Tracy Crum; Press, Hunt/Pucci Associates. CAST: Caroline Arnold (Sonia), Sully Boyar (Porfiry), Terence Burk (Chief Clerk/Lebezyatnikov/Bank Messenger/Crowd), Chad Burton (Marmeladov/Nikolay/Crowd), Jason Evans (Boy/Kolya), Michael Grodenchik (Waiter/Priest), David Jaffe (Razumikhin/Driver/Crowd), James Mathers (Svidrigaylov/Caretaker/Crowd), Eulalie Noble (Mrs. Raskolnikov/Crowd), Steven Patterson (Assistant Superintendent/Dr. Zossimov/Crowd), Matina Simmons (Polya/Crowd), Shan Sullivan (Raskolnikov), Diane Tarleton (Mrs. Marmeladov/Crowd), Gretchen Trapp (Lisavetta/Whore/Dunya), Barbara Sinclair (Pawnbroker/Landlady/Crowd), Donn Whyte (Luzhin/Crowd), Michael Grodenchik (Standby). A drama performed with one intermission. The action takes place in St. Petersburg, Russia, in 1860.

(Hartley House) Thursday, Nov. 7,–30, 1985 (20 performances) Playwrights Preview Productions (Frances Hill, Artistic Director; Rick Porter, Producer) presents:
AN OUNCE OF PREVENTION by Hal Corley; Director, Susann Brinkley; Set, David Birn; Lighting, Richard Comfort; Costumes, Lauryn Axelrod; Hairstylist, Tony Thoman; Production Assistants, Deborah Hobart, Linda Shary, Stuart Laurence; Stage Managers, Elaine O'Donnell, Judy Cummings; Press, Ann Hollywood, Joel Spinetti. CAST: Tonya Pinkins (Mona), Carole Lockwood (Bobbie), Cindy Adkins (April), Angelini Fiordellisi (Hilda), Charles Keating (Ergun). Performed without intermission. The action takes place at the present time in a junior high school classroom in the suburbs.

(Jack Lawrence Theatre) Thursday, Nov. 7,–Dec. 8, 1985 (6 performances and 30 previews) Ivan Bloch, Joanne L. Zippel, New Day Productions and Mary Fisher Productions present:
JUST SO based on Rudyard Kipling's Just So Stories; Book, Mark St. Germain; Lyrics, David Zippel; Music, Doug Katsaros; Conceived and Directed by Julianne Boyd; Choreography, David Storey; Sets, Atkin Pace; Costumes, Ann Hould-Ward; Lighting, Craig Miller; Musical Supervision/Direction, David Friedman; Vocal and Dance Arrangements/Orchestrations, Doug Katsaros; Sound, Tom Gould; General Management, McCann & Nugent Productions; Technical Supervisor, Tom Shilhanek; Props, Katherine Conklin; Wardrobe, Laura Castro; Stage Managers, Renee Lutz, Richard Hester; Press, Jacksina Company, Kevin Boyle. CAST: Andre DeShields (Eldest Magician), Keith Curran (Giraffe), Teresa Burrell (Camel), Tom Robbins (Rhino), Tina Johnson (Elephant Child), Tico Wells (Leopard), Jason Graae (Man). MUSICAL NUMBERS: Just So, The Whole World Revolves around You, Arm in Arm in Harmony, Chill Out!, Camel's Blues, Eat Eat Eat, Dessert Dessert, Itch Itch Itch, Everything under the Sun, The Gospel according to the Leopard, My First Mistake, Shadowy Forest of Garadufi Dance, Giraffe's Reprise, The Answer Song, I've Got to Know, I Have Changed, Lullaby. A musical in two acts. The action takes place on the world's first day.

Reizl Bozyk, Shifee Lovitt, David Montefiore, Eleanor Reissa, Monica Tesler in "A Match Made in Heaven" *(Martha Swope Photo)*

(One Sheridan Square) Thursday, Nov. 7, 1985–Feb. 27, 1986. The Ridiculous Theatrical Company (Artistic Director, Charles Ludlam; General Manager, Steven Samuels) presents:
SALAMMBO by Charles Ludlam; Freely adapted from the novel by Gustave Flaubert; Original Music, Peter Golub; Sets, Edgar Franceschi; Costumes, Everett Quinton; Lighting, Richard Currie; Director, Charles Ludlam; Production Manager, Rock Townsend; Assistant Director, Phillip Warner; Sound, Edward McGowan; Wardrobe, Carol Squadra; Props, Debra Griboff; Hairstylist, Ethyl Eichelberger; Press, Carolyn VanDusen. CAST: Charles Ludlam (Salammbo), Everett Quinton (Taanach), Philip Campanaro (Matho), Steven Samuels (Spendius), John Heys (Schahabarim), Katy Dierlam (Hanno), Ethyl Eichelberger (Hamilcar Barca), Daniel Sambula (Narr'Havas), Deborah Petti (Priest), Arthur Brady (Victim), Arthur Kraft (Iddibal), Barbarians: Pierre Asselin, John Germain, Jerry Reiner, Boubie, Jeffrey Steinberg, David Paul. An "erotic tragedy" in two acts. The action takes place in Carthage in 300 B.C.

(TOMI Terrace Theatre) Thursday, Nov. 7,–23, 1985 (16 performances) New Arts Theatre Co. presents:
THE WONDER YEARS by Simone Bloch; Director, Joshua Astrachan; Set, Derek McLane; Lighting, M. L. Costumes, Candice Donnelly; Sound, James M. Bay; Managing Director, Daniel Kanter; Cityscape Design, Jesse Hartland; Stage Manager, Loretta Scheer; Press, Patt Dale, Julianne Waldhelm. CAST: Fred Sanders (Steve), Ellen Mareneck (Helen), Ed Baran (Bob), Elaine Rinehart (Mary), Kathleen Milne (Joann). A comedy in two acts. The action takes place in New York City in 1981.

Charles Ludlam, Philip Campanaro in "Salammbo" *(Anita & Steve Shevett Photo)*

(Samuel Beckett Theatre) Thursday, Nov. 7, 1985–Jan. 19, 1986 (73 performances and 7 previews)
THE IMPORTANCE OF BEING EARNEST by Oscar Wilde; Director, Philip Campanella; Set, David R. Ballou; Costumes, Peggy Farrell; Lighting, Jackie Manassee; General Manager, Craig S. Dorfman; Company Manager, Richard Goodis; Technical Director, John L. Harrison; Wigs, Paul Huntley; Stage Managers, Lee Bloomrosen, Kelli Kruger; Press, Henry Luhrman, Terry M. Lilly, David Mayhew, Andrew P. Shearer; Presented by the Harold Clurman Theatre (Jack Garfein, Artistic Director) and Halcyon Productions (Carmella Ross/Ellen Oppenheim). CAST: A. D. Cover (Lane), Anthony Fusco (Algernon Moncrieff), Samuel Maupin (John Worthing), Dina Merrill succeeded by Peg Small (Lady Bracknell), Cynthia Dozier (Hon. Gwendolyn Fairfax), Carmella Ross (Miss Prism), Cherry Jones (Cecily Cardew), William Denis (Rev. Canon Chasuble), Robert North (Merriman), Kelli Kruger (Understudy). A comedy in three acts. The action takes place in 1895.

(Riverwest Theatre) Friday, Nov. 8,–Dec. 1, 1985 (16 performances and 4 previews) The Phoenix Ensemble presents:
CASUALTIES by Joe DiMiceli; Director, Carter Inskeep; Set, Billy Makuta; Costumes, Reenie Upchurch; Lighting, Peggy Eisenhauer; Stage Manager, Joseph E. Tully; Press, Maya Associates/Penny Landau. CAST: Ed Hyland (Harris), Hariet S. Miller (Ted), Stacey Gladstone (Terri), Margaret Hunt (Jean), Vicki Hirsch (Pappy), Mary Israel (Bev), Reenie Upchurch (Janice), Paul Ravich (Ramey), Understudy: Kerry Metzler. A drama in two acts. The action takes place between Tam Ky, Vietnam in 1971, and a veterans hospital today.

Cynthia Dozier, Samuel Maupin, Dina Merrill in "The Importance of Being Earnest" *(Martha Swope Photo)*

Trey Wilson, Dee Hoty, Nancy Opel, Laura Dean, Jeff Keller, Jason Alexander in "Personals" *(Martha Swope Photo)*

(Minetta Lane Theatre) Friday, Nov. 8, 1985–July 13, 1986 (265 performances and 19 previews). John-Edward Hill, Arthur MacKenzie, Jon D. Silverman in association with Fujisankei Communications Group present:
PERSONALS with Music by William Dreskin, Joel Phillip Friedman, Seth Friedman, Alan Menken, Stephen Schwartz, Michael Skloff; Written by and Lyrics by David Crane, Seth Friedman, Marta Kauffman; Director, Paul Lazarus; Choreography, D. J. Giagni; Set, Loren Sherman; Costumes, Ann Hould-Ward; Lighting, Richard Nelson; Sound, Otts Munderloh; Musical Director/Vocal Arrangements, Michael Skloff; Orchestrations, Steven Oirich; General Management, Weiler/Miller Associates; Casting, McCorkle; Props, Terrence Foster; Wardrobe, Cheryl Woronoff, Susan Manning; Production Assistant, Rod Caspers; Stage Managers, Tom Aberger, Lauren Class Schneider; Press, Fred Nathan, Glenna Freedman, Merle Frimark, Anne Abrams, Bert Fink, Marc Thibodeau, Dennis Crowley. CAST: Jason Alexander succeeded by Marcus Olson (Louis and Others), Jeff Keller (Sam and Others), Laura Dean succeeded by Liz Larsen (Kim and Others), Dee Hoty (Claire and Others), Nancy Opel (Louise and Others), Trey Wilson succeeded by Hal Robinson (Typesetter and Others). MUSICAL NUMBERS: Nothing to Do with Love, After School Special, Mama's Boys, A Night Alone, I Think You Should Know, Second Grade, Imagine My Surprise, I'd Rather Dance Alone, Moving in with Linda, A Little Happiness, I Could Always Go to You, The Guy I Love, Michael, Picking Up the Pieces, Some Things Don't End. A musical revue in two acts.

(Chelsea Center for the Arts) Saturday, Nov. 9–24, 1985 (14 performances) The Cab Theatre Company presents:
CARTOON by David Jones; Director, Joan Sitomer; Set/Costumes, Neal Bishop; Lighting, John Hickey; Sound, Mary MacDonald; Producers, Sherry Mandel, Joann C. Carollo; Music, Daniel McCleary; Lyrics, Lynne Sandy; Stage Manager, Mary MacDonald; Press, Bruce Paddock. CAST: Andrew Finney (He), Ashley Gardner (She), Daniel McCleary. A post-nuclear comedy in two acts and three scenes.

(Players Theatre) Sunday, Nov. 10,–Dec. 15, 1985 (21 performances and 16 previews) Robert Mansdorf presents:
INSIDE-OUT by James Van Lare; Director, Mr. Van Lare; Set, Donald Jensen; Lighting, John Michael Deegan; Costumes, Shell Walker; Associate Producer, Michael J. Kay; General Management, Next Wave; Production Associate, Lisa Young; Production Assistant, Robin Allan; Stage Managers, John Hodge, Michael J. Kay; Press, Jacksina Company, Marcy Granata, Kevin Boyle, Jane Steinberg, Darrel Joseph, Ted Killmer. CAST: John Kudan (Neil), Adam Oliensis (Rich), Jo Anna Rush (Alice), Sharon Talbot (Standby for Alice). A play in three scenes without intermission. The action takes place at the present time in Neil's apartment in New York City.

(Second Avenue Theatre) Monday, Nov. 11, 1985–July 13, 1986 (277 performances and 18 previews) Sherwin M. Goldman, Moishe Rosenfeld and Westport Productions present:
THE GOLDEN LAND created by Zalmen Mlotek and Moishe Rosenfeld; Director, Jacques Levy; Musical Staging, Donald Saddler; Musical Arrangements/Direction, Zalmen Mlotek; Orchestrations, Peter Sokolow; Associate Producer, William Twohill; Sound, Jack Weisberg; Casting, Deborah Brown; Lighting, John McLain; Costumes, Natasha Landau; Scenery, Lindsey Decker; Company Manager, Daryl T. Dodson; Dance Captain, Joanne Borts; Technical Director, John Griffith; Wardrobe, John Robelen; Production Assistant, Dorothy Chansky; Stage Managers, Deborah Clelland, Craig Butler, Lisa Welmer; Press, Milly Schoenbaum, Kevin Patterson. CAST: Bruce Adler, Phyllis Berk, Joanne Borts, Avi Hoffman, Marc Krause, Neva Small, and The Golden Land Klezmer Orchestra, Standbys: Jacob Ehrenreich, Ellen Gould. A musical in two acts and nine scenes.

Joanne Borts, Bruce Adler, Phyllis Berk, Marc Krause, Neva Small, Avi Hoffman in "The Golden Land" *(Martha Swope Photo)*

John Kudan, Jo Anna Rush in "Inside-Out" *(Martha Swope Photo)*

George Gerdes (kneeling), Al DeCristo, Louise Edeiken, Carol Hall, Gretchen Cryer, Guy Stroman, Kecia Lewis-Evans, Dylan Baker, Becky Gelke, Tamara Tunie, Jennifer Naimo in "To Whom It May Concern" *(Martha Swope Photo)*

(LaMama E.T.C.) Thursday, Nov. 14, 1985
HARM'S WAY by Mac Wellman; Director, George Ferencz; Music, Bob Jewett, Jack Maeby; Set, Patrick Kennedy; Costumes, Sally J. Lesser; Lighting, Blu; Performed by The Acting Company Cement; Stage Manager, Virlana Tkacz. CAST: Tom Costello (Mother/Blackmange), Sheila Dabney (Fisheye/Wizard), Stephen Mellor (Santouche), Deirdre O'Connell (Isle of Mercy), Zivia Flomenhaft (By Way of Being Hidden), Gregg Daniel (Crowsfoot), Jeff Shoemaker (President McKinley)

(Actors Outlet) Friday, Nov. 15,–Dec. 1, 1985 StageArts Theater Company (Artistic Directors, Nell Robinson, Ruth Ann Norris) presents:
MORTALLY FINE by William J. Sibley; Director, Cash Baxter; Set, Jack Bell Stewart; Costumes, Lewis D. Rampino; Lighting, Bob Bessoir; Casting, Jay Binder; Sound, Jesse Miller; Stage Managers, Jack Gianino, Annalee Van Kleeck; Press, Shirley Herz Associates, Pete Sanders, Peter Cromarty. CAST: Ruth Ann Norris (Irene Fondren), Helen Lloyd Breed (Alice Nunley), Arne Gundersen (Hobart Fondren), David Canary (Nub McKaty), Gil Rogers (Elvin Shoemaker), Kirsti Carnahan (Karin Ann/Arcy Peace), Dena Dietrich (Mary Nell Hubka), William G. Clark (Larry). A comedy in two acts. The action takes place at the present time in a small town in Texas.

(St. Stephen's Church) Tuesday, Nov. 19, 1985–March 23, 1986 (106 performances and 19 previews). The Bedda Roses Company presents:
TO WHOM IT MAY CONCERN by Carol Hall; Director, Geraldine Fitzgerald; Musical Supervision/Vocal Arrangements/Musical Direction/Staging, Michael O'Flaherty; Lighting, Christina Giannelli; General Management, Maria Productions; Assistant Musical Director, Mary Sugar; Costume Coordinator, Kenneth M. Yount; Wardrobe, Susan Shofner; Stage Managers, Noel Stern, Colleen Janich; Press, Patt Dale, Julianne Waldhelm. CAST: Michael O'Flaherty (Choir Master), Jennifer Naimo (Child), Dylan Baker (Priest), William Hardy (Grandad), Gretchen Cryer (Fay), Michael Hirsch (Bob), Carol Hall (Caroline), Louise Edeiken (Frederika), Tamara Tunie (Sister), Becky Gelke (Celia), Guy Stroman (Mike), Kecia Lewis-Evans (Deloris), Al DeCristo (Elliott), George Gerdes (Stranger), Robin Boudreau, Ellia English. "A musical celebration" performed without intermission. The action takes place at the present time in a church auditorium.

Top: Gil Rogers, David Canary, Dena Dietrich in "Mortally Fine" *(Carol Rosegg Photo)*

(Promenade Theatre) Friday, Nov. 22, 1985–June 1, 1986 (186 performances and 13 previews) Lewis Allen and Stephen Graham present:

A LIE OF THE MIND by Sam Shepard; Directed by Mr. Shepard; Set, Andy Stacklin; Costumes, Rita Ryack; Lighting, Anne E. Militello; Hairstylist/Makeup, Marlies Vallant; General Manager, Albert Poland; Company Manager, Marion Finkler; Assistant Director, Roxanne Rogers; Props, Katherine Conklin; Sound, Janet Kalas; Wardrobe, Susan Freel; Stage Managers, Ruth Kreshka, Jane Grey; Press, David Powers, Leo Stern. CAST: Harvey Keitel succeeded by Bill Raymond, David Straithorn (Jake), Aidan Quinn succeeded by Don Harvey (Frankie), Amanda Plummer succeeded by Deirdre O'Connell (Beth), Will Patton succeeded by John Griesemer, Steve Hofvendahl (Mike), Geraldine Page succeeded by Salome Jens, Sally Gracie (Lorraine), Karen Young succeeded by Betsy Aidem (Sally), James Gammon succeeded by Beeson Carroll (Baylor), Ann Wedgeworth succeeded by Louise Latham (Meg). A drama in three acts. Recipient of 1986 citation for Best Play by the New York Drama Critics Circle.

Martha Swope Photos

Right: Beeson Carroll, David Strathairn, Deirdre O'Connell, Louise Latham Top: Will Patton, Amanda Plummer

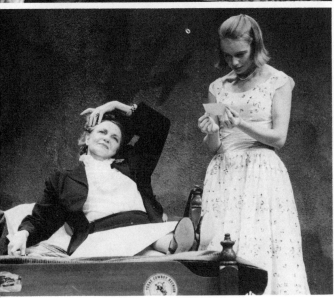

Geraldine Page, Karen Young
Above: Ann Wedgeworth, Aidan Quinn

James Gammon, Amanda Plummer
"A Lie of the Mind"

67

(South Street Theatre) Tuesday, Nov. 26, 1985–Feb. 2, 1986 (60 performances and 6 previews) Bernard E. Seeman presents The Orange Theatre Company's production of:

IN THE BOOM BOOM ROOM by David Rabe; Director, Jerrold Brody; Set, Victoria Nourafchan; Costumes, Hope Hanafin; Lighting, Heather Carson; Sound, Tom Gould; Music Coordination, M. Leslie Thompson; Assistant Producer, Deena Levy; General Management, Whitbell Productions; Casting, Slater/Willett; Technical Director, Mark Porter; Wardrobe, Chris Sanders; Stage Manager, Gerard J. Campbell; Production Assistants, Rachel S. Levine, Nan Siegmund, Jill Lummus; Press, Patt Dale, Julianne Waldhelm. CAST: Ron August (Harold), Victor D'Altorio (Guy), Val Hawk (Sally), Deena Levy (Vikki), Michael Farris-Manetta (Al), Liz McDonald (Chrissy), Polly O'Malley (Melissa), Curt Rayvis (Eric), M. Leslie Thompson (Susan), Marie Wallace (Helen), Kim Waltman (Ralphie), Robert Zukerman (Man), Understudies: Laurie Graff (Chrissy), Nan Gatewood (Susan/Vikki/Melissa/Sally/Helen), Robert Zukerman (Harold/Guy/Eric), Daniel Hutchison (Ralphie/Al/Man). A play in two acts with prologue and epilogue.

(Lamb's Theatre) Wednesday, Nov. 27, 1985–Jan. 5, 1986 (35 performances and 8 previews). The Lamb's Theatre Co. (Producing Director, Carolyn Rossi Copeland; Associate Director, Pamela Perrell) presents:

THE GIFTS OF THE MAGI based on the classic O'Henry Stories; Book/Lyrics, Mark St. Germain; Music/Lyrics, Randy Courts; Director, Christopher Catt; Choreography, Lynnette Barkley; Musical Direction/Incidental Music, Steven M. Alper; Set, Michael C. Smith; Costumes, Hope Hanafin; Lighting, Heather Carson; Technical Director, Tom Dale Keever; Props, Amy Darnton; Production Assistants, Chuck Cover, Tedrin Blair Lindsay, Elizabeth Navarre, Bill Petroni; Stage Managers, Steve Zorthian, Melissa L. Burdick; Press, Jacksina Co., Judy Jacksina, Marcy Granata, Kevin Boyle, Jane Steinberg, Darrel Joseph, Ted Kilmer. CAST: Glenn Mure (Him), Lynne Winterseller (Her), Michael Kelly Boone (Willy), John David Westfall (Jim), Leslie Hicks (Della), Bert Michaels (Soapy). MUSICAL NUMBERS: Star of the Night, Gifts of the Magi, More Than Enough, Christmas to Blame, How Much to Buy a Dream?, The Restaurant, Once More, Bum Luck, Greed, Pockets, The Same Girl. A musical performed without intermission. The action takes place in New York City from December 23 through 25, 1905.

(Cherry Lane Theatre) Tuesday, Dec. 3, 1985–Feb. 23, 1986; Moved to Sheridan Square Playhouse/Circle Rep. Theatre Feb. 27, 1986 and still playing at press time. The Nunsense Theatrical Company in association with Joseph Hoesl and Brill Crowder present:

NUNSENSE originally presented by the Baldwin Theatre; Written and Directed by Dan Goggin; Musical Staging/Choreography, Felton Smith; Set, Barry Axtell; Lighting, Susan A. White; Musical Direction, Michael Rice; General Management, Roger Alan Gindi; Company Manager, Jeffrey Capitola; Stage Managers, Trey Hunt, Susan Gordon-Clark; Press, Shirley Herz, Pete Sanders, Peter Cromarty, Irene Gandy, Gary Lawrence, David Roggensack. CAST: Marilyn Farina (Sister Mary Cardelia), Vicki Belmonte succeeded by Edwina Lewis (Sister Mary Hubert), Christine Anderson (Sister Robert Anne), Semina DeLaurentis (Sister Mary Amnesia), Suzi Winson (Sister Mary Leo), Susan Gordon-Clark (Understudy). MUSICAL NUMBERS: Nunsense Is Habit-Forming, A Difficult Transition, Benedicite, The Biggest Ain't the Best, Playing Second Fiddle, So You Want to Be a Nun, Turn Up the Spotlight, Lilacs Bring Back Memories, Tackle That Temptation with a Time Step, Growing Up Catholic, We've Got to Clean Out the Freezer, Just a Coupla Sisters, Soup's On/The Dying Nun Ballet, I Just Want to Be a Star, The Drive-In, I Could've Gone to Nashville, Gloria in Excelsis Deo, Holier Than Thou. A musical comedy in two acts. The action takes place at the present time in Mt. Saint Helen's School Auditorium.

Stephen Aucoin Photos

Cast of "The Gifts of the Magi"
Top: Liz McDonald, M. Leslie Thompson
in "In the Boom Boom Room" *(Martha Swope Photos)*

Christine Anderson, Suzi Winson, Marilyn Farina,
Vicki Belmonte, Semina DeLaurentis in "Nunsense"
also above *(Stephen Aucoin Photos)*

**Stephen Lehew, Roslyn Burrough, Keith Amos,
Stephanie Cotsirilos in "Sweet Will"**
(Peter Cunningham Photo)

(Provincetown Playhouse) Tuesday, Dec. 3, 1985–Jan. 5, 1986 in repertory with Vampire Lesbians of Sodom/Coma. (28 performances and 8 previews). Presented by Theatre in Limbo (Kenneth Elliott, Gerald A. Davis).
TIMES SQUARE ANGEL by Charles Busch; Director, Kenneth Elliott; Choreography, Jeff Veazey; Set, B. T. Whitehill; Costumes, Debra Tennenbaum; Lighting, Vivien Leone; General Management, David Lawlor/Thom Shovestull; Stage Manager/Wigs, Elizabeth Katherine Carr; Press, Shirley Herz, Pete Sanders. CAST: Andy Halliday (Eddie), Robert Carey (Johnny the Noodle/Georgie), Tom Aulino (Reporter/Mrs. Paine/Milton Keisler/Agnes), Arnie Kolodner (Abe Kesselman/Albert an angel), Charles Busch (Irish O'Flanagan), Meghan Robinson (Miss Ellerbee/Olive Sanborn/Old Mag), Ralph Buckley (Duke O'Flanagan/Chick LaFountain), Julie Halston (Mrs. Tooley/Stella), Theresa Marlowe (Cookie Gibbs/Valerie Waverly), Michael Belinger (Dexter Paine III), James Cahill (Voice of the Lord), Yvonne Singh (Peona), Understudies: Michael Belanger, Julie Halston. "A Hard-Boiled Christmas Fantasy" performed without intermission. The action takes place in New York City from 1938 to 1948, and in Heaven.

(18th Street Playhouse) Thursday, Dec. 5–20, 1985 (13 performances; Re-opened Thursday, Jan. 9–12, 1986 for 4 additional performances). Small Child Productions presents:
ALVARONE by Steven Sater; Directed by Mr. Sater; Costumes, Yuval Kaspin; Set, Christopher Holvenstot; Lighting, Richard Clausen; Makeup, Pauline White; Stage Manager, Tom Becker; Press, Bruce Cohen, Kathleen von Schmid. CAST: Steven Sater (Steven), Jo Ann Cunningham (Alvrone), Jeff Bender (Jeffrey), Kate Shein (Jill), Joel Rooks (Ronald). Performed without intermission. The action takes place one evening in a living room in Evansville, Indiana.

(Judith Anderson Theatre) Thursday, Dec. 5–21, 1985 (21 performances) Advantage Entertainment presents:
LOOSE CONNECTIONS by Bill Barnett; Director, Jack Betts; Set/Sound/Lighting, Rick Azar; Lighting, Élaine O'Donnel; Sound, Dave Dumere; Assistant to Producers, Ginger Tidwell; Executive Producer, Chip Cornelius; Associate Producers, Phillip Candler, Dennis D'Amico; Stage Manager, Rick Azar. CAST: Rosalie Gouletas (Stephanie Seiler), Mallory Danaher (Alma Rosenthal), Donald Silva (Warren P. Morgan), Michael Storm (Paul Slater). A comedy in two acts. The action takes place at the present time in Stephanie and Warren's New York City apartment.

(Theatre of the Riverside Church) Friday, Dec. 6–21, 1985 (12 performances)
THE LONG SMOLDERING by Harry Granick; World Premiere; Director, Rod Alexander; Stage Manager; Press, Shellie Bransford. CAST: David Coxwell, Julia Indichova, Joel Leffert, Bashia McCoy, Tom O'Brien, Les Shenkel. A drama in two acts. The action takes place in Poland ten years before the holocaust.

(Quaigh Theatre) Wednesday, Dec. 18–30, 1985 (12 performances) Quaigh Theatre in association with Monroe Productions, Ronald A. Rabinowitz, Philip Vasta present:
LIPPE by Ron Scott Stevens; Director, Mr. Stevens; Set, Don Jensen; Sound, George Jacobs; Lighting, Deborah Matlack; Stage Manager, George Anderson; Press, FLT/Francine L. Trevens, Terence Womble. CAST: William Hickey (Lippe), Gary Warner (Jack), Barbara J. Fox (Rose), Dick Turmail (Henry), Bob Jordan (Seymour), J. J. Johnson (Jason Johnson), Linda Roberts (Marie), Tom Hoover (Blackie Brown), Steve O'Brien (Commissioner), Bernard Feinerman (Al Mainetti), Herb Goldman (Reporter), Milton Langhorne (Understudy). A play in 2 acts and 13 scenes with prologue and epilogue. The action takes place in New York City.

(Douglas Fairbanks Theater) Thursday, Dec. 26, 1985–Jan. 7, 1986 (1 performance and 14 previews). David C. Gold presents:
BE HAPPY FOR ME by Jerry Sterner; Director, John Ferraro; Set, David Potts; Costumes, Abigail Murray; Lighting, Greg MacPherson; Music arranged by Margaret R. Pine; General Management, Dorothy Olim/George Elmer; Wardrobe, Jill Moray; Stage Managers, William Hare, Russ Pennington; Press, Bruce Cohen, Kathleen von Schmid. CAST: David Groh (Phil), Philip Bosco (Norman), Priscilla Lopez (Elizabeth), Russ Pennington (Casino Dealer/Cab Driver). A comedy in two acts. The action takes place at the present on Aruba, an island in the Caribbean.

(Joann's Silver Lining Cabaret Theatre) Thursday, Dec. 26, 1985–1/11/86 (22 performances). David Drummond presents:
SWEET WILL with Lyrics by William Shakespeare; Music, Lance Mulcahy; Director, John Olon; Musical Direction/Arrangements, Michael Ward; Musical Staging, Dennis Dennehy; Consultant, Desmond Heeley; Lighting, Michael Deegan; General Manager, Paul B. Berkowsky; Company Manager, Mark Saks; Production Assistant, John O'Neill; Stage Manager, Anita Ross; Press, Jeffrey Richards Associates, C. George Willard, Ben Morse, Susan Lee, Bill Shuttleworth. CAST: Keith Amos, Roslyn Burrough, Stephanie Cotsirilos, Stephen Lehew, Steve Postel, Scott Simpson. MUSICAL NUMBERS: Hey Ho the Wind and the Rain, When Icicles Hang by the Wall, Hark Hark the Lark, Where the Bee Sucks, Sigh No More Ladies, It Was a Lover and His Lass, Who Is Sylvia?, When Daisies Pied, All That Glisters, Venus and Adonis, Anon Comes Adonis, Thrice Fairer, Venus and Young Adonis, A Thousand Kisses, I Know Not Love, Graze on My Lips, The Premonition, Ah Me Poor Venus, Adonis Leaving Venus, If He Be Dead, She Looks Upon His Lips, Thus Weary of the World, Street Cries, Shall I Compare Thee, Some Glory in Their Birth, Why Is My Verse So Barren, When My Love Swears, How Heavy Do I Journey, Absent in the Spring, O Mistress Mine, Come into These Yellow Sands, Sea Song, Lo Here the Gentle Lark, Over Hill Over Dale, Now, Oh Take Those Lips Away, Full Fathom Five, Under the Greenwood Tree, Farewell Dear Love. A musical in two acts.

**David Groh, Philip Bosco, Priscilla Lopez
in "Be Happy for Me"** *(Carol Rosegg Photo)*

69

(Lucille Lortel Theatre) Friday, Dec. 27, 1985–Feb. 23, 1986 (68 performances). Lucille Lortel presents:
GERTRUDE STEIN AND A COMPANION by Win Wells; Director, Ira Cirker; Set, Bob Phillips; Costumes, Amanda J. Klein; Lighting, Richard Dorfman; Original Music, Jason Cirker; General Manager, Ben Sprecher; Company Manager, Susan Gustafson; Production Assistant, Dan Bauer; Wardrobe, Mary Lawson; Stage Manager, Robert Bennett; Press, Jeffrey Richards, C. George Willard, Ben Morse, Bill Shuttleworth, Susan E. Lee, Marie-Louise Silva. CAST: Jan Miner (Gertrude Stein), Marian Seldes (Alice B. Toklas). A play in two acts. The action takes place between 1907 and 1967.

(American Renaissance Theater) Thursday, January 9–12, 1986 (4 performances). The American Renaissance Theater presents:
PORTRAIT OF A MAN performed by Robert Elston; Director, Anita Khanzadian; Musical Director, Erica Kaplan; Set, Ernie Schenk; Lighting, David Shepherd. Performed with one intermission.

Jan Miner, Marian Seldes in "Gertrude Stein and a Companion" *(Peter Cunningham Photo)*

(Village Gate Downstairs) Friday, Jan. 10,–April 6, 1986 (86 performances). Ron Abbott, Susan Liederman, and Michael Tucker present:
EL GRANDE DE COCA-COLA by Ron House, Diz White, Alan Shearman, John Neville-Andrews; Directors, Ron House, Diz White, Alan Shearman; Set, Elwin Charles Terrel II; Lighting, Judy Rasmuson; Sound, Paul Garrity; Choreography, Anne Gunderson; General Manager, Albert Poland; Company Manager, Leonard A. Mulhern; Technical Director, Robbie Swanson; Wardrobe, Helen Wilson; Production Assistant, Alison Tucker; Stage Managers, Duane Mazey, Don Stitt; Press, Judy Jacksina, Marcy Granata, Kevin Boyle, Jane Steinberg, Darrel Joseph, Ted Killmer. CAST: Diz White (Consuela Hernandez), Rodger Bumpass (Juan Rodriguez), Alan Shearman (Miguel Hernandez), Ron House (Senor Don Pepe Hernandez), Olga Merediz (Maria Hernandez), Understudies: Emilio Del Pozo (Pepe), Don Stitt/Emilio Del Pozo (Miguel/Juan), Cecilia Arana (Consuela/Maria). A musical revue performed without intermission.

(CSC Repertory Theatre) Sunday & Monday, January 12–13, 1986 (2 performances). CSC in association with Nancy Richards and Robert Mooney presents:
ARTISTS AND ADMIRERS by Alexander Ostrovsky; Translated by David Leveaux, Hanif Kureishi; Director, Robert Mooney; Stage Manager, Andrea Schwartz. CAST: Estelle Kemler (Donma Pantelyevna), Herman Petras (Martyn Prokofyich Narokov), William Cain (Prince Irakly Stratonych Dulyebov), Robin Robson (Grigory Antonych Bakin), Nancy Richards (Alexandra Nikolavna), Kathleen M. Robbins (Nina Vasilyevna Smelskaya), Frank Muller (Ivan Semyonych Velikatov), F. Leslie (Pytor Yegoych Melusov), Randy Kelly (The Tragedian), Peter von Berg (Gavril Petrovich Migaev), Stephen Gleason (Vasya), Joel George, Frank Wood (Waiter/Guards/Porter). A drama in 4 acts performed with one intermission. The action takes place in the late 1870's in a provincial Russian town.

Alan Shearman (also above), Olga Merediz, Ron House, Diz White, Rodger Bumpass in "El Grande de Coca-Cola" *(Martha Swope Photos)*

(St. Clements) Tuesday, Jan. 14–Feb. 15, 1986 Music-Theatre Group/Lenox Arts Center presents the *World Premiere* of **AFRICANIS INSTRUCTUS** composed by Stanley Silverman; Written and Directed by Richard Foreman; Set, Nancy Winters; Costumes, Jim Buff; Lighting, Bill Armstrong; Producing Director, Lyn Austin; Managing Director, Diane Wondisford; Production Associate, Vanessa Palmer; Press, Shirley Herz, Peter Cromarty. CAST: Eve Bennett-Gordon (Rhoda), Susan Browning (Nurse), Keith David (Ben), Kate Dezina (Eleanor), Tommy Hollis (Black Max), David Sabin (Max), Alan Scarfe (Otto), Clarke Brown, Peter Davis, Gerald Gilmore, Charles Richardson, and musicians: Martha Caplin, William Moersch, Joe Tamosaitis, David Oei (Musical Director)

Alan Scarfe, Susan Browning in "Africanis Instructus"
(Carol Rosegg Photo)

(Palsson's Upstairs Supper Club) Monday, Jan. 20,–March 31, 1986 (11 performances on Mondays only). The Fresh Air Cab Company presents: **DON'T EVEN THINK OF PARKING HERE** by Peter Freedman; Director, Maura Tighe; Based on ideas by Betsy Beers, Michael Berliner, Peter Freedman; Developed under the direction of Fred Gorman; Music, Roger Leonard; Lyrics, Betsy Beers; Lights, Rebecca Bandiere, Todd Crosby; Stage Manager, Valerie Lindquist; Press, Becky Flora. CAST: Betsy Beers, Michael Berliner, Winnie Boone, Peter Freedman, Roger Leonard, Frank Lindquist (Pianist). Violations: Our Town Our Town, Identity Crisis in Midtown, That Awkward Silence, Existential Playhouse, Jack Dart, The Adventures of Urban Girl, Midnight in Manhattan, Existential Playhouse Revisited, A Drink with Lenny and Estelle, Fred! The Musical Tragedy, Finale. A comedy revue performed without intermission. The action takes place at the present time in New York City.

(American Folk Theater) Wednesday, Jan. 29,–March 2, 1986 (30 performances). American Folk Theater (Dick Garfield, Artistic Director) presents: **THE TOY FACTORY** by James Himelsbach; Director, Dick Gaffield; Set, Scott Stauffer; Lighting, Tony Giovannetti; Sound, Steven Menasche; Wardrobe, Vanessa Geter, Velma Simmons; Production Manager, Louis Hunt; Production Assistant, Dario Robertson; Stage Managers, Louis Hunt, Paul Spencer. CAST: Leon McMichael (Billy), Douglas Popper (Keller), John A. Bakos (Delbert). The action takes place at the present time in a toy factory in Lancaster, Pennsylvania.

(The Writers Theatre) Thursday, Jan. 30,–Feb. 15, 1986 (13 performances) The Writers Theatre (Joe Chart, Managing Director; Linda Laundra, Artistic Director) presents: **BEEF** by David Pownall; Inspired by the legends of Ireland; Director, Byam Stevens; Set, Cam Lorendo; Lighting, John Hickey; Costumes, Walker Hicklin; Sound/Original Music, Patricia Lee Stotter; Props, Steve Rosse; Wardrobe, M. A. Neff; Stage Managers, Brian Meister, Juliet Weber, Wendell Collins; Press, Byam Stevens, Mary Jane Gibbons. CAST: K. C. Wilson (Cusack), Michael Champagne (Con), Marko Maglich (Cuckoo), Stephen J. Brackley (Ali), Juanin Clay (Maeve), Anderson Matthews (Fergus), Dorothy Brooks (Janet). A play in 2 acts and 3 scenes. The action takes place in a Dublin slaughterhouse on Sept. 30, 1979, and in the monastery at Clonmacnois in 1180.

Olga Merediz, Diz White in "El Grande de Coca-Cola" *(Martha Swope Photo)*
Right Center: Michael Berliner, Peter Freedman, Winnie Boone, Betsy Beers in "Don't Even Think . . ." *(Christine Chang Photo)*

(front) Marko Maglich, Anderson Matthews, (back) Stephen Brackley, Dorothy Brooks, Michael Champagne, Juanin Clay in "Beef" *(David Laundra Photo)* **71**

**Geraldine Librandi, James Eckhouse
in "Emma" (Carl Paler Photo)**

(Courtyard Playhouse) Wednesday, Feb. 2–Mar. 16, 1986 (15 performances). The Original Cast presents:
DAYS AND NIGHTS OF AN ICE CREAM PRINCESS by Sandra Bertrand; Director, S. M. Deutschmann; Producer, Joanna Darski; Assistant Director/Stage Manager, Cal Saint John; Set, Dan Hubp; Lighting, Gerard MacMillan; Costumes, Blanche Blakeny; Sound/Music, John Houshmand. CAST: Jody Jensen (Younger Princess), Mary Kay Dean (Older Princess), Joanna Darski (Princess), Margo Whitcomb (BeeGee), Robert Simonton (President/Mugger), Steve Roy Rish (Donut), Margaret Ritchie (Mother/Psychiatrist/Teacher/Artist), Jack Anthony Rose (Writer/Fiance), J. D. Clarke (Daddy/Minister/Boss/Rich Gentleman/Gynecologist), Kevin McGinn (One Night Stand/Greyhound Cowboy). A play in two acts. "A kaleidoscopic journey" in which the past, present, and future overlap.

(ATA) Tuesday, Feb. 4–22, 1986 (12 performances). American Theatre of Actors presents:
VISIONS OF KEROUAC by Martin Bauml Duberman; Director, Bruce Kronenberg; Set/Lighting, John Jay; Costumes, James Ottaway; Sound, Marc Nastasi; Stage Manager, William P. Quinian; Press, Patricia Krawitz. CAST: Brian Zipin (TV Crew Member/Simon/Joey Rose), Daniel Troth (Cameron/Japhy Ryder), Kevin O'Rourke (Jack Kerouac), Steve Rapella (John Wiman/Raphael Urso), William Toddie (Conrad Carver/Trooper/Emil), John Flynn (Allen Moore/Will Hubbard), Donald Berman (Irwin Goldbook), Alice Barrett (Ruth Heaper), Scott Renderer (Cod Pomeray), Jodie Markell (Marylou/Tristessa/Princess/Stella Kerouac), Susan Boehm (Evelyn Pomeray), Helen Marcy (Gabrielle Kerouac). A play in two acts. The action takes place in various locations between 1944 and 1969.

(TOMI Theatre) Wednesday, Feb. 5–March 2, 1986 (20 performances and 3 previews). The MTA (Artistic Director, Paul Leavin) presents:
EMMA by Howard Zinn; Director, Maxine Klein; Set, Michael Anania; Costumes, Michael S. Schler; Lighting, Eric A. Hart; Production Supervisor, Richard Costabile; Arrangements, Andy Gaus; Musical Director, Eddie Korbich; Stage Managers, Kathi Guy, Nancy Wernick; Associate Producer, Little Flaggs Theater, Boston; Technical Director, Greg Haydock; Production Assistants, Gabriel Sonnino, Lori Joachim; Press, Bruce Cohen, Kathleen von Schmid. CAST: Robert J. Bennett (Vogel/Vito/Prisoner), Jay D. Blitzman (Levine/Sachs/Policeman/Monty), James Eckhouse (Sasha), Amy Jane Lauren (Rose/Helena/Sue/Matron), Richard Levine (Father/Most/Reitman), Geraldine Librandi (Emma), Ahvi Spindell (Fedya), Jo Twiss (Jenny/Mother/Mrs. Sachs/Maureen/Lizabeth), Lanie Zera (Dora/Anna). A drama in two acts. The action takes place in various locations in the Eastern United States, between 1887 and 1906.

(Actors Outlet) Friday, Jan. 31,–Feb. 16, 1986 (16 performances) The Working Theatre presents:
CROWN CORK CAFETERIA by William Wise; Sets, Johniene Papandreas; Lighting, Rita Ann Kogler; Costumes, Quina Fonseca; Sound, Edward Cosla; Director, Robert Owens Scott; Production Coordinator, Tommy Re; Technical Director, Stephen Cowles; Assistant Stage Manager/Props, Roni Schwartz; Stage Manager, Stan Friedman; Press, Bruce Cohen, Kathleen von Schmid. CAST: Bob Arcaro (Emil), James Carruthers (Marcus), Mary Daciuk (Gladys), Rich Ferguson (Jack), Greg Giordano (Lenny), Earl Hagan, Jr. (Don), Johnny Kline (Waldo), Jonathan Lipnick (Dutch), Bill Mitchell (Dave Wittkowski), Honour Molloy (Molly), Robin Polk (Honey), Marisa Redanty (Jan), Jack Schmidt (Klaus), Nelson Simon (Little Henry), Ron Stetson (Bob), Wendy Weill (Skipper). A play in 2 acts and 4 scenes. The action takes place in the lunch room of the Crown Cork bottle cap factory on the southwest side of Chicago in 1966, 1967, 1968.

(Ernie Martin Studio Theatre) Friday, Jan. 31–Feb. 17, 1986 (12 performances). The Actors Creative Theatre (Artistic Director, Ernie Martin) presents:
EXTRAORDINARY LIES by Mark DeGasperi; Director, Michael Schwartz; Set, Stephanie Kerley; Lighting, Martin Goldenberg; Stage Managers, Bill Barnes, David Nettles; Props/Sound, Al Geddes, Steve Ventin; Press, Jeffrey Richards Associates/Bill Shuttleworth. CAST: Michael Halata (Frank Conroy), Teresa Rossomando (Phyllis/Carol), Karin Huntzinger (Melissa), Marc Romeo (Carl/Sal), Lura Albee (Elizabeth Blake), W. J. Paterson (Petersen/Jack). A play in two acts. The action takes place in New York City, at the present time.

(Henry Lindenbaum Center) Saturday, Feb. 1–25, 1986 (16 performances) Theater of the Open Eye (Jean Erdman, Producing Artistic Director; Amie Brockway, Artistic Director) presents:
THE BONE RING by Donald Hall; Adapted from his memoirs "String Too Short to Be Saved"; Director, Kent Paul; Set, Jennifer Gallagher; Costume, Judy Ruskin Wong; Lighting, Karl E. Haas; Music, Michael Bacon; Production Manager/Technical Director, Adrienne J. Brockway; Managing Director, Richard Heeger; Marketing/Development, William C. Martin; Stage Manager, Susan Selig; Press, Bruce Cohen, Kathleen von Schmid. CAST: George Hall (Andrew Hunt/Samuel Potter), Lenka Peterson (Lucy Potter), Michael Kelly Boone (Andrew Hunt as a boy), Ian Blackman (Cedric Blasington/Billy Blasington), John Leighton (Washington Woodward). A lyrical play performed without intermission. The action takes place in New Hampshire at the present and in the early 1940's.

**George Hall, Lenka Peterson
in "The Bone Ring"
(Carol Rosegg Photo)**

**Sheila Dabney, Maritza Rivera
in "La Chunga"**
(Carol Rosegg Photo)

(INTAR Theatre) Wednesday, Feb. 5–March 9, 1986 (28 performances and 6 previews) INTAR Hispanic American Arts Center (Max Ferra, Artistic Director) presents the *World Premiere* of:
LA CHUNGA by Mario Vargas Llosa; Director, Max Ferra; Set, Ricardo Morin; Lighting, Beverly Emmons; Costumes, David Navarro Velasquez; Sound, Paul Garrity; Translation, Joanne Pottlitzer; Dramaturge, Jim Lewis; Music Consultant, Fernando Rivas; Technical Director, Beau Kennedy; Stage Manager, James DiPaola. CAST: Raul Aranas (Jose), Sheila Dabney succeeded by Michele Shay (La Chunga), Pepe Douglas (Lituma), Shawn Elliott (Josefino), Ralph Marrero (El Mono), Maritza Rivera (Meche). A drama set in northern Peru in 1945 inside a run-down bar on the outskirts of a town called Piura.

(Players Theatre) Tuesday, February 11–23, 1986 (8 performances and 8 previews). Shakespearewrights Players Theatre, in association with Donald H. Goldman, presents:
ANOTHER PARADISE by Donna Spector; Director, Licia Colombi; Set, Peter Harrison; Costumes, Donna Zakowska; Lighting, Jean Redmann; Music, Carolyn Dutton; Stage Manager, John Caywood; Press, Patricia Krawitz. CAST: Tom Ligon (Hiram), Cass Morgan (Birdie Mae), Arleigh Richards (Neva), Meg Van Zyl (Sal Henry), Mick Webber (Omer). A drama in two acts. The action takes place in Paradise, Kentucky, from 1903 to 1924.

(All Souls Church) Friday, Feb. 14–Mar. 2, 1986 (16 performances). The All Souls Players presents:
SILK STOCKINGS with Music and Lyrics by Cole Porter; Book, George S. Kaufman, Leueen McGrath, Abe Burrows; Suggested by *Ninotchka* by Melchior Lengyel; Director, Jeffery K. Neill; Musical Director/Orchestrations, Wendell Kindberg; Sets, Robert Edmonds; Costumes, Virginia Wood; Lighting, David Bean; Assistant Director/Tap Sequences, Suzanne Kaszynski; Associate Producer, Marlene Greene; Producers, Tran Wm. Rhodes, Howard Van Der Meulen; Stage Managers, Marlene Greene, Lawrence Bigbee, Sam Monchek; Props, Julie Otto; Technical Director, David Bean. CAST: Earl Aaron Levine (Peter Ilyitch Boroff), Donald Brooks Ford (Alexis/Bookseller), Jeff Paul (Hotel Manager/Assistant Director), Karol Richter (Flower Girl/Saleswoman), Cindy Stroud (Telephone Operator/Vera), James David Phillips (Ivanov), Tim McKanic (Brankov), Buck Hobbs (Bibinski), Joe Gram (Steve Canfield), William Walters (Commissar Markovitch), Kevin Halpin (Choreographer/Reporter/Grisha), Jean McClelland (Ninotchka Yoschenko), Richard Ambrose (Reporter), John S. Corker (Reporter/M. Fabour), Trudi Anne Posey (Janice Dayton), Billy Siegenfeld (Pierre Bouchard/Movie Director), Debra Lynn (Sonia), Kim Saunders (Anna), Steven Riddle (Boris). MUSICAL NUMBERS: Too Bad, *Art, Paris Loves Lovers, Stereophonic Sound, It's a Chemical Reaction, That's All, All of You, Satin and Silk, Without Love, Hail, Bibinski, As on through the Seasons We Sail, Josephine, Siberia, Silk Stockings, The Red Blues, *Give Me the Land, Finale (*cut from original production before New York opening). A musical in two acts. The action takes place in Paris and Moscow in 1954.

(Actors' Playhouse) Tuesday, Feb. 18–March 9, 1986 (9 performances and 14 previews). Brunnen Productions presents:
ANAIS NIN: THE PARIS YEARS by Lee Kessler; Based on the Writings of Anais Nin; Director, Spider Duncan Christopher; Original Production Directed by Tamara Long; Set, Keith Hein; Lighting, Robert Googooian; Costumes, Jean-Pierre Dorleac; Stage Manager, Denise Yaney; Associate Producer, Didi Gough; Press, Cindy Valk: Solters/Roskin/Friedman, Inc. CAST: Lee Kessler (Anais Nin). A play in two acts. The action takes place in a Brooklyn bank vault in the Spring of 1966, and in locations in and around Paris from 1931 to 1939.

(Vital Arts Center) Friday, Feb. 28–Mar. 16, 1986 (12 performances) The Foundation for the Vital Arts' Interaction Program (Executive Director, Victor Aikens) presents Quivira Production of:
SUDDEN MEMORY Written and Directed by Philip Alan Storck; Set, Chas Plummer; Lighting, John Parkinson; Costumes/Props, Maggie Finnin; Music, The American Folk Purists; Executive Producer, Lea Orth; Assistant Director, Stephanie Klapper; Assistant Producer, Sandy White; Press, Sandra Black. CAST: Michael J. Curran (Tchepka J. Krabbe), R. K. Greene (Michael Dobyns), Bump Heeter (Lloyd Niswonger), Scott Cain, Michael J. Curran, Wendy Feder, R. K. Greene, Lea Orth (The American Folk Purists). Understudy, Scott Cain. A serious comedy in two acts and an epilogue. The action takes place in the English Gardens, Munich, Germany, in the late Spring of 1968.

**Cass Morgan, Tom Ligon, Arleigh Richards
in "Another Paradise"**
(Bert Andrews Photo)

**Michael J. Curran, R. K. Greene
in "Sudden Memory"**

73

(Town Hall) Sunday, March 2–3, 1986 (2 performance limited engagement). The New Amsterdam Theatre Company (Artistic Director, Bill Tynes) presents a concert production of:
JUBILEE with Book by Moss Hart; Music and Lyrics, Cole Porter; Director/Choreographer, James Brennan; Musical Director, Gregory J. Dlugos; Orchestrations/Vocal Arrangements, Larry Moore; Producing Director, Marjorie E. Hassenfelt; Associate Conductor/Chorus Master, William Hicks; Stage Manager, Robert Bennett; Lighting Consultant, Peter M. Ehrhardt; Set Consultant, Roger LaVoie; Costume Consultant, David Toser; Wardrobe, Suzzane Brashaw; Press, Jeffrey Richards Associates. CAST: John Remme (King), Paula Laurence (Queen), Reed Jones (Prince James), Rebecca Luker (Princess Diana), Roderick Cook (Lord Wyndham), Patrick Quinn (Eric Dare), Alyson Reed (Karen O'Kane), Carole Shelley (Eva Standing) Davis Gaines (Charles "Mowgli" Rausmiller), Barbara Bornmann, Elizabeth Cangelosi, Catherine Anne Claxton, Elizabeth L. Henreckson, Sarah Knapp, Ilya Speranza, Rebecca Varon, Elissa Weiss, Scott Britton, Bill Fabris, John Horvath, Christopher Jon, Christopher O'Brien, David Perkins, Christopher Rogers, James Michael Vogel, Matthew Brennan, Michael Naselli. MUSICAL NUMBERS: Our Crown (National Anthem), Feathermore, Why Shouldn't I?, Entrance of Eric, The Kling-Kling Bird on the Divi-Divi Tree, When Love Comes Your Way, What a Nice Municipal Park, When Me, Mowgli, Love, My Lou-Lou, Begin the Begine, Good Morning Miss Standing, My Most Intimate Friend, There's Nothing Like Swimming, A Picture of Me Without You, Ev'rybod-ee Who's Anybod-ee, The Judgment of Paris, Swing That Swing, Sunday Morning, Breakfast Time, Mr. and Mrs. Smith, Six Little Wives, Me and Marie, Just One of Those Things, Jubilee Presentation. A musical comedy in two acts. The action takes place in a country threatened with an insurrection in 1935.

(Lamb's Little Theatre) Wednesday, March 5–30, 1986 (27 performances). The Lamb's Theatre Company (Producing Director, Carolyn Rossi Copeland; Associate Director, Pamela Perrell) presents:
BIG TIME by Steven Braunstein; Director, Tony Lo Bianco; Sets, Bob Phillips; Costumes, Eiko Yamaguchi, John McLain; Props, Deborah Alix Martin; Musical Supervision, Randy Courts; Sound, Aural Fixation, Marty Focazio; Stage Managers, Marjorie Horne, Melissa Burdick; Technical Directors, Ed Ramage, Marty Focazio; Ventriloquist Consultant, Stanley Burns; *Laugh with Us:* Music, Randy Courts/Lyrics, Steven Braunstein; Press, The Jacksina Company, Inc. CAST: Brent Collins (Spike), Melinda Keel (Molly), Tony Lo Bianco (Burgess). A play in two acts. The action takes place in the present at the Club Virtuoso, Atlantic City, New Jersey.

(Village Gate Upstairs) Tuesday, March 11–still playing May 31, 1986. Betmar and Charles Allen present:
BEEHIVE Created and Directed by Larry Gallagher; Set/Lighting, John Hickey; Costumes, David Dille; Hair/Makeup, J. Stanley Crowe; Musical Director/Arrangements, Skip Brevis; Choreography, Leslie Dockery; Vocal Adaptation, Claudia Brevis; Sound, Lewis Mead, Larry Zinn; General Management, Maria Productions, Inc.; Stage Manager, Brian Kaufman; Wardrobe, J. Stanley Crowe; Press, Hunt/Pucci Associates. CAST: Pattie Darcy, Alison Fraser, Jasmine Guy, Adriane Lenox succeeded by Lynne Maillard, Gina Taylor, Laura Theodore. Understudies: Andrea Petty, Jenny Douglas. MUSICAL NUMBERS: The Name Game, My Boyfriend's Back, Sweet Talkin' Guy, One Fine Day, I Sold My Heart to the Junkman, Academy Award, Will You Still Love Me Tomorrow, Give Him a Great Big Kiss, Remember (Walking in the Sand), I Can Never Go Home Again, Where Did Our Love Go?, Come See About Me, I Hear a Symphony, It's My Party, I'm Sorry, Rockin' Around the Christmas Tree, I Dream About Frankie, She's a Fool, You Don't Own Me, Judy's Turn to Cry, Where the Boy's Are, The Beehive Dance, The Beat Goes On, Downtown, To Sir with Love, Wishin' and Hopin', Don't Sleep in the Subway, You Don't Have to Say You Love Me, A Fool in Love, River Deep Mountain High, Proud Mary, Society's Child, Respect, A Natural Woman, Do Right Woman, Piece of My Heart, Try (Just a Little Bit Harder), Me and Bobby McGee, Ball and Chain, Make Your Own Kind of Music. A musical revue in two acts. A nostalgic tribute to the girl groups and the great female singers of the 60's.

Top Right: Tony Lo Bianco, Melinda Keel, Brent Collins in "Big Time"
(Carol Rosegg Photo)

Right Center: Jasmine Guy, Gina Taylor, Alison Fraser, Carol Maillard, Laura Theodore, Pattie Darcy in "Beehive"

Alison Fraser, Jasmine Guy, Laura Theodore, Gina Taylor, Carol Maillard, Pattie Darcy (seated) in "Beehive"

(Ernie Martin Studio Theatre) Friday, March 14–29, 1986 (11 performances). The Actors Creative Theatre (Artistic Director, Ernie Martin) presents:
THE KILLING TIME by Ronnie Paris; Director, Ernie Martin; Set/Costumes, Stephanie Kerley; Lighting, Martin Goldenberg; Stage Managers, Joseph Ditrinco, Bill Barnes, Dianna Martin; Props/Sound, A. J. Geddes, Shyron Lee, Steve Ventin. CAST: Frank Anderson (Harry), Allison Eikeren (Mary), Sara Emrie (Barbara-30's), Jessica Jones (Barbara-8), Judette Jones (Paula), Russell Rothberg (Lenny), Michael Schwartz (Santini), Ann Settel (Mrs. Bowen), Danae Torn (Barbara-14), Courtney Jones (Voice of William L. Shiver). A play in three acts. The action takes place in the workroom and backyard of a millinery shop, 1938–1944, and in a lecture hall in 1960.

(Lucille Lortel Theatre) Tuesday, March 18–April 13, 1986 (24 performances and 2 previews). Arthur Cantor and Edwin W. Schloss by arrangement with Lucille Lortel present:
ELISABETH WELCH: TIME TO START LIVING; Musical Director, Peter Howard; Scenic Supervision, Leo Meyer; Sound, Tony Meloa; Brian Ronan; Stage Manager, William Castleman; Press, Arthur Cantor Associates/Ken Mandelbaum. CAST: Elisabeth Welch, Peter Howard (Piano), Peter Barshay (Bass), Steve Singer (Drums). An evening of songs without intermission.

(don't tell mama) Tuesday, March 18–May 4, 1986 (32 performances and 7 previews). Pendleton Productions presents:
LIVING COLOR with Music and Lyrics by Scott Warrender; Director, Susan Skroman; Musical Director, Brad Garside; Set, Gregory W. Galway; Costumes, Robert DeMora; Stage Manager, Mark Ramont; Technical Design, Annette DiMeo; Concept: Davis Gaines, Susan Stroman, Scott Warrender; Press, Kevin P. McAnarney/Mark Goldstaub Public Relations, Philip Butler, Dan Kellachan. CAST: Davis Gaines, Jason Graae succeeded by Scott Bartlett, Nancy Johnston, Faith Prince. MUSICAL NUMBERS: Living Color, Life is Funny, Reruns, Parakeet Counselor by Day—Nightingale by Night, Bobby Bear, Texas Chainsaw Manicurist, Asia Avenue, Spirograph, I Will See You, Make It in L.A., Young Americans, Candy Bar, That Girl, Mr. Potato Head, Love for Four, My Barbie Was the Tramp of the Neighborhood, Waiting Game. An evening of songs subtitled "A Twisted Mnemonic Entertainment."

(Lamb's Theatre) Thursday March 20–May 4, 1986 (40 performances). Robert Cole and Bruce Rensing present:
THE ALCHEMEDIANS A Collaborative Work; Conception/Choreography: Bob Berky, Michael Moschen; Director, Ricardo Velez; Artistic Design/Construction, John Kahn; Music, David Van Tieghem; Lighting, Jan Kroeze; Costumes, Mei-Ling Louie; Sound, Jan Nebozenko, Craig Van Tassel; General Management, Kingwill & Goossen; Stage Managers, Dave Feldman, Allison Sommers; Assistant Lighting Designer, Debra Dumas; Press, Jeffrey Richards Associates/Elizabeth M. Ward. CAST: Michael Moschen, Bob Berky. An entertainment in two acts. The setting is a fanciful laboratory in which Berky and Moschen conduct wild and fantastic experiments.

Frank Anderson, Allison Eikeren, Judette Jones,
Sara Emrie, Michael Schwartz in "The Killing Time"
(Adam Newman Photo)

Bob Berky (top), Michael Moschen
in "The Alchemedians" *(Dan Wagner Photo)*

Jason Graae, Nancy Johnston, Faith Prince,
Davis Gaines in "Living Color"
(Martha Swope/Linda Alaniz Photo)

(Harold Clurman Theatre) Thursday, Mar. 20–April 13, 1986 (24 performances). UBU Repertory Theater presents:
THE EDEN CINEMA by Marguerite Duras; Translation, Barbara Bray; Director, Francoise Kourilsky; Music, Genji Ito; Set, Beth Kuhn; Lighting, Curt Ostermann; Costumes, Debra Stein; Sound, Phil Lee; Stage Managers, Marilyn Dampf, Mary-louise Burke; General Manager, Lisa M. Poyer; Company Manager, Meredity Portman; Props, John Knight; Press, Becky Flora. CAST: Marylouise Burke (Mother), Ryan Cutrona (Monsieur Jo), Josh Hamilton (Joseph), Brooke Shields (Suzanne), Ching Yeh (Corporal). The action of the play takes place in French Indochina in the early thirties.

(Westside Arts Theatre) Friday, March 21,–May 18, 1986 (53 performances and 13 previews). Margery Klain and Dan Fisher present:
DAUGHTERS by John Morgan Evans; Director, John Henry Davis; Set, Kevin Rupnik; Lighting, F. Mitchell Dana; Costumes, Donna Zakowska; Sound, Tom Gould; Casting, Ronnie Yeskel; General Management, Dorothy Olim, George Elmer, Thelma Cooper, Ken Novice; Assistant to Producers, Judith Baldwin; Props, Dale Dickey; Wardrobe, Chris Sanders; Stage Managers, Susan Whelan, Debra Cole; Press, P. R. Partners, Marilyn LeVine, Meg Gordean, Patricia Roberts, Allison Dixon. CAST: Marcia Rodd (Tessie), Bette Henritze (Mom), Mary Testa (Patty Ann), Miriam Phillips (Grandma), Marisa Tomei (Cetta). A play in 2 acts and 3 scenes. The action takes place at the present time in the kitchen of the DiAngelo home in Brooklyn, New York.

(Perry Street Theatre) Wednesday, March 26,–April 13, 1986 (17 performances) The New York Theatre Workshop (Jean Passanante, Artistic Director; Nancy Kassak Diekmann, Managing Director) presents:
BOSOMS AND NEGLECT by John Guare; Director, Larry Arrick; Set, Loy Arcenas; Costumes, Jeffrey Ullman; Lighting, David N. Weiss; Sound, Tommy Hawk; Technical Director, Glen F. Timpone; Props, Janice Kitchen; Wigs, Charles LoPresto; Company Manager, Arthur Catricala; Production Manager, Jon Widercrantz; Production Assistants, Elliot J. Cohen, Emily E. Klein, Nick Sanders; Stage Manager, Alan Fox. CAST: Anne Meara (Henny), Richard Kavanaugh (Scooper), April Shawhan (Deirdre). A comedy in two acts. The action takes place at the present time, in an apartment in Queens (prologue), an apartment in NYC's East Sixties, and in a room in Columbia Presbyterian Hospital in NYC.

(Musical Theatre Works) Wednesday, March 26–April 12, 1986 (12 performances and 2 previews). Musical Theatre Works (Artistic Director, Anthony J. Stimac) presents:
CHARLEY'S TALE with Book and Lyrics by Tricia Tunstall; Music, Donald Johnston; Director, Gideon Y. Schein; Choreographer, Marcia Milgrom Dodge; Musical Director, David Evans; Set, James Wolk; Costumes, Pamela Scofield; Lighting, Victor En Yu Tan; Stage Manager, Sondra R. Katz; Production Manager, Julie Nessen; Technical Supervisor, Jess M. Klarnet; Production Assistants, Lisa Contadino, Meryl Jacobs, Kim McNutt, Jordan Tinsley; Wardrobe, Joni George. CAST: Tim Ewing (Archibald/Schubert), Don Goodspeed (Jack), Beth Guiffre (Maggie), Rex D. Hays (Charley), Bjorn Johnson (Lucas/Liszt), Dan Kael (Danny), Lynne Kolber (Kit), Susan Long (Nona), Suzanne Lukather (Iris), Donna Lee Marshall (Jody), Sal Mistretta (Vic/Verdi), William Nabel (Max/Wagner), Kristine Nevins (Binky), Harold Shepard (Mr. Kelly/Schumann). Marianne Tatum (Susannah). MUSICAL NUMBERS: Deserto Sulla Terra/Come Out Tonight, Better Off Alone, Ain't Got Time, One of a Hundred Girls/I Like it Here, Close Your Eyes, Ain't Got Time At All, Mushrooms and Mozart, Longing/Dear Verdi, If I Weren't a Beast, We Can Do Better, Greenwich Village Girls, Wagner's Reprise, Love Me/To Kiss Your Eyes, Rag Doll Rag, Look At Me, Charley, Finale. A musical in two acts.

(Jack Lawrence Theatre) Friday, March 28,–May 18, 1986 (53 performances and 8 previews). Cheryl Crawford, Paul B. Berkowsky, Robert Franz in association with Maxine and Stanford Makover and J. Arnold Nickerson by special arrangement with Alliance Theatre Company present:
SO LONG ON LONELY STREET by Sandra Deer; Director, Kent Stephens; Set, Mark Morton; Costumes, Jane Greenwood; Lighting, Allen Lee Hughes; Production Supervisor, Roger Shea; General Manager, Paul Berkowsky; Company Manager, Richard Seader; Original Music, Hal Lanier; Management Associate, Sheala N. Berkowsky; Technical Director, Jack Magnifico; Wardrobe, Judy Dearing; Production Assistant, John O'Neill; Stage Manager, Michael Hartman; Press, Jeffrey Richards, C. George Willard, Ben Morse, Marie-Louise Silva, L. Glenn Poppleton III, Ken Mandlebaum. CAST: Ray Dooley (Raymond Brown), Lizan Mitchell (Annabel Lee), Pat Nesbit (Ruth Brown), Stephen Root (King Vaughnum III), Jane Murray (Clairice Vaughnum), Fritz Sperberg (Bobby Stack). A play in two acts. The action takes place at the present time in late August at Honeysuckle Hill, a few miles outside a small Southern town.

Ryan Cutrona, Brooke Shields, Josh Hamilton in "The Eden Cinema" *(Henry Grossman Photo)*

(Carnegie Recital Hall) Wednesday, April 2–6, 1986 (5 performance limited engagement). Carnegie Hall presents:
NO, NO, NANETTE (Concert Version) with Music by Vincent Youmans; Book, Otto Harbach, Frank Mandel; Lyrics, Irving Caesar, Otto Harbach; Director/Conductor, John McGlinn; Orchestrations, Emil Gerstenberger, Stephen O. Jones, Max Steiner, Hilding Anderson, Robert Russell Bennett, Larry Moore (Reconstruction). CAST: Jane Connell (Pauline), Leigh Beery (Sue Smith), Rebecca Luker (Nanette), Cris Groenendaal (Billy Early), George Dvorsky (Tom Trainor), Judy Kaye (Lucille Early), Robert Nichols (Jimmy Smith), Suzanne Briar (Betty), Maureen Brennan (Winnie), Jeanne Lehman (Flora), Heidi Albrecht, Deborah Brandt, Linda Milani, Carrie Wilder (The Maids and The Marrieds), Larry Hansen, Patrick Rogers, Bryan Landrine, Steven Moore (The Bachelors). MUSICAL NUMBERS: Overture, Opening Act One, The Call of the Sea, Too Many Rings Around Rosie, I've Confessed to the Breeze, I Want To Be Happy, Charleston Speciality, No No Nanette, Finale Act One, A Peach on the Beach, My Doctor, Fight over Me, Tea for Two, You Can Dance with Any Girl, Finale Act Two, Hello Hello Telephone Girlie, The Where-Has-My-Hubby-Gone Blues, Take a Little One-Step, Pay Day Pauline, Finale Ultimo. A concert version of the musical comedy in three acts. The time is Summer, 1925. The action takes place at the home of Jimmy Smith, Park Avenue, New York (Act One); The lawn of Chickadee Cottage, Atlantic City, the next day (Act Two); and the living room of Chickadee Cottage, later that evening.

(TOMI Terrace Theatre) Thursday, April 3–20, 1986 (16 performances) Murder to Go Legit presents:
DEEP SIX HOLIDAY by David Landau; Director, Kip Rosser; Producer, Nancy Richards; Set, Joseph V. Hupcey, Jr.; Lighting, Joe Degennaro; Wardrobe/Props, Penelope Robson; Stage Manager, Jane MacPherson. CAST: James Leach (James Whitman), Mary Lynn Hetsko (Julia Hammet), Dale Place (Detective Kane). A drama in two acts. The action takes place in a New England beach cottage during autumn of the present time.

Lizan Mitchell, Pat Nesbit in "So Long on Lonely Street" *(Michael Ramonos Photo)*

(Shakespeare Center) Thursday, April 3–27, 1986 (16 performances) The Classic Theatre (Artistic Director, Maurice Edwards) in association with Riverside Shakespeare Company (Producing Director, Robert Graham Small) presents: **THE SPANISH TRAGEDIE** or Hieronimo Is Mad Againe by Thomas Kyd; Director, Ron Daley; Producer, Nicholas John Stathis; Set, Bob Phillips; Lighting, Lisa Grossman; Costumes, Michael S. Schler; Sound, Deena Kaye; Stage Combat, Lawrence H. Lustberg, Todd Loweth; Production Manager, G. Douglas Ward; Technical Director, Steve Sitler; Wardrobe, Elizabeth Gill; Stage Managers, Kate Riddle, L. Robert Johnson. CAST: Allen Barone (Don Andrea), Jacqueline Chauvin (Bel-Imperial), Ronald Durling (King of Portugal), John Greenleaf (Lorenzo), Michael E. Hermanski (Alcario/Ambassador), Dan Johnson (Castile), Mary Tierney Kelly (Isabella), Todd Loweth (Horatio), Paul Mantell (Hieronimo), Paul McNair (Rogero/Jacques), Rik Montgomery (Balthazar), Greg Petroff (Lazarotto), Edmond Ramage (Pedringano), R. Sebastian Russ (King of Spain), James Sheerin (Don Pedro), Robert E. Wherry, Jr. (Alexandro). A drama in three acts. The action takes place on the Iberian Peninsula circa 1560.

(theatre Guinevere) Thursday, April 3,–27, 1986 (23 performances) Penguin Repertory Company (Joe Brancato, Artistic Director; Andrew M. Horn, Executive Director) presents: **TREATS** by Christopher Hampton; Director, Joe Brancato; Producer, Andrew M. Horn; Set, Alex Polner; Lighting, Vivien Leone; Costumes, Maryann D. Smith; Technical Director, Will Austen; Incidental Music by Johnny Clegg, and performed by Juluka; Props, Sue Doster, Karen Oberthal; Sound, Kathi Guy; Wardrobe, Patricia Sullivan; Stage Manager, William Hare; Press, Bruce Cohen, Kathleen von Schmid. CAST: Anne Barrett (Ann), S. Sherrard Hicks (Patrick), Bruce McDonnell (Dave). A comedy in two acts. The action takes place at the present time in London in Anne's flat.

(Common Ground) Friday, April 4–27, 1986 (12 performances) Common Ground Chekhov (Norman Taffel, Director) presents: **THE CHERRY ORCHARD** by Anton Chekhov; New Adaptation/Direction, Norman Taffel. CAST: Ginger Grace (Lyuba), Joseph Hunt (Gaev), Elizabeth Herring (Anya), Colleen Cosgrove (Varya), Anthony John Lizzul (Lopakhin), George Laney (Peter), Gerald Beyer (Pistchik), Ana Ramos (Charlotta), Bill Salem (Epihodoff), Kathleen Devine (Dunyasha), Howard Jensen (Fiers), Adrian Williams (Yasha), Gerald Beyer (Stranger), Gerry Hambel (Understudy).

Jossie de Guzman, Jesse Corti
in "Lovers and Keepers" *(Carol Rosegg Photo)*

(INTAR Theatre) Friday, April 4,–May 4, 1986 (33 performances) International Arts Relations (Max Ferra, Artistic Director; Dennis Ferguson-Acosta) presents: **LOVERS & KEEPERS** with Book and Lyrics by Maria Irene Fornes; Music for Tona and Nick by Tito Puente; Music for Fred and Fina by Fernando Rivas; Music for Tato, Elena, Clara by Francisco Rodriguez; Set, Ricardo Morin; Lighting, Anne E. Militello; Costumes, Gabriel Berry; Music Direction/Arrangements, Fernando Rivas; Casting, Janet Murphy; Director, Maria Irene Fornes; Technical Director, Beau Kennedy; Production Assistant, Brian O'Malley; Stage Managers, Marybeth Ward; Press, Bruce Cohen, Kathleen von Schmid. CAST: Jesse Corti (Fred), Jose Fong (Tato), Jossie de Guzman (Fina/Elena), Tomas Milian (Nick), Sheila Dabney (Clara/Tona), Nina Laboy (Understudy). MUSICAL NUMBERS: My House, Farewell, Now He's Looking, You Ruined It, Lovers Rag, When You Walk in the Shadows, Uncle Manny, I Think of You, Yes We Can, Tires in the Trunk, Chicken Soup, My Nick. A musical in two acts. The action takes place in Florida from 1939 to 1962.

(Rutgers Church) Tuesday, April 8–19, 1986 (12 performances). Theatre Rutgers (Rev. R. Mark Wallace Coonradt, Executive Producer) presents: **FAMILY PORTRAIT** by Leonore Coffee and William Joyce Cowen; Director, Robert Bruce Holley; General Manager, Carolyne A. Jones; Set, Simon Hooper; Lighting, William J. Cuddy; Technical Director, Kendall A. Barnes; Costume Coordinator, Rob Weisfeld; Props, Michael Schafer; Stage Managers, Roger Franklin, Howard P. Lev. CAST: Andrea Andresakis (Esther), Tony Andresakis (Daniel), Susan Bethany (Anna/Beulah), James Coromel (James), Ned Coulter (Joseph), Char' Fontane (Mary of Magdala), Roger Franklin (A Disciple), Eddie L. Furs (Amos/Mendel), Delphi Lawrence (Hepzibah), Stacie Linardos (A Woman of Jerusalem), Barbara Niles (Naomi), David Olive (Simon), Robyn O'Neill (Citizen), Charles Rule (Mordecai/Mathias/Appius Hadrian/Leban), Anne Russell (Mary), David Salovitz (Rabbi Samuel), Socorro Santiago (Reba), Christopher Scott (Juda), June Squibb (Selima), Ray Stephens (The Preacher), Maggie Task (Mary Cleophas), Eric Watkins (Eben/Nathan/Joshua). A play in 3 acts and 7 scenes. The action takes place in Nazareth and in Jerusalem.

Top Right: Jacqueline Chauvin, Todd Loweth
in "The Spanish Tragedie" *(Marbeth Photo)*

June Squibb, Anne Russell, Roger Franklin
in "Family Portrait"

77

(St. Clements) Monday, April 8,–May 3, 1986. The Music-Theatre Group/Lenox Arts Center (Lyn Austin, Producing Director; Diane Wondisford, Managing Director; Production Associate, Vanessa Palmer; Mark Jones, Associate Producing Director) and Robert de Rothschild present the *World Premiere* of:
VIENNA: LUSTHAUS conceived and directed by Martha Clarke; Text, Charles Mee, Jr.; Set/Costumes, Robert Israel; Lighting, Paul Gallo; Music composed by Richard Peaslee with the aid of Bach, Friesen, and Johann Strauss. CAST: Robert Besserer, Brenda Currin, Timothy Doyle, Marie Fourcaut, Lotte Goslar, Robert Langdon-Lloyd, Richard Merrill, Gianfranco Paoluzzi, Amy Spencer, Paola Styron, Lila York, with musicians: Carol Emanuel, Alyssa Hess Reit, Jill Jaffe, Matthias Naegele, Peter Reit, Steve Silverstein.

(Washington Square Methodist Church) Wednesday, April 9–27, 1986 (12 performances)
AS YOU LIKE IT by William Shakespeare; Director, Charles Barber; Set/Lighting, Donald L. Brooks; Costumes, Peter MacIver; Music, Lucy Cross; Choreography, Alan Jones; Associate Producer, Mari S. Schatz; Stage Managers, Arlene Mantek, JoLynn Sciarro. CAST: Steve Franklin (Oliver), Jason Brown (Orlando), Phillip George (Jacques/Mme. LaBeau/Lord), D. R. Fox (Adam/Lord), Chuck Stanley (Dennis/Amiens), Richard Bowden (Duke Frederick/Sir Oliver Martext), David Urrutia (Celia), Keith McDermott (Rosalind), Jeffrey D. Eiche (Touchstone), James Sterling (Charles/Lord), David Haugen (Lord/William), Frank Lowe (Duke Senior), Robin Tate (Jacques), Derek Conte (Corin), Arnie Burton (Silvius), George Gale (Phebe), David Klionsky (Audrey). Performed with one intermission.

(Westbeth Theatre Center) Wednesday, April 9–14, 1986 (6 performances/limited engagement)
MADRID, MADRID by Catherine Burns; Director, Adam Zahler; Set and Lighting, Leon Hopkins; Dramaturg, Jack Zetlin. CAST: Debra Neel (Riba Stern), Michael James Stratford (David Mitchum), Margot Avery (Ethyl Mitchum), Joe Zaloom (Ed Mitchum), Elizabeth Flynn-Jones (Nora Mitchum), Jerry Matz (Archie Rothman). A play in two acts. The action takes place in the early 1950's in the kitchen and back yard of the Mitchum's basement apartment in Greenwich Village in New York City.

(Colonnades Theatre) Wednesday, April 16–May 18, 1986 (25 previews and 5 performances). The Ark Theatre Company (Artistic Directors, Bruce Daniel, Donald Marcus; Managing Director, Robert Martin) presents:
EMERALD CITY by Donald Marcus; Director, Rebecca Guy; Set, Derek McLane; Costumes, Gene Lakin; Lighting, Betsy Adams; Sound, John Kilgore, Tsilke Pearlman; Stage Managers, Patrice Thomas, Suzanne Hauser; Technical Supervisors, Alfred Miller, John Crawford; Technical Consultant, Michael Pillinger; Assistant Costume Designer, Melissa Binder; Wardrobe, Carole Cuming; Scenic Artist, Vivienne Culwick; Press, The Jacksina Company/Ted Killmer. CAST: Marcia Cross (Bonnye), Steven J. Gefroh (Paul), Christine Estabrook (Harriet), John Jiler (Toddy), Don Chastain (Rip). A comedy in three acts. The action takes place on the veranda of the Chambers' house in Columbia County, 100 miles north of New York City, at the present time.

(Raft Theatre) Friday, April 18,–May 11, 1986 (12 performances)
DISAPPEARING ACTS by Phil Bosakowski; Producer-Director, Terry D. Kester; Associate Producer, Arden Bing; Set/Lighting, Jim Albert Hobbs; Costumes, Suzanne Spellen; Stage Manager, Amy Beers. CAST: Julia Levo (Corrie), Robert Nelson (Steve), Jennifer Rose (Kelly), Lois Markle (Terry), Al Sperduto (Dominic), Judith Mayes (Nina), Roger Rignack (Johnny). A play in 2 acts and 5 scenes. The action takes place on a Thanksgiving Weekend in the recent past in the informal dining nook of the Delicata's residence in Philadelphia, Pa.

"Vienna Lusthaus"
(Mimi Cotter Photo)

(Joyce Theater) Tuesday, April 22–May 25, 1986 (38 performances and 2 previews). ICM Artists presents:
MUMMENSCHANZ The New Show; General Manager, Larry Kapust; Stage Manager, Dino De Maio; Stage Assistants, Lee Dassler, Walter Flohr; Lighting, Beverly Emmons; Press, Marilynn LeVine/P. R. Partners, Meg Gordean, Patricia Robert, Ken Sherber, Darrel Joseph, Allison Dixon. CAST: Andres Bossard, Floriana Frassetto, Bernie Schurch. An entertainment in two acts.

(Off Center Theatre) Friday, April 23–May 5, 1986 (12 performances). Bandwagon (Producer, Jerry Bell) presents:
RAINBOW with Music by Vincent Youmans; Lyrics, Oscar Hammerstein 2nd; Original Book, Oscar Hammerstein 2nd, Laurence Stallings; Additional Lyrics, Harold Adamson, Buddy De Sylva, Edward Heyman, Bud McCreery, J. Russell Robbison; New Book, Conn Fleming; Director, Robert Brewer; Musical Director/Vocal-Dance Arrangements, James Followell; Choreographer/Musical Staging, David Storey; Costumes, Venustiano Borromeo; Sets, Holmes Easley; Lighting, Michael Grimes; Stage Managers, Peter Wolf, Jennie Ryan, Jaime J. Harris, Siobhan R. K. Gould; Orchestrations, The Band; Assistant Costumer, Deirdre Burke; Assistant Musical Director, Arthur Sweet; Technical Director, Michael Grimes; Props, Faith Houston, Herbert Jasmine; Production Assistants, Iris Corbett, Diane Crowder, Tyrone Henderson, Elaine Ktistes, Timmie Ross; Press, Audrey Ross. CAST: John Vincent Leggio (Private Potter), Dale O'Brien (Sergeant Major), Gabrielle Sinclair (Penny), Lee Lobenhofer (Capt. Singleton), Joseph Culliton succeeded by Andy Umberger (Mjr. Davolo/Thug #1), Teri Bibb (Virginia Brown), Debbie Shapiro (Lotta), Fred Barrows ("Nasty" Howell), David Roberts (Bartender/Drunk/Pvt. McAdams), David Staller (Hal Stanton), Joe Deer (Thug #2), Anthony Bova (Charlie/Larry/Pvt. Baker), Campbell Martin (Jenkins), Andrea Cohen, Diana Losk, Linda Paul, Alicia Miller, Patricia Martin (Frontier Sweethearts/Saloon Girls). MUSICAL NUMBERS: On the Golden Trail, I Want a Man, West Wind, I Like You As You Are, Rise 'n' Shine, The Primping Dance, Time on My Hands, Virginia, Let Me Give All My Love to Thee, The One Girl, He Came Along, Diamond in the Rough, Mean Man, You're Everywhere, Drums in My Heart. A romantic musical adventure in two acts. The action takes place in and around Fort Independence, Missouri, and in and around a small mining town in California, in 1849, during the California Gold Rush.

**Jennifer Rose, Lois Markle, Al Sperduto,
Judith Mayes, Julia Levo, Robert Nelson
in "Disappearing Acts"**

**Campbell Martin, Debbie Shapiro, David
Roberts in "Rainbow"** *(Sal Provenza Photo)*

(Stage Arts Theatre) Sunday, April 27, 1986—Aumont Productions presents:
BUSKERS with Book, Music, Lyrics and Direction by Howard Goldberg; Choreography, Lillo Way; Musical Director/Arrangements, Hillel Dolgenas; Sets, Chris J. Shriver; Costumes, Muriel Stockdale; Lighting, Betsy M. Pool; General Management, Michael Lonergan; Stage Managers, David Semonin, Nancy Rutter; Production Assistant, Leslie Utstein; Company Manager, John Dwyer; Magic, Friedhoffer, the Madman of Magic; Press, Shirley Herz Associates/David Roggensack. CAST: Tony Azito (Antoine), Timothy Bennett (Chris), Sasha Charnin (Carmen), Bob Flannigan (Stagehand/Author/Louie/Prof./Cop), Kimberly Hall (Mrs. C./Breitenbacher), JoAnn Hunter (Selena), Phil LaDuca (Frankie), Anthony Marciona (Hinton/Watchman), Krista Tesreau (Leonie), Lyn Vaux (Sally/Banjo), Jim Wagg (Johnny C), Kelly Woodruff (Didier). Understudies: Paul Amodeo (Dider/Frankie/Chris), Lyn Vaux (Leonie), Adam Phillipson (Johnny/Hinton), Wendy Yondorf (Sally/Mrs. C.). MUSICAL NUMBERS: Power in the Air, I Walk Alone, Movie Stars/Monday Mornings, Down to the Foodstore, All of My Love, Myrna P., Pain in My Heart, Selena, Born to Love, Love at First Sight, Hinton Went Down, My Parents' House, Alien Love, Soap is Good for You, I Know What Love Can Bring, Etude, Maybe I'm Lonely, Ice Cream. A musical in two acts. The action takes place in Central Park, in New York City at the present time.

**Stephen Geoffreys, Trini Alvarado
in "Maggie Magalita" *(Carol Rosegg Photo)***

(John-Michael Tebelak Theater/Cathedral of St. John the Divine) Wednesday, April 30–May 24, 1986 (15 performances). Cathedral Productions (Director, Elliott Sroka) presents:
FURIES based on the *Oresteia* of Aeschylus; Translation, Robert Lowell; Director, Paul Zimet; Associate Director, Richard Armstrong; Music, Jonathan Hart, Ellen Maddow, Harry Mann; Set, Jun Maeda; Lighting, Beverly Emmons; Costumes, Genevieve Sevin-Doering, Reinhard Doering, Sally Lesser; Stage Manager, Sabrina Hamilton; Production Coordinator, Susan Wendell; Sound Recording, Phil Lee, Full House Productions, Inc.; Production Assistant, Mike Kohler; Press, Bruce Cohen. CAST: Richard Armstrong (Clytemnestra), William Badgett (Agamemnon/Pylades), Jonathan Hart (Cassandra), Ellen Maddow (Herald), Harry Mann (Fury/Old Person/Slave Woman), Daniel Prieto (Aegisthus), Rosemary Quinn (Fury/Old Person/Slave), Rossignol (Watchman/Cilissa), Tina Shepard (Electra), Jack Wetherall (Orestes). An avant garde-experimental theatre/opera collaboration.

(South Street Theatre) Thursday, May 1–25, 1986 (12 performances and 4 previews). Beechwood Productions and Robert Buzzell present:
THE GOOD COMPANIONS by Betty Neustat; Director, Todd Peters; Set, Teresa M. Carriker; Costumes, Shelley A. Goldstein; Lighting, Robert W. Rosentel; Stage Managers, Carolyn Caldwell, Anne Veenstra; Props, Veronica Garvey; Production Coordinator, Alexis Genya; Music Consultant, Igor Shvachkin; Press, David Lipsky, Avivah Simon. CAST: Frances Chaney (Pearl Campbell), Jean Richards (Jane Braverman), Ben R. Kelman (Joe Goldman), Sylvia Kauders (Tillie Teitlebaum), Jeff Gendelman (Steve Marcus), Sam Locante (Vincent Milano), Mary Cooper (Peggy Bryant), John L. Bryan (John Bryant). A comedy-drama in two acts. The action takes place in Berksville, a small town in upstate New York, in December, 1985.

(Theater 22) Thursday, May 1–18, 1986 (16 performances). Actors For Themselves presents:
ONE FLEW OVER THE CUCKOO'S NEST by Dale Wasserman; Based on novel by Ken Kesey; Director, Richard Dent; Press, Marie Henderson. CAST: Richard Steinmetz (McMurphy), Beverly Bonner (Nurse Ratched), John M. Flood (Dale Harding), David Sotolongo (Aide Williams), Edward Joseph (Bibbit), and Forry Buckingham, David Connell, Mark Folger, A. J. Johnson, Charles Kashi, Timothy Kelleher, Mary Lisa Kinney, Teresa Longo, Robert McCaskill, Mansoor Najeellah, Essene R., Stewart Steinberg

(Lamb's Theatre) Friday, May 2 - June 14, 1986 (41 performances and 4 previews). The Lamb's Theatre Company (Producing Director, Carolyn Rossi Copeland; Associate Director, Pamela Perrell) presents:
MAGGIE MAGALITA by Wendy Kesselman; Director, Julianne Boyd; Set, Michael C. Smith; Costumes, Nan Cibula; Lighting, James F. Ingalls; Music, Tania Leon; Sound, Marty Focazio; Stage Managers, Renee F. Lutz, Richard Hester; Production Assistant, Elyn Braun; Props, Neal Bishop; Dialect Coach, Graciela Lecube; Scenic Artists, Joel Fontaine, Richard Ginzberg; Press, The Jacksina Company. CAST: Trini Alvarado succeeded by Chiara Peacock (Maggie), Stephen Geoffreys (Eric), Blanca Camacho (Elena), Teresa Yenque (Abuela). A play in two acts. The action takes place in New York City at the present time.

(Actors Outlet Theatre) Friday, May 2, 1986 and still playing May 31, 1986. Mainstage Productions, Ltd. and Harve Brosten in association with "Murray the Furrier" present:
OLYMPUS ON MY MIND with Book, Lyrics, and Direction by Barry Harmon; Music, Grant Sturiale; Suggested by *Amphitryon* by Heinrich Von Kleist; Choreographer, Pamela Sousa; Sets, Chris Stapleton; Costumes, Steven Jones; Lighting, Fabian Yeager; Assistant Director, Edward Marshall; Assistant Music Director, David Geist; Assistant Choreographer, Laurent Giroux; Stage Manager, Joseph A. Onorato; Sound Consultant, Greg Leone; Wardrobe, Winsome McCoy; Press, Henry Luhrman Associates/Terry M. Lilly, David Mayhew, Andrew P. Shearer. CAST: Peter Kapetan (Tom), Andy Spangler (Dick), Keith Bennett (Horace), Faith Prince succeeded by Elizabeth Austin (Delores), Ron Raines (Jupiter:a/k/a/Jove, Zeus), Jason Graae (Mercury), Peggy Hewett (Charis), Emily Zacharias (Alcmene), Lewis J. Stadlen (Sosia), George Spelvin (Amphitryon). MUSICAL NUMBERS: Welcome to Greece, Heaven on Earth, The Gods on Tap, Surprise!, Wait Til it Dawns, I Know My Wife, It Was Me, Back So Soon?, Wonderful, At Liberty in Thebes, Jupiter Slept Here, Back to the Play, Don't Bring Her Flowers, Generals' Pandemonium, Olympus Is a Lonely Town, A Star Is Born, Final Sequence. A musical comedy in two acts. "The play is set in the ancient Greek city of Thebes, during the course of a forty-one hour day."

**Tony Azito, Krista Tesreau, Sasha Charnin
in "Buskers" *(Adam Newman Photo)***

**Lewis J. Stadlen, Peggy Hewett, Jason Graae
in "Olympus on My Mind" *(Anita & Steve Shevett Photo)***

79

Bebe Neuwirth in "Waitin' in the Wings"
(Martha Swope/Carol Rosegg Photo)

(Triplex) Sunday, May 4, 1986. The third annual presentation of:
WAITIN' IN THE WINGS: The Night the Understudies Take Centerstage; Concept/Producer, William Spencer Reilly; Written by Scott Harris; Director, Peter Link; Musical Director, Keith Thompson; Lighting, Phil Monat; Sound, Jesse Plumley; Costume Coordinator, Isis Mussenden; Keyboard Orchestrations, Alan Smallwood; Stage Managers, Anita Ross, Donald Christy, Cyrille Vlamynck; Assistants, Charles Leighton, Dan Shaheen; Production Assistants, Jeffrey Collins, Les Riek, Pam Weinstein; Press, Becky Flora. CAST: James Brennan, Karen Curlee, Pattie Darcy, Kim Darwin, Jack Davison, Jenny Douglas, Bruce Falco, Romain Fruge, Susan Goodman, Cris Groenendaal, Betsy Joslyn, George Merritt, Maureen Moore, Brad Moranz, Bebe Neuwirth, Jackie J. Patterson, Andrea Petty, Deborah Phelan, Stephanie Pope, Brenda Pressley, Roumel Reaux, Christina Saffran, Don Stitt, Special Guests: Vincent Sardi (Host), Debbie Allen, Don Correia, Carmen deLavallade, Sandy Duncan, Geraldine Fitzgerald, Tammy Grimes, Maurice Hines, Cleo Laine, Dorothy Loudon, Ann Reinking. An evening of songs from current Broadway and Off-Broadway shows (*Sweet Charity, Song & Dance, Singin' in the Rain, A Chorus Line, Sunday in the Park with George, Jerry's Girls, El Grande de Coca Cola, Big River, The Mystery of Edwin Drood, La Cage aux Folles, Beehive, Cats, Big Deal*) as performed by current understudies and standbys.

(The Shakespeare Center) Friday, May 9, - June 1, 1986 (16 performances). The Riverside Shakespeare Co. (Robert Graham Small, Producing Director) presents: **AS YOU LIKE IT** by William Shakespeare; Director, Robert Mooney; Producer, Ron Daley; Production Manager, G. Douglas Ward; Technical Director, Steve Sitler; Scenery, James Wolk; Costumes, Marilyn Keith; Combat, Richard Raether; Choreography, Gillian Hemstead; Lighting, Sam Scripps; Music, Joseph Church; Musical Director, Cheryl Rosen; Props, Natalie Lardner, Edie Jud; Stage Managers, Andrea Nugit, Kate Riddle. CAST: Lisa Bansavage (Celia/Aliena), Karen Braga (Rosalind), James Burns (Charles/Williams/Jacques DeBoys), Richard Fay (Orlando), Stephen Gleason (LeBeau/Amiens), Eric Hoffmann (Touchstone), Randy Kelly (Oliver/Lord), Scott C. Krohn (Jacques), Peter A. Levine (Silvius/Dennis/Lord), Roy MacArthur (Duke Frederick/Sir Oliver Martext/Page), Vincent Niemann (Corin/Lord/Hymen), Herman Petras (Duke Senior), Kathryn Shield (Phebe/Lord), Patricia Tallman (Audrey), Howard Thoresen (Adam/Lord/Page). Performed with one intermission.

Olivia Laurel Mates, Christian Slater
in "Dry Land" *(Bob Marshak Photo)*

(All Souls Fellowship Hall) Friday, May 9 - 25, 1986 (16 performances). The All Souls Players present:
A CONNECTICUT YANKEE with Libretto by Herbert Fields; Music, Richard Rodgers; Lyrics, Lorenz Hart; Based on the novel *A Connecticut Yankee in King Arthur's Court* by Mark Twain; Director/Choreographer, Jeffrey K. Neill; Musical Director/Additional Orchestrations, Wendell Kindberg; Sets, Norb Joerder; Costumes, Virginia Wood; Lighting, Bruce A. Kraemer; Assistant to Director, Suzanne Kaszynski; Producers, Marie and Walter Landa, Harry Blum; Stage Manager/Technical Director, John W. Lant; Stage Managers, Shawn Jones, Gwen M. Hamilton; Sound, Hal Schuler; Costume Assistant, Jodi Fogel; Press, twr/Cathy Tague. CAST: Tim McKanic (Prof. Albert Kay/Sir Kay), Donald Brooks Ford (Prof. Martin Barrett/The Yankee), Norb Joerder (Prof. Gerald Gareth/Sir Galahad), William Walters (Prof. Arthur Pengrass/King Arthur), Bob Cuccioli (Prof. Lawrence Lake/Sir Lancelot), Jeff Paul (Prof. Mervin Ross/Merlin), Brian Bowman (Prof. Borenstein/Sir Bors/Knight), Lawrence Raben (Prof. Geoffery/Sir Geoffery/Knight), Andy Thain (Prof. Colby/Sir Colgrim/Knight), Kevin J. Usher (Prof. Tracy/Sir Tristan/Knight), Eric Walden (Prof. Seagram/Sir Sagamore/Knight), Mark Wilkening (Prof. Dunhill/Sir Dinidan/Knight), Anne Fisher (Alice Carter/Alisande-"Sandy"), Leslie Bates (Rose/Telephone Girl/Slave), Wendy Coles (Daisy/Slave), Carol Cornicelli (Iris/Slave), Marianne Ferrari (Violet/Slave), Susan Peterson (Lily/Slave), Laura Lee Prouty (Heather/Slave), Patricia Moline (Fay Ross/Queen Morgan Le Fay), Marlene Greene (Angelina/Maid Angela), Joseph Aronica (Pete/Pete the Vassal), Jonathan Ready (Page), Margaret Benczak (Queen Guinevere), Carol Leigh Stevens (Mistress Evelyn). MUSICAL NUMBERS: This is My Night to Howl, Thou Swell, At the Round Table, I Blush, On a Desert Island with Thee, To Keep My Love Alive, Watch the Magic, My Heart Stood Still, The Burning Song/Hymn, Camelot Is Learning Fast/The Camelot Samba, Can't You Do a Friend a Favor?, I Feel at Home with You, You Always Love the Same Girl, Someone Should Tell Them, Finale. A musical comedy in two acts. The action takes place in the Camelot Room of the New Haven Hilton Hotel, 1986, and in Camelot, 543 A.D.

(Harold Clurman Theatre) Wednesday, May 14–25, 1986 (6 performances and 7 previews). The Heartbreak Company and Victor Cannon present:
A PLACE CALLED HEARTBREAK by Robert S. Stokes; Director, Ellen Cannon; Set/Costumes, Michael Sharp; Lighting, Howell Binkley; Executive Producer, Frank Scardino; Company Manager, Tracy Danehy; Technical Supervisor, Randall Whitescarver; Combat, Jason Heller; Military Consultant, Dr. Edward M. Potoker; Stage Managers, Raymond Chandler, Michael Raynor; Press, Howard Atlee. CAST: Tom Felix (Navy Lt. Cmdr. Ralph Connor), Rony Clanton (Navy Lt. Cmdr. Rafferty), Patrick Kilpatrick (Army First Lt. Chadd), Jason Heller (Navy Capt. Tom Harrington), Frank Michael Liu (Col. Nu), Phil Harper (Fowler), Carlos Cestero (Fidel), Brian Patrick Clarke (Marine Lt. Col. Cord Blass), Neil Bonin (Navy Cmdr. Richard Marquette), Alexander Thomas, Michael Raynor (P.O.W.'s), Ray Moy (Vietnamese Guard). A drama in 2 acts and 4 scenes. The action takes place in February 1973, 24 hours before the repatriation of the first group of U.S. prisoners of War in Indochina, in a large barracks room of the Hoa Lo Prison in Hanoi, and in a corridor outside the room.

(New Heritage Repertory Theatre) Thursday, May 15, - June 8, 1986 (16 performances) National Black Touring Circuit presents:
BROTHER MALCOLM by Frank G. Greenwood; Producer, Woodie King, Jr.; Executive Director, Voza Rivera; Artistic Director, Andre Robinson, R.; Technical Director, Ric Rogers; Director, Ron Milner. CAST: Duane Shepard as Malcom X. Performed with one intermission. The action takes place at the present time in the Harlem Headquarters of the Organization of Afro-American Unity in the Hotel Teresa.

(Judith Anderson Theatre) Thursday, May 15, - June 8, 1986 (16 performances) New Arts Theatre Company (Joshua Astrachan, Artistic Director) presents:
DRY LAND by Cyndi Coyne; Director, Kay Matschullat; Set, Loy Arcenas; Lighting, Robert Wierzel; Costumes, Candice Donnelly; Sound, Tom Gould; Production Coordinator, Christina Giannelli; Stage Managers, Amy Fritz, Lisa Braden; Press, Bob Ganshaw. CAST: Caris Corfman (Mary McCarthy), Marylouise Burke (Trish), Amy Sohn (Mary Teresa McCarthy), Christian Slater succeeded by Scott Tiler (Stevie Tierney), Olivia Laurel Mates (Amy Pedrotti), Charles Cissel (Man on the dance floor). A play in two acts. The action takes place on the beach in South Boston; in and around the McCarthy house in the summer of 1966.

(West End Arts Theatre) Friday, May 16, - June 9, 1986 (16 performances) MZM Productions and Nonson Gallery Productions present:
DOROTHY PARKER: NO SONG OF AN INGENUE/OSCAR WILDE: SOLITAIRE conceived, compiled and directed by E. M. Christian; Executive Producer, Marion Z. Murphy; Costumes, Evanne Marie; Lighting, Ray Swagerty; Production Assistant, John M. Flood; Stage Manager, Kathleen M. McHugh; Press, Nancy Christian. CAST: "Dorothy Parker" with Wendy Matthews (Mrs. Parker), Nancy Lipschultz (Dorothy), Donna Foley (Dottie). "Oscar Wilde" with James Fleming (Oscar), George Holmes, Nancy Lipschultz, Donna Foley, Joseph Travers.

(Village Gate Downstairs) Friday, May 16, - July 6, 1986 (53 performances and 6 previews).
NATIONAL LAMPOON'S "CLASS OF '86"; A Matty Simmons-John Heyman Production; Associate Producer, Jodi Doff; Head Writer, Andy Simmons; Settings, Daniel Proett; Sound, Richard Dunning; Lighting, Robert Strohmeier; Costumes, Nancy Konrardy; Director, Jerry Adler; Musical Director, Michael Sansonia; General Manager, Richard Horner; Technical Director, John Griffith; Wardrobe, Sahra Henrickson; Hairstylist, Nancy L. Konrardy; Musical Staging, Nora Brennan; Stage Manager, Amy Stiller; Press, Jeffrey Richards, C. George Willard, Ben Morse, Susan Lee, Mary-Louise Silva, L. Glenn Poppleton III, Ken Mandelbaum. CAST: Rodger Bumpass, Veanne Cox, Annie Golden, John Michael Higgins, Tommy Koenig, Brian Brucker O'Connor, Understudies: Amy Stiller, Patrick Weathers. MUSICAL NUMBERS: Cocaine, Yuppie Love, They Lost the Revolution, Revolution, My Bod Is for God, I Got It, The President's Dream, Don't Drop the Bomb, Apartheid Lover, The Ticker. A musical revue in two acts.

(Town Hall) Saturday, May 17–19, 1986 (3 performance limited engagement). The New Amsterdam Theatre Company (Artistic Director, Bill Tynes) presents:
I MARRIED AN ANGEL with Music by Richard Rodgers; Lyrics, Lorenz Hart; Book, Richard Rodgers, Lorenz Hart; Adapted from the play by John Vaszary; Special Dialogue, Michael Colby; Director, Rick Lombardo; Choreography, Jacqi Loewy; Musical Direction/Vocal Arrangements, Gregory J. Dlugos; Orchestrations, Hans Spialek/Reconstruction, Russell Warner; Production Supervisor, Robert Bennett; Producing Director, Marjorie E. Hassenfelt; Stage Manager, Daniel R. Bauer; Lighting Consultant, Peter M. Ehrhardt; Scenic Consultant, Roger LaVoie; Costume Consultant, David Toser; Press, Jeffrey Richards Associates, Ben Morse, Susan E. Lee. CAST: Kurt Peterson (Count Willy Palaffi), Virginia Seidel (Angel), Phyllis Newman (Countess Peggy Palaffi), Karen Ziemba (Anna Murphy), David Wasson (Harry Mischka Szigetti), Maggie Task (Olga Madayn), Lee Lobenhofer (Peter Mueller), Ralph Farnworth (Gen. Lucash), Carol Baxter, Leslie Bixby, Dave Demke, Ida Rae Hirsh, Shari Krikorion, Robin Manning, Ruth Rose, Cheryl Ann Rossi, Eric Van Baars. MUSICAL NUMBERS: Did You Ever Get Stung?, I Married an Angel, The Modiste, I'll Tell the Man in the Street, How to Win Friends and Influence People, Spring Is Here, Angel without Wings, A Twinkle in Your Eye, At the Roxy Music Hall, Finale. A concert version of the 1938 musical comedy in two acts.

(Perry Street Theatre) Wednesday, May 20 - June 1, 1986 (12 performances) New York Theatre Workshop (Artistic Director, Jean Passanante; Managing Director, Nancy Kassak Diekmann) presents:
1951 conceived and directed by Anne Bogart; Text Adapted by Anne Bogart, Mac Wellman; Music, Michael S. Roth; Lyrics, Mac Wellman; Set, Sarah Bonnemaison; Costumes, Walker Hicklin; Sound, Karen Michael McPherson, Michael S. Roth; Lighting, Carol Mullins; Dramaturg, Anne Cattaneo; Technical Director, Peter Bendevski; Wardrobe, M. A. Neff; Props, Happy Massee; Stage Manager, Richard Costabile. CAST: Mark Austin (Reggie/Clifford Odets/Ronald Reagan), Edward Baran (Fred/Lionel Stander/Walt Disney/Harold), Catherine Coray (Anne/Jerome Robbins/Dorothy Parker/Molly), Ryan Cutrona (Phil Smith/Larry Parks/Richard), Karen Evans-Kandel (Lisa/Arthur M. Schlesinger, Jr./Hazel Scott/Gail Clooney/Louis Mandel), Jonathan Fried (Sterling Hayden/George Spelvin/Julian/Louella Parsons), Henry Stram (Ray/Bertoldt Brecht/Elia Kazan), Karen Trott (Yvonne/Lillian Hellman/Howard Hughes/Adele), Randolyn Zinn (Randi Jo/Zero Mostel/Ayn Rand/Susie, David Gaines (Piano), Richard Wasley (Clarinets). Performed with one intermission.

Marilyn Pasekoff, Kathy Morath, Meg Bussert,
(seated) Dennis Bailey, David Ardao, Hal Davis
in "Professionally Speaking" *(Ken Howard Photo)*

Kurt Peterson, Phyllis Newman, Virginia Seidel
in "I Married an Angel" *(Ilan Rubin Photo)*

(Royal Court Theatre) Wednesday, May 21–25, 1986 (6 performances) Theatre House presents:
SOUTHERN LIGHTS: five original one-act plays. "You're Invited" by Kerry Madden; Director, Dale Dickey; with Fred Fehrman (Red), Deborah Jordan (Yellow), Brenda K. Brown (Blue), Don Stephenson (Green), Craig Gillespie (Purple), Rebecca O'Brien (Pink). "The Garden of Eden" by David Torbett; Director, Tommy Keeney; with Mark Sturgeon (Junior), Eleanor Moseley (Student), Julie Jackson (Pixie), Fred Fehrmann (Boss), Robert Camden (Young Junior), Marla Machart (Woman), Mother (Arden Sampson), Brenda Slaughter (Sister). "Edward" by David Torbett; Director, Mr. Torbett; with Carl Thoma (Charles), Tommy Keeney (Edward). "All You Can" by Kerry Madden; Director, Julie Jackson; with Don Stephenson (Owne), Dale Dickey (Sarah), Brenda Slaughter (Molly). "The Squids Are Clouds" by Craig Gillespie; Director, Mr. Gillespie; with Steven Shaw (He), Carol Goans (She). Performed with one intermission.

(Theatre at St. Peter's Church) Thursday, May 22, - June 15, 1986 (37 performances and 7 previews) Frederic Block and Irving Welzer in association with Kate Harper present:
PROFESSIONALLY SPEAKING with Music and Lyrics by Peter Winkler, Ernst Muller, Frederic Block; Director, Tony Tanner; Set, Robert Alan Harper; Costumes, P. Chelsea Harriman; Lighting, Barry Arnold; Musical Direction/Additional Arrangements, Bruce W. Coyle; General Management, Kate Harper; Technical Manager, Seth Newfeld; Production Assistant, Bill Dietrich; Stage Manager, Doug Fogel; Press, Shirley Herz, Glenna Freedman, Peter Cromarty, Pete Sanders, Gary Lawrence, Jilana Devine. CAST: Marilyn Pasekoff, Dennis Bailey, Hal Davis, Meg Bussert, David Ardao, Kathy Morath, Understudies: Joan Jaffe, Sel Vitella. MUSICAL NUMBERS: The Doctor's Out Today, Malpractice, Patient's Lament, Three Doctor's Wives, A Doctor's Prayer, Guadalajara, Gastrointestinal Rag, Sibling Rivalry, The Lawyer's Out Today, Malpractice II, Equitable Distribution Waltz, Portia's Plan, Lawyerman, What Price Have I Paid?, I Professionisti, First Let's Kill All the Lawyers, The Teacher's Out Today, The Best Part-time Job in Town, Emmylou Lafayette and the Football Team, Tamara Queen of the Nile, Stupidly in Love, I Hate It, Mathematical Quartet, Remember There Was Me, Who the Hell Do These Wise Guys Think They Are?, Over the Hill, Finale. A musical revue in two acts.

(Joyce Theatre) Tuesday, May 27–31, 1986 (6 performances).
MISTERO BUFFO (Comic Mystery) written and directed by Dario Fo; Set/Lighting, Lino Avolio; Translation by Stuart Hood and Ron Jenkins; Company Manager, Maria Nadotti; Stage Manager, Walter Valeri; Actors' assistant, Mario Pirovano; Presented by Compagnia Teatrale LaComune Milan. CAST: Dario Fo with Ron Jenkins translating.

(Hartley House Theater) Thursday, May 29, - June 15, 1986 (16 performances)
VOICES IN THE HEAD by Neal Bell; Director, Thomas Babe; Assistant Directors, Brian McNicholl, John Moser; Scenic Designer, Reagan Cook; Stage Manager, Elaine O'Donnell. CAST: Ben Siegler, Willie Reale, Fred Burrell, Monica Moran, with L. A. FREEWHEELING by Lewis Black; Director, Mark Linn-Baker; with Rebecca Nelson and Sam McMurrey.

OFF-BROADWAY SERIES

THE ACTING COMPANY

Fifteenth Season

Producing Artistic Director, John Houseman; Executive Producer, Margot Harley; Artistic Director, Michael Kahn; Production Manager, T. Wiley Bramlett; Lighting, Gregory C. MacPherson; Wigs/Facial Hair, Charles LoPresto; General Manager, Mary Beth Carroll; Production Assistant, Lynn Johnson; Technical Director, Jeff Clark; Props, Christopher B. Higgins; Wardrobe, Laurel Frushour; Company Manager, Camara McKinnon-Miller; Stage Managers, Maureen F. Gibson, Susan B. Feltman; Staff Repertory Director, Rob Bundy; Press, Michael Mace, Fred Nathan, Marc Thibodeau, Dennis Crowley.

(Lucille Lortel Theatre) Sunday, April 20,–May 3, 1986 (16 performances)
ORCHARDS: Seven American Playwrights present dramatizations of stories by Anton Chekhov; Director, Robert Falls; Sets, Adrianne Lobel; Costumes, Laura Crow; Lighting, Paul Gallo; Original Music, Louis Rosen; Dramaturg, Anne Cattaneo; Stage Managers, Maureen F. Gibson, Susan B. Feltman.
PRODUCTIONS: "The Man in a Case" by Wendy Wasserstein; Adapted from translation by Marian Fell. Brian Reddy (Byelinkov), Mariangela Pino (Varinka). "Vint" by David Mamet; Adapted from translation by Avrahm Yarmolinsky. Craig Bryant (Porter), Terrence Caza (Commissioner Persolin), Joel Miller (Zvisdulin), Phil Meyer (Kulakevitch), Kevin Jackson (Nedkudov), Aled Davies (Psiulin) "The Talking Dog" by John Guare; Adapted from translation by Marian Fell of "Joke". Susan Finch (F), Michael McKenzie (M), Kevin Jackson (F's Hang Glider), Phil Meyer (M's Hang Glider). "Drowning" translated by Avrahm Yarmolinsky; Adapted by Maria Irene Fornes. Philip Goodwin (Pea), Anthony Powell (Roe), Aled Davies (Stephen). "A Dopey Fairy Tale" based on Avrahm Yarmolinsky's translation of Chekhov's short story "The Skit." Phil Meyer (Smile), Terrence Caza (Father Baker), Susan Finch (Mother Baker), Craig Bryant (Clarence), Joel Miller (Chatter the Dog), Kevin Jackson (Mayor), Anthony Powell (Magistrate), Philip Goodwin (Minister), Wendy Brennan (Female Frog), Brian Reddy (Male Frog), Laura Brutsman (Sad Princess Gladys). "Eve of the Trial" by Samm-Art Williams; Adapted from translation by April FitzLyon and Kyril Zinovieff. Susan Finch (Ma Lola), Brian Reddy (Lester Simmons), Laura Brutsman (Pearl Simmons), Joel Miller (Tate), Mariangela Pino (Lily), Wendy Brennan (Kitty), Philip Goodwin (Alex Buskin/Alexis Buskenov). "Rivkala's Ring" adapted by Spalding Gray from Constance Garnett's translation of "The Witch". A monologue by Aled Davies.

Saturday, May 10,–June 29, 1986 (58 performances and 10 previews)
TEN BY TENNESSEE: A Retrospective of Tennessee Williams' Short Plays; Director, Michael Kahn; Sets, Derek McLane; Costumes, Ann Hould-Ward; Lighting, Dennis Parichy; Original Music, Lee Hoiby; Hairstylist, Phyllis Della; Sound, Aural Fixation; Assistant Director, Rob Bundy; Animals, William Berloni; Stage Managers, Kathleen Boyette Bramlett, Michael S. Mantel. CAST: "The Lady of Larkspur Lotion" with Mary Lou Rosato (Mrs. Hardwicke-Moore), Lisa Banes (Mrs. Wire), Randle Mell (The Writer). "Talk to Me Like the Rain and Let Me Listen" with Derek D. Smith (Man), Laura Hicks (Woman). "Portrait of a Madonna" with Lisa Banes (Miss Lucretia Collins), Anderson Matthews (Porter), Richard Howard (Elevator Boy), Derek D. Smith (Doctor), Mary Lou Rosato (Nurse), Randle Mell (Abrams). "The Unsatisfactory Supper" with Anderson Matthews (Archie Lee), Mary Lou Rosato (Baby Doll), Laura Hicks (Aunt Rose). "The Long Goodbye" with Randle Mell (Joe), Derek D. Smith (Silva), Anderson Matthews, Richard Howard, David Manis, Tim White (Movers), Lisa Banes (Myra), Richard Howard (Bill), Laura Hicks (Mother). Program B: "Auto-da-Fe" Lisa Banes (Mme. Duvenet), Richard Howard (Eloi). "The Strangest Kind of Romance" with Mary Lou Rosato (Landlady), Derek D. Smith (Little Man), Anderson Matthews (Old Man), Richard Howard (Officer), Randle Mell (Boxer). "A Perfect Analysis Given by a Parrot" with Mary Lou Rosato (Bessie), Lisa Banes (Flora), Anderson Matthews (Waiter), David Manis, Randle Mell (Sons of Mars). "This Property Is Condemned" with Laura Hicks (Willie), Richard Howard (Tom). "I Can't Imagine Tomorrow" with Mary Lou Rosato (One), Randle Mell (Two). Connecting material supplied by Greg Leaming from works of Tennessee Williams.

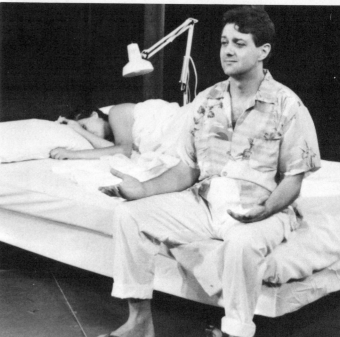

Top Right: Derek David Smith, Laura Hicks
in "Talk to Me Like the Rain . . ." *(Tony Triolo Photo)*
Center: Aled Davies in "Rivkala's Ring"
(Diane Gorodnitzki Photo)

Lisa Banes, Mary Lou Rosato in "A Perfect
Analysis Given by a Parrot" *(Tony Triolo Photo)*

AMAS REPERTORY THEATRE

October 24, 1985–May 4, 1986
Seventeenth Season

Founder/Artistic Director, Rosetta LeNoire; Associate Artistic Director, Billie Allen; Administrator/Business Manager, Gary Halcott; Administrator, Jerry Lapidus; Wardrobe, Howard Behar; Development, Richard Hunter; Press, Fred Nathan, Bert Fink, Dennis Crowley

Thursday, Oct. 24–Nov. 17, 1985 (16 performances)
BINGO with Book by Ossie Davis, Hy Gilbert; Music, George Fischoff; Lyrics, Hy Gilbert; Based on the "Bingo Long Travelling All-Stars and Motor Ings" by William Brashler; Director, Ossie Davis; Sets, Tom Barnes; Lighting, Jeffrey Schissler; Costumes, Christina Giannini; Technical Director, Alexander Herndon; Choreography/Musical Staging, Henry LeTang; Associate Choreographer, Ellie LeTang; Assistant Choreographer, Christian Holder; Musical Arrangements, Neal Tate, George Fischoff; Musical Director, Neal Tate; Stage Managers, Douglas R. Bergman, Kellie Williams, Femi Sarah Heggie, James McLaurin
CAST: Louis Baldonieri, David Winston Barge, Ethel S. Beatty, Ron Bobb-Semple, Brian Evaret Chandler, Joyce Dara, Melissa Haizlip, Christian Holder, Andy Hostettler, Donna Ingram-Young, David L. King, Norman Matlock, John R. McCurry, Monica Parks, Barbara Passolt, Jackie Patterson, James Randolph, Sharon E. Scott, Keith Tyrone, Ronald Wyche
A musical in 2 acts and 15 scenes with prologue. The action takes place in 1939.
Thursday, Feb. 13–Mar. 9, 1986 (16 performances)
LA BELLE HELENE with Book by John Fearnley; Adapted from A. P. Herbert's *Helen;* Music, Jacques Offenbach; Lyrics, David Baker; Adapted from *Helen;* Director, John Fearnley; Choreography, J. Randall Hugill; Sets, Donald L. Brooks; Lighting, Deborah Matlack, Costumes, Howard Behar; Technical Director, Jon Dewey; Musical Supervisor, David Baker; Musical Director, Patrick Holland; Props, Anthony Nugent; Hairstylist/Makeup, Ricardo Rodriguez, Brad Scott; Stage Managers, Jay McManigal, Bruce Greenwood, James McLaurin
CAST: Philip Anderson (Philicomus/Ajax II), Alexander Barton (Agamemmnon), Marcia Brushingham (Minerva), Beverly Burchett (Eleni), Larry Campbell (Menelaus), Cliff Hicklen (Mercury), Jozie Hill (Parthenis), Jay Aubrey Jones (Calchas), Francesca MacAaron (Calchas), Saundra McClain (Bacchis), Susan McDonnell (Leora), Kenneth McMullen (Hector), Steven Riedel (Pylades), Alex Santoriello (Paris), Brad Scott (Oresties), Vanessa Shaw (Helen), Ted Simmons, Jr. (Ajax I), Sunder (Venus), Marzetta Tate (Juno), Ivan Thomas (Achilles)
A musical in 3 acts and 8 scenes. The action begins in Sparta, some 3000 years ago.
Friday April 11–May 4, 1986 (16 performances)
SH-BOOM! with Book and Lyrics by Eric V. Tait, Jr.; Music, Willex Brown, Jr./Mr. Tait; Director, Stuart Warmflash; Choreography, Audrey Tischler; Sets, Janice Davis; Lighting, Eric Thomann; Technical Director, Jon Dewey; Musical Director/Arranger, Loni Berry; Costumes, Candace Warner; Musical Supervisor/Arranger, Mr. Brown; Assistant Musical Director, Edward Reichert; Stage Managers, Jay McManigal, Bruce Greenwood, James McLaurin
CAST: Michael Accardo (Half Note/Chuckle), Anthony Barone (Chico), Toni-Maria Chalmers (Charlene), Sarah Clarke (Diane), Barbara Warren-Cooke (Miss McIntosh), Ruthann Curry (Mrs. Antiamore), Deborah Davis (Grace), Anthony Dowdy (Danny/Chuckle), Gregory Harvey (Chip), Reginald Hobbs (Tony C.), Sue Judin (Dolores), Michael Kostroff (Teddy/Half Note), Jill Kotler (Jill), Daniel Neusom (Sandman/Billy), Peter J. Saputo (Antiamore), Julia Simpson (God/Mrs. Johnson), Crist Swann (Bob/Half Note), Casey Williams (Sheila/Grandmother)
A musical in two acts. The action takes place in a lower-middle-class New York City high school in 1954.

Ken Katz, JWL Photos

**Top Right: James Randolph, Norman Matlock, Monica
Parks, John R. McCurry in "Bingo"**
(Ken Katz Photo)
**Below: Peter J. Saputo, Julia Sampson, Barbara
Warren-Cooke in "Sh-Boom!"** *(JWL Photo)*

**Jay Aubrey Jones, Saundra McClain
in "La Belle Helene"** *(JWL Photo)*

83

AMERICAN PLACE THEATRE

November 13, 1985–June 1, 1986
Twenty-second Season

Director, Wynn Handman; Associate Director, Julia Miles; Production Manager, Carl Zutz; Business Manager, Joanna Vedder; Literary Adviser, Chris Bryer; Membership, Ron Spetrino; Women's Project Director, Julia Miles; Literary Manager, Suzanne Bennett; Development, Ellie Meglio; Press, Fred Nathan, Anne Abrams, Philip Rinaldi.

Wednesday, Nov. 13–Dec. 8, 1985 (26 performances). The Women's Project presents:

BREAKING THE PRAIRIE WOLF CODE by Lavonne Mueller; Director, Liz Diamond; Set, Richard Hoover; Lighting, Jane Reisman; Costumes, Mimi Maxmen; Original Score/Musical Director, Alice Eve Cohen; Assistant Director, Janna Gjesdal; Props, Andrea Odezynska; Wardrobe, Mara Williams; Wigs, Vito Mastrogiovanni; Stage Managers, Rebecca Green, Novella Nelson.

CAST: Keliher Walsh (Helen), Tenney Walsh (Amy), Robert Black (Schoolcraft/Bluster), James Lally (Skeeter/Capt. David Yeager), Judith Barcroft (Jenny Sturdevant/Mother), Novella Nelson (Esther)

A play in two acts. The action takes place on the Overland Trail to California in 1866.

Thursday, Dec. 5–15, 1985 (18 performances)

TIMES AND APPETITES OF TOULOUSE-LAUTREC by Jeff Wanshel; Lyrics, Michael Feingold based on French originals; Director, John Ferraro; Set, John Arnone; Costumes, Edi Giguere; Lighting, Stephen Strawbridge; Choreography, Priscilla Lopez; Musical Director, Russell Walden; Circus/Clown Consultant, Bill Irwin; Sound, Gary Harris; Casting, Jeffrey Passero; Musical Consultant/Accordionist, Bill Schimmel; Props, Leslie Weisberg; Stage Manager, Mark Baltazar.

CAST: Lonny Price (Count Henri de Toulouse-Lautrec Monfa), Lezlie Dalton (Leontine/Mamie/Dead Lady/Sewer-Grating/Mother Guilbert/Mayhilde Tarquini d'Or), MacIntyre Dixon (Dr. Bourges/Pere Abbe/Dogmouth/Ducarre/Doctor/Critic/Announcer), Ron Faber (Count Alphonse de Toulouse-Lautrec Monfa/Maurice Joyant/Vincent Van Gogh/Puffy Fellow/Oller/Lauradour), Susanna Frazer (Jane Avril/Clowness Cha-U-Kao/Little Girl/Whore), June Gable (Yvette Guilbert/Countess Adele Tapie de Celeyran/Something Fancy/Nini Leg-in-the-Air), Judith Hoag (Mireille/Jeanne D'Armagnac/Love-Tomato), Nicholas Kepros (Dr. Senelaigne/Jean Lorrain/Fernand Cormon/High-Class/Cheret/Tourist), Priscilla Lopez (La Goulue/Paulette), David Purdham (Aristide Bruant/Emile Bernard/Critic/Achille), Rocco Sisto (Dr. Gabriel Tapie de Celeyran/Valentin Desosse/Louis Anquetin/Neighbor/Critic), Carl Zutz (Clown/Announcer)

MUSICAL NUMBERS: Freckled Fanny, In Saint-Lazare, Can-Can, Dance, A Little Anisette, Under a Bridge at Night, Madame Arthur, Mademoiselle de Paris, It's Not as Good as Love, Along the Seine

A musical in two acts. The action takes place in and around Paris from Nov. 24, 1864 to Sept. 9. 1901.

David Purdham, Priscilla Lopez, Rocco Sisto,
Lonny Price in "Times and Appetites. . . ."
Top: Keliher Walsh, Tenney Walsh
in "Breaking the Prairie Wolf Code"

David Purdham, Susanna Frazer, Rocco Sisto,
Lonny Price, June Gable in "Times and
Appetites of Toulouse-Lautrec"

Tuesday, Jan. 1–Feb. 23, 1986 (31 performances) Jubilee! A Theatre Festival Celebrating the Black Experience:

CELEBRATION conceived and Directed by Shauneille Perry; Musical Director, Thomas Riggsbee; Costumes, Judy Dearing; Lighting, Marc D. Malamud; Stage Manager, David Horton Black; Associate Producer, Karen Baxter. A musical journey from the beginning of the African American tradition to the present with songs, poems excerpts and stories by Gwendolyn Brooks, Paul Laurence Dunbar, Langston Hughes, Zora Neal Hurston, Shauneille Perry, Dudley Randall, Carolyn Rodgers, Margaret Walker; Performed by Carolyn Byrd, Clebert Ford, Andre Robinson, Jr., Fran Salisbury

Wednesday, Jan. 15–April 27, 1986 (104 performances)

DRINKING IN AMERICA written and performed by Eric Bogosian; Director, Wynn Handman; Lighting, Marc Malamud; Sound, Richard Tattersall; Stage Manager, Rebecca Green

Performed by Mr. Bogosian without an intermission.

Thursday, Feb. 27–June 1, 1986 (87 performances) Presented by American Place Theatre and Henry Street Settlement's New Federal Theatre.

WILLIAMS & WALKER by Vincent D. Smith; Director, Shauneille Perry; Musical Director, Neal Tate; Choreographer, Lenwood Sloan; Set/Lighting, Marc D. Malamud; Costumes, Judy Dearing; Wardrobe, Ocakte; Props, Annalee Van Kleeck; Stage Manager, Lisa Blackwell; Henry Street Settlement's New Federal Theatre production.

CAST: Ben Harney (Bert Williams), Vondie Curtis-Hall (George Walker), Neal Tate (Pianist).

MUSICAL NUMBERS: Magnetic Rag, Constantly, Bon Bon Buddy, Somebody Stole My Gal, Let It Alone, Everybody Wants to See the Baby, Save Your Money John, Nobody, I'd Rather Have Nothin' All of the Time, I May Be Crazy but I Ain't No Fool, I'm a Jonah Man, Original Rag, Chocolate Drop

Performed without intermission. The action takes place on June 10, 1910 backstage in the Majestic Theatre in New York City in the dressing room of Bert Williams.

Friday, March 21–April 6, 1986 (24 performances) The Women's Project presents:

WOMEN HEROES: IN PRAISE OF EXCEPTIONAL WOMEN Series A: "Parallax (In Honor of Daisy Bates)" written and directed by Denise Hamilton performed by Michele Shay; "Personality" written by Gina Wendkos, Ellen Ratner; Directors, Gina Wendkos, Richard Press; Performed by Ellen Ratner; "How She Played the Game" by Cynthia Cooper; Director, Bryna Wortman; Musical Consultant, Paul Schubert; Performed by Susan Stevens; Series B: "Emma Goldman" written and performed by Jessica Litwak; Director, Anne Bogart; Original Music, Person-to-Person; Slides, Barry Schoenfeld; Production Supervisor, Terry Knickerbocker; "Millie" by Susan Kander; Director, Carol Tanzman; Performed by Louise Stubbs; "Colette in Love" by Lavonne Mueller; Director, Mirra Bank; Music, Alice Eve Cohen; Lyrics, Lavonne Mueller; Choreography, Joy Javits; Sets, Marc D. Malamud, Ina Mayhew; Costumes, Judy Dearing; Lighting, Marc D. Malamud; Projections, Charles E. Hoefler; Sound, Gary Harris; Stage Managers, Mary Fran Loftus, Pamela Singer;

CAST: Shirley Knight (Colette), John P. Connolly (Willie/Max/Missy), Terry Knickerbocker (Voice of announcer), Susan Stevens (Voice of Colette's Mother); Birds by William Berloni Theatrical Animals

Martha Holmes Photos

Top: Eric Bogosian in "Drinking in America"
Right: Vondie Curtis-Hall, Ben Harney
in "Williams & Walker"

Shirley Knight as Colette
in "Colette in Love"

85

AMERICAN JEWISH THEATRE

September 28, 1985–June 15, 1986
Sixth Season

Artistic Director, Stanley Brechner; Managing Director, Leda Gelles; Production Associate, Evanne Christian; Technical Director, Floyd R. Swagerty, Jr.; Development, Norman Golden; Resident Director, Dan Held; Literary Manager, Peter Gordon; Dramaturg, Susan Nanus; Sound, Gary Rehab; Wardrobe, Michelle Matland; Assistant Stage Manager, Nan Siegmund; Press, Helene Davis, Robert Resnikoff, Jeffrey Richards Associates

(92nd Street Y) Saturday, Sept. 28–Nov. 24, 1985 (47 performances and 3 previews) **GREEN FIELDS** by Peretz Hirshbein; Translation, Joseph Landis; Director, Stanley Brechner; Set, Eugene Gurlitz; Costumes, Donna Zakowska; Lighting, Robert Bessoir; Stage Manager, Noel Stern; Casting, Elissa Myers/Mark Teschner; Choreography, Ruth Goodman; Composer, Jonathan Firstenberg; Artistic Consultant, Sonia Zomina.
CAST: Rebecca Schull (Rokhel), Herbert Rubens (Dovid-Noyakh), Barbara Spiegel (Gittl), Norman Golden (Elkone), Robin Morse (Tsine), Rebecca Ellens (Stere), Matt deGanon (Hersh-Ber), Peter A. Smith (Avrom-Yankev), Michael Cerveris (Levi-Yitskhok)

Saturday, Dec. 14, 1985–Feb. 9, 1986 (33 performances and 17 previews) *World Premiere* of
TODAY I AM A FOUNTAIN PEN by Israel Horovitz; Based on stories by Morley Torgov; Director, Stephen Zuckerman; Set, James Fenhagen; Costumes, Mimi Maxmen; Lighting, Curt Osterman; Sound, Aural Fixation; Casting, Darlene Kaplan; Production Coordinator, Neal Fox; Stage Manager, Michael S. Mantel.
CAST: Josh Blake (Irving Yanover), Stephen Prutting (Emil Ilchak), Sol Frieder (Ardenshensky/Priest), Dana Keeler (Mrs. Ilchak), Marcia Jean Kurtz (Esther Yanover), Melissa Leo (Annie Ilchak), Sam Schacht (Moses Yanover), Grant Shaud (Pete Lisanti)

Saturday, Feb. 15–April 13, 1986 (51 performances) *World Premiere* of
A ROSEN BY ANY OTHER NAME by Israel Horovitz; Based on characters from Morley Torgov's book "A Good Place to Come From"; Director, Stephen Zuckerman; Set, James Fenhagen; Costumes, Mimi Maxmen; Lighting, Curt Ostermann; Sound, Aural Fixation; Stage Manager, Michael S. Mantel.
CAST: Maddie Corman (Fern), Barbara eda-Young (Pearl Rosen), Sol Frieder (Reb Brechtman/Ardenshensky/Pottstein/Judge Brown/Edelman/Kravitz/Clerk), Michael Ornstein (Manny Boxbaum), Peter Riegert (Barney Rosen), Peter Smith (Stanley Rosen), Cat (Toronto Rosen)

Monday, March 3–24, 1986 (4 performances Mondays only)
A RENDEZVOUS WITH GOD by Miriam Hoffman; Directed by Sue Lawless; Musical Direction, Malke Gottlieb; A solo performance by Avi Hoffman based on the life and works of Itsik Manger.

Saturday, May 3–June 15, 1986 (39 performances) *World Premiere* of
THE CHOPIN PLAYOFFS by Israel Horovitz; Based on stories by Morley Torgov; Director, Stephen Zuckerman; Set, James Fenhagen; Costumes, Mimi Maxmen; Lighting, Curt Ostermann; Sound, Aural Fixation; Production Coordinator, Elyse Barbell; Stage Managers, Neal Fox, Celestine.
CAST: Maddie Corman (Fern Phipps), Sol Frieder (Ardenshensky/Uncle Goldberg/Wong/Reb Brechtman), Marcia Jean Kurtz (Esther Yanover), Karen Ludwig (Pearl Rosen/voice of Mrs. Phipps), Richard Portnow (Barney Rosen/voice of Mr. Phipps/M.C.), Sam Schacht (Moses Yanover), Jonathan Marc Sherman (Irving Yanover), Nicholas Strouse (Stanley Rosen)

Gerry Goodstein Photos

Michael Cerveris, Rebecca Schull, Robin Morse, Herb Rubens in "Green Fields" Below: Peter Riegert, Barbara eda-Young in "A Rosen by Any Other Name"

Sam Schacht, Marcia Jean Kurtz, Sol Frieder in "Today I Am a Fountain Pen"

Sam Schact, Marcia Jean Kurtz, Sol Frieder, Karen Ludwig, Richard Portnow in "Chopin Playoffs"

APPLE CORPS THEATRE

June 19, 1985–June 22, 1986
Seventh Season

Artistic Director, John Raymond; Managing Director/Company Manager, Neal Arluck; Assistant Administrator, Bob Del Pazzo; Press, Aviva Cohen

Wednesday, June 19–July 14, 1985 (27 performances)
MAN ENOUGH by Patty Gideon Sloan; Director, Steve McCurdy; Set/Lighting, Clark Middleton; Costumes, Joy Alpern; Casting, Alan Coleridge/Professional Casting Associates; Presented in association with RSM Productions & Pequod Productions; Assistant Lighting Designer, Donalee Katz; Hairstylist, Tony Gueli; Operations Director, Scott Nelson; Stage Managers, Nereida Ortiz, Mary Lou Simo
CAST: Marilyn Chris succeeded by Aideen O'Kelly (Josie Delaney), Bruce Roberts King (Joey Delaney), Peter Noel Duhamel (Donal Delaney), Alissa Alban (Kit Delaney), David S. Howard (Jack Delany), Tudi Roche (Sheila McCardle), Richard Karn (Tom McCardle), Jay Keye (Frank Quinn), and UNDERSTUDIES: Jane Hamilton (Josie), Jay Keye (Donal), Richard Karn (Joey), Mary Lou Simo (Sheila/Kit), Tom Bade (Frank/Tom/Jack)
A drama in 2 acts and 4 scenes. The action takes place at the present time in the home of Josie and Jack Delaney in Flatbush, Brooklyn, NY.

Friday, Aug. 23–Sept. 22, 1985 (24 performances)
MURDER AT THE VICARAGE by Agatha Christie; Dramatized by Moie Charles, Barbara Toy; Director, John Raymond; Set, Diann Duthie; Lighting, Deborah Constantine; Costumes, MaryAnn D. Smith; Sound, Elliot Forrest; Technical Director, Alex LaBianca; Stage Manager, Kara Sheridan.
CAST: William Van Hunter (Rev. Clement), Anne Newhall (Griselda), Frank Dowd (Dennis), Lois Nelson (Mary), Keith Williams (Ronald Hawes), Mare Kenney (Lettice Protheroe), Martha Farrar (Miss Marple), Helen Marcy (Mrs. Ridley), Anne Barrett (Anne Protheroe), Peter Bubriskie (Lawrence Redding), Robert McFarland (Dr. John Haydock), Bob Del Pazzo (Inspector Slack).
A mystery in 2 acts and 5 scenes. The action takes place during the summer of 1949 in the study of a vicarage in the country.

Tuesday, Dec. 3, 1985–Jan. 26, 1986 (55 performances)
PLAY IT AGAIN, SAM by Woody Allen; Director, Jack Melanos; Set, Larry Brodsky; Lighting, William J. Plachy; Costumes, MaryAnn D. Smith; Sound, Elliot Forrest; Technical Director, Keith Hutchings; Stage Manager, Kara Sheridan.
CAST: Neal Arluck (Allan Felix), John Raymond (Bogey), Gary Richards (Dick Christie), Wendy Makkena (Linda Christie), Jacqueline Rowen (Sharon/Vanessa/Go-Go Girl/Intellectual Girl/Barbara), Mare Kenney (Nancy/Sharon Lake/Gina).
A comedy in 3 acts. The action takes place in the apartment of Allan Felix on West 10th Street in New York City during 1969.

Wednesday, May 14–June 22, 1986 (35 performances)
BLACK COFFEE by Agatha Christie; Director, John Raymond; Set, Larry Brodsky; Lighting, William J. Plachy; Costumes, MaryAnn D. Smith; Sound, Neal Arluck; Technical Director, Carmen Bau; Production Assistant, Jim Yrizarry; Stage Manager, Mark Baltazar.
CAST: Richard Voigts (Tredwell/Dr. Graham/Johnson), Anne Barrett (Lucia Amory), Helen Marcy (Miss Caroline Amory), Nick Kaledin (Richard Amory), Debra Whitfield (Barbara Amory), Neal Arluck (Edward Raynor), Peter Bubriski (Dr. Carelli), Bob Del Pazzo (Hercule Poirot), Stockman Barner (Sir Claud Amory/Insp. Japp), William Van Hunter (Capt. Arthur Hastings)
A mystery in three acts. The action takes place during 1934 in the library of Sir Claud Amory's house at Abbot's Cleve, about 25 miles from London.

Austin Trevett Photos

**Wendy Makkena, John Raymond
in "Play It Again, Sam"**

**Anne Barrett, Bob Del Pazzo
in "Black Coffee"**

87

CIRCLE REPERTORY COMPANY

September 24, 1985–April 13, 1986
Seventeenth Season

Artistic Director, Marshall W. Mason; Managing Director, Suzanne M. Sato; Associate Artistic Director, B. Rodney Marriott; Associate Literary Manager, Bill Hemming; Assistant to Artistic Director/Casting, Harry Newman; Business Manager, Vicki Rubin; Marketing, Lynn Landis; Production Manager, Kate Stewart; Stage Managers, Fred Reinglas, Jody Boese, Jane Sanders, Leslie Loeb, Richard Costable; Wardrobe, Abby Levin, Tom Miller; Props, Jay Corcoran; Technical Director, Bonnie B. Burnham; Press, Reva Cooper

(Circle Repertory Theatre) Tuesday, Sept. 24–Dec. 1, 1985 (41 performances in repertory)

TALLEY & SON by Lanford Wilson; Director, Marshall W. Mason; Set, John Lee Beatty; Costumes, Laura Crow; Lighting, Dennis Parichy; Sound, Chuck London Media/Stewart Werner; Wigs, Paul Huntley; Wigs/Hair, Joan Weiss.

CAST: Robert Macnaughton (Timmy), Farley Granger (Eldon), Trish Hawkins (Sally), Joyce Reehling Christopher (Lottie), Laura Hughes (Olive), Helen Stenborg (Netta), Lisa Emery (Viola Platt), Lindsey Richardson (Buddy), Steve Decker (Emmet Young), Richard Backus (Harley Campbell), Edward Seamon (Mr. Talley, Julie Bargeron (Avalaine Platt).

A drama in two acts. The action takes place on Independence Day, 1944, in the front parlor of the Talley Place, a farm near Lebanon, Missouri.

Opened Friday, Oct. 4–Nov. 24, 1985 (28 performances in repertory)

TOMORROW'S MONDAY by Paul Osborn; Director, Kent Paul; Set, John Lee Beatty; Costumes, Jennifer von Mayrhauser; Lighting, Dennis Parichy; Wigs, Paul Huntley; Wigs/Hair, Joan Weiss.

CAST: Amy Epstein (Mary Davis), Robert Macnaughton (John Allen), Trish Hawkins (Esther Allen), Edward Seamon (Dr. Nichols), Richard Backus (Richard Allen), Diane Venora (Lora Allen), Helen Stenborg (Mrs. Allen).

A play in three acts. The action takes place somewhere in the Midwest at sometime in the mid-1930's.

Thursday, Dec. 12, 1985–Feb. 2, 1986 (60 performances)

THE BEACH HOUSE by Nancy Donohue; Director, Melvin Bernhardt; Set, David Potts; Costumes, Jennifer von Mayrhauser; Lighting, Dennis Parichy, Mal Sturchio; Sound, Chuck London Media/Stewart Werner; Stage Manager, Ginny Martino; Production Manager, Benita Hoftstetter.

CAST: Robert Leonard (Chris), George Grizzard (John), Swoosie Kurtz (Annie), Paul Chalakani (Art), Angelo Tiffe (Dan).

A play in three acts. The action takes place at the present time in a beach house in Connecticut.

**Top Left: Farley Granger, Robert Macnaughton
in "Talley & Son"**
Gerry Goodstein Photos

Richard Backus, Diane Venora
in "Tomorrow's Monday"

George Grizzard, Robert Leonard, Swoosie Kurtz
in "The Beach House"

Ken Marshall, James McDaniel
in "Caligula"

(The Triplex) Saturday, Jan. 11–April 1, 1986 (28 performances in repertory)
CALIGULA by Albert Camus; Adapted from a translation by Stuart Gilbert; Director, Marshall W. Mason; Set, John Lee Beatty; Costumes, Jennifer von Mayrhauser; Lighting, Dennis Parichy; Sound, Chuck London Media/Stewart Werner; Stage Managers, Fred Reinglas, Leslie Loeb.
CAST: Jake Dengel (Octavius), Margaret Barker (Claudia), Sharon Schlarth (Lucia), Zane Lasky (Cassius), James McDaniel (Helicon), Jay Patterson (Cherea), Paul Martell (Scipio), Ken Marshall (Caligula), Stephanie Gordon (Caesonia), Kelly Connell (Intendant), Scott Phelps (Patricius), Trish Hawkins (Lepida), Bruce McCarty (Mucius), Alice King (Mucius' Wife), Edward Seamon (Mereia), Abby Levin (Metella), and Jay Corcoran, Alice King, Abby Levin, Tom Miller, Randy Noojin, Michael Quarry, Jane Sanders, Michael Swain.
A drama in two acts. The action takes place at the present time.
Tuesday, Jan. 14–April 4, 1986 (30 performances in repertory)
THE MOUND BUILDERS by Lanford Wilson; Director, Marshall W. Mason; Set, John Lee Beatty; Costumes, Jennifer von Mayrhauser; Lighting, Dennis Parichy; Original Music, Jonathan Hogan; Sound, Chuck London Media/Stewart Werner.
CAST: Jake Dengel (Prof. August Howe), Stephanie Gordon (Cynthia Howe), Bruce McCarty (Chad Jasker), Ken Marshall (Dr. Dan Loggins), Sharon Schlarth (Dr. Jean Loggins), Tanya Berezin (D. K. Delia Eriksen)
A drama in two acts. The action takes place in February in Champaign-Urbana, and the previous summer in Blue Shoals, Illinois.
Sunday, March 2–April 13, 1986 (26 performances in repertory)
QUIET IN THE LAND by Anne Chislett; Director, Daniel Irvine; Set, John Lee Beatty; Costumes, Jennifer von Mayrhauser; Lighting, Dennis Parichy; Sound, Chuck London Media/Stewart Werner.
CAST: Kelly Connell (Bishop Eli Frey), Bruce McCarty (Yock Bauman), Randy Noojin (Paddy O'Rourke), Zane Lasky (Zepp Brubacher), Tanya Berezin (Lydie Brubacher), Sharon Schlarth (Katie Brubacher), Paul Martell (Menno Miller), Margaret Barker (Hannah Bauman), Abby Levin (Martha Brubacher), Jane Sanders (Nancy Brubacher), Alice King (Esther Miller), Jay Patterson (Levi Miller), Edward Seamon (Christy Bauman), Ken Marshall (Mr. O'Rourke), Paul Butler (Recruitment Officer), and Danielle Acarino, Jay Corcoran, Tom Miller, Kristina Oster, Michael Swain.
A drama in two acts. The action takes place in an Amish farming community near Kitchener in Ontario, Canada, in the fall of 1917, and early summer to winter of 1918.

Gerry Goodstein Photos

**Top Right: Jay Patterson, Trish Hawkins
in "The Mound Builders"**

Tanya Berezin, Margaret Barker
in "Quiet in the Land"

89

CITY STAGE COMPANY/CSC

November 3, 1985–May 25, 1986
Nineteenth Season

Artistic Director, Craig D. Kinzer; Managing Director, Will Maitland Weiss; General Manager/Press, Bruce Allardice; Resident Designer, Rick Butler; Dramaturg, Laurence Maslon; Assistant Director, Tom Szentgyorgyi; Production Associate, Tonia Payne; Technical Director, David L. Bornstein; Assistant Designer, Gerry Lantaigne; Wardrobe, Sue Jane Stoker

COMPANY

Mike Atkin, Mark Ballora, David Friedlander, Janet Geist, Nicola Glick, Christina Heath, Nina Howes, Richard Johnson, Susan Keller, Kathryn Klvana, Katherine Marie Loague, Sandra McAllister, Michael McGuinness, John Ryker O'Hara, Richard Renzaneth, Dierdre Ryan, David Sennett, Lisa Shea, David Sherrick, Maria Wallace, Susan Bruce, John Camera, Sally Chamberlin, Frank Dwyer, Patrick Egan, Tom Gould, Michael Meyer, Erika Petersen, Whitney Quesenbery, Michael Rothhaar, Tom Spackman, Robert Stattel, Stephen Strawbridge, Patrick Tull, Catherine Zuber

PRODUCTIONS

"Brand" by Henrik Ibsen/Translated by Michael Meyer, "Frankenstein" by Mary Shelley/Adapted by Laurence Maslon, "A Medieval Mystery Cycle," "The Tempest" by William Shakespeare, "A Country Doctor" by Len Jenkins/Based on story by Franz Kafka, "The Divine Orlando" by William Luce/Music by Orlando di Lasso

Gerry Goodstein Photos

Stephen Mellor, Rocky Parker, Olek Krupa, Richard Merrell, Jayne Haynes, Laura Innes, Rocco Sisto in "A Country Doctor" Left Center: Robert Stattel, Erika Petersen in "Brand"

Susan Bruce, Tom Spackman
in "Frankenstein"

THE CLASSIC THEATRE

April 3–May 25, 1986
Eleventh Season

Executive Director, Nicholas John Stathis; Associate Producer, Adda C. Gogoris; Artistic Director, Maurice Edwards
(The Shakespeare Center) Thursday, April 3–27, 1986 (16 performances)
THE SPANISH TRAGEDIE by Thomas Kyd; Director, Ron Daley; Producer, Nicholas John Stathis; Produced in association with Riverside Shakespeare Company; Set, Bob Phillips; Costumes, Michael S. Schler; Lighting, Lisa Grossman; Sound, Deena Kaye; Stage Combat, Lawrence H. Lustberg, Todd Loweth; Choreography, Stuntworks, Producing Director of Riverside Shakespeare Co., Robert Graham Small; Production Manager, G. Douglas Ward; Technical Director, Steve Sitler; Wardrobe, Elizabeth Gill; Sound, David Lawson; Stage Managers, Kate Riddle, L. Robert Johnson.
CAST: Steve Sitler (King of Portugal), R. Sebastian Russ (King of Spain), Dan Johnson (Duke of Castile), Jacqueline Chauvin (Bel-Imperia), Edmond Ramage (Pedringano), James Sheerin (Don Pedro), Rik Montgomery (Balthazar), Paul Mantell (Hieronimo), Mary Tierney Kelly (Isabella), Lawrence H. Lustberg (Horatio), John Greenleaf (Lorenzo), Allen Barone (Don Andrea), Michael Hermanski (Alcario), Paul McNair (Rogero), Greg Petroff (Lazarotto/Villuppo), Robert E. Wherry, Jr. (Alexandro/Bazardo)
A drama in three acts. The action takes place on the Iberian Peninsula circa 1560.
(TOMI/Terrace Theatre) Thursday, May 1–8, 1986 (7 performances)
UNDER MILK WOOD by Dylan Thomas; Director, Saylor Creswell; Lighting, Debbie Gantert; Stage Manager, Kenneth R. Saltzman.
CAST: Frank Hamilton, Saylor Creswell, Stephen Gabis, Paul Meacham, Sylvia Gassell, Valerie Beaman.
A play for voices performed without intermission. The action takes place in a Welsh fishing village sometime earlier in this century.
Tuesday, May 13–18, 1986 (7 performances)
ESCOFFIER KING OF CHEFS written and performed by Owen S. Rackleff; Director, Laurence Carr; Lighting, Debbie Gantert.
CAST: Owen S. Rackleff (Georges Auguste Escoffier).
A play in two acts. The action takes place in the sitting room of Escoffier's villa in Monte Carlo in 1922
Thursday, May 22–May 25, 1986 (5 performances)
SONGS OF LOVE AND MONEY by Kurt Weill and Bertolt Brecht and their progeny; Lighting, Jane MacPherson; At the piano, Harry Huff. Performed by Marion Brasch and Maurice Edwards.

ENSEMBLE STUDIO THEATRE

September 30, 1985–June 16, 1986
Fourteenth Season

Artistic Director, Curt Dempster; Managing Director, Erik Murkoff; Producing Director, John McCormack; Literary Manager, D. S. Moynihan; Assistant to Artistic Director/Literary Associate, Monique Giroux; Casting, Risa Bramon, Billy Hopkins; Production Manager, James D'Asaro; Production Supervisor, Joseph Pabst; Technical Director, Alex LaBianca; Business Manager, Brian Berk; Press, Bruce Cohen, Kathleen von Schmid

Wednesday, Nov. 20–Dec. 22, 1985 (34 performances)
DENNIS by James Ryan; Director, Dan Bonnell; Set, James Wolk; Lighting, Karl Haas; Costumes, Deborah Shaw; Sound, Bruce Ellman; Stage Manager, Rickie Grosberg.
CAST: William Carden (Dennis Sweeney), Peter Friedman (Allard Lowenstein), and Frank Girardeau, Sam Gray, Richmond Hoxie, Michael Albert Mantel, Anne O'Sullivan, Myra Taylor, David Toney
A drama in two acts that traces the lives of Allard Lowenstein and his murderer Dennis Sweeney.

Tuesday, December 3–22, 1985 (18 performances)
BEEN TAKEN by Roger Hedden; Director, Billy Hopkins; Set, Bob Barnett; Lighting, Greg MacPherson; Costumes, Isis C. Mussenden; Sound, Bruce Ellman; Stage Manager, Susan Selig.
CAST: Perry Lang (Dennis), Tim Ransom (John), Mary Stuart Masterson (Margaret), Rick Martino (Steve), Helen Hunt (Jill), Lynn Goodwin (Waitress)
A play in two acts, the second being five years after the first act.

Tuesday, Feb. 18–March 1, 1986 (14 performances)
THE TALE OF MADAME ZORA with Book and Lyrics by Aishah Rahman; Music, Olu Dara; Choreography, Dianne McIntyre; Director, Glenda Dickerson; Set, Charles H. McClennahan; Lighting, Karl Haas; Costumes, Sydney Inis; Production Manager, Jim D'Asaro; Technical Director, Alex LaBianca; Wardrobe, Angelynn Bruno; Props, Mo Gilbride; Stage Managers, Ken Johnson, Lori Lundquist
CAST: Stephanie Berry (Happy Sweet), Keith David (Dr. Mo), Willie Barnes (Black Herman), Townspeople/Musicians: Jean-Paul Bourelly, Deborah Malone
A dramatization with music of the life of Zora Neal Hurston, folklorist, social scientist, and novelist during America's Renaissance. The action takes place on the porch of Joe Clark's General Store on a hot summer night during the annual Lie Swapping Contest in Hurstonville, Florida in the 1960's.
A musical based on the life of the prolific black novelist Zora Neale Hurston.

Wednesday, March 26–April 13, 1986 (18 performances)
ROSE COTTAGES by Bill Bozzone; Director, Risa Bramon; Set, Irene Kaufman; Lighting, Greg MacPherson; Costumes, Deborah Shaw; Sound, Bruce Ellman; Stage Manager, Denise Laffer.
CAST: Bill Cobbs (Rose), Lloyd Hollar (Ricky Knoll), Corey Parker (Lydell), Grace Zabriskie (Jessie), Anna Levine (Ginger), Bill Cwikowski (Vince)
A comedy in two acts. The action takes place during the present time just outside Orlando, Florida, over a period of four humid days in May.

Wednesday, May 7–June 16, 1986 (48 performances)
MARATHON'86: Series A: Sets, Daniel Proett; Lighting, Greg MacPherson; Costumes, Deborah Shaw; Sound, Bruce Ellman; Stage Manager, Pamela Edington.
"Sunday Morning Vivisection" by Elise Caitlin; Director, Leslie Ayvazian; with Katherine Cortez (Mary), Loren Brown (Woman), Patrick McCord (Man). "The Workers Life" by Brandon Cole with John Turturro; Director, Aidan Quinn; with John Spencer (Gus), Stanley Tucci (Vic), Bruce MacVittie (Bruno), John Turturro (Mac). "Blind Date" by Horton Foote; Director, Curt Dempster; with James Rebhorn (Robert), Kelly Wolf (Sarah Nancy), Deborah Hedwall (Dolores), Corey Parker (Felix). "Mink on a Gold Hook" by James Ryan; Director, Jack Gelber; with Paul Guilfoyle (Bobby), Lucinda Jenney (Laila), Pete Zapp (Harry), Michael Countryman (Wayne), Dan Ziskie (Frank).
Series B: "Vanishing Act" by Richard Greenberg; Director, Jeff Perry; with Patricia Clarkson (Minna), Kimi Morris (Anya), Leslie Lyles (Sasha), Joe Ponazecki (Clay), Jack Gilpin (Sky), Lenny von Dohlen (Spence), Mary Joy (Carla), Niki Scalera (Jenny). "The West Side Boys Will Rock You Anytime" by Shirley Kaplan; Director, Billy Hopkins; with Lisa Roxanne Walters (Raya), Noelle Parker (Izzie). "Comic Dialogue" by Alan Zweibel; with Mike Nussbaum (Stu Cooper), David (Michael Kaufman). "Terry Neal's Future" by Roger Hedden; Director, Billy Hopkins; with J. T. Walsh (Terry Neal), Elias Koteas (Billy Tune), Sarah Jessica Parker (Darlene Magnum), Patricia Mauceri (Gypsy), Carol Schneider (Waitress).

Carol Rosegg Photos

**Top Right: Peter Freedman, William Carden
in "Dennis" Below: Grace Zabriskie, Corey
Parker, Bill Cobbs in "Rose Cottages"**

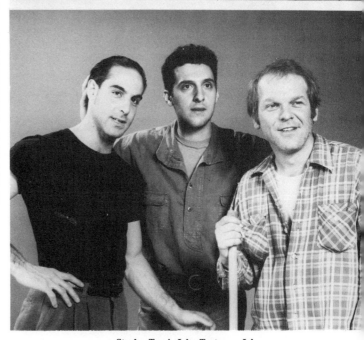

**Stanley Tucci, John Turturro, John
Spencer in "The Worker's Life"**

91

Daniel Marcus, David Pevsner, Susan Varon,
Andy Alsup, Samme Johnston, Michael Irwin,
Maggie Bilder, (kneeling) Kurt Ziskie, Wendy
Merritt, David Snizek, Suzanna Frazer (prone)
in "A Flash of Lightning"

Trish Weyenberg, Kenny Morris, Walt Mayfield,
Jean Kauffman, Peter Jensen, Drew Taylor, Lee Chew,
Carolyn DeLany, Roxanne Parker, Victoria Forster,
Keith Herron, Rick Porter, Mark Ankeny, Deborah
Bradshaw, Brent Michener in "She Loves Me"

Susan Sheppard, Malcolm Gets, Debbie Birch, David
Beris, Lisa Meryll, Andrew Gorman, Deborah Goletz,
Philip Carrubba, Braddon Harris, Amy DeMayo
in "They're Playing Our Song"

EQUITY LIBRARY THEATRE

September 26, 1985–June 8, 1986
Forty-third Season

Managing Director, George Wojtasik; Business Manager, Janice E. Sager; Office Manager, Amy Mattison; Assistant to Managing Director, Rebecca Kreinen; Development, Jan C. Greenwald; Associate Production Director, Randy Becker; Technical Directors, Eric Vennerbeck, Jason Townley; Costumer, Ken Brown; Production Coordinator, Adele Bove; Sound, Hal Schuler; Production Director, Lynn Montgomery; Press, Lewis Harmon

(Master Theatre) Thursday, Sept. 26–Oct. 13, 1985 (22 performances)
A FLASH OF LIGHTNING by Augustin Daly; Director, Stephen G. Hults; Set, Robert Klingelhoefer; Lighting, Renee Clark; Costumes, Sally Plum; Incidental Music composed by Wayne Barker; Choreography, Tim Zimmermann; Fight Choreography, Kurt Ziskie; Props, Barbara Grill; Wardrobe, Sharianne Fischer, Jill Jones; Stage Managers, Virginia Jones, Elizabeth Burgess, Steven Channell.
CAST: Andy Alsup (Charlie), Arnold W. Bankston III (Benedetto), Joanne Baum (Patsy), Maggie Bilder (Ann), Susanna Frazer (Bessie Fallon), Michael Iannucci (Sam), Michael Irwin (Fred Chauncey), Samme Johnston (Rose Fallon), Daniel Marcus (Skiffley), Wendy Merritt (Mary Fallon), David Pevsner (Terry), David Snizek (Garry Fallon), Susan Varon (Mrs. Dowderry), Douglas Willen (Yank), Kurt Ziskie (Jack Ryder)
MUSICAL NUMBERS: Come Away, Hip Hip Hurrah, Momma, Goodbye My Lady Love, Angelus, The Same Old Story, I Just Can't Make My Eyes Behave, The Night the 'Virginia' Went Down, He Goes to Church on Sunday, Keep on Smiling
A "blood and thunder" drama in 2 acts and 8 scenes. The action takes place in the 1860's.

Thursday, Oct. 31–Nov. 24, 1985 (30 performances and 2 previews)
SHE LOVES ME with Book by Joe Masteroff; Music, Jerry Bock; Lyrics, Sheldon Harnick; Based on play "The Little Shop around the Corner" by Miklos Laszlo; Director, Robert Bridges; Musical Direction, Paul Johnson; Set, Carl A. Baldasso; Costumes, Edi Giguere; Choreography, Jamie Stiller; Lighting, Tom Hennes; Associate Music Director, Edward C. Reichert; Hair/Wigs, Robin Gurin; Wardrobe, Jeanmarie Magrino, Tina Salks; Props, Sharon Henry.
CAST: Mark Ankeny (Clerk/Viktor/Paul), Deborah Bradshaw (Stefanie/Shopper/Customer), Lee Chew (Georg Nowack), Carolyn DeLany (Amalia Balash), Victoria Forster (Magda/Customer), Keith Herron (Arpad), Peter Jensen (Keller/Jascha), Jean Kauffman (Customer), Kenny Morris (Sipos), Roxann Parker (Ilona Ritter), Rick Porter (Busboy/Clerk), Fred Rivers (Waiter), Drew Taylor (Ferencz/Clerk), Todd Thurston (Kodaly), David Vogel (Maraczek), Trish Weyenberg (Nurse/Customer)
MUSICAL NUMBERS: Good Morning Good Day, Sounds While Selling, Days Gone By, No More Candy, Three Letters, Tonight at 8, I Don't Know His Name, Perspective Goodbye Georg, Will He Like Me, Ilona, I Resolve, A Romantic Atmosphere, Tango Tragique, Mr. Nowack Will You Please, Dear Friend, Try Me, Where's My Shoe, Vanilla Ice Cream, She Loves Me, A Trip to the Library, Grand Knowing You, Twelve Days to Christmas, Finale
A musical in 2 acts and 19 scenes. The action takes place in a European city during 1930.

Thursday, Dec. 5–22, 1985 (24 performances)
ANOTHER PART OF THE FOREST by Lillian Hellman; Director, Christian Angermann; Set, Roger Benischek; Lighting, Fabian Yeager; Costumes, Marla Speer; Wardrobe, Carole Cuming; Dialect Coach, Arden Kay Sampson; Stage Managers, Camille Calman, Steven Channell, Sue Jane Stoker.
CAST: Ward Asquith (Simon Isham), Juli Cooper (Birdie Bagtry), John Henry Cox (Benjamin Hubbard), Jack Mahoney (Oscar Hubbard), Delores Mitchell (Coralee), Margaret Nagle (Laurette Sincee), Casper Roos (Marcus Hubbard), Nicola Sheara (Lavinia Hubbard), James Watkins (Harold Penniman), Vincent Vogt (John Bagtry), Juanita Walsh (Regina Hubbard), DeForest Westry (Jake), Jack Wilkes (Gilbert Jugger)
A drama in three acts. The action takes place during June 1880 in the Alabama town of Bowden in the living room of the Hubbard home.

Thursday, Jan. 9–Feb. 2, 1986 (32 performances)
THEY'RE PLAYING OUR SONG with Book by Neil Simon; Music, Marvin Hamlisch; Lyrics, Carole Bayer Sager; Director, Philip Giberson; Choreographer, Dee Deringer; Musical Direction, Nathan Matthews; Set, Reagan Cook; Lighting, William J. Plachy; Costumes, Melina Root; Sound, Elliot Forrest; Props, Sharon Henry; Hairstylist, Laura Blood; Wardrobe, Tina Salaks; Stage Managers, Max Storch, Howard McBride, Lance LaShelle, Rick Lucero.
CAST: David M. Beris (Voice), Debbie Birch (Sonia Voice), Philip Carrubba (Voice), Amy DeMayo (Voice), Malcolm Gets (Voice), DeBorah Goletz (Voice), Andrew Gorman (Vernon Gersch), Braddon Harris (Voice), Lisa Meryll (Sonia Walsk), Susan Sheppard (Voice)
A musical in 2 acts and 13 scenes. The action takes place at the present time.

Thursday, Feb. 13–March 2, 1986 (22 performances and 2 previews)
THE CONSTANT WIFE by W. Somerset Maugham; Director, Howard Rossen; Set, Daniel Ettinger; Lighting, Maidie O. Greer; Costumes, John Deering; Music Coordinator, William Boswell; Props, Donna Linderman; Stage Managers, Sherrill Ann Moyer, Lillian Butler, Marjorie Ohie.
CAST: Kathryn Chilson (Martha Culver), Ray Collins (John Middleton), Stephen Cross (Bentley), Judy Frank (Mrs. Culver), Douglas Hayle (Mortimer Durham), Kathleen Huber (Barbara Fawcett), Roger Middleton (Bernard Kersal), Tina Smith (Marie-Louise Durham), Susan Tabor (Constance Middleton)
A comedy in three acts. The action takes place during 1927 in London in Constance Middleton's drawing room.

Thursday, March 13–April 6, 1986 (32 performances)
GIRL CRAZY with Music by George Gershwin; Lyrics, Ira Gershwin; Book, Guy Bolton, Jack McGowan; Director, Stephen Bonnell; Set, Lawrence Edward Nussbaum; Costumes, Isabel Rubio; Lighting, Anita Jorgensen; Musical Direction/Vocal & Dance Arrangements, Wayne Green; Choreography, Frank Ventura; Assistant Choreographer, Blake Atherton; Production Assistant, Mary Fremgen; Wardrobe, Amy Ginette Fritz; Stage Managers, Kate Mennone, Lisa Braden, Lyle Jones, John W. Calder III
CAST: Ciro Barbaro (Gieber Goldfarb), John Barone (Slick Fothergill), Stephen Brice (Jake/Sheriff), Gerry Burkhardt (Ensemble), Sally Doffer (Ensemble), Jaime Zee Eisner (Ensemble), Andrea Garfield (Flora), Russell Giesenschlag (Ensemble), Steve Goodwillie (Ensemble), Daniel Guzman (Ensemble), Tom Hafner (Danny Churchill), Peder Hansen (Sam Mason), Heidi Joyce (Molly Gray), Mary Ann Kelleher (Kate Fothergill), Alyson L. Lang (Ensemble), Kirsten Lind (Tess), Eria L. Paulson (Patsy), Ed Rubeo (Pete), Stuart Rudin (Lank), J. Scott Smith (Ensemble), Andy Spangler (Ensemble)
MUSICAL NUMBERS: Bidin' My Time, The Lonesome Cowboy Won't Be Lonesome Now, Could You Use Me?, Bronco Busters, You've Got What Gets Me, Barbary Coast, Embraceable You, Sam and Delilah, I Got Rhythm, Land of the Gay Caballero, But Not For Me, Treat Me Rough, Boy What Love Has Done to Me
A musical in 2 acts and 7 scenes.

Thursday, Apr. 17–May 4, 1986 (22 performances and 2 previews)
THREE SISTERS by Anton Chekov; Translated by Lanford Wilson; Director, Rena Down; Scenery, Calvin Morgan, Elizabeth A. Doyle; Costumes, Daphne Pascucci; Lighting, Daniel Brandes; Composer, Carolyn Dutton; Sound, Elliot Forrest; Wardrobe, Anona Williams; Stage Managers, Ellen Sontag, Jake Bell, Pam Hamilton, Danielle Gardner.
CAST: Sam Blackwell (Tuzenbach), Frank Deal (Rodez), Daydrie Hague (Natasha), Marc Jacobs (Solyony), Manny Kleinmuntz (Feraponmt), Sandra Laub (Masha), Arlene Lencioni (Irina), Alexander Peck (Musician/Soldier), Constance Morgan (Maid), Larry John Meyers (Fyodor Ilich Kulygin), James Goodwin Rice (Col. Vershinin), Rose Roffman (Anfisa), Maura Vaughn (Olga), John-David Wilder (Andrei), Richard Willis (Chebutykin), Scott Winters (Fedotik)
A drama in four acts with one intermission. The action takes place in a provincial town in Russia in 1900.

Thursday, May 15–June 8, 1986 (30 performances and 2 previews).
FUNNY GIRL with Music by Jule Styne; Lyrics, Bob Merrill; Book, Isobel Lennart; From an original story by Miss Lennart; Director, Alan Fox; Musical Direction, Bob McDowell; Choreography, David Storey; Scenery, Daniel Conway; Costumes, Ken Brown; Lighting, John McKernon; Hairstylists, Scott A. Mortimer, Robert Vincent; Wardrobe, Adele Bari, Heather West, Anona Williams; Dance Captain, Wyatt Townley; Stage Managers, Eve Sorel, Greta Minsky, John Sullivan, Laurel Smith.
CAST: Diane Boeki (Ensemble), Anthony Bova (Ensemble), Jayne Cacciatore (Maude/Ensemble), Norma Crawford (Mrs. O'Malley), Amy DeMayo (Ensemble), Larry French (Mr. Keeney/Ziegfeld Tenor), Brian James Grace (Ensemble), James Edward Kampf (Ensemble), Janet Kingsley (Emma), Lorna Lable (Mrs. O'Malley), Elizabeth Mozer (Ensemble), John Loder (Renaldi/Heckie/Ensemble), George McCulloch (Nick Arnstein), Christopher Nilsson (Ensemble), Richard Parrow (John/Stage Manager), Tracey Phelps (Mrs. Brice), Mari Phippen (Mimsey/Ensemble), Beverly Poltrack (Ensemble), Mary Rocco (Mrs. Strakosh), Carole Schweid (Fanny Brice), Frank Torren (Florenz Ziegfeld), Wyatt Townley (Jenny), Jeff Veazey (Eddie Ryan), Melodie Wolford (Ensemble)
MUSICAL NUMBERS: If a Girl Isn't Pretty, I'm the Greatest Star, Cornet Man, Who Taught Her Everything?, His Love Makes Me Beautiful, I Want to Be Seen with You Tonight, Henry Street, People, You Are Woman I Am Man, Don't Rain on My Parade, Sadie Sadie, Find Yourself a Man, Rat-Tat-Tat-Tat, Who Are You Now?, The Music that Makes me Dance.
A musical in two acts, based on incidents in the life of Fanny Brice shortly before and after World War I.

Ned Snyder Photos

Tina Smith, Kathleen Huber, Susan Tabor, Kathryn Chilson, Judy Frank in "The Constant Wife"

Jamie Lee Eisner, Daniel Guzman, Andrea Garfield, Gerry Burkhardt, Andy Spangler, Stephen Brice, Sally Doffer, Russell Giesenschlag, J. Scott Smith, Alyson Lang, Steve Goodwillie, Kirsten Lind in "Girl Crazy"

Anthony Bova, Amy DeMayo, Beverly Poltrack, Jeff Veazey, Jayne Caccitore, Carol Schweid, Wyatt Townley, Melodie Wolford, Richard Parrow in "Funny Girl"

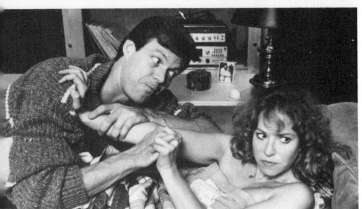

**Ivar Brogger, Susan Greenhill
in "Seascape with Sharks and Dancer"**
(Charles Marinaro Photo)

**J. R. Horne, Susan Wands, Dorothy Lancaster,
Mary Lou Rosato, Linda Kampley in "They
Dance Real Slow in Jackson"**

**Susan Wands, David Manis
in "They Dance Real Slow. . . ."**

HUDSON GUILD THEATRE

Oct. 16, 1985–June 22, 1986
Eleventh Season

Producing Director, David Kerry Heefner; Associate Director, James Abar; Production Manager/Technical Director, John B. Morean; Producing Assistant, Michael Kovaka; Business Manager, Laura L. Fowler; Sound, Aural Fixation; Stage Manager, John M. Atherlay; Press, Jeff Richards, C. George Willard, Ben Morse, Bill Shuttleworth, Susan E. Lee, Marie-Louise Silva
Wednesday, Oct. 16–Nov. 10, 1985 (28 performances)
SEASCAPE WITH SHARKS AND DANCER by Don Nigro; Director, David Kerry Heefner; Set, Daniel Conway; Costumes, Mary L. Hayes; Lighting, Phil Monat.
CAST: Susan Greenhill (Tracy), Ivar Brogger (Ben)
A comedy-drama in 2 acts and 5 scenes. The action takes place at the present time in a small decrepit beach house on Cape Cod in Massachusetts.
Wednesday, Dec. 4–22, 1985 (28 performances)
AND THEY DANCE REAL SLOW IN JACKSON by Jim Leonard, Jr. Director, David Kerry Heefner; Set/Lighting, Paul Wonsek; Costumes, Pamela Scofield; Original Music, Ivana Themmen; Performed by Sandra Miller; Props, Camille Costa; Production Assistant, Kenneth Elchert.
CAST: Susan Wands (Elizabeth Ann Willow), Dorothy Lancaster (Beth Willow), J. R. Horne (Ben Willow), David Manis (1st Man/Skeeter/Woody/Timmy/Rev. Peester/Boy/Bobby), Mary Lou Rosato (1st Woman/Nancy/Claranelle/Judith), Michael Countryman (2nd Man/Russel/Jeremy/Billy/Daddy/Kid), Linda Kampley (2nd Woman/Maddie/Emma/Cindy/Girl)
A drama in two acts. The action takes place in a fictitious Indiana town at the present time.
Wednesday, Feb. 5–March 28, 1986 (28 performances)
THE SECOND MAN by S. N. Behrman; Director, Thomas Gruenewald; Set/Lighting, Paul Wonsek; Costumes, Pamela Scofield; Production Assistant, Rochelle Elman; Hairstylist, Michael DiCesare; Props, Michael Allwine; Pianist, Allen Cohen.
CAST: Valerie Von Volz (Mrs. Kendall Frayne), Daniel Gerroll (Clark Storey), Ivar Brogger (Austin Lowe), Jane Fleiss (Monica Grey).
A comedy in 3 acts and 4 scenes. The action takes place in 1927 in Clark Storey's studio on the West Side of Manhattan, New York City.
Wednesday, April 2–27, 1986 (28 performances)
WRESTLERS by Bill C. Davis; Director, Geraldine Fitzgerald; Set/Lighting, Paul Wonsek; Costumes, Mary L. Hayes; Production Assistant, Rochelle Elman; Props, Rita M. Long.
CAST: Bill C. Davis (Monty), Dan Butler (Bobby), Elizabeth Berridge (Angie)
The action takes place in the present, here, and in the past, in upstate New York, and in New York City.
Wednesday, May 28–June 22, 1986 (27 performances)
WRITER'S CRAMP by John Byrne; Director, David Kerry Heefner; Setting/Lighting, Richard Harmon; Costumes, Patricia Adshead.
CAST: K. C. Kelly (F. S. McDade), Sullivan Brown (Narrator/Dr. Arthur Quigley/Charles Bentwood Brazil/Mrs. Thelma McDade), Brooks Baldwin (Sandy/Dermot Double-Davis/A Trusty/Mrs. Renee Ripper/David/Father Mannion)

Bob Marshak Photos

**Valerie Von Volz, Daniel Gerroll, Ivar Brogger,
Jane Fleiss in "The Second Man"**

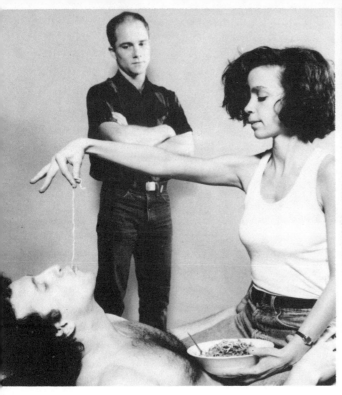

K. C. Kelly, Brooks Baldwin
in "Writer's Cramp" Left:
Bill C. Davis, Dan Butler,
Elizabeth Berridge in "Wrestlers"

LAKOTA THEATRE COMPANY

September 27, 1985–March 15, 1986
Third Season

Artistic Director, John Geter; Company Manager, Robert Cesario; Business Manager, Archie Harrison; Program Director, David Buffam; Development, Meg Peltier; Press, Gerry Bernardi.

(Clyde Vinson Studio) Friday, Sept. 27,–Oct. 17, 1985 (12 performances)
THE TROJAN WOMEN by Euripides; Director, John Geter; Translation, Richard Lattimore; Assistant Director, Robert Cesario; Production Coordinator, Anne Carney; Lighting, Tracy Dedrickson; Sound/Lights, Mark Anthony Taylor; Costumes, Archie Harrison; Set, Rick Simpson.
CAST: Barchevska (Hecuba), Gerry Bernardi (Talthybius), Anne Carney (Andromache), Gloria Duncan (Chorus), Christie Gaudet (Chorus), Andrew Kreiss (Soldier), Kate Loague (Athene/Chorus), Geoffrey Miller (Menelaus), Anne Marie Offer (Chorus), Meg Peltier (Helen), Jeanette Srubar (Cassandra), Beth Swartz (Chorus), Drew Tillotson (Poseidon), David A. Walker (Soldier).

Friday, December 6–22, 1985 (14 performances)
TWELFTH NIGHT by William Shakespeare; Director, Michael Landrum; Assistant Director, Andrew Kreiss; Coordinator/Lighting, Anne Carney; Sound/Lights, Jeanette Srubar; Costumes, Christie Gaudet; Stage Manager, Beth Swartz; Musical Direction, Lisa Wenzel.
CAST: David Buffam (Malvolio), Carole Bugge (Viola), Robert Foster (Curio), John Geter (Sir Andrew Aguecheek), Archie Harrison (Orsino), Geoffrey Miller (Sir Toby Belch), Rene Moreno (Fabian), Anne Marie Offer (Maria), Michael Pollis (Antonio), Meg Peltier (Olivia), William Snovell (Sea Captain/Priest), Mark Anthony Taylor (Valentine), Drew Tillotson (Feste), David Walker (Sebastian).

Friday, Feb. 21,–March 15, 1986 (12 performances)
THREE SISTERS by Anton Chekhov; Director, Madeline Barchevska; Painting, Ann Purcell; Piano/Original Music, Edith Alexis; Costumes, Anne Marie Offer; Lighting, Tracy Dedrickson; Production Manager, Joan Meehan; Sound, Archie Harrison, Drew Tillotson; Stage Manager, Gary Betsworth.
CAST: Gerry Bernardi (Solyony), Anne Carney (Olga), Robert Cesario (Tuzenbach), Mark Ethan (Chebutykin), Robert Foster (Ferapont), Mary Irwin (Natasha), Ben Lemon (Andrei), Geoffrey Miller (Vershinin), Anne Marie Offer (Anfisa), Jeanette Srubar (Irina), Beth Swartz (Masha), Mark Anthony Taylor (Kulygin).

Gilbert Johnson Photos

Gerry Bernardi, Anne Carney, Ben Lemon, Beth
Swartz, Jeanette Srubar, Geoffrey Miller,
Mark Ethan in "Three Sisters" (Lakota)

JEWISH REPERTORY THEATRE

June 29, 1985–June 19, 1986
Twelfth Season

Artistic Director, Ran Avni; Associate Director, Edward M. Cohen; Casting, Susan Haskins; Press, Shirley Herz, Pete Sanders, Peter Cromarty, David Roggensack, Gary Lawrence

Saturday, June 29–Aug. 1, 1985 (30 performances)
PEARLS a musical adaptation of Jacob Gordin's play "Mirele Efros"; Book, Music and Lyrics, Nathan Gross; Director, Ran Avni; Musical Staging, Haila Strauss; Sets, Jeffrey Schneider; Costumes, Karen Hummel; Lighting, Dan Kinsley; Musical Director, Andrew Howard; Orchestrations, Gene Scholtens; Props, Joanna Kourkounakis; Wardrobe, Arlene Mantek; Stage Managers, D. C. Rosenberg, David Lawrence Folender.
CAST: Gloria Hodes (Malka), Richard Frisch (Solomon), Stan Rubin (Nechemtse), Grace Roberts (Chana-Dvora), Rosalind Elias (Mirele Efros), Daniel Neiden (Yossel), Judy Kuhn succeeded by Susan Friedman (Sheyndele)
MUSICAL NUMBERS: Mud, A Promise Is a Promise, I Don't Like the Match, A Simple Child, Sweet Wine Sweet Spices, Wedding in the Rain, My Sabbath Bride, Live and Let Live, Friend, Jewels, Save Me, What's the Difference?, Mama's Boy, Ask for a Star, Across This Threshold, Can't You Find Forgiveness?, Look in the Mirror, Her Little Boy, Pearls, A Mother's Love
A musical in 2 acts and 4 scenes. The action takes place in Slutsch and Grodno in 1885.

Saturday, Oct. 19–Nov. 17, 1985 (27 performances)
THE SPECIAL with Music by Galt MacDermot; Book/Lyrics, Mike Gutwillig; Director, Ran Avni; Musical Staging, Haila Strauss; Musical Director/Arranger, Galt MacDermot; Conductor, Andrew Howard; Sets, Jeffrey Schneider; Costumes, Karen Hummel; Lighting, Dan Kinsley; Stage Managers, D. C. Rosenberg, Arlene Mantek; Wardrobe, Geraldine Teagarden.
CAST: Paul Ukena (Joe Rubinsky), Sam Stoneburner (Irving Levitt), Adam Heller (Hershie Levitt), Kenneth Bridges (Jacques Boucher), Patricia Ben Peterson (Manon Boucher), Simon Jutras (Claude Boucher), Olga Merediz (Therese Boucher), Annie Korzen (Esther Levitt), Mina Bern (Mollie Bernstein), Steve Sterner (Rabbi Wiser), Raymond Murcell (Pere LeBeau)
MUSICAL NUMBERS: What's So Special about a Special?, The Situation in Quebec, There Is an Old Tradition, Quebec Oui!, Non Merci!, Longue Vie a la Famille!, Cote St-Jacques, Will You Be My Yvette?, Married Yet, We Say Oui!, J'pas Capable!, A Ruling Is a Ruling, It Isn't Easy to Be a Jew, Alleluia Alleluia, On My Heart, A Special!, What Will People Think?, I Don't Want That You Don't Want, Notre Pere, Shema, God's Favorite Choice, Raise a Glass to Love, Ess ess Mein Kindt, Swing Your Heart to le Bon Dieu
A musical in 2 acts and 14 scenes. The action takes place in and around Montreal, Canada, during 1980.

**Chris Ceraso, Braden Danner, Mark Zeller
in "Lies My Father Told Me" Above: Gregg
Edelman, Lilia Skala in "Shop on Main Street"**

Saturday, Dec. 14, 1985–Jan. 12, 1986 (27 performances)
THE SHOP ON MAIN STREET based on the novel by Ladislav Grosman; Book/Lyrics, Bernard Spiro; Music, Saul Honigman; Set, James Leonard Joy; Costumes, Mardi Philips; Lighting, Phil Monat; Puppets, Jane Stein; Director, Fran Soeder; Choreography, Janet Watson; Musical Direction, Norman Weiss; Orchestrations, Scott Frankel; General Management, Theatre Now; Company Manager, Martin Guest; Wardrobe, Ernest Mossiah; Presented in association with Tanrydoon Productions and Dolph Browning; Stage Managers, Raymond Chandler, Heidi Joyce.
CAST: Chuck Brown (Narrator/Piti/Bachi/Joseph Katz), Gregg Edelman (Tono Brtko), Olga Talyn (Eveline), Nancy Callman (Rose), Kenneth Kantor (Marcus), Lawrence Weber succeeded by John Newton (Kuchar), Lilia Skala (Mrs. Lautman), John Roccosalva, Agatha Balek (Commissaries)
MUSICAL NUMBERS: Piti's Song, Tono Brtko, The Shop on Main Street, The Chatter of an Old Old Woman, Mark Me Tomorrow, Someone to Do For, Noon Sunday Promenade, Market Day, Shainele, I Feel Like a Woman, Better Days, Who Are They to Me?
A musical in 2 acts. The action takes place in the town of Sabinov in Eastern Czechoslovakia in mid-June of 1942.

Saturday, Feb. 8–March 9, 1986 (27 performances)
I, SHAW a double bill of two one-act plays; Director, Edward M. Cohen; Sets, Joel Fontaine; Costumes, Edi Giguere; Lighting, Dan Kinsley; Sound, Paul Garrity; Fight Director, Bo Walker; Hair/Makeup, Julio Piedra, Michelle Sullivan; Production Assistant, Ann Wright; Stage Managers, Betsy M. Martin, Catherine Natale. CAST: "The Shy and Lonely" by Irwin Shaw: Scott G. Miller (Lawrence Mosher), Rob Morrow (Peter Sirutis), Richard Gleason (Albert Sowers), Nealla Spano (Harriet Twist), Tracy Thorne (Madge Cornell), Angela Workman (Eleanor Kurloff). "Sailor Off the Bremen" by William Kramer; Based on stories by Irwin Shaw; with Tracy Thorne (Paulette), Rob Morrow (Charlie), Scott G. Miller (Harold), Angela Workman (Sally), Richard Gleason (Lueger), Catherine Natale (Lenore), Nealla Spano (Anita Kersey), Catherine Natale (Nurse)

Saturday, April 5–May 4, 1986 (27 performances)
LIGHT UP THE SKY by Moss Hart; Director, Robert Bridges; Set, Carl A. Baldasso; Costumes, Edi Giguere; Lighting, Tom Hennes; Sound, Laura Lampel; Technical Director, Stan Chandler; Wardrobe, Donna M. Villella; Title Song composed by Carleton Carpenter; Stage Managers, D. C. Rosenberg, Geraldine Teagarden, Williamson Vedder.
CAST: Margaret Harrington (Miss Lowell), Carleton Carpenter (Charleton Fitzgerald), Ilene Kristen (Frances Black), Joe Ponazecki (Owen Turner), Grace Roberts (Stella Livingston), Lee Chew (Peter Sloan), Stephen Pearlman (Sidney Black), Maeve McGuire (Irene Livingston), Edward Penn (Tyler Rayburn), William Gleason (William H. Gallegher), Williamson Vedder (Plainclothesman)
A comedy in three acts. The action takes place in 1948 in the living-room of Irene Livingston's Ritz-Carlton Hotel suite in Boston, Massachusetts.

Saturday, May 31–June 19, 1986 (27 performances)
LIES MY FATHER TOLD ME by Ted Allan; Director, Lynn Polan; Set, Ray Recht; Costumes, Debra Stein; Lighting, Dan Kinsley; Musical Staging, Helen Butleroff; Original Music/Arrangements/Direction, Margaret Rachlin Pine; Wardrobe, Julianne Flynn; Props, Patrick M. Latham; Technical Director, Alan Lampel; Stage Managers, D. C. Rosenberg, Arlene Mantek.
CAST: Chris Ceraso (David), Sophie (Annie), Stephen Singer (Harry), Braden Danner (Young David), Mark Zeller (Zaida), Gary Richards (Benny), Angela Pietropinto (Housewife/Mrs. Tanner/Edna/Mrs. Caruck/Benny's Wife), Bill Nelson (Baumgarten/Hasid/Horse Caller/Real Estate Agent/Policeman)
A play in two acts. The action takes place in David's home and courtyard, and in various locations in Montreal during the 1920's.

Adam Newman Photos

**Top: Daniel Neiden, Rosalind Elias
in "Pearls"**

LINCOLN CENTER THEATER

December 20, 1985–May 31, 1986
First Season

Director, Gregory Mosher; Executive Producer, Bernard Gersten; General Manager, Steven C. Callahan; Production Manager, Jeff Hamlin; Development, Barbara M. Groves; Scripts, Laura Jones; Casting, Billy Hopkins; Press, Merle Debuskey, Robert W. Larkin

(Mitzi E. Newhouse Theater) Friday, Dec. 20, 1985–Feb. 2, 1986 (48 performances and 4 previews) Lincoln Center Theater presents the double bill of:
PRAIRIE DU CHIEN/THE SHAWL two plays by David Mamet; Director, Gregory Mosher; Sets, Michael Merritt; Costumes, Nan Cibula; Lighting, Kevin Rigdon; Company Manager, Danielle Fenton; Wardrobe, Tony Karniewich; Stage Managers, Kate Stewart, Stephen Hamilton
CAST: "Prairie du Chien" with Tom Signorelli (Card Dealer), W. H. Macy (Gin Player), Paul Butler (Porter), Jerry Stiller (Story Teller), Brad Hall (Listener), Christopher Jennings (Listener's Son), Understudies: Stephen Hamilton, Evan Thompson
"The Shawl" with Mike Nussbaum (John), Lindsay Crouse (Miss A), Calvin Levels (Charles), Frederica Meister (Understudy for Miss A)

(Mitzi E. Newhouse Theater) Friday, Feb. 28–Apr. 20, 1986 (39 performances and 20 previews). The Lincoln Center Theater presents:
THE HOUSE OF BLUE LEAVES by John Guare; Words and Music, John Guare; Director, Jerry Zaks; Sets, Tony Walton; Costumes, Ann Roth; Lighting, Paul Gallo; Sound, Aural Fixation, Norman Frith; Hair, J. Roy Helland; Stage Managers, Kate Stewart, Peter J. Downing; Wardrobe, Tony Karniewich; Special Effects, Gary Zeller; Piano Music Arrangements/Recording, Rusty Magee; Assistant Lighting Designer, Robert W. Rosentel; Props, C. J. Simpson; Production Assistant, Erika Morrell
CAST: John Mahoney (Artie Shaughnessy), Ian Blackman (El Dorado Bartender/M.P.), Peter J. Downing (El Dorado Bartender/The White Man), Ben Stiller (Ronnie Shaughnessy), Stockard Channing (Bunny Flingus), Swoosie Kurtz (Bananas Shaughnessy), Julie Hagerty (Corrinna Stroller), Patricia Falkenhain (Head Nun), Jane Cecil (Second Nun), Ann Talman (Little Nun), Christopher Walken succeeded by Brian Evers (Billy Einhorn). Understudies: Ian Blackman (Ronnie), Jane Cecil (Head Nun), Kathleen McKiernan (Bananas/Little Nun), Melodie Somers (Bunny/Corrinna)
A comedy in two acts. The action takes place in the El Dorado Bar and Grill and in an apartment in Sunnyside, Queens, New York, on October 4, 1965.
This production moved to the Vivian Beaumont Theater. See Broadway calendar.

Brigitte Lacombe Photos

(Mitzi Newhouse Theater) Wednesday, April 23,–May 4, 1986 (16 performances). Lincoln Center Theater presents:
THE FLYING KARAMAZOV BROTHERS who conceived, wrote, and directed their performance; Company Manager, Bridget Jennings; Lighting, Eben Sprinsock; Props, Doug Nelson; Wardrobe, A. Devora; Sets, Seiza de Tarr; Stage Manager, Peter Dansky
CAST: Timothy Daniel Furst, Paul David Magid, Randy Nelson, Howard Jay Patterson, Sam Williams
"Juggling and Cheap Theatrics" performed with one intermission.
(Mitzi E. Newhouse Theater) Wednesday, May 14,–Aug. 3, 1986 (57 performances and 3 previews). Lincoln Center Theater presents:
SPALDING GRAY in three of his autobiographical monologues: Terrors of Pleasure, Sex and Death to the Age 14, and Swimming to Cambodia.

Lindsay Crouse, and above: Calvin Levels,
Mike Nussbaum in "The Shawl"

Spalding Gray

Swoosie Kurtz, Christopher Walken
in "The House of Blue Leaves"

97

Pamela Blair, George Gerdes, Larry Block, Keith
Reddin, (back) Nada Despotovich, William Newman,
James Lally in "The Hit Parade"

MANHATTAN PUNCH LINE

July 12, 1985–May 25, 1986
Eighth Season

Artistic Director, Steve Kaplan; Executive Director, Mitch McGuire; Managing Director, Patricia Baldwin; Production Manager, Pamela Singer; Press, Harold L. Marmon; Producing Directors, Steve Kaplan, Mitch McGuire

(TOMI Theatre) Friday, July 12,–Aug. 11, 1985 (23 performances)
THE HIT PARADE by Richard Dresser; Director, Don Scardino; Set, Daniel Conway; Costumes, David C. Woolard; Lighting, Joshua Dachs; Original Songs, Jim Wann; Sound, Phil Lee; Production Coordinator, Robert S. Johnson; Stage Manager, William Hare.
CAST: Pamela Blair (Cilla), Larry Block (Del Bates), Nada Despotovich (Susie), George Gerdes (Bobby Max), James Lally (Walt), William Newman (Dan Slack), Keith Reddin (Jerry Flynn)
A comedy in two acts. The action takes place in 1971 on a winter afternoon at the Heart of America Travel Lodge off Route 70 outside Bedford, Indiana.

(INTAR Theatre) Friday, Sept. 20,–Oct. 20, 1985 (24 performances)
GOODBYE FREDDY by Elizabeth Diggs; Director, Barbara Rosoff; Sets, Johniene Papandreas; Costumes, Martha Hally; Lighting, Jackie Manassee; Stage Manager, Thomas L. Clewell; Presented in association with Portland Stage Co. (Barbara Rosoff, Artistic Director; Patricia Egan, Managing Director)
CAST: Barbara eda-Young (Kate), Michael Murphy (Hank), Walter Bobbie (Paul), Carole Monferdini (Alice), Nicholas Cortland (Andy), Kit Flanagan (Nessa)
A comedy in two acts. The action takes place at the present time in the home of Kate and Hank in Kansas City, Missouri.

(INTAR Theatre) Thursday, Oct. 24,–Nov. 24, 1985 (24 performances)
LOVE AS WE KNOW IT by Gil Schwartz; Director, Josh Mostel; Sets, Randy Benjamin; Lighting, Greg MacPherson; Costumes, Mimi Maxmen; Sound Aural Fixation; Stage Manager, C. A. Clark.
CAST: Act I: "Perfect Lover" with John C. McGinely (Brad), Marek Johnson (Karen); "Want Ad" with Polly Draper (Lucy), Michael Countryman (Bruce), Karen Ludwig (Fish); "Folie A'Deux" with Polly Draper (Danny), Marek Johnson (Lil); "A Day to Remember" with Karen Ludwig (Amy); "Only a Woman" with John C. McGinley (Les), Polly Draper (Heather); "Plato's Retreat" with Karen Ludwig (Amy); "Dandruff of the Gods" with Michael Countryman (Butch), Marek Johnson (Suzi). Act II: "Separate Vacation/Grounds for Divorce/Sexual History" with Michael Countryman (Larry), Polly Draper (Lois), Marek Johnson (Betsy), John C. McGinley (Ted), Karen Ludwig (Amy), David Healy and Leslie Sergeant Wise (The Droids).
The action takes place at the present time in New York City.

(INTAR Theatre) Saturday, Nov. 30, 1985–Jan. 5, 1986 (37 performances)
FESTIVAL OF ORIGINAL ONE-ACT COMEDIES with Sets by Brian Martin; Lights, Scott Pinkney; Costumes, David C. Woolard (A), Marcy Grace Froehlich (B); Sound, Bruce Ellman; Composer, William Turner; Associate Producer, Robert S. Johnson; Stage Managers, Kate Mennone, Madeline S. Katz, Jessica C. Christie, Taylor Davidson, Diane B. Greenberg, Melissa Margolies, Monique Martin, Leslie C. Nemet, John Sullivan, Mary Tiefenbrunn, Annalee Van Kleeck.
COMPANY: Peter Basch, Fran Brill, Lee Bryant, Jill Choder, Taylor Davidson, Dennis Drew, Gillian Farrell, John Hallow, Francis Guinan, Frank Hamilton, Brian Keeler, Richard Long, Mitchell McGuire, Steve Maidment, Laura Neal, Lois Nelson, Sarah Newhouse, Matthew Penn, Richard Portnow, Peter Riegert, Fred Sanders, Kathrin King Segal, Diane Shakar, Steve Skrovan, Barbara Spiegal, Helene Spitzer, Toby Wherry PROGRAM A: "Alone at Last" by Gina Barnett; Director, Melodie Somers; "The Middle Kingdom" by Howard Korder; Director, Robert S. Johnson; "Powder" by Judy Engles; Director, Peter Glazer; "Square One" by Richard Aellen; Director, Robert S. Johnson; "Lip Service" by Howard Korder; Director, Robin Saex; PROGRAM B: "Smoke" by Laurence Klavan; Director, Steve Kaplan; "The Interrogation" by Murphy Guyer; Director, Pamela Singer; "The Art of Conversation" by Mark Malone; Director, Gavin Cameron-Webb; "The Job Search" by Brandon Toropov; Director, Jason Buzas; "Uncle Lumpy Comes to Visit" by Laurence Klavan; Director, Steve Kaplan

(Samuel Beckett Theatre) Friday, May 16,–25, 1986 (14 performances)
PRIME TIME PUNCH LINE with Brian Trust, Punch Line Players, Deb E. Kasper, Chicago City Limits National Touring Company, Women in Comedy, Phil Stein Vaudeville Show, Sylvanian Shakespearean Sircus, Steve Skrovan, For Play, Paranoids, John Ten Eyck, Susie Schneider, Personality, Ellen Ratner, Cafe Haha, Anita Hollander, Phil Nee Fools Nite, Scott Blakeman, Clown Festival

Cathryn Williams Photos

**Left Center: Brendan Conway, Mitch McGuire
in "Prime Time Punch Line" Above: John C.
McGinley, Karen Ludwig, Polly Draper, Marek
Johnson, Michael Countryman in "Love As We
Know It" Top: Barbara eda-Young, Kit Flanagan, Carole
Monferdini in "Goodbye Freddy"**

MANHATTAN THEATRE CLUB

October 29, 1985–June 15, 1986
Fourteenth Season

Artistic Director, Lynne Meadow; Managing Director, Barry Grove; General Manager, Victoria B. Bailey; Artistic Associate/Plays, Jonathan Alper; Artistic Associate/Production, Thomas Bullard; Artistic Associate/Administration, Michael Bush; Casting, Donna Isaacson, Jonathan Freund; Development, Janet M. Harris; Marketing/Press, Virginia Louloudes, Charles M. Gomes, Claudia Jacobs; Business Manager, Michael P. Naumann; Company Manager, Marina Sheriff; Production Manager, Michael R. Moody; Technical Director, Betsy Tanner; Costumiere, Debra Tennenbaum

(City Center Theater/Space) Tuesday, Oct. 29,–Dec. 1, 1985 (40 performances)
OLIVER OLIVER by Paul Osborn; Director, Vivian Matalon; Set, Tom Schwinn; Costumes, Albert Wolsky; Lighting, Richard Nelson; Hair/Wigs, Paul Huntley; Props, Marjorie Fedyszyn, Steven Corby; Wardrobe, Zorba Soteras; Production Assistant; Stage Managers, Don Walters, James Bernardi.
CAST: Joan Inwood (Gertrude), Frances Sternhagen (Constance Oakshot), Nicholas Kaledin (Carl Bridgewater), Alexander Reed (Williamson), Nancy Marchand (Judith Tiverton), Patricia Clarkson (Phyllis), Timothy Daly (Oliver Oliver), Kurt Knudson (Justin Stock)
A comedy in three acts. The action takes place in the late '20's before the Great Depression in the home of Constance Oakshot.

Tuesday, Dec. 17, 1985–Jan. 26, 1986 (47 performances)
IT'S ONLY A PLAY by Terrence McNally; A re-write of "Broadway Broadway" by Mr. McNally; Director, John Tillinger; Sets, John Lee Beatty; Costumes, Rita Ryack; Lighting, Pat Collins; Stan Metelits; Sound, Michael Valvano; Wardrobe, Zorba Soteras; Props, Shelly Barclay, Kate Dale; Stage Managers, Tracy B. Cohen, Anne Marie Kuehling.
CAST: Jihmi Kennedy (Gus Washington), James Coco (James Wicker), Joanna Gleason (Virginia Noyes), David Garrison (Frank Finger), Christine Baranski (Julia Budder), Paul Benedict (Ira Drew), Mark Blum (Peter Austin), Florence Stanley (Emma), Standbys: Steven Culp (Gus/Frank/Peter), Scott Robertson (James/Ira)
A comedy with one intermission. The action takes place in Julia Budder's townhouse in New York City.

Tuesday, Feb. 4,–March 15, 1986 (48 performances)
LOOT by Joe Orton; Director, John Tillinger; Sets, John Lee Beatty; Costumes, Bill Walker; Lighting, Richard Nelson; Fight Coordinator, J. Allen Suddeth; Production Assistant, Laura Michele; Wig, Paul Huntley/James Herrera; Props, Kate Dale; Dialect Coach, Timothy Monich; Stage Managers, Peggy Peterson, Jon Nakagawa.
CAST: Charles Keating (McLeavy), Zoe Wanamaker (Fay), Zeljko Ivanek (Hal), Kevin Bacon (Dennis), Joseph Maher (Truscott), Nick Ullett (Meadows/Standby for McLeavy and Truscott)
A comedy in two acts. The action takes place at the present time in a room in McLeavy's house on an afternoon.

Tuesday, March 26,–April 27, 1986 (40 performances)
PRINCIPIA SCRIPTORIAE by Richard Nelson; Director, Lynne Meadow; Sets, John Lee Beatty; Costumes, William Ivey Long; Lighting, Jennifer Tipton; Sound, Scott Lehrer; Wig/Hair, Paul Huntley, Pamela Bogert; Dialect Coach, Timothy Monich; Stage Managers, Don Walters, Steve Wappel.
CAST: Anthony Heald (Bill Howell), Joe Urla (Ernesto Pico), Shawn Elliott (Julio Montero), George Morfogen (Alberto Fava), Steven Gilborn (Norton Quinn), Mike Nussbaum (Hans Einhorn), Ernesto Gonzalez (Man in prison/Soldier), Standbys: Stefano Loverso (Ernesto/Julio/Man in prison/Soldier), David Ossian (Bill Howell)
A drama in two acts with coda. The action takes place in 1970 and 1985 in a country in Latin America.

Tuesday, May 13,–June 15, 1986 (40 performances)
WOMEN OF MANHATTAN by John Patrick Shanley; Director, Ron Lagomarsino; Sets, Adrianne Lobel; Costumes, Ann Emonts; Lighting, James F. Ingalls; Sound, Stan Metelits; Production Assistant, Brad Cottrill; Hair, Pamela Bogert; Stage Managers, Tom Aberger, Susi Mara.
CAST: Nancy Mette (Billie), J. Smith-Cameron (Rhonda Louise), Jayne Haynes (Judy), Keith Szarabajka (Bob), Tom Wright (Duke), Standbys: Michael Genet (Duke), Peter Mackenzie (Bob)
Performed without intermission.

Gerry Goodstein Photos

**Top Left: Frances Sternhagen, Nancy Marchand
in "Oliver Oliver" Below: James Coco, Christine
Baranski in "It's Only a Play"**

**Joe Urla, Anthony Heald in "Principia
Scriptoriae" Above: Jayne Haynes, J. Smith-Cameron,
Nancy Mette in "Women of Manhattan"**

THE MEAT & POTATOES COMPANY

June 27, 1985–May 4, 1986
Tenth Season

Artistic Director, Neal Weaver; Administrative Director, David Baum; Administrative Assistant, Terrence McDonnell; Lighting Designer, David L. Arrow

(The Alvina Krause Theatre) Thursday, June 27,–July 28, 1985 (20 performances)
THE BACCHAE by Euripides; Director, Neal Weaver; Costumes, Peter MacIver; Sound, George Choma; Set, Neal Weaver, Vernon Morris; Stage Managers, Andrew R. Rosenthal, Nancy Cross.
CAST: Tim Hart (Dionysus), Frances Robertson (Priestess of Dionysus/Chorus Leader), Vernon Morris (Tiresias the Prophet), Joel Parsons (Cadmus), Rick Giolito (Pentheus King of Thebes), Parlan McGaw (Pentheus' Messenger), Bill Phillips (Captain of the Guard), Joe Cattelona (Herdsman), Dorothy Stinnette (Queen Agave, Mother of Pentheus), Joe Cattelona/Andrew R. Rosenthal (Guards), Chorus of Bacchantes: Barbara Callander, Anthony DiPietro, Jim Egan, Patricia Hutson, Chris Polsonetti, Penny S. Rosen.

Wednesday, Aug. 7,–Sept. 1, 1985 (19 performances)
HEDDA GABLER by Henrik Ibsen; Director, Neal Weaver; Costume Coordinator, Kathleen Darcy; Set, Neal Weaver; Stage Manager, Nancy Cross.
CAST: Toni Brown (Julianna Tesman), Kathleen Darcy (Berta), Jerry Holste (George Tesman), Laura Neal (Hedda Gabler Tesman), Lindsay Frost (Thea Elvsted), Herbert DuVal (Judge Brack), Kurt Schlesinger (Eilert Lovborg)

Thursday, Sept. 12,–Oct. 13, 1985 (20 performances)
A DEFINITE MAYBE by Jean Shepard and John O'Leary; Director, Neal Weaver; Set, Jean Shepard, Neal Weaver; Stage Managers, Tom Farrell, George Choma.
CAST: Tanny McDonald (Katherine Wheeler), Lynne Matthew (Marnie), Tom Farrell (John), Tim Hart (Buddy), Vernon Morris (Dr. Rudder), Denis Lybe (Frank Wheeler), George Choma (Man), Herbert DuVal (Ted Wright), Mary Sharmat (Helen Cleveland), Elliott Landen (Ernie Cleveland), Lea Ann Johnson (Jane Cleveland), Veronica Beirne (Marguerita Wright).

Wednesday, Oct. 23,–Nov. 17, 1985 (20 performances)
THE GREEN BAY TREE by Mordaunt Sharp; Directed and Designed by Neal Weaver; Stage Managers, Nancy Cross, David Keats, Shelly Langefeld.
CAST: Tom Deming (Trump), Herbert DuVal (Mr. Dulcimer), Tim Hart (Julian), Margaret Dulaney succeeded by Jean Tafler (Leonora Yale), Ronald Willoughby (William Owen)

Friday, Nov. 29,–Dec. 22, 1985 (20 performances)
A MAN'S WORLD by Rachel Crothers; Director, Neal Weaver; Costume Coordinator, Georgea Pace; Set, Neal Weaver; Stage Manager, Jill Larmett.
CAST: Marc Anthony/Jeremy Schein (Kiddie), Ronald Willoughby (Fritz Bahn), Lenny Bart (Wells Trevor), John E. Brady (Emile Grimeaux), Elissa Napolin (Frank Ware), Rebecca Varon (Lione Brune), Jayne Chamberlin (Clara Oakes), Greg S. Ryan (Malcolm Gaskell)

Thursday, Jan. 9,–Feb. 9, 1986 (20 performances)
MURDER ON THE NILE by Agatha Christie. Director, Jon Teta; Set, Neal Weaver; Lighting, Janet Herzenberg; Costume Coordinator, Judy Kiwitt; Technical Director, Stephen Cowles; Production Manager, David Baum; Stage Managers, Eve Sorel, Ashish Gattegno.
CAST: Mark Cohen (Beadseller/McNaught), Mark Hamilton (Steward), Kate Britton (Miss ffoliot-ffoulkes), Valerie Beaman (Christina Grant), Charles Lynch (Smith), Rebecca Varon (Louise), Charles Fatone (Dr. Bessner), Lynn Weaver (Kay Mostyn), Paul Murray (Simon Mostyn), Vernon Morris (Canon Pennefather), Mary Parker (Jacqueline de Severac)

Thursday, Feb. 20,–March 23, 1986 (20 performances)
NIGHTMARE ABBEY by Thomas Love Peacock; Directed and Designed by Neal Weaver; Lighting, Janet Herzenberg; Stage Managers, Patti Whipple, Brian Popovics.
CAST: Toby O'Brien (Crow), Vernon Morris (Glowry), Stephan Yarian (Toobad), Henry Traeger (Raven), Lee Welch (Scythrop Glowry), Donald Pace (Hilary), James Egan (Listless), Oliver Dixon (Flosky), Patti McClenahan (Marionetta), Mark Cohen (Fatout), Darian Harris (Stella)

Thursday, April 3,–May 4, 1986 (20 performances)
A MIDSUMMER NIGHT'S DREAM by William Shakespeare; Designed and Directed by Neal Weaver; Choreography, Val Folly; Costume Coordinator, Barbara Lawrence; Original Music, David Meade; Stage Manager, Uriel Menson.
CAST: Alan Kitty (Theseus), Julienne Dallara (Hippolyta Queen of the Amazons), Barbara Lawrence (Her Attendant), Robert Michael Kane, Rey Lawrence, Jonathan Powers (Attendants to Theseus), Uriel Menson (Philostrate), Elliott Landen (Egeus), Barbara Callander (Hermia), Edward D. Griffith (Demetrius), Jason Broad (Lysander), Lynn Weaver (Helena), Henry Traeger (Peter Quince), Mark Cohen (Nick Bottom), Stephen Weihs (Frances Flute), Parlan McGaw (Robin Starveling), Tom G. O'Brien (Tom Snout), Toby O'Brien (Snug), Barbara Lawrence (Peaseblossom), Brian MacReady (Puck), Andrew Lamond (Oberon), M. Brauer (Titania), Jonathan Powers (Indian Boy), Robert Michael Kane (Cobweb), Rey Lawrence (Mustardseed), Jonathan Powers (Moth), Alan Kitty, Julienne Dallara, Elliott Landen (Attendants to Oberon)

Herbert Fogelson Photos

Tim Hart, Herbert DuVal in "Green Bay Tree"
Top: Elissa Napolin, Greg Ryan in "Man's World"

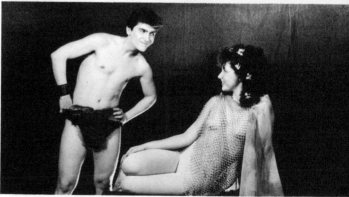

Brian MacReady, Barbara Lawrence in "Midsummer Night's Dream" Above: Dennis Lybe, Tanny MacDonald in "A Definite Maybe"

MIRROR REPERTORY COMPANY

October 29, 1985–March 23, 1986
Third Season

Artistic Director, Sabra Jones; Producing General Management, Weiler/Miller Associates; Scenery and Lighting, James Tilton; Costumes, Gail Cooper-Hecht; Directors, Tom Brennan, Austin Pendleton, Stephen Porter, Ellis Rabb, Peter Mark Schifter, Arthur Storch, John Strasberg, Porter Van Zandt; Associate Artistic Director, John Strasberg; Company Manager, Terry Byrne; Executive Coordinator, Kathleen Warnock; Technical Director, Jess Klarnet; Props, Charlie Eisenberg; Wardrobe, Frank Sabino; Dresser, Suzanne Westenhoeffer; Hairstylist, Teddy Jenkins; Production Assistant, Suzanne Munkelt; Sound, Rob Gorton; Crew, Brandon Doemling, Steve Jordan, Lauren Heller, Kim Gretchen; Stage Managers, Nicholas Dunn, Anne S. King, Kate Hancock; Press, Shirley Herz, David Roggensack.
  (Theatre at St. Peter's Church)
  COMPANY: F. Murray Abraham, Mason Adams, Haru Aki, Margaret Barker, Gabriel Barre, Kristofer Batho, Kim Beaty, Gina Belafonte, Loni Berry, Peter Bloch, Tom Brennan, Ivar Brogger, Scott Bryant, W. B. Brydon, Frank Camacho, Alexander D. Carney, Maxwell Caulfield, Randy William Charnin, Pat Ciserano, Bryan Clark, Judith Cohen, Matthew Cowles, David Cryer, John David Cullum, Marc Dietrich, Michael DiGioia, Brandon Doemling, William Driscoll, Nicholas Dunn, Eric Eisenberg, Frank Faranda, Tovah Feldshuh, Erica Ferszt, Terry Finn, Clement Fowler, Veronica Francis, Elizabeth Franz, Laura Galusha, Don Gigliotti, Francois de la Giroday, Rose Gregorio, Richard Grusin, Frank Hamilton, Kate Hancock, William Ha'o, Baxter Harris, Katharine Houghton, Ann Hilary, Anthony Hopkins, Meg Hosey, Anne Jackson, Timothy Jenkins, Erica Jennings, Sabra Jones, Rowan Joseph, Lilah Kan, Jose Kendall, Anne S. King, Shirley Knight, Jim Knobeloch, Sofia Landon, Richard Leighton, Valerie Leonard, Omar Lotayef, Joan MacIntosh, Deirdre Madigan, Richard Matthews, Thomas MacAteer, Gordon McConnell, Dina Merrill, Clark Middleton, Juliet Mills, David Moreland, Michael Moriarty, N. Janet Nichols, Carrie Nye, F. J. O'Neil, Jess Osuna, Geraldine Page, Jessica Poli, James Pritchett, Phillip Pruneau, James Rebhorn, Charles Regan, Kelly Roman, Donna Sacco, Paul Serson, Madeleine Sherwood, Fred G. Smith, Michael O. Smith, Victor Slezak, Denise Stephenson, John Strasberg, Neil Vipond, Thomas G. Waites, Todd Waring, Steven Weber, Nanette Werness, Helen Wheels, Jane White, Susan Willis
PRODUCTIONS IN REPERTORY: The Madwoman of Chaillot by Jean Giraudoux; Adapted by Maurice Valency; Directed by Stephen Porter; Opened Tuesday, Oct. 29, 1985 and played 37 performances. The Time of Your Life by William Saroyan; Director, Peter Mark Schifter; opened Wednesday, Dec. 18, 1985 and played 23 performances. Children of the Sun by Maxim Gorky; Translated by Ariadne Nicolaev; Director, Tom Brennan; Opened Wednesday, Dec. 25, 1985 and played 21 performances. The Circle by W. Somerset Maugham; Director, Stephen Porter; Opened Thursday, Feb. 20, 1986 and played 47 performances.

Martha Swope/Sara Cook Photos

**Right: Geraldine Page in "The Circle"
Above: Elizabeth Franz, Michael Moriarty
in "Children of the Sun" Top: Geraldine
Page, F. Murray Abraham in "The Madwoman
of Chaillot"**

**Mason Adams, Tovah Feldshuh
in "The Time of Your Life"**

**W. B. Brydon, Geraldine Page
in "The Circle"**

101

NEW FEDERAL THEATRE

October 10, 1985–June 8, 1986
Woodie King, Jr., Producer

(Harry DeJur Henry Street Settlement Playhouse) Thursday, Oct. 10,–Nov. 3, 1985

LONG TIME SINCE YESTERDAY by P. J. Gibson; Staged and Directed by Bette Howard; Set, Charles Henry McClennahan; Costumes, Judy Dearing; Lighting, William H. Grant III; Sound, Bernard Hall; Production Manager, Clarence Taylor; Company Manager, Linda Herring; Wardrobe, Okhute; Props, Melissa Lynne Stephenson; Stage Manager, Reginald Arthur; Press, Max Eisen, Madelon Rosen, Maria Somma.

CAST: Sabrina DePina (Young Laveer Swan), Ayana Phillips (Young Janeen Earl), Starletta DuPois (Laveer Swan), Petronia Paley (Babbs Wilkerson), Thelma Louise Carter (Alisa Myers-Reynolds), Emily Yancy (Thelma Carlson), Denise Nicholas (Panzi Lew McVain), Loretta Devine (Janeen Earl-Taylor).

A play in two acts. The action takes place at the present time in late summer, in Ewing Township, New Jersey

(Experimental Theatre) Thursday, Nov. 14–24, 1985 (12 performances)

NONSECTARIAN CONVERSATIONS WITH THE DEAD by Laurie Carlos; Directors, Miss Carlos and LaTanya Richardson; Choreographer, Jawole Willa Jo Zollar; Music, Don Meissner, Lorenzo LaRoche; Lyrics, Miss Carlos; Costumes, Amber Sunshower & Co.; Set, Erik Stephenson; Lighting, Richard Leu; Stage Manager, Deborah Artman.

CAST: Laurie Carols, Ruben S. Hudson, Jonathan Peck, LaTanya Richardson, Amber Villenueva, Marilyn Worrell.

Presented in three parts.

(Theatre Guinevere) Tuesday, Dec. 3,–22, 1985 (21 performances)

APPEAR AND SHOW CAUSE by Stephen Taylor; Director, Woodie King, Jr.; Based on story by Leon H. Gildin and Stephen Taylor; Set, Richard Harmon; Light, Leo Gambacorta; Costumes, Judy Dearing; Technical Director, Telton Ricards; Props, Doug Jewell; Wardrobe, Ali Davis; Props, Debbie DaVilla; Stage Manager, Casandra Scott.

CAST: Ronnie Newman (Capt. Philip Bresnick), Terry Rabine (Lt. Peter Carlsen), David E. Weinberg (Sgt. Andrew Smith), David Bryant (Mj. Evans Chandler), Robert S. Ryan (Sgt. Hugh Connor), Warner Schreiner (Col. Wheldon Kearns), Ken Laron (Lt. Joshua Harrow), Cliff Frazier (Rep. Noah Lincoln Keyes), Drew Eliot (General), Jack R. Marks (Col. Harlan Phillips).

A play in two acts. the action takes place in 1951 in Stuttgart, West Germany.

(Louis Abrons Arts for Living Center) Thursday, Dec. 5,–29, 1985 (24 performances)

IN THE HOUSE OF BLUES by David Charles; Directed and Staged by Buddy Butler; Musical Director, John McCallum; Set, Llewellyn Harrison; Lights, Buddy Butler; Costumes, Judy Dearing; Choreographer, Hope Clarke; Props/Assistant Stage Manager, Bonnie Garcia; Stage Manager, Wayne Elbert.

CAST: David Connell (Mr. Blues), Crystal Lilly (Melody), Larry Marshall (M. C.), Leslie Reuben (Man II) Katie Love (Woman I), Josie Waller (Woman II), Edna Chew (Woman III), Andre Morgan (Man I), Debra Byrd (Bessie Smith), Understudy: Wendy P. Bowers.

A play in two acts. The action takes place at the present time and from 1920 to 1937.

Emily Yancy, Petronia Paley
in "Long Time Since Yesterday"

Gilbert Lewis, Ken LaRon, David Bryant
in "Appear and Show Cause"

Katie Burnside, Larry Marshall, Chrystal Lilly
in "In the House of the Blues"
Bert Andrews Photos

Chequita Jackson, Bruce Strickland
in "I Have a Dream"

Herman LeVern Jones, James Curt Bergwall,
Chequita Jackson, Diane Weaver, Dwight
Witherspoon in "I Have a Dream"

(Louis Abrons Arts for Living Center) Sunday, Dec. 22, 1985–Jan. 12, 1986 (24 performances)

I HAVE A DREAM by Josh Greenfield; Director, Woodie King, Jr.; Musical Director, Lee Coward; Set/Slides, Ina Mayhew; Costumes, Judy Dearing; Light, Richard Lew; Stage Manager, Malik.

CAST: Dwight Witherspoon (Soloist/Ensemble), Diane Weaver (Rosa Parks/Deranged Woman/Ensemble), James Curt Bergwall (Bus Driver/John Kennedy/Ensemble), Bruce Strickland (Martin Luther King, Jr.), Herman Levern Jones (Abernathy/Martin L. King, Sr./A. Phillip Randolph/Ensemble), Chequita Jackson (Coretta Scott King/Ensemble).

A play with music in two acts.

ACT I: America in the 1950's: I Must Tell Jesus, I Cried and I Cried, The Storm Is Passing Over, Standing in the Need of Prayer, Thank You Lord, Sweet Hour of Prayer, His Eye Is on the Sparrow, We Shall Overcome, We Shall Not Be Moved, Freedom (Amen), Jesus Is My Captain, Lift Every Voice and Sing, Free At Last.

ACT II: America in the 1960's: Nearer My God to Thee, Over My Head, Yes I Thank You Thank You, I'm Going to Sit at the Welcome Table, Amazing Grace, Come Ye Disconsolate, I Will Trust in the Lord, I Woke Up This Morning with My Mind Stayed on Freedom, I Ain't Gonna Let Nobody Turn Me Around, We've Come This Far by Faith, It Is Well with My Soul, Precious Lord, I Don't Feel No Ways Tired, Abraham Martin & John.

(Theatre Guinevere) Sunday, Jan. 12,–Feb 2, 1986 (26 performances)

DECEMBER SEVENTH by George Rattner; Director, Gordon Edelstein; Assistant Director, Ellen T. White; Set, James Wolk; Costumes, David C. Woolard; Sound, Gary Harris; Lighting, Leo Gambacorta; Props, Tammy Taylor; Technical Director, Carle Atwater; Wardrobe, Andrea Nugit; Stage Managers, C. A. Clark, Kate Riddle.

CAST: Brian Backer (Danny Newman), Scott Burkholder (Kurt Steiner), David Jaffe (Jerrold Strauss), Brett Goldstein (Hal Fox), Humbert Allen Astredo (Dr. Dennis), Robin Morse (Beattie Patrick).

A play in two acts. The action takes place in the living room of Sigma Alph Delta fraternity house at Clinton College on December 7, 1941.

(New Federal Theatre) Friday, Feb. 14–23, 1986 (12 performances before moving to the American Place Theatre)

WILLIAMS & WALKER by Vincent D. Smith; Director, Shauneille Perry; Choreography, Lenwood Sloan; Set/Lighting, Marc D. Malamud; Costumes, Judy Dearing; Music, various composers from minstrel shows to Broadway.

CAST: Ben Harney (Bert Williams), Vondie Curtis-Hall (George Walker), Neal Tate (Pianist).

A musical play without intermission. The action takes place June 10, 1910 backstage of the Majestic Theatre in New York City.

(Louis Abrons Arts for Living Center) Wednesday, May 14,–June 8, 1986 (20 performances) Linda Herring presents:

STORIES ABOUT THE OLD DAYS by Bill Harris; Director, LaTanya Richardson; General Manager/Business Manager, Linda Herring; Associate Producer, Maritza Myers; Technical Director, Richard Arnold; Wardrobe, Harriet Foy; Stage Manager, Monique Martin.

CAST: Clebert Ford (Clayborn), Abbey Lincoln (Ivy).

A play in four scenes without intermission. The action takes place in a church on the east side of Detroit at some point in the 1970's.

Bert Andrews Photos

Robin Morse, Brian Backer, Humbert Allen Astredo
in "December 7th"

Clebert Ford, Abbey Lincoln
in "Stories about the Old Days"

NEGRO ENSEMBLE COMPANY

July 18, 1985–July 27, 1986
Nineteenth Season

Artistic Director, Douglas Turner Ward; Managing Director, Leon B. Denmark; General Manager, Stephanie S. Hughley; Company Manager, Larry K. Walden; Production Supervisor, John Harris; Marketing, Porcia Howard; Development, Dianne Aubry, Irene Gandy, Misani; Press, Burnham & Callaghan, David Lotz

(Theatre Four) Thursday, July 18,–Sept. 29, 1985 (86 performances)
EYES OF THE AMERICAN by Samm-Art Williams; Director, Walter Dallas; Set, Llewellyn Harrison; Lighting, Sylvester N. Weaver, Jr.; Costumes, Julian Asion; Sound, Bernard Hall.
CAST: Graham Brown, Glynn Turman, Seret Scott
   Friday, Jan. 24,–Feb. 16, 1986 (40 performances)
HOUSE OF SHADOWS by Steve Carter; Director, Clinton Turner Davis; Set, Daniel M. Proett; Lighting, Sylvester N. Weaver, Jr.; Original Music, Grenaldo; Sound, Bernard Hall; Costumes, Julian Asion; Portrait, Michael Anzalone; Technical Director, Richard Arnold; Production Assistant, James Carter; Wardrobe, Marcy Belton; Stage Managers, Lisa L. Watson, Jeffrey L. Pearl.
CAST: Teddy Abner (Eric), Frances Foster (Cassie), Daniel Barton (Aaron), Raymond Rosario (Hector), Joan Grant (Mary), Victor Steinback (Majeski)
   Friday Feb. 28,–March 30, 1986 (37 performances)
JONAH AND THE WONDER DOG by Judi Ann Mason; Director, Douglas Turner Ward; Assistant Director, LaTanya Richardson; Set, Charles H. McClennahan; Lighting, Sylvester N. Weaver, Jr.; Costumes, Judy Dearing; Sound, Bernard Hall; Stage Manager, Lisa L. Watson.
CAST: Kevin Hooks (Nick), Douglas Turner Ward (Jonah Howard)
   Friday, May 16,–July 27, 1986 (96 performances)
LOUIE AND OPHELIA by Gus Edwards; Director, Douglas Turner Ward; Set, Charles H. McClennahan; Lighting, Sylvester N. Weaver, Jr.; Costumes, Judy Dearing; Sound, Dennis Ogburn; Stage Manager, Lisa L. Watson.
CAST: Elain Graham (Ophelia), Douglas Turner Ward (Louie)

Bert Andrews Photos

**Right: Douglas Turner Ward, Kevin Hooks
in "Jonah and the Wonder Dog" Top: Glynn
Turman, Seret Scott, Graham Brown
in "Eyes of the American"**

**Victor Steinbach, Frances Foster
in "House of Shadows"**

**Douglas Turner Ward, Elain Graham
in "Louie and Ophelia"**

TNT/THE NEW THEATRE OF BROOKLYN

Deborah J. Pope, Artistic Director
Second Season

(The New Theatre of Brooklyn) Wednesday, Nov. 6,–Dec. 8, 1985 (20 performances)

THE DOUBLE BASS by Patrick Suskind; Translated by Eric Overmyer and Harry Newman; Director, Kent Paul; Set, William Barclay; Costumes, Jared Aswegan; Lighting, Phil Monat; Sound, Tom Gould; Technical Director, Michael J. Kondrat; Stage Manager, Louis D. Pietig.
CAST: Boyd Gaines (The Double Bassist).
A play in two acts. The action takes place at the present time in Germany.
Friday, Jan. 24,–Feb. 16, 1986 (12 performances and 3 previews)

NUCLEAR FOLLIES by Gregory Langdon and Joseph Peret; Director, Steve Settler; Musical Director, Hank Levy; Choreographer, Jay Tramel; Scenic Adviser, John Iacovelli; Lighting, Richard Moore; Costume Adviser, Jana Rosenblatt; Production Manager, Leslie Moore; Stage Manager, Liz Small.
CAST: Roger Chapman (The President/Stan Fertel), Larry Fishman (Gen. Stiff/K. C. Smith/WDUL Announcer), Hank Levy (Black Box Man/Vic Paradise), Daniel Neiden (Telephone Man/Rock Singer/Andreanana Pagaladadada), Rende Rae Norman (Nancy Fertel/Messenger/Tango Woman), Christopher Wells (Davey/Dick Fertel/Maurice Fertel).
Performed with one intermission. The action takes place sometime in the not-too-distant future, in the captial of a Western superpower.
Wednesday, March 5,–23, 1986 (14 performances)

COUNTESS MITZI or The Family Reunion by Arthur Schnitzler; Director, Deborah J. Pope; Set, Dan Conway; Lighting, Victor En Yu Tan; Costumes, Kenneth M. Yount; Sound, Tom Gould; Hairstylist, Kerri Lee Robbins; Assistant to Director, Cynthia Lynes; Dramaturg, David Olivenbaum; Production Manager, Leslie Moore; Technical Director, John Jensen; Stage Manager, Susan Selig.
CAST: Neal Randall (Count Arpad Pazmandy), Michael Sutton (Joseph/Wasner), Tom Loftis (Peter/Prof. Windhofer), David Reinhardsen (Prince Egon Ravenstein), Cynthia Lammel (Countess Mitzi), Sean Woods (Philip), Rosemary McNamara (Lolo Langhuber).
Performed without intermission. The action takes place at noon on June 23, 1909 on Count Arpad's estate just outside Vienna.
Thursday, April 24,–May 18, 1986 (20 performances)

WAITING FOR THE PARADE by John Murrell; Director, Melanie Joseph; Set, Dan Canway; Lighting, Michael Moody; Costumes, Melina Root; Sound, Tom Gould; Musical Direction, Jamie Bernstein; Choreography, Robert Buntzen; Assistant Director, Cynthia Lynes; Production Manager, Leslie Moore; Technical Director, Howard Stump; Stage Managers, Sherrill Ann Moyer, Marjorie Ohle.
CAST: Charlotte Colavin (Marta), Martha Horstman (Eve), Rica Martens (Margaret), Frederica Meister (Catherine), Joyce O'Brien (Janet).
A drama in two acts. The action takes place in Calgary, Alberta, Canada, During the Spring of 1940 and the Fall of 1945.

Jessica Katz Photos

Top Right: Boyd Gaines in "Double Bass"
Below: Frederica Meister, Martha Horstman,
Charlotte Calavin in "Waiting for the Parade"

Daniel Neiden, Christopher Wells, Larry Fishman,
Roger Chapman in "Nuclear Follies"

Cynthia Lammel, Rosemary McNamara
in "Countess Mitzi"

NEW YORK SHAKESPEARE FESTIVAL

Producer, Joseph Papp; General Manager, Laurel Ann Wilson; Company Manager, Robert Reilly; Press, Merle Debuskey, Richard Kornberg, Bruce Campbell, Don Anthony Summa, Barbara Carroll; Principal Director, Wilford Leach; Plays and Musicals Department, Gail Merrifield; Literary Manager, Bill Hart; Casting, Rosemarie Tichler; Development, Jane Gullong; Production Manager, Andrew Mihok; Technical Director, Mervyn Haines, Jr.; Props, James Gill, John Jewell

(Delacorte Theater/Central Park) Friday, June 21,–July 21, 1985 (36 performances) The NY Shakespeare Festival with the cooperation of the City of New York (Edward I. Koch, Mayor; Bess Myerson, Commissioner of Cultural Affairs; Henry Stern, Commissioner of Parks) in association with NY Telephone, with Joseph Papp (Producer) presents:

MEASURE FOR MEASURE by William Shakespeare; Director, Joseph Papp; Set, Robin Wagner; Costumes, Lindsay W. Davis; Lighting, Richard Nelson; Music, Allen Shawn; Wigs, Charles LoPresto; Associate Producer, Jason Steven Cohen; Stage Managers, James Bernardi, Tracy B. Cohen; Production Assistants, Janet Callahan, Pat Sosnow; Technical Director, Mitchell Yaven; Sound, David Schriniman, John Rude, Diane Hartdagen, Stuart Pyle; Props, Frances Smith, Evan Canary, John Doyle; Wardrobe, Hannah Murray; Hair, Nickolas Soccadato, James Post. CAST: John Getz (Vincentio), Joseph Warren (Escalus), Richard Jordan (Angelo), Gregory Salata (Lucio), Reg E. Cathey (Gentleman 1), John N. Cutler (Gentleman 2), Rosemary DeAngelis (Mistress Overdone), Nathan Lane (Pompey), Joe Urla (Claudio), Tom Mardirosian (Provost), John Wylie (Friar Thomas), Mary Elizabeth Mastrantonio (Isabella), Gretchen Taylor (Francisca), Tom Toner (Elbow), Robert Stanton (Froth), Steven Dawn (Justice), Mark Zeisler (Angelo's Servant), Elizabeth Perkins (Juliet), Laura MacDermott (Mariana), Antonio Fargas (Abhorson), William Duff-Griffin (Barnardine), Eldon Bullock (Friar Peter), Ralph Zito (Varrius), Kevin Dwyer, Ken Forman, Joseph Gargiulo, Rick Parks (Officers), Howard Samuelsohn (Young Friar), Erika Gregory (Townswoman), Teri Tirapelli (Nun/Widwife). Performed with one intermission. The action takes place in Vienna during 1910.

(Delacorte Theater/Central Park) Sunday, Aug. 4,–Sept. 1, 1985 (27 performances)

THE MYSTERY OF EDWIN DROOD by Rupert Holmes; Suggested by Charles Dickens' unfinished novel; Director, Wilford Leach; Choreography, Graciela Daniele; Musical Direction, Michael Starobin, Edward Strauss; Conductor, Michael Starobin; Scenery, Bob Shaw; Costumes, Lindsay W. Davis; Lighting, Paul Gallo; Sound, Otts Munderloh; Hair and Wigs, Paul Huntley; Associate Producer, Jason Steven Cohen; Production Assistants, Connie Drew, Diahnne Hill, Brendan Smith; Technical Director, Mitchell Yaven; Props, John Masterson; Wardrobe, Hannah Murray; Stage Managers, James Harker, Robin Herskowitz

CAST: George Rose (Mayor Thomas Sapsea/Your Chairman/William Cartwright), Howard McGillin (John Jasper/Clive Paget), Larry Shue (Rev. Crisparkle/Wilfred Barking-Smythe), Betty Buckley (Edwin Drood/Alice Nutting), Patti Cohenour (Rosa Bud/Deirdre Peregrine), Jana Schneider (Helena Landless/Janet Conover), John Herrera (Neville Landless/Victor Grinstead), Jerome Dempsey (Durdles/Nick Cricker), Don Kehr (Deputy/Robert Bascomb), Cleo Laine (Princess Puffer/Angela Prysock), Nicholas Gunn (Brothel Client/Harry Sayle), Brad Miskell (Brothel Client/Montague Pruitt), Francine Landes (Succuba/Gwendolyn Pynn), Karen Giombetti (Succuba/Sarah Cook), Donna Murphy (Succuba/Florence Gill), Judy Kuhn (Alice/Isabel Yearsley/Succuba), Donna Murphy (Beatrice/Florence Gill/Succuba), Stephen Glavin (Statue/Christopher Lyon), Charles Goff (Portrait/Brian Pankhurst/Horace), Robert Grossman (Brothel Client/James Throttle/Harold), Herndon Lackey (Brothel Client/Alan Eliot/Julian), Joe Grifasi (Bazzard/Phillip Bax), Dick Datchery. Understudies: Charles Goff (Bazzard/Crisparkle), Robert Grossman (Chairman/Durdles), Judy Kuhn (Drood/Rosa), Herndon Lackey (Jasper/Neville), Brad Miskell (Deputy), Donna Murphy (Helena/Puffer).

(Public/Delacorte/Circle in the Square Downtown) Thursday, August 8–18, 1985 **FESTIVAL LATINO:** the best of Latino theatre, film, music and dance, with productions from 15 Latin American countries, Europe and the U.S. Director, Oscar Ciccone; Associate Director, Cecilia Vega.

A musical in two acts.

**Richard Jordan, John Getz, Joseph Warren,
Mary Elizabeth Mastrantonio (kneeling)
in "Measure for Measure"**

**John Getz, Mary Elizabeth Mastrantonio
in "Measure for Measure"**
Martha Swope Photos

"La Verdadera Historia de Pedro Navaja"

**Jana Schneider, Howard McGillin, Cleo Laine, Larry
Shue, John Herrera, Patti Cohenour, Joe Grifasi
in "The Mystery of Edwin Drood"**

(Public/ Newman Theater) Tuesday, Oct. 1,–Nov. 24, 1985 (63 performances and 10 previews)

A MAP OF THE WORLD by David Hare; Directed by Mr. Hare; Scenery, Hayden Griffin; Costumes, Jane Greenwood; Lighting, Rory Dempster; Music, Nick Bicat; Production Assistant, Roger Smith; Props, Frances Smith; Wardrobe, Judith Holland; Sound, Don McKennan; Stage Managers, William Chance, Karen Armstrong
CAST: Zeljko Ivanek (Stephen Andrews), Alfre Woodard (Elaine Le Fanu), Roshan Seth (Victor Mehta), Ravinder Kumar (1st Waiter/Crew), Homi Hormasji (2nd Waiter/Crew), N. Erick Avari (3rd Waiter/Crew), Elizabeth McGovern (Peggy Whitton), Tom Klunis (Cameraman/Senior Diplomat), Erika Gregory (Script Girl), Joseph Hindy (Angelis), Joe Costa (Sleeping Man/Diplomat), Herb Downer (Sound Man/Man with feathers), Mike Starr (Clapper Boy/Man with flowers), Judith Moreland (Makeup Girl), Thomas Gibson (Paul/Diplomat/Crew), Richard Venture (Martinson), Ving Rhames (M'Bengue), Thomas Gibson (Stephen), Erika Gregory (Peggy), Tom Klunis (Martinson), Judith Moreland (Elaine)
A drama in two acts. The action takes place in Bombay, India, in 1978 and in the present.

(Public/Martinson Hall) Monday, Oct. 28, 1985–Jan. 26, 1986 (82 performances and 12 previews)

AUNT DAN AND LEMON by Wallace Shawn; Director, Max Stafford-Clark; Scenery, Peter Hartwell; Costumes, Jennifer Cook; Lighting, Christopher Toulmin, Gerard P. Bourcier; Sound, John del Nero, Andy Pink; Props, Lisa Venezia; Wardrobe, Carol Gant, Stage Managers, Bethe Ward, Janet P. Callahan. The Royal Court Theatre Production.
CAST: Kathryn Pogson (Lemon), Linda Bassett (Mother/June/Flora), Wallace Shawn (Father/Freddie/Jasper), Linda Hunt succeeded by Pamela Reed (Aunt Dan), Lynsey Baxter (Mindy), Larry Pine (Andy/Marty), Mario Arrambide (Raimondo)
A drama in two acts. The action takes place at the present time in a room in London.

Sunday, March 23,–June 29, 1986 (109 performances and 22 previews)

AUNT DAN AND LEMON by Wallace Shawn; Director, Max Stafford-Clark; Associate Director, Simon Curtis; Props, Lisa Venezia; Wardrobe, Judy Holland; Sound, Stuart Pyle; Fight Consultant, B. H. Barry; Stage Managers, Bethe Ward, Frank DiFilia
CAST: Kathy Whitton Baker succeeded by Pippa Pearthree (Lemon), Ellen Parker (Mother/June/Flora), Paul Perri (Father/Freddie/Jasper), Pamela Reed (Aunt Dan), Larry Pine (Andy/Marty), Margaret Whitton (Mindy), Kenneth Ryan (Ray), Understudies: Laura Hicks (Lemon/Mindy), Annalee Jeffries (Mother/Dan/Flora/June), Kenneth Ryan (Father/Freddie/Andy/Jasper/Marty), Joe Espinosa (Ray)

(Public/LuEsther Hall) Thursday, Nov. 14, 1985–Jan. 26, 1986 (46 performances and 47 previews)

JONIN' by Gerard Brown; Director, Andre Robinson, Jr.; Scenery, Wynn P. Thomas; Costumes, Karen Perry; Lighting, Ric Rogers; Music Supervision, Bill Toles; Choreography, Jerome Preston Bates; Props, John Masterson; Wardrobe, Michael DiFonzo; Stage Managers, Dwight R. B. Cook, Sheryl Nieren
CAST: Timothy Simonson (Steve), Jerome Preston Bates (Fred), Mark Vaughn (Constance), John Canada Terrell (Duffy), Eric A. Payne (Eddie), Greogry Holtz, Sr. (Greg), Jaime Perry (QT), Eriq LaSalle (Willie), Carla Brothers (Sheila), Understudies: Kent Gash (Fred/Greg/Willie), Victor Love (Constance/Steve/Eddie), Scot Robinson (QT), Toni Ann Johnson (Sheila)
A drama in two acts. The action takes place in a boys dormitory at the present time.

(Susan Stein Shiva Theater) Tuesday, Jan. 14,–Mar. 23, 1986 (64 performances and 16 previews)

RUM AND COKE by Keith Reddin; Director, Les Waters; Scenery, John Arnone; Costumes, Kurt Wilhelm; Lighting, Stephen Strawbridge; Projections, Wendall K. Harrington; Fight, B. H. Barry; Props, Evan Canary; Wardrobe, Bruce Brumage; Dialect Consultant, Timothy Monich; Stage Managers, Janet P. Callahan; David Lansky.
CAST: Peter MacNicol (Jake Seward), Michael Ayr (Rodger Potter/Ramon), John Bedford-Lloyd (Tod Cartmell/Fidel Castro/Com. Tyler), Frank Maraden (Bar Patron/Richard Nixon/Grandmother), Jose Ramon Rosario (Bar Waiter/Felix Duque), Polly Draper (Linda Seward), Larry Bryggman (Tom Tanner/Larry Peters), Robert Stanton (Bob Stanton/Waiter/Child 2/Soldier 1), Jose Fong (Jorge/Child 1), Tony Plana (Miguel)
A drama in two acts. The action takes place in various locations in the years between 1959 and 1961.

Zeljko Ivanek, Roshan Seth, Alfre Woodard,
Elizabeth McGovern in "A Map of the World"

Michael Ayr, John Bedford-Lloyd, Peter MacNicol
in "Rum and Coke" *(Susan Cook/Swope Associates)*

Ellen Parker, Kathy Whitton Baker, Pamela Reed,
Paul Perri in "Aunt Dan and Lemon"
Carol Rosegg Photos

Eric Payne, Jerome Preston Bates, Gregory
Holtz, Sr., Jaime Perry in "Jonin' "
(Susan Cook/Swope Associates)

NEW YORK SHAKESPEARE FESTIVAL

(Public/Newman Theater) Tuesday, Feb. 18,–May 11, 1986 (70 performances and 21 previews)

HAMLET by William Shakespeare. Director, Liviu Ciulei; Scenery, Bob Shaw; Costumes, William Ivey Long; Lighting, Jennifer Tipton; Fights, B. H. Barry; Vocal/Text Consultant, Elizabeth Smith; Wig/Hair, Paul Huntley; Production Assistant, Tony Blofson; Props, Frances Smith; Wardrobe, Carol Gant; Stage Managers, Alan Traynor, Pat Sosnow

CAST: David Adamson (Norwegian Capt./Danish Gen.), Mario Arrambide (Marcellus), Mary Barto (Lady-in-waiting/Flautist), Leonardo Cimino (Polonius), Lynn Cohen (Player Queen/Lady-in-waiting), David Cromwell (Guildenstern), Peter Crook (Francisco/Fortinbras), William Duell (2nd Gravedigger/5th Player/Old Gentleman), Ron Faber (Voltemand/4th Player), Kate Falk (Lady-in-waiting), Richard Frank (Horatio), Harriet Harris (Ophelia), Richard Michael Hughes (Bernardo/2nd Sailor), Garry Kemp (Cornelius), Kevin Kline (Hamlet), Sharon Laughlin (Lady-in-waiting), Randle Mell (Rosencrantz), Dan Nutu (Valet), David Pierce (Laertes), Marco St. John (1st Sailor/Danish Officer), Priscilla Smith (Gertrude), Peter Van Norden (Gentleman/1st Gravedigger/3rd Player), Paul Walker (Reynaldo/2nd Valet), Joseph Warren (Priest/Minister of Finance), Jeff Weiss (Ghost/Player King/Osric), Garo Yellin (Gentleman/Cellist), Harris Yulin (Claudius)

A tragedy performed with one intermission.

(Public/LuEsther Hall) Tuesday, March 4,–April 27, 1986 (40 performances and 24 previews)

LARGO DESOLATO by Vaclav Havel; Translation, Marie Winn; Director, Richard Foreman; Scenery, Richard Foreman; Costumes, Nancy Winters; Lighting, Heather Carson; Props, John Masterson; Wardrobe, John Calvert; Stage Managers, Karen Armstrong, Chris Fielder

CAST: Larry Block (Lada I), Michael Guido (Man II), Sally Kirkland (Zuzana), Matthew Locricchio (Man I), Tom Mardirosian (Olda), Burke Pearson (Lada II), Richard Russell Ramos (Fellow II), Josef Sommer (Leopold), Jodi Thelen (Marketa), Diane Venora (Lucy), Joseph Wiseman (Olbram), Edward Zang (Fellow I)

A drama in two acts. The action takes place in Leopold Kopriva's spacious apartment in contemporary Prague during a 36-hour period.

(Public/Susan Stein Shiva Theater) Tuesday, Apr. 22,–June 14, 1986 (24 performances and 19 previews)

CUBA AND HIS TEDDY BEAR by Reinaldo Povod; Director, Bill Hart; Set, Donald Eastman; Costumes, Gabriel Berry; Lighting, Anne E. Militello; Props, Evan Canary; Wardrobe, Bruce Brumage; Stage Managers, Ruth Kreshka, Joel Elins

CAST: Robert DeNiro (Cuba), Ralph Macchio (Teddy), Burt Young (Jackie), Nestor Serrano (Redlights), Wanda De Jesus (Lourdes), Michael Carmine (Che), Paul Calderon (Dealer)

A drama in two acts. The action takes place at the present time in Cuba's apartment in New York City.

Martha Swope Photos

Right: Burt Young, Ralph Macchio, Michael Carmine, Robert DeNiro in "Cuba and His Teddy Bear" Top: Josef Sommer, Diane Venora in "Largo Desolato"

David Pierce, Kevin Kline in "Hamlet"

Burt Young, Ralph Macchio, Robert DeNiro in "Cuba and His Teddy Bear"

PAN ASIAN REPERTORY THEATRE

October 8, 1985–June 7, 1986
Ninth Season

Artistic/Producing Director, Tisa Chang: Managing Director, Elizabeth A. Hyslop; Development/Marketing/Stage Manager, Jon Nakagawa; Press, G. Theodore Killmer; Technical Director, Nadine Charlsen; Wardrobe, Jenna Krempel; Sound, Raul Aranas; Costumes, Eiko Yamaguchi; Lighting, Victor En Yu Tan.

(Playhouse 46) Tuesday, Oct. 8,–Nov. 2, 1985 (26 performances)
ONCE IS NEVER ENOUGH by R. A. Shiomi, Marc Hayashi, Lane Kiyomi Nishikawa; Director, Raul Aranas; Set, Christopher Stapleton; Costumes, Eiko Yamaguchi.
CAST: Henry Yuk (Sam Shikaze), Carol A. Honda (Rosie), Alkis Papuchis (Pete), Glenn Kubota (Chuck Chan), Natsuko Ohama (Yoko), Richard Voights (Hubert Sloane), Ronald Nakahara (Jimmy Hayakawa), Sam Howell (Victor). A play in two acts. The action takes place in the late 1970's on Powell Street in Vancouver, Canada.

(Playhouse 46) Tuesday, Nov. 12,–Dec. 7, 1985 (24 performances)
GHASHIRAM KOTWAL by Vijay Tendulkar; Director, Tisa Chang; English translation, Eleanor Zelliot, Jayant Karve; Special Consultant, Satish Alekar; Choreography/Music, Rajika Puri; Original Music, Bhaskar Chandavarkar; Musical Director, Daniel Paul Karp; Set, Atsushi Moriyasu; Stage Managers, Dominick Balletta, David Lawrence Folender.
CAST: Allan Tung (Dancing Ganesh), Mathy Neda (Dancing Saraswati/Chandra), Arundhati Chattopadhyaya (Dancing Lakshmi/Gulabi), Norris M. Shimabuku (Sutradhar), Brahman Wall: Jose R. Andrews, Jeffrey Akaka, John Baray, Mauricio Bustamante, Michael G. Chin, Hirsh Diamant, Leroy Lessane, Chico Kasinoir, Henry Ravelo, Ennis Smith, Allan Tung, Brahmans: John Baray, Hirsh Diamant, Jose R. Andrews, Ennis Smith, Chico Kasinoir, Three Handsome Brahmans: Michael G. Chin, Henry Ravelo, Allan Tung, Tamasha Dancers: Ako, Kris Marie Chun, Mathy Neda, Jennie Yue, Mel Duane Gionson (Nana Phadnavis), Ismail Abou-El-Kanater (Ghashiram Kotwal), Hustling Brahmans: Jeffrey Akaka, Hirsh Diamant, Henry Ravelo, Leroy Lessane (Sahib), Jose R. Andrews/Michael G. Chin (Soldiers), Lynette Chun (Gauri), Leroy Lessane/Jennie Yue (7th Man and Wife), Kris Marie Chun (Woman with complaint), Jeffrey Akaka (Tortured Brahman), John Baray (Bhatji), Ako (Nana's Bride), Jose R. Andrews (Sardar Phakade), Strangers to Pune: Hirsh Diamant, Chico Kasinoir, Allan Tung, Henry Ravelo, Musicians: Bharatkumar Terphale, Daniel Paul Karp, Jamey Haddad. The action takes place in 1792 in Pune, in the Maharshtra state of India.

(Susan Bloch Theatre) Tuesday, Feb. 25,–March 22, 1986 (28 performances)
MEDEA by Euripides; Director, Alkis Papoutsis; Adaptation, Claire Bush; English translation, Claire Bush/Alkis Papoutsis; Lighting, Richard Dorfman; Set, Alex Polner; Stage Manager, Dominick Balletta.
CAST: Kati Kuroda (Nurse), Roger Chang (Older Boy), Randy Chang (Younger Boy), Christen Villamor (Woman 1), Lynette Chun (Woman 2), Mari Scott (Woman 3), Ching Valdes/Aran (Medea), Ismail Abou-El-Kanater (Creon/Jason), Norris M. Shimabuku (Tutor/Aegeus). Performed with one intermission.

(Playhouse 46) Tuesday, May 13,–June 7, 1986 (24 performances)
THE MAN WHO TURNED INTO A STICK by Kobo Abe; Director, Ron Nakahara; Lighting, Tina Charney; Set, Bob Phillips; Stage Manager, Dominick Balletta.
CAST: Donald Li (Hippie Boy), Mary Lee-Aranas (Hippie Girl), Ernest Abuba (The Man Who Turned into a Stick), Raul Aranas (Man from Hell), Kati Kuroda (Woman from Hell), with "Boxer" performed by Ernest Abuba, and "Suitcase" performed by Mary Lee-Aranas (Woman), Kati Kuroda (Visitor), Ernest Abuba (Suitcase).

Martha Swope/Carol Rosegg Photos

Ron Nakahara, Henry Yuk, Glenn Kubota
in "Once Is Never Enough"

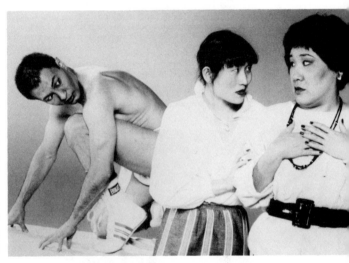

Ernest Abuba, Mary Lee-Aranas, Kati Kuroda
in "The Man Who Turned into a Stick"

Ismail Abou-El-Kanater, Ching Valdes/Aran
in "Medea"

Lynette Chun, Mel Duane Gionson
in "Ghashiram Kotwal"

PEARL THEATRE COMPANY

February 6,–June 15, 1986
Second Season

Artistic Director, Shepard Sobel; Producing Director, Christopher Warrick; Development, Juan C. Dandridge; Artistic Associate, Joanne Camp; Dramaturg, Dale Ramsey; Producing Consultant/Sound, Tarquin Jay Bromley
RESIDENT ACTING COMPANY Joel Bernstein, Robin Leslie Brown, Joanne Camp, Robert Emmet, Shelley Frew, Frank Geraci, Bonnie Horan, Laura Margolis, Pinkney Mikell, Anna Minot, James Nugent, Judith Reagan, Daniel Region, Dugg Smith, Rose Stockton, Patrick Turner, Richard Warner, Joseph Warren, Donnah Welby, Robin Westphal, Robert Zukerman, David Brazda, Jimi Foster, Rati Gorfien, Jan Maxwell, Garrison Phillips, Grover Zucker, Michael Hill, Stephen Lajoie
GUEST ARTISTS Douglas Simes, Stuart Lerch
(The Pearl Theatre) Thursday, Feb. 6,–March 1, 1986 (16 performances)
HER GREAT MATCH by Clyde Fitch; Director, Richard Warner; Set, Robert Joel Schwartz; Lighting, Ed Mattews; Costumes, C. L. Hundley; Stage Manager, Stuart Lerch.
Friday March 7–29, 1986 (16 performances)
TWO GENTLEMEN OF VERONA by William Shakespeare; Director, Shepard Sobel; Sets, Robert Joel Schwartz; Lighting, Edward Matthews; Costumes, Sharon DeRosa; Stage Manager, Mary Sue Gregson
Friday, April 4–26, 1986 (16 performances)
ANTIGONE by Sophocles; Director, Alkis Papoutsis; Sets, Robert Joel Schwartz; Costumes, Leslie Chilton; Lights, Edward R. F. Matthews; Special Movement Consultant, Alice Teirstein; Stage Managers, Jane Koch, Gary Miller
Friday, May 2–24, 1986 (16 performances)
THE LADY FROM THE SEA by Henrik Ibsen; Translated by Frances E. Archer; Set, Robert Joel Schwartz; Director, Shepard Sobel; Assistant Director, Joel Bernstein; Costumes, Murrey Nelson; Lights, Edward R. F. Matthews; Stage Managers, Laura Rathgeb, Rati Gorfien
Thursday, May 29,–June 15, 1986 (16 performances)
THE CONTRAST by Royall Tyler; Director, Joan Elizabeth Thiel; Set, Robert Joel Schwartz; Costumes, C. L. Hundley; Lighting, Edward R. F. Matthews; Stage Manager, Michael Durkin

Martha Swope/Carol Rosegg Photos

Joanne Camp, Laura Margolis, Pinkney Mikell, Donnah Welby in "The Contrast" Top: James Nugent, Robert Emmet, Rose Stockton in "Two Gentlemen of Verona"

PLAYWRIGHTS HORIZONS

June 26, 1985–June 15, 1986
Fifteenth Season

Artistic Director, Andre Bishop; Managing Director, Paul S. Daniels; General Manager, James F. Priebe; Development, Carolyn Stolper; Production Manager, Carl Mulert; Casting, John Lyons, Amy Introcaso; Technical Director, Robert Usdin; Costumer, Laurie Buehler; Literary Manager, Eric Overmyer; Resident Director, Ben Levit; Props, David Birn Press, Bob Ullman, Steven O'Neill.
Wednesday, June 26,–July 21, 1985 (15 performances and 16 previews)
RAW YOUTH by Neal Bell; Director, Amy Saltz; Set, Thomas Lynch; Costumes, Kurt Wilhelm; Lighting, Ann G. Wrightson; Sound, Scott Lehrer, Lia Vollack; Technical Director, Darlene Murray; Wardrobe, Maralyn Keith; Production Assistants, Julia Mayer, Winter Mead; Stage Manager, J. R. MacDonald
CAST: Ben Siegler (Sam in his 20's), John Seitz (Mel, Sam's father), James Ray (Congressman Gary). A drama in two acts. The action takes place in October of the present time in a single-room-occupant hotel in New York, and at a nearby beach.
(Mainstage Theatre) Wednesday, September 4–October 6, 1985 (14 performances and 21 previews).
PARADISE! with Book and Lyrics by George C. Wolfe; Music, Robert Forrest; Director/Choreographer, Theodore Pappas; Set, James Noone; Costumes, David C. Woolard; Lighting, Frances Aronson; Sound, Paul Garrity, Lia Volack; Special Effects, Jauchem & Meeh, Inc.; Orchestrations/Additional Arrangements, John McKinney; Program Director, Ira Weitzman; Musical Director, David Loud; Assistants, Nancy Schakel, Dennis Kralovec, Hillary Nelson; Wigs/Hair, Peg Schierholz; Wardrobe: Mary Jestice, Diane Swanson; Production Assistant, Jane Roth; Stage Managers: M. A. Howard, J. R. MacDonald
CAST: The Coupes: Janice Lynde (Grace), Steven Vinovich (Dan), Danielle Ferland (Caddy), Ben Wright (Toddie). The Mahaneyheyans: Tommy Hollis (Heath), Charlaine Woodard (Local)
MUSICAL NUMBERS: This Could Be the End, Rubber Plant Song, We're Needed Here, Take Me Away, Something's Gonna Happen Really Strange Tonight, On Mahaneyheya, Doom Is Due at Dawn, With the Dawn, Mama Will Be Waiting with the Dawn, This Must Be the End, Welcome to Paradise, Atlanta, Welcome to Paradise Part II, Inside, Who Is This Woman, Secrets Men Should Know, The Last Paradise, Dear Diary, The Uncle Dan Song, You've Got to Let Go, This Is Not the End
A musical in two acts. The action takes place "on an ocean and an island, this weekend."

Robin Westphal, Daniel Region, Laura Margolis in "Her Great Match" Above: Joanne Camp, Frank Geraci in "The Lady from the Sea"

Nov. 8,–Dec. 8, 1985 (22 performances and 15 previews)

ANTEROOM by Harry Kondoleon; Director, Garland Wright; Set, Adrianne Lobel; Costumes, Rita Ryack; Lighting, James F. Ingalls; Sound, Scott Lehrer; Wardrobe, Mary Jestice; Props, Betsy Spanbock; Production Assistant, John Daum; Stage Managers, Robin Rumpf, Corbey Rene Low.

CAST: Albert Macklin (Parker), Mitchell Lichtenstein (Wilson), Elizabeth Wilson (Fay), Susan Cash (Maya), Colin Fox (Craig), Janet Hubert (Joy), Crystal Field (Barbara). A comedy in two acts. The action takes place during the summer of the present time, in Fay's mansion in Southampton, L.I., N.Y.

Wednesday, Jan. 1,–Feb. 2, 1986 (39 workshop performances)

MIAMI with Book by Wendy Wasserstein; Music, Jack Feldman; Lyrics, Bruce Sussman, Jack Feldman; Director, Gerald Gutierrez; Choreography, Larry Hyman; Set, Heidi Landesman; Costumes, Ann Hould-Ward; Lighting, Richard Nelson; Sound, Scott Lehrer; Musical Direction/Vocal Arrangements, David Bishop; Associate Musical Director/Dance Arrangements, Henry Aronson; Keyboard and Percussion Arrangements, David Bishop, Henry Aronson; Musical Theatre Program Director, Ira Weitzman; Assistant Choreographer, Patti Mariano; Hairstylist, Peg Schierholz; Wardrobe, Mary Jestice, Brian James Grace; Production Assistant, Jenny Peek; Stage Managers, Suzanne Fry, Corbey Rene Low.

CAST: Royana Black (Cathy Maidman), Fisher Stevens (Jonathan Maidman), Phyllis Newman (Helen Maidman), Stephen Pearlman (Sam Maidman), John Aller (Maitre d'/Carlos de Goya), David Green (Vic Barry), Marcia Lewis (Kitty Katz), Chevi Colton (Erma Goldman), Cleve Asbury (Dirk/Waiter/Dr. English/Renaldo/Boy 2), Bill Badolato (Andy/Boy 1/Waiter), Catherine Wolf (Vita Weinstein), John Cunningham (Ted Fine), Jane Krakowski (Denise Fine), Joanna Glushak (Annette de Goya), Larry Keith (Murray Murray), Jerry Mayer (Luis Hernandez), Mary Anne Dorward (Yvette/Mrs. Cohen/Girl 1), Molly Wassermann (Nanette/Girl 2). A musical-in-progess set in Miami in the 1950's.

Wednesday, Feb. 12,–March 16, 1986 (22 performances and 15 previews)

LITTLE FOOTSTEPS by Ted Tally; Director, Gary Pearle; Set, Thomas Lynch; Costumes, Ann Hould-Ward; Lighting, Nancy Schertler; Sound, Scott Lehrer; Music, John McKinney; Fights, B. H. Barry; Props, Jenny Peek; Wardrobe, Mary Jestice; Stage Managers, M. A. Howard, J. R. MacDonald.

CAST: Mark Blum (Ben), Anne Lange (Joanie), Jo Henderson succeeded by Lenka Peterson (Charlotte), Thomas Toner (Gil). A comedy in two acts. The action takes place at the present time in Ben and Joanie's apartment.

Wednesday, March 19,–June 22, 1986 (94 performances and 16 previews)

THE PERFECT PARTY by A. R. Gurney, Jr.; Director, John Tillinger; Set, Steven Rubin; Costumes, Jane Greenwood; Lighting, Dan Kotlowitz; Sound, Gary Harris; Technical Director, Albert Webster; Wardrobe, Jennifer Smith; Props, Eleanor Trimble; Production Assistant, David Bass; Stage Managers, Suzanne Fry, Corbey Rene Low.

CAST: John Cunningham (Tony), Holland Taylor succeeded by Charlotte Moore (Lois), Debra Mooney (Sally), David Margulies succeeded by Stephen Pearlman (Wes), Kate McGregor-Stewart succeeded by June Gable, Marilyn Cooper (Wilma). A comedy in two acts. The action takes place at the present time in Tony's study.

Monday, May 21,–June 15, 1986 (14 performances and 17 previews)

THE NICE AND THE NASTY by Mark O'Donnell; Director, Douglas Hughes; Set, Loren Sherman; Costumes, Andrew B. Marlay; Lighting, Stephen Strawbridge; Sound, Scott Lehrer; Original Music, Paul Sullivan; Technical Director, Albert Webster; Wardrobe, Virginia Patton, Eleanor Trimble; Production Assistant, Jenny Peek; Stage Managers, Robin Rumpf, Lawrence Eaton.

CAST: Jane Adams (Tippy Blite), David O'Brien (Blade Crevvis), Marianne Owen (Cathexa Heitz), W. H. Macy (Junius Upsey), Jerry Mayer (Lesser Lawyer/Deus ex Machina), Lawrence Eaton (Lest Lawyer), Kurt Beattie (Smurgison), James McDonnell (Gad Allwyn), Bill Fagerbakke (Fanatic/Security Man/Simmons), Charles Bradley (Boyd Barnes), Jodi Thelen (Needa Heitz), Thomas Barbour (Hobart Heitz). A comedy in two acts. The action takes place "right now exactly in an absolutely enourmous American city."

Gerry Goodstein, Bob Marshak, Martha Swope/Susan Cook Photos

Danielle Ferland, Janice Lynde, Ben Wright, Stephen Vinovich in "Paradise!" Top: Elizabeth Wilson, Mitchell Lichtenstein, Colin Fox in "Anteroom"

Debra Mooney, Stephen Pearlman, Charlotte Moore, June Gable, John Cunningham in "The Perfect Party"

Jodi Thelen, Marianne Owen, W. H. Macy in "The Nice and the Nasty" Above: Mark Blum, Anne Lange in "Little Footsteps"

111

PUERTO RICAN TRAVELING THEATRE

Jan. 15–June 1, 1986
Nineteenth Season

Artistic Director, Miriam Colon Edgar; Managing Director, Ellen Scrimger Gordon; Community Coordinator, Julio E. Martinez; Technical Director, Alan Sporing; Props, Alane Brown; Press, Max Eisen, Maria Somma, Madelon Rosen, Barbara Glenn

Wednesday, Jan. 15,–Feb. 23, 1986 (42 performances)
BODEGA by Federico Fraguada; Director, Alba Oms; Translation by Freddy Valle; Set, Carl Baldasso; Costumes, Sue Ellen Rohrer; Lighting, Rachel Budin; Sound, Gary Harris; Fight, John Goodrum; Producer, Miriam Colon Edgar; Stage Manager, David Lawrence Folender
CAST: Puli Toro (Elena Toro), Jaime Tirelli (Maximo Toro), Millie Vega (Norma Toro), Antonio Aponte (Rafy Lopez), Olga Molina-Tobin (Dona Luz), Donald Silva (Michael Peterson), Alane Brown, Rudy Fort, Marnie Millington, Jaime Rodriguez (Bodega customers)
A drama in two acts. The action takes place at the present time in a bodega in the South Bronx of New York City.

Wednesday, March 5,–April 13, 1986 (42 performances)
THE BITTER TEARS OF PETRA VON KANT by Rainer Werner Fassbinder; English translation, Denis Calandra; Spanish translation, Fernando Masilorens, Federico Gonzalez del Pino; Director, Andre Ernotte; Set, Carl Baldasso; Costumes, Betsy Gonzalez; Lighting, Rachel Budin; Sound, Gary Harris; Producer, Miriam Colon Edgar; Technical Director, James T. Kirkpatrick; Props, Tina Salaks; Stage Manager, Lisa Rollins
CAST: Caroline Kava/Ilka Tanya Payan (Petra von Kant), Janne Peters (Marlene), Alicia Kaplan (Sidonie von Grasenabb), Barbara Wilder/Jeanette Mirabal (Karin Thimm), Arlene Roman (Gabriele von Kant), Monica Boyer (Valerie von Kant)
A drama in 2 acts and 5 scenes. The action takes place in the city of Cologne, Germany, in the interior of a fashion designer's loft.

Wednesday, April 23,–June 1, 1986 (42 performances)
THE BIRDS FLY OUT WITH DEATH by Edilio Pena; Translation, Asa Zatz; Director, Vicente Castro; Set/Costumes, Rafael Mirabal; Lighting, Craig Kennedy; Sound, Gary Harris; Producer, Miriam Colon Edgar; Stage Manager, Nan Siegmund
CAST: Bertila Damas (Daughter), Lillian Hurst (Mother)
A drama in two acts. The action takes place in an unidentified Latin American town at the present time.

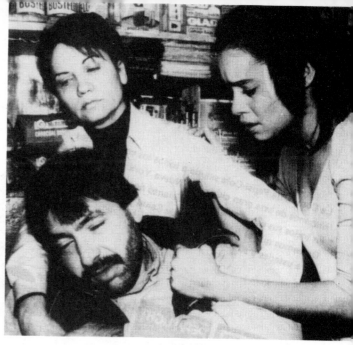

Jaime Tirelli, Puli Toro,
Millie Vega in "Bodega"

Monica Boyar (top), Caroline Kava, Arlene
Roman in "Bitter Tears of Petra Von Kant"
(Martha Swope Photo)

Lillian Hurst (top), Bertila Damas
in "Birds Fly Out with Death"
(Peter Krupenye Photo)

QUAIGH THEATRE

September 7, 1985–May 23, 1986

Artistic Director, Will Lieberson; Managing Director, Murray Mottner; Executive Directors, Peggy Ward, Albert Brower; Producers, Ruth Previn, Judith Rubin; Directors, Terence Cartwright, Dennis Lieberman, Ted Mornel; Sound, George Jacobs; Press, Francine L. Trevens

Saturday, September 7–29, 1985

THE ERUDITE by Spurgeon Crayton; Director, Don Durant; Lighting, Eddie Baker.
CAST: Tammy Heyward (Alethia), Jaunice Pryce (Alethia), Eartha Frederick (Dr. Sophia Warren), Michael DeLavallade (Dr. Hudson), Lee Storey (Vale Terrell), Tyree Lewis Pope (Dr. Bythos Hudson), Charles L. Norris, Jr. (Mark Hudson), Saundra Marsh (Dr. Sophia Warren)

Sunday, December 1–8, 1985 (9 performances)

BAD BAD JO-JO by James Leo Herlihy; Director, Len Silver. CAST: John Mudd, Tim Bass, Patrick Ferrara

Monday, December 30, 1985–January 1, 1986

DRAMATHON '85: A 36 hour non-stop theatrical entertainment produced by Ted Mornell and Will Lieberson; Sound, George Jacobs; Lighting, Deborah E. Matlack; Stage Managers, Ann Chitwood, Temoth Harvin, Deborah Baron, Robin Shwarz, Nikk Harmon, Sharon L. Reich, Jim Griffith.

THE ENTERTAINMENT: The Greatest Male Dancer in the World by Richard Garrick Bethell, Wedding Bell Blues and Bar Dreams by Steven Otfinoski, Playpen by Linda Andre, Dicks by Jules Feiler, The Sweetshoppe Myriam by Ivan Klima, Fantasy Impromptu by Hugh Dignon, Jonathan Littman and Mark Bennett, The Box by Sheldon Rosen, The Big Bang by Sheila Walsh, Joanna's My Name By Sheila Walsh, Present Company, Bruce Vernon Bradly, Bob Friedhoffer, Something Unspoken by Tennessee Williams, The Secret Dreams of Professor Isaac by John Minnigah, The Wedge by Steve Shilo Felson, Impromptu by Tad Mosel, No One Lives on the Moon Anymore by Tony Martinetti, Royal Flush by Dan Bottstein, Christian Follies by Peter Manos, Prescripted by Pat Schneider, Theatre of the Absurd by Mark Farnen, A Lady in Yellow Boucle by John W. Fiero, The Rock by Roxanne Shafer, Mutulation by Mark Troy, The Pumpkin Carvers by Peter Hedges, Talking With by Jane Martin, Encounter with the Gods by C. Dumas, Chateau Foirelacour by Mark Robson, Pelleas et Melisande by Maurice Maeterlinck, Walter Adkins & Antoinette Mille, Time Makes Everything a Memory by Copper Cunningham, Consenting Adults by Ralph Hunt, A Medieval Tapestry (scenes from Shakespeare), The Ties That Bind by Matthew Witten, Beanstock by David Shawn Klein, Liars by Joseph Yesutis, The Break by Fred Saunders, The Night We Lost Willie Nightingale by Dalene Young, Belinda Munsell, The Lovebirds by Pamela G. Bird, Jim Babb, Playtime by Gary Beck, 27 Wagons Fill of Cotton

Wednesday, Jan. 15,–Feb. 9, 1986 (20 performances)

NECKTIES: A COMIC TRILOGY OF LOVE-KNOTS by F. J. Hartland; Director, Peter M. Gordon; Set, John Geurts; Costumes, Claudia S. Anderson; Lighting, Nancy Blumstein; Stage Managers, Sue Jane Stoker, Steven Channell; Press, FLT/Francine L. Trevens, Terence E. Womble
CAST: "Neckties" with Jon Wool (Kevin), Paul Zappala (Joel), Risa Brainin (Janet). The action takes place on a Sunday morning in June in Kevin's studio apartment. "Subject to Change" with Jon Wool (Stuart), Paul Zappala (Kenny), Risa Brainin (Lilah). The action takes place at a college reunion and in a fraternity house ten years earlier. "Auto-Erotic Misadventure" with Paul Zappala (Cliff), Risa Brainin (Norma), Jon Wool (Brandon). The action takes place in Myrtle Beach, Minneapolis, and New York in the present, and in a townhouse in Washington, D.C. in the past.

Monday, April 28,–May 9, 1986 (12 performances)

THE FOURTH ONE by Mario Fratti; performed by Marie Costanza, Gayle Stahlhuth; with

THE TIES THAT BIND by Mathew Witten; performed by Nancy Stewart Hill, Dani Klein, Ken Myles

Monday, May 12–23, 1986 (10 performances)

EARLY BIRD by John Jiler; Director, Ted Mornel. No other details submitted

Adam Newman Photos

Top Right: Eleni Kelakos, Robert Boles in "To Feed Their Hopes" Below: Arthur French, Dianne Kirksey, Marcial Howard, Bennie Russell in "Time Makes Everything a Memory"

Harriette Bigus, J. H. Sharp in "Medieval Tapestries"

113

RIVERWEST THEATRE

June 20, 1985–March 30, 1986
Fifth Season

Producing Managers: Nat Habib, June Summers, Joseph Cahalan, Mike Burrows; Technical Director, Anthony Ross; Press, Maya Associates/Penny M. Landau, Mark Goldstaub, Dan Kellachan

(Riverwest Theatre) Thursday, June 20,–July 14, 1985 (16 performances and 4 previews)

FLY BY NIGHT by Ed Sala; Director, Jerry Grayson; Set, Anthony Ross; Lighting, Matt Ehlert; Costumes, Mary Gottlieb; Sound, David Lawson; Stage Managers, Marcia Simon, Shelley Ginsberg
CAST: Barbara Luna (Lenore Lundy Randolph), Gavin Troster (Dudley Randolph), K. Lype O'Dell (Broderick Robinson), Billie A. Stewart (Millie Robinson), William Pitts (Prof. Etheridge)
   A comedy in 2 acts and 5 scenes. The action takes place at the present time in Lenore Lundy Randolph's attic apartment.
   Friday, Aug. 30,–Sept. 29, 1985 (15 performances and 9 previews)

MEMORIES OF RIDING WITH JOE COOL by Christopher Gerard and Bill Hooey; Director, Christopher Gerard; Sets, Anthony Ross; Lighting, Dave Feldman; Costumes, Lisa Lo Curto; Hairstylist, Irene Smith; Stage Manager, Richard Fisher
CAST: P. J. Benjamin (Max), John Joseph Tribbie (Bill), Char Fontaine (Helen/Kate), Donna Drake (Lydia), Billie A. Stewart (Susan), David Gale (Bill, Sr.), Cassandra Malaxa (Gloria/Lois), Van Farrier (Brett)
   A play in two acts. The action passes between the present and the past.
   Friday, Oct. 11,–Nov. 3, 1985 (20 performances)

THE TROLL PALACE by John Martin and Dudley Stone; Director, Diane Miner; Set, Anthony Ross; Lighting, Donald Edmund Thomas; Costumes, Van Broughton Ramsey; Sound, David Lawson; Masks, Kathryn Ross; Stage Managers, Jonathan Shulman, Jeanne Ward; Presented by CHS Productions and Rodney Productions in association with Riverwest.
CAST: Richard Merrell (Bass), Tom Tammi (Julian Stratton), John Seidman (Andrew Stratton), Ron Randell (Col. Lionel Stratton), Kim Zimmer (Winifred Stratton), Lukas Skipitaris (Rashid Sham'oun), Ava Haddad (Razilee Sham'oun)
   A murder mystery in 3 acts and 5 scenes. The action takes place in 1975 in the drawing room of Biddington Hall in the county of Norfolk, England.
   Friday, Jan. 17,–Feb. 9, 1986 (21 performances)

THE CAMEL HAS HIS NOSE UNDER THE TENT by Andre Ernotte and Elliot Tiber; Directed by the authors; Lighting, Matt Ehlert; Sound, David Lawson; Scenery, Anthony Ross; Costumes, Vicki Davis
CAST: Burt Edwards, Drinda LaLumia, Richard Merrell, Katie C. Sparer, and the voice of June Summers.
   A comedy in two acts.
   Thursday, Feb. 20,–March 30, 1986 (32 performances)

DEAD WRONG by Nick Hall; Director, Bill Gile; Set, Anthony Ross; Costumes, Van Broughton Ramsey; Lighting, Matt Ehlert; Sound, David Lawson; Casting, Slater/Willett; Stage Managers, Jonathan Shulman, James Nantz
CAST: David Groh (Craig Blaisdell), Anita Gillette (Peggy Blaisdell), Michael Wilding (Allen Gauthier), Lachlan MacLeay (Detective Walter Scott)
   A suspense play in 2 acts and 3 scenes. The action takes place at the present time during early autumn in the living room of the Blaisdell cottage in Mt. Kisko, NY.

Anita & Steve Shevett Photos

Gavin Troster, Barbara Luna
in "Fly by Night"

John Joseph Tribbie, P. J. Benjamin
in "Memories of Riding with Joe Cool"
(Gerry Goodstein Photo)

Michael Wilding, Anita Gillette
in "Dead Wrong" Above: Richard Merrell,
Ron Randell, Kim Zimmer in "Troll Palace"

ROUNDABOUT THEATRE

August 1, 1985–July 13, 1986
Twentieth Season

Artistic Director, Gene Feist; Managing Director, Todd Haimes; General Manager, Ellen Richard; Development, Vicki Reiss; Marketing, Michael P. Lynch; Literary Manager, Eileen Cowel; Technical Director, Patrick Kelly; Costumes, Robert Pusilo, Lynn Hoffman, Debbie Larkin; Musical Director/Sound Design, Philip Campanella; Hairstylists, Tomo 'n' Tomo, Linda Wager; Stage Managers, K. Siobhan Phelan, Matthew Mundinger; Casting, David Tochterman; Press, Solters/ Roskin/ Friedman, Adrian Bryan-Brown, Joshua Ellis, Keith Sherman, Cindy Valk, Jackie Green, Andrew Hirshfield, Jim Sapp

(Christian C. Yegen Theatre) Thursday, Aug. 1,–Sept. 7, 1985 (55 performances)
SPRINGTIME FOR HENRY by Benn W. Levy; Director, Tony Tanner, Set, Holmes Easley; Lighting, Barry Arnold; Furs, Ben Kahn; Production Assistant, Jennifer J. Wollan
CAST: Peter Evans (Mr. Dewlip), George N. Martin (Mr. Jelliwell), Tovah Feldshuh (Mrs. Jelliwell), Jodi Thelen (Mrs. Smith)
A farce in three acts. The action takes place in the sitting room of Mr. Dewlip's flat in the spring of 1932.

Saturday, Oct. 12,–Nov. 10, 1985 (31 performances and 24 previews)
THE WALTZ OF THE TOREADORS by Jean Anouilh; Translation, Lucienne Hill; Director, Richard Russell Ramos; Set, Kate Edmunds; Lighting, Barry Arnold; Wigs, Bruce Geller; Stage Manager, Kathy J. Faul
CAST: Tammy Grimes (Mme. St. Pe), Lee Richardson (Gen. St. Pe), Eric Swanson (Gaston), Jane Jones (Sidonie), Amanda Carlin (Estelle), Alvin Epstein (Dr. Bonfant), Elizabeth Owens (Eugenie/ Mme. Dupont-Fredaine), Carole Shelley (Mlle. de Ste.-Euverte), Wyman Pendleton (Father Ambrose), Whitney Reis (Pamela)
A comedy in 3 acts and 5 scenes. The action takes place in the study of General St. Pe and in his wife's adjoining bedroom.

Wednesday, Nov. 27, 1985, moved to Haft Theatre Thursday, Jan. 23,–Feb. 9, 1986 (93 performances)
MRS. WARREN'S PROFESSION by George Bernard Shaw; Director, John Madden; Set, Andrew Jackness; Costumes, Nan Cibula; Lighting, Frances Aronson; Wigs, Bruce Geller, Hats, Rodney Gordon; Production Assistant, Galit Zimbalist
CAST: Pamela Reed (Vivie Warren), George Morfogen (Praed), Uta Hagen (Mrs. Kitty Warren), Harris Yulin (Sir George Crofts), William Converse-Roberts (Frank Gardner), Gordon Sterne (Rev. Samuel Gardner)
A play in four acts and one intermission. The action takes place in the garden of a rented cottage near Haslemere, Surrey, England; inside the cottage; the rectory garden; Honoria Fraser's chambers in Chauncery Lane, London.

Wednesday, Jan. 29,–March 23, 1986 (46 performances and 18 previews)
ROOM SERVICE by John Murray, Allen Boretz; Director, Alan Arkin; Set, Daniel Ettinger; Costumes, A. Christina Giannini; Lighting, Barry Arnold; Props, David Ellis; Production Assistant, Deborah J. Larkin; Stage Manager, Kathy J. Faul
CAST: Mark Hamill (Gordon Miller), Andrew Bloch (Harry Binion), Barbara Dana (Hilda Manney), MacIntyre Dixon (Simon Jenkins/Timothy Hogarth), Pierre Epstein (Sasha Smirnoff), Timothy Jerome (Dr. Glass/Senator Blake), Kurt Knudson (Gregory Wagner), Ann McDonough (Christine Marlowe), Lonny Price (Faker Englund), Keith Reddin (Leo Davis), Eugene Troobnick (Joseph Gribble), Anthony Arkin (Bank Messenger)
A farce in three acts. The action takes place in Gordon Miller's room in the White Way Hotel in New York.

Saturday, March 29,–May 11, 1986 (56 performances)
CHEAPSIDE by David Allen; Director, Carey Perloff; Set, Adrianne Lobel; Costumes, Susan Hilferty; Lighting, James F. Ingalls; Props, Patricia Bobo; Production Assistant, Ron Williams; Presented in association with Lucille Lortel
CAST: Daniel Gerroll (Robert Greene), Robert Stanton (William Shakespeare), Dennis Boutsikaris (Christopher Marlowe), Joe Morton (Cutting Ball), Susan Cash (Alice), Robin Bartlett (Mary Frith)
A drama in two acts. The action takes place in Sixteenth Century London.

Wednesday, May 21,–July 13, 1986 (60 performances)
MASTER CLASS by David Pownall; Director, Frank Corsaro; Set/Costumes, Franco Colavecchia; Lighting, Robert Wierzel; Original Compositions/ Arrangements, John White; Musical Director, Jack Lee; Wig, Paul Huntley; Props, Patricia Bobo; Choreography, John Montgomery; Stage Manager, Kathy J. Faul
CAST: Philip Bosco (Zhdanov), Werner Klemperer (Prokofiev), Austin Pendleton (Shostakovich), Len Cariou (Stalin)
A drama in two acts. The action takes place on an evening in January of 1984 in a room in the Kremlin.

Martha Swope Photos

**Top Right: Lee Richardson, Tammy Grimes
in "Waltz of the Toreadors" Daniel Gerroll,
Joe Morton in "Cheapside" Below: William
Converse-Roberts, Gordon Sterne, Uta Hagen,
Pamela Reed, Harris Yulin, George Morfogen
in "Mrs. Warren's Profession" Below: Barbara
Dana, Andrew Bloch, Keith Reddin, Lonny Price,
Mark Hamill in "Room Service"**

**Jodi Thelen, Peter Evans, Tovah Feldshuh,
George N. Martin in "Springtime for Henry"**

THE SECOND STAGE

June 25, 1985–July 15, 1986
Sixth Season

Artistic Directors, Robyn Goodman, Carole Rothman; Managing Director, Rosa I. Vega; Marketing, Laura Kaminker, John Thew; Literary Manager/Dramaturg, Kim Powers; Business Manager, Elizabeth McHugh; Production Supervisor, Lawrence Rosenthal; Casting, Simon/Kumin; Technical Director, David Crist; Press, Richard Kornberg

(McGinn/Cazale Theatre) Tuesday, June 25,–Aug. 11, 1985 (48 performances)
SISTER AND MISS LEXIE based on the works of Eudora Welty; Adapted by David Kaplan, Brenda Currin; Director, David Kaplan; Set/Costumes, Susan Hilferty; Lighting, Ken Tabachnick; Sound, Gary Harris; Hair, Antonio Soddu; Production Supervisor, Kim Novick; Technical Director, Tom Pavelka; Wardrobe, Clare Gosney; Stage Managers, Kathi Guy, Dominick Balletta
CAST: Brenda Currin, and pianists Karen Weingort, Katy Zhukov
  A solo performance without intermission.
  Sunday, Nov. 17, 1985–Jan. 19, 1986 (53 performances)
LEMON SKY by Lanford Wilson; Director, Mary B. Robinson; Set, G. W. Mercier; Costumes, Connie Singer; Lighting, Stephen Strawbridge; Sound, Gary Harris; Technical Director, Dave Morkal; Props, Elsbeth Collins; Stage Managers, Lawrence Eaton, Stephanie Burda
CAST: Jeff Daniels (Alan), Wayne Tippit (Douglas), Jill Eikenberry (Ronnie), Laura White (Penny), Cynthia Nixon (Carol), Cameron Charles Johann (Jerry), Patrick Koch (Jack)
  The action takes place in 1970 and the late 1950's in a suburb of San Diego.
  Monday, Feb. 3,–March 9, 1986 (35 performances)
BLACK GIRL by J. E. Franklin; Director, Glenda Dickerson; Choreography, Dianne McIntyre; Set, Charles H. McClennahan; Lighting, Marshall Williams; Costumes, Ellen Ellis Lee; Sound, Gary Harris; Hair, Antonio Soddu; Technical Directors, Scott C. Parker, Walter Ulasinsky; Props, Bill Lipscomb; Stage Managers, Pamela Edington, Roy Harris
CAST: Terry Alexander (Earl), Angela Bassett (Ruth Ann), Ann Marie Cavener (Sheryl), Arthur French (Mr. Herbert), Ernestine Jackson (Rosie), Shawn Judge (Netta), Herbert L. Newsome III (Little Earl), Kimberly Russell (Billie Jean), Myra Taylor (Norma Faye), Yvonne Warden (Mu'Dear)
  Performed without intermission. The action takes place in a small Texas town.
  Friday, April 4,–27, 1986 (26 performances)
RICH RELATIONS by David Hwang; Director, Harry Kondoleon; Set, Kevin Rupnik; Lighting, Pat Collins; Costumes, Candice Donnelly; Sound, Gary Harris; Props, Melissa L. Burdick, Judy Guralnick; Wardrobe, Stephanie Handler; Stage Managers, Robin Rumpf, Roy Harris
CAST: Joe Silver (Hinson), Keith Szarabajka (Keith), Phoebe Cates (Jill), Susan Kellermann (Barbara), Johann Carlo (Marilyn)
  A play in two acts. The action takes place at the present time in the second living room of a large home in the hills above Los Angeles.
  Tuesday, May 27,–July 15, 1986 (44 performances)
THE FURTHER ADVENTURES OF KATHY AND MO written and performed by Kathy Najimy and Mo Gaffney; Director, Don Scardino; Set, Andrew Jackness; Lighting, Joshua Dachs; Costumes, Gregg Barnes; Sound, Gary Harris; Hair/Makeup, Charles Joseph Berry; Musical Director, Steven Gunderson; Production Assistants, Robin Abrams, Drea Brandford, Jennifer Smul; Stage Managers, Pamela Edington, Roy Harris
  Performed with one intermission.

Stephanie Saia Photos

Angela Basset, Terry Alexander, Myra Taylor
in "Black Girl" Below: Wayne Tippit, Jeff
Daniels in "Lemon Sky"

Brenda Currin
in "Sister and Miss Lexie"

Kathy Najimy, Mo Gaffney
in "The Further Adventures
of Kathy and Mo"

116

SOHO REPERTORY THEATRE

February 14,–June 22, 1986
Eleventh Season

Artistic Directors, Jerry Engelbach, Marlene Swartz; Business Manager, Laurie J. Greenwald; Dramaturg, Victor Gluck

(Greenwich House) Friday, Feb. 14,–March 9, 1986 (20 performances)

THE TWO ORPHANS by Adolphe D'Ennery and Eugene Corma; Translation, John Oxenford; Additional Text, Julian Webber; Director, Julian Webber; Sets, Daniel Conway; Costumes, Patricia Adshead; Fight Director, Jim Manley; Lighting, David Noling; Musical Score, Marshall Coid; Stage Managers, Alice Permutter, Kimberly Van Dyke, Rita M. Long

CAST: Suzanne Ford (Henrietta), Ellen Mareneck (Louise), Richard Abernethy (Marquis de Presles), Edward Trotta (Count de Mailly/Policeman), David Pursley (LaFleur/Marais), Herbert DuVal (Martin/Doctor), Michael Sexton (Henchman/Policeman/Guest), Andy Thain (Henchman/Policeman/Guest), Mimi Bensinger (LaFrochard/Sister Genevieve), Bill Jacob (Pierre), Thomas G. Waites (Jacques), Laura Pierce (Marianne), Robert Hock (Count de Linieres), Lois Markle (Countess de Linieres), Victor Talmadge (Armand), Avrom Berel (Picard), Kathryn Shield (Florette), Audrey Anderson (Julie/Guest), Kimberly Van Dyke (Yvette/Guest)

A melodrama in two acts, set in Paris on the eve of the French Revolution.

(Greenwich House) Friday, April 4–27, 1986 (16 performances)

ONE FINE DAY by Nicholas Wright; Director, Tazewell Thompson; Sets, Joseph A. Varga; Costumes, Laura Drawbaugh; Lighting, David Noling; Dialect Coach, Zubeida Tumbo-Masabo; Stage Manager, Dian Hartdagen.

CAST: Jaison Walker (Starford), Gerald Gilmore (Frank), Scott Whitehurst (Nkwabi), LaDonna Mabry (Violet), Evan O'Meara (Steve Winter), Lex Monson (Kaduma), Todd Jackson (Mzoga).

American Premiere of an East African comedy. The action takes place in Tanzania at the present time.

(Greenwich House) Friday, May 30,–June 22, 1986 (16 performances)

THE GRUB-STREET OPERA by Henry Fielding; World Premiere of new score by Anthony Bowles; Director, Anthony Bowles; Music Director, Robert Grusecki; Sets, Alison Ford; Lighting, David Noling; Costumes, Gabriel Berry; Technical Director, Mark S. Henry; Stage Manager, Alice Permutter

CAST: Richard T. Alpers (Fielding/John), Ward Asquith (Apshones), Fred Winhorn (William), Colleen Fitzpatrick (Sweetissa), Avril Gentles (Apshinken), Peter Jensen (Master Owen), Nita Novy (Susan), David Pursley (Sir Owen), Steve Sterner (Robin), Sharon Watroba (Margery), Lee Winston (Puzzletext), Helen Zelon (Molly)

A musical comedy set in Wales in 1731.

Evan O'Meara, Jaison Walker, Scott Whitehurst in "One Fine Day"
Top Right: Ellen Mareneck, Suzanne Ford in "The Two Orphans"
Gerry Goodstein Photos

117

STARET. . . . THE DIRECTORS COMPANY

Artistic Director, Michael Parva; Producing/Managing Director, Victoria Lanman; Resident Master Director, Stephen Zuckerman; Production Manager, Kathy Uhler; Literary Manager, Michael Norton; Assistant to Producers, Jill Mackavey; Production Assistant, Jim Bumgardner

(Staret's Workshop Space 603) Monday, June 16,–July 11, 1985 (12 performances)

THE STRONGER and CREDITORS by August Strindberg; Director, Terry Dudley; Scenery, Gregory L. Haydock; Lighting, William J. Plachy; Costumes, S. L. Bornstein; Sound, Paul Winnicky; Technical Director, Beau Kennedy; Stage Manager, Nora Giessen

CAST: Peter Harris, Cathy Lind Hayes, Robert Hock, Elizabeth Pearson, Aviva Skell

Two one-act plays.

(Space 603) Saturday, June 22,–July 15, 1985 (12 performances)

MIRANDOLINA by Goldoni; Director, Tim Sanford; Scenery, Gregory L. Haydock; Lighting, William J. Plachy; Costumes, S. L. Bornstein; Technical Director, Beau Kennedy; Sound, Paul Winnicky; Stage Manager, Valerie Park

CAST: Bill Mesnik (Marquis of Forlipopali), Victor Talmadge (Count of Albafiorita), Dy Llowell (Fabrizio), Michael Hill (Baron Ripafratta), Patricia Triana (Mirandolina), Arnold Bankston (Baron's Servant)

An 18th Century Italian farce in 3 acts and 4 scenes. The action takes place in Mirandolina's inn in Florence, Italy, in 1753.

(Musical Theatre Works) Monday, July 15,–August 2, 1985 (13 performances)

A MIDSUMMER NIGHT'S DREAM by William Shakespeare; Director, Stephen Zuckerman; Set, James Fenhagen; Lighting, William Plachy; Costumes, Mimi Maxmen; Sound, Paul Winnicky; Choreographer, Alyce Bochette; Production Manager, Kathy Uhler; Technical Director, Beau Kennedy; Props, John Moser; Stage Managers, Michael S. Mantel, Valerie Park

CAST: Mark Metcalf (Theseus/Oberon), Kristin Griffith (Hippolyta/Titania), Kevin O'Rourke (Egeus/Snug/Peaseblossom), Janet Zarish (Hermia), Norman Snow (Demetrius), Ken Marshall (Lysander), Jodi Long (Helena), John Bowman (Bottom), Stephen Stout (Peter Quince), David Daly (Flute), Ann Janowsky (Robin Starveling/Mustardseed), Kathy Rossetter (Tina Snout/Cobweb), Barbara Garrick (Puck), Thea Dahlberg (1st Fairy/Phyllis Straight)

A comedy in two acts. The action takes place in and around a high school in America in 1963.

(Musical Theatre Works) Thursday, Aug. 8–31, 1985 (19 performances)

TALES OF TINSELTOWN with Music by Paul Katz; Libretto by Michael Colby; Director, Rick Lombardo; Staging, Dennis Dennehy, Rick Lombardo; Musical Direction, James Stenborg; Choreography, Dennis Dennehy; Scenery, Alexander Okun; Costumes, Michele Reisch; Lighting, Jason Kantrowitz; Musical Coordinator, Steven M. Alper; Wigs, Elizabeth Katherine Carr; Stage Managers, Karen L. Carpenter, Michael C. Naccari; Press, FLT/Francine L. Trevens

CAST: Elizabeth Austin (Ellie Ash), Alison Fraser (Lulu Beauveen), Greg Mowry (Tommy Burke), Olga Talyn (Adele DeRale), Jason Graae (Elmo Green), Bob Arnold (Norman G. Nertshmertz), Nora Mae Lyng (Bertha Powell), Nat Chandler (Antonio Toscanini), Laura Jaye-Greer (Standby)

MUSICAL NUMBERS: Tinseltown Tattletale, I Belong to Hollywood, Let's Go, N.G.N. Productions, Musical Melange, Full, I Can Sing, All over the Place, Hollywood Sign, The Tragedy of Miss Potato Sack, In Broken-Promise Land, I Knew It, Jungle Fever, So This Is the Movies, Alphabet Soup, At Sea, Just Laugh It Away, Hunchy, It's Mine, Oh the Scandal!, Nobody Shtomps on My Shtudio, Be Good, Bad!, Dream of Hollywood, I'll Stand by You, I'm Beautiful, Take Two, Ruin Them, Stars in My Eyes, Expose

A movieland musical in two acts.

Michael Holmes, Elizabeth Wolynski Photos
**Top Right: Alison Fraser, Bob Arnold
and below Bob Arnold, Olga Talyn
in "Tales of Tinseltown"**

**Ken Marshall, Janet Zarish, also above with
Norman Snow, Jodi Long in "Midsummer Night's Dream"**

VINEYARD THEATRE

June 11, 1985–June 29, 1986
Fifth Season

Executive Director, Barbara Zinn Krieger; Managing Director, Gary P. Steuer; General Manager, Susan Wilder; Artistic Director, Douglas Aibel; Press, Bruce Cohen, Kathleen von Schmid

Tuesday, June 11, 1985–July 5, 1985 (18 performances)
SOMEWHERES BETTER by William Wise; Director, Jeff Martin; Set, Johniene Papandreas; Lighting, Phil Monat; Costumes, Deborah Shaw; Sound, Aural Fixation; Production Manager, Susan Wilder; Assistant Director, Jane Slotin; Technical Director, David Raphel; Stage Managers, Crystal Huntington, Nancy Mutnick
CAST: Cameron Charles Johann (Evan Pickett), Stacey Glick (Annalee Pickett), Tom Stechschulte (Duff Pickett), Shelley Rogers (Wilma Pickett), Joseph D'Onofrio (Nicky Cordone), Robin Westphal (Robin Wells), Peter J. Saputo (Milt Goldstein)
A comedy-drama in two acts. The action takes place in the Yonkers apartment of the Picketts form October 1981 to January of 1982.

Thursday, Oct. 17,–Dec. 22, 1985 (58 performances) Re-opened at Circle in the Square Downtown on Wednesday, April 9, and closed June 29, 1986 (95 performances)
GOBLIN MARKET adapted by Peggy Harmon and Polly Pen from the poem by Christina Rossetti; Music, Polly Pen; Director, Andre Arnotte; Set, William Barclay; Lighting, Phil Monat; Costumes, Muriel Stockdale, Kitty Leech; Musical Direction, Lawrence Yurman; Choreography, Ara Fitzgerald; Orchestrations, James McElwaine; Production Manager, Susan Wilder; Hair, Marc Daniels; Technical Director, Scott Parker; Special Props, Amy Bock; Production Assistants, Kimbley Gilchrist, Lourdes Babauta; Stage Managers, Laura Heller, Shira Lynn Margulies
CAST: Terri Klausner succeeded by Sharon Scruggs (Laura), Ann Morrison (Lizzie)
MUSICAL NUMBERS: Come Buy, We Must Not Look, Mouth So Charmful, Do You Not Remember Jeanie, Sleep Laura Sleep, The Sisters, Some There Are Who Never Venture, Mirage, Passing Away, Here They Come, Like a Lilly, Lizzie Have You Tasted, Two Doves
A musical performed without intermission.

Thursday, Feb. 27,–March 23, 1986 (20 performances and 5 previews)
SORROWS AND SONS –three one-act plays by Stephen Metcalfe; Director, Peter Frisch; Set, James Wolk; Lighting, Richard Moore; Costumes, Jeffrey Ullman; Production Coordinator, Susan Wilder; Assistant to Director, Len Silver; Technical Director, Weng Ho; Props, Kathy Havemeyer; Wigs, Charles LoPresto; Stage Managers, Richard Costabile, Carol Fishman, Nancy Mutnick
CAST: "Sorrows and Sons" with Rafael Sbarge succeeded by Steven Flynn (Bucky), John Hallow (Edwin), Richard Thomsen (Burt). A college dorm room in Western Pennsylvania in October of 1974. "Spittin' Image" with Rafael Sbarge succeeded by Steven Flynn (Bucky), Dann Florek (Megs) The same room two months later. "Pilgrims: with Eddie Jones (Dee), Elizabeth Berridge (Jilly), Robert Tyler (Roy), Grant Shaud (Toole), Terri Hawkes (Marcia). The action takes place during June 1970 in a coffee shop in central Connecticut.

Thursday, May 29,–June 29, 1986 (20 performances and 3 previews)
LADY DAY AT EMERSON'S BAR & GRILL by Lanie Robertson; Director, Andre Ernotte; Musical Director, Danny Holgate; Set, William Barclay; Lighting, Phil Monat; Costumes, Muriel Stockdale; Sound, Phil Lee; Production Coordinator, Susan Wilder; Stage Manager, Crystal Huntington
CAST: Danny Holgate (Jimmy Powers), Lonette McKee (Billie Holiday), Rudy Stevenson (Buck Wilson), David Jackson (Frankie Lee Jones). Set in a seedy nightclub in Philadelphia in March of 1959, Billy Holiday is giving one of her last performances and singing 15 of her best known songs.

Carol Rosegg Photos

Stacey Glick, Shelley Rogers, Cameron Johann in "Somewheres Better"

Ann Morrison, Terri Klausner in "Goblin Market" *(Adam Newman Photo)*

Lonette McKee in "Lady Day at Emerson's Bar and Grill"

Terri Hawkes, Robert Tyler, Grant Shaud in "Soldiers and Sons"

119

WPA THEATRE

November 12, 1985–June 29, 1986
Ninth Season

Artistic Director, Kyle Renick; Managing Director, Wendy Bustard; Casting/Literary Adviser, Darlene Kaplan; Designer, Edward T. Gianfrancesco; Lighting, Craig Evans; Marketing, Nona Pipes; Technical Directors, David Caskie, Adam Hart; Props, Melissa Stephenson; Press, Milly Schoenbaum

Thursday, Nov. 12,–Dec. 8, 1985 (24 performances and 13 previews)
CRUISE CONTROL by Kevin Wade; Director, Norman Rene; Costumes, Walker Hicklin; Sound, Paul Garrity; Stage Manager, Mary Fran Loftus; Wardrobe, M. A. Neff; Hair/Makeup, David Banky
CAST: John Getz (Billy), Patricia Richardson (Linda), Derek D. Smith (Rick), Elizabeth Berridge (Suze)
A play in two acts. The action takes place during August of this year on an island off the mid-Atlantic coast.

Tuesday, Feb. 4,–March 2, 1986 (28 performances)
FRESH HORSES by Larry Ketron; Director, Dann Florek; Costumes, Don Newcomb; Sound, Aural Fixation; Assistant to Director, Kim Sharp; Stage Manager, Paul Mills Holmes
CAST: Suzy Amis (Jewel), Craig Sheffer (Larkin), Mark Benninghofen (Tipton), John Bowman (Sproles), Alice Haining (Christy), Haviland Morris (Ellen), Marissa Chibas succeeded by Cecilia Peck (Bobo)
A drama in two acts. The action takes place in and around a maintenance station abandoned by the railroad in a southern countryside during the spring.

Friday, April 4–27, 1986 (22 performances and 7 previews)
WASTED by Fred Gamel; Director, Clinton Turner Davis; Set, Charles H. McClennahan; Costumes, Don Newcomb; Sound, Paul Garrity; Military Adviser, Lee Russell; Stage Manager, David Lawrence Folender
CAST: Matt Mulhern succeeded by Burke Moses, Kevin Dwyer (Sgt. "Farm Boy" Kelly), Walter Allen Bennett, Jr. (1Cpl. "Spider" Evans), Eriq LaSalle (Cpl. "Hound" Bassett), Jace Alexander (LCpl. "Big Mac" MacNeill), Ramon Franco (Cpl. "Slick" Acevedo), Emil Herrera (Pfc. "Padre" Gomez), Alvin Alexis (Pfc. Earl Thomas), Erik King (Pfc. Roy Pruitt), Kevin Dwyer (Lt. Gary Blade)
A drama in two acts. The action takes place on April 6, 1968 in a coastal base camp near Chu Lai, Vietnam.

Tuesday, June 3,–29, 1986 (28 performances)
TRINITY SITE by Janeice Scarbrough; Director, William Ludel; Costumes, Don Newcomb; Stage Manager, David Lawrence Folender
CAST: Patricia Richardson (Lanell), Royana Black (Dale), Mark Metcalf (Marshall), Christopher Curry (Ingram)
A drama in two acts. The action takes place in New Mexico during the summer of 1945.

Martha Swope Photos

Right: Matt Mulhern, Walter Allen Bennett, Jr., Emil Herrera, Eriq LaSalle, Jace Alexander in "Wasted"
Top: Patricia Richardson, John Getz, Derek Smith, Elizabeth Berridge in "Cruise Control"

**Suzy Amis, Craig Sheffer
in "Fresh Horses"**

**Mark Metcalf, Patricia Richardson, Royana Black
in "Trinity Site"**

YORK THEATRE COMPANY

October 25, 1985–May 31, 1986
Seventeenth Season

Producing Director, Janet Hayes Walker; Managing Director, Molly Pickering Grose; Designer, James Morgan; Costumes, Martin Pakledinaz; Lighting, Christina Giannelli; Casting, Judy Henderson; Press, Keith Sherman

(Church of the Heavenly Rest) Friday, Oct. 25,–Nov. 17, 1985 (20 performances)
ON THE 20th CENTURY with Book and Lyrics by Betty Comden, Adolph Green; Based on play by Ben Hecht, Charles MacArthur and Bruce Millholland; Music, Cy Coleman; Direction/Choreography, Dennis Rosa; Musical Director, Lawrence W. Hill; Lighting, Mary Jo Dondlinger; Technical Director, Ed Bartosik; Wardrobe, Robert Swasey, Ivana Mestrovic; Props, Dejie Johnson, Steven McCloskey; Production Assistants, Mary Tokar, Kumi Tucker; Assistant Musical Director, Michael Mimbs; Stage Managers, Clifford Schwartz, Mark Menard
CAST: Jeff McCarthy (Oscar Jaffee), Victoria Brasser (Lily Garland), Tom Galantich (Bruce Granit), Leonard John Crofoot (Owen O'Malley), David Green (Oliver Webb), Robin Taylor (Letitia Primrose), Glenn Mure (Conductor/Congressman/Dr. Johnson), Ron Bohmer (Max Jacobs), Barbara McCulloh (Imelda Thornton), Mimi Bessette (Agnes), Deanna Wells (Anita), Steve Fickinger (Maxwell Finch/Cyril), Margaret Benczak (Nurse), John Blair (Attendant/Nigel), Tim Hunt (Lead Actor/Rodney), Ensemble: Margaret Benczak, Mimi Bessette, John Blair, Ron Bohmer, Steve Fickinger, Tim Hunt, Barbara McCulloh, Deanna Wells
MUSICAL NUMBERS: Stranded Again, On the 20th Century, I Rise Again, Indian Maiden's Lament, Veronique, I Have Written a Play, Together, Never, Our Private World, Repent, Mine, I've Got It All, Five Zeros, Sextet, She's a Nut, Max Jacobs, Babette, The Legacy, Lily Oscar
    A musical in two acts
    Friday, Jan. 17,–Feb. 2, 1986 (16 performances)
THE TIME OF THE CUCKOO by Arthur Laurents; Director, Stuart Howard; Original Music, David Evans; Sound, Tony Meola; Dialect Coach, Lilene Mansell; Technical Director, Deborah Alix Martin; Hair, Marc Daniels; Props, Carol Wiederrecht, Brynn Washington; Wardrobe, Robert Swasey, Joanna Ward; Stage Managers, Jane Neufeld, Brian Kaufman
CAST: Michael Learned (Leona Samish), Judith Roberts (Signora Fioria), Brent Barrett (Eddie Yeager), Debra Jo Rupp (June Yeager), Alexandra Gersten (Giovanna), Lois Markle (Mrs. McIlhenny), Wyman Pendleton (Mr. McIlhenny), Nickie Feliciano (Mauro), George Guidall (Renato DiRossi), Robert Cicchini (Vito)
    A play in two acts. The action occurs in the garden of Pensione Fioria, Venice, during the summer of 1952.
    (Paul Mazur Theatre) Wednesday, Feb. 12,–March 1, 1986 (16 performances)

MOBY DICK adapted from Herman Melville's novel of same title; Libretto, Mark St. Germain; Music/Musical Director, Doug Katsaros; Director, Thomas Gardner; Costumes, Sheila Kehoe; Lighting, Mary Jo Dondlinger; Technical Director, Deborah Alix Martin; Props, Steven McCloskey; Wardrobe, Robert Swasey; Assistant Musical Director, Mari Falcone; Stage Managers, Victor Lukas, Sandy Shannon
CAST: Richard Bowne (Boomer/Bildad/Mapple), Steven Blanchard (Capt. of Jeroboam/Bunger/Sailor), Victor Cook (Pip), Ed Dixon (Capt. Ahab), Michael Ingram (Stubb), Dennis Parlato (Starbuck), Buddy Rudolph (Ishmael), Gordon Stanley (Peleg/Capt. of Rachael), John Timmons (Elijah/Carpenter/Sailor), Louis Tucker (Queequeg)
MUSICAL NUMBERS: The Sea, The Sermon, What Makes Ye Go a Whaling?, Morning to Ye, Ahab, After Ye/Setting Sail, The Doubloon, Eight Bells, Stand By Me, Stubb's Song, The Whiteness, Every Morning, The Jeroboam, The Will, First Hunt, Pip's Song, White Whale, Thou Venerable Head, Boomer & Bunger, Queequeg Dying, Ahab and the Carpenter, My Boy, I Will Stay with You, Mild Day, Final Chase, Epilogue
    A musical in two acts.
    (Church of the Heavenly Rest) Friday, March 21,–April 13, 1986 (16 performances)
MACBETH by William Shakespeare; Director, Porter Van Zandt; Scenery/Graphics, James Morgan; Costumes, David Pearson; Lighting, Mary Jo Dondlinger; Sound, Keena Kaye; Fight Consultant, Nels Hennum; Assistant to Director, Gillian Shaw; Verse Coach, Maureen Clarke; Technical Director, Jim Jensen, Sally Smith; Props, Steven McCloskey; Wardrobe, Robert Swasey; Stage Managers, Lawrence Berrick, Angela Foster, Alice Farrell
CAST: J. Kenneth Campbell (Macbeth), Jude Ciccolella (Banquo), Gus Demos (Seyton/3rd Murderer/Servant), Norma Fire (1st Witch), Buck Hobbs (3rd Witch), Francesca James (Lady Macbeth), Chet London (King Duncan), Richard Marshall (Angus), Bill Mesnik (Porter/Old Siward), Kam Metcalf (Fleance/Messenger), Bob J. Mitchell (Ross), Vincent Niemann (Scottish Doctor/Old Man), Matt Penn (Murderer 1/Caithness), Noni Pratt (Witch 2), Jim Pratzon (Donalbain), Jay O. Sanders (MacDuff), Elizabeth A. Soukup (Lady MacDuff), Jim Stubbs (Malcolm), John Tillotson (Lenox), Carl Tyson (Little MacDuff), Ralph David Westfall (Murderer 2/Mentieth/Lord Chamberlain)
    Performed with one intermission.
    (Paul Mazur Theatre) Thursday, May 15–31, 1986 (15 performances)
TALLEY'S FOLLY by Lanford Wilson; Director, David Feldshuh; Set, Daniel Ettinger; Costumes, Carol Wiederrecht; Lighting, Michael Baumgarten; Sound, Bill Bradbury; Assistant Stage Manager/Wardrobe, Robert Swasey; Program Coordinator, Kate Grinnell; Technical Director, Jim Jensen; Stage Managers, Jessica Christie, Loretta Grande
CAST: Katie Grant (Sally), Eugene Troobnick (Matt)
    Performed without intermission. The action takes place in an old boathouse on the Talley Place near Lebanon, Missouri, on a July evening in 1944.

Dennis Parlato, Ed Dixon, Buddy Rudolph
in "Moby Dick" Top: George Guidall,
Michael Learned in "The Time of the Cuckoo"

Katie Grant, Eugene Troobnick in "Talley's Folly"
Above: J. Kenneth Campbell, Francesca James
in "Macbeth"

Carol Rosegg/Martha Swope Photos

121

NATIONAL TOURING COMPANIES
(Failure to meet deadline necessitated omissions)

ANNIE

Book, Thomas Meehan; Music, Charles Strouse; Lyrics, Martin Charnin; Director, Sam A. Jerris; Musical Director, Corinne Jerris Aquilina; Choreography, Carla Roetzer Vitale; Producer, James Vollertsen; Based on the comic strip "Little Orphan Annie"; Scenery/Props, Michael J. Hotopp, Paul DePass; Costumes, Theoni V. Aldredge; Lighting, Tom Hennes; Orchestrations, Philip Lang; Production Supervisor, Karl Lengel; Sound, Gary Dean Moeller; Animal Trainer, William Berloni; Company Manager, Sam A. Jerris; Props, Jon P. Sweet, Lenore Nalezny Shoults; Wardrobe, Barbara Oleszczuk; Hair/Makeup, Mary Jo Foresta; Stage Managers, Dale Kaufman, John Grimsley, Tom Kirk. Opened in the Auditorium Theatre, Rochester, NY, on Friday, January 3, 1986 and still touring May 31, 1986.

CAST

Molly	Erin Daly
Pepper	Kristen A. Schmitz
July	Allison Harvey
Tessie	Janna Robinson
Kate	Nicole Anthony
Duffy	Molly Beth Totten
Annie	Sarah Bethany Reynolds
Miss Hannigan	Teri Gibson
Bundles	Brett C. Rosborough
Apple Seller/Mrs. Pugh/Bonnie	Becky Garrett
Dog Catchers	Richard Bitsko, Tom Kirk
Sandy	Moose
Lt. Ward/Sound Effects Man/Hull	Tom Vazzana
Sophie/Mrs. Greer	Jane Strauss
Eddie/Honor Guard	Frank Stancati
Grace Farrell	Leslie Castay
Drake	Michael Oliver
Cecille/Perkins	Janetta Betz
Annette	Marilyn Kay Huelsman
Oliver Warbucks	Robert Tiffany
Star to Be/Connie Boylan	Nanette Gordon
Rooster Hannigan	Don Cohen
Lily St. Regis	Meryl Natter
Bert Healy/Howe	Brett C. Rosborough
Fred McCracken/Morganthau	Tom Kirk
Jimmy Johnson/Ickes	Richard Bitsko
Ronni Boylan	Marilyn Kay Huelsman
F.D.R.	Ron Wisniski

UNDERSTUDIES: Stephanie Kae Seeley (Annie), Michael Mulheren (Warbucks), Janetta Betz (Lily), Jane Strauss (Miss Hannigan), Richard Bitsko (F.D.R.), Frank Stancati (Rooster), Marilyn Kay Huelsman (Grace), Swings: Paula Betlem, Michael Mulheren

MUSICAL NUMBERS: Maybe, It's the Hard-Knock Life, Tomorrow, We'd Like to Thank You, Little Girls, I Think I'm Gonna Like It Here, N.Y.C., Easy Street, You Won't Be an Orphan For Long, You're Never Fully Dressed without a Smile, Something Was Missing, I Don't Need Anything But You, Annie, A New Deal for Christmas

A musical in 2 acts and 12 scenes. The action takes place from December 11–25, 1933 in NYC. For original Broadway production, see THEATRE WORLD Vol. 33.

(no photos available)

Top Right: (clockwise from top left) Simon Jones, Lise Hilboldt, George Ede, Claudette Colbert, Rex Harrison in "Aren't We All?"

AREN'T WE ALL?

By Frederick Lonsdale; Director, Clifford Williams; Sets, Finaly James; Costumes, Judith Bland; Lighting, Natasha Katz; Sound, Jan Nebozenko; Casting, Hughes/Moss; General Management, Kingwill & Goossen; Presented by Douglas Urbanski, Karl Allison, Bryan Bantry, James M. Nederlander, in association with Duncan C. Weldon, with Paul Gregg, Lionel Becker, Jerome Minskoff; Associate Producers, Robert Michael Geisler, John Roberdeau; Props, Liam Herbert; Wardrobe, James M. Kabel; Hairstylist, David H. Lawrence; Wigs and Hairstyles, Paul Huntley; Original Music, David Firman; Stage Managers, Warren Crane, William Weaver, David Silber; Press, Solters/Roskin/Friedman, Joshua Ellis, Cindy Valk, Adrian Bryan-Brown, Keith Sherman. Opened in the Curran Theatre San Francisco, Ca., September 24, 1985 and closed in Kennedy Center Opera House, Jan. 5, 1986.

CAST

Morton	Richard Neilson
Honorable William Tatham	Simon Jones †1
Lady Frinton	Claudette Colbert
Arthur Wells	Steven Sutherland †2
Martin Steele	John Patrick Hurley
Kitty Lake	Leslie O'Hara
Lord Grenham	Rex Harrison
Hon. Mrs. W. Tatham	Lise Hilboldt
Roberts	George Ede †3
Angela Lynton	Joyce Worsley
Reverend Ernest Lynton	George Rose †4
John Willocks	Ned Schmidtke

A comedy in 2 acts and 4 scenes. The action takes place in William Tatham's house in Mayfair, and in Grenham Court.
UNDERSTUDIES: Richard Neilson (Grenham), Leslie O'Hara (Mrs. Tatham), George Ede (Rev. Lynton), John Patrick Hurley (Willocks), Steven Sutherland (Tatham), David Silber (Morton/Roberts/Arthur/Martin), Betty Low (Lady Frinton/Mrs. Lynton)

†Succeeded by: 1. Steven Sutherland, 2. David Silber, 3. Leo Leyden, 4. George Ede, 5. Leo Leyden, 6. David Silver, 7. John Curless

Martha Swope Photos

BILOXI BLUES

By Neil Simon; Director, Gene Saks; Set, David Mitchell; Costumes, Ann Roth; Lighting, Tharon Musser; Presented by Emanuel Azenberg; Assistant Director, Bill Molloy; Sound, Tom Morse; Casting, Meg Simon/Fran Kumin; General Manager, Robert Kamlot; Technical Supervision, Theatrical Services; Props, Jan Marasek; Company Manager, Noel Gilmore; Consultant, Jose Vega; Props, Brian DeVerna; Wardrobe, Kathleen Sullivan; Stage Managers, Frank Marino, Greg Johnson, Linnea Sundsten; Press, Bill Evans, Sandra Manley, Jim Baldassare, Marlene DeSavino. Opened in the Fox Theatre in Atlanta, Ga., on Tuesday, May 27, 1986.

CAST

Roy Selridge	John Younger
Joseph Wykowski	David Warshofsky
Don Carney	John C. MacKenzie
Eugene Morris Jerome	William Ragsdale
Arnold Epstein	Andrew Polk
Sgt. Merwin J. Toomey	Ted Levine †
James Hennesey	Michael McNeill
Rowena	Kathy Danzer
Daisy Hannigan	Marita Geraghty

UNDERSTUDIES: David Nackman/Michael McNeill (Eugene), David Nackman (Epstein), Milton Elliott (Selridge/Wykowski/Hennesey), Michael McNeill (Carney), Kenneth Kay (Toomey), Linnea Sundsten (Rowena), Kelly Baker (Daisy)

A comedy in 2 acts and 14 scenes. The action takes place in Biloxi and Gulfport, Mississippi, in 1943.

†Succeeded by John Finn.

Martha Swope Photos

Top Right: Kathy Danzer, William Ragsdale in "Biloxi Blues"

Martha Traverse, Richard Harris in "Camelot"

CAMELOT

Book and Lyrics, Alan Jay Lerner; Music, Frederick Loewe; Staged and Directed by Richard Harris; Sets, Tom Barnes; Lighting, Ruth Roberts; Sound, Sherman F. Steadman; Costumes, Shirley Bird Gray; Choreography, Norb Joerder; Additional Costumes, Michael Bottari, Ronald Case; Musical Director, Terry James; Presented by Excaliber Productions; Associate Producer/General Manager, James M. Sullivan; Company Manager, Douglas C. Baker; Musical Director, Terry James; Props, Glenn F. Belfer; Wardrobe, Shirley Bird Gray; Stage Manager, Dianne Trulock; Press, Molly Smyth. Opened on June 4, 1985 in Minneapolis, Mn., and closed December 21, 1985 in Toronto, Canada.

CAST

Arthur	Richard Harris
Sir Sagramore	Gregg Busch
Merlyn/King Pellinore	James Valentine
Merlyn Sprites	Norb Joerder, John Nicoletti, Tony Lillo
Guenevere	Martha Traverse
Sir Dinadan	Patrick Godfrey
Nimue/Lady Sybil	Marcia Brushingham
Nimue's Nymphs	Karen Luschar, Nancy Meadows, Sally Stotts
Lancelot du Lac	Chip Huddleston
Mordred	Andy McAvin
Tom of Warwick/Young Arthur	William Thomas Bookmyer
Musician/Sir Castor	Dean G. Watts
Lady Anne	Mary Gaebler
Lady Margaret	Julie Ann Fogt
Sir Lionel	William James
Jester	S. Chris Pender
Squire Dap/Turquine	Roubert Ousley
Horrid	Sean Sable Belevedere
Herald	John Nicoletti
Sir Bliant/Forest Merlyn	John Deyle
Lord Chancellor	James Van Treuren
Court Dancer	Norb Joerder
Wenches	Darleigh Miller, Susan Van Cott

ENSEMBLE: Eric Alderfer, Marcia Brushingham, Gregg Busch, John Deyle, Julie Ann Fogt, Mary Gaebler, Patrick Godfrey, William James, Norb Joerder, Tony Lillo, Karen Luschar, Nancy Meadows, Darleigh Miller, John Nicoletti, Robert Ousley, S. Chris Pender, Tom Russell, Sally Stotts, Susan Van Cott, James Van Treuren, Dean G. Watts, Swings: Raymond Dragen, Karen Luschar

MUSICAL NUMBERS: Guenevere, I Wonder What the King Is Doing Tonight, The Simple Joys of Maidenhood, Camelot, Follow Me, Madrigal, C'Est Moi, The Lusty Month of May, Take Me to the Fair, How to Handle a Woman, The Jousts, Before I Gaze at You Again, If Ever I Would Leave You, Seven Deadly Virtues, Fie on Goodness, What Do the Simple Folk Do?, I Loved You Once in Silence

A musical in 2 acts and 16 scenes with a prologue.

CATS

Company Manager, Martin Cohen; Musical Directors, Tom Helm, Kristin Blodgett, Ross Allen, Tony Geralis; Dance Captain, Joseph Konicki, Richard Stafford; General Management, Gatchell & Neufeld; Wigs, Paul Huntley; Makeup, Candace Carell; Assistant Company Manager, Tony Magner; Stage Managers, Jake Bell, Dan Hild, Marbeth Abel; Press, Fred Nathan, Anne Abrams, Bert Fink, Dennis Crowley, Merle Frimark, Larry Reitzer. Opened in Boston's Shubert Theatre on Wednesday, December 21, 1983 and still touring May 31, 1986. For original creative credits, and musical numbers, see Broadway calendar.

CAST

Alonzo/Rumpus Cat .... Jamie Patterson †1
Bustopher Jones/Asparagus/Growltiger .... Sal Mistretta †2
Bombalurina .... Cindi Klinger
Cassandra .... Charlotte d'Amboise †3
Coricopat .... Allen Hidalgo †4
Demeter .... Pamela Blasetti †5
Grizabella .... Diane Fratantoni †6
Jellylorum .... Jennifer Butt
Jennyanydots .... Cindy Benson †7
Mistoffelees .... Jaime Torcellini †8
Mungojerrie .... Todd Lester
Munkustrap .... Mark Dovey †9
Old Deuteronomy .... Calvin E. Remsberg
Plato/Macavity .... Russell Warfield
Pouncival .... Barry K. Bernal †10
Rum Tum Tugger .... Rich Hebert †11
Rumpleteazer .... Kelli Ann McNally
Sillabub .... Tina Decker †12
Skimbleshanks .... Anthony Whigas †13
Tantomile .... Tori Brenno †14
Tumblebrutus .... Thomas McManus †15
Victoria .... Susan Zaguirre
Cats Chorus: Janene Lovullo †16, Susanna Wells †17, John Dewar †18, Bill Nolte †19

†Succeeded by: 1. Fred Anderson, 2. John Dewar, Bill Carmichael, 3. Jessica Northrup, Kim Noor, 4. Bob Amore, 5. Dorothy Tancredi, Diana Kavilis, 6. Janene Lovullo, 7. Sally Ann Swarm, 8. Marvin Engran, Mark Esposito, 9. Scott Dainton, 10. Brian Jay, 11. Paul Mack, 12. Joanne Baum, 13. Willie Rosario, Danny Rounds, 14. Stephanie McConlough, Patricia Forestier, 15. Mark Esposito, Tony Jaeger, 16. Sally Ann Swarm, Victoria Clark, 17. Anna Marie Gutierrez, 18. Bill Carmichael, Richard Poole, 19. Clent Bowers, R. F. Daley

CATS

Musical Director, Kevin Farrell; General Management, Gatchell & Neufeld; Production Supervisor, David Taylor; Dance Supervisor, T. Michael Reed; Company Manager, Barbara Seinfeld; Dance Captain, Greg Minahan; Assistant Conductor, John Berkman; Props, George Green, Jr., Edward Schnedk, John Alfredo, Jr.; Wardrobe, Dorothy Priest; Hairstylist, Leon Gagliardi, Wayne Herndon; Stage Managers, Scott Faris, J. A. Mayo, Maureen Donley; Press, Fred Nathan, Leslie Anderson, Anne Abrams, Bert Fink, Ted Killmer. Opened in the Shubert Theatre in Los Angeles, Ca., and still playing May 31, 1986.

CAST

Alonzo/Rumpus Cat .... Derryl Yeager
Bustopher Jones/Asparagus/Growltiger .... Norman A. Large †1
Bombalurina .... Edyie Fleming
Cassandra .... Leigh Webster
Coricopat .... Serge Rodnunsky †2
Demeter .... Sheri Cowart †3
Grizabella .... Kim Criswell
Jellylorum/Griddlebone .... Sally Spencer †4
Jennyanydots .... Marsha Mercant
Mistoffelees .... George de la Pena †5
Mungojerrie .... Don Johanson
Munkustrap .... Mark Morales
Old Deuteronomy .... George Anthony Bell
Plato/Macavity .... Jeff Adkins
Pouncival .... Phineas Newborn III
Rum Tum Tugger .... Michael Alan-Ross †6
Rumpleteazer .... Kristi Lynes
Sillabub .... Kathleen Dawson †7
Skimbleshanks .... Thom Keeling
Tantomile .... Andrea Gibbs Muldoon
Tumblebrutus .... Kenneth Jezek †8
Victoria .... J. Kathleen Lamb
Cats Chorus .... Vincent Pirillo, Lance Roberts, Rebecca Eichenberger, Deborah Shulman, Linden Waddell, Rachelle Ottley

For musical numbers and creative credits, see Broadway calendar listing.

†Succeeded by: 1. Peter Kevoian, Reece Holland, 2. Marc C. Oka, 3. April Ortiz, 4. Linden Waddell, 5. Jamie Torcellini, Marc C. Oka, 6. Gregory Donaldson, 7. Linda Hess, Susan Carr George, 8. David Reitman

Martha Swope Photos

Norman A. Large (kneeling), Mark Morales in "Cats"

A COUPLA WHITE CHICKS SITTING AROUND TALKING

By John Ford Noonan; Director, Dorothy Lyman; Set, Charles Cosler; Lighting, Russell Pyle; Costumes, Diana Eden; Original Songs, Loudon Wainwright III; Presented by PACE Theatrical Group and Roadworks Productions; Associate Producer, Christopher Santee; General Management, Gary Gunas; Company Manager, Connie Weinstein; Wardrobe, Jeane Frisbe; Stage Managers, Thomas P. Carr, Steve Wappel; Press, Smyth/Katzen, Art Katzen. Opened in the State Theatre, Cleveland, Ohio, on Tuesday, October 29, 1985.*

CAST

Maude Mix ....Susan Anton
Hannah Mae Bindler .... Elizabeth Ashley
Understudy: Polly Bourke

A comedy in 2 acts and 6 scenes. The action takes place in early June of the present time at 19 Charlemagne Lane in the town of Fox Hollow in a secluded corner of northern Westchester, NY.

*Closed Apr. 17, 1986 in Proctor's Theatre, Schenectady, NY. For original New York production see THEATRE WORLD Vol. 36.

**Susan Anton, Elizabeth Ashley
in "A Coupla White Chicks. . . ."**

CYRANO DE BERGERAC

By Edmond Rostand; Adapted by Emily Frankel; Director, Arthur Storch; Set, Victor A. Becker; Costumes, Jennifer von Mayrhauser; Lighting, Marc B. Weiss; Sound, Michael Jay; Fight Choreography, Erik Fredricksen; Presented by Columbia Artists Theatricals Corp. in association with Syracuse Stage; Casting, David Tochterman; Stage Managers, Robert C. Strickstein, Deirdre Sinnott; Music synthesized, performed, produced and engineered by Michael Jay. Opened Saturday, Sept. 14, 1985 in the Ulster Performing Arts Center, Kingston, NY, and closed Feb. 1, 1986 in the Mechanic Theatre, Baltimore, Md.

CAST

Bellerose/1st Gentleman .... Bernie Passeltiner
Ragueneau ....John Perkins
Marquis/Musketeer ....Dan Diggles
Valvert ....Timothy Davis-Reed
Orange Girl/Page/Sister Claire .... Lisa Merrill McCord
Mme. Aubrey/Lise/Sister Anne ....Christine Hunter
Busybody/2nd Gentleman ....John Tillotson
DeGuiche ....Richard Cottrell
Christian .... Marcus Smythe
Ligniere/Monk ....Lance Davis
Brissaille ....Anthony Spiner
LeBret ....Sean G. Griffin
Roxane .... Megan Gallagher
Duenna/Mother Margaret ....Shirl Bernheim
Montfleury ....Joseph Culliton
Cyrano de Bergerac ....John Cullum
Gascons .... Joseph Culliton, Lance Davis, Bernie Passeltiner,
John Tillotson, Timothy Davis-Reed, Dan Diggles

UNDERSTUDIES: Sean G. Griffin (Cyrano), Timothy Davis-Reed (Christian), Lisa Merrill McCord (Roxane), Lance Davis (LeBret), Joseph Culliton (DeGuiche/Brissaille), Anthony Spina (Ragueneau/Bellerose), Christine Hunter (Duenna/Orange Girl/Mother Margaret), Bernie Passeltiner (Ligniere/Cadet), Dan Diggles (Valvert/Cadet), Lisa Merrill McCord (Lise), John Tillotson (Montfleury/Marquis/Cadet)

Susan Piper Kublick Photo

**John Cullum, Timothy Davis-Reed
in "Cyrano de Bergerac"**

DREAMGIRLS

Book and Lyrics, Tom Eyen; Music, Henry Krieger; Direction/Choreography, Michael Bennett; Co-Choreographer, Michael Peters; Production Supervisor, Bob Avian; Scenery, Robin Wagner; Costumes, Theoni V. Aldredge; Lighting, Tharon Musser; Sound, Otts Munderloh; Musical Supervision/Orchestrations, Harold Wheeler; Musical Coordinator, Yolanda Segovia; Musical Director, Randy Booth; Vocal Arrangements, Cleavant Derricks; Hairstylist, Ted Azar; Casting, Johnson-Liff; Presented by Marvin A. Krauss and Irving Siders; General Management, Marvin A. Krauss Associates; Company Manager, Allan Williams; Technical Coordinator, Arthur Siccardi; Props, Charles Zuckerman, Greg Martin, Joe Schwarz; Wardrobe, Alyce Gilbert, Walter Douglas, Marilyn Knotts; Wigs, Michael Robinson; Hair, Steven Coy, David Dunn, John James; Dance Captain, Brenda Braxton; Stage Managers, Peter B. Mumford, Carmen Albanese, Thomas A. Bartlett; Press, Diane Judge, Norman Zagier. Opened in the Providence (R.I.) Performing Arts Center on Tuesday, Oct. 8, 1985.*

CAST

The Stepp Sisters	Rhetta Hughes, Johnnie Teamer, Lauren Velez, LueCinda Ramseur
Charlene	Yvette Louise Cason
Joanne	Susan Beaubian
Marty	Larry Stewart
Curtis Taylor, Jr.	Weyman Thompson, Jr.
Deena Jones	Deborah Burrell
The M.C./Mr. Morgan	Vernon Spencer
Tiny Joe Dixon/Jerry/Security Guard	Roy L. Jones
Lorrell Robinson	Arnetia Walker
C. C. White	Lawrence Clayton
Effie Melody White	Sharon Brown
Little Albert & the Tru-Tones	Bobby Daye, Robert Clater, Vincent M. Cole, Thomas Scott Gordon, Kevyn Morrow
James Thunder Early	Herbert L. Rawlings, Jr.
Edna Burke	Fuschia Walker
James Early Band	Robert Clater, Vincent M. Cole, Bobby Daye, Thomas Scott Gordon, Kevyn Morrow, Steve Marder
Wayne	Milton Craig Nealy
Dave & the Sweethearts	Paul Binotto, Pat Heaven, Lauren Velez
Frank, a press agent	Tim Cassidy
Dwight, a tv director	Steve Marder
Television Stage Manager	Paul Binotto
Michelle Morris	LueCinda Ramseur
Carl, a piano player	Bobby Daye
Film Executives	Paul Binotto, Bobby Daye, Kevyn Morrow
Five Tuxedos	Robert Clater, Vincent M. Cole, Bobby Daye, Thomas Scott Gordon, Kevyn Morrow
Les Style	Susan Beaubian, Yvette Louise Cason, Pat Heaven, Johnnie Teamer

UNDERSTUDIES: Yvette Louise Cason, Arnetia Walker, Fuschia Walker (Effie), Susan Beaubian, LueCinda Ramseur (Deena Jones), Susan Beaubian, Rhetta Hughes (Lorrell), Susan Beaubian, Johnnie Teamer (Michelle), Lawrence Clayton, Larry Stewart (Curtis), Phillip Gilmore, Milton Craig Nealy (Thunder), Bobby Daye (C. C.), Roy L. Jones, Milton Craig Nealy, Vernon Spencer (Marty), Phillip Gilmore, Thomas Gordon, Kevyn Morrow (Wayne), Steve Marder (Frank), Vernon Spencer (Jerry), Tim Cassidy (Dave), Milton Nealy (M.C.), Vernon Spencer (Morgan), Phillip Gilmore, Darryl Eric Tribble (Tiny Joe), Brenda Braxton, B. J. Jefferson (Charlene/Joanne/Edna)

MUSICAL NUMBERS: I'm Looking for Something, Goin' Downtown, Takin' the Long Way Home, Move, Fake Your Way to the Top, Cadillac Car, Steppin' to the Bad Side, Party Party, I Want You Baby, Family, Dreamgirls, Press Conference, Only the Beginning, Heavy, It's All Over, And I'm Telling You I'm Not Going, Love Love You Baby, I Am Changing, One More Picture Please, When I First Saw You, Got to Be Good Times, Ain't No Party, I Meant You No Harm, Quintette, The Rap, I Miss You Old Friend, One Night Only, I'm Somebody, Faith in My Self, Hard to Say Goodbye My Love

*Still touring May 31, 1986. For original Broadway production, see *Theatre World* Vol. 38.

Martha Swope Photos

Top Right: LueCinda Ramseur, Deborah Burrell, Arnetia Walker, and below with Herbert L. Rawlings, Jr.

LueCinda Ramseur, Deborah Burrell, Sharon Brown, Arnetia Walker

42nd STREET

Book, Michael Stewart/Mark Bramble; Based on novel by Bradford Ropes; Music, Harry Warren; Lyrics, Al Dubin; Choreography, Gower Champion; Reproduced by Karin Baker/Randy Skinner; Director, Lucia Victor from Gower Champion's original; Set, Robin Wagner; Musical Direction, Stephen Bates; Vocal Arrangements, John Lesko; Lighting, Tharon Musser; Costumes, Theoni V. Aldredge; Orchestrations, Philip J. Lang; Hairstylists, Anne Sampogna, Suzy Mazzarese, Ron Scott, Sherri Bramiett; Props, Leo Herbert, Michael Gallagher; Wardrobe, Robin B. Robillard; Furs, Oscar Loewy; General Manager, Leo K. Cohen; Company Manager, Kim Sellon; Dance Captain, Christopher Lucas; Presented by David Merrick; Stage Managers, Harold Goldfaden, Pat Trott, David Hansen, John Salvatore; Press, Solters/Roskin/Friedman, Joshua Ellis, Cindy Valk, Adrian Bryan-Brown, Keith Sherman, Jackie Green, Morris Yuter. Opened in the Forrest Theatre, Philadelphia, Pa., on Tuesday Nov. 9, 1983 and closed July 26, 1986 in the Queen Elizabeth Theatre, Vancouver, Canada. For original Broadway production, see *Theatre World* Vol. 37.

CAST

Andy Lee	Barry Preston
Oscar	Chuck Hunnicut
Mac/Thug/Doctor	Igors Gavon †1
Annie	Beth Leavel †2
Maggie Jones	Bibi Osterwald †3
Bert Barry	Don Potter
Billy Lawlor	Jim Walton †4
Peggy Sawyer	Clare Leach †5
Lorraine	Sandra Yarish †6
Phyllis	Bonnie Patrick †7
Julian Marsh	Barry Nelson
Dorothy Brock	Dolores Gray
Abner Dillon	J. Frank Lucas
Pat Denning	Randy Phillips
Thug	Al Micacchion

ENSEMBLE: Linda Marie Brenz, Marietta Clark, T. Michael Dalton, Debbie DiBiase, Deanna Dys, Suzie Jary, Monica Kelly, Wade Laboissonniere, Kim Larese, Rosemary Loar, Laura Menhart, Al Micacchion, Steven Minning, Ann Nieman, Vicky Nitchie, Doug Okerson, Tina Parise, Chris Peterson, Russell Rhodes, Richard Lee Ruth, Anne Rutter, Greg Schanuel, Jeanna Schweppe, Robin Stephens, Elizabeth Stover, Karen Toto, Mary Chris Wall, James Walski, Melodie Wolford, Carol Lynn Worcell, Michael Worcell

MUSICAL NUMBERS: see Broadway Calendar.

Succeeded by: 1. Lew Resseguie, 2. Sandra Yarish, 3. Denise Lor, 4. Kevin Daly, 5. Gail Benedict, 6. Anne Rutter, 7. Ann Nieman

Martha Swope Photos

Top Right: Dolores Gray, Barry Nelson

Gail Benedict

GLENGARRY GLEN ROSS

By David Mamet; Director, Gregory Mosher; Sets, Michael Merritt; Costumes, Nan Cibula; Lighting, Kevin Rigdon; Presented by Elliot Martin, James M. Nederlander, Arnold Bernhard, The Goodman Theatre; General Management, Joseph Harris; Company Manager, Mitchell Brower; Props, Paul Biega, Bob Curry; Wardrobe, Anthony Karniewich; Stage Managers, Daniel Miller Morris, Joel Bloom; Press, Jeffrey Richards, C. George Willard, Ben Morse, Bill Shuttleworth, Susan E. Lee. Opened in the Curran Theatre in San Francisco, Ca., on Tuesday, October 22, 1985.*

CAST

Shelly Levene	Peter Falk
John Williamson	J. T. Walsh
Dave Moss	J. J. Johnston
George Aaronow	Alan Manson
Richard Roma	Joe Mantegna
James Lingk	Chuck Stransky
Baylen	Jack Wallace

UNDERSTUDIES: Robert Hackman (Levene/Aaronow), Richard Holden (Williamson/Lingk/Baylen), Alfred Karl (Moss/Roma/Baylen)

A drama in two acts. The action takes place at the present time in a Chinese restaurant, and in a real estate office.

*Closed in Chicago, Il., on March 29, 1986. For original Broadway production, see THEATRE WORLD Vol. 40.

(no photos available)

LA CAGE AUX FOLLES

See creative credits in Broadway listing; Musical Director, Donald W. Chan; General Management, Marvin A. Krauss Associates; Company Managers, Mark Andrews, Michael Sanfilippo; Management Associates, Allan Williams, Jeff Capitola; Dance Captain, Shannon Lee Jones; Props, Charles Zuckerman, Paul Mazarek, Colleen Mazurek, Alan Steiner; Wardrobe, Gayle Patton, Jerry Wolf, Mario Brera, Santos Ramos; Hairstylist, Lamara Jackson; Music Coordinator, John Monaca; Associate Conductor, James May; Assistant Choreographers, Richard Balestrino, Linda Haberman; Makeup, Max Factor; Stage Managers, Kathleen A. Sullivan, Jeanne Fornadel, Allan Sobek; Press, Shirley Herz, Peter Cromarty, Pete Sanders, Gary Lawrence. Opened Thursday, Dec. 27, 1984 in Theatre for Performing Arts, Miami Beach, Fl., and still touring May 31, 1986. For original Broadway production, see *Theatre World* Vol. 40.

CAST

Georges	Peter Marshall
Les Cagelles:	
Clo Clo	Harrison Beal
Bitelle	Deborah Roshe
Odette	John Clonts
Dermah	Louie M. Trisoliere
Monique	John Anzalone
Hanna	Keith Allen
Chantal	Philip Clayton
Angelique	Karen Byers
Nicole	Andrew A. Currie
Phaedra	Thomas C. Stoehr
Francis	Joseph L. Taylor
Jacob	Ronald Dennis
Albin	Keene Curtis
Jean-Michel	Peter Reardon
Anne	Juliette Kurth †1
Jacqueline	le Clanche du Rand †2
M. Renaud	Mace Barrett
Mme. Renaud	Melody Jones
Paulette	Leslie Ellis
Hercule	Joe Joyce
Etienne	Scott Sigler
Colette	Mary Ellen Thomas
Pepe	Bryce Ward
Mme. Dindon	Pamela Hamill
Edouard Dindon	Bob Carroll

For musical numbers, see Broadway Calendar.
†Succeeded by: 1. Lynn Rose, 2. Lisa McMillan

Martha Swope Photos
Left: (C) Peter Marshall, Keene Curtis
Above: Mace Barrett, Melody Jones, Keene
Curtis, Peter Marshall Top: Peter
Marshall with Les Cagelles

Peter Marshall, Keene Curtis

LEGENDS!

By James Kirkwood; Director, Clifford Williams; Set, Douglas Schmidt; Costumes, Freddy Wittop; Lighting, Thomas Skelton; Presented by Ahmet M. Ertegun, Kevin Eggers, Robert Regester, Cheryl Crawford, Pace Theatrical Group; General Management, Alan Wasser/Douglas C. Baker; Company Manager, Alexander Holt; Props, Robert Saltzman; Wardrobe, James Kabel; Production Assistant, Keith A. Baumgartner; Specialty Music, Jeremy Lubbock, Randy Waldman; Sound, Jan Nebozenko; Hairstylist, Paul Huntley; Stage Managers, Steve Meyer, James Bernardi; Press, Gifford Wallace Inc. Opened in the Majestic Theatre, Dallas, Tx., Wednesday, January 8, 1986, and still touring May 31, 1986.*

CAST

Sylvia Glenn	Carol Channing
Leatrice Monsee	Mary Martin
Aretha Thomas	Annie-Joe
Martin Klemmer	Gary Beach
Policeman	Don Howard
Young Man	Eric Riley
Earl	Tim Johnson

STANDBYS & UNDERSTUDIES: Barbara Sohmers (Leatrice/Sylvia), Gwendolyn Shepherd (Aretha), Don Howard (Klemmer), Tim Johnson (Young Man/Policeman)

A comedy in 2 acts and 3 scenes. The action takes place at the present time in New York City.

Kenn Duncan Photos

Left: Mary Martin, Carol Channing
Center: Don Howard, Carol Channing
Right Center: Gary Beach

Carol Channing, Eric Riley, Annie-Joe

Mary Martin, Carol Channing

MY ONE AND ONLY

Music, George Gershwin; Lyrics, Ira Gershwin; Book, Peter Stone, Timothy S. Mayer; Directed and Choreographed by Thommie Walsh and Tommy Tune; Settings, Adrianne Lobel/Tony Walton; Costumes, Rita Ryack; Lighting, Marc B. Weiss; Sound, Otts Munderloh; Musical Concept/Dance Arrangements, Wally Harper; Orchestrations, Michael Gibson; Dance Arrangements, Peter Larson; Casting, Hughes/Moss; Hairstylist, Alan Schubert; Musical Consultant, Michael Feinstein; Musical/Vocal Direction, Jack Lee; Associate Choreographer, Baayork Lee; Associate Director, Phillip Oesterman; Presented by Barry and Fran Weissler in association with The One and Only Joint Venture, and Pace Theatrical Group; General Manager, National Artists Management Co.; Production Assistant, David Wolfe; Technical Supervisor, Arthur Siccardi; Props, Joseph Harris, Jr., Clyde Churchill, Jr.; Dance Captain, Niki Harris, Patti D'Beck; Wardrobe, Irene Ferrari; Stage Managers, Peter von Mayrhauser, Robert Kellogg, Betty Lynd; Press, Judy Jacksina, Glenna Freedman, Marcy Granata, Marc P. Thibodeau, Kevin Boyle, Jane Steinberg, Darrel Joseph. Opened in JFK Center, Washington, DC, on Friday, March 8, 1985.*

CAST

The New Rhythm Boys	David Jackson †1, Ken Leigh Rogers, Glenn Turner
Capt. Billy Buck Chandler	Tommy Tune
Mickey	Peggy O'Connell
Prince Nicolai Erraclyovitch Tchatchavadse	Don Amendolia
Prawn	Susan Hartley †2
Sturgeon	Debi A. Monahan
Kipper	Sandra Menhart
Flounder	Kerry Casserly †3
Minnow	Niki Harris
Anchovie	Eileen Casey
Edith Herbert	Sandy Duncan †4
Rt. Rev. J. D. Montgomery	Tiger Haynes
Reporter	Kerry Casserly †3
Mr. Magix	Charles "Honi" Coles
Ritz Quartet	Mark East, Walter Hook, Adam Petroski, Casper Roos
Stage Doorman	Adam Petroski
Achmed	Don Amendolia

DANCING GENTLEMEN: Adrian Bailey, Shaun Baker-Jones, James Ervin, Luther Fontaine, David Jackson, Jan Mickens

STANDBYS & UNDERSTUDIES: Ronald Young (Chandler/Magix), Judd Jones/Ken Leigh Rogers (Montgomery), Susan Hartley (Edith), Kerry Casserly (Mickey), Walter Hook (Prince), Luther Fontaine (Magix), Swings: Patti D'Beck, Ciscoe Bruton II, Bobby Walker, Merrilee Magnuson, Ruddy L. Garner, Kevyn Burrows

MUSICAL NUMBERS: I Can't Be Bothered Now, Blah Blah Blah, Boy Wanted, Soon, High Hat, Sweet and Low-Down, He Loves and She Loves, 'S Wonderful, Strike Up the Band, In the Swim, What Are We Here For, Nice Work if You Can Get It, My One and Only, Funny Face, Kickin' the Clouds Away, How Long Has This Been Going On?

A musical in 2 acts and 14 scenes. The action takes place in 1927.

*Closed March 29, 1986 at the Forrest Theatre in Philadelphia, Pa. For original Broadway production, see *Theatre World* Vol. 39.

†Succeeded by: 1. Bobby Walker, 2. Kaylyn Dillehay, 3. Karen Prunczik, 4. Lucie Arnaz

Kenn Duncan Photos

Sandy Duncan, Tommy Tune, and
above with Don Amendolia

Lucie Arnaz, Tommy Tune

**Richard Perloff, Dan Snow, Austin Butler
in "The Merchant of Venice" Right: Peter
Barbieri, Todd Loweth in "The Comedy of
Errors"**

NATIONAL SHAKESPEARE COMPANY

Executive Director, Elaine Sulka; Artistic Director/Director, Ron Daley; Scenic
Designer, Richard Kendrick; Costume Designer, Michael S. Schler; Lighting De-
signer, David Higham; Sound Design/Composer, Deena Kaye; Stage Combat, Todd
Loweth; Business Manager, Bruce Piper; Company Manager, Mechele Leon; Pro-
duction Manager, Austin Butler; Technical Director, Peter Barbieri, Jr.; Tour Direc-
tor, Marjorie A. Rubins; Stage Managers, G. Douglas Ward, Peter Barbieri, Jr.;
Press, Robert Campbell. Opened Wednesday, July 24, 1985 in Dickinson College,
Carlisle, Pa., and closed May 18, 1986 in The Cubiculo, New York City.

COMPANY: Peter Barbieri, Jr., Ezra Barnes, Alice Bergmann, Austin Butler, Rufus
Collins, Bruce Hamilton, R. Paul Hamilton, Mechele Leon, Todd Loweth, Amy
McLellan, Richard Perloff, William Richert, Dan Snow

PRODUCTIONS: Othello directed by Elowyn Castle, The Comedy of Errors directed
by Raymond David Marciniak, The Merchant of Venice directed by Ron Daley

**Alice Bergmann, Dan Snow
in "Othello"**

131

NOISES OFF

By Michael Frayn; Director, Michael Blakemore; Settings/Costumes, Michael Annals; Lighting, Martin Aronstein; Production Supervisor, Susie Cordon; Wardrobe, John Dunn; Presented by Tom Mallow, James Janek and Pace Theatrical Group, by arrangement with James Nederlander, Robert Fryer, Jerome Minskoff, in association with Jonathon Farkas and MTM Enterprises; General Management, American Theatre Productions; Company Manager, Alan Ross Kosher; Props, Gary Moreland; Wardrobe, Jeanne C. Smolens; Stage Managers, Mark S. Krause, Scott Glenn; Press, Max Eisen, Barbara Glenn. Opened in the Hershey Theatre, Hershey, Pa., on Thursday, September 5, 1985 and still playing May 31, 1986. For original Broadway production, see *Theatre World* Vol. 40.

CAST

Dotty Otley	Patricia Kilgarriff
Lloyd Dallas	Noel Harrison
Garry Lejeune	John Rensenhouse
Brooke Ashton	Lydia Laurans
Poppy Norton-Taylor	Mary Portser
Frederick Fellowes	Hugh A. Rose
Belinda Blair	Carolyn Porter
Tim Allgood	Berry Cooper
Selsdon Mowbray	Moultrie Patten

UNDERSTUDIES: Patricia Michael (Dotty/Belinda), Kathleen Helmer (Brooke/Poppy), Ian Thomson (Selsdon/Frederick), Richard Stack (Lloyd/Garry/Tim)

A comedy in 3 acts.

Martha Swope Photos

Right: Patricia Kilgarriff, Noel Harrison

Lydia Laurans, Noel Harrison, Mary Portser, Carolyn Porter, Moultrie Patten, Berry Cooper (in door), Hugh A. Rose, John Rensenhouse, Patricia Kilgarriff

SUGAR BABIES

Conceived by Ralph G. Allen, Harry Rigby; Book, Ralph G. Allen; Based on traditional material; Music, Jimmy McHugh; Lyrics, Dorothy Fields, Al Dubin; Additional Music and Lyrics, Arthur Malvin; Staged/Choreographed by Ernest O. Flatt; Sketches directed by Rudy Tronto; Production Supervision, Ernest O. Flatt; Scenery/Costumes, Raoul Pene du Bois; Lighting, Gilbert V. Hemsley, Jr.; Vocal Arrangements, Arthur Malvin, Hugh Martin, Ralph Blane; Music Director, Sherman Frank; Orchestrations, Dick Hyman; Dance Music Arrangements, Arnold Gross; Presented by Terry Allen Kramer and Harry Rigby in association with Columbia Pictures; Associate Producers, Frank Montalvo, Thomas Walton Associates; General Management, Alan Wasser; Assistant Choreographer, Eddie Pfeiffer; Associate Conductor, Jon Olson; Wardrobe, Lyn Gilsbach; Hairstylists, Stephen LoVullo, Antonio Belo, Frank Kocontes; Company Managers, Alexander Holt, Mitzi Harder; Stage Managers, Kay Vance, Bill Braden, Thom Mitchell; Press, Henry Luhrman, Bill Miller, Terry M. Lilly. Opened in the Airie Crown Theatre in Chicago, Il., on Monday, November 8, 1982, and closed in the Spartanburg, SC, Memorial Auditorium on April 20, 1986. For original Broadway production, see *Theatre World* Vol. 36.

CAST

Mickey	Mickey Rooney
Jay	Jay Stuart
Julie	Julie Miller †1
Mickey D	Mickey Deems
Phil	Phil Ford †2
Ann	Ann Miller †3
Frank	Frank Olivier †4
Jeff	Jeff Dunham
Gaiety Quartet	Jonathan Aronson †5, Dale Hensley, Gary Kirsch, Barry Woodruff, Hank Brunjes (Alternate)

SUGAR BABIES: Dani Brownlee, Carole Cotter, Kimberly Dean, Millie Garvey †6, Katherine Hopkins, Meridith Johnson †7, Kym Kaminsky †8, Melanie Montana, Kate Murtagh †9, Susie Nelson, Terry Nelson †10, Andrea Rose, Kathy Skizlak, Barbara Tobias, Joan Aslund (Alternate) †11, Kris Mooney

SKITS & MUSICAL NUMBERS: A Good Old Burlesque Show, Let Me Be Your Sugar Baby, I Want a Girl, In Louisiana, I Feel a Song Comin' On, Goin' Back to New Orleans, Broken Arms Hotel, Sally, Scenes from Domestic Life, Don't Blame Me, Monkey Business, Orientale, Little Red Schoolhouse, Mme. Rentz and Her All Female Minstrels, Down at the Gaiety Burlesque, Mr. Banjo Man, Candy Butcher, I'm Keepin' Myself Available for You, Exactly Like You, Court of Last Resort, I'm in the Mood for Love, Presenting Mme. Alla Gazaza, Cuban Love Song, Cautionary Tales, I'm Shootin' High, When You and I Were Young Maggie Blues, On the Sunny Side of the Street, Frank Olivier, You Can't Blame Your Uncle Sammy

A musical in 2 acts and 24 scenes.

†Succeeded by: 1. Lucianne Buchanan, 2. Rudy Tronto, William Linton, Jack Fletcher, 3. Jane Summerhays during Miss Miller's recovery from knee injury, 4. Daniel Rosen, 5. Bubba Dean Rambo, Chris Peterson, 6. Carol Ann Basch, Millene Michel, 7. Joan Aslund, 8. Meridith Johnson, 9. Laura Quinn, 10. Susan Trainor, 11. Sandra Turner, and during the year, additions to the cast were Kay McClelland, Daniel Rosen, and Senor Wences.

Martha Swope Photos

Ann Miller

Ann Miller, Mickey Rooney
(also at top)

133

WEST SIDE STORY

Book, Arthur Laurents; Based on a Jerome Robbins conception; Music, Leonard Bernstein; Lyrics, Stephen Sondheim; Original Direction and Choreography by Jerome Robbins; Reproduced by Ruth Mitchell and Tommy Abbott; Presented by Diana Corto, Francine LeFrak in association with LeFrak Entertainment Co.; Scenery, Peter Wolf; Lighting, Marc B. Weiss; Costumes, Stanley Simmons after originals by Irene Sharaff; Sound, Jack Mann; Musical Director, Milton Rosenstock; Hairstylist, Phyllis Della; Production Coordinator, Jay Norman; General Management, Theatre Now; Dance Captain, Christopher Cotten; Assistant Musical Director, Doug Lutz; Production Supervisor, Jeremiah J. Harris; Props, Robert Curry, Ron Korker; Wardrobe, Barrett Hong; Production Associates, Lois Cohen, Bud Burrell, Joseph Corcoran; Stage Managers, Larry Forde, Barbara Schneider, Kerri Knight; Press, Fred Nathan, Bert Fink, Anne Abrams, Glenna Freedman, Marc Thibodeau, Dennis Crowley, Larry Reitzer. Opened in JFK Center Opera House, Washington DC, on Saturday, August 31, 1985, and closed there on September 3, 1985. For original Broadway production, see *Theatre World* Vol. 14.

CAST

The Jets:
Riff, the leader .... Kevin Neil McCready
Tony, his friend .... Rex Smith
Action .... Rick Negron
A-Rab .... Thomas LoMonaco
Baby John .... Jim Soriero
Snowboy .... Kelly Woodruff
Big Deal .... Joe Locarro
Diesel .... John Schiappa
Gee-Tar .... William Sutton
Their Girls:
Graziella .... Anne-Marie Gerard
Velma .... Rebecca Timms
Minnie .... Liisa Lee
Clarice .... Tracy Galvin
Anybodys .... Liza Balkan
The Sharks:
Bernardo, the leader .... Luis Perez
Maria, his sister .... Katharine Buffaloe
Anita, his girl .... Leilani Jones
Chino, his friend .... Guillermo Gonzalez
Pepe .... Nick Garzillo
Indio .... John Saucier
Anxious .... Porfirio Figueroa
Nibbles .... James Rivera
Juano .... Jorge Noa
Toro .... Rob Parker
Their Girls:
Rosalia .... Marilu Morreale
Francisca .... Terri Garcia
Teresita .... Joann M. Hunter
Marguerita .... Pam Nahal
Doc .... Elek Hartman
Schrank .... Daniel P. Hannafin
Krupke .... Ron Orbach
Gladhand .... Jake Turner
Consuela .... Amelia Marshall

MUSICAL NUMBERS: Prologue, Jet Song, Something's Coming, The Dance at the Gym, Maria, Tonight, America, Cool, One Hand One Heart, The Rumble, I Feel Pretty, Somewhere, Gee Officer Krupke, A Boy Like That, I Have a Love, Finale

A musical in 2 acts and 15 scenes with a prologue. The action takes place on the West Side of New York City during the last days of summer in 1957.

Sheldon Secunda Photos

Top Right: Katharine Buffaloe, Rex Smith

Rex Smith, Katharine Buffaloe

ZORBA

Book, Joseph Stein; Based on novel by Nikos Kazantzakis; Lyrics, Fred Ebb; Music, John Kander; Original Direction, Michael Cacoyannis; Production Supervised by Joel Grey; Choreography, Graciela Daniele; Scenery, David Chapman, Marck Haack; Costumes, Hal George; Lighting, Marc B. Weiss; Sound, T. Richard Fitzgerald; Hairstylist/Makeup, Steve Atha; Casting, Hughes/Moss; Musical Supervisor, Paul Gemignani; Musical Director, Al Cavaliere; Orchestrations, Don Walker; Dance Arrangements, Thomas Fay; Associate Producer, Alecia Parker; Musical Coordinator, John Monaco; Cast album by RCA Records; Presented by Barry and Fran Weissler, Kenneth-John Productions. Opened in JFK Center, Washington, D.C., on Wednesday, Sept. 5, 1984 and closed at Westbury, NY, Music Fair, Aug. 3, 1986.

CAST

The Leader	Donna Theodore
Niko	Paul Harman
Zorba	Anthony Quinn
Konstandi/Turkish Dancer/Russian Admiral	Frank DeSal
Despo/Crow	Panchali Null
Thanassi/French Admiral	Lee Mathis
Constable	Raphael LaManna
Sister/Crow	Leila Martin
Mariki/Crow	Loretta Toscano
Katina/Cafe Whore	Sharon Lawrence
Vassilakas/Monk	George Kmeck
Marinakos/Monk	James Sbano †1
Mimiko	Aurelio Padron
Katapolis/Monk	John Norman
Yorgo/Italian Admiral	Richard Warren Pugh
Sophia/Crow	Wysandria Woolsey
Maria/Crow	Laurie Crochet
Mavrodani	Charles Karel †2
Pavli	Thomas David Scalise
Manolakas	David Brummel
The Widow	Angelina Fiordellisi
Priest/English Admiral	Paul Straney
Marsalias	Frank Cava
Anagnosti/Monk	Morgan Richardson
Madame Hortense	Lila Kedrova

STANDBYS & UNDERSTUDIES: Charles Karel/James Lockhart (Zorba), Leila Martin (Hortense), Wysandria Woolsey (Leader), James Sbano (Niko), Loretta Toscano (Widow), Raphael LaManna (Mavrodani), Lee Mathis (Mimiko), George Kmeck (Manolakas), Swings: John Mineo (Dance Captain), Charles Bari, Anna Villa

MUSICAL NUMBERS: Life Is, The First Time, The Top of the Hill, No Boom Boom, Vive La Difference, The Butterfly, Goodbye Canavaro, Grandpapa, Only Love, The Bend of the Road, Yassou, Woman, Why Can't I Speak, That's a Beginning, Easter Dance, Miner's Dance, The Crow, Happy Birthday, I Am Free

†Succeeded by: 1. Luke Lynch, 2. Walter Hook. For original Broadway production, see *Theatre World* Vol. 40.

Martha Swope Photos

Anthony Quinn, Lila Kedrova in "Zorba"

PRODUCTIONS THAT OPENED AND CLOSED BEFORE SCHEDULED BROADWAY DEBUT

THE NIGHT OF THE IGUANA

By Tennessee Williams; Director, Arthur Sherman; Set, Oliver Smith; Costumes, Lucinda Ballard; Lighting, Feder; Sound, Jack Mann; Casting, Hughes/Moss; Presented by Fred Walker, Michael Lonergan, Jacqueline de la Chaume; General Management, Michael Lonergan; Company Manager, Mary Ellyn Devery; Hairstylist, Esther Teller; Props, Al Steiner; Wardrobe, Ellen Lee; Stage Managers, Alan Hall, Ruth E. Rinklin; Press, Solters/Roskin/Friedman, Joshua Ellis, Keith Sherman, Cindy Valk, Adrian Bryant-Brown, Jackie Green, Andrew Hirshfield. Opened in Morris Mechanic Theatre, Baltimore, Md. on Tuesday, October 15, 1985 and closed there on November 10, 1985.

CAST

Pancho	Julian Reyes
Maxine Faulk	Eileen Brennan
Pedro	Kevin Gray
Rev. T. Lawrence Shannon	Michael Moriarty
Wolfgang	Brad Greenquist
Hilda	Carrie Nygren
Herr Fahrenkopf	C. M. Gampel
Frau Fahrenkopf	M'El Dowd
Hank	Martin Shakar
Miss Judith Fellowes	Penelope Allen
Hannah Jelkes	Jeanne Moreau
Charlotte Goodall	Marita Geraghty
Nonno (Jonathan Coffin)	Roy Dotrice
Jake Latta	Sam J. Coppola

UNDERSTUDIES: Penelope Allen (Maxine), Tom Brennan (Nonno/Jake/Fahrenkopf), Richard James Perry (Wolfgang/Pedro/Pancho/Hank), Martin Shakar (Shannon), Katherine Udall (Judith/Frau Fahrenkopf), Phoebe Underer (Charlotte/Hilda)

A drama in 2 acts and 3 scenes. The action takes place in the summer of 1940 in the Costa Verde Hotel in Puerto Barrio, on the west coast of Mexico.

Martha Swope Photos

Eileen Brennan, Michael Moriarty, Jeanne Moreau, Roy Dotrice in "The Night of the Iguana"

PROFESSIONAL REGIONAL COMPANIES

ACT/A CONTEMPORARY THEATRE

Seattle, Washington
May 2, 1985–May 25, 1986
Twenty-first Season

Producing Director, Gregory A. Falls; Producing Manager, Phil Schermer; Administrative Manager, Susan Trapnell Moritz; Communications Asst, Sarah E. Meyer; Stage Managers, Michael Wise, James Verdery, Jorie Wackerman, Sarah S. Mixson, Karen Brilliande

PRODUCTIONS & CASTS

KING LEAR by William Shakespeare; Director, Arne Zaslove; Asst. Director, Craig Huisenga; Musical Director, Shelley Henze Schermer; Costumes, Julie James; Lighting, Phil Schermer; Stage Manager, Michael Wise; Co-produced by The Bathhouse Theatre. CAST: Rex. E. Allen, Mark Anders, Carolyn Ayres, John Aylward, Kelly Cresap, Mark Crusch, Robert Ellis, Susan Finque, Allen Galli, Eric Hangerman, Randy Hoffmeyer, Kevin Lynch, David Mainer, Dylan Marshall, Daniel Mayes, David Mong, Joyce Mycka-Steller, Eric Newman, Gretchen Orsland, Micha Rice, Michael V. Schauermann, Frank Smith, David Stettler, Eric Sumerall, Robert E. Taeschner, G. Valmont Thomas, Rich Tutor, Jo Vetter, Carolyn Ayres

TRUE WEST by Sam Shepard; Director, John Dillon, Set, Michael Olich; Costumes, Liz Covey; Lighting, Jody Briggs; Sound, Lindsay Smith; Stage Manager, James Verdery. CAST: Laurence Ballard, Marjorie Nelson, Richard Riehle, Peter Silvert. Understudies: David Debesse, Bruce Ellsperger, Beth Gilles

MAYDAYS by David Edgar; *American Premiere;* Co-Directors, Jeff Steitzer, Anne-Denise Ford; Asst. Director, Peggy Shannon; Set/Lighting, Bill Forrester; Costumes, Liz Covey; Sound, James Verdery; Stage Manager, Jorie Wackerman. CAST: Laurence Ballard, Kurt Beattie, Richard M. Davidson, Richard Farrell, Sandra M. Galeota, Lizabeth Hinton, Randy Hoffmeyer, Paul Hostetler, David S. Klein, Diana LaMar, Martin LaPlatney, Lori Larsen, Susan Ludlow, Brian Martin, Rex McDowell, David Pichette, Demetra Pittman, Richard Riehle, Clark Sanford, Paul Anthony Weber, David P. Whitehead, R. Hamilton Wright, Roald Berton Wulff. Understudies: John Lee, Peggy Shannon

OTHER PLACES by Harold Pinter. Director, Gregory A. Falls; Set, Bill Raoul; Costumes, Rose Pederson; Lighting, Donna Grout; Sound, David Hunter Koch; Stage Manager, James Verdery. CAST: "Victoria Station": Clayton Corzatte, R. Hamilton Wright. "One for the Road": Laurence Ballard, Shane Clark, Mark Drusch, Rebecca Stucki. "A Kind of Alaska": Clayton Corzatte, Zoaunne LeRoy, Susan Ludlow. Understudies: Mark Branom, Thomas Diggs, Katie Forgette, David S. Klein, Ruth McRee

END OF THE WORLD (WITH SYMPOSIUM TO FOLLOW) by Arthur Kopit; Director, Jeff Steitzer; Set, Scott Weldin; Costumes, Sally Richardson; Lighting, Rick Paulsen; Sound, David Hunter Koch; Stage Manager, Jorie Wackerman. CAST: Sarah Brooke, George Catalano, Clayton Corzatte, Mark Drusch, Randy Hoffmeyer, Susan Ludlow, Daniel Milder, Tony Mockus, David Mong, Rod Pilloud, R. Hamilton Wright. Understudies: Lynne Devin, John Conescu, Derek Longbrek, John Pribyl

QUARTERMAINE'S TERMS by Simon Gray; Director, Jeff Steitzer; Set, Shelley Henze Schermer; Costumes, Anne Thaxter Watson; Lighting, A. W. Nelson; Sound, David Hunter Koch; Stage Manager, James Verdery. CAST: Clayton Corzatte, Richard Farrell, Joyce Harris, Dianne Benjamin Hill, David Mong, Jack Sydown, Rick Tutor. Understudies: Bill Crossett, Scott Kaiser, Gwynne Rhynedance, David Mong, Roald Berton Wulff

A CHRISTMAS CAROL by Charles Dickens; Adapted by Gregory A. Falls & Kurt Beattie; Music, Robert MacDougal; Director, Anne-Denise Ford; Set, Bill Forrester; Costumes, Nanrose Buchman; Lighting, Jody Briggs; Choreographer, Ursula Meyer; Stage Manager, Jorie Wackerman. CAST: Tobias Anderson, Allison Barcott, Ariel Basom, Sarah Brooke, Colleen Carey, Philip Davidson, Richard Farrell, Melissa Bray, Jo Leffingwell, Peter Lohnes, Kevin C. Loomis, Christopher Marks, Daniel Milder, Tony Pasqualini, Rex Rabold, Jeff Sellers, Judith Shahn, Tony Soper, Casey Trupin. Understudies: Allison Barcott, Melissa Bray, B. J. Douglas, Bill terKuile, Casey Trupin, Noah Marks, Amber Taylor, Sarah Brooke

JUGGLE & HYDE, A Play with Words, Written and Directed by The Flying Karamazov Brothers; *World Premiere*. CAST: Randy Nelson, Paul David Magid, Howard Jay Petterson, Sam Williams, Timothy Daniel Furst

THESEUS AND THE MINOTAUR by Gregory A. Falls; *World Premiere;* Director, Gregory A. Falls; Set, Richard J. Harris; Costumes, Rose Pederson; Lighting, Donna Grout; Sound, David Hunter Koch; Stage Manager, James Verdery. CAST: Steve Brush (Theseus), Craig Kenyon Menteer (Damysus/Androgeous/Cretan Wrestler), Paul T. Mitri (Scamander/Medeus/Sinis), Annette Romano (Ariadne/Medea/Perifites), Paul Shapiro (Pittheus/Minos), Bill terKuile (Aegeus/Minotaur/Procrustes), Laurel Anne White (Aethra/Nymphea/Phytalus' Daughter)

A WRINKLE IN TIME by Gregory A. Falls; Based on the book by Madeline L'Engle; Director, Anne-Denise Ford; Set, Jennifer Lupton; Costumes, Sarah Campbell; Lighting, Peter W. Allen; Music/Sound, David Hunter Koch; Stage Manager, Sarah S. Mixson. CAST: Thomas Diggs (Charles Wallace Murry), Marceline Hugot (Mrs. Whatsit), Gregg Thomas Johnson (Boy/Postman/Calvin O'Keefe), Kathryn Mesney (Mrs. Murry/Camazotz #4/Man with Red Eyes/Beast), Tawnya Pettiford-Wates (Girl/Mrs. Which/Paper Girl's Mom/Camazotz #3/Aunt Beast), Bill terKuile (Principal/Camazotz #1/Mr. Murry Jerri Lee Young (Meg Murry)

THE NAVIGATOR, A STORY OF MICRONESIA by Michael Cowell; Producing Director, Gregory A. Falls; Director, John Kauffman; Set, Joseph Dodd; Costumes, Laura Crow; Lighting, Lloyd S. Riford, III; Consultant on Micronesia, Lino Olopai; Stage Manager, Karen Brilliande. CAST: Loretta Ables (Mother/Ilaemal), Ray Bumatai (Crash/Solang/Captain Herring), Christine Merino (Liteirang), Don Nahaku (Guts/Tilifag), James Pestana (Gabby), Gregory P. Suenaga (Bugolimar/Storm), Tremaine Tamayose (Samal Garor)

ON THE RAZZLE by Tom Stoppard; adapted from Johann Nestroy's "Einen Jux will er sich machen"; Director, Jeff Steitzer; Asst. Director, Jon Kretzu; Set, Shelley Henze Schermer; Costumes, Sally Richardson; Lighting, Phil Schermer; Sound/Musical Director, David Hunter Koch; Stage Manager, James Verdery. CAST: Mark Drusch (Weinberl), Judy Ford Taylor (Christopher), Tony Soper (Sonders), Suzanne Irving (Marie), John Aylward (Zangler), Jill C. Klein (Gertrud), Dan Daily (Belgian Foreigner), R. Hamilton Wright (Melchior), Rex McDowell (Hupfer), Himself (Lightning), Jill C. Klein (Philippine), Jo Vetter (Madame Knorr), Diane Benjamin Hill (Frau Fischer), David Mong (Coachman), Rex McDowell (Waiter #1), David Prichette (Waiter #2), Edward R. Williams (Waiter #3), Rex McDowell (Constable), Dan Daily (Fraulein Blumenblatt), Jill C. Klein (Lisette), Casey Trupin (Ragamuffin)

Chris Bennion Photos

Laurence Ballard (standing) with Marjorie Nelson, Richard Riehle, Peter Silbert in "True West"

Top: John Aylward, Joyce Mycka-Stettler in "King Lear"

ACTORS THEATRE OF LOUISVILLE

Louisville, Kentucky
September 1985–May 1986
Twenty-second Season

Producing Director, Jon Jory; Administrative Director, Alexander Speer; Associate Director, Marilee Slater; Stage Directors: Conrad Bishop, Tom Bullard, Larry Deckel, Ray Fry, Jon Jory, Mladen Kiselov, Frazier Marsh, Laszlo Marton, Adale O'Brien, Jackson Phippin, Mary Robinson, Rob Spera; Set Designers: Paul Owen, Elmon Webb, Virginia Dancy, James Joy, Jim Sanderfur; Costumes: Marcia Dixcy, Marie Chiment, Holly Jenkins-Evans, Karen Anderson-Fields, Anne Wallace; Lighting: Jeffrey Hill, Geoff Korf, Paul Owen; Props, Diann Fay; Sound, David S. Strang; Tech Director, Tom Rupp; Production Manager, Frazier Marsh; Press, Jenan Dorman; Development, Jim Luigs; Literary, Julie Crutcher; Stage Managers: Craig Weindling, Rick Cunningham, Cynthia Hood, Debra Acquavella, Dan Kanter, March Field, Matt Sweigart, Bob Hornung, Suzanne Fry
COMPANY: Andy Backer, Jonathon Bolt, Robert Brock, Melody Combs, Beth Dixon, Ray Fry, George Gerdes, Suzanna Hay, Patrick Husted, Jeffrey Hutchinson, Jane Ives, Christine Jansen, Lee Kissman, Kevin Kling, Bruce Kuhn, Larry Larson, Levy Lee, Fred Major, Bill McNulty, Dana Mills, Debra Monk, Adele O'Brien, Peggity Price, Steve Rankin, Elizabeth Ruscio, John Shepard, Wayne Turney, Bill Verderber, Basil Wallace, Janet Zarish, Julie Boyd, June Ballinger, Veronica Castang, Christian Kaufman, John Leighton, Bram Lewis, Richard Ziman, Christine Baskous, Alan Brasington, Bob Burrus
PRODUCTIONS: *Traveler in the Dark, Cloud 9, And a Nightingale Sang, A Christmas Carol, Gift of the Magi, The Royal Comedians, The Misanthrope, Educating Rita, The Illuminati, 21A, A Streetcar Named Desire, Master Harold . . . and the Boys,* WORLD PREMIERES: *Shorts '85* (One-Act Play Festival), Humana Festival of New American Plays: *How to Say Goodbye, The Shaper, Smitty's News, To Culebra, No Mercy, How Gertrude Stormed the Philosophers' Club*

David S. Talbott Photos

**Right: Debra Monk, John Shepard
in "Astronauts"**

Larry Larson, Levi Lee in "Some Things You Need to Know before the World Ends"

ACTORS THEATRE OF ST. PAUL

St. Paul, Minnesota
October 25, 1985–May 11, 1986

Artistic Director, Michael Andrew Miner; Associate Artistic Director, David Ira Goldstein; Composer, Randall Davidson; Design Associate, Chris Johnson; Resident Costumer/Designer, Nanya Ramey; Designer, Janie Geiser; Stage Manager, Jeff Couture; Asst. Stage Manager, Janet Hall; Managing Director, Jan Miner; Business Manager, Christopher Marquardt; Development, Martha Sloca Richards; Marketing, Andrew Brolin
RESIDENT COMPANY: Paul Boesing, D. Scott Glasser, Tim Goodwin, David M. Kwiat, David Lenthall, Dolores Noah, John Seibert
GUEST ARTISTS: George C. White (Director), Dawn Renee Jones (Director), Dick Leerhoff (Designer), Steven Deitz (Playwright), John Einwech (Composer), James Cada. ACTORS: James Cada, Mary Anne Dempsey, Ben Krielkamp, Margit Moe, Nanci Olesen, Terry Heck, Annie Enneking, Alan Woodward, Carole Jean Anderson, Craig Johnson, Sally Wingert, Bart Tinapp, Mari Rovang, Charlotte Gibson, Lizanne Wilson, James Craven
PRODUCTIONS: *Much Ado About Nothing* by William Shakespeare, *And a Nightingale Sang . . .* by C. P. Taylor, *Blood Knot* by Athol Fugard, *The Barber of Seville* by Beaumarchais
WORLD PREMIERES: *Joyous Noel! A Noel Coward Music Hall* compiled by David Ira Goldstein, *More Fun Than Bowling* by Steven Deitz, *Trakker's Tel* a collaboration by Director D. Scott Glasser/Composer Randall Davidson/Puppeteer Janie Geiser/and Actors Theatre Company

Connie Jerome Photos

Right: James Craven in "Blood Knot"
Top: Cast of "Joyous Noel!"

ALASKA REPERTORY THEATRE

Anchorage, Alaska
June 21, 1985–February 8, 1986

Artistic Director, Paul Brown; Producing Director, Ben Taber; General Manager, Alice Chebba; Fiscal Manager, Jim Woodard; Company Manager, Dennis Booth; Technical Director, Patricia Eckert; Marketing, Steven L. Bennett; Sound, Gretchen Van Horne; Stage Managers, Gretchen Van Horne, Michael Paul
PRODUCTIONS & CASTS
PUMP BOYS AND DINETTES: Musical Director, Mark Hardwick; Staging, Maggie La Mee; Set, Connie Lutz; Costumes, Jennifer Svenson; Sound, Bruce Crouch; Lighting, Lauren Miller; Stage Manager, Carol Chiavetta. CAST: Richard Perrin, Guy Strobel, Joel Lockman, Donn Ruddy, Brooks Almy, Christine Ranck, Frances Asher
TWELFTH NIGHT: Director, Roy Brocksmith; Set, Michael Olich; Costumes, Carrie Robbins; Lighting, Spencer Mosse; Music, Grant Sturiale. CAST: Ethan Phillips, Richard Ryder, Susan Diol, David Whitehead, Diana Van Fossen, Stephen Pelinski, Christine Andreas, Andy McCutcheon, Kevin Hills, David Fuller, Lawrence Overmire, Peter Josephson, John Bauer, Marc Cohen, Beth Gilles, Will Folsom, Therese Hayes, E. D. Bourgeois, Susanne Ward, Karen Hoins
WATCH ON THE RHINE: Director, Robert J. Farley; Set, Karen Gjelsteen; Costumes, Jennifer Svenson; Lighting, Spencer Mosse. CAST: Mitchell Edmonds, Lucy Flynn, June Gibbons, Sherrie Heginbotham, Phillip Lindsay, Alan Mixon, Etain O'Malley, Reno Roop, Mary Nell Santacroce, Raymond Wiberg, Janet Zarish
GREATER TUNA: Director, Robert J. Farley; Set, Karen Gjelsteen; Costumes, Jennifer Svenson; Lighting, Spencer Mosse. CAST: Richard Riehle, Larry Paulsen
TINTYPES: Director, Walton Jones; Musical Director, Uel Wade; Staging & Choreography, Susan Rosenstock; Set, Michael Olich; Costumes, Deborah Dryden; Lighting, Spencer Mosse. CAST: Carolyn DeLany, James Hindman, Mark McGrath, Eleanor Reissa, Corliss Taylor-Dunn

Chris Arend Photos

Mary Nell Santacroce, Mitchell Edmonds, Reno Roop in "Watch on the Rhine" Above: Christine Andreas, Stephan Pelinski in "Twelfth Night"

ALLEY THEATRE

Houston, Texas
October 10, 1985–June 8, 1986
Thirty-ninth Season

Artistic/Executive Director, Pat Brown; Associate Artistic Director, George Anderson; Assistant to the Artistic Director, Trent Jenkins; Resident Director, Beth Sanford; Young Company/Staff Director, James Martin; Literary Associate, Edwin Carl Erwin; Secretary, Maxine Smith; Company Manager, Charles Sanders; Production Manager, Bettye Fitzpatrick; Assistant Production Manager, Carol Hickle; Marketing, Carl Davis; Marketing, Jeffrey E. Orth; Press, Julie Devane; Development, Sharon McDonald-Tiknis

RESIDENT COMPANY: Ruth Adams, Timothy Arrington, James Belcher, Jeff Bennett, Bettye Fitzpatrick, Scott Fults, Sandra M. Galeota, Kayce Glasse, Cynthia Gorman, Paul Hope, Jack Stubblefield Johnson, Charles Krohn, Kristin Norton, James Ream, Charles Sanders, Leigh Selting, Brandon Smith, Robert Strane, Susan Welby, John Wylie. Young Company: Jensie Anderson, Ken Bahn, Christopher Combest, Sarah Hill, Derek Horton, Stephen O'Dwyer, Greg Williams, Timothy Hanlon, Chalethia Williams

GUEST ARTISTS: Gerald J. Quimby, K. Lype O'Dell, Holly Barron, Jim Bernhard, Kristina Friman, Jill Tanner, Jess Richards, Janet Williams Adderley, K. K. Preece, Marilyn J. Johnson, Kevin Ramsey, William Rohrig, Bob Marich, Paul Polk, Elizabetta Melchiori, Paula Abbott, J. Brent Alford, David Ray Bartee, Dolores Baum, Steven Blair, Jonathan Charles, Ann Forgy, Tito Hernandez, Lou Ann Miles, Georganna Mills, Floyd T. Nash, Pam Ritter, Frank Vega, Jennie Welch, Denton Yockey, Marilyn McIntyre, Ambrosio Guerra, David Gregory, Bruce Nozick, Dennis Wells, Alexandra Neil, Steven Marcus, Mark Hymen, Luisa Amaral-Smith, Ntozake Shange, Peter Angel Garcia, Jim McQueen, Harold Suggs, Holly Villaire, Melody Kay Coker, Marijane Vandivier, Marietta Marich, Richard C. Brown, Bobo Lewis, Victoria Boothby, Nancy Boykin, Charlene Bigham

PRODUCTIONS:

EXECUTION OF JUSTICE by Emily Mann; Director, Pat Brown; Asst. Director, Beth Sanford; Set, Charles S. Kading; Costumes, Barbara A. Bell; Lighting, Greg Sullivan; Sound, Art Yelton; Media Specialist, John Yavel; Video Co-ordinator, Andy Mann

KISS ME, KATE, music & lyrics by Cole Porter, book by Samuel and Bella Spewack; Director, Charles Abbott; Choreographer, Bick Goss; Musical Director, Art Yelton; Set, Charles S. Kading; Costumes, Lewis Brown; Lighting, Frances Aronson

THE MISS FIRECRACKER CONTEST by Beth Henley; Director, Pat Brown; Asst. Director, Beth Sanford; Set, Richard Ellis; Costumes, Barbara A. Bell; Lighting, Richard W. Jeter; Sound, Jan Cole

PACK OF LIES by Hugh Whitemore; Director, Malcolm Morrison, Set, Michael Ryan; Lighting, Richard W. Jeter; Costumes, Sarajane Milligan; Sound, Art Yelton

SPRING AWAKENING by Frank Wedekind, translated by Edward Bond; Director, Pat Brown; Asst. Director, James Martin; Set, Charles S. Kading; Costumes, Howard Tsvi Kaplan; Lighting, James Sale; Sound, Art Yelton; Puppet Designer/Consultant, Erminio Pinque

THE FOREIGNER by Larry Shue; Director, James Martin; Set, Charles S. Kading; Costumes, Howard Tsvi Kaplan; Lighting, Richard W. Jeter; Sound, Art Yelton

PAINTING CHURCHES by Tina Howe; Director, Josephine R. Abady; Set, Richard Ellis; Lighting, Richard W. Jeter; Costumes, Barbara A. Bell; Sound, John Michener

BALM IN GILEAD by Lanford Wilson; Director, George Anderson; Set, Charles S. Kading; Costumes, Howard Tsvi Kaplan; Lighting, Pamela A. Gray; Music, Jan Cole

THE TRAVELING LADY by Horton Foote; Director, Beth Sanford; Set, Richard Ellis; Costumes, Patricia E. Doherty; Lighting, Richard Jeter; Sound, Art Yelton

ORPHANS by Lyle Kessler; Director, George Anderson; Set, Richard Ellis; Costumes, Barbara A. Bell; Lighting, Pamela A. Gray; Sound, Art Yelton

**Top Right: Paul Hope, Gerald J. Quimby
in "Execution of Justice" Below: Peter
Garcia, Alexandra Neil, Mark Hymen
in "Balm in Gilead"**

**Jeff Bennett, Richard C. Brown
in "The Foreigner"**

139

ALLIANCE THEATRE COMPANY

Atlanta, Georgia
September 4, 1985–June 15, 1986
Seventeenth Season

Managing Director, Edith H. Love; Associate Director, Kent Stephens; Literary Manager, Sandra Deer; Artistic Assistant/Casting, Adam Muzzy; General Manager, William B. Duncan; Assistant Manager, Daniel M. Posener; Production Manager, Billings Lapierre; Assistant Production Manager, Rixon Hammond; Marketing, Kim Resnik; Publicity, Ruthie Ervin; Development, Betty Blondeau-Russell; Technical Director, Stephen Reardon; Scenic Artist/Chargeperson, Nancy Branton; Costume Manager, Carol Hammond; Props, Sharon Braunstein; Electrics, Pete Shinn; Sound, David M. Lyons; Stage Operations, Bill Harrison; Stage Managers, Dale C. Lawrence, Kathy E. Richardson, Seth R. Ghitelman, John Kirman, Rixon Hammond, John Kirman

PRODUCTIONS & CASTS

SO LONG ON LONELY STREET by Sandra Deer; Director, Kent Stephens; Set, Mark William Morton; Costumes, Joyce Andrulot; Lighting, Allen Lee Hughes; Composer, Hal Lanier. CAST: Daren Kelly, Lizan Mitchell, Pat Nesbit, Stacy Ray, Stephen Root, Ken Strong

THE IMPORTANCE OF BEING EARNEST by Oscar Wilde; Director, Kent Stephens; Set, Kate Edmunds; Costumes, Pierre DeRagon; Lighting, Marilyn Rennagel. CAST: Brad Bellamy, Charlotte Booker, John F. Degen, Frank Groseclose, Henry J. Jordon, Laura MacDermott, Rosemary Murphy, John Purcell, Linda Stephens

GUYS AND DOLLS with Music and Lyrics by Frank Loesser; Book by Jo Swerling and Abe Burrows; A Musical Fable of Broadway based on the characters and stories of Damon Runyon; Director, Scott Harris; Musical Director, Michael Fauss; Choreographer, Terry Rieser; Set, Mark William Morton; Costumes, Susan Hirschfeld; Lighting, Jason Kantrowitz. CAST: Amanda Beason, Evan Bell, Wade Benson, Arleen Floyd Black, Tracy Lynn Buckner, Earnest L. Dixon, Dennis Durrett-Smith, Crystal Fox, Joy Franz, Glenn B. Gordon, Rex Hays, Felicia Hernandez, James Horvath, Patrick Hutchinson, Bryan Curtis Jones, Betsy Joslyn, Jon Kohler, Scott Martin, Thomas J. Miller, Jill Powell, Richard Warren Pugh, Lawrence Raiken, Jeffrey Roberts, Jude Wido, Carol Williams, David Alan Willoughby, Iggie Wolfington

FLINT AND ROSES by Jim Pect; *World Premiere;* Director, Skip Foster; Set, Victor Becker; Costumes, Susan Mickey; Lighting, Paulie Jenkins. CAST: Michael Bruce Boehlke, Lisa Emery, Edmond Genest, Al Hamacher, Earl Hindman, Tom McKeon, Diane Tarleton, Peter Thomasson

GREAT EXPECTATIONS by Charles Dickens, adapted by Sandra Deer; *World Premiere;* Director, Fred Chappell; Set, Charles Caldwell; Costumes, Kathleen Blake; Lighting, Marilyn Rennagel; Composer, Scott Depoy. CAST: Brian Cousins, Stanton Cunningham, Alison Day, Skip Foster, Al Hamacher, Christian Hesler, I. M. Hobson, Pat Hurley, Terrence Markovich, John Noonan, Pamella O'Connor, Gavin Reed, Alan Ripley, Mary Nell Santacroce, Peter Thomasson, Laura Tietjen

HAMLET by William Shakespeare; Director, Tony Tanner; Set, Kate Edmunds; Costumes, Susan Hirschfeld; Lighting, Barry Arnold; Composers, Martin Silvestri, Jeremy Stone; Fight Choreography, Skip Foster. CAST: Lloyd Battista, David Brizzolara, Haynes Brooke, Mark Chavis, John Clark, Hugh D. Cobb, Lynn Todd Craig, Teresa DeBerry, Gwyllum Evans, Allen Evitts, Jeroy Hannah, Pat Hurley, Eddie King, George Lawes, Charles L. Major, Kenneth L. Marks, Gregory Martyn, Allen O'Reilly, Wyman Pendleton, Simon Reynolds, Sarah Rice, Jim Shadburne, Linda Stephens, Ken Strong, Peter Thomasson, Ian Trigger, David Wasman, Neal Williams

'NIGHT MOTHER by Marsha Norman; Director, Fred Chappell; Set, Lynne Monterey Hiett; Costumes, Susan Mickey; Lighting, Peter H. Shinn. CAST: Eileen Heckart, Joyce Reehling

BLUE WINDOW by Craig Lucas; Director, William Partlan; Set, Dennis C. Maulden; Costumes, Susan Mickey; Lighting, Liz Lee. CAST: Dennis Bailey, Brenda Bynum, John Foley, Eddie King, Nancy Mette, Tambra Smith, Chondra Wolle

LADY DAY AT EMERSON'S BAR AND GRILL by Lanie Robertson; *World Premiere;* Director, Woodie King, Jr.; Musical Director, Neal Tate; Set, Stephen Reardon; Costumes, Joyce Andrulot; Lighting, David Brewer. CAST: George Grier, Neal Tate, Reenie UpChurch

THROUGH LINE by Tom Huey; *World Premiere;* Director, Kent Stephens; Set, Michelle Bellavance; Costumes, Susan Mickey; Lighting, William B. Duncan. CAST: Catherine Cox, Skip Foster

PINOCCHIO story by Carlo Collodi, adapted by Sandra Deer; *World Premiere;* Director, Skip Foster; Set, Charles Caldwell; Costumes, Susan Hirschfeld; Lighting, Marilyn Rennagel; Composer, David Smadbeck. CAST: John Ammerman, Lynn Brown, Marianne Fraulo, Amanda Graham, Al Hamacher, John Kirman, Iris Little-Roberts, Jon Ludwig, Kelvin R. Shepard, Brad Sherrill

TALES FROM EDGAR ALLAN POE adapted by Tom Huey; *World Premiere;* Director, Kent Stephens; Choreography, Dee Wagner; Set, Nancy Margaret Orr; Costumes, Joyce Andrulot; Lighting, Paulie Jenkins; Sound/Music, Michael Keck. CAST: John Ammerman, Raul Aportela, Michael Keck, Buck Newman, Jr., Bill Nunn, John Purcell, Kelvin R. Shepard, Brad Sherrill, Ken Strong

FINDING HOME by Michael Bigelow Dixon, Jerry Patch, Diane King; Director, Michael W. Nelson; Musical Director, Bryan Mercer; Choreography, James F. Sturgell; Set, Mark S. Edlund; Costumes, Judy Winograd. CAST: Lynn Brown, Pat Flick, Michael Meredith, Donna Nelson

Charles Rafshoon Photos

William Paterson, Joan Stuart-Morris in "Opera Comique" Above: Joyce Reehling, Eileen Heckart in " 'night, Mother" Top: Earl Hindman, Lisa Emery in "Flint and Roses"

AMERICAN CONSERVATORY THEATRE

San Francisco, California
October 9, 1985–May 17, 1986
Twentieth Season

Artistic Director, Edward Hastings; Conservatory Director, Lawrence Hecht; Communications, Dennis Powers; General Manager, Dianne M. Prichard; Administrative Director, Pamela Simi; Company Manager, Mary Garrett; Press/Public Relations, Ralph Hoskins; Stage Directors: William Ball, Eugene Barcone, Joy Carlin, Sabin Epstein, Edward Hastings, Lawrence Hecht, Janice Hutchins, Nagle Jackson, Laird Williamson; Stage Managers, James Haire, Eugene Barcone, Duncan W. Graham, Alice Elliott Smith; Costumes, Regina Cate, Jeannie Davidson, Fritha Knudsen, Katharine E. Kraft, Warren Travis; Lighting, Richard Devin, Derek Duarte; Sets, Jesse Hollis, Warren Travis; Sound, Christopher Moore; Stylist/Props, Oliver C. Olsen

COMPANY: Linda Aldrich, Jim Baker, Joseph Bird, Scot Bishop, Kate Brickley, Joy Carlin, Michelle Casey, John Castellanos, Peter Donat, Nike Doukas, Geoffrey Elliott, Sabin Epstein, Drew Eshelman, Jill Fine, Dean Goodman, Wendell J. Grayson, Rick Hamilton, Lawrence Hecht, Elizabeth Huddle, Janice Hutchins, Johanna Jackson, Peter Jacobs, John Loschmann, David Haier, Dakin Matthews, William McKeregahan, Mark Murphey, Fredi Olster, Frank Ottiwell, Elizabeth Padilla, William Paterson, Marcia Pizzo, John Stuart-Morris, Deborah Sussel, Bernard Vash, Marrian Walters, Kenn Watt, Henry Watt, Henry Woronicz, Daniel Zippi
Lance Baker, Heather Bostian-Vash, Peter Bradbury, Sandy Bull, Julia Elliott, John Erlendson, Cynthia Fujikawa, Tim Greer, Tom Harmon, Ian Hewitt, Kimberley LaMarque, Robin Nordli, Shanti Reinhardt, Stephen Rockwell, Katherine Stanford, Lannyl Stephens

PRODUCTIONS: *The Majestic Kid* by Mark Medoff, WORLD PREMIERE: *Opera Comique* by Nagle Jackson, *'night, Mother* by Marsha Norman, *You Never Can Tell* by George Bernard Shaw, *A Christmas Carol* by Charles Dickens, *Private Lives* by Noel Coward, *The Passion Cycle* by Anonymous, *Woolgatherer* by William Mastrosimone

Larry Merkle Photos

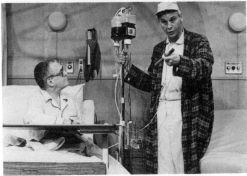

Jeremy Geidt, John Bottoms in "The Day Room"
Above: Marrian Walters (L) in " 'night, Mother"

AMERICAN REPERTORY THEATRE

Cambridge, Massachusetts
November 27, 1985–May 11, 1986

Artistic Director, Robert Brustein; Managing Director, Robert J. Orchard; Literary Director, Jonathan Marks; Production Manager, Jonathan Miller; Marketing, Lynn Garvin; Press, Jan Geidt; Graphics, Freelow Crummett; Technical Director, Jeff Muskovin; Stage Managers, John Grant-Phillips, Abbie H. Katz, Michele Steckler

PRODUCTIONS & CASTS

THE CHANGELING by Thomas Middleton; Director, Robert Brustein; Sets/Costumes, Michael H. Yeargan; Lighting, Richard Riddell; Music, Karl Lundeberg; Vocal and text consultant, Elizabeth Smith. CAST: Harry S. Murphy, Rodney Hudson, Jeremy Geidt, Diane D'Aquila, Thomas Derrah, Jack Stehlin, John Bottoms, Elizabeth Norment
THE JUNIPER TREE; Music by Philip Glass and Robert Moran; Libretto by Arthur Yorinks; Based on a tale by the Brothers Grimm; *World Premiere;* Director, Andrei Serban; Musical Director/Conductor, Richard Pittman; Sets/Costumes, Michael H. Yeargan; Lighting, Jennifer Tipton; Projections, Wendall K. Harrington, Bo Eriksson. CAST: Jane West, Sanford Sylvan or S. Mark Aliapoulios, Lynn Torgove or Lisa Saffer, Ruby Hinds or Valerie Walters, Janet Brown or Sue Ellen Kuzma, David Stoneman, Thomas Derrah, William Cotten
THE BALCONY by Jean Genet; Translation by Jean-Claude van Itallie; Director, JoAnne Akalaitis; Sets, George Tsypin; Costumes, Kristi Zea; Lighting, Jennifer Tipton; Music, Ruben Blades; Choreography, Johanna Boyce; Sound, Peter Michael Sullivan; Wigs/Makeup, Bobby Miller; Assistant Director, Peter Confalone. CAST: John Bottoms, Joan MacIntosh, Rodney Hudson, Eric Menyuk, Ben Halley Jr., Diane D'Aquila, Harry S. Murphy, Elizabeth Norment, Jack Stehlin, Tim McDonough, Jeremy Geidt, Thomas Derrah
ALCESTIS; *World Premiere;* Adapted by Robert Wilson from a play by Euripides as translated by Dudley Fitts and Robert Fitzgerald; Additional text, Heiner Muller; *Description of a Picture* translated by Carl Weber; Japanese Kyogen *The Birdcatcher in Hell* translated by Mark Oshima; Music, Laurie Anderson; Conceived, Directed, Designed by Robert Wilson; Set, Tom Kamm, Robert Wilson; Costumes, John Conklin; Lighting, Jennifer Tipton, Robert Wilson; Movement, Suzushi Hanayagi; Audio Environment, Hans Peter Kuhn; Assistant Director, Ann-Christin Rommen. CAST: Rodney Hudson, Diane D'Aquila, Seth Goldstein, Harry S. Murphy, Shirley Wilber, Christopher Moore, Eric D. Menyuk, Paul Rudd, Jeremy Geidt, Thomas Derrah, Tim McDonough, John Bottoms
OLYMPIAN GAMES book and lyrics by Kenneth Cavander and Barbara Damashek; Music, Barbara Damashek; Based on Ovid's *Metamorphoses;* Director, Barbara Damashek. Sets/Costumes, Alexander Okun; Lighting, Spencer Moss. CAST: Christopher Moore, Harry S. Murphy, John Bottoms, Thomas Derrah, Lynn Torgove, Rodney Hudson, Diane D'Aquila, Jeremy Geidt, Elizabeth Norment, Karen MacDonald
T DAY ROOM by Don DeLillo; *World Premiere;* Director, Michael Bloom; Set, Loy Arcenas; Costumes, Karen Eister; Lighting, Richard Riddell. CAST: Jeremy Geidt, Thomas Derrah, Harry S. Murphy, Gayle Keller, Charles Weinstein
MISTERO BUFFO (A Comic Mystery) Written, Staged, and Performed by Dario Fo; *American Premiere;* English Supertitle Translation, Stuart Hodd, Ron Jenkins, Walter Valeri; Onstage Translator, Ron Jenkins; Set/Lighting, Lino Avolio. CAST: Dario Fo
TUTTA CASA, LETTO, E CHIESA (It's All Bed, Board, and Church) by Dario Fo and Franca Rame; *American Premiere* Director, Dario Fo; Onstage Translator, Maria Consagra; Set/Lighting, Lino Avolio. CAST: Franca Rame

Richard M. Feldman Photos

Top: Diane D'Aquila, Bonnie Zimering,
Paul Rudd in "Alcestis"

141

AMERICAN MUSICAL THEATRE

New London, Connecticut
January 9, 1985–May 3, 1986
First Season

Producer, Charles S. Peckham; Associate Producer/Technical Director, Daniel C. Morse; Musical Director, Glen Clugston; Stage Managers, John Brigleb, Regan Morse, Deborah L. Moignard; Development, Marion H. Bigelow; Company Manager, Arthur A. Pignataro; Wardrobe, Celeste Giommi, Lynn Poirot, Kathy Williams; Props, Chrissy Mitchell, James Warykas, Hazel Tal, Lynn Hill; Scenic Artists, Suzy Abbott, Daniel Truth, Elaine Mills, Donna Wieters, Kathleen Fillion, Nancy Gibson, Bernice M. Rosenthal; Assistant Conductor, Stephen Hinnenkamp; Make-up/Hair, James Stidfole, Wayne Beebe, John Driscoll, Alan Mitchell, Mae Awad; Production Manager, Victor Panciera; Press, Evelyn R. Warner/The Communications Group
RESIDENT COMPANY: Darla Allen, Kirk Barnes, Virginia Bundonis, Leon Charboneau, Sidney Charbonneau, Karen Dearborn, Jean De Grooth, Jeff Dutton, Eva Engman, Holly Evers, Stephen Fickinger, Diane Foster, Mark Foster, Rita Herbert, Julie Johnson, Brett Larson, Molly Loughlin, Chris Mahn, Mike Mosher, Ted Robin McKnight, Judy Anne Nelson, James Boyd Parker, Wendy Piper, Robert Vaughan-Porter, Carol Rood, Cheryl Swift, Tony Tenuto, Cecile Thompson, John Tobin, Michaele Blake Tapley, Michael DiFonzo, Anne Gunderson, Chris Harrison, Kristine Kepright, Marion Markham, Rosejean Goddard, Jenny Cunningham, Gary Baillargeon, Christine Bialowans, April Dickenson, David Dorman, Donald Hall, Peter Marcus, Mary Norris, Amy Norris, Jason Siegel, Kristin Havrilla, Ron Bohmer, Kevin Coleman, Valerie DePena, Joe DeVito, Mark Foster, Donald Hall, Steve Hill, Kathleen Hare, Marisa Manthey, Amy Mazurek, Matthew Padden, Deborah Rastall, Christopher Scott, Stacey Spartz, Doug Tompos, Paul Anderson, Gary Barker, Brian Harvey, Tony Szerszen, Mike Packewicz, Carol Ann Robey, Julie Schroll, Richard Schuh, Marla Snitkin, Patricia Uguccioni, Amy Mazurek, Stefan Ambrosch, Revell Carr, Lisa DeVito, Michael Hall, Martha Jenssen, Patrick Loughlin, Jason Siegel, Andy Slater, Michael Slater, Travis Sullivan, Ryan Zemanek, Celeste Furman, Seth Posner, Doug Bjorn, Ryan Zemanec, Elizabeth Clouthier, Terri D. Dagitz, Bridget Elliott, Kimberly Gould, Walter Hughes, Dale Shanholtzer, Julia Wardlaw, Tricia Mitchell, Bob Perry, Erin Lynn Windle, Ryan Zemanec, Kathy Hershey, Kathy Williams, Lisa Rue, Margaret S. Ayer, Helen Bodman, Pauline DeMarco, Pat Durham, Margaret Gerlipp, Ellie Grasso, Linda Hudson, Anne Ilson, Corie Lanning, Dorothy L. Sayers, Dorothy Sayers, Dorothy Scanlon, Mimi Seed, Judith Strickland, Lucille Tourville, Hanne Waldschmidt, Joan Weigle, John Driscoll, Marge Gerlib, Lisa Rue

PRODUCTIONS & CASTS

MY FAIR LADY with book and lyrics by Alan Jay Lerner; Music, Frederick Lowe; Director/Choreographer, Don Price; Set, Daniel Morse; Costumes, H. Victor Panciera; Lighting, Susan White. CAST: Paige O'Hara (Eliza Doolittle), Gary Krawford (Henry Higgins), George Holmes (Col. Pickering), Gary Baillargeon (Freedy Eynsford-Hill), John Clarkson (Alfred P. Doolittle)

**Paige O'Hara, Bryon Nease
in "Annie Get Your Gun"**

ANNIE GET YOUR GUN with Music and Lyrics by Irving Berlin; Book, Herbert and Dorothy Fields; Director, Jerry Heymann; Choreographer, Leo Muller; Set, Ernest Allen Smith; Lighting, Greg MacPherson; Costumes, H. Victor Panciera. CAST: Paige O'Hara (Annie Oakley), Byron Nease (Frank Butler), Martin J. Walsh (Col. William F. Cody/Buffalo Bill), Jared Matesky (Charlie Davenport), Judith Bro (Dolly Tate), Dick Decareau (Foster Wilson/Waiter/Major Gordon Lillie/Pawnee Bill), Robert Irwin (Little Jake), Ashley Aimetti (Nellie), Julie E. Schroll (Jessie), Anne Graboski (Minnie)
KISS ME KATE with Music and Lyrics by Cole Porter; Book, Sam and Bella Spewack; Director, Charles Maryan; Choreographer, Jerry Fires; Set, Ernest Allen Smith; Costumes, Lana Fritz; Lighting, Greg MacPherson. CAST: Ron Raines (Fred Graham/Petruchio), Susan Long (Lilli Vanessi/Katherine), Ellyn Arons (Lois Lane/Bianca), Mark Martino (Bill Calhoun/Lucentio), John Bennes, Michael McCarty (Gangsters), Rosejean Goddard (Hattie)
THE MUSIC MAN with Music and Lyrics by Meredith Willson; Book, Meredith Willson, Franklin Lacey; Director, James R. Lee; Choreographer, Sally Lee; Set, Kent Goetz; Costumes, Lana Fritz; Lighting, Greg MacPherson. CAST: Gary Krawford (Harold Hill), Rebecca Luker (Marian Paroo), Gibby Brand (Marcellus Washburn), Christopher Scott (Tommy Djilas), Holly Evers (Zaneeta Shinn), Irwin Charone (Mayor Shinn), Justine Johnston (Eulalie Mackecknie Shinn), Carol Ann Robey (Mrs. Paroo).
HOW TO SUCCEED . . . with Music and Lyrics by Frank Loesser; Book, Abe Burrows, Jack Weinstock, Willie Gilbert; Director, Leslie B. Cutler; Choreographer, Leo Muller; Set, Ernest Allen Smith; Costumes, Lana Fritz; Lighting, Greg MacPherson. CAST: Matthew Padden (J. Pierrepont Finch), Marion Markham (Smitty), G. Wayne Hoffman (Frump), Karen Looze (Miss Jones), Alec Murphy (Mr. Twimble/Womper), Kathleen Jaworski (Hedy)
MAME with Book by Jerome Lawrence and Robert E. Lee; Music and Lyrics, Jerry Herman; Based on the Novel by Patrick Dennis and the Play *Auntie Mame* by Lawrence and Lee; Director/Choreographer, Don Price; Set, Ernest Allen Smith; Costumes, Susanna Douthit; Lighting, Greg MacPherson. CAST: Jo Ann Cunningham (Mame Dennis), John Almberg (Beauregard Jackson Pickett Burnside), Janie Kelly (Vera Charles), Barbara Marineau (Agnes Gooch), Isao Sato (Ito), Christopher Unger (Patrick Dennis), David Miles (M. Lindsey Woolsey/Uncle Jeff), Eva Engman (Gloria Upson), Kathy Yates (Pegeen Ryan), Ken Nagy (Junior Babcock), Carol Ann Robey (Mother Burnside).
THE SOUND OF MUSIC with Music by Richard Rodgers; Lyrics by Oscar Hammerstein II; Book, Howard Lindsay, Russel Crouse; Choreographer, Leo Muller; Set, Ernest Allen Smith; Lighting, Greg Mac Pherson. CAST: Jeanne Lehman (Maria), Arne Gundersen (Capt. von Trapp), Marsha Bagwell (Mother Abbess), JoAnn Cuningham (Elsa Schrader), Alec Murphy (Max Detweiler), Lisa Pompa (Liesel), Scott Bluefoote (Rolf Gruber), Jean Baker (Sister Berthe), James Boyd Parker (Franz), Rosejean Goddard (Frau Schmidt), Reid MacLean (Fredrich), Lisa Devito (Louisa), Richard Blake (Kurt), Amy Kunen (Brigitta), Julie Schroll (Marta), Samantha Jordan (Gretl), Charles Cagle (Admiral von Schreiber)

Photos by William Burrows

**Arne Gundersen, Marsha Bagwell, Jeanne Lehman
in "The Sound of Music"**

ARENA STAGE

Washington, D.C.
October 4, 1985–June 4, 1986
Thirty-fifth Season

Producing Director, Zelda Fichandler; Associate Producing Director, Douglas C. Wager; Managing Director, William Stewart; Artistic Associate, Garland Wright; Production Coordinator, Guy Bergquist; Producing Associate, James C. Nicola; Development, David Copelin; Technical Directors, David Glenn, James Glendinning; Scenic Artist, Michael Franklin-White; Props, Charles Fox; Lighting, Nancy Schertler; Sound, Susan R. White; Costumes, Marjorie Slaiman; Stage Managers, Jeffery Alspaugh, Maxine Krasowski Bertone, Melissa Davis, Martha Knight, Eric Osbun, Wendy Streeter, Sarah Whitham; Composer, John McKinney; Sets, Adrianne Lobel; Lighting, Paul Gallo; Vocal Consultant, Timothy Monich; Public Relations/Marketing, Patricia Nicholson, Mary Elizabeth Rutkowski
COMPANY: Stanley Anderson, Richard Bauer, Casey Biggs, Ralph Cosham, Terrence Currier, Randy Danson, Heather Ehlers, John Gegenhuber, Mark Hammer, Tom Hewitt, Tana Hicken, John Leonard, Thomas Anthony Quinn, Cary Anne Spear, Kim Staunton, Henry Strozier, Halo Wines, Maggie Winn-Jones
GUESTS ARTISTS: Jorge Abreu, Alvin Alexis, Richard Bertone, Charles Bortell, Doug Brown, Michael Chaban, Kevin Davis, Richard Dix, Abraham Dobkin, Franchelle Stewart Dorn, Avner Eisenberg, Rebecca Ellens, Dave W. Esguerra, Jeffrey Fignar, E'Dior FitzGerald, Mary Beth Flournoy, Laurie Franks, Joe Glenn, Martin Goldsmith, Ann Guilbert, Dorothea Hammond, Jeffrey Hayenga, Terry Hinz, Pete Holm, Robert Honeygosky, Seymour Horowitz, Bill Irwin, Keith Johnson, Ben Kapen, Rosemary Knower, Jeanette Landis, David MacDonald, Walt MacPherson, Charles C. Mark, Mercedes McCambridge, Christopher McCann, Lori Cope McGuin, Lesa McLaughlin, John Millar, Scott Morgan, Donald Neal, M. C. O'Connor, LaFontaine Oliver, Bernie Papure, Lawrence Redmond, Yohance Richards, Laila Robins, Michael Russotto, Scott Schofield, Doug Skinner, Chris Stanzione, Thomas Tillotson, Warren K. Travis, Stephen Wade, Robert W. Westenberg

PRODUCTIONS

THE GOOD PERSON OF SETZUAN by Bertholt Brecht; Music, John McKinney; Director, Garland Wright; Set, John Arnone; Costumes, Marjorie Slaiman; Lighting, Nancy Schertler; Stage Manager, Benita Hofstetter
'NIGHT MOTHER by Marsha Norman; Director, James C. Nicola; Set, Russell Metheny; Costumes, Noel Borden; Lighting, Frances Aronson; Stage Manager, Pat Cochran
WOMEN AND WATER by John Guare; Director, Douglas C. Wager; Set, Tony Straiges; Costumes, Marjorie Slaiman; Lighting, Allen Lee Hughes; Stage Manager, M. A. Howard; Puppets, Julie Taymor, Robert Flanagan; Fight Direction, Terry Hinz
RESTORATION by Edward Bond; Director, Sharon Ott; Set, Thomas Lynch; Costumes, Marjorie Slaiman; Lighting, Paul Gallo; Stage Manager, Robin Rumpf; Musical Direction, David Loud; Music, Nick Bicat, John McKinney
THE WILD DUCK by Henrik Ibsen; Translated by David Westerfer; Stage Version by Lucian Pintilie; Director, Lucian Pintilie; Set, Radu Boruzescu; Costumes, Miruna Boruzescu; Lighting, Beverly Emmons; Stage Manager, Melissa Davis
THE PHILADELPHIA STORY by Philip Barry; Director, Douglas C. Wager; Set, Adrianne Lobel; Costumes, Ann Hould-Ward; Lighting, Allen Lee Hughes; Stage Manager, Martha Knight
OLD TIMES by Harold Pinter; Director, Garland Wright; Set, Douglas O. Stein; Costumes, Marjorie Slaiman; Lighting, Nancy Schertler; Stage Manager, Wendy Streeter
THE TAMING OF THE SHREW by William Shakespeare; Director, Douglas C. Wager; Set, Adrianne Lobel; Costumes, Martin Pakledinaz; Lighting, Paul Gallo; Stage Manager, Martha Knight; Movement Consultant, Lesa McLaughlin
SPECIAL EVENTS: Stephen Wade in *Banjo Dancing or the 48th Annual Squitters Mountain Song Dance Folklore Convention . . . and how I lost*, Avner the Eccentric, *The Regard of Flight, Stray Dogs* by Julie Jensen, *PlayLab*
LIVING STAGE THEATRE COMPANY: Director, Robert Alexander; Managing Director, Catherine Irwin; Associate Artistic Director, Jennifer Nelson; Music Director, Mark Novak; Performing Company: Fracaswell Hyman, Ezra Knight, Jennifer Nelson, Oran Sandel, Brenda Wooley-Gonzalez; Production Coordinator, Kelly Jerome

Joan Marcus, Shawn Fraser Photos

Top Right: Henry Strozier, Casey Biggs, Randy Danson in "The Taming of the Shrew" Below: Richard Bauer, Rebecca Ellens, Mark Hammer in "The Wild Duck"

ARKANSAS REPERTORY THEATRE

Little Rock, Arkansas
September 12, 1985–June 15, 1986

Artistic Director, Cliff Fannin Baker; Managing Director, Andrew C. Gaupp; Associate Director, Cathey Crowell Sawyer; Business Manager, Lynn Frazier; Production Manager, Terry Sneed; Marketing, Beth A. Jasper; Touring Manager, Guy Couch; Office Manager, Melanie Strange; Technical Director/Scenic Designer, Mike Nichols; Lighting/Electrician, Kathy Gray; Costumes, Marcy Bethel; Carpenter, Paul Brooks; Apprentices: Jeffrey Bailey, Sarah Farmer Earll, Barry Mines; Interns: Amy Jo Barker, Molly Marie Davis, Brad Fry, Karen Heck, Robert A. Jones, Lisa K. Martley, Maggie Murphy, Pamela Jennings Nunnelley, Sonja Young
COMPANY: Ronald J. Aulgur, Cathey Crowell Sawyer, Terry Sneed, Caroline Pugh,
GUEST ARTISTS: Scott Edmonds, Mercedes McCambridge, Frank Bonner, Sally Sockwell, Mark Johnson, Ron Himes, Maureen Shannon, Steve Wilkerson, Patrick McCarthy, Terry Kennedy, Diane Tack
PRODUCTIONS: *The Night of the Iguana, Agnes of God, The Foreigner, Quartermaine's Terms, Home, 'night Mother, Quilters*, WORLD PREMIER: *The Good Woman of Setzuan* translated by Eric Bentley; Music and Lyrics by Michael Rice

Barry Arthur Photos

Above: Cathey Crowell Sawyer, Mercedes McCambridge in " 'night, Mother"

143

ARIZONA THEATRE COMPANY

Tucson/Phoenix, Arizona
November 2, 1985–June 22, 1986

Artistic Director, Gary Gisselman; Resident Director, Walter Schoen; Associate Artistic Director, Ken Ruta; Guest Director, Edward Payson Call; Costume Director, Bobbi Culbert; Production Manager, Don Hooper; Managing Director, Richard Bryant; General Manager, Nancy Thomas; Marketing/Public Relations, Gary Bacal; Development, Barbara R. Levy; Company Manager, Becky Schwartz; Sound, Jeff Ladman; Wardrobe, Maggi Shaw; Props, Vicki L. Dittemore; Production Assistant, James Smith

PRODUCTIONS & CASTS
FOOL FOR LOVE by Sam Shepard; Director, Gary Gisselman; Set, Vicki Smith; Costumes, Bobbi Culbert; Lighting, Kent Dorsey; Sound, Jeff Ladman; Stage Managers, Jay Rabins, Kent Conrad. CAST: Stephen Yoakam (Eddie), Jenifer Parker (May), Paul Ballantyne (The Old Man), Tony DeBruno (Martin)
THE REAL THING by Tom Stoppard; Director, Ken Ruta; Set, Sam Kirkpatrick, Don Hooper; Costumes, Diane Fargo; Lighting, Don Darnutzer; Sound, Jeff Ladman; Stage Manager, Nancy Thomas. CAST: Charles Gregory (Max), Jeanne Cullen (Charlotte), Ron Siebert (Henry), Kandis Chappell (Annie), Gregory Welch (Billy), Katy Boyer (Debbie), Sean Michael Kelly (Brodie)
GALILEO by Bertolt Brecht; Translation, Charles Laughton; Director, Gary Gisselman; Set, Vicki Smith; Costumes, Gene David Buck; Lighting, Don Darnutzer; Music, Roberta Carlson; Sound, Jeff Ladman; Stage Manager, Jay Robins. CAST: Bain Boehlke, To-Ree-Nee Keiser, Ken Ruta, Michael Angiulo, Jenifer Parker, Marco Barricelli, Paul C. Thomas, W. Francis Walters, Julian Gamble, Don West, Eduardo Martin, Larry Paulsen, Francesca Jarvis, Joe Horvath, Adam E. Graham, Michael Ellison, Tony DeBruno, Melinda McCrary, Jason David, Elsie C. Wagner, Roberta Carlson, Michael Blaisus
THE GOVERNMENT INSPECTOR by Nikolai Gogol; Director, Walter Schoen; Set, Vicki Smith; Costumes, David Mickelsen; Lighting, Don Darnutzer; Sound, Bob Bish; Stage Manager, Kent Conrad CAST: Peder Melhuse, Tony DeBruno, Adam E. Graham, Paul C. Thomas, W. Francis Walters, Joe Horvath, Michael Ellison, Marco Barricelli, Eduardo Martin, Julian Gamble, Jenifer Parker, Melinda McCrary, To-Ree-Nee Keiser, Don West, Bain Boehlke, Elsie C. Wagner, Francesca Jarvis, James Breining
PRIVATE LIVES by Noel Coward; Director, Edward Payson Call; Set, Don Hooper; Costumes, Christopher Beesley; Lighting, Don Hooper; Sound, Jeff Ladman; Musical Direction, Sandi Shroads; Stage Manager, Jay Rabins. CAST: Jordan R. Baker (Sibyl Chase), Rudolph Willrich (Elyot Chase), Julian Gamble (Victor Prynne), Margery Murray (Amanda Prynne), Sherilyn Forrester (Louise)
MY FAIR LADY with Book and Lyrics by Alan Jay Lerner; Music by Frederick Loewe; Adapted from George Bernard Shaw's Play and Gabrial Pascal's motion picture *Pygmalion;* Director, Gary Gisselman; Choreographer, Myron Johnson; Musical Director, Anita Ruth; Set, Kent Dorsey, Thomas Buderwitz; Costumes, Gene Davis Buck; Lighting, Don Darnutzer; Sound, Jeff Ladman; Stage Manager Kent Conrad. CAST: Charlotte Adams, Bain Boehlke, Gary Briggle, Oliver Cliff, Carl Craig, John Jellison, Patricia E. Kennedy, Wendy Lehr. Eduardo Martin, Bruce Nelson, Delrae Novak, Marion Primont, Alba R. Quezada, Philip Ross, Don West
A CIRCULAR FUNCTION by Michael Grady; *World Premiere*

Tim Fuller Photos

Curzon Dobell as "Hamlet"

Ken Ruta as "Galileo"

ASOLO STATE THEATER

Sarasota, Florida
June 1, 1985–May 31, 1986

Executive Director, Richard G. Fallon; Associate Executive Director, Stephen Rothman; Artistic Director, John Ulmer; General Manager, Robert A. Rosenbaum; Assistant Artistic Director, John Gulley; Press, Edith N. Anson; Sets, Jeffrey Dean, John Ezell, Bennet Averyt, Kenneth N. Kurtz, Kevin Lock, Holmes Easley, Charles T. Parsons; Costumes, Catherine King, Mitchell Bloom; Lighting, Martin Petlock, Mark Noble; Technical Director, Victor Meyrich; Stage Managers, Marian Wallace, Stephanie Moss, Dan Carter, Marlie Cordon; Guest Directors: Susan Gregg, Porter Van Zandt, Jamie Brown, Robert Miller, Bill Levis, Alan Arkin; Fight Director for *Hamlet,* Jamie Smith; Original Music for *Forgive Me, Evelyn Bunns,* John Franceschina
COMPANY: Donald Buka, A. D. Cover, Stephen Daley, Douglas Jones, Jack Koenig, Carolyn Michel, Karl Redcoff, Barbara Sohmers, Georgia Southcotte, Eric Tavares, Isa Thomas, Bradford Wallace, Kathryn Riedman, Mark Ciokajlo, Jody Kielbasa, Susan Jones Mannino, Carol Martini, Michael Piontek, Kenn Rapczynski, Karen Rasch, Jennifer Riggs, Steve Spencer, Donna Anderson, Karen Bair, Nancy Hartman, Michael Lariscy, Mary E. Launder, David B. Levine, Lynne Perkins, Parry B. Stewart, Vince Williams. Kay Daphne, Michael O. Smith, John Thomas Waite, Nora Chester, Marc Durso, Dane Knell, Terry Layman, Lisa Barnes, Sheridan Crist, Mac Crowell, Curzon Dobell, Arthur Hanket, Mark Hattan, Rory Kelly, Richard Maynard, Rupert Ravens, Adam Arkin, Anthony Arkin, Barbara Dana, Yvette Hawkins, Tresa Hughes, Diane Kamp, Dolores Sutton, Linda Cook, Ann Ducati, Suzanne Grodner, Bill Levis, Peter Gregory Thompson, Donna A. DeLonay, Laurel Casey, Art Dohany, Jeffrey Herbst, Elizabeth Herron, Michael Laird, Beth Lane, Kyndal May, Robb Pruitt, Christine Sloane, Richard Smolendki, Alex C. Thayer, Jill Ann Womack.
PRODUCTIONS: *A Month in the Country, You Can't Take it With You, Twice Around the Park, A Christmas Carol, Greater Tuna, Moon for the Misbegotten, A Life in the Theater, Sleuth, Orphans, Spoon River Anthology, Tartuffe, How the Other Half Loves, As Is,* WORLD PREMIER: *Forgive Me, Evelyn Bunns* by Janet Couch; AMERICAN PREMIERE of the A. L. Rowse edition of *Hamlet*

Gary W. Sweetman Photos

BARTER THEATRE

Abingdon, Virginia
June 1, 1985–May 31, 1986
Fifty-third Season

Artistic Director/Producer, Rex Partington; Business Manager, Pearl Hayter; Press, Christan Whittington; Directors, Judith Haskell, William Van Keyser, Rex Partington, Ken Costigan, Trip Plymale; Sets, Gary Aday, Daniel Ettinger, John C. Larrance, Jim Stauder; Costumes, Sigrid Insull, Barbara Forbes, Karen Brewster, Martha Hally, Lisa C. Michaels; Lighting, Al Oster; Stage Managers, Champe Leary, Don Buschmann, Robert I. Cohen, Tony Partington

PRODUCTIONS & CASTS

AND A NIGHTINGALE SANG by C. P. Taylor. CAST: Marlene Bryon, John FitzGibbon, Gavin Reed, Carol Schultz, Edward Stevlingson, Darrold Strubbe, Deborah Van Nostrand
AGNES OF GOD by John Pielmeier. CAST: Cleo Holladay, Sarah Melici, Ann Newhall
MY FAT FRIEND by Charles Laurence. CAST: Stephen Gabis, Ross Bickell, Helen Zelen, David Licht
PAINTING CHURCHES by Tina Howe. CAST: Marjorie Lovett, Gwyllum Evans, Beverly Jensen
THE GUARDSMAN by Ferenc Molnar. CAST: Sarah Melici, Ross Bickell, McKee Anderson, Frank Lowe, Kathryn Ballard, Rex Partington
GREATER TUNA by Jaston Williams, Joe Sears, Ed Howard. CAST: Trip Plymale, Richard Kinter
TWICE AROUND THE PARK by Murray Schisgal. CAST: Donald Christopher, Cleo Holladay
BILLY BISHOP GOES TO WAR by John Gray with Eric Peterson. CAST: Ross Bickell, Byron Grant
SEA MARKS by Gardner McKay. CAST: John FitzGibbon, Beverly Jensen
EDUCATING RITA by Willy Russell. CAST: Stratton Walling, Laura Mellencamp
I OUGHT TO BE IN PICTURES by Neil Simon. CAST: Lorraine Morgan, Larry Sharp, June Daniel White

Charles Beatty, Dave Grace Photos

**Top Right: Laura Mellencamp, Stratton
Walling in "Educating Rita"**

**Doug Holmes, Brian Horton, Nancy Carroll
in "Fiddler on the Roof" Above: Walter
Willison, Suzanne Stark in "Carousel"**

BEEF AND BOARDS DINNER THEATRE

Indianapolis, Indiana
June 1, 1985–May 31, 1986

Artistic Director, Douglas E. Stark; Managing Djirector, Robert D. Zehr; Musical Director, Richard Laughlin; Sets/Lighting, Michael Layton; Costumes, Debby Shively, JoAnn Jankowski, Livingston; Public Press Relations, Karen Marchesseault; Choreographers, Stephen Essner, William Alan Coats; Stage Manager, Edward Stockman; Stage Directors, Douglas E. Stark, Robert D. Zehr

PRODUCTIONS & CASTS

ON GOLDEN POND by Ernest Thompson; CAST: Albert Helmer Ratcliffe (Norman Thayer, Jr.), Fiona Hale (Ethel Thayer), Brian Horton (Charlie Martin), Debby Shively (Chelsea Thayer Wayne), Gavin Inglis (Billy Ray), Doug Holmes (Bill Ray)
GYPSY with Book by Arthur Laurents; Lyrics, Stephen Sondheim; Music, Jule Stein; CAST: Shelly Wald (Rose), Sally Woodson (Louise), Laurie Walton (June), Richard Pruitt (Herbie), Debby Shively (Tessie Tura), Joyce Moody (Mazeppa), Natalie Jakowlew (Electra), Brian Horton (Uncle Jocko/Weber/Cigar), Heather Hussey (Baby Louise), Matt Clark (Tulsa), Kori McOmber (Baby June), Michael D. Cupp (Pop/Kringelein/Pastey), George Evans (Yonkers), Andy Spangler (LA), Graham Cox (Mr. Goldstone), Colleen Campbell (Agnes), and Scott Potasnik, Rebecca Vargas, Rob Constantine
FIDDLER ON THE ROOF with Book by Joseph Stein; Music, Jerry Bock; Lyrics, Sheldon Harnick; CAST: Douglas Edward Stark (Tevye), Annabelle Weenick (Golde), Nancy E. Carroll (Tzeitel), Mary Ann Marek (Hodel), Laurie Walton (Chava), Michelle Miller (Shprintze), Melissa Schott (Bielke), Jacqueline Rohrbacker (Yente), Doug Holmes (Motel), Stephen W. Essner (Perchik), Richard Pruitt (Lazar Wolf), Donald Sherrill (Mordcha), Brian Horton (Rabbi/Sasha), George Evans (Mendel), Judy Johnson (Fruma-Sarah/Shandel), Dan Scharbrough (Constable), Andy Spangler (Fyedka)
WEST SIDE STORY with Book by Arthur Laurents; Music, Leonard Bernstein; Lyrics, Stephen Sondheim; CAST: Gary Harger (Tony), Teresa DeZarn (Maria), Rhonda Farer (Anita), Stephen Bourneuf (Riff), Richard Loreto (Bernardo), Greg Garrison (Action), Andy Spangler (A-Rab), Ned Hannah (Baby John), Michele Humphrey (Anybodys), Tom Mason (Doc), Donald Sherrill (Officer Krupke), Brian Horton (Glad Hand), Phillip H. Colglazier (Chino), Nolan Hines (Pepe), Thea Mann (Velma/Francisca), Cathy Sessions (Graziella/Rosalia)
SHAME with Book & Lyrics by David Blomquist; Music, Douglas Benge & Peter Schmutte; *World Premiere;* CAST: Ann Heinricher, Brian Horton, Doug Holmes, Richard Pruitt, Leslie Esser, Patrick Parker, Jacqueline Rohrbacker, Priscilla Quimby, Donald Sherrill, Melissa Schott
A FUNNY THING HAPPENED ON THE WAY TO THE FORUM with Book by Burt Shevelove and Larry Gelbart; Music and Lyrics, Stephen Sondheim; CAST: Richard Pruitt (Pseudolus), Doug Holmes (Hysterium), Jacqueline Rohrbacker (Domina), Whit Reichert (Senex), Patrick Parker (Hero), Leslie Esser (Philia), Brian Horton (Lycus), Donald Sherrill (Milos Gloriosus), Mahlon Sharp (Erronius), Jennifer Campbell (Tintinnabula), Priscilla Quimby (Panacea), Michelle Humphrey (Vibrata), Thea Mann (Gymnasia), Christopher Zunner (Proteans), Nolan Hines (Proteans)
CAROUSEL with Book and Lyrics by Oscar Hammerstein II; Music, Richard Rodgers; CAST: Walter Willison (Billy Bigelow), Suzanne L. Stark (Julie Jordan), Laurie Walton (Carrie Pipperidge), Doug Holmes (Starkeeper/David Bascombe), Paula Leggett (Mrs. Mullins), Dee Etta Rowe (Nettie Fowler), Skip Harris (Enoch Snow), Brian Horton (Jigger Craigin), Cassey Nicholaw (Heavenly Friend), Ruth Anne Farrelly (Louise), Mark Knowles (Carnival Boy/Policeman), Christopher Zunner (Enoch Snow, Jr.), Leslie Esser (Bessie)

D. Todd Moore Photos

145

CENTER THEATRE GROUP

AHMANSON THEATRE

Los Angeles, California
September 26, 1985–May 24, 1986

Artistic Director, Robert Fryer; Associate Artistic Director, James H. Hansen; General Managers, Arline Chambers, Tom Jordan; Press, Rick Miramontez; Management Associate, Michelle McGrath; Executive Associate, Joyce Zaccaro; Production Manager, Ralph Beaumont; Technical Director, Robert Routolo; Administrative Assistants, Alan Cummings, John Traub; Props, Steve Rapollo

PRODUCTIONS & CASTS

THE UNVARNISHED TRUTH by Royce Ryton; *American Premiere;* Director, Robert Drivas; Set, Richard Seger; Costumes, Robert Blackman; Lighting, Martin Aronstein; Stage Managers, Bob Borod, Joe Cappelli, Kathleen Horton. CAST: John Ritter (Tom Bryce), James Coco (Bill Carlisle), Beth Howland (Annabel Bryce), Dody Goodman (Mrs. Cartwright), Paul Benedict (Lt. Drew), Ruth Jaroslow (Mrs. Plimpton-Strutt), Carol Morley (Isabel Fanton), Liz Sheridan (Dr. Sarah Hedley), Arthur Grethel (Policeman #1), George Spelvin (Policeman #2)

FOXFIRE by Susan Cooper and Hume Cronyn; Director, David Trainer; Set, David Mitchell; Costumes, Robert Blackman; Lighting, Ken Billington; Stage Managers, Martha Knight, James M. Arnemann. CAST: Jessica Tandy (Annie Nations), Hume Cronyn (Hector Nations), Keith Carradine (Dillard Nations), Donna Bullock (Holly Burrell), Jack Davidson (Doctor), Tom Stechschulte (Prince Carpenter)

LEGENDS by James Kirkwood; Director, Clifford Williams; Set, Douglas Schmidt; Costumes, Freddy Wittop; Lighting, Thomas Skelton; Stage Managers, Randall Buck, James Bernardi. CAST: Mary Martin (Leatrice Monsee), Carol Channing (Sylvia Glenn), Gary Beach (Martin Klemmer), Annie-Joe (Aretha Thomas), Eric Riley (A Young Man), Don Howard (Policeman), Tim Johnson (Earl)

PICNIC by William Inge; Director, Marshall W. Mason; Set, John Lee Beatty; Costumes, Madeline Ann Graneto; Lighting, Dennis Parichy; Dance Movement, Ralph Beaumont; Stage Managers, Bob Borod, Joe Cappelli, Kathleen Horton. CAST: Gregory Harrison (Hal Carter), Jennifer Jason Leigh (Madge Owens), Rue McClanahan (Flo Owens), Dick Van Patten (Howard Bevens), Dana Hill (Millie Owens), Timothy Shelton (Alan Benson), Michael Learned (Rosemary Sydney), Conchata Ferrell (Helen Potts), Brady Rubin (Christine Schoenwalder), Beth Grant (Irma Kronkite), Morgan Englund (Bomber), Ellen Crawford (Olive), Gary Berner (Poopdeck McCullough)

Jay Thompson, Kenn Duncan Photos

Jennifer Jason Leigh, Gregory Harrison
in "Picnic" Above: Jessica Tandy, Keith
Carradine in "Foxfire"

MARK TAPER FORUM

Los Angeles, California
August 29, 1985–July 13, 1986
Nineteenth Season

Artistic Director/Producer, Gordon Davidson; Executive Managing Director/CTG, William P. Wingate; Associate Artistic Director, Kenneth Brecher; Associate Producer, Madeline Puzo; Resident Director, Robert Egan; General Manager, Stephen J. Albert; Staff Director for ITP, Peter C. Brosius; Dramaturg, Jack Viertel, Jessica Teich; Literary Manager, William Storm; Development, Robert J. Schlosser; Directors, TV/Film Department, Elizabeth Daley, Judith Rutherford James; Lighting, Tharon Musser, Arden Fingerhut, Martin Aronstein, Frances Aronson, Paulie Jenkins; Production Administrator, Don Winton; Technical Director/TCG, Robert Routolo; Production Coordinator/Supervisor, Frank Bayer; Stage Managers, Jonathan Barlow Lee, Mary Michele Miner, Richard Winnie, Michael Wolf, Arlene Grayson, Mireya Hepner, James T. McDermott, Tami Toon; Press, Nancy Hereford, Phyllis Moberly, Ken Werther, Elizabeth Franklin.

PRODUCTIONS & CASTS

THE BEAUTIFUL LADY Book by Elizabeth Swados and Paul Schmidt; Poems translated by Paul Schmidt; Music and Lyrics, Elizabeth Swados; Director, Elizabeth Swados; Co-Choreographer/Assistant Director, Gary Mascaro; Set, Karl Eigsti; Costumes, Marianna Elliott; Lighting, Arden Fingerhut, Assistant Director, Tony Scheitinger; CAST: JoAnne Worley (Boris Pronin), Natasha Lutov (Natalia Pavlovna), Karen Trott (Akhmatova/Anna), Michael Hoit (Mayakovsky/Vladimir), Michael A. Shaner (Mandelstam/Osip), Daniel McDonald (Yesenin/Sergei), Kathy Sagal (Tsvetaeva/Marina), Don Sparks (Khlebnikov/Velemir), Donn Simione (Blok/Alexander); Patrons, Party Members (also Understudies:) Mark Bradford, Stephen Breithaupt, Sally Champlin, Randy Hamilton, Gary Imhoff, Karon Kearney, Lisa Michelson, James Rich, Kathryn Skatula

ROMANCE LANGUAGE by Peter Parnell; Director, Sheldon Larry; Set, Loren Sherman; Costumes, Sheila McLamb-Wilcox; Music, Conrad Susa; Sound, Jon Gottlieb, Scott Lehrer; Song, Jonathan Sheffer; Fight Choreography, Anthony De Longis; Choreography, Joann DiVito; Assistant Director, Gillian Eaton; Wigs, Bill Fletcher; Co-Production with The Old Globe Theatre, San Diego (Artistic Director, Jack O'Brien). CAST: Dakin Matthews (Walt Whitman), Jon Matthews (Huckleberry Finn), Carl Weintraub (Policeman/Lt. Varnum), Frances Conrow (Louisa May Alcott), Kevin Gray (Kooloo/Raincloud), Billy Barthy (Alcott/Lonesome Charley), Concetta Tomei (Charlotte Cushman), Jacque Lynn Colton (Emma Stebbins/Ellen Emerson/Dancehall Girl), Howard Shangraw (Tommy), Ben Siegler (Autie Reed), Valerie Mahaffey (Emily Dickinson), Kay E. Kuter (Ralph Waldo Emerson/Mitch Bouyer), John Vickery (Henry David Thoreau/George Armstrong Custer), Eric Schiff (Tom Sawyer), Howard Shangraw (Mme. Nash), Ralph Dreyfuss (Piano Catch Randy), Gregory Michaels (Bloody Knife), and Scott Brittingham, Timothy Dang, Matthew Dunn, Lynne Griffin, H. David C. Gunderman, Rion Hunter, Miguel Marcott, Gregory Michaels, Richardson Morse, Dan Speaker, Robert S. Telford

'night, Mother by Marsha Norman; Director, Tom Moore; Set, Richard Seger; Costumes, Heidi Landesman, Ann Bruice; Assistant Director, Michael Kyle. CAST: Anne Pitoniak, Kathy Bates. Understudies: Susan Barnes, Elizabeth Hoffman

GREEN CARD Written and Directed by JoAnne Akalaitis; Set, Douglas Stein; Costumes, Marianna Elliott; Choreography, Carolyn Dyer; Sound, Jon Gottlieb; Slide Projections/Photography, Craig Collins; Associate Producer, Madeline Puzo; Assistant Director, Linda Callahan; Puppet, Christina Haatainen; Films, Steve Brown, Chris Squires; Wigs/Hair, Bill Fletcher. CAST: Raye Birk, Jesse Borrego, Rosalind Chao, George Calvan, Castulo Guerra, Jim Ishida, Josie Kim, Dana Lee, Alma Martinez, Jessica Nelson, Mimi Seton. Understudies: Becky Gonzalez, Tony Simotes

THE REAL THING by Tom Stoppard; Director, Gordon Davidson; Set, David Jenkins; Costumes, Robert Blackman; Sound, Daniel Birnbaum; Assistant Director, Brian Kulick; CAST: Dakin Matthews (Max), Kate Mulgrew (Charlotte), Michael Gross (Henry), Linda Purl (Annie), Tony Goldwyn (Billy), Amy Resnick (Debbie), Tuck Milligan (Brodie). Understudies: George Deloy, Jonathan Emerson, Joan Foley, Richard Gould, Michele Seyler

HEDDA GABLER by Henrik Ibsen; In a version by Christopher Hampton; Director, Robert Egan; Set, David Jenkins; Costumes, Robert Blackman; Music/Sound, Daniel Birnbaum; Assistant Director, Brian Kulick; Wigs, Bill Fletcher; Hair, Christopher Richards; Production Assistants, Kathy Ogilvie, Mark L. Shanks. Kate Mulgrew (Hedda Gabler), Diana Douglas (Aunt Julia Tesman), Julianna McCarthy (Berte), Michael Gross (George Tesman), Linda Purl (Mrs. Elvsted), Dakin Matthews (Judge Brack), George Deloy (Eilert Lovborg). Understudies: Joan Foley, Richard Gould, Tuck Milligan, Dinah Anne Rogers, Michele Seyler

THE DREAM COAST Written and Directed by John Steppling; *World Premiere;* Set, John Ivo Gilles; Costumes, Terry Soon; Music, Don Preston; Sound, Daniel Birnbaum; Assistant Director, Brian Kulick. CAST: Bob Glaudini (Weldon), Louis R. Plante (Wilson), Elizabeth Ruscio (Marliss), Michael Collins (Drew), Tina Preston (Lana), John Pappas (Gary), Lee Kissman (Penny), Robert Hummer (Bill/Mr. Goodwrench), Sharon Madden (Woman's Voice)

**Kate Mulgrew, Dakin Matthews, Michael Gross
in "The Real Thing"**

MRS. CALIFORNIA by Doris Baizley; *World Premiere;* Director, Warner Shook; Set, John Ivo Gilles; Costumes, Deborah Dryden; Sound, Daniel Birnbaum; Dramaturg, Corey Beth Madden; Assistant Director, Ellen Krout. CAST: Deborah May (Dot), Fred Applegate (Dudley), Jean Smart (Babs), Gregory Itzin (Stage Manager), Frances Conroy (Mrs. San Francisco), Susan Krebs (Mrs. San Bernadino), Sharon Madden (Mrs. Modesto)

PLANET FIRES by Thomas Babe; Director, John Henry Davis; Set, Dan Dryden; Costumes, Susan Denison; Music, John Franceschina; Sound, Daniel Birnbaum; Fight Choreography, Greg Michaels; Dramaturg, William Storm; Assistant Director, Russell Bekins. CAST: Stephen Joyce (Bartholomew Van Amburg), Judd Nelson (Henry Hitchcock), Grand L. Bush (Will Dickens Hill), J. C. Quinn (Man/Abraham Lincoln), Tom Henschel (Dime Raffles), Shanna Reed (Tina Rubens), Rob Miller (Hippodrome Music Master)

SLEEPING DOGS by Neal Bell; *World Premiere;* Director, Jody McAuliffe; Set, Dan Dryden; Costumes, Ann Bruice; Sound, Daniel Birnbaum; Assistant Director, James Slowiak. CAST: Michael McGuire (Park), Judd Nelson (Sling/Bartender), Leigh Taylor-Young (Sally), Shanna Reed (Nana), J. C. Quinn (Miner), Julie Payne (Evelyn), Stephen Joyce (Capp)

LEGENDS by Kendrew Lascelles; Director, Robert Egan; Set, Michael Devine; Costumes, Grania O'Connor; Sound, Daniel Birnbaum; Production Assistant, Carole Beams; Assistant Director, Brian Kulick. CAST: Howard Witt (Gurk), Frances Lee McCain (Goodman), Monique Mannen (Seynab), J. C. Quinn (Walsh)

THE WASH by Philip Ken Gotanda; *World Premiere;* Director, Barbara Damashek; Set, Michael Devine; Costumes, Elizabeth Palmer; Music, Barbara Damashek; Sound, Daniel Birnbaum; Dramaturg, Corey Beth Madden; Production Assistant, Alicia C. Heffernan; Assistant Director, Nancy Simon. CAST: Mako (Nobu), Shizuko Hoshi (Masi), Kim Miyori (Marsha), Rosalind Chao (Judy), Keone Young (Blackie), June Kim (Kiyoko), Sab Shimono (Sadao), Momo Yashima (Chiyo), Daniel Kuramoto (Musician)

AN EVENING OF MICRO-OPERAS: *For Under The Volcano* Music, Carla Bley, Text, Malcolm Lowry, Carla Bley; *A Madrigal Opera* Music, Philip Glass, Text, Len Jenkin; *Slow Fire* Music, Paul Dresher, Text, Rinde Eckert

TAPER, TOO

ON THE VERGE or the Geography of Yearning by Eric Overmyer; Director, Jackson Phippin; Music, Roger Trefousse; Choreography, Gary Mascaro; Set, Larry Fulton; Costumes, Susan Denison; Lighting, Liz Stillwell; Sound, Jon Gottlieb; CAST: Susan Barnes (Fanny), Libby Boone (Alex), Paddi Edwards (Mary), James McDonnell (The Man)

SEE BELOW MIDDLE SEA by Mimi Seton; *World Premiere;* Conceived, Composed, Directed by Mimi Seton; Choreography, Eddie Glickman; Musical Director, David Anglin; Set, Nancy Seruto; Costumes, Sylvia Moss; Lighting, Liz Stillwell; Slide Projections/Photography, Craig Collins. CAST: Tony Abatemarco, Tony Duran, Daisietta Kim, Susan Kohler, Roxanne Mayweather, Deborah Nishimura, Graciela Onetto, William Pasley, Gregory Thirloway, Bradd Wong

RAT IN THE SKULL by Ron Hutchinson; Director, Dana Elcar; Set, Clare. Scarpulla; Costumes, Durinda Wood; Lighting, Peter Maradudin; Stage Manager, Caryn Shick. CAST: David Marshall Grant (Roche), William Glover (Harris), Christopher Grove (Naylor), Charles Hallahan (Nelson)

IMPROVISATIONAL THEATRE PROJECT: *Newcomer* by Janet Thomas; *World Premiere;* Director, Peter C. Brosius; Choreography, Gary Mascaro; Music/Sound, Daniel Birnbaum; Set, Rob Murphy; Costumes, Armand Coutu; Coordinators, Sarah McArthur, Barbara Leonard; Stage Managers, Tom Allard, Kerry Hirschberg; Production Assistants, Patty Toy, James W. Quinn. CAST: Karen Maruyama (Aurora), Miho (Mai Li), Jerry Tondo (Benny/Boatman/Guard), Jay Varela (Jesus Escamilla/Johnson), Virginia Wing (Mai Li's mother). Understudies: Patty Toy, James W. Quinn

SUNDAYS AT THE ITCHEY FOOT: *Poets in Their Youth* by Eileen Simpson; Adaption, Jeremy Lawrence; Director, William Woodman; Producer, William Storn; CAST: Bruce French, Tom Henschel, John de Lancie, Suzanne Lederer, Marnie Mosiman. *The Damned Thing* by Ambrose Bierce and *The Facts in the Case of M. Valdemar* and *Berenice* by Edgar Allan Poe; Adapted and Produced by Madeline Puzo; Director, Dakin Matthews; CAST: Raye Birk, Carl Lumbly, Dakin Matthews. *Souvenir* Two Stories by Jayne Anne Phillips; Adapted and Produced by Jessica Teich; Director, Jody McAuliffe; CAST: Barbara Tarbuck, Mary Crosby, Lynne Griffin.

IN DREAMS BEGIN RESPONSIBILITIES by Delmore Schwartz; Conceived by Jack Viertel, Jon Robin Baitz, Peter Frechette; Adapted and Directed by Jon Robin Baitz; Music, Randolph Dreyfuss, William Bolcom; Producer, Jack Viertel; CAST: Peter Frechette, Randolph Dreyfuss

Rob Brown, Joy Thompson, Richard Feldman Photos

**Left Center: Anne Pitoniak, Kathy Bates
in " 'night, Mother" Above: Billy Barty,
Kay E. Kuter, Howard Shangraw in "Romance
Language" Top: Rosalind Chao, Mimi Seton,
Alma Martinez, Jessica Nelson, Josie Kim
in "Green Card"**

BURT REYNOLDS JUPITER THEATRE

Jupiter, Florida
June 11, 1985–June 22, 1986

Executive Director, Elaine Price; Producer, Karen Poindexter; Production Manager, Linda Bryant; Artistic Coordinator, Michael Deal; Public Relations, Peggy Sheffield
GUEST ARTISTS: Judd Nelson, Pat Hingle, Betsy Palmer, Vera Miles, Deborah Raffin, Jeff Conaway, Monte Markham, Sue Ann Langdon, Marilyn McCoo, Donna Pescow, David Holliday
PRODUCTIONS: A Chorus Line, WORLD PREMIERE: The News, Ain't Misbehavin', The Foreigner, Man of La Mancha, Orphans, Taken In Marriage, Alone Together, A . . . My Name is Alice, Dancin'

(No photos submitted)

CAPITAL REPERTORY COMPANY

Albany, New York
October 12, 1985–May 18, 1986

Producing Directors, Bruce Bouchard, Peter H. Clough; Business Manager, Barbara H. Smith; Marketing/Publicity, Hilde Schuster; Development, Mary Laub; Literary Manager, Robert Meiksins; Stage Managers, Patricia Frey, C. A. Fitzpatrick; Technical Director, David Yergan; Stage Directors: Pamela Berlin, Michael J. Hume, Gilbert Moses, Bruce Bouchard, Gloria Muzio, Peter H. Clough; Sets: Jeffrey Schneider, Rick Dennis, Dale F. Jordan, Leslie Taylor; Costumes: Martha Hally, Heidi Hollmann, Lloyd Waiwaiole, Catherine Zuber; Lighting, Jackie Manassee, Lary Opitz, Dale F. Jordan, David Yergan; Masks, Willa Shalit; Sound, Kevin Bartlett

PRODUCTIONS & CASTS
PLAYBODY OF THE WESTERN WORLD by John Millington Synge; CAST: Jean McNally (Pegeen Mike), Adam LeFevre (Shawn Keogh), Richard Maynard (Philly Cullen), Cullen Johnson (Jimmy Farrell), Frederick Walters (Michael James), Stephen Hamilton (Christopher Mahon), Barbara Sohmers (Widow Quin), Dermot McNamara (Old Mahon), and Michele Ortlip, Linda Caldwell, Helen Lesnick, Murphy Davis, Will McGarrahan
WHAT THE BUTLER SAW by Joe Orton; CAST: Rand Bridges (Dr. Prentice), Emily Heebner (Geraldine Barclay), Tudi Wiggins (Mrs. Prentice), Terrance Vorwald (Nicholas Beckett), Gwyllum Evans (Dr. Rance), Adam LeFevre (Sgt. Match)
DREAMING EMMETT by Toni Morrison; *World Premiere;* CAST: Joseph C. Phillips (Emmett), Peggy Cowles (Princess), Mel Winkler (Eustace), Herb Downer (George), Beatrice Winde (Ma), Frank Stoeger (Major), Larry Golden (Buck), Lorraine Toussaint (Tamara), and Richard Zobel (Major), Olivia Virgil Harper (Tamara)
GOODBYE FREDDY by Elizabeth Diggs; CAST: Janni Brenn (Kate), Tom Bloom (Hank), Larry Golden (Paul), Mary Baird (Alice), Richard Zoble (Andy), Kate Kelly (Nessa)
NOVEMBER by Don Nigro; *World Premiere;* CAST: Mary Fogarty (Aunt Liz), Jane Welch (Aunt Dor), Phyllis Gottung (Aunt Moll), Jen Jones (Mrs. Prikosovits), Nicola Sheara (Becky), Christopher Wynkoop (Rooks), Sherman Lloyd (Mr. Kafka), Kymberly Dakin (Nurse Jane), Thomas Schall (Ben)
THE PHANTOM OF THE OPERA or, The Passage of Christine; Book and Lyrics, Kathleen Masterson; Music, David Bishop; Adapted from the novel by Gaston Leroux; *World Premiere;* CAST: Yvette deBotton (Christine Daae), Patti Perkins (Usbek), Al DeCristo (The Phantom), John Barone (Firmin Richard), Robert Ousley (Armand Moncharmin), Malita Barron (Giulietta Giannini), Joseph Kolinski (Vicomte Raoul de Chagny), Jan Buttram (Mame Giry), Spencer Cherashore (Carolus Faust/Faust/Fireman), and Tracy Daniels, Dyann Arduini, Nicole Stokes, Carlotta Chang (Corps de Ballet), Will McGarrahan (Stanislav Kotyza/Mephisto/Ratcatcher), Helen Lesnick (Fraulein Krauss/Valentin/Fireman), Michele Ortlip (Madame Valla/Marthe/Fireman)

Skip Dickstein Photos

**Top Right: Sherman Lloyd, Kymberly Dakin
in "November" Below: Lorraine Toussaint,
Joseph C. Phillips, Beatrice Winde in
"Dreaming Emmett"**

**Kurt Peterson, Suellen Estey
in "Marry Me a Little"
(Cincinnati Playhouse)**

CINCINNATI PLAYHOUSE IN THE PARK

Cincinnati, Ohio
September 24, 1985–June 29, 1986

Artistic Director, Worth Gardner; Managing Director, Katherine Mohylsky; Artistic Associate, D. Lynn Meyers; Associate Director, Leonard Mozzi; Production Manager, Patricia Ann Speelman; Stage Managers, Kimberly Osgood, Tom Lawson, Bruce E. Coyle; Press, Charlaine Martin; Media, Sue Ann Stein; Development, David Hagar

PRODUCTIONS & CASTS

THE GLASS MENAGERIE by Tennessee Williams; Director, Steven Schacter; Set, Paul Shortt; Lighting, Jay Depenbrock; Costumes, William Schroder; Music, Alaric 'Rokko' Jans; Stage Managers, Kimberly Osgood, Tom Lawson. CAST: Annabel Armour, Robert Clinton, Joan Hotchkis, Mark McConnell

PAINTING CHURCHES by Tina Howe; Director, Mary B. Robinson; Set, Johniene Papandreas; Lighting, Joseph P. Tilford; Costumes, Rebecca Senske; Stage Manager, Tom Lawson. CAST: Anne Shropshire, Lynn Greene, William Cain

CARNIVAL with Music and Lyrics by Bob Merrill; Book, Michael Stewart; Based on Material by Helen Deutsch; Director/Choreographer, Worth Gardner; Set, Paul Shortt; Lighting, Kirk Bookman; Costumes, Kurt Wilhelm; Music Direction, Scot Woolley; Stage Managers, Kimberly Osgood, Tom Lawson, Bruce Coyle. CAST: Walter Willison (Paul Berthalet), Judith Blazer (Lili), Todd Heughens (Jacquot), Naz Edwards (Rosalie), Steven Berger (Marco), Patrick Farrelly (Mr. Schlegel), and Stan Chandler, F. Keith Cox, Michael Gruber, Danny Matalon, Darren Matthias, Michael McCauley, Catherine Moore, Michael Pappa, Lynnette Perry, Sarah Simon, Laurie Walton

TWO CAN PLAY by Trevor Rhone; Director, Clinton Turner Davis; Set, Llewellyn Harrison; Lighting, Sylvester N. Weaver, Jr.; Costumes, Julian Asion; Stage Managers, Janice Lane, Tom Lawson. CAST: Hazel J. Medina, Sullivan H. Walker. A Production of The Negro Ensemble Company

MARRY ME A LITTLE with Songs by Stephen Sondheim; Conceived and Developed by Craig Lucas and Norman Rene; Director/Musical Director, Worth Gardner; Set, Joseph P. Tilford; Lighting, Jay Depenbrock; Costumes, Barbara Kay; Stage Manager, Bruce E. Coyle. CAST: Kurt Peterson, Suellen Estey

TOP GIRLS by Caryl Churchill; Director, Steven D. Albrezzi; Set, James Leonard Joy; Lighting, Kirk Bookman; Costumes, Linda Fisher; Stage Managers, Kimberly Osgood, Tom Lawson. CAST: Glynis Bell, Mary Dierson, Elaine Hausman, Yolanda Lloyd, Christina Moore, Amelia White, Judith Yerby

TRAVELER IN THE DARK by Marsha Norman; Director, D. Lynn Meyers; Set, Joseph P. Tilford; Lighting, Spencer Mosse; Costumes, Rebecca Senske; Stage Manager, Bruce E. Coyle. CAST: Wanda Cannon, Dennis Parlato, Addison Powell, Jerry Taylor

HAMLET by William Shakespeare; Director, Leonard Mozzi; Set, James C. Fenhagen; Lighting, Judy Rasmuson; Costumes, Kurt Wilhelm, Rebecca Senske; Stage Managers, Tom Lawson, Kimberly Osgood. CAST: Robert Burns, Darryl Croxton, Hamilton Gillett, David Goldsmith, John Hardy, Hugh Hodgin, Jane Jones, Peter Messaline, Etain O'Malley, Joe Palmieri, Dennis Predovic, Jay E. Raphael, Charles Shaw Robinson, Ahvi Spindell, Robert Stocker, Lawrence Dorrell, Marilyn Dryden, Mark Alan Gordon, Dick Hagerman, Todd Louiso, Christopher Mixon, JoAnn Tahtinen, Ben Whitson, Melinda Wood

ROSENCRANTZ AND GUILDENSTERN ARE DEAD by Tom Stoppard; Director, Michael Hankins; Set, James C. Fenhagen; Lighting, Judy Rasmuson; Costumes, Kurt Wilhelm, Rebecca Senske; Stage Managers, Bruce E. Coyle, Maura J. Murphy

... AND A NIGHTINGALE SANG by C. P. Taylor; Director, Michael Murray; Set, Karl Eigsti; Lighting, Spencer Mosse; Costumes, Mariann S. Verheyen; Stage Managers, Tom Lawson, Kimberly Osgood. CAST: Maggie Baird, Franklin Brown, Stephen Coulter, Kathleen McCall, Edward McPhillips, Miriam Newhouse, Patrick O'Connell

Sandy Underwood Photos

**Walter Willison, Judith Blazer
in "Carnival" (Cincinnati Playhouse)**

(front to back) Myra Taylor, Vickilyn, Arnold Bankston, Robert Jason, Olivia Virgil Harper in "The Colored Museum" (Crossroads)

CROSSROADS THEATRE COMPANY

New Brunswick, New Jersey

Founder/Artistic Director, Lee Richardson; Founder/Executive Director, Rich Khan; General Manager, Elizabeth Bulluck; Development, Louise H. Gorham, Talvin W. Wilks; Office Manager, Elizabeth A. Shultis; Stage Managers, Kenneth Johnson, Cheri Bogdan-Kechely; Technical Director, Sue Barr; Costumes, Anita Ellis; Props, Neil Jacob, Gene Kish; Press, Cummins, MacFail & Nutry, Inc.

PRODUCTIONS & CASTS

ONE MO' TIME conceived by Vernel Bagneris; Director, Rick Khan; Set, Dan Proett; Costumes, Judy Dearing; Lights, Shirley Prendergast; Musical Director, Lillette E. Jenkins; Choreography, Bernard J. Marsh. CAST: Roumel Reaux (Papa Du), Lynne Clifton Allen (Thelma), Ellia English (Ma Reed), Sandra Reeves-Phillips (Bertha), Charles Woolfolk (Theatre Owner)

TAMER OF HORSES by William Mastrosimone; *World Premiere;* Director, Lee Richardson; Set, Dan Proett; Costumes, Nancy Konrardy; Lights, Susan A. White; Sound, Rob Gorton. CAST: Joe Morton (Ty Fletcher), Michele Shay (Georgiane Fletcher), Tony Moundroukas (Hector)

BLACK NATIVITY by Langston Hughes; Director/Choreographer, Mike Malone; Set, Felix E. Cochren; Costumes, Fontella Boone; Lights, Shirley Prendergast; Musical Director, Tony Booker. CAST: Carolyn Campbell, Germaine Edwards, Gina Ellis, Tina Fabrique, Gwen Nelson-Fleming, L. Michael Gray, James Arthur Johnson, Andre Smith, Katherine Smith, Tony Terry, Lee Truesdale, Kathi Walker, Neil Whitehead

ROADS OF THE MOUNTAINTOP by Ron Milner; *World Premiere;* Director, Rick Khan; Set, Dan Proett; Costumes, Anita Ellis; Lights, Shirley Prendergast; Sound, Rob Gorton; Projections, Anton Nelessen. CAST: James Pickens, Jr. (Dr. Martin Luther King, Jr.), Elizabeth Van Dyke (Coretta Scott King), Helmar Augustus Cooper (Ray), Tommy Hicks (Howard), Jeff Mooring (Abe), Michael Genet (Aaron), Marvin Jefferson (Josh)

THE COLORED MUSEUM with Book and Lyrics by George C. Wolfe; Music, Kysia Bostic; Director, Lee Richardson; Set, Brian Martin; Costumes, Nancy Konrardy; Lights, William Grant III; Sound, Rob Gorton; Choreography, Hope Clarke; Musical Director, Daryl Waters; Projections, Anton Nelessen. CAST: Arnold Bankston, Olivia Virgil Harper, Robert Jason, Myra Taylor, Vickilyn, Natasha Durant (Regional Award: Foundation of the Dramatists' Guild/CBS New Plays Program)

AGNES OF GOD by John Pielmeier; Director, Harold Scott; Set, Brian Martin; Costumes, Judy Dearing; Lights, Shirley Prendergast. CAST: Erica Gimpel (Agnes), Lorraine Toussaint (Dr. Martha Livingstone), Petie Trigg Seale (Mother Miriam Ruth)

Ed Birch Photos

149

DALLAS THEATER CENTER

Dallas, Texas
October 15, 1985–May 15, 1986

Artistic Director, Adrian Hall; Executive Managing Director, Peter Donnelly; Sets, Eugene Lee; Costumes, Donna M. Kress.
PRODUCTIONS: *The Skin of Our Teeth, A Christmas Carol, The Marriage of Bette and Boo, The Glass Menagerie, The Tavern.* PREMIERES: *The Ups and Downs of Theophilus Maitland, A Folk Tale,* and *Kith and Kin* by Oliver Hailey No other information submitted.

Linda Blase Photos

Right: Robert Black, Jim Fields, Bill Bolender in "Kith and Kin" Top: Linda Gehringer, Jack Willis in "Marriage of Bette and Boo"

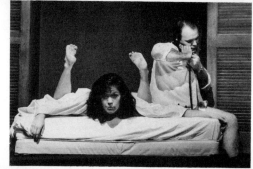

DELAWARE THEATRE COMPANY

Wilmington, Delaware
November 21, 1985–April 20, 1986
Seventh Season

Artistic Director, Cleveland Morris; Managing Director, Dennis Luzak; Business Manager, Ray Barto; Development, Ann G. Schenck; Marketing, Wendy S. Baird; Office Manager, Roberta Adams; Assistant Artistic Director, Danny Peak; Administrative Assistant, Cheri Friedman; Coordinator, Carolyn Hoan; Secretary, Jeane Laushey; Stage Managers, Patricia Christian, Rebecca G. Frederick; Technical Director, Eric Schaeffer; Lighting, Bruce K. Morriss; Props, Della L. Johnson; Sound, Alan Gardner; Costumes, Holly Whitney; Technical Assistant, Tammy Swisher.

PRODUCTIONS & CASTS
COME BACK, LITTLE SHEBA by William Inge; Director, Cleveland Morris; Set, Eric Schaeffer; Costumes, E. Lee Florance. CAST: John Herzog (Doc), Catherine Christianson (Marie), Laura Gardner (Lola), Gavin Troster (Turk), Andy Zimmerman (Postman), Sarah Burke (Mrs. Coffman), Hank Winchester (Milkman), Martin Willeford (Messenger), Clay Warnick (Bruce), Tom Stapleford (Ed Anderson), Robert Balick (Elmo Huston)
FALLEN ANGELS by Noel Coward; Director, Kent Thompson; Set, James F. Pyne, Jr.; Costumes, E. Lee Florance. CAST: Pamela Lewis (Julia Sterroll), Wesley Stevens (Fred Sterroll), Mary Ed Porter (Saunders), James Jenner (Willy Banbury), Marianne Tatum (Jane Banbury), Greg Tigani (Maurice Duclos)
K2 by Patrick Meyers; Director, Francis X. Kuhn; Set, David Potts; Sound, Alan Gardner, Bruce K. Morriss; Music, Alan Gardner. CAST: Eric Booth (Taylor), Allen Fitzpatrick (Harold)
THE MAJESTIC KID by Mark Medoff; Director, Derek Wolshonak; Set, Eric Schaeffer; Costumes, Barbara Forbes; Music, Dean Johnson. CAST: Michael Cullen (Judge William S. Hart Finlay), Juliette Kurth (Lisa Belmondo), Amy VanNostrand (Ava Jean Pollard), Alex Wipf (The Laredo Kid), Stuart Zagnit (Aaron Weiss)
THE GRAND DUCHESS OF GEROLSTEIN with Music by Charles Offenbach; Libretto, Ludovic Halevy; New Adaption, Cleveland Morris, Judy Brown; Director, Cleveland Morris; Musical Director, Judy Brown; Set, Lewis Folden; Costumes, Catherine Adair. CAST: Scott Waara (Fritz), Lorraine Goodman (Wanda), Allen Fitzpatrick (General Boum), Daryl Kroken (Baron Puck), Connie Coit (The Grand Duchess of Gerolstein), Mark Baker (Prince Paul), David Van Der Veen (Baron Grog), Gary Newcomb, John Heffron, Richard Coombs, Sarah Hill, Deborah De-Hart, Kristine Miller, Stephen Lashbrook, David Wright

Richard C. Carter Photos

Top Left: Gavin Troster, John Herzog, Laura Gardner, Catherine Christianson in "Come Back, Little Sheba" Below: Eric Booth, Allen Fitzpatrick in "K2"

Connie Coit, Mark Baker in "The Grand Duchess of Gerolstein"

DENVER CENTER THEATRE COMPANY

Denver, Colorado
September 30, 1985–April 12, 1986
Seventh Season

Artistic Director, Donovan Marley; Associate Artistic Director/Development, Peter Hackett; Associate Artistic Director/Design, Richard L. Hay; Casting, Randal Myler; Associate Artistic Director/Repertoire and Ensemble, Laird Williamson; Executive Director, Sarah Lawless; Administrative Director, Karen Knudsen; Producing Director, Barbara Sellers; Technical Director, Dan McNeil; Assistant Producing Director, Rodney J. Smith; Stage Managers: Lyle Raper, Paul Jefferson, Joseph F. Martin, Christopher C. Ewing, Jessica Evans, D. Adams; Props, Mary Jo Hamilton, Victoria Stasica, Judith Bergquist; Composer, Larry Delinger; Music Director, Bruce K. Sevy; Stage Directors: Peter Hackett, Sari Ketter, Roberta Leviton, Donovan Marley, Donald McKayle, James Moll, Randal Myler, Bruce K. Sevy, J. Steven White, Garland Wright, Laird Williamson; Artistic Associate, Cleo Parker Robinson; Choreographer, Donald McKayle; Sets: Robert Blackman, John Dexter, Pavel Dobrusky, Richard L. Hay, Catherine Poppe, Kevin Rupnik, Douglas Stein, Bill Curley, Judy Lowey, Dan Reeverts; Costumes: Robert Blackman, Ann Hould-Ward, Janet S. Morris, Andrew V. Yelusich, Kitty Murphy, Patricia A. Whitelock; Lighting: Wendy Heffner, Peter Maradudin, Michael W. Vennerstrom, Charles MacLeod; Costume Director, Janet S. Morris; Sound, John Pryor; Press, Susan Goodell.
COMPANY: Stephen Anderson, Benny Bell, Annette Bening, Donnie L. Betts, Henri Bolzon, Jack Casperson, Craig Diffenderfer, Kay Doubleday, Richard K. Gardner, Frank Georgianna, Ann Guilbert, Carol Halstead, Mark Harelik, Wiley Harker, Barta Heiner, Jamie Horton, Robert Jacobs, Byron Jennings, Sandra Ellis Lafferty, Kate Levy, Lory Marie, Michael X. Martin, Allen McCowan, James Newcomb, Luis Oropeza, Caitlin O'Connell, Art Andre Palmer, Dougald Park, Rachael Patterson, Guy Raymond, Robynn Rodriquez, Renee Rose, Archie Smith, Adrienne Thompson, Fredye Jo Williams, Michael Winters, James H. (Buddy) Zimmer.
GUESTS ARTISTS: Barbara Andres, Harvy Blanks, Frank Borgman, Roslyn Brisco, Bataki Cambrelen, Kathleen Chalfant, Pi Douglass, Alfred L. Dove, Antonio Fargas, Clebert Ford, Curtis Fraser, Marceline Freeman, Lita Gaithers, David Gale, Wenelin H. Harston, Delane Hill, Elizabeth Hill, John Hutton, Joanne Jackson, Beryl Jones, Leslie Lyles, Warren "Juba" Lucas, Renee Rose, Judith T. Smith, Avery Sommers
PRODUCTIONS: The Stage: *The Petrified Forest* by Robert E. Sherwood; *Christmas Miracles* by Laird Williamson, Dennis Powers, World Premiere; *The Emperor Jones* by Eugene O'Neill, *The Cherry Orchard* by Anton Chekhov. The Space: *Pygmalion* by George Bernard Shaw; *Purlie* with Music by Gary Geld, Lyrics by Peter Udell, Book by Ossie Davis, Phillip Rose, Peter Udell; *The Immigrant: A Hamilton County Album; Circe & Bravo* by Donald Freed. The Source: World Premieres: *A Woman Without a Name* by Romulus Linney, *When the Sun Slides* by Stephen Davis Parks, *Pleasuring Ground* by Frank X. Hogan, *Hope of the Future* by Shannon Keith Kelley
PRIMAFACIE II: Staged readings of 12 unproduced American works: *American Dreamer* by Carol K. Mack, *Rachel's Fate* by Larry Ketron, *Reunion* by Sybille Pearson, *Heathen Valley* by Romulus Linney, *Cal and Sally* by Robert Clyman, *Watch Your Back* by Gary Leon Hill, *Fat Men on Thin Ice* by Roger Cornish, *Telling Time* by Laura Shamas, *Goodnight, Texas* by Terry Dodd, *The World of Mirth* by Murphy Guyer, *Hoopla* by Molly Newman, *The Ballad of the El Gimpo Cafe* by Jeff Carey

Nicholas De Sciose Photos

**Mark Bishop, John Swain, Cornell Markham,
Fran Washington, Nelson Phillips, Von Washington
in "A Touch of the Poet" (Detroit)**

**Dee Andrus, Booker Hinton
in "Mendola's Rose" (Detroit)**

DETROIT REPERTORY THEATRE

Detroit, Michigan
November 1, 1985–June 22, 1986
Twenty-eighth Season

Artistic Director, Bruce E. Millan; Executive Director, Robert Williams; Advertising/Marketing Director, Reuben Yabuku; Development/Press, Dee Andrus; Literary Manager, Barbara Busby; Costumes, Anne Saunders; Music Director, Kelly Smith; Administrative Assistant, Kim Davis; Sets, Bruce E. Millan, Marylynn Kacir; Scenic Artists, John Knox, Peter Knox; Stage Managers, William Boswell, Dee Andrus, Robert Williams-Vogue; Lighting, Kenneth R. Hewitt, Jr.; Sound, Reuben Yabuku; Props, William Boswell, Dee Andrus; Production Assistants, William Boswell, Cornell Markham, John R. Swain, Mack Palmer; Graphics, Barbara Weinberg-Barefield

PRODUCTIONS & CASTS
MENDOLA'S ROSE by Robert Unger; Director, Von H. Washington. CAST: Booker Hinton, Dee Andrus
SOUVENIRS by Sheldon Rosen; Director, Barbara Busby. CAST: John R. Swain, Mack Palmer, Reuben Yabuku, Ruth Allen, Don Weingust, Divina Cook, William Boswell
THE ADVENTURES OF STANLEY TOMORROW by Alan Foster Friedman; Director, Divina Cook. CAST: Cornell Markham, Vito Guerra, William Boswell, Mack Palmer, Barbara Busby, Dee Andrus
A TOUCH OF THE POET by Eugene O'Neill; Director, Bruce E. Millan. CAST: Michael Kelley, Nelson Phillips, Fran L. Washington, Barbara Busby, Von H. Washington, Cornell Markham, Mark Bishop, John R. Swain, Kimberly S. Newberry, William Boswell

Bruce E. Millan, Rita K. Tinetti Photos

**Frank Georgianna, Jack Casperson
in "Pleasuring Ground"
(Denver Center)**

FOLGER THEATRE

Washington, D.C.
October 1, 1985–July 20, 1986
Sixteenth Season

Artistic Producer, John Neville-Andrews; Managing Director, Mary Ann de Barbieri; Production Manager, Jack Mulligan; Technical Director, Tom Whittington; Development, Michael Darling; Business Manager, Elizabeth Hamilton; Costume Manager, Paige Southard; Dramaturg, Genie Barton; Stage Managers, Debra Acquavella, Pat A. Flora, B. Laurie Hunt; Press, Regan M. Byrne.

COMPANY: Emery Battis, Jim Beard, Orlagh Cassidy, Alessandro Cima, Edward Gero, Richard Hart, Michael Howell, Floyd King, Michael Kramer, Mikel Lambert, Krystov Lindquist, Sybil Lines, Michael Tolaydo, John Wylie.
GUEST ARTISTS: Howard Bass, Scott Bryan, Marilyn Caskey, Andrew Clemence, Roger Cox, Lou Dickey, Diane Falk, Catherine Flye, Anthony Giaimo, Annette Helde, Jyl Hewston, Elmore James, Hilary Kacser, Celeste Lawson, Rita Litton, Marty Lodge, Mark Mendez, Melanie Metzger, Robert Morse, John Neville-Andrews, Nick Newlin, Nicole Orth-Pallavicini, Robert Max Ramsey, Sherry Skinker, Grady Smith, Clay Warnick, Mary Kay Wulf.
PRODUCTIONS
OTHELLO by William Shakespeare; Director, Mikel Lambert; Set, Russell Metheny; Costumes, Ann Hould-Ward; Lighting, Stuart Duke.
THE MERRY WIVES OF WINDSOR by William Shakespeare; Director, John Neville-Andrews; Set, Michael Layton; Costumes, Holly Cole; Lighting, Daniel M. Wagner.
THE CHERRY ORCHARD by Anton Chekhov; Translator, John PiRoman; *World Premiere;* Director, John Neville-Andrews; Set, Ursula Belden; Costumes, Mark Pirolo; Lighting, Stuart Duke; Russian Consultant, Irina Levin; Choreographer, Virginia Freeman.
THE MISER by Jean-Baptiste Moliere; Translator, Miles Malleson; Director, John Going; Set/Costumes, William Schroeder; Lighting, F. Mitchell Dana; Composer, Steven Rydbert; Mask Movement, Jack Guidone.
TWELFTH NIGHT by William Shakespeare; Director, Gavin Cameron-Webb; Set, Russell Metheny; Costumes, Gail Brassard; Lighting, Allen Hughes.

Joan Marcus Photos

**Top Right: John Wylie, Jim Beard
in "The Miser" (Folger)**

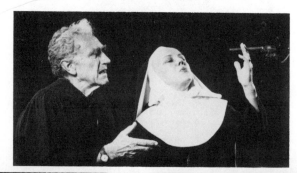

**Cast of "Little Me" Above: James
Whitmore, Audra Lindley in "Handy Dandy"
(Ford's Theatre)**

FORD'S THEATRE

Washington, D.C.
September 21, 1985–May 31, 1986

Executive Producer, Frankie Hewitt; Artistic Director, David H. Bell; Press, Larisa Wanserski.

PRODUCTIONS & CASTS

HANDY DANDY by William Gibson; Director, Arthur Storch; Set, Victor A. Becker; Costumes, Maria Marrero; Lighting, Judy Rasmuson; A Production of ESIPA, Inc. (Producing Director, Patricia B. Snyder); Stage Manager, Robin Horowitz; Production Supervisor, Peter Davis; Production Assistants, Joe Ventura, Douglas A. Lange; Sound, Steve Shapiro, Pryce Arwin Mandel; Press, Patricia Gioia, Ron Nicoll; Assistant to Producers, Olga Delorey, Renee Hariton, Bonnie Bruce; General Manager, Alan Wasser; Associate General Manager, Alexander Holt. CAST: James Whitmore (Henry Pulaski), Audra Lindley (Molly Egan).
BARBARA COOK: A BROADWAY EVENING; Director, Thommie Walsh; Musical Director/Conductor, Wally Harper; Associate Director, Baayork Lee; Lighting, Richard Winkler; Stage Manager, John Bonanni; Costumes, Dona Granata; *Gladys* written by Seth Olinka; Lighting Assistants, Steven Gerri, Scott Pinkney; Presented in Association with Jerry Kravat; General Management, Maria Productions, Inc. CAST: Barbara Cook, Julie Nicholas, Sheilah Glover, Willow Wray.
LITTLE ME with Book by Neil Simon; Lyrics, Carolyn Leigh; Music, Cy Coleman; Based on a novel by Patrick Dennis; Director/Choreographer, David H. Bell; Musical Director, Rob Bowman; Set, Daniel Proett; Costumes, Doug Marmee; Lighting, Susan A. White, Renee Clark; Stage Managers, Carroll McKee, Terrence Witter; Assistant Choreographer, Ann-Marie Gerard; Props, Allison Campbell; Assistant Director, David Courier; Wigs, Hilary Paul. CAST: James W. Sudik (Patrick Dennis/Noble Eggleston/Mr. Pinchley/Val du Val/Fred Poitrine/Otto Schnitzler/Prince Cherney), Beth Williams (Older Belle), Carol Dilley (Young Belle), Mark Bove (George Musgrove), and Michael McCarty, Teri Bibb, Anne-Marie Gerard, William P. Leonard, Connie Kunkle, Bruce Moore, Tim Roberts, Dee Amerio Sudik, Edward Tyler, Christopher Wells, Beth Blatt, Randy Pitts, Charles Abel, William P. Leonard.
JEEVES TAKES CHARGE by P. G. Wodehouse; Conceived and Adapted by Edward Duke; Director, Gillian Lynne; Designer, Carl Toms; Lighting, Peter Hanson; Costumes, Una-Mary Parker; Choreography, Susan Holderness; Stage Manager, Cosmo P. Hanson; Presented in Association with Lawrence N. Dykun, Michael J. Needham, Robert L. Sachter. CAST: Edward Duke (Bertie Wooster/Reginald Jeeves).
HOT MIKADO Adapted from Gilbert and Sullivan's *Mikado;* Director/Choreographer, David H. Bell; Set, Daniel Proett; Costumes, Carol Oditz; Lighting, Susan A. White; Musical Supervision/Arrangements, Rob Bowman; Orchestrations, George Hummel; Stage Managers, Carroll McKee, Terrence Witter; Assistant Choreographer/Dance Captain, Tim Roberts; Assistants, Allison Campbell, Carol Kunz, Renee Clark, Ed Peterson; Hair, Vito Mastrogiovanni; Casting, Jeffrey Solis. CAST: Robin Baxter (Pitti-Sing), Raymond Bazemore (Pooh-Bah), Steve Blanchard (Nanki-Poo), Merwin Foard (Pish-Tush), Lawrence Hamilton (Mikado), Frank Kopyc (Ko-Ko), Kathleen Mahony-Bennett (Yum-Yum), Val Scott (Peep-Bo), Helena-Joyce Wright (Katisha), Steven Cates, Bill Derifield, Mamie Duncan-Gibbs, Greg Hellems, Todd Heughens, Michael S. Lynch, Tim Roberts, Mona Wyatt. Understudies: Mona Wyatt, Steven Cates, Mamie Duncan-Gibbs, Todd Heughens, Michael S. Lynch.

Joan Marcus Photos

GEORGE STREET PLAYHOUSE

New Brunswick, New Jersey
October 23, 1985–May 11, 1986

Producing Director, Eric Krebs; General Manager, Geoffrey Cohen; Associate Artistic Director, Maureen Heffernan; Production Manager, Carol Andrew; Technical Director, John Griffith; Literary Manager, Alexis Greene; Press, Sharon Rothe

PRODUCTIONS: *The Price* by Arthur Miller; *Cabaret* with Book by Joseph Masteroff; Music, John Kander; Lyrics, Fred Ebb; *Glengarry Glen Ross* by David Mamet; *Greater Tuna* by Joe Sears, Jaston Williams and Ed Howard; *Mrs Warren's Profession* by George Bernard Shaw; *The Rise of David Levinsky* with Book & Lyrics by Isaiah Sheffer; Music, Bobby Paul.
    No further details submitted

Suzanne Karp Krebs Photos

Top Right: Marilyn Cooper, Laurence Luckinbill, Eileen Valentino, Danette Cuming, Cheryl Stern in "The Rise of David Levinsky" Below Left: Peter Moran, Mary Munger in "Cabaret" (George Street)

Ron Canada, Lou Myers in "Fences"
Above: Denise Bessette, Judith Tillman
in "The Importance of Being Earnest" (GeVa)

GeVa THEATRE

Rochester, N.Y.
October 26, 1985–July 7, 1986

Producing Director, Howard J. Millman; Managing Director, Thomas Pechar; Assistant to the Directors, Christine Orr Pohlig; Business Manager, Dorinda Dean Goggin; Development, Sarah L. Booher; Literary Director, Ann Patrice Carrigan; Press/Marketing, Adele Fico-McCarthy; Stage Managers: Catherine Norberg, James Stephen Sulanowski; Casting, David Tochterman, Alexa Fogel

PRODUCTIONS & CASTS
BLACK COFFEE by Agatha Christie; Director, Barbara Redmond; Set, Bob Barnett; Lighting, Nicholas Minetor; Costumes, Martha Kelly; Hair, Paul Lyons. CAST: Patrick Egan, Bernerd Engel, Brad Fullagar, Polly Holliday, Matthew Kimbrough, Philip LeStrange, Devora Millman, John Quinn, Walter Rhodes, Thomas Schall, Eberle Thomas, Lauren Thompson
AIN'T MISBEHAVIN' Based on an idea by Murray Horwitz and Richard Maltby, Jr.; Directed by Arthur Faria; Musical Direction, William Foster McDaniel; Orchestrations/Arrangements, Luther Henderson; Vocal/Musical Concepts, Jeffrey Gutcheon; Arrangements, Jeffrey Gutcheon, William Elliott; Set, John Lee Beatty; Lighting, Barry Arnold; Costumes, Eaves-Brooks Costume Co, Inc.; Co-Producer, Citibank (NYS), N.A. CAST: Leslie Barlow, Doug Eskew, Stanley Ramsey, Wendy E. Taylor, Terri White
A CHRISTMAS CAROL by Charles Dickens; Adaption, Eberle Thomas; Music, John Franceschina; Director, Howard J. Millman; Set, William Barclay; Lighting, Phil Monat; Costumes, Pamela Scofield; Sound, Nicholas Minetor; Choreography, Jim Hoskins; Hair, Paul Lyons; Co-Producer, Sibley's. CAST: Cynthia L. Anderson, Steve Barley, John Keene Bolton, Jill Nicole Braverman, Thomas Lee Carson, Robert Colston, Lucia Fontana Ennocenti, Peggy Fleche, Brad Fullagar, Elaine Good, John Greenleaf, Steve Hendrickson, Ellen Herzman, Leonard Kelly-Young, Philip LeStrange, Gracen Porreca, Barbara Redmond, Gerald Richards, Cecelia Riddett, Michael Rogers, David Runzo, Eliza Schneider, Charles M. Scott, Julie Snyder, Mary Stark, Jessica Stone, Frankie Michael Storace, Eberle Thomas, Time Winters, Jason E. Zwetsch
ISN'T IT ROMANTIC? by Wendy Wasserstein; Director, Terence Lamude; Set, Duke Durfee; Lighting, Ann Wrightson; Costumes, Barbara Forbes; Sound, Tom Gould; Co-Producer, Bausch and Lomb, Inc. CAST: Franklin Brown, Robin Leslie Brown, George Collins, Eleanor Garth, Eve Johnson, James Secrest, Dan Strickler, Anne Swift
FENCES by August Wilson; Director, Claude Purdy; Set, David Potts; Lighting, Phil Monat; Costumes, Thom Coates; Co-Producers, Rochester Telephone Corp., Rollins Container Corp. CAST: Ron Canada, D'Shawna Dupree, Robert Gossett, Carol Jean Lewis, Lou Myers, David A. Shakes, Trina Waller, Lanyard A. Williams
THE IMPORTANCE OF BEING EARNEST by Oscar Wilde; Director, Thomas Gruenewald; Set, Charles Cosler, Raymond Kluga; Lighting, Craig Miller; Costumes, Thom Coates; Co-Producer, Eastman Kodak Company. CAST: Nick Bakay, Denise Bessette, Mary Chalon, Robertson Dean, Brad Fullagar, Donald C. Moore, Sylvia Short, Judith Tillman, Ronald Wendschuh
DIMINISHED CAPACITY by Tom Dulack; *World Premiere;* Director, Allen R. Belknap; Set, James Fenhagen; Lighting, Curt Ostermann; Costumes, Pamela Scofield. CAST: Eve Bennett-Gordon, O. L. Duke, Mart Hulswit, Allan Wasserman, Peter Webster, Anthony Zerbe
THE LION IN WINTER by James Goldman; Director, Howard J. Millman; Sets, William Barnett; Lighting, Phil Monat; Costumes, Pamela Scofield. CAST: David Little, Maeve McGuire, Devora Millman, Matthew Kimbrough, John Greenleaf, Steven McCloskey, David Bryant

Brad Bliss Photos

153

GOODMAN THEATRE

Chicago, Illinois
October 4, 1985–June 29, 1986

Artistic Director, Robert Falls; Producing Director, Roche Schulfer

PRODUCTIONS & CASTS

THE GOVERNMENT INSPECTOR by Nikolai Gogol; Director, Frank Galati; Set, Michael Merritt; Lighting, Kevin Rigdon; Costumes, Virgil Johnson; Stage Managers, Joseph Drummond, Malcolm Ewen. CAST: Laurel M. Cronin, Nathan Davis, Frank Farrell, Glendon Gabbard, Tim Halligan, I. M. Hobson, B. J. Jones, Kathy Joosten, Bernie Landis, Ruth Landis, Harry J. Lennix, Polly Liontis, Lawrence McCauley, John Mohrlein, Bradley Mott, Judy O'Malley, Lucina Paquet, Keith Reddin, John Starrs, Jack Wallace

KING LEAR by William Shakespeare; A Stratford Shakespearean Festival Production; Director, John Hirsch; Designer, Chris Dyer; Costumes, Judy Peyton Ward; Set: Frank Holte, Chris Dyer, Christina Poddubiuk; Music/Sounds, Stanley Silverman; Lighting, Michael J. Whitfield, Elizabeth Asselstine; Assistant Director, Brian Rintoul; Fight Supervision, John Broome; Stage Managers, Michael Shamata, Victoria Klein, Peter McGuire; Sound, John Hazen. CAST: Douglas Campbell (King Lear), Patricia Collins, Maria Ricossa, Seana McKenna, Nicholas Pennell, James Blendick, Michael Shepherd, John Bourgeois, David Renton, Lewis Gordon, Richard McMillan, Benedict Campbell, Mervyn Blake, Roger Forbes, Colm Feore, Nolan Jennings, Ernest Harrop, Stephen Russell, Jefferson Mappin, John Bourgeois, Simon Bradbury, Brian Paul, William Dunlop, Brent Stait, Charles Kerr, Howard Rosenstein, Kelly Bricker, Julie Khaner, Eric McCormack, Elizabeth McDonald, Susan Morgan, Eric Zivot, Keith Dinicol.

TWELFTH NIGHT by William Shakespeare; A Stratford Shakespearean Festival Production; Directors, David Giles, John Hirsch; Set/Costumes, Christina Poddubiuk; Music, Louis Applebaum; Lighting. Michael J. Whitfield, Elizabeth Asseltine; Assistant Director, Jeannette Aster; Fights/Dance Supervision, John Broome; Stage Managers, Margaret Palmer, Victoria Klein, Peter McGuire; Assistant Designer, Jennifer Carroll. CAST: Colm Feore, Brent Stait, David Renton, Seana McKenna, Michael Shepherd, James Blendick, Patricia Collins, Richard McMillan, Edward Atienza, Maria Ricossa, Nicholas Pennell, Benedict Campbell, Ernest Harrop, Keith Dinicol, Simon Bradbury, William Dunlop, Nolan Jennings, Charles Kerr, Eric McCormack, Brian Paul, Kelly Bricker, Julie Khaner, Elizabeth McDonald, Howard Rosenstein, Eric Zivot, Eric McCormack

A CHRISTMAS CAROL by Charles Dickens; Adaption, Larry Sloan; Director, Sandra Grand; Music, Larry Schanker; Set, Joseph Nieminski; Costumes, Christina Scholtz; Lighting, Robert Christen; Sound, Robert Neuhaus; Stage Managers, Joseph Drummond, Alden Vasquez. CAST: Jamie Baron, Paul Barrosse, Joshua Bartz, Ramiro Carrillo, Jason Cole, Vannesa Cooksey, John Copeland, Gary Davidson, Helen Eigenberg, Kit Falsgraf, Linda Kimbrough, Lawrence McCauley, Rugaivah Morris, Roger Mueller, Maura Ann Murphy-Barrosse, Ernest Perry, Jr., Michael Rassel, Jo Ann Rome, Ross Salinger, Nina Siemaszko, David Smith, Brian K. Spivey, Daniel Allyn Swope, Cherise Thruman, Frank J. Vizen

FENCES by August Wilson; In association with Yale Repertory Theatre; Director, Lloyd Richards; Sets, James D. Sandefur; Costumes, Candice Donnelly; Lighting, Danianne Mizzy; Stage Managers, Joseph Drummond, Chuck Henry. CAST: Mary Alice, Ray Aranha, Charles Brown, Frankie Faison, James Earl Jones, Courtney Michelle Megginson, Courtney B. Vance

HAPPY DAYS by Samuel Beckett; Director, Andrei Belgrader; Set, Douglas Stein; Costumes, Candice Donnelly; Lighting, Frances Aronson; Stage Managers, Joseph Drummond, Chuck Henry. CAST: Jo Henderson, Richard Spore

ORCHARDS (See The Acting Company under National Tours)

William B. Carter, David Cooper, Lisa Ebright, Diane Gorodnitzki, Kevin Horan Photos

Right Center: Charles Brown, James Earl Jones, Mary Alice, Ray Aranha in "Fences" Above: Richard Spore, Jo Henderson in "Happy Days" Top: Daniel Allyn Swope, Ruqaiyah Morris, Linda Kimbrough (standing), Roger Mueller (seated), Maura Ann Murphy-Barrosse, Nina Siemaszko in "A Christmas Carol"

I. M. Hobson, Lawrence McCauley, Bradley Mott, Nathan Davis in "The Government Inspector"

GOODSPEED OPERA HOUSE

East Haddam, Connecticut
July 3, 1985–June 27, 1986
Twenty-third Season

Executive Director, Michael P. Price; Associate Producer, Warren Pincus; Musical Director, Lynn Crigler; Producing Associate, Sue Frost; Press, Kay McGrath

PRODUCTIONS & CASTS

FIORELLO! with Music by Jerry Bock; Lyrics, Sheldon Harnick; Book, Jerome Weidman, George Abbott; Director, Gerald Gutierrez; Choreographer, Peter Gennaro; Set, Douglas Stein; Lighting, Pat Collins; Costumes, Ann Hould-Ward; Stage Manager, Kate Pollock. CAST: Cleve Asbury, Larry Cahn, Randy Graff, Jack Hallett, Philip Hoffman, Kiel Junius, Laura Kenyon, Terry Kirwin, George Kmeck, Tom Robbins, Raymond Thorne, Todd Thurston, Kenneth H. Waller, Lynne Wintersteller, Bill Badolato, Scott Breitbart, Andrea Cohen, Michael Craig, Andrea Goodman, Andrea Leigh-Smith, Patricia Lockery, Wendy Oliver, Susan Rosenstock

LEAVE IT TO JANE with Book and Lyrics by Guy Bolton, P. G. Wodehouse; Music, Jerome Kern; Based on the play *The College Widow* by George Ade; Director, Thomas Gruenewald; Choreographer, Walter Painter; Set, James Leonard Joy; Lighting, Craig Miller; Costumes, John Carver Sullivan; Stage Manager, Michael Brunner. CAST: Tom Batten, Nick Corley, Jack Doyle, Gary Gage, Rebecca Luker, Patrick McCord, Robert Nichols, Dale O'Brien, Michael O'Steen, Faith Prince, Iris Revson, David Staller, Michael Waldron, Paul Cira, Patricia Forestier, Mercedes Perez, Lisa Pompa, Donna M. Pompei, Brian Quinn, Keith Savage

IRMA LA DOUCE with Music by Marguerite Monnot; Original Book and Lyrics, Alexandre Breffort; English Book and Lyrics, Julian More, David Heneker, Monty Norman; Director, Fran Soeder; Choreographer, Janet Watson; Set, James Leonard Joy; Lighting, Craig Miller; Costumes, Mariann Verheyen. CAST: Stephen Bourneuf, Chuck Brown, Kevin Gray, Andy Hostettler, Richard Korthaze, Tony Marino, Bob Morissey, Gary Moss, John L. Nicoletti, Barry Phillips, Nikki Sahagen, Kevin Sweeney, Paul Ukena, Jr.

(NORMA TERRIS THEATRE/Musicals-in-progress)

GEORGIA AVENUE with Music by Howard Marren; Book, Joe Masteroff; Based on *Imitation of Life* by Fannie Hurst; Director, Fran Soeder; Music Direction/Arrangements, Uel Wade; Set, James Leonard Joy; Lighting, Curt Osterman; Costumes, Andrew B. Marlay; Stage Manager, Peter J. Taylor. CAST: Teresa Bowers, Chuck Brown, Kim Crosby, Louise Edeiken, Gregg Edelman, Tim Ewing, Beth Fowler, Jaime Leigh, Staci Love, Rosemary McNamara, Patricia Ben Peterson, Louis Tucker

Wilson H. Brownell, Diane Sobolewski Photos

Right: Jack Hallett as "Fiorello!"
**Top: Marianne Tatum, Rex D. Hays
in "You Never Know"**

**Teresa Bowers, Beth Fowler
in "Georgia Avenue"**

Rebecca Luker in "Leave It to Jane"

GUTHRIE THEATRE

Minneapolis, Minnesota
June 1, 1985–March 22, 1986
Twenty-third Season

Artistic Director, Liviu Ciulei; Associate Artistic Director, Stephen Kanee; Managing Director, Donald Schoenbaum; General Manager, Dennis Babcock; Stage Directors: Liviu Ciulei, Howard Dallin, William Gaskill, Edward Gilbert, Stephen Kanee, Emily Mann, Timothy Near; Costumes: Deirdre Clancy, John Conklin, Jack Edwards, Jennifer von Mayrhauser, Beni Montresor, Jeff Struckman; Lighting: Dawn Chiang, Pat Collins, Marcus Dilliard, John Gisondi, Craig Miller, Beni Montresor, Judy Rasmuson; Sound: Tom Bolstad, Timothy Near; Composers: Thomas Fay, Philip Glass, Hiram Titus; Musical Directors: David Bishop, Paul Goldstaub; Choreographer, Loyce Houlton; Stage Managers: Mimi Apfel, Andrew Feigin, Russell Johnson, Christine Nelson, Jill Rendall; Sets: Jack Barkla, Ming Cho Lee, Deirdre Clancy, John Conklin, Kate Edwards, Beni Montresor; Literary Manager/Dramaturg, Mark Bly; Dramaturgs: Robert Cowgill, Michael Lupu; Press Director, Dennis Behl.

RESIDENT COMPANY Daniel Ahearn, Julian Bailey, Gerry Bamman, Mark Benninghofen, Robert Breuler, James Cada, Helen Carey, Lynn Chausow, Camille D'Ambrose, Stephen D'Ambrose, Charles Dean, Kathryn Dowling, Don R. Fallbeck, Peter Francis-James, Warren Frost, Thomas Glynn, Allen Hamilton, Brian Hargrove, Harriet Harris, James Horswill, Richard Howard, Suzy Hunt, Richard S. Iglewski, Matthew Kimbrough, Barbara Kingsley, Jacqueline Knapp, James Lawless, Darrie Lawrence, Katherine Leask, Mitchell Lichtenstein, MaryAnn Lippay, Ray Lonergan, Peter MacNicol, Ann-Sara Matthews, John McCluggage, Jack McLaughlin-Gray, Meg Merkens, Peter Moore, W. Alan Nebelthau, Pamela Nyberg, Richard Ooms, Edwin Owens, Jay Patterson, Deirdre Peterson, David Pierce, Faye Price, Gary Rayppy, Gary Reineke, Mari Rovang, Kurt Schweickhardt, John Spencer, Peter Thoemke, Barbara Tirrell, Lorraine Toussaint, John Madden Towey, Henrietta Valor, Peter Vogt, Timothy Wahrer, Eric Weitz, Jack Wetherall, Claudia Wilkens, Sally Wingert.

PRODUCTIONS: *Great Expectations* by Charles Dickens/Adaptation by Barbara Field (National Touring production); *Cyrano de Bergerac* by Edmond Rostand; *A Midsummer Night's Dream* by William Shakespeare; *Execution of Justice* by Emily Mann; *Candida* by George Bernard Shaw, *A Christman Carol* by Charles Dickens/Adaptation by Barbara Field, *On The Razzle* adaptation by Tom Stoppard, *The Rainmaker* by N. Richard Nash

Joe Giannetti Photos

**Top Right: Peter Thoemke, Peter Francis-James,
Katherine Leask (kneeling), John Spencer
in "Execution of Justice"**

**Mitchell Lichenstein, Henrietta Valor
in "Great Expectations"**

**Harriet Harris, Jay Patterson
in "A Midsummer Night's Dream"**

HARTFORD STAGE COMPANY

Hartford, Connecticut
October 1, 1985–May 25, 1986
Twenty-third Season

Artistic Director, Mark Lamos; Managing Director, David Hawkanson; Resident Playwright/Literary Manager, Constance Congdon; Dramaturg, Greg Leaming; Business Manager, Vera Furdas; Marketing, Jeffrey Woodward; Press, Howard Sherman; Production Manager, Candice Chirgotis; Technical Director, Clayton Austin

PRODUCTIONS & CASTS

TWELFTH NIGHT, OR What You Will by William Shakespeare; Director, Mark Lamos; Set, Michael H. Yeargan; Costumes, Jess Goldstein; Lights, Stephen Strawbridge; Sound, David Budries; Music, Marvin Jones; Stage Manager, Katherine M. Goodrich. CAST: Robert Burke (Orsino), Marcia Cross (Olivia), June Gable (Maria), Patrick Garner (Sir Andrew Aguecheek), Davis Hall (Feste), Arthur Hanket (Fabian), Scott Kanoff (Sebastian), Jerome Kilty (Sir Toby Belch), Martin LaPlatney (Captain/Antonio), Mary Layne (Viola), Benjamin Stewart (Malvolio), and Michael Alicia, Charles Johnson, Mimi Savage, Cynthia Stuart, F. Allan Tibbetts

A SHAYNA MAIDEL: *The Life of a Family* by Barbara Lebow; Director, Robert Kalfin; Set, Wolfgang Roth; Costumes, Eduardo Sicangco; Lights, Curt Ostermann; Sound, David Budries; Stage Manager, Alice Dewey. CAST: Maggie Burke (Mama), Ray Dooley (Duvid), Kate Fuglei (Hanna), Mark Margolis (Mordechai Weiss), Gordana Rashovich (Lusia Weiss Pechenik), Lindsey Margo Smith (Rose Weiss)

ANDROCLES AND THE LION by George Bernard Shaw; Director, Jerome Kilty; Set, Lowell Detweiler; Costumes, Jess Goldstein; Lighting, John McLain; Sound, David Budries; Stage Manager, Katherine M. Goodrich. CAST: Robert Burke (The Captain), Alvin Epstein (Androcles), Brian Evers (Centurion), Jerome Kilty (George Bernard Shaw/Caesar), Gary Lahti (Metellus), Robert Langdon-Lloyd (Spintho), Mary Layne (Lavinia), Katherine McGrath (Megaera), Mark Wayne Nelson (The Retiarius), Kevin O'Donnell (Menagerie Keeper), Edward O'Neill (Ferrovius), Jeff Paris (Call Boy), Morgan Strickland (Lentulus/Secutor), Tom Zemon (The Lion), and Stacey Burton, Stuart Ian Evans, Ken Festa, Garland Fitzpatrick, Robert James, Nathalie G. Jerardi, Ruth Lanzer, Richard Luciano, Melissa Mauro, Priscilla Moore, John Moser, John Sabovik, Hellen Snyder, John Tindall

THE TOOTH OF CRIME by Sam Shepard; Director, David Petrarca; Set, John Conklin; Costumes, Eduardo Sicangco; Lighting, Vivien Leone; Music, Sync66; Sound, David Budries; Stage Managers, Alice Dewey, Katherine M. Goodrich. CAST: Michael Cerveris (Crow), Bill Fagerbakke (Cheyenne), Zach Grenier (Galactic Jack/Referee), David Patrick Kelly (Hoss), Park Overall (Becky Lou), John Remme (Star-Man), George Riddle (Doc)

DISTANT FIRES by Kevin Heelan; *World Premiere;* Director, Mark Lamos; Set, Marjorie Bradley Kellogg; Costumes, G. W. Mercier; Lighting, Stephen Strawbridge; Stage Manager, Liz Small. CAST: Scott Dimalante (Beauty), Leo V. Finnie III (Foos), David Alan Grier (Thomas), Art Kempf (General), Barry Lee (Angel), Ellis E. Williams (Raymond)

ON THE VERGE, OR The Geography of Yearning by Eric Overmyer; Director, Mark Lamos; Set, Derek McLane; Costumes, Dunya Ramicova; Lighting, Robert Wierzel; Sound, David Budries; Stage Manager, Katherine M. Goodrich. CAST: Kate Burton (Alexandra), Arthur Hanket (Alphonse/Grover/The Yeti/The Gorge Troll/Mr. Coffee/Madame Nhu/Gus/Nicky Paradise), Laurie Kennedy (Fanny), Pamela Payton-Wright (Mary)

T. Charles Erickson, Lanny Nagler Photos

Right Center: Ellis E. Williams, Leo V. Finnie III, Barry Lee, Scott Dimalante, David Alan Grier in "Distant Fires" Above: Gordana Rashovich, Ray Dooley in "A Shayna Maidel" Top: Laurie Kennedy, Kate Burton, Pamela Payton-Wright in "On the Verge"

David Patrick Kelly, Michael Cerveris in "The Tooth of Crime"

HARTMAN THEATRE

Stamford, Connecticut
October 11, 1985–June 15, 1986
Eleventh Season

Artistic Director, Margaret Booker; Managing Director, Timothy Brennan; Associate Artistic Director, Michael Bloom; Production Manager, Katharyn Davies; Stage Managers, Kevin Mangan, Kathleen Iacobacci; Press/Marketing, William Sharek, Susan Aronson; Assistant to Managing/Artistic Directors, Amy Germano; Props, Timothy Whitney, Linda Misenheimer; Sound, Stephanie Burda; Casting, Jay Binder

PRODUCTIONS & CASTS

THE IMAGINARY INVALID by Moliere; Adaptation, Miles Malleson; Director, Pat Patton; Set, Michael Miller; Costumes, John Carver Sullivan; Lighting, James Sale. CAST: Tom Aldredge, Denny Dillon, Leonard Drum, Richard Esterbrook, Jonathan Fuller, Rex D. Hays, Leslie Hicks, Malcolm Hillgartner, Joe Palmieri, Judith Roberts, Barry Snider, Terres Unsoeld

THE PHILADELPHIA STORY by Philip Barry; Director, Ron Lagomarsino; Set, John Lee Beatty; Costumes, Elizabeth Covey; Lighting, James Sale; Stage Manager, Don Enoch. CAST: Scotty Bloch, Richard Esterbrook, George Hamlin, Timothy Landfield, Arden Lewis, John Bedford-Lloyd, Sam McMurray, Katherine Elizabeth Neuman, Sam Robards, Sam Stoneburner, Jane Summerhays, Anne Twomey, Ronald Wendschuh

FALLEN ANGELS by Noel Coward; Director, Nagle Jackson; Set, Kate Edmunds; Costumes, Kurt Wilhelm; Lighting, Jeff Davis. CAST: Richard Esterbrook, Richmond Hoxie, Henry J. Jordan, Gilles Kohler, Jane Murray, Susan Pellegrino, Debora Weston, Mary Catherine Wright

THE THREE SISTERS by Anton Chekhov; Translation, Randall Jarrell; Director, Margaret Booker; Set, David Potts; Costumes, John Carver Sullivan; Lighting, Jeff Davis; Sound, David A. Schnirman. CAST: Robert Adamo, Kate Burton, Jay Doyle, Richard Esterbrook, Michele Farr, Bruce Gooch, Paul Hecht, Patricia A. Hodges, Vera Johnson, Jerome Kilty, John Martinuzzi, James Maxwell, Stacy Ray, John C. Vennema, Debora Weston

CARELESS LOVE by John Olive; Director, Margaret Booker; Set, David Potts; Costumes, Kurt Wilhelm, Cecilia Friederichs; Lighting, Jeff Davis; Sound, David Schnirman. CAST: Kelly Curtis, Bruce Gooch. Understudies: Richard Esterbrook, Bernadette Wilson

Gerry Goodstein Photos

**Anne Twomey, John Bedford-Lloyd
in "The Philadelphia Story"**

**Mariana Rence, Mary Leigh Stahl, Linda Jane
Ammon, Janet Hayes in "Carry On"**

HERITAGE ARTISTS, LTD.

Cohoes, New York
November 15, 1985–June 7, 1986

Producing Director, Robert W. Tolan; Business Manager, Catherine B. Ryan; Marketing/Press, Sarah S. Burke; Assistant to Producing Director, Donna J. Gagnon; Sets: Duke Durfee, James M. Youmans, David Finley, Gary English; Lighting: Rachel Bickel, James Parsons, Debra Dumas; Costumes: Nancy Palmatier, Chelsea Harriman, Amanda Aldridge; Stage Managers: Jonathan D. Secor, Karen Terry

PRODUCTIONS & CASTS

THE WONDER YEARS with Music and Lyrics by David Levy; Book, David Levy, Steve Liebman, David Holdgrive, Terry LaBolt; *World Premiere;* Director/Choreographer, David Holdgrive; Musical Direction, Keith Thompson. CAST: Scott Banfield, David Beditz, Deb G. Girdler, Larry Hirschorn, Nona Waldeck, Susanna Wells

BILLY BISHOP GOES TO WAR: Director, William S. Morris, CAST: Robin Haynes (Billy Bishop), T. O. Sterrett (Piano Player/Musical Director

BABY: Director, Robert W. Tolan; Musical Director, Jeremy Kahn; Musical Staging, David Holdgrive. CAST: Linda Jane Ammon, David Beditz, Susan Cicarelli, Dolores Farrell, Laura Gardner, Richard Gervais, W. M. Hunt, Andre H. Montgomery, Tim Pinckney, Mariana Rence, Tonia Rowe

GODSPELL; Director/Choreographer, Vincent Telesco; Musical Director, Jeremy Kahn. CAST: Linda Jane Ammon, Sam Calandrino, Jim Charles, Susan Cicarelli, Richard Gervais, Gerry McCarthy, Andre H. Montgomery, Tim Pinckney, Mariana Rence, Tonia Rowe

SOMETHING'S AFOOT; Directors, Gary Gage, Robert W. Tolan; Musical Director, Marty Jones; Dance Staging, Constance Valis Hill. CAST: Linda Jane Ammon, Jim Charles, David Edwards, Gary Gage, Janet Hayes, John Newton, Tim Pinckney, Mariana Rence, Luke Sickle, Mary Leigh Stahl

Skip Dickstein, Cynthia Morse, Ed Schultz Photos

**Left Center: Robin Haynes, T. O. Sterrett
in "Billy Bishop Goes to War"**

HUNTINGTON THEATRE COMPANY

Boston, Massachusetts
September 28, 1985–June 15, 1986
Fourth Season

Producing Director, Peter Altman; Managing Director, Michael Maso; Board President, Gerald Gross.

PRODUCTIONS & CASTS

SULLIVAN & GILBERT by Kenneth Ludwig; Director, Larry Carpenter; Sets, John Falabella; Costumes, David Murin; Lighting, Marcia Madeira; Orchestrations/Musical Supervision, John Clifton; Musical Director, Herbert Kaplan; Stage Managers, Karen Carpenter, K. Margit Hartmann. CAST: Thomas Toner (William Schwenck Gilbert), Michael Allinson (Sir Arthur Sullivan), Thomas Carson (Richard D'Oyly Carte), Etain O'Malley (Lucy Turner "Kitty" Gilbert), Munson Hicks (Alfred, Duke of Edinburgh), Regina O'Malley (Violet Russell), John Clifton (Francois Cellier), Michael Connolly (George Grossmith), Terry Runnels (Rutland Barrington), Anthony Emeric (Durward Lely), Kevin Dearinger (Courtice Pounds), Diane Armistead (Rosina Brandram), Joanna Glushak (Jessie Bond), Catherine Gaines (Sybil Grey).
THE MISANTHROPE by Moliere; Director, Edward Gilbert; Set/Costumes, John Conklin; Lighting, Beverly Emmons; Stage Managers, Liza C. Stein, K. Margit Hartmann. CAST: Stephen Markle (Alceste), Munson Hicks (Philinte), James Harper (Oronte), Catherine Cox (Celimene) Monica Merryman (Eliante), Jennifer Harmon (Arsinoe), Thomas Schall (Clitandre) James Bodge (Basque), Scott Kealey (Dubois).
THE BIRTHDAY PARTY by Harold Pinter; Director, Ben Levit; Set, James Leonard Joy; Costumes, Mariann Verheyen; Lighting, Frances Aronson; Stage Managers, Karen L. Carpenter, Sarah Donnelly. CAST: James Greene (Petey), Mary Louise Wilson (Meg), Gary Sloan (Stanley), Mary Beth Fisher (Lulu), Gordon Chater (Goldberg), Pat McNamara (McCann).
SAINT JOAN by George Bernard Shaw; Director, Jacques Cartier; Set, Karl Eigsti; Costumes, Robert Morgan; Lighting, Roger Meeker; Stage Managers, Karen L. Carpenter, Sarah E. Donnelly. CAST: Joseph Costa (Robert de Baudricourt), Ted Davis (Steward), Maryann Plunkett (Joan), John Conley (Bertrand de Poulengey), Earle Edgerton (Archbishop of Rheims), Donald Christopher (La Tremouille/Canon de Courcelles), Henry J. Jordan (Giles de Rais: "Bluebeard"), Leonard Kelly-Young (Captain La Hire), Charles Jansz (The Dauphin), Stephen Markle (Dunois), Jack Ryland (Richard de Beauchamp), Ross Bickell (Chaplain de Stogumber), Louis Turenne (Peter Cauchon), Michael Pereira (Page), Thomas Barbour (Inquisitor), Henry J. Jordan (D'Estivet), David Silber (Brother Martin Ladvenu), Leonard Kelly-Young (Executioner), and Joseph Costa, Ted Davis, Frank T. Graham, Martin Hanley, Bob Knapp, Skip Maloney, Jack McCullough, William Strempek.
ON THE VERGE OR The Geography of Yearning by Eric Overmyer; Director, Pamela Berlin; Set, Franco Colavecchia; Costumes, Lindsay Davis; Lighting, Jackie Manassee; Music, Louis Rosen; Choreography, Martha Bowers; Stage Managers, Karen L. Carpenter, Karin Hartmann. CAST: Roberta Maxwell (Mary), Cristine Rose (Fanny), Julie White (Alex), A. C. Weary (The Others).

(No photos submitted)

Fred Zimmerman (prone), Brian Leo
in "Sherlock's Last Case"

ILLINOIS THEATRE CENTER

Park Forest, Illinois
September 27, 1985–May 4, 1986

Artistic Director, Steve S. Billig; Sets, Jonathan Roark; Lighting, Richard Peterson; Costumes, Henriette Swearingen.

PRODUCTIONS & CASTS

QUILTERS by Molly Newman and Barbara Damashek; Music and Lyrics, Barbara Damashek; CAST: Claudia Lee Dalton, Karen Wheeler, Iris Lieberman, Lorian Stein, Etel Billig, Diane Fishbein, Lynne Clayton.
MESSIAH by Martin Sherman; CAST: Marlene DuBois, Michael Myers, Sharon Carlson, Etel Billig, Rosalind Hurwitz, Steve Billig, Drew Gold.
110 IN THE SHADE by Tom Jones and Harvey Schmidt; CAST: Iris Lieberman, Tony Stokes, David Lewman, Jim Hinton, Lorian Stein, Fred Zimmerman, Steve Billig.
PAINTING CHURCHES by Tina Howe; CAST: Eileen Vorbach, Etel Billig, Steve Billig.
GREATER TUNA by Joe Sears and Jaston Williams; CAST: Steve Billig, Fred Zimmerman.
SHERLOCK'S LAST CAST by Charles Marowitz; CAST: Richard Lavin, Cathy Bieber, Etel Billig, Fred Zimmerman, Brian Leo.
HANGIN' 'ROUND by Steve S. Billig; *World Premiere;* CAST: Judy McLaughlin, Laura Collins, Scott Brigham, Etel Billig, Dave Katz, Steve Billig, Vivian O'Brien.

Lloyd De Grane Photos

**Marlene DuBois, Michael Myers
in "Messiah"**

INDIANA REPERTORY THEATRE

Indianapolis, Indiana
October 25, 1985–June 31, 1986

Artistic Director, Tom Haas; Managing Director, Jessica L. Andrews; Associate Artistic Director, Paul Moser; Dramaturg, Janet Allen; General Manager, Robert A. Gillman; Marketing Director, William "Butch" Coyne; Press, Kim Montgomery; Development, Marita Scherer; Production Manager, Donald R. Youngberg; Stage Manager, Joel Grynheim

RESIDENT COMPANY: Frederick Farrar, Craig Fuller, Bernadette Galanti, Mark Goetzinger, Bella Jarrett, Howard Jensen, Ron Keaton, Michael Lipton, Karen Nelson, Kurt Owens, Amelia Penland, Howard Pinhasik, Frank Raiter, David Williams. Interns: Ken Triwush, Matthew Harrington, Barbara Garren, David Connelly

PRODUCTIONS & CASTS

THE FRONT PAGE by Charles MacArthur and Ben Hecht; Director Tom Haas: Costumes, Nancy Pope; Set, Christopher H. Barreca; Lighting, Stuart Duke. CAST: Dan Desmond (Hildy Johnson), Michael Lipton (Walter Burns), David Connelly (Policeman 1), Frederick Farrar (McCue), Craig Fuller (Kruger), Bernadette Galanti (Mrs. Schlosser), Barbara Garren (Jenny), Mark Goetzinger (Murphy), Matthew Harrington (Woodenshoes Eichorn), Bella Jarrett (Mrs. Grant), Howard Jensen (Mr. Pincus), Linda Lee Johnson (Molly Malloy), Norman M. Leger (Diamond Louis), John MacKay (The Mayor), Jerry Mayer (Sheriff Hartman), Larry John Meyers (Schwartz), Karen Nelson (Peggy Grant), Howard Pinhasik (Endicott), Frank Raiter (Bensinger), Ken Triwush (Wilson), Phil A. Tunnah (Frank)

VIRGINIA by Edna O'Brien; Director, Paul Moser; Costumes, Connie Singer; Set, Christopher H. Barreca; Lighting, Stuart Duke. CAST: Christine Healy (Virginia Woolf), Amelia Penland (Vita), William Perley (Virginia's Father/Leonard Woolf)

PETER PAN by J. M. Barrie; Director, Tom Haas; Costumes, Bobbi Owen; Set, Christopher H. Barreca; Lighting, Rachel Budin; Music, T. O., Sterrett. CAST: Frank Raiter (J. M. Barrie), Michael Lipton (Mr. Darling/Captain Hook), Amelia Penland (Wendy), David Connelly (First Twin), Frederick Farrar (John), Craig Fuller (Slightly), Barbara Garren (Liza/Tiger Lily), Mark Goetzinger (Cecco), Matthew Harrington (John), Howard Jensen (Smee), Russ Jolly (Curly), Ron Keaton (Noodler), Norman M. Leger (Gentleman Starkey), Julia Meade (Mrs. Darling), Kurt Owens (Tootles), Howard Pinhasik (Nibs), Ken Triwush (Second Twin), Phil A. Tunnah (Pirate), David Williams (Bill Jukes)

SISTER MARY IGNATIUS EXPLAINS IT ALL FOR YOU/THE ACTOR'S NIGHTMARE by Christopher Durang; Director, Ben Cameron; Costumes, Connie Singer; Set, Christopher H. Barreca; Lighting, Stuart Duke. CAST: Joshua Bringle (Thomas), Bernadette Galanti (Ellen Terry/Philomena Rostovish), Patrick Garner (George Spelvin/Aloysius Benheim), Bella Jarrett (Sarah Siddons/Sister Mary Ignatius), Karen Nelson (Meg/Diane Symonds), Victor Talmadge (Henry Irving/Gary Sullavan)

DRACULA by Bram Stoker; Adaptation, Tom Haas; Director, Gavin Cameron-Webb; Costumes, Gail Brassard; Set, Alison Ford; Lighting, Rachel Budin. CAST: Bernadette Galanti (Violet Walker), Howard Jensen (Dr. Leonard Seward), Frederick Farrar (Renfield), Matthew Harrington (Jacob Simmons), Craig Fuller (Lt. Jonathan Harker), Karen Nelson (Lucy Seward), Frank Raiter (Prof. Arthur Van Helsing), Richard Ryder (Count Dracula), Jean Childers (Maid)

THE BOYS IN AUTUMN: HUCK 'N' TOM GROW'D UP by Bernard Sabath; Director, Paul Moser; Costumes, Gail Brassard; Set, Russell Metheny; Lighting, Stuart Duke. CAST: Nesbitt Blaisdell (Henry Finnegan), Frank Raiter (Thomas Gray)

MOURNING BECOMES ELECTRA by Eugene O'Neill; Director, Tom Haas; Costumes, Gail Brassard; Set, Christopher H. Barreca; Lighting, Rachel Budin. CAST: Matthew Harrington (Seth Beckwith), Janet Sarno (Christine Mannon), Amelia Penland (Lavinia Mannon), Craig Fuller (Peter Niles), Marylou DiFilippo (Hazel Niles), Martin LaPlatney (Capt. Adam Brant), Michael Lipton (Brigadier-General Ezra Mannon), Frederick Farrar (Orin Mannon)

DIAL "M" FOR MURDER by Frederick Knott; Director, Paul Moser; Costumes, Gail Brassard; Set, Russell Metheny; Lighting, Michael Lincoln. CAST: Matthew Harrington (Thompson), John Herzog (Capt. Lesgate), Seth Jones (Tony), Michael Minor (Mas), Karen Nelson (Margot), Frank Raiter (The Inspector)

ROMEO AND JULIET by William Shakespeare; Director, Tom Haas; Costumes, Bill Walker; Set, G. W. Mercier; Lighting, Stephen Strawbridge; Fight Choreography, Randy Kovitz; Choreographer, Michael O'Gorman. CAST: Tony Carlin (Mercutio), Michael Cerveris (Romeo), Frederick Farrar (Paris), Matthew Harrington (Peter), Bella Jarrett (Nurse), Michelle Joyner (Juliet), Priscilla Lindsay (Lady Capulet), Lowry Miller (Capulet), Viggo Mortensen (Tybalt), Michael O'Gorman (Escalus), Frank Raiter (Friar Laurence), Malcolm Smith (Benvolio/Friar John), Ken Triwush (Balthasar), David Williams (Montague/Apothecary)

TORCH SONG TRILOGY by Harvey Fierstein; Director, Paul Moser; Costumes, Connie Singer; Set, Christopher H. Barreca; Lighting, Stuart Duke. CAST: Donald Berman (Arnold), Craig Fuller (Ed), Judith Granite (Mrs. Beckoff), Mark Grindey (David), Karen Nelson (Laurel), Sean Woods (Alan)

CABARET SEASON: *The Jerome Kern Song Book,* Director, Tom Haas, with Frederick Farrar, Bernadette Galanti, Howard Pinhasik, Lynne Wieneke; *Greater Tuna,* Director, Paul Moser, with Ron Keaton, Kurt Owens; *Season's Greetings,* Director, Paul Moser, with Jane Henley, Jeff Johnson, Rose Malague, David Olive; *Magic Child: An Evening With Teresa Burrell* with Teresa Burrell, Darryl Waters (Musical Director); *Some Enchanted Evenings: The Songs of Rodgers and Hammerstein,* Director, Frederick Farrar, with Bernadette Galanti, Mark Goetzinger, Robert Vincent, Lynne Wieneke; *Bullshot Crummond,* Director, Paul Moser, with C. J. Critt, Bernadette Galanti, Mark Goetzinger, Ron Keaton, Kurt Owens; *A Little Sondheim Music,* Director, Tom Haas, with Brigid Brady, Frederick Farrar, Bernadette Galanti, Mark Goetzinger; *Together Again,* Director, Tom Haas, with Bernadette Galanti, Mark Goetzinger

**Karen Nelson, Craig Fuller, Frank Raiter
in "Dracula"**

JOHN F. KENNEDY CENTER FOR THE PERFORMING ARTS

May 18, 1985–July 5, 1986
Washington, D.C.

Chairman, Roger L. Stevens; Artistic Director, Marta Istomin; Operations, Thomas R. Kendrick; Development, Jillian H. Poole; Communications, Laura Longley, Tiki Davies

(Eisenhower Theater) Saturday, May 18,–June 22, 1985. The American National Theater presents:

THE COUNT OF MONTE CRISTO by Alexandre Dumas and Auguste Maquet; Dramatized by Mr. Dumas; Translated and adapted by Charles Fechter, assisted by Arthur Leclercq; Revised and immortalized by James O'Neill; Additions from the King James Bible and from the writings of Lord Byron; Restored and assembled by Davies King; Director, Peter Sellars; Sets, George Tsypin; Costumes, Kurt Wilhelm; Lighting, James F. Ingalls; Music, Beethoven, Schnittke; Sound, Lenny Will; Casting, Meg Simon/Fran Kumin; Stage Manager, Ellen Raphael. CAST: Tony Azito (Danglars), Roscoe Lee Browne (M. Noirtier), Anne Beresford Clarke (Mlle. Sophie Danglars), Joaquim de Almeida (Fernand/Count de Morcerf), Earl Hindman (Gaspard Caderousse), Leo Leyden (Edouard Denis Morel), Patti LuPone (Mercedes Mondego), Michael O'Keefe (Albert Mondego/Viscont de Morcerf), Brian McCue (Germain de Beauchamp), Ernie Meier (Emile de Chateau-Renaud), Zakes Mokae (M. Gerard de Villefort), Isabell Monk (Madeleine Caderousse/La Charconte), Richard Thomas (Edmund Dantes/Count of Monte Cristo), David Warrilow (Old Dantes/Abbe Faria)

(Terrace Theater) Wednesday, June 12,–Juy 6, 1985. American National Theater presents the Steppenwolf Theatre Company in **COYOTE UGLY** by Lynn Siefert; Director, John Malkovich; Sets/Lights, Kevin Rigdon; Costumes, Erin Quigley; Sound, Gregg M. Winters; Stage Manager, Cindy Jo Savitski. CAST: Laurie Metcalf (Scarlet), Moira Harris (Andreas), Francis Guinan (Red), Randall Arney (Dowd), Kathleen Sykora (Penny), Understudies: Amy Morton, Alan Wilder

(Free Theatre) Wednesday, June 12,–July 29, 1985. American National Theater presents Wisdom Bridge Theatre in

IN THE BELLY OF THE BEAST: LETTERS FROM PRISON by Jack Henry Abbott; Director, Robert Falls; Set, Robert Falls/Michael S. Philippi; Lighting, Michael S. Philippi; Sound, Jim Kusyk; Stage Manager, Karl W. Sullivan. CAST: Tim Halligan, Peter Aylward and William L. Petersen as Jack Henry Abbott.

(Terrace Theater) Tu July 9,–Aug. 3, 1985. The Wisdom Bridge Theatre production of

KABUKI MEDEA freely adapted from Euripides' Medea by Bill Strieb and Lou Anne Wright; Edited by A. Doyle Moore; Conceived, Designed, Directed by Shozo Sato; Lighting, Michael S. Philippi; Electronic Music Composer, Michael Cerri; Stage Managers, T. Paul Lynch, Todd Little. CAST: Dean Fortunato (King of Korea/Jason), Roone O'Donnell (Princess), Barbara E. Robertson (Medea), Christine McHugh (Nurse), Kokens: Jim Brooks, Margo Buchanan, Chorus: Nathalie Cunningham, Judith Easton, Henry Godines, Elizabeth Kelly, Travis Lawhon, Neil Maffin, Jody Naymik, Rick Sparks

(Free Theater) Wednesday, July 24,–Aug. 10, 1985. The Steppenwolf Theatre Company production of

STREAMERS by David Rabe; Director, Terry Kinney; Set/Lights, Kevin Rigdon; Costumes, Nan Cibula. CAST: Randall Arney (MP Lt.), Vito D'Ambrosio (PFC Hinson/MP), Afram Duende (PFC Clark/MP), Dennis Farina (Cokes), Erik King (Roger), Ron McLarty (Rooney), Jeff Perry (Richie), Ving Rhames (Carlyle), Gary Sinise (Billy), Alan Wilder (Martin)

(Eisenhower Theater) Wednesday, July 31,–Sept. 14, 1985

THE ICEMAN COMETH by Eugene O'Neill; Director, Jose Quintero. For cast and other credits, see Broadway Calendar.

(Terrace Theater) Monday, Aug. 5,–Sept. 14, 1985. Actors Theatre of Louisville production of

TENT MEETING by Larry Larson, Levi Lee, Rebecca Alworth Wackler; Director, Patrick Tovatt; Set/Lighting, Paul Owen; Costumes, Marcia Dixcy; Sound, James M. Bay; Props, Diann Fay; Stage Manager, Craig Weindling. CAST: Levi Lee (Reverend Ed), Larry Larson (Darrell), Rebecca Alworth Wackler (Becky Ann)

(Opera House) Wednesday, Aug. 31,–Sept. 21, 1985

WEST SIDE STORY with Book by Arthur Laurents; Music, Leonard Bernstein; Lyrics, Stephen Sondheim; Director, Ruth Mitchell. For other credits and cast, see National Touring Companies section.

(New Playwrights Theatre) Thursday, Nov. 7,–30, 1985. American National Theater presents

SOLO VOYAGES adapted by Joseph Chaikin from plays of Adrienne Kennedy; Director, Mr. Chaikin; Music composed and performed by Skip LaPlante and Edwina Lee Tylor; Movement choreographed and performed by Jawole Willa Jo Zollar; Assistant Director, David Willinger; Set, Jun Maeda; Lighting, Beverly Emmons, Rachel Budin; Costume, Gwen Fabricant; Supervising Producer, Melody Brooks; Company Manager, Joel Bassin; Performed by Robbie McCauley.

IS THIS REAL? by Ronnie Gilbert, Mira Rafalowicz; Directors, Ronnie Gilbert, Dianne Houston; Lighting, Rachel Budin. CAST: Joseph Chaikin, Ronnie Gilbert, Harvey Perr, Skip LaPlante (Musician)

(Terrace Theater) Monday, Nov. 25–Dec. 14, 1985

ZOE CALDWELL AS LILLIAN a play by William Luce; Based on the autobiographical works of Lillian Hellman; Director, Robert Whitehead. For additional credits, see Broadway Calendar.

(New Playwrights Theater) Saturday, Dec. 7–22, 1985. American National Theater presents the Wooster Group production of

NORTH ATLANTIC with Text by Jim Strahs; Director, Elizabeth LeCompte; Music, Eddy Dixon; Design, Jim Clayburgh; Technical Directors, Michael Nishball, Jeff Webster; Sound, Bob Cardelli; General Manager, Linda Chapman. CAST: Willem Dafoe (Col. Lloyd Lud), Spalding Gray (Gen. Lance Benders), Anna Kohler (Nurse Pvt. Wendy-Owen Clark), Nancy Reilly (Cpl. Nurse Jane Babcock), Peyton Smith (MSgt. Mary Brysynsky), Michael Stumm (Pvt. Guy Doberman), Kate Valk (Ens. Ann Pusey), Ron Vawter (Capt. Roscoe Chizzum)

(Eisenhower Theater) Monday, Dec. 9, 1985–Jan. 11, 1986

A SEAGULL by Anton Chekhov; Translated by Maria M. Markof-Belaeff; Director, Peter Sellars; Music, Alexander Scriabin; Sets, George Tsypin; Costumes, Kurt Wilhelm; Lights, James F. Ingalls; Stage Manager, Frank Marino. CAST: Colleen Dewhurst (Arkadina), Kevin Spacey (Konstantin), Henderson Forsythe (Nikolayevich), Kelly McGillis (Nina), Tony Mockus (IlyaShamrayev), Kathleen Nolan (Polina), Priscilla Smith (Masha), David Strathairn (Boris), Paul Winfield (Dorn), Jan Triska (Semyon), Walter Atamaniuk (Yakov), Marlena Lustik (Cook), Jan Maxwell (Chambermaid), Leslie Amper (Pianist)

(Eisenhower Theater) Monday, Feb. 17,–March 22, 1986 The American National Theater presents

IDIOT'S DELIGHT by Robert Sherwood; Director, Peter Sellars; Sets, George Tsypin; Costumes, Kurt Wilhelm; Lighting, James F. Ingalls; Sound, Bruce Odland; Choreography, Baayork Lee; Dance/Vocal Arrangements, Randolph Mauldin; Stage Manager, Lani Ball; Director, Peter Sellars. CAST: Paul Stolarsky (Dumpsty), Marc Epstein (Donald Navadel), Merwin Goldsmith (Pittaluga), Jan Triska (Capt. Locicero), Richard Woods (Dr. Waldersee), Sam Robards (Mr. Cherry), Anne Beresford Clarke (Mrs. Cherry), Stacy Keach (Van Harry), Barbara Sharma (Shirley), Jaclyn Ross (Beulah), Helen Schneider (Bebe), Tim Choate (Quillery), Nick Mathwick (Signor Rossi), Brian McCue (Auguste/Signora Rossi/Anna), Werner Klemperer (Achille Weber), JoBeth Williams (Irene) Understudies: Karma Camp, Anne Beresford Clarke, Brian McCue, Nick Mathwick, Jaclyn Ross, Stephen Yoakam, Stephen Willems

(Eisenhower Theater) Tuesday, May 13,–17, 1986. Haifa Municipal Theatre of Israel productions of

GHETTO by Joshua Sobol; Director, Gedalia Besser; Set, Adrian Vaux; Costumes, Edna Sobol; Music, Yoni Rechter; Choreography, Nava Zuckerman; Lighting, Yehiel Orgal. CAST: Youssef Abu Warda (Gens), Riki Gal (Hayyah), Ami Weinberg (Dummy), Rami Danon (Weiskopf), Shmuel Wolff (Judge), Eli Gorenstein (Srulik), Michael Kfir (Dr. Wiener), Alex Munte (Rabbi/Hassid), Gury Segal (Ilya), Dor Zweigenbom (Yankel), Erez Shafrir (Gaivush), Viki Moran (The Lady), Dalya Shimko (Leibele), Giora Shammai (Gottlieb/Dessler), Doron Tavori (Kittel/Dr. Paul), Ilan Toren (Kruk/Ghetto Librarian)

THE SOUL OF A JEW by Joshua Sobol; Director, Gedalia Besser; Set, Adrian Vaux; Costumes, Edna Sobol; Music, Yoni Rechter. CAST: Doron Tavori (Otto Weininger), Giora Shammai/Alex Munte (Leopold), Leora Rivlin (Adelaide/Adela), Gury Segal (Berger), Dalya Shimko (Clara), Youssef Abu Warda/Ilan Toren (Tietz/Strindberg/Moebius), Michael Kfir (Freud), Tchia Danon (The Double), Tchia Danon, Gury Segal (Prostitutes)

(Eisenhower Theatre) Wednesday, May 28,–July 5, 1986

THE CAINE MUTINY COURT-MARTIAL by Herman Wouk; Director, Charlton Heston; Set, Saul Radomsky; Lighting, Martin Aronstein. CAST: Ben Cross (Lt. Barney Greenwald), John Corey (Lt. Stephen Maryk), Stephen Macht (Lt. Com. John Challee), Robert Rockwell (Capt. Blakely), Charlton Heston (Lt. Com. Philip Francis Queeg), William Wright (Lt. Thomas Keefer), Karl Wiedergott (Signalman 3rd Class Junius Urban), Michael Thoma (Lt. jg. Willis Seward Keith), Frank Aletter (Capt. Randolph Southard), Joe George (Dr. Forrest Lundeen), Vincent Marzello (Dr. Bird), Bryan Burch-Worch (Stenographer), Loren Lester (Orderly), Court: Tony Campisi, Paul Laramore, Robert Legionaire, Mark McIntire, Henry Sutton, B. J. Theus, Ben Wilson

Joan Marcus Photos

**Top: Charlton Heston, Ben Cross
in "The Caine Mutiny Court-Martial"**

**Top Right of preceding page: Richard Thomas,
Michael O'Keefe in "The Count of Monte Cristo"
Below: Werner Klemperer, JoBeth Williams
in "Idiot's Delight"**

161

LONG ISLAND STAGE

Rockville Centre, New York
October 15, 1985–June 22, 1986

Artistic Director, Clinton J. Atkinson; Managing Director, Andrew Cohn; Executive Director, Sally Cohen; Production Coordinator, Tom Pavelka; Press, Doris Meadows; Development, Norma Ackerman; Stage Manager, David Wahl; Lighting, John Hickey, Vivian Leone; Sets, Dan Conway, Mark Fizgibbons, James Singelis, Charles Cosler, Dan Ettinger; Costumes, Jose Lengson, Don Newcomb, David Navarro Velasquez; Choreographer, Dennis Dennehy; Music Director, Edward Reichert; Casting, Slater/Willett

PRODUCTIONS & CASTS

THE PLAY'S THE THING by Ferenc Molnar; Adaptation, P. G. Wodehouse. CAST: J. B. Adams, Peter Bartlett, Alexander Carney, Claudine Cassan-Jellison, George Cavey, Michael Drucker, Larry Grey, John High, John R. Little
A FUNNY THING HAPPENED ON THE WAY TO THE FORUM with Music and Lyrics by Stephen Sondheim; Book, Larry Gelbart, Burt Shevelove. CAST: Arthur D'Alessio, Lydia Alfred, Yvette Alfred, David-Cameron Anderson, Peter Bartlett, Harry Bennett, James Brochu, George Cavey, Leonard Drum, Lorrie Harrison, Carey Hern, Donna Marie Milian, Evelyn Page, Joe Posa, Dick Richards, Lisa Semel, Steven Smeltzer, Gina Trano
RE-VIEWING SAROYAN (3 one-act plays) by William Saroyan. CAST: Mark Arnott, Lenisha D. Brown, Joseph D. Giardina, Bjorn Johnson, Bertram Prosser, Don Reeves, Tracy Sallows, Kendred T. Smith, Roxana Stuart
WARS OF ATTRITION by Patricia Goldstone; *World Premiere.* CAST: Cynthia Belgrave, Pamela Burrell, Cara Duff-MacCormick, Jack Parrish, Virginia Robinson, Ed Setrakian
A LESSON FROM ALOES by Athol Fugard. CAST: Pamela Burrell, Peter Matthey, Tyrone Wilson
YOU NEVER CAN TELL by George Bernard Shaw. Peter Bartlett, Veronica Castang, Emily Heebner, John High, Jim Hillgartner, Ben Lemon, Philip LeStrange, Tracy Sallows, Steven Smeltzer, Jerry Smith-Niles

Cathy Blaivas Photos

**James Naughton, Joanne Woodward, Treat Williams,
Karen Allen in "The Glass Menagerie"**

LONG WHARF THEATRE

New Haven, Connecticut
October 4, 1985–June 1, 1986
Twenty-First Season

Artistic Director, Arvin Brown; Executive Director, M. Edgar Rosenblum; Literary Manager, John Tillinger; Associate Artistic Director, Kenneth Frankel; General Manager, John K. Conte; Assistant to the Directors, Janice Muirhead; Literary, Margaret Van Sant, Ruth Grdseloff; Communications, Jay Drury; Development, Jacqueline J. Smaga; Stage Managers, Beverly J. Androeozzi, Anne Keefe, Robin Kevrick, Ellen Schafroth; Technical Director, Randy Engels; Scenic Artist, Keith Hyatte; Props, David Fletcher, Fred Thompson, Joseph P. Hoey; Sound, Rich Shrout, Brent Paul Evans; Wigs, Paul Huntley; Wardrobe, Margaret Jane Morgan, Maggie L. Normand; Casting Deborah Brown; Press, David Mayhew

PRODUCTIONS & CASTS

PARIS BOUND by Philip Barry; Director, John Tillinger; Sets, Steven Rubin; Costumes, Bill Walker; Lighting, Judy Rasmuson; Music, Tom Fay. CAST: Linda McGuire (Julie), Richard Bekins (Jim Hutton), Fran Brill (Mary Hutton), Ann McDonough (Nora Cope), Joyce Ebert (Helen White), Anne Swift (Fanny Shippan), Rex Robbins (James Hutton), W. H. Macy (Peter Cope), Nancy Mette (Noel Farley), Peter Friedman (Richard Parish)
PRIDE AND PREJUDICE by David Pownall; Based on the novel by Jane Austen; Director, Kenneth Frankel; Sets, John Conklin; Costumes, Dunya Ramicova; Lighting, Pat Collins; Music, Tom Fay; Dance/Movement, Dan Siretta. CAST: Richard Kiley (Mr. Bennet), Marge Redmond (Mrs. Bennet), Nancy Paul (Jane Bennet), Jane Kaczmarek (Lizzy Bennet), Jane Fleiss (Lydia Bennet), Jayne Atkinson (Charlotte Lucas), Peter Gallagher (Mr. Darcy), Tony Goldwyn (Mr. Bingley), Michele Farr (Caroline Bingley), David Cromwell (Rev. Collins), David Brizzolara (George Wickham), Patricia Falkenhain (Lady Catherine De Bourgh), Carey Cromelin (Anne De Bourgh)
CRYSTAL CLEAR *American Premiere;* Devised and Directed by Phil Young; Sets, Hugh Landwehr; Costumes, Linda Fisher; Lighting, Ronald Wallace; Technical Consultation, Maureen Scanlon; Originally created through improvisation by Anthony Allen, Diana Barrett, Philomena McDonagh. CAST: Jack Coulter (Richard), Jessica Harper (Thomasina), Sofia Landon (Jane)
THE NORMAL HEART by Larry Kramer; Director, Arvin Brown; Sets, D. Martyn Bookwalter; Costumes, Bill Walker, Lighting, Ronald Wallace; Dialect Coach, Tim Monich. CAST: Peter MacKenzie (Craig Donner/Grady/Orderly II), David Proval (Mickey Marcus), Thomas Hulce (Ned Weeks), Robertson Dean (David/Hiram Keebler/ Examining Doctor/Orderly I), Joyce Ebert (Dr. Emma Brookner), Ted Leplat (Bruce Niles), Richard Bekins (Felix Turner), Norman Parker (Ben Weeks), Eric Swanson (Tommy Boatwright)
THE GLASS MENAGERIE by Tennessee Williams; Director, Nikos Psacharopoulos; Set, Andrew Jackness; Costumes, Jess Goldstein; Lighting, Pat Collins; Music, Paul Bowles; Arrangements, Michael O'Flaherty, F. Wade Russo; Dialect Coach, Robert Williams. CAST: Treat Williams (Tom Wingfield), Joanne Woodward (Amanda Wingfield), Karen Allen (Laura Wingfield), James Naughton (Gentleman Caller)
FUGUE by Leonora Thuna; Director, Kenneth Frankel; Set, David Jenkins; Costumes, Jess Goldstein; Lighting, Judy Rasmuson; Music, Tom Fay. CAST: Barbara Barrie (Mary), Peggy Cosgrave (Zelda), Jess Osuna (Dr. Oleander), Richard Backus (Danny), Rebecca Schull (Mother), John Bowman (Noel), Alexandra O'Karma (Liz), Laura White (Tammy)
LOST IN THE STARS by Maxwell Anderson and Kurt Weill; Based on Alan Paton's novel, *Cry, The Beloved Country;* Director, Arvin Brown; Musical Director, Tom Fay; Sets, Michael Yeargan; Costumes, Jennifer von Mayrhauser; Lighting, Ronald Wallace; Dialect Consultant, Elizabeth Smith; Movement Consultant, Wesley Fata; Stage Managers, Anne Keefe, Jerry Cleveland; Conducting Assistants, Carol Crawford, James Luse. CAST: Thomas Young (Leader), Iralene Swain (Answerer/Young Woman), Wendell Pierce (Answeree/Matthew Kumalo), Michael V. Smartt (Stephen Kumalo), Thyli Dumakude (Grace Kumalo), Tamara Tunie (Nita/Rose), Walter Hudson (Stationmaster/Mark Eland), Jimmy Rivers (Young Man/Hlabeni), William Swetland (James Jarvis), Joel Stedman (Arthur Jarvis), Thomas Brand/Nicholas Tamarkin (Edward Jarvis), Tommy Hollis (John Kumalo), Thomas Young (Paulus), Jeffrey Smith (William/Servant), Jack Waddell (Jared/Guard), Kobie Powell (Alex Kumalo), Alex Wipf (Foreman/White Man/Judge), Phyllis Bash (Mrs. Mkize), Ebony Jo-Ann (Linda), Ellis Williams (Johannes Pafuri), Michael Wright (Absalom Kumalo), Janet Hubert (Irina), Peter Graham (Policeman/Burton), Gayton Scott (White Woman), Beth Allen, Karen Burlingame (Townspeople)

Photos by T. Charles Erickson

**Left Center: Mark Arnott, Tracy Sallows
in "Hello, Out There" (Long Island Stage)**

LOS ANGELES THEATRE CENTER

Los Angeles, California
September 12, 1985–June 15, 1986

Artistic Producing Director, Bill Bushnell; Producers, Diane White, Phillip Esparza; Sets: Timian Alsaker, Andy Stacklin, Douglas D. Smith, Russell Pyle, D. Martyn Bookwalter, Nicole Morin, Karl Eigsti; Costumes: Timian Alsaker, Ardyss L. Golden, Susan Nininger, Nicole Morin, Marianna Elliott, Armand Coutu, Heidi Kaczenski, Noel Taylor; Lighting: Timian Alsaker, Kurt Landisman, Russell Pyle, Kathy A. Perkins, Martin Aronstein, Lawrence Metzler, Todd Jered, Karl Eigsti, Tom Ruzika; Dramaturgs: Adam Leipzig, Mame Hunt; Sound: Jon Gottlieb, J. A. Deane, Stephen Shaffer; Stage Managers: Charles McEwan, Michelle E. Tatum, Donald David Hill, Nancy Ann Adler, Joan Toggenburger, Jill Johnson, Mark McDougal, Vicky Barlow, Susan Bougetz, Edward DeShae

PRODUCTIONS & CAST

THREE SISTERS by Anton Chekhov; Translation, Michael Frayn; *American Premiere;* Director, Stein Winge; Music Direction, Fredric Myrow. CAST: Angela Paton (Anfisa), Robbin Margurite Harvey (Maid), Kim Cattrall (Marsha), Ann Hearn (Irina), Meg Foster (Olga), Stephen Tobolowsky (Lt. Baron Tusenbach), Gerald Hiken (Dr. Chebutykin), Bruce Rodgers-Wright (Jr. Capt. Solyony), Hal Bokar (Farapont), Cliff DeYoung (Lt.-Col Vershinin), Gregory Wagrowski (Andrey Prozorov), Barry Michlin (Kulgin/Fyodor), Caitlin O'Heaney (Natasha), Arye Gross (2nd Lt. Rode), Cameron Thor (2nd Lt. Fedotik). Standbys: Janis Ward, Allegra Swift, Hal Bokar, Arye Gross, Cameron Thor
FOOL FOR LOVE by Sam Shepard; Director, Julie Herbert. CAST: Richard Lawson (Eddie), Pam Grier (May), Henry G. Sanders (Martin), Moses Gunn (Old Man). Standbys: Shabaka, Barry Henley, Tyra Farrell
NANAWATAI bY William Mastrosimone; Director, Lamont Johnson; *English Language Premiere;* Music/Collages, Fredric Myrow; Special Effects, Russell Pyle. CAST: Gina Gershon (Sherina), Philip Baker Hall (Georgi Daskal), Tommy Swerdlow (Anton Golikov), Adam Arkin (Nikolai Kaminisi), Gerald Papasian (Samad), Bill Pullman (Koverchenko), Edwin Gerard (Shahzaman), Steven Bauer (Taj Mohamud), Stefan Gierasch (Akbar), Mark Petrakis (Iskander), Rene Assa (Moustafa), Arlana Delawari, Setara Begum, Rahila Delawari, Soraya Delawari, Yasmine Delawari, Roya Fahmy, Khorshied Machalle Nusratty, Zarmina Popal. Standbys: Kevin Bash, Edwin Gerard, Carmine Iannaconne, Khorshied Machalle Nusratty, Gerald Papasian, Mark Petrakis

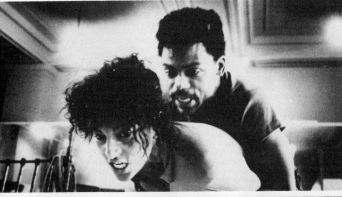

**Robert Beltram, James Victor, Patti Yasutake,
Anne Betancourt in "I Don't Have to Show You . . ."
Above: Pam Grier, Richard Lawson in "Fool for Love"**

THE TRIUMPH OF THE SPIDER MONKEY by Joyce Carol Oates; Director, Al Rossi; Music Score/Arrangements/Direction, Fredric Myrow; Songs: Music, Shaun Cassidy; Music Myrow; Lyrics, Joyce Carol Oates; Music Produced & Recorded by Michael Lloyd. CAST: Shaun Cassidy (Bobbie Gotteson), Dudley Knight (Voice of Judge), Paul Makley, Thomas Nixon (Baliffs), Rick Hamilton (Defense Attorney), James Siering (Prosecutor), Molly Cleator (Woman), Jonathan Palmer (Man), Doris Dowling (Melva), Kerry Noonan (Doreen), Peggy Schoditsch (Therapist), Gerald Hiken (Danny Minx), Paul Mackley, Thomas Nixon (College Boys), Allan Kolman (Vlad J), Patricia Estrin (Louise), Christine Avila (Rosalind). Standbys: Paul Mackley, Jonathan Palmer, Laura Skill, Hunt Burdick, Marily Alex, Molly Cleator, Al Rossi
A RICH FULL LIFE by Mayo Simon; *World Premiere;* Director, Alan Mandell. CAST: Lois Nettleton (Doris), Rhoda Gemignani (Christine), Frank McCarthy (Neil), Peter Haskell (Ted), Rebecca Patterson (Alice), Malcolm Danare (Bob). Standby: Annie Murray
THE PETRIFIED FOREST by Robert E. Sherwood; Director, Charles Marowitz. CAST: Armin Shimerman (Lineman), David Stenstrom (Lineman), Christopher McDonald (Boze Herzlinger), Jim B. Baker (Jason Maple), Judith Hansen (Gabby Maple), John McLiam (Gramp Maple), Alma Beltran (Paula), Rene Auberjonois (Alan Squier), Jack Axelrod (Herb), John C. Becher (Mr. Chisholm), Ronnie Claire Edwards (Mrs. Chisholm), Leland P. Smith (Joseph), Oz Tortora (Jackie), Philip Baker Hall (Duke Mantee), Frank Collison (Ruby), Earl Billings (Pyles), Stanley Grover (Legion Commander), David Stenstrom (Legionnaire), Charles Parks (Sheriff), Bob Devin Jones (Deputy), Armin Shimerman (Deputy). Standbys: Bob Devin Jones, David Stenstrom, Stanley Grover, Jennifer Parsons, Jack Axelrod, Dan Mason, Michael Abrams, Annie Murray, Jennifer Parsons, Armin Shimerman
HELP WANTED *(Steps, Conversation, Christmas Death, Negative Balance, Last Judgement, Poor Poet, Promises, Homecoming, English as a Second Language, Time Out)* by Franz Xaver Kroetz; Translation, Gitta Honegger; Director, Robert Harders. CAST: Dennis Redfield, Elizabeth Ruscio, Sasha von Schoeler, Brent Jennings
BOESMAN AND LENA by Athol Fugard; Director, Bill Bushnell. CAST: Moses Gunn, Madge Sinclair, Shabaka. Standbys: Tyra Farrell, Davis Roberts, Shabaka
THE QUARTERED MAN by Donald Freed; *World Premiere;* Conceptualized by Mark W. Travis & Bill Bushnell; Director, Mark W. Travis; Multimedia Coordination, R. S. Bailey; Video Photography Direction, John Cannaday; Slide/Still Photography, Victoria Wendell. CAST: Brock Peters (Father Carl Cruze), John Carter (George O'Connor), Patti Yasutake (Reporter), Dianne Turley Travis (Sister Mary Agnes Cassidy), William Glover (Grahmn Jones), Robert Beltran (Julio Ortez), Nora Ekserjan (Maria), Ricardo T. Lopez (Ernesto), Charles Parks (Buddy Heubing), Nancy Kwan (Mai O'Connor). Standbys: Nora Ekserjan, Gerald Hiken, Patti Johns, John Lassell, Ricardo Lopez, John Vargas
AS THE CROW FLIES *(World Premiere)* and **THE SOUND OF A VOICE** by David Hwang; Director, Reza Abdoh; Musical Direction, Carl Stone. CAST: *As the Crow Flies:* Phyllis Applegate (Hannah), Nobu McCarthy (Chan), Sab Shimono (P.K.); *The Sound of a Voice:* Sab Shimono (Man), Gerielani Miyazaki (Woman), Sarvi Shevbany (Little Girl). Standbys: Emily Kuroda, Nelson Mashita
THE BIRTHDAY PARTY by Harold Pinter; Director, Alan Mandell. CAST: Basil Langton (Petey), Erica Yohn (Meg), Robert Phalen (Stanley), Rhonda Aldrich (Lulu), Stefan Gierasch/Harold Gould (Goldberg), Colm Meaney (McCann). Standbys: Angela Paton, Phil Roth, Tracy Shaffer, Don Sparks
I DON'T HAVE TO SHOW YOU NO STINKING BADGES Written and Directed by Luis Valdez; *World Premiere;* Assistant Director, Tony Curiel; Videographer, Bill Swadley. CAST: Anne Betancourt (Connie Villa), James Victor (Buddy Villa), Robert Beltran (Sonny Villa), Patti Yasutake (Anita Sakai). Standbys: Geoff Rivas, Diane Rodriguez, Ray Victor, Marilyn Tokuda, Sam Vlahos
DIARY OF A HUNGER STRIKE; Written and Directed by Peter Sheridan; *American Premiere.* CAST: Tony Maggio (Liam Staunton), James Scally (Warden McClay), Jerry Hardin (Governor), Jim Piddock (Lord Rothleigh), Colm Meaney (Patrick O'Connor), Shaun Cassidy (Sean Crawford), Mike Genovese (Warden Maxwell), Bairbre Dowling (Bernadette Maguire). Standbys: Laura Drake, Tom Fuccello, W. Dennis Hunt, Tony Maggio
THE FAIR PENITENT; Adapted and Directed by Charles Marowitz; *American Premiere;* Fight Director, Erik Fredricksen. CAST: Maria Mayenzet (Calista), Franklyn Seales (Lothario), Oliver Csizmas (Horatio), Christopher McDonald (Altamont), Jack Swillim (Sciolto), Frank Collison (Rossano), Lynn Ann Leveridge (Lucilla), Tania Myren (Lavinia), John Lasell (Priest/Servant), Carmine Iannaccone, Joan Pirkle, David Prather, Allegra Swift. Standbys: J. Michael Flynn, Carmine Iannaccone, John Lasell, Joan Pirkle, David Prather, Allegra Swift
TUMBLEWEED by Adele Edling Shank; *World Premiere;* Director, Theodore Shank. CAST: Rudy Ramos (Chavo), Michael De Lorenzo (Fanny), Ruth Manning (Alice), Ann Hearn (Anemone), Gregory Wagrowski (Paul), Margaret Klenck (Lynn), Bette Ford (Jean), Frank McCarthy (Ray). Standbys: J. Edmundo Araiza, Terry Beaver, Theresa Karanik, Tony Maggio, Annie Murray
ALL MY SONS by Arthur Miller; Director, Bill Bushnell. CAST: Jim Jansen (Dr. Jim Bayliss), Philip Baker Hall (Joe Keller), Jon Menick (Frank Lubey), Sheila Shaw (Sue Bayliss), Ruth de Sosa (Lydia Lubey), Bill Pullman (Chris Keller), Eric Ratican (Bert), Nan Martin (Kate Keller), Julie Fulton (Ann Deever), Gregory Wagrowski (George Deever). Standbys: Ann Hearn, Gerald Hiken
INTERMEDIA PERFORMANCE SERIES: *The King and Queen of Bingo Surrounded by Swift Nudes, Joan of Compton/Joan of Arcadia, Autoscape: New Year's Eve, Passing Through*

A. Buck, R. Kaufman, Meridian Photos

MARRIOTT'S LINCOLNSHIRE THEATRE

Lincolnshire, Illinois
June 5, 1985–October 12, 1986

Producer, Kary M. Walker; Artistic Director, Dyanne Earley; Marketing, Peter Grigsby; Musical Director, Kevin Stites; Sets: Jeffrey Harris, Thomas Ryan, John Doepp; Costumes, Nancy Missimi; Lighting, John Williams, Terry Jenkins; Sound, William Wood, Todd Seisser.

PRODUCTIONS & CASTS

A CHORUS LINE: Director, Dominic Missimi; Choreographer, Candace Tovar. CAST: Ray Frewen (Zach), Dana Sweeney (Larry), Candace Tovar (Cassie), Judith T. Smith (Sheila), Beverly Britton (Val), Linda Leonard (Diana), Katherine Lynn Condit (Judy), Joan Schwenk (Kristine), Laurie Stephenson (Maggie), Robyn Peterman (Bebe), Michelle Kelly (Connie), William Akey (Mike), Kenny Ingram (Richie), Mark Hobee (Don), Todd Hueghens (Paul), Peter Anderson (Mark), Owen Frank (Greg), Don Franklin (Bobby), Jordan Leeds (Al), Michael Halpin (Frank), Allyson Rice (Tricia)

HELLO, DOLLY!: Director, Dominic Missimi; Choreographer, Rudy Hogenmiller. CAST: Alene Robertson (Dolly Levi), Ann Arvia (Ernestina), James Kall (Ambrose Kemper), Dale Benson (Horace Vandergelder), Sally Nurphy (Ermengarde), Richard Casper (Cornelius Hackl), William Akey (Barnaby Tucher), Paula Scrofano (Irene Malloy), Michelle Kelly (Minnie Fay), Dale Morgan (Rudolph), Peter Anderson, Michael Bartsch, Jeffrey Clonts, Jeanne Croft, Kenny Ingram, Chuck Lubeck, Phil Masterson, Susan McGhee, Debra Sandlund, Leslie Trayer, Rob Walther

CAMELOT: Director, Dyanne Earley; Choreographer, Richard Casper. CAST: George Lee Andrews (Arthur), Marti Morris (Guenevere), Robert Frisch (Lancelot), Larry McCauley (Pellinore), Kevin McCollum (Mordred), Neil Freidman (Sir Dinadan), Susan McGhee (Lady Anne), Ann Arvia (Nimue), Tim Mathistad (Dap), James McCammond (Sir Lionel), James Braet (Sir Sagramore), Adam Arvidson (Tom of Warwick), Michael Bartsch, Jeanne Croft, Kent Kane, Karen Rahn, Debra Sandlund, R. F. Daley

BABY: Director, Richard Maltby, Jr.; Choreographer, Mark Hoebee. CAST: Liz Callaway (Lizzie Fields), Dan Foster (Danny Hooper), Kathy Taylor (Arlene McNally), Joe Lauck (Alan McNally), Shannon Cochran (Pam Sakarian), Russell Reneau (Nick Sakarian), Jeanne Croft (Nurse), R. F. Daley (Doctor/Dean Webber), Jordan Leeds (Mr. Weiss), Beth Williams (Ms. Hart)

Lisa Ebright, J. Verser Englehard Photos

Alene Robertson (c) in "Hello, Dolly!"
Top: "A Chorus Line" (Lincolnshire)

Randy Lilly, Greg Thornton, Jerome Butler,
Mary Martello in "Christmas Gifts"

McCARTER THEATRE

Princeton, New Jersey
December 19, 1985–June 29, 1986

Artistic Director, Nagle Jackson; Managing Director, Alison Harris; Special Programming, W. W. Lockwood, Jr.; Associate Artistic Director, Robert Lanchester; Assistant to Directors, Megan Miller-Shields; Production Manager, John Herochik; Technical Director, David R. York; Business Manager, Timothy J. Shields; Administrative Director, Laurence Capo; Development, Pamela Vevers Sherin; Communications, Linda S. Kinsey; Press, Jamie Saxon; Sales, James Olson; Props, Jennifer Sliwinski; Sound, Rob Gorton

PRODUCTIONS & CASTS

CHRISTMAS GIFTS Adapted and Directed by Robert Lanchester; Set, Robert Little; Costumes, Barb Taylorr; Musical Director, Richard M. Loatman; Lighting, Don Ehman; Stage Managers, Francis X. Kuhn, Carol Boland; Music, Greg Thornton; Songs by various authors. CAST: Jerome Butler, Randy Lilly, Mary Martello, Cynthia Martells, Penelope Reed, Greg Thornton

AS YOU LIKE IT by William Shakespeare; Director, Robert Lanchester; Set, Peter Harrison; Costumes, Elizabeth Covey; Lighting, Don Ehman; Composer, Richard Hobson; Choreographer, Nancy Thiel; Fight Master, Stephen Kazakoff; Wigs, Denise O'Brien; Stage Managers, Jeanne Anich Stives, Peter C. Cook. CAST: Stephen Schnetzer (Orlando), Eric Conger (Oliver), Nat Warren-White (Adam), M. Austin Hargrove (Dennis/Outlaw), Richard Leighton (Duke Frederick/Duke Senior), Gerald Gilmore (Le Beau/William/Outlaw), Gerald Lancaster (Charles/Corin), Jerome Butler (Touchstone), Mary Martello (Celia), Michele Farr (Rosalind), Zivia Flomenhaft (Gentlewoman/Amiens), Mary Hatch (Gentlewoman/Outlaw), Mark Zaki (Violinist/Fiddler), Carlyle B. Owens (Sergeant/Outlaw), John Criscitiello, C. Peter Kauzmann (Dragoons/Outlaws), Henson Keys (First Lord/Brother), Richmond Hoxie (Jaques), Scott G. Miller (Silvius), Jay Doyle (Sir Oliver Martext/Hymen), Cynthia Martells (Audrey), Judith Dewey (Phebe), Matthew Goida (Drummer)

THE BOYS NEXT DOOR by Tom Griffin; *World Premiere;* Director, Nagle Jackson; Set, John Jensen; Costumes, Marie Miller; Lighting, F. Mitchell Dana; Casting, Jay Binder, Jack Boudan; Stage Managers, Jeanne Anich Stives, Carol Boland. CAST: Bob Balaban (Arnold Wiggins), William Jay (Lucien P. Smith), David Schramm (Norman Bulansky), Alan Ruck (Barry Klemper), Ray Baker (Jack), Christine Estabrook (Sheila), Jay Doyle (Mr. Klemper), Peggy Cowles (Mrs. Fremus/Mrs. Warren/Clara), Henson Keys (Mr. Hedges/Mr. Corbin/Senator Clarke)

Cliff Moore Photos

Left Center: David Schramm, Peggy Cowles,
Alan Ruck in "The Boys Next Door"

MEADOW BROOK THEATRE

Rochester, Michigan
October 10, 1985–May 18, 1986

Artistic/General Director, Terence Kilburn; Assistant to General Director/Tour Director, James Spittle; Stage Directors: Terence Kilburn, Charles Nolte, Carl Schurr, David Regal; Sets: Peter W. Hicks, Barry Griffith; Lighting, Reid Johnson, Daniel Jaffe; Stage Managers, Terry W. Carpenter, Robert Herrle; Technical Director, Daniel Jaffe; Master Carpenter, Douglas Osborne/Greg Utech; Scenic Artists: Rebecca Castle, Elaine Sutherland; Sound, Tony Vaillancourt; Costume Coordinator, Mary Lynn Bonnell; Wardrobe, Paul Kalevas; Props, Mary Chmelko-Jaffe, Ellen MacRae; Set Technicians, Bradley Burke, Neil Patterson

PRODUCTIONS & CASTS

ROMEO AND JULIET: with Jeanne Arnold, Barbara Barringer, Arthur Beer, David Fox, George Gitto, Joey L. Golden, Thom Haneline, Paul Hopper, Jayne Houdyshell, John Michael Manfredi, Peter Moore, Wayne David Parker, Glen Allen Pruett, Joseph Reed, Dona Werner, Jerry Bacik, Cynthia Betley, Jenie Lyn Dahlmann, Heidi Guthrie, Eric M. Johnson, Lisamarie Kaleita, Frederick Karn, Sandi Litt, Richard Marlatt, David Miller, D. C. Moons, Neil Patterson, Susann Powell, Mar Riehl

PRESENT LAUGHTER: with Curtis Armstrong, Barbara Barringer, Cynthia Carle, Christopher Darga, George Gitto, Joey L. Golden, Robert Herrle, Jayne Houdyshell, Jillian Lindig, Jane Lowry, Carl Schurr, Jeanne Taylor

A CHRISTMAS CAROL: with Barbara Barringer, Booth Colman, Joey L. Golden, Thom Haneline, Paul Hopper, Jayne Houdyshell, William Kux, Phillip Locker, Wayne David Parker, Glen Allen Pruett, Joseph Reed, Mar Riehl, Ron Melnik, Jenie Lyn Dahlmann, Kevin Skiles, Sarah Jayne Huber, J. Luke Huber, Tom Cucheran, Melanie Hansen, Terry G. Hunt, Brett Lashuay, Sandi Litt, Nora McGowan, Rebekka Parker, Susann Powell, Brian Schulz, Michelle Slanda, Bryan Syzdek

ANGEL STREET: with Barbara Barringer, Bethany Carpenter, Richert Easley, George Gitto, Liz Zweifler, Gerald Hart Hoy, D. C. Moons

84 CHARING CROSS ROAD: with Jeanne Arnold, Barbara Barringer, Paul Hopper, Margaret Ingraham, Wil Love, Wayne David Parker, Liz Zweifler

THE MISER: with George Gitto, Paul Hopper, Jayne Houdyshell, William Le Massena, Ron Martell, Wayne David Parker, Joseph Reed, Mar Riehl, Dona Werner, Michael Patterson, Sandi Litt, Ted Moniak

THE GOOD DOCTOR: with James Anthony, Donald Ewer, Joey L. Golden, Paul Hopper, Juliet Randall, Dona Werner

SING FOR YOUR SUPPER: with Pi Douglass, Karen Eubanks, Joy Franz, Paul Hopper, Bev Larson, Jess Richards, Steve Steiner, Sandi Litt

Richard Hunt Photos

Dona Werner, Mar Riehl, Jayne Houdyshell,
William LeMassena, Michael Patterson in "The Miser"
Top: Carl Shurr, Jillian Lindig in "Present Laughter"

Peter Moore, Dona Werner
in "Romeo and Juliet"

Jeanne Arnold, Wil Love
in "84 Charing Cross Road"

MERRIMACK REPERTORY THEATRE

Lowell, Massachusetts
November 15, 1985–April 13, 1986

Producing Director, Danial L. Schay; Administrative Director, Helene Desjarlais; Marketing/Development, Keith E. Stevens; Business Manager, Jacqueline A. Normand; Production Manager, Richard Rose; Stage Managers, Hazel Youngs, Eliza Townsend; Costumes, Amanda Aldridge, Joan St. Germain; Lighting, Kendall Smith; Sound, Martha Domine; Props, Gregg Watts; Production Assistant, Robert Welch

PRODUCTIONS & CASTS
THE SCHOOL FOR WIVES bY Moliere; Translation, Richard Wilbur; Director, Daniel L. Schay; Set, Leslie Taylor; Lighting, Sid Bennett; Costumes, Barbara Forbes. CAST: Marissa Chibas, Roger Curtis, Gary-Thomas Keating, Kenneth L. Marks, Joe Ponazecki, M. Lynda Robinson, David Rothauser
A CHRISTMAS CAROL by Charles Dickens; Adapatation, Larry Carpenter; Director, Thomas Clewell; Set, Leslie Taylor; Lighting, David "Sparky" Lockner; Costumes, Amanda Aldridge. CAST: Robin Chadwick, Pat Dougan, Karl Heist, Gary-Thomas Keating, Richard Maynard, William Miller, Tammy Richards, Alice White
EDUCATING RITA by Willy Russell; Director, Richard Rose; Set, Leslie Taylor. CAST: Cynthia Babak, Robin Chadwick
REQUIEM FOR A HEAVYWEIGHT by Rod Serling; Director, Daniel L. Schay; Set, Gary English; Sound, Michael Wilson. CAST: Frank Biancamano, James Bodge, Joseph Costa, Dawn Davis, Kirsten Giroux, Jerry Goodwin, Richard Hancock, Patrick Kilpatrick, Jack Neary, Mark H. Rogers, Spiro Veloudos, John Haynes Walker
CRIMES OF THE HEART by Beth Henley; Director, Judy Braha; Set, Leslie Taylor; Music, Vin Costanzo. CAST: Becky Borczon, Ken Cheeseman, Dawn Davis, Pat Dougan, Paris Klopp, David Zoffoli
SOMETHING'S AFOOT with Book, Music and Lyrics by James McDonald, David Vos, Robert Gerlach; Additional Music, Ed Linderman; Director/Choreographer, Richard Rose; Musical Director, John Mulcahy; Set, Gary English; Effects Construction, Gregg Watts. CAST: Taina Elg (Miss Tweed), Eleanor Barbour, Ron Bohmer, Leslie Hicks, Nancy Hudson, James Judy, Bill McDonald, George Riddle, Casper Roos, Gary-Thomas Keating

Kevin Harkins Photos

Eleanor Barbour, Casper Roos in "Something's Afoot"
Top: Dawn Davis, Becky Borczon, Paris Klopp
in "Crimes of the Heart" (Merrimack)

NORTHLIGHT THEATRE

Evanston, Illinois
September 19, 1985–June 22, 1986

Artistic Director, Michael Maggio; Managing Director, Susan Medak; Production Manager, Greg Murphy; Assistant Artistic Director, Jimmy Bickerstaff; Assistant Set Designer, Rick Penrod; Technical Director, Greg Murphy; Props, Alan Donahue; Wardrobe, Kitty Norton; Marketing, E. R. Schuenemann, Robert Bays; Stage Managers, Rick Berg, Amy Anson; Press, Marilyn Perlman

PRODUCTIONS & CASTS
THE REAL THING by Tom Stoppard; Director, Michael Maggio; Set, Gary Baugh; Costumes, Kaye Nottbusch; Lighting, Robert Shook. CAST: David Darlow, Barbara Gaines, Keven Gudahl, Katherine Lynch, John Mueller, Kristine Thatcher, Joe Van Slyke
QUILTERS by Molly Newman and Barbara Damashek; Director, Kyle Donnelly; Set, Linda Buchanan; Costumes, Jessica Hahn; Lighting, Rita Pietraszek. CAST: Margo Buchanan, Caitlan Hart, Anne Hills, Jeanne Morick, Roon O'Donnell, Kathy Taylor, Natalie West
BOESMAN AND LENA by Athol Fugard; Director, Woodie King; Set, Michael Philippi; Costumes, Colleen Muscha; Lighting, Bob Christen. CAST: Trazana Beverley, John Cothran, Jr., Robert L. Curry
WEST MEMPHIS MOJO by Martin Jones *(World Premiere);* Director, Michael Maggio; Set, Gary Baugh; Costumes, Kay Nottbusch; Lighting, Robert Shook. CAST: Gregory Alan-Williams, John Cothran, Jr., Lisa Dodson, Don Franklin
SISTER AND MISS LEXIE by Brenda Currin; Director, David Kaplan; Set/Costumes, Susan Hilferty; Lighting, Ken Tabachnik. CAST: Brenda Currin, Annbritt Gemmer, Patricia A. Lee-Matijevic

Jennifer Girard Photos

Trazana Beverley, Robert Curry
in "Boesman and Lena"

Left Center: Kristine Thatcher, David Darlow
in "The Real Thing"

166

PAPER MILL PLAYHOUSE

Millburn, New Jersey
September 18, 1985–June 29, 1986
Forty-sixth Year

Executive Director, Angelo Del Rossi; Artistic Director, Robert Johanson; General Manager, Wade Miller; Administrative Director, Jim Thesing; Musical Director, Jim Coleman; Sets, Michael Anania; Costumes: Guy Geoly, Alice S. Hughes; Lighting, Jeff Davis, Brian MacDevitt; Production Manager/Lighting, David Kissel; Musical Director, Jim Coleman; Archivist, Joseph McConnell; Stage Managers: Roy Meachum, J. Andrew Burgreen, Jeffry George

PRODUCTIONS & CASTS

WINDY CITY with Book and Lyrics by Dick Vosburg; Music, Tony Macaulay; Based on *The Front Page* by Ben Hecht and Charles MacArthur; Director/Choreographer, David H. Bell; Musical Arrangements, Kevin Stites; Orchestrations, David Siegel; with Gary Sandy (Hildy Johnson), Ronald Holgate (Walter Burns), Judy Kay (Molly Malloy), Pamela Clifford, Alan Sues, James W. Sudik, Frank Kopyc, MacIntyre Dixon

CAROUSEL with Music by Richard Rodgers; Book and Lyrics, Oscar Hammerstein II; Based on the play *Liliom* by Ferenc Molnar as adapted by Benjamin F. Glaser; Director, Robert Johanson; Choreographer, Sharon Halley; with Judith McCauley, Richard White, Maureen Brennan, Tom Ligon, Monte Ralstin, Mary Jay, Sam Kressen, Louise Hickey, David Loring, Marsha Bagwell

RUN FOR YOUR WIFE; Director, Chris Johnston; with David McCallum, Michael Connolly, William Denis, Tom Fervoy, Mitchell Greenberg, Frank Kopyc, Jana Robbins, Kay Walbye

THE FOREIGNER by Larry Shue; Director, David Saint; with Bob Denver, Jane Connell, Harley Venton, Leah Doyle, Sam Stoneburner, Mike Starr, Greg Germann

THE 1940'S RADIO HOUR written by Walton Jones; Director/Choreographer, Robert Johanson; Assistant Director, Philip Wm McKinley; Assistant Choreographer, Ruth Gottschall; Sound, David R. Paterson; with Robert Cenedella, David Chaney, Larry Grey, Donna Kane, Kenneth Kantor, Ken Lundie, Melodee Savage, John Scherer, Susan Elizabeth Scott, Dorothy Stanley, Bob Walton, Lenny Wolpe

CANDIDE with Music by Leonard Bernstein; Book, Hugh Wheeler, adapted from Voltaire; Lyrics, Richard Wilbur; Additional Lyrics, Stephen Sondheim, John LaTouche; Director-Choreographers, Robert Johanson, Philip Wm. McKinley; Sound, David R. Paterson; Hair, Paul Germano; with Maureen Brennan, Robert Johanson, Sal Mistretta, Mary Jay, Jack Harrold, Patrick Quinn, Patti Allison, Kenneth Kantor, Marsha Bagwell, Rebecca Spencer

Jerry Dalia, Gerry Goodstein Photos

**Ronald Holgate, Gary Sandy, Judy Kaye,
James W. Sudik in "Windy City" (Paper Mill)**

PENNSYLVANIA STAGE COMPANY

Allentown, Pennsylvania
October 11, 1985–July 20, 1986

Producing Director, Gregory S. Hurst; General Manager, Daniel B. Fallon; Associate Director/Literary Manager, Pam Petter; Press, Lisa K. Higgins; Development, Mary Ann Confar; Business Manager, Kathleen kund Nolan; Production Manager, Peter Wrenn-Meleck; Stage Managers, Peter S. Del Vecho, Thomas M. Kauffman; Technical Director, Bill Kreider; Costumer, Marianne Faust

PRODUCTIONS & CASTS

PUMP BOYS AND DINETTES by John Foley, Mark Hardwick, Debra Monk, Cass Morgan, John Schimmel, Jim Wann; Director, Debra Monk; Musical Director, John Foley; Sets, Christopher J. Shriver; Costumes, Deborah Shippee O'Brien; Lighting, John Gisondi; Sound, Daryl Bornstein. CAST: Bruce Conner, Jason Edwards, John Lenehan, Caroline Peyton, Steven Riddle, Marcie Shaw

THE CRUCIBLE by Arthur Miller; Director, Gregory S. Hurst; Sets/Lighting, Bennet Averyt; Costumes, Barbara Forbes. CAST: Jean Barker, Laura Carney, Donna Davis, Susan Decker, Scott Edmiston, Leslie Feagan, Monique Fowler, Lorey Hayes, James Hilbrandt, Edward Kendall, Will Lyman, Paul Milikin, John O'Hara, Keith Perry, Linda Pritts, Lennie Shaw, Edward Stevlingson, Tom Teti, Bonnie Thomas, Mary Ward

PAINTING CHURCHES by Tina Howe; Director, Pam Pepper; Sets/Lighting, Curtis Dretsch; Costumes, Marianne Faust. CAST: Deborah Allison, Russell Nype, Elizabeth Perry

THE CLUB by Eve Merriam; Songs Arranged by Alexandra Ivanoff; Director/Choreographer, Bick Goss; Musical Director, Memrie Innerarity; Sets, Harry Feiner; Costumes, Susan Hirschfeld; Lighting, Quentin Thomas; Hats, Rodney Gordon. CAST: Gwen Arment, Gloria Hodes, Memrie Innerarity, Judith Moore, Dana Vance, Terry White, Nancy Holcombe-Auffarth

BILLY BISHOP GOES TO WAR by John Gray with Eric Peterson; Director, Mitchell Ivers; Musical Director, David Loud; Sets, Patricia Woodbridge; Costumes, Myra Bumgarner; Lighting, Jackie Manassee. CAST: Scott Ellis, David Loud

GREATER TUNA by Jaston Edwards, Joe Sears, Ed Howard; Director, Stephen Rothman, Sets, Kevin Lock; Costumes, Catherine King; Lighting, Linda Sechrist; Sound, Bert Taylor. CAST: John Thomas Waite, Michael O. Smith

QUALITY TIME by Barbara Field; *World Premiere;* Director, Gregory S. Hurst; Sets, Atkin Pace; Costumes, Karen Gerson; Lighting, Curtis Dretsch; Video/Computer-Aided Productions, Robin Miller, Filmaker, Inc. CAST: Roscoe Born, Joanne Camp, Barry Cullison

Gregory M. Fota Photos

Barry Cullison, Joanne Camp in "Quality Time"

**Left Center: Mary Ward, Edward Kendall
in "The Crucible"**

THE PEOPLE'S LIGHT & THEATRE COMPANY

Malvern, Pennsylvania
April 17, 1985–December 29, 1985

Producing Director, Danny S. Fruchter; General Manager, Greg T. Rowe; Associate Artistic Director, Abigail Adams; Development, Judy Nicholson Asselin; Coordinator/Casting Assistant, Andrea Beaver; Sales, Sandy Blackman; Literary, Alda Cortese; Dramaturg, Lee Devin; Press, Hoan C. Homick; Technical Director, Cecil Johnson; Playwright-in-Residence, Louis Lippa; Administrative Services, Nancy Lippa; Production Manager, Ken Marini; Stage Managers, Katherine Pierce, Deborah Teller; Associate Artistic Director, Joe Ragney; Business Manager, Don Tritt; Marketing, Linda L. White
GUESTS ARTISTS: Directors: Steven Kaplan, Michael Nash; Musical Consultant/Music Director, Adam Wernick; Costumes, Barbara Forbes; Sound, Charles Cohen
PRODUCTIONS & CASTS
AWAKE & SING by Clifford Odets; CAST: Lee Golden, Carol Gustafson, Louis Lippa, Liza Balkan, Scott G. Miller, Viet Shchaeffer, Tom Teti, Dick Boccelli, Stephen Novelli
TAKEN IN MARRIAGE by Thomas Babe; CAST: Donna Daley, Denise Bessette, Susan Wilder, Joan Stanley, Alda Cortese
5th ANNUAL NEW PLAY FESTIVAL: *The Love Suicide at Schofield Barracks* by Romulus Linney, with Steve Skrovan, Douglas Wing, Lee Devin, Natsuko Ohama, Bill Smitrovich, Joan Stanley, Murphy Guyer, Alda Cortese, Gerald Richards; *Sleeping Beauty* by Laurence Klavan, with Amy Beth Williams, Brad Bellamy, Murphy Guyer, Steve Skrovan; *The Tattler* by Terri Wagener, with Greg Alexander, Carla Belver, Jessie K. Jones, Sean McKinley, Stephen Novelli, Shaw Purnell; WORLD PREMIERE: *The Defector* by Louis Lippa, with Gerald Richards, Douglas Wing; *What Leona Figured Out* by David J. Hill, with Alda Cortese, Carla Belver
BOESMAN & LENA by Athol Fugard; CAST: A. Dean Irby, Trazana Beverley, Mats Suber
YOU NEVER CAN TELL by George Bernard Shaw; CAST: Stephen Novelli, Denise Bessette, Greg Alexander, Margery Murray, Carla Belver, Louis Lippa, Jarlath Conroy, Douglas Wing, Lee Devin, Alda Cortese

Gerry Goodstein, Ken Kaufman Photos

Stephen Novelli, Margery Murray in "You Never Can Tell" Top: Trazana Beverley, A. Dean Irby in "Boesman and Lena" (People's)

PHILADELPHIA DRAMA GUILD

Philadelphia, Pennsylvania
October 18, 1985–May 25, 1986

Producing Director, Gregory Poggi; Business Manager, Mark D. Bernstein; Marketing, Barbara Konik; Directors: Patrick Tovatt, Edmund J. Cambridge, Charles Karchmer, Michael Murray; Sets: Kevin Rupnik, Daniel P. Boylen, John Falabella, John Jensen; Costumes: Kevin Rupick, Frankie Fehr, Jess Goldstein; Lighting: James L. Leitner, William H. Grant, III, Jeff Davis; Sound: Charles Cohen, Jeff Ghestek; Production Manager, Edward Johnson; Stage Managers: Ralph Batman, Donna E. Curci; Playwright's Project Coordinator, Charles Conwell; Guest Director, John A. Allen

PRODUCTIONS & CASTS
TENT MEETING by Larry Larson, Levi Lee and Rebecca Wackler; Director, Patrick Tovatt; with Larry Larson, Levi Lee, Rebecca Wackler
A RAISIN IN THE SUN by Lorraine Hansberry; Director, Edmund J. Cambridge; with S. Epatha Merkerson, Michael Jefferson, David Downing, Charlaine Woodard, Rosanna Carter, Erik Kilpatrick, Michael Genet, Vaughn Dwight Morrison, Don Auspitz, Ronal Stepney, Floyd W. Green, III
ABSURD PERSON SINGULAR by Alan Ayckbourn; Director, Charles Karchmer; with Jill Rose, Jeff Brooks, Jonathan Farwell, Delphi Harrington, Randy Graff, Mark Capri
A DELICATE BALANCE by Edward Albee; Director, Michael Murray; with Rosemary Prinz, John Carpenter, Tudi Wiggins, Gloria Cromwell, John Newton, Robin Moseley
THE HOT L BALTIMORE by Lanford Wilson; Director, Charles Karchmer; with Robert Gossett, Kate McNeil, Georgia Southcotte, Mary Diveny, Kathryn Gay Wilson, Joseph Daly, Lynn Chausow, David Schachter, Allen Fitzpatrick, Lynne Clifton Allen, Brian Ungar, Stephen Hamilton, Maggie Flynn, Richard Salter

Kenneth Kauffman Photos

Michael Jefferson, Rosanna Carter, S. Epatha Merkerson in "A Raisin in the Sun" (PDG)

Left Center: Rosemary Prinz, John Carpenter in "A Delicate Balance"

PITTSBURGH PLAYHOUSE

Pittsburgh, Pennsylvania
November 20, 1985–June 1, 1986
Fiftieth Season

General Director, Mark Lewis; Producer, James O. Prescott; Executive Assistant, Roderick Carter; Administrative Assistant, Carole Berger; Press, Burton White; Production Manager, Alan Forino; Technical Director, Brian Fitzmorris; Sets: Mary Burt, Norene Walworth; Costumes, Don DiFonso, Joan Markert, Mary M. Turner; Lighting: Alan Forino, Jennifer L. Ford; Props: Mary Burt, Cassandra Ross

PRODUCTIONS & CASTS

A CHORUS LINE conceived by Michael Bennett; Book, James Kirkwood, Nicholas Dante; Music, Marvin Hamlisch; Lyrics, Edward Kleban; Directed, Staged, Choreographed by Danny Herman; Associate Directors: Kenneth Gargara, Ron Tassone; Musical Director, Kenneth Gargaro; Stage Manager, Burton White; Set/Lighting, Alan Forino; Costumes, Joan Markert. CAST: Lenora Nemetz (Cassie), Michael Ragan (Zach), James McCrum (Don), Kathryn McCombs (Maggie), Joseph Bowerman (Mike), Anna Simonelli (Connie), Brien Fisher (Greg), Diane French (Shiela), Preston Simpson (Bobby), Pam Bradley (Bebe), Heather Berman (Judy), Tome' Cousin (Richie), James Athens (Al), Kristin Thornburg (Kristine), Kathleen Marshall (Val), Jeffrey Sherin (Mark), Rob Davis (Paul), Linda E. Gabler (Diana), Kurt Bartol, Lisa Beatty, Trish Boehm, Kathy Cristell, Colleen Dunn, Angela Garrison, Tom Rocco, Michael Rudge, Iris Sherman, Lauri Stallings, Maura White, Monica Farrell (Guest Vocalist). Understudies: Kathleen Marshall, Angela Garrison, Iris Sherman, Kurt Bartol, Marc Acito.

MARAT/SADE by Peter Weiss; Music, Richard Peaslee; Director, James Prescott; Assistant Director, Mark Thompson; Musical Director, Kenneth Gargaro; Stage Manager, Sheila McKenna; Dramaturg, Michael McGovern; Lighting, Jennifer L. Ford; Set/Props, Mary Burt; Costumes, Mary Turner. CAST: John Amplas (Marat), Raymond Laine (DeSade), Maria Barney (Corday), Don Wadsworth (Herald), Thom McLaughlin (Roux), Marti Ranii (Simonne), Rob Roznowski (Duperret), Kate Young (Rossignol), Brian Kelly (Cucurucu), David Doepken (Polpoch/Lavoisier), John Gresh (Kokol/Military Representative), Sarah Worthington (Antoinette), Jane Scutieri (Catherine), Gene Kail (Mr. Coulmier), Mary K. Chess (Mm. Coulmier), Cathy Yonek (Mlle. Coulmier), Donna Meeham (Abbess), Linwood Harcum (A Mad Animal), Jack Boslett (Schoolmaster), Beth Walters (Mother), Chuck Baker (Father), Deborah Sale (Scientist), Karen Sarp (Rich Lady), Mark Thompson (Voltaire), Angela Eckard (DeSade's Pet), Kurt Carley, Joseph Hartung (Nuns), Patrick O'Hara, Scott Small, James Eddy (Nurses). Understudy: Chris Josephs

GODSPELL Conceived and Adapted by John-Michael Tebelak; Music/Lyrics, Stephen Schwartz; Associate Director, Burton White; Director/Musical Director, Kenneth Gargaro; Choreographer, Judith Leifer; Stage Manager, Mary Vehec; Set, Norene Walworth; Costumes, Joan Markert; Lighting, Jennifer L. Ford. CAST: James McCrum (Jesus), Tom Rocco (Judas), Lisa Beatty, Dierdre Berry, Beverly Billin, Maureen Boren, Kim Cea, Kathy Connolly, Kate Cordaro, Richard Costantino, Jim Critchfield, Tome' Farrell, Angela Garrison, James Hicks, Janice Jarabeck, Michael Jones, Linda Lopata, Katie Ludwig, Michelle Maceio, Elizabeth Matthews, Mia Miyares, Laura Ponzio, Janet Ross, Rob Roznowski, Dan Silford, Sara Stock, Maura White, Anne Zachary, Stacy Zahradnik

LITTLE SHOP OF HORRORS with Book and Lyrics by Howard Ashman; Music, Alan Menken; Vocal Arrangements, Robert Billig; Orchestrations, Bobby Merkin, Based on the Film by Roger Corman/Screenplay, Charles Griffith; Re-Created/Staged by Edie Cowan; Acting Producer/Musical Director, Kenneth Gargaro; Stage Manager, Teri McIntyre; Set, Mary Burt; Lighting, Jennifer L. Ford; Puppet Design, Martin P. Robinson; Puppet Construction, Jim Martin; Costumes, Don DiFonso; Props, Cassandra Ross. CAST: Linda E. Gabler (Audrey), Tom Rocco (Seymour), Richard Rauh (Mr. Mushnik), James McCrum (Orin et al.), Monica C. Farrell (Ronette), Dina Eiger (Crystal), Iris Brown (Chiffon), Eric Parham (Audrey II Voice), Holly A. Koenig, Kurt Carley (Audrey II Manipulation)

Drew Yenchak, Ray Gilmore Photos

**Left Center: Katie Ludwig, Tom Rocco,
James McCrum in "Godspell"
Top: "A Chorus Line"**

**Richard Rauh, Dina Eiger, Tom Rocco, Iris
Brown in "Little Shop of Horrors"**

PITTSBURGH PUBLIC THEATER

Pittsburgh, Pennsylvania
June 4, 1985–June 29, 1986
Eleventh Season

Producing Director, William T. Gardner; Literary Manager, Mary G. Guaraldi; Comptroller, Cynthia J. Tutera; Marketing, Roz Ruch; Press, Curt Powell; Technical Director, A. D. Carson; Costume Shop, Flozanne A. John; Development, Sylvia Smith-Middleman

PRODUCTIONS & CASTS

PRIVATE LIVES by Noel Coward; Director, Philip Minor; Music, Clay Zambo; Set, Allen D. Cornell; Costumes, Jeffrey Ullman; Lighting, Ann G. Wrightson; Stage Manager, Jack Mulligan. CAST: Charlotte Booker (Sybil), Susan Martinelli (Louise), Robert Moberly (Elyot), Paul Perri (Victor), Margo Skinner (Amanda)
THE REAL THING by Tom Stoppard; Director, Lee Sankowich; Set, Ray Recht; Costumes, Mary Mease Warren; Lighting, Kirk Bookman; Stage Manager, Roy W. Backes. CAST: Steven Culp (Billy), Don Fishcer (Brody), Mary Beth Fisher (Charlotte), Robert Moberly (Max), Mary O'Sullivan (Debbie), Helena Ruoti (Annie), Thomas A. Stewart (Henry).
LIFE WITH FATHER by Howard Lindsay and Russel Crouse; Director, Susan Einhorn; Set, Frank J. Boros; Costumes, David Murin; Lighting, Ann G. Wrightson; Stage Manager, Stephen McCorkle. CAST: Leta Anderson (Cora), Patti Booth (Maggie), Robert Desmond (Harlan), Geoff Garland (Rev. Dr. Lloyd), Katherine Hiler (Mary), Denise Huot (Margaret), Jill Larson (Vinnie), Ruth Lesko (Nora), Maura Minteer (Annie), Victor Raider-Wexler (Father), David Shuman (Whitney), Robert Stanton (Clarence), Mary Stein (Delia), Ben Tatar (Dr. Humphreys), Bill Thunhurst (Dr. Somers), Whit Wales (John)
MASTER HAROLD and the boys by Athol Fugard; Director, Larry Arrick; Set, Ursula Belden; Costumes, Flozanne A. John; Lighting, Kristine L. Bick; Stage Manager, Roy W. Backes. CAST: J. Mark Diamond (Hally), Robert Jason (Willie), William Jay (Sam).
SHE STOOPS TO CONQUER by Oliver Goldsmith; Director, Phillip Minor; Music, Richard Cumming; Set, John Jensen; Costumes, David Toser; Lighting, Kristine L. Bick; Stage Manager, Roy W. Backes. CAST: William Cameron (Diggory), James Carruthers (Stingo/Sir Charles Marlow), Mark Chamberlin (Hastings), Mary K. Chess (Pimple), David L. Doepken (Aminadab/Roger), Don Fischer (Tony Lumpkin), Michel R. Gill (Marlow), Jeff Monahan (Jack Slang/Dick/Jeremy), Carmen Mathews (Mrs. Hardcastle), Sarah Rush (Kate Hardcastle), William Swetland (Mr. Hardcastle), Sarah Trubey Walker (Miss Neville), Thomas Mills Wood (Dick Muggins/Thomas)
GARDENIA by John Guare; Director, Stephen McCorkle; Set, Ray Recht; Costumes, David Murin; Lighting, Kirk Bookman; Stage Manager, Clayton Phillips. CAST: William Carden (Joshua Hickman), Steven Culp (Dan Grady), Robert Desmond (Jeremiah Grady), Sean G. Griffin (O'Malley), Frank Hankey (Amos Mason), Caryn West (Lydie Bjreeze)
THE SHOW-OFF by George Kelly; Director, Philip Minor; Set, Allen D. Cornell; Costumes, Jeffrey Ullman; Lighting, Ann. G. Wrightson; Stage Manager, Roy W. Backes. CAST: Charlotte Booker (Amy), Gregory Chase (Frank Hyland), Donald Christopher (Mr. Fisher), Timothy Donoghue (Mr. Gill), Lance Lewman (Joe), Roberert Moberly (Aubrey Piper), Patricia O'Connell (Mrs. Fisher), Rose Stockton (Clara)

Ric Evans Photos

Robert Moberly, Helena Ruoti, Mary Beth Fisher, Thomas A. Stewart in "The Real Thing"

(clockwise from left) Jill Larson, Whit Wales, Robert Stanton, Victor Raider-Wexler, David Stewart Shuman, Robert Desmond, (in back) Maura Minteer, Denise Huot in "Life with Father"

PLAYMAKERS REPERTORY COMPANY

Chapel Hill, North Carolina
September 28, 1985—April 27, 1986

Executive Producer, Milly S. Barranger; Artistic Director, David Hammond; Managing Director, Jonathan L. Giles; Sets, Linwood Taylor; Costumes, Bobbi Owen; Lighting, Robert Wierzel; Stage Directors, Douglas Johnson, Evan Yionoulis, John C. Fletcher; Stage Managers, Dean Robinson, Rebecca Symonds, Norman Ussery; Voice Coach, Carol Pendergrast; Movement Coach, Craig Turner; Literary Manager, Ben Cameron; Development, Sharon Herr, Sharon Fowler
RESIDENT COMPANY: Pat Barnett, Constance Conover, Kimball Crossley, Michael Cumpsty, John Feltch, Tom Fitzsimmons, David Gottlieb, Bill Goulet, Joseph C. Haj, Kate Haris, Peter Hertsgaard, Brian Hotaling, Wanda Melocci, Robert Murphy, Ilya Parenteau, Melissa Proctor, Becket Royce, Dave Whalen, Shelley Williams, Deborah Winstead-Mann
GUEST ARTISTS: Dick Beebe, Mimi Carr, Tandy Cronyn, John C. Fletcher, Steve Hendrickson, Douglas Johnson, Tom Nahrwold, James Pritchett, James Scholes, Paul Tourtillotte, Evan Yionoulis
PRODUCTIONS: *She Stoops to Conquer* by Oliver Goldsmith; Director, Douglas Johnson. *The Storm* by Alexander Ostrovsky; Adapted and Directed by David Hammond.
PLAYFEST '86: *The Dining Room* by A. R. Gurney, Jr.; Director, Ben Cameron. *The Guiteau Burlesque* by Dick Beebe; *World Premiere;* Director, Evan Yionoulis. *Clarence Darrow* by David W. Rintels; Director, John C. Fletcher. *Much Ado About Nothing* by William Shakespeare; Director, David Hammond

Steve Hendrickson, Tandy Cronyn in "Much Ado about Nothing"

PORTLAND STAGE COMPANY

Portland, Maine
October 31, 1985–April 20, 1986

Artistic Director, Barbara Rosoff; Managing Director, Patricia Egan; Stage Directors: Mitchell Ivers, Barbara Rosoff, Alma Becker, Munson Hicks, Mel Marvin; Sets: Patricia Woodbridge, John Falabella, Tim Thomas, John Doepp, John Jensen, Georgi Tsypin, Bryon Taylor; Costumes: Deborah Shippee O'Brien, David Murin, Martha Hally; Lighting: Jackie Manassee, Jeff Davis, Arden Fingerhut, Francis Aronson; Stage Managers: Rheatha Forster, Diana Krauss; Musical Director, David Loud; Composer, Mel Marvin; Choreographer, Daniel McCusker

PRODUCTIONS & CASTS

BILLY BISHOP GOES TO WAR by John Gray with Eric Peterson. CAST: David Loud, Scott Ellis

HOLIDAY by Philip Barry. CAST: Shaw Purnell, E. Z. Trask, Aaron Kjenaas, Thomas A. Stewart, Charlotte Maier, Susanna Burney, Patrick Clear, Joseph Warren, Robert Szatkowski, Sally Stockwell, Jeff Brooks, Lucinda Hitchcock Cone

MASTER HAROLD and the boys by Athol Fugard. CAST: Dennis Green, Gregory Daniel, Lennie Loftin

LEVITATION by Timothy Mason. CAST: Timothy Mason, Donald Symington, Kathryn Eames, Michael Paneka, Scott Kanoff, Innes-Fergus McDade, Hope Cameron, Joseph Daly, Daniel Reidman

CURSE OF THE STARVING CLASS by Sam Shepard. CAST: Jordan Roberts, Phyllis Somerville, Mary O'Sullivan, David Combs, Michael Murphy, Michael Cannis, James Donovan, Paul McCrillis

THE CHERRY ORCHARD by Anton Chekov; English version by Trevor Griffiths. CAST: James Eckhouse, Mary Catherine Wright, Aaron Kjenaas, John Scanlan, Lydia Bruce, Diane Dreux, Charlotte Maier, P. L. Carling, Leon B. Stevens, Mona Stiles, Karen Leiner, Michael Eugene O'Brien, Paul McCrillis, Jordan Roberts, Rob G. Richards

Steven B. Nichols Photos

Joseph Daly, Kathryn Eames, Hope Cameron,
Timothy Mason, Donald Symington in "Levitation"
Top: Phyllis Somerville, Jordan Roberts, David
Combs in "Curse of the Starving Class"

REPERTORY THEATRE OF ST. LOUIS

St. Louis, Missouri
September 4, 1985–April 11, 1986

Producing Director, David Chambers; Associate Producing Director, Russell Vandenbroucke; Managing Director, Steven Woolf; NEA director fellow, Tony Kushner; Technical Director/Lighting, Max DeVolder; Playwright-in-residence, James Nicholson; Stage Managers: Glenn Dunn, Rachael Lindhart, T. R. Martin
GUESTS ARTISTS: Jeffrey King, Kurt Beattie, Rocky Carroll
PRODUCTIONS: Mainstage: *Twelfth Night* by William Shakespeare; Director, David Chambers; Set, Oliver Smith; Costumes, Mary Anne Chiment; Music, Mel Marvin.
WORLD PREMIERE: *Under Statements* by Susan Rivers; Director, Irene Lewis; Set, Kevin Rupnik; Lighting, Jennifer Tipton; Costumes, Marie Anne Chiment. *Little Shop of Horrors* by Howard Ashman and Alan Menken; Director, M. Burke Walker; Choreographer, Marcia Wilgrom Dodge; Music Director, Byron Grant; Set/Costumes, Carolyn L. Ross; Lighting, Peter Sargent. *The Mighty Gents* by Richard Wesley; Director, Hal Scott; Set, Charles Henry McClennahan; Costumes, Judy Dearing; Lighting, Allen Lee Hughes. *Golden Boy* by Clifford Odets; Director, Tony Kushner; Set, Jim Sandefur; Costumes, Jim Buff. *A Streetcar Named Desire* by Tennessee Williams; Set, Carolyn L. Ross; Costumes, Marie Anne Chiment.
STUDIO THEATRE: *The Marriage of Bette and Boo* by Christopher Durang; Director, Jackson Phippin; Set, Bill Schmiel; Costumes, Elizabeth Eisloffel. *Tom and Viv* by Michael Hastings; Director, Peter Farago; Set, John Roslevich, Jr.; Costumes, Elizabeth Eisloeffel.
WORLD PREMIERE: *Miss Julie Bodiford* by James Nicholson; Director, Susan Gregg; Set, John Roslevich, Jr.; Costumes, Dorothy L. Marshall; Lighting, Glenn Dunn.
IMAGINARY THEATRE COMPANY: *Yes Yes No No: The Solace-of-Solstice, Apogee/Perigee, Bestial/Celestial Holiday Show* Written and Directed by Tony Kushner; Stage Manager, M. George Murphy; with Kari Ely, Maggie Lerian, Lisa Raziq, Jeanne Trevor. *The Baseball Show* by James Nicholson, Directed by Wayne Solomon; *Actors on Acting* by Tony Kushner, Directed by Wayne Solomon; *Crossroads* Written and Directed by Rhonnie Washington; Company Manager, M. Gregory Murphy; with Kari Ely, Jeanne Trevor, Patrick Siler, Norman McGowan
No other information submitted.

Scott Dine Photos

Jarlath Conroy, Yusef Bulos, William Duff-Griffin
in "Twelfth Night"

Left Center: April Shawhan, Stephen Mendillo
in "The Marriage of Bette and Boo"

171

SEATTLE REPERTORY THEATRE

Seattle, Washington
October 23, 1985–June 8, 1986

Managing Director, Benjamin Moore; Artistic Directors, Daniel Sullivan, Douglas Hughes; Technical Director, Robert Scales; Production Manager, Rita Calabro; Press, Marnie Andrews; Marketing, Jerry Sando; Development, Frank Self; Wardrobe, Sally Roberts; Stage Manager, Mary Hunter

PRODUCTION & CASTS

THE MERRY WIVES OF WINDSOR by William Shakespeare; Director, Daniel Sullivan; Sets, Ralph Funicello; Costumes, Laura Crow; Lighting, Pat Collins; Music, Norman Durkee; Sound, Michael Holten. CAST: Barney O'Sullivan (Shallow), Paul Redford (Slender), Glenn Mazen (Sir Hugh Evans), John Aylward (Page), William Biff McGuire (Sir John Falstaff), Daniel Mayes (Pistol), Douglas Newel (Nym), Michael Santo (Bardolph), William P. Ontiveros (Simple), Kate Skinner (Anne Page), John Procaccino (Host of the Garter Inn), Bobo Lewis (Mistress Quickly), Donald Matt (Rugby), Daniel Sullivan (Dr. Caius), Mark Arnott (Fenton), Jeannie Carson (Mistress Page), Patricia Conolly (Mistress Ford), Woody Eney (Ford), Thomas Diggs (Robin), Eric Anderson (John), Floyd Van Buskirk (Robert), J. Cody Clark/John Sullivan (Boy), Emily Sweeny-Samuelson/Jenny Zappala (Girl), Edward Christian, Laura Kenny, Susan Rolfe Peck, Gretchen Rumbaugh, Steve Springston

ALL MY SONS by Arthur Miller; Director, Edward Hastings; Sets, Hugh Landwehr; Costumes, Robert Wojewodski; Lighting, Dennis Parichy; Sound, Lindsay Smith. CAST: Michael Santo (Dr. Jim Bayliss), William Biff McGuire (Joe Keller), Paul Redford (Frank Lubey), Patricia Conolly (Sue Bayliss), Jane Bray (Lydia Lubey), Mark Arnott (Chris Keller), Shane Clark (Bert), Betty Miller (Kate Keller), Kate Skinner (Ann Deever)

THE REAL THING by Tom Stoppard; Director, Paxton Whitehead; Sets, Robert A. Dahlstrom; Costumes, Laura Crow; Lights, Neil Peter Jampolis; Sound, Steven M. Klein. CAST: Woody Eney (Max), Deborah May (Charlotte), George Deloy (Henry), Holly Palance (Annie), Tony Soper (Billy), Tenney Walsh (Debbie), John Lee (Brodie)

THE FOREST by Alexander Ostrovsky; Adaptation, Douglas Hughes; From a translation by Maria Coachman-Tarlinskaja, Vicki Yehling; Director, Douglas Hughes; Sets, Loren Sherman; Costumes, Kurt Wilhelm; Lighting, James F. Ingalls. CAST: Judith Cohen (Pianist) Denis Arndt (Gennady Demyanich Goormizhsky), Michael Santo (Arkady), Kate Skinner (Aksinja Danilovna), Barney O'Sullivan (Karp Savelich), R. Hamilton Wright (Aleksei Sergeyich Bulanov), Bobo Lewis (Oolita), Patricia Conolly (Raissa Pavlovna Goormizhkaya), Woody Eney (Father Grigory), John Aylward (Uar Kirilich Bodayev), Glenn Mazen (Ivan Petrovich Vosmibratov), Paul Redford (Pyotr), Shane Clark (Terenka), Charles Bedoian, Katie Forgette, Ken Hicks, Rick Hinkson

FENCES by August Wilson; Director, Lloyd Richards; Associate Director, Diane Wynter; Sets, Jim Sandefur; Costumes, Candice Donnelly; Lighting, Danianne Mizzy; Sound, Michael Holten. CAST: Gilbert Lewis (Troy Maxson), Robert Colston (Jim Bono), Frances Foster (Rose), Samuel L. Jackson (Lyons), William Jay (Gabriel), Keith Amos (Cory), Tralenea Givens/Zene Olivia Latrice Simpson (Raynell)

GIRL CRAZY with Music by George Gershwin; Lyrics, Ira Gershwin; Original Book, Guy Bolton, John McGowan; Adaptation/Director, Daniel Sullivan; Choreographer, D. J. Giagni; Musical Director, Stan Keen; Orchestrator, Peter Matz; Dance Music Arrangements, John McKinney; Creative Consultant, Herb Gardner; Sets, Ralph Funicello; Costumes, Laura Crow; Lighting, Pat Collins; Sound, Mac Perkins. CAST: Harry Groener (Dickie Wentworth), Gale McNeeley (Dr. Schnitzel/Butch), Joanne Klein (Betty), Carla Farnsworth-Webb (Lucille), Carol Schuberg (Secretary/Show Girl), Richard Farrell (Spottiswode Wentworth), Kenston Ames (Assistant), Lisa Leguillou (Renata/Consuela), Tara Tyrrell (Joyce), Karen E. Fraction (Francine) Bradford Minkoff (Desert Crawler/Slick Sampson), Tom Robbins (Eugene Hackett), Michael J. Smith (Lank), Tudi Roche (Molly Bingham), Jason Kincaid (Zachary Randolph), Randy Rogel (Pete), Susan Terry (Kate Parker), Al Micacchion (Minister), Geoffrey Haberer, Rick Emery, Christopher Cotten, Bobby Clark, Lawrence Motall, Karen Harvey, Mary Wanamaker, Karen Paskow

PONCHO FORUM: *Endgame* by Samuel Beckett; Director, Douglas Hughes; Sets, Ralph Funicello; Costumes, Laura Crow; Lighting, Dennis Parichy. CAST: Denis Arndt, Bill Cobbs, Glenn Mazen, Jeannie Carson. *Cat's-Paw* by William Mastrosimone; Director, Daniel Sullivan; Sets, Thomas Fichter; Costumes, Sally Richardson; Lighting, Rick Paulsen; Sound, Michael Holten. CAST: John Procaccino, Mark Jenkins, Amy Caton-Ford, Kit Flanagan.

THE SEARCH FOR SIGNS OF INTELLIGENT LIFE IN THE UNIVERSE by Jane Wagner; *World Premiere*; starring Lily Tomlin

NEW-PLAYS-IN-PROCESS SERIES: *The Understanding* by William Mastrosimone; Director, John Schwab; Fight Director, Robert Macdougall; with John Aylward, Tim Streeter, Becca Rauscher. *A Peep into the Twentieth Century* by Christopher Davis; Director, Jon Dichter; with Michael Santo, Brian Faker, Barry Press, Rod Pilloud, David Mong, Whitey Shapiro, Ken Hicks, Gary Taylor, Nick Flynn. *Remote Conflict* by Kathleen Tolan; Director, John Schwab; with Ben Prager, Salvador Rivas, Nathan Haas, Lori Larsen, Barry Press, Dawn Didawick, Rod Pilloud, Shona Curley, Sets, Kurt Walls; Costumes, Rose Pederson; Lighting, Rick Paulsen; Sound, Steven M. Klein.

THE DOLLAR THEATRE: *Thanatophobia: Fear of Death* with Kirk Charles. *Krapp's Last Tape* by Samuel Beckett; Director, John Schwab with David S. Klein; *Theatresports;* Producer, Barry Press. *Ruth;* director, Roald Simonson; with the Alazais Azema Theatre Company

MOB TOUR: *HomeGirl* Written, Directed, and with Lyrics by Kevin Tighe; Scoring, Orchestrations, Leonard Goldsmith; Co-Producer, Daniel Moore; Sets, Kurt Walls; Costumes, Sarah Gates; Musical Direction, Beth Chandler; Choreography, Mary Anne Claire; with Christine Deaver, Christy Prestridge, Wesley Rice, Sam Strange, Clayton Wilcox

Chris Bennion Photos

**Frances Foster, Gilbert Lewis
in "Fences"**

Top: "Girl Crazy" Below: Holly Palance,
George Deloy in "The Real Thing"

SOUTH COAST REPERTORY

Costa Mesa, California
September 10, 1985–June 29, 1986
Twenty-first Season

Producing Artistic Director, David Emmes; Artistic Director, Martin Benson; Literary Managers, Jerry Patch, John Glore; Voice Director, James Wilson; Composer, Diane King; Artistic Coordinator, Donna Ruzika; General Manager, Timothy Brennan; Business Manager, Paula Tomei; Development, Bonnie Brittain Hall, JayneRobin Ruane, Nancy Gill; Marketing/Communications, John Mouledoux; Press, Cristofer Gross; Production Coordinator, Martin Benson; Production Manager, Paul Hammond; Lighting, Tom Ruzika; Sound, Stephen Shaffer; Stage Managers: Bill Venom, Julie Haber, Bonnie Lorenger, Andy Tighe; Props, Michael Mora, Heather McLarty, David Ward; Technical Director, Ted Carlsson; Scenic Artists, Abby Selman-Pait, Mary Zerbst; Wardrobe, Nancy Hamann

PRODUCTIONS & CASTS

GALILEO by Bertolt Brecht; Director, Martin Benson; Set, Susan Tuohy; Costumes, Robert Blackman; Lighting, Tom Ruzika; Music, Diane King. CAST: Dana Elcar (Galileo), Ron Boussom, Martha McFarland, Tom Shelton, James E. Brodhead, Richard Doyle, Don Took, Hal Landon Sr., Anni Long, Walter Daly, George Pelling, George Woods, Hal Landon Jr., Jack Holland, Art Koustik, Greg Atkins, Gary Weissbrot, Steve Beazley, Nigel Neale, Betsy Klingelhoefer, Melissa Smith, Nathan Adler, William Bartram, Wortham Krimmer, John Ellington, John-David Keller, Julie Kuhlman, Donnie Jeffcoat, Kris Barton, Martin Noyes
BEFORE I GOT MY EYE PUT OUT by Timothy Mason; *World Premiere;* Director, David Emmes; Set, Cliff Faulkner; Costumes, Barbara Cox; Lighting, Cameron Harvey. CAST: James Olson, Pamela Dunlap, Rick Najera, Richard Doyle, Timothy Shelton, Jessica Drake, Mark Del Castillo-Morante
THE FOREIGNER by Larry Shue; Director, Ron Lagomarsino; Set, Robert Blackman; Costumes, Susan Denison; Lighting, Peter Maradudin; Sound, Stephen Shaffer. CAST: Jeffrey Alan Chandler (Charlie), Don Took, Angela Paton, Ann Gillespie, Michael Tulin, Art Koustik, Robert Macnaughton, William Bartram, Nigel Neale
AS YOU LIKE IT by William Shakespeare; Director, Lee Shallat; Set, Cliff Faulkner; Costumes, Shigeru Yaji; Lighting, Peter Maradudin; Music, Chuck Estes. CAST: Monique Fowler (Rosalind), Anni Long, David Chemel, Ron Boussom, William Kerr, Greg Atkins, Larry Drake, Robert Machray, John-David Keller, Hal Landon Jr., Carl Reggiardo, Benjamin Stewart, Don Took, John Ellington, Jonathan McMurtry, Cheryl Crabtree, Kristen Lowman, Jonathan Palmer, William Bartram, Robert Blomgren, Ken Jensen, Pat Massoth, Nigel Neale, Jeff Newman
BURIED CHILD by Sam Shepard; Director, Sam Weisman; Set, Ralph Funicello; Costumes, Dwight Richard Odle; Lighting, Tom Ruzika; Music, J.A.C. Redford. CAST: Ralph Waite, Nan Martin, Raymond J. Barry, Hal Landon Jr., Anthony Starke, Jennifer Parsons, John-David Keller

**Sally Klein, Karen Hensel in "Unsuitable
for Adults" Top: Michael Canavan holding
Anthony Forkush, Sally Kemp in "Jitters"**

JITTERS by David French; Director, Martin Benson; Set, Michael Devine; Costumes, Sylvia Moss; Lighting, Paulie Jenkins. CAST: Sally Kemp, George Sperdakos, Anthony Forkush, Michael Canavan, Benjamin Stewart, Susan Isaacs, Robert Machray, Anni Long, Ron Boussom
A CHRISTMAS CAROL by Charles Dickens; Adaptation, Jerry Patch; Director, John-David Keller; Set, Cliff Faulkner; Costumes, Dwight Richard Odle; Lighting, Tom & Donna Ruzika. CAST: Hal Landon Jr. (Scrooge), Anni Long, Art Koustik, William Bartrum, Betsy Klingelhoefer, Terey Summers, John Ellington, Richard Doyle, Ron Boussom, Martha McFarland, Don Took, Michelle Wallen, Howard Shangraw, Nigel Neale, Ron Michaelson, Marilyn Fox, Greg Atkins, Jay Novick, Corbett Hart Bufton, Cameron Bourboulis, Gavin Tomalas, Sara Waskow, Jill Thirlwall, Kris Barton, Scott Simon, Arielle Lawson, Lisa Spiritus, Saul Wheeler, Morgan Lang
BLUE WINDOW by Craig Lucas; Director, Norman Rene; Set, Cliff Faulkner; Costumes, Shigeru Yaji; Lighting, Paulie Jenkins. CAST: Jane Galloway, Tuck Milligan, Chris Mulkey, Brad O'Hare, Lisa Pelikan, Maureen Silliman, Barbara Tarbuck (Moved to New Mayfair Theatre, Santa Monica, California, for five-month run)
PAINTING CHURCHES by Tina Howe; Director, Lee Shallat; Set, Mark Donnelly; Costumes, Shigeru Yaji; Lighting, Peter Maradudin. CAST: Patricia Fraser, Joan McMurtrey, Ford Rainey
DRIVING AROUND THE HOUSE by Patrick Smith; Director, Martin Benson; Set, John Ivo Gilles; Costumes, Charles Tomlinson; Lighting, Brian Gale; Sound, Stephen Shaffer. CAST: Timothy Donoghue, Jane Atkins, Michael Canavan, Joe Dahman, Tom Rosqui, Gabrielle Sinclair, Richard Doyle
UNSUITABLE FOR ADULTS by Terry Johnson; *American Premiere*; Director, David Emmes; Set, Michael Devine; Costumes, Susan Denison; Lighting, Cameron Harvey. CAST: Karen Hensel, Wayne Grace, Sally Klein, Richard Doyle, Troy Evans, John Napierala
VIRGINIA by Edna O'Brien; Director, Robert Berlinger; Set, Cliff Faulkner; Costumes, Sally Cleveland; Lighting, Paulie Jenkins. CAST: Megan Cole (Virginia), Bruce French, Nataliz Nogulich
TOMFOOLERY by Tom Lehrer; Written by Cameron Macintosh, Robin Ray; Director, John-David Keller; Set/Costumes, Charles Tomlinson; Lighting, Donna Ruzika; Choreography, Diane Doyle. CAST: Richard Doyle, John Ellington, John-David Keller, Diane King, Martha McFarland, Bo Efford

Ron M. Stone

**James Olson in "Before I
Got My Eye Put Out"**

**Left Center: Bruce French, Megan
Cole in "Virginia"**

STAGEWEST

Springfield, Massachusetts
October 9, 1985–May 23, 1986

Artistic Director, Gregory Boyd; Managing Director, Marvin E. Weaver; Production Manager, David Alan Stach; Marketing/Development, Sheldon Wolf; Press, Mark G. Auerbach; Stage Managers, Patricia Noto, Tree O'Halloran, Sue Ruocco; Stage Directors, Gregory Boyd, Eric Hill, Douglas Johnson, Nancy Niles Sexton; Sets: Peter David Gould, Jeffrey Struckman; Costumes: Sam Fleming, Jeffrey Struckman, V. Jane Suttell; Lighting, Robert Jared; Music Director, Martin Erskine

RESIDENT COMPANY/GUEST ARTISTS: David Asher, Robert Boardman, Barry Boys, Rick Casorla, Dillon Evans, Eric Hill, Karen Ingenthron, Kimberly King, Ellen Lauren, Christiane McKenna, Kathryn Meisle, William Meisle, Anne Pitoniak, Noble Shropshire, John Straub, Ron Vernan, Charles Michael Wright
PRODUCTIONS: *As You Like It* by William Shakespeare, *Peter Pan or The Boy Who Wouldn't Grow Up* by J. M. Barrie. *Courage* by John Pielmeier, *Painting Churches* by Tina Howe, *Happy Days* by Samuel Beckett, *U.S.A.* by Paul Shyre and John Dos Passos, *A Flea in Her Ear* by Georges Feydeau; Translated by Douglas Johnson

Carl Bartels, Gerry Goodstein Photos

Anne Pitoniak, John Straub in "Painting Churches"
Left Top: Noble Shropshire in "Courage"

STUDIO ARENA THEATRE

Buffalo, New York
September 19, 1985–May 25, 1986
Twenty-first Season

Artistic Director, David Frank; Managing Director, Raymond Bonnard; Associate Director/Dramaturg, Kathryn Long; Development, Anne E. Hayes; Marketing, Anne E. Conable; Press, Blossom Cohan; Creative Director, Daniel J. Wasinger; Company Manager, Anne Marie Fedele; Technical Director, Brett Thomas; Stage Managers, Christine Michael, Glenn Bruner; Costumiere, Mary Ann Powell; Sound, Rick Menke; Props, Jolene Obertin

PRODUCTIONS & CASTS
THE FOREIGNER by Larry Shue; Director, Nick Faust; Set, Gary C. Eckhart; Costumes, John Carver Sullivan; Lighting, Dan Kotlowitz; Music, Bob Volkman. CAST: David Hyde-Lamb ("Froggy" LeSueur), Jeff Brooks (Charlie Baker), Mary Fogarty (Betty Meeks), David Glen (Rev. David Marshall Lee), Donna Snow (Catherine Simms), Earl Hindman (Owen Musser), Christopher Shaw (Ellard Simms), Arlene Clement, Beverly Murray Kobee, Rick Makowski, Dave Mancuso, Daryl Rittiman, George Woolston
CHILDREN OF A LESSER GOD by Mark Medoff; Director, Kathryn Long; Set/Lighting, Victor Becker; Costumes, Mary Ann Powell; Sign Language Adviser, Alan Champion; Interpreter, Aaron Brace. CAST: Janis I. Cole (Sarah Norman), W. T. Martin (James Leeds), Larry Bazzell (Orin Dennis), Stephen McKinley Henderson (Mr. Franklin), Jen Jones (Mrs. Norman), Jodene Marie Anicello (Lydia), Edna Dix (Edna Klein)
SLEUTH by Anthony Shaffer; Director, David Frank; Set, Lewis Folden; Costumes, Mary Ann Powell; Lighting, Curt Ostermann. CAST: David Main (Andrew Wyke), Steven Crossley (Milo Tindle), Arthur M. Grayson (Inspector Doppler), Evan Truxall (Det. Sgt. Tarrant), Geoffrey Parker (Constable Higgs)
AIN'T MISBEHAVIN' based on an idea by Murray Horwitz & Richard Maltby, Jr.; Director, Arthur Faria; Musical Director, William Foster McDaniel; Set, John Lee Beatty; Lighting, Barry Arnold. CAST: Leslie Barlow, Doug Eskew, Boncellia Lewis, Stanley Ramsey, Terri White, William Foster McDaniel
THE IMPORTANCE OF BEING EARNEST by Oscar Wilde; Director, David Frank; Set, Robert Morgan; Costumes, Mary Ann Powell; Lighting, Curt Ostermann. CAST: John Bennes (Lane), John Abajian (Algernon Moncrieff), David Manis (John Worthing) Mary Jay (Lady Bracknell), Bonnie Black (Gwendolen Fairfax), Anne Gayley (Miss Prism), Donna Snow (Cecily Cardew), John Bennes (Rev. Canon Chasuble), Walter Barrett (Merriman)
GREATER TUNA by Jaston Williams, Joe Sears, Ed Howard; Director, Kathryn Long; Set, Curtis Trout; Costumes, Mary Ann Powell; Lighting, Michael Orris Watson; Sound, Rick Menke; Music, Bob Volkman. CAST: Wil Love, Robert Spencer
ARSENALS by Jeremy Lawrence; *World Premiere;* Director, Gwen Arner; Set, D. Martyn Bookwalter; Costumes, Bill Walker; Lighting, Brett Thomas. CAST: Laurinda Barrett (Frances Berman), Tanny McDonald (Joanne Berman), Matthew Lewis (Andrew Tobin), Mark Arnott (Mike Schwartz), Richard Ryder (Larry Berman)

K. C. Kratt Photos

John Abajian, Bonnie Black, Mary Jay, Donna Snow in "The Importance of Being Earnest"

Left Center: Tanny McDonald, Richard Ryder in "Arsenals"

SYRACUSE STAGE

Syracuse, New York
October 11, 1985–May 4, 1986
Thirteenth Season

Producing Artistic Director, Arthur Storch; Managing Director, James A. Clark; Business Manager, Diana Coles; Development, Shirley Lockweed; Press, Zoe Tolone; Marketing, Barbara Beckos; Dramaturg, Tom Walsh; Company Manager, Donna Inglima; Stage Managers: Cynthia Poulson, Don Buschmann, Barbara Beeching, Avy Cuomo, Kenneth R. Bolinsky; Technical Director, Jeff Vandeyacht; Scenic Artist, Gary May; Sound, Margi B. Heiple; Props, Susan Baker, Roger Anderson, Mark Wenderlick; Costumer, Maria Marrero; Casting, David Tochterman

PRODUCTIONS & CASTS

THE FOREIGNER by Larry Shue; Director, Charles Karchmer; Set, Timothy Galvin; Costumes, Maria Marrero; Lighting, Ann G. Wrightson. CAST: Richard Poe ("Froggy" LeSueur), Bill Kux (Charlie Baker), Elizabeth Moore (Betty Meeks), Robert Curtis-Brown (Rev. David Marshall Lee), Stacy Huntington (Catherine Simms), Richard Fitzpatrick (Owen Musser), Mark Morocco (Ellard Simms), David Cooley, Kevin Hackett, J. Lentner, Neal McDonough, Ilo Orleans, Bill Ullman
GLENGARRY GLEN ROSS by David Mamet; Director, Tony Giordano; Set, Hugh Landwehr; Costumes, Maria Marrero; Lighting, Dennis Parichy. CAST: Roger Serbagi (Shelly Levene), Barry Cullison (John Williamson), Madison Arnold (Dave Moss), Joseph Rose (George Aaronow), Michael Fischetti (Richard Roma), George Hosmer (James Lingk), Walter Innes (Baylen)
AIN'T MISBEHAVIN' based on an idea by Murray Horwitz and Richard Maltby Jr.; Director, Arthur Faria; Musical Director, William Foster McDaniel; Set, John Lee Beatty; Lighting, Barry Arnold; Costumes, Eaves-Brooks; CAST: Leslie Barlow, Ellia English, Doug Eskew, Stanley Ramsey, Terri White, William Foster McDaniel
ROMEO AND JULIET by William Shakespeare; Concept/Direction, Arthur Storch; Set, Victor A. Becker; Costumes, Nanzi Adzima; Lighting, Ralph Dressler; Fight Choreography, Norm Beauregard; Choreography, Linda Sabo; Voice/Verse Coach, Beverly Bluem; Music/Sound, Arthur Storch/Margi B. Heiple. CAST: Gary Armagnac (Lord Capulet), Nick Bakay (Paris), Beverly Bluem (Lady Montague), James Clow (Romeo), Sally Dunn (Lady Capulet), Dick Harris (Lord Montague), Alan Mixon (Chorus/Prince), Al Rodriguez (Tybalt), J. Smith-Cameron (Juliet), Mitchell Sugarman (Mercutio), Brenda Thomas (Nurse), Ted Van Griethuysen (Friar Laurence), Suzanne Bayles, Carrie Chantler, Stephen Christian, John Demicco, Roger Durling, Sunshine Frateschi, Karen Fuller, Sam Goldsman, Kevin Hackett, Adrienne Hampton Smith, Amy Hausman, Kathleen Horrigan, Tracy Katz, Antonia Noble Ludwig, Eric Mills, Patrick Mulcahy, Jennifer Pauly, Sarah J. Pickett, Kevin Richardson, Jody Rowell, Helen Sacher, Susan Shimer, Chris Walz, Jenifer L. Weber, Erick Weiss
LUV by Murray Schisgal; Director, Terry Schreiber; Set, Michael Miller; Costumes, Gregg Barnes; Lighting, Victor A. Becker. CAST: Jim Shankman (Harry Berlin), Stephan Weyte (Milt Manville), Staci Swedeen (Ellen Manville)
BENT by Martin Sherman; Director, Tom Walsh; Set/Costumes/Lighting, Victor A. Becker. CAST: William Fichtner (Max), Christopher Wells (Rudy), Gary Lahti (Wolf), Noel Craig (Greta), Walter Flanagan (Uncle Freddie), Kenneth Meseroll (Horst), James Gingeleski (Officer/Kapo), Joel Ancowitz, Steven Capone, Ilo Orleans, Kevin Smith (Prisoners), James B. Hagerman, Patrick Mulcahy (Guards)

Susan Piper Kublick Photos

Entire company of "Romeo and Juliet"
Top: Staci Swedeen, Stephan Weyte,
Jim Shankman in "Luv" (Syracuse)

TACOMA ACTORS GUILD

Tacoma, Washington
October 4, 1985–March 29, 1986

Artistic Directors, Rick Tutor; Assistant Artistic Director, Bill Becvar; Stage Managers, Hal Meng, Pamela Guion; Technical Director, Jeffrey Noyes; Scenic Artist, Richard Harris; Wardrobe, Heidi A. Hermiller; Press, Jim Paddleford; Sets: Jerry S. Hooker, Jennifer Lupton; Costumes: Frances Kenny, Anne Thaxter Watson, Sarah Campbell; Lighting: James Berdery, Richard Davin; Music/Sound, Jim Ragland; Assistant Director, Madge Montgomery; Stage Directors: Anne-Denise Ford, John Schwab, Rita Giomi

PRODUCTIONS & CASTS

THE REAL INSPECTOR HOUND and DOGG'S HAMELT by Tom Stoppard. CAST: Rose E. Cano, Rex Rabold, Peter Lohnes, Victoria Otto, Ki Gottberg, Tony Soper, Frank Corrado, Richard Riner
A COUPLA WHITE CHICKS SITTING AROUND TALKING by John Ford Noonan. CAST: Cheri Sorenson, Susan Ronn
A CHILD'S CHRISTMAS IN WALES by Dylan Thomas and
A CHRISTMAS MEMORY by Truman Capote. CAST: Craig English, Gail McNeeley, Helen Machin-Smith, David Mong, Paul Shapiro, Richard Riner, Lyn Tyrrel, Jerri Lee Young
THE PRICE by Arthur Miller. CAST: Frank Corrado, Jo Ann Johnson, David S. Klein, Rod Pilloud
FINAL PASSAGES by Robert Schenkkan. CAST: Kevin Hugh Lynch, James Kelly, Coby Scheldt, W. Earl Ray, Rod Pilloud, Eric Anderson, Andy Taylor, W. Huston Dougharty, Wendy Robie
HOME by Samm-Art Williams. CAST: W. Earl Ray, Jacqueline Moscou, Tamu Gray

Fred Andrews Photos

Andy Taylor, Wendy Robie
in "Final Passages"

175

THEATRE BY THE SEA

Portsmouth, New Hampshire
October 3, 1985–May 24, 1986

Artistic Director, Tom Celli; Managing Director, Janet Wade; Company Manager/Assistant to the Directors, Sharon Fentiman; Development, Donna Meeks; Marketing, Allyn Sweet; Press, Michael Reznicek; Business Manager, Sarah Coco; Associate Director, Paul Mroczka; Stage Managers, John Lawrence Becker, Dori Eskenazi; Technical Director/Sets, James P. Murphy, Gary English; Lighting, Jon Terry, David "Sparky" Lockner; Props, Kim Miskell; Costumes, Lisa Micheels, Judianne Sisson

PRODUCTIONS: *I'll Be back Before Midnight* by Peter Colley (WORLD PREMIERE); Director, Tom Celli; with John Hickok (Greg Sanderson), Kate Phelan (Jan Sanderson), Frank T. Wells (George Willowhy), Maxine Taylor-Morris (Laura Sanderson), Robert Spelvin (Robert Willowhy). *What the Butler Saw* by Joe Orton. *'night, Mother* by Marsha Norman. *A Day in Hollywood/A Night in the Ukraine* with Book and Lyrics by Dick Vosburgh; Music, Frank Lazarus. *Romeo and Juliet* by William Shakespeare

Andrew Edgar, Thomas O. Kreigsmann Photos

Right: Terry Urdang in "Godspell"
Top: "Pump Boys and Dinettes"

THEATRE/THEATRO

Los Angeles, California
June 1, 1985–May 31, 1986
Seventh Season

A program of the Bilingual Foundation of the Arts (Leo Trujillo, Chairman); Managing Producer/President, Carmen Zapata; Artistic Director, Margarita Galban; Productions Manager, Estela Scarlata; Executive Director, Sue Welsh; Press, Martin Quiroz; Development, Rosalind Lane; Office Managers, Mary Repass, Rosaura Ramires.

PRODUCTIONS & CASTS

THE YOUNG LADY FROM TACNA by Mario Vargas Llosa; Translated and Directed by Joanne Pottlitzer; Producer, Carmen Zapata; Set, Estela Scarlata; Lighting, Robert Frommer; Costumes, Richard Smart; Stage Manager, Roy Conboy. CAST: Irene de Bari (Mame-E), Diane Rodriguez (Amelia), Henry Darrow (Belisario), Louis Cruz Beltran (Joaquin), Evelina Fernandez (Grandmother Carmen), Sam Vlahos (Grandfather Pedro), Angela Moya (Carlota), Sal Lopez (Ceaser), Richard German (Agustin), Standbys: Michael Sandoval, Angela Moya, Kathleen Salamone

BLOOD WEDDING/BODAS DE SANGRE by Federico Garcia Lorca; New England Translation, Michael Dewell, Carmen Zapata; Director, Margarita Galban; Music, Ian Krouse; Choreography, Linda Dangcil; Sets, Estala Scarlata; Lighting, Octavio Ramirez; Costumes, Richard Smart; Props, Mark Measures. CAST: Angela Moya (Death), Michael Bernal (Woodcutter), Mary Bermudez (Moon), Armando Di Lorenzo (Bridegroom), Carmen Zapata (Mother), Roz Bosley (Neighbor), Tina Bacon (Mother-in-law), Marie Saint-Clair (Wife), John Vargas (Leonardo), Benita Martinez (Girl), Angelina Estrada (Maid), Richard German (Father), Roxanne Cordova (Bride), Rico Ortiz (First Youth), Herberto Guillen (Second Youth), Standbys: William Marquez, Benita Marquez, Benita Martinez, Lina Montalvo, Nikko Rey

THE SHOEMAKER'S PRODIGIOUS WIFE by Federico Garcia Lorca; New English Translation, Michael Dewell, Carmen Zapata; Director, Margarita Galban; Music, F. Garcia Lorca and Adapted by Ian Krouse; Sets, Estela Scarlata; Lighting, Magda Gonzalez; Costumes, Armand Coutu; Choreography, Angela Moya; Stage Manager, Frankie Hernandez. CAST: Heberto Guillen (Author), Hector Hernandez (Author-English), Maria Richwine (Zapatera-English), Sandra Nelson (Zapatera-Spanish), Pete Leal (Zapatero-Spanish), Raul Espinosa (Zapatero-English), Lorena Gonzalez, Angela Estrada, Lenette Rico (Ninas-children), Christina Castro (Vecina-Neighbor #2), Rosita Ojeda (Vecina-Neighbor #3), Angelina Estrada (Vecina-Neighbor #1), Hecmar Lugo (Alcalde-Spanish), Richard Leos (Alcalde-English), Herberto Guillen (Don Mirlo), Hector Hernandez (Mozo #1), Nikko Rey (Mozo #2), Understudies: Armando Di Lorenzo, Berta Holguin

Christina Castro, Angelina Estrada, Bertha Holguin,
Rosita Ojeda in "The Shoemaker's Prodigious Wife"

Left Center: Bob Kokol, Victoria Racimo
in "The Death of Rosendo"

THEATRE THREE

Dallas, Texas
May 31, 1985–May 4, 1986

Founding/Artistic Director, Norman Young; Executive Producer/Director, Jac Alder; Associate Producer, Charles Howard; Associate Director, Laurence O'Dwyer; Operations, John Briggs; Development, Susan P. Swan; Press, Gary Yawn; Literary, Sharon Bunn; Musical Director, Terry Dobson; Stage Manager, Jimmy Mullen; Production Coordinator, Cheryl Denson

PRODUCTIONS & CASTS

ANYTHING GOES by Cole Porter; Director/Sets, Jac Alder; Costumes, Cheryl Denson; Lighting, Michael Murray; Choreography, Betty Ferguson; Musical Direction, Terry Dobson. CAST: Jac Alder, Andi Allen, Peppy Biddy, Peggy Billo, Scott Bradford, Sharon Bunn, Jim Caruso, Terry Dobson, Doug Jackson, Jim McQueen, Amy Mills, Laurence O'Dwyer, Peggy Townsley, Holly K. Watts
A . . .MY NAME IS ALICE conceived by Joan Micklin Silver and Julianne Boyd; Director, Maureen Shea; Set, Cheryl Denson; Costumes, Sally Lynn Askins; Lighting, Shari Melde; Musical Direction, Terry Dobson. CAST: Kim Kassira, Leslie Evans Leach, Amy Mills, Connie Nelson, Sally Soldo
THE LIFE SHE LED by T. Y. Hill; Director, John Briggs; Set/Costumes, Cheryl Denson; Lighting, Michael G. Moynihan. CAST: Norma Young
INFIDELITIES by Pierre De Marivaux; Director, Laurence O'Dwyer; Set, Harland Wright; Costumes, Patricia Greer McGarity; Lighting; Wayne Lambert. CAST: Cheryl Black, Bradley Campbell, Georgia Clinton, Jerry Crow, Scott Everhart, Suzanne Hayes, Terry Vandivort, Robert Bartley, Kerry Cole, Bruce Coleman, Cynthia Hestand
HOME FRONT by James Duff; Director, Laurence O'Dwyer; Sets, Jac Alder; Costumes, Bruce R. Coleman; Lighting, Shari Melde. CAST: Vince Davis, Hugh Feagin, Gloria Hocking, Victoria Wright
SEASON'S GREETINGS by Alan Ayckbourn; Director, John Briggs; Sets, Michael G. Moynihan; Costumes, Bruce R. Coleman; Lighting, Ken Hudson. CAST: Sharon Bunn, Traber Burns, Kerry Cole, Hugh Feagin, Ryland Merkey, Thurman Moss, Connie Nelson, John Rainone, Judith Townsend
LITTLE SHOP OF HORRORS with Book and Lyrics by Howard Ashman; Music, Alan Menken; Based on the film by Roger Corman/Screenplay, Charles Griffith; Directors, Laurence O'Dwyer, Jac Alder; Musical Director, Terry Dobson; Sets, Harland Wright; Lighting, Ken Hudson; Costumes, Cheryl Denson; Puppets, Martin P. Robinson. CAST: Sa'mi Chester, Melvin O. Dacus, Doug Jackson, Lynn Mathis, Connie Nelson, Leon Newman, Tami Ward, Gabrielle Suzette West, Yolanda Williams, Jerry Haynes
1986 FESTIVAL OF NEW PLAYS: *Small Nights of Terror* by Jack Bonham; Director, Robin Stanton. *On Weddings and Divorces* by James Serpento; Director, Thurman Moss. *Safety* by Patricia Griffith; Director, Ester Benson. *Mud in Your Eye* by Gerald Stuebben; Director, Richard Roberts.

Susan Kandell Photos

**Top Right: Doug Jackson, Connie Nelson
in "Little Shop of Horrors"**

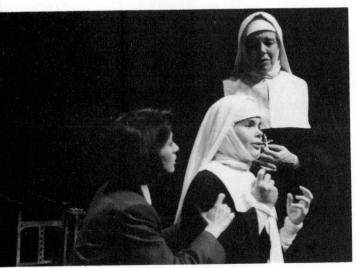

**Ellen Fiske, Catherine Christianson, Sylvia
Short in "Agnes of God" (Virginia)**

THEATRE VIRGINIA

Richmond, Virginia
October 3, 1985–May 3, 1986

Artistic Director, Terry Burgler; General Manager, Edward W. Rucker; Operations, Robb Mackenzie; Company Manager, Maren Swenson; Press/Marketing, E. Frazier Millner; Development, David E. Johnson; Literary, Bo Wilson; Casting, Wendy Dana; Production Manager, Deborah Simon; Sets/Costumes, Charles Caldwell, David M. Crank; Scenic Artists: Ann E. Gumpper, Jennifer C. DeBell; Technical Director, Terry Cermak; Props: Susan Senita, Leland Lew; Lighting, Lynne M. Hartman, Jennifer Lockwood, Terry Cermak, Jackie Manassee, Richard Moore Sound, Christy A. Perry; Stage Managers, Doug Flinchum, Donna Stanley.

PRODUCTIONS & CASTS

STAGE STRUCK by Simon Gray; Director, Terry Burgler; Costumes, Barbara Forbes; CAST: Tom Rolfing (Robert), Stewart Finlay-McLennan, Chris Casady (Anne), Jim Hillgartner (Widdecombe)
MAN OF LA MANCHA with Book by Dale Wasserman; Music, Mitch Leigh; Lyrics, Joe Darion; Director/Choreographer, Terry Burgler; Musical Director, Ted Kociolek. CAST: Stephan Foster (Don Quixote/Cervantes), Steve Liebman (Sancho), Jerry Guarino (Captain), Barbara Turvett (Aldonza), Jim Fleetwood (Innkeeper/Governor), Lance Hewett (Dr. Carrasco/Duke), Gordon Stanley (Padre), Lora Martens (Antonia), Marie Goodman Hunter (Housekeeper), Jerome Butler (Pedro), Jerry Bradley (Anselmo), Gilbert Olin (Jose), Maury Erickson (Juan), Greg Baber (Paco/Horse), Bev Appleton (Tenorio), Marie Goodman Hunter (Maria), Catherine Shaffner (Fermina), Robert Throckmorton (Barber), Cliff Abramson (Guitarist), Darly Cobb (Horse), Jerry L. Dagenhart, Paul Howard, J. Roo Huigen, Christy A. Perry, Pia Sexton, Charlene Thompson, Martin A. Tyler
A CHRISTMAS CAROL by Charles Dickens; Adaptation, Tom Markus; Director, Bev Appleton; Costumes, Lana Fritz; CAST: Donald Christopher (Scrooge), Bev Appleton, Jerry Bradley, Susan Brandner, Terry Burgler, Amanda Di Girolamo, Lucien Douglas, Heather Elizabeth Dunville, Christy Michelle Fairman, Robert Foley, Tracy O'Neil Heffernan, Jim Hillgartner, Steven Journey, Joe Terrill Murphy, Jessica Printz, Adrian Rieder, Todd Rodriguez, Ed Sala, Catherine Shaffner, Rob Storrs, Robert L. Townes, Nan Wray, Dexter Zollicoffer
AGNES OF GOD by John Pielmeier; Director, Dan Hamilton; CAST: Ellen Fiske (Dr. Martha Livingstone), Sylvia Short (Mother Miriam Ruth), Catherine Christianson (Agnes)
TRUE WEST by Sam Shepard; Director, Bill Gregg; Costumes, Catherine Szari; CAST: Will Osborne (Austin), James Mathers (Lee), Jim Hillgartner (Saul Kimmer), Anne Sheldon (Mom)
THE GLASS MENAGERIE by Tennessee Williams; Director, Terry Burgler; CAST: Will Osborne (Tom), Anne Sheldon (Amanda), Catherine Christianson (Laura), Clifford Fetters (Male Companion/Gentleman Caller), Tami Desiree Bick/Maren Swenson (Female Companion), Al Waters (Musician)
ARMS AND THE MAN by George Bernard Shaw; Director, Terry Burgler; Costumes, Susan Tsu; CAST: Kathryn Meisle (Raina), Victoria Boothby (Catherine Petkoff), Jeanine Morick (Louka), Graeme Malcolm (Capt. Bluntschli), Terry Burgler (Russian Officer), Bev Appleton (Nicola), Dion Anderson (Maj. Paul Petkoff), David Fuller (Maj. Sergius Saranoff)
THE FOREIGNER by Larry Shue; Director, Terry Burgler; Costumes, Susan Griffin; Stage Manager, Bo Wilson. CAST: Terry Burgler (S/Sgt. "Froggy" LeSueur), Davis Hall (Charlie Baker), Lalla Rolfe (Betty Meeks), David Fuller (Rev. David Marshall Lee), Kathryn Meisle (Catherine Simms), Ed Sala (Owen Musser), Bev Appleton (Ellard Simms), David E. Johnson, Robb Mackenzie, Tom Muza, Sharon O'Neille, David Wilt. Understudy: Bev Appleton

Ron Jennings Photos

TRINITY SQUARE REPERTORY COMPANY

Providence, Rhode Island
June 28, 1985–May 25, 1986
Twenty-Second Season

Artistic Director, Adrian Hall; Managing Director, E. Timothy Langan; Assistant to Mr. Hall, Marion Simon; Composer, Richard Cumming; Designer, Eugene Lee; Sets, Robert D. Soule; Lighting, John F. Custer; Costumes, William Lane; Production Manager, William Radka; Stage Managers: Wendy Cox, Ruth Sternberg, Wendy Chapin; Technical Directors: David Rotondo, Michael McGarty; Props, Robert Schleinig; Press/Marketing, Anne Marden; Press, Jeannie MacGregor-Jochim; Development, Simone Joyaux; Operations, Gene Minkow; Stage Directors: Adrian Hall, Richard Jenkins, Tony Giordano, Philip Minor, Neal Baron, William Damkoehler, David Wheeler, George Martin.

RESIDENT COMPANY: Richard Kneeland, Richard Kavanaugh, Peter Gerety, Barbara Orson, Ed Hall, Barbara Meek, Richard Jenkins, Tom Griffin, David C. Jones, Timothy Crowe, Keith Jochim, Richard Ferrone, Becca Lish, Anne Scurria, Howard London, Daniel Von Bargen, Barbara Blossom, Brenda Jean Corwin, William Damkoehler, Cynthia Strickland, Margot Dionne, Steven Jermanovich, David Kennett, Margaret Marx, Ruth Maynard, Brian McEleny, Derek Meader, Ricardo Pitts-Wiley, Stella Reed, David PB Stephens, Patricia Thomas, Jennifer Van Dyck, Akin Babatunde, Geraldine Librandi, Frederick Sullivan, Jr., Stephen Berenson, Andrew Mutnick, Dee Hennigan, Nicolas Mize, Andrew Polk, David Sabin, Margo Skinner, Deborah Strang, Stephen Burleigh.
PRODUCTIONS: *The Marriage of Bette and Boo* by Christopher Durang; *Cat on a Hot Tin Roof* by Tennessee Williams; *The Beauty Part* by S. J. Perelman; *A Christmas Carol* by Charles Dickens, Adapted by Adrian Hall and Richard Cumming; *The Crucible* by Arthur Miller; *The Tavern* by George M. Cohan; *Life and Limb* by Keith Reddin; *Pasta* by Tom Griffin (WORLD PREMIERE); *The Country Girl* by Clifford Odets; *Baby* by Sybille Pearson, David Shire, Richard Maltby Jr.; *Not By Bed Alone* by Georges Feydeau.

Ron Manville, Mark Morelli Photos

Right: Cynthia Strickland, William Damkoehler,
Tom Griffin in "The Crucible" Top: Anne Scurria,
Peter Gerety, Nicolas Mize in "Pasta"

178

Richard Kneeland, Margot Dionne
in "The Country Girl"

Richard Ferrone, Anne Scurria
in "The Marriage of Bette and Boo"

VIRGINIA STAGE COMPANY

Norfolk, Virginia
October 11, 1985–April 19, 1986
Seventh Season

Artistic Director, Charles Towers; Associate Artistic Director, Christopher Hanna; Managing Director, Dan J. Martin; Assistant to Directors, Marimar Lucks; General Manager, Caroline F. Turner; Production Manager, Dan Sedgwick; Stage Managers, Dan Sedgwick, Nancy Kay Uffner, Suzanne Averitt; Development, Stuart Gordon; Press/Marketing, Stacey Milcos; Business Manager, Robert Bullington; Company Manager, Deborah Shumate; Technical Director, Christopher Buckley; Costumes, Candice Cain; Lighting/Sound, Dirk Kuyk; Props, Gretchen Gregg

PRODUCTIONS & CASTS

THE BEASTLY BEATITUDES OF BALTHAZAR B by J. P. Donleavy; *American Premiere;* Director, Charles Towers; Set, John Lee Beatty; Lighting, Roger Morgan; Costumes, Kurt Wilhelm; Scenic Artist, Rick Jordan; Voice/Dialect Consultant, Tim Monich. CAST: Wendy Barrie, Bille Brown, Maureen Garrett, Kathleen Mahony-Bennett, Pam Manning, Gary Montgomery, Ed Morgan, Derek Murcott, Emmett O'Sullivan-Moore, Harriet Rogers, G. F. Rowe, Patrick Ryecart, Peg Small

MASTER HAROLD . . . and the boys by Athol Fugard; Director, Alex Dmitriev; Set, Lewis Folden; Choreographer, Lisa Brailoff; Scenic Artist, Deborah Jasin. CAST: John David Cullum, Lou Ferguson, Ennis Dexter Locke

PAINTING CHURCHES by Tina Howe; Director, Jamie Brown; Set, Michael Miller; Lighting, Jim Sale. CAST: Jordan R. Baker, Avril Gentles, Wyman Pendleton

WETTER THAN WATER by Deborah Pryor; (Workshop); Director, Charles Towers. CAST: Helen Harrelson, Dorrie Joiner, Casper Roos, George L. Topper

GREEN WITCH by Jeannie Lee; (Staged Reading); Director, Paul Hildebrand, Jr. CAST: Lisa Brailoff, Kay Buchanan, Helen Harrelson, Kathryn James, Dorrie Joiner, Edward Morgan

HAUT GOUT by Allan Havis; (Staged Reading); Director Christopher Hanna. CAST: Scott Forbes Elliott, Rex Ellis, Helen Harrelson, Gordana Rashovich, Casper Roos, John Gould Rubin

JITTERS by David French; Director, Pamela Berlin; Set, Rick Dennis; Stage Manager, Bonnie L. Becker. CAST: Joe Barrett, Barry Boys, John Capodice, Patricia Gage, Emily Heebner, Geoffrey Nauffts, Anne O'Sullivan, John Seidman, Larry Singer

THE GLASS MENAGERIE by Tennessee Williams; Director, Christopher Hanna; Set, Lewis Folden; Lighting, Spencer Moss. CAST: Brenda Daly, David Fuller, Stephen Plienski, Jennifer Sternberg

BILLY BISHOP GOES TO WAR by John Gray with Eric Peterson; Director, Mitchell Ivers; Set, Pat Woodbridge; Lighting, Jackie Manassee. CAST: Scott Ellis, David Loud

Ellen Forsyth Photos

**Billie Brown, Patrick Ryecart
in "The Beastly Beatitudes of Balthazar B"
(Virginia Stage Co.)**

THE WHOLE THEATRE

Montclair, New Jersey
October 29, 1985–April 20, 1986

Artistic Director, Olympia Dukakis; Managing Director, Laurence N. Feldman; Press/Marketing, Clifford R. Scott; Stage Managers: Kathleen Cunneen, Travis DeCastro, Edward Neuret; Sets: Randy Benjamin, Michael Miller, Ricardo F. Morin; Costumes: Judy Dearing, Karen Gerson, Sigrid Insull; Lighting: Richard Moore, Carol Rubinstein, Ann G. Wrightson; Directors: Billie Allen, Romulus Linney, Austin Pendleton, Amy Saltz, Kent Thompson; Musical Directors: Richard Reiter, Richard Cohen; Choreographer, Elise Lynch; Vocal Coach, Dan Levitan

PRODUCTIONS AND CASTS

A MIDSUMMER NIGHT'S DREAM by William Shakespeare; Adaptation, Amy Saltz. CAST: Paul Bates, Jossie de Guzman, Mary Irey, Victor Love, Chris Odo, Lonny Price, Daniel Southern, Ching Valdes/Aran

SEASON'S GREETINGS by Alan Ayckerbourn. CAST: Ross Bickell, Cynthia Mace, Yolanda Childress, Leslie Barrett, Apollo Dukakis, Innes-Fergus McDade, Stephen Root, Tiina Cartmell, Stephen Temperley

HOME by Samm-Art Williams. CAST: S. Epatha Merkerson, Elain Graham, Samuel L. Jackson

SAND MOUNTAIN by Romulus Linney (Two one-act plays); *Sand Mountain Matchmaking* (WORLD PREMIERE) and *Why the Lord Come to Sand Mountain.* CAST: Kari Jenson, Kevin Carrigan, William Hardy, Ron Lee Savin, Kathleen Chalfant, Damon Dukakis, Leon Russom

ELECTRA: THE LEGEND by Michael Sayers; *World Premiere.* CAST: Humbert Allen Astredo, Michael Grieco, Tom Klunis, Elizabeth J. Ross, Maria Tucci, Beth McDonald, Ruth Ann Roberts, Andrew Black, Daniel Southern, Jeff Dunston, William Schroeder, Kate Collins, Novella Nelson, Marvin Forney, Chase Sterling, Nel Evan Nussbaum, Terrence O'Brien, Mark Phelan, Daniel Kahn, Suzanne Clare, Maria Romano

Jerry Dalia, Jeffrey Sestilio Photos

**William Schroeder, Dan Southern, Maria Tucci,
Humbert Allen Astredo, (kneeling) Tom Klunis,
Beth McDonald in "Electra" (Whole Theatre)**

YALE REPERTORY THEATRE

New Haven, Connecticut
September 17, 1985–May 24, 1986

Artistic Director, Lloyd Richards; Managing Director, Ben Mordecai; Literary Managers: Barbara Davenport, Gitta Honegger, Joel Schechter; Press, Rosalind Heinz; Production Manager, Bronislaw Sammler; Set Design Adviser, Ming Cho Lee; Costume Design Adviser, Jane Greenwood; Lighting Adviser, Deborah Hecht; Movement Adviser, Wesley Fata; Sets, Michael H. Yeargan; Costumes, Dunya Ramicova; Lighting, William B. Warfel; Musical Director, Dwight Andrews

PRODUCTIONS & CASTS

THE BLOOD KNOT Written and Directed by Athol Fugard; 25th Anniversary Production; Set, Rusty Smith; Costumes, Susan Hilferty. CAST: Athol Fugard, Zakes Mokae
LITTLE EYOLF by Henrik Ibsen; Director, Travis Preston; Sets, Elina Kasioula; Costumes, Arnall Downs; Lighting, Jennifer Tipton. CAST: Susan Gibney, Stephen McHattie, Rebecca Nelson, Pamela Payton-Wright, John Gould Rubin
MARRIAGE by Nikolai Gogol; Director, Andrei Belgrader; Set Pamela Peterson; Lighting, Danianne Mizzy. CAST: Kitty Crooks, Abba Elfman, Warren Manzi, Frank Maraden, Jared Matesky, Theresa Merritt, Karen Shallo, Richard Spore, Ian Trigger, Jeannie Ventriss
WINTERFEST SIX: Four New American Plays in Repertory;
WORLD PREMIERES: *A Child's Tale* by Carl Capotorto; Director, Dennis Scott; Set, Tim Saternow; Costumes, Scott Bradley; Lighting, Donald Holder; CAST: Amy Aquino, Kimberleigh Burroughs, Patrick Kerr, Leonard Parker, Ching Valdes. *Crazy From the Heart* by Edit Villarreal; Director, Mark Brokow; Set, Tina Navarro; Costumes, Arnall Downs; Lighting, Donald Holder; CAST: Cosmo F. Allegretti, Hortensia Colorado, Peter Crombie, Randolph Mantooth, Theresa McElwee, David Officer. *Stitchers and Starlight Talkers* by Kathleen Betsko. Director, William Partlan; Set, Michael H. Yeargan; Costumes, Dunya Ramicova; Lighting, Michael Chybowski; CAST: Constance Ball, Kitty Crooks, Leigh Curran, Aloysius Gigl, Kirk Jackson, Bruce Katzman, Susan Kellermann, Mary McDonnell, Mark Rafael, Rudolph Willrich. *Union Boys* by James Yoshimura; Director, Steven Robman; Set, Rosario Provenza; Costumes, Charles McCarry; Lighting, Michael Giannitti; CAST: Spencer Beglarian, Jon DeVries, Stanford Egi, Giancarlo Esposito, Marcus Giamatti, Michael Hagerty, Delroy Lindo, Sam McMurray.
OTHELLO by William Shakespeare; Director, Dennis Scott, Set, David Peterson; Costumes, Rusty Smith; Lighting, Michael Chybowski. CAST: Spencer Beglarian, Pearce Bunting, Robert Burns, Stephen Burks, Daniel Chance, Martin Donegan, John Doolittle, Charles S. Sutton, Marcus Giamatti, Aloysius Gigl, James Glossman, Robin Groves, Kirk Jackson, Henson Keys, Benjamin Lloyd, Pirie MacDonald, Edwin J. McDonough, Tom McGowan, Devora Millman, Philip Moon, Brennan Murphy, David Officer, Mark Rafael, Dana Smith
THE IMPORTANCE OF BEING EARNEST by Oscar Wilde; Director, Alvin Epstein; Set, Charles E. McCarry; Costumes, Tina Cantu Navarro; Lighting, Donald Holder. CAST: William Atherton, Tom Brennan, Kitty Crooks, Alice Drummond, Holly Felton, Tammy Grimes, Ben Halley Jr., David Officer, Eric Swanson
JOE TURNER'S COME AND GONE by August Wilson; *World Premiere;* Director, Lloyd Richards; Set, Scott Bradley; Costumes, Pamela Peterson; Lighting, Michael Giannitti; Musical Director, Dwight Andrews. CAST: Angelea Bassett, Kimberleigh Burroughs, L. Scott Caldwell, Charles S. Dutton, Ed Hall, Bo Rucker, Raynor Scheine, Kimberly Scott, Mel Winkler, Casey Lydell Badger, Cristal Coleman, Lamar James Federick, LaJara Henderson

William B. Carter, Paul J. Penders Photos

**Right: Susan Gibney, Pamela Payton-Wright,
Stephen McHattie in "Little Eyolf" Top:
Tammy Grimes in "The Importance of Being Earnest"**

Devora Millman, Charles S. Dutton
in "Othello"

LaJara Henderson, Charles S. Dutton
in "Joe Turner's Come and Gone"

ANNUAL SHAKESPEARE FESTIVALS

ALABAMA SHAKESPEARE FESTIVAL

Montgomery, Alabama
December 12, 1985–August 16, 1986
Premier Season at Wynfield

Artistic Director, Martin L. Platt; Managing Director, Jim Volz; Chairman of the Board, Winton M. Blount; General Manager, Doug Perry; Development, Barbara W. Larson; Marketing, Larry T. Stafford; Company Manager, Joseph Cowperthwaite; Production Manager, Mark D. Loigman; Sets, Philipp Jung, Mark Morton, Michael Stauffer; Costumes, Philipp Jung, Susan Rheaume, Kristine A. Kearny; Lighting, Paul Ackerman, Michael Stauffer, Michael Watson; Music Coordinator, Jim Conley; Stage Manager; Production Stage Manager, Sherrill DeWitt-Howard; Press, M. P. Wilkerson, Jay Drury

COMPANY: Charles Antalosky, Kermit Brown, Robert Browning, Evelyn Carol Case, Edward Conery, Bruce Cromer, James Donadio, Shannon Eubanks, Greta Lambert, Betty Leighton, Brian Martin, John Milligan, John Morrow, David O. Petersen, Harvey Phillips, Philip Pleasants, Paul Thomas, Peter Jack Tkatch, Joan Ulmer

PRODUCTIONS: Festival Theatre: A Midsummer Night's Dream by William Shakespeare, Death of a Salesman by Arthur Miller, Pygmalion by George Bernard Shaw, A Flea in Her Ear by Georges Feydeau with translation by John Mortimer, The School for Scandal by Richard Brinsley Sheridan, the Merry Wives of Windsor by William Shakespeare, Richard II by William Shakespeare, Octagon Theatre: The Glass Menagerie by Tennessee Williams, Betrayal by Harold Pinter, The Imaginary Heir by Jean-Francois Regnard adapted and translated by Freday Thomas (World Premiere)

Right: Bruce Cromer, A. D. Cover, Andrew Barnicle in "She Stoops to Conquer" Top: Lisa McMillan, Jack Wetherall in "Macbeth"

Theodore Swetz, Jim Stubbs, John Aden in "The Merry Wives of Windsor"

AMERICAN PLAYERS THEATRE

Spring Green, Wisconsin
June 25,–October 13, 1985
Sixth Season

Artistic Director, Randall Duk Kim; Managing Director, Charles Bright; General Manager, Francis X. Tobin; Literary Director, Ann Occhiogrosso; Set/Props, William Gleave; Lighting, Mark Nash; Music, Tim Schirmer, Douglas Brown; Fight Choreography, Brad Waller; Directors, Anne Occhiogrosso, Fred Ollerman, Sandra Reigel-Ernst, Theodore Swetz, Charles Bright; Stage Managers, Rhoda Nathan, Dana Graham, Colleen D. Lewis; Press, Dixie Legler

COMPANY Harvey Phillips, Steven A. Helmeke, David Cecsarini, Jim Stubbs, Karl Stoll, John Aden, Jonathan Herold, Randall Duk Kim, Jonathan Smoots, Theodore Swetz, Thomas Winslow, William Schlaht, Paul Bentzen, Lee Elmer Ernst, James Hulin, Brad Waller, Stephen Hemming, John Fionte, Drew C. Noll, Joel Hooks, Oksana Fedunyszyn, Alexandra Mitchell, Lucas G. Hendrickson, Rebecca Russell, Laurie Shaman, Anne Occhiogrosso, Fred Ollerman, Lisa Lawrence, Asa Wyatt Derks, Terry Kerr, Andrew Joel Notbohm, Jonathan Herold, Melissa Allen, Bethany Notbohm

PRODUCTIONS The Tragedy of Julius Caesar, The Comedy of Errors, The Merry Wives of Windsor, The Merchant of Venice, Three One-Act Plays by Chekhov: On the Harmfulness of Tobacco, The Bear, The Proposal

Zane Williams Photos

Left Center: Randall Duk Kim in "The Merchant of Venice"

BERKELEY SHAKESPEARE FESTIVAL

Berkeley, California
July 12,–September 22, 1985

Artistic Director, Dakin Matthews; Artistic Associate, Tessa Ross; Production Manager, Michael Cook; Technical Director, Dan Sweeney; Wardrobe, Rick Austin; Props, Eric Landisman, Melanie Chang; Managing Director/Press, John Maynard, Jr.; Stage Managers, Michael Cook, Carolyn Grigsby, Michael Cawelti; Lighting, Brad Belleville; Choreographer, Janet D. Bryant; Costumes, Barbara Bush, Frances Kenny, Patricia Polen; Sets, Eric Landisman, Peggy McDonald, Ron Pratt, Gene Angell; Music Director/Composer, Linda LaFlamme, Carl Smith

ACTING COMPANY: Chiron Alston, Richard Butterfield, Nancy Carlin, Mark Castillo, Michael Cawelti, Lura Dolas, Mike Doukas, Ann Houle, Peter Jacobs, Douglas Leach, Julian Lopez-Morillas, Louis Lotorto, Sandra Mackenzie, Dakin Matthews, Jarion King Monroe, Mykael O'Sruitheain, Tom Ramirez, Robert Sicular, Bob B. Hobbs, Kira LaFlamme, Andrew Matthews, Anne Matthews, Joey Pruger, Ron Sipes, Apprentices: Walter Brown, Lise Bruno, Cheryl DiCostanzo, Fred Franklin, Tracy Grant, Kathryn Knotts, Noel Phipps, Jacqueline Ravel, Blancett Reynolds, Tamra Shelley, Mare Skipper, Glenn Smith
PRODUCTIONS: A Midsummer Night's Dream by William Shakespeare; Director, Richard E. T. White; Two Noble Kinsmen by William Shakespeare and John Fletcher; Director, Julian Lopez-Morillas; Richard III by William Shakespeare; Director, Anne McNaughton

Allen Nomura Photos

Nancy Carlin, Robert Sicular, Jarion King Monroe in "Two Noble Kinsmen" Below: "A Midsummer Night's Dream" Left Center: Dakin Matthews, Nike Doukas in "Richard III" (Berkeley)

CHAMPLAIN SHAKESPEARE FESTIVAL

Burlington, Vermont
July 3,–August 10. 1985
Twenty-seventh Season

Producer/Artistic Director, Judith W. B. Williams; Associate Producer, William M. Schenk; Administrative Director, Judy Hallberg; Assistant to Producer, Kelly C. Morgan; Sets, Gary Eckhart, Patrick Orr; Costumes, Martin Thaler; Lighting Charles Schmidt; Props, Sandra Fleishman; Fight Choreographer, David Leong; Technical Director, Ross Keim; Music Director, George Bedell; Press, Mary Kerr, Marc Todd

COMPANY: Ray Chapman, Dale Ducko, Tom Fervoy, Hamilton Gillett, Jane Macfie, Dennis McIernon, Kelly C. Morgan, Catherine Nix, Gayton Scott, Bob Stanfield, Michelle Steckler, and David Borror, Paul-Andrew Cooley, Jonathan Hadley, Jeannie Hill, Nancy Hodgkins, Ellen Hulkower, Stephen O'Dwyer, Tom Watson, Eban Young
JUNIOR COMPANY: Herb Allen, Reinhard Bichsel, Anne Black, Valerie Cutko, Hope Davis, Frederique Destribats, Mary-Pat Farell, Sean Haberle, Diane Heller, Caitlin Hughes, Jim Kanelos, Greg Konzal, Julia Matthews, Becky Mode, Julie Mondin, Mary Neudecker, Matthew Norris, Ursula Oure, Kyran O'Dwyer, Olivia Parry, Neil Pepe, Michelle Rogosky, Lynn Seymour, Caroline Shrank, Jennifer Silver, Amanda Sloan, Laura Solinger, Will Warren
PRODUCTIONS: Hamlet by William Shakespeare; Director, Dudley Swetland; Man of La Mancha by Dale Wasserman; Director, Judith W. B. Williams; Charley's Aunt by Brandon Thomas; Director, Robert L. Hobbs

Rob Swanson Photos

Catherine Nix, Anne Black, Dennis McLernon in "Hamlet" (Champlain)

COLORADO SHAKESPEARE FESTIVAL

Boulder, Colorado
July 11,–August 24, 1985
Twenty-eighth Season

Producing Director, Daniel S. P. Yang; Directors, Robert Cohen, Leslie Reidel, James M. Symons; Scenery, Douglas-Scott Goheen, Richard M. Isackes, Randy McMullen; Costumes, James-Berton Harris, Anne Thaxter Watson, Lorraine Venberg; Lighting, Richard Devin; Press, Patti McFerran

COMPANY: Irwin Appel, Judith Aplon, Holly Baumgardner, William Charlton, Jack Cirillo, James DeVita, Tim Douglas, James Drevescraft, Christopher Duncan, Edith Elliot, Linda Edmond, Tom Ford, Thomas Freeland, Gregg Henry, Bill Higham, David Hirvela, Tim Hopper, Bruce Lecuru, Tim Loughrin, Lynn Mathis, William Michie, Carlton Miller, Frank Nall, Samuel Sandoe, Maggie Stewart, Robert Stormont, James Symons
PRODUCTIONS: Antony and Cleopatra directed by Libby Appel; Scenery, Robert Schmidt; Costumes, David A. Busse; The Merry Wives of Windsor directed by Paul Gaffney; Scenery, Robert Schmidt; Costumes, Gwendolyn Nagle; Romeo and Juliet directed by Will York; Scenery, Thrim Paulsen; Costumes, Lee Hodgson

Jerry Stowall Photos

Right: Carlton Miller in "Antony and Cleopatra"
Top: Lynn Mathis, Tom Ford in "Merry Wives of Windsor"

HOUSTON SHAKESPEARE FESTIVAL

Houston, Texas
August 2–17, 1985
Eleventh Season

Producing Director, Sidney Berger; Director, Charles Krohn; Set Designer, Keith Belli; Costume Designer, Barbara Medlicott; Lighting Designer, John A. Gow; Combat Director, Claude Caux; Music Coordinator/Composer, Robert Nelson; Production Manager, Jonathan Middents; Stage Managers, David Fitzgerald, Elizabeth A. Gross; Technical Director, Leo Schlosser; Special Effects/Makeup, Philip L. Nichols, Jr.; Props, Lori-Jo Brandafino; Press, Miriam Strane

PRODUCTIONS & CASTS

RICHARD III with Rita G. Oldham (Duchess of York), James Gale (Duke of Clarence), Frank Barrie (Richard III), Mary Agen Cos (Queen Elizabeth), Aaron Korhn (Edward Plantagenet), Cary Winscott (Richard), Katherine Hallowell (Lady Anne), Suzi Williams (Margaret), Bruce Ellis (Lord Rivers), Logan Bazar (Lord Grey), Kenneth Kyle Hudgins (Sir Thomas Vaughan), Rutherford Cravens (Duke of Buckingham), Timothy Hanson (Lord Hastings), Wayne Swallows (Bishop of Ely), James Black (Sir William Catesby), Michael Foster (Sir Richard Ratcliffe), Harry Booker (Sir James Tyrrel), Dennis Wells (Sir Robert Brakenbury/Lord Stanley), David Born (Duke of Norfolk), Sheila Plaisance (Lady Faulkenbridge), W. Ruth Kingsberry (Lady Pembroke)
MEASURE FOR MEASURE with James Black (Vincentio), Dennis Wells (Escalus), James Gale (Angelo), Timothy Hanson (Lucio), Vaughn Johnson, Jared Cooley (Friends to Lucio), Suzi Williams (Mistress Overdone), Bruce Ellis (Pompey), Michael Foster (Claudio), Wayne Swallows (Provost), Katherine Hallowell (Isabella), Rita G. Oldham (Francisca), Vaughn Johnson (Froth), Allison Pennel (Juliet), Mary Agen Cox (Mariana), Aaron Kroh (Boy), Logan Bazar (Friar Thomas/Abhorson), Harry Booker (Elbow/Barnardine), Jared Cooley (Friar Peter); Officers/Attendants: David Born, Kenneth Kyle Hudgins, Sheila Plainsance, Ruben Stubblefield

Jim Caldwell Photos

Frank Barrie as "Richard III"
Above: "Measure for Measure"
(Houston)

NEW JERSEY SHAKESPEARE FESTIVAL

Madison, New Jersey
June 26,–September 22, 1985
Twenty-first Season

Artistic Director/Stage Director, Paul Barry; Producing Director, Ellen Barry; Scenery, S. Mark Evancho; Costumes, Mitchell S. Bloom, Robin Borts, Jim Buff, Heidi Hollmann; Musical Director, Deborah Martin; Choreography, Caroline Worth-Tyrrell; Technical Director, Allan Abrams; Assistant to Producing Director, Gregory W. Cesear

EQUITY COMPANY: Dion Anderson, Neville Aurelius, N. Erick Avari, Ellen Barry, Paul Barry, Catherine Bayers, Brendan Burke, Ned Coulter, Regina David, Margaret Emory, David S. Howard, J. C. Hoyt, Vivien Landau, Robert Machray, Paul Meacham, Jane Moore, Frank Nastasi, Patrick T. O'Brien, Daniel O'Donnell, Don Perkins, William Preston, Cindy Rosenthal, Geddeth Smith, Thea Ruth White, Cal Winn
SUPPORTING COMPANY: Joanna Bache, John Blau, Catherine Bulger, Richard Carson, Na'ama Caspi, Adrienne Cuginia, Edward DeFord, Michael Dundon, Roxanne Eldred, Maureen Fagan, Dianne Fannell, Kate Forlenza, Jonathan Freiman, Domenica Galati, Kimberly Grieger, Jennifer Holan, Gretchen Holz, Valorie Hubbard, Linda Iannella, James Iorio, Thomas Jaeger, Karen Jones, Robert Michael Kane, Beverly Knox, Betha A. Kucharczyk, Gail Lelyveld, Debbie Lewisohn, Michael Mararian, Lindsay Millard, Deian Miller, Stephen Moser, Dorothy Pelovitz, Tom Pennacchini, Julie Potter, Kate Preston, Sophia Ransom, Carin Rose, George Ryan, Nada Salib, Matthew Samels, Tony Scoles, Anne Sussman, Brock-David Stovall, Diane Sykes, Elizabeth Van Tine, Catherine Verow, Mary Vining, Cece von der Heyde, Stephen Waldrup, Joseph Whelan, Nancy Wilkening, Alec Bauer, Andrew Black
PRODUCTIONS: Henry VIII by William Shakespeare, A Man for All Seasons by Robert Bolt, The Merry Wives of Windsor by William Shakespeare

Jim Chambers, Jim Del Guidice Photos

Regina David, Robert Machray in "Merry Wives of Windsor" Top: Ellen Barry in "A Lesson from Aloes" (NJSF)

D. B. Novak, Neil Alan Tadken, Peter Crook, Dawn Didawick, George Deloy, Kandis Chappell, David Ogden Stiers in "A Midsummer Night's Dream"

OLD GLOBE THEATRE

San Diego, California
June 7,–September 22, 1985
Fiftieth Season

Executive Producer, Craig Noel; Artistic Director, Jack O'Brien; Managing Director, Thomas Hall; Production Manager, Erica Young; Assistant Production Manager, Debbie Smaw; Production Coordinator/Lighting Design, John B. Forbes; Composer, Conrad Susa; Dramaturge, Diana Maddox; Scenic Designers, Fred M. Duer, Alan K. Okazaki; Douglas W. Schmidt, Richard Seger, Robert Morgan; Costumes, Lewis Brown, Sally Cleveland, Deborah M. Dryden, Robert Morgan; Lighting, Kent Dorsey, Greg Sullivan; Sound, Michael Holten, Michael Winston; Wardrobe, Cassandra Carpenter; Props, Ruth Long; Wigs/Makeup, Frank Bowers; Stage Managers, Douglas Pagliotti, Maria Carrera, Raul Moncada, Tamara Boutcher, Robert Drake, Peter Van Dyke; Press, William B. Eaton, Charlene Baldridge

ACTING COMPANY: Jacqueline Brookes, Helena Carroll, Kandis Chappell, Ludi Claire, Oliver Cliff, Jeffrey Combs, Frances Conroy, Peter Crook, George Deloy, Dawn Didawick, Larry Drake, Mitchell Edmonds, Jody Gelb, Margaret Gibson, Laurance Hugo, Charles Janasz, Richard Kneeland, Tom Lacy, Katherine McGrath, Jonathan McMurty, Deborah May, Thomas S. Oleniacz, Philip Reeves, William Roesch, Tom Rosqui, Janie Sell, David Ogden Stiers, Ian Trigger, Paxton Whitehead, James R. Winkler
YOUNG GLOBE COMPANY: Michael Gerald Barnhart, Craig Cavanah, Susan Gosdick, Ken Hicks, Mark Hofflund, Todd Jackson, Don R. McManus, Leah Maddrie, Reed C. Martin, Alison Stair Neet, D. B. Novak, Marsha June Robinson, James Schendel, Christine Sevec, Neil Alan Tadken
PRODUCTIONS: A Midsummer Night's Dream by William Shakespeare, directed by Jack O'Brien; Fallen Angels by Noel Coward, directed by Jack O'Brien and Tom Moore; Greater Tuna by Jaston Williams, Joe Sears and Ed Howard, directed by David McClendon; Painting Churches by Tina Howe, directed by Robert Berlinger; London Assurance by Dion Boucicault, directed by Craig Noel; Richard III by William Shakespeare, directed by John Houseman

John Peter Weiss Photos

Left Center: Tom Rosqui, Paxton Whitehead, Larry Drake, Frances Conroy in "Richard III"

OREGON SHAKESPEAREAN FESTIVAL

Ashland, Oregon
February 19,–October 27, 1985
Fiftieth Season

Artistic Director, Jerry Turner; Executive Director, William Patton; Associate Director, Pat Patton; General Manager, Paul Nicholson; Costumes, Jeannie Davidson, Deborah M. Dryden, Claudia Everett, Frances Kenny; Fights, David I. Boushey; Lighting, Robert Peterson, Gregg Sulivan; Music, Todd Barton; Scenery, William Bloodgood, Richard L. Hay, Jesse Hollis; Production Manager, Tom Knapp; Hairstylist, Ranny Beyer; Wardrobe, Lynn M. Ramey; Props, Paul-James Martin; Sound, Douglas K. Faerber; Stage Managers, Lee Alan Byron, Kirk M. Boyd, Kimberley Jean Barry, Peggy I. Fantozzi; Press, Margaret Rubin, Sally K. White, Cynthia Fuhrman

ACTING COMPANY: Tobias Andersen, Denis Arndt, Wayne Ballantyne, Gloria Biegler, Wesley Grant Bishop, John David Castellanos, Philip Davidson, Corky Dexter, Milan Dragicevich, James Edmondson, Richard Elmore, Bill Geisslinger, Skip Greer, Torrey Hanson, Dan Dremer, Priscilla Hake Lauris, Dee Maaske, Douglas Markkanen, Steven Martin-Beck, Michael McCarrell, William McKereghan, Penny Metropulos, Paul V. O'Connor, Shirley Patton, Jeanne Paulsen, Larry Paulsen, Daniel Renner, Paul Roland, Margaret Rubin, Nancy Ryan, Stephanie Shine, Philip Charles Sneed, Carla Spindt, Joan Stuart-Morris, Kamella Tate, David Thompson, Brian Tyrrell, Elizabeth Ury, Joe Vincent
PRODUCTIONS: The Tragedy of King Lear by William Shakespeare, directed by Jerry Turner; Light Up the Sky by Moss Hart, directed by Pat Patton; Trelawny of the "Wells" by Arthur Wing Pinero, directed by James Edmondson; Crimes of the Heart by Beth Henley, directed by James Moll; An Enemy of the People directed by Jerry Turner; The Merchant of Venice by Shakespeare, directed by Albert Takazauckas; King John by Shakespeare, directed by Pat Patton; All's Well That Ends Well J. Traister; *World Premieres* of The Majestic Kid by Mark Medoff, directed by Edward Hastings; Lizzie Borden in the Late Afternoon by Cather MacCallum, directed by Lou Salerni

Hank Kranzler Photos

Left: Denis Arndt as "King Lear"

Priscilla Hake Lauris, Joan Stuart-Morris, Kamella Tate in "Crimes of the Heart"

Terri McMahon, Dan Kremer in "The Tempest"

185

SHAKESPEARE & COMPANY

Lenox, Massachusetts
July 6,–August 31, 1985
Eighth Season

Artistic Director, Tina Packer; Director of Training, Kristin Linklater; Associate Director, Dennis Krausnick; Costumes, Kiki Smith; Production Manager/Sets/Lighting, Bill Ballou; Props, Katherine Conklin, Debra Schutt; Sound, Janet Kalas; Wardrobe, Georgia Carney, Leslie Miller; General Manager, Ann Olson; Development, Beth Logan Balmuth; Stage Managers, J. P. Elins, Jane Hubbard; Press, Susannah Rake, Kate Maguire, Jared Waye.

PRODUCTIONS & CASTS

THE COMEDY OF ERRORS by William Shakespeare; Director, Tina Parker; Music Composer, Bruce Odland; Clownmaster, Merry Conway; Text Analyst, Neil Freeman. CAST: William Denis (Egeon), John Michalski (Solinus), Brian Calloway (Jailer), John Hadden (Antipholus of Syracuse), Jon Matthews (Dromio of Syracuse), Cliff Abramson (1st Merchant), James Newcomb (Dromio of Ephesus), Patricia Norcia (Adriana), Christine Adaire (Luciana), Michael Hammond (Antipholus of Ephesus), Charles M. Geyer (Balthazar), Michael Mauldin (Angelo), Earle Edgerton (2nd Merchant), Kathryn Wilson (Courtesan), Victor Love (Dr. Pinch), Louis Colaianni (Luce), Kristin Linklater (Emilia), Lawrence Nathanson (Servant to Adriana), and Gregory Allen, Rafael Baez, Wesley Clark, Suzanne Dudley, Robert Jimenez, Ezra Knight, Patricia Knowlton, Michaela Murphy, Oliver Platt, Kenneth Ransom, Gus Rogerson, Amy Smukler, Andrew Wilce, Lon Withers

MUCH ADO ABOUT NOTHING by William Shakespeare; Director, Derek Goldby; Scenery/Costumes, John Pennoyer; Assistant Designer, Kiki Smith; Music composed and directed by Eric Alexander; Choreography, Susan Dibble. CAST: William Denis (Leonato), James Newcomb (1st Messenger/1st Watch), Victor Love (Don Pedro), Elaine Bromka (Beatrice), Michael Mauldin (Don John), Jon Matthews (Claudio), James McDonnell (Benedick), Earle Edgerton (Antonio), Charles M. Geyer (Conrade), Michael Hammond (Borachio), Cliff Abramson (Balthazar), Patricia Norcia (Hero), Kathryn Wilson (Margaret), Christine Adaire (Ursula), Hamish Linklater (Boy), John Michalski (Verges), Louis Colaianni (2nd Watch), Lawrence Nathanson (3rd Watch), Delroy Lindo (Friar Francis), John Hadden (Sexton), Gregory Alle, Rafael Baez, Wesley Clark, Suzanne Dudley, Robert Jimenez, Ezra Knight, Patricia Knowlton, Michaela Murphy, Oliver Platt, Kenneth Ransom, Gus Rogerson, Amy Smukler, Andrew Wilce, Lon Withers

Robert D. Lohbauer Photos

Susan Coyne, Sada Thompson
in "The Glass Menagerie"

Nicholas Pennell, Douglas Campbell
in "King Lear"

Michael Hammond, Natsuko Ohama
in "Romeo and Juliet" (Shakespeare & Co.)

STRATFORD FESTIVAL

Stratford, Ontario, Canada
May 26,–October 13, 1985
Thirty-third Season

Artistic Director, John Hirsch; Executive Director, Gerry Eldred; Artistic Director Designate/Director Young Company, John Neville; Producer, Peter Roberts; Communications, Elizabeth Bradley; Director of Production, Richard C. Dennison; Literary Manager, Michal Schonberg; Production Manager, Dwight Griffin; Technical Directors, Neil McLeod, Peter Lamb; Company Manager, Robert Beard; Directors/Choreographers, Michael Bogdanov, John Broome, Laura Burton, Ronald Eyre, David Giles, John Hirsch, Brian Macdonald, John Neville, Edwin Stephenson, Paula Thomson, David William; Designers, Polly Scranton Bohdanetzky, Chris Dyer, Ralph Funicello, Lesley Macaulay, Suzanne Mess, Tanya Moiseiwitsch, Christina Poddubiuk, Phillip Silver, Judy Peyton Ward; Lighting, Harry Frehner, Louis Guinand, Michael J. Whitfield; Composers/Writers, Louis Applebaum, Jim Betts, Berthold Carriere, Gary Kulesha, Erika Ritter, Michal Schonberg, Stanley Silverman; Stage Managers, Margaret Palmer, Penelope Sharp, Meg Westley; Press, Ann Selby

COMPANY: Wendy Abbott, Donald Adams, Marion Adler, Edward Atienza, Stephen Beamish, Michael Beattie, Mervyn Blake, James Blendick, John Bourgeois, Simon Bradbury, James Bradford, Jay Brazeau, Kelly Bricker, Benedict Campbell, Douglas Campbell, Brent Carver, Douglas Chamberlain, Kim Coates, Joy Coghill, Patricia Collins, Caro Coltman, Patricia Conolly, Susan Coyne, Timothy Cruikshank, Keith Dinicol, Peter Donat, Eric Donkin, William Dunlop, Ted Dykstra, Aggie Cekuta Elliot, Colm Feore, Don Fiore, Sharry Flett, Roger Forbes, David Gale, Pat Galloway, Richard Gilbert-Hill, Maurice Godin, Lewis Gordon, Allison Grant, Nigel Hamer, Mary Haney, Ernest Harrop, James Haworth, Max Helpmann, Scott Hurst, Jeff Hyslop, Nolan Jennings, David Keeley, Charles Kerr, Julie Khaner, Elizabeth Leigh-Milne, Janet MacDonald, Larry Mannell, Jefferson Mappin, Barbara March, Richard March, Robert McClure, Eric McCormack, Elizabeth McDonald, Seana McKenna, Richard McMillan, Kevin McNulty, Dale Mieske, John Moffat, Susan Morgan, William Needles, Rith Nichol, Brian Paul, Lucy Peacock, Ted Pearson, Nicholas Pennell, Jeffrey Prentice, Max Reimer, David Renton, Lindsay Richardson, Maria Ricossa, Howard Rosenstein, Hane Roth-Casson, Bradley C. Rudy, Stephen Russell, Larry Russo, Alan Scarfe, Michael Shepherd, Karen Skidmore, Brent Stait, Keith Thomas, Sada Thompson, Caralyn Tomlin, William Vickers, Gwynyth Walsh, Scott Wentworth, Tim Whelan, Jim White, Mark Wilson, Karen Wood, Joseph Ziegler, Eric Zivot

PRODUCTIONS: King Lear, Twelfth Night, Measure for Measure by William Shakespeare, The Government Inspector by Nikolai Gogol, The Pirates of Penzance by Gilbert and Sullivan, She Stoops to Conquer by Oliver Goldsmith, The Glass Menagerie by Tennessee Williams, Antigone by Sophocles, The Beaux Strategem by George Farquhar

David Cooper Photos

Left Center: Peter Donat, Richard McMillan
in "The Government Inspector"; Lucy Peacock,
Janet Macdonald in "Beaux Stratagem"

PULITZER PRIZE PRODUCTIONS

1918-Why Marry? **1919-**No award, **1920-**Beyond the Horizon, **1921-**Miss Lulu Bett, **1922-**Anna Christie, **1923-**Icebound, **1924-**Hell-Bent fer Heaven, **1925-**They Knew What They Wanted, **1926-**Craig's Wife, **1927-**In Abraham's Bosom, **1928-**Strange Interlude, **1929-**Street Scene, **1930-**The Green Pastures, **1931-**Alison's House, **1932-**Of Thee I Sing, **1933-**Both Your Houses, **1934-**Men in White, **1935-**The Old Maid, **1936-**Idiot's Delight, **1937-**You Can't Take It with You, **1938-**Our Town, **1939-**Abe Lincoln in Illinois, **1940-**The Time of Your Life, **1941-**There Shall Be No Night, **1942-**No award, **1943-**The Skin of Our Teeth, **1944-**No award, **1945-**Harvey, **1946-**State of the Union, **1947-**No award, **1948-**A Streetcar Named Desire, **1949-**Death of a Salesman, **1950-**South Pacific, **1951-**No award, **1952-**The Shrike, **1953-**Picnic, **1954-**The Teahouse of the August Moon, **1955-**Cat on a Hot Tin Roof, **1956-**The Diary of Anne Frank, **1957-**Long Day's Journey into Night, **1958-**Look Homeward, Angel, **1959-**J. B., **1960-**Fiorello!, **1961-**All the Way Home, **1962-**How to Succeed in Business without Really Trying, **1963-**No award, **1964-**No award, **1965-**The Subject Was Roses, **1966-**No award, **1967-**A Delicate Balance, **1968-**No award, **1969-**The Great White Hope, **1970-**No Place to Be Somebody, **1971-**The Effect of Gamma Rays on Man-in-the-Moon Marigolds, **1972-**No award, **1973-**That Championship Season, **1974-**No award, **1975-**Seascape, **1976-**A Chorus Line, **1977-**The Shadow Box, **1978-**The Gin Game, **1979-**Buried Child, **1980-**Talley's Folly, **1981-**Crimes of the Heart, **1982-**A Soldier's Play, **1983-**'night Mother, **1984-**Glengarry Glen Ross, **1985-**Sunday in the Park with George, **1986-**No award

NEW YORK DRAMA CRITICS CIRCLE AWARDS

1936-Winterset, **1937-**High Tor, **1938-**Of Mice and Men, Shadow and Substance, **1939-**The White Steed, **1940-**The Time of Your Life, **1941-**Watch on the Rhine, The Corn is Green, **1942-**Blithe Spirit, **1943-**The Patriots, **1944-**Jacobowsky and the Colonel, **1945-**The Glass Menagerie, **1946-**Carousel, **1947-**All My Sons, No Exit, Brigadoon, **1948-**A Streetcar Named Desire, The Winslow Boy, **1949-**Death of a Salesman, The Madwoman of Chaillot, South Pacific, **1950-**The Member of the Wedding, The Cocktail Party, The Consul, **1951-**Darkness at Noon, The Lady's Not for Burning, Guys and Dolls, **1952-**I Am a Camera, Venus Observed, Pal Joey, **1953-** Picnic, The Love of Four Colonels, Wonderful Town, **1954-**Teahouse of the August Moon, Ondine, The Golden Apple, **1955-**Cat on a Hot Tin Roof, Witness for the Prosecution, The Saint of Bleecker Street, **1956-**The Diary of Anne Frank, Tiger at the Gates, My Fair Lady, **1957-**Long Day's Journey into Night, The Waltz of the Toreadors, The Most Happy Fella, **1958-**Look Homeward Angel, Look Back in Anger, The Music Man, **1959-**A Raisin in the Sun, The Visit, La Plume de Ma Tante, **1960-**Toys in the Attic, Five Finger Exercise, Fiorello! **1961-**All the Way Home, A Taste of Honey, Carnival, **1962-**Night of the Iguana, A Man for All Seasons, How to Succeed in Business without Really Trying, **1963-**Who's Afraid of Virginia Woolf?, **1964-**Luther, Hello Dolly!, **1965-**The Subject Was Roses, Fiddler on the Roof, **1966-**The Persecution and Assassination of Marat as Performed by the Inmates of the Asylum of Charenton under the Direction of the Marquis de Sade, Man of La Mancha, **1967-**The Homecoming, Cabaret, **1968-**Rosencrantz and Guildenstern Are Dead, Your Own Thing, **1969-**The Great White Hope, 1776, **1970-**The Effect of Gamma Rays on Man-in-the-Moon Marigolds, Borstal Boy, Company, **1971-**Home, Follies, The House of Blue Leaves, **1972-**That Championship Season, Two Gentlemen of Verona, **1973-**The Hot l Baltimore, The Changing Room, A Little Night Music, **1974-**The Contractor, Short Eyes, Candide, **1975-**Equus, The Taking of Miss Janie, A Chorus Line, **1976-**Travesties, Streamers, Pacific Overtures, **1977-**Otherwise Engaged, American Buffalo, Annie, **1978-**Da, Ain't Misbehavin', **1979-**The Elephant Man, Sweeney Todd, **1980-**Talley's Folly, Evita, Betrayal, **1981-**Crimes of the Heart, A Lesson from Aloes, Special Citation to Lena Horne, "The Pirates of Penzance, **1982-**The Life and Adventures of Nicholas Nickleby, A Soldier's Play, (no musical honored), **1983-**Brighton Beach Memoirs, Plenty, Little Shop of Horrors, **1984-**The Real Thing, Glengarry Glen Ross, Sunday in the Park with George, **1985-**Ma Rainey's Black Bottom, (no musical), **1986-**A Lie of the Mind, Benefactors, no musical, Special to Lily Tomlin and Jane Wagner

AMERICAN THEATRE WING ANTOINETTE PERRY (TONY) AWARD PRODUCTIONS

1948-Mister Roberts, **1949-**Death of a Salesman, Kiss Me, Kate, **1950-**The Cocktail Party, South Pacific, **1951-**The Rose Tattoo, Guys and Dolls, **1952-**The Fourposter, The King and I, **1953-**The Crucible, Wonderful Town, **1954-**The Teahouse of the August Moon, Kismet, **1955-**The Desperate Hours, The Pajama Game, **1956-**The Diary of Anne Frank, Damn Yankees, **1957-**Long Day's Journey into Night, My Fair Lady, **1958-**Sunrise at Campobello, The Music Man, **1959-**J. B., Redhead, **1960-**The Miracle Worker, Fiorello! tied with The Sound of Music, **1961-**Becket, Bye Bye Birdie, **1962-**A Man for All Seasons, How to Succeed in Business without Really Trying, **1963-**Who's Afraid of Virginia Woolf?, A Funny Thing Happened on the Way to the Forum, **1964-**Luther, Hello Dolly!, **1965-**The Subject Was Roses, Fiddler on the Roof, **1966-**The Persecution and Assassination of Marat as Performed by the Inmates of the Asylum of Charenton under the Direction of the Marquis de Sade, Man of La Mancha, **1967-**The Homecoming, Cabaret, **1968-**Rosencrantz and Guildenstern Are Dead, Hallelujah Baby!, **1969-**The Great White Hope, 1776, **1970-**Borstal Boy, Applause, **1971-**Sleuth, Company, **1972-**Sticks and Bones, Two Gentlemen of Verona, **1973-**That Championship Season, A Little Night Music, **1974-**The River Niger, Raisin, **1975-**Equus, The Wiz, **1976-**Travesties, A Chorus Line, **1977-**The Shadow Box, Annie, **1978-**Da, Ain't Misbehavin', Dracula, **1979-**The Elephant Man, Sweeney Todd, **1980-**Children of a Lesser God, Evita, Morning's at Seven, **1981-**Amadeus, 42nd Street, The Pirates of Penzance, **1982-**The Life and Adventures of Nicholas Nickleby, Nine, Othello, **1983-**Torch Song Trilogy, Cats, On Your Toes, **1984-**The Real Thing, La Cage aux Folles, **1985-**Biloxi Blues, Big River, Joe Egg, **1986-**I'm Not Rappaport, The Mystery of Edwin Drood, Sweet Charity

PREVIOUS THEATRE WORLD AWARD WINNERS

1944-45: Betty Comden, Richard Davis, Richard Hart, Judy Holliday, Charles Lang, Bambi Linn, John Lund, Donald Murphy, Nancy Noland, Margaret Phillips, John Raitt

1945-46: Barbara Bel Geddes, Marlon Brando, Bill Callahan, Wendell Corey, Paul Douglas, Mary James, Burt Lancaster, Patricia Marshall, Beatrice Pearson

1946-47: Keith Andes, Marion Bell, Peter Cookson, Ann Crowley, Ellen Hanley, John Jordan, George Keane, Dorothea MacFarland, James Mitchell, Patricia Neal, David Wayne

1947-48: Valerie Bettis, Edward Bryce, Whitfield Connor, Mark Dawson, June Lockhart, Estelle Loring, Peggy Maley, Ralph Meeker, Meg Mundy, Douglass Watson, James Whitmore, Patrice Wymore

1948-49: Tod Andrews, Doe Avedon, Jean Carson, Carol Channing, Richard Derr, Julie Harris, Mary McCarty, Allyn Ann McLerie, Cameron Mitchell, Gene Nelson, Byron Palmer, Bob Scheerer

1949-50: Nancy Andrews, Phil Arthur, Barbara Brady, Lydia Clarke, Priscilla Gillette, Don Hanmer, Marcia Henderson, Charlton Heston, Rick Jason, Grace Kelly, Charles Nolte, Roger Price

1950-51: Barbara Ashley, Isabel Bigley, Martin Brooks, Richard Burton, Pat Crowley, James Daly, Cloris Leachman, Russell Nype, Jack Palance, William Smothers, Maureen Stapleton, Marcia Van Dyke, Eli Wallach

1951-52: Tony Bavaar, Patricia Benoit, Peter Conlow, Virginia de Luce, Ronny Graham, Audrey Hepburn, Diana Herbert, Conrad Janis, Dick Kallman, Charles Proctor, Eric Sinclair, Kim Stanley, Marian Winters, Helen Wood

1952-53: Edie Adams, Rosemary Harris, Eileen Heckart, Peter Kelley, John Kerr, Richard Kiley, Gloria Marlowe, Penelope Munday, Paul Newman, Sheree North, Geraldine Page, John Stewart, Ray Stricklyn, Gwen Verdon

1953-54: Orson Bean, Harry Belafonte, James Dean, Joan Diener, Ben Gazzara, Carol Haney, Jonathan Lucas, Kay Medford, Scott Merrill, Elizabeth Montgomery, Leo Penn, Eva Marie Saint

1954-55: Julie Andrews, Jacqueline Brookes, Shirl Conway, Barbara Cook, David Daniels, Mary Fickett, Page Johnson, Loretta Leversee, Jack Lord, Dennis Patrick, Anthony Perkins, Christopher Plummer

1955-56: Diane Cilento, Dick Davalos, Anthony Franciosa, Andy Griffith, Laurence Harvey, David Hedison, Earle Hyman, Susan Johnson, John Michael King, Jayne Mansfield, Sara Marshall, Gaby Rodgers, Susan Strasberg, Fritz Weaver.

1956-57: Peggy Cass, Sydney Chaplin, Sylvia Daneel, Bradford Dillman, Peter Donat, George Grizzard, Carol Lynley, Peter Palmer, Jason Robards, Cliff Robertson, Pippa Scott, Inga Swenson

1957-58: Anne Bancroft, Warren Berlinger, Colleen Dewhurst, Richard Easton, Tim Everett, Eddie Hodges, Joan Hovis, Carol Lawrence, Jacqueline McKeever, Wynne Miller, Robert Morse, George C. Scott

1958-59: Lou Antonio, Ina Balin, Richard Cross, Tammy Grimes, Larry Hagman, Dolores Hart, Roger Mollien, France Nuyen, Susan Oliver, Ben Piazza, Paul Roebling, William Shatner, Pat Suzuki, Rip Torn

1959-60: Warren Beatty, Eileen Brennan, Carol Burnett, Patty Duke, Jane Fonda, Anita Gillette, Elisa Loti, Donald Madden, George Maharis, John McMartin, Lauri Peters, Dick Van Dyke

1960-61: Joyce Bulifant, Dennis Cooney, Sandy Dennis, Nancy Dussault, Robert Goulet, Joan Hackett, June Harding, Ron Husmann, James MacArthur, Bruce Yarnell

1961-62: Elizabeth Ashley, Keith Baxter, Peter Fonda, Don Galloway, Sean Garrison, Barbara Harris, James Earl Jones, Janet Margolin, Karen Morrow, Robert Redford, John Stride, Brenda Vaccaro

1962-63: Alan Arkin, Stuart Damon, Melinda Dillon, Robert Drivas, Bob Gentry, Dorothy Loudon, Brandon Maggart, Julienne Marie, Liza Minnelli, Estelle Parsons, Diana Sands, Swen Swenson

1963-64: Alan Alda, Gloria Bleezarde, Imelda De Martin, Claude Giraud, Ketty Lester, Barbara Loden, Lawrence Pressman, Gilbert Price, Philip Proctor, John Tracy, Jennifer West.

1964-65: Carolyn Coates, Joyce Jillson, Linda Lavin, Luba Lisa, Michael O'Sullivan, Joanna Pettet, Beah Richards, Jaime Sanchez, Victor Spinetti, Nicolas Surovy, Robert Walker, Clarence Williams III

1965-66: Zoe Caldwell, David Carradine, John Cullum, John Davidson, Faye Dunaway, Gloria Foster, Robert Hooks, Jerry Lanning, Richard Mulligan, April Shawhan, Sandra Smith, Leslie Ann Warren

1966-67: Bonnie Bedelia, Richard Benjamin, Dustin Hoffman, Terry Kiser, Reva Rose, Robert Salvio, Sheila Smith, Connie Stevens, Pamela Tiffin, Leslie Uggams, Jon Voight, Christopher Walken

1967-68: David Birney, Pamela Burrell, Jordan Christopher, Jack Crowder (Thalmus Rasulala), Sandy Duncan, Julie Gregg, Stephen Joyce, Bernadette Peters, Alice Playten, Michael Rupert, Brenda Smiley, Russ Thacker

1968-69: Jane Alexander, David Cryer, Blythe Danner, Ed Evanko, Ken Howard, Lauren Jones, Ron Leibman, Marian Mercer, Jill O'Hara, Ron O'Neal, Al Pacino, Marlene Warfield

1969-70: Susan Browning, Donny Burks, Catherine Burns, Len Cariou, Bonnie Franklin, David Holliday, Katharine Houghton, Melba Moore, David Rounds, Lewis J. Stadlen, Kristoffer Tabori, Fredricka Weber

1970-71: Clifton Davis, Michael Douglas, Julie Garfield, Martha Henry, James Naughton, Tricia O'Neil, Kipp Osborne, Roger Rathburn, Ayn Ruymen, Jennifer Salt, Joan Van Ark, Walter Willison

1971-72: Jonelle Allen, Maureen Anderman, William Atherton, Richard Backus, Adrienne Barbeau, Cara Duff-MacCormick, Robert Foxworth, Elaine Joyce, Jess Richards, Ben Vereen, Beatrice Winde, James Woods

1972-73: D'Jamin Bartlett, Patricia Elliott, James Farentino, Brian Farrell, Victor Garber, Kelly Garrett, Mari Gorman, Laurence Guittard, Trish Hawkins, Monte Markham, John Rubinstein, Jennifer Warren, Alexander H. Cohen (Special Award)

1973-74: Mark Baker, Maureen Brennan, Ralph Carter, Thom Christopher, John Driver, Conchata Ferrell, Ernestine Jackson, Michael Moriarty, Joe Morton, Ann Reinking, Janie Sell, Mary Woronov, Sammy Cahn (Special Award)

1974-75: Peter Burnell, Zan Charisse, Lola Falana, Peter Firth, Dorian Harewood, Joel Higgins, Marcia McClain, Linda Miller, Marti Rolph, John Sheridan, Scott Stevensen, Donna Theodore, Equity Library Theatre (Special Award)

1975-76: Danny Aiello, Christine Andreas, Dixie Carter, Tovah Feldshuh, Chip Garnett, Richard Kelton, Vivian Reed, Charles Repole, Virginia Seidel, Daniel Seltzer, John V. Shea, Meryl Streep, A Chorus Line (Special Award)

1976-77: Trazana Beverley, Michael Cristofer, Joe Fields, Joanna Gleason, Cecilia Hart, John Heard, Gloria Hodes, Juliette Koka, Andrea McArdle, Ken Page, Jonathan Pryce, Chick Vennera, Eva LeGallienne (Special Award)

1977-78: Vasili Bogazianos, Nell Carter, Carlin Glynn, Christopher Goutman, William Hurt, Judy Kaye, Florence Lacy, Armelia McQueen, Gordana Rashovich, Bo Rucker, Richard Seer, Colin Stinton, Joseph Papp (Special Award)

1978-79: Philip Anglim, Lucie Arnaz, Gregory Hines, Ken Jennings, Michael Jeter, Laurie Kennedy, Susan Kingsley, Christine Lahti, Edward James Olmos, Kathleen Quinlan, Sarah Rice, Max Wright, Marshall W. Mason (Special Award)

1979-80: Maxwell Caulfield, Leslie Denniston, Boyd Gaines, Richard Gere, Harry Groener, Stephen James, Susan Kellermann, Dinah Manoff, Lonnie Price, Marianne Tatum, Anne Twomey, Dianne Wiest, Mickey Rooney (Special Award)

1980-81: Brian Backer, Lisa Banes, Meg Bussert, Michael Allen Davis, Giancarlo Esposito, Daniel Gerroll, Phyllis Hyman, Cynthia Nixon, Amanda Plummer, Adam Redfield, Wanda Richert, Rex Smith, Elizabeth Taylor (Special Award)

1981-82: Karen Akers, Laurie Beechman, Danny Glover, David Alan Grier, Jennifer Holliday, Anthony Heald, Lizbeth Mackay, Peter MacNicol, Elizabeth McGovern, Ann Morrison, Michael O'Keefe, James Widdoes, Manhatten Theatre Club (Special Award)

1982-83: Karen Allen, Suzanne Bertish, Matthew Broderick, Kate Burton, Joanne Camp, Harvey Fierstein, Peter Gallagher, John Malkovich, Anne Pitoniak, James Russo, Brian Tarantina, Linda Thorson, Natalia Makarova

1983-84: Martine Allard, Joan Allen, Kathy Whitton Baker, Mark Capri, Laura Dean, Stephen Geoffreys, Todd Graff, Glenne Headly, J. J. Johnston, Bonnie Koloc, Calvin Levels, Robert Westenberg, Ron Moody

1984-85: Kevin Anderson, Richard Chaves, Patti Cohenour, Charles S. Dutton, Nancy Giles, Whoopi Goldberg, Leilani Jones, John Mahoney, Laurie Metcalf, Barry Miller, John Turturro, Amelia White

Betty Comden

David Carradine

Carol Lawrence

James Earl Jones

Meryl Streep

John Rubinstein

1986 THEATRE WORLD AWARD WINNERS
(Outstanding New Talent)

SUZY AMIS
of "Fresh Horses"

ALEC BALDWIN
of "Loot"

ALED DAVIES
of "Orchards"

FAYE GRANT
of "Singin' in the Rain"

JULIE HAGERTY
of "House of Blue Leaves"

ED HARRIS
of "Precious Sons"

MARK JACOBY
of "Sweet Charity"

DONNA KANE
of "Dames at Sea"

CLEO LAINE
of "Edwin Drood"

HOWARD McGILLIN
of "Edwin Drood"

JOE URLA
of "Principia Scriptoriae"

MARISA TOMEI
of "Daughters"

191

THEATRE WORLD AWARDS presentations, Thursday, May 29, 1986. Top: Maureen Stapleton, Bernadette Peters, George Grizzard, Blythe Danner, John Shea, Patricia Neal; Laurie Beechman, Walter Willison; Fredricka Weber, Colleen Dewhurst, Peter Gallagher, Dorothy Loudon, Michael Rupert Below: Alec Baldwin, Christine Andreas; George Grizzard, Julie Hagerty; Michael Rupert, Anita Gillette, John McMartin Bottom: Mark Jacoby, Lynn Meadow, Marisa Tomei, John Shea, Donna Kane Above: Marilyn Fried (for Suzy Amis), Howard McGillin, Blythe Danner, Joe Urla, Colleen Dewhurst, John McMartin, Eric Shepard (for Faye Grant)

Michael Viade, Van Williams Photos

Top: John Springer (for Ed Harris); Patricia Neal, Maureen Stapleton, Dina Merrill; Spalding Gray (for Aled Davies), Risa Bramen (for Ensemble Studio Theatre); **Below:** Stuart Klein, Colleen Dewhurst; Dorothy Loudon, Peter Gallagher, Cleo Laine **Bottom:** Michael Rupert; Bernadette Peters, George Grizzard, Blythe Danner; Fredricka Weber Above: Lucille Lortel, Drew Eliot; Karen Allen, John Shea, Blythe Danner, Barry Landau, Patricia Neal; Bernadette Peters

Michael Viade, Van Williams Photos

193

Caroline
Aaron

Danny
Aiello

Karen
Akers

Robert
Arcaro

Margaret
Barker

Stockman
Barner

BIOGRAPHICAL DATA ON THIS SEASON'S CASTS

AARON, CAROLINE. Born Aug. 7, 1954 in Richmond, Va. Graduate Catholic U. Bdwy debut 1982 in "Come Back to the 5 & Dime, Jimmy Dean," followed by "The Iceman Cometh," OB in "Flying Blind," "Last Summer at Bluefish Cove," "Territorial Rites," "Good Bargains," "The House of Bernarda Alba," "Tribute."

AARON, JACK. Born May 1, 1933 in NYC. Attended Hunter Col., Actors Workshop. OB in "Swim Low Little Goldfish," "Journey of the 5th Horse," "The Nest," "One Flew Over the Cuckoo's Nest," "The Birds," "The Pornographer's Daughter," "Love Death Plays," "Unlikely Heroes," "Taking Steam," "Mark VIII: xxxvi."

ABERLIN, BETTY. Born Dec. 30, 1942 in NYC. Graduate Bennington Col. Debut 1954 OB in "Sandhog," followed by "Upstairs at the Downstairs," "I'm Getting My Act Together," "Alice in Concert," "Yours Anne," Bdwy 1964 in "Cafe Crown."

ABRAHAM, F. MURRAY. Born Oct. 24, 1939 in Pittsburgh, PA. Attended UTx. Debut OB 1967 in "The Fantasticks," followed by "An Opening in the Trees," "14th Dictator," "Young Abe Lincoln," "Tonight in Living Color," "Adaptation," "Survival of St. Joan," "The Dog Ran Away," "Fables," "Richard III," "Little Murders," "Scuba Duba," "Where Has Tommy Flowers Gone?," "Miracle Play," "Blessing," "Sexual Perversity in Chicago," "Landscape of the Body," "The Master and Margarita," "Biting the Apple," "The Seagull," "Caretaker," "Antigone," "Uncle Vanya," "The Golem," "Madwoman of Chaillot," "Twelfth Night," Bdwy in "Man in the Glass Booth"(1968), "6 Rms Riv Vu," "Bad Habits," "The Ritz," "Legend," "Teibele and Her Demon."

ABUBA, ERNEST. Born Aug. 25, 1947 in Honolulu, HI. Attended Southwestern Col. Bdwy debut 1976 in "Pacific Overtures," followed by "Loose Ends." OB in "Sunrise," "Monkey Music," "Station J.," "Yellow Fever," "Pacific Overtures," "Empress of China," "Man Who Turned into a Stick."

ADAMS, MASON. Born Feb. 26, 1919 in NYC. UWisc. graduate. Bdwy credits include "Get Away Old Man," "Public Relations," "Career Angel," "Violet," "Shadow of My Enemy," "Tall Story," "Inquest," "Trial of the Catonsville 9," "The Sign in Sidney Brustein's Window," OB in "Meegan's Game," "Shortchanged Review," "Checking Out," "The Soft Touch," "Paradise Lost," "The Time of Your Life."

ADAMSON, DAVID. Born May 30, 1940 in Orange, NJ. Graduate Bucknell, Yale. Bdwy debut 1971 in "Unlikely Heroes," followed by "Full Circle," "Hamlet," "Hide and Seek," "Children of a Lesser God," OB in "Isadora Duncan Sleeps with the Russian Navy," "Sister Aimee," "Hamlet," "Happy Birthday Wanda June," "Henry V," "Ice Bridge."

ADAMSON, ELLEN. Born in Atlanta, Ga., July 13, 1956. Neighborhood Playhouse, Stanford U. graduate. Debut 1983 OB in "The Triptych," followed by "The Park," "Midsummer Night's Dream."

ADLER, BRUCE Born Nov. 27, 1944 in NYC. Attended NYU. Debut 1957 OB in "It's a Funny World," followed by "Hard to Be a Jew," "Big Winner," "The Golden Land," Bdwy in "A Teaspoon Every Four Hours" (1971), "Oklahoma" (1979), "Oh, Brother!", "Sunday in the Park with George."

AIDEM, BETSY. Born Oct. 28, 1957 in Eastmeadow, NY. Graduate NYU. Debut 1981 OB in "The Trading Post," followed by "A Different Moon," "Balm in Gilead," "Crossing the Bar."

AIELLO, DANNY. Born June 20, 1935 in NYC. Bdwy debut 1975 in "Lamppost Reunion" for which he received a Theatre World Award, followed by "Wheelbarrow Closers," "Gemini," "Knockout," "The Floating Light Bulb," "Hurlyburly," "House of Blue Leaves."

AKERS, KAREN. Born Oct. 13, 1945 in NYC. Hunter College graduate. Bdwy debut 1982 in "Nine" for which she received a Theatre World Award.

ALEXANDER, JACE. Born Apr. 7, 1964 in NYC. Attended NYU. Bdwy debut 1983 in "The Caine Mutiny Court Martial," OB in "I'm Not Rappaport," followed by "Wasted."

ALEXANDER, JASON. Born Sept. 23, 1959 in Irvington, NJ. Attended Boston U. Bdwy bow 1981 in "Merrily We Roll Along," OB in "Forbidden Broadway." "Stop the World . . . ," "D.," "Personals."

ALEXANDER, TERRY. Born Mar. 23, 1959 in Detroit, Mi. Graduate Wayne State U. Bdwy debut 1971 in "No Place to Be Somebody," OB in "Rashomon," "The Glass Menagerie," "Breakout," "Naomi Court," "Streamers," "Julius Caesar," "Nongogo," "Sus."

ALEXIS, ALVIN. Born July 5 in NYC. Debut 1976 OB in "In the Wine of Time," followed by "Rear Column," "Class Enemy," "Zooman and the Sign," "Painting a Wall," "The Flatbush Faithful," "The Amen Corner," "Teens Today," "In the Wine Time," "Wasted."

ALICE, MARY. Born Dec. 3, 1941 in Indianola, Ms. Debut 1967 OB in "Trials of Brother Jero," followed by "The Strong Breed," "Duplex," "Thoughts," "Miss Julie," "House Party," "Terraces," "Heaven and Hell's Agreement," "In the Deepest Part of Sleep," "Cockfight," "Julius Caesar," "Nongogo," "Second Thoughts," "Spell #7," "Zooman and the Sign," "Glasshouse," "The Ditch," "Take Me Along," "Departures," "Marathon 86," Bdwy in "No Place to Be Somebody" (1971).

ALLARD, MARTINE. Born Aug. 24, 1970 in Brooklyn, NY. Bdwy debut 1983 in "The Tap Dance Kid" for which she received a Theatre World Award.

ALLEN, DEBBIE (a.k.a. Deborah) Born Jan. 16, 1950 in Houston, Tx. Graduate Howard U. Debut 1972 OB in "Ti-Jean and His Brothers," followed by "Anna Lucasta," "Louis," Bdwy in "Raisin" (1973), "Ain't Misbehavin'," "West Side Story," "Sweet Charity."

ALLEN, ELIZABETH. Born Jan. 25, 1934 in Jersey City, NJ. Attended Rutgers U. Bdwy debut 1957 in "Romanoff and Juliet," followed by "The Gay Life," "Do I Hear a Waltz?," "Sherry!," "42nd Street."

ALLEN, JOAN. Born Aug. 20, 1956 in Rochelle, IL. Attended E. Ill. U., W. ILL. U. Debut 1983 OB in "And a Nightingale Sang" for which she received a Theatre World Award, followed by "The Marriage of Bette and Boo," "Marathon '86."

ALLEN, SETH. Born July 13, 1941 in Brooklyn, NY. Attended AMTA. OB in "Viet Rock," "Futz," "Hair," "Candaules Commissioner," "Mary Stuart," "Narrow Road to the Deep North," "More Than You Deserve," "Split Lip," "The Misanthrope," "Hard Sell," "The Wild Duck," "Jungle of Cities," "Egyptology," "The Lisbon Traviata," Bdwy in "Jesus Christ Superstar," "Accidental Death of an Anarchist."

ALLER, JOHN. Born July 5, 1957 in Cuba. Graduate Hofstra U. Debut 1985 OB in "Pacific Overtures," followed by "Encore," "Miami."

ALMQUIST, GREGG. Born Dec. 1, 1948 in Minneapolis, Mn. Graduate UMinn. Debut 1974 OB in "Richard III," followed by "A Night at the Black Pig," "Mother Courage," "King Lear," Bdwy in "I'm Not Rappaport" (1986).

ALVARADO, TRINI. Born in NYC in 1967. Bdwy debut 1978 in "Runaways," OB in "Yours Anne," "Maggie Magalita."

AMENDOLIA, DON. Born Feb. 1, 1945 in Woodbury, NJ. Attended Glassboro State Col., AADA. Debut 1966 OB in "Until the Monkey Comes," followed by "Park," "Cloud 9," Bdwy 1984 in "My One and Only."

AMIS, SUZY. Born Jan. 5, 1958 in Oklahoma City, Ok. Attended Actors Studio. Debut 1986 OB in "Fresh Horses," for which she received a Theatre World Award.

AMOS, KEITH. Born Oct. 26, 1963 in Annapolis, Md. Attended Howard U. Bdwy debut 1983 in "Amen Corner," followed by OB in "Sweet Will."

ANDERMAN, MAUREEN. Born Oct. 26, 1946 in Detroit, Mi. Graduate UMich. Bdwy debut 1970 in "Othello," followed by "Moonchildren" for which she received a Theatre World Award, "An Evening with Richard Nixon . . . ," "The Last of Mrs. Lincoln," "Seascape," "Who's Afraid of Virginia Woolf?," "A History of the American Film," "The Lady from Dubuque," "The Man Who Came to Dinner," "Einstein and the Polar Bear," "You Can't Take It with You," "Macbeth," "Benefactors," OB in "Hamlet," "Elusive Angel," "Out of Our Father's House," "Sunday Runners."

ANDERSON, CHRISTINE. Born Aug. 6 in Utica, NY. Graduate UWi. Bdwy debut in "I Love My Wife" (1980), OB in "I Can't Keep Running in Place," "On the Swing Shift," "Red, Hot and Blue," "A Night at Texas Guinan's," "Nunsense."

ANDERSON, KEVIN. Born Jan. 13, 1960 in Illinois. Attended Goodman School. Debut 1985 OB in "Orphans" for which he received a Theatre World Award.

ANDERSON, SYDNEY. Born Apr. 4 in Tacoma, WA. Graduate UWa. Debut 1978 OB in "Gay Divorce," Bdwy in "A Broadway Musical" (1978), followed by "Charlie and Algernon," "Oklahoma!," "La Cage aux Folles."

ANDREWS, GEORGE LEE. Born Oct. 13, 1942 in Milwaukee, Wi. Debut OB 1970 in "Jacques Brel Is Alive and Well . . .," followed by "Starting Here Starting Now," "Vamps and Rideouts," "The Fantasticks," Bdwy in "A Little Night Music" (1973), "On the 20th Century," "Merlin."

ANKENY, MARK. Born Oct. 9, 1958 in Austin, Mn. Attended UMinn. Debut 1985 OB in "She Loves Me," followed by "Murder Game."

ANTON, SUSAN. Born Oct. 12, 1950 in Yucaipa, Ca. Attended Bernardino Col. Bdwy debut 1985 in "Hurlyburly."

ARANAS, RAUL. Born Oct. 1, 1947 in Manilla, PI. Graduate Pace U. Debut 1976 OB in "Savages," followed by "Yellow Is My Favorite Color," "49," "Bullet Headed Birds," "Tooth of Crime," "Teahouse," "Shepard Sets," "Cold Air," "La Chunga," "The Man Who Turned into a Stick," Bdwy in "Loose Ends" (1978).

ARCARO, ROBERT (a.k.a. Bob) Born Aug. 9, 1952 in Brooklyn, NY. Graduate Wesleyan U. Debut 1977 OB in "New York City Street Show," followed by "Working Theatre Festival."

ARDAO, DAVID. Born July 24, 1951 in Brooklyn, NY. Graduate Rutgers U. Bdwy debut 1981 in "Joseph and the Amazing Technicolor Dreamcoat," followed OB by "Professionally Speaking" (1986).

ARLISS, DIMITRA. Born in Lorain, Oh. Attended Miami U., Goodman Theatre. Debut 1963 OB in "The Trojan Women," followed by "Antigone," "Queen of Greece," "Pericles," "Arms and the Man," Bdwy in "Indians" (1970).

ARLUCK, NEAL. Born Dec. 4, 1946 in Brooklyn, NY. Graduate Lehigh U., NYU, AADA. Debut 1981 OB in "Catch 22" followed by "Dead Giveaway," "The Hooch," "Something Old Something New," "Crazy Arnold," "Black Coffee."

ARNOLD, BOB. Born Dec. 12, 1948 in Cleveland, Oh. Graduate Bowling Green State U. Debut OB 1983 in "An Evening of Adult Fairy Tales," followed by "Tales of Tinseltown."

ARNOLD, MADISON. Born Feb. 7, 1935 in Allentown, Pa. Attended Columbia U., UVienna, UBerlin. OB in "Lower Depths," "Much Ado about Nothing," "The Gamblers," "The Marriage," "Macbeth," "Basic Training of Pavlo Hummel," "Jungle of Cities," "Ride a Black Horse," "In the Boom Boom Room," "The Good Life," Bdwy in "Man in the Glass Booth" (1968).

ARONS, ELLYN. Born Oct. 29, 1956 in Philadelphia, Pa. Graduate Temple U. Debut 1979 OB in "Plain and Fancy," Bdwy in "Camelot" (1980), "Mame" (1983), "Jerry's Girls."

ARRAMBIDE, MARIO. Born Mar. 1, 1953 in San Antonio, Tx. Attended RADA. Debut 1985 OB in "The Golem," followed by "Aunt Dan and Lemon," "Hamlet."

ASHLEY, ELIZABETH. Born Aug. 30, 1939 in Ocala, Fl. Attended Neighborhood Playhouse. Bdwy debut 1959 in "The Highest Tree," followed by "Take Her She's Mine" for which she received a Theatre World Award, "Barefoot in the Park," "Ring Round the Bathtub," "Cat on a Hot Tin Roof," "The Skin of Our Teeth," "Legend," "Caesar and Cleopatra," "Hide and Seek," "Agnes of God."

ASQUITH, WARD. Born March 21 in Philadelphia, Pa. Graduate UPa., Columbia U. Debut 1979 OB in "After the Rise," followed by "Kind Lady," "Incident at Vichy," "Happy Birthday Wanda June," "Another Part of the Forest."

ASTREDO, HUMBERT ALLEN. Born in San Francisco, Ca. Attended SanFranU. Debut 1967 OB in "Arms and the Man," followed by "Fragments," "Murderous Angels," "Beach Children," "End of Summer," "Knuckle," "Grand Magic," "Big and Little," "Jail Diary of Albie Sachs," "Breakfast Conversations in Miami," "December 7th," Bdwy in "Les Blancs" (1970), "An Evening with Richard Nixon . . .," "The Little Foxes" (1981).

AUBERJONOIS, RENE. born June 1, 1940 in NYC. Graduate Carnegie Inst. With LCRep in "A Cry of Player," "King Lear," and "Twelfth Night," Bdwy in "Fire," "Coco," "Tricks," "The Good Doctor," "Break a Leg," "Every Good Boy Deserves Favor," "Big River," BAM. Co. in "The New York Idea," "Three Sisters," "The Play's the Thing" and "Julius Caesar."

AUGUST, RON. Born Dec. 25, 1942 in NYC. Attended Brigham Young U. Debut 1983 OB in "Anna Christie," followed by "American Dreams," "In the Boom Boom Room."

AUSTIN, BETH. (a.k.a. Elizabeth) Born May 23, 1952 in Philadelphia, Pa. Graduate Point Park Col., Pittsburgh Playhouse. Debut 1977 OB in "Wonderful Town," followed by "The Prevalence of Mrs. Seal," "Engaged," "Pastoral," "Head over Heels," "A Kiss Is Just a Kiss," "Tales of Tinseltown," "Olympus on My Mind," Bdwy in "Sly Fox" (1977), "Whoopee!," "Onward Victoria!"

AUSTIN, MARK. Born May 22, 1964 in Murray, Ky. Graduate NYU. Debut 1986 OB in "1981."

AVARI, N. ERICK. Born Apr. 13, 1952 in Calcutta, IN. Graduate Col. of Charleston, SC. Debut 1983 OB in "Bhutan," followed by "Comedy of Errors," "Map of the World."

AYR, MICHAEL. Born Sept. 8, 1953 in Great Falls, MT. Graduate SMU. Debut 1976 OB in "Mrs. Murray's Farm," followed by "The Farm," "Ulysses in Traction," "Lulu" "Cabin 12," "Stargazing," "The Deserter," "Hamlet," "Mary Stuart," "Save Grand Central," "The Beaver Coat," "Richard II," "Great Grandson of Jedediah Kohler," "Domestic Issues," "Time Framed," "The Dining Room," "The Sea Gull," "Love's Labour's Lost," "Rum And Coke," Bdwy in "Hide and Seek" (1980), "Piaf."

AZITO, TONY. Born July 18, 1948 in NYC. Attended Juilliard. Debut 1971 OB in "Red White and Black," followed by "Players Project," "Secrets of the Citizens Correction Committee," "Threepenny Opera," "Buskers," "Twelfth Night," Bdwy in "Happy End" (1977), "Pirates of Penzance."

BABATUNDE, OBBA. Born in Jamaica, NY. Attended Brooklyn Col. Debut OB 1970 in "The Secret Place" followed by "Guys and Dolls," "On Toby Time," "The Breakout," "Scottsborough Boys," "Showdown Time," "Dream on Monkey Mt.," "Sheba," "George White's Scandal," Bdwy in "Timbuktu" (1978), "Reggae," "It's So Nice to Be Civilized," "Dreamgirls," "Grind."

BACKER, BRIAN. Born Dec. 5, 1956 in NYC. Attended Neighborhood Playhouse. Bdwy debut 1981 in "The Floating Light Bulb," for which he received a Theatre World Award, OB in "December 7th."

BACKUS, RICHARD. Born Mar. 28, 1945 in Goffstown, NH Harvard graduate. Bdwy debut 1971 in "Butterflies Are Free," followed by "Promenade All," for which he received a Theatre World Award, "Ah, Wilderness!," "Camelot" (1981), OB in "Studs Edsel," "Gimme Shelter," "Sorrows of Stephen," "Missing Persons," "Henry V," "Talley and Son," "Tomorrow's Monday."

BACON, KEVIN. Born July 8, 1958 in Philadelphia, PA. Debut 1978 OB in "Getting Out," followed by "Glad Tidings," "Album," "Flux," "Poor Little Lambs," "Slab Boys," "Men without Dates," "Loot."

BAILEY, DENNIS. Born Apr. 12, 1953 in Grosse Point Woods, MI. UDetroit graduate. Debut 1977 OB in "House of Blue Leaves," followed by "Wonderland," "Head over Heels," "Preppies," "Professionally Speaking," Bdwy in "Gemini" (1978), "Leader of the Pack," "Figaro."

BAIRD, QUIN. Born Nov. 21, 1950 in Seattle, Wa. Graduate UCalDavis. Bdwy debut 1968 in "The Happy Time," followed by "Sweet Charity" (1986).

BAKER, KATHY WHITTON. Born June 8, 1950 in Midland, Tx. Graduate UCalBerkeley. Debut 1983 OB in "Fool for Love" for which she received a Theatre World Award, followed by "Desire under the Elms," "Aunt Dan and Lemon."

BAKER, RAYMOND. Born July 9, 1948 in Omaha, NE. Graduate UDenver. Debut 1972 OB in "The Proposition," followed by "Are You Now or Have You Ever Been . . .," "Character Lines," "Lunch Hour," "Legends of Arthur," "War Babies," "Bathroom Plays," "I'm Not Rappaport," Bdwy in "Crimes of the Heart," "Division Street," "Is There Life After High School?," "Torch Song Trilogy."

BALDINO, MISSY. Born June 13, 1959 in Philadelphia, Pa. Graduate St. Francis Col. Debut 1985 OB in "What's a Nice Country Like You Doing in a State Like This?"

BALDWIN, ALEC. Born Apr. 3, 1958 in Massapequa, NY. Attended George Washington U, NYU, Lee Strasberg Inst. Bdwy debut 1986 in "Loot."

BALOU, BUDDY. Born in 1953 in Seattle, WA. Joined American Ballet Theatre in 1970, rising to soloist. Joined Dancers in 1977. Bdwy debut 1980 in "A Chorus Line," followed by "Song and Dance."

BAMMAN, GERRY. Born Sept. 18, 1941 in Independence, Ks. Graduate Xavier U, NYU. Debut 1970 OB in "Alice in Wonderland," followed by "All Night Long," "Richard III," "Oedipus Rex," "A Midsummer Night's Dream," "He and She," "Johnny on the Spot," "Museum," "Henry V," "Our Late Night," "The Seagull," "Endgame," Bdwy in "Accidental Death of an Anarchist" (1984), "Execution of Justice."

BANES, LISA. Born July 9, 1955 in Chagrin Falls, OH. Juilliard grad. Debut OB 1980 in "Elizabeth I," followed by "A Call from the East," "Look Back in Anger" for which she received a Theatre World Award, "My Sister in This House," "Antigone," "Three Sisters," "The Cradle Will Rock," "Isn't It Romantic," "Fighting International Fat," "Ten by Tennessee."

BANKSTON, ARNOLD. Born June 2, 1955 in Los Angeles, Ca. Graduate LACC. Debut 1985 OB in "Mirandolina," followed by "The Journal of Albion Moonlight," "A Flash of Lightning."

BANSAVAGE, LISA. Born Mar. 22, 1953 in Syracuse, NY. Graduate Carnegie-Mellon U, UPittsburgh. Debut 1983 OB in "The Changeling," followed by "As You Like It."

BARAN, EDWARD. Born May 18, 1950 in Minneapolis, Mn. Graduate Williams Col. Debut 1984 OB in "A Fool's Errand," followed by "The Wonder Years," 1951.

BARANSKI, CHRISTINE. Born May 2, 1952 in Buffalo, NY. Graduate Juilliard Sch. Debut OB 1978 in "One Crack Out," followed by "Says I Says He," "The Trouble with Europe," "Coming Attractions," "Operation Midnight Climax," "Sally and Marsha," "A Midsummer Night's Dream," Bdwy in "Hide and Seek." (1980), "The Real Thing," "Hurlyburly," "It's Only a Play," "Marathon '86," "House of Blue Leaves."

BARAY, JOHN. Born Nov. 29, 1944 in San Antonio, TX. Graduate Trinity U. Debut 1981 OB in "The Red Mill," followed by "Babes in Toyland," "Mikado," "Pirates of Penzance," "Pacific Overtures," "Ghashiram."

BARBARO, CIRO. Born March 6, 1952 in Brooklyn, NY. Attended Hunter Col. Debut 1986 OB in "Girl Crazy."

BARBEE, VICTOR. Born in 1954 in Raleigh, NC. Attended School of American Ballet. Joined NYC Ballet where he rose principal. Bdwy debut 1983 in "Woman of the Year," followed by "Song and Dance."

BARBOUR, THOMAS. Born July 25, 1921 in NYC. Graduate Princeton, Harvard. Bdwy debut 1968 in "Portrait of a Queen," followed by "Great White Hope," "Scratch," "Lincoln Mask," "Kingdoms," OB in "Twelfth Night," "Merchant of Venice," "Admirable Bashful," "The Lady's Not for Burning," "The Enchanted," "Antony and Cleopatra," "The Saintliness of Margery Kemp," "Dr. Willy Nilly," "Under the Sycamore Tree," "Epitaph for George Dillon," "Thracian Horses," "Old Glory," "Sjt. Musgrave's Dance," "Nestless Bird," "The Seagull," "Wayside Motor Inn," "Arthur," "The Grinding Machine," "Mr. Simian," "Sorrows of Frederick," "Terrorists," "Dark Ages," "Royal Bob," "Relatively Speaking," "The Nice and the Nasty."

BARKER, CHRISTINE. Born Nov. 26 in Jacksonville, FL. Attended UCLA. Bdwy debut 1979 in "A Chorus Line."

BARKER, JEAN. Born Dec. 20 in Philadelphia, Pa. Attended UPa., AmThWing. Debut 1953 OB in "The Bald Soprano," followed by "Night Shift," "A Month in the Country," "Portrait of Jenny," "Knucklebones," "About Iris Berman," "Goodnight Grandpa," "Victory Bonds," "Cabbagehead," Bdwy in "The Innkeepers" (1956).

BARKER, MARGARET. Born Oct. 10, 1908 in Baltimore, Md. Attended Bryn Mawr. Bdwy debut 1928 in "Age of Innocence," followed by "The Barretts of Wimpole Street," "The House of Connelly," "Men in White," "Gold Eagle Guy," "Leading Lady," "Member of the Wedding," "Autumn Garden," "See the Jaguar," "Ladies of the Corridor," "The Master Builder," OB in "Wayside Motor Inn," "The Loves of Cass McGuire," "Three Sisters," "Details without a Map," "The Inheritors," "Caligula," "The Mound Builders," "Quiet in the Land."

BARNER, STOCKMAN. Born July 26, 1921 in New London, Ct. Graduate UIowa. Bdwy debut 1945 in "Othello," OB in "The Hollow," "Revenger's Tragedy," "The Miser," "Hound of the Baskervilles," "Black Coffee."

BARON, EVALYN. Born Apr. 21, 1948 in Atlanta, GA. Graduate Northwestern., UMinn. Debut 1979 OB in "Scrambled Feet," followed by "Hijinks," "I Can't Keep Running in Place," "Jerry's Girls," "Harvest of Strangers," "Quilters," Bdwy in "Fearless Frank" (1980), "Big River."

BARONE, JOHN. Born March 14, 1954 in Staten Island, NY. Graduate Wagner Col. Debut 1982 OB in "Robin Hood," followed by "The Music Man," "Flesh, Flash & Frank Harris," "Consenting Adults," "Blessed Event," "Girl Crazy."

BARRE, GABRIEL. Born Aug. 26, 1957 in Brattleboro, VT. Graduate AADA. Debut 1977 OB in "Jabberwock," followed by "T.N.T.," "Bodo," "The Baker's Wife," "The Time of Your Life," "Children of the Sun."

BARRETT, BRENT. Born Feb 28, 1957 in Quinter, KS. Graduate Carnegie-Mellon. Bdwy debut 1980 in "West Side Story," followed by "Dance a Little Closer," OB in "March of the Falsettos," "Portrait of Jenny," "The Death of Von Richthofen," "Sweethearts in Concert," "What's a Nice Country like You . . .," "Time of the Cuckoo."

BARRETT, JOE. Born Nov. 30, 1950 in Webster, NY. Graduate URochester. Debut 1975 OB in "Boy Meets Boy," followed by "The Great American Backstage Musical," "Personals."

BARRON, DOUGLAS. Born Oct. 27, 1953 in Topeka, Ks. Attended AzStateU. Debut OB 1985 in "Stud Silo," followed by "Dance of the Mayfly."

BARRY, KATHERINE. Born Sept. 19, 1956 in Washington, DC. Graduate Northwestern U. Debut 1982 OB in "After the Fall," followed by "The Legend of Sleepy Hollow."

BARTENIEFF, GEORGE. Born Jan. 24, 1933 in Berlin, Ger. Bdwy debut 1947 in "The Whole World Over," followed by "Venus Is," "All's Well That Ends Well," "Quotations from Chairman Mao Tse-Tung," "The Death of Bessie Smith," "Cop-Out," "Room Service," "Unlikely Heroes," OB in "Walking to Waldheim," "Memorandum," "The Increased Difficulty of Concentration," "Trelawny of the Wells," "Charley Chestnut Rides the IRT," "Radio (Wisdom): Sophia Part I," "Images of the Dead," "Dead End Kids," "The Blonde Leading the Blonde," "The Dispossessed," "Growing Up Gothic," "Rosetti's Apologies," "On the Lam," "Samuel Beckett Trilogy," "Quartet," "Help Wanted," "A Matter of Life and Death."

BARTLETT, LISABETH. Born Feb. 28, 1956 in Denver, CO. Northwestern U. Graduate. Bdwy debut 1981 in "The Dresser," followed by "Execution of Justice," OB in "The Lady's Not for Burning," "The Rachel Plays."

BARTLETT, ROBIN. Born Apr. 22, 1951 in NYC. Graduate Boston U. Bdwy debut 1975 in "Yentl," followed by "The World of Sholem Aleichem," OB in "Agamemnon," "Fathers and Sons," "No End of Blame," "Living Quarters," "After the Fall," "Cheapside."

BARTO, MARY. Born Sept. 27 in Easton, Md. Graduate Peabody Conservatory, Juilliard, Neighborhood Playhouse. Bdwy debut 1980 in "Annie," followed by "The King and I," OB in "A Marriage Proposal," "The Blue Hour," "Hamlet."

BARTON, DANIEL. Born Jan. 23, 1949 in Buffalo, NY. Attended Buffalo State, Albany State. Bdwy debut 1976 in "The Poison Tree," followed by "Timbuktu," OB in "The House of Shadows."

BARTON, FRED. Born Oct. 20, 1958 in Camden, NJ. Graduate Harvard. Debut 1982 OB in "Forbidden Broadway."

BASCH, PETER. Born May 11, 1956 in NYC. Graduate Columbia Col., UCalBerkeley. Debut 1984 OB in "Hackers," followed by "Festival of One Acts."

BASSETT, ANGELA. Born Aug. 16, 1958 in NYC. Graduate YaleU. Debut 1982 OB in "Colored People's Time," followed by "Antigone," "Black Girl" (1986), Bdwy in "Ma Rainey's Black Bottom" (1985).

BATES, JEROME PRESTON. Born July 20, 1954 in Augusta, Ga. Attended Knoxville Col., UTn, LAMDA. Debut 1985 OB in "Jonin'."

BATES, KATHY. Born June 18, 1948 in Memphis, TN, Graduate S. Methodist U. Debut 1976 OB in "Vanities," followed by "The Art of Dining," "Curse of the Starving Class," Bdwy in "Goodbye Fidel" (1980), "5th of July," "Come Back to the 5 & Dime, Jimmy Dean," " 'night, Mother."

BAUM, JOANNE. Born June 30, 1960 in New Jersey. Graduate Boston Conservatory. Debut OB 1984 in "Kuni-Leml," followed by "A Flash of Lightning."

BAXTER, KEITH. Born Apr. 29, 1935 in Newport, Wales. Graduate RADA. Bdwy debut 1961 in "A Man for All Seasons" for which he received a Theatre World Award, followed by "The Affair," "Avanti," "Sleuth," "A Meeting by the River," "Romantic Comedy," "Corpse," OB in "The Penultimate Problem of Sherlock Holmes.";

BAYLESS, ANITA. Born May 6 in Blue Mound, Il. Attended Millikin U, AmThWing. Debut 1970 OB in "Barefoot in the Park," followed by "Mornings at 7," "The Skaters," "The Foreigner."

BEACH, GARY. Born Oct. 10, 1947 in Alexandria, Va. Graduate NCSch. of Arts. Bdwy debut 1971 in "1776," followed by "Something's Afoot," "Moony Shapiro Songbook," "Annie," "Doonesbury," OB in "Smile Smile Smile," "What's a Nice Country Like You. . . .," "Ionescpade," "By Strouse," "A Bundle of Nerves."

BEAN, REATHEL. Born Aug. 24, 1942 in Missouri. Graduate Drake U. OB in "America Hurrah," "San Francisco's Burning," "Love Cure," "Henry IV," "In Circles," "Peace," "Journey of Snow White," "Wanted," "The Faggot," "Lovers," "Not Back with the Elephants," "Art of Coarse Acting," "The Trip Back Down," Bdwy in "Doonesbury" (1983), "Big River."

BEDFORD-LLOYD, JOHN. Born Jan. 2, 1956 in New Haven, CT. Graduate Williams Col., Yale. Debut OB 1983 in "Vieux Carre," followed by "She Stoops to Conquer," "The Incredibly Famous Willy Rivers," "Digby," "Rum and Coke."

BEECHMAN, LAURIE. Born Apr. 4, 1954 in Philadelphia, Pa. Attended NYU. Bdwy debut 1977 in "Annie," followed by "Pirates of Penzance," "Joseph and the Amazing Technicolor Dreamcoat" for which she received a Theatre World Award. "Some Enchanted Evening" (OB), "Pal Joey in Concert," "Cats."

BELL, VANESSA. Born Mar. 20, 1957 in Toledo. OH. Graduate OhioU. Bdwy debut 1981 in "Bring Back Birdie," followed by "El Bravo!," "Dreamgirls," OB in "Take me Along," "A . . . My Name Is Alice."

BELMONTE, VICKI. Born Jan. 20, 1947 in U.S.A. Bdwy debut 1960 in "Bye Bye Birdie," followed by "Subways Are for Sleeping," "All American," "Annie Get Your Gun" (LC), OB in "Nunsense."

BENJAMIN, P. J. Born Sept. 2, 1951 in Chicago, IL. Attended Loyola U., Columbia U. Bdwy debut 1973 in "Pajama Game," followed by "Pippin," "Sarava," "Charlie and Algernon," "Sophisticated Ladies," "Torch Song Trilogy," "Wind in the Willows," OB in "Memories of Riding with Joe Cool."

BENNETT, HARRY. Born Dec. 25 in Ridgefield, Ct. Graduate UCt, Catholic U. Debut 1982 OB in "Not Now Darling," followed by "Kiss Me Kate," OB in "The Legend of Sleepy Hollow."

BENSINGER, MIMI. Born May 5 in Pottsville, PA. Attended Penn State, AmThWing. Debut OB 1961 in "Electra," followed by "Hadrian's Wall," "The Doctor in spite of Himself," "The Eye of a Bird," "A Doll's House," "Two Orphans."

BENTLEY, JOHN. Born Jan. 31, 1940 in Jackson Heights, NY. Graduate AADA. Debut 1961 OB in "King of the Dark Chamber," followed by "As to the Meaning of Words," "West Side Story" (JB), "Short Eyes," Bdwy in "Mike Downstairs" (1968), "Lysistrata," "The Selling of the President," "A Funny Thing Happened on the Way to the Form" (1972), "West Side Story" (1980).

BEREZIN, TANYA. Born Mar. 25, 1941 in Philadelphia, PA. Attended Boston U. Debut OB 1967 in "The Sandcastle," followed by "Three Sisters," "Great Nebula in Orion," "him," "Amazing Activity of Charlie Contrare," "Battle of Angels," "Mound Builders," "Serenading Louie," "My Life," "Brontosaurus," "Glorious Morning," "Mary Stuart," "The Beaver Coat," "Balm in Gilead," "Caligula," "Quiet in the Land," Bdwy in "5th of July" (1981), "Angels Fall."

BERGER, STEPHEN. Born May 16, 1954 in Philadelphia, PA. Attended UCinn. Bdwy debut 1982 in "Little Me," OB in "Nite Club Confidential," "Mowgli," "Isn't It Romantic."

BERIS, DAVID M. Born Sept. 29, 1958 in Elizabeth, NJ. Graduate Emerson Col. Debut 1986 OB in "They're Playing Our Song."

BERK, PHYLLIS. Born Aug. 8 in NYC. Graduate Fordham U. Debut 1985 OB in "The Golden Land."

BERMAN, DONALD F. Born Jan. 23, 1954 in NYC. Graduate USyracuse. Debut 1977 OB in "Savages," followed by "Dona Rosita," "The Lady or the Tiger," "The Overcoat," "Steel on Steel," "Visions of Kerouac," "The Normal Heart."

BERNSTEIN, DOUGLAS. Born May 6, 1958 in NYC. Amherst graduate. Debut 1982 OB in "Upstairs at O'Neals," followed by "Backer's Audition," "Mayor."

BERRIDGE, ELIZABETH. Born May 2, 1962 in Westchester, NY. Attended Strasberg Inst. Debut 1984 OB in "The Vampires," followed by "The Incredibly Famous Willy Rivers," "Ground Zero Club," "Outside Waco," "Cruise Control," "Sorrows and Sons."

BESSETTE, MIMI. Born Jan. 15, 1956 in Midland, Mi. Graduate TCU, RADA. Debut 1978 OB in "The Gift of the Magi," followed by "Bugles at Dawn," "On the 20th Century," Bdwy in "The Best Little Whorehouse in Texas" (1981).

BETHANY, SUSAN. Born Sept. 9, 1957 in Jamaica, Queens, NY. Graduate Queens Col. Debut 1984 OB in "Balm in Gilead," followed by "Ice," "Murder One!," "Family Portrait."

BEVAN, ALISON. Born Nov. 20, 1959 in Cincinnati, Oh. Attended NYU. Debut 1980 OB in "Trixie True Teen Detective," followed by "Brigadoon" (LC).

BEVELANDER, NANNETTE. Born Jan. 19, 1956 in Holland. Graduate Canadian College of Dance. Bdwy debut 1983 in "Oh! Calcutta!"

BIAGINI, SAL. Born Apr. 13, 1952 in Brooklyn, NY. Graduate USFla. Debut 1984 OB in "Sing Me Sunshine," followed by "On the Brink," "Three One Acts."

BIRNEY, DAVID. Born Apr. 23, 1939 in Washington, DC. Graduate Dartmouth, UCLA. OB in "Comedy of Errors," "Titus Andronicus," "King John," "MacBird," "Crime of Passion," "Ceremony of Innocence," "Lincoln Center's Summertree" for which he received a Theatre World Award, "The Miser," "Playboy of the Western World," "Good Woman of Setzuan," "An Enemy of the People and Antigone," Bdwy in "Amadeus" (1983), "Benefactors."

BIRNEY, REED. Born Sept. 11, 1954 in Alexandria, Va. Attended Boston U. Bdwy debut 1977 in "Gemini," OB in "The Master and Margarita," "Bella Figura," "Winterplay," "The Flight of the Earls," "Filthy Rich."

BLACK, ROYANA. Born March 1, 1973 in Poughkeepsie, NY. Bdwy debut 1984 in "Brighton Beach Memoirs." OB in "Miami," "Trinity Site."

BLACKMAN, IAN. Born Sept. 2, 1959 in Toronto, Can. Attended Bard Col. Debut 1982 OB in "Herself as Lust," followed by "Sister Mary Ignatius Explains It All," "The Actor's Nightmare," "Nuclear Follies," "The Bone Ring."

BLAIR, PAMELA. Born Dec. 5, 1949 in Arlington, Vt. Attended Ntl. Acad. of Ballet. Bdwy debut 1972 in "Promises Promises," followed by "Sugar," "Seesaw," "Of Mice and Men," "Wild and Wonderful," "A Chorus Line," "The Best Little Whorehouse in Texas," "King of Hearts," OB in "Ballad of Boris K," "Split," "Real Life Funnies," "Double Feature," "Hit Parade."

BLAISDELL, NESBITT. Born Dec. 6, 1928 in NYC. Graduate Amherst, Columbia U. Debut 1978 OB in "Old Man Joseph and His Family," followed by "Moliere in spite of Himself," "Guests of the Nation," "Ballad of Soapy Smith," "Custom of the Country."

BLANC, JENNIFER. Born Apr. 21, 1971 in NYC. Attended Professional Children's School. Bdwy debut 1985 in "Brighton Beach Memoirs."

BLANCHARD, STEVEN. Born Dec. 4, 1958 in York, PA. Attended UMd. Bdwy debut 1984 in "The Three Musketeers," OB in "Moby Dick."

BLOCK, LARRY. Born Oct. 30, 1942 in NYC. Graduate URI. Bdwy bow 1966 in "Hail Scrawdyke," followed by "La Turista," OB in "Eh?," "Fingernails Blue as Flowers," "Comedy of Errors," "Coming Attractions," "Henry IV Part 2," "Feuhrer Bunker," "Manhattan Love Songs," "Souvenirs," "The Golem," "Responsible Parties," "Hit Parade," "Largo Desolato."

BLOOM, STUART. Born July 13, 1958 in Brooklyn, NY. Attended Wesleyan U, NYU. Debut 1981 OB in "Side Street Scenes," followed by "Next Please!"

BLOOM, VERNA Born Aug 7 in Lynn, MA. Graduate Boston U. Bdwy debut 1967 in "Marat/deSade," followed by "Brighton Beach Memoirs," OB's "Kool Aid," "The Cherry Orchard," "Bits and Pieces," "Barbary Shore," "Messiah."

BLUM, MARK. Born May 14, 1950 in Newark, NJ. Graduate UPa., UMinn. Debut OB 1976 in "The Cherry Orchard," followed by "Green Julia," "Say Goodnight, Gracie," "Table Settings," "Key Exchange," "Loving Reno," "Messiah," "It's Only a Play," "Little Footsteps."

BOBBIE, WALTER. Born Nov. 18, 1945 in Scranton, Pa. Graduate UScranton, Catholic U. Bdwy debut 1971 in "Frank Merriwell," followed by "The Grass Harp," "Grease," "Tricks," "Going Up," "History of the American Film," OB in "Drat!," "She Loves Me," "Up from Paradise," "Goodbye Freddy."

BODIN, JAY. Born Mar. 20, 1965 in Yonkers, NY. Attended Bard Col., AMDA. Debut 1985 OB in "What's a Nice Country Like You Doing in a State Like This?"

BODLE, JANE. Born Nov 12 in Lawrence KS. Attended UUtah. Bdwy debut 1983 in "Cats."

BOGOSIAN, ERIC. Born Apr. 24, 1953 in Woburn, Ma. Graduate Oberlin Col. Debut 1982 OB in "Men Inside/Voices of America," followed by "Funhouse," "Drinking in America."

BOLES, ROBERT. Born July 27, 1953 in Cincinnati, Oh. Attended Memphis State U, AMDA. Debut 1984 OB in "Richard II," followed by "Pericles," "To Feed Their Hopes."

BONDS, R. J. Born Nov. 30, 1946 in Detroit, MI. Attended MSU, Neighborhood Playhouse. Debut 1980 OB in "Home of the Brave," followed by "Bury the Dead," "In Pursuit of Liberty," "Icebridge," "Tracers."

BOONE, MICHAEL KELLY. Born Mar. 13, 1957 in Abingdon, Va. Graduate UTn. Bdwy debut 1985 in "Take Me Along," OB in "The Merry Widow," "Gifts of the Magi," "The Bone Ring."

BORDO, EDWIN. Born Mar. 3, 1931 in Cleveland OH. Graduate Allegheny Col., LAMDA. Bdwy debut 1964 in "The Last Analysis," followed by "Inquest," "Zalmen or the Madness of God," "Annie," OB in "The Dragon," "Waiting for Godot," "Saved," "Ten Little Indians," "King Lear."

BORTS, JOANNE. Born June 12, 1961 in Syosset, NY. Graduate SUNYBinghamton. Debut 1985 OB in "The Golden Land."

BOSCO, PHILIP. Born Sept. 26, 1930 in Jersey City, NJ. Graduate Catholic U. Credits: "Auntie Mame," "Rape of the Belt," "Ticket of Leave Man," "Donnybrook," "Man for All Seasons," "Mrs. Warren's Profession," with LCRep in "The Alchemist," "East Wind," "Galileo," "St. Joan," "Tiger at the Gate," "Cyrano," "King Lear," "A Great Career," "In the Matter of J. Robert Oppenheimer," "The Miser," "The Time of Your Life," "Camino Real," "Operation Sidewinder," "Amphitryon," "Enemy of the People," "Playboy of the Western World," "Good Woman of Setzuan," "Antigone," "Mary Stuart," "Narrow Road to the Deep North," "The Crucible," "Twelfth Night," "Enemies," "Plough and the Stars," "Merchant of Venice," and "A Streetcar Named Desire," "Henry V," "Threepenny Opera," "Streamers," "Stages," "St. Joan," "The Biko Inquest," "Man and Super-man," "Whose Life Is It Anyway," "Major Barbara," "A Month in the Country," "Bacchae," "Hedda Gabler," "Don Juan in Hell," "Inadmissible Evidence," "Eminent Domain," "Mis-alliance," "Learned Ladies," "Some Men Need Help," "Ah, Wilderness!," "The Caine Mutiny Court Martial," "Heartbreak House," "Come Back, Little Sheba," "Love of Anatole," "Be Happy for Me," "Master Class."

BOUDREAU, ROBIN. Born Nov. 7 in Pittsburgh, Pa. Graduate NYU. Bdwy debut 1981 in "Pirates of Penzance," followed by OB in "To Whom It May Concern."

BOUTSIKARIS, DENNIS. Born Dec. 21, 1952 in Newark, NJ. Graduate Hampshire Col. Debut 1975 OB in "Another Language," followed by "Funeral March for a One-Man Band," "All's Well That Ends Well," "A Day in the Life of the Czar," "Nest of the Wood Grouse," "Cheapside," "Rum and Coke," Bdwy in "Filumena" (1980), "Bent," "Amadeus."

BOVA, JOSEPH. Born May 25 in Cleveland, OH. Graduate Northwestern U. Debut 1959 OB in "On the Town," followed by "Once Upon a Mattress," "House of Blue Leaves," "Comedy," "The Beauty Part," "Taming of the Shrew," "Richard III," "Comedy of Errors," "Invitation to a Beheading," "Merry Wives of Windsor," "Henry V," "Streamers," Bdwy in "Rape of the Belt," "Irma La Douce," "Hot Spot," "The Chinese," "American Millionaire," "St. Joan," "42nd Street."

BOWNE, RICHARD L. Born Nov. 12, 1949 in Bronxville, NY. Graduate UCt. Bdwy debut 1979 in "Snow White and the Seven Dwarfs," followed by "Showboat" (1983), OB in "Moby Dick."

BOYAR, MONICA. Born Dec. 20 in the Dominican Republic. Bdwy debut 1948 in "Summer and Smoke," followed by "Thirteen Daughters," OB in "The Bitter Tears of Petra Von Kant."

BOZYK, REIZL (ROSE). Born May 13, 1914 in Poland. Star of many Yiddish productions before 1966 Bdwy debut in "Let's Sing Yiddish," followed by "Sing, Israel, Sing," "Mirele Efros," "The Jewish Gypsy," OB in "Light, Lively and Yiddish," "Rebecca the Rabbi's Daughter," "Wish Me Mazel-Tov," "Roumanian Wedding," "The Showgirl," "Match Made in Heaven."

BRADLEY, CHARLES. Born Oct. 22, 1975 in NYC. Debut 1986 OB in "The Nice and the Nasty."

BRASSER, VICTORIA. Born May 13, 1959 in Rochester, NY. Graduate Eastman Sch. of Music. Bdwy debut in "Sunday in the Park with George" (1985), OB in "On the 20th Century."

BRAZDA, DAVID. Born Sept. 28, 1954 in Weisbaden, Ger. Attended UVa., Circle in the Square. Debut 1985 OB in "Onlyman," "Two Gentelmen of Verona."

BREED, HELEN LLOYD. Born Jan. 27, 1911 in NYC. Debut 1956 OB in "Out of This World," followed by "Winners," "Exiles," "Something Unspoken," "You Never Can Tell," "Liliom," "The Hollow," "The Chalk Garden," "Ring Round the Moon," "Richard II," "Kind Lady," "A Little Night Music," "The Holly and the Ivy," "For the Use of the Hall," "Mortally Fine," "The Affair."

BREEN, J. PATRICK. Born Oct. 26, 1960 in Brooklyn, NY. Graduate NYU. Debut 1982 OB in "Epiphany," Bdwy in "Brighton Beach Memoirs" (1983).

BREITBARTH, DAVID. Born Nov. 3, 1957 in NYC. Graduate Hamilton Col. Debut 1984 OB in "It's Hard to Be a Jew," followed by "Short Change."

BRENNAN, TOM. Born Apr. 16, 1926 in Cleveland, OH. Graduate Oberlin, Western Reserve. Debut 1958 OB in "Synge Trilogy," followed by "Between Two Thieves," "Easter," "All in Love," "Under Milkwood," "An Evening with James Purdy," "Golden Six," "Pullman Car Hiawatha," "Are You Now or Have You . . .," "Diary of Anne Frank," "Milk of Paradise," "Transcendental Love," "The Beaver Coat," "The Overcoat," "Summer," "Asian Shade," "Inheritors," "Paradise Lost," "Madwoman of Chaillot," "The Time of Your Life" Bdwy in "Play Memory" (1984).

BRETT, JEREMY. Born Nov. 3, 1933 in Berkswell, Eng. Attended Eaton. Bdwy debut 1956 with Old Vic's "Troilus and Cressida," "Macbeth," "Richard II," and "Romeo and Juliet," followed by "The Deputy," "Dracula," "Aren't We All?"

BRIAN, MICHAEL. Born Nov. 14, 1958 in Utica, NY. Attended Boston Consv. Debut 1979 OB in "Kennedy's Children," followed by "Street Scene," "The Death of Von Richthofen as Witnessed from Earth," "Lenny and the Heartbreakers," "Gift of the Magi," "Next Please!," Bdwy in "Baby" (1983), "Big River."

BRIGGS, RICHARD. Born May 28, 1919 in Los Angeles, CA. Graduate College of Pacific, Neighborhood Playhouse. OB in "Blue Is for Boys," "The Cherry Orchard," "Twelfth Night," "Mirrors," "Subway to the Moon."

BRILL, FRAN. Born Sept. 30 in PA. Attended Boston U. Bdwy debut 1969 in "Red, White and Maddox," OB in "What Every Woman Knows," "Scribes," "Naked," "Look Back in Anger," "Knuckle," "Skirmishes," "Baby with the Bathwater," "Holding Patterns," "Festival of One Acts."

BRODERICK, MATTHEW. Born Mar. 21, 1963 in NYC. Debut OB 1981 in "Torch Song Trilogy," Bdwy 1983 in "Brighton Beach Memoirs" for which he received a Theatre World Award, followed by "Biloxi Blues."

BROGGER, IVAR. Born Jan. 10, in St. Paul, Mn. Graduate UMn. Debut 1979 OB in "In the Jungle of Cities," followed by "Collected Words of Billy the Kid," "Magic Time," "Cloud 9," "Richard III," "Clarence," "Madwoman of Chaillot," "Seascape with Sharks and Dancer," "Second Man," Bdwy in "Macbeth" (1981).

BROOKES, JACQUELINE. Born July 24, 1930 in Montclair, NJ. Graduate UIowa, RADA. Bdwy debut 1955 in "Tiger at the Gates," followed by "Watercolor," "Abelard and Heloise," OB in "The Cretan Woman" for which she received a Theatre World Award, "The Clandestine Marriage," "Measure for Measure," "Duchess of Malfi," "Ivanov," "Six Characters in Search of an Author,"

"An Evening's Frost," "Come Slowly, Eden," "The Increased Difficulty of Concentration," "The Persians," "Sunday Dinner," "House of Blue Leaves," "A Meeting by the River," "Owners," "Hallelujah," "Dream of a Blacklisted Actor," "Knuckle," "Mama Sang the Blues," "Buried Child," "On Mt. Chimorazo," "Winter Dancers," "Hamlet," "Old Flames," "The Diviners," "Richard II," "Vieux Carre," "Full Hookup."

BROOKS, ALAN. Born July 11, 1950 in Bakersfield, CA. Graduate Occidental Col., FlaStateU. Debut 1978 OB in "Porno Stars at Home," followed by "Dr. Faustus," "Merchant of Venice," "Don Juan," "The Cuchulain Cycle," "The Changeling," "Night Must Fall," "Foreigner."

BROOKS, DOROTHY. Born May 23 in Des Moines, IO. Graduate Buffalo State Col., Fla StateU. Debut 1979 OB in "The Underlings," followed by "Hoffman and Co.," "Pigeons on the Walk," "Night Must Fall," "Murder on the Nile," "Beef."

BROWN, CHUCK. Born Oct. 16, 1959 in Cleveland, OH. Attended Baldwin-Wallace Col. Debut 1984 OB in "Pacific Overtures," followed by "The Shop on Main Street."

BROWN, CLARK. Born Mar. 26, 1958 in Mt. Kisco, NY. Graduate Hampshire Col. Debut OB 1984 in "Magic Time," followed by "Cherokee County," "Africanis Instructus."

BROWN, GRAHAM. Born Oct. 24 in NYC. Graduate Howard U. OB in "Widower's Houses" (1959), "The Emperor's Clothes," "Time of Storm," "Major Barbara," "Land Beyond the River," "The Blacks," "Firebugs," "God Is a (Guess What?)," "An Evening of One-Acts," "Man Better Man," "Behold! Cometh the Vanderkellans," "Ride a Black Horse," "The Great MacDaddy," "Eden," "Nevis Mountain Dew," "Season Unravel," "The Devil's Tear," "Sons and Fathers of Sons," "Abercrombie Apocalypse," "Ceremonies in Dark Old Men," "Eyes of the American," Bdwy in "Weekend" (1968), "Man in the Glass Booth," "River Niger," "Pericles," "Black Picture Show," "Kings."

BROWN, LOREN. Born Dec. 15, 1952 in Kansas City, Mo. Graduate Stanford, AADA. Debut 1978 OB in "The Grinding Machine," followed by "Sunday Morning Vivisection," Bdwy in "The Survivor" (1980).

BROWN, SULLIVAN. Born Jan. 11, 1952 in Biloela, Australia. Graduate UQueensland. Debut 1986 OB in "Writer's Cramp."

BROWNING, SUSAN. Born Feb. 25, 1941 in Baldwin, NY. Penn State graduate. Bdwy debut 1963 in "Love and Kisses," followed by "Company" for which she received a Theatre World Award, "Shelter," "Goodtime Charley," "Big River," OB in "Jo," "Dime a Dozen," "Seventeen," "Boys from Syracuse," "Collision Course," "Whiskey," "As You Like It," "Removalists," "Africa-nis Instructus."

BRUMMEL, DAVID. Born Nov. 1, 1942 in Brooklyn, NY. Bdwy debut 1973 in "The Pajama Game," followed by "Music Is," "Oklahoma!," OB in "Cole Porter," "The Fantasticks."

BRUNS, PHILIP. Born May 2, 1931 in Pipestone, Mn. Graduate Augustana Col., Yale. Bdwy bow 1964 in "The Deputy," followed by "Lysistrata," OB in "Mr. Simian," "The Cradle Will Rock," "He Who Gets Slapped," "Dr. Willy Nilly," "Come Play with Me," "Listen to the Mocking Bird," "The Bald Soprano," "Jack of the Submission," "Endgame," "Servant of Two Masters," "Pantomania," "Square in the Eye," "Butter and Egg Man," "Spitting Image," "Henry V," "A Dream Out of Time," "Two," "The Electric Man."

BRUTSMAN, LAURA. Born July 31, 1961 in Cheyenne, WY. Graduate Juilliard. Debut 1984 OB in "Pieces of Eight," followed by "The Skin of Our Teeth," "As You Like It," "A New Way to Pay Old Debts," "Orchards."

BRYANT, CRAIG. Born Sept. 13, 1961 in Aurora, Il. Graduate NYU. Debut 1986 OB in "Orchards."

BRYANT, DAVID. Born May 26, 1936 in Nashville, Tn. Attended TnStateU. Bdwy debut 1972 in "Don't Play Us Cheap," followed by "Bubbling Brown Sugar," "Amadeus," OB in "Up in Central Park," "Elizabeth and Essex," "Appear and Show Cause."

BRYDON, W. B. Born Sept. 20, 1933 in Newcastle, Eng. Debut 1962 OB in "The Long, the Short and the Tall," followed by "Live Like Pigs," "Sjt. Musgrave's Dance," "The Kitchen," "Come Slowly Eden," "The Unknown Soldier and His Wife," "Moon for the Misbegotten," "The Orphan," "Possession," "Total Abandon," "Madwoman of Chaillot," "The Circle," Bdwy in "The Lincoln Mask," "Ulysses in Nighttown," "The Father."

BRYGGMAN, LARRY. Born Dec. 21, 1938 in Concord, Ca. Attended CCSF, AmThWing. Debut 1962 OB in "A Pair of Pairs," followed by "Live Like Pigs," "Stop," "You're Killing Me," "Mod Donna," "Waiting for Godot," "Ballymurphy," "Marco Polo Sings a Solo," "Brownsville Raid," "Two Small Bodies," "Museum," "Winter Dancers," "The Resurrection of Lady Lester," "Royal Bob," "Modern Ladies of Guanabacoa," "Rum and Coke," Bdwy in "Ulysses in Nighttown" (1974), "Checking Out," "Basic Training of Pavlo Hummel," "Richard III."

BRYNE, BARBARA. Born Apr. 1, 1929 in London, Eng. Graduate RADA. NY debut 1981 OB in "Entertaining Mr. Sloane," Bdwy in "Sunday in the Park with George" (1984), "Hay Fever."

BUBRISKI, PETER. Born Aug. 20, 1953 in Bennington, Vt. Graduate Yale U., Webber Douglas Academy. Debut OB 1980 in "Dark of the Moon," followed by "Androcles and the Lion," "Murder at the Vicarage," "Black Coffee."

BUCKLEY, BETTY. Born July 3, 1947 in Big Spring, TX. Graduate TCU. Bdwy debut 1969 in "1776," followed by "Pippin," "Cats," OB in "Ballad of Johnny Pot," "What's a Nice Country Like You . . . ," "Circle of Sound," "I'm Getting My Act Together . . .", "Juno's Swans," "The Mystery of Edwin Drood (OB and Bdwy)."

BUCKLEY, MELINDA. Born Apr. 17, 1954 in Attleboro, MA. Graduate UMa. Bdwy debut 1983 in "A Chorus Line," OB in "Damn Yankees," "Pal Joey."

BUDD, JULIE. Born May 7, 1954 in Brooklyn, New York. Debut 1985 OB in "Options," followed by "America Kicks Up Its Heels."

BUFFALOE, KATHARINE. Born Nov. 7, 1953 in Greenville, SC. Graduate NCSch. of Arts. Bdwy debut 1981 in "Copperfield," followed by "Joseph and the Amazing Technicolor Dream-coat," OB in "Non Pasquale," "Charley's Tale."

BURGE, GREGG. Born in NYC in 1959. Juilliard graduate. Bdwy debut 1975 in "The Wiz," followed by "Sophisticated Ladies," "Song and Dance."

BURK, TERENCE. Born Aug. 11, 1947 in Lebanon, IL. Graduate S.Ill.U. Bdwy debut 1976 in "Equus," OB in "Religion," "The Future," "Sacred and Profane Love," "Crime and Punishment."

BURKE, MAGGIE. Born May 2, 1936 in Bay Shore, NY. Graduate Sarah Lawrence Col. OB in "Today Is Independence Day," "Lovers and Other Strangers," "Jules Feiffer's Cartoons," "Fog," "Home Is the Hero," "King John," "Rusty & Rico & Lena & Louie," "Friends," "Butterfaces," "Old Times," Bdwy debut 1985 in "Brighton Beach Memoirs."

BURKHARDT, GERRY. Born June 14, 1946 in Houston, Tx. Attended Lon Morris Col. Bdwy debut 1968 in "Her First Roman," followed by "The Best Little Whorehouse in Texas," OB in "Girl Crazy."

BURKS, DONNY. Born in Martinsville, VA. Graduate St. John's U. Debut 1964 OB in "Dutchman," followed by "Billy Noname" for which he received a Theatre World Award, "Miracle Play," Bdwy in "Hair" (1968), "The American Clock," "The Tap Dance Kid."

BURNS, CATHERINE. Born Sept. 25, 1945 in NYC. Attended AADA. Bdwy 1968 in "The Prime of Miss Jean Brodie," OB in "Dream of a Blacklisted Actor," "The Disintegration of James Cherry," "Operation Sidewinder," "Dear Janet Rosenberg, Dear Mr. Kooning" for which she received a Theatre World Award, "Two Small Bodies," "Voices," "Jungle of Cities," "One Wedding," "Metamorphosis," "Within the Year."

BURRELL, FRED. Born Sept. 18, 1936. Graduate UNC, RADA. Bdwy debut 1964 in "Never Too Late," followed by "Illya Darling," OB in "The Memorandum," "Throckmorton," "Texas," "Voices in the Head."

BURRELL, PAMELA. Born Aug. 4, 1945 in Tacoma, WA. Bdwy debut 1966 in "Funny Girl," followed by "Where's Charley?," "Strider," "Sunday in the Park with George," OB in "Arms and the Man" for which she received a Theatre World Award, "Berkeley Square," "The Boss," "Biography: A Game," "Strider: Story of a Horse," "A Little Madness."

BURRELL, TERESA (formerly Terry). Born Feb. 8, 1952 in Trinidad, WI. Attended Pace U. Bdwy debut 1977 in "Eubie!," followed by "Dreamgirls," OB in "That Uptown Feeling," "They Say It's Wonderful," "George White's Scandals," "Just So."

BURROWS, VINIE. Born Nov. 15, 1928 in NYC. Graduate NYU. Bdwy in "The Wisteria Trees," "Green Pastures," "Mrs. Patterson," "The Skin of Our Teeth," "The Ponder Heart," OB in "Walk Together Children," "Sister! Sister!."

BURTON, KATE. Born Sept. 10, 1957 in Geneva, Switz. Graduate Brown U., Yale. Bdwy debut 1982 in "Present Laughter," followed by "Alice in Wonderland," "Doonesbury," OB in "Winners" for which she received a Theatre World Award, "Romeo and Juliet," "The Accrington Pals," "Playboy of the Western World."

BUSSERT, MEG. Born Oct. 21, 1949 in Chicago, Il. Attended UIll. Bdwy debut 1980 in "The Music Man for which she received a Theatre World Award," followed by "Brigadoon," "Camelot," "New Moon," "The Firefly," OB in "Lola" (1982), "Professionally Speaking."

BUSTAMANTE, MAURICIO. Born Jan. 14, 1948 in Mexico City, Mx. Attended Loretto Heights Col., Strasberg Inst. Debut 1980 OB in "Annie Get Your Gun," followed by "Ghashiram."

BYERS, RALPH. Born Jan. 10, 1950 in Washington, DC. Graduate William & Mary Col., Catholic U. Debut 1975 OB in "Hamlet," followed by "Julius Caesar," "Rebel Women," "No End of Blame," "Henry IV Part I," "Sunday in the Park with George," Bdwy in "Herzl" (1976), "Goodbye Fidel," "Big River."

CACCIATORE, JAYNE. Born May 31, 1961 in Denver, Co. Graduate Point Park Col., Utah. Debut 1985 OB in "Downriver," followed by "Funny Girl."

CADY, DAVID. Born Nov. 21, 1960 in NYC. Attended NYU. Debut 1979 OB in "The City Suite," followed by "Yours, Anne," Bdwy in "Merrily We Roll Along" (1981).

CAFFEY, MARION J. Born Jan. 11, 1955 in Hempstead, TX. OB in "Come with Us," "Seeds," "Blackberries," "Dreams of Becoming," "Mayor."

CAHILL, JAMES. Born May 31, 1940 in Brooklyn, NY. Bdwy debut 1967 in "Marat/deSade," followed by "Break a Leg," "The Marriage of Figaro," OB in "The Hostage," "The Alchemist," "Johnny Johnson," "Peer Gynt," "Timon of Athens," "An Evening for Merlin Finch," "The Disintegration of James Cherry," "Crimes of Passion," "Rain," "Screens," "Total Eclipse," "Entertaining Mr. Sloane," "Hamlet," "Othello," "The Trouble with Europe," "Lydie Breeze," "Don Juan," "Bathroom Plays," "Wild Life," "Uncle Vanya."

CAIN, WILLIAM B. Born May 27, 1931 in Tuscaloosa, Al. Graduate UWash, Catholic U. Debut 1962 OB in "Red Roses for Me," followed by "Jericho Jim Crow," "Henry V," "Antigone," "Relatively Speaking," "I Married an Angel in Concert," Bdwy in "Wilson in the Promise Land" (1970), "Of the Fields Lately," "You Can't Take It with You."

CALL, ANTHONY D. Born Aug. 31, 1940 in Los Angeles, Ca. Attended UPa. Debut 1969 OB in "The David Show," followed by "Frequency," "Countess Mitzi," Bdwy in "Crown Matrimonial" (1973)," "The Trip Back Down," "Suspenders."

CALLMAN, NANCY. Born Apr. 12, 1949 in Buffalo, NY. Graduate SUNY/Binghamton, Manhattan Sch. of Music. Bdwy debut 1976 in "1600 Pennsylvania Avenue," followed by "Sweeney Todd," "Nine," OB in "Circa 1900," "Broadway a la Carte," "Hit Tunes from Flop Shows," "The Shop on Main Street."

CAMACHO, BLANCA. Born Nov. 19, 1956 in NYC. Graduate NYU. Debut 1984 OB in "Sarita," followed by "Maggie Magalita."

CAMP, JOANNE. Born Apr. 4, 1951 in Atlanta, GA. Graduate FlAtlanticU, Geo WashU. Debut 1981 OB in "The Dry Martini," followed by "Geniuses," for which she received a Theatre World Award, "June Moon," "Painting Churches," "Merchant of Venice," "Lady from the Sea," "The Contrast."

CAMPBELL, GRAEME. Born Nov. 30, 1940 in Australia. Attended Christian Brothers Col. Bdwy debut 1982 in "Othello," followed by "Oliver!"

CANARY, DAVID. Born Aug. 25 in Elwood, IN. Graduate UCin, CinConservatory. Debut 1960 OB in "Kittywake Island," followed by "The Fantastiks," "The Father," "Hi, Paisano," "Summer," "Blood Moon," "Sally's Gone, She Left Her Name," "Mortally Fine," Bdwy in "Great Day in the Morning," "Happiest Girl in the World," "Clothes for a Summer Hotel."

CAPLIN, JEREMY O. Born Mar. 17, 1955 in Albemarle County, Va. Graduate Wesleyan U, UVa. Bdwy debut 1983 in "Marilyn: An American Fable," followed by "Execution of Justice."

CAPRI, MARK. Born July 19, 1951 in Washington, DC. Graduate Stanford U, RADA. Debut 1984 OB in "On Approval" for which he received a Theatre World Award, followed by "An Enemy of the People."

CARDEN, WILLIAM. Born Feb. 2, 1947 in NYC. Attended Lawrence U., Brandeis U. Debut 1974 OB in "Short Eyes," followed by Leaving Home," "Back in the Race," "Thin Ice," "Bloodletters," "Dennis."

CARIOU, LEN. Born Sept. 30, 1939 in Winnipeg, Can. Bdwy debut 1968 in "House of Atreus," followed by "Henry V" and "Applause" for which he received a Theatre World Award, "Night Watch," "A Little Night Music," "Cold Storage," "Sweeney Todd," "Dance a Little Closer," OB in "A Sorrow Beyond Dreams," "Up from Paradise," "Master Class."

CARLIN, AMANDA. Born Dec. 12 in Queens, NY. Graduate Tufts U. Bdwy debut 1980 in "Major Barbara," followed by "The Man Who Came to Dinner," OB in "The Dining Room," "Twelfth Night," "The Accrington Pals," "Comedy of Errors," "Playboy of the Western World," "Waltaz of the Toreadors."

CARLING, P. L. Born Mar. 31. Graduate Stanford, UCLA. Debut 1955 OB in "The Chairs," followed by "In Good King Charles' Golden Days," "Magistrate," "Picture of Dorian Gray," "The Vise," "Lady from the Sea," "Booth Is Back in Town," "Ring Round the Moon," "Philadelphia Here I Come," "Sorrows of Frederick," "Biography," "Murder on the Nile," "3 Lost Plays of O'Neill," "Verdict," "The Dispute," Bdwy in "The Devils" (1965), "Scratch," "Shenandoah."

CARLO, JOHANN. Born May 21, 1957 in Buffalo, NY. Attended Webber-Douglas Academy. Debut 1978 OB in "Grand Magic," followed by "Artichoke," "Don Juan Comes Back from the War," "The Arbor," "Cinders," "Rich Relations," Bdwy in "Plenty (1983)."

CARMINE, MICHAEL. Born Mar. 6, 1959 in Brooklyn, NY. Attended Cal.Inst.of Arts. Debut 1984 OB in "Sarita," followed by "Cuba and His Teddy Bear."

CARNAHAN, KIRSTI. Born June 29 in Evanston, Il. Attended UCincinnati. Bdwy debut 1983 in "Baby," followed by "The Three Musketeers," OB in "Hang on to the Good Times," "Mortally Fine."

CARPENTER, CARLETON. Born July 10, 1926 in Bennington, Vt. Attended Northwestern U. Bdwy debut 1944 in "Bright Boy," followed by "Career Angel," "Three to Make Ready," "Magic Touch," "John Murray Anderson's Almanac," "Hotel Paradiso," "Box of Watercolors," "Hello, Dolly!," OB in "Stage Affair," "Boys in the Band," "Dylan," "The Greatest Fairy Story Ever Told," "A Good Old Fashioned Revue," "Miss Stanwyck Is Still in Hiding," "Rocky Road," "Apollo of Bellac," "Light Up the Sky."

CARRICART, ROBERTSON Born Dec. 28, 1947 in Norfolk, VA. Graduate UCLA. Debut 1974 OB in "Private Ear/Public Eye," followed by "Cromwell," "Out of the Night," "Dr. Faustus," Bdwy in "Oklahoma " (1979), "Design for Living," "Figaro."

CARROLL, DANNY. Born May 30, 1940 in Maspeth, NY. Bdwy bow in 1957 "The Music Man," followed by "Flora the Red Menace," "Funny Girl," "George M!," "Billy," "Ballroom," "42nd Street," OB in "Boys from Syracuse," "Babes in the Woods."

CARROLL, DAVID-JAMES. Born July 30, 1950 in Rockville Centre, NY. Graduate Dartmouth Col. Debut 1975 OB in "A Matter of Time," followed by "Joseph and the Amazing Technicolor Dreamcoat," "New Tunes," "La Boheme," Bdwy in "Rodgers and Hart" (1975), "Where's Charley?," "Oh, Brother!," "7 Brides for 7 Brothers," "Roberta in Concert," "The Wind in the Willows."

CARRUBBA, PHILIP. Born May 3, 1951 in San Francisco, Ca. Graduate SFStateU. Bdwy debut 1981 in "Joseph and the Amazing Technicolor Dreamcoat," followed by OB in "They're Playing Our Song."

CARRUTHERS, JAMES. Born May 26, 1931 in Morristown, NJ. Attended Lafayette Col., HB Studio. Debut 1959 OB in "Our Town," followed by "Under the Sycamore Tree," "Misalliance," "The Hostage," "Telemachus Clay," "Shadow of a Gunman," "Masks," "Biography: A Game," "Lulu," "Salt Lake City Skyline," "Journey to Gdansk," "Crown Cork Cafeteria," Bdwy in "Poor Murderer" (1976).

CARTER, ROSANNA. Born Sept. 20 in Rolle Town, Bahamas. Bdwy debut 1980 in "The American Clock," followed by "Inacent Black," OB in "Lament of Tasta Fari," "Burghers of Callais," "Scottsboro Boys," "Les Femmes Noires," "Killings on the Last Line," "Under Heaven's Eye," "Marathon '86."

CARTER, THELMA LOUISE. Born July 16 in Gary, IN. Debut 1975 OB in "Liberty Call," followed by "The Crucible," "Between Rails," "Long Time Since Yesterday."

CASH, SUSAN. Born Dec. 21, 1956 in Delaware County, PA. Attended Carnegie-Mellon U. Debut 1983 OB in "Talking With," followed by "Almost in Vegas," "Cheapside," "Anteroom."

CASS, PEGGY. Born May 21, 1926 in Boston, MA. Attended Wyndham Sch. Credits include "Touch and Go," "Live Wire," "Bernardine," "Othello," "Henry V," "Auntie Mame" for which she received a Theatre World Award, "A Thurber Carnival," "Children from Their Games," "Don't Drink the Water," "Front Page" (1969), "Plaza Suite," "Once a Catholic," "42nd Street," "The Octette Bridge Club," OB in "Phoenix '55," "Are You Now or Have You Ever Been," "One Touch of Venus," "George White's Scandals."

CASSERLY, KERRY. Born Oct. 26, 1953 in Minneapolis, MN. Attended UMinn. Bdwy debut 1980 in "One Night Stand," followed by "A Chorus Line," "My One and Only."

CASSIDY, TIM. Born March 22, 1952 in Alliance, OH. Attended UCincinnati. Bdwy debut 1974 in "Good News," followed by "A Chorus Line."

CASTANG, VERONICA. Born Apr. 22 1938, in London, Eng. Attended Sorbonne. Bdwy debut 1964 in "How's the World Treating You?," followed by "The National Health," "Whose Life Is It Anyway?," OB in "The Trigon," "Sjt. Musgrave's Dance," "Saved," "Water Hens," "Self-Accusation," "Kaspar," "Ionescapade," "Statements After and Arrest under the Immorality Act," "Ride a Cock Horse," "Banana Box," "Bonjour La Bonjour," "A Call from the East," "Close of Play," "Cloud 9," "After the Prize," "David and Paula," "The Accrington Pals."

CAZA, TERRENCE. Born Mar. 26, 1958 in Detroit, Mi. Graduate UMi, UWash. Debut 1984 OB in "Pieces of Eight," followed by "As You Like It," "A New Way to Pay Old Debts," "Orchards."

CELLARIO, MARIA. Born June 19, 1948 in Buenos Aires, Arg. Graduate Ithaca Col. Bdwy debut 1975 in "The Royal Family," followed by OB in "Fugue in a Nursery," "Declassee," "Equinox," "Flatbush Faithful."

CERVERIS, MICHAEL. Born Nov. 6, 1960 in Bethesda, MD. Graduate Yale U. Debut 1983 OB in "Moon," followed by "Macbeth," "Life Is a Dream," "Total Eclipse," "Green Fields."

CHALAKANI, PAUL. Born Feb. 12, 1955 in Hastings-on-Hudson, NY. Graduate Rider Col., George Washington U. Debut 1985 OB in "The Beach House."

CHALMERS, TONI-MARIA. Born July 11, 1966 in Washington, DC. Attended Philadelphia Col. Bdwy debut 1986 in "Uptown It's Hot," followed by OB in "Sh-Boom!."

CHAMBERLIN, SALLY. Born Dec. 26 in Cambridge, Ma. Graduate Sarah Lawrence Col. Bdwy debut 1949 in "Twelfth Night," followed by OB in "Julius Caesar," "Behind a Mask," "Brand."

CHAMPAGNE, MICHAEL. Born Apr. 10, 1947 in New Bedford, MA. Graduate SMU., MSU. Debut 1975 OB in "The Lieutenant," followed by "Alinsky," "The Hostage," "Livingstone and Sechele," "A Christmas Carol," "Penelope," "An Occasion of Sin," "Beef."

CHANDLER, NAT. Born Dec. 16, 1957 in LaGrange, Ga. Graduate Furman U., Northwestern U. Debut 1985 OB in "Tales of Tinseltown."

CHANNING, CAROL. Born Jan. 31, 1921 in Seattle, Wa. Attended Bennington Col. Bdwy debut 1941 in "No for an Answer," followed by "Let's Face It," "Proof through the Night," "Lend an Ear" for which she received a Theatre World Award, "Gentlemen Prefer Blondes," "Wonderful Town," "The Vamp," "Show Girl," "Hello, Dolly!" (1964/1978), "Four on a Garden," "Lorelei."

CHANNING, STOCKARD. Born in 1944 in NYC. Attended Radcliffe Col. Debut 1970 OB in "Adaptation/Next," followed by "The Lady and the Clarinet," "The Golden Age," Bdwy in "Two Gentlemen of Verona," "They're Playing Our Song," "The Rink," "Joe Egg," "House of Blue Leaves."

CHAPMAN, GARY. Born Apr. 20, 1953 in Brooklyn, NY. Attended CalInst of Arts. Bdwy debut 1979 in "Dancin'," followed by "Sophisticated Ladies," "Big Deal."

CHARLES, WALTER. Born Apr. 4, 1945 in East Stroudsburg, PA. Graduate Boston U Bdwy debut 1973 in "Grease," followed by "1600 Pennsylvania Avenue," "Knickerbocker Holiday," "Sweeney Todd," "Cats," "La Cage aux Folles."

CHAVES, RICHARD. Born Oct. 9, 1951 in Jacksonville, FL. Attended Occidental Col. Debut 1985 OB in "Tracers" for which he received a Theatre World Award.

CHEW, LEE. Born Feb. 8 in Roanoke, Va. Graduate VaComU. Debut 1978 OB in "Can-Can," followed by "Light Up the Sky," "She Loves Me."

CHIBAS, MARISSA. Born June 13, 1961 in NYC. Graduate SUNY/Purchase. Debut OB 1983 in "Asian Shade," followed by "Sudden Death," "Total Eclipse," Bdwy in "Brighton Beach Memoirs" (1983), "Fresh Horses."

CHILSON, KATHRYN. Born Jan. 31, 1955 in Louisiana, Mo. Graduate Webster U. Debut 1982 OB in "The Cherry Orchard," followed by "The Constant Wife."

CHODER, JILL. Born Dec. 14, 1948 in Pittsburgh, Pa. Attended NYU. Bdwy debut 1962 in "Bye Bye Birdie," followed by "Stop the World I Want to Get Off," "The Roar of the Greasepaint," OB in "Best Foot Forward" (1963), "Your Own Thing," "Boccaccio," "Festival of One Acts."

CHRIS, MARILYN. Born May 19, 1939 in NYC. Bdwy in "The Office" (1966), "Birthday Party," "7 Descents of Myrtle," "Lenny," OB in "Nobody Hears a Broken Drum," "Fame," "Juda Applause," "Junebug Graduates Tonight," "Man Is Man," "In the Jungle of Cities," "Good Soldier Schweik," "The Tempest," "Ride a Black Horse," "Screens," "Kaddish," "Lady from the Sea," "Bread," "Leaving Home," "Curtains," "Elephants," "The Upper Depths," "Man Enough," "Loose Connections."

CHRYST, GARY. Born in 1959 in LaJolla, Ca. Joined Joffrey Ballet in 1968, Bdwy debut in "Dancin' " (1979), followed by "A Chorus Line," OB in "One More Song, One More Dance," "Music Moves Me."

CHUN, LYNETTE. Born Sept. 13 in Hilo, Hi. Graduate Rockford Col., UAuckland. Debut 1972 OB in "Return of the Phoenix," followed by "Legend of Wu Chang," "Monkey Music," "Yellow Is My Favorite Color," "Sunrise," "Bullet-Headed Birds," "Rohwer," "Station J," "Teahouse," "Yellow Fever," "American Dreams," "Ghashiram Kotwal," "The Lady Aoi," "Medea."

CILENTO, WAYNE. Born Aug. 25, 1949 in The Bronx, NY. Graduate SUNY/Brockport. Bdwy debut 1973 in "Irene," followed by "Rachel Lily Rosenbloom," "Seesaw," "A Chorus Line," "The Act," "Dancin'," "Perfectly Frank," "Big Deal."

CLARK, BRYAN E. Born Apr. 5, 1929 in Louisville, KY. Graduate Fordham U. Bdwy debut 1978 in "A History of the American Film," followed by "Bent," OB in "Winning Isn't Everything," "Put Them All Together," "Red Rover," "Paradise Lost," "Clarence," "A Step Out of Line," "Madwoman of Chaillot," "The Circle."

CLARK, CHERYL. Born Dec. 7, 1950 in Boston, MA. Attended Ind. U., NYU. Bdwy debut 1972 in "Pippin," followed by "Chicago," "A Chorus Line."

CLARK, JOSH. Born Aug. 16, 1955 in Bethesda, Md. Attended NCSch. of Arts. Debut 1976 OB in "The Old Glory," followed by "Molly," "Just a Little Bit Less Than Normal," "Rear Column," "The Browning Version," "Accounts," Bdwy in "The Man Who Came to Dinner" (1980), "Alice in Wonderland," "Execution of Justice."

CLARK, WILLIAM G. Born Feb. 27, 1939 in Okolona, Ms. Graduate UWFla/Pensacola. Debut 1985 OB in "Mortally Fine."

CLARKE, CAITLIN. Born May 3, 1952 in Pittsburgh, PA. Graduate Mt. Holyoke Col., Yale. Debut 1981 OB in "No End of Blame," followed by "Lorenzaccio," "Summer," "Quartermaine's Terms," "Thin Ice," "Total Eclipse," Bdwy in "Teaneck Tanzi" (1983), "Strange Interlude," "Arms and the Man," "Figaro."

CLEMENTE, RENE. Born July 2, 1950 in El Paso, TX. Graduate WestTxStateU. Bdwy debut 1977 in "A Chorus Line," followed by "Dancin'," "Play Me a Country Song," "Cats."

CLOSE, GLENN. Born May 19, 1947 in Greenwich, CT. Graduate William & Mary Col. Bdwy debut 1974 with Phoenix Co. in "Love for Love," "Member of the Wedding," and "Rules of the Game," followed by "Rex," "Crucifer of Blood," "Barnum," "The Real Thing," "Benefactors," OB in "The Crazy Locomotive," "Uncommon Women and Others," "Wine Untouched," "The Winter Dancers," "The Singular Life of Albert Nobbs," "Joan of Arc at the Stake," "Childhood."

COCO, JAMES. Born Mar. 21, 1930 in NYC. Debut 1956 OB in "Salome," followed by "Moon in the Yellow River," "Squat Betty/The Sponge Room," "That 5 a.m. Jazz," "Lovey," "The Basement," "Fragments," "Witness," "Next," "Monsters/The Transfiguration of Benno Blimpie," "It's Only a Play," Bdwy in "Hotel Paradiso," "Everybody Loves Opal," "Passage to India," "Arturo Ui," "The Devils," "Man of LaMancha," "The Astrakian Coat," "Here's Where I Belong," "Last of the Red Hot Lovers," "Wally's Cafe," "Little Me," "You Can't Take It with You."

COHEN, LYNN. Born Aug. 10 in Kansas City, MO. Graduate Northwestern U. Debut 1979 OB in "Don Juan Comes Back from the Wars," followed by "Getting Out," "The Arbor," "The Cat and the Canary," "Suddenly Last Summer," "Bella Figura," "The Smash," "Chinese Viewing Pavilion," "Isn't It Romantic," "Total Eclipse," "Angelo's Wedding," "Hamlet."

COHENOUR, PATTI. Born Oct. 17, 1952 in Albuquerque, NMx. Attended UNMx. Bdwy debut 1982 in "A Doll's Life," followed by "Pirates of Penzance," "Big River," "The Mystery of Edwin Drood." OB in "La Boheme" for which she received a Theatre World Award.

COLBERT, CLAUDETTE. Born Sept. 13, 1903 in Paris. Bdwy debut 1925 in "Wild Westcotts," followed by "Ghost Train," "A Kiss in a Taxi," "The Barker," "The Mulberry Bush," "La Gringa," "Tin Pan Alley," "Dynamo," "See Naples and Die," "Janus," "The Marriage-Go-Round," "Jake, Julia and Uncle Joe," "Irregular Verb to Love," "The Kingfisher," "A Talent for Murder," "Aren't We All?"

COLBY, CHRISTINE. Born Feb. 27 in Cincinnati, Oh. Attended UCincinnati. Bdwy debut 1978 in "Dancin'," followed by "Sweet Charity."

COLE, KAY. Born Jan. 13, 1948 in Miami, FL. Bdwy debut 1961 in "Bye Bye Birdie," followed by "Stop the World I Want to Get Off," "Roar of the Greasepaint . . .," "Hair," "Jesus Christ Superstar," "Words and Music," "Chorus Line," OB in "The Cradle Will Rock," "Two If By Sea," "Rainbow," "White Nights," "Sgt. Pepper's Lonely Hearts Club Band," "On the Swing Shift," "Snoopy," "Road to Hollywood," "One-man Band."

COLEMAN, DESIREE. Born in NYC in 1968. Debut OB 1983 in "Mama I Want to Sing," Bdwy in "Big Deal" (1986).

COLES, CHARLES HONI. Born Apr. 2, 1911 in Philadelphia, PA. Debut 1933 OB in "Humming Sam," Bdwy in "Gentlemen Prefer Blondes" (1949), "Black Broadway," "My One and Only."

COLKER, JERRY. Born Mar. 16, 1955 in Los Angeles, CA. Attended Harvard U. Debut 1975 OB in "Tenderloin," followed by "Pal Joey," "3 Guys Naked from the Waist Down," Bdwy in "West Side Story," "Pippin," "A Chorus Line."

COLLINS, RAY. Born July 20, 1949 in London, Eng. Attended LAMDA. Debut 1985 OB in "Roundheads and Peakheads," followed by "The Constant Wife."

CONAWAY, JEFF. Born Oct. 5, 1950 in NYC. Attended NYU. Bdwy debut 1960 in "All the Way Home," followed by "Grease," "The News."

CONNELL, DAVID. Born Nov. 24, 1935 in Cleveland, Oh. Bdwy debut 1968 in "The Great White Hope," followed by "Don't Play Us Cheap," OB in "Ballet Behind the Bridge," "Miracle Play," "Time Out of Time," "Champeen!," "One Flew over the Cuckoo's Nest," "In the House of the Blues."

CONNELL, GORDON. Born Mar. 19, 1923 in Berkeley, CA. Graduate UCal, NYU. Bdwy debut 1961 in "Subways Are for Sleeping," followed by "Hello, Dolly!," "Lysistrata," "The Human Comedy," "Big River," OB in "Beggar's Opera," "The Butler Did It," "With Love and Laughter."

CONNELL, JANE. Born Oct. 27, 1925 in Berkeley, CA. Attended UCal. Bdwy debut in "New Faces of 1956," followed by "Drat! The Cat!," "Mame" (1966/'83), "Dear World," "Lysistrata," OB in "Shoestring Revue," "Threepenny Opera," "Pieces of Eight," "Demi-Dozen," "She Stoops to Conquer," "Drat!," "The Real Inspector Hound," "The Rivals," "The Rise and Rise of Daniel Rocket," "Laughing Stock," "The Singular Dorothy Parker," "No No Nanette in Concert."

CONNOLLY, JOHN P. Born Sept. 1, 1950 in Philadelphia, PA. Graduate Temple U. Debut 1973 OB in "Paradise Lost," followed by "The Wizard of Oz," "Fighting Bob," "For the Use of the Hall," "The Golem," "A Step Out of Line," "For Sale," "Filthy Rich."

COOK, RODERICK. Born in 1932 in London, Eng. Attended Cambridge U. Bdwy debut 1961 in "Kean," followed by "Roar Like a Dove," "The Girl Who Came to Supper," "Noel Coward's Sweet Potato," "The Man Who Came to Dinner," "Woman of the Year," "Eileen," OB in "A Scent of Flowers," "Oh, Coward!," "Sweethearts in Concert," "Jubilee in Concert."

COOPER, JULI. Born June 21, 1957 in Washington, DC. Graduate UVa., LAMDA, RADA. Bdwy debut 1985 in "Pack of Lies," followed by OB in "Another Part of the Forest."

COOPER, MARILYN. Born Dec. 14, 1936 in NYC. Attended NYU. Appeared in "Mr. Wonderful," "West Side Story," "Brigadoon," "Gypsy," "I Can Get It for You Wholesale," "Hallelujah Baby!," "Golden Rainbow," "Mame," "A Teaspoon Every 4 Hours," "Two by Two," "On the Town," "Ballroom," "Woman of the Year," "The Odd Couple" (1985), OB in "The Mad Show," "Look Me Up," "The Perfect Party."

CORCORAN, MARY. Born Oct. 10, 1959 in Washington, DC. Graduate Regis Col. Debut 1986 OB in "To Feed Their Hopes."

CORFMAN, CARIS. Born May 18, 1955 in Boston, Ma. Graduate FlaStateU, Yale. Debut 1978 OB in "Wings," followed by "Fish Riding Bikes," "Filthy Rich," "Dry Land," Bdwy in "Amadeus" (1980).

CORNTHWAITE, ROBERT. Born Apr. 18, 1917 in St. Helens, Or. Graduate USCal. Bdwy debut 1978 in "The Devil's Disciple," OB in "And a Nightingale Sang," "Season's Greetings."

CORREIA, DON. Born Aug. 28, 1951 in San Jose, CA. Attended SanJoseStateU. Bdwy debut 1980 in "A Chorus Line," followed by "Perfectly Frank," "Little Me," "Sophisticated Ladies," "5–6–7–8 Dance," "My One and Only," "Singin' in the Rain."

CORTEZ, KATHERINE. Born Sept. 28, 1950 in Detroit, MI. Graduate UNC. Debut 1979 OB in "The Dark at the Top of the Stairs," followed by "Corners," "Confluence," "The Great Grandson of Jedediah Kohler," "A Think Piece," "The Sea Gull," "Dysan," "Fool for Love," "For Sale," "Sunday Morning Vivisection," Bdwy in "Foxfire" (1982).

CORTLAND, NICHOLAS. Born Oct. 10, 1946 in NYC. Graduate Hofstra U. Debut 1984 in "Suzanna Andler," followed by "Goodbye Freddy."

COSTA, JOSEPH. Born June 8, 1946 in Ithaca, NY. Graduate Gettysburg Col., Yale. Debut 1978 OB in "The Show-Off," followed by "The Tempest," "The Changeling," "A Map of the World."

COTSIRILOS, STEPHANIE. Born Feb. 24, 1947 in Chicago, Il. Graduate Brown U., Yale. Debut 1973 OB in "The Little Mahagonny," followed by "Sweet Will," Bdwy in "A Kurt Weill Cabaret" (1980), followed by "Goodbye Fidel," "Nine."

COUNTRYMAN, MICHAEL. Born Sept. 15, 1955 in St. Paul, Mn. Graduate Trinity Col, AADA. Debut 1983 OB in "Changing Palettes," followed by "June Moon," "Terra Nova," "Mink on a Gold Hook," "Custom of the Country," "Love as We Know It," "And They Dance Real Slow in Jackson."

COVER, A. D. Born in 1928 in Stamford, Ct. Attended Wesleyan, Yale, UVt., AADA. Debut 1985 OB in "The Importance of Being Earnest."

COX, CATHERINE. Born Dec. 13, 1950 in Toledo, OH. Wittenberg U. graduate. Bdwy debut 1976 in "Music Is," followed by "Whoopee!" "Oklahoma!," "Shakespeare's Cabaret," "Barnum," "Baby," OB in "By Strouse," "It's Better With a Band," "In Trousers," "Crazy Arnold."

CRABTREE, DON. Born Aug. 21, 1928 in Borger, TX. Attended Actors Studio. Bdwy bow 1959 in "Destry Rides Again," followed by "Happiest Girl in the World," "Family Affair," "Unsinkable Molly Brown," "Sophie," "110 In the Shade," "Golden Boy," "Pousse Cafe," "Mahagonny" (OB), "The Best Little Whorehouse in Texas," "42nd Street."

CRAIG, BETSY. Born Jan. 5, 1952 in Hopewell, VA. Attended Berry Col. Bdwy debut 1972 in "Ambassador," followed by "Smith," "Brigadoon," "La Cage aux Folles."

CRAIG, NOEL. Born Jan. 4 in St. Louis, MO. Attended Northwestern U., Goodman Theatre, London Guildhall. Bdwy debut 1967 in "Rosencrantz and Guildenstern Are Dead," followed by "A Patriot for Me," "Conduct Unbecoming," "Vivat! Vivat Regina!," "Going Up," "Dance a Little Closer," "A Chorus Line," OB in "Pygmalion," "Promenade," "Family House," "Inn at Lydda."

CRESWELL, SAYLOR. Born Nov. 18, 1939 in Pottstown, Pa. Graduate Brown U. Debut 1968 OB in "Carving a Statue," followed by "Room Service," "Savages," "Under Milk Wood," Bdwy in "Herzl" (1976).

CRIVELLO, ANTHONY. Born Aug. 2, 1955 in Milwaukee, Wi. Bdwy debut 1982 in "Evita," followed by "The News," OB in "The Juniper Tree."

CROFOOT, LEONARD JOHN. Born Sept. 20, 1948 in Utica, NY. Bdwy debut 1968 in "The Happy Time," followed by "Come Summer," "Gigi," "Barnum," "Grind," OB in "Circus," "Joseph and the Amazing Technicolor Dreamcoat," "On the 20th Century."

CROMWELL, DAVID. Born Feb. 16, 1946 in Cornwall, NY. Graduate Ithaca Col. Debut 1968 OB in "Up Eden," followed by "In the Boom Boom Room," "Hamlet," Bdwy in "A History of the American Film" (1978).

CRONYN, HUME. Born July 18, 1911 in London, Can. Bdwy debut 1934 in "Hipper's Holiday," followed by "Boy Meets Girl," "High Tor," "Room Service," "There's Always a Breeze," "Escape This Night," "Off to Buffalo," "Three Sisters," "Weak Link," "Retreat to Pleasure," "Mr. Big," "Survivors," "The Fourposter," "The Honeys," "A Day by the Sea," "Man in Dog Suit," "Triple Play," "Big Fish Little Fish," "Hamlet," "The Physicists," "A Delicate Balance," "Hadrian VII," "Promenade All," "Noel Coward in Two Keys," "The Gin Game," "Foxfire," "The Petition," OB in "Krapp's Last Tape," "Madam Will You Walk," "Happy Days," "Act Without Words."

CROOK, PETER. Born Mar. 17, 1958 in Houston, Tx. Graduate Juilliard. Debut 1982 OB in "A Midsummer Night's Dream," followed by "Zones of the Spirit," "Hamlet," Bdwy in "Amadeus" (1983).

CROSBY, KIM. Born July 11, 1960 in Ft. Smith, Ar. Attended SMU, ManSch of Music. Bdwy debut 1985 in "Jerry's Girls."

CROSS, STEPHEN. Born Aug. 23, 1959 in Halifax, NS, Can. Attended Ryerson PolyInst. Debut 1986 OB in "The Constant Wife."

CROUSE, LINDSAY. Born May 12, 1948 in NYC. Graduate Radcliffe Col. Bdwy debut 1972 in "Much Ado about Nothing," OB in "The Foursome," "Fishing," "Long Day's Journey into Night," "Total Recall," "Father's Day," "Hamlet," "Reunion," "Twelfth Night," "Childe Byron," "Richard II," "Serenading Louie," "Prairie/Shawl."

CROXTON, DARRYL. Born Apr. 5, 1946 in Baltimore, Md. Attended AADA. Bdwy debut 1969 in "Indians," followed by "Sly Fox," OB in "Volpone," "Murder in the Cathedral," "The Taking of Miss Janie," "Old Glory," "Divine Comedy," "Jack Gelber's New Play," "Cabal of Hypocrites," "Julius Caesar."

CRYER, GRETCHEN. Born Oct. 17, 1935 in Indianapolis, In. Graduate DePauw U. Bdwy debut 1962 in "Little Me," followed by "110 in the Shade," OB in "Now Is the Time for All Good Men," "Gallery," "Circle of Sound," "I'm Getting My Act Together . . .," "Blue Plate Special," "To Whom It May Concern."

CUERVO, ALMA. Born Aug. 13 1951 in Tampa, FL. Graduate Tulane U, Yale U. Debut 1977 in "Uncommon Women and Others," followed by "A Foot in the Door," "Put Them All Together," "Isn't It Romantic," "Miss Julie," "Quilters," "Bdwy in Once in a Lifetime," "Bedroom Farce," "Censored Scenes from King Kong," "Is There Life after High School?"

CULLIVER, KAREN. Born Dec. 30, 1959 in Florida. Attended Stetson U. Bdwy debut 1983 in "Show Boat," followed by OB in "The Fantasticks."

CULLUM, JOHN. Born Mar. 2, 1930 in Knoxville, TN. Graduate UTn. Bdwy debut 1960 in "Camelot," followed by "Infidel Caesar," "The Rehearsal," "Hamlet," "On a Clear Day You Can See Forever" for which he received a Theatre World Award, "Man of La Mancha," "1776," "Vivat! Vivat Regina!," "Shenandoah," "Kings," "The Trip Back Down," "On the 20th Century," "Deathtrap," "Doubles," "The Boys in Autumn," OB in "Three Hand Reel," "The Elizabethans," "Carousel," and "The King and I" (JB), "In the Voodoo Parlor of Marie Leveau," "Whistler."

CUNNINGHAM, JOHN. Born June 22, 1932 in Auburn, NY. Graduate Yale, Dartmouth. OB in "Love Me a Little," "Pimpernel," "The Fantasticks," "Love and Let Love," "The Bone Room," "Dancing in the Dark," "Father's Day," "Snapshot," "Head over Heels," "Quartermaine's Terms," "Wednesday," "On Approval," "Miami," "A Perfect Party," Bdwy in "Hot Spot" (1963), "Zorba," "Company," "1776," "Rose."

CURRY, CHRISTOPHER. Born Oct. 22, 1948 in Grand Rapids, Mi. Graduate UMi. Debut 1974 OB in "When You Comin' Back Red Ryder?," followed by "The Cherry Orchard," "Spelling Bee," "Ballymurphy," "Isadora Duncan Sleeps with the Russian Navy," "The Promise," "Mecca," "Soul of the White Ant," "Strange Snow," "Love Letters on Blue Paper," "Kennedy at Colonus," "The Foreigner," Bdwy in "Crucifer of Blood" (1978).

CURTIS, KEENE. Born Feb. 15, 1925 in Salt Lake City, UT. Graduate UUtah. Bdwy bow 1949 in "Shop at Sly Corner," with APA in "School for Scandal," "The Tavern," "Anatole," "Scapin," "Right You Are," "Importance of Being Earnest," "Twelfth Night," "King Lear," "Seagull," "Lower Depths," "Man and Superman," "Judith," "War and Peace," "You Can't Take It With You," "Pantagleize," "Cherry Orchard," "Misanthrope," "Cocktail Party," "Cock-a-Doodle Dandy," and "Hamlet," "A Patriot for Me," "The Rothschilds," "Night Watch," "Via Galactica," "Annie," "Division Street," "La Cage aux Folles," OB in "Colette," "Ride Across Lake Constance."

CWIKOWSKI, BILL. Born Aug. 4, 1945 in Newark, NJ. Graduate Smith and Monmouth Col. Debut 1972 OB in "Charlie the Chicken," followed by "Summer Brave," "Desperate Hours," "Mandrogola," "Two by Noonan," "Soft Touch," "Innocent Pleasures," "3 From the Marathon," "Two Part Harmony," "Bathroom Plays," "Little Victories," "Dolphin Position," "Cabal of Hypocrites," "Split Second," "Rose Cottages."

DACIUK, MARY. Born July 7, 1951 in Toronto, Can. Graduate York U. Debut 1984 OB in "The Undefeated Rhumba Champ," followed by "Crown Cork Cafeteria," "The Person I Once Was," "A Flight of Angels."

DALE, JIM. Born Aug 15, 1935 in Rothwell, Eng. Debut 1974 OB with Young Vic Co. in "Taming of the Shrew," "Scapino" that moved to Bdwy, followed by "Barnum," "Joe Egg."

DALTON, LEZLIE. Born Aug. 12, 1952 in Boston, MA. Attended Pasadena Playhouse, UCLA. Debut 1980 OB in "Annie and Arthur" followed by "After Maigret," "Blessed Event," "Times and Appetites of Toulouse-Lautrec."

D'ALTORIO, VICTOR. Born Jan. 10, 1957 in Garfield Heights, Oh. Graduate Northwestern U. Debut 1982 OB in "The Coarse Acting Show," followed by "In the Boom Boom Room."

d'AMBOISE, CHRISTOPHER. Born in 1963 in NYC. Debut 1983 OB in Non Pasquale, followed by Bdwy in "Song and Dance" (1985).

DANA, BARBARA. Born Dec. 28, 1940 in NYC. Bdwy debut 1963 in "Enter Laughing," followed by "Who's Afraid of Virginia Woolf?," "Where's Daddy?," "Room Service," OB in "A Clearing in the Woods," "A Worm in the Horseradish," "Angels of Anadarko," "Second City," "Joan of Lorraine," "Room Service."

DANEK, MICHAEL. Born May 5, 1955 in Oxford, Pa. Graduate Columbia Col. Bdwy debut 1978 in "Hello, Dolly!" followed by "A Chorus Line," "Copperfield," "Woman of the Year," OB in "Big Bad Burlesque," "Dreams."

DANIELLE, MARLENE. Born Aug. 16 in NYC. Bdwy debut 1979 in "Sarava," followed by "West Side Story," "Marlowe," "Damn Yankees" (JB), "Cats," OB in "Little Shop of Horrors."

DANIELLE, SUSAN. Born Jan. 30, 1949 in Englewood, NJ. Graduate Wm. Patterson Col. Debut 1979 OB in "Tip-Toes," Bdwy in "A Chorus Line" (1985).

DAVIES, ALED. Born June 29, 1953 in Freeport, Il. Graduate UManchester, UCalSanDiego. Debut 1986 OB in "Orchards" for which he received a Theatre World Award.

DAVIS, BILL C. Born Aug. 24, 1951 in Ellenville, NY. Graduate Marist Col. Debut 1980 OB in "Mass Appeal," followed by "Wrestlers," both of which he wrote.

DAVIS, BRUCE ANTHONY. Born Mar. 4, 1959 in Dayton, Oh. Attended Juilliard. Bdwy debut 1979 in "Dancin'," followed by "Big Deal."

DAVIS, HAL. Born Mar. 30, 1950 in Wichita, Ks. Graduate WichitaStateU, LAMDA. Debut 1976 OB in "Rosewood," followed by "Handy Dandy," "Professionally Speaking."

DAVIS, SHEILA KAY. Born May 30, 1956 in Daytona, FL. Graduate Spelman Col. Debut 1982 OB in "Little Shop of Horrors."

DeACUTIS, WILLIAM. Born Sept. 17, 1957 in Bridgeport, CT. Juilliard graduate. Debut 1979 OB in "Spring Awakening," followed by "The Normal Heart."

DEAL, FRANK. Born Oct. 7, 1958 in Birmingham, Al. Attended Duke U. Debut 1982 OB in "The American Princess," followed by "Richard III," "Ruffian on the Stair," "A Midsummer Night's Dream," "We Shall Not All Sleep," "The Legend of Sleepy Hollow," "Three Sisters."

DEAN, LAURA. Born May 27, 1963 in Smithtown, NY. Debut 1973 OB in "The Secret Life of Walter Mitty," followed by "A Village Romeo and Juliet," "Carousel," "Hey Rube," "Landscape of the Body," "American Passion," "Feathertop," "Personals," Bdwy in "Doonesbury" (1983) for which she received a Theatre World Award.

DeANGELIS, ROSEMARY. Born Apr. 26, 1933 in Brooklyn, NY. Graduate FIT. Debut 1959 OB in "Time of Vengeance," followed by "Between Two Thieves," "To Be Young Gifted and Black," "In the Summerhouse," "Monsters," "Rocky Road," "Nest of the Wood Grouse," "Measure for Measure."

DECKER, STEVE. Born Dec. 15, 1960 in Provo, Ut. Graduate UUtah. Debut 1985 OB in "Talley and Son."

DeCRISTO, AL. Born Aug. 14, 1953 in Providence, RI. Graduate URI, AMDA. Bdwy debut 1982 in "Evita," OB in "Women of Fortune" (1983), "To Whom It May Concern."

DeGANON, MATT. Born July 10, 1962 in NYC. Graduate SUNY/Purchase. Debut 1985 OB in "A New Way to Pay Old Debts," followed by "As You Like It," "The Skin of Our Teeth," "Green Fields."

de LA GIRODAY, FRANCOIS. Born Mar. 18, 1952 in Oxford, Eng. Attended Queens Col., Marymount Manhattan Col. Bdwy debut 1982 in "Monday after the Miracle," OB in "Paradise Lost" (1983), followed by "Loot," "The Tempest," "Antigone," "Rashomon," "Moby Dick," "The Dwarfs," "Woyzeck," "Out to Lunch," "Dracula," "Rats," "The Hasty Heart," "The Time of Your Life."

deLAVALLADE, CARMEN. Born Mar. 6, 1931 in New Orleans, La. Bdwy debut 1954 in "House of Flowers," followed by "Josephine Baker and Company," OB in "Othello," "Departures."

DeMIRJIAN, DENISE. Born July 8, 1952 in Los Angeles, Ca. Graduate CalInst of Arts. Debut 1978 OB in "Cartoons," followed by "No Strings," "Oh," "Baby!," "To Feed Their Hopes."

DEMPSEY, JEROME. Born Mar. 1, 1929 in St. Paul, Mn. Graduate Toledo U. Bdwy debut 1959 in "West Side Story," followed by "The Deputy," "Spofford," "Room Service," "Love Suicide at Schofield Barracks," "Dracula," "Whodunit," "You Can't Take It with You," "The Mystery of Edwin Drood," OB in "Cry of Players," "The Year Boston Won the Pennant," "The Crucible," "Justice Box," "Trelawny of the Wells," "Old Glory," "Six Characters in Search of an Author," "Threepenny Opera," "Johnny on the Spot," "The Barbarians," "he and she," "A Midsummer Night's Dream," "The Recruiting Officer," "Oedipus the King," "The Wild Duck," "The Fuehrer Bunker," "Entertaining Mr. Sloane," "The Clownmaker."

DENGEL, JAKE. Born June 19, 1933 in Oshkosh, Wi. Graduate Northwestern U. Debut OB in "The Fantasticks," followed by "Red Eye of Love," "Fortuna," "Abe Lincoln in Illinois," "Dr. Faustus," "An Evening with Garcia Lorca," "The Shrinking Bride," "Where Do We Go from Here?," "Woyzeck," "Endgame," "Measure for Measure," "Ulysses in Traction," "Twelfth Night," "The Beaver Coat," "The Great Grandson of Jedediah Kohler," "Caligula," "The Mound Builders," "Quiet in the Land," Bdwy in "The Royal Hunt of the Sun," "Cock-a-Doodle Dandy," "Hamlet," "The Changing Room."

DeNIRO, ROBERT. Born Aug. 17, 1943 in NYC. Studied with Stella Adler. Debut 1970 OB in "One Night Stands of a Noisy Passenger," followed by "Kool Aid (LC)," "Cuba and His Teddy Bear."

DePINA, SABRINA. Born Apr. 23, 1969 in NYC. Attended AADA. Debut 1985 OB in "A Long Time Since Yesterday," followed by "Six Characters in Search of an Author."

DERRA, CANDACE. Born Jan. 4 in Chicago, Il. Graduate UCLA. Debut 1980 OB in "The Ladder," followed by "Valentine," "Two by One," "A Visit," "Daughter of Venice."

DeSAL, FRANK. Born Apr. 14, 1943 in White Plains, NY. Attended AmThWing. Credits include "110 in the Shade," "Marco Millions," "Sherry!," "Sweet Charity," "How Now, Dow Jones," "Fig Leaves Are Falling," "Bring Back Birdie," "Zorba" (1983), OB in "Anything Goes."

DeSHIELDS, ANDRE. Born Jan. 12, 1946 in Baltimore, MD. Graduate UWi. Bdwy debut 1973 in "Warp," followed by "Rachel Lily Rosenbloom," "The Wiz," "Ain't Misbehavin'," "Haarlem Nocturne," "Just So.," OB in "2008½," "Jazzbo Brown," "The Soldier's Tale," "The Little Prince," "Haarlem Nocturne."

DEVINE, LORETTA. Born Aug. 21 in Houston, TX. Graduate UHouston, Brandeis U. Bdwy debut 1977 in "Hair," followed by "A Broadway Musical," "Dreamgirls," "Big Deal," OB in "Godsong," "Lion and the Jewel," "Karma," "The Blacks," "Mahalia," "Long Time Since Yesterday."

Robin
Bartlett

Joe
Barrett

Katherine
Barry

Peter
Basch

Angela
Bassett

John
Bedford-Lloyd

P. J.
Benjamin

Olga
Bellin

David
Beris

Pamela
Blair

Jay
Bodin

Laura
Brutsman

Jayne
Cacciatore

James
Cahill

Nancy
Callman

Robertson
Carricart

Rosanna
Carter

Terrence
Caza

Paul
Chalakani

Jill
Choder

Gary
Chryst

Lynette
Chun

Josh
Clark

Kay
Cole

Kim
Crosby

Bill
Cwikowski

Mary
Daciuk

Michael
Danek

Rosemary
DeAngelis

Francois
de la Giroday

DEVLIN, JOHN. Born Jan. 26, 1937 in Cleveland, Oh. Graduate Carnegie Tech. Bdwy debut 1964 in "Poor Bitos," followed by "Billy," "Vivat! Vivat Regina!," OB in "Richard III," "King Lear," "Boys in the Band," "Blue Alley Jazz."

DeVRIES, JON. Born Mar. 26, 1947 in NYC. Graduate Bennington Col., Pasadena Playhouse. Debut 1977 OB in "The Cherry Orchard," followed by "Agamemnon," "The Ballad of Soapy Smith," Bdwy in "The Inspector General," "Devour the Snow," "Major Barbara," "Execution of Justice."

DIETRICH, DENA. Born Dec. 4, 1928 in Pittsburgh, Pa. Attended AADA. Debut 1962 OB in "Out of This World," followed by "Cindy," "Rimers of Eldritch," "Mortally Fine," Bdwy in "Funny Girl," "Here's Where I Belong," "Freaking Out of Stephanie Blake," "Prisoner of Second Avenue."

DIETRICH, MARC. Born Nov. 12, 1951 in Fontana, CA. Graduate CSU/San Bernardino. Debut 1985 OB in "The Madwoman of Chaillot."

DiGIOIA, MICHAEL. Born July 26, 1962 in Niles, IL. Graduate SUNY/Purchase. Debut 1984 OB in "Cricket on the Hearth," followed by "Madwoman of Chaillot," "Vivat! Vivat Regina!" "The Time of Your Life."

DILLION, MIA. Born July 9, 1955 in Colorado Springs, CO. Graduate Penn State U. Bdwy debut 1977 in "Equus," followed by "Da," "Once a Catholic," "Crimes of the Heart," "The Corn Is Green," "Hay Fever," OB in "The Crucible," "Summer," "Waiting for the Parade," "Crimes of the Heart," "Fables for Friends," "Scenes from La Vie de Boheme," "Three Sisters." "Wednesday," "Roberta in Concert," "Come Back, Little Sheba," "Vienna Notes," "George White's Scandals."

DILLON, MATT. Born Feb. 18, 1964 in Larchmont, NY. Attended AADA. Bdwy debut 1985 in "Boys of Winter."

DiPASQUALE, FRANK J. Born July 15, 1955 in Whitestone, NY. Graduate USC. Bdwy debut 1983 in "La Cage aux Folles."

DIXON, ED. Born Sept. 2, 1948 in Oklahoma. Attended OkU. Bdwy in "The Student Prince," followed by "No, No, Nanette," "Rosalie in Concert," "The Three Musketeers," OB in "By Bernstein," "King of the Schnorrers," "Rabboni," "Moby Dick."

DIXON, MacINTYRE. Born Dec. 22, 1931 in Everett, Ma. Graduate Emerson Col. Bdwy debut 1965 in "Xmas in Las Vegas," followed by "Cop-Out," "Story Theatre," "Metamorphosis," "Twigs," "Over Here!," "Once in a Lifetime," "Alice in Wonderland," OB in "Quare Fellow," "Plays for Bleecker Street," "Stewed Prunes," "Cat's Pajamas," "Three Sisters," "3 X 3," "Second City," "Mad Show," "Meow!," "Lotta," "Rubbers," "Conjuring an Event," "His Majesty the Devil," "Tomfoolery," "A Christmas Carol," "Times and Appetites of Toulouse-Lautrec," "Room Service."

DIXON, OLIVER. Born Dec. 9 in Colquitt, Ga. Graduate FlaStateU. Bdwy debut 1983 in "The Caine Mutiny Court-Martial," followed by OB in "Nightmare Alley."

DOEMLING, BRANDON E. Born Dec. 17, 1958 in Philadelphia, PA. Graduate Westchester State Col. Debut 1985 OB in "Madwoman of Chaillot," followed by "Vivat! Vivat Regina!"

DONNELL, PATRICE. Born Dec. 24, in St. Paul, Mn. Graduate NKyU, UIll. Debut 1985 OB in "Jackson Pollock A Portrait and a Dream," followed by "An Evening of Chekhov."

DONNELLY, DONAL. Born July 6, 1931 in Bradford, Eng. Bdwy debut 1966 in "Philadelphia Here I Come," followed by "A Day in the Death of Joe Egg," "Sleuth," "The Faith Healer," "The Elephant Man," "Execution of Justice," OB in "My Astonishing Self," "The Chalk Garden," "Big Maggie."

DORWARD, MARY ANNE. Born June 29, 1958 in Berkeley, Ca. Graduate UBerkeley. Debut 1982 OB in "T.N.T.," followed by "Transformations," "Snoopy," "Miami."

DOTRICE, ROY. Born May 26, 1925 in Guernsey, Channel Islands. Bdwy debut 1967 in "Brief Lives," a return engagement in 1974, "Mr. Lincoln," "A Life," "Hay Fever," OB in "An Enemy of the People."

DOUGLASS, PI. Born in Sharon, CT. Attended Boston Consv. Bdwy debut 1969 in "Fig Leaves Are Falling," followed by "Hello, Dolly!," "Georgy," "Purlie," "Ari," "Jesus Christ Superstar," "Selling of the President," "The Wiz," "La Cage aux Folles," OB in "Of Thee I Sing," "Under Fire," "The Ritz," "Blackberries," "Dementos."

DRAKE, DONNA. Born May 21, 1953 in Columbia, SC. Attended USC, Columbia. Bdwy debut 1975 in "A Chorus Line," followed by "It's So Nice to Be Civilized," "1940's Radio Hour," "Woman of the Year," "Sophisticated Ladies," "Wind in the Willows," OB in "Memories of Riding with Joe Cool."

DUDLEY, CRAIG. Born Jan. 22, 1945 in Sheepshead Bay, NY. Graduate AADA, AmThWing. Debut 1970 OB in "Macbeth," followed by "Zou," "Othello," "War and Peace," "Dial 'M' for Murder."

DUELL, WILLIAM. Born Aug. 30 1923 in Corinth, NY. Attended IllWesleyan, Yale. OB in "Portrait of an Artist. . .," "Barroom Monks," "A Midsummer Night's Dream," "Henry IV," "Taming of the Shrew," "The Memorandum," "Threepenny Opera," "Loves of Cass McGuire," "Romance Language," "Hamlet," Bdwy in "A Cook for Mr. General," "Ballad of the Sad Cafe," "Ilya, Darling," "1776," "Kings," "Stages," "The Inspector General," "The Marriage of Figaro."

DUFF-MacCORMICK, CARA. Born Dec. 12 in Woodstock, Can. Attended AADA. Debut 1969 OB in "Love Your Crooked Neighbor," followed by "The Wager," "Macbeth," "A Musical Merchant of Venice," "Ladyhouse Blues," "The Philanderer," "Bonjour, La, Bonjour," "Journey to Gdansk," "The Dining Room," "All the Nice People," "Faulkner's Bicycle," "Earthworms," "The Acting Lesson," "Craig's Wife," Bdwy in "Moonchildren" (1972) for which she received a Theatre World Award, "Out Cry," "Animals."

DUKAKIS, OLYMPIA. Born in Lowell, MA. Debut 1960 OB in "The Breaking Wall," followed by "Nourish the Beast," "Curse of the Starving Class," "Snow Orchid," "The Marriage of Bette and Boo," Bdwy in "The Aspern Papers" (1962), "Abraham Cochrane," "Who's Who in Hell," "Social Security."

DUNCAN, SANDY. Born Feb. 20, 1946 in Henderson, TX. Attended Len Morris Col. Debut 1965 in CC's revivals of "The Music Man," "Carousel," "Finian's Rainbow," "Sound of Music," "Wonderful Town" and "Life with Father," OB in "Ceremony of Innocence" for which she received a Theatre World Award, "Your Own Thing," Bdwy in "Canterbury Tales" (1969), "Love Is a Time of Day," "The Boy Friend" (1970), "Peter Pan" (1979), "5–6–7–8 Dance," "My One and Only."

DUTTON, CHARLES S. Born Jan. 30, 1951 in Baltimore, MD. Graduate Yale U. Debut 1983 OB in "Richard III," Bdwy in "Ma Rainey's Black Bottom" (1984) for which he received a Theatre World Award.

DuVAL, HERBERT. Born May 4, 1941 in Schenectady, NY. Graduate UMich. Debut 1977 OB in "Arsenic and Old Lace," followed by "Prairie Avenue," "Once More with Feeling," "The Devil's Disciple," "The Green Bay Tree," "A Definite Maybe," "Two Orphans," Bdwy in "Hide and Seek" (1980).

DWYER, FRANK. Born Feb. 1, 1945 in Kansas City, Mo. Graduate NYU, SUNY. Debut 1970 OB in "Moby Dick," followed by "Hamlet," "Bacchai," "A Streetcar Named Desire," "Darkness at Noon," "Vatzlav," "Brand," "Frankstein."

EASTLEY, KEELY. Born Feb. 18, 1957 in New Albany, In. Attended UNev. Debut 1981 OB in "The Lesson," followed by "I Am a Camera," "Flesh Flash and Frank Harris," "Journal of Albion Moonlight."

ECKHOUSE, JAMES. Born Feb. 14, 1955 in Chicago, IL. Graduate Juilliard. Bdwy debut 1982 in "Beyond Therapy," OB in "The Rise and Rise of Daniel Rocker," "Geniuses," "In the Country," "Sister Mary Ignatius Explains It All," "Dubliners," "The Ballad of Soapy Smith," "Emma."

eda-YOUNG, BARBARA. Born Jan. 30, 1945 in Detroit, Mi. Bdwy debut 1968 in "Lovers and Other Strangers," OB in "The Hawk," LCRep's "The Time of Your Life," "Camino Real," "Operation Sidewinder," "Kool Aid and A Streetcar Named Desire," "The Gathering," "The Terrorists," "Drinks Before Dinner," "Shout across the River," "After Stardrive," "Birdbath," "Crossing the Crab Nebula," "Maiden Stakes," "Come Dog Come Night," "Two Character Play," "Mensch Meier," "Glory in the Flower," "Goodbye Freddy," "A Rosen by Any Other Name."

EDEIKEN, LOUISE. Born June 23, 1956 in Philadelphia, PA. Graduate GeoWashU. Bdwy debut 1982 in "Nine," OB in "Weekend," "Jacques Brel Is Alive . . .," "Ladies and Gentlemen, Jerome Kern," "To Whom It May Concern."

EDELHART, YVETTE. Born Mar. 26, 1928 in Oak Park, Il. Attended Wright Col. Debut 1984 OB in "Office Mishegoss," followed by "Home Movies," "Night Must Fall," "The Miser."

EDELMAN, GREGG. Born Sept. 12, 1958 in Chicago, Il. Graduate Northwestern U. Bdwy debut 1982 in "Evita," followed by "Oliver!," OB in "Weekend," "Shop on Main Street."

EDENFIELD, DENNIS. Born July 23, 1946 in New Orleans, LA. Debut 1970 OB in "The Evil That Men Do," followed by "I Have Always Believed in Ghosts," "Nevertheless They Laugh," Bdwy in "Irene" ('73), "A Chorus Line."

EDMEAD, WENDY. Born July 6, 1956 in NYC. Graduate NYCU. Bdwy debut 1974 in "The Wiz," followed by "Stop the World . . .," "America," "Dancin'," "Encore," "Cats."

EDWARDS, BRANDT. Born Mar. 22, 1947 in Holly Springs, MS. Graduate UMiss. NY debut off and on Bdwy 1975 in "A Chorus Line."

EDWARDS, BURT. Born Jan. 11, 1928 in Richmond, VA. Graduate UVa. Debut 1949 OB in "Fifth Horseman of the Apocalypse," followed by "Cenci," "The Camel Has His Nose under the Tent," Bdwy 1985 in "The King and I."

EDWARDS, RANDALL. Born June 15 in Atlanta, Ga. Attended CalInst of Arts. Debut 1983 OB in "Upstairs at O'Neal's." Bdwy 1985 in "Biloxi Blues."

EICHE, JEFFREY D. Born Mar. 28, 1955 in San Diego, Ca. Graduate SanDiegoStateU. Debut 1983 OB in "The Taming of the Shrew," followed by "Nude with Violin," "As You Like It."

ELIAS, ROSALIND. Born in Lowell, Ma. Graduate New England Conservatory. Debut 1985 OB in "Pearls," Bdwy in "Sweeney Todd (LC)."

ELIOS, TOM. Born July 28, 1946 in Brooklyn, NY. Graduate NYU, AADA. OB credits include "The Sea Gull," "The Visit/The Mousetrap," "Sell-Out."

ELIOT, DREW. Born in Newark, NJ. Graduate Columbia, RADA. OB in "The Fairy Garden," "Dr. Faustus," "Servant of Two Masters," "Henry V," "Stephen D," "Sjt. Musgrave's Dance," "Deadly Game," "Taming of the Shrew," "Appear and Show Cause," Bdwy in "Elizabeth the Queen," "The Physicists," "Romulus."

ELLENS, REBECCA. Born Apr. 24, 1959 in Bad Kreuznach, Ger. Graduate Calvin Col. Debut 1985 OB in "Green Fields."

ELLIS, FRASER. Born May 1, 1957 in Boulder, CO. Graduate UCo. Bdwy debut 1982 in "A Chorus Line."

ELLIS, WILLIAM. Born Dec. 5, 1929 near Cincinnati, OH. Graduate Goodman School, Columbia, NYU. Debut 1953 OB in "One Foot to the Sea," followed by "Murder in the Cathedral," "Hill of Beans," "Rags to Ruebens," "Hidden Away in Stores," "Today's Children," "The Marriage Proposal," "Much Ado about Nothing," "Writers," "A Doll's House," "Legend of Sleepy Hollow."

ELMORE, STEVE. Born July 12, 1936 in Niangua, MO. Debut 1961 in "Madame Aphrodite," followed by "Golden Apple," "Enclave," Bdwy in "Camelot," "Jenny," "Fade in Fade Out," "Kelly," "Company," "Nash at 9," "Chicago," "42nd St."

EMMET, ROBERT. Born Oct. 3, 1952 in Denver, CO. Graduate UWash. Debut 1976 OB in "The Mousetrap," followed by "The Seagull," "Blue Hotel," "Miss Jairus," "Hamlet," "Deathwatch," "Much Ado About Nothing," "Songs and Ceremonies," "Mass Appeal, "Macbeth," "Bell, Book and Candle," "Comes the Happy Hour," "The Gift." "Merchant of Venice," "Arms and the Man," "The Lady from the Sea," "Two Gentlemen from Verona."

ENGEL, DAVID. Born Oct. 19, 1959 in Orange, CA. Attended UCal/Irvine. Bdwy debut 1983 in "La Cage aux Folles."

EPSTEIN, ALVIN. Born May 14, 1925 in NYC. Attended Queens Col. Appeared on Bdwy with Marcel Marceau, and in "King Lear," "Waiting for Godot" (1956), "From A to Z," "No Strings," "Passion of Josef D," "Postmark Zero," "A Kurt Weill Cabaret," OB in "Purple Dust," "Pictures in a Hallway," "Clerambard," "Endgame," (1958/1984), "Whores, Wares and Tin Pan Alley," "A Place without Doors," "Crossing Niagara," "Beckett Plays," "Kurt Weill Cabaret," "Waltz of the Toreadors."

EPSTEIN, PIERRE. Born July 27, 1930 in Toulouse, FR. Graduate UParis; Bdwy debut 1962 in "A Shot in the Dark," followed by "Enter Laughing," "Bajour," "Black Comedy," "Thieves," "Fun City," "Filumena," "Plenty," OB in "Incident in Vichy," "Threepenny Opera," "Too Much Johnson," "Second City," "People vs Ranchman," "Promenade," "Cake with Wine," "Little Black Sheep," "Comedy of Errors," "A Memory of Two Mondays," "They Knew What They Wanted," "Museum," "The Bright and Golden Land," "Manny," "God Bless You, Mr. Rosewater," "The Itch," "Breakfast Conversations in Miami," "The Ballad of Soapy Smith," "Room Service."

EVANS, PETER. Born May 27, 1950 in Englewood, NJ. Graduate Yale, London Central School of Speech. Debut OB 1975 in "Life Class," followed by "Streamers," "A Life in the Theatre," "Don Juan Comes Back From the War," "The American Clock," "Geniuses," "Transfiguration of Benno Blimpie," "Endgame," "Total Eclipse," "Springtime for Henry," Bdwy in "Night and Day" (1979) "Children of a Lesser God."

EVANS-KANDEL, KAREN. Born Aug. 11 in NYC. Graduate Queens Col. Debut 1977 OB in "Nightclub Cantata," followed by "1951," "The Making of Americans," "Underfire," "Alice in Concert," "Dispatches," Bdwy in "Runaways" (1978).

EVERS, BRIAN. Born Feb. 14, 1942 in Miami, FL. Graduate Capital U, UMiami. Debut 1979 OB in "How's the House?," followed by "Details of the 16th Frame," "Divine Fire," "Silent Night, Lonely Night," "Uncommon Holidays," "The Tamer Tamed," Bdwy in "House of Blue Leaves" (1986).

EWING, J. TIMOTHY (a.k.a. Tim) Born Apr. 3, 1954 in Evansville, In. Graduate OklaStateU. Debut 1972 OB in "Colette Collage," followed by "Promenade," "Pacific Overtures," "Good Times," "Charley's Tale."

FABER, RON. Born Feb. 16, 1933 in Milwaukee, Wi. Graduate Marquette U. Debut OB 1959 in "An Enemy of the People," followed by "The Exception and the Rule," "America Hurrah," "They Put Handcuffs on Flowers," "Dr. Selavy's Magic Theatre," "Troilus and Cressida," "The Beauty Part," "Woyzeck," "St. Joan of the Stockyards," "Jungle of Cities," "Scenes from Everyday Life," "Mary Stuart," "3 by Pirandello," "Times and Appetites of Toulouse-Lautrec," "Hamlet," Bdwy in "Medea" (1973)," "First Monday in October."

FAIRSERVIS, ELF. Born May 19, 1957 in Mt. Kisco, NY. Graduate Bennett Col. Debut 1982 OB in "Independent Study," followed by "Our Town," "A Little More Wine with Lunch," "Dick Deterred," "Shakespeare Marathon," "3 One Acts."

FALKENHAIN, PATRICIA. Born Dec. 3, 1926 in Atlanta, GA. Graduate Carnegie-Mellon, NYU. Debut 1946 OB in "Juno and the Paycock," followed by "Hamlet," "She Stoops to Conquer," "Peer Gynt," "Henry IV," "The Plough and the Stars," "Lysistrata," "Beaux Stratagem," "The Power and the Glory," "M. Amilcar," "Home," "The Marriage of Bette and Boo," Bdwy in "Waltz of the Toreadors," "The Utter Glory of Morrissey Hall," "Once a Catholic," "House of Blue Leaves."

FARINA, MARILYN J. Born Apr. 9, 1947 in NYC. Graduate Sacred Heart Col. Debut 1985 OB in "Nunsense."

FARR, KIMBERLY. Born Oct. 16, 1948 in Chicago, Il. Graduate UCLA. Bdwy debut 1972 in "Mother Earth," followed by "The Lady from the Sea," "Going Up," "Happy New Year," OB in "More Than You Deserve," "The S. S. Benchley," "At Sea with Benchley," "Suffragett," "Brownstone," "The Golden Windows."

FARRAR, MARTHA. Born Apr. 22, 1928 in Buffalo, NY. Graduate Smith Col. Bdwy debut 1953 in "A Pin to See the Peepshow," OB in "The Cretan Woman," "Easter," "Half-Life," "Touched," "Between Us," "Murder in the Vicarage."

FARRELL, GILLIAN. Born Feb. 21, 1951 in NYC. Attended Northwestern U. Debut 1985 OB in "Square One."

FELDSHUH, TOVAH. Born Dec. 27, 1953 in NYC. Graduate Sarah Lawrence Col., UMn. Bdwy debut 1973 in "Cyrano," followed by "Dreyfus in Rehearsal," "Rodgers and Hart," "Yentl" for which she received a Theatre World Award, "Sarava," OB in "Yentl the Yeshiva Boy," "Straws in the Wind," "Three Sisters," "She Stoops to Conquer," "Springtime for Henry," "The Time of Your Life," "Children of the Sun."

FICKINGER, STEVEN. Born Apr. 29, 1960 in Chicago, Il. Graduate UCLA. Debut 1982 OB in "Louisiana Summer," followed by "The Robber Bridegroom," "Judy Garland of Songs," "On the 20th Century."

FIELD, CRYSTAL. Born Dec. 10, 1942 in NYC. Attended Juilliard, graduate Hunter Col. Debut OB in "A Country Scandal (1960)," and most recent appearance was in "A Matter of Life and Death."

FIERSTEIN, HARVEY. Born June 6, 1954 in Brooklyn, NY. Graduate Pratt Inst. Debut 1971 OB in "Pork," followed by "International Stud," "Figure In a Nursery," Bdwy 1982 in "Torch Song Trilogy," for which he received a Theatre World Award.

FINCH, SUSAN. Born Aug. 30, 1959 in Germantown, Pa. Attended Juilliard. Debut 1986 OB in "Orchards."

FINKEL, FYVUSH. Born Oct. 9, 1922 in Brooklyn, NY. Bdwy debut 1970 in "Fiddler On the Roof" (also 1981 revival), OB in "Gorky," "Little Shop of Horrors."

FIORDELLISI, ANGELINA. Born Mar. 15, 1955 in Detroit, MI. Graduate UDetroit. Bdwy debut 1983 in "Zorba," OB in "An Ounce of Prevention."

FISH, STEVE ROY. Born Sept. 26, 1951 in Heidelburg, Ger. Attended UWisc. Debut 1978 OB in "Candida," followed by "Gravest Insult of Them All," "Days and Nights of an Ice Cream Princess," "Four by Eight."

FITCH, ROBERT. Born Apr. 29, 1934 in Santa Cruz, Ca. Attended USantaClara. Bdwy debut 1961 in "Tenderloin," followed by "Do Re Me," "My Fair Lady," "The Girl Who Came to Supper," "Flora the Red Menace," "Baker Street," "Sherry," "Mack and Mabel," "Henry Sweet Henry," "Mame," "Promises Promises," "Coco," "Lorelei," "Annie," "Do Black Patent Leather Shoes Really Reflect Up?," OB in "Lend an Ear," "Half-Past Wednesday," "Anything Goes," "Crystal Heart," "Broadway Dandies," "One Cent Plain," "Sweet Thighs of New England Women," "Dames at Sea."

FLANAGAN, KIT. Born July 6 in Pittsburgh, PA. Graduate Northwestern U. Debut 1979 OB in "The Diary of Anne Frank," followed by "An Evening with Dorothy Parker," "Still Life," "Cloud 9," "Alto Part," "A Step Out of Line," "Goodbye Freddy."

FLANAGAN, PAULINE. Born June 29, 1925 in Sligo, Ire. Debut 1958 OB in "Ulysses in Nighttown," followed by "Pictures in the Hallway," "Later," "Antigone," "The Crucible," "The Plough and the Stars," "Summer," "Close of Play," "In Celebration," Bdwy in "God and Kate Murphy," "The Living Room," "The Innocents," "The Father," "Medea," "Steaming," "Corpse."

FLANAGAN, WALTER. Born Oct. 4, 1928 in Ponta, Tx. Graduate Houston U. Bdwy in "Once for the Asking," "A Texas Trilogy," "A Touch of the Poet," "The Iceman Cometh," OB in "Bedtime Story," "Coffee and Windows," "Opening of a Window," "The Moon Is Blue," "Laughwind," "The Dodo Bird."

FLEISS, JANE. Born Jan. 28 in NYC. Graduate NYU. Debut 1979 OB in "Say Goodnight, Gracie," followed by "Grace," "The Beaver Coat," "The Harvesting," "D.," "Second Man," Bdwy in "5th of July" (1981), "Crimes of the Heart."

FLESS, SCOTT. Born Oct. 13, 1952 in The Bronx, NYC. Graduate Queens Col. Bdwy debut 1980 in "Onward Victoria," followed by "Evita," OB in "Road to Hollywood," "Hamlin."

FLODEN, LEA. Born Feb. 13, 1958 in Rockford, Il. Graduate IndianaU. Debut 1980 OB in "The Ladder," followed by "Cherokee County," "Short Change."

FLOREK, DAVE. Born May 19, 1953 in Dearborn, MI. Graduate Eastern MiU. Debut 1976 OB in "The Collection," followed by "Richard III," "Much Ado About Nothing," "Young Bucks," "Big Apple Messenger," "Death of a Miner," "Marvelous Gray," "Journey to Gdansk," "The Last of Hitler," "Thin Ice," "The Incredibly Famous Willy Rivers," "Responsible Parties," "For Sale," "The Foreigner," Bdwy 1980 in "Nuts."

FOLEY, BRENDA. Born Apr. 19, 1960 in Jacksonville, Fl. Graduate USantaClara, CalifInst. of Arts. Debut 1985 OB in "Playboy of the Western World."

FONG, JOSE. Born Mar. 19, 1959 in Santiago, Cuba. Graduate UMiami. Debut 1986 OB in "Rum and Coke."

FORBES, FRANCINE. Born Apr. 25, 1960 in Brooklyn, NY. Graduate URochester, RADA. Debut 1982 OB in "No Time for Tears," followed by "As You Like It," "Home Free," "A Doll's House," Bdwy in "The Marriage of Figaro (1985)."

FORD, CLEBERT. Born Jan 29, 1932 in Brooklyn, NY. Graduate CCNY, Boston U. Bdwy debut 1960 in "The Cool World," followed by "Les Blancs," "Ain't Supposed to Die a Natural Death," "Via Galactica," "Bubbling Brown Sugar," "The Last Minstrel Show," OB in "Romeo and Juliet," "The Blacks," "Antony and Cleopatra," "Ti-Jean and His Brothers," "Ballad for Bimshire," "Daddy," "Gilbeau," "Coriolanus," "Before the Flood," "The Lion and the Jewel," "Branches from the Same Tree," "Dreams Deferred," "Basin Street," "20 Year Friends," "Celebration," "Stories about the Old Days."

FORD, FRANCES. Born Nov. 10, 1939 in Appleton, WI. Graduate UWis. Debut 1964 OB in "A Midsummer Night's Dream," followed by "The Importance of Being Earnest," "She Stoops to Conquer," "The Maids," "Howling in the Night," "The Marquise," "Lulu," "36/47 and Every Other One," Bdwy in "The Stingiest Man in Town" (1971).

FORD, SPENCE. Born Feb. 25, 1954 in Richmond, VA. Attended UVa. Debut 1976 OB in "Follies," followed by "Pal Joey," Bdwy in "King of Hearts," "Carmelina," "Peter Pan," "Copperfield," "Dancin'," "Merlin," "La Cage aux Folles."

FORD, SUZANNE. Born Sept. 22, 1949 in Auburn, NY. Attended Ithaca Col., Eastman Sch. Debut 1973 OB in "Fashion," followed by "El Grande de Coca-Cola," "Tenderloin," "A Man between Twilights," "Under the Gaslight," "Mandrake," "Crimes of Vautrin," "Two Orphans."

FORD, SYDNEY. Born Feb. 28, 1938 in London, Eng. NY debut OB 1953 in "Private Secretary," followed by "The Bells," "Silver Nails," "Trilby," "Heloise," "Enemy of the People," "Hedda Gabler."

FORSTER, VICTORIA. Born Nov. 2 in NYC. Graduate Wesleyan U. Debut 1982 OB in "Lullabye and Goodnight," followed by "Lies and Legends," "She Loves Me."

FOSTER, FRANCES. Born June 11 in Yonkers, NY. Bdwy debut 1955 in "The Wisteria Trees," followed by "Nobody Loves an Albatross," "Raisin in the Sun," "The River Niger," "First Breeze of Summer," OB in "Take a Giant Step," "Edge of the City," "Tammy and the Doctor," "The Crucible," "Happy Ending," "Day of Absence," "An Evening of One Acts," "Man Better Man," "Brotherhood," "Akokawe," "Rosalee Pritchett," "Sty of the Blind Pig," "Ballet Behind the Bridge," "Good Woman of Setzuan" (LC), "Behold! Cometh the Vanderkellans," "Origin," "Boesman and Lena," "Do Lord Remember Me," "Henrietta," "Welcome to Black River," "House of Shadows."

FOWLER, CLEMENT. Born Dec. 27, 1924 in Detroit, MI. Graduate Wayne State U. Bdwy debut 1951 in "Legend of Lovers," followed by "The Cold Wind and the Warm," "Fragile Fox," "The Sunshine Boys," "Hamlet (1964), OB in "The Eagle Has Two Heads," "House Music," "Transfiguration of Benno Blimpie," "The Inheritors," "Paradise Lost," "The Time of Your Life," "Children of the Sun."

FOX, COLIN. Born Nov. 20, 1938 in Aldershot, Can. Attended UWestern Ontario. Bdwy debut 1968 in "Soldiers," followed by "Pack of Lies," OB in "The Importance of Being Earnest," "Declassee," "Love's Labour's Lost," "Anteroom."

FRANCIS, JOSEPH V. Born in Detroit, Mi. Graduate CCNY. Debut OB 1985 in "Mark VIII: xxxvi," followed by "Four Loves in Three Acts."

FRANCO, RAMON. Born Sept. 12, 1963 in Caguas, PR. Attended Bard Col. Debut 1979 OB in "Sancocho," followed by "Mio," "The Sun Always Shines for the Cook," "Pizza King," "The Lunch Girls," "Wasted."

FRANK, JUDY. Born Nov. 26, 1936 in Cincinnati, Oh. Graduate IndU, Yale. Bdwy debut in "Mary Mary (1962)," followed by "Xmas in Las Vegas," "Spoon River Anthology," OB in "Six Characters in Search of an Author," "Now Is the Time for All Good Men," "The Constant Wife."

FRANK, RICHARD. Born Jan. 4, 1954 in Boston, Ma. Graduate UMich. Debut 1978 OB in "Spring Awakening," followed by "Salt Lake City Skyline," "Hamlet," Bdwy in "The Dresser" (1981).

FRANZ, ELIZABETH. Born June 18, 1941 in Akron, OH. Attended AADA. Debut 1965 OB in "In White America," followed by "One Night Stands of a Noisy Passenger," "The Real Inspector Hound," "Augusta," "Yesterday Is Over," "Actor's Nightmare," "Sister Mary Ignatius Explains It All," "The Time of Your Life," "Children of the Sun," Bdwy in "Rosencrantz and Guildenstern Are Dead," "The Cherry Orchard," "Brighton Beach Memoirs," "The Octette Bridge Club."

FRASER, ALISON. Born July 8, 1955 in Natick, Ma. Attended Carnegie-Mellon U., Boston Conservatory. Debut 1979 OB in "In Trousers," followed by "March of the Falsettos," "Beehive," "Four One-Act Musicals," "Tales of Tinseltown," "Next Please!"

FRAZER, SUSANNA. Born Mar. 28 in NYC. Debut 1980 OB in "Kind Lady," followed by "The Enchanted," "A Doll's House," "Scenes from American Life," "Old Friends and Roommates," "Something Old, Something New," "Times and Appetites of Toulouse-Lautrec," "A Flash of Lightning."

FRENCH, ARTHUR. Born in NYC. Attended Brooklyn Col. Debut 1962 OB in "Raisin' Hell in the Sun," followed by "Ballad of Bimshire," "Day of Absence," "Happy Ending," "Jonah," "Ceremonies in Dark Old Men," "An Evening of One Acts," "Man Better Man," "Brotherhood," "Perry's Mission," "Rosalee Pritchett," "Moonlight Arms," "Dark Tower," "Brownsville Raid," "Nevis Mt. Dew," "Julius Caesar," "Friends," "Court of Miracles," "The Beautiful LaSalles," "Blues for a Gospel Queen," "Black Girl," Bdwy in "Ain't Supposed to Die a Natural Death," "The Iceman Cometh," "All God's Chillun Got Wings," "The Resurrection of Lady Lester," "You Can't Take It With You," "Design for Living," "Ma Rainey's Black Bottom."

FRENCH, LARRY D. Born Nov. 4, 1951 in Dallas, Tx. Graduate SMU. Bdwy debut 1982 in "Pirates of Penzance," followed by "Brigadoon," OB in "Funny Girl."

FRIED, JONATHAN. Born Mar. 3, 1959 in Los Angeles, Ca. Graduate Brown U, UCalSan-Diego. Debut 1986 OB in "1951."

FRIEDMAN, PETER. Born Apr. 24, 1949 in NYC. Debut 1971 OB in "James Joyce Memorial Liquid Theatre," followed by "Big and Little," "A Soldier's Play," "Mr. and Mrs.," "And a Nightingale Sang," "Dennis," Bdwy in "The Visit," "Chemin de Fer," "Love for Love," "Rules of the Game," "Piaf!," "Execution of Justice."

FRISCH, RICHARD. Born May 9, 1933 in NYC. Graduate Juilliard. Bdwy debut 1964 in "The Passion of Josef D," followed by "Fade Out-Fade In," OB in "Jonah," "Antigone," "The Mother of Us All," "Up from Paradise," "Pere Goriot," "Pearls."

FURS, EDDIE L. Born July 23, 1957 in Brooklyn, NY. Graduate NYU. Debut 1986 OB in "Dance of Death," followed by "Night Must Fall," "Squaring the Circle," "The Miser," "Harpo," "Family Portrait."

GABLE, JUNE. Born June 5, 1945 in NYC. Graduate Carnegie Tech. OB in "Macbird," "Jacques Brel Is Alive and Well . . .," "A Day in the Life of Just About Everyone," "Mod Donna," "Wanted," "Lady Audley's Secret," "Comedy of Errors," "Chinchilla," "Beggar's Opera," "Shoe Palace Murray," "Star Treatment," "Coming Attractions," "Times and Appetites of Toulouse-Lautrec," "The Perfect Party," Bdwy in "Candide" (1974),

GAINES, BOYD. Born May 11, 1953 in Atlanta, Ga. Graduate Juilliard. Debut 1978 OB in "Spring Awakening," followed by "A Month in the Country" for which he received a Theatre World Award, "BAM Theatre Co.'s Winter's Tale," "The Barbarians and Johnny on a Spot," "Vikings," "Double Bass."

GALE, DAVID. Born Oct. 2, 1936 in England. NY debut 1958 OB in "Elizabeth the Queen," followed by "Othello," "White Devil," "Baal," "What Do They Know about Love Uptown?," "Joe Egg," "The Trial," "Buy the Bi and Bye," "Dumbwaiter," "The Dodge Boys," "Biko Inquest," "Orpheus Descending," "The Price," "Memories of Riding with Joe Cool," Bdwy in "Of Mice and Men (1974)," "Sweet Bird of Youth."

GALLAGHER, PETER. Born Aug. 19, 1955 in NYC. Graduate Tufts U. Bdwy debut 1977 in "Hair," followed by "A Doll's Life" for which he received a Theatre World Award, "The Corn Is Green," "The Real Thing," "Long Day's Journey into Night."

GALLIGAN, ZACH. Born in 1963 in NYC. Attended Columbia U. Bdwy debut 1986 in "Biloxi Blues."

GAMMON, JAMES. Born Apr. 20, 1940 in Newman, Il. Debut 1978 OB in "Curse of the Starving Class," followed by "A Lie of the Mind."

GARFIELD, DAVID. Born Feb. 6, 1941 in Brooklyn, NY. Graduate Columbia, Cornell U. Debut 1964 OB in "Hang Down Your Head and Die," followed by "Government Inspector," "Old Ones," "Family Business," "Ralph Roister Doister," "Actors Deli," Bdwy in "Fiddler on the Roof," "The Rothschilds."

GARMAN, CARRIE. Born Apr. 4, 1975 in NYC. Debut 1985 OB in "Cabbagehead."

GARRISON, DAVID. Born June 30, 1952 in Long Branch, NJ. Graduate Boston U. Debut OB in "Joseph and the Amazing Technicolor Dreamcoat," followed by "Living At Home," "Geniuses," "It's Only a Play," Bdwy in "A History of the American Film," "A Day in Hollywood/A Night in the Ukraine," "Pirates of Penzance," "Snoopy," "Torch Song Trilogy," "One Touch of Venus."

GARSIDE, BRAD. Born June 2, 1958 in Boston, MA. Graduate NorthTexState U. Debut 1983 OB in "Forbidden Broadway."

GARZA, TROY. Born Aug. 20, 1954 in Hollywood, Ca. Attended RADA. Bdwy debut 1977 in "A Chorus Line," followed by "Got Tu Go Disco," OB in "Fourtune," "Paris Lights."

GASSELL, SYLVIA. Born July 1, 1923 in NYC. Attended Hunter Col. Bdwy debut 1952 in "The Time of the Cuckoo," followed by "Sunday Breakfast," "Fair Game for Lovers," "Inquest," OB in "U.S.A.," "Romeo and Juliet," "Electra," "A Darker Flower," "Fragments," "Goa," "God Bless You, Harold Fineberg," "Philosophy in the Boudoir," "Stag Movie," "The Old Ones," "Where Memories Are Magic," "Jesse's Land," "Under Milk Wood."

GAVON, IGORS. Born Nov. 14, 1937 in Latvia. Bdwy bow 1961 in "Carnival," followed by "Hello Dolly!" "Marat/deSade," "Billy," "Sugar," "Mack and Mabel," "Musical Jubilee," "Strider," "42 St," OB in "Your Own Thing," "Promenade," "Exchange," "Nevertheless They Laugh," "Polly," "The Boss," "Biography: A Game," "Murder in the Cathedral."

GEFFNER, DEBORAH. Born Aug. 26, 1952 in Pittsburgh, PA. Attended Juilliard, HB Studio. Debut 1978 OB in "Tenderloin," Bdwy in "Pal Joey," "A Chorus Line."

GELFER, STEVEN. Born Feb. 21, 1949 in Brooklyn, NY. Graduate NYU, IndU. Debut 1968 OB and Bdwy in "The Best Little Whorehouse in Texas," followed by "Cats."

GELKE, BECKY. Born Feb. 17, 1953 in Ft. Knox, Ky. Graduate Western Ky. U. Debut 1978 OB/Bdwy in "The Best Little Whorehouse in Texas," OB in "Altitude Sickness," "John Brown's Body," "Chamber Music," "To Whom It May Concern."

GEOFFREYS, STEPHEN. Born Nov. 22, 1964 in Cincinnati, Oh. Attended NYU. Bdwy debut 1984 in "The Human Comedy" for which he received a Theatre World Award, OB in "Maggie Magalita."

GERDES, GEORGE. Born Feb. 23, 1948 in NYC. Graduate Carnegie Tech. Debut 1979 OB in "Modigliani," followed by "The Idolmakers," "The Doctor and the Devils," "The Hit Parade," "A Country for Old Men," "Fool for Love," "To Whom It May Concern."

GERROLL, DANIEL. Born Oct. 16, 1951 in London, Eng. Attended Central Sch. of Speech. Debut 1980 OB in "The Slab Boys," followed by "Knuckle" and "Translations" for which he received a Theatre World Award," "The Caretaker," "Scenes from La Vie de Boheme," "The Knack," "Terra Nova," "Dr. Faustus," "Second Man," "Cheapside," Bdwy in "Plenty" (1982).

GETER, JOHN. Born Sept. 22, 1957 in Wenoka, OK. Graduate Hanover Col. Debut 1980 OB in "The Diviners," followed by "Billy Liar," "Twelfth Night," Bdwy in "Gemini" (1980).

GIANNINI, CHERYL. Born June 15 in Monessen, PA. Bdwy debut 1980 in "The Suicide," followed by "Grownups," OB in "Elm Circle," "I'm Not Rappaport."

GIBSON, THOMAS. Born July 3, 1962 in Charleston, SC. Graduate Juilliard. Debut 1985 OB in "Map of the World," followed by "Twelfth Night," Bdwy in "Hay Fever (1985)."

GIELLA, DAVID. Born Sept. 17, 1962 in Suffern, NY. Attended Rutgers U. Bdwy debut 1985 in "The Marriage of Figaro."

GIESENSCHLAG, RUSSELL. Born July 8, 1959 in San Diego, Ca. Attended SanDiegoStateU. Bdwy debut 1982 in "Seven Brides for Seven Brothers," OB in "Girl Crazy."

GILBERT, ALAN. Born Mar. 4, 1949 in Seneca, Ky. Graduate USyracuse. Debut 1972 OB in "No Strings," followed by "Follies," "Charley's Tale," Bdwy in "My Fair Lady" (1981), "The Little Prince and the Aviator."

GILBORN, STEVEN. Born in New Rochelle, NY. Graduate Swarthmore, Col., Stanford U. Bdwy debut 1973 in "Creeps," followed by "Basic Training of Pavlo Hummel," "Tartuffe," OB in "Rosmersholm," "Henry V," "Measure for Measure," "Ashes," "The Dybbuk," "Museum," "Shadow of a Gunman," "It's Hard to Be a Jew," "Isn't It Romantic," "Principia Scriptoriae."

GILES, NANCY. Born July 17, 1960 in Queens, NYC. Graduate Oberlin Col. Debut 1985 OB in "Mayor" for which she received a Theatre World Award.

GILLETTE, ANITA. Born Aug. 16, 1938 in Baltimore, MD. Debut 1960 OB in "Russell Patterson's Sketchbook" for which she received a Theatre World Award, followed by "Rich and Famous," "Dead Wrong," Bdwy in "Carnival," "All American," "Mr. President," "Guys and Dolls," "Don't Drink the Water," "Cabaret," "Jimmy," "Chapter Two," "They're Playing Our Song," "Brighton Beach Memoirs."

GILPIN, JACK. Born May 31, 1951 in Boyce, Va. Graduate Harvard. Debut 1976 OB in "Goodbye and Keep Cold," followed by "Shay," "The Soft Touch," "Beyond Therapy," "The Lady or the Tiger," "The Middle Ages," "The Rise of Daniel Rocket," "No Happy Ending," "Strange Behavior," "The Foreigner," "Marathon '86," Bdwy in "Lunch Hour" (1980).

GIOMBETTI, KAREN. Born May 24, 1955 in Scranton, PA. Graduate NYU. Bdwy debut 1978 in "Stop the World, I Want to Get Off," followed by "The Most Happy Fella," "Woman of the Year," "Zorba" (1983), "The Mystery of Edwin Drood."

GIONSON, MEL. Born Feb. 23, 1954 in Honolulu, HI. Graduate UHi. Debut 1979 OB in "Richard II," followed by "Sunrise," "Monkey Music," "Behind Enemy Lines," "Station J," "Teahouse," "A Midsummer Night's Dream," "Empress of China," "Chip Shot," "Manoa Valley," "Ghashiram."

GIRARDEAU, FRANK. Born Oct. 19, 1942 in Beaumont, TX. Attended Rider Col, HB Studio. Debut 1972 OB in "22 Years," followed by "The Soldier," "Hughie," "An American Story," "El Hermano," "Dumping Ground," "Daddies," "Accounts," "Shadow Man," "Marathon '84," "Dennis."

GLEASON, JAMES. Born Sept. 30, 1952 in NYC. Graduate Santa Fe Col. Debut 1982 OB in "Guys in the Truck," followed by "Corkscrews!," "Patrick Pearse Motel," "Taboo in Revue," "Curse of the Starving Class," "Curse of the Starving Class," Bdwy in "Guys in the Truck" (1983).

GLEASON, JOANNA. Born June 2, 1950 in Toronto, CAN. Graduate UCLA. Bdwy debut 1977 in "I Love My Wife" for which she received a Theatre World Award, followed by "The Real Thing," "Social Security," OB in "A Hell of a Town." "Joe Egg," "It's Only a Play."

GLUSHAK, JOANNA. Born May 27, 1958 in NYC. Attended NYU. Debut 1983 OB in "Lenny and the Heartbreakers," followed by "Lies and Legends," "Miami," Bdwy in "Sunday in the Park with George" (1984).

GNAT, MICHAEL. Born Dec. 13, 1955 in NYC. Graduate Syracuse U. Debut 1980 OB in "The Interview," followed by "The Ballad of Bernie Babcock," "Lord Alfred's Lover," "This Property Is Condemned," "Engaged," "Courtship," "Briss," "One Night Stand," "The Tiger," "Becoming Strangers."

GODFREY, THOMAS H. Born Aug. 25, 1949 in NYC. Graduate Tufts U. Debut 1985 OB in "Mark VIII: xxxvi."

GOETZ, PETER MICHAEL. Born Dec. 10, 1941 in Buffalo, NY. Graduate SUNY/Fredonia, Southern ILU. Debut 1980 OB in "Jail Diary of Albie Sachs," "Before the Dawn," followed by Bdwy in "Ned and Jack" (1981), "Beyond Therapy," "The Queen and the Rebels," "Brighton Beach Memoirs."

GOLD, FAY. Born Oct. 15, 1907. Attended Art Students League, HB Studio. Debut 1981 OB in "What a Life," followed by "Soupstone Project."

GOLDBERG, WHOOPI. Born Nov. 13, 1949 in NYC. Graduate H.S. of Performing Arts. Bdwy debut 1984 in "Whoopi Goldberg" for which she received a Theatre World Award.

GOLDEN, ANNIE. Born Oct. 19, 1951 in Brooklyn, NY. Bdwy debut 1977 in "Hair," followed by "Leader of the Pack," OB in "Dementos," "Dr. Selavy's Magic Theatre," "A . . . My Name Is Alice," "Little Shop of Horrors," "Class of '86."

GOLDSMITH, MERWIN. Born Aug. 7, 1937 in Detroit, MI. Graduate UCLA, Old Vic. Bdwy debut 1970 in "Minnie's Boys," followed by "The Visit," "Chemin de Fer," "Rex," "Chickencoop Chinaman," "Wanted," "Comedy," "Rubbers," "Yankees 3 Detroit 0," "Trelawny of the Wells," "Chinchilla," "Real Life Funnies," "Big Apple Messenger," "La Boheme," "Yours, Anne."

GONZALEZ, ERNESTO. Born Apr. 8, 1940 in San Juan, PR. Bdwy debut 1953 in "Camino Real," followed by "The Saint of Bleecker Street," "The Innkeepers," "Cut of the Axe," "Ride the Winds," "The Strong Are Lonely," "Oh, Dad, Poor Dad . . .," "The Leaf People," OB in "The Kitchen," "Secret Concubine," "Life Is a Dream," "The Marquise," "Principia Scriptoriae."

GOODMAN, JOHN. Born June 20, 1952 in St. Louis, MO. Graduate Southwest MoStateU. Debut 1978 OB in "A Midsummer Night's Dream," followed by "The Chisholm Trail," "Henry IV Part II," "Ghosts of the Loyal Oaks," "Half a Lifetime," "Marathon '84," Bdwy in "Big River" (1985).

GOODMAN, LISA. Born in Detroit, MI. Attended UMi. Debut 1982 OB in "Talking With," followed by "The First Warning," "The Show-Off," "Escape from Riverdale," "Jesse's Land," "State of the Union," "The Wonder Years."

GOODSPEED, DON. Born Apr. 1, 1958 in Truro, NS, Can. Bdwy debut 1983 in "The Pirates of Penzance," OB in "Diamonds," "Charley's Tale."

GOODWILLIE, STEVE. Born July 12, 1961 in Minneapolis, Mn. Attended SMU, NYU. Debut 1986 OB in "Girl Crazy."

GOODWIN, LYNN. Born Sept. 17, 1958 in Adak, Ak. Graduate Yale U. Debut 1982 OB in "The Gnostics," followed by "Baseball Wives," "The Ninth Step," "Been Taken."

GORMAN, ANDREW. Born May 16, 1951 in Chicago, Il. Graduate KanStateU. Debut 1983 OB in "The Buck Stops Here," followed by "A Touch of the Poet," "They're Playing Our Song."

GORMAN, BREON. Born Aug. 30, 1954 in Washington, DC. Attended Princeton U, Juilliard. Debut 1974 OB in "The Basement," followed by "The Foreigner," Bdwy in "Tricks of the Trade" (1980).

GORMAN, CLIFF. Born Oct. 13, 1936 in NYC. Attended UCLA. Debut 1965 OB in "Hogan's Goat," followed by "Boys in the Band," "Ergo," "Angelo's Wedding," Bdwy in "Lenny" (1971), "Chapter Two," "Doubles."

GOTLIEB, BEN. Born June 27, 1954 in Kfar Saba Israel. Attended RADA, CUNY, Brooklyn Col. Bdwy debut 1979 in "Dogg's Hamlet and Cahoot's Macbeth," OB in "Kohlhass," "Relatively Speaking," "The Underlings," "A Match Made in Heaven."

GOULETAS, ROSALIE. Born Jan. 9, 1958 in Chicago, Il. Graduate Columbia U. Debut 1985 OB in "Loose Connections."

GRAAE, JASON. Born May 15, 1958 in Chicago, IL. Graduate Cincinnati Consv. Debut 1981 OB in "Godspell," followed by "Snoopy," "Heaven on Earth," "Promenade," "Feathertop," "Tales of Tinseltown," "Living Color," "Just So," "Olympus on My Mind," Bdwy 1982 in "Do Black Patent Leather Shoes Really Reflect Up?"

GRACIE, SALLY. Born in Little Rock, Ar. Attended Neighborhood Playhouse. Bdwy debut 1942 in "Vickie," followed by "At War with the Army," "Dinosaur Wharf," "Goodbye Again," "Major Barbara," "Fair Game," "But Seriously," OB in "Naomi Court," "Dream Come True," "A Lie of the Mind."

GRANAU, PATTY. Born Aug. 26, 1958 in Freeport, NY. Graduate Hofstra U. Debut 1985 OB in "What's a Nice Country Like You Doing in a State Like This?"

GRANGER, FARLEY. Born July 1, 1928 in San Jose, CA. Bdwy debut 1959 in "First Impressions," followed by "The Warm Peninsula," "Advise and Consent," "The King and I" (CC), "Brigadoon" (CC), "The Seagull," "The Crucible," "Deathtrap," OB in "The Carefree Tree," "A Month in the Country," "Sailing," "Outward Bound," "Tally and Son."

GRANITE, JUDITH. Born Apr. 22, 1936 in Rochester, NY. Graduate Syracuse U, NYU. Bdwy debut 1965 in "The Devils," followed by "Criss-Crossing," OB in "Lovers in the Metro," "So Who's Afraid of Edward Albee?," "Macbird," "The World of Gunter Grass," "The Survival of St. Joan," "Equinox," "Savings," "The Flatbush Faithful."

GRANT, FAYE. Born July 16, in Detroit, Mi. Bdwy debut 1985 in "Singin' in the Rain" for which she received a Theatre World Award.

GRANT, JOAN. Born May 30, 1946 in San Francisco, Ca. Graduate San FranStateU. Debut 1986 OB in "House of Shadows."

GRANT, KATIE. Born Jan. 5, 1955 in Philadelphia, Pa. Juilliard graduate. Debut 1978 OB in "Spring Awakening," followed by "A Month in the Country," "Talley's Folly."

GRAVES, RUTHANNA. Born Sept. 14, 1957 in Philadelphia, Pa. Attended NYU. Debut 1980 OB in "Mother Courage," followed by "Boogie-Woogie Rumble," Bdwy in "Uptown It's Hot" (1986).

GRAY, DOLORES. Born June 7, 1924 in Hollywood, Ca. Bdwy debut 1944 in "Seven Lively Arts," followed by "Are You with It?," "Annie Get Your Gun," "Two on the Aisle," "Carnival in Flanders," "Destry Rides Again," "Sherry!," "42nd Street."

GRAY, SAM. Born July 18, 1923 in Chicago, IL. Graduate Columbia U. Bdwy debut 1955 in "Deadfall," followed by "Six Fingers in a Five Finger Glove," "Saturday, Sunday, Monday," "Golda," "A View from the Bridge," OB in "Ascent of F-6," "Family Portrait," "One Tiger on a Hill," "Shadow of Heroes," "The Recruiting Officer," "The Wild Duck," "Jungle of Cities," "3 Acts of Recognition," "Returnings," "A Little Madness," "The Danube," "Dr. Cook's Garden," "Child's Play," "Kafka Father and Son," "D," "Dennis."

GREEN, DAVID. Born June 16, 1942 in Cleveland, OH. Attended KanStateU. Bdwy debut 1980 in "Annie," followed by "Evita," OB in "Once on a Summer's Day," "Miami," "On the 20th Century."

GREEN, MELISSA ANN. Born Mar. 22, 1956 in NYC. Graduate Bennington Col, Columbia U. Debut 1978 OB in "Cheaters," followed by "What the Hell Nell," "A Little Night Music," "Roberta," "The Magnetic Lady Bug."

GREENBERG, MITCHELL. Born Sept. 19, 1950 in Brooklyn, NY. Graduate Harpur Col., Neighborhood Playhouse. Debut 1979 OB in "Two Grown Men," followed by "Scrambled Feet," "A Christmas Carol," "A Thurber Carnival," "Isn't It Romantic," "Crazy Arnold," Bdwy in "A Day in Hollywood/A Night in the Ukraine" (1980), "Can-Can" (1981), "Marilyn."

GREENE, JAMES. Born Dec. 1, 1926 in Lawrence, MA. Graduate Emerson Col. OB in "The Iceman Cometh," "American Gothic," "The King and the Duke," "The Hostage," "Plays for Bleecker Street," "Moon in the Yellow River," "Misalliance," "Government Inspector," "Baba Goya," LCRep 2 years, "You Can't Take It With You," "School for Scandal," "Wild Duck," "Right You Are," "The Show-Off," "Pantagleize," "Festival of Short Plays," "Nourish the Beast," "One Crack Out," "Artichoke," "Othello," "Salt Lake City Skyline," "Summer," "The Rope Dancers," "Frugal Repast," "Bella Figura," "The Freak," "Park Your Car in the Harvard Yard," "Pigeons on the Walk," "Endgame," "Great Days," "Playboy of the Western World," Bdwy in "Romeo and Juliet," "Girl on the Via Flaminia," "Compulsion," "Inherit the Wind," "Shadow of a Gunman," "Andersonville Trial," "Night Life," "School for Wives," "Ring Round the Bathtub," "Great God Brown," "Don Juan," "Foxfire," "Play Memory," "The Iceman Cometh."

GREENHILL, SUSAN. Born Mar. 19 in NYC. Graduate UPa., Catholic U. Bdwy debut 1982 in "Crimes of the Heart," followed OB by "Hooters," "Our Lord of Lynchville," "September in the Rain," "Seascape with Sharks and Dancer."

GREENHOUSE, MARTHA. Born June 14 in Omaha, NE. Attended Hunter Col., AmThWing. Bdwy debut 1942 in "Sons and Soldiers," followed by "Dear Me, the Sky Is Falling," "Family Way," "Woman Is My Idea," "Summer Brave," OB in "Clerambord," "Our Town," "3 by Ferlinghetti," "No Strings," "Cackle," "Philistines," "Ivanov," "Returnings," "Love Games," "Dancing to Dover," "Pushing the D Train Back to Brooklyn."

GREGORY, MICHAEL ALAN. Born Feb. 1, 1955 in Coral Gables, Fl. Graduate Wheaton Col., UWash. Debut 1985 OB in "Season's Greetings," followed by "Dracula," "Kiss Me Kate."

GREY, JOEL. Born Apr. 11, 1932 in Cleveland, Oh. Attended Cleveland Play House. Bdwy debut 1951 in "Borscht Capades," followed by "Come Blow Your Horn," "Stop the World—I Want to Get Off," "Half a Sixpence," "Cabaret," "George M!," "Goodtime Charley," "Grand Tour," OB in "The Littlest Revue," "Harry Noon and Night," "Marco Polo Sings a Solo," "The Normal Heart."

GRIESEMER, JOHN. Born Dec. 5, 1947 in Elizabeth, NJ. Graduate Dickinson Col., URI. Debut 1981 OB in "Turnbuckle," followed by "Death of a Miner," "Little Victories," "Macbeth," "A Lie of the Mind."

GRIFFITH, EDWARD D. Born Jan. 8, 1949 in Osaka, Japan. Graduate Georgetown U. Debut 1980 OB in "Fugue in a Nursery," followed by "Death Takes a Holiday," "Behind a Mask."

GRIFFITH, KRISTIN. Born Sept. 7, 1953 in Odessa, Tx. Juilliard Graduate. Bdwy debut 1976 in "A Texas Trilogy," OB in "Rib Cage," "Character Lines," "3 Friends/2 Rooms," "A Month in the Country," "Fables for Friends," "The Trading Post," "Marching to Georgia," "American Garage," "A Midsummer Night's Dream."

GRIMES, TAMMY. Born Jan. 30, 1934 in Lynn, Ma. Attended Stephens Col., Neighborhood Playhouse. Debut 1956 OB in "The Littlest Revue," followed by "Clerambard," "Molly Trick," "Are You Now or Have You Ever Been," "Father's Day," "A Month in the Country," "Sunset," "Waltz of the Toreadors," Bdwy in "Look after Lulu" (1959), for which she received a Theatre World Award,

GRIZZARD, GEORGE. Born Apr. 1, 1928 in Roanoke Rapids, Va. Graduate UNC. Bdwy debut 1954 in "All Summer Long," followed by "The Desperate Hours," "The Happiest Millionaire"

GROENENDAAL, CRIS. Born Feb. 17, 1948 in Erie, PA. Attended Allegheny Col, Exeter U, HB Studio. Bdwy debut 1979 in "Sweeney Todd," followed by "Sunday in the Park with George," "Brigadoon" (LC), OB in "Francis," "Sweethearts in Concert," "Oh, Boy " "No No Nanette in Concert."

GROENER, HARRY. Born Sept. 10, 1951 in Augsburg, Ger. Graduate UWash. Bdwy debut 1979 in "Oklahoma!," for which he received a Theatre World Award, followed by "Oh, Brother!," "Is There Life after High School," "Cats," "Harrigan 'n Hart," "Sunday in the Park with George," OB in "Beside the Seaside."

GROH, DAVID. Born May 21, 1939 in NYC. Graduate Brown U., LAMDA. Debut 1963 OB in "The Importance of Being Earnest," followed by "Elizabeth the Queen" (CC), "The Hot l Baltimore," "Be Happy for Me," "Dead Wrong," Bdwy in "Chapter Two" (1978).

GROOME, MALCOLM. Born Aug. 16, 1949 in Greensboro, NC. Graduate UNC. Debut 1971 OB in "Dionysus Wants You!," followed by "So Long My Tottie," "Billy Irish," "Heat," "The Normal Heart," Bdwy in "Grease" (1973).

GRUENEBERG, WILLIAM. Born Mar. 8, 1955 in Santa Monica, Ca. Attended CalStateU. Debut 1983 OB in "Twelfth Night," followed by "King Stag," "Comedy of Errors."

GRUSIN, RICHARD. Born Nov. 2, 1946 in Chicago, IL. Graduate Goodman School, Yale U. Debut 1978 OB in "Wings," followed by "Sganarelle," "Heat of Re-Entry," "For Sale," "The Time of Your Life."

GUIDALL, GEORGE. Born June 7, 1938 in Plainfield, NJ. Attended UBuffalo, AADA. Bdwy debut 1969 in "Wrong Way Light Bulb," followed by "Cold Storage," OB in "Counsellor-at-Law," "Taming of the Shrew," "All's Well That Ends Well," "The Art of Dining," "Biography," "After All," "Henry V," "Time of the Cuckoo," "Yours Anne."

GUIDO, MICHAEL. Born Jan. 13, 1950 in Woodside, NY. Graduate USFla., Brandeis U. Debut 1982 OB in "The Workroom," followed by "Strictly Dishonorable," "Flatbush Faithful," "Largo Desolato."

GUNN, NICHOLAS. Born Aug. 28, 1947 in Brooklyn, NY. Appeared with Paul Taylor Dance Co. before Bdwy debut in "The Mystery of Edwin Drood" (1985).

GUNTON, BOB. Born Nov. 15, 1945 in Santa Monica, CA. Attended UCal. Debut 1971 OB in "Who Am I?," followed by "The Kid," "Desperate Hours," "Tip-Toes," "How I Got That Story," "Hamlet," "Death of Von Richthofen," "The Man Who Could See Through Time," Bdwy in "Happy End" (1977), "Working," "King of Hearts," "Evita," "Passion," "Big River."

HACK, STEVEN. Born Apr. 20, 1958 in St. Louis, MO. Attended CalArts, AADA, Debut 1978 OB in "The Coolest Cat in Town," followed by Bdwy in "Cats" (1982).

HADARY, JONATHAN. Born Oct. 11, 1948 in Chicago, IL. Attended Tufts U. Debut 1974 OB in "White Nights," followed by "El Grande de Coca-Cola," "Songs from Pins and Needles," "God Bless You, Mr. Rosewater," "Pushing 30," "Scrambled Feet," "Coming Attractions," "Tomfoolery," "Charley Bacon and Family," Bdwy in "Gemini," (1977/also OB), "Torch Song Trilogy, "As Is."

HAGEN, UTA. Born June 11, 1919 in Goettingen, Ger. Bdwy debut 1938 in "The Seagull," followed by "The Happiest Years," "Key Largo," "Vickie," "Othello," "A Streetcar Named Desire," "Country Girl," "St. Joan," "The Whole World Over," "In Any Language," "The Magic and the Loss," CC's "Angel Street" and "Tovarich," "Who's Afraid of Virginia Woolf?," "The Cherry Orchard," "Charlotte," OB in "A Month in the Country," "Good Woman of Setzuan," "Mrs. Warren's Profession."

HAGERTY, JULIE. Born June 15, 1955 in Cincinnati, Oh. Attended Juilliard. Debut 1979 OB in "Mutual Benefit Life," followed by "Wild Life," "House of Blue Leaves" (1979), Bdwy in "House of Blue Leaves" (1986) for which she received a Theatre World Award.

HAGUE, DAYDRIE. Born Aug. 1, 1954 in New London, Ct. Graduate SUC/Potsdam, UWash. Debut 1981 OB in "Americana," followed by "Four of a Kind," "Three Sisters."

HALL, GEORGE. Born Nov. 19, 1916 in Toronto, Can. Attended Neighborhood Playhouse. Bdwy bow 1946 in "Call Me Mister," followed by "Lend an Ear," "Touch and Go," "Live Wire," "The Boy Friend," "There's a Girl in My Soup," "An Evening with Richard Nixon .," "We Interrupt This Program," "Man and Superman," "Bent," "Noises Off," OB in "The Balcony," "Ernest in Love," "A Round with Rings," "Family Pieces," "Carousel," "The Case Against Roberta Guardino," "Marry Me!" "Arms and the Man," "The Old Glory," "Dancing for the Kaiser," "Casualties," "The Seagull," "A Stitch in Time," "Mary Stuart," "No End of Blame," "Hamlet," "Colette Collage," "The Homecoming," "And a Nightingale Sang," "The Bone Ring."

HALL, KIMBERLY. Born Apr. 19, 1953 in Chicago, Il. Graduate UCLA. Debut 1986 OB in "Buskers."

HALLIDAY, ANDY. Born Mar. 31, 1953 in Orange, Ct. Attended USIU/San Diego. Debut OB 1985 in "Vampire Lesbians of Sodom," followed by "Times Square Angel."

HALLOW, JOHN. Born Nov. 28, 1924 in NYC. Attended Neighborhood Playhouse. Bdwy debut 1954 in "Anastasia," followed by "Ross," "Visit to a Small Planet," "Foxy," "Oh, Dad, Poor Dad . . .," "Ben Franklin in Paris," "Three Bags Full," "Don't Drink the Water," "Hadrian VII," "Tough to Get Help," "Ballroom," "A New York Summer," "The Man Who Came to Dinner," OB in "Hamlet," "Do I Hear a Waltz?," "Kind Lady," "The Butler Did It," "Festival of One Acts," "Sorrows and Sons."

HAMILL, MARK. Born Sept. 25, 1952 in Oakland, CA. Attended LACC. Bdwy debut 1981 in "The Elephant Man," followed by "Amadeus," "Harrigan 'n Hart," OB in "Room Service."

HAMILTON, LAWRENCE. Born Sept. 14, 1954 in Ashdown, AR. Graduate Henderson State U. Debut 1981 OB in "Purlie," Bdwy in "Sophisticated Ladies" (1982), followed by "Porgy and Bess," "The Wiz," "Uptown It's Hot."

HANAN, STEPHEN. Born Jan 7, 1947 in Washington, DC. Graduate Harvard, LAMDA. Debut 1978 OB in "All's Well That Ends Well," followed by "Taming of the Shrew," "Rabboni," Bdwy in "Pirates of Penzance" (1978),"Cats."

HANSEN, PEDER. Born Sept. 23, 1947 in NYC. Graduate SUNY/Cortland, George Washington U., Catholic U. Debut 1986 OB in "Girl Crazy."

HARA, DOUGLAS M. Born Dec. 14, 1968 in NYC. Debut 1983 OB in "My Heart's in the Highlands," followed by "Sometimes I Wake Up in the Middle of the Night," Bdwy in "Boys of Winter" (1985).

HARDING, JAN LESLIE. Born 1956 in Cambridge, MA. Graduate Boston U. Debut 1980 OB in "Album," followed by "Sunday Picnic," "Buddies," "The Lunch Girls," "Marathon '86."

HARDY, WILLIAM. Born Jan. 19, 1933 in Houston, Tx. Attended UHouston. Debut 1983 OB in "Joan of Lorraine," followed by "To Whom It May Concern."

HARNEY, BEN. Born Aug. 29, 1952 in Brooklyn, NY. Bdwy debut 1971 in "Purlie," followed by "Pajama Game," "Tree-Monisha," "Pippin," "Dreamgirls," OB in "Don't Bother Me I Can't Cope," "The Derby," "The More You Get," "Williams & Walker."

HARRAN, JACOB. Born July 23, 1955 in NYC. Graduate Hofstra U. Debut 1984 OB in "Balm in Gilead," followed by "Awake and Sing," "Crossing Delancey," "Romeo and Juliet," "Cabbage-head."

HARRINGTON, MARGARET. Born Jan. 25 in NYC. Graduate Marymount Manhattan Col. Debut 1978 OB in "Fefu and Her Friends," followed by "Life Is a Dream," "Four Corners," "Light Up the Sky."

HARRIS, BRADDON. Born Oct. 1, 1954 in Exeter, Ca. Graduate USIU/San Diego. Debut 1986 OB in "They're Playing Our Song."

HARRIS, ED. Born Nov. 28, 1950 in Tenafly, NJ. Attended ColumbiaU, UOkla. Debut 1983 OB in "Fool for Love," Bdwy in "Precious Sons" (1986) for which he received a Theatre World Award.

HARRIS, ROSEMARY. Born Sept. 19, 1930 in Ashby, Eng. Attended RADA. Bdwy debut 1952 in "Climate of Eden" for which she received a Theatre World Award, followed by "Troilus and Cressida," "Interlock," "The Disenchanted," "The Tumbler," APA's "The Tavern," "School for Scandal," "The Seagull," "The Importance of Being Earnest," "War and Peace," "Man and Superman," "Judith," and "You Can't Take It With You," "Lion in Winter," "Old Times," "Merchant of Venice," "A Streetcar Named Desire," "The Royal Family," "Pack of Lies," "Hay Fever," OB in "The New York Idea," "Three Sisters," "The Seagull."

HARRISON, REX. Born Mar. 5, 1908 in Huyten, Eng. Attended Liverpool Col. Bdwy debut 1936 in "Sweet Aloes," followed by "Anne of a Thousand Days," "Bell, Book and Candle," "Venus Observed," "Love of Four Colonels," "My Fair Lady" (1956/1981), "Fighting Cock," "Emperor Henry IV," "In Praise of Love," "Caesar and Cleopatra," "The Kingfisher," "Heartbreak House," "Aren't We All?"

HARRISON, STANLEY EARL. Born Sept. 17, 1955 in Cheverly, Md. Graduate MorganStateU. Debut 1978 OB in "The Phantom," followed by "The Boogie-Woogie Rumble of a Dream Deferred," "The Medium," "Mud," "The Mighty Gents," Bdwy in "The King and I" (1985).

HARUM, EIVIND. Born May 24, 1944 in Stavanger, Norway. Attended Utah State U. Credits include "Sophie," "Foxy," "Baker Street," "West Side Story" ('68),"A Chorus Line," "Woman of the Year."

HATCHER, ROBYN. Born Sept. 8, 1956 in Philadelphia, Pa. Graduate Adelphi U. Debut 1983 OB in "Macbeth," followed by "Edward II," "Deep Sleep," "Flatbush Faithful."

HAUSER, KIM. Born Mar. 11, 1974 in Lowell, Ma. Bdwy debut 1984 in "The Rink," followed by "Brighton Beach Memoirs," OB in "Opal."

HAWKINS, TRISH. Born Oct. 30, 1945 in Hartford, CT. Attended Radcliffe, Neighborhood Playhouse. Debut OB 1970 in "Oh! Calcutta!" followed by "Iphigenia," "The Hot 1 Baltmore" for which she received a Theatre World Award, "him," "Come Back, Little Sheba," "Battle of Angels," "Mound Builders," "The Farm," "Ulysses in Traction," "Lulu," "Hogan's Folly," "Twelfth Night," "A Tale Told," "Great Grandson of Jedediah Kohler," "Time Framed," "Levitations." "Love's Labour's Lost," "Talley & Son," "Tomorrow's Monday," "Caligula," "Quiet in the Land," Bdwy (1977) in "Some of My Best Friends," "Talley's Folly" (1979).

HAYESON, JIMMY. Born June 27, 1924 in Carthage, NC. Graduate NCCol. Debut 1969 OB in "Black Quartet," followed by "Black Girl," "Mark VIII:xxxvi," Bdwy in "Ain't Supposed to Die a Natural Death" (1971).

HAYLE, DOUGLAS. Born Jan. 11, 1942 in Trenton, NJ. Graduate AADA. OB in "Henry IV," "Romeo and Juliet," "King Lear," "A Cry of Players," "In the Matter of J. Robert Oppenheimer," "The Miser," "Trelawny of the Wells," "Oh Lady! Lady!," "The Desperate Hours," "Panama Hattie," "The Constant Wife."

HAYNES, TIGER. Born Dec. 13, 1907 in St. Croix, VI. Bdwy bow 1956 in "New Faces," followed by "Finian's Rainbow," "Fade Out-Fade In," "Pajama Game," "The Wiz," "A Broadway Musical," "Comin' Uptown," "My One and Only," OB in "Turns," "Bags," "Louis," "Taking My Turn."

HAYS, REX. Born June 17, 1946 in Hollywood, Ca. Graduate SanJoseStateU, Brandeis U. Bdwy debut 1975 in "Dance with Me," followed by "Angel," "King of Hearts," "Evita," "Onward Victoria," "Woman of the Year," OB in "Charley's Tale."

HEALD, ANTHONY. Born Aug. 25, 1944 in New Rochelle, NY. Graduate MiStateU. Debut 1980 OB in "The Glass Menagerie," followed by "Misalliance" for which he received a Theatre World Award, "The Caretaker," "The Fox," "Quartermaine's Terms," "The Philanthropist," "Henry V," "Digby," "Principia Scriptoriae," Bdwy in "The Wake of Jamey Foster" (1982), "Marriage of Figaro."

HEALY, DAVID. Born Dec. 17, 1960 in NYC. Graduate George Washington U. Debut 1985 OB in "Love as We Know It."

HELLER, ROBERT. Born Dec. 26, 1930 in Brooklyn, NY. Attended Actors Studio. Debut 1955 OB in "Terrible Swift Sword," followed by "The Cradle Will Rock," "My Prince My King," "Waiting for Lefty," "Upside-Down on the Handlebars," "Briss," "Cabal of Hypocrites," "Common Ground," Bdwy in "Marathon '33" (1963).

HENDERSON, JO. Born in Buffalo, NY. Attended WMiU. OB in "Camille," "Little Foxes," "An Evening with Merlin Finch," "20th Century Tar," "A Scent of Flowers," "Revival," "Dandelion Wine," "My Life," "Ladyhouse Blues," "Fallen Angels," "Waiting for the Parade," "Threads," "Bella Figura," "Details without a Map," "The Middle Ages," "Time Framed," "Isn't It Romantic," "Little Footsteps," Bdwy in "Rose" (1981), "84 Charing Cross Road," "Play Memory."

HENIG, ANDI. Born May 6 in Washington, DC. Attended Yale. Debut 1978 OB in "One and One," followed by "Kind Lady," "Downriver," Bdwy in "Oliver!" (1984), "Big River."

HENRITZE, BETTE. Born May 23 in Betsy Layne, KY. Graduate UTenn. OB in "Lion in Love," "Abe Lincoln in Illinois," "Othello," "Baal," "Long Christmas Dinner," "Queens of France," "Rimers of Eldritch," "Displaced Person," "Acquisition," "Crime of Passion," "Happiness Cage," "Henry VI," "Richard III," "Older People," "Lotta," "Catsplay," "A Month in the Country," "The Golem," "Daughters," Bdwy in "Jenny Kissed Me" (1948), "Pictures in the Hallway," "Giants, Sons of Giants," "Ballad of the Sad Cafe," "The White House," "Dr. Cook's Garden," "Here's Where I Belong," "Much Ado about Nothing," "Over Here," "Angel Street," "Man and Superman," "Macbeth" (1981), "Present Laughter," "The Octette Bridge Club."

HERMAN, DANNY. Born Nov. 2, 1960 in Pittsburgh, PA. Debut 1979 OB in "Big Bad Burlesque," Bdwy in "A Chorus Line" (1981), "Leader of the Pack."

HERNDON, JAN LEIGH. Born Apr. 9, 1955 in Raleigh, NC. Graduate ValntermontCol. Bdwy debut 1982 in "A Chorus Line," followed by "La Cage aux Folles," "The Mystery of Edwin Drood," OB in "Joan and the Devil."

HERRERA, JOHN. Born Sept. 21, 1955 in Havana, Cuba. Graduate Loyola U. Bdwy debut 1979 in "Grease," followed by "Evita," "Camelot," "The Mystery of Edwin Drood," OB in "La Boheme," "Lies and Legends."

HERRMANN, EDWARD. Born July 21, 1943 in Washington, DC. Graduate Bucknell U, LAMDA. Debut 1970 OB in "The Basic Training of Pavlo Hummel," followed by "A Midsummer Night's Dream," "Tom and Viv," "Not about Heroes," Bdwy in "Moonchildren" (1971), "Mrs. Warren's Profession," "The Philadelphia Story."

HERRON, KEITH. Born Dec. 5, 1958 in Lexington, Ky. Graduate IndU. Debut 1985 OB in "She Loves Me."

HICKEY, WILLIAM. Born in 1928 in Brooklyn, NY. Bdwy debut 1951 in "St. Joan," followed by "Tovarich," "Miss Lonelyhearts," "Body Beautiful," "Make a Million," "Not Enough Rope," "Moonbirds," "Step on a Crack," "Thieves," OB in "On the Town," "Next," "Happy Birthday, Wanda June," "Small Craft Warnings," "Mourning Becomes Electra," "Siamese Connections," "Troilus and Cressida," "Sunday Runners," "Romance Language," "Angelo's Wedding," "Lippe."

HICKS, LAURA. Born Nov. 17, 1956 in NYC. Graduate Juilliard. Debut 1978 OB in "Spring Awakening," followed by "Talking With," "The Cradle Will Rock," "Paducah," "10 by Tennessee."

HICKS, LESLIE. Born Oct. 21, 1955 in Providence, RI. Attended CalStateU/Northridge, ACT. Bdwy debut 1983 in "Merlin," OB in "The Gifts of the Magi."

HILLARY, ANN. Born Jan 8, 1931 in Jellico, TN. Attended Northwestern U., AADA. Bdwy debut 1953 in "Be Your Age," followed by "Separate Tables," "The Lark," OB in "Dark of the Moon," "Paradise Lost," "Total Eclipse," "The Circle."

HINES, MAURICE. Born in 1944 in NYC. Bdwy debut 1954 in "The Girl in Pink Tights," followed by "Eubie!," "Guys and Dolls," "Bring Back Birdie," "Sophisticated Ladies," "Uptown It's Hot."

HINGLE, PAT. Born July 19, 1923 in Denver, Co. Graduate UTx. Bdwy debut 1953 in "End as a Man," followed by "Festival," "Cat on a Hot Tin Roof," "Girls of Summer," "The Dark at the Top of the Stairs," "J.B.," "Deadly Game," "Strange Interlude," "Blues for Mr. Charlie," "A Girl Could Get Lucky," "The Glass Menagerie," "Johnny No Trump," "The Price," "Child's Play," "Selling of the President," "That Championship Season," "Lady from the Sea," "A Life," OB in "Reflections of a Genius."

HIRSCH, JUDD. Born Mar. 15, 1935 in NYC. Attended AADA. Bdwy debut 1966 in "Barefoot in the Park," followed by "Chapter Two," "Talley's Folly," OB in "On the Necessity of Being Polygamous," "Scuba Duba," "Mystery Play," "Hot 1 Baltimore," "Prodigal," "Knock Knock," "Life and/or Death," "Talley's Folly," "The Sea Gull," "I'm Not Rappaport."

HIRSCH, MICHAEL. Born Jan. 1, 1947 in Brooklyn, NY. Graduate Ithaca Col. Debut 1978 OB in "Company," followed by "Tip-Toes," "To Whom It May Concern."

HIRSCH, VICKI. Born Feb. 22, 1951 in Wilmington, DE. Graduate UDel, Villanova U. Debut 1985 OB in "Back County Crimes," followed by "Casualties."

HODES, GLORIA. Born Aug. 20 in Norwich, Ct. Bdwy debut 1969 in Gantry, OB in "The Club" for which she received a Theatre World Award, "Cycles of Fancy," "The Heroine," "Pearls."

HOFFMAN, AVI. Born Mar. 3, 1958 in The Bronx, NY. Graduate UMiami. Debut 1983 OB in "The Rise of David Levinsky," followed by "It's Hard to Be a Jew," "A Rendezvous with God," "The Golden Land."

HOFFMAN, G. WAYNE. Born Dec. 13, 1951 in Strasburg, Va. Graduate AADA. Debut 1985 OB in "Hamelin."

HOFVENDAHL, STEVE. Born Sept. 1, 1956 in San Jose, Ca. Graduate USantaClara, Brandeis U. Debut 1986 OB in "A Lie of the Mind."

HOLGATE, DANNY. Born July 9, 1933 in Boston, Ma. Attended Berklee and Manhattan Schools of Music. Debut 1986 OB in "Lady Day at Emerson's Bar & Grill."

HOLLAND, DOROTHY. Born Feb. 11, 1945 in Indianapolis, In. Attended HB Studio. Bdwy debut 1980 in "Onward Victoria," followed by "Brighton Beach Memoirs," OB in "Amidst the Gladiolas."

HOLLIDAY, JENNIFER. Born Oct. 19, 1960 in Houston, TX. Bdwy debut 1980 in "Your Arms Too Short to Box with God," followed by "Dreamgirls" for which she received a Theatre World Award.

HOLLIS, TOMMY. Born Mar. 27, 1954 in Jacksonville, TX. Graduate UHouston. Debut 1985 OB in "Diamonds," followed by "Secrets of the Lava Lamp," "Paradise," "Africanus Instructus."

HOLM, CELESTE. Born Apr. 29, 1919 in NYC. Attended UCLA, UChicago. Bdwy debut 1938 in "Glorianna," followed by "The Time of Your Life," "Another Sun," "Return of the Vagabond," "8 O'Clock Tuesday," "My Fair Ladies," "Papa Is All," "All the Comforts of Home," "Damask Cheek," "Oklahoma!," "Bloomer Girl," "She Stoops to Conquer," "Affairs of State," "Anna Christie," "The King and I," "His and Hers," "Interlock," "Third Best Sport," "Invitation to a March," "Mame," "Candida," "Habeas Corpus," "The Utter Glory of Morrissey Hall," OB in "A Month in the Country," "Paris Was Yesterday," "With Love and Laughter," "A Christmas Carol."

HOLMES, GEORGE. Born June 3, 1935 in London, Eng. Graduate ULondon. Debut 1978 OB in "The Changeling," followed by "Love from a Stranger," "The Hollow," "The Story of the Gadsbys," "Learned Ladies," "The Land Is Bright," "Something Old, Something New," "Oscar Wilde Solitaire."

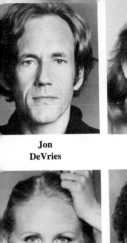
Jon
DeVries

Patrice
Donnell

Craig
Dudley

Keely
Eastley

Dennis
Edenfield

Karen
Evans-Kandel

Kimberly
Farr

Steve
Fickinger

Crystal
Field

Harvey
Fierstein

Kit
Flanagan

Scott
Fless

Jose
Fong

Judy
Frank

Arthur
French

Carrie
Garman

David
Giella

Fay
Gold

Lisa
Goodman

Andrew
Gorman

Rosalie
Gouletas

John
Griesemer

Kristin
Griffith

Andy
Halliday

Lawrence
Hamilton

Margaret
Harrington

Stanley Earl
Harrison

Leslie
Hicks

Michael
Hirsch

Gloria
Hodes

207

HOLMES, SCOTT. Born May 30, 1952 in West Grove, PA. Graduate Catawba Col. Bdwy debut 1979 in "Grease," followed by "Evita," "The Rink," "Jerome Kern Goes to Hollywood," OB in "Diamonds."

HOMBERG, TERRI. Born Jan. 5, 1959 in Jacksonville, Fl. Attended SanJoseStateU, Neighborhood Playhouse. Bdwy debut 1982 in "Joseph and the Amazing Technicolor Dreamcoat," followed by "Jerry's Girls."

HONDA, CAROL A. Born Nov. 20 in Kealakekua, HI. Graduate UHi. Debut 1983 OB in "Yellow Fever," followed by "Empress of China," "Manoa Valley," "Once Is Never Enough."

HOPKINS, ROSEMARY. Born in Nashville, Tn. Graduate OhioU. Debut 1972 OB in "Born Yesterday," followed by "Special Consideration," "Nirvana Manor," "Mapa," "A Double Scoop," "Dance of the Mayfly."

HORAN, BONNIE. Born Aug. 20, 1928 in Dayton, TX. Graduate UHouston, UParis, Geo.Wash.U. Debut 1980 OB in "The Devil's Disciple," followed by "The Meehans," "Arms and the Man," "Her Great Match."

HORMASJI, HOMI. Born June 14, 1948 in Poona, India. Graduate USussex. Debut 1985 OB in "A Map of the World."

HORVATH, JAN. Born Jan. 31, 1958 in Lake Forrest, IL. Graduate Cin.Consv. Bdwy debut 1983 in "Oliver!," followed by "Sweet Charity," OB in "Sing Me Sunshine." "Jacques Brel Is Alive and Well.."

HOTY, DEE. Born Aug. 16, 1952 in Lakewood, Oh. Graduate Otterbein Col. Debut 1979 OB in "The Golden Apple," followed by "Ta-Dah!," "Personals," Bdwy in "The Five O'Clock Girl" (1981), "Shakespeare Cabaret."

HOUGHTON, KATHARINE. Born Mar 10, 1945 in Hartford, CT. Graduate Sarah Lawrence Col. Bdwy debut 1965 in "A Very Rich Woman," followed by "The Front Page" (1969), OB in "A Scent of Flowers" for which she received a Theatre World Award, "To Heaven in a Swing," "Madwoman of Chaillot," "Vivat Vivat Regina " "The Time of Your Life," "Children of the Sun."

HOUSE, RON. Born in Chicago, Il. Attended Wilson Col., Roosevelt U. Debut 1973 OB in "El Grande de Coca Cola," followed by "Bullshot Drummond," 1986 revival of "El Grande de Coca Cola."

HOXIE, RICHMOND. Born July 21, 1946 in NYC. Graduate Dartmouth Col., LAMDA. Debut 1975 OB in "Shaw for an Evening," followed by "The Family," "Justice," "Landscape with Waitress," "3 from the Marathon," "The Slab Boys," "Vivien," "Operation Midnight Climax," "The Dining Room," "Daddies," "To Gillian on Her 37th Birthday," "Dennis."

HUBER, KATHLEEN. Born Mar. 3, 1947 in NYC. Graduate UCal. Debut 1969 OB in "A Scent of Flowers," followed by "The Virgin and the Unicorn," "The Constant Wife."

HUFFMAN, CADY. Born Feb. 2, 1965 in Santa Barbara, Ca. Debut 1983 OB in "They're Playing Our Song," Bdwy 1985 in "La Cage aux Folles," followed by "Big Deal."

HUGHES, BARNARD. Born July 16, 1915 in Bedford Hills, NY. Attended Manhattan Col. OB in "Rosmersholm," "A Doll's House," "Hogan's Goat," "Lime," "Older People," "Hamlet," "Merry Wives of Windsor," "Pericles," "Three Sisters," "Translations," Bdwy in "The Ivy Green," "Dinosaur Wharf," "Teahouse of the August Moon," "A Majority of One," "Advise and Consent," "The Advocate," "Hamlet," "I Was Dancing," "Generations," "How Now Dow Jones?," "Wrong Way Light Bulb," "Sheep on the Runway," "Abelard and Heloise," "Much Ado about Nothing," "Uncle Vanya," "The Good Doctor," "All Over Town," "Da," "Angels Fall," "End of the World," "The Iceman Cometh."

HUGHES, LAURA. Born Jan. 28, 1959 in NYC. Graduate Neighborhood Playhouse. Debut 1980 OB in "The Diviners," followed by "A Tale Told," "Time Framed," "Fables for Friends," "Talley and Son."

HULL, BRYAN. Born Sept. 12, 1937 in Amarillo, TX. Attended UNMx, Wayne State U. Bdwy debut 1976 in "Somethin's Afoot," OB in "The Fantasticks."

HUNT, LINDA. Born Apr. 2, 1945 in Morristown, NJ. Attended Goodman Theatre. Debut 1975 OB in "Down by the River," followed by "The Tennis Game," "Metamorphosis in Miniature," "Little Victories," "Top Girls," "Aunt Dan and Lemon," Bdwy in "Ah, Wilderness!" (1975), "End of the World."

HURLEY, JOHN PATRICK. Born May 7, 1949 in Salt Lake City, UT. Graduate UUtah. Debut 1982 OB in "Inserts," followed by "Sharing," Bdwy in "Aren't We All?" (1985).

HURST, LILLIAN. Born Aug. 13, 1949 in San Juan, PR. Attended UPR. Debut 1983 OB in "The Great Confession," followed by "The Cuban Swimmer/Dog Lady," "The Birds Fly Out with Death," Bdwy in "The Cuban Thing" (1968).

HURT, MARY BETH. Born in Marshalltown, Ia. in 1948. Attended UIa, NYU. Debut 1972 OB in "More Than You Deserve," followed by "As You Like It," "Trelawny of the Wells," "The Cherry Orchard," "Love for Love," "Member of the Wedding," "Boy Meets Girl," "Secret Service," "Father's Day," "Nest of the Wood Grouse," Bdwy in "Crimes of the Heart" (1981), "The Misanthrope," "Benefactors."

HYMAN, EARLE. Born Oct. 11, 1926 in Rocky Mount, NC. Attended New School, AmThWing. Bdwy debut 1943 in "Run Little Chillun," followed by "Anna Lucasta," "Climate of Eden," "Merchant of Venice," "Othello," "Julius Caesar," "The Tempest," "No Time for Sergeants," "Mr. Johnson" for which he received a Theatre World Award, "St. Joan," "Hamlet," "Waiting for Godot," "The Duchess of Malfi," "Les Blancs," "The Lady from Dubuque," "Execution of Justice," OB in "The White Rose and the Red," "Worlds of Shakespeare," "Jonah," "Life and Times of J. Walter Smintheus," "Orrin," "The Cherry Orchard," "House Party," "Carnival Dreams," "Agamemnon," "Othello," "Julius Caesar," "Coriolanus," "Remembrance," "Long Day's Journey into Night," "Sleep Beauty."

IANNUCCI, MICHAEL. Born Feb. 3, 1956 in Philadelphia, PA. Graduate Temple U, RADA. Debut 1983 OB in "Waiting for Lefty," followed by "Writers," "A Flash of Lightning."

INGE, MATTHEW. Born May 29, 1950 in Fitchburg, MA. Attended Boston U., Harvard. Bdwy debut 1976 in "Fiddler on the Roof," followed by "A Chorus Line."

INNES, LAURA. Born Aug. 16, 1957 in Pontiac, MI. Graduate Northwestern U. Debut 1982 OB in "Edmond," followed by "My Uncle Sam," "Life Is a Dream," "Alice and Fred," "A Country Doctor."

INWOOD, JOAN. Born Apr. 8, 1950 in South Bend, In. Graduate Stephens Col., FlaStateU. Debut 1985 OB in "Oliver Oliver," followed by "Burlesque."

IRWIN, MICHAEL. Born Aug. 31, 1953 in Baltimore, Md. Graduate VaComU. Debut 1985 OB in "A Flash of Lightning," followed by "A New York Summer," "Borders."

ISRAEL, MARY. Born in Seattle, Wa. Graduate Queens Col, NYU. Debut 1957 OB in "Candida," followed by "Casualties," "Murder in the Cathedral," "Distortions," "Pinter Revue Sketches," "A Perfect Analysis Given by a Parrot," "36/47 + Every Other One."

IVANEK, ZJELKO. Born Aug. 15, 1957 in Lujubljana, Yugo. Graduate Yale U., LAMDA. Bdwy debut 1981 in "The Survivor," followed by "Brighton Beach Memoirs," "Loot," OB in "Cloud 9," "A Map of the World."

IVEY, DANA. Born Aug. 12, in Atlanta, GA. Graduate Rollins Col. LAMDA. Bdwy debut 1981 in "Macbeth" (LC), followed by "Present Laughter," "Heartbreak House," "Sunday in the Park with George," "Pack of Lies," "Marriage of Figaro," OB in "A Call from the East," "Vivien," "Candida in Concert," "Major Barbara in Concert," "Quartermaine's Terms," "Baby with the Bathwater."

JABLONS, KAREN. Born July 19, 1951 in Trenton, NJ. Juilliard graduate. Debut 1969 OB in "The Student Prince," followed by "Sound of Music," "Funny Girl," "Boys from Syracuse," "Sterling Silver," "People in Show Business Make Long Goodbyes," "In Trousers," Bdwy in "Ari," "Two Gentlemen of Verona," "Lorelei," "Where's Charley?," "A Chorus Line."

JACKS, SUSAN J. Born Nov. 5, 1953 in Brooklyn, NY. Graduate SUNY. Debut 1983 OB in "Forbidden Broadway."

JACKSON, ERNESTINE. Born Sept. 18 in Corpus Christi, TX. Graduate Del Mar Col., Juilliard. Debut 1966 in "Show Boat" (LC), followed by "Finian's Rainbow," "Hello Dolly!," "Applause," "Jesus Christ Superstar," "Tricks," "Raisin" for which she received a Theatre World Award, "Guys and Dolls," "Bacchae," OB in "Louis," "Some Enchanted Evening," "Money Notes," "Jack and Jill," "Black Girl."

JACOB, STEVEN. Born May 11, 1959 in Lynne, Ma. Graduate NYU. Debut 1981 OB in "Florodora," followed by "Bodo," "Hamlin," Bdwy in "Merrily We Roll Along" (1981).

JACOBS, KATE. Born Jan. 11, 1959 in Alexandria, Va. Graduate Oberlin Col. Debut OB 1985 in "Big Pocket," followed by "Sell-Out," "Fitcher's Bird."

JACOBS, MARC RUSTY. Born July 10, 1967 in NYC. Debut 1979 OB in "Tripletale," followed by "Glory Hallelujah!," "What a Life!," "Three Sisters," Bdwy in "Peter Pan" (1979).

JACOBY, MARK. Born May 21, 1947 in Johnson City, Tn. Graduate GaStateU, FlaStateU, St. John's U. Debut 1984 OB in "Bells Are Ringing," Bdwy 1986 in "Sweet Charity" for which he received a Theatre World Award.

JAMES, ELMORE. Born May 3, 1954 in NYC. Graduate SUNY/Purchase. Debut 1970 OB in "Moon on a Rainbow Shawl," followed by "The Ups and Downs of Theopholus Maitland," "Carnival," "Until the Real Thing Comes Along," "A Midsummer Night's Dream," "The Tempest," Bdwy in "But Never Jam Today" (1979), "Your Arms Too Short to Box with God," "Big River."

JAMES, FRANCESCA. Born Jan. 23 in Montebello, Ca. Attended Carnegie-Mellon U. Bdwy debut 1971 in "The Rothschilds," OB in "The Father," "Life of Galileo," "The Truth," "Macbeth."

JENKINS, KEN. Born in Kentucky in 1940. Bdwy debut 1986 in "Big River."

JENNEY, LUCINDA. Born Apr. 23, 1954 in Long Island City, NY. Graduate Sarah Lawrence Col. Debut 1981 OB in "Death Takes a Holiday," followed by "Ground Zero Club," "True to Life," Bdwy in "Gemini" (1981).

JENNINGS, KEN. Born Oct. 10, 1947 in Jersey City, NJ. Graduate St. Peter's Col. Bdwy debut 1975 in "All God's Chillun Got Wings," followed by "Sweeney Todd" for which he received a Theatre World Award, "Present Laughter," OB in "Once on a Summer's Day," "Mayor," "Rabboni."

JENS, SALOME. Born May 8, 1935 in Milwaukee, Wi. Bdwy debut 1956 in "Sixth Finger in a Five Finger Glove," followed by "The Disenchanted," "A Far Country," "Night Life," "I'm Solomon," "A Patriot for Me," OB in "Bald Soprano," "Jack," "Deidre of the Sorrows," "USA," "Balcony," "Desire under the Elms," "Posterity for Sale," "Moon for the Misbegotten," "After the Fall," "But For Whom Charlie," "Tartuffe," "Mary Stuart," "Ride across Lake Constance," "Departures," "A Lie of the Mind."

JEROME, TIMOTHY. Born Dec. 29, 1943 in Los Angeles, CA. Graduate Ithaca Col. Bdwy debut 1969 in "Man of La Mancha," followed by "The Rothschilds," "Creation of the World . . . ," "Moony Shapiro Songbook," "Cats," OB in "Beggar's Opera," "Pretzels," "Civilization and Its Discontents," "The Little Prince," "Colette Collage," "Room Service."

JETER, MICHAEL. Born Aug. 26, 1952 in Lawrenceburg, TN. Graduate Memphis State U. Bdwy debut 1978 in "Once in a Lifetime," OB in "The Master and Margarita," "G. R. Point" for which he received a Theatre World Award, "Alice in Concert," "El Bravo," "Cloud 9," "Greater Tuna."

JILER, JOHN. Born Apr. 4, 1946 in NYC. Graduate UHartford. Debut 1982 OB in "The Frances Farmer Story," followed by "Trouble/Idle Hands," "One Room with Bath," "Emerald City."

JILLETTE, PENN. Born in 1955 in Greenfield, Ma. Debut 1985 OB in "Penn and Teller."

JOHANNES, MARK. Born Aug. 9, 1956 in Norfolk, Neb. Graduate WayneStateU. Debut 1983 OB in "Behind a Mask," followed by "Julius Caesar."

JOHNSON, DANIEL T. Born Aug. 13, 1947 in Cass County, Mi. Graduate WMiU, UOr. Debut 1980 OB in "Romeo and Juliet," followed by "The Scarecrow," "Meetings with Ben Franklin," "Edward II," "Two Wills," "Julius Caesar," "Porter's Brandy."

JOHNSON, MEL, JR. Born Apr. 16, 1949 in NYC. Graduate Hofstra U. Debut 1972 OB in "Hamlet," followed by "Love! Love! Love!," "Shakespeare's Cabaret," "The Peanut Man," "The Lottery," "Spell #7," "Do Lord Remember Me," Bdwy in "On the 20th Century," "Eubie!," "The Rink," "Big Deal."

JOHNSON, PAGE. Born Aug. 25, 1930 in Welch, WV. Graduate Ithaca Col. Bdwy bow 1951 in "Romeo and Juliet," followed by "Electra," "Oedipus," "Camino Real," "In April Once," for which he received a Theatre World Award, "Red Roses for Me," "The Lovers," "Equus," "You Can't Take It With You," OB in "The Enchanted," "Guitar," "4 in 1," "Journey of the Fifth Horse," APA's "School for Scandal," "The Tavern," and "The Seagull," "Odd Couple," "Boys In The Band," "Medea," "Deathtrap," "Best Little Whorehouse in Texas," "Fool for Love."

JOHNSON, SCOTT L. Born June 11, 1959 in Evansville, In. Graduate BallStateU. Debut 1985 OB in "The Making of Americans," followed by Bdwy in "The Marriage of Figaro" (1985).

JOHNSON, TINA. Born Oct. 27, 1951 in Wharton, Tx. Graduate NTxStateU. Debut 1979 OB in "Festival," followed by "Blue Plate Special," "Just So," Bdwy in "The Best Little Whorehouse in Texas."

JOHNSTON, J. J. Born Oct. 24, 1933 in Chicago, IL. Debut 1981 OB in "American Buffalo," and Bdwy 1983 in "American Buffalo" for which he received a Theatre World Award, followed by "Glengarry Glen Ross."

JOHNSTON, SAMME. Born Jan. 11, 1956 in Needham, Ma. Graduate Wellesley Col. Debut 1985 OB in "A Flash of Lightning," followed by "Theatre Olympics," "Time and the Conways," "Hedda Gabler."

JOLLY, RUSS. Born Sept. 23, 1961 in Bossier City, La. Graduate NCSchool of Arts. Bdwy debut 1986 in "Big River."

JONES, EDDIE. Born in Washington, PA. Debut 1960 OB in "Dead End," followed by "Curse of the Starving Class," "The Ruffian on the Stairs," "An Act of Kindness," "Big Apple Messenger," "The Skirmishers," "Maiden Stakes," "The Freak," "Knights Errant," "Slacks and Tops," "Burkie," "Curse of the Starving Class" (1985), "Sorrows and Sons," Bdwy in "That Championship Season" (1974), "Devour the Snow."

JONES, FRANZ. Born Nov. 11, 1951 in Washington, DC. Graduate TxChristianU. Debut 1974 OB in "Holocaust," followed by "Trade-Offs," "Brainwashed," "Pepperwine," "Things of the Heart," Bdwy in "Big River" (1985).

JONES, JANE. Born Aug. 7, 1954 in Petersburg, Va. Attended VaComU. Debut 1982 OB in "The Rise of Daniel Rocket," followed by "The Dolly," "The Dining Room," "Waltz of the Toreadors."

JONES, JAY AUBREY. Born Mar. 30, 1954 in Atlantic City, NJ. Graduate Syracuse U. Debut 1981 OB in "Sea Dream," followed by "Divine Hysteria," "Inacent Black and the Brothers," "La Belle Helene."

JONES, LEILANI. Born May 14, in Honolulu, HI. Graduate UHi. Debut 1981 OB in "El Bravo," followed by "The Little Shop of Horrors," Bdwy (1985) in "Grind" for which she received a Theatre World Award.

JONES, REED. Born June 30, 1953 in Portland, OR. Graduate USIU. Bdwy debut 1979 in "Peter Pan," followed by "West Side Story," "America," "Play Me a Country Song," "Cats," "Loves of Anatole," OB in "Music Moves Me," "Jubilee in Concert."

JONES, SABRA. Born Mar. 22, 1951 in California. Debut 1982 OB in "Joan of Lorraine," followed by "Inheritors," "Paradise Lost," "Ghosts," "Clarence," "Madwoman of Chaillot," "Vivat! Vivat Regina," "Children of the Sun."

JONES, SIMON. Born July 27, 1950 in Wiltshire, Eng. Attended Trinity Hall. Debut 1984 OB in "Terra Nova," followed by Bdwy in "The Real Thing" (1984), "Benefactors."

JONES, TAD. Born May 5, 1955 in Stuttgart, Ger. Graduate AADA. Debut 1983 OB in "The Inheritors," followed by "Paradise Lost," "Rain," "The Hasty Heart," "The Time of Your Life," "Children of the Sun."

JORDAN, BOB. Born May 2, 1926 in Boston, Ma. Graduate MoU, NorthwesternU. OB in "The American Cantata," "Lippe," "The Warm Heart," "Murder among Friends," "Changing Roles," "To Feed Their Hopes."

JORDAN, RICHARD. Born July 19, 1938 in NYC. Attended Harvard U. Bdwy debut 1961 in "Take Her She's Mine," followed by "Bicycle Ride to Nevada," "War and Peace," "Generation," "A Patriot for Me," OB in "Judith," "All's Well That Ends Well," "Trial of the Catonsville 9," "Three Acts of Recognition," "A Private View," "Measure for Measure."

JORDAN, SUSAN. Born Apr. 14, 1955 in Norman, Ok. Graduate UOk, NYU. Debut 1981 in "We Won't Pay!," followed by "Dusa Fish Stas & Vi," "Sweeney Agonistes," "Dear Friends," "The Amazing Spear of Destiny."

JOSEPH, ROWAN. Born Nov. 16, 1956 in Pottsville, Pa. Debut 1985 OB in "The Time of Your Life."

JOSHUA, LAWRENCE "LARRY". Born Feb. 12, 1954 in NYC. Debut 1979 OB in "Tooth of Crime," followed by "Sunday Runners in the Rain," "Middleman Out," "Kid Champion," "One Tiger to a Hill," "Ground Zero Club," "Savage in Limbo."

JOY, ROBERT. Born Aug. 17, 1951 in Montreal, Can. Graduate Nfd. Memorial U. Oxford U. Debut 1978 OB in "The Diary of Anne Frank," followed by "Fables for Friends," "Lydie Breeze," "Sister Mary Ignatius Explains It All," "Actor's Nightmare," "What I Did Last Summer," "The Death of Von Richthofen," "Lenny and the Heartbreakers," "Found a Peanut," "Field Day," "Life and Limb," Bdwy in "Hay Fever" (1985).

JOYCE, HEIDI. Born Sept. 12, 1960 in Cleveland, Oh. Graduate IndU. Debut 1986 OB in "Girl Crazy," followed by "The Shop on Main Street."

JUDE, PATRICK. Born Feb. 25, 1951 in Jersey City, NJ. Bdwy debut 1972 in "Jesus Christ Superstar," (also 1977 revival), followed by "Got Tu Go Disco," "Charlie and Algernon," "Marlowe," "The News," OB in "The Haggadah," "Dementos."

JULIA, RAUL. Born Mar. 9, 1940 in San Juan, PR. Graduate UPR. OB in "Macbeth," "Titus Andronicus," "Theatre in the Streets," "Life Is a Dream," "Blood Wedding," "Ox Cart," "No Exit," "Memorandum," "Frank Gagliano's City Scene," "Your Own Thing," "Persians," "Castro Complex," "Pinkville," "Hamlet," "King Lear," "As You Like It," "Emperor of Late Night Radio," "Threepenny Opera," "The Cherry Orchard," "Taming of the Shrew," "Othello," "The Tempest," "A Christmas Carol," Bdwy in "The Cuban Thing," "Indians," "Two Gentlemen of Verona," "Via Galactica," "Where's Charley?," "Dracula," "Betrayal," "Nine," "Design for Living," "Arms and the Man."

KALEDIN, NICHOLAS. Born Jan. 25, 1956 in Boston, Ma. Graduate Bowdoin Col, AmConsTh. Bdwy debut 1985 in "The Octette Bridge Club," followed by OB in "Oliver Oliver," "Becoming Memories," "Black Coffee."

KAMPLEY, LINDA. Born Sept. 18, 1944 in Des Moines, Ia. Attended San Diego State Col. Bdwy debut 1968 in "Rosencrantz and Guildenstern Are Dead," OB in "Maggie Flynn," "Living at Home," "Come Back to the 5 & Dime Jimmy Dean," "And They Dance Real Slow in Jackson."

KANE, BRADLEY. Born Sept. 29, 1973 in New Rochelle, NY. Debut 1982 OB in "Scraps," followed by "A Winter's Tale," "Sunday in the Park with George," Bdwy in "Evita (1983)."

KANE, DONNA. Born Aug. 12, 1962 in Beacon, NY. Graduate Mt. Holyoke Col. Debut 1985 OB in "Dames at Sea" for which she received a Theatre World Award.

KANSAS, JERI. Born Mar. 10, 1955 in Jersey City, NJ. Debut 1978 OB in "Gay Divorce," Bdwy 1979 in "Sugar Babies," followed by "42nd Street."

KANTOR, KENNETH. Born Apr. 6, 1949 in The Bronx, NY. Graduate SUNY, Boston U. Debut 1974 OB in "Zorba," followed by "Kiss Me Kate," "A Little Night Music," "Buried Treasure," "Sounds of Rodgers and Hammerstein," "Shop on Main Street," "Bdwy in The Grand Tour" (1979), "Brigadoon" (1980), "Mame" (1983).

KAPLAN, ALICIA. Born. Oct. 29, 1952 in NYC. Attended Adelphi U. Debut 1970 OB in "The Terrible Angels," followed by "Blood Wedding," "Yerma," "Rome Rome," "Letters Home," "The Bitter Tears of Petra Von Kant."

KATCHER, HOPE. Born June 22, 1951 in Brooklyn, NY. Graduate Boston U. Bdwy debut 1976 in "Fiddler on the Roof," OB in "King David and His Wives," "The Spare Seraphim."

KAUFFMAN, JEAN. Born Feb. 5, 1957 in NYC. Attended CalStateU/Northridge. Debut 1979 OB in "The Beggar's Soap Opera," followed by "Before the Flood," "She Loves Me."

KAUFMAN, MICHAEL. Born July 28, 1950 in Washington, DC. Graduate UWi. Debut 1978 OB in "Hooters," followed by "First Thirty," "Warriors from a Long Childhood," "Scenes from La Vie de Boheme," "Man Overboard," "Marathon '86," Bdwy in "Gemini" (1980).

KAVA, CAROLINE. Born in Chicago, IL. Attended Neighborhood Playhouse. Debut 1975 OB in "Gorky," followed by "Threepenny Opera," "The Nature and Purpose of the Universe," "Disrobing the Bride," "Marching Song," "Domestic Issues," "Little Victories," "Cloud 9," "Playboy of the Western World," "The Bitter Tears of Petra Von Kant." Bdwy in "Stages" (1978).

KAVANAUGH, RICHARD. Born in 1943 in NYC. Bdwy debut 1977 in "Dracula," followed "Hothouse," OB in "Learned Ladies," "Bosoms and Neglect."

KAYE, JUDY. Born Oct. 11, 1948 in Phoenix, AZ. Attended UCLA, Ariz. State U. Bdwy debut 1977 in "Grease," followed by "On the 20th Century" for which she received a Theatre World Award, "Moony Shapiro Songbook," "Oh, Brother!," OB in "Eileen in Concert," "Can't Help Singing," "Four to Make Two," "Sweethearts in Concert," "Love," "No No Nanette in Concert."

KEATING, CHARLES. Born Oct. 22, 1941 in London, Eng. Bdwy debut 1969 in "Arturo Ui," followed by "The House of Atreus," "Loot," OB in "An Ounce of Prevention."

KEHR, DON. Born Sept. 18, 1963 in Washington, DC. Bdwy debut 1976 in "Legend," followed by "The Human Comedy," "The Mystery of Edwin Drood," OB in "American Passion," "She Loves Me."

KEITH, LAWRENCE (LARRY). Born Mar. 4, 1931 in Brooklyn, NY. Graduate Brooklyn Col., IndU. Bdwy debut 1960 in "My Fair Lady," followed by "High Spirits," "I Had a Ball," "Best Laid Plans," "Mother Lover," OB in "The Homecoming," "Conflict of Interest," "The Brownsville Raid," "M. Amilcar," "The Rise of David Levinsky," "Miami."

KELLER, JEFF. Born Sept. 8, 1947 in Brooklyn, NY. Graduate Monmouth Col. Bdwy debut 1974 in "Candide," followed by "Fiddler on the Roof," "On the 20th Century," "The 1940's Radio Show," "Dance a Little Closer," OB in "Bird of Paradise," "Charlotte Sweet," "Roberta in Concert," "Personals."

KELLERMANN, SUSAN. Born July 4. Attended Neighborhood Playhouse. Bdwy debut 1979 in "Last Licks" for which she received a Theatre World Award, followed by "Whose Life Is It Anyway?," "Lunch Hour," OB in "Wine Untouched," "Crab Quadrille," "Country Club," "Cinque and the Jones Man," "Rich Relatives."

KELLY, JULIA. Born July 9, 1954 in Washington, DC. Graduate Webster Col. Debut 1976 OB in "A Taste of Honey," followed by "Still Love," "Cornered," "Revue Sketches," "A Conflict of Fragrances," "Incoming," "Crystal Clear."

KELLY, K. C. Born Nov. 12, 1952 in Baraboo, Wi. Attended UWis. Debut 1976 OB in "The Chicken Ranch," followed by "Last of the Knucklemen," "Young Bucks," "Writer's Cramp," Bdwy in "Romeo and Juliet" (1977), "The Best Little Whorehouse in Texas."

KEMP, GARRY. Born Aug. 28, 1934 in London, Eng. NY Debut 1986 OB in "Hamlet."

KENNY, JACK. Born Mar. 9, 1958 in Chicago, Il. Attended Juilliard. Debut 1983 OB in "Pericles," followed by "Tartuffe," "Play and Other Plays," "A Normal Heart."

KEPROS, NICHOLAS. Born Nov. 8, 1932 in Salt Lake City, Ut. Graduate UUt., RADA. Debut 1958 OB in "The Golden Six," followed by "Wars of Roses," "Julius Caesar," "Hamlet," "Henry IV," "She Stoops to Conquer," "Peer Gynt," "Octaroon," "Endicott and the Red Cross," "The Judas Applause," "Irish Hebrew Lesson," "Judgment at Havana," "The Millionairess," "Androcles and the Lion," "The Redemptor," "Othello," "Times and Appetites of Toulouse-Lautrec," Bdwy in "St. Joan" (1968), "Amadeus," "Execution of Justice."

KERNS, LINDA. Born June 2, 1953 in Columbus, Oh. Attended Temple U, AADA, Debut 1981 OB in "Crisp," Bdwy in "Nine" (1982), "Big River."

KERSEY, BILLYE. Born Oct. 15, 1955 in Norfolk, VA. Bdwy debut 1981 in "42nd Street."

KERSHAW, WHITNEY. Born Apr. 10, 1962 in Orlando, FL. Attended Harkness Joffrey Ballet Schools. Debut 1981 OB in "Francis," Bdwy in "Cats."

KESSLER, LEE. Born in Wellsville, NY. Graduate UWisc. Debut 1986 OB in "Anais Nin: The Paris Years."

KILPATRICK, PATRICK. Born Aug. 20 in Orange, VA. Graduate URichmond. Debut 1984 OB in "Linda Her and the Fairy Garden," followed by "A Place Called Heartbreak."

KIMBROUGH, CHARLES. Born May 23, 1936 in St. Paul. MN. Graduate IndU, Yale. Bdwy bow 1969 in "Cop-Out," followed by "Company," "Love for Love," "Rules of the Game," "Candide," "Mr. Happiness," "Same Time, Next Year," "Sunday in the Park with George," "Hay Fever," OB in "All in Love," "Struts and Frets," "Troilus and Cressida," "Secret Service," "Boy Meets Girl," "Drinks Before Dinner," "The Dining Room."

KING, ALICE. Born Jan. 26, 1957 in Monteray, Ca. Graduate U.S.Ala. Debut 1982 OB in "The Caucasian Chalk Circle," followed by "Romeo and Juliet," "Macbeth," "The Flatbush Faithful," "Edward II."

KING, ERIK. Born Aug. 18 in Washington, DC. Graduate Towson State U. Debut 1985 OB in "Balm in Gilead," followed by "Streamers," "Wasted."

KING, GINNY. Born May 12, 1957 in Atlanta, GA. Attended NCSch of Arts. Bdwy debut 1980 in "42nd Street."

KIRKLAND, SALLY. Born Oct. 31, 1944. Bdwy debut 1961 in "Step on a Crack," followed by "Bicycle Ride to Nevada," "Marathon 33," OB in "A Midsummer Night's Dream," "Fitz," "Bitch of Waverly Place," "Tom Paine," "Futz," "Sweet Eros," "Witness," "One Night Stands of a Noisy Passenger," "Justice Box," "Delicate Champions," "Where Has Tommy Flowers Gone?," "Chickencoop Chinaman," "Largo Desolato."

KIRSCH, CAROLYN. Born May 24, 1942 in Sheveport, LA. Bdwy debut 1963 in "How to Succeed . . . ," followed by "Follies Bergere," "La Grosse Valise," "Skyscraper," "Breakfast at Tiffany's," "Sweet Charity," "Hallelujah, Baby!," "Dear World," "Promises, Promises," "Coco," "Ulysses in Nighttown," "A Chorus Line," OB in "Silk Stockings," "Telecast."

KITTY, ALAN J. Born July 27, 1948 in Harrisburg, Pa. Graduate Suffolk U. Debut 1986 OB in "A Midsummer Night's Dream."

KLATT, DAVID. Born July 15, 1958 in Martins Ferry, OH. Attended West Liberty State Col. Bdwy debut 1984 in "La Cage aux Folles."

KLEIN, ROBERT. Born Feb. 8, 1942 in NYC. Graduate Alfred U., Yale. OB in "Six Characters in Search of an Author," "Second City Returns," "Upstairs at the Downstairs," Bdwy in "The Apple Tree," "New Faces of 1968," "Morning Noon and Night," "They're Playing Our Song," "The Robert Klein Show," "Robert Klein on Broadway."

KLEINMUNTZ, MANNY. Born Dec. 22, 1922 in Cologne, Ger. Graduate LACC, LAStateU. Debut 1986 OB in "Three Sisters."

KLINE, KEVIN. Born Oct. 24, 1947 in St. Louis, MO. Graduate IndU, Juilliard. Debut 1970 OB in "Wars of Roses," followed by "School for Scandal," "Lower Depths," "The Hostage," "Women Beware Women," "Robber Bridegroom," "Edward II," "The Time of Your Life," "Beware of the Jubjub Bird." "Dance on a Country Grave," "Richard III," "Henry V," "Hamlet," Bdwy in "Theee Sisters," "Measure for Measure," "Beggar's Opera," "Scapin," "On the 20th Century," "Loose Ends," "Pirates of Penzance," "Arms and the Man."

KLUNIS, TOM. Born in San Francisco, Ca. Bdwy debut 1961 in "Gideon," followed by "The Devils," "Henry V," "Romeo and Juliet," "St. Joan," "Hide and Seek," "Bacchae," "Plenty," OB in "The Immoralist," "Hamlet," "Arms and the Man," "Potting Shed," "Measure for Measure," "Romeo and Juliet," "The Balcony," "Our Town," "The Man Who Never Died," "God Is My Ram," "Rise Marlow," "Iphigenia in Aulis," "Still Life," "The Master and Margarita," "As You Like It," "The Winter Dancers," "When We Dead Awaken," "Vieux Carre," "The Master Builder," "Richard III," "A Map of the World."

KNIGHT, SHIRLEY. Born July 5, 1937 in Goessel, Ks. Attended Phillips U, Wichita U. Bdwy debut 1936 in Goessel, Ks. Attended Phillips U, Wichita U. Bdwy debut 1964 in "The Three Sisters," followed by "We Have Always Lived in a Castle," "The Watering Place," "Kennedy's Children," OB in "Journey to the Day," "Rooms," "Happy End," "Landscape of the Body," "A Lovely Sunday for Creve Coeur," "Losing Time," "Come Back Little Sheba," "Women Heroes."

KNUDSON, KURT. Born Sept. 7, 1936 in Fargo, ND. Attended NDStateU, UMiami. Debut 1976 OB in "The Cherry Orchard," followed by "Geniuses," "Room Service," Bdwy in "Curse of an Aching Heart" (1982), "Sunday in the Park with George," "Take Me Along."

KOKA, JULIETTE. Born Apr. 4, 1930 in Finland. Attended Helsinki School of Dramatic Arts. Debut 1977 OB in "Piaf . . . A Remembrance" for which she received a Theatre World Award, followed by "Ladies and Gentlemen Jerome Kern."

KOLBER, LYNNE. Born in Montreal, Can. Graduate Vassar Col. Debut OB 1983 in "Robin Hood," followed by "Nightingale," "Senor Discretion," "Charley's Tale."

KOLOC, BONNIE. Born Feb. 6, 1946 in Waterloo, IA. Attended U.Northern Iowa. Debut 1983 on and off Broadway in "The Human Comedy" for which she received a Theatre World Award.

KOPACHE, THOMAS. Born Oct. 17, 1945 in Manchester, NH. Graduate San Diego State, Cal. Inst. of Arts. Debut 1976 OB in "The Architect and the Emperor of Assyria," followed by "Brontosaurus Rex," "Extravagant Triumph," "Caligula," "The Tempest," "Macbeth," "Measure for Measure," "Hunting Scenes from Lower Bavaria," "The Danube," "Friends Too Numerous to Mention," "Twelfth Night," "A Winter's Tale."

KORZEN, ANNIE. Born Nov. 8, 1938 in NYC. Graduate Bard Col. Debut 1976 OB in "Fiorello," followed by "Intermission," "I Can't Keep Running in Place," "Pearls," "The Special."

KOTLER, JILL. Born Oct. 3, 1952 in Chicago, Il. Graduate USCal. OB in "The Piaglies," "Goatman," "Willie," "Play with an Ending," "Sh-Boom!"

KUDAN, JOHN. Born Sept. 13, 1955 in White Plains, NY. Graduate Adelphi U. Debut 1985 OB in "Inside Out," followed by "Oscar Wilde: Solitaire," "Titus Andronicus," "An Ideal Husband," "Nick Dad and the Elephant."

KUHN, JUDY. Born May 20, 1958 in NYC. Graduate Oberlin Col. Debut 1985 OB in "Pearls," followed by "The Mystery of Edwin Drood (OB & Bdwy)."

KUROWSKI, RON. Born Mar. 14, 1953 in Philadelphia, Pa. Attended Temple U., RADA. Bdwy debut 1977 in "A Chorus Line."

KURTZ, MARCIA JEAN. Born in The Bronx, NY. Juilliard graduate. Debut 1966 OB in "Jonah," followed by "America Hurrah," "Red Cross," "Muzeeka," "The Effects of Gamma Rays. . .," "The Year Boston Won the Pennant," "The Mirror," "The Orphan," "Action," "The Dybbuk," "Ivanov," "What's Wrong with This Picture?," "Today I Am a Fountain Pen," "The Chopin Playoffs," Bdwy in "The Chinese and Dr. Fish," "Thieves," "Execution of Justice."

KURTZ, SWOOSIE. Born Sept. 6 in Omaha, Ne. Attended USCal, LAMDA. Debut 1968 OB in "The Firebugs," followed by "The Effect of Gamma Rays . . .," "Enter a Free Man," "Children," "Museum," "Uncommon Women and Others," "Wine Untouched," "Summer," "The Beach House," Bdwy in "Ah, Wilderness!" (1975), "Tartuffe," "A History of the American Film," "5th of July," " House of Blue Leaves."

LaDUCA, PHIL. Born Dec. 10, 1954 in Chicago, Il. Attended DePaul U., Goodman School. Bdwy debut 1980 in "Brigadoon," followed by "Pirates of Penzance," "Singin' in the Rain," OB in "Buskers."

LaGRECA, PAUL. Born June 23, 1962 in The Bronx, NY. Graduate AADA. Debut 1983 OB in "Barnum's Last Life," followed by "Really Rosie."

LAHTI, CHRISTINE. Born Apr. 4, 1950 in Detroit, MI. Graduate UMich, HB Studio. Debut 1979 OB in 'The Wood" for which she received a Theatre World Award followed by "Landscape of the Body," "The Country Girl," Bdwy in "Loose Ends" (1980), followed by "Division Street," "Scenes and Revelations," "Present Laughter."

LAINE, CLEO. Born Oct. 28, 1927 in Southall, Eng. Bdwy debut 1985 in "The Mystery of Edwin Drood" for which she received a Theatre World Award.

LALLY, JAMES. Born Oct. 2, 1956 in Cleveland, Oh. Attended Sarah Lawrence Col. Debut 1977 OB in "The Mandrake," followed by "The Taming of the Shrew," "All's Well That Ends Well," "As You Like It."

LAMB, MARY ANN. Born July 4, 1959 in Seattle, Wa. Attended Neighborhood Playhouse. Bdwy debut 1985 in "Song and Dance."

LANCASTER, DOROTHY. Born Sept. 4, 1936 in Louisville, Ky. Attended ULouisville. Debut 1966 OB with "American Savoyards," followed by "The Diary of Anne Frank," "The Admirable Crichton," "Who's Happy Now?," "The Disintegration of James Cherry," "The Penultimate Problem of Sherlock Holmes," "And They Dance Real Slow in Jackson."

LANDES, FRANCINE. Born July 30, 1953 in San Francisco, Ca. Graduate Juilliard, Columbia U. Bdwy debut 1985 in "The Mystery of Edwin Drood."

LANDON, SOFIA. Born Jan 24, 1949 in Montreal, Can. Attended Northwestern U. Debut 1971 OB in "Red, White and Black," followed by "Gypsy," "Missouri Legend," "Heartbreak House," "Peg o' My Heart," "Scenes and Revelations," "The Hasty Heart,""Blue Window," "Flatbush Faithful."

LANE, NATHAN. Born Feb. 3, 1956 in Jersey City, NJ. Debut 1978 OB in "A Midsummer Night's Dream," followed by "Love," "Measure for Measure," Bdwy in "Present Laughter" (1982), "Merlin," "Wind in the Willows."

LANGE, ANN. Born June 24, 1953 in Pipestone, MN. Attended Carnegie-Mellon U. Debut 1979 OB in "Rat's Nest," followed by "Hunting Scenes from Lower Bavaria," "Crossfire," "Linda Her and the Fairy Garden," "Little Footsteps," Bdwy in "The Survivor" (1981).

LANNING, JERRY. Born May 17, 1943 in Miami, Fl. Graduate USCal. Bdwy debut 1966 in "Mame" for which he received a Theatre World Award, followed by "1776," "Where's Charley?," "My Fair Lady," OB in "Memphis Store Bought Teeth," "Berlin to Broadway," "Sextet," "Isn't It Romantic," "Paradise."

LANSING, ROBERT. Born June 5, 1929 in San Diego, CA. Bdwy debut 1951 in "Stalag 17," followed by "Cyrano de Bergerac," "Richard III," "Charley's Aunt," "The Lovers," "Cue for Passion," "Great God Brown," "Cut of the Axe," "Finishing Touches," OB in "The Father," "The Cost of Living," "The Line."

LARSEN, LIZ. Born Jan. 16, 1959 in Philadelphia, PA. Attended Hofstra U, SUNY/Purchase. Bdwy debut 1981 in "Fiddler on the Roof," OB in "Kuni Leml," "Hamlin," "Personals."

LAUB, SANDRA. Born Dec. 15, 1956 in Bryn Mawr, Pa. Graduate Northwestern U. Debut 1983 OB in "Richard III," followed by "Young Playwrights Festival," "Domestic Issues," "Say Goodnight Gracie," "Les Mouches," "Three Sisters."

LAUDICINO, DINO. Born Dec. 22, 1939 in Brooklyn, NY. Bdwy debut 1960 in "Christine," followed by "Rosencrantz and Guildenstern Are Dead," "Indians," "Scratch," "The Innocents," "Animals," OB in "King of the Dark Chamber," "Dollar," "Occupations," "The Tempest."

LAUGHLIN, SHARON. Graduate UWVa. Bdwy debut 1964 in "One by One," followed by "The Heiress," OB in "Henry IV," "Huui Huui," "Mod Donna," "Subject to Fits," "The Minister's Black Veil," "Esther," "Rag Doll," "Four Friends," "Heartbreak House," "Marching Song," "Declassee," "Frozen Assets," "Hamlet."

LAURENCE, PAULA. Born Jan. 25 in Brooklyn, NY. Bdwy debut 1936 in "Horse Eats Hat," followed by "Dr. Faustus," "Junior Miss," "Something for the Boys," "One Touch of Venus," "Cyrano de Bergerac," 'The Liar," "Season in the Sun," "Tovarich," "The Time of Your Life," "Beggar's Opera," "Hotel Paradiso," "Night of the Iguana," "Have I Got a Girl for You," "Ivanov," "Rosalie in Concert," OB in "7 Days of Mourning," "Roberta in Concert," "One Touch of Venus," "Coming of Age in SoHo," "George White's Scandals."

LAURENSON, DIANA. Born Sept. 25, 1957 in Elmont, NY. Graduate UMass/Amherst. Debut 1981 OB in "Manhattan Rhythm," Bdwy 1981 in "The Little Prince and the Aviator," followed by "Big Deal."

LAWLESS, RICK. Born Dec. 31, 1960 in Bridgeport, Ct. Graduate Fairfield U. Debut 1985 OB in "Dr. Faustus," followed by "The Foreigner."

LAWRENCE, DELPHI. Born Mar. 23, 1932 in London, Eng. Attended RADA. Debut 1972 OB in "The Divorce of Judy and Jane," followed by "Dylan," "The Elizabethans," "Souvenirs," "Family Portrait," Bdwy in "The Constant Wife" (1975).

LAWRENCE, WILLIAM A. Born Sept. 9, 1923 in Brooklyn, NY. Graduate St. Peter's Col., Hofstra U. Debut 1983 OB in "June Moon," followed by "Cabbagehead."

LEACH, JAMES. Born Oct. 2, 1954 in Colon, Panama. Graduate Ithaca Col. Debut 1980 OB in "Romeo and Juliet," followed by "The Lady's Not for Burning," "Deep Six Holiday."

LEE, IRVING ALLEN. Born Nov. 21, 1948 in NYC. Graduate Boston U. Debut 1969 OB in "Kiss Now," followed by "Ride the Winds," "A Visit with Death," "Changes," Bdwy in "Pippin" (1973), "Rockabye Hamlet," "A Broadway Musical," "Sweet Charity" (1986).

LEE, JENNIFER. Born July 19, 1967 in Chicago, Il. Attended UTx. Debut 1985 OB in "The Fantasticks."

LEE-ARANAS, MARY. Born Sept. 23, 1959 in Taipei, Taiwan. Graduate UOttawa. Debut 1984 OB in "Empress of China," followed by "A State without Grace," "Return of the Phoenix," "Yellow Is My Favorite Color," "The Man Who Turned into a Stick."

LEFFERT, JOEL. Born Dec. 8, 1951 in NYC. Graduate Brown U. Debut 1976 OB in "Orphee," followed by "Heroes," "The Last Burning," "Relatively Speaking," "The Bachelor," "Scaramouche," "Macbeth," "Don Juan in Hell," "Village Wooing," "The Long Smouldering."

LEHMAN, JEANNE. Born Sept. 14 in Woodland, Ca. Graduate UCal/San Francisco. Debut 1972 OB in "The Drunkard," followed by "Leave It to Jane," "Oh Lady Lady!," "Zip Goes a Million," "Oh Boy!," "No No Nanette," Bdwy in "Irene" (1973), "Rodgers and Hart," "Going Up," "A Musical Jubilee," "Jerome Kern Goes to Hollywood."

LEIGHTON, JOHN. Born Dec. 30 on Staten Island, NY. Attended NYU, Columbia U. Debut 1954 OB in "In Splendid Error," followed by "Juno and the Paycock," "A Christmas Carol," "Quare Fellow," "Brothers Karamazov," "Montserrat," "Othello," "Merchant of Venice," "Enter a Free Man," "The Bone Ring," Bdwy in "Of the Fields Lately" (1980).

LEIGHTON, RICHARD. Born Jan. 27, 1945 in Lakeland, Fl. Graduate Hunter Col. Bdwy debut in "Talent 1965," followed by "To Broadway with Love," OB in "Shadow of a Gunman," "The Long Christmas Dinner," "Rats," "Gypsies," "Color of the Wind," "Tuba Players," "Miss Jairus," "The Dark at the Top of the Stairs," "Julius Caesar," "The Tempest," "A Month in the Country," "The Devil's Disciple," "Modigliani," "It's Only a Play," "Buck," "The Time of Your Life," "Children of the Sun."

LEMMON, JACK. Born Feb. 8, 1925 in Boston, Ma. Harvard graduate. Bdwy debut 1953 in "Room Service," followed by "Face of a Hero," "Tribute," "Long Day's Journey into Night."

LEMON, BEN. Born May 21, 1955 in Tarrytown, NY. Graduate Brown U. Debut 1980 OB in "Dulcy," followed by "Love's Labour's Lost," "Three Sisters."

LENCIONI, ARLENE. Born Jan. 22, 1951 in Chicago, Il. Graduate Catholic U. Debut 1986 OB in "Three Sisters."

LENOX, ADRIANE. Born Sept. 11, 1956 in Memphis, TN. Graduate Lambuth Col. Bdwy debut 1979 in "Ain't Misbehavin'," followed by "Dreamgirls," OB in "Beehive."

LEO, MELISSA. Born Sept. 14, 1960 in NYC. Attended SUNY/Purchase. Debut 1984 OB in "Cinders," followed by "Out of Gas on Lover's Leap," "Today I Am a Fountain Pen."

LEONARD, ROBERT. Born Feb. 28, 1969 in Westwood, NJ. Debut 1985 OB in "Sally's Gone, She Left Her Name," followed by "Coming of Age in SoHo," "The Beach House," Bdwy in "Brighton Beach Memoirs" (1985).

LEONE, MARIANNE. Born Jan. 2, 1952 in Boston, Ma. Graduate UMa. Debut 1986 OB in "Save the Loopholes," followed by "Suicide in B Flat," "Key Largo," "What the Butler Saw," "The Hostage."

LESLIE, BETHEL. Born Aug. 3, 1929 in NYC. Bdwy debut 1944 in "Snafu," followed by "Years Ago," "The Wisteria Trees," "Goodbye My Fancy," "Time of the Cuckoo," "Mary Rose," "The Brass Ring," "Inherit the Wind," "Catch Me if You Can," "But Seriously," "Long Day's Journey into Night."

LESSANE, LEROY. Born Aug. 5, 1942 in NYC. Debut 1970 OB in "Gandhi," followed by "Snowbound King," "Ballad of Johnny Pot," "A Man Is a Man," "The Last Days of British Honduras," "Ghashiram," Bdwy in "Capt. Brassbound's Conversion (1972)."

LEVELS, CALVIN. Born Sept. 30, 1954 in Cleveland, OH. Graduate CCC. Bdwy debut 1984 in "Open Admissions" for which he received a Theatre World Award, OB in "Prairie du Chien," "The Shawl," "Common Ground."

LEVINE, ANNA. Born Sept. 18, 1957 in NYC. Debut 1975 OB in "Kid Champion," followed by "Uncommon Women and Others," "City Sugar," "A Winter's Tale," "Johnny-on-the-Spot," "The Wedding," "American Days," "The Singular Life of Albert Nobbs," "Cinders," "Rose Cottages."

LEVINE, RICHARD S. Born July 16, 1954 in Boston, Ma. Juilliard graduate. Debut 1978 OB in "Family Business," followed by "Magic Time," "It's Better with a Band," "Emma," Bdwy in "Dracula," "Rock 'n' Roll: The First 5000 Years."

LEWIS, GILBERT. Born Apr. 6, 1941 in Philadelphia, Pa. Attended Morgan State Col. Bdwy debut 1969 in "The Great White Hope," OB in "Who's Got His Own," "Transfers," "Ballet behind the Bridge," "Coriolanus," "Appear and Show Cause."

LEWIS, MARCIA. Born Aug. 18, 1938 in Melrose, MA. Attended UCin. OB in "The Impudent Wolf," "Who's Who, Baby," "God Bless Coney," "Let Yourself Go," "Romance Language," "Miami," Bdwy in "The Time of Your Life," "Hello, Dolly!," "Annie."

LEWIS, TODD. Born May 26, 1952 in Chicago, IL. Graduate Lewis U. Debut 1979 OB in "Flying Blind," followed by "Willy and Sahara," "Sawney Bean," "A Perfect Diamond," "Blood."

LEWIS, VICKI. Born Mar. 17, 1960 in Cincinnati, Oh. Graduate CinConsv. Bdwy debut 1982 in "Do Black Patent Leather Shoes Really Reflect Up?," followed by "Wind in the Willows," OB in "Snoopy," "A Bundle of Nerves."

LIBERATORE, LOU. Born Aug. 4, 1959 in Jersey City, NJ. Graduate Fordham U. Debut 1982 OB in "The Great Grandson of Jedediah Kohler," followed by "Threads," "Black Angel," "Richard II," "Thymus Vulgaris," "As Is," Bdwy "As Is" (1985).

LIND, KIRSTEN. Born Feb. 12, in Delft, Holland. Graduate NYU. Debut 1982 OB in "Deep in the Heart," followed by "Very Warm for May," "Girl Crazy."

LIPMAN, DAVID. Born May 12, 1938 in Brooklyn, NY. Graduate LIU, Brooklyn Col. Debut 1973 OB in "Moonchildren," followed by "The Devil's Disciple," "Don Juan in Hell," "Isn't It Romantic," Bdwy in "Fools" (1981).

LITTLE, CLEAVON. Born June 1, 1939 in Chickasha, OK. Attended San Diego State U., AADA. Debut 1967 OB in "Macbird," followed by "Hamlet," "Someone's Coming Hungry," "Ofay Watcher," "Scuba Duba," "Narrow Road to the Deep North," "Great MacDaddy," "Joseph and the Amazing Technicolor Dreamcoat," "Resurrection of Lady Lester," "Keyboard," "I'm Not Rappaport," Bdwy in "Jimmy Shine," "Purlie," "All over Town," "The Poison Tree."

LITTLE, DAVID. Born Mar. 21, 1937 in Wadesboro, NC. Graduate Wm. & Mary Col., Catholic U. Debut 1967 OB in "MacBird," followed by "Iphigenia in Aulis," "Antony and Cleopatra," "Antigone," "An Enemy of the People," "Three Sons," "Les Blancs," "Almost in Vegas," "The Wisteria Trees," Bdwy in "Thieves," "Zalmen, or the Madness of God."

LIZZUL, ANTHONY JOHN. Born Jan. 11 in the Bronx, NYC. Graduate NYU. Debut 1977 OB in "The Cherry Orchard," followed by "The Prophets," "Lady Windermere's Fan," "Revenger's Tragedy," "Twelfth Night," "Night Talk," "The Butterfingers Angel," "Consenting Adults," "The Cherry Orchard."

LLOWELL, DY. Born Mar. 6, 1960 in Philadelphia, Pa. Graduate Temple U. Debut 1983 OB in "Loose Ends," followed by "Gingham Dog," "Safe," "Mirandolina."

LoBIANCO, TONY. Born Oct. 19, 1936 in NYC. Bdwy debut 1966 in "The Office," followed by "Royal Hunt of the Sun," "The Rose Tattoo," "90 Day Mistress," "The Goodbye People," "A View from the Bridge," OB in "Threepenny Opera," "Answered the Flute," "Camino Real," "O, Dad, Poor Dad. . . .," "Journey to the Day," "Zoo Story," "Nature of the Crime," "Incident at Vichy," "Tartuffe," "Yankees 3 Detroit O," "Big Time."

LOCRICCHIO, MATTHEW. Born June 3, 1947 in Detroit, Mi. Attended EMiU. Debut 1983 OB in "Fool for Love," followed by "Largo Desolato."

LODER, JOHN. Born Apr. 16, 1954 in Spencer, Ia. Graduate UCol. Debut 1986 OB in "Funny Girl."

LONDON, CHET. Born Apr. 8, 1931 in Boston, Ma. Attended St. Alselm's Col. Bdwy debut 1961 in "First Love," followed by "Calculated Risk," OB in "The Shoemaker and the Peddler," "Romeo and Juliet," "A Midsummer Night's Dream," "Hamlet," "The Deadly Game," "Macbeth."

LONG, SUSAN. Born Feb. 1, 1947 in Salina, Ks. Graduate UCol. Debut OB 1971 in "Do It Again!," followed by "Skye," "Carolyn," "Charley's Tale."

LOPEZ, MICHAEL. Born Oct. 10, 1956 in NYC. Graduate Marquette U. Debut 1978 OB in "The Cradle Will Rock," followed by "Merry-Go-Round," "The Rape of Bunny Stuntz," "Baal," "A Midsummer Night's Dream."

LOPEZ, PRISCILLA. Born Feb. 26, 1948 in The Bronx, NY. Bdwy debut 1966 in "Breakfast at Tiffany's," followed by "Henry, Sweet Henry," "Lysistrata," "Company," "Her First Roman," "The Boy Friend," "Pippin," "A Chorus Line," "A Day in Hollywood/A Night in the Ukraine," "Nine," OB in "What's a Nice Country Like you . . . ," "Key Exchange," "Buck," "Extremities," "Non Pasquale," "Be Happy for Me," "Times and Appetites of Toulouse-Lautrec."

LOTAYEF, OMAR. Born Nov. 7, 1957 in Cairo, Egypt. Attended UToronto, AADA. Debut 1985 OB in "Vivat! Vivat Regina!," followed by "Madwoman of Chaillot," "Children of the Sun."

LOUDON, DOROTHY. Born Sept. 17, 1933 in Boston, MA. Attended Emerson Col., Syracuse U. Debut 1961 in "World of Jules Feiffer," Bdwy 1963 in "Nowhere to Go but Up" for which she received a Theatre World Award followed by "Noel Coward's Sweet Potato," "Fig Leaves Are Falling," "Three Men on a Horse," "The Women," "Annie," "Ballroom," "West Side Waltz," "Noises Off," "Jerry's Girls."

LUCAS, ROXIE. Born Aug. 25, 1951 in Memphis, TN. Attended UHouston. Bdwy debut 1981 in "The Best Little Whorehouse in Texas," followed by "Harrigan 'n Hart," OB in "Forbidden Broadway."

LUDWIG, KAREN. Born Oct. 9 in San Francisco, CA. Bdwy debut 1964 in "The Deputy," followed by "The Devils," "Bacchae," OB in "The Trojan Women," "Red Cross," "Muzeeka," "Huui, Huui," "Our Last Night," "Seagull," "Museum," "Nasty Rumors," "Daisy," "Gethsemene Springs," "After the Revolution," "Before She Is Even Born," "Exiles," "Messiah," "Love as We Know It," "The Chopin Playoffs."

LUKATHER, SUZANNE. Born Mar. 22 in Sacramento, Ca. Graduate UCal. Bdwy debut 1976 in "Rockabye Hamlet," followed by OB in "The Music Man," "Broadway Jukebox," "Charley's Tale."

LuPONE, ROBERT. Born July 29, 1956 in Brooklyn, NY. Juilliard graduate. Bdwy debut 1970 in "Minnie's Boys," followed by "Jesus Christ Superstar," "The Rothschilds," "Magic Show," "A Chorus Line," "St. Joan," OB in "Charlie Was Here," "Twelfth Night," "In Connecticut," "Snow Orchid," "Lennon," "Black Angel," "The Quilling of Prue," "Time Framed."

LYND, BETTY. Born In Los Angeles, CA. Debut 1968 OB in "Rondelay," followed by "Love Me, Love My Children," Bdwy in "The Skin of Our Teeth" (1975), "A Chorus Line."

LYNDE, JANICE. Born Mar. 28, 1947 in Houston, Tx. Attended UInd. Bdwy debut 1971 in "The Me Nobody Knows," followed by "Applause," "Butterflies Are Free," OB in "Sambo," "Paradise."

LYNG, NORA MAE. Born Jan. 27, 1951 in Jersey City, NJ. Debut 1981 OB in "Anything Goes," followed by "Forbidden Broadway," "Road to Hollywood," "Tales of Tinseltown," Bdwy in "Wind in the Willows" (1985).

MACCHIO, RALPH. Born in Huntington, NY in 1962. Debut 1986 OB in "Cuba and His Teddy Bear," and Bdwy debut in same play and year.

MACKAY, LIZBETH. Born March 7 in Buffalo, NY. Graduate Adelphi U., Yale. Bdwy debut 1981 in "Crimes of the Heart" for which she received a Theatre World Award.

MACKLIN, ALBERT. Born Nov. 18, 1958 in Los Angeles, Ca. Graduate Stanford U. Debut 1981 OB in "Ten Little Indians," followed by "Poor Little Lambs," "Anteroom," Bdwy in "Doonesbury" (1983).

MACLEAY, LACHLAN. Born Dec. 4, 1952 in St. Louis, Mo. Graduate UTx. Debut 1984 OB in "Romantic Arrangements," followed by "The Albino," "Moondance," "Dead Wrong."

MACNAUGHTON, ROBERT. Born Dec. 19, 1966 in NYC. Debut 1980 OB in "The Diviners," followed by "Henry V," "Tally & Son," "Tomorrow's Monday."

MacNICOL, PETER. Born April 10 in Dallas, TX. Attended UMn. Bdwy debut 1981 in "Crimes of the Heart" for which he received a Theatre World Award, OB in "Found a Peanut," "Rum and Coke," "Twelfth Night."

MacVITTIE, BRUCE. Born Oct. 14, 1956 in Providence, RI. Graduate Boston U. Bdwy debut 1983 in "American Buffalo," followed by "California Dog Fight," "The Worker's Life."

MACY, W. H. Born Mar. 13, 1950 in Miami, Fl. Graduate Goddard Col. Debut 1980 OB in "The Man in 605," followed by "Twelfth Night," "The Beaver Coat," "A Call from the East," "Sittin'," "Sunshine," "The Dining Room," "Speakeasy," "Wild Life," "Flirtations," "Baby with the Bathwater," "Prairie/Shawl," "The Nice and the Nasty."

MAHAFFEY, VALERIE. Born June 16, 1953 in Sumatra, Indonesia. Graduate UTx. Debut 1975 OB in "Father Uxbridge Wants to Marry," followed by "Bus Stop," "Black Tuesday," "Scenes and Revelations," (also Bdwy), "Twelve Dreams," "Translations," "Butter and Egg Man," "Top Girls," "Romance Language," "The Custom of the Country," Bdwy in "Rex," "Dracula," "Fearless Frank," "Play Memory," "Loves of Anatole."

MAHER, JOSEPH. Born Dec. 29, 1933 in Westport, Ire. Bdwy debut 1964 in "The Chinese Prime Minister," followed by "The Prime of Miss Jean Brodie," "Henry V," "There's One in Every Marriage," "Who's Who in Hell," "Days in the Trees," "Spokesong," "Night and Day," "84 Charing Cross Road," "Loot," OB in "The Hostage," "Live Like Pigs," "The Importance of Being Earnest," "Eh?," "Local Stigmatic," "Mary Stuart," "The Contractor," "Savages," "Entertaining Mr. Sloane," "Loot."

MAHONEY, JOHN. Born June 20, 1940 in Manchester, Eng. Attended Quincy Col., W.Ill.U. Debut 1985 OB in "Orphans" for which he received a Theatre World Award, Bdwy in "House of Blue Leaves" (1986).

MAILLARD, CAROL LYNN. Born Mar. 4, 1951 in Philadelphia, Pa. Graduate Catholic U. Debut 1977 OB in "The Great MacDaddy," followed by "It's So Nice to Be Civilized," "A Photograph," "Under Fire," "Zooman and the Sign," "Beehive," Bdwy in "Eubie!" (1979), "It's So Nice to Be Civilized."

MAIS, MICHELE. Born July 30, 1954 in NYC. Graduate CCNY. Debut 1975 OB in "Godspell," followed by "Othello," "Superspy," "Yesterday Continued," "We'll Be Right Back," "Que Ubo?," "El Bravo!," "Opening Night," "Surrender/a flirtation," "Catch of the Day," Bdwy in "Zoot Suit" (1979).

MALKOVICH, JOHN. Born Dec. 9, 1953 in Christopher, IL. Attended EastIllU, IllStateU. Debut 1982 OB in "True West" for which he received a Theatre World Award, Bdwy in "Death of a Salesman" (1984).

MANIS, DAVID. Born Nov. 24, 1959 in Ann Arbor, Mi. Graduate UWash. Debut 1983 OB in "Pericles," followed by "Pieces of 8," "A New Way to Pay Old Debts," "As You Like It," "The Skin of Our Teeth," "And They Dance Real Slow in Jackson."

MANSON, ALLISON RENEE. Born July 21, 1958 in NYC. Attended Queens Col. Bdwy debut 1979 in "Comin' Uptown," followed by "Sweet Charity" (1986).

MANTEL, MICHAEL ALBERT. Born Dec. 30, 1952 in Cleveland, Oh. Graduate Pratt Inst. Debut 1980 OB in "Success Story," followed by "Incident at Vichy," "Awake and Sing," "King John," "The Dolphin Position," "Welcome to the Moon," "Extenuating Circumstances," "Dennis."

MANTELL, PAUL. Born Nov. 21, 1953 in Brooklyn, NY. Graduate Carnegie-Mellon U. Debut 1975 OB in "The Mikado," followed by "Don Juan," "Little Malcolm," "Richard II," "Line," "Moving Day," "Merchant of Venice," "The Key and the Wall," "Lush Life," "Pushcart Peddlers," "Dreamboats," "Beagelman and Brackett," "Walk the Dog, Willie," "The Affair."

MARCIONA, ANTHONY. Born Sept. 27, 1961 in The Bronx, NY. Debut 1965 OB in "The Survival of St. Joan," followed by "Chickencoop Chinaman," "Good Citizen," "Landscape of the Body," "Buskers," Bdwy in "Zorba (1967)," "Georgy," "Gypsy" (1974).

MARCUS, DANIEL. Born May 26, 1955 in Redwood City, CA. Graduate Boston U. Bdwy debut 1981 in "The Pirates of Penzance," followed OB in "La Boheme," "Kuni Leml," "A Flash of Lightning."

MARCUS, JEFFREY. Born Feb. 21, 1960 in Harrisburg, Pa. Attended Carnegie-Mellon U. Bdwy debut 1982 in "Almost an Eagle," OB in "Short Change."

MARCY, HELEN. Born June 3, 1920 in Worcester, MA. Attended Yale U. Bdwy in "Twelfth Night," "In Bed We Cry," "Dream Girl," "Love and Let Love," OB in "Lady Windermere's Fan," "Verdict," "Hound of the Baskervilles," "Appointment with Death," "Ladies in Retirement," "Dr. Cook's Garden," "Murder in the Vicarage," "Black Coffee."

MARGOLIS, LAURA. Born Sept. 17, 1951 in Kansas City, MO. Graduate Catholic U. Debut 1978 OB in "Laura," followed by "Getting Ready," "Mantikee," "Arms and the Man," "Merchant of Venice," "Her Great Match," "The Contrast."

MARGULIES, DAVID. Born Feb. 19, 1937 in NYC. Graduate CCNY. Debut 1958 OB in "Golden Six," followed by "Six Characters in Search of an Author." "Tragical Historie of Dr. Faustus," "Tango," "Little Murders," "Seven Days of Mourning," "Last Analysis," "An Evening with the Poet Senator," "Kid Champion," "The Man with the Flower in His Mouth," "Old Tune," "David and Paula," "Cabal of Hypocrites," "The Perfect Party," Bdwy in "The Iceman Cometh" (1973), "Zalmen or the Madness of God," "Comedians," "Break a Leg," "West Side Waltz," "Brighton Beach Memoirs."

MARKS, JACK R. Born Feb. 28, 1935 in Brooklyn, NY. Debut 1975 OB in "Hamlet," followed by "A Midsummer Night's Dream," "Getting Out," "Basic Training of Pavlo Hummel," "We Bombed in New Haven," "Angel Street," "Birthday Party," "Tarzan and Boy," "Goose and Tomtom," "The Carpenters," "Appear and Show Cause," Bdwy in "The Queen and the Rebels" (1982).

MARSHALL, AMELIA. Born Apr. 2, 1958 in Albany, GA. Graduate UTex. Debut 1982 OB in "Applause," Bdwy in "Harrigan 'n Hart" (1985), "Big Deal."

MARSHALL, DONNA LEE. Born Feb. 27, 1958 in Mt. Holly, NJ. Attended AADA. Debut 1978 OB in "By Strouse," followed by "The Human Comedy," "Sidewalkin'," "Charley's Tale," Bdwy in "The Pirates of Penzance" (1981).

MARSHALL, KEN (Kenneth). Born in 1953 in Cleveland, OH. Graduate UMi, Juilliard. Debut 1973 OB in "Pericles," followed by "Becoming Memories," "Playboy of the Western World," "Hamlet," "A Midsummer Night's Dream," "Caligula," "The Mound Builders," "Quiet in the Land," Bdwy in "West Side Story" (1980).

MARSHALL, LARRY. Born Apr. 3, 1944 in Spartanburg, SC. Attended Fordham U. NewEngConsv. Bdwy debut in "Hair," followed by "Two Gentlemen of Verona," "A Midsummer Night's Dream," "Rockabye Hamlet," "Porgy and Bess," "A Broadway Musical," "Comin' Uptown," "Oh, Brother!," "Big Deal," OB in "Spell #7," "Jus' Like Livin'," "The Haggadah," "Lullabye and Goodnight," "Aladin," "In the House of the Blues."

MARSHALL, ROB. Born Oct. 17, 1960 in Madison, Wi. Graduate Carnegie-Mellon U. Debut 1982 OB in "Boogie-Woogie Rumble of a Dream Deferred," Bdwy in "The Mystery of Edwin Drood" (1985).

MARTENS, RICA. Born Jan. 8, 1925 in Eliasville, Tx. Graduate NTxU. Bdwy debut 1947 in "Laura," followed by "The Shrike," OB in "Assent of F6," "The Bird the Bear and the Actress," "Edward My Son," "Oedipus and Jocasta," "Beckett," "My Great Dead Sister," "Tied by the Leg," "Saved," "Ah, Wilderness!," "Naomi Court," "Gods in Summer," "Manners," "Waiting for the Parade."

MARTIN, GEORGE N. Born Aug. 15, 1929 in NYC. Bdwy debut 1970 in "Wilson in the Promise Land," followed by "The Hothouse," "Plenty," "Total Abandon," "Pack of Lies," "The Mystery of Edwin Drood," OB in "Painting Churches," "Henry V," "Springtime for Henry."

MARTIN, MARY. Born Dec. 1, 1913 in Weatherford, Tx. Attended Ward-Belmont Col. Bdwy debut 1938 in "Leave It to Me," followed by "One Touch of Venus," "Lute Song," "Annie Get Your Gun," "South Pacific," "Kind Sir," "Peter Pan," "The Skin of Our Teeth," "The Sound of Music," "Jennie," "Hello, Dolly!," "I Do! I Do!," "Do You Turn Somersaults?"

MARTIN, MILLICENT. Born June 8, 1934 in Romford, Eng. Attended Atalia Conti Sch. Bdwy debut 1954 in "The Boy Friend," followed by "Side by Side by Sondheim," "King of Hearts," "42nd Street."

MARTINO, MARK. Born Aug. 26, 1953 in Indianapolis, In. Graduate Wm and Mary Col. Bdwy debut 1981 in "Broadway Follies," followed by "Oh, Brother!," OB in "Forbidden Broadway."

MASTRANTONIO, MARY ELIZABETH. Born Nov. 17, 1958 in Chicago, IL. Attended UIll. Bdwy debut 1980 in "West Side Story," followed by "Copperfield," "Oh, Brother!," "The Marriage of Figaro," OB in "Henry V," "A Christmas Carol," "Measure for Measure."

MATES, OLIVIA LAUREL. Born Sept. 19, 1970 in NYC. Debut 1981 OB in "Twelve Dreams," followed by "Dry Land."

MATHERS, JAMES. Born Oct. 31, 1936 in Seattle, WA. Graduate UWA., Beverly Col. Debut 1983 OB in "Happy Birthday, Wanda June," followed by "Uncommon Holidays," "Harvest of Strangers," "Crime and Punishment."

MATTHEWS, ANDERSON. Born Oct. 21, 1950 in Springfield, Oh. Graduate Carnegie-Mellon U. Bdwy debut 1975 in "The Robber Bridegroom," followed by "Edward II," "The Time of Your Life," "Ten by Tennessee," "Beef."

MATZ, JERRY. Born Nov. 15, 1935 in NYC. Graduate Syracuse U. Debut 1965 OB in "The Old Glory," followed by "Hefetz," "A Day out of Time," "A Mad World My Masters," "The Rise of David Levinsky," "The Last Danceman," "Madrid Madrid."

MAY, DAVID. Born Sept. 24, 1953 in Dallas, Tx. Graduate Trinity U. Debut 1983 OB in "Paradise Lost," followed by "The Inheritors," "Rain," "The Hasty Heart," "Rockbound."

MAYER, JERRY. Born May 12, 1941 in NYC. Graduate NYU. Debut 1968 OB in "Alice in Wonderland," followed by "L'Ete," "Marouf," "Trelawny of the Wells," "King of the Schnorrers," "Mother Courage," "You Know Al," " Goose and Tomtom," "The Rivals," "For Sale," "Miami," "The Nice and the Nasty," Bdwy in "Much Ado about Nothing" (1972), "Play Memory."

MAYES, JUDITH. Born in Caruthersville, Mo. Graduate Columbia U. Debut 1973 OB in "Montipasse," followed by "Traveler without Luggage," "Victoria's House," "Medea," "Hamlet," "Volpone," "All's Well That Ends Well," "Ceremony," "Disappearing Acts."

MAZZIE, MARIN. Born Oct. 9, 1960 in Rockford, Il. Graduate WMiU. Debut 1983 OB in "Where's Charley?," Bdwy in "Big River" (1986).

McATEER, KATHRYN. Born Sept. 4, 1949 in Englewood, NJ. Graduate Montclair State Col. Debut 1983 OB in "Upstairs at O'Neal's," followed by "Mayor," (and Bdwy 1985).

McCANN, CHRISTOPHER. Born Sept. 29, 1952 in NYC. Graduate NYU. Debut 1975 OB in "The Measures Taken," followed by "Ghosts," "Woyzzeck," "St. Joan of the Stockyards," "Buried Child," "Dwelling in Milk," "Tongues," "3 Acts of Recognition," "Don Juan," "Michi's Blood," "Five of Us," "Richard III," "The Golem," "Kafka Father and Son," "Flatbush Faithful."

McCARTHY, ANDREW. Born in 1963 in NYC. Bdwy debut 1985 in "Boys of Winter."

McCLINTOCK, JODIE LYNNE. Born Apr. 7, 1955 in Pittsburgh, Pa. Graduate Westminster Col. Debut 1983 OB in "As You Like It," Bdwy in "Long Day's Journey into Night" (1986).

McCORD, PATRICK. Born July 19, 1950 in Ann Arbor, Mi. Attended UMi. Debut 1986 OB in "Sunday Morning Vivisection."

McCOY, BASIA. Born Dec. 15, 1916 in Plains, Pa. Graduate Carnegie-Mellon U. Debut 1948 OB in "The Fifth Horseman," followed by "Mary Stuart," "The Crucible," "Knitters in the Sun," "The Trojan Women," "Family Portrait," "The Bacchae," "Knitters in the Sun," "The Silver Years," "The Long Smouldering."

McCRANE, PAUL. Born Jan. 19, 1961 in Philadelphia, Pa. Debut 1977 OB in "Landscape of the Body," followed by "Dispatches," "Split," "Hunting Scenes," "Crossing Niagara," "Hooters," "Fables for Friends," Bdwy in "Runaways" (1978), "Curse of an Aching Heart," "The Iceman Cometh" (1985).

McCULLOH, BARBARA. Born Mar. 5 in Washington, DC. Graduate Wm & Mary Col., UMd. Debut 1984 OB in "Up in Central Park," followed by "On the 20th Century."

McDERMOTT, KEITH. Born in Houston, TX. Attended LAMDA. Bdwy debut 1976 in "Equus," followed by "A Meeting by the River," "Harold and Maude," OB in "Heat of Re-entry," "Misalliance," "The Poker Session," "As You Like It."

McDONALD, TANNY. Born Feb. 13 in Princeton, NJ. Graduate Vassar Col. Debut 1961 OB with "American Savoyards," followed by "All in Love," "To Broadway with Love," "Carricknabauna," "The Beggar's Opera," "Brand," "Goodbye Dan Bailey," "Total Eclipse," "Gorky," "Don Juan Comes Back from the War," "Vera with Kate," "Francis," "On Approval," "A Definite Maybe," Bdwy in "Fiddler on the Roof," "Come Summer," "The Lincoln Mask," "Clothes for a Summer Hotel."

McDONNELL, MARY. Born in 1952 in Ithaca, NY. Graduate SUNY/Fredonia. Debut 1978 OB in Buried Child, followed by "Letters Home," "Still Life," "Death of a Miner," "Black Angel," "A Weekend Near Madison," "All Night Long," "Savage in Limbo," Bdwy in "Execution of Justice" (1986).

McDONOUGH, ANN. Born in Portland, ME. Graduate Towson State U. Debut 1975 OB in "Trelawny of the Wells," followed by "Secret Service," "Boy Meets Girl," "Scribes," "Uncommon Women," "City Sugar," "Fables for Friends," "The Dining Room," "What I Did Last Summer," "The Rise of Daniel Rocket," "The Middle Ages," "Fighting International Fat," "Room Service."

McFARLAND, ROBERT. Born May 7, 1931 in Omaha, NE. Graduate UMi, Columbia U. Debut 1978 OB in "The Taming of the Shrew," followed by "When the War Was Over," "Divine Fire," "Ten Little Indians," "The Male Animal," "Comedy of Errors," "Appointment with Death," "The Education of One Miss February," "Murder in the Vicarage."

McGAW, PARLAN. Born Dec. 14, 1955 in Cleveland, Oh. Attended San Francisco State U. Debut 1982 OB in "Behind Enemy Lines," followed by "The Bacchae," "Aspersions Cast," "The Book of Elroy," "The Golem," "A Midsummer Night's Dream."

McGILLIN, HOWARD. Born Nov. 5, 1953 in Los Angeles, Ca. Graduate UCal/Santa Barbara. Debut 1984 OB in "La Boheme," followed by Bdwy in "Sunday in the Park with George," "The Mystery of Edwin Drood" for which he received a Theatre World Award.

McGINLEY, JOHN C. Born Aug. 3, 1959 in NYC. Graduate NYU. Debut 1984 OB in "Danny and the Deep Blue Sea," followed by "The Ballad of Soapy Smith," "Jesse and the Games," "Love as We Know It."

McGOVERN, ELIZABETH. Born July 18, 1961 in Evanston, IL. Attended Juilliard. Debut 1981 OB in "To Be Young, Gifted and Black," followed by "Hotel Play," "My Sister in This House" for which she received a Theatre World Award, "Painting Churches," "Hitch-Hikers," "Map of the World."

McGREEVEY, ANNIE. Born in Brooklyn, NY. Graduate AADA. Bdwy debut 1971 in "Company," followed by "The Magic Show," "Annie," OB in "Booth Is Back in Town," "Tatterdemalion."

McGREGOR-STEWART, KATE. Born Oct. 4, 1944 in Buffalo, NY. Graduate Beaver Col., Yale U. Bdwy debut 1975 in "Travesties," followed by "A History of the American Film," "Beyond Therapy," OB in "Titanic," "Vienna Notes," "Beyond Therapy," "Baby with the Bathwater," "The Perfect Party."

McGUIRE, MAEVE. Born in Cleveland, Oh. Graduate Sarah Lawrence Col., Cleveland Playhouse. Debut 1968 with LCRep in "Cyrano de Bergerac," followed by "The Miser," "Charades," OB in "Vera with Kate," "Light Up the Sky."

McGUIRE, MITCHELL. Born Dec. 26, 1936 in Chicago, IL. Attended Goodman Theatre, Santa Monica City Col. OB in "The Rapists," "Go, Go, God Is Dead," "Waiting for Lefty," "The Bond," "Guns of Carrar," "Oh! Calcutta!," "New York! New York!," "What a Life!," "Butter and Egg Man," "Almost in Vegas," "Festival of One Acts," "Prime Time Punch Line."

McKENZIE, BRANICE WILLIAMS. Born July 23, 1952 in Pittsburgh, Pa. Graduate Brown U., NYU. Debut 1984 OB in "Shades of Harlem," followed by "Tambourines to Glory."

McMURRAY, SAM. Born Apr. 15, 1952 in NYC. Graduate UWash. Debut 1975 OB in "The Taking of Miss Janie," followed by "Merry Wives of Windsor," "Clarence," "Ballymurphy," "The Connection," "Translations," "Man Overboard," "Comedians," "Kid Purple," "L.A. Freewheeling."

McNAMARA, PAT. Born July 22, 1938 in Astoria, NY. Attended Columbia U., AADA. Debut 1961 OB in "Red Roses for Me," followed by "Crystal and Fox," "Nobody Hears a Broken Drum," "The Passing Game," "Killings on the Last Line," Bdwy in "The Poison Tree" (1976), "Brothers," "The Iceman Cometh" (1985).

McNAMARA, ROSEMARY. Born Jan. 7, 1943 in Summit, NJ. Attended Newark Col. OB in "The Master Builder," "Carricknabuana," "Rocket to the Moon," "The Most Happy Fella," "Matchmaker," "Anyone Can Whistle," "Facade," "Marya," "A Good Year for the Roses," "Countess Mitzi," "Quilters," Bdwy in "The Student Gypsy" (1963).

Terri Homberg	Homi J. Hormasji	Katharine Houghton	Earle Hyman	Joan Inwood	Michael Irwin
Steven Jacob	Salome Jens	Page Johnson	Leilani Jones	Stephen Joyce	Heidi Joyce
Linda Kampley	Don Kehr	Susan Kellermann	Erik King	Juliette Koka	Ron Kurowski
Phil LaDuca	Jennifer Lee	Lou Liberatore	Susan Long	Robert LuPone	Janice Lynde
Lizbeth Mackay	Lachlan Macleay	Helen Marcy	David May	Jodie Lynne McClintock	Parlan McGaw

McNICKLE, JIM. Born Apr. 14, 1952 in Ashland, Ks. Graduate UKs. Debut 1982 OB in "Red Hot & Blue," followed by "The Buck Stops Here," "A Thurber Carnival."

McQUEEN, ARMELIA. Born Jan 6, 1952 in North Carolina. Attended HB Studio, Bklyn Consv. Bdwy debut 1978 in "Ain't Misbehavin'" for which she received a Theatre World Award, followed by "Harrigan 'n Hart," OB in "Can't Help Singing," "5-6-7-8 Dance."

McROBBIE, PETER. Born Jan. 31, 1943 in Hawick, Scot. Graduate Yale U. Debut 1976 OB in "The Wobblies," followed by "The Devil's Disciple," "Cinders," "The Ballad of Soapy Smith," Bdwy in "Whose Life Is It Anyway?" (1979), "Macbeth" (1981) "The Mystery of Edwin Drood."

MEACHAM, PAUL. Born Aug. 5, 1939 in Memphis, Tn. Graduate UTn, MiStateU. Debut 1973 OB in "Twelfth Night," followed by "The Homecoming," "The Tempest," "Moby Dick," "The Crucible," "The Passion of Dracula," "Fighting Bob," "Lineman and Sweet Lightnin'," "Under Milk Wood," "Blood Relations."

MEDINA, HAZEL J. Born Oct. 8 in Colon, Panama. Attended LACC. Debut 1982 OB in "Brixton Recovery," followed by "Time out of Time," "Street Sounds," "The Beautiful LaSalles," "State of the Union," "Two Can Play."

MEISTER, FREDERIKKE. Born Aug. 18, 1951 in San Francisco, Ca. Graduate NYU. Debut 1978 OB in "Museum," followed by "Dolphin Position," "Waiting for the Parade."

MELLOR, STEPHEN. Born Oct. 17, 1954 in New Haven, CT. Graduate Boston U. Debut 1980 OB in "Paris Lights," followed by "Coming Attractions," "Plenty," "Tooth of Crime," "Shepard Sets," "A Country Doctor," "Harm's Way."

MELOCHE, KATHERINE. Born June 1, 1952 in Detroit, MI. Bdwy debut 1976 in "Grease," followed by "Dancin'," OB in "Street Scene," "Little Shop of Horrors."

MEREDITH, JAN. Born Sept. 21, 1949 in Birmingham, AL. Graduate UAla. Debut 1982 OB in "The Raspberry Picker," followed by "The Ritz," "A Summer of Education," "Night Must Fall," "Vieux Carre."

MERRELL, RICHARD. Born July 6, 1925 in NJ. Graduate Neighborhood Playhouse. Debut 1953 OB in "Which Way Is Home," followed by "The Investigation," "Feathered Serpent," "Scenes and Revelations," "Busybody," "Family Comedy," "Patrick Pearse Motel," "King Lear," "The Troll Palace," "The Camel Has Its Nose under the Tent," "A Country Doctor." Bdwy in "Viva Madison Avenue" (1960).

MERRILL, DEBORAH. Born June 22, 1960 in Yonkers, NY. Graduate Dade Col. Bdwy debut 1985 in "The Marriage of Figaro."

MERRILL, DINA. Born Dec. 29, 1925 in NYC. Attended AADA, AMDA, George Washington U. Bdwy in "My Sister Eileen," "Mermaids Singing," "Major Barbara," "Misalliance," "Angel Street," "On Your Toes," OB in "Are You Now or Have You Ever Been," "Suddenly Last Summer," "The Importance of Being Earnest."

MERRITT, GEORGE. Born July 10, 1942 in Raleigh, NC. Graduate CatholicU. Bdwy debut 1976 in "Porgy and Bess," followed by its 1983 revival, "Ain't Misbehavin'," "Big River."

METCALF, LAURIE. Born June 16, 1955 in Edwardsville, IL. IllStateU graduate. Debut 1984 OB in "Balm in Gilead" for which she received a Theatre World Award.

METCALF, MARK. Born Mar. 11 in Findlay, OH. Attended UMi. Debut 1973 OB in "Creeps," followed by "The Tempest," "Beach Children," "Hamlet," "Patrick Henry Lake Liquors," "Streamers," "Salt Lake City Skyline," "Mr. & Mrs.," "Romeo and Juliet," "Blue Window," "A Midsummer Night's Dream," "Trinity Site."

METTE, NANCY. Born Jan. 22, 1955 in Pennsylvania. Graduate NCSch. of Arts. Debut 1982 OB in "The Good Parts," followed by "The Alto Part," "Chopin in Space," "Women of Manhattan."

MEYER, PHIL. Born in Mar. 6, 1956 in Napoleon, OH. Graduate Bowling Green State U., Temple U. Debut 1984 OB in "Pieces of Eight," followed by "The Cradle Will Rock," "As You Like It," "The Skin of Our Teeth," "New Way to Pay Old Debts," "Orchards."

MICHAELS, BERT. Born Dec. 22, 1943 in NYC. Attended UMiami. Bdwy debut 1965 in "Baker Street," followed by "La Grosse Valise," "Half a Sixpence," "Cabaret," "Man of La Mancha," "Canterbury Tales," "Ulysses in Nighttown," "Mack and Mabel," "On Your Toes," OB in "The Red Eye of Love," "Gifts of the Magi."

MIDDLETON, ROGER. Born Dec. 14, 1940 in Detroit, Mi. Graduate ColStateU. Debut 1969 OB in "Getting Married," followed by "The Ragdoll," "Hard Times."

MILLER, ANNETTE. Born Sept. 29, 1956 in Buffalo, NY. Debut 1979 OB in "Fantasy Children," Bdwy in "Five O'Clock Girl" (1981), followed by "The Odd Couple" (1985).

MILLER, BARRY. Born Feb. 6, 1958 in Los Angeles, CA. Debut 1981 OB in "Forty Deuce," followed by "The Tempest," Bdwy in "Biloxi Blues" (1985) for which he received a Theatre World Award.

MILLER, PENELOPE ANN. Born Jan. 13, 1964 in Santa Monica, CA. Attended Menlo Col., HB Studio. Bdwy debut 1985 in "Biloxi Blues."

MILLER, SCOTT GORDON. Born Jan. 21, 1956 in Cleveland, OH. Attended London's Drama Centre. Debut 1983 OB in "Ah, Wilderness!" followed by "City Boy," "I, Shaw."

MINER, JAN. Born Oct. 15, 1917 in Boston, Ma. Debut 1958 OB in "Obligato," followed by "Decameron," "Dumbbell People," "Autograph Hound," "A Lovely Sunday for Creve Coeur," "The Music Keeper," "Gertrude Stein and Companion," Bdwy in "Viva Madison Avenue" (1960), "Lady of the Camelias," "The Freaking Out of Stephanie Blake," "Othello," "The Milk Train Doesn't Stop Here Anymore," "Butterflies Are Free," "The Women," "Pajama Game," "Saturday Sunday Monday," "The Heiress," "Romeo and Juliet," "Watch on the Rhine," "Heartbreak House."

MIRABAL, JEANNETTE. Born Dec. 5, 1958 in Havana, Cuba. Graduate NYU. Debut 1984 OB in "Cuban Swimmer/Dog Lady," followed by "The Bitter Tears of Petra Von Kant."

MIRATTI, TONY. Born Dec. 6 1934 in Santa Barbara, CA. Attended SBCC, Pasadena Playhouse. Debut 1976 OB in "The Shortchanged Review," followed by "Jump, I'll Catch You!"

MISTRETTA, SAL. Born Jan. 9, 1945 in Brooklyn, NY. Graduate Ithaca Col. Bdwy debut 1976 in "Something's Afoot," followed by "On the 20th Century," "Evita," "The King and I," OB in "Charley's Tale."

MITCHELL, GREGORY. Born Dec. 9, 1951 in Brooklyn, NY. Juilliard graduate. Principal with Feld Ballet Co. before 1983 Bdwy debut in "Merlin," followed by "Song and Dance," OB in "One More Song, One More Dance."

MIZELLE, VANCE. Born Aug. 6, 1934 in Atlanta, Ga. Graduate Davidson Col., UGa. Debut 1975 OB in "Hamlet," followed by "On a Clear Day You Can See Forever," "Love's Labour's Lost," "Julius Caesar," Bdwy in "Canterbury Tales" (1980).

MOFFAT, DONALD. Born Dec. 26, 1930 in Plymouth, Eng. Attended RADA. Bdwy debut 1957 in "Under Milk Wood," followed by "Much Ado about Nothing," "The Tumbler," "Duel of Angels," "Passage to India," "The Affair," "Father's Day," "Play Memory," "The Wild Duck," "Right You Are," "You Can't Take It with You," "War and Peace," "The Cherry Orchard," "Cock-a-Doodle Dandy," "Hamlet," "The Iceman Cometh," OB in "The Bald Soprano," "Jack," "The Caretaker," "Misalliance," "Painting Churches."

MOKAE, ZAKES. Born Aug. 5, 1935 in Johannesburg, SAf. Attended St. Peter's Col., RADA. Debut 1970 OB in "Boesman and Lena," followed by "Fingernails Blue as Flowers," "The Cherry Orchard," Bdwy in "A Lesson for Aloes," "Master Harold. . .and the boys," "Blood Knot."

MOLINA-TOBIN, OLGA. Born Oct. 26, 1934 in NYC. Attended Hunter Col., Brooklyn Col. Debut 1974 OB in "Scribbles," followed by "The Guest," "Bodega."

MONFERDINI, CAROLE. Born in Eagle Lake, Tx. Graduate NorthTxStateU. Debut 1973 OB in "The Foursome," followed by "The Club," "The Alto Part," "Goodbye Freddy."

MONK, ISABELL. Born Oct. 4, 1952 in Washington, DC. Graduate Towson State U., Yale. Debut 1981 OB in "The Tempest," followed by "The Gospel at Colonus," Bdwy in "Execution of Justice" (1986).

MOONEY, DEBRA. Born in Aberdeen SD. Graduate Auburn, UMn. Debut 1975 OB in "Battle of Angels," followed by "The Farm," "Summer and Smoke," "Stargazing," "Childe Byron," "Wonderland," "A Think Piece," "What I Did Last Summer," "The Dining Room," "The Perfect Party," Bdwy in "Chapter 2" (1978), "Talley's Folly," "The Odd Couple" (1985).

MOOR, BILL. Born July 13, 1931 in Toledo, OH. Attended Northwestern, Denison U. Bdwy debut 1964 in "Blues for Mr. Charlie," followed by "Great God Brown," "Don Juan," "The Visit," "Chemin de Fer," "Holiday," "P.S. Your Cat Is Dead," "Night of the Tribades," "Water Engine," "Plenty," "Heartbreak House," "The Iceman Cometh," OB in "Dandy Dick," "Love Nest," "Days and Nights of Beebee Fenstermaker," "The Collection," "The Owl Answers," "Long Christmas Dinner," "Fortune and Men's Eyes," "King Lear," "Cry of Players," "Boys in the Band," "Alive and Well in Argentina," "Rosmersholm." "The Biko Inquest," "A Winter's Tale," "Johnny on a Spot," "Barbarians," "The Purging," "Potsdam Quartet," "Zones of the Spirit," "The Marriage of Bette and Boo."

MOORE, CHARLOTTE. Born July 7, 1939 in Herrin, Il. Attended Smith Col. Bdwy debut 1972 in "The Great God Brown," followed by "Don Juan," "The Visit," "Chemin de Fer," "Holiday," "Love for Love," "A Member of the Wedding," "Morning's at 7," OB in "Out of Our Father's House," "A Lovely Sunday for Creve Coeur," "Summer," "Beside the Seaside," "The Perfect Party."

MOORE, KIM. Born Jan. 11, 1956 in Wheaton, Mn. Graduate MoorheadStateU, LAMDA. Debut 1985 OB in "The Fantasticks."

MOORE, MAUREEN. Born Aug. 12, 1951 in Wallingford, Ct. Bdwy debut 1974 in Gypsy, followed by "Do Black Patent Leather Shoes Really Reflect Up?," "Amadeus," "Song and Dance," OB in "Unsung Cole," "By Strouse."

MORAN, DANIEL. Born July 31, 1953 in Corcoran, CA. Graduate NYU. Debut 1980 OB in "True West," followed by "The Vampires," "Tongues and Savage Love," "Life Is a Dream," "The Filthy Rich."

MORANZ, BRAD. Born Aug. 29, 1952 in Houston, TX. Bdwy debut in "A Day in Hollywood/A Night in the Ukraine" (1981), OB in "Little Shop of Horrors."

MORATH, KATHRYN (a.k.a Kathy) Born Mar. 23, 1955 in Colorado Springs, Co. Graduate Brown U. Debut 1980 OB in "The Fantasticks," followed by "Dulcy," "Snapshot," "Alice in Concert," "A Little Night Music," "The Little Prince," "Professionally Speaking," Bdwy in "Pirates of Penzance" (1982)."

MORELAND, DAVID. Born Feb. 26, 1961 in Buffalo, NY. Attended UMich. Debut 1985 OB in "The Madwoman of Chaillot."

MORENO, RITA. Born Dec. 11, 1931 in Humacao, PR. Bdwy debut 1945 in "Skydrift," followed by "West Side Story," "The Sign in Sidney Brustein's Window," "Last of the Red Hot Lovers," "The National Health," "The Ritz," "She Loves Me," "Wally's Cafe," "The Odd Couple."

MORFOGEN, GEORGE. Born Mar. 30, 1933 in NYC. Graduate Brown U., Yale. Debut 1957 OB in "The Trial of D. Karamazov," followed by "Christmas Oratorio," "Othello," "Good Soldier Schweik," "Cave Dwellers," "Once in a Lifetime," "Total Eclipse," "Ice Age," "Prince of Homburg," "Biography: A Game," "Mrs. Warren's Profession," "Principia Scriptoriae," Bdwy in "The Fun Couple," "Kingdoms," "Arms and the Man."

MORGAN, CONSTANCE. Born July 9 in Winston-Salem, NC. Graduate UMo, Stephens Col. Debut 1986 OB in "Three Sisters."

MORIARTY, MICHAEL. Born Apr. 5, 1941 in Detroit, Mi. Graduate Dartmouth, LAMDA. Debut 1963 OB in "Anthony and Cleopatra," followed by "Peanut Butter and Jelly," "Long Day's Journey into Night," "Henry V," "Alfred the Great," "Our Father's Failing," "G. R. Point," "Love's Labour's Lost," "Dexter Creed," "Children of the Sun," Bdwy in "Trial of the Catonsville 9," "Find Your Way Home" for which he received a Theatre World Award, "Richard III," "The Caine Mutiny Court-Martial."

MORRIS, KENNY. Born Nov. 4, 1954 in Brooklyn, NY. Graduate UNC/Chapel Hill. Debut 1981 OB in "Francis," followed by "She Loves Me," Bdwy in "Joseph and the Amazing Technicolor Dreamcoat" (1983).

MORRISON, ANN LESLIE. Born Apr. 9, 1956 in Sioux City, IA. Attended Boston Consv., Columbia U. Debut 1980 OB in "Dream Time," followed by "All of the Above," "Forbidden Broadway," " Goblin Market," Bdwy in "Merrily We Roll Along" (1981) for which she received a Theatre World Award.

MORSE, ROBIN. Born July 8, 1963 in NYC. Bdwy debut 1981 in "Bring Back Birdie," followed by "Brighton Beach Memoirs," OB in "Green Fields," "Dec. 7th."

MORTON, JOE. Born Oct. 18, 1947 in NYC. Attended Hofstra U. Debut 1968 OB in "A Month of Sundays," followed by "Salvation," "Charlie Was Here and Now He's Gone," "G. R. Point," "Crazy Horse," "A Winter's Tale" "Johnny on a Spot," "Midsummer Night's Drean," "The Recruiting Officer," "Oedipus the King," "The Wild Duck," "Rhinestone," "Souvenirs," "Cheapside," Bdwy in "Hair," "Two Gentlemen of Verona," "Tricks," "Raisin" for which he received a Theatre World Award, "Oh, Brother!"

MOSIEJ, JAMES E. Born Dec. 14, 1965 in Chicago, IL. Graduate IllWesternU. Debut 1983 OB in "Water Music," Bdwy in "Oh! Calcutta!" (1984).

MUNSEL, PATRICE. Born May 14, 1925 in Spokane, Wa. Operatic debut 1943 at Met in Mignon, Bdwy debut 1964 in "The Merry Widow," followed by "Musical Jubilee," OB in "George White's Scandals."

MURE, GLENN. Born Dec. 26, 1950 in NYC. Graduate Yale U. Debut 1972 OB in "Crazy Now," followed by "Gershwin!," "Breasts of Tiresias," "Very Warm for May," "On the 20th Century," "Gifts of the Magi."

MURRAY, JANE. Born May 10, 1954 in Santa Monica, Ca. Graduate Occidental Col. Bdwy debut 1982 in "Ghosts," followed by OB in "Custom of the Country," "So Long on Lonely Street."

MYERS, PAULENE. Born Nov. 9 in Ocilla, Ga. Attended New Theatre School. Bdwy debut 1933 in "Growin' Pains," followed by "Plumes in the Dust," "The Willow and I," "The Naked Genius," "Dear Ruth," "Take a Giant Step," "Anniversary Waltz," OB in "Goodnight Ms. Calabash."

NAGLE, MARGARET. Born Jan. 12, 1961 in Berkeley, Ca. Graduate Northwestern U. Debut 1985 OB in "Another Part of the Forest."

NAIMO, JENNIFER. Born Oct. 2, 1962 in Oaklawn, Il. Graduate NYU. Debut 1985 OB in "Jack and Jill," followed by "Bachelor's Wife," "And the Beat Goes On," "To Whom It May Concern."

NAJIMY, KATHY. Born Feb. 6, 1957 in San Diego, Ca. Attended SanDiegoStateU. Debut 1986 OB in "The Kathy and Mo Show."

NAKAHARA, RON. Born July 20, 1947 in Honolulu, HI. Attended UHI. Tenri U. Debut 1981 OB in "Danton's Death," followed by "Flowers and Household Gods," "A Few Good Men," "Rohwer," "A Midsummer Night's Dream," "Teahouse," "Song for Nisei Fisherman," "Eat a Bowl of Tea," "Once Is Never Enough."

NEAL, LAURA. Born Nov. 26 in Dallas, TX. Graduate UTex. Debut 1983 OB in "Under the Gaslight," followed by "A Doll's House," "Why Marry?," "Uncle Lumpy Comes to Visit," "Hedda Gabler," "Festival of One Acts," "Vieux Carre."

NEIDEN, DANIEL. Born July 9, 1958 in Lincoln, Ne. Graduate Drake U. Debut 1980 OB in "City of Life," followed by "Ratman and Wilbur," "Nuclear Follies," "Pearls."

NELSON, BARRY. Born in 1920 in Oakland, Ca. Bdwy debut 1943 in Winged Victory," followed by "Light Up the Sky," "The Moon Is Blue," "Wake Up Darling," "Rat Race," "Mary Mary," "Nobody Loves an Albatross," "The Cactus Flower," "Everything in the Garden," "Only Game in Town," "Fig Leaves Are Falling," "Engagement Baby," "Seascape," "The Norman Conquests," "The Act," "42nd Street."

NELSON, LOIS. Born Aug. 18, 1929 in Sioux City, Ia. Graduate UNe, Syracuse U. Debut 1985 OB in "Dr. Cook's Garden," followed by "Murder at the Vicarage," "Festival of One Acts."

NELSON, MARK. Born Sept. 26, 1955 in Hackensack, NJ. Graduate Princeton U. Debut 1977 OB in "The Dybbuk," followed by "Green Fields," "The Keymaker," Bdwy in "Amadeus" (1981), "Brighton Beach Memoirs," "Biloxi Blues."

NESTOR, GEORGE. Born Jan. 16, 1935 in NYC. Attended CCNY. Bdwy debut 1957 in "The Greatest Man Alive," followed by "Her First Roman," OB in "The Lesson," "Red Roses for Me," "Shadow of Heroes," "Carnival" (CC), "The First Night of Pygmalion."

NEUBERGER, JAN. Born Jan. 21, 1953 in Amityville, NY. Attended NYU. Bdwy debut 1975 in "Gypsy," OB in "Silk Stockings," "Chase a Rainbow," "Anything Goes," "A Little Madness," "Forbidden Broadway."

NEUSOM, DANIEL. Born June 19, 1962 in Detroit, Mi. Attended UToledo, Interlochen Arts Acad. Debut 1982 OB in "The Sun Gets Blue," followed by "Sh-Boom!"

NEWMAN, PHYLLIS. Born Mar. 19, 1935 in Jersey City, NJ. Attended Western Reserve U. Bdwy debut 1953 in "Wish You Were Here," followed by "Bells Are Ringing," "First Impressions," "Subways Are for Sleeping," "The Apple Tree," "On the Town," "Prisoner of Second Avenue," "Madwoman of Central Park West," "Miami," "I Married an Angel in Concert," OB in "I Feel Wonderful," "Make Someone Happy," "I'm Getting My Act Together," "Red River," "The New Yorkers."

NEWMAN, WILLIAM. Born June 15, 1934 in Chicago, Il. Graduate UWVa, Columbia U. Debut 1972 OB in "Beggar's Opera," followed by "Are You Now . . .?," "Conflict of Interest," "Mr. Runaway," "Uncle Vanya," "One Act Play Festival," "Routed," "The Great Divide," "Come Back Little Sheba," "Hit Parade," Bdwy in "Over Here" (1974), "Rocky Horror Show," "Strangers."

NICHOLAS, DENISE. Born July 12, 1944 in Detroit, Mi. Attended UMi. Debut 1966 OB in "Viet Rock," followed by "Ceremonies in Dark Old Men," "Dame Lorraine," "Long Time Since Yesterday."

NICHOLS, ROBERT. Born July 20, 1924 in Oakland, CA. Attended Pacific Col., RADA. Debut 1978 OB in "Are You Now . . .," followed by "Heartbreak House," "Ah, Wilderness!," "Oh, Boy!," "No No Nanette in Concert," Bdwy in "Man and Superman," "The Man Who Came to Dinner," "Einstein and the Polar Bear," "Take Me Along."

NILES, MARY ANN. Born May 2, in NYC. Attended Miss Finchley's Ballet Acad. Bdwy debut in "Girl from Nantucket," followed by "Dance Me A Song," "Call Me Mister," "Make Mine Manhattan," "La Plume de Ma Tante," "Carnival," "Flora the Red Menace," "Sweet Charity," "George M!," "No, No, Nanette," "Irene," "Ballroom," OB in "The Boys from Syracuse," CC's "Wonderful Town" and "Carnival."

NILSSON, CHRISTOPHER. Born Sept. 7, 1960 in Huntington, NY. Graduate SUNY/Fredonia. Debut OB in "Funny Girl" (1986/ELT).

NIXON, CYNTHIA. Born Apr. 9, 1966 in NYC. Debut 1980 in "The Philadelphia Story"(LC) for which she received a Theatre World Award, OB in "Lydie Breeze," "Hurlyburly," "Sally's Gone, She Left Her Name," "Lemon Sky," Bdwy in "The Real Thing" (1983), "Hurlyburly."

NIXON, JAMES. Born Oct. 12, 1957 in Jersey City, NJ. Attended Kean Col. Debut 1982 OB in "The Six O'Clock Boys," followed by "Holy Junkie," "Fresh Fatigues."

NORMAN, RENDE RAE. Born Apr. 1, 1958 in Pryor, Ok. Graduate Emporia State U, Southwest MoStateU. Debut 1985 OB in "Rabboni," followed by "Nuclear Follies."

NORRIS, BRUCE. Born May 16, 1960 in Houston, Tx. Graduate Northwestern U. Bdwy debut 1985 in "Biloxi Blues."

NORRIS, RUTH ANN. Born in Ada, Ok. Graduate UOk. Debut 1967 OB in "Where People Gather," followed by "Mortally Fine."

NOTO, LORE. Born June 9, 1923 in NYC. Attended AADA. Debut 1940 OB in "The Master Builder," followed by "Chee Chee," "Time Predicted," "Bomb Shelter," "Armor of Light," "Truce of the Bear," "Shake Hands with the Devil," "The Italian Straw Hat," "The Failures," "The Fantastiks" (continuously since 1972).

NUSSBAUM, MIKE. Born Dec. 29, 1923 in Chicago, Il. Attended UWisc. Bdwy debut 1984 in "Glengarry Glen Ross," followed by OB in "The Shawl," "Principa Scriptoriae," "Marathon '86."

NUTE, DON. Born Mar. 13, in Connellsville, PA. Attended Denver U. Debut OB 1965 in "The Trojan Women" followed by "Boys in the Band," "Mad Theatre for Madmen," "The Eleventh Dynasty," "About Time," "The Urban Crisis," "Christmas Rappings," "The Life of a Man," "A Look at the Fifties."

NYE, CARRIE. Born in Mississippi, attended Stephens Col., Yale U. Bdwy debut 1960 in "Second String," followed by "Mary, Mary," "Half a Sixpence," "A Very Rich Woman," "Cop-Out," "The Man Who Came to Dinner," OB in "Ondine," "Ghosts," "The Importance of Being Earnest," "The Trojan Women," "The Real Inspector Hound," "a/k/a Tennessee," "The Wisteria Trees," "Madwoman of Chaillot."

NYGREN, CARRIE. Born Nov. 26, 1961 in Sweden. Attended Lee Strasberg Inst. Bdwy debut 1986 in "Sweet Charity."

O'BRIEN, DAVID. Born Oct. 1, 1935 in Chicago, Il. Graduate Stanford U, LAMDA. Bdwy debut 1962 in "A Passage to India," followed by "Arturo Ui," "A Time for Singing," "End of the World," OB in "Under Milk Wood," "A Month in the Country," "Henry IV," "The Boys in the Band," "The Nice and the Nasty."

O'CONNOR, KEVIN. Born May 7, 1938 in Honolulu, HI. Attended UHi., Neighborhood Playhouse. Debut 1964 OB in "Up to Thursday," followed by "Six from La Mama," "Rimers of Eldritch," "Tom Paine," "Boy on the Straightback Chair," "Dear Janet Rosenberg," "Eyes of Chalk," "Alive and Well in Argentina," "Duet," "Trio," "The Contractor," "Kool Aid," "The Frequency," "Chucky's Hutch," "Birdbath," "The Breakers," "Crossing the Crab Nebula," "Jane Avril," "Inserts," "3 by Beckett," "The Dicks," "A Kiss Is Just a Kiss," "Last of the Knucklemen," "Thrombo," "The Dark and Mr. Stone," Bdwy in "Gloria and Esperanza," "The Morning after Optimism," "Figures in the Sand," "Devour the Snow," "The Lady from Dubuque."

O'HARA, JENNY. Born Feb. 24 in Sonora, CA. Attended Carnegie-Tech U. Bdwy debut 1964 in "Dylan," followed by "The Odd Couple" (1985), OB in "Hang Down Your Head and Die," "Play with a Tiger," "Arms and the Man," "Sambo," "My House Is Your House," "The Kid," "The Fox."

O'HARA, PAIGE. Born May 10, 1956 in Ft. Lauderdale, FL. Debut 1975 OB in "The Gift of the Magi," followed by "Company," "The Great American Backstage Musical," "Oh, Boy!," "Rabboni," Bdwy in "Show Boat" (1983).

OLIENSIS, ADAM. Born Mar. ww, 1960 in Passaic, NJ. Graduate UWisc. Debut 1985 OB in "Inside-Out."

OLSON, MARCUS. Born Sept. 21, 1955 in Missoula, Mt. Graduate Amherst Col. Debut 1986 in "Personals."

O'ROURKE, KEVIN. Born Jan. 25, 1956 in Portland, OR. Graduate Williams Col. Debut 1981 OB in "Declassee," followed by "Sister Mary Ignatius . . .," "Submariners," "A Midsummer Night's Dream," "Visions of Kerouac," Bdwy in "Alone Together" (1984).

O'SHEA, MILO. Born June 2, 1926 in Dublin, IRe. Bdwy debut 1968 in "Staircase," followed by "Dear World," "Mrs. Warren's Profession," "Comedians," "A Touch of the Poet," "Mass Appeal," "Corpse," OB in "Waiting for Godot," "Mass Appeal," "The Return of Herbert Bracewell."

O'SULLIVAN, ANNE. Born Feb. 6, 1952 in Limerick City, Ire. Debut 1977 OB in "Kid Champion," followed by "Hello Out There," "Fly Away Home," "The Drunkard," "Dennis," "The Three Sisters," "Another Paradise," "Living Quarters," "Welcome to the Moon."

OSUNA, JESS. Born May 28, 1933 in Oakland, CA. OB in "Blood Wedding," "Come Share My House," "This Side of Paradise," "Bugs and Veronica," "Monopoly," "The Infantry," "Hamp," "The Biko Inquest," "The American Clock," "Roads to Home," "The Inheritors," "Rain," "The Madwoman of Chaillot," "Children of the Sun," Bdwy in "The Goodbye People," "That Championship Season," "An Almost Perfect Person."

OWEN, MARIANNE. Born Sept. 5, 1952 in Hollis Depot, NH. Debut 1978 OB in "Sganarelle," followed by "Wings," "The Nice and the Nasty."

OWENS, ELIZABETH. Born Feb. 26, 1938 in NYC. Attended New School, Neighborhood Playhouse. Debut 1955 OB in "Dr. Faustus Lights the Lights," followed by "Chit Chat on a Rat," "The Miser," "The Father", "The Importance of Being Earnest," "Candida," "Trumpets and Drums," "Oedipus," "Macbeth," "Uncle Vanya," "Misalliance," "The Play's the Thing," "The Rivals," "Death Story," "The Rehearsal," "Dance on a Country Grave," "Othello," "Little Eyolf," "The Winslow Boy," "Playing with Fire," "The Chalk Garden," "The Entertainer," "The Killing of Sister George," "Waltz of the Toreadors," Bdwy in "The Lovers," "Not Now Darling," "The Play's the Thing."

OYSTER, JIM. Born May 3, 1930 in Washington, DC. OB in "Coriolanus," "The Cretan Woman," "Man and Superman," "Fallen Angels," "The Underlings," Bdwy in "Cool World" (1960), "Hostile Winners," "The Sound of Music," "The Prime of Miss Jean Brodie," "Who's Who in Hell."

PAGANO, GIULIA. Born July 9, 1949 in NYC. Attended AADA. Debut 1977 OB in "The Passion of Dracula," followed by "Heartbreak House," "The Winslow Boy," "Miss Julie," "Playing with Fire," "Out of the Night," "Snow Leopards," "Zoology," Bdwy in "Medea" (1982).

PAGE, GERALDINE. Born Nov. 22, 1924 in Kirksville, MO. Attended Goodman Theatre. Debut 1945 OB in "Seven Mirrors," followed by "Yerma," "Summer and Smoke," "Macbeth," "Look Away," "The Stronger," "The Human Office," "The Inheritors," "Paradise Lost," "Ghosts," "Madwoman of Chaillot," "Clarence," "Vivat! Vivat Regina!," "A Lie of the Mind," "The Circle," Bdwy in "Midsummer" (1953) for which she received a Theatre World Award, "The Immoralist," "The Rainmaker," "Innkeepers," "Separate Tables," "Sweet Bird of Youth," "Strange Interlude," "Three Sisters," "P.S. I Love You," "The Great Indoors," "White Lies," "Black Comedy," "The Little Foxes," "Angela," "Absurd Person Singular," "Clothes for a Summer Hotel." "Agnes of God."

PAGE, KEN. Born Jan. 20, 1954 in St. Louis, MO. Attended Fontbonne Col. Bdwy debut 1976 in "Guys and Dolls" for which he received a Theatre World Award followed by "Ain't Misbehavin'," "Cats," OB in "Louis," "Can't Help Singing."

PAIS, JOSH. Born June 21, 1958 in Princeton, NJ. Graduate Syracuse U., LAMDA. Debut 1985 OB in "Short Change," followed by "I'm Not Rappaport," "The Lower Depths," "The Survivor," "Untitled Play."

PALEY, PETRONIA. Born May 31, in Albany, Ga. Graduate Howard U. Debut 1972 OB in "Us vs Nobody," followed by "The Cherry Orchard," "The Corner," "Three Sisters," "Frost of Renaissance," "Long Time Since Yesterday," Bdwy in "The First Breeze of Summer" (1975).

PALMINTERI, CHAZZ. Born May 15, 1951 in The Bronx, NY. Graduate BronxComCol. Debut 1982 OB in "The Guys in the Truck," followed by "The King's Men," "22 Years," "The Flatbush Faithful," Bdwy in "The Guys in the Truck" (1983).

PANARO, HUGH. Born Feb. 19, 1964 in Philadelphia, Pa. Graduate Temple U. Debut 1985 OB in "What's a Nice Country Like You Doing in a State Like This?"

PARADY, RON. Born Mar. 12, 1940 in Columbus, Oh. Graduate Ohio Wesleyan U, Ohio State U. Bdwy debut 1981 in "Candida," OB in "Uncle Vanya," "The Father," "The New Man," "For Sale."

PARKER, COREY. Born July 8, 1965 in NYC. Attended NYU. Debut 1984 OB in "Meeting the Winter Bikerider," followed by "Red Storm Flower," "Been Taken," "Losing Battles," "The Bloodletters," "Orphans," "Blind Date," "Rose Cottages."

PARKER, ELLEN. Born Sept. 30, 1949 in Paris, Fr. Graduate Bard Col. Debut 1971 OB in "James Joyce Liquid Theatre," followed by "Uncommon Women and Others," "Dusa, Fish, Stas and Vi," "A Day in the Life of the Czar," "Fen," "Isn't It Romantic," "The Winter's Tale," "Aunt Dan and Lemon," Bdwy in "Equus," "Strangers," "Plenty."

PARKER, ROCHELLE ROCKY. Born Feb. 26, 1940 in Brooklyn, NY. Attended Neighborhood Playhouse. Bdwy debut 1980 in "The Survivor," OB in "Five Points," "Sheepskin," "Side Street Scenes," "Ruby and Pearl," "Within the Year," A Country Doctor."

PARKER, ROXANN. Born Apr. 24, 1948 in Los Angeles, CA. Graduate USCal. Debut 1979 OB in "Festival," followed by "New Faces of 1952," "Looking for Love," "She Loves Me."

PARLATO, DENNIS. Born Mar. 30, 1947 in Los Angeles, Ca. Graduate Loyola U. Bdwy debut 1979 in "A Chorus Line," followed by "The First," OB in "Beckett," "Elizabeth and Essex," "The Fantasticks," "Moby Dick."

PARRIS, STEVE. Born Nov. 25 in Athens, Greece. Graduate CCNY. Debut 1964 OB in "The Comforter," followed by "Consider the Lilies," "A Christmas Carol," "The Man with the Flower in His Mouth," "King David and His Wives," "3 by Pirandello," "Nymph Errant," "The Tamer Tamed."

PARROW, RICHARD. Born in NJ. Graduate Pace U. Debut 1980 OB in "Sky High," followed by "Funny Girl."

PASEKOFF, MARILYN. Born Nov. 7, 1949 in Pittsburgh, PA. Graduate Boston U. Debut 1975 OB in "Godspell," followed by "Words," "Forbidden Broadway," "Professionally Speaking."

PATTERSON, JAY. Born Aug. 22 in Cincinnati, Oh. Attended Ohio U. Bdwy debut 1983 in "K-2," followed by OB in "Caligula," "The Mound Builders," "Quiet in the Land."

PATTERSON, KELLY. Feb. 22, 1964 in Midland, TX. Attended Southern Methodist U. Debut 1984 OB in "Up in Central Park," followed by "Manhattan Serenade," Bdwy in "Sweet Charity" (1986).

PATTISON, LIANN. Born Apr. 12, 1957 in Chico, Ca. Attended CalStateU/Chico, UWash. Debut 1985 OB in "I'm Not Rappaport."

PATTON, WILL. Born June 14, 1954 in Charleston, SC. OB in "Kingdom of Earth," "Scenes from Country Life," "Cops," "Pedro Paramo," "Limbo Tales," "Tourists and Refugees," "Rearrangements," "Dark Ride," "Salt Lake City Skyline," "The Red Snake," "Goose and Tomtom," "Joan of Lorraine," "Fool for Love," "A Lie of the Mind."

PAYAN, ILKA TANYA. Born Jan. 7, 1943 in Santo Domingo, DR. Attended Peoples Col. of Law. Debut 1969 OB in "The Respectful Prostitute," followed by "Francesco Cenci," "The Effect of Gamma Rays . . .," "Blood Wedding," "Miss Margarida's Way," "The Bitter Tears of Petra Von Kant," "The Servant."

PEAHL, SUSAN. Born Jan. 18, 1959 in Minneapolis, Mn. Graduate UIl. Debut 1985 OB in "What's a Nice Country Like You Doing in a State Like This?"

PEARLMAN, STEPHEN. Born Feb. 26, 1935 in NYC. Graduate Dartmouth Col. Bdwy bow 1964 in "Barefoot in the Park," followed by "La Strada," OB in "Threepenny Opera," "Time of the Key," "Pimpernel," "In White America," "Viet Rock," "Chocolates," "Bloomers," "Richie," "Isn't It Romantic," "Bloodletters," "Light Up the Sky," "The Perfect Party."

PEARSON, ELIZABETH. Born Jan. 4 in Cincinnati, OH. Graduate NYU, CalStateU. Debut 1985 OB in "Comedy of Errors," followed by "The Stronger," "Creditors."

PEARSON, SCOTT. Born Dec. 13, 1941 in Milwaukee, WI. Attended Valparaiso U, UWisc. Bdwy debut 1966 in "A Joyful Noise," followed by "Promises, Promises," "A Chorus Line."

PEARTHREE, PIPPA. Born Sept. 23, 1956 in Baltimore, Md. Attended NYU. Bdwy debut 1977 in "Grease," followed by "Whose Life Is It Anyway?," OB in "American Days," "Hunting Scenes from Lower Bavaria," "And I Ain't Finished Yet," "The Dining Room," "The Singular Life of Albert Nobbs," "Hamlet," "Aunt Dan and Lemmon."

PECK, ALEXANDER. Born Sept. 5, 1956 in Vancouver, Can. Attended Brandon U, Camosun Col. Debut 1986 OB in "Three Sisters."

PENDLETON, WYMAN. Born Apr. 18, 1916 in Providence, RI. Graduate Brown U. Bdwy in "Tiny Alice" (1964), "Malcolm," "Quotations from Chairman Mao Tse-Tung," "Happy Days," "Henry V," "Othello," "There's One in Every Marriage," "Cat on a Hot Tin Roof," "Scenes and Revelations," OB in "Gallows Humor," "American Dream," "Zoo Story," "Corruption in the Palace of Justice," "Giant's Dance," "Child Buyer," "Happy Days," "Butter and Egg Man," "Othello," "Albee Directs Albee," "Dance for Me, Simeon," "Mary Stuart," "The Collyer Brothers at Home," "Period Piece," "A Bold Stroke for a Wife," "Hitch-hikers," "Waltz of the Toreadors," "Time of the Cuckoo."

PENN, EDWARD. Born in Washington, DC. Debut 1965 OB in "The Queen and the Rebels," followed by "My Wife and I," "Invitation to a March," "Of Thee I Sing," "The Fantasticks," "Greenwillow," "One for the Money," "Dear Oscar," "Speed Gets the Poppys," "Man with a Load of Mischief," "Company," "The Constant Wife," "Tune the Grand Up!," "Reflected Glory," "Taking My Turn," "Yours Anne," "Light up the Sky," Bdwy in "The Music Man," "Dear Oscar," "Shenandoah."

PENNINGTON, GAIL. Born Oct. 2, 1957 in Kansas City, MO. Graduate SMU. Bdwy debut 1980 in "The Music Man," followed by "Can-Can," "America," "Little Me" (1982), "42nd Street," OB in "The Baker's Wife."

PEREZ, LUIS. Born July 28, 1959 in Atlanta, Ga. With Joffrey Ballet before 1986 debut in "Brigadoon" (LC).

PERKINS, ELIZABETH. Born Nov. 18, 1960 in Queens, NYC. Attended Goodman Theatre. Bdwy debut 1984 in "Brighton Beach Memoirs," OB in "The Arbor," "Life and Limb," "Measure for Measure."

PERRI, PAUL. Born Nov. 6, 1953 in New Haven, CT. Attended Elmira Col., UMe., Juilliard. Debut 1979 OB in "Say Goodnight, Gracie," followed by "Henry VI," "Agamemnon," "Julius Caesar," "Waiting for Godot," "Home," Bdwy in "Bacchae," "Macbeth," "A View from the Bridge," "Aunt Dan and Lemon."

PERRY, JAIME. Born June 1, 1958 in Brooklyn, NYC. Attended Manhattan Col. Debut 1978 OB in "Runaways," followed by "The Hooch," "The Mugger," "Jonin'," Bdwy in "Runaways" (1978).

PERRY, JEFF. Born Aug. 16, 1955 in Highland Park, Il. Attended IlStateU. Debut 1984 OB in "Balm in Gilead," Bdwy in "The Caretaker" (1986).

PERRY, KEITH. Born Oct. 29, 1931 in Des Moines, IA. Graduate Rice U. Bdwy debut 1965 in "Pickwick," followed by "I'm Solomon," "Copperfield," OB in "Epicene, the Silent Woman," "Hope with Feathers," "Ten Little Indians."

PERRYMAN, STANLEY. Born June 19, 1953 in Seattle, Wa. Attended UWa. Appeared with Alvin Ailey American Dance Theatre before 1977 Bdwy debut in "Your Arms Too Short to Box with God," followed by "Sweet Charity" (1986).

PESATURO, GEORGE. Born July 29, 1949 in Winthrop, MA. Graduate Manhattan Col. Bdwy debut 1976 in "A Chorus Line," OB in "The Music Man" (JB).

PETERS, BERNADETTE. Born Feb. 28, 1948 in Jamaica, NY. Bdwy debut in "Girl in the Freudian Slip," followed by "Johnny No-Trump," "George M!" for which she received a Theatre World Award, "La Strada," "On the Town," "Mack and Mabel," "Sunday in the Park with George," "Song and Dance," OB in "Curley McDimple," "Penny Friend," "Most Happy Fella," "Dames at Sea," "Nevertheless They Laugh," "Sally and Marsha."

PETERS, JANNE. Born Nov. 2, 1949 in Minneapolis, Mn. Graduate MankatoStateU. Debut OB in "The Bitter Tears of Petra Von Kant" (1986).

PETERS, MARK. Born Nov. 20, 1952 in Council Bluffs, Ia. Yale graduate. Debut 1977 OB in "The Crazy Locomotive," followed by "The Legend of Sleepy Hollow."

PETERSEN, ERIKA. Born Mar. 24, 1949 in NYC. Attended NYU. Debut 1963 OB in "One Is a Lonely Number," followed by "I Dreamt I Dwelt in Bloomingdale's," "F. Jasmine Addams," "The Dubliners," "P.S. Your Cat Is Dead," "The Possessed," "Murder in the Cathedral," "The Further Inquiry," "State of the Union," "Brand," "Frankenstein."

PETERSON, KURT. Born Feb. 12, 1948 in Stevens Point, Wi. Attended AMDA. Bdwy debut 1969 in "Dear World," followed by "Follies," "Knickerbocker Holiday," OB in "An Ordinary Miracle," "West Side Story" (LC), "Dames at Sea," "By Bernstein," "I Married an Angel in Concert."

PETERSON, LENKA. Born Oct. 16, 1925 in Omaha, NE. Attended UIowa. Bdwy debut 1946 in "Bathsheba," followed by "Harvest of Years," "Sundown Beach," "Young and Fair," "The Grass Harp," "The Girls of Summer," "The Time of Your Life," "Look Homeward, Angel," "All the Way Home," "Nuts," OB in "Mrs. Minter," "American Night Cry," "Leaving Home," "The Brass Ring," "Father Dreams," "El Bravo," "Levitations," "Cliffhanger," "Quilters," "Custom of the Country," "Bone Ring," "Little Footsteps."

PEVSNER, DAVID. Born Dec. 31, 1958 in Skokie, Il. Graduate Carnegie-Mellon U. Debut 1985 OB in "A Flash of Lightning."

PHELAN, DEBORAH. Born Apr. 15 in New Haven, CT. Graduate Point Park Col. Bdwy debut in "Pippin" (1973), followed by "King of Hearts," "A Chorus Line," "Dancin'," "Encore," "La Cage aux Folles," "Jerry's Girls."

PHILLIPS, GARRISON. Born Oct. 8, 1929 in Tallahasee, Fl. Graduate UWVa. Debut 1956 OB in "Eastward in Eden," followed by "Romeo and Juliet," "Time of the Cuckoo," "Triptych," "After the Fall," "Two Gentlemen of Verona," Bdwy in "Clothes for a Summer Hotel" (1980).

PHILLIPS, MIRIAM. Born May 28, 1899 in Philadelphia, Pa. Graduate UPa. Bdwy debut 1926 in "Spring Song," followed by "Half a Widow," "Waltz of the Toreadors," "Legend of Lizzie," "Filumena," OB in "A House Remembered," "Evenings with Chekhov," "Lion in Love," "Hamlet of Stepney Green," "Daughters."

PIERCE, DAVID. Born Apr. 3, 1959 in Albany, NY. Graduate Yale U. Debut 1982 on Bdwy in "Beyond Therapy," followed by OB in "Summer," "That's It, Folks!," "The Three Sebs," "Donuts," "Hamlet."

PIETROPINTO, ANGELA. Born Feb. 5, in NYC. Graduate NYU. OB credits include "Henry IV," "Alice in Wonderland," "Endgame," "Our Late Night," "The Sea Gull," "Jinx Bridge," "The Mandrake," "Marie and Bruce," "Green Card Blues," "3 by Pirandello," "The Broken Pitcher," "A Midsummer Night's Dream," "The Rivals," "Cap and Bells," "Thrombo," "Lies My Father Told Me," Bdwy in "The Suicide" (1980).

PINKINS, TONYA. Born May 30, 1962 in Chicago, Il. Attended Carnegie-Mellon U. Bdwy debut 1981 in "Merrily We Roll Along," followed by OB in "Five Points," "A Winter's Tale," "An Ounce of Prevention."

PINO, MARIANGELA. Born Aug. 15, 1953 in Philadelphia, Pa. Graduate Temple U., UCal/SanDiego. Debut 1986 OB in "Orchards."

PITONIAK, ANNE. Born Mar. 30, 1922 in Westfield, MA. Attended UNC Women's Col. Debut 1982 OB in "Talking With," followed by Bdwy in "'night, Mother" (1983) for which she received a Theatre World Award, "The Octette Bridge Club."

PLACE, DALE. Born Feb. 27, 1950 in Hastings, Mi. Graduate Oakland U. Debut 1983 OB in "Starstruck," followed by "Happy Birthday Wanda June," "Lady Windermere's Fan," "Sell-Out," "Deep 6 Holiday."

PLANA, TONY. Born Apr. 19, 1953 in Havana, Cuba. Attended Loyola U, RADA. Bdwy debut 1979 in "Zoot Suit," followed by "Boys of Winter," OB in "Rum and Coke."

PLANK, SCOTT. Born Nov. 11, 1958 in Washington, DC. Attended NCSch of Arts. Bdwy debut 1981 in "Dreamgirls," followed by "A Chorus Line."

PLAYTEN, ALICE. Born Aug. 28, 1947 in NYC. Attended NYU. Bdwy debut 1960 in "Gypsy" followed by "Oliver," "Hello, Dolly!," "Henry Sweet Henry," for which she received a Theatre World Award, "George M!," OB in "Promenade," "The Last Sweet Days of Isaac," "National Lampoon's Lemmings," "Valentine's Day," "Pirates of Penzance," "Up from Paradise," "A Visit," "Sister Mary Ignatius Explains It All," "An Actor's Nightmare," "That's It, Folks."

PLUMMER, AMANDA. Born Mar. 23, 1957 in NYC. Attended Middlebury Col., Neighborhood Playhouse. Debut 1978 OB in "Artichoke," followed by "A Month in the Country," "A Taste of Honey" for which she received a Theatre World Award, "Alice in Concert," "A Stitch in Time," "Life under Water," "A Lie of the Mind," Bdwy in "A Taste of Honey," "Agnes of God," "The Glass Menagerie."

POE, RICHARD. Born Jan. 25, 1946 In Portola, Ca. Graduate USanFrancisco, UCal/Davis. Debut 1971 OB in "Hamlet," followed by "Seasons Greetings."

POLTRACK, BEVERLY. Born Apr. 1, 1956 in Greenwich, CT. Graduate Boston Consv. Debut 1983 OB in "Skyline," followed by "Eugene," "Stardust," "The Mikado," "Very Warm for May," "Funny Girl."

PONAZECKI, JOE. Born Jan. 7, 1934 in Rochester, NY. Attended Rochester U, Columbia U. Bdwy debut 1959 in "Much Ado about Nothing," followed by "Send Me No Flowers," "A Call on Kuprin," "Take Her She's Mine," "Fiddler on the Roof," "Xmas in Las Vegas," "3 Bags Full," "Love in E-Flat," "90 Day Mistress," "Harvey," "Trial of the Catonsville 9," "The Country Girl," "Freedom of the City," "Summer Brave," "Music Is," "The Little Foxes," OB in "The Dragon," "Muzeeka," "Witness," "All Is Bright," "The Dog Ran Away," "Dream of a Blacklisted Actor," "Innocent Pleasures," "Dark at the Top of the Stairs," "36," "After the Revolution," "The Raspberry Picker," "Raisin' in the Sun," "Light Up the Sky," "Marathon '86."

POPE, STEPHANIE. Born Apr. 8, 1964 in NYC. Debut 1983 OB in "The Buck Stops Here," followed by "Shades of Harlem," Bdwy in "Big Deal" (1986).

PORTER, RICK. Born Jan. 21, 1951 in Fall River, Ma. Graduate Bates Col., Brandeis U. Debut OB 1981 in "Catch 22," followed by "Philco Blues," "Tallulah," "Silverlake," "She Loves Me."

POWELL, ANTHONY. Born Dec. 13, 1958 in San Mateo, CA. Graduate UCLA, Temple U. Debut 1984 OB in "Pieces of Eight," followed by "A New Way to Pay Old Debts," "As You Like It," "The Skin of Our Teeth," "Orchards."

PREDOVIC, DENNIS. Born Sept. 14, 1950 in Cleveland, Oh. Attended OhU. Debut 1973 OB in "Broadway," followed by "Romanov," "King of Hearts," "Emma."

PRICE, GILBERT. Born Sept. 10, 1942 in NYC. Attended AmThWing. Debut 1962 OB in "Fly Blackbird," followed by "Jerico-Jim Crow" for which he received a Theatre World Award, "Promenade," "Slow Dance on the Killing Ground," "Six," "Melodrama Play," "The Crucifixion," "Throw Down," Bdwy in "Roar of the Greasepaint . . ." (1965), "Lost in the Stars," "The Night That Made America Famous," "1600 Pennsylvania Avenue," "Timbuktu!"

PRICE, LONNY. Born Mar. 9, 1959 in NYC. Attended Juilliard. Debut 1979 OB in "Class Enemy" for which he received a Theatre World Award, followed by "Up from Paradise," "Rommel's Garden," "Times and Appetites of Toulouse-Lautrec," "Room Service," Bdwy 1980 in "The Survivor," followed by "Merrily We Roll Along," "Master Harold and the boys," "The Time of Your Life," "Children of the Sun."

PRUNEAU, PHILLIP. Born July 10 in Chicago, IL. Attended New School. Bdwy debut 1949 in "The Cellar and the Well" which he wrote, followed by "Sabrina Fair," "The Winner," "The Bad Seed," "There Was A Little Girl," "Sophie" (which he wrote), OB in "The Last Analysis," "The Madwoman of Chaillot," "Clarence," "Vivat! Vivat Regina!," "A Little Bit Less Than Normal," "Legendary Star Dust Boys," "The Time of Your Life," "Children of the Sun."

PURDHAM, DAVID. Born June 3, 1951 in San Antonio, TX. Graduate UMd., UWa. Debut 1980 OB in "Journey's End," followed by "Souvenirs," "Once on a Summer's Day," "Twelfth Night," "Maneuvers," "The Times and Appetites of Toulouse-Lautrec," "The Winter's Tale," Bdwy in "Piaf" (1981).

PURSLEY, DAVID. Born July 13, 1938 in Lewisburg, Pa. Graduate Harvard U, Baylor U. Debut 1969 OB in "Peace," followed by "The Faggott," "Wings," "The Three Musketeers," Bdwy in "Happy End" (1977), "Snow White."

QUINN, AIDAN. Born March 8, 1959 in Chicago, IL. Debut 1984 OB in "Fool for Love," "A Lie of the Mind."

QUINN, ANTHONY. Born Apr. 21, 1915 in Chihuahua, Mex. Bdwy debut 1947 in "The Gentleman from Athens," followed by "Borned in Texas," "A Streetcar Named Desire," "Becket," "Chin Chin," "Born Yesterday," "Zorba" (1983).

QUINN, HENRY J. Born Aug. 6, 1928 in Boston, Ma. Graduate Catholic U. Debut 1979 OB in "The Sound of Music," followed by "Mrs. Warren's Profession," "Towards Zero," "Among the Fallen."

QUINN, PATRICK. Born Feb. 12, 1950 in Philadelphia, PA. Graduate Temple U. Bdwy debut 1976 in "Fiddler on the Roof," followed by "A Day in Hollywood/A Night in the Ukraine," OB in "It's Better with a Band," "By Strouse," "Forbidden Broadway," "A Little Night Music."

RACKLEFF, OWEN S. Born July 16, 1934 in NYC. Graduate Columbia U, London U. Bdwy debut 1977 in "Piaf," OB in "The Lesson" (1978), "Catsplay," "Arms and the Man," "Escoffier: King of Chefs," "New Way to Pay Old Debts," "Samson Agonistes," "Enter Laughing."

RAINES, RON. Born Dec. 2, 1949 in Texas City, Tx. Graduate OkCityU, Juilliard. Bdwy debut 1983 in "Show Boat," followed by OB in "Olympus on My Mind" (1986).

RAMOS, RICHARD RUSSELL. Born Aug. 23, 1941 in Seattle, Wa. Graduate UMn. Bdwy debut 1968 in "House of Atreus," followed by "Arturo Ui," OB in "Adaptation," "Screens," "Lotta," "The Tempest," "A Midsummer Night's Dream," "Gorky," "The Seagull," "Entertaining Mr. Sloane," "Largo Desolato."

RAMSEY, MARION. Born May 10 in Philadelphia, PA. Bdwy debut 1969 in "Hello, Dolly!," followed by "The Me Nobody Knows," "Rachel Lily Rosenbloom," "Eubie!," "Rock 'n' Roll," "Grind," OB in "Soon," "Do It Again," "Wedding of Iphigenia," "2008½," "Uptown It's Hot."

RANDEL, MELISSA. Born June 16, 1955 in Portland, ME. Graduate UCal/Irvine. Bdwy debut 1980 in "A Chorus Line."

RANDELL, RON. Born Oct. 8. 1920 in Sydney, Aust. Attended St. Mary's Col. Bdwy debut 1949 in "The Browning Version," followed by "Harlequinade," "Candida," "World of Suzie Wong," "Sherlock Holmes," "Mrs. Warren's Profession," "Measure for Measure," "Bent," "The Troll Palace," OB in "Holy Places," "After You've Gone," "Patrick Pearse Motel," "Maneuvers."

RAPHAEL, GERRIANNE. Born Feb. 23, 1935 in NYC. Attended New School, Columbia U. Bdwy debut 1941 in "Solitaire," followed by "A Guest in the House," "Violet," "Goodbye My Fancy," "Seventh Heaven," "Li'l Abner," "Saratoga," "Man of LaMancha," "King of Hearts," OB in "Threepenny Opera," "The Boy Friend," "Ernest in Love," "Say When," "The Prime of Miss Jean Brodie," "The Butler Did It," "The Ninth Step," "Whining and Dining."

RASCHE, DAVID. Born Aug. 7, 1944 in St. Louis, Mo. Graduate Elmhurst Col., UChicago. Debut 1976 OB in "John," followed by "Snow White," "Isadora Duncan Sleeps with the Russian Navy," "End of the War," "A Sermon," "Routed," "Geniuses," "Dolphin Position," "To Gillian on Her 37th Birthday," "Custom of the Country," Bdwy in "Shadow Box (1977)," "Loose Ends," "Lunch Hour."

RAVELO, HENRY. Born Aug. 14, 1958 in Manila, Phil. Attended UWis. Debut 1984 OB in "Pacific Overtures," followed by "Ghashiram."

RAY, JAMES. Born July 4, 1932 in Calgra, Ok. Attended Ok A&M. Bdwy debut 1957 in "Compulsion," followed by "J. B.," "The Wall," "Dylan," "The Glass Menagerie" (1965), "All Over," OB in "The Dreditors," "The Collection," "Love's Labour's Lost," "Henry IV," "The Basement," "Sensations," "The Disintegration of James Cherry," "Amphitryon," "Ray Youth."

REAMS, LEE ROY. Born Aug. 23, 1942 in Covington, KY. Graduate U. Cinn. Cons. Bdwy debut 1966 in "Sweet Charity," followed by "Oklahoma!" (LC), "Applause," "Lorelei" "Show Boat" (JB), "Hello, Dolly!" (1978), "42nd Street," OB in "Sterling Silver," "Potholes," "The Firefly in Concert."

REBHORN, JAMES. Born Sept. 1, 1948 in Philadelphia, PA. Graduate Wittenberg U, Columbia U. Debut 1972 OB in "Blue Boys," "Are You Now Or Have You Ever Been," "Trouble with Europe," "Othello," "Hunchback of Notre Dame," "Period of Adjustment," "The Freak," "Half a Lifetime," "Touch Black," "To Gillian on Her 37th Birthday," "Rain," "The Hasty Heart," "Husbandry," "Isn't It Romantic," "Blind Date."

REBICH, CISSY. Born May 20, 1952 in Aliquippa, Pa. Graduate Duquesne U. Debut 1980 OB in "Annie Get Your Gun," followed by "Bugout," Bdwy in "Mame" (1983).

REDFIELD, ADAM. Born Nov. 4, 1959 in NYC. Attended NYU. Debut 1977 OB in "Hamlet," followed by "Androcles and the Lion," "Twelfth Night," "Reflected Glory," "Movin' Up," "The Unicorn," Bdwy 1980 in "A Life" for which he received a Theatre World Award, followed by "Beethoven's Tenth," "Execution of Justice."

REDINGER, PAULA. Born Feb. 9 in Portland, Or. Graduate UNe. Bdwy debut 1985 in "The Marriage of Figaro."

REED, PAMELA. Born Apr. 2, 1949 in Tacoma, WA. Graduate UWa. Bdwy debut 1978 in "November People," OB in "The Curse of the Starving Class," "All's Well That Ends Well," "Seduced," "Getting Out," "The Sorrows of Stephen," Standing on My Knees," "Criminal Minds," "Fen," "Mrs. Warren's Profession," "Aunt Dan and Lemon."

REEVE, CHRISTOPHER. Born Sept. 25, 1952 in NYC. Graduate Cornell U, Juilliard. Debut 1975 OB in "Berkeley Square," followed by "My Life," Bdwy in "A Matter of Gravity (1976)," "5th of July," "The Marriage of Figaro."

REGAN, CHARLES. Born Sept. 21, 1934 in New Haven, Ct. Debut 1969 OB in "Make Me Disappear," followed by "The Killer Thing," "The Frankenstein Affair," "Joan of Lorraine," "Paradise Lost," "The Wig Lady," "The Time of Your Life," "The Circle."

REGION, DANIEL. Born Nov. 11, 1948 in Sandwich, IL. Debut 1981 OB in "Cowboy Mouth," followed by "Widows and Children First," "A Midsummer Night's Dream," "Beyond Therapy," "Taming of the Shrew," "Her Great Match," Bdwy in "Torch Song Trilogy" (1982).

REINHARDSEN, DAVID. Born Jan. 13, 1949 in NYC. Graduate Westminster Col. Bdwy debut 1976 in "Zalmen or the Madness of God," OB in "Altar Boys," "Extenuating Circumstances," "The Spare Seraphim," "Countess Mitzi."

REISSA, ELEANOR. Born May 11 in Brooklyn, NY. Graduate Brooklyn Col. Debut 1979 OB in "Rebecca the Rabbi's Daughter," followed by "That's Not Funny That's Sick," "The Rise of David Levinsky," "Match Made in Heaven."

REMME, JOHN. Born Nov. 21, 1935 in Fargo, ND. Attended UMn. Debut 1972 OB in "One for the Money," followed by "Anything Goes," "The Rise of David Levinsky," "Jubilee in Concert," Bdwy in "The Ritz" (1975), "The Royal Family," "Can-Can," "Alice in Wonderland."

REPOLE, CHARLES. Born May 24, 1945 in Brooklyn, NY. Graduate Hofstra U. Bdwy debut 1975 in "Very Good Eddie," for which he received a Theatre World Award, followed by "Finian's Rainbow," "Whoopee!," "Doubles," OB in "Make Someone Happy," "George White's Scandals."

RHODES, JENNIFER. Born June 27 in Rosiclare, IL. Attended S. Ill. U. Debut 1984 OB in "Lester Sims Retires Tomorrow," followed by "Donogoo," "The Crucible," "Madwoman of Chaillot."

RICE, SARAH. Born Mar. 5, 1955 in Okinawa. Attended AzStateU. Debut 1974 OB in "The Fantasticks," followed by "The Enchantress," "The Music Man," Bdwy 1979 in "Sweeney Todd" for which she received a Theatre World Award.

RICHARDS, CAROL. Born Dec. 26 in Aurora, IL. Graduate Northwestern U, Columbia U. Bdwy debut 1965 in "Half a Sixpence," followed by "Mame," "Last of the Red Hot Lovers," "Company," "Cats."

RICHARDS, GARY. Born Dec. 16, 1953 in NYC. Graduate Union Col. Debut 1981 OB in "Catch-22," followed by "Ladies in Retirement," "My Three Angels," "Play It Again Sam," "Lies My Father Told Me."

RICHARDS, JEAN. Born in NYC. Attended Yale U. Debut 1969 OB in "The Man with the Flower in His Mouth," followed by "Madwoman of Chaillot," "Poor Old Simon," "Whining and Dining."

RICHARDSON, LEE. Born Sept. 11, 1926 in Chicago, Il. Graduate Goodman Theatre. Debut 1952 OB in "Summer and Smoke," followed by "St. Joan," "Volpone," "The American Dream," "Bartleby," "Plays for Bleecker Street," "Merchant of Venice," "King Lear," "Thieves Carnival," "Waltz of the Toreadors," Bdwy in "The Legend of Lizzie" (1959), "Lord Pengo," "House of Atreus," "Find Your Way Home," "Othello," "The Jockey Club Stakes."

RICHARDSON, PATRICIA. Born Feb. 23 in Bethesda, MD. Graduate SMU. Bdwy debut 1974 in "Gypsy," followed by "Loose Ends," "The Wake of Jamey Foster," OB in "Coroner's Plot," "Vanities," "Hooters," "The Frequency," "Fables for Friends," "The Miss Firecracker Contest," "Cruise Control."

RICHERT, WANDA. Born Apr. 18, 1958 in Chicago, IL. Bdwy debut 1980 in "42nd Street" for which she received a Theatre World Award, followed by "Nine," "A Chorus Line."

RICKETTS, JIM. Born May 11, 1948 in NYC. Attended IllWesleyanU, AMDA. Debut 1977 OB in "Peg O My Heart," followed by "The Flatbush Faithful."

RIEGERT, PETER. Born Apr. 11, 1947 in NYC. Graduate UBuffalo. Debut 1975 OB in "Dance with Me," followed by "Sexual Perversity in Chicago," "Sunday Runners," "Isn't It Romantic," "La Brea Tarpits," "A Hell of a Town," "Festival of One Acts," "A Rosen by Any Other Name."

RIEHLE, RICHARD. Born May 12, 1948 in Menomonee Falls, Wi. Graduate UNotreDame, UMn. Bdwy debut 1986 in "Execution of Justice."

RIGNACK, ROGER. Born Sept. 24, 1962 in NYC. Graduate Emerson Col. Debut 1985 OB in "Dead! A Love Story," followed by "Disappearing Acts."

RILEY, LARRY. Born June 21, 1952 in Memphis, TN. Graduate Memphis State U. Bdwy debut 1978 in "A Broadway Musical," followed by "I Love My Wife," "Night and Day," "Shakespeare's Cabaret," "Big River," OB in "Street Songs," "Amerika," "Plane Down," "Sidewalkin'," "Frimbo," "A Soldier's Play," "Maybe I'm Doing It Wrong," "Diamonds."

RINGHAM, NANCY. Born Nov. 16, 1954 in Minneapolis, Mn. Graduate St. Olaf Col, Oxford U. Bdwy debut 1954 in "My Fair Lady (also 1981)," OB in "That Jones Boy," "Bugles at Dawn," "Not-So-New-Faces of '82," "Trouble in Tahiti," "Lenny and the Heartbreakers," "Four One-Act Musicals."

RITCHIE, MARGARET. Born May 31 in Madison, WI. Graduate UWis., NYU. Debut 1981 OB in "Last Summer at Bluefish Cove," followed by "Who's There," "Telling Tales," "All Soul's Day," "Days and Nights of an Ice Cream Princess."

RIVERA, CHITA. Born Jan. 23, 1933 in Washington, DC. Bdwy debut 1950 in "Guys and Dolls," followed by "Call Me Madam," "Can-Can," "Seventh Heaven," "Mr. Wonderful," "West Side Story," "Bye Bye Birdie," "Bajour," "Chicago," "Bring Back Birdie," "Merlin," "The Rink," "Jerry's Girls," OB in "Shoestring Revue."

RIVERS, FRED. Born Dec. 4, 1947 in NYC. Debut 1970 OB in "Tarot," followed by "The Price of Genius," "The Royal Hunt of the Sun," "She Loves Me."

ROBARDS, JASON. Born July 26, 1922 in Chicago, Il. Attended AADA. Bdwy debut 1947 with D'Oyly Carte, followed by "Stalag 17," "The Chase," "Long Day's Journey into Night" for which he received a Theatre World Award, "The Disenchanted," "Toys in the Attic," "Big Fish Little Fish," "A Thousand Clowns," "Hughie," "The Devils," "We Bombed in New Haven," "The Country Girl," "Moon for the Misbegotten," "A Touch of the Poet," "You Can't Take It with You," "The Iceman Cometh," OB in "American Gothic," "The Iceman Cometh," "After the Fall," "But For Whom Charlie," "Long Day's Journey into Night."

ROBARE, MARY C. Born May 23, 1959 in Havelock, NC. Bdwy debut 1982 in "Little Me," followed by "On Your Toes," "Wind in the Willows," OB in "Emperor of My Baby's Heart."

ROBERTS, GRACE. Born Nov. 9, 1935 in NYC. Debut 1956 OB in "Out of This World," followed by "Affairs of Anatol," "Beethoven/Karl," "Friends Too Numerous to Mention," "Applesauce," "A . . . My Name is Alice," "Briss," "Light Up the Sky," "Pearls."

ROBERTS, TONY. Born Oct. 22, 1939 in NYC. Graduate Northwestern U. Bdwy debut 1962 in "Something about a Soldier," followed by "Take Her, She's Mine," "Last Analysis," "Never Too Late," "Barefoot in the Park," "Don't Drink the Water," "How Now, Dow Jones," "Play It Again, Sam," "Promises Promises," "Sugar," "Absurd Person Singular," "Murder at the Howard Johnson's," "They're Playing Our Song," "Doubles," "Brigadoon" (LC), OB in "The Cradle Will Rock," "Losing Time," "The Good Parts," "Time Framed."

ROBERTSON, DEBORAH (formerly Bauers). Born July 19, 1953 in Nashville, TN. Graduate UCol., Smith Col. Bdwy debut 1982 in "Oh! Calcutta!"

ROBINSON, ANDREW. Born Feb. 14, 1942 in NYC. Graduate New School, LAMDA. Debut 1967 OB in "Macbird," followed by "Cannibals," "Futz," "Young Master Dante," "Operation Sidewinder," "Subject to Fits," "Mary Stuart," "Narrow Road to the Deep North," "In the Belly of the Beast."

ROBINSON, HAL. Born in Bedford, IN. Graduate IndU. Debut 1971 OB in "Memphis Store-Bought Teeth," followed by "From Berlin to Broadway," "The Fantasticks," "Promenade," "The Baker's Wife," "Yours Anne," "Personals."

ROBINSON, ROGER. Born May 2, 1941 in Seattle, Wa. Attended USCal. Bdwy debut 1969 in "Does a Tiger Wear a Necktie?," followed by "Amen Corner," "The Iceman Cometh," OB in "Walk in Darkness," "Jericho-Jim Crow," "Who's Got His Own," "Trials of Brother Jero," "The Miser," "Interrogation of Havana," "Lady Day," "Do Lord Remember Me."

ROCCO, MARY. Born Sept. 12, 1933 in Brooklyn, NY. Graduate Queens Col., CCNY. Debut 1976 OB in "Fiorello!," followed by "The Constant Wife," "Archy and Mehitabel," "Sweethearts," "Funny Girl," Bdwy in "Show Boat" (1983).

RODD, MARCIA. Born July 8, in Lyons, Ks. Attended Northwestern U, Yale U. Bdwy debut 1964 in "Love in E-Flat," followed by "Last of the Red Hot Lovers," "Shelter," OB in "O Say Can You See L.A.," "Cambridge Circus," "Mad Show," "Merry Wives of Windsor," "I Can't Keep Running in Place," "Daughters."

RODERICK, CONNIE. Born Jan. 7 in Dayton, Oh. Attended Northwestern U, Goodman Theatre. Bdwy debut 1983 in "The Corn Is Green," followed by "The Marriage of Figaro."

RODGERS, GABY. Born in Germany. Bdwy debut 1955 in "Heavenly Twins," followed by "Mister Johnson" for which she received a Theatre World Award, "The Hidden River," OB in "Cock-a-Doodle Dandy," "Under the Sycamore Tree," "A Pair of Pairs," "The Golden Window."

ROFFMAN, ROSE. Has appeared OB in "La Madre," "Harold Pinter Plays," "Arthur Miller Double Bill," "Happy Hypocrite," "Under Gaslight," "Beaux Stratagem," "Tea Party," "The Boy Friend," "Marlon Brando Sat Here," "Sing Me Sunshine," "Three Sisters."

ROGERS, ANNE. Born July 29, 1933 in Liverpool, Eng. Attended St. John's Col. Bdwy debut 1957 in "My Fair Lady," followed by "Zenda," "Half a Sixpence," "42nd Street."

ROGERS, GIL. Born Feb. 4, 1934 in Lexington, Ky. Attended Harvard U. OB in "The Ivory Branch," "Vanity of Nothing," "Warrior's Husband," "Hell-Bent fer Heaven," "Gods of Lightning," "Pictures in a Hallway," "Rose," "Memory Bank," "A Recent Killing," "Birth," "Come Back Little Sheba," "Life of Galileo," "Remembrance," "Mortally Fine," Bdwy in "The Great White Hope," "The Best Little Whorehouse in Texas," "The Corn Is Green" (1983).

ROMAN, ARLENE. Born Mar. 21, 1959 in The Bronx, NY. Attended NYU. Debut 1986 OB in "The Bitter Tears of Petra Von Kant."

ROOS, CASPER. Born Mar. 21, 1925 in The Bronx, NY. Attended Manhattan School of Music. Bdwy debut 1959 in "First Impressions," followed by "How to Succeed in Business . . . ," "Mame," "Brigadoon," "Shenandoah," "My One and Only," OB in "Street Scene," "Another Part of the Forest."

ROSE, GEORGE. Born Feb. 19, 1920 in Bicester, Eng. Bdwy debut with Old Vic 1946 in "Henry IV," followed by "Much Ado About Nothing," "A Man for All Seasons," "Hamlet," "Royal Hunt of the Sun," "Walking Happy," "Loot," "My Fair Lady," (CC'68) "Canterbury Tales," "Coco," "Wise Child," "Sleuth," "My Fat Friend," "My Fair Lady" (1976), "She Loves Me," "Peter Pan," BAM's "The Play's the Thing," "The Devil's Disciple," and "Julius Caesar," "The Kingfisher," "Pirates of Penzance," "Dance a Little Closer," "You Can't Take It with You," "Beethoven's Tenth," "Aren't We All?" "The Mystery of Edwin Drood."

ROSS, DYLAN. Born June 10, 1930 in Racine, Wi. Debut 1979 OB in "The Frankenstein Affair," followed by "Period of Adjustment," "Mark VIII:xxxvi."

ROSS, JAMIE. Born May 4, 1939 in Markinch, Scot. Attended RADA. Bdwy debut 1962 in "Little Moon of Alban," followed by "Moon Beseiged," "Ari," "Different Times," "Woman of the Year," "La Cage aux Folles," "42nd Street," OB in "Penny Friend," "Oh, Coward!"

ROSWELL, MAGGIE. Born Nov. 14 in Los Angeles, Ca. Attended LACC. Debut 1986 OB in "Sills & Co."

ROTHHAAR, MICHAEL. Born June 22, 1953 in Pittsburgh, Pa. Graduate Catholic U. Debut 1982 OB in "Who'll Save the Plowboy?," followed by "Dispatches from Hell," "Frankenstein," Bdwy in "The Corn Is Green" (1983).

ROWE, STEPHEN. Born June 3, 1948 in Johnstown, PA. Graduate Emerson Col., Yale. Debut 1979 OB in "Jungle Coup," followed by "A Private View," "Cinders," "Coming of Age in SoHo," "The Normal Heart."

RUBEO, ED. Born Oct. 20, 1956 in Yonkers, NY. Graduate SUNY/New Paltz. Debut 1983 OB in "Richard III," followed by "Girl Crazy."

RUBIN, STAN. Born Jan. 7, 1938 in The Bronx, NYC. Attended Fashion Inst. Debut 1974 OB in "You Can't Take It With You," followed by "The Sign in Sidney Brustein's Window," "A Slight Case of Murder," "Witness for the Prosecution," "Damn Yankees," "Kiss Me Kate," "Gingerbread Lady," "Pearls."

RUBINSTEIN, JOHN. Born Dec. 8, 1946 in Los Angeles, CA. Attended UCLA. Bdwy debut 1972 in "Pippin" for which he received a Theatre World Award, followed by "Children of a Lesser God," "Fools," "The Soldier's Tale." "The Caine Mutiny Court-Martial," "Hurlyburly."

RUCKER, BO. Born Aug. 17, 1948 in Tampa, FL. Debut 1978 OB in "Native Son" for which he received a Theatre World Award, followed by "Blues for Mr. Charlie," "Streamers," "Forty Deuce," "Dustoff."

RUDOLPH, BUDDY. Born Nov. 18, 1956 in Trenton, NJ. Attended Bucks County Com. Col. Debut 1986 OB in "Moby Dick."

RULE, CHARLES. Born Aug. 4, 1928 in Springfield, Mo. Bdwy debut 1951 in "Courtin' Time," followed by "Happy Hunting," "Oh Captain!," "Conquering Hero," "Donnybrook," "Bye Bye Birdie," "Fiddler on the Roof," "Henry Sweet Henry," "Maggie Flynn," "1776," "Cry for Us All," "Gypsy," "Goodtime Charley," "On the 20th Century," OB in "Family Portrait."

RUPERT, MICHAEL. Born Oct. 23, 1951 in Denver Co. Attended Pasadena Playhouse. Bdwy debut 1968 in "The Happy Time," for which he received a Theatre World Award, followed by "Pippin," "Sweet Charity" (1986), OB in "Festival," "Shakespeare's Cabaret," "March of the Falsettos."

RUSH, JO ANNA. (formerly Lehmann) Born Nov. 13, 1947 in Montclair, NJ. Bdwy debut 1966 in "Pousse Cafe," followed by "Shirley MacLaine at the Palace," OB in "Love Me Love My Children," "Broadway Scandals of 1928," "Options," "Inside Out."

RUSSELL, CATHY. Born Aug. 6, 1955 in New Canaan, CT. Graduate Cornell U. Debut 1980 OB in "City Sugar," followed by "Miss Schuman's Quartet," "A Resounding Tinkle," "Right to Life," "Collective Choices," "The Lunch Girls," "Home on the Range."

RYAN, STEVEN. Born June 19, 1947 in NYC. Graduate Boston U., UMn. Debut 1978 OB in "Winning Isn't Everything," followed by "The Beethoven," "September in the Rain," "Romance Language," Bdwy in I'm Not Rappaport" (1986).

SABELLICO, RICHARD. Born June 29, 1951 in NYC. Attended C. W. Post Col. Bdwy debut 1974 in "Gypsy," followed by "Annie," "The Magic Show," OB in "Gay Divorce," "La Ronde," "Manhattan Breakdown," "From Brooks with Love," "Dames at Sea."

St. JOHN, MARCO. Born May 7, 1939 in New Orleans, La. Graduate Fordham U. Bdwy debut 1964 in "Poor Bitos," followed by "And Things That Go Bump in the Night," "The Unknown Soldier and His Wife," "Weekend," "40 Carats," "We Comrades Three," "War and Peace," OB in "Angels of Anadarko," "Man of Destiny," "Timon of Athens," "Richard III," "Awake and Sing," "Desire under the Elms," "Hamlet," "Twelfth Night."

SALAMONE, NICK. Born Nov. 25, 1954 in Conshohocken, Pa. Graduate Tufts U. Debut OB 1979 in "Nightshift," followed by "The Sea Gull," "Design for Living," "Preggin and Liss," "The Open Meeting," "Kennedy's Children," "We Bombed in New Haven."

SALATA, GREGORY. Born July 21, 1949 in NYC. Graduate Queens Col. Bdwy debut 1975 in "Dance with Me," followed by "Equus," "Bent," OB in "Piaf: A Remembrance," "Sacraments," "Measure for Measure."

SAMPSON, ARDEN K. Born Apr. 4, 1946 in Nashville, Tn. Graduate UTn. Debut 1986 OB in "Southern Lights."

SANDERS, FRED. Born Feb. 24, 1955 in Philadelphia, PA. Yale graduate. Debut 1981 OB in "Coming Attractions," followed by "The Tempest," "Responsible Parties," "An Evening with Lenny Bruce," "Green Fields," "Incident at Vichy," "The Wonder Years," "Festival of One Acts."

SANDERS, JAY O. Born Apr. 16, 1953 in Austin, TX. Graduate SUNY/Purchase. Debut 1976 OB in "Henry V," followed by "Measure for Measure," "Scooping," "Buried Child," "Fables for Friends," "In Trousers," "Girls Girls Girls," "Twelfth Night," "Geniuses," "The Incredibly Famous Willy Rivers," "Rommel's Garden," "Macbeth," Bdwy in "Loose Ends" (1979), "The Caine Mutiny Court Martial."

SANTELL, MARIE. Born July 8 in Brooklyn, NY. Bdwy debut 1957 in "Music Man," followed by "A Funny Thing Happened on the Way . . . ," "Flora, the Red Menace," "Pajama Game," "Mack and Mabel," "La Cage aux Folles," OB in "Hi, Paisano!," "Boys from Syracuse," "Peace," "Promenade," "The Drunkard," "Sensations," "The Castaways," "Fathers and Sons."

SANTIAGO, SOCORRO. Born July 12, 1957 in NYC. Attended Juilliard. Debut 1977 OB in "Crack," followed by "Poets from the Inside," "Unfinished Women," "Family Portrait," Bdwy in "The Bacchae" (1980).

SAPUTO, PETER J. Born Feb. 2, 1939 in Detroit, MI. Graduate EMiU, Purdue U. Debut 1977 OB in "King Oedipus," followed by "Twelfth Night," "Bon Voyage," "Happy Haven," "Sleepwalkers," "Humulus the Mute," "The Freak," "Promises, Promises," "The Last of Hitler," "A Touch of the Poet," "Theatre Olympics," "Rude Time," "Shboom!," "Somewhere Better," Bdwy in "Once in a Lifetime."

SAVIOLA, CAMILLE. Born July 16, 1950 in The Bronx, NY. Debut 1970 OB in "Touch," followed by "Rainbow," "Godspell," "Starmites," "Battle of the Giants," "Dementos," "Spookhouse," "A Vaudeville," "Road to Hollywood," "Hollywood Opera," "Secrets of the Lava Lamp," Bdwy in "Nine" (1982).

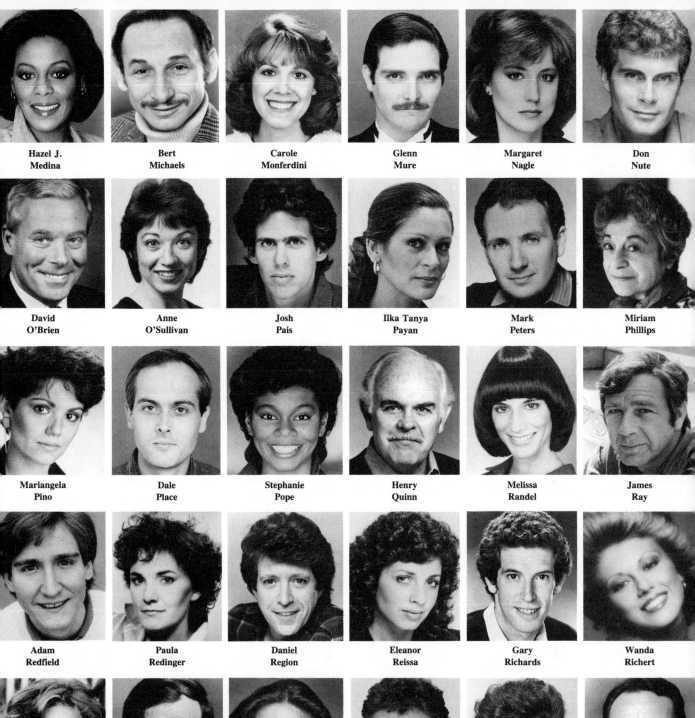

Hazel J. Medina	Bert Michaels	Carole Monferdini	Glenn Mure	Margaret Nagle	Don Nute
David O'Brien	Anne O'Sullivan	Josh Pais	Ilka Tanya Payan	Mark Peters	Miriam Phillips
Mariangela Pino	Dale Place	Stephanie Pope	Henry Quinn	Melissa Randel	James Ray
Adam Redfield	Paula Redinger	Daniel Region	Eleanor Reissa	Gary Richards	Wanda Richert
Nancy Ringham	Hal Robinson	Cathy Russell	Richard Sabellico	Arden Sampson	Peter J. Saputo

SBARGE, RAPHAEL. Born Feb. 12, 1964 in NYC. Attended HB Studio. Debut 1981 OB in "Henry IV Part I," followed by "The Red Snake," "Hamlet," "Short Change," Bdwy in "The Curse of an Aching Heart."

SCALERA, NIKI. Born Aug. 26, 1976 in New Milford, Ct. Debut 1986 OB in "Vanishing Act" (Marathon '86).

SCALISE, THOMAS DAVID. Born Mar. 12, 1953 in Conneaut, OH. Attended Kent State U. Bdwy debut 1981 in "Fiddler on the Roof," followed by "Zorba" (1983).

SCHACT, SAM. Born Apr. 19, 1936 in The Bronx, NY. Graduate CCNY. OB in "Fortune and Men's Eyes," "Cannibals," "I Met a Man," "The Increased Difficulty of Concentration," "One Night Stands of a Noisy Passenger," "Owners," "Jack Gelber's New Play," "The Master and Margarita," "Was It Good for You?," "True West," "Today I Am a Fountain Pen," "The Chopin Playoffs," Bdwy in "The Magic Show," "Golda."

SCHLARTH, SHARON. Born Jan. 19 in Buffalo, NY. Graduate SUNY/Fredonia. Debut 1983 OB in "Full Hookup," followed by "Fool for Love," "Love's Labour's Lost," "Caligula," "The Mound Builders," "Quiet in the Land."

SCHMIDT, JACK. Born Sept. 19, 1927 in San Francisco, CA. Attended UCLA, MexCityCol. Bdwy debut 1976 in "Something's Afoot," OB in "The Fantasticks," "Little Shop of Horrors," "Episode 26," "Crown Cork Cafeteria."

SCHMIDTKE, NED. Born June 19, 1942 in St. Louis, MO. Graduate Beloit Col., Carnegie-Mellon U. Bdwy debut 1985 in "Aren't We All?"

SCHNABEL, STEFAN. Born Feb. 2, 1912 in Berlin, Ger. Attended UBonn, Old Vic. Bdwy debut 1937 in "Julius Caesar," followed by "Shoemaker's Holiday," "Glamour Preferred," "Land of Fame," "The Cherry Orchard," "Around the World in 80 Days," "Now I Lay Me Down to Sleep," "Idiot's Delight," "Love of Four Colonels," "Plain and Fancy," "Small War on Murray Hill," "A Very Rich Woman," "A Patriot for Me," "Teibele and Her Demon," "Social Security," OB in "Tango," "In the Matter of J. Robert Oppenheimer," "Older People," "Enemies," "Little Black Sheep," "Rosmersholm," "Passion of Dracula," "Biography," "The Firebugs," "Twelve Dreams."

SCHNEIDER, JANA. Born Oct. 24, 1951 in McFarland, Wi. Graduate UWis. Debut 1976 OB in "Women Behind Bars," followed by "Telecast," "Just Like the Lions," Bdwy in "The Robber Bridegroom," "The Mystery of Edwin Drood."

SCHREINER, WARNER. Born Sept. 24, 1923 in Washington, DC. Graduate Geo.Wash.U. Debut 1960 OB in "Paths of Glory," followed by "Hooray for Paul," "Crawling Arnold," "Daydreams," "The Education of One Miss February," "Tail of the Tiger," "Appear and Show Cause," Bdwy in "The Skin of Our Teeth" (1961), "Can Can" (CC'62).

SCHULL, REBECCA. Born Feb. 22 in NYC. Graduate NYU. Bdwy debut 1976 in "Herzl," followed by "Golda," OB in "Mother's Day," "Fefu and Her Friends," "On Mt. Chimborazo," "Mary Stuart," "Balzamov's Wedding," "Before She Is Ever Born," "Exiles," "Nest of the Wood Grouse," "Green Fields."

SCHWEID, CAROLE. Born Oct. 5, 1946 in Newark, NJ. Graduate BostonU, Juilliard. Bdwy debut 1970 in "Minnie's Boys," followed by "A Chorus Line," "Street Scene," OB in "Love Me Love My Children," "How to Succeed in Business . . .," "Silk Stockings," "Children of Adam," "Upstairs at O'Neil's," "Not-So-New Faces of '82," "Unreasonable Expectations," "Funny Girl."

SCOTT, GEORGE C. Born Oct. 18, 1927 in Wise, Va. Debut 1957 OB in "Richard III," for which he received a Theatre World Award, followed by "As You Like It," "Children of Darkness," "Desire under the Elms," Bdwy in "Comes a Day," "The Andersonville Trial," "The Wall," "General Seegar," "The Little Foxes," "Plaza Suite," "Uncle Vanya," "Death of a Salesman," "Sly Fox," "Tricks of the Trade," "Present Laughter," "Boys in Autumn."

SCOTT, SERET. Born Sept. 1, 1949 in Washington, DC. Attended NYU. Debut 1969 OB in "Slave Ship," followed by "Ceremonies in Dark Old Men," "Black Terror," "Dream," "One Last Look," "My Sister My Sister," "Weep Not for Me," "Meetings," "The Brothers," "Eyes of the American."

SCOTT, SUSAN ELIZABETH. Born Aug. 9 in Detroit, MI. Graduate UDenver. Debut 1971 OB in "The Drunkard," followed by "Mother," Bdwy in "Music Is" (1976), "On the 20th Century," "Fearless Frank," "1940's Radio Hour," "Dames at Sea."

SEALE, DOUGLAS. Born Oct. 28, 1913 in London, Eng. Graduate Washington Col., RADA. Bdwy debut 1974 in "Emperor Henry IV," followed by "Frankenstein," "The Dresser," "Noises Off."

SEAMON, EDWARD. Born Apr. 15, 1937 in San Diego, CA. Attended San Diego State Col. Debut 1971 OB in "The Life and Times of J. Walter Smintheous," followed by "The Contractor," "The Family," "Fishing," "Feedlot," "Cabin 12," "Rear Column," "Devour the Snow," "Buried Child," "Friends," "Extenuating Circumstances," "Confluence," "Richard II," "Great Grandson of Jedediah Kohler," "Marvelous Gray," "Rime Framed," "The Master Builder," "Full Hookup," "Fool for Love," "The Harvesting," "A Country for Old Men," "Love's Labour's Lost," "Caligula," "The Mound Builders," "Quiet in the Land," "Talley and Son," "Tomorrow's Monday," Bdwy in "The Trip Back Down," "Devour the Snow," "The American Clock."

SEGAL, KATHRIN KING. Born Dec. 8, 1947 in Washington, DC. Attended HB Studio. Debut 1969 OB in "Oh! Calcutta!," followed by "The Drunkard," "Alice in Wonderland," "Pirates of Penzance," "Portfolio Revue," "Philomen," "Butter and Egg Man," "Art of Self-Defense," "Festival of One Acts."

SEIDEL, VIRGINIA. Born July 26 in Hervey, Il. Attended Roosevelt U. Bdwy debut 1975 in "Very Good Eddie" for which she received a Theatre World Award, OB in Hoofers, "Charlotte Sweet," "Where's Charley?," "I Married an Angel in Concert."

SEIDMAN, JOHN. Born Oct. 11, 1949 in Miami, Fl. Graduate NYU. Debut 1982 on Bdwy in "Alice in Wonderland," OB in "The Troll Palace."

SELDES, MARIAN. Born Aug. 23, 1928 in NYC. Attended Neighborhood Playhouse. Bdwy debut 1947 in "Medea," followed by "Crime and Punishment," "That Lady," "Tower Beyond Tragedy," "Ondine," "On High Ground," "Come of Age," "The Chalk Garden," "The Milk Train Doesn't Stop Here Anymore," "The Wall," "A Gift of Time," "A Delicate Balance," "Before You Go," "Father's Day," "Equus," "The Merchant," "Deathtrap," OB in "Different," "Ginger Man," "Mercy Street," "Isadora Duncan Sleeps with the Russian Navy," "Painting Churches," "Gertrude Stein and Companion."

SERRANO, NESTOR. Born Nov. 5, 1955 in The Bronx, NYC. Attended Queens Col. Debut 1983 OB in "Union City Thanksgiving," followed by "Diamonds," "Cuba and His Teddy Bear."

SESMA, THOM. Born June 1, 1955 in Sasebo, Japan. Graduate UCal. Bdwy debut 1983 in "La Cage aux Folles."

SHAWHAN, APRIL. Born Apr. 10, 1940 in Chicago, IL. Debut 1964 OB in "Jo," followed by "Hamlet," "Oklahoma!," "Mod Donna," "Journey to Gdansk," "Almost in Vegas," "Bosoms and Neglect," Bdwy in "Race of Hairy Men," "3 Bags Full" (1966) for which she received a Theatre World Award, "Dinner at 8," "Cop-Out," "Much Ado about Nothing," "Over Here," "Rex," "A History of the American Film."

SHEARA, NICOLA. Born May 23 in NYC. Graduate USyracuse. Debut 1975 OB in "Another Language," followed by "Sananda Sez," "All the Way Home," "Inadmissible Evidence," "Another Part of the Forest."

SHEARMAN, ALAN. Born in London, Eng. NYC debut 1973 OB in "El Grande Coca Cola," followed by "Bullshot Crummond," "El Grande" revival in 1986.

SHEIN, KATE. Born Oct. 13, in Tarrytown, NY. Graduate San Francisco State U. Debut 1985 OB in "Alvrone."

SHELLEY, CAROLE. Born Aug. 16, 1939 in London, Eng. Bdwy debut 1965 in "The Odd Couple," followed by "The Astrakhan Coat," "Loot," "Noel Coward's Sweet Potato," "Hay Fever," "Absurd Person Singular," "The Norman Conquests," "The Elephant Man," "The Misanthrope," "Noises Off," OB in "Little Murders," "The Devil's Disciple," "The Play's the Thing," "Double Feature," "Twelve Dreams," "Pygmalion in Concert," "A Christmas Carol," "Jubilee in Concert," "Waltz of the Toreadors."

SHEPARD, JOHN. Born Dec. 9, 1952 in Huntington Park, CA. Graduate UCal/Irvine. Debut 1982 OB in "Scenes from La Vie de Boheme," "Crimes of Vautrin," "Dr. Faustus," "Fabiola," Bdwy in "A View From the Bridge" (1983), followed by "American Buffalo."

SHEPARD, KATHERINE. Born Oct. 15, 1932 in Newark, NJ. Attended Vassar, UMo. Debut 1983 OB in "The King Trilogy," followed by "Blood."

SHEPPARD, SUSAN. Born Sept. 21, 1957 in Johannesburg, SAf. Graduate UMi. Bdwy debut 1981 in "Fiddler on the Roof," followed by OB in "They're Playing Our Song."

SHERMAN, JONATHAN MARC. Born Oct. 10, 1968 in Morristown, NJ. Attended Carnegie-Mellon U, AADA. Debut 1986 OB in "The Chopin Playoffs."

SHERWIN, MIMI. Born in NYC. Graduate UMi. Bdwy debut 1980 in "Canterbury Tales," followed by OB in "Street Scene," "American Gothics."

SHERWOOD, TOBA. Born Sept. 28, 1934. Bdwy debut 1956 in "The Most Happy Fella," OB in "27 Wagons Full of Cotton," "The Stronger," "The Madwoman of Chaillot," "The Lower Depths," "Ladies and Gentlemen Jerome Kern."

SHIELDS, BROOKE. Born May 31, 1965 in NYC. Attended Princeton U. Debut 1986 OB in "Eden Cinema."

SHORT, JOHN. Born July 3, 1956 in Christopher, IL. Graduate Hanover Col. Debut 1981 OB in "Unfettered Letters," followed by "Sister Mary Ignatius . . .", Bdwy in "Big River" (1985).

SHROPSHIRE, NOBLE. Born Mar. 2, 1946 in Cartersville, GA. Graduate LaGrange Col., RADA. Debut 1976 OB in "Hound of the Baskervilles," followed by "The Misanthrope," "The Guardsman," "Oedipus Cycle," "Gilles de Rais," "Leonce and Lena," "King Lear," "Danton's Death," "Tartuffe," "The Maids," "Midsummer Night's Dream," "Henry IV," "Richard II," "Marquis of Keith," "Wozzeck," "Peter Gynt," "The Cherry Orchard," "Ghost Sonata," "Faust," "Hamlet," "Big and Little," "Chopin in Space."

SHULTZ, PHILIP. Born July 24, 1953 in NYC. Graduate NYU. Debut 1974 OB in "Patience," followed by "Rehearsal," "The Coolest Cat in Town," "Basement Skylight," "Guys and Dolls," "Bugles at Dawn," "The Coarse Acting Show," "Red Hot and Blue," "Bugout."

SIEGLER, BEN. Born Apr. 9, 1958 in Queens, NY. Attended HB Studio. Debut 1980 OB in "Innocent Thoughts, Harmless Intentions," followed by "Threads," "Many Happy Returns," "Snow Orchid," "The Diviners," "What I Did Last Summer," "Time Framed," "Gifted Children," "Levitations," "Elm Circle," "Romance Language," "Raw Youth," "Voices in the Head," Bdwy 1981 in "5th of July."

SIGNORELLI, TOM. Born Oct. 19, 1939 in Brooklyn, NY. Attended UCLA. Debut 1960 OB in "Look Back in Anger," followed by "Bury the Dead," "Scapin," "Pretenders," "Prairie/Shawl," Bdwy in "General Seegar" (1958), "Borstal Boy," "Death of a Salesman" (1984).

SILLS, PAWNEE. Born in Castalia, NC. Attended Brooklyn Col. Debut OB 1962 in "Raisin Hell in the Sun," followed by "Mr. Johnson," "Black Happening," "One Last Look," "NY And Who to Blame It On," "Cities in Bezique," "I'd Go to Heaven if I Was Good," "Oakville U.S.A.," "Hocus-Pocus," "And So to Bed," "Marathon '86," Bdwy 1977 in "Caesar and Cleopatra."

SILVA, DONALD. Born Feb. 7, 1949 in Gloucester, Ma. Graduate Brandeis U. Debut 1985 OB in "Loose Connections," followed by "Bodega."

SILVER, JOE. Born Sept. 28, 1922 in Chicago, IL. Attended UIl., AmThWing. Bdwy bow 1942 in "Tobacco Road," followed by "Doughgirls," "Heads or Tails," "Nature's Way," "Gypsy," "Heroine," "Zulu and the Zayda," "You Know I Can't Hear You . . . ," "Lenny," "The Roast," "World of Sholom Aleichem," OB in "Blood Wedding," "Lamp at Midnight," "Joseph and His Brethern," "Victors," "Shrinking Bride," "Family Pieces," "Cakes with Wine," "The Homecoming," "Cold Storage," "Rich Relatives."

SILVER, RON. Born July 2, 1946 in NYC. Graduate SUNY, St. John's U. Debut OB in "El Grande de Coca Cola," followed by "Lotta," "Kaspar," "More Than You Deserve," "Emperor of Late Night Radio," "Friends," Bdwy in "Hurlyburly" (1984), "Social Security."

SILVERMAN, JONATHAN. Born Aug. 5, 1966 in Los Angeles, CA. Attended USCal. Bdwy debut 1983 in "Brighton Beach Memoirs."

SIMES, DOUGLAS. Born Apr. 21, 1949 in New Salem, NY. Graduate Lehigh U., Yale U. Debut 1974 OB in "The Lady's Not for Burning," followed by "The Dumb Waiter," "The Revenger's Tragedy," "The Lady from the Sea."

SIMONS, LESLIE A. Born Aug. 8, 1957 in Hatboro, PA. Graduate Beaver Col. Bdwy debut 1983 in "La Cage aux Folles."

SINGER, MARLA. Born Aug. 2, 1957 in Oklahoma City, OK. Graduate OkCityU. Debut 1981 OB in "Seesaw," followed by Bdwy's "42nd Street" (1985).

SISTO, ROCCO. Born Feb. 8, 1953 in Bari, Italy. Graduate UIll., NYU. Debut 1982 OB in "Hamlet," followed by "The Country Doctor," "The Times and Appetites of Toulouse-Lautrec."

SKAGGS, MARSHA. Born Aug. 23, 1949 in Bedford, Oh. Attended Purdue U, AADA. Bdwy debut 1981 in "They're Playing Our Song," followed by "Einstein and the Polar Bear," OB in "Little Shop of Horrors."

SKALA, LILIA. Born in Vienna and graduated from UDresden. Bdwy debut 1941 in "Letters to Lucerne," followed by "With a Silk Thread," "Call Me Madam," "Diary of Anne Frank," "Threepenny Opera," "Zelda," "40 Carats," "The Survivor," OB in "Medea and Jason," "Gorky," "Shop on Main Street."

SKELL, AVIVA. Born July 17, 1956 in State College, Pa. Graduate Sarah Lawrence Col., AADA. OB credits include "The Women at the Tomb," "A Dream of Freedom," "Cross Currents," "Who Says I Can't Drink," "Mayberry's Revenge," "Capt. Brassbound's Conversion," "Brecht on Brecht," "Exterminating Angel," "Uninvited Family," "The Stronger."

SKINNER, RANDY. Born Mar. 5, 1952 in Columbus, Oh. Graduate OhStateU. Debut 1976 OB in "The Boys from Syracuse," followed by "George White's Scandals."

SKIPTARIS, LOUKAS. Born Dec. 7, in Thessaloniki, Greece. Bdwy debut 1967 in "Illya Darling," followed by "Zorba," OB in "Wonderful Town," "The Troll Palace."

SLATER, CHRISTIAN. Born Aug. 18, 1969 in NYC. Bdwy debut 1980 in "The Music Man," followed by "Copperfield," "Macbeth," "Merlin," OB in "Between Daylight and Boonville," "Landscape of the Body," "Dry Land."

SLEZAK, VICTOR. Born July 7, 1957 in Youngstown, Oh. Debut 1979 OB in "The Electra Myth," followed by "The Hasty Heart," "Ghosts," "Alice and Fred."

SLOMAN, JOHN. Born June 23, 1954 in Rochester, NY. Graduate SUNY/Genasco. Debut 1977 OB in "Unsung Cole," Bdwy in "Whoopee!," "The 1940's Radio Show," "A Day in Hollywood/A Night in the Ukraine," "Mayor."

SMALL, LARRY. Born Oct. 6, 1947 in Kansas City, MO. Attended Manhattan School of Music. Bdwy debut 1971 in "1776," followed by "La Strada," "Wild and Wonderful," "A Doll's Life," OB in "Plain and Fancy," "Forbidden Broadway."

SMALL, NEVA. Born Nov. 17, 1952 in NYC. Bdwy debut 1964 in "Something More," followed by "The Impossible Years," "Henry Sweet Henry," "Frank Merriwell," "Something's Afoot," OB in "Ballad for a Firing Squad," "Show Me Where the Good Times Are," "How Much How Much," "F. Jasmine Addams," "Macbeth," "Yentl and the Yeshiva Boy," "Life Is Not a Doris Day Movie," "The Golden Land."

SMITH, J. SCOTT. Born July 10, 1960 in Oak Park, Il. Attended UCincinnati, UNC. Debut 1986 OB in "Girl Crazy."

SMITH, JENNIFER. Born Mar. 9, 1956 in Lubbock, TX. Graduate TxTechU. Debut 1981 OB in "Seesaw," followed by "Suffragette," Bdwy in "La Cage aux Folles" (1983).

SMITH, LOUISE. Born Feb. 8, 1955 in NYC. Graduate Antioch Col. Debut 1981 OB in "The Haggadah," followed by "Salt Speaks," "The Tempest."

SMITH, REX. Born Sept. 19, 1955 in Jacksonville, Fl. Bdwy debut 1978 in "Grease," followed by "The Pirates of Penzance" for which he received a Theatre World Award, "The Human Comedy."

SMITH-CAMERON, J. Born Sept. 7 in Louisville, KY. Attended FlaStateU. Bdwy debut 1982 in "Crimes of the Heart," OB in "Asian Shade," followed by "The Knack," "Second Prize: 2 Weeks in Leningrad," "The Great Divide," "The Voice of the Turtle," "Women of Manhattan," "Alice and Fred."

SNOW, DONNA. Born March 23 in Philadelphia, Pa. Graduate UWash. Debut 1985 OB in "Private Scenes."

SOMMER, JOSEF. Born June 26, 1934 in Griefswald, Ger. Graduate Carnegie Tech. Bdwy debut 1970 in "Othello," followed by "Children Children," "Trial of the Catonsville 9," "Full Circle," "Who's Who in Hell," "Shadow Box," "Spokesong," "The 1940's Radio Show," "Whose Life Is It Anyway?," OB in "Enemies," "Merchant of Venice," "The Dog Ran Away," "Drinks before Dinner," "Lydie Breeze," "Black Angel," "The Lady and the Clarinet," "Love Letters on Blue Paper," "Largo Desolato."

SPACEY, KEVIN. Born July 26, 1959 in South Orange, NJ. Attended LACC, Juilliard. Debut 1981 OB in "Henry IV Part I," followed by "Barbarians," "Uncle Vanya," "The Robbers," "Life and Limb," Bdwy in "Ghosts" (1982), "Hurlyburly," "Long Day's Journey into Night."

SPACKMAN, TOM. Born Oct. 4, 1950 in Binghamton, NY. Graduate WayneStateU. Debut 1981 OB in "Peer Gynt," followed by "King Lear," "Ghost Sonata," "Faust," "Wild Oats," "I Am a Camera," "Dance of Death," "Flirtations," "Memories of an Immortal Spirit," "Brand," "Frankenstein."

SPAISMAN, ZIPORA. Born Jan. 2, 1920 in Lublin, Poland. Debut 1955 OB in "Lonesome Ship," followed by "In My Father's Court," "Thousand and One Nights," "Eleventh Inheritor," "Enchanting Melody," "Fifth Commandment," "Bronx Express," "The Melody Lingers On," "Yoshke Muzikant," "Stempenyu," "Generations of Green Fields," "Shop," "A Play for the Devil," "Broome Street America."

SPANO, NEALLA. Born Sept. 26, 1958 in NYC. Graduate Northwestern U. Debut 1981 OB in "Lady Windermere's Fan," followed by "The Night Is Young," "The Coarse Acting Show," "Serious Bizness," "Found a Peanut," "I Shaw."

SPARER, KATHRYN C. Born Jan. 5, 1956 in NYC. Graduate UChicago. Debut 1982 OB in "Beside the Seaside," followed by "About Iris Berman," "The Rise of Daniel Rocket," "Ladies in Retirement," "The Camel Has His Nose under the Tent."

SPEROS, TIA. Born May 3, 1959 in San Francisco, Ca. Graduate San Jose State U. Debut 1985 OB in "Tatterdemalion."

SPIEGEL, BARBARA. Born March 12 in NYC. Debut 1969 in LCRep's "Camino Real," "Operation Sidewinder" and "Beggar on Horseback," OB in "The Disintegration of James Cherry," "Feast for Fleas," "Museum," "Powder," "The Bleachers," "Nightshift," "Cassatt," "Rope Dancers," "Friends Too Numerous to Mention," "Rope Dancers," "Bronx Dreams," "Green Fields," "Festival of One Acts."

SPINDELL, AHVI. Born June 26, 1954 in Boston, Ma. Attended Ithaca Col., UNH, Juilliard. Bdwy debut 1977 in "Something Old Something New," OB in "Antony and Cleopatra," "Forty Deuce," "Alexandriad," "Emma."

SQUIBB, JUNE. Born Nov. 6 in Vandalia, Il. Attended Cleveland Play House. Debut 1956 OB in "Sable Brush," Followed by "The Boy Friend," "Lend an Ear," "Another Language," "Castaways," "Funeral March for a One-man Band," "Gorey Stories," "Blues for Mr. Charlie," "The Workroom," "Family Portrait," "Bdwy in Gypsy" (1960), "The Happy Time," "Gorey Stories."

STADLEN, LEWIS J. Born Mar. 7, 1947 in Brooklyn, NY. Attended Stella Adler Studio. Bdwy debut 1970 in "Minnie's Boys" for which he received a Theatre World Award, followed by "The Sunshine Boys," "Candide," "The Odd Couple," OB in "The Happiness Cage," "Heaven on Earth," "Barb-A-Que," "Don Juan and Non Don Juan," "Olympus on My Mind."

STAHLHUTH, GAYLE. Born Aug. 11, 1950 in Indianapolis, In. Graduate InCentralU. Debut 1981 OB in "Lou," followed by "Sholom Aleichem," "Jimmy the Veteran," "Cries and Whispers," "The Fourth One."

STANLEY, DOROTHY. Born Nov. 18 in Hartford Ct. Graduate Ithaca Col., Carnegie-Mellon U. Debut 1978 OB in "Gay Divorce," followed by "Dames at Sea," Bdwy in "Sugar Babies" (1980), "Annie," "42nd Street."

STANLEY, FLORENCE. Born July 1 in Chicago, IL. Graduate Northwestern U. Debut 1960 OB in "Machinal," followed by "Electra," "What's Wrong with This Picture?," "It's Only a Play," Bdwy in "The Glass Menagerie" (1965), "Fiddler on the Roof," "A Safe Place," "Prisoner of Second Avenue," "Secret Affairs of Mildred Wild."

STANLEY, GORDON. Born Dec. 20, 1951 in Boston, Ma. Graduate Brown U., Temple U. Debut 1977 OB in "Lyrical and Satirical," followed by "Allegro," "Elizabeth and Essex," "Red Hot and Blue," "Two on the Isles," "Moby Dick," Bdwy in "Onward Victoria," (1980), "Joseph and the Amazing Technicolor Dreamcoat."

STANTON, ROBERT. Born Mar. 8, 1963 in San Antonio, Tx. Graduate George Mason U, NYU. Debut 1985 in "Measure for Measure," followed by "Rum and Coke," "Cheapside."

STATTEL, ROBERT. Born Nov. 20, 1937 in Floral Park, NY. Graduate Manhattan Col. Debut 1958 OB in "Heloise," followed by "When I Was a Child," "Man and Superman," "The Storm," "Don Carlos," "Taming of the Shrew," "Titus Andronicus," "Henry IV," "Peer Gynt," "Hamlet," LCRep's "Danton's Death," "The Country Wife," "The Caucasian Chalk Circle," and "King Lear," "Iphigenia in Aulis," "Ergo," "The Persians," "Blue Boys," "The Minister's Black Veil," "Four Friends," "Two Character Play," "The Merchant of Venice," "Cuchulain," "Oedipus Cycle," "Gilles de Rais," "Woyzeck," "King Lear," "The Fuehrer Bunker," "Learned Ladies," "Domestic Issues," "Great Days," "The Tempest," "Brand."

STEHLIN, JACK. Born July 21, 1956 in Allentown, PA. Juilliard graduate. Debut 1984 OB in "Henry V," followed by "Gravity Shoes."

STEINBACH, VICTOR. Born Jan. 1, 1944 in USSR. Graduate Leningrad-Gorky School. Debut 1986 OB in "House of Shadows," followed by "My Life in Art."

STEINBERG, ROY. Born Mar. 24, 1951 in NYC. Graduate Tufts U, Yale U. Debut 1974 OB in "A Midsummer Night's Dream," followed by "The Firebugs," "The Doctor in Spite of Himself," "Romeo and Juliet," "After the Rise," "Our Father," "Zeks," "In Agony," "Merchant of Venice," "Macbeth," Bdwy in "Wings" (1979).

STENBORG, HELEN. Born Jan. 24, 1925 in Minneapolis, MN. Attended Unter Col. OB in "A Doll's House," "A Month in the Country," "Say Nothing," "Rosmersholm," "Rimers of Eldritch," "Trial of the Catonsville 9," "The Hot l Baltimore," "Pericles," "Elephant in the House," "A Tribute to Lili Lamont," "Museum," "5th of July," "In the Recovery Lounge," "The Chisolm Trail," "Time Framed," "Levitations," "Enter a Free Man," "Talley and Son," "Tomorrow's Monday," Bdwy in "Sheep on the Runway" (1970), "Da," "A Life."

STEPHENSON, DON. Born Sept. 10, 1964 in Chattanooga, Tn. Graduate UTn. Debut 1986 OB in "Southern Lights."

STERN, ARLENE. Born March 23 in Boston, Ma. Graduate Northeastern U. Debut 1981 OB in "Final Curtain," followed by "The First Night of Pygmalion."

STERNER, STEVE. Born May 5, 1951 in NYC. Attended CCNY. Bdwy debut 1980 in "Clothes for a Summer Hotel," followed by "Oh, Brother!," OB in "Lovesong," "Vagabond Stars," "The Fabulous '50's," "My Heart Is in the East," "Mandrake," "The Special."

STEVENS, FISHER. Born Nov. 27, 1963 in Chicago, IL. Attended NYU. Bdwy debut 1982 in "Torch Song Trilogy," followed by "Brighton Beach Memoirs," OB in "Out of Gas on Lover's Leap," "Miami."

STEVENS, SUSAN. Born in 1942 in Louisville, Ky. Attended Jackson Col., AMDA. Debut 1978 OB in "The Price of Genius," followed by "Dream Play," "Zeks," "Philistines," "The Last of Hitler," "Brass Birds Don't Sing," "Women Heroes."

STILLER, JERRY. Born June 8, 1931 in NYC. Graduate USyracuse. Debut 1953 in "Coriolanus," followed by "The Power and the Glory," "Golden Apple," "Measure for Measure," "Taming of the Shrew," "Carefree Tree," "Diary of a Scoundrel," "Romeo and Juliet," "As You Like It," "Two Gentlemen of Verona," "Passione," "Hurlyburly," "Prairie/Shawl," Bdwy in "The Ritz," "Unexpected Guests," "Passione."

STOUT, STEPHEN. Born May 19, 1952 in Berwyn, Il. Graduate SMU. Bdwy debut 1981 in "Kingdoms," followed by OB in "Cloud 9," "A Midsummer Night's Dream."

STROMAN, GUY. Born Sept. 11, 1951 in Terrell, Tx. Graduate TxChristianU. Bdwy debut 1979 in "Peter Pan," followed by "Annie," OB in "After the Rain," "Berlin to Broadway," "Jerome Moross Revue," "Close Your Eyes," "Juno and the Paycock," "Glory Hallelujah!," "To Whom It May Concern."

STROUSE, NICHOLAS. Born Dec. 11, 1968 in NYC. Debut 1980 OB in "Raft of Medusa," followed by "Table Settings," "The Chopin Playoffs," Bdwy in "Brighton Beach Memoirs" (1986).

STRUTHERS, SALLY. Born July 28, 1948 in Portland, OR. Attended Pasadena Playhouse. Bdwy debut 1981 in "Wally's Cafe," followed by "The Odd Couple" (1985).

STUBBS, JIM. Born Mar. 19, 1949 in Charlotte, NC. Graduate UNCSchool of Arts. Bdwy debut 1975 in "Dance with Me," followed by OB in "The Passion of Dracula," "Willie," "Macbeth."

SULLIVAN, KIM. Born July 21, 1952 in Philadelphia, Pa. Graduate NYU. Debut 1972 OB in "The Black Terror," followed by "Legend of the West," "Deadwood Dick," "Big Apple Messenger," "Dreams Deferred," "A Raisin in the Sun," "The Tempest."

SWANN, ELAINE. Born May 9 in Baltimore, Md. Attended UNC. Bdwy debut 1957 in "The Music Man," followed by "Greenwillow," "A Thurber Carnival," "My Mother My Father and Me," "Jennie," "Agatha Sue I Love You," OB in "Miss Stanwyck Is Still in Hiding," "Oh, Boy!," "Vieux Carre," "Big Apple Cabaret."

SWETOW, JOEL. Born Dec. 30, 1951 in Kew Gardens, NY. Graduate Hamilton Col. Debut 1982 OB in "Shenandoah," followed by "Songs of the Religious Life," "Tiger at the Gates," "Switching Channels," "Three One-act Plays."

SWIFT, ALLEN. Born Jan. 16, 1924 in NYC. Debut 1961 OB in "Portrait of the Artist," followed by "A Month of Sundays," "Where Memories Are Magic," "My Old Friends," "Divine Fire," "Royal Bob," "The New Yorkers," Bdwy in "The Student Gypsy" (1963), "Checking Out," "The Iceman Cometh."

SWIT, LORETTA. Born Nov. 4 in Passaic, NJ. Attended AADA. Bdwy debut 1986 in "The Mystery of Edwin Drood."

SZARABAJKA, KEITH. Born Dec. 2, 1952 in Oak Park, IL. Attended Trinity U, UChicago. Bdwy debut 1973 in "Warp!," followed by "Doonesbury," OB in "Bleacher Bums," "Class Enemy," "Digby," "Rich Relations," "Women of Manhattan."

SZYMANSKI, WILLIAM. Born May 16, 1949 in Omaha, Ne. Attended UNe. Debut 1979 OB in "Big Bad Burlesque," followed by "Little Shop of Horrors."

TABOR, SUSAN. Born May 28, 1939 in Detroit, Mi. Graduate NYU. Debut 1962 OB in "Electra," followed by "What Every Woman Knows," "The Constant Wife," Bdwy in "Inadmissible Evidence" (1965), "California Suite."

TACKABERRY, CELIA. Born Sept. 17 in St. Louis, MO. Graduate Southwest MoStateU. Bdwy debut 1980 in "A Day in Hollywood/A Night in the Ukraine," followed by "Sweet Charity," OB in "The Desk Set" (1984).

TALMAN, ANN. Born Sept. 13, 1957 in Welch, WVa. Graduate PaStateU. Debut 1980 OB in "What's So Beautiful about a Sunset over Prairie Avenue?," followed by "Louisiana Summer," "Winterplay," "Prairie Avenue," "Broken Eggs," "Octoberfest," "We're Home," "Yours Anne," Bdwy in "The Little Foxes" (1981), "House of Blue Leaves."

TALYN, OLGA. Born Dec. 5 in West Germany. Attended Syracuse U, UBuffalo. Debut 1973 OB in "The Proposition," followed by "Corral," "Tales of Tinseltown," "Shop on Main Street," Bdwy in "A Doll's Life" (1982).

TANDY, JESSICA. Born June 7, 1909 in London, Eng. Attended Greet Acad. Bdwy debut 1930 in "The Matriarch," followed by "Last Enemy," "Time and the Conways," "White Steed," "Geneva," "Jupiter Laughs," "Anne of England," "Yesterday's Magic," "A Streetcar Named Desire," "Hilda Crane," "The Fourposter," "The Honeys," "A Day by the Sea," "Man in the Dog Suit," "Triple Play," "Five Finger Exercise," "The Physicists," "A Delicate Balance," "Home," "All Over," "Camino Real," "Not I," "Happy Days," "Noel Coward in Two Keys," "The Gin Game," "Rose," "Foxfire," "The Glass Menagerie," "Salonika," (OB), "The Petition."

TARANTINA, BRIAN. Born Mar. 27, 1959 in NYC. Debut 1980 OB in "Innocent Thoughts and Harmless Intentions," followed by "Time Framed," "Fables for Friends," "Balm in Gilead," Bdwy in "Angels Fall" (1983), for which he received a Theatre World Award, "Biloxi Blues," "Boys of Winter."

TARBUCK, BARBARA. Born Jan. 15, 1942 in Detroit, MI. Graduate UMich, LAMDA. Debut 1970 OB in "Landscape"/"Silence," followed by "Amphitryon," "Birthday Party," "The Crucible," "The Carpenters," "The Great American Refrigerator," "An Evening with Sylvia Plath," "Biography for a Woman," "Hot-House," "The Water Engine," Bdwy in "Brighton Beach Memoirs" (1984).

TARLETON, DIANE. Born Oct. 25, in Baltimore, MD. Graduate UMd. Bdwy debut 1965 in "Anya," followed by "A Joyful Noise," "Elmer Gantry," "Yentl," "Torch Song Trilogy," OB in "A Time for the Gentle People," "Spoon River Anthology," "International Stud," "Too Much Johnson," "To Bury a Cousin," "A Dream Play," "Crime and Punishment."

TASK, MAGGIE. Born July 4 in Marion, Oh. Attended Wright Col. Bdwy debut 1960 in "Greenwillow," followed by "A Family Affair," "Tovarich," "Most Happy Fella," "Carousel," "Funny Girl," "Kelly Anya," "A Time for Singing," "Darling of the Day," "The Education of Hyman Kaplan," "The Sound of Music," "Coco," "Sweeney Todd," OB in "Sing Melancholy Baby," "Road to Hollywood," "Family Portrait," "I Married an Angel in Concert."

TATUM, MARIANNE. Born Feb. 18, 1951 in Houston, TX. Attended Manhattan School of Music. Debut 1971 OB in "Ruddigore," followed by "The Sound of Music," "The Gilded Cage," "Charley's Tale," Bdwy in "Barnum" (1980), for which she received a Theatre World Award, "The Three Musketeers."

TAYLOR, DREW. Born Mar. 9, 1955 in Milwaukee, Wi. Attended AADA. Debut 1985 OB in "She Loves Me," followed by "Kiss Me Kate."

TAYLOR, HOLLAND. Born Jan. 14, 1943 in Philadelphia, Pa. Graduate Bennington Col. Bdwy debut 1965 in "The Devils," followed by "Butley," "We Interrupt This Program," "Something Old Something New," "Moose Murders," OB in "Poker Session," "The David Show," "Tonight in Living Color," "Colette," "Fashion," "Nightlight," "Children," "Breakfast with Les and Bess," "A Perfect Party."

TAYLOR, MYRA. Born July 9, 1960 in Ft. Motte, SC. Graduate Yale U. Debut 1985 OB in "Dennis," followed by "The Tempest," "Black Girl," "Marathon '86."

TAYLOR, ROBIN. Born May 28 in Tacoma, Wa. Graduate UCLA. Debut 1979 OB in "Festival," followed by "On the 20th Century," Bdwy in "A Chorus Line" (1985).

TEITEL, CAROL. Born Aug. 1, 1929 in NYC. Attended AmThWing. Bdwy debut 1957 in "The Country Wife," followed by "The Entertainer," "Hamlet," "Marat/deSade," "A Flea in Her Ear," "Crown Matrimonial," "All Over Town," "The Little Foxes," "The Marriage of Figaro," OB in "Way of the World," "Juana La Loca," "An Evening with Ring Lardner," "The Misanthrope," "Shaw Festival," "A Country Scandal," "The Bench," "Colombe," "Under Milk Wood," "7 Days of Mourning," "Long Day's Journey into Night," "The Old Ones," "Figures in the Sand," "The World of Sholom Aleichem," "Big and Little," "Duet," "Trio," "Every Good Boy Deserves Favor" (LC), "Fallen Angels," "A Stitch in Time," "Faces of Love," "The Keymaker," "Learned Ladies," "Major Barbara in Concert," "Baseball Wives," "Flight of the Earls."

TELLER. Born in 1948 in Philadelphia, Pa. Graduate Amherst Col. Debut 1985 OB in "Penn & Teller."

TERRY, SUSAN. Born May 30, 1953 in New Haven, Ct. Graduate UNH. Bdwy debut 1979 in "Evita," followed by "Zorba," OB in "Insert Foot," "Follies in Concert," "Forbidden Broadway" (1985).

TESTA, MARY. Born June 4, 1955 in Philadelphia, Pa. Attended URI. Debut 1979 OB in "In Trousers," followed by "Company," "Life Is Not a Doris Day Movie," "Not-So-New Faces of '82," "American Princess," "Mandrake," "4 One-act Musicals," "Next Please!," "Daughters," Bdwy in "Barnum" (1980), "Marilyn," "The Rink."

THELEN, JODI. Born June 12, 1962 in St. Cloud, Mn. Bdwy debut 1983 in "Brighton Beach Memoirs," OB in "Before the Dawn," "Springtime for Henry," "Largo Desolato," "The Nice and the Nasty."

THEODORE, DONNA. Born July 25, 1945 in Oakland, Ca. Debut 1974 OB in "Oh, Lady Lady," followed by "Dance on a Country Grave," Bdwy (1975) in "Shenandoah" for which she received a Theatre World Award.

THEODORE, LAURA. Born Dec. 11, 1957 in Cleveland, Oh. Attended OhU. Debut 1986 OB in "Beehive."

THOMA, CARL. Born Aug. 29, 1947 in Manila, PI. Attended SUNY/Buffalo. Bdwy debut 1970 in "The Me Nobody Knows," followed by OB in "Southern Lights."

THOMAS, MARLO. Born Nov. 21, 1938 in Detroit, Mi. Graduate USCal. Bdwy debut 1974 in "Thieves," followed by "Social Security."

THOMAS, WILLIAM, JR. Born Nov. 8 in Columbus, OH. Graduate OhStateU. Debut 1972 OB in "Touch," followed by "Natural," "Godspell," "Poor Little Lambs," "Loose Joints," "Not-So-New Faces of '81," Bdwy in "Your Arms Too Short to Box with God" (1976), "La Cage aux Folles."

THOMPSON, EVAN. Born Sept. 3, 1931 in NYC. Graduate UCal. Bdwy bow 1969 in "Jimmy," followed by "1776," OB in "Mahagonny," "Treasure Island," "Knitters in the Sun," "Half-Life," "Fasnacht Dau," "Importance of Being Earnest," "Under the Gaslight," "Henry V," "The Fantasticks," "Walk the Dog, Willie," "Macbeth."

THOMPSON, JEFFREY V. Born Mar. 21, 1952 in Cleveland, Oh. Graduate OhU. Debut 1976 OB in "Homeboy," followed by "Macbeth," "Season's Reasons," "Helen," "Louis," "Edward II," "Take Me Along," Bdwy in "Eubie!" (1978), "Amen Corner," "Uptown It's Hot."

THURSTON, TODD. Born May 29, 1956 in Baltimore, Md. Graduate UWa/Seattle. Debut 1985 OB in "She Loves Me."

TIPPIT, WAYNE. Born Dec. 19, 1932 in Lubbock, TX. Graduate UIowa. Bdwy debut 1959 in "Tall Story," followed by "Only in America," "Gantry," OB in "Dr. Faustus," "Under the Sycamore Tree," "Misalliance," "The Alchemist," "MacBird," "Trainor, Dean Liepolt & Co.," "Young Master Dante," "Boys in the Band," "Wayside Motor Inn," "For Sale," "Lemon Sky."

TIRELLI, JAIME. Born Mar. 4, 1945 in NYC. Attended UMundial, AADA. Debut 1975 OB in "Rubbers/Yanks 3 Detroit 0," followed by "The Sun Always Shines on the Cool," "Body Bags," "Bodega."

TOMEI, CONCETTA. Born Dec. 30, 1945 in Kenosha, WI. Graduate UWisc, Goodman School. Debut 1979 OB in "Little Eyolf," followed by "Cloud 9," "Lumiere," "Richard III," "A Private View," "Fen," "The Normal Heart," Bdwy in "The Elephant Man" (1979), "Noises Off."

TOMEI, MARISA. Born Dec. 4, 1964 in Brooklyn, NY. Attended Boston U., NYU. Debut 1986 OB in "Daughters" for which she received a Theatre World Award.

TOMLINSON, ROBERT MICHAEL. Born Aug. 29, 1953 in Brooklyn, NYC. Graduate Temple U. Debut 1984 OB in "Delirious," followed by "Mirandolina," "Hedda Gabler," "Gravity Shoes."

TONER, THOMAS. Born May 25, 1928 in Homestead, Pa. Graduate UCLA. Bdwy debut 1973 in "Tricks," followed by "The Good Doctor," "All Over Town," "The Elephant Man," "California Suite," "A Texas Trilogy," "The Inspector General," OB in "Pericles," "The Merry Wives of Windsor," "A Midsummer Night's Dream," "Richard III," "My Early Years," "Life and Limb," "Measure for Measure," "Little Footsteps."

TORO, PULI. Born in San Juan, PR. Attended NewEngConsv. Debut 1974 OB in "The Merry Widow," followed by "Union City Thanksgiving," "Festival Latino '86," "Bodega."

TORREN, FRANK. Born Jan. 5, 1939 in Tampa, FL. Attended UTampa, AADA. Debut 1964 OB in "Jo," followed by "No Corner in Heaven," "Treasure Island," "Open Season for Butterflies," "The Brownstone Urge," "The Meehans," "Where's Charley?," "Ladies and Gentlemen, Jerome Kern," "Funny Girl."

TOWLER, LAURINE. Born Oct. 19, 1952 in Oberlin, OH. Graduate Stanford U., UCal. Debut 1981 OB in "Godspell," followed by "The Tempest," "Something Old, Something New."

TOWNLEY, WYATT. Born in Kansas City, Mo. Graduate SUNY/Purchase. Debut 1986 OB in "Funny Girl."

TOY, CHRISTINE. Born Dec. 26, 1959 in Scarsdale, NY. Graduate Sarah Lawrence Col. Debut 1982 OB in "Oh, Johnny!," followed by "Pacific Overtures."

TROOBNICK, GENE. Born Aug. 23, 1926 in Boston, MA. Attended Ithaca Col., Columbia U. Bdwy debut 1960 in "Second City," followed by "The Odd Couple," "Before You Go," "The Time of Your Life," "Requiem for a Heavyweight," OB in "Dynamite Tonight," "A Gun Play," "Tales of the Hasidim," "Wings," "Sganarelle," "Damien," "The Workroom," "Room Service," "Talley's Folley."

TROY, LOUISE. Born Nov. 9 in NYC. Attended AADA. Debut 1955 OB in "The Infernal Machine," followed by "Merchant of Venice," "Conversation Piece," "Salad Days," "O, Oysters!," "A Doll's House," "Last Analysis," "Judy and Jane," "Heartbreak House," "Rich Girls," Bdwy in "Pipe Dream" (1955), "A Shot in the Dark," "Tovarich," "High Spirits," "Walking Happy," "Equus," "Woman of the Year," "Design for Living," "42nd St."

TRURO, VICTOR. Born Feb. 7, 1940 in Boston, Ma. Graduate Harvard, Columbia U, AADA. Debut 1975 OB in "Crack," followed by "After the Revolution," "Broken Borders," "Tribe of the People," "S.W.A.K."

TULL, KAREN. Born Jan. 22 in Metuchen, NJ. Graduate Boston U. Debut 1984 OB in "The Vampires," followed by "The 9th Step," "Baal," "Curse of the Starving Class."

TULL, PATRICK. Born July 28, 1941 in Sussex, Eng. Attended LAMDA. Bdwy debut 1967 in "The Astrakhan Coat," OB in "Ten Little Indians," "The Tamer Tamed," "Brand," "Frankenstein."

TUNE, TOMMY. Born Feb. 28, 1939 in Wichita Falls, TX. Graduate UTX. Bdwy debut 1965 in "Baker Street," followed by "A Joyful Noise," "How Now Dow Jones," "Seesaw," "My One and Only," OB in "Ichabod."

TURKEN, GRETA. Born Nov. 23, 1959 in NYC. Graduate Sarah Lawrence Col. Debut 1984 OB in "Cinders," followed by "The Merchant of Venice."

TURNER, GLENN. Born Sept. 21, 1957 in Atlanta, GA. Bdwy debut 1984 in "My One and Only."

TURNER, PATRICK. Born Dec. 2, 1952 in Seattle, WA. Attended UWash., AmConsTheatre. Debut 1984 OB in "The Merchant of Venice," followed by "Double Inconstancy," "The Taming of the Shrew," "Lady from the Sea," "Two Gentlemen of Verona," "The Contrast."

TURTURRO, JOHN. Born Feb. 28, 1957 in Brooklyn, NYC. Graduate SUNY/New Paltz, Yale U. Debut 1984 OB in "Danny and the Deep Blue Sea" for which he received a Theatre World Award, followed by "Men without Dates," "Chaos and Hard Times," "Steel on Steel," "Tooth of Crime," "Of Mice and Men," "Jamie's Gang," "Marathon '86," Bdwy in "Death of a Salesman" (1984).

UGGAMS, LESLIE. Born May 25, 1943 in NYC. Bdwy debut 1967 in "Hallelujah, Baby!" for which she received a Theatre World Award, followed by "Her First Roman," "Blues in the Night," "Jerry's Girls."

ULLETT, NICK. Born Mar. 5, 1947 in London, Eng. Graduate Cambridge U. Debut 1967 OB in "Love and Let Love," followed by "The Importance of Being Earnest," Bdwy in "Loot" (1986).
ULLRICK, SHARON. Born Mar. 18, 1947 in Dallas, TX. Graduate SMU. Debut 1980 OB in "Vanities," followed by "Jump, I'll Catch You!," Bdwy in "Crimes of the Heart" (1981).
URLA, JOE. Born Dec. 25, 1958 in Pontiac, Mi. Graduate UMi, Yale U. Debut 1985 OB in "Measure for Measure," followed by "Henry V," "Principia Scriptoriae" for which he received a Theatre World Award.
UTLEY, BYRON. Born Nov. 4, 1954 in Indianapolis, In. Attended UDC. Bdwy debut 1977 in "Hair," followed by "Reggae," "Big Deal," OB in "Bones," "The Trojan Women," "Sweet Will Shakespeare."
VACCARO, BRENDA. Born Nov. 18, 1939 in Brooklyn, NY. Attended Neighborhood Playhouse. Bdwy debut 1961 in "Everybody Loves Opal" for which she received a Theatre World Award, followed by "The Affair," "Children from Their Games," "Cactus Flower," "The Natural Look," "How Now Dow Jones," "The Goodbye People," "Father's Day," "The Odd Couple" (1985).
VAN HUNTER, WILLIAM. Born Feb. 1, 1947 in Worcester, MA. Graduate Nassau Col., Syracuse U. Debut 1975 OB in "The Three Musketeers," followed by "Lenz," "Couple of the Year," "Stage Door," "Outpost," "Black Coffee," "Murder at the Vicarage."
VAN NORDEN, PETER. Born Dec. 16, 1950 in NYC. Graduate Colgate U, Neighborhood Playhouse. Debut 1975 OB in "Hamlet," followed by "Henry V," "Measure for Measure," "A Country Scandal," "Hound of the Baskervilles," "Tartuffe," "Antigone," "Bingo," "Taming of the Shrew," "The Balcony," "Shadow of a Gunman," "Jungle of Cities," "Shakespeare's Cabaret," "Hamlet" (1986), Bdwy in "Romeo and Juliet" (1977), "St. Joan," "The Inspector General," "Macbeth," "Little Johnny Jones."
VARON, SUSAN. Born May 5, 1952 in The Bronx, NY. Attended Hofstra U. Debut 1977 OB in "The Madwoman of Chaillot," followed by "The Way of the World," "The Anniversary," "The Seahorse," "The Cabbagehead," "Red Cross," "Remember the Sun," "A Flash of Lightning."
VAUGHN, MAURA. Born Oct. 27, 1958 in Boston, Ma. Graduate NYU. Debut 1983 OB in "Big Maggie," followed by "Three Sisters."
VEAZEY, JEFF. Born Dec. 6 in New Orleans, La. Bdwy debut 1975 in "Dr. Jazz," followed by "The Grand Tour," "Sugar Babies," "Sophisticated Ladies," OB in "Speakeasy," "Trading Places," "Nightclub Confidential," "Funny Girl."
VENNEMA, JOHN C. Born Aug. 24, 1948 in Houston, TX. Graduate Princeton U, LAMDA. Bdwy debut 1976 in "The Royal Family," followed by "The Elephant Man," "Otherwise Engaged," OB in "Loot" (1973), "Statements after an Arrest. . . ," "The Biko Inquest," "No End of Blame," "In Celebration," "Custom of the Country."
VENORA, DIANE. Born in 1952 in Hartford, CT. Graduate Juilliard. Debut 1981 OB in "Penguin Touquet," followed by "A Midsummer Night's Dream," "Hamlet," "Uncle Vanya," "Messiah," "Tomorrow's Monday," "Largo Desolato."
VEREEN, BEN. Born Oct. 10, 1946 in Miami, FL. Debut 1965 OB in "Prodigal Son," followed by Bdwy's "Sweet Charity," "Golden Boy," "Hair," "Jesus Christ Superstar" for which he received a Theatre World Award, "Pippin," "Grind."
VINOVICH, STEVE. Born Jan. 22, 1945 in Peoria, IL. Graduate UIl, UCLA, Juilliard. Debut 1974 OB in "The Robber Bridegroom," follwed by "King John," "Father Uxbridge Wants to Marry," "Hard Sell," "Ross," "Double Feature," "Tender Places," "A Private View," "Love," "Poker Session," "Paradise," Bdwy in "Robber Bridegroom" (1976), "The Magic Show," "The Grand Tour," "Loose Ends," "A Midsummer Night's Dream."
VIPOND, NEIL. Born Dec. 24, 1929 in Toronto, Can. Bdwy debut 1956 in "Tamburlaine the Great," followed by "Macbeth," OB in "Three Friends," "Sunday Runners," "Hamlet," "Routed," "Mr. Joyce is Leaving Paris," "The Time of Your Life," "Children of the Sun."
VIVIANO, SAL. Born July 12, 1960 in Detroit, Mi. Graduate EIllU. Bdwy debut 1948 in "The Three Musketeers," OB in "Hot Times and Suicide," "Miami."
VOET, DOUG. Born Mar. 1, 1951 in Los Angeles, CA. Graduate BYU. Bdwy debut in "Joseph and the Amazing Technicolor Dreamcoat" (1982), OB in "Forbidden Broadway."
VOGEL, DAVID. Born Oct. 19, 1922 in Canton, Oh. Attended UPa. Bdwy debut 1984 in "Ballet Ballads," followed by "Gentlemen Prefer Blondes," "Make a Wish," "Desert Song," OB in "How to Get Rid of It," "The Fantasticks," "Miss Stanwyck Is Still in Hiding," "Marya," "She Loves Me."
VOIGTS, RICHARD. Born Nov. 25, 1934 in Streator, IL. Graduate InU, Columbia U. Debut 1979 OB in "The Constant Wife," followed by "Company," "The Investigation," "Dune Road," "The Collection," "Miracle Man," "As Time Goes By," "Silence," "Station J," "Frozen Assets," "Happy Birthday, Wanda June," "My Three Angels," "Child's Play," "Once Is Never Enough," "Black Coffee."
VON DOHLEN, LENNY. Born Dec. 22, 1958 in Augusta, Ga. Graduate Loretto Heights Col. Debut 1982 OB in "Cloud 9," followed by "Twister," "Asian Shade," "Desire under the Elms," "Marathon '86."
WAARA, SCOTT. Born June 5, 1957 in Chicago, Il. Graduate SMU. Debut 1982 OB in "The Rise of Daniel Rocket," followed by "The Dining Room," Bdwy in "The Wind in the Willows" (1985).
WALD, KAREN. Born Sept. 5, 1959 in NYC. Graduate Hofstra U. Debut 1985 OB in "A Little Night Music."
WALDREN, PETER. Born Sept. 7, 1933 in Manila, PI. Graduate Colgate U. Debut 1962 OB in "Bell, Book and Candle," followed by "When the War Was Over," "Napoleon's Dinner," "Open Meeting," "Cabin Fever," "Zen Boogie," "Father Uxbridge Wants to Marry," "Outward Bound," "The Affair," "Crazy Arnold."
WALDROP, MARK. Born July 30, 1954 in Washington, DC. Graduate Cincinnati Consv. Debut 1977 OB in "Movie Buff," Bdwy in "Hello, Dolly!" (1978), "The Grand Tour," "Evita," "La Cage aux Folles."
WALKEN, CHRISTOPHER. Born Mar. 31, 1943 in Astoria, NY. Attended Hofstra U. Bdwy debut 1958 in "J.B.," followed by "High Spirits," "Baker Street," "The Lion in Winter," "Measure for Measure," "The Rose Tattoo" for which he received a Theatre World Award, "The Unknown Soldier and His Wife," "Rosencrantz and Guildenstern Are Dead," "Scenes from American Life," "Cymbeline," "Enemies," "The Plough and the Stars," "Merchant of Venice," "The Tempest," "Troilus and Cressida," "Macbeth," "Sweet Bird of Youth," OB in "Best Foot Forward" (1963), "Iphigenia in Aulis," "Lemon Sky," "Kid Champion," "The Seagull," "Cinders," "Hurlyburly," "House of Blue Leaves."
WALKER, CHET. Born June 1, 1954 in Stuttgart, Ar. Bdwy debut 1972 in "On the Town," followed by "The Ambassador," "Pajama Games," "Lorelei," "Pippin," "Sweet Charity" (1986).
WALLACE, MARIE. Born May 19, 1939 in NYC. Attended NYU. Credits include OB in "Electra," "Harlequinade," "Bell Book and Candle," "Mert and Phil," "In the Boom Boom Room," Bdwy in "Gypsy," "The Beauty Part," "Nobody Loves an Albatross," "The Right Honourable Gentleman," "The Women," "Sweet Charity," "Last Licks."
WALSH, JUANITA. Born May 3, 1951 in Milwaukee, Wi. Graduate Stephens Col. Debut 1980 OB in "Mo' Tea Miss Ann," followed by "The Land Is Bright," "Modern Statuary," "All on Her Own," "The Bookworm," "Another Part of the Forest."
WALTERS, KELLY. Born May 28, 1950 in Amarillo, TX. Graduate UWash. Debut 1973 OB in "Look, We've Come Through," followed by "The Tempest," Bdwy in "Candide" (1975), "Canterbury Tales," "Barnum," "Grind."
WALTZ, LISA. Born Aug. 31, 1961 in Limerick, Pa. Graduate Carnegie-Mellon U. Debut 1983 OB in "Femme Fatale," followed by "Early Girl," "Opal," Bdwy in "The Rink" (1984), "Brighton Beach Memoirs" (1986).
WANAMAKER, ZOE. Born May 13, 1949 in NYC. Attended London Central Sch. of Speech & Drama. Bdwy debut 1981 in "Piaf," followed by "Loot" (1986).
WANDS, SUSAN. Born Oct. 20 in Denver, Co. Graduate UWa. Debut 1985 OB in "Whining and Dining," followed by "And They Dance Real Slow in Jackson."
WARD, DOUGLAS TURNER. Born May 5, 1930 in Burnside, LA. Attended UMi. Bdwy debut 1959 in "A Raisin in the Sun," followed by "One Flew over the Cuckoo's Nest," "Last Breeze of Summer," OB in "The Iceman Cometh," "The Blacks," "Pullman Car Hiawatha," "Bloodknot," "Happy Ending," "Day of Absence," "Kongi's Harvest," "Ceremonies in Dark Old Men," "The Harangues," "The Reckoning," "Frederick Douglass through His Own Words," "River Niger," "Brownsville Raid," "The Offering," "Old Phantoms," "The Michigan," "About Heaven and Earth," "Louie and Ophelia."
WARDEN, YVONNE. Born Jan. 16, 1928 in NYC. Attended UCLA, NYU. Debut 1967 OB in "Trials of Brother Jero," followed by "The Strong Breed," "Macbeth," "Waiting for Godot," "Welfare," "Where Have All the Dreamers Gone," "Calalou," "Masque and Dacha," "Black Girl."
WARREN, JENNIFER LEIGH. Born Aug. 29 in Dallas TX. Graduate Dartmouth Col. Debut 1982 OB in "Little Shop of Horrors," followed by "Next, Please!" Bdwy in "Big River" (1985).
WARREN, JOSEPH. Born June 5, 1916 in Boston, MA. Graduate UDenver. Bdwy debut 1951 in "Barefoot in Athens," followed by "One Bright Day," "Love of Four Colonels," "Hidden River," "The Advocate," "Philadelphia, Here I Come," "Borstal Boy," "Lincoln Mask," OB in "Brecht on Brecht," "Jonah," "Little Black Sheep," "Black Tuesday," "The Show-Off," "Big Apple Messenger," "The Ballad of Soapy Smith," "Her Great Match," "Measure for Measure," "Hamlet."
WARRILOW, DAVID. Born Dec. 28, 1934 in Stone, Eng. Graduate UReading. Debut 1970 OB in "The Red Horse Animation," followed by "Penguin Touquet," "A Piece of Monologue," "Three Plays by Samuel Beckett," "Messiah," "Golden Windows."
WASSERMANN, MOLLY. Born Feb. 11 in Toledo, Oh. Graduate UCincinnati. Debut 1982 OB in "Nymph Errant," followed by "Miami," Bdwy in "Show Boat" (1983).
WATERSTON, SAM. Born Nov. 15, 1940 in Cambridge, Ma. Yale graduate. Bdwy debut 1963 in "Oh Dad Poor Dad. . . . ," followed by "First One Asleep Whistle," "Halfway Up the Tree," "Indians," "Hay Fever," "Much Ado about Nothing," "A Meeting by the River," "Lunch Hour," "Benefactors," OB in "As You Like It," "Thistle in My Bed," "The Knack," "Fitz," "Biscuit," "La Turista," "Posterity for Sale," "Ergo," "Muzeeka," "Red Cross," "Henry IV," "Spitting Image," "I Met a Man," "Brass Butterfly," "Trial of the Catonsville 9," "Cymbeline," "Hamlet," "The Tempest," "A Doll's House," "Measure, for Measure Chez Nous," "Waiting for Godot," "Gardenia," "The Three Sisters."
WATKINS, JAMES. Born June 6, 1933 in Harrisburg, Pa. Debut 1957 OB in "The Beggar's Opera," followed by "Paths of Glory," "Faust," "Another Part of the Forest," "The Front Page," "Electra," "Arms and the Man," "Julius Caesar," "Up in Giovanni's Room," "The Inspector General."
WEAVER, FRITZ. Born Jan. 19, 1926 in Pittsburgh, Pa. Graduate UChicago. Bdwy debut 1955 in "The Chalk Garden," for which he received a Theatre World Award, followed by "Protective Custody," "Miss Lonelyhearts," "All American," "Lorenzo," "The White House," "Baker Street," "Child's Play," "Absurd Person Singular," "Angels Fall," OB in "The Way of the World," "White Devil," "The Doctor's Dilemma," "Family Reunion," "The Power and the Glory," "The Great God Brown," "Peer Gynt," "Henry IV," "My Fair Lady" (CC), "Lincoln," "The Biko Inquest," "The Price," "Dialogue for Lovers," "A Tale Told," "Time Framed," "A Christmas Carol."
WEAVER, LYNN. Born May 17 in Paris, Tn. Graduate UTn, Neighborhood Playhouse. Debut 1981 in "The Italian Straw Hat," followed by "Tiger at the Gates," "The Cherry Orchard," "Murder on the Nile," "A Midsummer Night's Dream."
WEBER, LAWRENCE. Born Sept. 10, 1918 in NYC. Attended NYU, Columbia U. Bdwy debut 1948 in "My Romance." No other credits submitted.
WEBSTER, PETER. Born Apr. 11 in Los Angeles, Ca. Attended UTx, UHouston, UCol. Bdwy debut 1979 in "The Elephant Man," OB in "Pericles," "Sleeping Beauty."
WEDGEWORTH, ANN. Born Jan. 21, 1935 in Abilene, Tx. Bdwy debut 1958 in "Make a Million," followed by "Blues for Mr. Charlie," "The Last Analysis," "Thieves," "Chapter 2," OB in "Chapparal," "The Crucible," "The Days and Nights of Beebee Fenstermaker," "Ludlow Fair," "Line," "Elba," "A Lie of the Mind."
WEINER, JOHN. Born Dec. 17, 1954 in Newark, NJ. Graduate Wm. & Mary Col. Bdwy debut 1983 in "La Cage aux Folles."
WEISS, JEFF. Born in 1940 in Allentown, Pa. Debut 1986 OB in "Hamlet."
WELBY, DONNAH. Born May 4, 1952 in Scranton, PA. Graduate Catholic U. Debut 1981 OB in "Between Friends," followed by "Double Inconstancy," "Taming of the Shrew," "The Contrast."
WELLS, CRAIG. Born July 2, 1955 in Newark, NJ. Graduate Albion Col. Debut 1985 OB in "Forbidden Broadway."
WELLS, DEANNA. Born Aug. 7, 1962 in Milwaukee, Wi. Graduate Northwestern U. Debut 1985 OB in "On the 20th Century."
WESTENBERG, ROBERT W. Born Oct. 26, 1953 in Miami Beach, FL. Graduate UCal/Fresno. Debut 1981 OB in "Henry IV Part I," followed by "Hamlet," "The Death of von Richthofen," Bdwy in "Zorba" (1983) for which he received a Theatre World Award, "Sunday in the Park with George."

WESTFALL, RALPH DAVID. Born July 2, 1934 in North Lewisburg, Oh. Graduate OhWesleyanU, SUNY/New Paltz. Debut 1977 OB in "Richard III," followed by "The Importance of Being Earnest," "Anyone Can Whistle," "A Midsummer Night's Dream," "Macbeth."
WESTON, JACK. Born Aug. 21, 1915 in Cleveland, OH. Attended Cleveland Play House, AmThWing. Bdwy debut 1950 in "Season in the Sun," followed by "South Pacific," "Bells Are Ringing," "California Suite," "The Ritz," "Cheaters," "The Floating Light Bulb," OB in "The Baker's Wife."
WESTPHAL, ROBIN. Born Nov. 24, 1953 in Salt Lake City, UT. Graduate UUtah. Debut 1983 OB in "June Moon," followed by "Taming of the Shrew," "Merchant of Venice," "Somewheres Better," "Lady from the Sea," "Her Great Match," "Antigone."
WEYENBERG, TRISH. Born Oct. 21, 1949 in Little Chute, Wi. Graduate UWi. Debut 1982 OB in "Lysistrata," followed by "She Loves Me."
WHALEN, PAMELA. Born Nov. 18, 1959 in NYC. Graduate Northwestern U. Debut 1982 OB in "Changing Interiors," followed by "The Great White Hope," "The Murder Game."
WHITE, AMELIA. Born Sept. 14, 1954 in Nottingham, Eng. Attended London's Central School of Speech & Drama. Debut 1984 OB in "The Accrington Pals" for which she received a Theatre World Award.
WHITE, LAURA. Born Sept. 1, 1964 in Rowayton, Ct. Attended IndU, NYU. Debut 1985 OB in "Lemon Sky."
WHITE, RICHARD. Born Aug. 4, 1953 in Oak Ridge, Tn. Graduate Oberlin Col. Bdwy debut 1979 in "The Most Happy Fella," followed by "Brigadoon" (LC), OB in "Elizabeth and Essex."
WHITFIELD, DEBRA. Born July 1, 1957 in Charlotte, NC. Graduate OhStateU, KentStateU. Debut 1983 OB in "Brandy Before Breakfast," followed by "Dr. Jekyll and Mr. Hyde," "Bravo," "Appointment with Death," "Hound of the Baskervilles," "The Land Is Bright," "Black Coffee."
WHITTON, MARGARET. (formerly Peggy) Born Nov. 30 Philadelphia, Pa. Debut 1973 OB in "Baba Goya," followed by "Arthur," "The Wager," "Nourish the Beast," "Another Language," "Chinchilla," "Othello," "The Art of Dining," "One Tiger to a Hill," "Henry IV Parts I & II," "Don Juan," "My Uncle Sam," "Aunt Dan and Lemon," Bdwy in "Steaming" (1982).
WHYTE, DONN. Born Feb. 23, 1941 in Chicago, Il. Attended Northwestern U. Debut 1969 OB in "The Brownstone Urge," followed by "Foreplay," "One Flew over the Cuckoo's Nest," "Crime and Punishment."
WIERNEY, J. THOMAS. (a.k.a. Tom) Born Jan. 11, 1953 in Honolulu, Hi. Graduate Syracuse U. Debut 1976 OB in "Panama Hattie," followed by Bdwy in "Sweet Charity" (1986).
WILDER, ALAN. Born Sept. 24, 1953 in Chicago, Il. Graduate IlStateU. Bdwy debut 1986 in "The Caretaker."
WILDING, MICHAEL. Born Jan. 6, 1955 in Los Angeles, Ca. Debut 1986 OB in "Dead Wrong."
WILKOF, LEE. Born June 25, 1951 in Canton, OH. Graduate UCincinnati. Debut 1977 OB in "Present Tense," followed by "Little Shop of Horrors," "Holding Patterns," Bdwy in "Sweet Charity" (1986).
WILLIAMS, ALLISON. Born Sept. 26, 1958 in NYC. Debut 1977 OB in "Guys and Dolls," followed by "Young Gifted and Broke," Bdwy in "The Wiz" (1977), "Dreamgirls," "Sweet Charity" (1986).
WILLIAMS, KEITH. Born Oct. 2, 1954 in Scranton, PA. Graduate Mansfield Col., Catholic U. Debut 1983 OB in "Lady Windermere's Fan," followed by "Verdict," "My Three Angels," "Something Old, Something New," "Murder at the Vicarage."
WILLIS, RICHARD. Born in Dallas, Tx. Graduate CornellU, NorthwesternU. Debut 1986 OB in "Three Sisters."
WILLIS, SUSAN. Born in Tiffin, Oh. Attended Carnegie Tech, Cleveland Play House. Debut 1953 OB in "The Little Clay Cart," followed by "Love and Let Love," "Glorious Age," "The Guardsman," "Dangerous Corners," "Children of the Sun," Bdwy in "Take Me Along" (1959), "Gypsy," "Dylan," "Come Live with Me," "Cabaret," "Oliver!"
WILLISON, WALTER. Born June 24, 1947 in Monterey Park, Ca. Bdwy debut 1970 in "Norman, Is That You?," followed by "Two by Two" for which he received a Theatre World Award, "Wild and Wonderful," "A Celebration of Richard Rodgers," "Pippin," "A Tribute to Joshua Logan," "A Tribute to George Abbott," OB in "They Say It's Wonderful," and "Broadway Scandals of 1928," "Options," both of which he wrote.
WILLOUGHBY, RONALD. Born June 3, 1937 in Boss, MS. Graduate Millsaps Col., Northwestern U. Debut 1963 OB in "Walk in Darkness," followed by "Little Eyolf," "Anthony and Cleopatra," "Balm in Gilead," "Dracula: Sabbat," "The Faggot," "King of the U.S.," "Twelfth Night," "Black People's Party," "Mrs. Warren's Profession," "Why Marry?" "The Green Bay Tree," "Julius Caesar," "A Man's World."
WILSON, ELIZABETH. Born Apr. 4, 1925 in Grand Rapids, MI. Attended Neighborhood Playhouse. Bdwy debut 1953 in "Picnic," followed by "The Desk Set," "Tunnel of Love," "Big Fish, Little Fish," "Sheep on the Runway," "Sticks and Bones," "Secret Affairs of Mildred Wild," "The Importance of Being Earnest," "Morning's at 7," "You Can't Take It with You," OB in "Plaza 9," "Eh?," "Little Murders," "Good Woman of Setzuan," "Uncle Vanya," "Threepenny Opera," "All's Well That Ends Well," "Taken in Marriage," "Salonika," "Anteroom."
WILSON, K. C. Born Aug. 10, 1945 in Miami, Fl. Attended AADA. Debut 1973 OB in "Little Mahagonny," followed by "The Tempest," "Richard III," "Macbeth," "Threepenny Opera," "The Passion of Dracula," "Francis," "Robin Hood," "Tatterdemalion," "Beef."
WILSON, MARY LOUISE. Born Nov. 12, 1936 in New Haven, CT. Graduate Northwestern U. Bdwy debut 1963 in "Hot Spot," followed by "Flora the Red Menace," "Criss-Crossing," "Promises, Promises," "The Women," "The Gypsy," "The Royal Family," "Importance of Being Earnest," "Philadelphia Story," "Fools," "Alice in Wonderland," "The Odd Couple," OB in "Our Town," "Upstairs at the Downstairs," "Threepenny Opera," "A Great Career," "Whispers on the Wind," "Beggar's Opera," "Buried Child," "Sister Mary Ignatius Explains It All," "Actor's Nightmare," "Baby with the Bathwater."
WILSON, TREY. Born Jan. 21, 1948 in Houston, Tx. Bdwy debut 1979 in "Peter Pan," followed by "Tintypes," "The First," "Foxfire," OB in "Personals," "Custom of the Country."
WINDE, BEATRICE. Born Jan. 6 in Chicago, Il. Debut 1966 OB in "In White America," followed by "June Bug Graduates Tonight," "Strike Heaven on the Face," "Divine Comedy," "Crazy Horse," "My Mother My Father and Me," "Steal Away," "The Actress," Bdwy in "Ain't Supposed to Die a Natural Death" (1971) for which she received a Theatre World Award.
WINSON, SUZI. Born Feb. 28, 1962 in NYC. Bdwy debut 1980 in "Brigadoon," followed by OB in "Moondance," "Nunsense."
WINTERS, SCOTT. Born Dec. 5, 1959 in Newark, NJ. Graduate Northwestern U. Debut 1986 OB in "Three Sisters."
WINTERSTELLER, LYNNE. Born Sept. 18, 1955 in Sandusky, OH. Graduate UMd. Bdwy debut 1982 in "Annie," OB in "Gifts of the Magi" (1984).
WISE, LESLIE SERGEANT. Born Oct. 26, 1957 in Rochester, NY. Graduate CtCol. Debut 1985 OB in "Leverage," followed by "Reckonings," "Love as We Know It."
WISE, WILLIAM. Born May 11 in Chicago, Il. Attended Bradley U., NorthwesternU. Debut 1970 OB in "Adaptation/Next," followed by "Him," "The Hot 1 Baltimore," "Just the Immediate Family," "36," "For the Use of the Hall," "Orphans," "Working Theatre Festival."
WISNISKI, RON. Born Aug. 11, 1957 in Pittsburgh, Pa. Graduate UPittsburgh. Debut 1983 OB in "Promises Promises," followed by "Tatterdemalion."
WOLF, CATHERINE. Born May 25 in Abington, Pa. Attended Carneigie-Tech, Neighborhood Playhouse. Bdwy debut 1976 in "The Innocents," followed by "Otherwise Engaged," OB in "A Difficult Borning," "I Can't Keep Running in Place," "Cloud 9," "The Importance of Being Earnest," "Miami."
WOLPE, LENNY. Born Mar. 25, 1951 in Newburgh, NY. Graduate Geo. Wash. U, UMn. Debut 1978 OB in "Company," followed by "Brownstone," "Mayor," Bdwy in "Onward Victoria" (1980), "Copperfield," "Mayor."
WOODARD, ALFRE. Born Nov. 8 in Tulsa, Ok. Graduate Boston U. Bdwy debut 1976 in "Me and Bessie," OB in "So Nice They Named It Twice," "Two by South," "A Map of the World."
WOODARD, CHARLAINE. Born Dec. 29 in Albany, NY. Graduate Goodman Sch., SUNY. Debut 1975 OB in "Don't Bother Me, I Can't Cope," followed by "Dementos," "Under Fire," "A . . . My Name Is Alice," "Twelfth Night," "Hang on to the Good Times," "Paradise," Bdwy in "Hair" (1977), "Ain't Misbehavin'."
WOODRUFF, KELLY. Born Aug. 12, 1957 in Johnson City, TN. Attended FlaStateU. Debut 1984 OB in "Bells Are Ringing," followed by "Buskers," "George White's Scandals."
WRIGHT, TOM. Born Nov. 29, 1952 in Englewood, NJ. Attended Westchester State Col. Debut 1981 OB in "A Taste of Honey," followed by "Turnbuckle," "The Box," "Women of Manhattan," Bdwy in "A Taste of Honey" (1981).
YANCEY, KIM. Born Sept. 25, 1959 in NYC. Graduate CCNY. Debut 1978 OB in "Why Lillie Won't Spin," followed by "Escape to Freedom," "Dacha," "Blues for Mr. Charlie," "American Dreams," "Ties That Bind," "Walking Through."
YANCY, EMILY. Born in 1947 in NYC. Attended Brooklyn Col. Bdwy debut 1967 in "Hello Dolly!," followed by "Man of LaMancha," "1600 Pennsylvania Avenue," OB in "Your Own Thing," "Long Time Since Yesterday."
YEOMAN, JOANN. Born Mar. 19, 1948 in Phoenix, AZ. Graduate AzStateU, Purdue U. Debut 1974 OB in "The Boy Friend," followed by "Texas Starlight," "Ba Ta Clan," "A Christmas Carol."
YOUNG, KAREN. Born Sept. 29 in Pequonnock, NJ. Attended Douglass Col. Rutgers U. Debut 1982 OB in "Three Acts of Recognition," followed by "A Lie of the Mind."
YOUNG, WILLIAM ALLEN. Born Jan. 24, 1954 in Washington, DC. Graduate USCal, CalStateU. Debut 1985 OB in "In the Belly of the Beast."
YULIN, HARRIS. Born Nov. 5, 1937 in Calif. Attended USCal. Debut 1963 OB in "Next Time I'll Sing to You," followed by "A Midsummer Night's Dream," "Troubled Waters," "Richard III," "King John," "The Cannibals," "Lesson from Aloes," "Hedda Gabler," "Barnum's Last Life," "Hamlet," "Mrs. Warren's profession," "Marathon '86," Bdwy in "Watch on the Rhine" (1980).
ZACHARIAS, EMILY. Born July 27, 1953 in Memphis, Tn. Graduate Northwestern U. Debut 1980 OB in "March of the Falsettos," followed by "America Kicks Up Its Heels," "Crazy He Calls Me," "Olympus on My Mind," Bdwy in "Perfectly Frank" (1980).
ZAGNIT, STUART. Born Mar. 28, 1952 in New Brunswick, NJ. Graduate Montclair State Col. Debut 1978 OB in "The Wager," followed by "Manhattan Transference," "Women in Tune," "Enter Laughing," "Kuni Leml," "Tatterdemalion."
ZALOOM, PAUL. Born Dec. 14, 1951 in Brooklyn, NY. Graduate Goddard Col. Debut 1979 OB in "Fruit of Zaloom," followed by "Zalooming Along," "Zaloominations," "Crazy as Zaloom," "Return of the Creature from the Blue Zaloom," "Theatre of Trash.," "Madrid Madrid."
ZANARINI, TOM. Born Oct. 16, 1956 in Peru, IL. Graduate IllStateU. Debut 1984 OB in "Balm in Gilead," followed by "The Caretaker."
ZANG, EDWARD. Born Aug. 19, 1934 in NYC. Graduate Boston U. OB in "The Good Soldier Schweik," "St. Joan," "Boys in the Band," "The Reliquary of Mr. and Mrs. Potterfield," "The Last Analysis," "As You Like It," "More Than You Deserve," "Polly," "Threepenny Opera," "Largo Desolato," "The NY Idea," "The Misanthrope," "Banana Box," "The Penultimate Problem of Sherlock Holmes," Bdwy in "Crucifer of Blood" (1978), "Amadeus," "Alice in Wonderland."
ZEISLER, MARK. Born Mar. 23, 1960 in NYC. Graduate SUNY/Purchase. Debut 1984 OB in "Crime and Punishment," followed by "Measure for Measure."
ZELLER, MARK. Born Apr. 20, 1932 in NYC. Attended NYU. Bdwy debut 1956 in "Shangri-La," followed by "Happy Hunting," "Wonderful Town" (CC), "Saratoga," "Ari," OB in "Candle in the Wind," "Margaret's Bed," "Freud," "Kuni Leml," "Lies My Father Told Me."
ZIEMBA, KAREN. Born Nov. 12, 1957 in St. Joseph, MO. Graduate UAkron. Debut 1981 OB in "Seesaw," followed by "I Married an Angel in Concert," Bdwy in "A Chorus Line" (1982), "42nd Street."
ZINN, RANDOLYN. Born Aug. 23, 1952 in Hamilton, Oh. Graduate Sawyer Col. Bdwy debut 1971 in "The Rothschilds," OB in "1951" (1986).
ZISKIE, KURT. Born Apr. 16, 1956 in Oakland, Ca. Graduate Stanford U, Neighborhood Playhouse. Debut 1985 OB in "A Flash of Lightning."
ZORICH, LOUIS. Born Feb. 12, 1924 in Chicago, IL. Attended Roosevelt U. OB in "Six Characters in Search of an Author," "Crimes and Crimes," "Henry V," "Thracian Horses," "All Women Are One," "Good Soldier Schweik," "Shadow of Heroes," "To Clothe the Naked," "Sunset," "A Memory of Two Mondays," "They Knew What They Wanted," "The Gathering," "True West," "The Tempest," "Come Dog, Come Night," Bdwy in "Becket," "Moby Dick," "The Odd Couple," "Hadrian VII," "Moonchildren," "Fun City," "Goodtime Charley," "Herzl," "Death of a Salesman" (1984), "Arms and the Man." "The Marriage of Figaro."

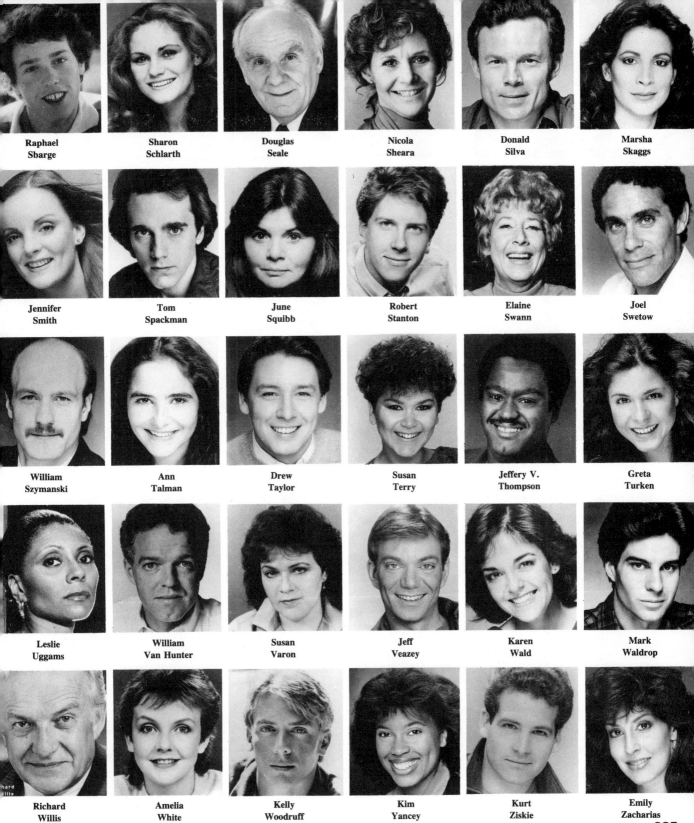

Raphael Sbarge	Sharon Schlarth	Douglas Seale	Nicola Sheara	Donald Silva	Marsha Skaggs
Jennifer Smith	Tom Spackman	June Squibb	Robert Stanton	Elaine Swann	Joel Swetow
William Szymanski	Ann Talman	Drew Taylor	Susan Terry	Jeffery V. Thompson	Greta Turken
Leslie Uggams	William Van Hunter	Susan Varon	Jeff Veazey	Karen Wald	Mark Waldrop
Richard Willis	Amelia White	Kelly Woodruff	Kim Yancey	Kurt Ziskie	Emily Zacharias

225

Brian
Aherne

Robert
Alda

Ann
Andrews

Edith
Atwater

Anne
Baxter

Marie
Bell

OBITUARIES

BRIAN AHERNE, 83, British-born stage and film actor, died of heart failure on February 10, 1986, in Venice, Fla. He made his acting debut at the age of 8 in a pantomime show in England with Noel Coward. Bdwy debut 1931 in "The Barretts Of Wimpole Street" with Katharine Cornell. He also appeared in "Romeo and Juliet," St. Joan," and "Lucrece" (all with Cornell), "Quadrille," National Company of "My Fair Lady," and "Dear Liar." His first marriage, to Joan Fontaine, ended in divorce. Survived by his second wife.

ROBERT ALDA, 72, NYC-born stage, film, and television actor, died on May 3, 1986 at his home in Los Angeles, CA, after a long illness. He won the Tony, Drama Critics Circle and Donaldson Awards for his Bdwy debut in "Guys and Dolls." Other Bdwy appearances include "Harbor Lights," "What Makes Sammy Run?," "My Daughter, Your Son," and "Front Page." Survived by his second wife, Flora; two sons, actors Alan and Antony. a brother, a sister, and four grandchildren.

RICHARD ALDRICH, Boston-born producer, died on March 31, 1986, in Williamsburg, Va. He was 83 years old and lived in East Dennis, Mass. He produced more than 30 plays on Bdwy, including "The Moon Is Blue," "Goodbye My Fancy," "The Playboy of the Western World," "Springtime for Henry," "Dear Charles," and "Pygmalion" starring his first wife, Gertrude Lawrence. Survived by his second wife, four children, and several grandchildren.

MATTHEW ANDEN, 42, Germany-born actor, died July 19, 1985 in New York, after a lengthy illness. He made his stage debut in the 1965 City Center production of "The Threepenny Opera," and appeared Off-Broadway in "Futz." Survived by his adoptive mother, actress Yoshi Schreiner, and his mother.

ANN ANDREWS, 95, Los Angeles-born actress, died Jan. 23, 1986 in New York City. Bdwy debut in 1917 in "Nju," followed by "Two Married Men," "The Hottentot," "The Champion," "Her Temporary Husband," "The Captive," "The Royal Family," "Dinner at Eight," "Oliver Oliver," "Dark Victory," "De Luxe," "First Love," "Reflected Glory," "Three Waltzes," "When We Are Married," "Spring Again," "Public Relations," and "Four Winds." No reported survivors.

HAROLD ARLEN, 81, Buffalo, NY-born composer of popular songs for film and theatre, died of cancer on April 23, 1986 in his New York apartment. He composed the scores for such Bdwy shows as "Bloomer Girl," "St. Louis Woman," "House of Flowers," and "Jamaica." Survived by a brother, Jerry, and a son, Samuel.

EDITH ATWATER, 74, Chicago-born stage, film, and television actress died March 14, 1986 of cancer in Los Angeles. Bdwy debut in "Springtime for Henry," followed by "Brittle Heaven," "This Our House," "The Country Wife," "The Masque of Kings," "Susan and God," "Retreat to Pleasure," "Johnny On A Spot," "Broken Journey," "R. U. R.," "Parlor Story," "State of The Union," "The Gentleman From Athens," "Metropole," "King Lear," "Flahooley," "Time Out for Ginger," "Two's Company," "The Best Man," and "The Child Buyer." No immediate survivors.

JAMES AWE, 66, Wisconsin-born company manager, died of cardio-pulmonary arrest on June 11, 1985, after being struck by two cars while walking on a New York street. He began his career as assistant to Joshua Logan on "Mister Roberts," "Annie Get Your Gun," and "South Pacific." He was company manager for Bdwy shows including "Sweet Bird of Youth," "I Do I Do," "Coco," "Belle of Amherst," "Dancin'," "Oklahoma," and "Camelot." Survived by a sister and brother.

ALEKSEI ARBUZOV, 77, Soviet playwright, died on April 20, 1986 in Moscow. His plays produced in the US include "The Promise," "An Irktsk Story," "Confession at Night," and "Do You Turn Somersaults?" starring Mary Martin in 1978. No reported survivors.

KENNY BAKER, 72, stage, film, and television actor-singer, died of a heart attack on Aug. 10, 1985 at his home in Solvang, CA. He made his Bdwy debut in 1943 in "One Touch of Venus." No reported survivors.

STUART BAKER-BERGEN, 40, actor, playwright, composer, died in his hometown of New Orleans, LA on May 9, 1986 after a long illness. He appeared on Bdwy in "Purlie," and in Public Theatre's "Agamemnon," "Umbrellas Of Cherbourg," and "Alice in Concert." Survived by a sister.

EDWARD BARTON, 43, Ohio-born dancer, choreographer, actor died Dec. 20, 1985 in New York of cancer. He appeared on Bdwy in "Jesus Christ Superstar" and "Sergeant Pepper's Lonely Hearts Club Band On The Road." Survived by his mother, four brothers and two sisters.

CHARITA BAUER, 62, stage, radio, film, and television actress, died Feb. 28, 1985 at her home in New York City, following a long illness. She appeared on Bdwy in "Thunder On The Left," "The Women," "Life Of Riley," and "Good Morning Corporal." She joined the radio series of "Guiding Light" in the late 1940s and played the role of Bert Bauer, moving from radio to television, for more than 35 years. In 1983, the Academy of Television Arts and Sciences honored her with its Lifetime Achievement Award. Survived by her father, son, and grandson.

ANNE BAXTER, 62, Indiana-born stage, film, and television actress, died Dec. 12, 1985 after suffering a stroke Dec. 4 in New York City. She made her Bdwy debut at 13 in "Seen But Not Heard," followed by "There's Always a Breeze," "Mme. Capet," "Square Root of Wonderful," "Applause," and "Noel Coward in Two Keys." She was an Academy Award winner for "The Razor's Edge," and nominee for "All About Eve." Survived by three daughters.

JULIAN BECK, 60, avant-garde actor-director, died Sept. 14, 1985 in his native New York of cancer. He and his wife, Judith Malina, co-founded the Living Theatre in 1947. Survived by his wife, a son and a daughter.

MARIE BELL, 84, French stage and screen actress, died Aug. 15, 1985 in Neuilly, France. One of the great French tragediennes, she made her Bdwy debut in 1963 with her own company in "Phedre" and "Bernice." No reported survivors.

ELISABETH BERGNER, 85, Vienna-born actress who was an international stage and screen star, died on May 12, 1986 at her home in London, after a long illness. Bdwy debut 1933 in "Escape Me Never," followed by "The Two Mrs. Carrolls," for which she won the Delia Austrian Medal given by the Drama League of New York, "The Overtons," "The Duchess Of Malfi," and "The Cup of Trembling." Her husband, Dr. Paul Czinner, died several years ago. They had no children and there are no survivors.

HERSCHEL BERNARDI, 62, New York-born stage, film, and television actor, died May 9, 1986 in Los Angeles of a heart attack. He began his career at age 3 and later played Tevye in "Fiddler On The Roof" for 702 Bdwy performances. He was also on Bdwy in "The World of Sholom Aleichem," "Bajour," "Zorba," "The Goodbye People," and 1981 revival of "Fiddler." Survived by his wife, Terry, their infant son, Michael, a son, Adam, and two daughters, Beryl and Robin, from an earlier marriage, and two brothers, Jack and Sam.

ALLEN BORETZ, 85, New York City-born playwright and screenwriter, died May 21, 1986 of cancer in Branford, Conn. He began his career as a songwriter and later wrote Bdwy revues for Billy Rose. In 1937 he collaborated with John Murray to write "Room Service." Survived by his wife, two sons, a daughter, two stepsons and a sister.

NELLIE BREEN, 88, Bdwy dancer-comedienne of the 20's and 30's, died April 26, 1986 in San Jose, CA. Bdwy debut in 1919 at New York Hippodrome, followed by George White's "Scandals of 1921," "The Perfect Fool," "The Passing Show of 1922," "Take A Chance," "Mercenary Mary," "Golden Dawn," and "The Desert Song." In 1922 she performed the first tap dance on radio. Survived by a brother.

KENNETH BRYAN, 32, New Jersey-born stage and television actor, died March 3, 1986 in Walnut Creek, CA., after a long illness. Bdwy debut 1981 in "Joseph and the Amazing Technicolor Dreamcoat," followed by "The Human Comedy." Survived by his mother and two brothers.

YUL BRYNNER, 65, Japan-born stage and film actor, died Oct. 10, 1985 in New York, after a long bout with cancer. Bdwy debut 1946 in "Lute Song," followed by "The King and I" (1951/1977/1984), and "Home Sweet Homer." He became identified with his role in "King and I," and gave 4,635 performances as The King over the course of 30 years, winning an Oscar for his role in the 1956 film version. Survived by his wife, Kathy, a son, Rock, and three daughters, Victoria, Mia, and Melody.

JOHN BUBBLES, 84, Kentucky-born entertainer who invented rhythm tap dancing and portrayed the original Sportin' Life in "Porgy and Bess," died May 18, 1986 at his home in Baldwin Hills, CA. He began performing at age 7, and appeared in minstrels, carnivals, circuses, nightclubs, and Bdwy in "Ziegfeld Follies," "Carmen Jones," "George White's Varieties," "Show Time," "Laugh Time," "Curtain Time," "At Home at the Palace," and "Black Broadway." One of his last appearances was in 1979 at the Newport Jazz Festival in New York. No reported survivors.

HAL BUCKLEY, 49, Connecticut-born stage, screen, and television performer, died March 17, 1986 in Los Angeles, CA. He appeared Off-Bdwy in "The Cradle Will Rock," "The Imaginary Invalid," "Ernest In Love," and "Upstairs At The Downstairs," and on Bdwy in "Love In E-Flat." He is survived by his parents and two brothers.

GEORGIA BURKE, 107, Georgia-born character actress, died November 28, 1985 in New York City. Made Bdwy debut in Lew Leslie's "Blackbirds," followed by "Five Star Final," "Savage Rhythm," "In Abraham's Bosom," "Old Man Satan," "They Shall Not Die," "Mamba's Daughters," "Cabin in the Sky," "No Time for Comedy," "Sun Fields," "Anna Lucasta," "The Wisteria Trees," "The Grass Harp," "Porgy and Bess" (revival), "Bohikee Creek" (Off-Bdwy), and "Decision," for which she won the Donaldson Award in 1944. There are no known survivors.

PESACH BURSTEIN, 89, Polish-born international star of the Yiddish stage, died April 6, 1986 in New York City, after suffering a heart attack the previous Monday. He was known in the early years of his career as Paul Burstein. He made his Bdwy debut in 1923 in "The Jolly Tailors," and returned to Bdwy in 1968 with his wife, actress Lillian Lux, and his son, actor Mike Burstein, in "The Megilla of Itzik Manger," and appeared Off-Bdwy in 1982 in "My Lifetime in the Theatre." He is survived by his wife and two sons.

ADOLPH CAESAR, 52, New York City-born actor, died March 6, 1986 in Los Angeles after collapsing from an apparent heart attack on the set of the film "Tough Guys." Bdwy appearances include "The River Niger" and "A Soldier's Play," for which he won an Obie and the New York Drama Desk Award. He received an Oscar nomination and an Image Award for his role in the film "A Soldier's Story." Survived by his wife and three children.

JAMES CAGNEY, 86, New York City-born dancer, and quintessential tough guy who became one of Hollywood's greatest actors and stars, died March 30, 1986 at his Duchess County farm in Stanfordville, NY after a long series of illnesses. He made his Bdwy debut in 1920 in "Pitter Patter," where he met and wed chorus girl Frances Willard (Willie) Vernon. In 1921 he and his wife appeared in "Dot's My Boy" and Les Fields' "Ritz Girls," followed by "Outside Looking In," "Broadway," "Women Go On Forever," "The Grand Street Follies of 1928," "The Grand Street Follies of 1929," "Maggie the Magnificent," and "Penny Arcade," in which he was paired for the first time with Joan Blondell. He went on to appear in 64 films, and to win an Oscar for his portrayal of George M. Cohan in "Yankee Doodle Dandy." The Cagney's adopted son, Jimmy Jr., died last year. He is survived by his wife, brother, sister, and adopted daughter.

RAFAEL CAMPOS, 49, Dominican Republic-born stage, film, and television actor, died July 9, 1985 of stomach cancer in Woodland Hills, CA. He made his Bdwy debut in "Infidel Caesar," and was discovered for films while appearing in "Heavenly Express" at ELT. Married to and divorced from Dinah Washington and model Sally Boyd, he is survived by two daughters by Boyd, and by his nine brothers and sisters.

PHILIP NORMAN CLARKE, 81, British-born stage, radio, and television actor, died Sept. 27, 1985 at his home in Dothan, Ala. His Bdwy appearances include "Native Son" and "On Whitman Avenue." Survived by his wife, and three daughters.

MAURICE COPELAND, 74, Arkansas-born stage and film actor, died Oct. 3, 1985 in New Rochelle, NY, after a long illness. Bdwy debut 1974 in "The Freedom of the City," followed by "First Monday In October," "Morning's at 7," "Travesties," "The Royal Family," and Off-Bdwy in "Henry V," "Blood Relations," and "Richard III." He is survived by his wife, a son and two daughters.

BRODERICK CRAWFORD, 74, Academy Award-winning actor for "All The Kings Men" and star of the popular TV series "Highway Patrol," died April 26, 1986 in Rancho Mirage, CA. He had suffered a series of strokes since Dec. 31, 1984. Bdwy debut in 1935 in "Point Valaine," followed by "Punches and Judy," "Sweet Mystery of Life," and as Lennie in "Of Mice And Men." He is survived by his fourth wife and two sons.

JOEL CROTHERS, 44, stage and television actor, died Nov. 6, 1985 of cancer in Los Angeles. He made his Bdwy debut at 12 in "The Remarkable Mr. Pennypacker," followed by "A Case Of Libel," "Barefoot In The Park," "The Jockey Club Stakes," "The Office Murders," and "Torch Song Trilogy." At the time of his death he was the popular star of the TV series Santa Barbara. He is survived by his parents and a brother.

SARAH CUNNINGHAM, 67, South Carolina-born actress, died March 24, 1986 from an asthmatic attack in the lobby of the Dorothy Chandler Pavilion in Los Angeles, Ca., while attending the Academy Awards. She made her Bdwy debut in 1948 in "The Respectful Prostitute," followed by "A Happy Journey," "Blood Wedding," "The Young and Fair," "Fair Game," "The Visit," "Toys in the Attic," "The Zulu and the Zayda," "Mme. Colombe," and "My Sweet Charlie," and OB in "Portrait of the Artist . . .," "Barroom Monks," "Christy," "Oh, Pioneers," and "Present Tense." She and her husband, actor John Randolph, were founders of the Ensemble Theater. She is survived by her husband, a son and daughter.

HOWARD DA SILVA, 76, Ohio-born actor, director, producer, and author, died of lymphoma Feb. 16, 1986 at his home in Ossining, NY. Bdwy debut with Civic Rep Co., followed by "Ten Million Ghosts," "Golden Boy," "The Cradle Will Rock," "Casey Jones," "Abe Lincoln in Illinois," "Summer Night," "Two on an Island," "Oklahoma !," "Shootin' Star," "Burning Bright," "The Unknown Soldier and His Wife," "Compulsion," "Fiorello," "Romulus," "In the Counting House," "Dear Me the Sky Is Falling," "Hamlet" (CP), "1776," and OB "The World of Sholom Aleichem," "The Adding Machine," "Diary of A Scoundrel," and "Volpone." He directed shows on Bdwy including "Purlie Victorious," and with Felix Leon he co-wrote "The Zulu and the Zayda." He made over 40 films, and won an Emmy Award in 1978 for his performance in the television film "Verna: U.S.O. Girl." He is survived by his wife, two sons, and three daughters.

RICK DAVIS, 71, stage, film, and television actor, died Aug. 28, 1985 of heart failure in Los Angeles. He made his Bdwy debut in 1924 in "Dracula." At the time of his death he had been administrative director for Theatre Rapport, Los Angeles, for 15 years. No reported survivors.

OLIVE DEERING, 67, New York-born stage, screen, and television actress, died March 22, 1986 in New York of cancer. Bdwy debut 1932 in "Girls in Uniform," followed by Moss Hart's "Winged Victory," "Growing Pains," "Searching the Sun," "Daughters of Atreus," "Richard II," "Medicine Show," "They Walk Alone," "Nathan the Wise," "Skydrift," "Front Page," "Dark Legend," "The Devil's Advocate," "Marathon '33," "Vieux Carre," "Counselor-at-Law," OB in "Ceremony of Innocence," "Two by Tennessee," "Winter Chicken," and "Two Character Play." She is survived by a brother, actor Alfred Ryder.

DORIS DUDLEY, 68, eccentric Bdwy actress known for the night in the '30's when she crashed a plane in Boston and still made it to the theater on time, died Aug. 14, 1985 in Jacobia, TX (population: 21). Daughter of Bide Dudley, drama critic for the New York Evening World and WOR Radio, she made her Bdwy debut in 1935 in S. N. Berman's "End of Summer." Other Bdwy appearances include "The Smiling Visitor," "Battle of Angels," and "My Dear Children" with John Barrymore. She was the mother of MGM child star Jackie "Butch" Jenkins.

ETHEL DWYER MCCADY, 86, stage and silent film actress, died Sept. 2, 1985 in Pittsburg, PA. She made her Bdwy debut in "Fiddlers Three," followed by "Lombardi Limited," "Abie's Irish Rose," and as Jane in the 1921 Bdwy production of "Tarzan." Surviving are two children, six grandchildren, and a great-grandson.

DAVID ELLIN, 61, Montreal-born actor, died May 27, 1986 in New York City of a heart attack. Bdwy debut 1946 in "Swan Song," followed by "West Side Story," "Education of Hyman Kaplan," "Light Lively and Yiddish," OB in "Trees Die Standing," "Mirele Efros," "End of All Things Natural," "Yoshe Kalb," "Fiddler on the Roof" (JB), "Rebecca the Rabbi's Daughter," "Wish Me Mazel-Tov," "Roumanian Wedding," "The Showgirl," and "The Jewish Gypsy." Survived by his wife and son.

IDA LUBLENSKI EHRLICH, 99, Russia-born playwright, producer, and author, died Feb. 22, 1986 in Carmel, NY. Her first produced play was "Helena's Boys," on Bdwy in 1924, followed by "Dr. Johnson," "The Magic Carpet," and "Alice in Fableland." In 1940 she founded Everyman's Theatre, Off-Bdwy. She is survived by three children.

WILLIAM ELLIOTT, 41, composer, arranger, and conductor, died of cancer on Oct. 22, 1985 in his Los Angeles home. He was resident musical director of La Mama Experimental Theatre Club from 1971 to 1978; won an Obie Award in 1974 for his score for "C.O.R.F.A.X.;" composed music for NY Shakespeare Festival productions of "Othello," "Henry V," "Mother Courage" and "Summer Evening," conducted and adapted "Non Pasquale," "Pirates of Penzance," and "La Boheme;" supplied vocal arrangements for "Ain't Misbehavin'." He is survived by his mother.

LEIF ERICKSON, 74, California-born stage, film, and television actor, died Jan. 29, 1986 of cancer in Pensacola, Fla. He made his debut in Max Reinhardt's production of "A Midsummer Night's Dream," and played trombone for Olson & Johnson's "Hellzapoppin'." His more than 75 films include "Tea and Sympathy," in which he recreated his Bdwy role. He is survived by his wife and daughter.

CHESTER ERSKINE, 80, New York-born stage and screen producer and director, died April 7, 1986 in Beverly Hills, CA. His first success came in 1929, when he adapted, produced and directed "Harlem," followed by "Subway Express" and, in 1930, "The Last Mile" starring Spencer Tracy in the pivotal theatre performance that sent him to Hollywood. He is survived by his wife and two sisters.

PEGGY FEURY, 61, New Jersey-born actress and drama coach, died Nov. 20, 1985 in Los Angeles, CA in an automobile accident. Her Bdwy credits include "Enter Laughing," "Turn of the Screw," "Peer Gynt," "Tonight in Samarkand," "Grass Harp," "The Three Sisters," and Franco Zeffirelli's production of "The Lady of the Camellias." She was a charter member of the Actor's Studio in New York. She is survived by her husband, actor William Taylor, and two daughters.

NEIL FLANAGAN, 52, Illinois-born stage and television actor, died June 4, 1985, in North Hollywood, Ca., following a long illness. He made his debut Off-Bdwy in "Fortune and Men's Eyes," followed by "Haunted Host," "Madness of Lady Bright" (for which he received an Obie Award), "Dirtiest Show in Town," "The Play's the Thing," "As You Like It," "Hedda Gabler," "Design for Living," "him," "Partnership," "Down by the River," "Lisping Judas," "Elephant in the House," "Exiles," and Bdwy in "Sheep on the Runway," "Secret Affairs of Mildred Wild," "Knock Knock," and "Beethoven's Tenth." He won his second Obie in 1976 for his 10-year contributions to Off-Off Bdwy. He is survived by his wife, mother, and brother.

| Martin Gabel | Don Gantry | Virginia Gilmore | Ruth Gordon | Grayson Hall | Richard Haydn |

ALLEN FLETCHER, 63, director, died Aug. 28, 1985 in Denver, Col., following a long battle with a rare blood disease. After graduating from Stanford U., he became artistic director of the Seattle Repertory Theatre, and in 1967 joined ACT in San Francisco, where he staged 35 plays. He also staged shows at Oregon Shakespeare Festival, San Diego's Old Globe, New York City and San Francisco opera companies, American Shakespeare Festival in Conn., and Pacific Conservatory of Performing Arts in Solvang, Ca. He was made head of the National Theatre Conservatory at the Denver Center Theatre Co. last year. Surviving are his wife, actress Anne Lawder, a son and a daughter.

JACK FORD, 81, Massachusetts-born song and dance man of the 20's and 30's, died March 2, 1986 of cancer in Largo, Fla. Bdwy debut in "Kosher Kitty Kelly," followed by "Side Kicks," and the "James C. Morton Revue" in 1929. In '32 he teamed with his brother Ben as the Ford Bros., playing the vaudeville circuits, and in '36 the pair founded the Ford Theatrical Agency in Boston, Mass. Surviving are his wife, two brothers and a sister.

PHIL FOSTER, 72, Brooklyn-born stand-up comedian who later became a stage and television actor, died July 8, 1985 in Rancho Mirage, Ca., after having a heart attack. He appeared OB in 1965 in "The Day the Whores Came Out to Play," and in National tour of "The Odd Couple." He is best known for his role as Laverne's father on the TV series "Laverne and Shirley." He is survived by two sons.

MARTIN GABEL, 73, Philadelphia-born stage, film, and radio actor and producer, died May 22, 1986 of a heart attack in New York. Bdwy debut in '32 in "Man Bites Dog," followed by "The Sky's the Limit," "Dead End," "Ten Million Ghosts," "Julius Caesar," "Danton's Death," "Medicine Show," "King Lear," "The Little Blue Light," "Reclining Figure," "Will Success Spoil Rock Hunter?," "The Rivalry," "Children from Their Games," "Baker Street," "Sheep on the Runway," and "Big Fish, Little Fish," for which he won a 1961 Tony Award. He co-produced such Bdwy shows as "Twentieth Century" (1951), "Tiger at the Gates," "Cafe Crown," "The Survivors," "Men of Distinction," "Reclining Figure," "The Hidden River," "Once More with Feeling," "Sweet Love Remember'd," and "Mrs. Dally." Survived by his wife, actress and broadcaster Arlene Francis, and a son.

DONALD GANTRY, 52, Philadelphia-born stage, film, and TV actor, died Nov. 16, 1985 in New York of cancer. Bdwy debut 1961 in "One More River," followed by "Ah, Wilderness," "The Queen and the Rebels," "Moon for the Misbegotten," "Chapter Two," OB in "The Iceman Cometh," "Children of Darkness," "Here Come the Clowns," "Seven at Dawn," "Long Day's Journey into Night," "The Enclave," and "Bags." He had continuing roles on various TV soap operas, most recently, "All My Children." He is survived by his wife and daughter.

JAMES GELB, 79, production stage manager for the Group Theatre and many other Bdwy and OB productions, died Oct. 17, 1985 in New York City. A member of the Civic Repertory Co. in the early years of his career, he later was PSM for such producers as Robert Whitehead, Kermit Bloomgarten, and Arthur Laurents. Survived by his wife, and three sisters.

JEAN GENET, 75, Paris-born playwright, novelist, poet and one of the revolutionary artists of the 20th century, died April 15, 1986 in the Paris hotel where he lived. His plays include "Deathwatch," "The Maids," "The Balcony," "The Blacks," and "The Screens." There are no survivors.

BETTY GILLETT, 58, Philadelphia-born actress, died Aug. 13, 1985 of lymphoma in Lakeland, Fla. Bdwy appearances include "South Pacific," "Pal Joey," "Wonderful Town," and "Miss Liberty." Survived by two sisters.

SAM GILMAN, 70, Massachusetts-born actor, died Dec. 3, 1985 at his N. Hollywood, Ca. home after a long bout with cancer. Bdwy appearances include "How Long 'Til Summer," and on tour with Marlon Brando in "Arms and the Man." Survived by his wife and son.

VIRGINIA GILMORE, 66, California-born stage and film actress, died March 28, 1986 of complications from emphysema in Santa Barbara, Ca. Bdwy debut in 1943 in "Those Endearing Young Charms," followed by "The World's Full of Girls," and "Dear Ruth." She acted in more than 40 films. She was married to actor Yul Brynner from 1944 to 1960, and is survived by their son, Rock Brynner.

CHARLES GNYS, 51, former Bdwy company manager and managing director of the Playwrights Unit in the '60's and '70's, died of cancer on March 13, 1986 at his home in New York City. For the last 10 years he served as President of Curtis Brown Management. He is survived by his parents, a brother and a sister.

RUTH GORDON, 88, Massachusetts-born stage, film, TV actress, playwright, screenwriter, and novelist, died Aug. 28, 1985 of a stroke in her sleep at her summer home in Edgartown, Mass. Bdwy debut (1915) as one of the Lost Boys in "Peter Pan" with Maude Adams, followed by "Seventeen," "Picadilly Jim," "Clarence," "Tweedles," "Holding Helen," "Saturday's Children," "Serena Blandish," "Hotel Universe," "The Violet," "The Wiser They Are," "A Church Mouse," "Here Today" (original and revival), "They Shall Not Die," "A Sleeping Clergyman," "Ethan Frome," "The Country Wife," "A Doll's House," "The Strings, My Lord, Are False," "The Three Sisters," "The Smile of the World," "The Matchmaker," "The Good Soup," and "My Mother, My Father and Me." She wrote "Years Ago," and wrote and starred in "Over Twenty-One," "The Leading Lady," and "A Very Rich Woman." In 1942 she married writer-director Garson Kanin, and began collaborating with her husband on some of the most successful screenplays of the '40's. With many films to her credit, she won an Oscar in 1968 for her performance in "Rosemary's Baby." She is most identified with her role in the 1971 black comedy "Harold and Maude." In 1979 she won an Emmy for her performance on TV's "Taxi." She is survived by her husband, and her son Jones Harris Kanin.

TOM GREENWAY, 75, stage and film actor, died Feb. 8, 1985 of a heart attack at his home in Los Angeles, Ca. He appeared on Bdwy in "American Holiday," "Murder in the Cathedral," and "It Can't Happen Here" (all in 1936), and "The Sun and I" (1937). Survived by his wife, and daughter.

JERRY GRIMES, 39, dancer and choreographer, died March 31, 1985 of spinal meningitis in Los Angeles, Ca. He made his Bdwy debut in "I'm Solomon," and was Joe Layton's assistant director-associate choreographer for "2000 Years of Rock 'n' Roll." He staged shows for many well known performers, and danced in films and on television. He is survived by his mother, father, three sisters, and four brothers.

GRAYSON HALL, 58, Philadelphia-born stage, film, and television actress, died Aug. 7, 1985 of cancer in New York. Debut 1953 OB in "Man and Superman," followed by "La Ronde," "Six Characters in Search of an Author," "The Balcony," "Buskers," "The Love Nest," "Shout from the Rooftops," "The Last Analysis," "Friends and Relatives," "The Screens," "Secrets of the Citizens Correction Committee," "The Sea," "What Every Woman Knows," "Jack Gelber's New Play," "Happy End," "Madwoman of Chaillot," and on Bdwy in "Subways Are for Sleeping," "Those That Play the Clowns," "Leaf People," "Happy End," and "Suicide." Oscar nominated in 1964 for "Night of the Iguana," she is best remembered for her role of Dr. Julia Hoffman on the TV series "Dark Shadows." She is survived by her husband, writer Sam Hall, and a son.

JAMES HANLEY, 84, Dublin-born playwright, lyricist, and novelist, died Nov. 11, 1985 in London. He wrote book and lyrics for "No Foolin'" (1926), "Honeymoon Lane" (1926), "Sidewalks of New York" (1927), and lyrics for "Keep It Clean" (1927). His plays include "Say Nothing" (1965), and "The Inner Journey" (1969). There are no reported survivors.

PAUL HARRIS, 67, stage, film and television actor and singer, died Aug. 25 1985 of cancer in Los Angeles, Ca. He appeared on Bdwy in "Show Boat" and "Free and Easy." Survived by his wife and two daughters.

PATRICK HINES, 55, Texas-born stage, film, and television actor and director died Aug. 12, 1985 of a heart attack in his New York City apartment. He made his OB debut in "Duchess of Malfi," followed by "Lysistrata," "Peer Gynt," "Henry IV," "Richard III," "Hot Grog," BAM'S "A Winter's Tale," "Johnny on a Spot," "Barbarians," and "The Wedding." He appeared on Bdwy in "The Great God Brown," "Passage to India," "The Devils," "Cyrano," "The Iceman Cometh," "A Texas Trilogy," "Caesear and Cleopatra," "1776," and "Amadeus." He also appeared in the film versions of the latter two shows. His directing credits include plays at the American Shakespeare Festival Theatre in Stratford. He is survived by his mother and stepmother.

RICHARD HAYDN, 80, British stage and film actor, died April 25, 1985 at his home in Pacific Palisades, Ca. He made his Bdwy debut in Noel Coward's "Set To Music" (1939), followed by "Two for the Show" (1940). He appeared in over 30 films, including "Charley's Aunt" and "The Sound of Music." There are no reported survivors.

HILDA HAYNES, 72, New York City-born actress and longtime member of the Council of AEA, died March 4, 1986 in New York City. She made her Bdwy debut 1948 in "A Streetcar Named Desire," followed by "Anna Lucasta," "King of Hearts," "Wisteria Trees," "Lost in the Stars," "The Long Dream," "Irregular Verb to Love," "Blues for Mr. Charlie," "Golden Boy," "Great White Hope," "Purlie Victorious," and OB in "Monday Heroes," "Trouble in Mind," "Take A Giant Step," and "Wedding Band." Survived by a brother.

WILLIAM HILLPOT, 79, New Jersey-born singer on radio, in films, and on Bdwy in the 30's and 40's, died Feb. 25, 1985 of pneumonia in New York City. He starred on Bdwy in "The Ziegfeld Follies," as well as in many early movies. Survived by his wife and a sister.

LOIS HOLMES, 86, Ohio-born stage and television actress, died March 12, 1986 in New York after a long illness. Her Bdwy appearances include "The White Steed," "I Remember Mama," "The Cherry Orchard," "The Autumn Garden," "I've Got Sixpence," "The Lark," "Easter," "Winesburg, Ohio," "Journey With Strangers," "Enemy of the People," "Hedda Gabler," OB in "Curate's Play," "Hooray!! It's a Glorious Day . . . And All That," "The Penny Wars." "Becoming Madness, (1984)." She was the widow of actor Wendell Holmes. There are no reported survivors.

CHRISTOPHER ISHERWOOD, 81, England-born playwright, novelist, and writer of short stories, died Jan. 4, 1986 of cancer in Los Angeles, Ca. He wrote 25 books, including his most popular work, "The Berlin Stories" (expanded from the 1939 novel "Goodbye To Berlin"), which inspired the 1952 John Van Druten play "I Am a Camera," and the 1966 musical "Cabaret." During the '30's he collaborated with W. H. Auden on the plays "Dog Beneath the Skin," "The Ascent of F6," and "On The Frontier." In 1967 he collaborated with Don Bachardy on the Bdwy play "A Meeting by the River." He left Britain for the US in '39 and became a naturalized US citizen in '46. He is survived by his long-time companion, artist Don Bachardy. There are no other reported survivors.

DAVID KANTER, 76, Philadelphia-born producer, production manager, and director, died Dec. 8, 1985 in Philadelphia, Pa. Bdwy directorial credits include "The Tenth Man," "Billy Budd," "Take A Giant Step," "Once More With Feeling," and "Will Success Spoil Rock Hunter?" He served as production manager for 22 Bdwy shows, including "Call Me Mister," "The Boy Friend," "Fanny," "Lend An Ear," "Alive and Kicking," and "Milk and Honey." He produced "The Medium," "The Telephone," and "The Consul." He is survived by two sons and a daughter.

ALEXA KENIN, 23, New York City-born stage, film, and television actress, died Sept. 10, 1985 at her home in New York City from causes unknown. Debut 1977 OB in "Landscape of the Body," followed by "Elusive Angel," and "Life Under Water." She is survived by her parents and two step-sisters.

GEORGE KONDOLF, 85, stage, radio, and television producer and director, died Dec. 25, 1985 of a stroke at his home in Locust, NY. He was director of the Federal Theatre Project in New York from '37 to '39, producing plays including "One Third of a Nation," "Prologue to Glory," "Big Blow," and "The Swing Mikado." On Bdwy he produced "Hangman's Whip," "The Wind and the Rain," "Hell Freezes Over," "A Room in Red and White," "Morning Star," "The Fifth Season," and "The 49th Cousin." He is survived by his wife, a son and a daughter.

JOHN (RED) KULLERS, early 70's, stage and film actor, died in July, 1985 in Connecticut of unknown causes. His Bdwy credits include "Devils Galore," "Mister Roberts," and "The Fifth Season." He is survived by a brother.

HAROLD LANG, 64, California-born stage actor and dancer who achieved his greatest success in the title role of "Pal Joey" (1952), died July 26, 1985 in Chico, Ca. after a long illness. He appeared with Ballet Russe de Monte Carlo and Ballet Theatre before making his Bdwy bow in 1945 in "Mr. Strauss Goes to Boston," followed by "Three To Make Ready," "Look, Ma, I'm Dancin'," "Kiss Me, Kate," "Make A Wish," "Pal Joey," "The Time Of Your Life," "Shangri-La," "Ziegfeld Follies" (1957), "I Can Get It For You Wholesale," and OB in "On the Town," "Once Upon a Mattress," and "The Decline and Fall of the Entire World As Seen Through the Eyes of Cole Porter, Revisited." Surviving is a brother.

PHILIP J. LANG, 74, New York City-born musician, composer and orchestrator, died Feb. 22, 1986 in Branford, Ct. He was the orchestrator of more than 50 Bdwy musicals, including "42nd Street," "My Fair Lady," "Camelot," "Annie Get Your Gun," "Applause," "Hello, Dolly!," and "Carnival." He wrote scores for the Boston Pops, Radio City Music Hall, films, television and ballet, and was an orchestrator for the Metropolitan Opera. He is survived by his wife, two sons, and a daughter.

PAUL LATCHAW, 38, stage and film actor, died Oct. 31, 1985 in New York after a long illness. A graduate of Princeton, he made his debut OB in 1972 in "Yoshe Kalb," followed by "Out of this World," and on Bdwy in "42nd Street." He is survived by his sister.

EMMET LAVERY, 83, New York-born playwright and screenwriter, died Jan. 1, 1986 after suffering apparent cardiac arrest in Los Angeles, Ca. His plays include "The First Legion," "The Magnificent Yankee," "The Gentleman From Athens," and "Dawn's Early Light." No reported survivors.

CARL LEE, 52, stage, film, and television actor, died April 17, 1986 in New York City. Debut 1959 in the Living Theater's production of "The Connection," followed by "Deep are the Roots," "Decision," "The Respectful Prostitute," "Wedding in Japan," "Othello," "God Bless," "The Odd Couple," "No Time For Sergeants," "The Marrying Maiden," "Ceremonies in Dark Old Men," and "Dunbar." Survived by his mother.

CHARLES LE MAIRE, 88, costume designer for stage and films, died June 8, 1985 in Palm Springs, Ca. He first became a success on Bdwy in 1921, designing costumes for musicals of Florenz Ziegfeld and Oscar Hammerstein 2nd, and went on to films, winning three Oscars. He is survived by two step-children.

MARK LINTON, 28, Massachusetts-born actor, and musician, died in New York (date not reported) of heart failure, having entered a hospital with pneumonia. His New York appearances include "Cloud 9," "Gemini," "Pippin," "El Grande de Coca-Cola," "My Child," and "The Great American Backstage Musical." He is survived by his parents, and two sisters.

JON LORMER, 80, stage, film and television actor, died of cancer March 19, 1986 in Burbank, Ca. One-time director at the American Theater Wing in New York, he appeared on Bdwy in "Summer and Smoke," "The Big Knife," "Treasure Island," and "American Holiday." No reported survivors.

DON MACLAUGHLIN, 79, stage and television actor, died May 28, 1986 in Goshen, Conn. He appeared on Bdwy in "The Fifth Column," "Virginia Reel," and "The Happy Journey to Trenton and Camden." He portrayed attorney Chris Hughes in the TV soap opera "As the World Turns" for 30 years. He is survived by a daughter.

GORDON MacRAE, 64, New Jersey-born stage, film, and television star, died Jan. 24, 1986 at Bryan Memorial Hospital in Lincoln, Neb., where he had been undergoing treatment for cancer of the mouth and jaw as well as pneumonia. He made his Bdwy debut as a child actor in 1927 in "John," followed by "Our Betters" (1928), "Exceeding Small" (1928), "The Trojan Horse" (1940), "Three to Make Ready" (1946), and "I Do, I Do" (1967). He starred in a number of films, and is best remembered for his performances as Curly in "Oklahoma," and Billy Bigelow in "Carousel." He is survived by his wife, Elizabeth, their daughter, and two sons, actor-musicians Garr and Bruce, and two daughters, actresses Meredith and Heather, from his first marriage to actress Sheila MacRae.

PHILIP MAGDALANY, 49, Brooklyn-born playwright, died July 22, 1985 in New York City after a long illness. His plays "Criss-Crossing" and "Watercolor" were shown as a double bill on Bdwy in 1970. OB productions include "Boo Hoo" (1976), and "Rich Girls" (1984). His play "Section Nine" was staged in London, and under the nom de plume Phil Phillips he wrote the book for the Bdwy musical "Wild and Wonderful" (1971). There are no reported survivors.

PAUL MANN, 77, Toronto-born actor and director, died of a stroke Sept. 24, 1985 in Bronxville, NY. Bdwy debut 1935 in "Bitter Oleander." He also acted with the Neighborhood Playhouse, the Group Theatre, and the Playwrights Company in various productions. He is survived by his wife, the actress Lenore Harris, a son and a brother.

MARGO, 68, Mexico City-born stage and film actress, died July 17, 1985 at her home in Pacific Palisades, Ca. of a brain tumor. Bdwy debut 1934 in "Sunday Nights at Nine," followed by "Winterset," "The Masque of Kings," "Faust," "The World We Make," "Tanyard Street," "A Bell for Adano," and "ANTA Album." She is best remembered for her recreation of her stage role in the 1936 film adaption of "Winterset," and for her role in the 1937 "Lost Horizon." She survived by her husband, actor Eddie Albert, a daughter, and a son, actor Edward Albert.

MARION MARTIN, 76, stage and film actress, died of natural causes on August 13, 1985 in Santa Monica, Ca. She made her Bdwy debut in "Lombardi, Ltd." in 1927, followed by "Shady Lady" (1933), "Ziegfeld Follies of 1933," "George White's Scandals," and "New Faces of 1936." She was brought to Hollywood in 1938 by Universal and made numerous films. Surviving are her husband and a brother.

JOE MASIELL, 45, Bronx-born stage and film actor-singer, died Sept. 13, 1985 in New York City of bone cancer. He made his debut OB in 1964 in "Cindy," followed by "Jacques Brel is Alive and Well, and Living in Paris," "Sensations," "Leaves of Grass," "How to Get Rid of It," "A Matter of Time," "Tickles by Tucholsky," "Not at the Palace," and "Non Pasquale." Bdwy debut in 1969 in "Dear World," followed by "Different Times," "Got Tu Go Disco," and "Jacques Brel" (revival). He is best remembered for his performance in Jacques Brel which he repeated in the film. He is survived by his mother and two sisters.

ROBERT MEADOWS, 29, stage, film, and television actor-dancer, died May 17, 1986 in New York City after a brief illness. He made his Bdwy debut in 1983 in "On Your Toes." He was in the national companies of "Chicago," "Oklahoma," and "Cats," and danced with American Ballet Theatre II. Survived by his parents, a brother and a sister.

UNA MERKEL, 82, Kentucky-born stage, film, and television actress, died Jan. 2, 1986 at her home in Los Angeles, Ca. She made her Bdwy debut in 1922 in "Montmarte," followed by "Two by Two," "The Poor Nut," "Pigs," "The Gossipy Sex," "Two Girls Wanted," "Coquette," "Salt Water," "Three's a Family," "The Remarkable Mr. Pennypacker," "The Ponder Heart," and "Take Me Along." She won a Tony Award for her performance in "The Ponder Heart" on Bdwy. She appeared in more than 100 films, including such memorable performances as the wise-cracking chorus girl in "42nd Street," and the mother in "Summer and Smoke," which earned her an Oscar nomination. No immediate survivors reported.

BETH MERRILL, 93, Wisconsin-born actress, died Feb. 22, 1986 at a nursing home in Tenafly, NJ. She made her Bdwy debut in 1922 in "Fashions for Men," followed by "White Desert," "Ladies of the Evening," "Lily Sue," "Hidden," "Lazybones," "Christmas Eve," "The Lady Who Came to Stay," "Autumn Hill," "Uncle Harry," and "All My Sons." She retired in 1947. There are no immediate survivors.

RAY MILLAND, 81, Wales-born stage, film, and television actor, died March 10, 1986 in Torrance, Ca. of cancer. He made his Bdwy debut in 1966 in "Hostile Witness," his only Bdwy appearance. He appeared in 170 films, including an Oscar winning performance in "The Lost Weekend." Survived by his wife, and a daughter.

NORMA MILLAY ELLIS, 92, Maine-born actress, died May 14, 1986 at Steepletop, the Millay farm in Austerlitz, NY. She made her Bdwy debut in 1924 in "The Saint," followed by "Desire Under the Elms," "Patience," "Love for Love," "Me, Not Herbert," "La Finta Giardiniera," and "Key Largo." She was a sister of the poet Edna St. Vincent Millay. There are no reported survivors.

COURT MILLER, 34, Connecticut-born stage, film, and television actor, died March 7, 1986 in Portland, after a long illness. He made his Bdwy debut in 1982 in "The First," followed by "Torch Song Trilogy," and appeared OB in "Elizabeth and Essex," "Welded," and "Spookhouse." He is survived by his parents, a brother and a sister.

FRANK MILTON, 66, producer and actor, died of cancer July 14, 1985 in his native New York City. He appeared on Bdwy in "All in Fun," "Dream With Music," "On the Town," "If the Shoe Fits," "Happy as Larry," "Out of this World," "Gentlemen Prefer Blondes," "Bells Are Ringing," and "Tonight at 8:30." He won a 1975 Tony as associate producer of "Equus," and subsequently co-produced "Bedroom Farce," "Otherwise Engaged," and "No Man's Land." He is survived by two brothers.

GREGORY MORTON, 74, New York City-born stage, film, and television actor, musician, and writer, died Jan. 28, 1986 of a massive stroke in Los Angeles. He appeared on Bdwy in "Bitter Stream," "The Eternal Road," "Nathan the Wise," "A Flag is Born," "Montserrat," "Now I Lay Me Down to Sleep," "Sherlock Holmes," "Sands of the Negev," and "Who Was That Lady I Saw You With?." He is survived by his wife, two daughters, and a son.

KATE MOSTEL, 67, actress and author, died Jan. 22, 1986 at her apartment in New York City. The widow of actor Zero Mostel, she began her theatrical career as a child actress and dancer, appearing as Katherine Harkin. Bdwy credits include "The Bird Cage," "The Ladies of the Corridor," and "Three Men on a Horse" (revival). She is survived by two sons, Tobias and actor Joshua.

RENA MURPHY, 104, who performed on Bdwy in the 1920's as "The Queen of Vaudeville," died May 28, 1986 at a nursing home in Waterford, Ct. Known as Rena Arnold, she introduced George Burns to Gracie Allen, her roommate, in the 20's.

JAMES F. NOLAN, 69, San Francisco-born stage, film, and television actor, died July 29, 1985 in Woodland Hills, Ca. His Bdwy credits include "Sunday Breakfast," and "Lunatics and Lovers." He also appeared in 40 films. There are no reported survivors.

LLOYD NOLAN, 83, San Francisco-born stage, film, and television actor, died of lung cancer Sept. 27, 1985 at his home in Los Angeles. He made his Bdwy debut in 1929 in "Cape Cod Follies," followed by "The Blue and the Gray," "Sweet Stranger," "Reunion in Vienna," "Americana," "One Sunday Afternoon," "Ragged Army," "Gentlewoman," "One More River," and "The Caine Mutiny Court-Martial," in which he created his best-remembered role as Capt. Queeg. He is survived by his second wife, and a daughter.

LILLI PALMER, 71, Austria-born stage, film, and television actress and writer, died Jan. 27, 1986 at her home in Los Angeles, Ca., apparently of cancer. She made her Bdwy debut in 1949 in "My Name is Aquilon," followed by "Caesar and Cleopatra," "ANTA Album," "Bell, Book and Candle," "Venus Observed," "The Love of Four Colonels," "Song at Twilight," "Shadows of the Evening" and "Come into the Garden, Maud." She is survived by her husband, Argentine-born actor, producer and writer Carlos Thompson, her son (by first husband Rex Harrison), and two sisters.

JERRY PARIS, 60, San Francisco-born stage, television and film actor, director, producer and writer died March 31, 1986 of complications from a brain tumor in Los Angeles, Ca. He made his Bdwy debut in 1952 in "Anna Christie." In 1964 he won an Emmy for his direction of The Dick Van Dyke tv series. He is survived by two sons, a daughter and two sisters.

TODD PATTERSON, 54, Massachusetts-born stage, film, and television actor, died Feb. 1, 1986 in Phoenix, Ariz., after a brief illness. His Bdwy credits include "The Devil's Disciple," "Good As Gold," "Auntie Mame," and "No Time For Sergeants." He is survived by his father, stepmother, a brother and sister.

STEPHEN PENDER, 35, Boston-born stage and television actor-singer, died March 15, 1986 in Los Angeles, Ca. His Bdwy credits include "It's So Nice To Be Civilized," and "Sarava," and OB in "Portrait of Jenny" and "Shakespeare and the Indians." Survived by his mother and three brothers.

ELAINE PERRY, 64, New York City-born actress and daughter of Antoinette Perry, died Jan. 30, 1986 at her home in Buena Vista, Col. She began her acting career as understudy to Ingrid Bergman in "Liliom," and later appeared on Bdwy in "Glamour Preferred," "No for an Answer," "The Trojan Women," and "Pillar to Post." She directed and produced "A Race of Hairy Men!," and also produced "Touchstone," "King of Hearts," "Anastasia," "How's the World Treating You?" and "The Late Christopher Bean." She is survived by a sister.

JOHN PRATT, 74, Canada-born scenic and costume designer, died March 26, 1986 in St. Louis, Mo. His Bdwy credits include "The Swing Mikado," "American Legend," "Look, Ma, I'm Dancin'," and "Fourth Avenue North." He is survived by his wife, choreographer and ethnologist Katherine Dunham, a daughter, a brother and a sister.

TED PRITCHARD, 49, Ohio-born stage and television actor, died Nov. 7, 1985 of a heart attack in Champaign, Ill. He made his Bdwy debut in 1974 in "Music!Music!" (CC) followed by OB 1975 in "Tuscaloosa's Calling Me But I'm Not Going." He is survived by his wife, two sons and a sister.

JIMMY RITZ, 81, Brooklyn-born stage, film, and television performer, died Nov. 17, 1985 of heart failure in Los Angeles. With his brothers Al and Harry, he formed the Ritz Brothers comedy team, appearing on Bdwy in Casino Varieties, and various editions of Earl Carroll's Vanities. Survivors include brother Harry, a sister and a daughter.

BARRY ROBINS, 41, Brooklyn-born stage, film, and television actor, died April 1, 1986 in Los Angeles after a long illness. He made his Bdwy debut in 1964 in "The King and I," in which he played the Crown Prince. He is best known for his portrayal of Paul Muni in the TV musical-bio, "Actor." He is survived by his parents, brother and sister.

BARTLETT ROBINSON, 73, New York City-born stage, radio, film, and television actor, died March 26, 1986 in Fallbrook, Ca. after a long bout with cancer. He appeared on Bdwy in "Naughty Naught '00," "Fireman's Flame," "Merchant of Yonkers," "Dear Ruth," "Another Part of the Forest," "Light Up the Sky," "Point of No Return," "Room Service," "South Pacific," and "The Prescott Proposals." He is survived by his wife, and two sons.

MORRIE RYSKIND, 89, Brooklyn-born playwright, lyricist, screenwriter, and columnist, died Aug. 24, 1985 in Washington, DC, of an apparent stroke. He appeared in Ned Wayburn's "Gambols" in 1929; wrote lyrics for "Buds of 1927," and "Merry-Go-Round;" and was musical director for "The Gang's All Here." His works as a playwright include books for the musicals "The 49'ers," "Garrick Gaieties," "Ned Wayburn's Gambols," "Pardon My English," "Bring on the Girls," "Louisiana Purchase," "Merry-Go-Round," with Howard Dietz, and "The Coconuts," "Animal Crackers," "Strike Up the Band," "Let 'Em Eat Cake," and "Of Thee I Sing," all with George S. Kaufman. He received the Pulitzer Prize in 1933 for his collaboration on "Of Thee I Sing." He is survived by his wife, a daughter, and a son.

GLORIA SAFIER, 63, Ohio-born theatrical and literary agent, died Oct. 9, 1985 in her New York City apartment. She opened her own office on Bdwy in 1948, representing clients ranging from Ethel Merman to Liz Smith. She is survived by her mother and sister.

MARY SARGENT, 90, actress, died July 24, 1985 in Manchester, Mass. She made her Bdwy debut in 1917 in "Lord and Lady Algy," followed by "No More Ladies," "Post Road," "Times Have Changed," "Fresh Fields," "One Good Year," "And Stars Remain," "Sea Legs," "A Case of Youth," "My Fair Ladies," "Sweet Charity" (1942), "Ask My Friend Sandy," "Love on Leave," and "Calico Wedding." A son survives.

JOEL W. SCHENKER, 81, Bdwy producer, actor, real-estate developer, builder and philanthropist, died Aug. 3, 1985 in New York City after a long illness. He produced plays on Bdwy including "Right You Are (If You Think You Are)," "The Shadow of a Gunman," "The Rivalry," "The Long Dream," "Kukla,Burr and Ollie," "A Far Country," "The Captains and the Kings," "Venus at Large," "Seidman and Son," "A Case of Libel," "Darling of the Day," "Indians," "Oedipus Rex," "The Mayor of Zalamea," "The Royal Hunt of the Sun," and "Homecoming," and he co-wrote and acted in "This Our House." He is survived by his wife, and four daughters.

MARTHA SCHLAMME, 60, Austria-born singer-actress, died Oct. 6, 1985 in Jamestown, NY, two months after suffering a stroke on stage. She made her debut OB in 1963 in "The World of Kurt Weill," followed by "A Month of Sundays," "Mata Hari," "Beethoven and Karl," "Aspirations," "God of Vengeance," "Twilight Cantata," "Mrs. Warren's Profession," and on Bdwy in "Fiddler on the Roof," "Threepenny Opera," "Solitaire/Double Solitaire," and "A Kurt Weill Cabaret." There are no reported survivors.

GLEN BYAM SHAW, 81, London-born actor and director, died April 29, 1986 in London. His Bdwy appearances include "And So To Bed," "The Cherry Orchard," "The Lady of the Camellias," "The Winslow Boy," "Queen of Scots," and "The Merchant of Venice." His Bdwy directing credits include "Dear Octopus," "The Winslow Boy," "Henry V," "Antony and Cleopatra," "The Merchant of Venice," "Richard III," "Macbeth," "King Lear," "The Complaisant Lover," "Ross," and "The Dance of Death." His wife, actress Angela Baddeley, whom he married in 1929, died 10 years ago. There are no reported survivors.

LARRY SHUE, 38, New Orleans-born playwright and actor, was killed in an airplane crash on Sept. 23, 1985 at Weyers Cave, Va. He made his debut OB in 1984 in his play "The Foreigner," followed by "The Mystery of Edwin Drood." His plays include "Grandma Duck Is Dead," "Wenceslas Square," "The Nerd," and "The Foreigner," which won two Obies and two NY Drama Critics Circle Awards. He is survived by his parents and a sister.

PHIL SILVERS, 73, Brooklyn-born stage, film, and television actor, died in his sleep Nov. 1, 1985 at his home in Los Angeles, Ca. of natural causes. He made his Bdwy debut in 1939 in "Yokel Boy," followed by "High Button Shoes," "Top Banana," "Do Re Mi," and the 1972 revival of "A Funny Thing Happened on the Way to the Forum," winning a Tony Award for his role. He is best remembered for his portrayal of Master Sgt. Ernie Bilko in the 1950's TV series The Phil Silvers Show. He is survived by his wife and five daughters.

JUSTIN SMITH, 66, New York-born actor, drama coach, and writer-director, died Feb. 27, 1986 in Santa Monica, Ca., after a long illness. He made his Bdwy debut in "The Common Sin" in 1928. His acting students included Keith Carradine and Lesley Ann Warren, among others. Survivors include a sister.

Elisabeth
Bergner

Herschel
Bernardi

Kenneth
Bryan

Yul
Brynner

Adolph
Caesar

James
Cagney

Rafael
Campos

Maurice
Copeland

Joel
Crothers

Sarah
Cunningham

Howard
DaSilva

Olive
Deering

David
Ellin

Peggy
Feury

Neil
Flanagan

Hilda
Haynes

Harold
Lang

Gordon
MacRae

Margo

Joe
Masiell

Una
Merkel

Court
Miller

Lloyd
Nolan

Lilli
Palmer

Todd
Patterson

Phil
Silvers

Gale
Sondergaard

Burr
Tillstrom

Orson
Welles

Audrey
Wood

231

KENT SMITH, 78, New York City-born stage, film, and television actor, died April 23, 1986 of congestive heart failure in Woodland Hills, Ca. He made his Bdwy debut in 1932 in "Men Must Fight," followed by "Spring in Autumn," "The Drums Begin," "Dodsworth," "Mad Morning," "The Lambent Flame," "Caesar and Cleopatra," "Saint Joan," "Seen But Not Heard," "The Wingless Victory," "Candida," "Idiot's Delight," "The Star-Wagon," "How to Get Tough About It," "Herod and Mariamne," "Jeremiah," "Christmas Eve," "An International Incident," "Old Acquaintance," "The Story of Mary Surratt," "Antony and Cleopatra," "Good Housekeeping," "The Wisteria Trees," "Burning Bright," "Richard II," "The Autumn Garden," "The Wild Duck," "Charley's Aunt," "What Every Woman Knows," "Measure for Measure," "Bus Stop," "Saint Joan," and "The Child Buyer." He is survived by his second wife, actress Edith Atwater, and a daughter.

MURIEL BURRELL SMITH, 62, actress-singer, died Sept. 13, 1985 in Richmond, Va. She made her Bdwy debut in 1943, creating the title role in "Carmen Jones," followed by "Our Lan'," "The Cradle Will Rock," "Sojourner Truth," "Hippolytus," "South Pacific," "The King and I," and as "Carmen Jones" again in 1956. She received the arts award of the National Council of Negro Women in 1984. There are no reported survivors.

GALE SONDERGAARD, 86, Minnesota-born stage, film, and television actress, died Aug. 14, 1985 in Woodland Hills, Ca. after an illness of several years. She made her Bdwy debut in 1923 in "What's Your Wife Doing?," followed by "Faust," "Major Barbara," "Strange Interlude," "Karl and Anna," "Red Dust," "Alison's House," "American Dream," "Dr. Monica," "Invitation to a Murder," "Cue for Passion," and "Goodbye Fidel," and OB in "The Woman," "Kicking the Castle Down," and "John Gabriel Borkman." She won an Oscar in 1936 for her film debut in "Anthony Adverse." She is survived by a sister.

LEONARD SPIGELGASS, 76, Brooklyn-born playwright and screenwriter, died Feb. 14, 1986 at his home in Los Angeles, Ca. He wrote 75 film scripts before scoring on Bdwy with "A Majority of One." His other plays include "Dear Me," "The Sky is Falling," "The Playgirls," "The Wrong Way Light Bulb," and "Look to the Lillies." He is survived by a sister.

CHARLES STARRETT, 82, Massachusetts-born stage and film actor, died March 22, 1986 of cancer in Borrego Springs, Ca. He made his Bdwy debut in 1929 in "Star of Bengal," followed by "Claire Adams." He is best known for having played The Durango Kid in 66 pictures. He is survived by his wife and two sons.

PAUL STEWART, 77, New York City-born stage, film, and television actor, director, and playwright, died of heart failure Feb. 17, 1986 in Los Angeles, Ca. He appeared on Bdwy in 1920 in "The Fall of Susan Lenox," followed by "Two Seconds," "East of Broadway," "Bulls, Bears and Asses," "Wine of Choice," "Native Son," and "Mister Roberts." He was a member of Orson Welles Mercury Theatre group in 1938, and later performed in more than 50 films. He also appeared in or directed some 5,000 radio and TV shows. On Bdwy he directed "Alternate Current," "Twilight Walk," and "Sing Me No Lullaby," and he wrote "Miss Temple Is Willing." He is survived by his wife.

SIDNEY STONE, 83, stage and television actor, died of heart failure Jan. 12, 1986 in his native New York City. A vaudevillian, he made his Bdwy debut in 1921 in "The Three Musketeers," followed by "Summer Night," "An International Incident," "Mr. Big," "Three Men on a Horse," "Allah Be Praised!," "Hilarities," "Damn Yankees," and "Sugar Babies." He gained his widest recognition as the "Tell ya what I'm gonna do!" pitchman on Milton Berle's TV series, Texaco Star Theater. He is survived by his wife and a daughter.

BENJAMIN STROBACH JR., 61, actor and stage manager, died April 25, 1985 in Santa Monica, Ca. of viral pneumonia. He stage managed such Bdwy shows as "Stop the World—I Want to Get Off," "Superman," "Follies," "A Little Night Music," "A Matter of Gravity," "Harold and Maude," "West Side Waltz," and "Side by Side by Sondheim." He is survived by his father.

CLAUDE STROUD, 78, character actor and one of the Stroud Twins in vaudeville, died Oct. 16, 1985 in Santa Monica, Ca. His Bdwy appearances include "Heaven on Earth" in 1948. He is survived by his wife, the former Gloria Brewster of the performing Brewster Twins, and two daughters.

MARION TANNER, 94, Buffalo-born actress known as "the ultimate Greenwich Village eccentric," died Oct. 30, 1985 in New York City. Her Bdwy appearances include "Fires of Spring," "The Cat and the Canary," "Knickerbocker Holiday," and "Tobacco Road." She was immortalized as the apparent model for the madcap fictional character in the novel Auntie Mame, written by her nephew, Edward Everett Tanner 3rd, using the pen name Patrick Dennis, which was adapted by Lawrence & Lee into the play "Auntie Mame" and musical "Mame." There are no immediate survivors.

SONNY TERRY, 74, Georgia-born blues vocalist and harmonica player, died March 11, 1986 in Mineola, LI. He appeared on Bdwy in "Finian's Rainbow" and "Cat on a Hot Tin Roof." He is survived by his wife.

BURR TILLSTROM, 68, Chicago-born stage and television entertainer, puppeteer, and writer, died December 6, 1985 at his home in Palm Springs, Ca. from natural causes. In 1960 he conceived, wrote, and performed on Bdwy in "Kukla, Burr and Ollie," featuring the cast of Kuklapolitan Players immortalized on his 1947–1957 TV series "Kukla, Fran, and Ollie," with Fran Allison. He also appeared on Bdwy, with Kukla and Ollie, in "Side by Side by Sondheim" in 1978. He won more than 50 major awards, including five Emmy's. On March 23, 1986 he was posthumously inducted into the Television Academy Hall of Fame. He is survived by a brother.

JIM TUSHAR, 56, singer-actor, was killed in his New York City apartment on April 9, 1986 by an unknown assailant. He appeared on Bdwy in "All in One," "Juno," "Trouble in Tahiti," and "The Rink." There were no reported survivors.

EDITH VAN CLEVE, 90, actress and one of the most respected of Bdwy's theatrical agents, died October 10, 1985 in Boston, following complications from a blood clot in her leg. She made her Bdwy debut in 1923 with the Jane Cowl repertory theatre, in "Romeo and Juliet," followed by such plays as "Malvaloca," "Antony and Cleopatra," "The Depths," "The New Gallantry," "Broadway," "Little Accident," "The Channel Road," "Wild Waves," "American Dream," "June Moon," "Three and One," "Three Men on a Horse," "Angel Island," "All That Glitters," "What a Life," "Ring Two," and "Goodbye in the Night." For several years she was assistant to George Abbott, and at one time appeared in two of his plays, "The Front Page" and "Boy Meets Girl," concurrently, in theaters across the street from each other. She became a theatrical agent and discovered and represented many well known actors, including Marlon Brando, Grace Kelly, and Montgomery Clift. She is survived by a sister.

LUCIA VICTOR, 74, Iowa-born director, producer, playwright, and production stage manager, died March 22, 1986 at her home in Chappaqua, NY. She was long associated with producer David Merrick, and stage managed his productions including "Take Me Along," "Becket," "The Rehearsal," "and "Carnival." She was Gower Champion's assistant on "Hello, Dolly!" and "42nd Street," and directed touring companies of those shows, among others. On Bdwy, she directed "Billy Noname," "Exodus," and "Heathen," and produced "The Milky Way," "Boy Meets Girl," and two plays that she wrote, "Detour After Dark" and "Eye for an I," were produced. There are no immediate survivors.

DENNIS WARNING, 34, St. Louis-born actor, died Sept. 2, 1985 in New York City. He made his Bdwy debut in 1976 in "The Robber Bridegroom," followed by "The Most Happy Fella," "The Pirates of Penzance," and "Baby," and OB in "Jimmy and Billy." He is survived by his mother, brother, and two sisters.

ROBERT WARNERS, 29, Oakland, Ca.-born stage, film, and television singer-dancer, died April 17, 1986 in New York City after a long illness. He made his Bdwy debut in 1979 in "Dancin'," followed by "Woman of the Year," "Merlin," and OB in "One More Song/One More Dance." He is survived by his parents and two brothers.

ORSON WELLES, 70, Wisconsin-born stage, film, radio, and television actor, director, playwright, screenwriter, and producer, died Oct. 10, 1985 at his home in Hollywood, Ca., apparently of natural causes. He made his Bdwy debut in 1934 with Katharine Cornell in "Romeo and Juliet," followed by his involvement as either actor, director, producer (or all three) in such plays as "Panic," "Horse Eats Hat," "Doctor Faustus," "Julius Caesar," "Heartbreak House," "Danton's Death," "Five Kings," "Around the World," "Macbeth," "Moby Dick," "King Lear," "The Shoemaker's Holiday," "Native Son," and "Rhinoceros." In 1937, with John Houseman, he founded the Mercury Theatre, and the same year was appointed a director of the Federal Theatre Project in NY, responsible for productions including "The Cradle Will Rock." He is best remembered for his 1938 radio broadcast of "The War of the Worlds," and his film classic "Citizen Kane." He is survived by his widow, Paola Mori, and his daughters Christopher (by Virginia Nicholson), Rebecca (by Rita Hayworth), and Beatrice (by Mori).

PATRICIA WHEEL, 61, stage, film, and television actress, died June 3, 1986 in her native New York City after a long illness. She appeared on Bdwy in "Cyrano de Bergerac," "Charley's Aunt," "The Tempest," "Arms and the Man," "Little Brown Jug," "Stars Weep," "The Browning Version," "Cry of the Peacock," "Gertie," "Sacred Flame," "Soldiers," "Butterflies Are Free," "Voices," "The Women," and OB in "Grass Widows." She is survived by two sons and a sister.

CYPRIENNE GABEL WHELAN, 61, dancer-actress, died Oct. 10, 1985 in Boston, Mass. after a long illness. She appeared on Bdwy in "Annie Get Your Gun," "Finian's Rainbow," and "On the Town," among others. In later years, she was a director of the American Academy of Dramatic Arts. She is survived by two sons, a daughter, actress Susan Whelan, and two brothers.

CLINTON WILDER, 65, Pennsylvania-born theatrical producer, died Feb. 14, 1986 at his home in Bedford, NY, after a long illness. Together with his partners Richard Barr and Edward Albee, he produced Mr. Albee's early plays "The American Dream," "Who's Afraid of Virginia Woolf," "Tiny Alice," "A Delicate Balance," and "All Over." He also produced or co-produced such plays as "The Tender Trap," "Visit to a Small Planet," "Bartleby," "The Death of Bessie Smith," "Gallows Humor," "Happy Days," "Bertha," "Endgame," "Whisper Into My Good Ear," "Mrs. Dally Has a Lover," "The Zoo Story," "Tiny Alice," "Johnny No-Trump," "Everything in the Garden," "The Butter and Egg Man," "Home and Regina." With Mr. Albee and Mr. Barr, he established The Playwright's Unit Off Off Bdwy, which mounted the first New York productions of writers Sam Shepard and Lanford Wilson, among others. He is survived by two brothers.

KURT WILHELM, 41, Cincinnati-born theatrical costume designer, died Mar. 24, 1986 in Louisville, Ky., after suffering a heart attack. His designs were seen in the NYSF productions of "Rum and Coke" and "My Uncle Sam," and OB in "Raw Youth," "Through the Leaves," and "Getting Out." He is survived by his wife.

AUDREY WOOD, 80, New York City-born legendary theatrical agent, died on December 27, 1985 in Fairfield, Conn., after being in a coma since suffering a stroke in her New York City home on April 30, 1981. In 1937 she founded an agency with her husband to be, William Liebling. She discovered and nurtured the careers of such writers as Tennessee Williams, William Inge, Robert Anderson, Carson McCullers, Arthur Kopit, Studs Terkel, Brian Friel, Murray Schisgal, and Preston Jones, and her only acting client, Eva Le Gallienne. She was a strong force in the theatre and films, and responsible for seeing such plays produced on Bdwy as "Room Service," "Porgy and Bess," "The Member of the Wedding," "Finian's Rainbow," "The Glass Menagerie," "Summer and Smoke," "A Streetcar Named Desire," "The Rose Tattoo," "Cat on a Hot Tin Roof," "Come Back, Little Sheba," "Picnic," "Bus Stop," "The Dark at the Top of the Stairs," "Tea and Sympathy," "I Never Sang for My Father," "The Texas Trilogy," "Indians," and "Wings," to name but a few. There are no immediate survivors.

INDEX

A . . . My Name Is Alice, 148, 177
Aaron, Caroline, 12, 38, 194
Aaron, Jack, 61, 194
Abady, Josephine R., 139
Abajian, John, 174
Abar, James, 94
Abatemarco, Tony, 147
Abbott, Charles, 139
Abbott, George, 155
Abbott, Jack Henry, 60, 161
Abbott, Paula, 139
Abbott, Ron, 70
Abbott, Suzy, 142
Abbott, Tommy, 134
Abbott, Wendy, 186
Abdoh, Reza, 163
Abe Lincoln in Illinois, 187
Abe, Kobo, 109
Abel, Charles, 152
Abel, Marbeth, 124
Abel, Timothy, 13
Abele, Jim, 61
Aberger, Tom, 65, 99
Aberlin, Betty, 61, 194
Abernethy, Richard, 117
Abiko, Tadashi, 8
Ables, Loretta, 136
Abner, Teddy, 104
Abou-El-Kanater, Ismail, 109
Abraham, F. Murray, 101, 194
Abrams, Allan, 184
Abrams, Anne, 11, 26, 27, 37, 39, 48, 65, 84, 124, 134
Abrams, Diane, 49
Abrams, Michael, 163
Abrams, Robin, 116
Abrams, Ron, 34
Abramson, Cliff, 177, 186
Abreu, Jorge, 143
Absurd Person Singular, 168
Abuba, Ernest, 109, 194
Acarino, Danielle, 89
Accardo, Michael, 83
Acito, Marc, 169
Ackerman, Norma, 162
Ackerman, Paul, 181
Acquavella, Debra, 137, 152
Actor's Nightmare, The, 160
Actors on Acting, 171
Adair, Catherine, 150
Adaire, Christine, 186
Adamo, Robert, 158
Adams, Abigail, 168
Adams, Betsy, 78
Adams, Charlotte, 144
Adams, D., 151
Adams, Donald, 186
Adams, Edie, 188
Adams, J. B., 162
Adams, Jane, 111
Adams, Mason, 101, 194
Adams, Roberta, 150
Adams, Ruth, 139
Adamson, David, 59, 108, 194
Adamson, Ellen, 194
Adamson, Harold, 78
Aday, Gary, 145
Adderley, Janet Williams, 139
Aden, John, 181
Adkins, Cindy, 64
Adkins, Jeff, 124
Adkins, Walter, 113
Adler, Bruce, 66, 194
Adler, Jay, 16, 50
Adler, Jerry, 81
Adler, Marion, 186
Adler, Nancy Ann, 163
Adler, Nathan, 173
Adshead, Patricia, 62, 94, 117
Adventures of Stanley Tomorrow, The, 151
Adzima, Nanzi, 175
Aellen, Richard, 98
Affair and Bubbe Adelstein, The, 61
Africanis Instructus, 71
Agar, Sam, 57
Agnes of God, 143, 145, 149, 177
Ahearn, Daniel, 156
Aherne, Brian, 226
Aibel, Douglas, 119
Aidem, Betsy, 67, 194
Aiello, Danny, 43, 188, 194
Aikens, Victor, 73
Aimetti, Ashley, 142
Ain't Misbehavin', 148, 153, 174, 175, 187
Akaka, Jeffrey, 109
Akalaitis, JoAnne, 141, 146
Akers, Karen, 188, 194
Akey, William, 164
Aki, Haru, 101
Ako, 109
Alan-Ross, Michael, 124
Alan-Williams, Gregory, 166
Alban, Alissa, 87
Albanese, Carmen, 126
Albee, Edward, 168
Albee, Lura, 72
Albert, Stephen J., 60, 146
Albertine, Charles, 58
Albrecht, Heidi, 76
Albrezzi, Steven D., 149
Alcestis, 141
Alchemedians, The, 75
Alda, Alan, 188
Alda, Robert, 226
Alder, Jac, 177
Alderfer, Eric, 123
Aldredge, Theoni V., 45, 49, 50, 122, 126, 127
Aldredge, Tom, 158, 158
Aldrich, Linda, 141
Aldrich, Rhonda, 163
Aldrich, Richard, 226
Aldridge, Amanda, 158, 166
Alekar, Satish, 109
Alessandrini, Gerard, 53
Aletter, Frank, 161
Alex, Marily, 163
Alexander, Adinah, 64
Alexander, Cheryl, 16
Alexander, Eric, 186
Alexander, Greg, 168
Alexander, Jace, 18, 57, 120, 194
Alexander, Jane, 188
Alexander, Jason, 65, 194
Alexander, Robert, 143
Alexander, Rod, 69
Alexander, Terry, 116, 194
Alexis, Alvin, 60, 120, 143, 194
Alexis, Edith, 95
Alford, J. Brent, 139
Alford, Larry, 24
Alfred, Lydia, 162
Alfred, Yvette, 162
Alfredo, John, Jr., 124
Aliapoulios, S. Mark, 141
Alice and Fred, 62
Alice, Mary, 154, 194
Alicia, Michael, 157
Alison's House, 187
All My Sons, 163, 172, 187
All the Way Home, 187
All's Well That Ends Well, 185
Allan, Robin, 66
Allan, Ted, 96
Allard, Martine, 188, 194
Allard, Tom, 147
Allardice, Bruce, 90
Alle, Gregory, 186
Allegretti, Cosmo F., 180
Allen, Andi, 177
Allen, Anthony, 162
Allen, Beth, 162
Allen, Billie, 83, 179
Allen, Charles, 74
Allen, Clint, 46
Allen, Darla, 142
Allen, David, 115
Allen, Debbie, 40, 41, 80, 194
Allen, Elizabeth, 194
Allen, Gregory, 186
Allen, Herb, 182
Allen, Janet, 160
Allen, Joan, 188, 194
Allen, John A., 168
Allen, Jonelle, 188
Allen, Karen, 162, 188, 193
Allen, Keith, 128
Allen, Lewis, 12, 18, 57, 67
Allen, Lynne Clifton, 149, 168
Allen, Mana, 58
Allen, Melissa, 181
Allen, Penelope, 135
Allen, Peter W., 136
Allen, Ralph G., 133
Allen, Rex E., 136
Allen, Richard, 61
Allen, Ross, 124
Allen, Ruth, 151
Allen, Seth, 57, 194
Allen, Woody, 87
Alleni, Betmar, 74
Allentuck, Max, 39
Aller, John, 111, 194
Allinson, Michael, 159
Allison, Deborah, 167
Allison, Karl, 122
Allison, Patti, 167
Allison, W. Scott, 58
Allwine, Michael, 94
Almberg, John, 142
Almquist, Gregg, 18, 194
Almy, Brooks, 138
Alone Together, 148
Alper, I., 64
Alper, Jonathan, 99
Alper, Steven M., 68, 118
Alperin, Yankele, 64
Alpern, Joy, 87
Alpers, Richard T., 117
Alpert, Michael, 32
Alsaker, Timian, 163
Alspaugh, Jeffery, 143
Alston, Chiron, 182
Alsup, Andy, 59, 92
Altman, Peter, 159
Altshuld, Alan, 63
Alvarado, Trini, 61, 79, 194
Alvarone, 69
Alyson, Eydie, 55
Amadeus, 187
Amaral-Smith, Luisa, 139
Ambrosch, Stefan, 142
Ambrose, Richard, 73
Amendola, Kate, 60, 62
Amendolia, Don, 130, 194
Amenta, Davida, 58
American Buffalo, 187
American Dreamer, 151
American Gothics, 62
Ames, Kenston, 26, 172
Amirante, Robert, 45
Amis, Suzy, 120, 189, 192, 194
Ammerman, John, 140
Ammon, Linda Jane, 158
Amodeo, Paul, 79
Among The Fallen, 63
Amore, Bob, 124
Amos, Keith, 69, 172, 194
Amper, Leslie, 161
Amplas, John, 169
Anais Nin: The Paris Years, 73
Anania, Michael, 72, 167
Ancowitz, Joel, 175
And a Nightingale Sang, 137, 138, 145, 149
And They Dance Real Slow in Jackson, 94
Anden, Matthew, 226
Anderman, Maureen, 27, 38, 188, 194
Anders, Mark, 136
Andersen, Tobias, 185
Anderson, Audrey, 117
Anderson, Carole Jean, 138
Anderson, Christine, 68, 195
Anderson, Claudia S., 113
Anderson, Craig, 64
Anderson, Cynthia L., 153
Anderson, Dale, 57
Anderson, David-Cameron, 162
Anderson, Dion, 177, 184
Anderson, Donna, 144
Anderson, Eric, 172, 175
Anderson, Frank, 75
Anderson, Fred, 124
Anderson, George, 69, 139
Anderson, Hilding, 76
Anderson, Jensie, 139
Anderson, Kevin, 188, 195
Anderson, Laurie, 141
Anderson, Leslie, 6, 47, 124
Anderson, Leta, 170
Anderson, Maxwell, 162
Anderson, McKee, 145
Anderson, Paul, 142
Anderson, Peter, 164
Anderson, Philip, 83
Anderson, Roger, 175
Anderson, Stanley, 143
Anderson, Stephen, 151
Anderson, Sue, 24
Anderson, Sydney, 50, 195
Anderson, Tobias, 136
Anderson-Fields, Karen, 137
Andes, Keith, 188
Andoniadis, George, 62
Andre, Linda, 113
Andreas, Christine, 138, 188, 192
Andreopoulous, Dennis, 59
Andres, Barbara, 151
Andresakis, Andrea, 77
Andresakis, Tony, 77
Andrew, Carol, 153
Andrews, Ann, 226
Andrews, Brian, 48
Andrews, Dwight, 180
Andrews, George Lee, 52, 164, 195
Andrews, Jennifer Lee, 52
Andrews, Jessica L., 160
Andrews, Jose R., 109
Andrews, Julie, 188
Andrews, Mark, 128
Andrews, Marnie, 172
Andrews, Nancy, 188
Andrews, Tod, 188
Andreyko, Helena, 61
Andriuk, Andy, 62
Androcles and the Lion, 157
Androeozzi, Beverly J., 162
Andrulot, Joyce, 140
Andrus, Dee, 151
Angel Street, 165
Angell, Gene, 182
Angermann, Christian, 92
Angiulo, Michael, 144
Anglim, Philip, 188
Anglin, David, 147
Angulo, Dennis, 49
Anicello, Jodene Marie, 174
Ankeny, Mark, 92, 195
Anna Christie, 187
Annals, Michael, 27, 132
Annie Get Your Gun, 142
Annie, 122, 129
Annie-Joe, 129, 73
Another Paradise, 73
Another Part of the Forest, 92
Anouilh, Jean, 115
Anson, Amy, 166
Anson, Edith N., 144
Antalosky, Charles, 181
Anteroom, 111
Anthony, James, 165
Anthony, Marc, 100
Anthony, Nicole, 122
Antigone, 110, 186
Anton, Susan, 125, 195
Antonio, Candido, 60, 61
Antonio, Lou, 188
Antony and Cleopatra, 183
Anything Goes, 177
Anzalone, John, 128
Anzalone, Michael, 104
Apfel, Mimi, 156
Aplon, Judith, 183
Apogee/Perigee, 171
Aponte, Antonio, 112
Aportela, Raul, 140
Appear and Show Cause, 102
Appel, Irwin, 183
Appel, Libby, 183
Applause, 187
Applebaum, Louis, 154, 186
Applegate, Fred, 147
Applegate, Phyllis, 163
Appleton, Bev, 177
Aquilina, Corinne Jerris, 122
Aquino, Amy, 180
Araiza, J. Edmundo, 163
Aran, 109
Arana, Cecilia, 70
Aranas, Raul, 73, 109, 195
Aranha, Ray, 154
Arbuzov, Aleksei, 226
Arcaro, Robert, 72, 194, 195
Arcenas, Loy, 76, 80, 141
Archer, Frances E., 110
Archie, Wilbur, 58
Ard, Kenneth, 11
Ardao, David, 6, 81, 195
Arduini, Dyann, 148
Aren't We All?, 122
Ariel, Raymond, 64
Arkin, Adam, 144, 163
Arkin, Alan, 115, 144, 188
Arkin, Anthony, 115, 144
Arlen, Harold, 226
Arlen, Steeve, 50
Arliss, Dimitra, 195
Artt, Lewis, 27
Arluck, Neal, 62, 87, 195
Armagnac, Gary, 175
Arment, Gwen, 167
Armistead, Diane, 159
Armour, Annabel, 149
Arms and the Man, 177
Armstrong, Bill, 71
Armstrong, Cody, 32
Armstrong, Curtis, 165
Armstrong, Karen, 107, 108
Armstrong, Richard, 79
Arnaz, Lucie, 130, 188
Arndt, Denis, 172, 185
Arnemann, James M., 146
Arner, Gwen, 174
Arney, Randall, 161
Arnold, Barry, 81, 115, 140, 153, 174, 175
Arnold, Bob, 118, 195
Arnold, Caroline, 64
Arnold, Jeanne, 165
Arnold, Madison, 175, 195
Arnold, Richard, 103, 104
Arnone, John, 84, 107, 143
Arnott, Mark, 162, 172, 174
Arnotte, Andre, 119
Aronica, Joseph, 80
Arons, Ellyn, 24, 142, 195
Aronson, Frances, 110, 115, 139, 143, 146, 154, 159, 171
Aronson, Henry, 111
Aronson, Jonathan, 133
Aronson, Susan, 158, 158
Aronstein, Martin, 27, 132, 146, 161, 163
Arrambide, Mario, 107, 108, 195
Arrick, Larry, 76, 170
Arrington, Timothy, 139
Arrow, David L., 100
Arrow, Max, 61
Arsenals, 174
Arthur, Phil, 188
Arthur, Reginald, 102
Artists and Admirers, 70
Artman, Deborah, 102
Arvia, Ann, 164
Arvidson, Adam, 164
As Is, 144
As You Like It, 78, 80, 164, 173, 174
As the Crow Flies, 163
Asbell, Ronnie, 60
Asbury, Cleve, 111, 155
Asher, David, 174
Asher, Frances, 138
Ashley, Barbara, 188
Ashley, Elizabeth, 125, 188, 195
Ashman, Howard, 55, 169, 171, 177
Asion, Julian, 104, 149
Askins, Sally Lynn, 177
Askler, David, 7
Aslund, Joan, 133
Aspden, Craig, 55
Aspinall, Jennifer, 64
Asquith, Ward, 92, 117, 195
Assa, Rene, 163
Asselin, Judy Nicholson, 168
Asselin, Pierre, 65
Aster, Jeannette, 154
Astrachan, Joshua, 65, 80
Astredo, Humbert Allen, 103, 179, 195
Astronauts, 137
Aswegan, Jared, 105
Atamaniuk, Walter, 161
Atha, Steve, 135
Athens, James, 169
Atherlay, John M., 57, 94
Atherton, Blake, 93
Atherton, William, 180, 188
Atienza, Edward, 154, 186
Atkin, Mike, 90
Atkins, Greg, 173
Atkins, Jane, 173
Atkinson, Clinton J., 162
Atkinson, Jayne, 162
Atkinson, Susan D., 63
Atlee, Barbara, 58, 61, 62
Atlee, Howard, 57, 58, 61, 62, 80
Atwater, Carle, 103
Atwater, Edith, 226
Auberjonois, Rene, 46, 163, 195
Aubry, Dianne, 104
Auerbach, Mark G., 174
August, Ron, 68, 195
Aulgur, Ronald J., 143
Aulino, Tom, 59
Aulisi, Joseph G., 34
Aunt Dan And Lemon, 107
Auntie Mame, 142
Aurelius, Neville, 184
Auspitz, Don, 168
Austen, Jane, 162
Austen, Will, 77
Austin, Clayton, 157
Austin, Elizabeth, 79, 118, 195
Austin, Lee, 58
Austin, Lyn, 71, 78
Austin, Mark, 81, 195
Austin, Paul, 12, 59
Austin, Rick, 182
Auto-Erotic Misadventure, 113
Autoscape: New Year's Eve, 163
Avari, N. Erick, 107, 184, 195
Avedon, Doe, 188
Averitt, Suzanne, 179
Avery, Margot, 63, 78
Averyt, Bennet, 144, 167
Avian, Bob, 45, 126
Avila, Christine, 163
Avner the Eccentric, 143
Avni, Ran, 96
Avolio, Lino, 81, 141
Awad, Mae, 142
Awake & Sing, 168
Awe, James, 226
Axelrod, Jack, 163
Axelrod, Lauryn, 64
Axtell, Barry, 68
Ayckbourn, Alan, 59, 168, 177, 179
Aycock, Janet, 58
Ayer, Margaret S., 142
Ayler, Ethel, 60
Aylward, John, 136, 172
Aylward, Peter, 161
Ayr, Michael, 107, 195
Ayres, Carolyn, 136
Ayvazian, Leslie, 91
Azar, Rick, 69
Azar, Ted, 49, 50, 126
Azenberg, Emanuel, 6, 42, 47, 123
Azito, Tony, 79, 161, 195
Babak, Cynthia, 166
Babatunde, Akin, 178
Babatunde, Obba, 195
Babauta, Lourdes, 119
Babb, Jim, 113
Babcock, Debra, 63
Babcock, Dennis, 156
Babe, Thomas, 81, 147, 168
Baber, Greg, 177
Baby, 158, 164, 178
Bacal, Gary, 144
Bacchae, The, 100
Bache, Joanna, 184
Bacik, Jerry, 165
Backer, Andy, 137
Backer, Brian, 103, 188, 195
Backes, Roy W., 170
Backus, Richard, 88, 162, 188, 195
Bacon, Kevin, 99, 195
Bacon, Michael, 72
Bacon, Tina, 176
Bad Bad Jo-Jo, 113
Bade, Tom, 87
Badger, Casey Lydell, 180
Badgett, William, 79
Badolato, Bill, 111, 155
Badolato, Dean, 64
Baez, Rafael, 186
Bagneris, Vernel, 149
Bagwell, Marsha, 142, 167
Bahn, Ken, 139
Baier, Frank, 16
Bailey, Adrian, 130
Bailey, Dennis, 81, 14, 140, 195
Bailey, Jeffrey, 143
Bailey, Julian, 156
Bailey, R. S., 163
Bailey, Victoria B., 99
Baillargeon, Gary, 142
Bair, Karen, 144
Baird, Maggie, 12, 149
Baird, Mary, 148
Baird, Quin, 40, 195
Baird, Wendy S., 150
Baitz, Jon Robin, 147
Baizley, Doris, 147
Bakay, Nick, 153, 175
Baker, Chuck, 169
Baker, Cliff Fannin, 143
Baker, Dana, 34, 63
Baker, David, 83
Baker, Douglas C., 30, 123, 129
Baker, Dylan, 62, 66
Baker, Eddie, 113
Baker, Henry, 60
Baker, Jean, 142
Baker, Jim, 141, 163
Baker, Jordan R., 144, 179
Baker, Karin, 127
Baker, Kathy Whitton, 107, 188, 195
Baker, Kelly, 123
Baker, Kenny, 226
Baker, Lance, 141
Baker, Leslie, 61
Baker, Mark, 150, 188

Baker, Raymond, 57, 164, 195
Baker, Susan, 175
Baker, Word, 52
Baker-Bergen, Stuart, 226
Baker-Jones, Shaun, 130
Bakos, John A., 71
Balaban, Bob, 164
Balcony, The, 141
Baldassare, Jim, 6, 22, 23, 38, 42, 47, 123
Baldasso, Carl A., 92, 96, 112
Baldino, Missy, 195
Baldonieri, Louis, 83
Baldridge, Charlene, 184
Baldwin, Alec, 36, 189, 192, 195
Baldwin, Brooks, 94, 95
Baldwin, Bryant, 37
Baldwin, Judith, 76
Baldwin, Patricia, 98
Baldwin, Phillip, 62
Baldwin, Robert W., 64
Balek, Agatha, 96
Balestrino, Richard, 50, 128
Balian, Rick, 58
Balick, Robert, 150
Balin, Ina, 188
Balkan, Liza, 134, 168
Ball, Constance, 180
Ball, Lani, 40, 161
Ball, William, 141
Ballad of the El Gimpo Cafe, The, 151
Ballantyne, Paul, 144
Ballantyne, Wayne, 185
Ballard, Kathryn, 145
Ballard, Laurence, 136
Ballard, Lucinda, 135
Balletta, Dominick, 109, 116
Ballinger, June, 137
Ballora, Mark, 90
Ballou, Bill, 186
Ballou, David R., 65
Balm in Gilead, 139
Balmuth, Beth Logan, 186
Balou, Buddy, 11, 45, 195
Baltazar, Mark, 84, 87
Bam, Sheila, 59
Bamford, George, 34
Bamman, Gerry, 33, 156, 195
Bancroft, Anne, 188
Bandiere, Rebecca, 71
Banes, Lisa, 82,, 188, 195
Banfield, Scott, 158
Banjo Dancing or the 48th Annual Squitters Mountain Song Dance Folklore Convention . . . and how I lost, 143
Bank, Mirra, 85
Bankey, Christopher, 15, 24
Bankston, Arnold, 92, 118, 149, 195
Banky, David, 120
Banninger, Carole, 49
Bansavage, Lisa, 80, 195
Bantry, Bryan, 122
Baran, Edward, 65, 81, 195
Barandes, Janice, 16
Barandes, Martin, 16
Baranski, Christine, 43, 99, 195
Baray, John, 109, 195
Barbara Cook: A Broadway Evening, 152
Barbaro, Ciro, 93, 195
Barbeau, Adrienne, 188
Barbee, R. Nelson, 29
Barbee, Victor, 11, 195
Barbell, Elyse, 86
Barber of Seville, The, 138
Barber, Charles, 78
Barbieri, Peter, 131
Barbour, Eleanor, 166
Barbour, Thomas, 111, 159, 195
Barcelo, Randy, 15
Barchevska, Madeline, 95
Barclay, Shelly, 99
Barclay, William, 105, 119, 153
Barcone, Eugene, 141
Barcott, Allison, 136
Barcroft, Judith, 57, 84
Barge, David Winston, 83
Bargeron, Julie, 88
Bari, Adele, 93
Bari, Charles, 135
Barker, Amy Jo, 143
Barker, Christine, 195
Barker, Gary, 142
Barker, Jean, 61, 167, 195
Barker, Margaret, 89, 101, 194, 195
Barker, Sheila D., 32
Barker, Wayne, 92
Barkla, Jack, 156
Barkley, Lynnette, 68
Barley, Steve, 153
Barlow, Leslie, 153, 174, 175
Barlow, Vicky, 163
Barner, Stockman, 87, 194, 195
Barnes, Bill, 72, 75
Barnes, Ezra, 131
Barnes, Gregg, 116, 175
Barnes, Irving, 26
Barnes, Kendall A., 77
Barnes, Kirk, 142
Barnes, Lisa, 144
Barnes, Susan, 146, 147
Barnes, Tom, 83, 123
Barnes, Willie, 91
Barnett, Bill, 69
Barnett, Bob, 91, 153
Barnett, Gina, 98
Barnett, Pat, 170
Barnett, William, 153
Barney, Maria, 169
Barnhart, Michael Gerald, 184
Barnicle, Andrew, 181
Baron, Deborah, 113
Baron, Evalyn, 46, 195
Baron, Jamie, 154
Baron, Neal, 178
Baron, Sheldon, 52
Barone, Allen, 77, 90
Barone, Anthony, 83
Barone, John, 62, 93, 148, 195
Barr, Sue, 149
Barranger, Milly S., 170
Barre, Gabriel, 101, 196
Barreca, Christopher H., 160
Barrett, Alice, 72
Barrett, Anne, 77, 87
Barrett, Brent, 121, 196
Barrett, Diana, 162
Barrett, Florence, 57
Barrett, Joe, 59, 179, 196, 201
Barrett, Laurinda, 174
Barrett, Leslie, 179
Barrett, Mace, 128
Barrett, Walter, 174
Barricelli, Marco, 144
Barrie, Barbara, 162
Barrie, Frank, 183
Barrie, J. M., 160, 174
Barrie, Wendy, 179
Barringer, Barbara, 165
Barron, Douglas, 61, 62, 196
Barron, Holly, 139
Barron, Malita, 148
Barrosse, Paul, 154
Barrows, Fred, 78
Barry, B. H., 17, 18, 46, 57, 107, 108, 111
Barry, Ellen, 184
Barry, Katherine, 196, 201
Barry, Kimberley Jean, 185
Barry, Paul, 184
Barry, Philip, 143, 158, 158, 162, 171
Barry, Raymond J., 173
Barsha, Debra, 57
Barshay, Peter, 75
Bart, Lenny, 100
Bartee, David Ray, 139
Bartenieff, George, 196
Bartlett, Bill, 61
Bartlett, D'Jamin, 188
Bartlett, Kevin, 148
Bartlett, Lisabeth, 33, 196
Bartlett, Peter, 162
Bartlett, Robin, 115, 196, 201
Bartlett, Scott, 75
Bartlett, Thomas A., 126
Bartley, Robert, 177
Barto, Mary, 108, 196
Barto, Ray, 150
Bartol, Kurt, 169
Barton, Alexander, 83
Barton, Daniel, 104, 196
Barton, Edward, 226
Barton, Fred, 53, 196
Barton, Genie, 152
Barton, Kris, 173
Barton, Steve, 48
Barton, Todd, 185
Bartosik, Ed, 121
Bartram, William, 173
Bartsch, Michael, 164
Barty, Billy, 146, 147
Bartz, Joshua, 154
Basch, Carol Ann, 133
Basch, Peter, 60, 98, 196, 201
Baseball Show, The, 171
Bash, Kevin, 163
Bash, Phyllis, 162
Baskous, Christine, 137
Basom, Ariel, 136
Bass, David, 111
Bass, Howard, 152
Bass, Leah, 58
Bass, Tim, 113
Bassett, Angela, 116, 180, 196, 201
Bassett, Linda, 107
Bassin, Joel, 58, 60, 161
Batchelder, Lisa, 63
Bates, Jerome Preston, 107, 196
Bates, Kathy, 59, 146, 147, 196
Bates, Leslie, 80
Bates, Paul, 179
Bates, Stephen, 127
Batho, Kristofer, 101
Batman, Ralph, 168
Batten, Tom, 155
Battis, Emery, 152
Battista, Lloyd, 57, 140
Batutis, Dennis, 49
Bau, Carmen, 87
Bauer, Alec, 184
Bauer, Charita, 226
Bauer, Daniel R., 70, 81
Bauer, John, 138
Bauer, Richard, 143
Bauer, Steven, 163
Baugh, Gary, 166
Baum, David, 100
Baum, Dolores, 139
Baum, Joanne, 92, 124, 196
Baum, Roberta, 64
Baumgardner, Holly, 183
Baumgarten, Lisa, 60
Baumgarten, Michael, 121
Baumgartner, Keith A., 129
Bavaar, Tony, 188
Baxter, Anne, 226
Baxter, Carol, 81
Baxter, Cash, 66
Baxter, Charles, 57
Baxter, Karen, 85
Baxter, Keith, 29, 188, 196
Baxter, Lynsey, 107
Baxter, Robin, 152
Bay, James M., 65, 161
Bayer, Ethel R., 24
Bayer, Frank, 146
Bayer, Patricia, 16
Bayers, Catherine, 184
Bayles, Suzanne, 175
Bayless, Anita, 54, 196
Bays, Robert, 166
Bazar, Logan, 183
Bazemore, Raymond, 152
Bazian, Menachem, 63
Bazzell, Larry, 174
Be Happy For Me, 69
Beach House, The, 88
Beach, Gary, 129, 146, 196
Beal, Harrison, 128
Beaman, Valerie, 90, 100
Beamish, Stephen, 186
Beams, Carole, 147
Bean, David, 63, 73
Bean, Orson, 188
Bean, Reathel, 46, 196
Beanstock, 113
Bear, The, 181
Beard, Jim, 152
Beard, Robert, 186
Beason, Amanda, 140
Beastly Beatitudes of Balthazar B, The, 179
Beattie, Kurt, 111, 136, 171
Beattie, Michael, 186
Beatty, Ethel S., 83
Beatty, John Lee, 36, 56, 88, 89, 99, 146, 153, 158, 174, 175, 179
Beatty, Lisa, 169
Beatty, Warren, 188
Beaty, Kim, 101
Beaubian, Susan, 126
Beaumarchais, Pierre Augustin, 14, 138
Beaumont, Ralph, 146
Beauregard, Norm, 175
Beautiful Lady, The, 146
Beauty Part, The, 178
Beaux Stratagem, The, 186
Beaver, Andrea, 168
Beaver, Terry, 163
Beazley, Steve, 173
Becher, John C., 163
Beck, Gary, 113
Beck, Julian, 226
Beck, Michelle, 39
Becker, Alma, 171
Becker, Bonnie L., 179
Becker, John Lawrence, 176
Becker, Lionel, 122
Becker, Randy, 92
Becker, Tom, 69
Becker, Victor A., 125, 140, 152, 174, 175
Becket, 187
Beckett, Samuel, 154, 172, 174
Beckler, Steven, 34
Beckos, Barbara, 175
Beckwith, Tobias, 51
Becoming Strangers, 63
Becvar, Bill, 175
Beddow, Margery, 26
Bedelia, Bonnie, 188
Bedell, George, 182
Bedford-Lloyd, John, 107, 158, 196, 201
Beditz, David, 158
Bedoian, Charles, 172
Beebe, Dick, 170
Beebe, Wayne, 142
Beeching, Barbara, 175
Beechman, Laurie, 48, 188, 192, 196
Beef, 71
Beehive, 74
Been Taken, 91
Beer, Arthur, 165
Beers, Amy, 78
Beers, Betsy, 71
Beery, Leigh, 76
Beesley, Christopher, 144
Before I Got My Eye Put Out, 173
Beglarian, Spencer, 180
Begum, Setara, 163
Behar, Howard, 59, 83
Behl, Dennis, 156
Behrman, S. N., 94
Beirne, Veronica, 100
Bekins, Richard, 162
Bekins, Russell, 147
Belafonte, Gina, 101
Belafonte, Harry, 188
Belanger, Michael, 59, 69
Belcher, James, 139
Belden, Ursula, 152, 170
Belevedere, Sean Sable, 123
Belfer, Glenn F., 123
Belgrader, Andrei, 154, 180
Belgraier, Bernett, 58
Belgrave, Cynthia, 162
Belinger, Michael, 69
Belknap, Allen R., 153
Bell, Barbara A., 139
Bell, Benny, 151
Bell, David H., 152, 167
Bell, Evan, 140
Bell, George Anthony, 124
Bell, Glynis, 149
Bell, Jake, 93, 124
Bell, Jerry, 78
Bell, Marie, 226
Bell, Marion, 188
Bell, Marty, 34
Bell, Nancy Hall, 48
Bell, Neal, 81, 110, 147
Bell, Vanessa, 196
Bellamy, Brad, 140, 168
Bellavance, Michelle, 140
Belletieri, Beverly, 33
Belleville, Brad, 182
Belli, Keith, 183
Bellin, Olga, 201
Belmonte, Vicki, 68, 196
Belo, Antonio, 133
Belton, Marcy, 104
Beltram, Robert, 163
Beltran, Alma, 163
Beltran, Louis Cruz, 176
Belver, Carla, 168
Belzer, Rick, 64
Benczak, Margaret, 80, 121
Bender, Jeff, 69
Bendevski, Peter, 81
Benedict, Gail, 127
Benedict, Paul, 99, 146
Benefactors, 27, 187
Benge, Douglas, 145
Bening, Annette, 151
Benischek, Roger, 92
Benitez, Felipe A., 57
Benjamin, P. J., 26, 114, 196, 201
Benjamin, Paul, 22, 59
Benjamin, Randy, 98, 179
Benjamin, Richard, 188
Benjamin, Shell M., 26
Bennes, John, 142, 174
Bennett, Harry, 162, 196
Bennett, Jeff, 139
Bennett, Keith, 79
Bennett, Mark, 113
Bennett, Michael, 45, 126, 169
Bennett, Reggie, 59
Bennett, Robert Russell, 76
Bennett, Robert, 70, 72, 74, 81
Bennett, Rudolph, 50
Bennett, Sid, 166
Bennett, Steven L., 138
Bennett, Suzanne, 84
Bennett, Timothy, 79
Bennett, Walter Allen, Jr., 120
Bennett-Gordon, Eve, 71, 153
Benninghofen, Mark, 120, 156
Benoit, Patricia, 188
Bensinger, Mimi, 117, 196
Benson, Cindy, 124
Benson, Dale, 164
Benson, Ester, 177
Benson, Martin, 173
Benson, Ray, 7
Benson, Wade, 140
Bent, 175
Bentley, Eric, 143
Bentley, John, 196
Benton, Robert, 51
Bentzen, Paul, 181
Berdery, James, 175
Berel, Avrom, 117
Berenice, 147
Berenson, Stephen, 178
Berezin, Tanya, 89, 196
Berg, Richard, 23
Berg, Rick, 166
Berger, Carole, 169
Berger, Sidney, 183
Berger, Stephen, 196
Berger, Steven, 149
Bergman, Andrew, 38
Bergman, Douglas R., 83
Bergmann, Alice, 131
Bergner, Elisabeth, 226, 231
Bergquist, Guy, 143
Bergquist, Judith, 151
Bergwall, James Curt, 103
Beris, David M., 92, 196, 201
Berk, Brian, 91
Berk, Phyllis, 66, 196
Berkman, John, 124
Berkowsky, Paul B., 76, 69
Berkowsky, Sheala N., 76
Berky, Bob, 75
Berlin, Irving, 142
Berlin, Pamela, 148, 159, 179
Berlind, Roger, 34, 37, 42
Berliner, Michael, 71
Berlinger, Robert, 173, 184
Berlinger, Warren, 188
Berlingieri, Osvaldo, 13
Berloni, William, 82, 85, 122
Berman, Donald, 72, 160, 196
Berman, Heather, 169
Bermudez, Mary, 176
Bern, Mina, 96
Bernal, Barry K., 48, 124
Bernal, Michael, 176
Bernardi, Gerry, 95
Bernardi, Herschel, 226, 231
Bernardi, James, 99, 106, 129, 146
Berner, Gary, 146
Bernhard, Arnold, 127
Bernhard, Jim, 139
Bernhardt, Melvin, 88
Bernheim, Shirl, 125
Bernstein, Douglas, 15, 196
Bernstein, Jamie, 105
Bernstein, Joel, 110
Bernstein, Leonard, 134, 145, 161, 167
Bernstein, Mark D., 168
Beron, Elba, 13
Beroza, Janet, 9
Berrick, Lawrence, 121
Berridge, Elizabeth, 94, 95, 119, 120, 196
Berry, Charles Joseph, 116
Berry, Dierdre, 169
Berry, Gabriel, 77, 108, 117
Berry, Loni, 101, 83
Berry, Stephanie, 91
Bertish, Suzanne, 188
Bertone, Maxine Krasowski, 143
Bertone, Richard, 143
Bertrand, Sandra, 72
Besser, Gedalia, 161
Besserer, Robert, 78
Bessette, Denise, 153, 168
Bessette, Mimi, 121, 196
Bessoir, Robert, 66, 86
Besthoff, Jane, 63
Bestial/Celestial Holiday Show, 171
Betancourt, Anne, 163
Bethany, Susan, 77, 196
Bethel, Marcy, 143
Bethell, Richard Garrick, 113
Betlem, Paula, 122
Betley, Cynthia, 165
Betrayal, 181, 187
Betsko, Kathleen, 180
Betsworth, Gary, 95
Bettis, Valerie, 188
Betts, Donnie L., 151
Betts, Jack, 69
Betts, Jim, 186
Betz, Janetta, 122
Beusman, Sue Ann, 7
Bevan, Alison, 196
Bevelander, Nannette, 51, 196
Beverley, Trazana, 166, 168, 188
Beyer, Gerald, 77
Beyer, Ranny, 185
Beyond the Horizon, 187
Biagini, Sal, 196
Bialowans, Christine, 142
Biancamano, Frank, 166
Bibb, Teri, 78, 152
Bicat, Nick, 107, 143
Bichsel, Reinhard, 182
Bick, Kristine L., 170
Bick, Tami Desiree, 177
Bickel, Rachel, 158
Bickell, Ross, 145, 159, 179
Bickerstaff, Jimmy, 166
Biddy, Peppy, 177
Bieber, Cathy, 159
Biega, Paul, 27, 37, 40, 127
Biegler, Gloria, 185
Bierce, Ambrose, 147
Big Bang, The, 113
Big Deal, 37
Big River, 46, 187
Big Time, 74
Bigbee, Lawrence, 73
Bigelow, Marion H., 142
Biggs, Casey, 143
Bigham, Charlene, 139
Bigley, Isabel, 188
Bigus, Harriette, 113
Bilder, Maggie, 92
Billig, Etel, 159
Billig, Pamela Caren, 57
Billig, Robert, 7, 55, 169
Billig, Steve S., 159
Billin, Beverly, 169
Billings, Carol, 62
Billings, Earl, 163
Billington, Ken, 31, 146
Billo, Peggy, 177
Billy Bishop Goes to War, 145, 167, 179
Biloxi Blues, 47, 123, 187
Binder, Jay, 66, 158,, 164
Binder, Melissa, 78
Bing, Arden, 78
Bingo, 83
Binkley, Howell, 80
Binotto, Paul, 126
Birch, Debbie, 92
Bircher, Betsy, 25
Bird, Joseph, 141
Bird, Pamela G., 113
Birdcatcher, in Hell, The, 141
Birds Fly Out With Death, The, 112
Birk, Raye, 146, 147
Birkenhead, Susan, 62
Birn, David, 64, 110
Birnbaum, Daniel, 146, 147
Birney, David, 27, 188, 196
Birney, Reed, 61, 196
Birthday Party, The, 159, 163
Bish, Bob, 144
Bishop, Andre, 110
Bishop, Conrad, 137
Bishop, David, 111, 148, 156
Bishop, Kelly, 34, 45
Bishop, Mark, 151
Bishop, Neal, 66, 79
Bishop, Scot, 141
Bishop, Wesley Grant, 185
Bitsko, Richard, 122
Bitter Tears of Petra Von Kant, The, 112
Bixby, Leslie, 81
Bjorn, Doug, 142
Black Coffee, 87, 153
Black Girl, 116
Black Nativity, 149
Black, Andrew, 179, 184
Black, Anne, 182
Black, Arleen Floyd, 140
Black, Bonnie, 174
Black, Cheryl, 177
Black, David Horton, 85
Black, Don, 11
Black, James, 183
Black, Lewis, 81
Black, Robert, 84, 150
Black, Royana, 111, 120, 196
Black, Sandra, 73
Blackman, Ian, 43, 72, 97, 196
Blackman, Robert, 146, 151, 173
Blackman, Sandy, 168
Blackwell, Byeager, 58
Blackwell, Charles, 47
Blackwell, David, 40
Blackwell, Lisa, 85
Blackwell, Sam, 93
Blades, Ruben, 141
Blair, John, 121
Blair, Pamela, 98, 196, 201
Blair, Steve 3
Blaisdell, Nesbitt, 60, 160, 196
Blaisus, Michael, 144
Blake, Josh, 57, 86
Blake, Kathleen, 140
Blake, Mervyn, 154, 186
Blake, Richard, 142
Blakeman, Scott, 98
Blakemore, Michael, 27, 132
Blakeny, Blanche, 72
Blanc, Jennifer, 196
Blanchard, Steven, 121, 152, 196
Bland, Judith, 122
Blane, Ralph, 133
Blankenship, Hal, 62
Blankenship, Paul, 52
Blanks, Harvy, 151
Blasetti, Pamela, 124
Blatt, Beth, 152
Blau, John, 184
Blazer, Judith, 149
Bleezarde, Gloria, 188
Blendick, James, 154, 186
Bley, Carla, 147
Blithe Spirit, 187
Blitzman, Jay D., 72
Bloch, Andrew, 115
Bloch, Ivan, 17, 64
Bloch, Peter, 101
Bloch, Scotty, 158, 158
Bloch, Simone, 65
Block, Frederic, 81

Block, Larry, 98, 108, 196
Blodgett, Kristin, 124
Blofson, Tony, 108
Blomgren, Robert, 173
Blomquist, David, 145
Blondeau-Russell, Betty, 140
Blood Knot, The, 22, 138, 180
Blood Wedding/Bodas De Sangre, 176
Blood, Laura, 92
Bloodgood, William, 185
Bloom, Joel, 127
Bloom, Meg, 55
Bloom, Michael, 141, 158, 158
Bloom, Mitchell S., 144, 184
Bloom, Stuart, 59, 196
Bloom, Tom, 148
Bloom, Verna, 196
Bloomquist, David, 60
Bloomrosen, Jay, 60
Bloomrosen, Lee, 60, 65
Blossom, Barbara, 178
Blount, Winton M., 181
Blue Window, 140, 173
Bluefoote, Scott, 142
Bluem, Beverly, 175
Blum, Harry, 80
Blum, Mark, 99, 111, 196
Blumenfeld, Robert, 62
Blumstein, Nancy, 113
Bly, Mark, 156
Bly, Richard, 34
Boardman, Robert, 174
Bobb-Semple, Ron, 83
Bobbie, Walter, 98, 196
Bobby, Anne Marie, 34
Bobo, Patricia, 115
Boccelli, Dick, 168
Bochette, Alyce, 118
Bock, Amy, 119
Bock, Jerry, 92, 145, 155
Bodebe, Moketsi, 59
Bodega, 112
Bodge, James, 159, 166
Bodibe, Moketsi, 59
Bodin, Jay, 196, 201
Bodle, Jane, 48, 196
Bodman, Helen, 142
Boehlke, Bain, 144
Boehlke, Michael Bruce, 140
Boehm, Susan, 72
Boehm, Trish, 169
Boeki, Diane, 93
Boese, Jody, 88
Boesing, Paul, 138
Boesman and Lena, 163, 166, 168
Bogart, Anne, 81, 85
Bogazianos, Vasili, 188
Bogdan-Kechely, Cheri, 149
Bogdanov, Michael, 186
Bogert, Pamela, 99
Bogosian, Eric, 85, 196
Bohdanetzky, Polly Scranton, 186
Bohmer, Ron, 121, 142, 166
Bokar, Hal, 163
Boland, Carol, 164
Bolcom, William, 147
Bolender, Bill, 150
Boles, Robert, 113, 196
Bolinsky, Kenneth R., 175
Bolstad, Tom, 156
Bolt, Jonathon, 137
Bolt, Robert, 184
Bolton, Guy, 93, 155, 172
Bolton, John Keene, 153
Bolzon, Henri, 151
Bonanni, John, 152
Bond, Edward, 139, 143
Bond, Sudie, 54
Bonds, R. J., 196
Bone Ring, The, 72
Bonham, Jack, 177
Bonin, Neil, 80
Bonnard, Raymond, 174
Bonnell, Dan, 91
Bonnell, Mary Lynn, 165
Bonnell, Stephen, 93
Bonnemaison, Sarah, 81
Bonner, Beverly, 79
Bonner, Frank, 143
Booher, Sarah L., 153
Booker, Charlotte, 140, 170
Booker, Harry, 183
Booker, Margaret, 158
Booker, Tony, 149
Bookman, Kirk, 149, 170
Bookmyer, William Thomas, 123
Bookwalter, D. Martyn, 162, 163, 174
Boone, Fontella, 149
Boone, Libby, 147
Boone, Michael Kelly, 68, 72, 197
Boone, Winnie, 71
Booth, Dennis, 138
Booth, Eric, 150
Booth, Patti, 170
Booth, Randy, 126
Boothby, Victoria, 139, 177
Borczon, Becky, 166
Borden, Noel, 143
Bordo, Edwin, 197
Boren, Maureen, 169
Boretz, Allen, 115, 226
Borgman, Frank, 151
Born, David, 183
Born, Roscoe, 167
Bornmann, Barbara, 74
Bornstein, Daryl, 167
Bornstein, David L., 90
Bornstein, S. L., 118
Borod, Bob, 146
Boros, Frank J., 170
Borrego, Jesse, 146
Borromeo, Venustiano, 78
Borror, David, 182
Borstal Boy, 187
Bortell, Charles, 143
Borts, Joanne, 66, 197
Borts, Robin, 184
Boruzescu, Miruna, 143
Boruzescu, Radu, 143
Bosakowski, Phil, 78
Bosco, Philip, 69, 115, 197
Boslett, Jack, 169
Bosley, Roz, 176
Bosoms and Neglect, 76
Bossard, Andres, 78
Bostian-Vash, Heather, 141
Bostic, Kysia, 149
Boswell, William, 93, 151
Both Your Houses, 187
Bottari, Michael, 123
Bottoms, John, 141
Bottstein, Dan, 113
Boubie, 65
Bouchard, Bruce, 148
Boucicault, Dion, 184
Boudan, Jack, 164
Boudreau, Robin, 66, 197
Bougetz, Susan, 163
Bourboulis, Cameron, 173
Bourcier, Gerard P., 107
Bourelly, Jean-Paul, 91
Bourgeois, E. D., 138
Bourgeois, John, 154, 186
Bourneuf, Stephen, 145, 155
Boushey, David I., 185
Boussom, Ron, 173
Boutcher, Tamara, 184
Boutsikaris, Dennis, 115, 197
Bova, Anthony, 64, 78, 93
Bova, Joseph, 49, 197
Bove, Adele, 92
Bove, Mark, 45, 152
Bowden, Charles, 9
Bowden, Jonny, 64
Bowden, Richard, 78
Bowerman, Joseph, 169
Bowers, Clent, 48, 124
Bowers, Faubion, 8
Bowers, Frank, 184
Bowers, Martha, 159
Bowers, Teresa, 155
Bowers, Wendy P., 102
Bowles, Anthony, 117
Bowles, Paul, 162
Bowman, Brian, 80
Bowman, John, 118, 120, 162
Bowman, Rob, 152
Bowne, Richard L., 121, 197
Box, The, 113
Boxer, 109
Boyar, Monica, 112, 197
Boyar, Sully, 64
Boyce, Johanna, 141
Boyd, Gregory, 174
Boyd, Julianne, 64, 79, 177
Boyd, Julie, 137
Boyd, Kirk M., 185
Boyer, Katy, 144
Boyer, Monica, 112
Boykin, Nancy, 139
Boyle, Kevin, 17, 64, 66, 68, 70, 130
Boylen, Daniel P., 168
Boys Next Door, The, 164
Boys in Autumn, The: Huck 'N' Tom Grow'd Up, 44, 160
Boys of Winter, The, 17
Boys, Barry, 174, 179
Bozyk, Reizl (Rose), 64, 197
Bozzone, Bill, 91
Brace, Aaron, 174
Brackley, Stephen J., 71
Bradbury, Bill, 121
Bradbury, Peter, 141
Bradbury, Simon, 154, 186
Bradbury, Stephen, 59
Braden, Bill, 133
Braden, Lisa, 64, 80, 93
Bradford, James, 186
Bradford, Mark, 146
Bradford, Scott, 177
Bradley, Charles, 111, 197
Bradley, Elizabeth, 186
Bradley, Jerry, 177
Bradley, Marjorie, 157
Bradley, Pam, 169
Bradley, Scott, 57, 180
Bradly, Bruce Vernon, 113
Bradshaw, Deborah, 92
Brady, Arthur, 65
Brady, Barbara, 188
Brady, Brigid, 160
Brady, Dan Patrick, 59
Brady, John E., 100
Braet, James, 164
Braga, Karen, 80
Braha, Judy, 166
Brailoff, Lisa, 179
Brainin, Risa, 113
Bramble, Mark, 49, 127
Bramen, Risa, 193
Bramlett, Sherri, 127
Bramlett, Kathleen Boyette, 82
Bramlett, T. Wiley, 82
Bramon, Risa, 91
Brancato, Joe, 77
Brand, 90
Brand, Gibby, 142
Brand, Thomas, 162
Brandafino, Lori-Jo, 183
Brandes, Daniel, 93
Brandford, Drea, 116
Brandmer, Gerhard, 60
Brandner, Susan, 177
Brando, Marlon, 188
Brandt, Deborah, 76
Branom, Mark, 136
Bransford, Shellie, 69
Branton, Nancy, 140
Brasch, Marion, 90
Brashaw, Suzanne, 61, 74
Brashler, William, 83
Brasington, Alan, 137
Brassard, Gail, 152, 160
Brasser, Victoria, 121, 197
Brauer, M., 100
Braun, Elyn, 79
Braunstein, Steven, 74, 140
Braverman, Jill Nicole, 153
Brawer, Jacques, 63
Braxton, Brenda, 126
Bray, Barbara, 76
Bray, Jane, 172
Bray, Melissa, 136
Brazda, David, 110, 197
Brazeau, Jay, 186
Break, The, 113
Breaking The Prairie Wolf Code, 84
Brecher, Kenneth, 146
Brechner, Stanley, 86
Brecht, Bertolt, 90, 143, 144, 173
Breed, Helen Lloyd, 66, 197
Breen, J. Patrick, 197
Breen, Nellie, 226
Breen, Patrick, 46
Breffort, Alexandre, 155
Breining, James, 144
Breitbart, Scott, 155
Breitbarth, David, 60, 197
Breithaupt, Stephen, 146
Brenn, Janni, 148
Brennan, Eileen, 135, 188
Brennan, James, 26, 74, 80
Brennan, Matthew, 74
Brennan, Maureen, 76, 167, 188
Brennan, Nora, 48, 81
Brennan, Timothy, 158, 173
Brennan, Tom, 101, 135, 180, 197
Brennan, Wendy, 82
Brenno, Tori, 124
Brenz, Linda Marie, 127
Brera, Mario, 128
Brett, Jeremy, 197
Breuler, Robert, 156
Brevis, Claudia, 74
Brevis, Skip, 74
Brewer, David, 140
Brewer, Robert, 78
Brewster, Karen, 145
Brian, Michael, 46, 59, 197
Briar, Suzanne, 62, 76
Brice, Stephen, 93
Bricker, Kelly, 154, 186
Brickley, Kate, 141
Bridewell, Sandra, 64
Bridges, Kenneth, 96
Bridges, Mark, 51, 64
Bridges, Rand, 148
Bridges, Robert, 92, 96
Bridwell, Thom, 32
Brigadoon, 187
Briggle, Gary, 144
Briggs, Jody, 136
Briggs, John, 177
Briggs, Richard, 197
Brigham, Scott, 159
Bright, Charles, 181
Brighton Beach Memoirs, 187
Brigleb, John, 142
Brill, Fran, 98, 162, 197
Brilliande, Karen, 136
Brimm, Thomas Martell, 12
Bringle, Joshua, 160
Brinkley, Susann, 64
Brisco, Roslyn, 151
Britten, Bill, 61
Brittingham, Scott, 146
Britton, Beverly, 164
Britton, Kate, 100
Britton, Scott, 74
Brizzolara, David, 140, 162
Bro, Judith, 142
Broad, Jason, 100
Brochu, James, 162
Brock, Lee, 58
Brock, Robert, 137
Brocksmith, Roy, 138
Brockway, Adrienne J., 72
Brockway, Amie, 72
Broderick, Matthew, 47, 188, 197
Brodhead, James E., 173
Brodsky, Larry, 87
Brody, Jerrold, 68
Brogger, Ivar, 94, 101, 197
Brogyanyi, Eugene, 57
Brohn, William D., 26
Brokow, Mark, 180
Brolaski, Carol, 60
Brolin, Andrew, 138
Bromka, Elaine, 18, 186
Bromley, Tarquin Jay, 110
Brongo, Laurie, 15
Brooke, Haynes, 140
Brooke, Sarah, 136
Brookes, Jacqueline, 184, 188, 197
Brooks, Alan, 54, 197
Brooks, Donald L., 78, 83
Brooks, Dorothy, 71, 197
Brooks, Gwendolyn, 85
Brooks, Hewitt, 63
Brooks, Jeff, 54, 168, 171, 174
Brooks, Jim, 161
Brooks, Martin, 188
Brooks, Melody, 58, 60, 161
Brooks, Paul, 143
Broome Street, America, 63
Broome, John, 154, 186
Brosius, Peter C., 146, 147
Brother Malcolm, 80
Brothers, Carla, 107
Brower, Albert, 113
Brower, Mitchell, 127
Brown, Alane, 112
Brown, Arvin, 162
Brown, Barry, 50
Brown, Billie, 179
Brown, Brenda K., 81
Brown, Charles, 154
Brown, Chuck, 96, 155, 197
Brown, Clark, 197
Brown, Clarke, 71
Brown, Deborah, 54, 66, 162
Brown, Douglas, 143, 181
Brown, Franklin, 149, 153
Brown, Geoffrey, 52
Brown, Gerard, 107
Brown, Graham, 104, 197
Brown, Heidi, 62
Brown, Iris, 169
Brown, Jamie, 144, 179
Brown, Janet, 141
Brown, Jason, 78
Brown, Judy, 150
Brown, Ken, 92, 93
Brown, Kermit, 181
Brown, Lenisha D., 162
Brown, Lenora, 55
Brown, Lewis, 139, 184
Brown, Loren, 91, 197
Brown, Lynn, 140
Brown, Mr., 83
Brown, Nacio Herb, 7
Brown, Pat, 59, 139
Brown, Paul, 138
Brown, Richard C., 139
Brown, Robin Leslie, 110, 153
Brown, Sharon, 126
Brown, Steve, 146
Brown, Sullivan, 94, 197
Brown, Toni, 100
Brown, Walter, 182
Brown, Willex, Jr., 83
Browne, Roscoe Lee, 161
Browning, Dolph, 96
Browning, Robert, 181
Browning, Susan, 46, 71, 188, 197
Brownlee, Dani, 133
Brubach, Karen, 63
Brubach, Robert, 50
Bruce, Bonnie, 152
Bruce, Cheryl Lynn, 59
Bruce, Lydia, 171
Bruce, Susan, 90
Bruders, Janet, 62
Bruice, Ann, 146, 147
Brumage, Bruce, 107, 108
Brummel, David, 135, 197
Bruner, Glenn, 59, 174
Brunjes, Hank, 133
Brunner, Michael, 155
Bruno, Angelynn, 91
Bruno, Lise, 182
Bruns, Philip, 197
Brush, Steve, 136
Brushingham, Marcia, 83, 123
Brustein, Robert, 141
Bruton, Ciscoe II, 37, 130
Brutsman, Laura, 82, 197, 201
Bryan, Jennifer, 37
Bryan, John L., 79
Bryan, Kenneth, 226, 231
Bryan, Scott, 152
Bryan-Brown, Adrian, 34, 36, 46, 49, 56, 115, 122, 127
Bryant, Craig, 82, 197
Bryant, David, 102, 153, 197
Bryant, Janet D., 182
Bryant, Lee, 98
Bryant, Linda, 148
Bryant, Mary, 64
Bryant, Richard, 144
Bryant, Scott, 101
Bryant-Brown, Adrian, 135
Bryce, Edward, 188
Brydon, W. B., 101, 197
Bryer, Chris, 84
Bryggman, Larry, 107, 197
Bryne, Barbara, 23, 197
Brynner, Yul, 226, 231
Bryon, Marlene, 145
Bubbles, John, 227
Buberl, Doris J., 51
Bubriski, Peter, 87, 197
Bucciarelli, Rene, 57
Buchanan, Kay, 179
Buchanan, Linda, 166
Buchanan, Lucianne, 133
Buchanan, Margo, 161, 166
Buchman, Nanrose, 136
Buck, Gene David, 144
Buck, John, Jr., 30
Buck, Randall, 146
Buckingham, Forry, 79
Buckley, Betty, 11, 20, 21, 48, 106, 197
Buckley, Christopher, 179
Buckley, Hal, 227
Buckley, Melinda, 197
Buckley, Ralph, 59, 69
Buckner, Tracy Lynn, 140
Budd, Julie, 58, 197
Buderwitz, Thomas, 144
Budin, Rachel, 112, 160, 161
Budries, David, 157
Buehler, Laurie, 110
Bufalino, Brenda, 58
Buff, Jim, 71, 171, 184
Buffaloe, Katharine, 134, 197
Buffam, David, 95
Bufman, Zev, 16, 24
Bufton, Corbett Hart, 173
Bugbee, Charles, 3rd, 64
Bugge, Carole, 95
Buka, Donald, 144
Bulger, Catherine, 184
Bulifant, Joyce, 188
Bull, Sandy, 141
Bullard, Thomas, 99, 137
Bullard, Walter, 20
Bullington, Robert, 179
Bullock, Donna, 146
Bullock, Eldon, 106
Bullshot Crummond, 160
Bulluck, Elizabeth, 149
Bulos, Yusef, 171
Bumatai, Ray, 136
Bumgardner, Jim, 118
Bumgarner, Myra, 167
Bumpass, Rodger, 70, 81
Bunch, Barbara, 62
Bundonis, Virginia, 142
Bundy, Rob, 82
Bunis, Irene, 50
Bunn, Sharon, 177
Bunting, Pearce, 180
Buntzen, Robert, 105
Burch-Worch, Bryan, 161
Burchett, Beverly, 83
Burda, Stephanie, 116, 158, 158
Burdick, Hunt, 163
Burdick, Melissa L., 68, 74, 116
Burge, Gregg, 11, 197
Burgess, Elizabeth, 92
Burgess, Phyllis, 58
Burgler, Terry, 177
Burgreen, J. Andrew, 167
Buried Child, 173, 187
Burk, Terence, 64, 197
Burke, Bradley, 165
Burke, Brendan, 184
Burke, Deirdre, 78
Burke, Georgia, 227
Burke, Maggie, 157, 197
Burke, Marylouise, 76, 80
Burke, Robert, 157
Burke, Sarah S., 150, 158
Burkhardt, Gerry, 93, 198
Burkholder, Scott, 103
Burks, Donny, 188, 198
Burks, Stephen, 180
Burleigh, Stephen, 178
Burlingame, Karen, 162
Burnell, Peter, 188
Burnett, Carol, 188
Burnett, Robert, 48
Burney, Harry L., III, 46
Burney, Susanna, 171
Burnham, Bonnie B., 88
Burns, Catherine, 63, 78, 188, 198
Burns, James, 80
Burns, Ralph, 37, 40
Burns, Robert, 149, 180
Burns, Ron, 57
Burns, Stanley, 74
Burns, Traber, 177
Burnside, Katie, 102
Burrell, Bud, 134
Burrell, Deborah, 126
Burrell, Fred, 81, 198
Burrell, Pamela, 162, 188, 198
Burrell, Teresa, 64, 160, 198
Burrichter, Robert, 60
Burrough, Roslyn, 69
Burroughs, Kimberleigh, 180
Burrows, Abe, 73, 140, 142
Burrows, Kevyn, 130
Burrows, Mike, 114
Burrows, Vinie, 198
Burrus, Bob, 137
Burstein, Pesach, 227
Burt, Mary, 169
Burton, Arnie, 78
Burton, Chad, 64
Burton, Kate, 157, 158, 188, 198
Burton, Laura, 186
Burton, Richard, 188
Burton, Stacey, 157
Bury, John, 39
Busby, Barbara, 151
Busch, Charles, 59, 69
Busch, Gregg, 123
Buschmann, Don, 145, 175
Bush, Barbara, 182
Bush, Claire, 109
Bush, Grand L., 147
Bush, Michael, 99
Busheme, Joseph, 46
Bushnell, Bill, 163
Buskers, 79
Bussanich, Rachele, 48
Bussard, Larry, 24
Busse, David A., 183
Bussert, Meg, 81, 188, 198
Bustamante, Mauricio, 109, 198
Bustard, Wendy, 120
Butcher, Cheri, 7
Butler, Austin, 131
Butler, Buddy, 102
Butler, Craig, 66
Butler, Dan, 94, 95
Butler, Jerome, 164, 177
Butler, Leslie, 42, 47
Butler, Lillian, 93
Butler, Paul, 89, 97
Butler, Philip, 8, 75
Butler, Rick, 90
Butleroff, Helen, 96
Butt, Jennifer, 124
Butterfield, Patricia, 56
Butterfield, Richard, 182
Buttram, Jan, 148
Buzas, Jason, 98
Buzzell, Robert, 79
Bye Bye Birdie, 187
Byers, Bill, 45
Byers, Karen, 128
Byers, Michael, 26
Byers, Ralph, 46, 198
Bynum, Brenda, 140
Byrd, Carolyn, 85
Byrd, Debra, 102
Byrne, John, 94
Byrne, Regan M., 152
Byrne, Terry, 101
Byron, Lee Alan, 185
Cabalero, Roxann, 45
Cabaret, 153, 187
Cabbagehead, The, 61
Cacciatore, Jayne, 93, 198, 201
Cacoyannis, Michael, 135
Cada, James, 138, 156
Caddick, David, 11
Cadiff, Andrew, 57
Cady, David, 61, 198
Caesar, Adolph, 227, 231
Caesar, Irving, 76
Caffey, Marion J., 15, 198
Cagelles, Les, 50
Cagelles, The, 128
Cagle, Charles, 142
Cagney, James, 227, 231
Cahalan, Joseph, 114
Cahill, James, 14, 69, 198, 201
Cahn, Larry, 155
Cahn, Sammy, 188
Cahn-Puiter, Naomi, 62
Cain, Candice, 179
Cain, Scott, 73
Cain, William, 44, 70, 149, 198
Caine Mutiny Court-Martial, The, 161

Caine, David, 50
Cal and Sally, 151
Calabro, Rita, 172
Calandra, Denis, 112
Calandrino, Sam, 158
Calavin, Charlotte, 105
Calder, John W., III, 93
Calderon, Paul, 108
Caldwell, Carolyn, 79
Caldwell, Charles, 140, 177
Caldwell, L. Scott, 180
Caldwell, Linda, 148
Caldwell, Zoe, 30, 188
Caligula, 89
Call, Anthony D., 198
Call, Edward Payson, 144
Callahan, Bill, 188
Callahan, Dennis, 50
Callahan, Janet, 106, 107
Callahan, Linda, 146
Callahan, Steven C., 43, 97
Callander, Barbara, 100
Callaway, Liz, 164
Callman, Nancy, 96, 198, 201
Calloway, Brian, 186
Calman, Camille, 92
Calvan, George, 146
Calvert, John, 108
Camacho, Blanca, 79, 198
Camacho, Frank, 101
Camas, Rosemary, 60
Cambrelen, Bataki, 151
Cambridge, Edmund J., 168
Camden, Robert, 81
Camel Has His Nose Under the Tent, The, 114
Camelot, 123, 164
Camera, John, 90
Cameron, Ben, 160, 170
Cameron, Dennis, 60
Cameron, Hope, 171
Cameron, William, 170
Cameron-Webb, Gavin, 98, 152, 160
Camp, Joanne, 110, 167, 188, 198
Camp, Karma, 161
Campanaro, Philip, 65
Campanella, Philip, 65, 115
Campbell, Allison, 59, 152
Campbell, Benedict, 154, 186
Campbell, Bradley, 177
Campbell, Bruce, 20, 106
Campbell, Carolyn, 149
Campbell, Colleen, 145
Campbell, Douglas, 154, 186
Campbell, Gerard J., 68
Campbell, Graeme, 198
Campbell, J. Kenneth, 17, 121
Campbell, Jennifer, 145
Campbell, Larry, 83
Campbell, Robert, 131
Campbell, Sally, 24, 59
Campbell, Sarah, 136, 175
Campisi, Tony, 161
Campos, Rafael, 227, 231
Camus, Albert, 89
Canada, Ron, 153
Canary, David, 66, 198
Canary, Evan, 106, 107, 108
Canavan, Michael, 173
Candida, 156
Candide, 167, 187
Candler, Phillip, 69
Cane, Marianne, 46
Cangelosi, Elizabeth, 74
Cannaday, John, 163
Cannis, Michael, 171
Cannon, Ellen, 80
Cannon, Richard E., 58
Cannon, Wanda, 149
Cano, Rose E., 175
Cantor, Arthur, 31, 75
Capitola, Jeffrey, 68, 128
Caplin, Jeremy O., 33, 198
Caplin, Martha, 71
Caplin, Mortimer, 33
Capo, Laurence, 164
Capodice, John, 179
Capone, Steven, 175
Capote, Truman, 175
Capotorto, Carl, 180
Cappelli, Joe, 146
Capri, Mark, 168, 188, 198
Caracciolo, 59
Cardelli, Bob, 161
Carden, William, 91, 170, 198
Careless Love, 158
Carell, Candace, 48, 124
Caretaker, The, 28
Carey, Colleen, 136
Carey, Darrell, 50
Carey, Helen, 156
Carey, Jeff, 151
Carey, Robert, 59, 69
Carey-Jones, Selena, 36
Caringi, Rudy, 60
Cariou, Len, 115, 188, 198
Carle, Cynthia, 165
Carley, Kurt, 169
Carlin, Amanda, 115, 198
Carlin, Joy, 141
Carlin, Nancy, 182
Carlin, Tony, 160
Carling, P. L., 60, 171, 198
Carlo, Johann, 116, 198
Carlos, Laurie, 102
Carlson, Roberta, 144
Carlson, Sandra, 46
Carlson, Sharon, 159
Carlsson, Ted, 173
Carlyon, David, 59
Carmichael, Bill, 124
Carmine, Michael, 108
Carnahan, Kirsti, 66, 198
Carney, Alexander D., 101, 162
Carney, Anne, 95
Carney, Georgia, 186
Carney, Laura, 167
Carnival, 149, 187
Caro, Bruce, 64
Carol Rosegg Photos, 107
Carollo, Joann C., 66
Carols, Laurie, 102
Carousel, 145, 167, 187
Carpenter, Bethany, 165
Carpenter, Brian, 63
Carpenter, Carleton, 96, 198
Carpenter, Cassandra, 184
Carpenter, John, 168
Carpenter, Karen L., 118, 159
Carpenter, Larry, 159, 166
Carpenter, Terry W., 165
Carr, Allan, 50
Carr, Elizabeth Katherine, 59, 69, 118
Carr, Laurence, 90
Carr, Mimi, 170
Carr, Revell, 142
Carr, Thomas P., 125
Carradine, David, 188
Carradine, Keith, 146
Carrafa, John, 7
Carrera, Maria, 184
Carricart, Robertson, 14, 198, 201
Carrier and the Box, 59
Carriere, Berthold, 186
Carrigan, Ann Patrice, 153
Carrigan, Kevin, 179
Carriker, Teresa M., 79
Carrillo, Ramiro, 154
Carroll, Barbara, 20, 106
Carroll, Beeson, 67
Carroll, Bob, 128
Carroll, Danny, 49, 198
Carroll, David, 26
Carroll, David-James, 198
Carroll, Edward P., 57
Carroll, Helena, 184
Carroll, Jennifer, 154
Carroll, Mary Beth, 82
Carroll, Nancy E., 145
Carroll, Rocky, 171
Carrubba, Philip, 92, 198
Carruthers, James, 72, 170, 198
Carry On, 158
Carson, A. D., 170
Carson, Heather, 68, 108
Carson, Jean, 188
Carson, Jeannie, 172
Carson, Richard, 184
Carson, Thomas, 153, 159
Carter, Dan, 51, 58, 144
Carter, Dixie, 188
Carter, James, 104
Carter, John, 163
Carter, Nell, 188
Carter, Ralph, 188
Carter, Roderick, 169
Carter, Rosanna, 168, 198, 201
Carter, Steve, 104
Carter, Thelma Louise, 102, 198
Cartier, Jacques, 159
Cartmell, Tina, 179
Cartoon, 66
Cartwright, Terence, 113
Caruso, Arlene, 61
Caruso, Jim, 177
Caruso, John, 61
Carver, Brent, 186
Casady, Chris, 177
Case, Evelyn Carol, 181
Case, Ronald, 123
Casey, Eileen, 130
Casey, Laurel, 144
Casey, Michelle, 141
Cash, Susan, 111, 115, 198
Caskey, Marilyn, 152
Caskie, David, 120
Cason, Yvette Louise, 126
Casorla, Rick, 174
Casper, Richard, 164
Caspers, Rod, 65
Casperson, Jack, 151
Caspi, Na'ama, 184
Cass, Peggy, 49, 188, 198
Cassan-Jellison, Claudine, 162
Casserly, Kerry, 45, 130, 198
Cassidy, Orlagh, 152
Cassidy, Shaun, 163
Cassidy, Tim, 126, 198
Castang, Veronica, 137, 162, 198
Castay, Leslie, 122
Castellanos, John David, 141, 185
Castillo, Mark, 182
Castle, Elowyn, 131
Castle, Rebecca, 165
Castleman, William, 75
Castro, Christina, 176
Castro, Laura, 64
Castro, Lauro, 58
Castro, Vicente, 112
Casualties, 65
Cat on a Hot Tin Roof, 178, 187
Cat's-Paw, 172
Catalano, George, 136
Catanese, Charles, 64
Cate, Regina, 141
Cater, Robert, 126
Cates, Phoebe, 116
Cates, Steven, 152
Cathey, Reg E., 106
Caton-Ford, Amy, 172
Catricala, Arthur, 76
Cats, 48, 124, 187
Catt, Christopher, 68
Cattaneo, Anne, 81, 82
Cattelona, Joe, 100
Cattrall, Kim, 163
Caulfield, Maxwell, 101, 188
Caux, Claude, 183
Cava, Frank, 135
Cavaliere, Al, 135
Cavanah, Craig, 184
Cavander, Kenneth, 141
Cavener, Ann Marie, 116
Cavey, George, 162
Cavise, Joe Antony, 48
Cawelti, Michael, 182
Caywood, John, 73
Caza, Terrence, 82, 198, 201
Cea, Kim, 169
Cecil, Jane, 43, 97
Cecil, Pamela, 50
Cecsarini, David, 181
Celebration, 85
Celestine, 86
Cellario, Maria, 60, 198
Celli, Tom, 176
Cenedella, Robert, 167
Cennamo, Jack, 50
Ceraso, Chris, 96
Cermak, Terry, 177
Cerri, Michael, 161
Cerveris, Michael, 86, 157, 160, 198
Cesario, Robert, 95
Cesear, Gregory W., 184
Cestero, Carlos, 80
Chaban, Michael, 143
Chadman, Christopher, 37
Chadwick, Robin, 166
Chaikin, Joseph, 60, 161
Chalakani, Paul, 88, 198, 201
Chalfant, Kathleen, 151, 179
Chalmers, Toni-Maria, 32, 83, 198
Chalon, Mary, 153
Chamberlain, Douglas, 186
Chamberlin, Jayne, 100
Chamberlin, Mark, 170
Chamberlin, Sally, 90, 198
Chambers, Arline, 146
Chambers, David, 171
Champagne, Michael, 71, 198
Champion, Alan, 174
Champion, Gower, 49, 127
Champlin, Sally, 146
Chan, Donald W., 128
Chance, Daniel, 180
Chance, William, 107
Chandavarkar, Bhaskar, 109
Chandler, Beth, 172
Chandler, Brian Evaret, 83
Chandler, Chan, 22
Chandler, Jeffrey Alan, 173
Chandler, Nat, 118, 198
Chandler, Raymond, 80, 96
Chandler, Stan, 96, 149
Chaney, David, 167
Chaney, Frances, 79
Chang, Carlotta, 148
Chang, Melanie, 182
Chang, Randy, 109
Chang, Roger, 109
Chang, Tisa, 109
Changeling, The, 141
Changing Room, The, 187
Channell, Steven, 92, 113
Channing, Carol, 129, 146, 188, 199
Channing, Stockard, 43, 97, 199
Chansky, Dorothy, 66
Chantler, Carrie, 175
Chao, Rosalind, 146, 147
Chapin, Wendy, 178
Chaplin, Clive, 31
Chaplin, Sydney, 188
Chapman, David, 135
Chapman, Gary, 37, 199
Chapman, Linda, 161
Chapman, Ray, 182
Chapman, Roger, 105
Chappell, Fred, 140
Chappell, Kandis, 144, 184
Charboneau, Leon, 142
Charbonneau, Sidney, 142
Charisse, Zan, 188
Charles, David, 102
Charles, Jim, 52, 158
Charles, Jonathan, 139
Charles, Kirk, 172
Charles, Moie, 87
Charles, Walter, 50, 199
Charley's Aunt, 182
Charley's Tale, 76
Charlsen, Nadine, 109
Charlton, William, 183
Charmin, Randy William, 101
Charney, Tina, 109
Charnin, Martin, 122
Charnin, Sasha, 79
Charone, Irwin, 142
Chart, Joe, 71
Chase, Gregory, 170
Chaskin, Rob, 62
Chastain, Don, 49, 78
Chateau Foirelacour, 113
Chater, Gordon, 159
Chattopadhyaya, Arundhati, 109
Chausow, Lynn, 156, 168
Chauvin, Jacqueline, 77, 90
Chaves, Richard, 188, 199
Chavis, Mark, 140
Cheapside, 115
Chebba, Alice, 138
Cheeseman, Ken, 166
Chekhov, Anton, 77, 82, 95, 151, 152, 158, 161, 163
Chekov, Anton, 93, 171
Chemel, David, 173
Cherashore, Spencer, 148
Cherry Orchard, The, 77, 151, 152, 171
Chess, Mary K., 169, 170
Chester, Nora, 144
Chester, Sa'mi, 177
Chew, Edna, 102
Chew, Lee, 92, 96, 199
Chiang, Dawn, 156
Chiavetta, Carol, 138
Chibas, Marissa, 120, 166, 199
Chiel, Daniel, 63
Child's Christmas in Wales, A, 175
Child's Tale, A, 180
Childers, Jean, 160
Children of a Lesser God, 174, 187
Children of the Sun, 101
Childress, Yolanda, 179
Childs, Kirsten, 24, 40
Chilson, Kathryn, 93, 199
Chilton, Leslie, 110
Chiment, Marie Anne, 137, 171
Chin, Michael G., 109
Chirgotis, Candice, 157
Chislett, Anne, 89
Chitwood, Ann, 113
Chmelko-Jaffe, Mary, 165
Choate, Tim, 161
Choder, Jill, 98, 199, 201
Choen, Mimi, 57
Choma, George, 100
Chopin Playoffs, The, 86
Chorus Line, A, 45, 148, 164, 169, 187, 188
Chris, Marilyn, 87, 199
Christen, Robert, 154, 166
Christian Follies, 113
Christian, E. M., 80
Christian, Edward, 172
Christian, Evanne, 86
Christian, Nancy, 80
Christian, Patricia, 150
Christian, Stephen, 175
Christianson, Catherine, 150, 177
Christie, Agatha, 87, 100, 153
Christie, Barbara, 61
Christie, Jessica C., 98, 121
Christmas Carol, A, 136, 137, 141, 144, 150, 153, 154, 156, 165, 166, 173, 177
Christmas Death, 163
Christmas Gifts, 164
Christmas Memory, A, 175
Christmas Miracles, 151
Christopher, Donald, 145, 159, 170, 177
Christopher, Jordan, 188
Christopher, Joyce Reehling, 88
Christopher, Spider Duncan, 73
Christopher, Thom, 188
Christy, Donald, 57, 80
Christy, Roberta, 34
Chryst, Gary, 45, 199, 201
Chun, Kris Marie, 109
Chun, Lynette, 109, 199, 201
Church, Joseph, 80
Churchill, Caryl, 149
Churchill, Clyde, Jr., 130
Chute, Susan, 61
Chybowski, Michael, 180
Ciaccio, Tom, 32
Cibula, Nan, 79, 97, 115, 127, 161
Cicarelli, Susan, 158
Cicchini, Robert, 121
Ciccolella, Jude, 59, 121
Ciccone, Oscar, 106
Ciesla, Diane, 61
Cilento, Diane, 188
Cilento, Wayne, 24, 37, 199
Cima, Alessandro, 152
Cimino, Leonardo, 12, 108
Ciokajlo, Mark, 144
Cira, Paul, 155
Circe & Bravo, 151
Circle, The, 101
Cirillo, Jack, 183
Cirker, Ira, 70
Cirker, Jason, 70
Ciroux, Monique, 91
Ciserano, Pat, 101
Cissel, Charles, 80
Ciulei, Liviu, 108, 156
Claiborne, Cary, 61
Claire, Ludi, 184
Claire, Mary Anne, 172
Clancy, Deirdre, 156
Clanton, Rony, 80
Clare, Suzanne, 179
Clarence Darrow, 170
Clark, Bobby, 172
Clark, Brian, 39
Clark, Bryan, 101, 199
Clark, C. A., 98, 103
Clark, Cheryl, 199
Clark, China, 60
Clark, J. Cody, 172
Clark, James A., 175
Clark, Jeff, 82
Clark, John, 140
Clark, Josh, 33, 199, 201
Clark, Marietta, 127
Clark, Matt, 145
Clark, Paul, 58
Clark, Renee, 92, 152
Clark, Shane, 136, 172
Clark, Victoria, 124
Clark, Wesley, 186
Clark, William G., 66, 199
Clarke, Anne Beresford, 161
Clarke, Brian Patrick, 80
Clarke, Caitlin, 14, 199
Clarke, Hope, 102, 149
Clarke, J. D., 72
Clarke, Lydia, 188
Clarke, Martha, 78
Clarke, Maureen, 59, 121
Clarke, Michael A., 51, 64
Clarke, Philip Norman, 227
Clarke, Richard, 23
Clarke, Sarah, 83
Clarkson, John, 142
Clarkson, Patricia, 43, 91, 99
Clater, Robert, 126
Clausen, Richard, 62, 69
Claxton, Catherine Anne, 74
Clay, Juanin, 71
Clayburgh, Jim, 161
Claypool, Kathleen, 54
Claypool, Veronica, 9
Clayton, Lawrence, 126
Clayton, Lynne, 159
Clayton, Philip, 128
Clear, Patrick, 171
Cleator, Molly, 163
Clegg, Johnny, 77
Clelland, Deborah, 66
Clemence, Andrew, 152
Clement, Arlene, 174
Clemente, Rene, 48, 199
Cleveland, Jerry, 32, 162
Cleveland, Sally, 173, 184
Clewell, Thomas L., 98, 166
Cliff, Oliver, 144, 184
Clifford, Pamela, 167
Clifton, John, 159
Cline, Perry, 37
Clinton, Georgia, 177
Clinton, Robert, 149
Clonts, Jeffrey, 164
Clonts, John, 128
Close, Glenn, 27, 199
Cloud 9, 137
Clough, Lancey, 18
Clough, Peter H., 148
Clouthier, Elizabeth, 142
Clow, James, 175
Club, The, 167
Clugston, Glen, 142
Clyman, Robert, 151
Coachman-Tarlinskaja, Maria, 172
Coates, Carolyn, 188
Coates, Kim, 186
Coates, Norman, 16
Coates, Thom, 153
Coats, William Alan, 145
Cobb, Darly, 177
Cobb, Hugh D., 140
Cobbs, Bill, 91, 172
Cochran, Pat, 143
Cochran, Shannon, 164
Cochrane, James, 20
Cochren, Felix E., 61, 149
Cocktail Party, The, 187
Coco, James, 99, 146, 199
Coco, Sarah, 176
Codron, Michael, 27
Coffee, Leonore, 77
Coghill, Joy, 186
Cohan, Blossom, 174
Cohan, George M., 178
Cohen, Alexander H., 188
Cohen, Alice Eve, 84, 85
Cohen, Allen, 94
Cohen, Andrea, 78, 155
Cohen, Arthur W., 62
Cohen, Aviva, 87
Cohen, Bruce, 62, 63, 69, 72, 77, 79, 91, 119
Cohen, Buzz, 60
Cohen, Charles, 168
Cohen, Don, 122
Cohen, Edward M., 96
Cohen, Elliot J., 76
Cohen, Geoffrey, 153
Cohen, Jason Steven, 20, 45, 106
Cohen, Judith, 101, 172
Cohen, Leo K., 36, 49, 127
Cohen, Lois, 134
Cohen, Lynn, 108, 199
Cohen, Marc, 138
Cohen, Mark, 100
Cohen, Martin, 124
Cohen, Michael, 61
Cohen, Richard, 179
Cohen, Robert I., 16, 145, 183
Cohen, Sally, 162
Cohen, Sherry, 48
Cohen, Tracy B., 99, 106
Cohenour, Patti, 20, 21, 46, 106, 188, 199
Cohn, Andrew, 162
Coid, Marshall, 117
Coit, Connie, 150
Coker, Melody Kay, 139
Colaianni, Louis, 186
Colavecchia, Franco, 61, 115, 159
Colavin, Charlotte, 105
Colbert, Claudette, 122, 199
Colby, Christine, 40, 199
Colby, Michael, 81, 118
Cole, Brandon, 91
Cole, Debra, 76
Cole, Holly, 152
Cole, Jan, 59, 139
Cole, Janis I., 174
Cole, Jason, 154
Cole, Kay, 57, 199, 201
Cole, Kerry, 177
Cole, Megan, 173
Cole, Robert, 75
Cole, Steve, 31
Cole, Vincent M., 37, 126
Coleman, Bruce R., 177
Coleman, Cristal, 180
Coleman, Cy, 40, 121, 152
Coleman, Desiree, 37, 199
Coleman, Jim, 167
Coleman, Kevin, 142
Coleridge, Alan, 87
Coles, Charles "Honi", 130, 199
Coles, Deborah, 54
Coles, Diana, 175
Coles, Wendy, 80
Colette in Love, 85
Colglazier, Phillip H., 145
Colker, Jerry, 199
Colley, Peter, 176
Collins, Brent, 74
Collins, Craig, 146, 147
Collins, Elsbeth M., 61, 116
Collins, Elsbeth, 116
Collins, George, 153
Collins, Jeffrey, 80
Collins, Kate, 179
Collins, Laura, 159
Collins, Mary, 58
Collins, Michael, 146
Collins, Pat, 17, 18, 33, 57, 99, 116, 155, 156, 162, 172
Collins, Patricia, 154, 186
Collins, Ray, 93, 199
Collins, Rufus, 131
Collins, Wendell, 71
Collins, Zebedee, 59
Collison, Frank, 163
Collodi, Carlo, 140
Colman, Booth, 165
Colombi, Licia, 73
Colorado, Hortensia, 180

Colored Museum, The, 149
Colston, Robert, 49, 153, 172
Coltman, Caro, 186
Colton, Chevi, 111
Colton, Jacque Lynn, 146
Colton, Richard, 7
Colyer, Austin, 7
Combest, Christopher, 139
Combs, David, 171
Combs, Jeffrey, 184
Combs, Melody, 63, 137
Comden, Betty, 7, 121, 188
Come Back, Little Sheba, 150
Comedy of Errors, The, 131, 181, 186
Comfort, Richard, 64
Company, 187
Compton, Gardner, 51
Conable, Anne E., 174
Conaway, Jeff, 16, 148, 199
Conboy, Roy, 176
Condit, Katherine Lynn, 164
Cone, Lucinda Hitchcock, 171
Conery, Edward, 181
Conescu, John, 136
Confalone, Peter, 141
Confar, Mary Ann, 167
Congdon, Constance, 157
Conger, Eric, 164
Conklin, John, 141, 156, 157, 159, 162
Conklin, Katherine, 64, 67, 186
Conklin, Mary, 60
Conley, Jim, 181
Conley, John, 159
Conlow, Peter, 188
Conn, William, 14, 25, 44
Connecticut Yankee, A, 80
Connell, David, 79, 102, 199
Connell, Gordon, 46, 199
Connell, Jane, 76, 167, 199
Connell, Kelly, 89
Connell, Thomas, 8
Connelly, David, 160
Conner, Bruce, 167
Connolly, John P., 46, 57, 61, 85, 199
Connolly, Kathy, 169
Connolly, Michael, 159, 167
Connor, Whitfield, 188
Conolly, Patricia, 172, 186
Conover, Constance, 170
Conrad, Kent, 144
Conrow, Frances, 146, 147
Conroy, Frances, 184
Conroy, Jarlath, 168, 171
Consagra, Maria, 141
Consenting Adults, 113
Constant Wife, The, 93
Constantine, Deborah, 62, 87
Constantine, Rob, 145
Consul, The, 187
Contadino, Lisa, 76
Conte, Derek, 78
Conte, John K., 162
Contractor, The, 187
Contrast, The, 110
Conversation, 163
Converse-Roberts, William, 115
Conway, Brendan, 98
Conway, Daniel, 93, 94, 98, 105, 117, 162
Conway, Merry, 186
Conway, Shirl, 188
Conwell, Charles, 168
Cook, Barbara, 152, 188
Cook, Divina, 151
Cook, Dwight R. B., 107
Cook, James, 52
Cook, Jennifer, 107
Cook, Linda, 144
Cook, Michael, 182
Cook, Peter C., 164
Cook, Reagan, 81, 92
Cook, Roderick, 74, 199
Cooksey, Vannesa, 154
Cookson, Peter, 188
Cooley, David, 175
Cooley, Jared, 183
Cooley, Paul-Andrew, 182
Coombs, Richard, 150
Cooney, Dennis, 188
Coonradt, R. Mark Wallace, Rev., 77
Cooper, Berry, 132
Cooper, Cynthia, 85
Cooper, Helmar Augustus, 149
Cooper, Juli, 92, 199
Cooper, Marilyn, 6, 111, 153, 199
Cooper, Mary, 79
Cooper, Neil, 63
Cooper, Reva, 88
Cooper, Susan, 146
Cooper, Thelma, 76
Cooper-Hecht, Gail, 101
Copeland, Carolyn Rossi, 74, 79, 68
Copeland, John, 154
Copeland, Maurice, 227, 231
Copelin, David, 143
Copes, Juan Carlos, 13
Coppola, Sam J., 135
Coray, Catherine, 81
Corbett, Iris, 78
Corby, Steven, 99
Corcoran, Jay, 88, 89
Corcoran, Joseph, 134
Corcoran, Mary, 199
Cordaro, Kate, 169
Cordon, Marlie, 144
Cordon, Susie, 132
Cordova, Roxanne, 176
Corey, John, 161
Corey, Wendell, 188
Corfman, Caris, 61, 80, 199
Corker, John S., 73
Corley, Hal, 64
Corley, Nick, 58, 155
Corma, Eugene, 117
Corman, Maddie, 86
Corman, Roger, 55
Cormier, Tony, 63
Corn is Green, The, 187
Cornelius, Chip, 69
Cornell, Allen D., 170
Cornell, Jeffrey, 49
Cornicelli, Carol, 80
Cornish, Roger, 151
Cornthwaite, Robert, 59, 199
Coromel, James, 77
Corpse!, 29
Corrado, Frank, 175
Correia, Don, 7, 80, 199
Corsaro, Frank, 115
Cortese, Alda, 168
Cortez, Katherine, 57, 91, 199
Corti, Jesse, 77
Cortland, Nicholas, 98, 199
Corto, Diana, 134
Corwin, Brenda Jean, 178
Corzatte, Clayton, 136
Cos, Mary Agen, 183
Cosgrave, Peggy, 162
Cosgrove, Colleen, 77
Cosham, Ralph, 143
Cosla, Edward, 72
Cosler, Charles, 125, 153, 162
Cost of Living, The, 57
Costa, Camille, 94
Costa, Joseph, 107, 159, 166, 199
Costabile, Richard, 72, 81, 88, 119
Costantino, Richard, 169
Costanza, Marie, 113
Costanzo, Vin, 166
Costello, Tom, 66
Costigan, Ken, 145
Cote, Joe, 59
Cothran, John, Jr., 166
Cotsirilos, Stephanie, 69, 199
Cotten, Christopher, 134, 172
Cotten, William, 141
Cotter, Carole, 133
Cottrell, Richard, 125
Cottrill, Brad, 99
Couch, Guy, 143
Couch, Janet, 144
Coulter, Carl, 162
Coulter, Ned, 77, 184
Coulter, Stephen, 149
Council, Richard E., 18
Count of Monte Cristo, The, 161
Countess Mitzi, 105
Country Doctor, A, 90
Country Girl, The, 178
Countryman, Michael, 60, 91, 94, 98, 199
Coupla White Chicks Sitting Around Talking, A, 125, 175
Courage, 174
Courier, David, 152
Courts, Randy, 68, 74
Cousin, Tome', 169
Cousins, Brian, 140
Coutu, Armand, 147, 163, 176
Couture, Jeff, 138
Cover, A. D., 65, 144, 181, 199
Cover, Chuck, 68
Covey, Elizabeth, 158, 158, 164
Covey, Liz, 136
Cowan, Edie, 55, 169
Coward, Lee, 103
Coward, Noel, 23, 141, 144, 150, 158, 170, 184
Cowart, Sheri, 124
Cowel, Eileen, 115
Cowell, Michael, 136
Cowen, William Joyce, 77
Cowgill, Robert, 156
Cowles, David, 64
Cowles, Matthew, 101
Cowles, Peggy, 148, 164
Cowles, Stephen, 72, 100
Cowperthwaite, Joseph, 181
Cox, Alice Everett, 40
Cox, Barbara, 173
Cox, Catherine, 62, 140, 159, 199
Cox, F. Keith, 149
Cox, Graham, 145
Cox, John Henry, 92
Cox, Mary Agen, 183
Cox, Roger, 152
Cox, Veanne, 81
Cox, Wendy, 178
Coxwell, David, 69
Coy, Steven, 126
Coyle, Bruce E., 149
Coyle, Bruce W., 81
Coyne, Cyndi, 80
Coyne, Susan, 186
Coyne, William "Butch", 160
Coyote Ugly, 161
Crabtree, Cheryl, 173
Crabtree, Don, 49, 199
Craig's Wife, 187
Craig, Betsy, 50, 199
Craig, Carl, 144
Craig, Jerry, 58
Craig, Lynn Todd, 140
Craig, Michael, 155
Craig, Noel, 175, 199
Crane, David, 65
Crane, Robert J., 63
Crane, Warren, 122
Crank, David M., 177
Craven, James, 138
Cravens, Rutherford, 183
Crawford, Broderick, 227
Crawford, Carol, 162
Crawford, Cheryl, 76, 129
Crawford, Ellen, 146
Crawford, John, 78
Crawford, Norma, 93
Crayton, Spurgeon, 113
Crazy Arnold, 62
Crazy From the Heart, 180
Cresap, Kelly, 136
Creswell, Saylor, 90, 200
Crigler, Lynn, 155
Crime and Punishment, 64
Crimes of the Heart, 166, 187
Criscitiello, John, 164
Crist, David, 116
Crist, Sheridan, 144
Cristell, Kathy, 169
Cristofer, Michael, 188
Criswell, Kim, 124
Critchfield, Jim, 169
Critt, C. J., 64, 160
Crivello, Anthony, 16, 200
Crochet, Laurie, 135
Crofoot, Leonard John, 121, 200
Croft, Jeanne, 164
Croft, Paddy, 29
Cromarty, Peter, 7, 24, 50, 57, 60, 61, 66, 68, 71, 81, 96, 128
Crombie, Peter, 63, 180
Cromelin, Carey, 162
Cromer, Bruce, 181
Cromwell, David, 108, 162, 200
Cromwell, Gloria, 168
Cronin, Laurel M., 154
Cronyn, Hume, 39, 146, 200
Cronyn, Tandy, 170
Crook, Peter, 108, 184, 200
Crooks, Kitty, 180
Crosby, Kim, 24, 155, 200, 201
Crosby, Mary, 147
Crosby, Todd, 71
Cross, Ben, 161
Cross, Lucy, 78
Cross, Marcia, 78, 157
Cross, Nancy, 100
Cross, Richard, 188
Cross, Stephen, 93, 200
Crossett, Bill, 136
Crossley, Kimball, 170
Crossley, Steven, 174
Crossroads, 171
Crothers, Joel, 227, 231
Crothers, Rachel, 100
Crothers, Sam, 15
Crouch, Bruce, 138
Crouse, Lindsay, 97, 200
Crouse, Russel, 142, 170
Crow, Jerry, 177
Crow, Laura, 82, 88, 136, 172
Crowder, Brill, 68
Crowder, Diane, 78
Crowder, Jack, 188
Crowe, J. Stanley, 74
Crowe, Timothy, 178
Crowell, Mac, 144
Crowley, Ann, 188
Crowley, Dennis, 11, 26, 27, 37, 39, 48, 65, 82, 83, 124, 134
Crowley, Pat, 188
Crown Cork Cafeteria, 72
Croxton, Darryl, 60, 149, 200
Crucible, The, 167, 178, 187
Cruikshank, Timothy, 186
Cruise Control, 120
Crum, Tracy, 64
Crummett, Freelow, 141
Crusch, Mark, 136
Crutcher, Julie, 137
Cruze, Josh, 17
Cryer, David, 101, 188
Cryer, Gretchen, 66, 200
Crystal Clear, 162
Csizmas, Oliver, 163
Cuba and His Teddy Bear, 108
Cuccioli, Bob, 80
Cucheran, Tom, 165
Cuddy, William J., 77
Cuervo, Alma, 200
Cuginia, Adrienne, 184
Culbert, Bobbi, 144
Culbert, John, 57
Culbreath, Lloyd, 37
Cullen, David, 11, 48
Cullen, Jeanne, 144
Cullen, Michael, 150
Cullison, Barry, 167, 175
Culliton, Joseph, 78, 125
Culliver, Karen, 52, 200
Cullum, John David, 101, 179
Cullum, John, 44, 125, 188, 200
Culp, Steven, 57, 99, 170
Culwick, Vivienne, 78
Cuming, Carole, 78, 92
Cuming, Danette, 153
Cumming, Richard, 170, 178
Cummings, Alan, 146
Cummings, Judy, 64
Cumpsty, Michael, 170
Cuningham, JoAnn, 142
Cunneen, Kathleen, 179
Cunningham, Copper, 113
Cunningham, Jenny, 142
Cunningham, Jo Ann, 69, 142
Cunningham, John, 111, 200
Cunningham, Nathalie, 161
Cunningham, Rick, 137
Cunningham, Sarah, 227, 231
Cunningham, Stanton, 140
Cuomo, Avy, 175
Cupo, Steve, 58
Cupp, Michael D., 145
Curci, Donna E., 168
Curiel, Tony, 163
Curlee, Karen, 45, 80
Curletto, Lida, 13
Curley, Bill, 151
Curley, Shona, 172
Curran, Keith, 64
Curran, Leigh, 180
Curran, Michael J., 73
Currie, Andrew A., 128
Currie, Richard, 65
Currier, Terrence, 143
Currin, Brenda, 78, 116
Curry, Bob, 127
Curry, Christopher, 54, 120, 200
Curry, Robert, 134, 166
Curry, Ruthann, 83
Curse of the Starving Class, 59, 171
Curtis, Keene, 128, 200
Curtis, Kelly, 158
Curtis, Roger, 166
Curtis, Simon, 107
Curtis-Brown, Robert, 175
Curtis-Hall, Vondie, 85, 103
Cusack, Philip, 6
Custer, John F., 178
Custom of the Country, The, 60
Cutko, Valerie, 182
Cutler, John N., 106
Cutler, Leslie B., 142
Cutrona, Ryan, 76, 81
Cwikowski, Bill, 91, 200, 201
Cyrano de Bergerac, 125, 156
D'Agnese, John, 58
D'Alessio, Arthur, 162
D'Altorio, Victor, 68, 200
d'Amboise, Charlotte, 11, 48, 124
d'Amboise, Christopher, 11, 200
D'Ambrose, Camille, 156
D'Ambrose, Stephen, 156
D'Ambrosio, Vito, 161
D'Amico, Dennis, 69
D'Andrea, Al, 63
D'Aquila, Diane, 141
D'Arcy, Mary, 7
D'Arinzo, Bob, 64
D'Asaro, James, 58, 91
D'Beck, Patti, 130
D'Ennery, Adolphe, 117
D'Onofrio, Joseph, 119
Da, 187
DaSilva, Howard, 227, 231
DaVilla, Debbie, 102
Dabney, Sheila, 66, 73, 77
Dachs, Joshua, 98, 116
Daciuk, Mary, 72, 200, 201
Dacus, Melvin O., 177
Dafoe, Willem, 161
Dagenhart, Jerry L., 177
Dagitz, Terri D., 142
Dahlberg, Thea, 118
Dahlmann, Jenie Lyn, 165
Dahlstrom, Robert A., 172
Dahman, Joe, 173
Daily, Dan, 136
Daily, Patricia, 59
Dainton, Scott, 124
Dakin, Kymberly, 148
Dale, Jim, 200
Dale, Kate, 99
Dale, Patt, 65, 66, 68
Daley, Donna, 168
Daley, Elizabeth, 146
Daley, R. F., 124, 164
Daley, Ron, 77, 80, 90, 131
Daley, Stephen, 28, 144
Dallara, Julienne, 100
Dallas, Walter, 104
Dallin, Howard, 156
Dalton, Claudia Lee, 159
Dalton, Lezlie, 84, 200
Dalton, T. Michael, 127
Daly, Augustin, 92
Daly, Brenda, 179
Daly, David, 118
Daly, Erin, 122
Daly, James, 188
Daly, Joseph, 168, 171
Daly, Kevin, 127
Daly, Timothy, 99
Daly, Walter, 173
Damas, Bertila, 112
Damashek, Barbara, 141, 147, 159, 166
Dames At Sea, 58, 190
Damkoehler, William, 178
Damn Yankees, 187
Damned Thing, The, 147
Damon, Stuart, 188
Dampf, Marilyn, 76
Dana, Barbara, 115, 144, 200
Dana, F. Mitchell, 76, 152, 164
Dana, Paige, 48
Dana, Wendy, 177
Danaher, Mallory, 69
Danare, Malcolm, 163
Dance of the Mayfly, 62
Dancy, Virginia, 137
Dandridge, Juan C., 110
Daneel, Sylvia, 188
Danehy, Tracy, 80
Danek, Michael, 45, 200, 201
Dang, Timothy, 146
Dangcil, Linda, 176
Daniel, Bruce, 78
Daniel, Gregg, 66
Daniel, Gregory, 171
Daniele, Graciela, 20, 106, 135
Danielle, Marlene, 48, 200
Danielle, Susan, 45, 200
Daniels, David, 188
Daniels, Jeff, 116
Daniels, Marc, 119, 121
Daniels, Paul S., 110
Daniels, Tracy, 148
Danjuro, Ichikawa XII, 8
Dann, Elonzo, 39
Danner, Blythe, 188, 192, 193
Danner, Braden, 96
Danon, Rami, 161
Danon, Tchia, 161
Dansicker, Michael, 7
Dansky, Peter, 35, 97
Danson, Randy, 143
Dante, Nicholas, 45, 169
Danzer, Kathy, 123
Daphne, Kay, 144
Dara, Joyce, 83
Dara, Olu, 91
Darcy, Kathleen, 100
Darcy, Pattie, 74, 80
Darga, Christopher, 165
Darion, Joe, 177
Darkness at Noon, 187
Darling, Michael, 152
Darlow, David, 166
Darnton, Amy, 68
Darnutzer, Don, 144
Darrow, Harry Silverglat, 51
Darrow, Henry, 176
Darski, Joanna, 72
Dart, Jack, 71
Darveris, George, 54
Darwin, Kim, 37, 80
Dassler, Lee, 78
Daughters, 76, 111
Davalos, Dick, 188
Davenport, Barbara, 180
David, Jason, 144
David, Keith, 71, 91
David, Regina, 184
David, Steven H., 37
Davidson, Gary, 154
Davidson, Gordon, 60, 146
Davidson, Jack, 146
Davidson, Jeannie, 141, 185
Davidson, John, 188
Davidson, Philip, 136, 185
Davidson, Randall, 138
Davidson, Richard M., 136
Davidson, Taylor, 98
Davies, Aled, 82, 189, 193, 200
Davies, Irving, 31
Davies, Katharyn, 158, 158
Davies, Tiki, 161
Davin, Richard, 175
Davis, Ali, 102
Davis, Bill C., 94, 95, 200
Davis, Bruce Anthony, 11, 37, 200
Davis, Carl, 139
Davis, Christopher, 172
Davis, Clifton, 188
Davis, Clinton Turner, 104, 120, 149
Davis, Dawn, 166
Davis, Deborah, 83
Davis, Donna, 167
Davis, Gerald A., 69
Davis, Hal, 81, 200
Davis, Helene, 86
Davis, Hope, 182
Davis, Janice, 83
Davis, Jeff, 158, 167, 168, 171
Davis, John Henry, 76, 147
Davis, Kevin, 143
Davis, Kim, 151
Davis, Lance, 125
Davis, Lindsay W., 20, 106, 108, 159
Davis, Luther, 62
Davis, Melissa, 15, 143
Davis, Merlyn, 48
Davis, Michael Allen, 188
Davis, Molly Marie, 143
Davis, Murphy, 148
Davis, Nathan, 154
Davis, Ossie, 18, 19, 83, 151
Davis, Penny, 6, 42
Davis, Peter, 71, 152
Davis, Richard, 188
Davis, Rick, 227
Davis, Rob, 169
Davis, Sheila Kay, 200
Davis, Ted, 159
Davis, Vicki, 114
Davis, Vince, 177
Davis-Reed, Timothy, 125
Davison, Jack, 50, 80
Dawn, Steven, 106
Dawson, Kathleen, 124
Dawson, Mark, 188
Day in Hollywood/A Night in the Ukraine, A, 176
Day Room, The, 141
Day, Alison, 140
Day, Connie, 49
Daye, Bobby, 126
Days and Nights of an Ice Cream Princess, 72
de Almedia, Joaquim, 161
de Barbieri, Mary Ann, 152
de Bari, Irene, 176
De Grooth, Jean, 142
de Guzman, Jossie, 77, 179
De Jager, Lisa, 60
De Jesus, Wanda, 108
de la Chaume, Jacqueline, 135
de la Giroday, Francois, 101, 200, 201
de la Pena, George, 124
de Lancie, John, 147
De Longis, Anthony, 146
De Lorenzo, Michael, 163
de Luce, Virginia, 188
De Maio, Dino, 78
De Marivaux, Pierre, 177
De Martin, Imelda, 188
de Rothschild, Robert, 78
de Sosa, Ruth, 163
de Tarr, Seiza, 35, 97
DeAcutis, William, 200
DeAngelis, Rosemary, 106, 200, 201
DeBaer, Jean, 63
DeBell, Jennifer C., 177
DeBerry, Teresa, 140
deBotton, Yvette, 148
DeBruno, Tony, 144
deBuys, Laura, 27
DeCarlo, Thomas, 60
DeCastro, Travis, 57, 179
DeCristo, Al, 66, 148, 200
DeFord, Edward, 184
DeGanon, Matt, 86, 200
DeGasperi, Mark, 72
DeHart, Deborah, 150
DeLany, Carolyn, 92, 138
DeLaurentis, Semina, 68
deLavallade, Carmen, 80, 200
DeLavallade, Michael, 113
DeLillo, Don, 141
DeLonay, Donna A., 144
DeMarco, Pauline, 142
DeMayo, Amy, 92, 93
DeMirjian, Denise, 200
DeMora, Robert, 75
DeNiro, Robert, 24, 108, 200
DePass, Paul, 122
DePena, Valerie, 142
DePina, Sabrina, 102, 200
DeRagon, Pierre, 140

DeRosa, Sharon, 110
DeSal, Frank, 135, 200
DeSavino, Marlene, 22, 38, 42, 123
DeShae, Edward, 163
DeShields, Andre, 64, 200
DeSylva, Buddy, 31, 78
DeVerna, Brian, 123
DeVita, James, 183
DeVito, Joe, 142
DeVito, Karla, 46
DeVito, Lisa, 142
DeVito, Ronny, 49
DeVolder, Max, 171
DeVries, Jon, 33, 180, 202, 207
DeWitt-Howard, Sherrill, 181
DeYoung, Cliff, 163
DeZarn, Teresa, 145
Dead Wrong, 114
Deal, Dennis, 64
Deal, Frank, 93, 200
Deal, Michael, 148
Dean, Charles, 156
Dean, Jacque, 7
Dean, James, 188
Dean, Jeffrey, 144
Dean, Kimberly, 133
Dean, Laura, 65, 188, 200
Dean, Mary Kay, 72
Dean, Michael-Pierre, 45
Dean, Robertson, 153, 162
Deane, J. A., 163
Deane, Michael Howell, 57
Dearborn, Karen, 142
Dearing, Judy, 76, 85, 102, 103, 104, 149, 171, 179
Dearinger, Kevin, 159
Death of Rosendo, The, 176
Death of a Salesman, 181, 187
Deaver, Christine, 172
Debesse, David, 136
Debuskey, Merle, 14, 20, 25, 28, 35, 43, 44, 45, 97, 106, 142
December 7th, 103
Deckel, Larry, 137
Decker, Lindsey, 66
Decker, Steve, 88, 200
Decker, Susan, 167
Decker, Tina, 124
Dedrickson, Tracy, 95
Deegan, John Michael, 66, 69
Deems, Mickey, 133
Deep Six Holiday, 76
Deer, Joe, 78
Deer, Sandra, 76, 140
Deering, John, 93
Deering, Olive, 227, 231
Defector, The, 168
Definite Maybe, A, 100
Degen, John F., 140
Degennaro, Joe, 76
Deitz, Steven, 138
Del Castillo-Morante, Mark, 173
Del Giudice, Judy, 61
del Nero, John, 107
del Pino, Federico Gonzalez, 112
Del Pazzo, Bob, 87
Del Pozo, Emilio, 70
Del Rossi, Angelo, 167
Del Vecho, Peter S., 167
Delawari, Arlana, 163
Delawari, Rahila, 163
Delawari, Soraya, 163
Delawari, Yasmine, 163
Delicate Balance, A, 168, 187
Delinger, Larry, 151
Della, Phyllis, 9, 24, 40, 82, 134
Delmar, Elaine, 31
Delorey, Olga, 152, 146, 172, 184
Demicco, John, 175
Deming, Tom, 100
Demke, Dave, 81
Demos, Gus, 121
Dempsey, Jerome, 20, 21, 106, 200
Dempsey, Mary Anne, 138
Dempster, Curt, 91
Dempster, Rory, 107
Dengel, Jake, 89, 200
Denis, William, 65, 167, 186
Denison, Susan, 147, 173
Denmark, Leon B., 104
Dennehy, Dennis, 69, 118, 162
Dennis, 91
Dennis, Carol, 46
Dennis, Patrick, 142, 152
Dennis, Rick, 148, 179
Dennis, Robert, 51, 63
Dennis, Ronald, 128
Dennis, Sandy, 188
Dennison, Richard C., 186
Denniston, Leslie, 188
Denson, Cheryl, 177
Dent, Richard, 79
Denver, Bob, 167
Departures, 58
Depenbrock, Jay, 149
Depoy, Scott, 140
Derifield, Bill, 152
Deringer, Dee, 92
Derks, Asa Wyatt, 181
Derr, Richard, 188
Derra, Candace, 200
Derrah, Thomas, 141
Derricks, Cleavant, 37, 126
Description of a Picture, 141
Desimone, Richard, 64
Desjarlais, Helene, 165
Desmond, Dan, 160
Desmond, Robert, 170
Desperate Hours, The, 187
Despotovich, Nada, 98
Destribats, Frederique, 182
Detweiler, Lowell, 29, 157
Deutchman, Lois, 57
Deutsch, Helen, 149
Deutschmann, S. M., 72
Devane, Julie, 139
Devery, Mary Ellyn, 135
Devin, Lee, 168
Devin, Lynne, 136
Devin, Richard, 141, 183
Devine, Erick, 48
Devine, Jilana, 81
Devine, Kathleen, 77
Devine, Loretta, 37, 102, 200
Devine, Michael, 147, 173
Devito, Lisa, 142
Devlin, John, 202
Devora, A., 35, 97
Dewar, John, 124
Dewell, Michael, 176
Dewey, Alice, 157
Dewey, Jon, 83
Dewey, Judith, 164
Dewhurst, Colleen, 161, 188, 192, 193
Dexter, Corky, 185
Deyle, John, 123, 151
Dezina, Kate, 71
Di Girolamo, Amanda, 177
di Lasso, Orlando, 90
Di Lorenzo, Armando, 176
DiBiase, Debbie, 127
DiCesare, Michael, 94
DiCostanzo, Cheryl, 182
DiDia, Maria, 51
DiFilia, Frank, 107
DiFilippo, Marylou, 160
DiFonso, Don, 169
DiGioia, Michael, 101, 107, 142, 202
DiMaggio, Phil, 34
DiMeo, Annette, 75
DiMiceli, Joe, 65
DiPaola, James, 73
DiPasquale, Frank, 50, 200
DiPietro, Anthony, 100
DiRenzo, Denise, 48
DiVito, Joann, 146
Dial "M" for Murder, 160
Diamant, Hirsh, 109
Diamond, J. Mark, 170
Diamond, Liz, 84
Diary of Anne Frank, The, 187
Diary of a Hunger Strike, 163
Dibble, Susan, 186
Dichter, Jon, 172
Dickens, Charles, 106, 136, 140, 141, 153, 154, 156, 166, 173, 178
Dickenson, April, 142
Dickerson, Glenda, 91, 116
Dickey, Dale, 76, 81
Dickey, Lou, 152
Dickinson, Clay, 63
Dicks, 113
Didawick, Dawn, 172, 184
Diekmann, Nancy Kassak, 76, 81
Diener, Joan, 188
Dierlam, Katy, 65
Dierson, Mary, 149
Dietrich, Bill, 81
Dietrich, Dena, 66, 202
Dietrich, Marc, 101, 202
Diffenderfer, Craig, 151
Diggles, Dan, 125
Diggs, Elizabeth, 98, 148
Diggs, Thomas, 136, 172
Dignon, Hugh, 113
Dille, David, 74
Dillehay, Kaylyn, 130
Dilley, Carol, 152
Dilliard, Marcus, 156
Dillman, Bradford, 188
Dillon, Denny, 158, 158
Dillon, John, 136
Dillon, Matt, 17, 202
Dillon, Melinda, 188
Dillon, Mia, 23, 202
Dimalante, Scott, 157
Diminished Capacity, 153
Dimou, Fotini, 59
Dinicol, Keith, 154, 186
Dining Room, The, 170
Diol, Susan, 138
Dionne, Margot, 178
Disappearing Acts, 78
Dispute, The, 60
Distant Fires, 157
Ditrinco, Joseph, 75
Dittemore, Vicki L., 144
Diveny, Mary, 168
Dix, Edna, 174
Dix, Richard, 143
Dixcy, Marcia, 137, 161
Dixon, Allison, 76, 78
Dixon, Beth, 137
Dixon, Earnest L., 140
Dixon, Ed, 121, 161, 202
Dixon, MacIntyre, 84, 115, 167, 202
Dixon, Michael Bigelow, 140
Dixon, Oliver, 100, 202
Dixon, Robert, 60
Dlugos, Gregory J., 74, 81
Dmitriev, Alex, 179
Dobell, Curzon, 144
Dobkin, Abraham, 143
Dobrusky, Pavel, 151
Dobson, Terry, 177
Dockery, Leslie, 74
Dodd, Joseph, 136
Dodd, Terry, 151
Dodds, William, 39
Dodge, Marcia Milgrom, 76, 171
Dodson, Daryl T., 66
Dodson, Lisa, 166
Doemling, Brandon E., 101, 202
Doepken, David L., 169, 170
Doepp, John, 164, 171
Doering, Reinhard, 79
Doff, Jodi, 81
Doffer, Sally, 93
Dogg's Hamlet, The, 175
Dohany, Art, 144
Doherty, Patricia E., 139
Dolan, Judith, 61
Dolas, Lura, 182
Dolby, Cheryl, 9
Dolf, John, 50
Dolgenas, Hillel, 79
Doll Dance, 7
Domine, Martha, 166
Domvito, Jean-Luc, 13
Don't Even Think of Parking Here, 71
Donadio, James, 181
Donahue, Alan, 166
Donald, Donald K., 13
Donaldson, Gregory, 124
Donat, Peter, 141, 186, 188
Dondlinger, Mary Jo, 121
Donegan, Martin, 180
Donen, Stanley, 7
Donkin, Eric, 186
Donleavy, J. P., 179
Donley, Maureen, 124
Donnell, Patrice, 202, 207
Donnelly, Candice, 65, 80, 116, 154, 172
Donnelly, Donal, 33, 202
Donnelly, Kyle, 166
Donnelly, Mark, 173
Donnelly, Peter, 150
Donnelly, Sarah E., 159
Donoghue, Timothy, 170, 173
Donohue, Nancy, 88
Donovan, James, 171
Dooley, Ray, 76, 157
Doolittle, John, 180
Dorfman, Craig S., 60, 65
Dorfman, Richard, 70, 109
Dorleac, Jean-Pierre, 73
Dorman, David, 142
Dorman, Jenan, 137
Dorn, Franchelle Stewart, 143
Dorothy Parker: No Song of an Ingenue, 80
Dorrell, Lawrence, 149
Dorsey, Kent, 144, 184
Dorward, Mary Anne, 111, 202
Dos Passos, John, 174
Doster, Sue, 77
Dostoyevsky, Fyodor, 64
Dotrice, Roy, 23, 135, 202
Dotson, Deborah, 55
Double Bass, The, 105
Doubleday, Kay, 151
Dougall, Bernard, 31
Dougan, Pat, 166
Dougharty, W. Huston, 175
Douglas, B. J., 136
Douglas, Diana, 146
Douglas, Jerry, 59, 74, 80
Douglas, Lucien, 177
Douglas, Michael, 188
Douglas, Paul, 188
Douglas, Pepe, 73
Douglas, Suzzanne, 55
Douglas, Tim, 183
Douglas, Walter, 126
Douglass, Charles, 60
Douglass, Pi, 50, 151, 165, 202
Doukas, Nike, 141, 182
Douthit, Susanna, 142
Dove, Alfred L., 151
Dovey, Mark, 124
Dowd, Frank, 87
Dowd, M'El, 135
Dowdy, Anthony, 83
Dowling, Bairbre, 163
Dowling, Doris, 163
Dowling, Kathryn, 156
Down, Rena, 93
Downer, Herb, 107, 148
Downing, David, 168
Downing, Peter J., 43, 97
Downs, Arnall, 180
Doyle, Diane, 173
Doyle, Elizabeth A., 93
Doyle, Jack, 155
Doyle, Jay, 158, 164
Doyle, John, 106
Doyle, Kathleen, 6
Doyle, Leah, 167
Doyle, Richard, 173
Doyle, Timothy, 78
Dozier, Cynthia, 65
Dracula, 160, 187
Dragen, Raymond, 123
Dragicevich, Milan, 185
Drake, Donna, 26, 55, 114, 202
Drake, Jessica, 173
Drake, Laura, 163, 173, 184
Drake, Robert, 184
Dramathon '85, 113
Dramaturg, 117
Draper, Debra Ann, 49
Draper, Polly, 98, 107
Draper, Rob, 49
Dratfield, Melanie N., 64
Drawbaugh, Laura, 60, 117
Dream Coast, The, 146
Dreamgirls, 126
Dreaming Emmett, 148
Dremer, Dan, 185
Dresher, Paul, 147
Dreskin, William, 65
Dresser, Richard, 98
Dressler, Ralph, 175
Dretsch, Curtis, 167
Dreux, Diane, 171
Drevescraft, James, 183
Drew Yenchak, 169
Drew, Connie, 20, 106
Drew, Dennis, 98
Dreyfuss, Ralph, 146
Dreyfuss, Randolph, 147
Drill, Marine, 17
Drinking in America, 85
Driscoll, John, 142
Driscoll, William, 101
Drivas, Robert, 146, 188
Driver, John, 188
Driving Around the House, 173
Drucker, Michael, 162
Drum, Leonard, 158, 162
Drummond, Alice, 180
Drummond, David, 69
Drummond, Joseph, 154
Drury, Jay, 162, 181
Drusch, Mark, 136
Dry Land, 80
Dryden, Dan, 147
Dryden, Deborah M., 138, 147, 184, 185
Dryden, Marilyn, 149
du Bois, Raoul Pene, 133
du Rand, le Clanche, 128
DuBois, Marlene, 159
DuPois, Starletta, 102
DuVal, Herbert, 100, 117, 202
Duarte, Derek, 141
Duberman, Martin Bauml, 72
Dubin, Al, 49, 127, 133
Ducati, Ann, 144
Ducko, Dale, 182
Dudley, Craig, 202, 207
Dudley, Doris, 227
Dudley, Suzanne, 186
Dudley, Terry, 118
Duell, William, 14, 108, 202
Duende, Afram, 161
Duer, Fred M., 184
Dufallo, Basil John, 60
Duff, James, 177
Duff, Michael, 16
Duff-Griffin, William, 106, 171
Duff-MacCormick, Cara, 57, 162, 188, 202
Duhamel, Peter Noel, 87
Dukakis, Apollo, 179
Dukakis, Damon, 179
Dukakis, Olympia, 38, 179, 202
Duke, Edward, 152
Duke, O. L., 153
Duke, Patty, 188
Duke, Stuart, 152, 160
Dulack, Tom, 153
Dulaney, Margaret, 100
Dumakude, Thyli, 162
Dumas, Alexandre, 161
Dumas, C., 113
Dumas, Debra, 75, 158
Dumere, Dave, 69
Dunaway, Faye, 188
Dunayer, Denise, 63
Dunbar, Brian, 6
Dunbar, June, 63
Dunbar, Paul Laurence, 85
Duncan, Christopher, 183
Duncan, Diane, 7
Duncan, Gloria, 95
Duncan, Kenn, 11
Duncan, Sandy, 80, 130, 188, 202
Duncan, William B., 140
Duncan-Gibbs, Mamie, 152
Dundon, Michael, 184
Dunham, Jeff, 133
Dunlap, Pamela, 173
Dunleavey, Barry, 60
Dunlop, William, 154, 186
Dunn, Colleen, 169
Dunn, David, 126
Dunn, Glenn, 171
Dunn, John, 27, 132
Dunn, Matthew, 146
Dunn, Nicholas, 101
Dunn, Sally, 175
Dunning, Richard, 81
Dunston, Jeff, 179
Dunville, Heather Elizabeth, 177
Dupree, D'Shawna, 153
Duran, Tony, 147
Durang, Christopher, 160, 171, 178
Durant, Don, 113
Durant, Natasha, 149
Duras, Marguerite, 76
Durfee, Duke, 153, 158
Durham, Pat, 142
Durkee, Norman, 172
Durkin, Michael, 110
Durling, Roger, 175
Durling, Ronald, 77
Durnin, Eric, 26
Durnin, Michael, 26
Durrett-Smith, Dennis, 140
Durso, James, 55
Durso, Marc, 144
Dussault, Nancy, 188
Duthie, Diann, 87
Dutra, Jayne, 60
Dutton, Carolyn, 73, 93
Dutton, Charles S., 180, 188, 202
Dutton, Jeff, 142
Dutton, Yvonne, 7
Dvorsky, George, 58, 76
Dwyer, Ethel McCady, 227
Dwyer, Frank, 90, 202
Dwyer, John, 79
Dwyer, Kevin, 106, 120
Dwyer, Linda, 64
Dyer, Carolyn, 146
Dyer, Chris, 154, 186
Dykstra, Ted, 186
Dykun, Lawrence N., 152
Dys, Deanna, 127
Eames, Kathryn, 171
Earle, Carla, 49
Earley, Dyanne, 164
Earll, Sarah Farmer, 143
Early Bird, 113
Easley, Holmes, 78, 115, 144
Easley, Richert, 165
East, Mark, 130
Eastley, Keely, 202, 207
Eastman, Donald, 108
Easton, Judith, 161
Easton, Richard, 188
Eaton, Daniel, 20
Eaton, Gillian, 146
Eaton, Lawrence, 111, 116
Eaton, William B., 184
Eaves-Brooks, 175
Ebb, Fred, 135, 153
Ebert, Joyce, 162
Eck, Tracy, 63
Eckard, Angela, 169
Eckert, Patricia, 138
Eckert, Rinde, 147
Eckhart, Gary C., 174, 182
Eckhouse, James, 72, 171, 202
eda-Young, Barbara, 86, 98, 202
Eddy, James, 169
Ede, George, 122
Edeiken, Louise, 57, 66, 155, 202
Edelhart, Yvette, 202
Edelman, Gregg, 48, 96, 155, 202
Edelstein, Gordon, 103
Edelstein, Stephen, 57
Eden Cinema, The, 76
Eden, Diana, 125
Edenfield, Dennis, 202, 207
Edgar, David, 136
Edgar, Miriam Colon, 112
Edgerton, Earle, 159, 186
Edington, Pamela, 91, 116
Edlund, Mark S., 140
Edmead, Wendy, 202
Edmiston, Scott, 167
Edmond, Linda, 183
Edmonds, Mitchell, 138, 184
Edmonds, Robert, 73
Edmonds, Scott, 143
Edmondson, James, 185
Edmunds, Kate, 60, 115, 140, 158
Educating Rita, 137, 145, 166
Edwards, Ben, 12, 30
Edwards, Brandt, 49, 202
Edwards, Burt, 114, 202
Edwards, David, 158
Edwards, Germaine, 149
Edwards, Gus, 104
Edwards, Jack, 156
Edwards, Jason, 167
Edwards, Kate, 156
Edwards, Maurice, 77, 90
Edwards, Naz, 149
Edwards, Paddi, 147
Edwards, Randall, 47, 202
Edwards, Ronnie Claire, 163
Effect of Gamma Rays on Man-in-the-Moon Marigolds, The, 187
Efford, Bo, 173
Egan, James, 100
Egan, Patricia, 90, 98, 153, 171
Egan, Robert, 146, 147
Eggers, Kevin, 129
Egi, Stanford, 180
Ehlers, Heather, 143
Ehlert, Matt, 114
Ehman, Don, 164
Ehrenreich, Jacob, 66
Ehrhardt, Peter M., 74, 81
Ehrler, Anita, 24
Ehrlich, Ida Lublenski, 227
Ehrlich, Judy, 49
Eiche, Jeffrey D., 78, 202
Eichelberger, Ethyl, 65
Eichenberger, Rebecca, 124
Eigenberg, Helen, 154
Eiger, Dina, 169
Eigsti, Karl, 146, 149, 159, 163
84 Charing Cross Road, 165
Eikenberry, Jill, 116
Eikeren, Allison, 75
Einhorn, Abe, 11
Einhorn, Susan, 170
Einsele, Marc, 11
Einwech, John, 138
Eisen, Max, 29, 64, 102, 112, 132, 29
Eisenberg, Avner, 143
Eisenberg, Charlie, 57, 101
Eisenberg, Eric, 101
Eisenhauer, Peggy, 65
Eisloffel, Elizabeth, 171
Eisner, Jamie Lee, 93
Eister, Karen, 141
Ekserjan, Nora, 163
El Grande de Coca-Cola, 70, 71
Elber, Steve, 63
Elbert, Wayne, 102
Elcar, Dana, 147, 173
Elchert, Kenneth, 94
Eldred, Gerry, 186
Eldred, Roxanne, 184
Electra: The Legend, 179
Elephant Man, The, 187
Elfman, Abba, 180
Elg, Taina, 166
Elias, Leila, 63
Elias, Rosalind, 96, 202
Elins, J. P., 186
Elins, Joel, 108
Elios, Tom, 202
Eliot, Drew, 102, 193, 202
Elisabeth Welch: Time to Start Living, 75
Elkins, Hillard, 51
Ellens, Rebecca, 86, 143, 202
Ellentuck, Dan, 62
Ellin, David, 64, 227, 231
Ellin, Ruth V., 64
Ellington, John, 173
Ellington, Mercedes, 32
Elliot, Aggie Cekuta, 186
Elliot, Edith, 183
Elliot, Mark, 57
Elliott, Bridget, 142
Elliott, Geoffrey, 141
Elliott, Harvey, 31
Elliott, Julia, 141
Elliott, Kenneth, 59, 69
Elliott, Marianna, 146, 163
Elliott, Milton, 123
Elliott, Patricia, 188
Elliott, Scott, 58, 179
Elliott, Shawn, 73, 99
Elliott, William, 153, 227
Ellis, Anita D., 57, 149
Ellis, Bruce, 183
Ellis, David, 115
Ellis, Fraser, 45, 202
Ellis, Gina, 149

Ellis, Joshua, 34, 36, 46, 49, 56, 115, 122, 127, 135
Ellis, Leslie, 128
Ellis, Rex, 179
Ellis, Richard, 139
Ellis, Robert, 136
Ellis, Scott, 167, 171, 179
Ellis, William, 202
Ellison, Michael, 144
Ellman, Bruce, 57, 91, 98
Ellsperger, Bruce, 136
Ellstein, Abraham, 63
Elman, Rochelle, 94
Elmer, George, 16, 69, 76
Elmore, Richard, 185
Elmore, Steve, 49, 202
Elrod, Susan, 28
Elston, Robert, 70
Ely, Kari, 171
Emanuel, Carol, 78
Emerald City, 78
Emeric, Anthony, 159
Emerson, Jonathan, 146
Emery, Lisa, 88, 140
Emery, Rick, 172
Emma, 72
Emmes, David, 173
Emmet, Robert, 110, 202
Emmons, Beverly, 60, 61, 73, 78, 79, 143, 159, 161
Emonts, Ann, 99
Emory, Margaret, 184
Emotte, Andre, 114
Emperor Jones The, 151
Emrie, Sara, 75
En Yu Tan, Victor, 76, 105, 109
Encounter with the Gods, 113
End of the World (With Symposium to Follow), 136
Endgame, 172
Enemy of the People, An, 185
Eney, Woody, 172
Engel, Bernerd, 153
Engel, David, 50, 202
Engelbach, Jerry, 117
Engels, Randy, 162
Engles, Judy, 98
English as a Second Language, 163
English, Craig, 175
English, Ellia, 149, 175
English, Gary, 158, 166, 176
Englund, Morgan, 146
Engman, Eva, 142
Engran, Marvin, 124
Enneking, Annie, 138
Ennocenti, Lucia Fontana, 153
Enoch, Don, 158, 158
Epstein, Alvin, 115, 157, 180, 202
Epstein, Amy, 88
Epstein, Marc, 161
Epstein, Paul, 44
Epstein, Pierre, 115, 202
Epstein, Robert, 33
Epstein, Sabin, 141
Equus, 187
Erdman, Jean, 72
Erickson, Leif, 227
Erickson, Maury, 177
Erickson, Mitchell, 12
Eriksson, Bo, 141
Erlendson, John, 141
Ernotte, Andre, 112, 119
Ernst, Lee Elmer, 181
Erskine, Chester, 227
Erskine, Martin, 174
Ertegun, Ahmet M., 129
Erudite, The, 113
Ervin, James, 130
Ervin, Ruthie, 140
Erwin, Edwin Carl, 139
Escoffier King of Chefs, 90
Esguerra, Dave W., 143
Eshelman, Drew, 141
Eskenazi, Dori, 176
Eskew, Doug, 153, 174, 175
Eskolsky, Alan, 22
Esparza, Phillip, 163
Espinosa, Joe, 107
Espinosa, Raul, 176
Esposito, Giancarlo, 180, 188
Esposito, Mark, 124
Esser, Leslie, 145
Essner, Stephen W., 145
Estabrook, Christine, 78, 164
Esterbrook, Richard, 158
Estes, Chuck, 173
Estevez, Aramis, 46
Estey, Suellen, 148, 149
Estrada, Angelina, 176
Estrin, Patricia, 163
Ethan, Mark, 95
Etters, Elizabeth, 52
Ettinger, Daniel, 93, 115, 121, 145, 162
Eubanks, Karen, 165
Eubanks, Shannon, 181
Evanko, Ed, 188
Evans, Bill, 6, 22, 23, 38, 42, 47, 123
Evans, Brent Paul, 162
Evans, Craig, 55, 120
Evans, David, 50, 76, 121
Evans, Dillon, 174
Evans, George, 145
Evans, Gwyllum, 140, 145, 148
Evans, Jason, 64
Evans, Jessica, 151
Evans, John Morgan, 76
Evans, Leon, 32
Evans, Lillian, 59
Evans, Peter, 115, 202
Evans, Stuart Ian, 157
Evans, Troy, 173
Evans-Kandel, Karen, 81, 203, 207
Evening of Micro-Operas, An, 147
Everett, Claudia, 185
Everett, Tim, 188
Everhart, Scott, 177
Evers, Brian, 43, 97, 157, 203
Evers, Holly, 142
Evita, 187
Evitts, Allen, 140
Ewen, Malcolm, 154
Ewer, Donald, 165
Ewing, Christopher C., 151
Ewing, J. Timothy, 203
Ewing, Tim, 76, 155
Execution of Justice, 33, 139, 156
Extraordinary Lies, 72
Eyck, John Ten, 98
Eyen, Tom, 126
Eyes of the American, 104
Eyre, Ronald, 186
Ezell, John, 144
Faber, Ron, 84, 108, 203
Fabricant, Gwen, 60, 161
Fabrique, Tina, 149
Fabris, Bill, 74
Facts in the Case of M. Valdemar, 147
Faerber, Douglas K., 185
Fagan, Maureen, 184
Fagerbakke, Bill, 157
Fahey, Jack, 62
Fahmy, Roya, 163
Fair Penitent, The, 163
Fairman, Christy Michelle, 177
Fairservis, Elf, 203
Faison, Frankie, 154
Faker, Brian, 172
Falabella, John, 159, 168, 171
Falana, Lola, 188
Falco, Bruce, 11, 80
Falk, Diane, 152
Falk, Kate, 108
Falk, Peter, 127
Falkenhain, Patricia, 43, 97, 162, 203
Fallbeck, Don R., 156
Fallen Angels, 150, 158
Fallon, Richard G., 144
Falls, Gregory A., 136
Falls, Robert, 82, 161
Falsgraf, Kit, 154
Family Portrait, 77
Fancy, Richard, 7
Fannell, Dianne, 184
Fantasticks, The, 52
Fantozzi, Peggy I., 185
Farago, Peter, 171
Faranda, Frank, 101
Farell, Mary-Pat, 182
Farentino, James, 188
Farer, Rhonda, 145
Fargas, Antonio, 106, 151
Fargo, Diane, 144
Faria, Arthur, 153, 174, 175
Farina, Dennis, 161
Farina, Marilyn, 68, 203
Faris, Scott, 124
Farkas, Jonathan, 37, 50, 132
Farley, Robert J., 138
Farnsworth-Webb, Carla, 172
Farnworth, Ralph, 81
Faro, Lynn, 50
Farone, Felicia, 58
Farquhar, George, 186
Farr, Kimberly, 203, 207
Farr, Michele, 158, 162, 164
Farrar, Frederick, 160
Farrar, Martha, 87, 203
Farrell, Brian, 188
Farrell, Dolores, 158
Farrell, Frank, 154
Farrell, Gillian, 98, 203
Farrell, Kevin, 48, 124
Farrell, Monica C., 169
Farrell, Peggy, 65
Farrell, Richard, 136, 172
Farrell, Tom, 59, 100
Farrell, Tome', 169
Farrell, Tyra, 163
Farrelly, Patrick, 149
Farrelly, Ruth Anne, 145
Farrier, Van, 55
Farris-Manetta, Michael, 68
Farwell, Jonathan, 168
Fat Men on Thin Ice, 151
Fata, Wesley, 16, 162, 180
Fatone, Charles, 100
Faulkner's Bicycle, 57
Faulkner, Cliff, 173
Fauss, Michael, 140
Faust, Marianne, 167
Faust, Nick, 174
Fay, Diann, 137, 161
Fay, Richard, 80
Fay, Thomas, 135, 156
Fay, Tom, 162
Faye, Denise, 11
Feagan, Leslie, 167
Feagin, Hugh, 177
Fearnley, John, 83
Fechter, Charles, 161
Fedele, Anne Marie, 174
Feder, Wendy, 73
Federick, Lamar James, 180
Fedigan, Michael, 46
Fedunyszyn, Oksana, 181
Fedyszyn, Marjorie, 99
Fehr, Frankie, 168
Fehrmann, Fred, 81
Feiffer, Jules, 51
Feigin, Andrew, 156
Feiner, Harry, 167
Feinerman, Bernard, 69
Feingold, Michael, 84
Feinstein, Michael, 130
Feld, Kenneth, 30
Felder, David, 57, 75
Feldman, Laurence N., 179
Feldshuh, Tovah, 101, 115, 188, 203
Felix, Tom, 80
Fell, Marian, 82
Feller, Katherine, 42
Feller, Peter, 6, 47
Felt, Sherri, 64
Feltch, John, 170
Feltman, Susan B., 82
Felton, Holly, 180
Fences, 154, 172
Fenhagen, James, 86, 149, 153
Fentiman, Sharon, 176
Fenton, Danielle, 97
Feore, Colm, 154, 186
Ferencz, George, 66
Ferguson, Betty, 177
Ferguson, Lou, 179
Ferguson, Rich, 72
Ferguson-Acosta, Dennis, 77
Ferland, Danielle, 111
Fernandez, Evelina, 176
Ferra, Max, 73, 77
Ferrari, Irene, 130
Ferrari, Marianne, 80
Ferraro, John, 69, 84
Ferrell, Conchata, 146, 188
Ferris, Chet, 53
Ferrone, Richard, 178
Ferszt, Erica, 101
Fervoy, Tom, 167, 182
Festa, Ken, 157
Festival Latino, 106
Festival of Original One-Act Comedies, 98
Fetters, Clifford, 177
Feuer, Howard, 17, 27, 37, 40
Feury, Peggy, 227, 231
Feydeau, Georges, 174, 178, 181
Fichandler, Zelda, 143
Fichter, Thomas, 172
Fichtner, William, 175
Fickett, Mary, 188
Fickinger, Steve, 203, 207
Fico-McCarthy, Adele, 153
Fiddler on the Roof, 145, 187
Field, Barbara, 156, 167
Field, Crystal, 203, 207
Field, March, 137
Fielder, Chris, 46, 108
Fields, Dorothy, 31, 40, 133, 142
Fields, Herbert, 80, 142
Fields, Jim, 150
Fields, Joe, 188
Fierstein, Harvey, 50, 160, 188, 203, 207
Figa, Stewart, 64
Fignar, Jeffrey, 143
Figueroa, Porfirio, 134
Filling the Hole, 62
Fillion, Kathleen, 142
Filthy Rich, 61
Final Passages, 175
Finch, Susan, 82, 203
Finding Home, 140
Fine, Jill, 141
Fingerhut, Arden, 23, 57, 146, 171
Fink, Bert, 11, 26, 27, 37, 39, 48, 65, 83, 124, 134
Finkel, Fyvush, 55, 203
Finkler, Marion, 67
Finlay-McLennan, Stewart, 177
Finley, David, 158
Finn, Terry, 101
Finnell, Jan, 64
Finney, Andrew, 66
Finnie, Leo V., III, 157
Finnin, Maggie, 73
Finque, Susan, 136
Fionte, John, 181
Fiordellisi, Angelini, 64, 135, 203
Fiore, Don, 186
Fiorello!, 155, 187
Fire, Norma, 59
Fires, Jerry, 142
Firestone, I. W., 63
Firman, David, 122
Firstenberg, Jonathan, 86
Firth, Peter, 188
Fischer, Don, 170
Fischer, Sharianne, 92
Fischetti, Michael, 175
Fischoff, George, 83
Fish, Steve Roy, 203
Fishbein, Diane, 159
Fishcer, Don, 170
Fisher, Anne, 80
Fisher, Brien, 169
Fisher, Dan, 76
Fisher, Jules, 11, 37, 50
Fisher, Linda, 62, 149, 162
Fisher, M. Anthony, 46
Fisher, Mary Beth, 159, 170
Fisher, Mary, 64
Fishman, Larry, 105
Fiske, Ellen, 177
Fitch, Clyde, 110
Fitch, Robert, 58, 203
Fite, Mark, 59
Fitts, Dudley, 141
FitzGerald, E'Dior, 143
FitzGibbon, John, 145
FitzLyon, April, 82
Fitzgerald, Peter J., 50
Fitzgerald, David, 183
Fitzgerald, Geraldine, 66, 80, 94
Fitzgerald, Peter J., 17, 24
Fitzgerald, Richard, 49, 135
Fitzgerald, Robert, 141
Fitzmorris, Brian, 169
Fitzpatrick, Allen, 150, 168
Fitzpatrick, Bettye, 59, 139
Fitzpatrick, C. A., 148
Fitzpatrick, Colleen, 48
Fitzpatrick, Garland, 157
Fitzpatrick, Richard, 175
Fitzsimmons, Tom, 170
Five Finger Exercise, 187
Fizgibbons, Mark, 162
Flanagan, Kit, 98, 172, 203, 207
Flanagan, Neil, 227, 231
Flanagan, Pauline, 29, 203
Flanagan, Robert, 143
Flanagan, Walter, 12, 175, 203
Flannigan, Bob, 79
Flash of Lightning, A, 92
Flatbush Faithful, The, 60
Flatt, Ernest O., 133
Flaubert, Gustave, 65
Flaxman, John, 61
Flea in Her Ear, A, 174, 181
Fleche, Peggy, 153
Fleetwood, Jim, 177
Fleishman, Sandra, 182
Fleiss, Jane, 94, 162, 203
Fleming, Conn, 78
Fleming, Cynthia, 45
Fleming, Edyie, 124
Fleming, James, 80
Fleming, Sam, 174
Flender, Nicole, 64
Flesher, Mark Allen, 61
Fless, Scott, 64, 203, 207
Fletcher, Allen, 228
Fletcher, Bill, 146
Fletcher, David, 162
Fletcher, Jack, 133
Fletcher, John, 170, 182
Flett, Sharry, 186
Flick, Pat, 140
Flinchum, Doug, 177
Flint and Roses, 140
Floden, Lea, 60, 203
Flohr, Walter, 78
Flomenhaft, Zivia, 66, 164
Flood, John M., 79, 80
Flora, Becky, 53, 60, 61, 64, 71, 76, 80
Flora, Pat A., 152
Florance, E. Lee, 150
Florek, Dave, 54, 57, 203
Flournoy, Mary Beth, 143
Fly by Night, 114
Flye, Catherine, 152
Flying Doctor, The, 60
Flying Karamazov Brothers, The, 35, 97, 136
Flynn, J. Michael, 163
Flynn, John, 72
Flynn, Julianne, 96
Flynn, Lucy, 138
Flynn, Maggie, 168
Flynn, Nick, 172
Flynn, Patricia, 62
Flynn, Steven, 63
Flynn-Jones, Elizabeth, 63, 78
Fo, Dario, 81, 141
Foard, Merwin, 152
Focazio, Marty, 74, 79, 148, 174
Fogel, Alexa, 153
Fogel, Doug, 81
Fogel, Jodi, 80
Fogt, Julie Ann, 123
Folden, Lewis, 150, 174, 179
Folender, David Lawrence, 96, 109
Foley, Brenda, 203
Foley, Donna, 80
Foley, Joan, 146
Foley, John, 140, 167
Foley, Robert, 177
Folger, Mark, 79
Folk Tale, A, 150
Follies, 187
Followell, James, 78
Folly, Val, 100
Folsom, Will, 138
Fonda, Jane, 188
Fonda, Peter, 188
Fong, Jose, 77, 107, 203, 207
Fonseca, Quina, 72
Fontaine, Joel, 79, 96
Fontaine, Luther, 130
Fontane, Char, 77
Fool for Love, 144, 163
Foote, Horton, 91, 139
For Sale, 57
For Under The Volcano, 147
Forbes, Barbara, 145, 150, 153, 166, 167, 168, 177
Forbes, Francine, 14, 203
Forbes, John B., 184
Forbes, Roger, 154, 186
Forbidden Broadway, 53
Ford, Alison, 160
Ford, Anne-Denise, 136, 175
Ford, Bette, 163
Ford, Clebert, 85, 103, 151, 203
Ford, Donald Brooks, 73, 80
Ford, Frances, 203
Ford, Jack, 228
Ford, Jennifer L., 169
Ford, Phil, 133
Ford, Spence, 203
Ford, Suzanne, 117, 203
Ford, Sydney, 203
Ford, Tom, 183
Forde, Larry, 134
Foreigner, The, 54, 139, 143, 148, 167, 173, 174, 175, 177
Foreman, Richard, 71, 108
Forest, The, 172
Forestier, Patricia, 124, 155
Forgette, Katie, 136, 172
Forgive Me, Evelyn Bunns, 144
Forgy, Ann, 139
Forino, Alan, 169
Forkush, Anthony, 173
Forlenza, Kate, 184
Forman, Ken, 106
Fornadel, Jeanne, 128
Fornes, Maria Irene, 77, 82
Forney, Marvin, 179
Forrest, Elliot, 87, 92, 93
Forrester, Bill, 136
Forrester, Sherilyn, 144
Forster, Rheatha, 171
Forster, Victoria, 92, 203
Forsythe, Henderson, 161
Fortunato, Dean, 161
42nd Street, 49, 127, 187
Fosse, Bob, 37, 40
Foster, Dan, 164
Foster, Diane, 142
Foster, Frances, 104, 172, 203
Foster, Gloria, 188
Foster, Jimi, 110
Foster, Mark, 142
Foster, Meg, 163
Foster, Michael, 183
Foster, Phil, 228
Foster, Robert, 95
Foster, Skip, 140
Foster, Stephan, 177
Foster, Terrence, 65
Fourcaut, Marie, 78
Fourposter, The, 187
Fowler, Beth, 155
Fowler, Clement, 101, 203
Fowler, Laura L., 94
Fowler, Molly, 33
Fowler, Monique, 167, 173
Fowler, Robert H., 32
Fowler, Sharon, 170
Fox, Alan, 76, 93
Fox, Barbara J., 69
Fox, Charles, 143
Fox, Colin, 111, 203
Fox, Crystal, 140
Fox, D. R., 78
Fox, David, 165
Fox, Marilyn, 173
Fox, Neal, 86
Fox, Robert, 29
Foxfire, 146
Foxworth, Robert, 188
Foy, Harriet, 103
Fraction, Karen E., 172
Fradkin, Philip, 49
Franceschi, Edgar, 65
Franceschina, John, 144, 147, 153
Franciosa, Anthony, 188
Francis, Allan, 33
Francis, Joseph V., 61, 203
Francis, Veronica, 101
Francis-James, Peter, 156
Franco, Ramon, 203
Frank, Anne, 61
Frank, David, 174
Frank, Judy, 93, 203, 207
Frank, Owen, 164
Frank, Richard, 108, 203
Frank, Sherman, 133
Frankel, Emily, 125
Frankel, Kenneth, 162
Frankel, Richard, 56
Frankel, Scott, 96
Frankenstein, 90
Franklin, Al, 60
Franklin, Bonnie, 188
Franklin, Don, 164, 166
Franklin, Elizabeth, 146
Franklin, Fred, 182
Franklin, Roger, 77
Franklin, Steve, 78
Franklin-White, Michael, 143
Franks, Laurie, 143
Franks, Michael, 32
Franz, Elizabeth, 101, 203
Franz, Joy, 140, 165
Franz, Robert, 76
Fraser, Alison, 59, 74, 118, 203
Fraser, Curtis, 151
Fraser, Patricia, 42, 173
Frassetto, Floriana, 78
Fratantoni, Diane, 124, 203
Frateschi, Sunshine, 175
Fraulo, Marianne, 140
Frawley, Bernard, 29
Frawley, Craig, 7
Frawley, Terrence, 63
Frayn, Michael, 27, 132, 163
Frazer, Susanna, 84, 92, 203
Frazier, Cliff, 102
Frazier, Lynn, 143
Frechette, Peter, 147
Frederick, Rebecca G., 150
Frederick, Ron, 57
Fredricksen, Erik, 125, 163
Freed, Arthur, 7
Freed, Donald, 151, 163
Freed, Morris, 45
Freedman, Glenna, 11, 26, 27, 50, 65, 81, 130, 134
Freedman, Peter, 71, 91
Freedman, Robert M., 62
Freek, George, 63
Freel, Susan, 67
Freeland, Thomas, 183
Freeman, Marceline, 151
Freeman, Neil, 186
Freeman, Virginia, 152
Freeman, Yvette, 57
Frehner, Harry, 186
Freidman, Neil, 164
Freiman, Jonathan, 184
Fremgen, Mary, 93
French, Arthur, 113, 203, 207
French, Bruce, 147, 173
French, David, 173, 179
French, Diane, 169
French, Larry, 93, 203
Fresh Horses, 120, 189
Fressola, Steven, 57
Freund, Jonathan, 99
Frew, Shelley, 110
Frewen, Ray, 164
Frey, Patricia, 148
Freydberg, James B., 22
Fried, Jonathan, 81, 204
Fried, Marilyn, 192
Frieder, Sol, 86
Friederichs, Cecilia, 158
Friedheim, Eric, 31
Friedlander, David, 90
Friedman, Alan Foster, 151
Friedman, Cheri, 150
Friedman, David, 64
Friedman, Janet, 49
Friedman, Joel Phillip, 65
Friedman, Peter, 33, 91, 162, 204
Friedman, Phil, 37, 40
Friedman, Seth, 65
Friedman, Stan, 72
Friedman, Susan, 96
Friman, Kristina, 139
Frimark, Merle, 13, 26, 27, 29, 48, 65, 124
Frisbe, Jeane, 125
Frisch, Richard, 96, 204

Frisch, Robert, 164
Frith, Norman, 97
Fritz, Amy Ginette, 93
Fritz, Amy, 80
Fritz, Lana, 142, 177
Froehlich, Marcy Grace, 98
Frommer, Robert, 176
Front Page, The, 160
Frost, Lindsay, 100
Frost, Sue, 155
Frost, Warren, 156
Fruchter, Danny S., 168
Fruge, Romain, 46, 80
Frushour, Laurel, 82
Fry, Brad, 143
Fry, Ray, 137
Fry, Suzanne, 137
Fryer, Robert, 27, 132, 146
Fuccello, Tom, 163
Fugard, Athol, 22, 138, 162, 163, 166, 168, 170, 171, 179, 180
Fuglei, Kate, 157
Fugue, 162
Fuhrman, Cynthia, 185
Fujikawa, Cynthia, 141
Fullagar, Brad, 153
Fuller, Craig, 160
Fuller, David, 138, 177, 179
Fuller, Jonathan, 158
Fuller, Karen, 175
Fulton, Julie, 163
Fulton, Larry, 147
Fults, Scott, 139
Funicello, Ralph, 172, 173, 186
Funny Girl, 93
Funny Thing Happened on the Way to the Forum, A, 145, 162, 187
Fuqua, Joseph, 61
Furdas, Vera, 157
Furies, 79
Furman, Celeste, 142
Furs, Eddie L., 77, 204
Furst, Timothy Daniel, 35, 97, 136
Furth, George, 34
Further Adventures of Kathy and Mo, The, 116
Fusco, Anthony, 65
Futterman, Enid, 61
Fyfe, Jim, 47
Gabbard, Glendon, 154
Gabel, Martin, 228
Gabis, Stephen, 90, 145
Gable, June, 84, 111, 157, 204
Gabler, Linda E., 169
Gaebler, Mary, 123
Gaffield, Dick, 71
Gaffney, Mo, 116
Gaffney, Paul, 183
Gage, Gary, 155, 158
Gage, Patricia, 179
Gagliardi, Leon, 11, 48, 124
Gagnon, Donna J., 158
Gaines, Barbara, 166
Gaines, Boyd, 105, 188, 204
Gaines, Catherine, 159
Gaines, David, 81
Gaines, Davis, 74, 75
Gaithers, Lita, 151
Gal, Riki, 161
Galanti, Bernadette, 160
Galantich, Tom, 121
Galati, Domenica, 184
Galati, Frank, 154
Galban, Margarita, 176
Gale, Brian, 173
Gale, David, 114, 151, 186, 204
Gale, George, 78
Gale, James, 183
Galeota, Sandra M., 136, 139
Galileo, 144
Galindo, Ramon, 11, 48
Gallagher, Jennifer, 72
Gallagher, Kathleen, 33
Gallagher, Larry, 74
Gallagher, Megan, 125
Gallagher, Michael, 127
Gallagher, Peter, 42, 162, 188, 192, 193, 204
Gallant, Frank, 62
Galli, Allen, 136
Galligan, Zach, 47, 204
Gallo, Paul, 20, 43, 54, 78, 82, 97, 106, 143
Galloway, Don, 188
Galloway, Jane, 173
Galloway, Pat, 186
Galusha, Laura, 101
Galvin, Timothy, 175
Galvin, Tracy, 134
Galway, Gregory W., 75
Gamache, Laurie, 45
Gambacorta, Leo, 102, 103
Gamble, Julian, 144
Gamel, Fred, 120
Gammon, James, 67, 204
Gampel, C. M., 135
Gandy, Irene, 68, 104
Ganshaw, Bob, 80
Gant, Carol, 107, 108
Gantert, Debbie, 90
Gantry, Donald, 228
Garber, Robert S., 59
Garber, Victor, 188
Garcia, Bonnie, 102
Garcia, Peter Angel, 139
Garcia, Terri, 134
Gardenia, 170
Gardner, Alan, 150
Gardner, Ashley, 23, 66
Gardner, Danielle, 93
Gardner, Herb, 18, 57, 172
Gardner, Laura, 150, 158
Gardner, Richard K., 151
Gardner, Thomas, 121
Gardner, William T., 170
Gardner, Worth, 149
Garfein, Jack, 65
Garfield, Andrea, 93
Garfield, David, 204
Garfield, Dick, 71
Garfield, Julie, 188
Gargaro, Kenneth, 169
Gargiulo, Joseph, 106
Gari, Angela, 26, 46
Garland, Geoff, 170
Garland, Marc, 56
Garman, Carrie, 61, 204, 207
Garner, Jay, 50
Garner, Patrick, 157, 160
Garner, Ruddy L., 130
Garnett, Chip, 188
Garnett, Constance, 82
Garren, Barbara, 160
Garrett, Becky, 122
Garrett, Kelly, 188
Garrett, Mary, 141
Garrett, Maureen, 179
Garrick, Barbara, 118
Garrison, Angela, 169
Garrison, David, 99, 204
Garrison, Greg, 145
Garrison, Sean, 188
Garrity, Paul, 70, 73, 96, 110, 120
Garside, Brad, 75, 204
Garth, Eleanor, 153
Gartin, Christopher, 34
Garvey, Millie, 133
Garvey, Veronica, 79
Garvin, Lynn, 141
Gary, Glen, 61, 64
Garza, Troy, 45, 204
Garzillo, Nick, 134
Gash, Kent, 107
Gaskill, William, 156
Gassell, Sylvia, 90, 204
Gatchell, R. Tyler, Jr., 11, 48
Gates, Sarah, 172
Gatewood, Nan, 68
Gati, Kathi, 62
Gattegno, Ashish, 100
Gaudet, Christie, 95
Gaupp, Andrew C., 143
Gaus, Andy, 72
Gavon, Igors, 127, 204
Gayley, Anne, 174
Gazzara, Ben, 188
Geddes, A. J., 75
Geddes, Al, 72
Geddes, Barbara Bel, 188
Geer, Kevin, 54
Geffen, David, 38, 48, 55
Geffner, Deborah, 204
Gefroh, Steven J., 78
Gegenhuber, John, 143
Gehringer, Linda, 150
Geidt, Jan, 141
Geidt, Jeremy, 141
Geiger, Mary Louise, 57
Geiser, Janie, 138
Geisler, Robert Michael, 122
Geisslinger, Bill, 185
Geist, David, 79
Geist, Janet, 90
Gelb, James, 228
Gelb, Jody, 184
Gelbart, Larry, 145, 162
Gelber, Jack, 91
Geld, Gary, 151
Gelfer, Steven, 48, 204
Gelke, Becky, 66, 204
Geller, Bruce, 115
Gelles, Leda, 86
Gemignani, Paul, 135
Gemignani, Rhoda, 163
Gemmer, Annbritt, 166
Gendelman, Jeff, 79
Genest, Edmond, 140
Genet, Jean, 141, 228
Genet, Michael, 99, 149, 168
Gennaro, Peter, 155
Genovese, Mike, 163
Gentles, Avril, 117, 179
Gentry, Bob, 188
Gentry, Minnie, 59
Genuardi, Nancy C., 63
Genuardi, Nancy, 51
Genya, Alexis, 79
Geoffreys, Stephen, 79, 188, 204
Geoly, Guy, 167
George, Hal, 135
George, Jeffry, 167
George, Joe, 161
George, Joel, 70
George, Joni, 76
George, Lovette, 32
George, Phillip, 78
George, Susan Carr, 124
Georger, Diana, 62
Georgia Avenue, 155
Georgianna, Frank, 151
Geraci, Drew, 50
Geraci, Frank, 110
Geraghty, Marita, 123, 135
Geralis, Tony, 124
Gerard, Anne-Marie, 134, 152
Gerard, Christopher, 114
Gerard, Edwin, 163
Gerber, Charles E., 51
Gerber, Jonathan S., 16
Gerdes, George, 66, 98, 137, 204
Gere, Richard, 188
Gerety, Peter, 178
Gerlach, Robert, 166
Gerlib, Marge, 142
Gerlipp, Margaret, 142
Germain, John, 65
German, Richard, 176
Germann, Greg, 62, 167
Germano, Amy, 158, 158
Germano, Paul, 167
Gero, Edward, 152
Gerri, Steven, 152
Gerroll, Daniel, 60, 94, 115, 188, 204
Gerry Goodstein Photos, 88
Gershon, Gina, 163
Gershwin, George, 93, 130, 172
Gershwin, Ira, 31, 93, 130, 172
Gerson, Karen, 63, 167, 179
Gersten, Alexandra, 121
Gersten, Bernard, 35, 45, 97
Gerstenberger, Emil, 76
Gertrude Stein and a Companion, 70
Gervais, Richard, 158
Geter, John, 95, 204
Geter, Vanessa, 71
Gets, Malcolm, 92
Getz, John, 106, 120
Geurts, John, 113
Gewurz, Laura, 61
Geyer, Charles M., 186
Ghashiram Kotwal, 109
Ghestek, Jeff, 168
Ghetto, 161
Ghitelman, Seth R., 140
Giagni, D. J., 65, 172
Giaimo, Anthony, 152
Giamatti, Marcus, 180
Gianfrancesco, Edward T., 55, 120
Gianino, Jack, 66
Giannelli, Christina, 66, 80, 121
Giannini, Cheryl, 18, 57, 204
Giannini, Christina, 83, 115
Giannini, Evadne, 64
Giannitti, Michael, 180
Gianono, Joseph, 24
Giardina, Joseph D., 162
Gibbons, June, 138
Gibbons, Mary Jane, 71
Gibbs, Nancy Nagel, 55
Giberson, Philip, 92
Gibney, Susan, 180
Gibson, Charlotte, 138
Gibson, David Warren, 40
Gibson, Judy, 57
Gibson, Karen, 61
Gibson, Margaret, 184
Gibson, Maureen F., 82
Gibson, Michael, 130
Gibson, Nancy, 142
Gibson, P. J., 102
Gibson, Teri, 122
Gibson, Thomas, 23, 107, 204
Gibson, William, 152
Giella, David, 14, 204, 207
Gierasch, Stefan, 163
Giesenschlag, Russell, 93, 204
Giessen, Nora, 118
Gift of the Magi, 137
Gifts of the Magi, The, 68
Gigl, Alyosius, 180
Gigliotti, Don, 101
Giguere, Edi, 84, 92, 96
Gilb, Melinda, 7
Gilbert and Sullivan, 186
Gilbert, Alan, 204
Gilbert, Alyce, 45, 126
Gilbert, Edward, 156, 159
Gilbert, Hy, 83
Gilbert, Ronnie, 161
Gilbert, Stuart, 89
Gilbert, Willie, 142
Gilbert-Hill, Richard, 186
Gilborn, Steven, 99, 204
Gilbride, Mo, 91
Gilchrist, Kimbley, 119
Gildin, Leon H., 102
Gile, Bill, 114
Giles, David, 154, 186
Giles, Jonathan L., 170
Giles, Nancy, 15, 188, 204
Gill, Elizabeth, 77, 90
Gill, James, 106
Gill, Michel R., 170
Gill, Nancy, 173
Gilleland, LouAnne, 59
Gilles, Beth, 136, 138
Gilles, John Ivo, 60, 146, 147, 173
Gillespie, Ann, 173
Gillespie, Craig, 81
Gillett, Betty, 228
Gillett, Hamilton, 149, 182
Gillette, Anita, 114, 188, 192, 204
Gillette, Priscilla, 188
Gilliam, Gwendolyn M., 32
Gilliam, Roscoe, 45
Gillman, Robert A., 160
Gilman, Sam, 228
Gilmore, Gerald, 71, 117, 164
Gilmore, Noel, 6, 123
Gilmore, Phillip, 126
Gilmore, Virginia, 228
Gilpin, Jack, 54, 91, 204
Gilsbach, Lyn, 133
Gimpel, Erica, 149
Gin Game, The, 187
Gindi, Roger Alan, 68
Gindi, Roger, 11
Gingeleski, James, 175
Ginnosuke, Ichikawa, 8
Ginsberg, Jeremiah, 58
Ginsberg, Shelley, 114
Ginzberg, Richard, 79
Gioia, Patricia, 152
Giolito, Rick, 100
Giombetti, Karen, 20, 106, 204
Giomi, Rita, 175
Giommi, Celeste, 142
Gionson, Mel Duane, 109
Gionson, Mel, 204
Giordano, Greg, 72
Giordano, Tony, 175, 178
Giovannetti, Tony, 71
Girardeau, Frank, 91, 204
Giraud, Claude, 188
Giraudoux, Jean, 101
Girdler, Deb G., 158
Girl Crazy, 93, 172
Giroux, Kirsten, 166
Giroux, Laurent, 20, 79
Gisondi, John, 156, 167
Gisselman, Gary, 144
Gitto, George, 165
Giuffre, Joseph, 58
Givens, Tralenea, 172
Gjelsteen, Karen, 138
Gjesdal, Janna, 84
Gladstone, Stacey, 65
Gladys, 152
Glaser, Benjamin F., 167
Glaser, John, 59
Glasner, Katie, 7
Glass Menagerie, The, 149, 150, 162, 177, 179, 181, 186, 187
Glass, Philip, 141, 147, 156
Glasse, Kayce, 139
Glasser, D. Scott, 138
Glaudini, Bob, 146
Glavin, Stephen, 20, 106
Glaze, Susan, 46
Glazener, Janet, 24
Glazer, Peter, 46, 98
Gleason, James, 59, 204
Gleason, Joanna, 38, 99, 188, 204
Gleason, Richard, 96
Gleason, Stephen, 70, 80
Gleason, William, 96
Gleave, William, 181
Glen, David, 174
Glendinning, James, 143
Glengarry Glen Ross, 127, 175, 187
Glenn, Barbara, 29, 112, 132
Glenn, David, 143
Glenn, Joe, 143
Glenn, Scott, 132
Glick, Nicola, 90
Glick, Stacey, 119
Glickman, Eddie, 147
Gliniewicz, Patty, 62
Glore, John, 173
Glossman, James, 180
Glover, Danny, 188
Glover, Sheilah, 152
Glover, William, 147, 163
Gluck, Victor, 117
Glushak, Joanna, 111, 159, 204
Glynn, Carlin, 188
Glynn, Thomas, 156
Gnat, Karen, 63
Gnat, Michael, 63, 204
Gnys, Charles, 228
Goans, Carol, 81
Goblin Market, 119
Goddard, Rosejean, 142
Godfrey, Patrick, 123
Godfrey, Thomas Hoyt, 61, 204
Godin, Maurice, 186
Godines, Henry, 161
Godspell, 158, 169, 176
Goethals, Rosalind, 63
Goetz, Kent, 142
Goetz, Peter Michael, 204
Goetzinger, Mark, 160
Goff, Charles, 20, 106
Goggin, Dan, 68
Goggin, Dorinda Dean, 153
Gogol, Nikolai, 144, 154, 180, 186
Gogoris, Adda C., 90
Goheen, Douglas-Scott, 183
Goida, Matthew, 164
Going, John, 152
Gold, David C., 69
Gold, Drew, 159
Gold, Fay, 204, 207
Gold, Martin, 6, 23
Gold, Robert Alan, 52
Goldberg, Bob, 57
Goldberg, Howard, 79
Goldberg, Marcia, 49
Goldberg, Michael, 64
Goldberg, Whoopi, 188, 204
Goldby, Derek, 186
Golden Apple, The, 187
Golden Boy, 171
Golden Land, The, 66
Golden Rose Productions, 64
Golden, Annie, 55, 81, 204
Golden, Ardyss L., 163
Golden, Joey L., 165
Golden, Larry, 148
Golden, Lee, 168
Golden, Norman, 86
Goldenberg, Martin, 72, 75
Goldfaden, Harold, 49, 127
Goldman, Donald H., 73
Goldman, Herb, 69
Goldman, James, 153
Goldman, Sherwin M., 57, 66
Goldoni, 118
Goldsman, Sam, 175
Goldsmith, David, 149
Goldsmith, Leonard, 172
Goldsmith, Martin, 143
Goldsmith, Merwin, 61, 161, 204
Goldsmith, Oliver, 170, 186
Goldstaub, Mark, 8, 75, 114
Goldstaub, Paul, 156
Goldstein, Brett, 103
Goldstein, David Ira, 138
Goldstein, Jess, 157, 162, 168
Goldstein, Seth, 141
Goldstein, Shelley A., 79
Goldstick, Oliver, 61
Goldstone, Patricia, 162
Goldwyn, Tony, 146, 162
Goletz, DeBorah, 92
Goloborotko, Sheila, 61
Golub, Peter, 65
Gomes, Charles M., 99
Gonneau, George, 57
Gonzalez, Becky, 146
Gonzalez, Betsy, 112
Gonzalez, Ernesto, 99, 204
Gonzalez, Guillermo, 134
Gonzalez, Lorena, 176
Gonzalez, Magda, 176
Gooch, Bruce, 158
Good Companions, The, 79
Good Doctor, The, 165
Good Woman of Setzuan, The, 143
Good, Elaine, 153
Goodbye Freddy, 98, 148
Goodell, Susan, 151
Goodfellow, Joan, 47
Gooding, David, 30
Goodis, Richard, 65
Goodman, Andrea, 155
Goodman, Dean, 141
Goodman, Dody, 146
Goodman, John, 46, 204
Goodman, Lisa, 204, 207
Goodman, Lorraine, 150
Goodman, Robyn, 116
Goodman, Ruth, 86
Goodman, Susan, 20, 80
Goodnight, Texas, 151
Goodrich, Frances, 61
Goodrich, Katherine M., 157
Goodrum, John, 112
Goodspeed, Don, 76, 204
Goodwillie, Steve, 93, 204
Goodwin, Jerry, 166
Goodwin, Lynn, 91, 204
Goodwin, Philip, 82
Goodwin, Tim, 138
Goodzeit, Andrea, 63
Googooian, Robert, 73
Goor, Carolyn, 64
Goossen, Larry, 17
Gordean, Meg, 13, 76, 78
Gordin, Jacob, 96
Gordon, Ellen Scrimger, 112
Gordon, Geoffrey, 60
Gordon, Glenn B., 140
Gordon, Lewis, 154, 186
Gordon, Mark Alan, 149
Gordon, Miriam, 63
Gordon, Nanette, 122
Gordon, Paula, 58
Gordon, Peter, 86, 113
Gordon, Rodney, 115, 167
Gordon, Ruth, 228
Gordon, Stephanie, 89
Gordon, Stuart, 179
Gordon, Thomas Scott, 126
Gordon-Clark, Susan, 68
Gorel, David, 39
Gorenstein, Eli, 161
Gorfien, Rati, 110
Gorham, Louise H., 149
Gorky, Maxim, 101, 204
Gorman, Andrew, 92, 207
Gorman, Breon, 54, 204
Gorman, Cliff, 38, 204
Gorman, Cynthia, 139
Gorman, Fred, 71
Gorman, Mari, 188
Gorton, Rob, 58, 101, 149, 164
Gosdick, Susan, 184
Goslar, Lotte, 78
Gosney, Clare, 64, 116
Goss, Bick, 139, 167
Gossett, Robert, 153, 168
Gotanda, Philip Ken, 147
Gotlieb, Ben, 64, 205
Gottberg, Ki, 175
Gottfried, Michael, 57, 58
Gottlieb, David, 170
Gottlieb, Jon, 146, 147, 163
Gottlieb, Malke, 86
Gottlieb, Mary, 114
Gottschall, Ruth, 167
Gottung, Phyllis, 148
Gough, Didi, 73
Gould, Ellen, 66
Gould, Harold, 163
Gould, Kimberly, 142
Gould, Peter David, 174
Gould, Richard, 146
Gould, Siobhan R. K., 78
Gould, Tom, 64, 68, 76, 80, 90, 105, 153
Goulet, Bill, 170
Goulet, Robert, 188
Gouletas, Rosalie, 69, 205, 207
Goutman, Christopher, 188
Government Inspector, The, 144, 154, 186
Gow, John A., 183
Graae, Jason, 64, 75, 79, 118, 205
Graboski, Anne, 142
Grace, Brian James, 93, 111
Grace, Ginger, 77
Grace, Wayne, 173
Gracie, Sally, 67, 205
Grady, Michael, 144
Graff, Laurie, 68
Graff, Randy, 155, 168
Graff, Todd, 188
Graham, Adam E., 144
Graham, Amanda, 140
Graham, Dana, 181
Graham, Duncan W., 141
Graham, Elain, 104, 179
Graham, Frank T., 159
Graham, John, 63
Graham, Peter, 162
Graham, Robert, 60
Graham, Ronny, 188
Graham, Stephen, 12, 67
Gram, Joe, 73
Granata, Dona, 58, 152
Granata, Marcy, 17, 66, 68, 70, 130
Granau, Patty, 205
Grand Duchess of Gerolstein, The, 150
Grand Kabuki, The, 8
Grand, Sandra, 154
Grande, Loretta, 121
Graneto, Madeline Ann, 146
Granger, Farley, 88, 205
Granick, Harry, 69
Granite, Judith, 60, 160, 205
Grant, Allison, 186
Grant, Beth, 146
Grant, Byron, 145, 171
Grant, David Marshall, 147
Grant, Faye, 7, 43, 189, 192, 205
Grant, Joan, 104, 205
Grant, Katie, 121, 205
Grant, Tracy, 182
Grant, William H., III, 102, 149, 168
Grant-Phillips, John, 141

Grasso, Ellie, 142
Graves, Ruthanna, 32, 205
Graves, Yolanda, 32
Gray, Dolores, 49, 127, 205
Gray, John, 145, 167, 171, 179
Gray, Kathy, 143
Gray, Kevin, 135, 146, 155
Gray, L. Michael, 149
Gray, Pamela A., 139
Gray, Sam, 91, 205
Gray, Shirley Bird, 123
Gray, Simon, 136, 177
Gray, Spalding, 82, 97, 161, 193
Gray, Tamu, 175
Grayson, Arlene, 146
Grayson, Arthur M., 174
Grayson, Jerry, 114
Grayson, Milton B., Jr., 57
Grayson, Wendell J., 141
Grdseloff, Ruth, 162
Great Expectations, 140, 156
Great White Hope, The, 187
Greater Tuna, 138, 144, 145, 153, 159, 160, 167, 174, 184
Greco, Cathy, 49
Green Bay Tree, The, 100
Green Card, 146, 147
Green Fields, 86
Green Pastures, The, 187
Green, Adolph, 121
Green, David, 111, 121, 205
Green, Dennis, 171
Green, Floyd W., III, 168
Green, George T., 43
Green, George, Jr., 11, 34, 48, 124
Green, Jackie, 36, 46, 49, 115, 127, 135
Green, Melissa Ann, 205
Green, Rebecca, 84, 85
Green, Scott, 29
Green, Wayne, 93
Greenberg, Diane B., 98
Greenberg, Faye, 59
Greenberg, Mitchell, 62, 167, 205
Greenberg, Richard, 91
Greenberg, Rocky, 58
Greenblatt, Kenneth D., 50
Greenburg, Dan, 51
Greenburg, Mitchell, 62
Greene, Alexis, 153
Greene, Arthur M., 48
Greene, James, 12, 159, 205
Greene, Kim Morgan, 40
Greene, Lynn, 149
Greene, Marlene, 63, 73, 80
Greene, R. K., 73
Greene, Romaine, 37
Greenfield, Josh, 103
Greenhill, Susan, 94, 205
Greenhouse, Martha, 205
Greenleaf, John, 77, 90, 153
Greenlee, Susan, 62
Greenquist, Brad, 135
Greenwald, Jan C., 92
Greenwald, Laurie J., 117
Greenway, Tom, 228
Greenwood, Bruce, 83
Greenwood, Frank G., 80
Greenwood, Jane, 12, 30, 76, 107, 111, 180
Greer, Maidie O., 93
Greer, Skip, 185
Greer, Tim, 141
Gregg, Bill, 177
Gregg, Gretchen, 179
Gregg, Julie, 188
Gregg, Paul, 122
Gregg, Susan, 144, 171
Gregorio, Rose, 101
Gregory, Charles, 144
Gregory, David, 139
Gregory, Erika, 106, 107
Gregory, Michael Alan, 59, 205
Gregory, Michael Scott, 48
Gregory, Virginia, 52
Gregson, Mary Sue, 110
Grenaldo, 104
Grenier, Zach, 157
Gresh, John, 169
Gretchen, Kim, 101
Grethel, Arthur, 146
Grey, Jane, 67
Grey, Joel, 135, 205
Grey, Larry, 162, 167
Grianti, Gary, 64
Griboff, Debra, 65
Grieco, Michael, 179
Grieger, Kimberly, 184
Grier, David Alan, 157, 188
Grier, George, 140
Grier, Pam, 163
Grifasi, Joe, 20, 67, 106, 205, 207
Griffin, Dwight, 186
Griffin, Hayden, 107
Griffin, Lynne, 146, 147
Griffin, Sean G., 125, 170
Griffin, Susan, 177
Griffin, Tom, 164, 178
Griffith, Andy, 188
Griffith, Barry, 165
Griffith, Charles, 55, 169, 177
Griffith, Edward D., 100, 205
Griffith, Jim, 113
Griffith, John, 66, 81, 153
Griffith, Kristin, 118, 205, 207
Griffith, Patricia, 177
Griffiths, Trevor, 171
Grigsby, Carolyn, 182
Grigsby, Peter, 164
Grill, Barbara, 92
Grimes, Jerry, 228
Grimes, Michael, 78
Grimes, Tammy, 80, 115, 180, 188, 205
Grimsley, John, 122
Grindey, Mark, 160
Grinnell, Kate, 121
Grizzard, George, 88, 188, 192, 193, 205
Grodenchik, Michael, 64
Grodner, Suzanne, 144
Groenendaal, Cris, 76, 80, 205
Groener, Harry, 172, 188, 205
Groh, David, 69, 114, 205
Groome, Malcolm, 205
Grosberg, Rickie, 91
Grose, Molly Pickering, 121
Groseclose, Frank, 140
Grosman, Ladislav, 96
Gross, Arnold, 31, 133
Gross, Arye, 163
Gross, Cristofer, 173
Gross, Elizabeth A., 183
Gross, Gerald, 159
Gross, Michael, 146, 147
Gross, Nathan, 96
Grossenbacher, Maxey R., 54
Grossman, Bill, 48
Grossman, Gideon, 57
Grossman, Lisa, 77, 90
Grossman, Robert, 106
Grout, Donna, 136
Grove, Barry, 99
Grove, Christopher, 147
Grover, Stanley, 163
Groves, Barbara M., 97
Groves, Robin, 180
Grub-Street Opera, The, 117
Gruber, Michael, 149
Grueneberg, William, 205
Gruenewald, Thomas, 94, 153, 155
Grusecki, Robert, 117
Grusin, Richard, 57, 101, 205
Gruson, Harris, 60
Grynheim, Joel, 160
Guaraldi, Mary G., 170
Guardsman, The, 145
Guare, John, 43, 76, 82, 97, 143, 170
Guarino, Jerry, 177
Gudahl, Keven, 166
Gueli, Tony, 87
Guerra, Ambrosio, 139
Guerra, Castulo, 146
Guerra, Vito, 151
Guerrasio, John, 61
Guest, Martin, 96
Guidall, George, 61, 121, 205
Guido, Michael, 60, 108, 205
Guidone, Jack, 152
Guiffre, Beth, 76
Guilbert, Ann, 143, 151
Guilfoyle, Paul, 91
Guillen, Heberto, 176
Guinan, Francis, 98, 161
Guinand, Louis, 186
Guion, Pamela, 175
Guiteau Burlesque, The, 170
Guiteras, John, 47
Guittard, Laurence, 188
Gulley, John, 144
Gullong, Jane, 106
Gumpper, Ann E., 177
Gunas, Gary, 125
Gunderman, H. David C., 146
Gundersen, Arne, 66, 70, 142
Gunderson, Steven, 116
Gunn, Moses, 163
Gunn, Nicholas, 20, 106, 205
Gunton, Bob, 46, 205
Guralnick, Judy, 116
Gurin, Robin, 92
Gurkoff, Jeffrey, 57
Gurlitz, Eugene, 86
Gurney, A. R., Jr., 111, 170
Gustafson, Carol, 168
Gustafson, Susan, 34, 70
Gutcheon, Jeffrey, 153
Guthrie, Heidi, 165
Gutierrez, Anna Marie, 124
Gutierrez, Gerald, 111, 155
Gutknecht, Marianne L., 32
Gutwillig, Mike, 96
Guy, Jasmine, 74
Guy, Kathi, 72, 77, 116
Guy, Rebecca, 78
Guyer, Murphy, 98, 151, 168
Guys and Dolls, 140, 187
Guzman, Daniel, 93
Gypsy, 145
Gyse, Alisa, 32
Ha'o, William, 101
Haack, Marck, 135
Haas, Karl, 72, 91
Haas, Nathan, 172
Haas, Tom, 160
Haatainen, Christina, 146
Haber, Julie, 173
Haberer, Geoffrey, 172
Haberle, Sean, 182
Haberman, Linda, 50, 128
Habib, Nat, 114
Hack, Steven, 48, 205
Hacker, Sander, 51
Hackett, Albert, 61
Hackett, Joan, 188
Hackett, Kevin, 175
Hackett, Peter, 151
Hackman, Robert, 127
Hadary, Jonathan, 205
Haddad, Ava, 114
Haddad, Jamey, 109
Hadden, John, 186
Hadley, Jonathan, 182
Hafner, Tom, 93
Hagan, Earl, Jr., 72
Hagar, David, 149
Hagen, Uta, 115, 205
Hager, Max, 24
Hagerman, Dick, 149
Hagerman, James B., 175
Hagerty, Julie, 43, 97, 190, 192, 205
Hagerty, Michael, 180
Hagman, Larry, 188
Hague, Daydrie, 93, 205
Hahn, Jessica, 166
Haier, David, 141
Hailey, Oliver, 150
Haimes, Todd, 115
Haimsohn, George, 58
Haines, Mervyn, Jr., 106
Haining, Alice, 120
Haire, James, 141
Haizlip, Melissa, 83
Haj, Joseph C., 170
Halata, Michael, 72
Halcott, Gary, 83
Hale, Fiona, 145
Halevy, Ludovic, 150
Hall, Adrian, 60, 150, 178
Hall, Alan, 135
Hall, Bernard, 102, 104
Hall, Bonnie Brittain, 173
Hall, Brad, 97
Hall, Carol, 66
Hall, Davis, 157, 177
Hall, Delores, 57
Hall, Donald, 72, 142
Hall, Ed, 178, 180
Hall, George, 72, 205
Hall, Grayson, 228
Hall, Janet, 138
Hall, Kimberly, 79, 205
Hall, Michael, 142
Hall, Nick, 114
Hall, Peter, 39
Hall, Philip Baker, 163
Hall, Thomas, 184
Hall, William, Jr., 18, 57
Hallahan, Charles, 147
Hallberg, Judy, 182
Hallelujah Baby!, 187
Hallett, Jack, 155
Halley, Ben, Jr., 141, 180
Halley, Sharon, 167
Halliday, Andy, 59, 69, 205, 207
Halligan, Tim, 154, 161
Hallow, John, 98, 119, 205
Hallowell, Katherine, 183
Hally, Martha, 98, 145, 148, 171
Halpin, Kevin, 73
Halpin, Michael, 164
Halstead, Carol, 151
Halston, Julie, 69
Hamacher, Al, 140
Hamann, Nancy, 173
Hambel, Gerry, 77
Hamelin, 64
Hamer, Nigel, 186
Hamill, Mark, 115, 205
Hamill, Pamela, 128
Hamilton, Allen, 156
Hamilton, Bruce, 131
Hamilton, Dan, 177
Hamilton, Denise, 85
Hamilton, Elizabeth, 152
Hamilton, Frank, 90, 98, 101
Hamilton, Gwen M., 80
Hamilton, Jane, 87
Hamilton, Josh, 76
Hamilton, Lawrence, 32, 152, 205, 207
Hamilton, Mark, 100
Hamilton, Mary Jo, 151
Hamilton, Mitzi, 45
Hamilton, Pam, 93
Hamilton, Patrick, 64
Hamilton, R. Paul, 131
Hamilton, Randy, 146
Hamilton, Rick, 141, 163
Hamilton, Sabrina, 79
Hamilton, Stephen, 97, 148, 168
Hamlet, 108, 140, 144, 149, 182
Hamlin, George, 158, 158
Hamlin, Jeff, 43, 97
Hamlisch, Marvin, 45, 92, 169
Hammer, Mark, 143
Hammerstein, Oscar II, 31, 78, 142, 145, 167
Hammond, Carol, 140
Hammond, David, 170
Hammond, Dorothea, 143
Hammond, Michael, 42, 186
Hammond, Paul, 173
Hammond, Rixon, 140
Hampton, Christopher, 77, 146
Hanafin, Hope, 68
Hanan, Stephen, 206
Hanayagi, Suzushi, 141
Hancock, Kate, 101
Hancock, Richard, 166
Handler, Stephanie, 116
Handman, Wynn, 84, 85
Handy Dandy, 152
Handy, John, 12
Haneline, Thom, 165
Haney, Carol, 188
Haney, Mary, 186
Hangerman, Eric, 136
Hangin' 'Round, 159
Hanket, Arthur, 144, 157
Hankey, Frank, 170
Hankins, Michael, 149
Hanley, Ellen, 188
Hanley, James, 228
Hanley, Martin, 159
Hanlon, Timothy, 139
Hanmer, Don, 188
Hannafin, Daniel P., 134
Hannah, James, 57
Hannah, Jeroy, 140
Hannah, Ned, 145
Hannibal, Lydia, 59
Hansberry, Lorraine, 168
Hansen, Arthur, 60
Hansen, David, 127
Hansen, James H., 146
Hansen, Judith, 163
Hansen, Larry, 76
Hansen, Melanie, 165
Hansen, Peder, 93, 206
Hanson, Cosmo P., 152
Hanson, Fredric, 33
Hanson, Kenneth, 37
Hanson, Peter, 152
Hanson, Timothy, 183
Hanson, Torrey, 185
Happy Days, 154, 174
Hara, Douglas M., 17, 206
Harbach, Otto, 31, 76
Harburg, E. Y., 31
Harder, Mitzi, 133
Harders, Robert, 163
Hardin, Jerry, 163
Harding, Jan Leslie, 206
Harding, June, 188
Hardwick, Mark, 138, 167
Hardy, John, 149
Hardy, William, 44, 66, 179, 206
Hare, David, 107
Hare, Kathleen, 142
Hare, William, 69, 77, 98
Harelik, Mark, 151
Harewood, Dorian, 188
Harger, Gary, 145
Hargrove, Brian, 156
Hargrove, M. Austin, 164
Haris, Kate, 170
Hariton, Renee, 152
Harker, James, 20, 106
Harker, Wiley, 151
Harley, Margot, 82
Harm's Way, 66
Harman, Paul, 135
Harmon, Barry, 79
Harmon, Jennifer, 159
Harmon, Lewis, 92
Harmon, Nikk, 113
Harmon, Peggy, 46, 119
Harmon, Richard, 59, 94, 102
Harmon, Tom, 141
Harney, Ben, 85, 103, 206
Harnick, Sheldon, 92, 145, 155
Harper, James, 159
Harper, Jessica, 162
Harper, Kate, 81
Harper, Olivia Virgil, 148, 149
Harper, Phil, 80
Harper, Robert Alan, 81
Harper, Wally, 130, 152
Harran, Jacob, 61, 206
Harrell, G., 50
Harrell, Gordon Lowry, 37
Harrelson, Helen, 179
Harriman, Chelsea, 81, 158
Harrington, Delphi, 168
Harrington, Margaret, 96, 160, 206, 207
Harrington, Nancy, 58
Harrington, Wendall K., 107, 141
Harris, Albert, 57
Harris, Alison, 164
Harris, Andrew B., 59
Harris, Barbara, 188
Harris, Baxter, 101
Harris, Bill, 103
Harris, Braddon, 92, 206
Harris, Darian, 100
Harris, Dick, 175
Harris, Ed, 34, 190, 193, 206
Harris, Edna, 14
Harris, Elinor, 49
Harris, Gary, 57, 84, 85, 103, 111, 112, 116
Harris, Harriet, 108, 156
Harris, Jaime J., 78
Harris, James, 63
Harris, James-Berton, 183
Harris, Janet M., 99
Harris, Jeffrey, 164
Harris, Jeremiah J., 27, 37, 134
Harris, Joe, Jr., 24
Harris, John, 104
Harris, Joseph, 27, 37, 40, 127, 130
Harris, Joyce, 136
Harris, Julie, 188
Harris, Moira, 161
Harris, Niki, 130
Harris, Paul, 228
Harris, Peter, 118
Harris, Richard, 123, 136, 175
Harris, Rosemary, 23, 188, 206
Harris, Roy, 116
Harris, Scott, 80, 140
Harris, Skip, 145
Harrison, Archie, 61, 95
Harrison, Bill, 140
Harrison, Chris, 142
Harrison, Gregory, 146
Harrison, John L., 65
Harrison, Llewellyn, 102, 104, 149
Harrison, Lorrie, 162
Harrison, Noel, 132
Harrison, Peter, 73, 164
Harrison, Rex, 122, 206
Harrison, Stanley Earl, 206, 207
Harrold, Jack, 167
Harrop, Ernest, 154, 186
Harston, Wenelin H., 151
Hart, Adam, 120
Hart, Bill, 106, 108
Hart, Caitlan, 166
Hart, Cecilia, 188
Hart, Christopher, 22
Hart, Dolores, 188
Hart, Eric A., 72
Hart, J. Richard, 45
Hart, Jonathan, 79
Hart, Lorenz, 80, 81
Hart, Moss, 74, 96, 185
Hart, Richard, 152, 188
Hart, Tim, 100
Hartdagen, Diane, 106, 117
Hartenstein, Frank, 46
Hartland, F. J., 113
Hartland, Jesse, 65
Hartley, Cheryl, 51
Hartley, Susan, 130
Hartman, Elek, 134
Hartman, Lynne M., 177
Hartman, Michael, 76
Hartman, Nancy, 144
Hartmann, Karin, 159
Hartung, Joseph, 169
Hartwell, Peter, 107
Harum, Eivind, 45, 206
Harvey, 187
Harvey, Allison, 122
Harvey, Brian, 142
Harvey, Cameron, 173
Harvey, Christopher, 59
Harvey, Don, 67
Harvey, Gregory, 83
Harvey, Karen, 172
Harvey, Laurence, 188
Harvey, Robbin Margurite, 163
Harvin, Temoth, 113
Haskell, Judith, 145
Haskell, Peter, 163
Haskins, Susan, 96
Hassenfelt, Marjorie E., 74, 81
Hastings, Edward, 141, 172, 185
Hastings, Michael, 171
Hatch, Mary, 164
Hatcher, Robyn, 60, 206
Hattan, Mark, 144
Haugen, David, 78
Hauptman, William, 46
Hauser, Frank, 14, 25, 44
Hauser, Kim, 206
Hauser, Suzanne, 78
Hausman, Amy, 175
Hausman, Elaine, 149
Haut Gout, 179
Havel, Vaclav, 108
Havemeyer, Kathy, 119
Havis, Allan, 179
Havrilla, Kristin, 142
Hawk, Tommy, 76
Hawk, Val, 68
Hawkanson, David, 157
Hawkes, Terri, 119
Hawkins, Trish, 88, 89, 188, 206
Hawkins, Yvette, 144
Haworth, James, 186
Hay Fever, 23
Hay, Richard L., 151, 185
Hay, Suzanna, 137
Hayashi, Marc, 109
Haydn, Richard, 228
Haydock, Gregory L., 72, 118
Hayenga, Jeffrey, 143
Hayes, Anne E., 174
Hayes, Cathy Lind, 118
Hayes, Janet, 158
Hayes, Lorey, 167
Hayes, Mary L., 94
Hayes, Suzanne, 177
Hayes, Therese, 138
Hayeson, Jimmy, 206
Hayle, Douglas, 93, 206
Haynes, Hilda, 224, 231
Haynes, Jayne, 61, 90, 99
Haynes, Jerry, 177
Haynes, Robin, 158
Haynes, Tiger, 130, 206
Hays, Rex, 76, 140, 155, 158, 206
Hayter, Pearl, 145
Hazen, John, 154
Head, Monroe, 61
Headly, Glenne, 188
Heald, Anthony, 14, 54, 99, 188, 206
Healy, Christine, 160
Healy, David, 98, 206
Heard, John, 188
Hearn, Ann, 163
Hearn, George, 50
Heath, Christina, 90
Heathen Valley, 151
Heaven, Pat, 126
Hebert, Rich, 124
Hebron, Paul, 59
Hecht, Ben, 121, 160
Hecht, Deborah, 180
Hecht, Lawrence, 141
Hecht, Paul, 158
Heck, Karen, 143
Heck, Terry, 138
Heckart, Eileen, 140, 188
Hedda Gabler, 100, 146
Hedden, Roger, 91
Hedges, Peter, 113
Hedison, David, 188
Hedwall, Deborah, 61, 91
Heebner, Emily, 148, 162, 179
Heefner, David Kerry, 94
Heeger, Richard, 72
Heelan, Kevin, 157
Heeley, Desmond, 69
Heeschen, Tamara K., 57
Heeter, Bump, 73
Heffernan, Alicia C., 147
Heffernan, Maureen, 153
Heffernan, Tracy O'Neil, 177
Heffner, Wendy, 151
Heffron, John, 150
Heggie, Femi Sarah, 83
Heginbotham, Sherrie, 138
Hein, Keith, 73
Heiner, Barta, 151
Heinfling, Martin, 18, 50, 57
Heinricher, Ann, 145
Heinsohn, Elisa, 49
Heinz, Rosalind, 180
Heiple, Margi B., 175
Heisey, David, 51
Heist, Karl, 166
Held, Dan, 86
Helde, Annette, 152
Hell-Bent fer Heaven, 187
Helland, J. Roy, 26, 38, 43, 97
Hellems, Greg, 152
Heller, Adam, 96
Heller, Diane, 182
Heller, Jason, 80
Heller, Lauren, 101, 119
Heller, Robert, 206
Hellman, Lillian, 30, 92, 161
Hello Dolly!, 164, 187
Hello, Out There, 162
Helm, Tom, 124
Helmeke, Steven A., 181
Helmer, Kathleen, 132
Help Wanted, 163
Helpmann, Max, 186
Helward, Dale, 59
Hemming, Bill, 88

Hemming, Stephen, 181
Hemsley, Gilbert V., Jr., 133
Hemstead, Gillian, 80
Henderson, Jo, 111, 154, 206
Henderson, Judy, 121
Henderson, LaJara, 180
Henderson, Luther, 153
Henderson, Marcia, 188
Henderson, Marie, 79
Henderson, Stephen McKinley, 174
Henderson, Tyrone, 78
Hendrickson, Benjamin, 57
Hendrickson, Lucas G., 181
Hendrickson, Steve, 153, 170
Heneker, David, 155
Henig, Andi, 46, 206
Henley, Barry, 163
Henley, Beth, 139, 166, 185
Henley, Jane, 160
Hennes, Tom, 58, 92, 96, 122
Hennigan, Dee, 178
Hennum, Nels, 121
Henreckson, Elizabeth L., 74
Henrickson, Sahra, 81
Henritze, Bette, 76, 206
Henry VIII, 184
Henry, Chuck, 154
Henry, Gregg, 183
Henry, Joan, 58
Henry, Mark S., 117
Henry, Martha, 188
Henry, Sharon, 92
Henschel, Tom, 147
Hensel, Karen, 173
Hensley, Dale, 133
Hepburn, Audrey, 188
Hepner, Mireya, 146
Her Great Match, 110
Herber, Peter, 59
Herbert, Diana, 188
Herbert, Heather, 49
Herbert, Julie, 163
Herbert, Leo, 36, 49, 127
Herbert, Liam, 12, 17, 122
Herbert, Rita, 142
Herbst, Jeffrey, 144
Hereford, Nancy, 60, 146
Herlihy, James Leo, 113
Herman, Danny, 45, 169, 206
Herman, Jerry, 24, 50, 142
Hermann, Elizabeth, 53
Hermanski, Michael, 77, 90
Hermiller, Heidi A., 175
Hermus, Gary Paul, 57
Hern, Carey, 162
Hernandez, Felicia, 140
Hernandez, Frankie, 176
Hernandez, Hector, 176
Hernandez, Tito, 139
Herndon, Alexander, 83
Herndon, Jan Leigh, 50, 206
Herndon, Wayne, 124
Herochik, John, 164
Herold, Jonathan, 181
Herr, Sharon, 170
Herrera, Emil, 120
Herrera, James, 99
Herrera, John, 20, 106, 206
Herring, Elizabeth, 77
Herring, Linda, 102, 103
Herrmann, Edward, 62, 165, 204
Herrmann, Keith, 48
Herron, Elizabeth, 144
Herron, Keith, 92, 206
Hersey, David, 48
Hershey, Kathy, 142
Herskowitz, Robin, 20, 106
Hertsgaard, Peter, 170
Herz, Shirley, 7, 24, 50, 60, 61, 66, 68, 69, 71, 79, 81, 96, 101, 128
Herzenberg, Janet, 100
Herzer, Martin, 42
Herzman, Ellen, 153
Herzog, John, 150, 160
Hesler, Christian, 140
Hess, Linda, 124
Hestand, Cynthia, 177
Hester, Richard, 64, 79
Heston, Charlton, 161, 188
Hetsko, Mary Lynn, 76
Heughens, Todd, 149, 152
Hewett, Lance, 177
Hewett, Peggy, 79
Hewitt, Frankie, 152
Hewitt, Ian, 141
Hewitt, Kenneth R., Jr., 151
Hewitt, Tom, 143
Hewston, Jyl, 152
Heyman, Edward, 78
Heyman, John, 81
Heymann, Jerry, 142
Heys, John, 65
Heyward, Tammy, 113
Hicken, Tana, 143
Hickey, John, 66, 71, 74, 162
Hickey, Louise, 167
Hickey, William, 69, 206
Hickle, Carol, 139
Hicklen, Cliff, 83
Hicklin, Walker, 71, 81, 120
Hickman, Annie, 57
Hickok, John, 176
Hicks, James, 169
Hicks, Ken, 172, 184
Hicks, Laura, 82, 107, 206
Hicks, Leslie, 68, 158, 166, 206, 207
Hicks, Munson, 159, 171
Hicks, Peter W., 165
Hicks, S. Sherrard, 77
Hicks, Tommy, 149
Hicks, William, 74
Hidalgo, Allen, 124
Hiett, Lynne Monterey, 140
Higgins, Christopher B., 82
Higgins, Joel, 188
Higgins, John Michael, 81
Higgins, Lisa K., 167
High Tor, 187
High, John, 162
Higham, Bill, 183
Higham, David, 131
Hiken, Gerald, 163
Hilary, Ann, 101
Hilboldt, Lise, 122
Hilbrandt, James, 167
Hild, Dan, 124
Hildebrand, Paul, Jr., 179
Hiler, Katherine, 170
Hilferty, Susan, 22, 115, 116, 166, 180
Hill, Constance Valis, 158
Hill, Dana, 146
Hill, David J., 168
Hill, Delane, 151
Hill, Diahnne, 106
Hill, Diane Benjamin, 136
Hill, Donald David, 163
Hill, Elizabeth, 151
Hill, Eric, 174
Hill, Frances, 64
Hill, Gary Leon, 151
Hill, Jeannie, 182
Hill, Jeffrey, 137
Hill, John Edward, 65
Hill, Jozie, 83
Hill, Lawrence W., 121
Hill, Lucienne, 115
Hill, Lynn, 142
Hill, Michael, 110, 118
Hill, Nancy Stewart, 113
Hill, Sarah, 139, 150
Hill, Steve, 142
Hill, T. Y., 177
Hillary, Ann, 206
Hillgartner, Jim, 162, 177
Hillgartner, Malcolm, 158, 158
Hillpot, William, 229
Hills, Anne, 166
Hills, Kevin, 138
Himelsbach, James, 71
Himes, Ron, 143
Hindman, Earl, 140, 161, 174
Hindman, James, 138
Hinds, Ruby, 141
Hindy, Joseph, 107
Hines, Gregory, 188
Hines, Maurice, 32, 80, 206
Hines, Nolan, 145
Hines, Patrick, 228
Hingle, Pat, 148, 206
Hinkson, Rick, 172
Hinnenkamp, Stephen, 142
Hinton, Booker, 151
Hinton, Jim, 159
Hinton, Lizabeth, 136
Hinz, Terry, 143
Hippen, Lynn, 55
Hirsch, Judd, 4, 18, 19, 57, 154, 186, 206
Hirsch, Michael, 66, 206, 207
Hirsch, Vicki, 65, 206
Hirschberg, Kerry, 147
Hirschfeld, Susan, 140, 167
Hirschorn, Larry, 158
Hirsh, Ida Rae, 81
Hirshbein, Peretz, 86
Hirshfield, Andrew, 36, 115, 135
Hirvela, David, 183
Hit Parade, The, 98
Hitchcock, Jane Stanton, 60
Ho, Weng, 119
Hoag, Judith, 84
Hoan, Carolyn, 150
Hobart, Deborah, 64
Hobbs, Bob B., 182
Hobbs, Buck, 73, 121
Hobbs, Jim Albert, 78
Hobbs, Reginald, 83
Hobbs, Robert L., 182
Hobee, Mark, 164
Hobson, I. M., 140, 154
Hobson, Richard, 164
Hochman, Larry, 57
Hock, Robert, 117, 118
Hocking, Gloria, 177
Hodd, Stuart, 141
Hodes, Gloria, 96, 167, 188, 206, 207
Hodge, John, 66
Hodges, Dale, 27
Hodges, Eddie, 188
Hodges, Patricia A., 158
Hodgin, Hugh, 149
Hodgkins, Nancy, 182
Hodgson, Lee, 183
Hoebee, Mark, 164
Hoefler, Charles E., 85
Hoesl, Joseph, 68
Hoey, Joseph P., 162
Hofflund, Mark, 184
Hoffman, Avi, 66, 86, 206
Hoffman, Dustin, 188
Hoffman, Elizabeth, 146
Hoffman, G. Wayne, 64, 142, 206
Hoffman, Lynn, 115
Hoffman, Miriam, 86
Hoffman, Philip, 155
Hoffmann, Eric, 80
Hoffmann, Virginia, 63
Hoffmeyer, Randy, 136
Hofsiss, Jack, 57
Hofvendahl, Steve, 67, 206
Hogan, Frank X., 151
Hogan, Jonathan, 89
Hogan, Tessie, 57
Hogenmiller, Rudy, 164
Hoiby, Lee, 82
Hoigate, Danny, 119
Hoins, Karen, 138
Hoit, Michael, 146
Holan, Jennifer, 184
Holcombe, Gary, 46
Holcombe-Auffarth, Nancy, 167
Holden, Brenna Krupa, 24
Holden, Richard, 127
Holder, Christian, 83
Holder, Donald, 180
Holderness, Susan, 152
Holdgrive, David, 158
Holgate, Danny, 119, 206
Holgate, Ronald, 167
Holguin, Bertha, 176
Holiday, 171
Holladay, Cleo, 145
Holland, Dorothy, 206
Holland, Jack, 173
Holland, Judith, 107
Holland, Patrick, 83
Holland, Reece, 124
Hollander, Anita, 98
Hollar, Lloyd, 91
Holley, Robert Bruce, 77
Holliday, David, 148, 188
Holliday, Jennifer, 188, 206
Holliday, Judy, 188
Holliday, Polly, 153
Hollis, Jesse, 141, 185
Hollis, Tommy, 71, 110, 162, 206
Hollmann, Heidi, 148, 184
Hollywood, Ann, 64
Holm, Celeste, 206
Holm, Pete, 143
Holmes, Doug, 145
Holmes, George, 80, 142, 206
Holmes, Lois, 229
Holmes, Martha, 85
Holmes, Paul Mills, 120
Holmes, Rupert, 20, 106
Holmes, Scott, 31, 208
Holste, Jerry, 100
Holt, Alexander, 129, 133, 152
Holt, Fritz, 50
Holt, Michael, 59
Holte, Frank, 154
Holten, Michael, 172, 184
Holtz, Gregory, Sr., 107
Holvenstot, Christopher, 69
Holz, Gretchen, 184
Homberg, Terri, 24, 208, 213
Home Front, 177
Home, 143, 175, 179, 187
HomeGirl, 172
Homecoming, 163
Homecoming, The, 187
Homick, Hoan C., 168
Honchaurk, Peter, 60
Honda, Carol A., 109, 208
Honegger, Gitta, 163, 180
Honeygosky, Robert, 143
Hong, Barrett, 134
Honigman, Saul, 96
Hood, Cynthia, 137
Hood, Stuart, 81
Hooey, Bill, 114
Hook, Walter, 130, 135
Hooker, Jerry S., 175
Hooks, Joel, 181
Hooks, Kevin, 104
Hooks, Robert, 188
Hoolahan, Lyn, 62
Hoon, Barbara, 7
Hooper, Don, 144
Hooper, Simon, 77
Hoopla, 151
Hoover, Richard, 84
Hoover, Tom, 69
Hope of the Future, 151
Hope, Paul, 139
Hope, Stephen, 58
Hopkins, Anthony, 101
Hopkins, Billy, 97
Hopkins, Katherine, 133
Hopkins, Leon, 63, 78
Hopkins, Rosemary, 62, 208
Hopper, Paul, 165
Hopper, Tim, 183
Horan, Bonnie, 110, 208
Horiuchi, Gen, 11
Hormann, Nicholas, 33
Hormasji, Homi, 107, 208, 213
Horn, Andrew M., 77
Horne, J. R., 94
Horne, Lena, 187
Horne, Marjorie, 74
Horner, Richard, 62, 81
Hornung, Bob, 137
Hornung, Richard, 16
Horovitz, Israel, 86
Horowitz, Robin, 152
Horowitz, Seymour, 143
Horrigan, Kathleen, 175
Horrigan, Patrick, 24
Horstman, Martha, 105
Horswill, James, 156
Horton, Brian, 145
Horton, Derek, 139
Horton, Jamie, 151
Horton, Kathleen, 146
Horvath, James, 140
Horvath, Jan, 40, 208
Horvath, Joe, 144
Horvath, John, 74
Horwitz, Murray, 153, 174, 175
Hosey, Meg, 101
Hoshi, Shizuko, 147
Hoskins, Jim, 153
Hoskins, Ralph, 141
Hosmer, George, 175
Hostetler, Paul, 136
Hostettler, Andy, 83, 155
Hot L Baltimore, The, 168, 187
Hot Mikado, 152
Hotaling, Brian, 170
Hotchkis, Joan, 149
Hotopp, Michael J., 122
Hott, Jordan, 58
Hoty, Dee, 65, 208
Houdina, Mary Jane, 62
Houdyshell, Jayne, 165
Houghton, Katharine, 101, 188, 208, 213
Hould-Ward, Ann, 64, 65, 82, 111, 143, 151, 152, 155
Houle, Ann, 182
Houlton, Loyce, 156
House of Blue Leaves, The, 43, 97, 187, 190
House of Shadows, 104
House, Ron, 70, 208
Houseman, John, 82, 184
Houshmand, John, 72
Houston, Dianne, 60, 161
Houston, Faith, 78
Hovis, Joan, 188
How Gertrude Stormed the Philosophers' Club, 137
How the Other Half Loves, 144
How to Say Goodbye, 137
How to Succeed in Business without Really Trying, 187
Howard, Andrew, 96
Howard, Bette, 102
Howard, Charles, 177
Howard, David S., 87, 184
Howard, Don, 129, 146
Howard, Ed, 145, 153, 167, 174, 184
Howard, Ken, 188
Howard, M. A., 110, 111, 143
Howard, Marcial, 113
Howard, Mel, 13
Howard, Paul, 177
Howard, Peter, 31, 62, 75
Howard, Porcia, 104
Howard, Richard, 33, 82, 156
Howard, Stuart, 50, 121
Howe, Tina, 139, 145, 149, 159, 167, 173, 174, 179, 184
Howell, Michael, 152
Howell, Sam, 109
Howes, Nina, 90
Howie, Betsy, 63
Howland, Beth, 146
Hoxie, Richmond, 91, 158, 164, 208
Hoy, Gerald Hart, 165
Hoylen, Anthony, 16
Hoyt, J. C., 184
Hubbard, Alison, 59
Hubbard, Jane, 186
Hubbard, Valorie, 184
Huber, J. Luke, 165
Huber, Kathleen, 93, 208
Huber, Sarah Jayne, 165
Hubert, Janet, 111, 162
Hubp, Dan, 72
Huddle, Elizabeth, 141
Huddleston, Chip, 123
Hudgins, Kenneth Kyle, 183
Hudson, Ken, 177
Hudson, Linda, 142
Hudson, Nancy, 166
Hudson, Rodney, 141
Hudson, Ruben S., 102
Hudson, Walter, 162
Hueghens, Todd, 164
Huelsman, Marilyn Kay, 122
Huey, Tom, 140
Huff, Gordon, 56
Huff, Harry, 90
Huffman, Cady, 37, 208
Hughes, Alice S., 167
Hughes, Allen Lee, 76, 140, 143, 152, 171
Hughes, Barnard, 12, 208
Hughes, Caitlin, 182
Hughes, Douglas, 111, 172
Hughes, Langston, 85, 149
Hughes, Laura, 88, 208
Hughes, Rhetta, 126
Hughes, Richard Michael, 108
Hughes, Tresa, 144
Hughes, Walter, 142
Hughley, Stephanie S., 104
Hugill, J. Randall, 83
Hugo, Laurance, 184
Hugot, Marceline, 136
Huigen, J. Roo, 177
Huisenga, Craig, 136
Hulce, Thomas, 162
Hulin, James, 181
Hulkower, Ellen, 182
Hull, Bryan, 52, 208
Hull, Robert, 60
Hulswit, Mart, 153
Hults, L. R., 62
Hults, Stephen G., 92
Hume, Michael J., 148
Hummel, George, 152
Hummel, Karen, 96
Hummel, Mark, 24
Hummer, Robert, 146
Humphrey, Michelle, 145
Humphreys, James, 60
Hundley, C. L., 57, 110
Hunnicut, Chuck, 127
Hunt, B. Laurie, 152
Hunt, Betty Lee, 33
Hunt, Emera, 32
Hunt, Helen, 91
Hunt, Joseph, 77
Hunt, Linda, 107, 208
Hunt, Louis, 71
Hunt, Mame, 163
Hunt, Margaret, 65
Hunt, Ralph, 113
Hunt, Suzy, 33, 156
Hunt, Terry G., 165
Hunt, Tim, 121
Hunt, Trey, 62, 68
Hunt, W. Dennis, 163
Hunt, W. M., 158
Hunt, William E., 57
Hunter, Christine, 125
Hunter, JoAnn, 79
Hunter, Joann M., 134
Hunter, Kim, 57
Hunter, Marc, 48
Hunter, Marie Goodman, 177
Hunter, Mary, 172
Hunter, Richard, 83
Hunter, Rion, 146
Huntington, Crystal, 119
Huntington, Stacy, 175
Huntley, Paul, 7, 14, 20, 23, 26, 29, 30, 36, 42, 48, 65, 88, 89, 106, 108, 115, 122, 124, 129, 162
Huntzinger, Karin, 72
Huot, Denise, 170
Hupcey, Joseph V., Jr., 76
Huppeler, Cindia, 59
Hurlbert, Carolyn, 57
Hurley, John Patrick, 122, 208
Hurley, Pat, 140
Hurst, Gregory S., 167
Hurst, Lillian, 112, 208
Hurst, Scott, 186
Hurston, Zora Neal, 85
Hurt, Mary Beth, 27, 208
Hurt, William, 188
Hurwitz, Jill, 46
Hurwitz, Rosalind, 159
Husmann, Ron, 188
Hussey, Heather, 145
Husted, Patrick, 137
Hutchings, Keith, 87
Hutchins, Janice, 141
Hutchinson, Jeffrey, 137
Hutchinson, Patrick, 140
Hutchinson, Ron, 147
Hutchison, Daniel, 68
Hutson, Patricia, 100
Hutton, John, 151
Hwang, David, 116, 163
Hyatte, Keith, 162
Hyde-Lamb, David, 174
Hyland, Ed, 65
Hyman, Dick, 133
Hyman, Earle, 33, 188, 208, 213
Hyman, Fracaswell, 143
Hyman, Larry, 111
Hyman, Phyllis, 188
Hymen, Mark, 139
Hyslop, Elizabeth A., 109
Hyslop, Jeff, 186
I Am a Camera, 187
I Don't Have to Show You No Stinking Badges, 163
I Have a Dream, 103
I Married an Angel, 81
I Ought to Be in Pictures, 145
I'll Be Back Before Midnight, 176
I'm Not Rappaport, 4, 57, 187
I, Shaw, 96
Iacobacci, Kathleen, 158,
Iacovelli, John, 105
Iannaconne, Carmine, 163
Iannella, Linda, 184
Iannucci, Michael, 92, 208
Ibsen, Henrik, 90, 100, 110, 143, 146, 180
Icebound, 187
Iceman Cometh, The, 12, 161
Idiot's Delight, 161
Ikeda, Thomas, 17
Illuminati, The, 137
Ilo, Angelique, 45
Ilson, Anne, 142
Imaginary Heir, The, 181
Imaginary Invalid, The, 158
Imhoff, Gary, 146
Immigrant, The: A Hamilton Country Album, 151
Importance of Being Earnest, The, 65, 140, 153, 174, 180
Impromptu, 113
In Abraham's Bosom, 187
In Dreams Begin Responsibilities, 147
In The Boom Boom Room, 68
In the Belly of the Beast: Letters From Prison, 60, 161
In the House of the Blues, 102
Indichova, Julia, 69
Infidelities, 177
Ingalls, James F., 79, 99, 111, 115, 161, 172
Inge, Matthew, 208
Inge, William, 146, 150
Ingenthron, Karen, 174
Inglima, Donna, 175
Inglis, Gavin, 145
Ingraham, Margaret, 165
Ingram, Kenny, 164
Ingram, Michael, 121
Ingram-Young, Donna, 83
Inis, Sydney, 91
Innerarity, Memrie, 167
Innes, K. Craig, 50
Innes, Laura, 62, 90, 208
Innes, Walter, 175
Inside-Out, 66
Inskeep, Carter, 65
Insull, Sigrid, 145, 179
Introcaso, Amy, 110
Inwood, Joan, 99, 208, 213
Ionesco, Eugene, 63
Iorio, James, 184
Irby, A. Dean, 168
Iredale, Jane, 26
Irey, Mary, 179
Irma La Douce, 155
Irvine, Daniel, 89
Irving, Suzanne, 136
Irwin, Bill, 84, 143
Irwin, Catherine, 143
Irwin, Mary, 95
Irwin, Michael, 92, 208, 213
Irwin, Robert, 142
Is This Real?, 161
Isaacs, Susan, 173
Isaacson, Donna, 99
Isackes, Richard M., 183
Isherwood, Christopher, 229
Ishida, Jim, 146
Isn't It Romantic?, 153
Israel, Mary, 65, 208
Israel, Robert, 44, 78
Isreal, Zangwill, 62
Istomin, Marta, 161
It's Only a Play, 99
Ito, Genji, 76
Itzin, Gregory, 147
Ivanek, Zeljko, 36, 99, 107, 208
Ivanoff, Alexandra, 167
Ivers, Mitchell, 167, 171, 179
Ives, Jane, 137
Ivey, Dana, 14, 208
Ivey, Judith, 34
J. B., 187
Jablons, Karen, 208
Jackness, Andrew, 34, 115, 116, 162
Jacks, Susan J., 208

Jacksina, Judy, 17, 68, 70, 130
Jackson, Anne, 101
Jackson, Cameron, 60
Jackson, Chequita, 103
Jackson, David, 50, 119, 130
Jackson, Doug, 177
Jackson, Ernestine, 116, 188, 208
Jackson, Joanne, 151
Jackson, Johanna, 141
Jackson, Julie, 81
Jackson, Kevin, 82
Jackson, Kirk, 180
Jackson, Lamara, 128
Jackson, Nagle, 141, 158, 164
Jackson, Samuel L., 172, 179
Jackson, Todd, 117, 184
Jacob, Abe, 37
Jacob, Bill, 117
Jacob, Jere, 58
Jacob, Neil, 149
Jacob, Steven, 208, 213
Jacobowsky and the Colonel, 187
Jacobs, Abe, 45
Jacobs, Claudia, 99
Jacobs, Craig, 40
Jacobs, George, 69, 113
Jacobs, Kate, 208
Jacobs, Marc, 93, 208
Jacobs, Meryl S., 26, 76
Jacobs, Peter, 141, 182
Jacobs, Robert, 151
Jacobs, Sally J., 48
Jacobson, Jay B., 17
Jacobus, James, 63
Jacoby, Mark, 40, 190, 192, 208
Jaeger, Thomas, 184
Jaeger, Tony, 124
Jaffe, Daniel, 165
Jaffe, David, 64, 103
Jaffe, Jill, 78
Jaffe, Joan, 81
Jaffe, Ruth, 32
Jakowlew, Natalie, 145
Jalenak, Jan, 64
James, Elmore, 46, 152, 208
James, Finaly, 122
James, Francesca, 121, 208
James, John, 126
James, Judith Rutherford, 146
James, Julie, 136
James, Kathryn, 179
James, Mary, 188
James, Robert, 157
James, Stephen, 188
James, Terry, 123
James, William, 123
Jamiaque, Yves, 57
Jampolis, Neil Peter, 9, 172
Janasz, Charles, 184
Jane Wagner, 187
Janek, James, 132
Janich, Colleen, 66
Janis, Conrad, 188
Jankowski, JoAnn, 145
Jankowski, John E., 61
Janowsky, Ann, 118
Jans, Alaric "Rokko", 149
Jansen, Christine, 137
Jansen, Jim, 163
Jansz, Charles, 159
Jarabeck, Janice, 169
Jarboe, Richard, 64
Jared, Robert, 174
Jaris, Richard, 61
Jaroslow, Ruth, 146
Jarrell, Randall, 158
Jarrett, Bella, 160
Jarvis, Francesca, 144
Jary, Suzie, 49, 127
Jasin, Deborah, 179
Jasmine, Herbert, 78
Jason, Rick, 188
Jason, Robert, 149, 170
Jasper, Beth A., 143
Javits, Joy, 85
Jaworski, Kathleen, 142
Jay, Brian, 124
Jay, John, 72
Jay, Mary, 174
Jay, Michael, 125
Jay, William, 164, 170, 172
Jaye-Greer, Laura, 118
Jeeves Takes Charge, 152
Jeffcoat, Donnie, 173
Jefferson, B. J., 126
Jefferson, Marvin, 149
Jefferson, Michael, 168
Jefferson, Paul, 151
Jeffries, Annalee, 107
Jellison, John, 26, 144
Jenkins, Daniel, 46, 146
Jenkins, David, 146, 162
Jenkins, Elizabeth, 62
Jenkins, Ken, 46, 208
Jenkins, Len, 90, 147
Jenkins, Lillette E., 149
Jenkins, Mark, 172
Jenkins, Paulie, 60, 140, 146, 173
Jenkins, Richard, 178
Jenkins, Ron, 81, 141
Jenkins, Teddy, 101
Jenkins, Terry, 164
Jenkins, Timothy, 101
Jenkins, Trent, 59, 139
Jenkins-Evans, Holly, 137
Jenner, James, 150
Jenney, Lucinda, 91, 208
Jennings, Brent, 35
Jennings, Bridget, 97, 163
Jennings, Byron, 151
Jennings, Christopher, 62, 97
Jennings, Erica, 101
Jennings, Ken, 15, 188, 208
Jennings, Nolan, 154, 186
Jens, Salome, 58, 67, 208, 213
Jensen, Beverly, 145
Jensen, Donald, 66, 69
Jensen, Howard, 77, 160
Jensen, Jim, 121
Jensen, Jody, 72
Jensen, John, 105, 164, 168, 170, 171
Jensen, Julie, 143
Jensen, Ken, 173
Jensen, Peter, 92, 117
Jenson, Kari, 179
Jenssen, Martha, 142
Jerardi, Nathalie G., 157
Jered, Todd, 163
Jermanovich, Steven, 178
Jerome Kern Goes to Hollywood, 31
Jerome Kern Song Book, The, 160
Jerome, Timothy, 48, 115, 143, 208
Jerris, Sam A., 122
Jerry's Girls, 24
Jestice, Mary, 58, 110, 111
Jeter, Michael, 188, 208
Jeter, Richard W., 59, 139
Jewell, Doug, 102
Jewell, John, 106
Jewett, Bob, 66
Jezek, Kenneth, 124
Jiler, John, 78, 113, 208
Jillette, Penn, 56, 208
Jillson, Joyce, 188
Jimenez, Robert, 186
Jitters, 173, 179
Jo-Ann, Ebony, 162
Joachim, Lori, 72
Joan of Compton/Joan of Arcadia, 163
Joanna's My Name, 113
Jochim, Keith, 178
Joe Egg, 187
Joe Turner's Come and Gone, 180
Joerder, Norb, 80, 123
Johann, Cameron Charles, 116, 119
Johannes, Mark, 60, 208
Johanson, Don, 124
Johanson, Robert, 167
John, Flozanne A., 170
Johns, Patti, 163
Johnsen, Walter, 56
Johnson, A. J., 79
Johnson, Ardis, 61
Johnson, Bjorn, 76, 162
Johnson, Cecil, 168
Johnson, Charles, 157
Johnson, Chris, 138
Johnson, Craig, 138
Johnson, Cullen, 148
Johnson, Dan, 77, 90
Johnson, Daniel T., 208
Johnson, David E., 177
Johnson, David-Michael, 7
Johnson, Dean, 150
Johnson, Dejie, 121
Johnson, Della L., 150
Johnson, Douglas, 170, 174
Johnson, Edward, 168
Johnson, Eric M., 165
Johnson, Eve, 153
Johnson, Greg, 123
Johnson, Gregg Thomas, 136
Johnson, J. J., 69
Johnson, Jack Stubblefield, 139
Johnson, James Arthur, 149
Johnson, Jeff, 160
Johnson, Jill, 163
Johnson, Jo Ann, 175
Johnson, Jodi, 51
Johnson, Judy, 145
Johnson, Julie, 142
Johnson, Keith, 143
Johnson, Kenneth, 91, 149
Johnson, Kenya, 58
Johnson, L. Robert, 77, 90
Johnson, Lamont, 163
Johnson, Lea Ann, 100
Johnson, Linda Lee, 160
Johnson, Lynn, 82
Johnson, Marek, 98
Johnson, Marilyn J., 139
Johnson, Mark, 143
Johnson, Mary Lea, 15
Johnson, Mel, Jr., 208,
Johnson, Meridith, 133
Johnson, Myron, 144
Johnson, Page, 188, 208, 213
Johnson, Paul, 92
Johnson, Reid, 165
Johnson, Richard, 90
Johnson, Robert S., 98
Johnson, Russell,, 156
Johnson, Scott Lindsay, 14, 208
Johnson, Susan, 188
Johnson, Terry, 173
Johnson, Tim, 129, 146
Johnson, Tina, 64, 208
Johnson, Tommi, 32
Johnson, Toni Ann, 107
Johnson, Van, 50
Johnson, Vaughn, 183
Johnson, Vera, 158
Johnson, Virgil, 154
Johnson-Liff, 11, 33
Johnson, Chris, 167
Johnston, Donald, 49, 76
Johnston, J. J., 127, 188, 209
Johnston, Justine, 142
Johnston, Nancy, 75
Johnston, Samme, 92, 209
Joiner, Dorrie, 179
Joji, Takeshiba, 8
Jolly, Russ, 46, 160, 209
Jon, Christopher, 74
Jonah and the Wonder Dog, 104
Jones, Alan, 78
Jones, Annette, 61
Jones, B. J., 154
Jones, Beryl, 151
Jones, Bob Devin, 163
Jones, Bradley, 45
Jones, Bryan Curtis, 140
Jones, Carolyne A., 77
Jones, Cherry, 65
Jones, Courtney, 75
Jones, David, 66, 178
Jones, Dawn Renee, 138
Jones, Douglas, 144
Jones, Eddie, 59, 119, 209
Jones, Franz, 46, 209
Jones, Gib, 45
Jones, Herman LeVern, 103
Jones, James Earl, 154, 188
Jones, Jane, 115, 149, 209
Jones, Jay Aubrey, 83, 209
Jones, Jen, 148, 174
Jones, Jessica, 75
Jones, Jessie K., 168
Jones, Jill, 92
Jones, John Christopher, 12
Jones, Judd, 130
Jones, Judette, 75
Jones, Karen, 184
Jones, Laura, 97, 188
Jones, Leilani, 134, 188, 209, 213
Jones, Lyle, 93
Jones, Mark, 78
Jones, Martin, 166
Jones, Marty, 158
Jones, Marvin, 157
Jones, Melody, 128
Jones, Michael, 169
Jones, Neal, 46
Jones, Reed, 74, 209
Jones, Robert A., 143
Jones, Roy L., 126
Jones, Sabra, 101, 209
Jones, Seth, 160
Jones, Shannon Lee, 50, 128
Jones, Shawn, 80
Jones, Simon, 27, 122, 209
Jones, Stephen O., 76
Jones, Steven, 79
Jones, Tad, 209
Jones, Tom, 52, 159
Jones, Virginia, 92
Jones, Walton, 138, 167
Jonin', 107
Joosten, Kathy, 154
Jordan, Bob, 69, 209
Jordan, Dale F., 62, 148
Jordan, Henry J., 140, 158, 159
Jordan, John, 188
Jordan, Richard, 106, 209
Jordan, Rick, 179
Jordan, Samantha, 142
Jordan, Steve, 101
Jordan, Susan, 209
Jordan, Tom, 146
Jorgensen, Anita, 93
Jory, Jon, 137
Joseph, Darrel, 17, 66, 68, 70, 78, 130
Joseph, Edward, 79
Joseph, Melanie, 105
Joseph, Nathan, 39
Joseph, Rowan, 101, 209
Josephs, Chris, 169
Josephson, Peter, 138
Joshua, Lawrence, 61, 209
Joshua, Shirl, 62
Joslyn, Betsy, 80, 140
Journey, Steven, 177
Joy, James Leonard, 96, 137, 149, 155, 159
Joy, Mary, 91
Joy, Robert, 23, 209
Joyaux, Simone, 178
Joyce, Elaine, 188
Joyce, Heidi, 93, 96, 213
Joyce, Joe, 128
Joyce, Stephen, 147, 188, 209, 213
Joyner, Michelle, 160
Joyous Noel! A Noel Coward Music Hall, 138
Jubak, John, 62
Jubilee, 74
Jud, Edie, 80
Jude, Patrick, 16, 209
Judge, Diane, 126
Judge, Shawn, 116
Judin, Sue, 83
Judy, James, 166
Juel, Gordon A., 63
Juggle & Hyde, 136
Julia, Raul, 209
Jung, Philipp, 57, 181
Juniper Tree, The, 141
Junius, Kiel, 155
Jurrist, Charles, 59
Just So, 64
Jutras, Simon, 96
Juzo, Kataoka VI, 8
K2, 150
Kabel, James, 122, 129
Kabuki Medea, 161
Kacir, Marylynn, 151
Kacser, Hilary, 152
Kaczenski, Heidi, 163
Kaczmarek, Jane, 162
Kading, Charles S., 139
Kadison, Michele, 64
Kael, Dan, 76
Kafka, Franz, 90
Kahn, Ben, 40, 115
Kahn, Daniel, 179
Kahn, Gus, 31
Kahn, Jeremy, 158
Kahn, John, 75
Kahn, Michael, 82
Kail, Gene, 169
Kaiser, Scott, 136
Kalas, Janet, 67, 186
Kaledin, Nicholas, 87, 99, 209
Kaleita, Lisamarie, 165
Kalember, Patricia, 54
Kalevas, Paul, 165
Kalfin, Robert, 157
Kall, James, 164
Kaller, Sheryl A., 59
Kallman, Dick, 188
Kamezo, Kataoka IV, 8
Kaminker, Laura, 116
Kaminsky, Kym, 133
Kamlot, Robert, 6, 23, 38, 42, 47, 123
Kamm, Tom, 141
Kamp, Diane, 34, 144
Kampf, James Edward, 93
Kampley, Linda, 94, 209, 213
Kan, Lilah, 101
Kanai, Shunichiro, 8
Kandel, Lenore, 51
Kander, John, 135, 153
Kander, Susan, 85
Kane, Bradley, 63, 209
Kane, Donna, 58, 167, 190, 192, 209
Kane, Kent, 164
Kane, Robert Michael, 100, 184
Kanee, Stephen, 156
Kanelos, Jim, 182
Kanoff, Scott, 157, 171
Kansas, Jeri, 49, 209
Kanter, Dan, 137
Kanter, Daniel, 65
Kanter, David, 229
Kantor, Kenneth, 96, 167, 209
Kantrowitz, Jason, 118, 140
Kapen, Ben, 143
Kapetan, Peter, 79
Kaplan, Alicia, 112, 209
Kaplan, Darlene, 86, 120
Kaplan, David, 116, 166
Kaplan, Erica, 70
Kaplan, Herbert, 159
Kaplan, Howard Tsvi, 139
Kaplan, Shirley, 91
Kaplan, Steven, 98, 168
Kapust, Larry, 78
Karanik, Theresa, 163
Karchmer, Charles, 168, 175
Karel, Charles, 135
Karl, Alfred, 127
Karn, Frederick, 165
Karn, Richard, 87
Karniewich, Anthony, 127
Karniewich, Tony, 43, 97
Karp, Daniel Paul, 109
Karve, Jayant, 109
Kashi, Charles, 79
Kasinoir, Chico, 109
Kasioula, Elina, 180
Kasper, Deb E., 98
Kaspin, Yuval, 69
Kassira, Kim, 177
Kaszynski, Suzanne, 73, 80
Katcher, Hope, 61, 209
Katsaros, Doug, 64, 121
Katz, Abbie H., 141
Katz, Arthur, 46
Katz, Dave, 159
Katz, Donalee, 87
Katz, Ken, 83
Katz, Kristina, 63
Katz, Madeline S., 98
Katz, Natascha, 57, 122
Katz, Paul, 118
Katz, Sondra R., 76
Katz, Steven, 60
Katz, Tracy, 175
Katz, Zev, 25
Katzen, Art, 125
Katzman, Bruce, 180
Kauders, Sylvia, 79
Kauffman, Jean, 92, 209
Kauffman, John, 136
Kauffman, Marta, 65
Kauffman, Thomas M., 167
Kaufman, Brian, 74, 121
Kaufman, Christian, 137
Kaufman, Dale, 122
Kaufman, George S., 73
Kaufman, Irene, 91
Kaufman, Michael, 209
Kauzmann, C. Peter, 164
Kava, Caroline, 112, 209
Kavanaugh, Richard, 76, 178, 209
Kavilis, Diana, 124
Kay, Barbara, 149
Kay, Hershy, 45
Kay, Kenneth, 123
Kay, Michael J., 66
Kay, Stanley, 32
Kaye, Deena, 77, 90, 131
Kaye, Judy, 76, 167, 188, 209
Kaye, Keena, 121
Kazakoff, Stephen, 164
Kazantzakis, Nikos, 135
Keach, Stacy, 161
Keal, Anita, 61
Kealey, Scott, 159
Kean, Norman, 51
Keane, George, 188
Kearney, Karon, 146
Kearns, Daniel, 13
Kearny, Kristine A., 181
Kearsley, Barry, 37
Keating, Charles, 36, 64, 99, 209
Keating, Gary-Thomas, 166
Keaton, Ron, 160
Keats, David, 100
Keck, Michael, 140
Kedrova, Lila, 135
Keefe, Anne, 162
Keel, Melinda, 74
Keeler, Brian, 98
Keeler, Dana, 86
Keeley, David, 186
Keeling, Thom, 124
Keen, Stan, 172
Keeney, Tommy, 81
Keever, Tom Dale, 68
Kehoe, Sheila, 121
Kehr, Don, 106, 209, 213
Keim, Ross, 182
Keiser, To-Ree-Nee, 144
Keitel, Harvey, 67
Keith, Larry, 111, 209
Keith, Maralyn, 110
Keith, Marilyn, 80
Kelakos, Eleni, 113
Kellachan, Daniel, 8, 75, 114
Kelleher, Mary Ann, 93
Kelleher, Timothy, 79
Keller, Gayle, 141
Keller, Jeff, 65, 209
Keller, John-David, 173
Keller, Susan, 90
Kellermann, Susan, 116, 180, 188, 209, 213
Kelley, Dan, 57
Kelley, Michael, 151
Kelley, Peter, 188
Kelley, Shannon Keith, 151
Kellogg, Mary Ann, 7
Kellogg, Robert, 130
Kelly, Brian, 50, 169
Kelly, Daren, 140
Kelly, David Patrick, 157
Kelly, Elizabeth, 161
Kelly, Gene, 7
Kelly, George, 170
Kelly, Grace, 188
Kelly, James, 175
Kelly, Janie, 142
Kelly, Julia, 209
Kelly, K. C., 94, 95, 209
Kelly, Kate, 148
Kelly, Kieran, 22
Kelly, Martha, 153
Kelly, Mary Tierney, 77, 90
Kelly, Michelle, 164
Kelly, Monica, 127
Kelly, Patrick, 115
Kelly, Randy, 70, 80
Kelly, Rory, 144
Kelly, Sean Michael, 144
Kelly, Thomas A., 18, 57
Kelly-Young, Leonard, 153, 159
Kelman, Ben R., 79
Kelton, Richard, 188
Kemler, Estelle, 70
Kemp, Garry, 108, 209
Kemp, Sally, 173
Kempf, Art, 61, 157
Kendall, Edward, 167
Kendall, Jose, 101
Kendrick, Richard, 131
Kendrick, Thomas R., 161
Kenin, Alexa, 229
Kennedy, Adrienne, 60, 161
Kennedy, Beau, 73, 77, 118
Kennedy, Craig, 112
Kennedy, Jihmi, 99
Kennedy, Laurie, 157, 188
Kennedy, Patricia E., 144
Kennedy, Patrick, 66
Kennedy, Terry, 143
Kennett, David, 178
Kenney, Daniel, 58
Kenney, Mare, 87
Kennison, Kevin, 63
Kenny, Frances, 175, 182, 185
Kenny, Jack, 209
Kenyon, Laura, 155, 172
Kenyon, Neal, 58
Kepright, Kristine, 142
Kepros, Nicholas, 33, 84, 209
Kerle, Trish, 58
Kerley, Stephanie, 72, 75
Kern, Jerome, 31, 155
Kernan, David, 31
Kerns, Linda, 46, 209
Kerr, Charles, 154, 186
Kerr, John, 188
Kerr, Mary, 182
Kerr, Patrick, 180
Kerr, Terry, 181
Kerr, William, 173
Kersey, Billye, 49, 209
Kersey, Robin, 24
Kershaw, Whitney, 209
Kerwin, Shawn, 186
Kerzman, Robert, 62
Kesey, Ken, 79
Kesselman, Wendy, 79
Kessler, Lee, 73, 209
Kessler, Lyle, 139
Kessler, Michael, 59
Kester, Terry D., 78
Ketron, Larry, 120, 151
Ketter, Sari, 151
Kevoian, Peter, 124
Kevrick, Robin, 162
Keye, Jay, 87
Keys, Henson, 164, 180
Keysar, Franklin, 29
Kfir, Michael, 161
Khan, Rick, 149
Khaner, Julie, 154, 186
Khanzadian, Anita, 70
Kielbasa, Jody, 144
Kilburn, Terence, 165
Kiley, Richard, 162, 188
Kilgarriff, Patricia, 132
Kilgore, John, 46, 78
Killing Time, The, 75
Killmer, G. Theodore, 58, 109
Killmer, Ted, 17, 66, 68, 70, 78, 124
Kilpatrick, Erik, 168
Kilpatrick, Patrick, 80, 166, 209
Kilty, Jerome, 157, 158
Kim, Daisietta, 147
Kim, Josie, 146, 147
Kim, June, 147
Kim, Randall Duk, 181
Kim, Willa, 11, 42
Kimbrough, Charles, 23, 209
Kimbrough, Linda, 154
Kimbrough, Matthew, 153, 156
Kincaid, Jason, 172
Kind of Alaska, A, 136
Kindberg, Wendell, 73, 80
Kindl, Charles, 18, 57
Kindred, Lloyd, 15
King and I, The, 187
King and Queen of Bingo Surrounded by Swift Nudes, The, 163
King of the Sehnorrers, The, 62
King John, 185
King Lear, 136, 185, 186
King, Alice, 60, 89, 209
King, Anne S., 101
King, Bruce Roberts, 87

King, Catherine, 144, 167
King, David L., 83
King, Davies, 161
King, Diane, 140, 173, 140
King, Eddie, 140
King, Erik, 120, 161, 209, 213
King, Floyd, 152
King, Ginny, 209
King, Jeffrey, 171
King, John Michael, 188
King, Kimberly, 174
King, Woodie, 80, 102, 103, 140, 166
Kingsberry, W. Ruth, 183
Kingsley, Barbara, 156
Kingsley, Janet, 93
Kingsley, Susan, 188
Kingwill, Jay, 17
Kinney, Mary Lisa, 79
Kinney, Terry, 161
Kinsey, Linda S., 164
Kinsley, Dan, 96
Kinter, Richard, 145
Kinzer, Craig D., 90
Kipling, Rudyard, 64
Kirby, Earl, 38
Kirk, Tom, 122
Kirkland, Sally, 108, 209
Kirkman, Tamara, 63
Kirkpatrick, James T., 112
Kirkpatrick, Sam, 26, 144
Kirksey, Dianne, 113
Kirkwood, James, 45, 129, 146, 169
Kirman, John, 140
Kirsch, Carolyn, 209
Kirsch, Gary, 133
Kirwin, Terry, 155
Kiselov, Mladen, 137
Kiser, Terry, 188
Kiser, Tony, 60
Kish, Gene, 149
Kismet, 187
Kiss Me Kate, 139, 142, 187
Kissel, David, 167
Kissman, Lee, 137, 146
Kitchen, Janice, 76
Kith and Kin, 150
Kitty, Alan, 100, 210
Kiwitt, Judy, 100
Kjenaas, Aaron, 171
Klain, Margery, 76
Klapper, Stephanie, 73
Klarnet, Jess, 76, 101
Klatt, David, 50, 210
Klausmeyer, Charles, 51
Klausner, Terri, 119
Klavan, Laurence, 98, 168
Kleban, Edward, 45, 169
Kleigel, Frank, 45
Klein, Amanda J., 70
Klein, Carol, 14, 28, 44
Klein, Dani, 54, 113
Klein, David S., 113, 136, 172, 175
Klein, Emily E., 76
Klein, Jill C., 136
Klein, Joanne, 172
Klein, Maxine, 72
Klein, Randi, 59
Klein, Robert, 25, 210
Klein, Sally, 173
Klein, Steven M., 172
Klein, Stuart, 193
Klein, Victoria, 154
Kleinman, Marsha, 17
Kleinmuntz, Manny, 93, 210
Kleiser, Steve C., 64
Klemperer, Werner, 115, 161
Klenck, Margaret, 163
Kliegel, Frank, 45
Klima, Ivan, 113
Kline, Johnny, 72
Kline, Kevin, 108, 137, 210
Klingelhoefer, Betsy, 173
Klingelhoefer, Robert, 92
Klinger, Cindi, 124
Klinger, Pam, 45
Klionsky, David, 78
Klopp, Paris, 166
Klotz, Florence, 24
Kluga, Raymond, 153
Klump, Karen, 49
Klunis, Tom, 107, 179, 210
Klvana, Kathryn, 90
Kmeck, George, 135, 155
Knapp, Bob, 159
Knapp, Jacqueline, 156
Knapp, Sarah, 74
Knapp, Tom, 185
Kneeland, Richard, 178, 184
Knell, Dane, 144
Knickerbocker, Terry, 85
Knight, Dudley, 163
Knight, Ezra, 143, 186
Knight, John, 76
Knight, Kerri, 134
Knight, Martha, 143, 146
Knight, Shirley, 85, 101, 210
Knobeloch, Jim, 101
Knott, Frederick, 160
Knotts, Kathryn, 182
Knotts, Marilyn, 126
Knower, Rosemary, 143
Knowles, Mark, 145
Knowlton, Patricia, 186
Knox, Beverly, 184
Knox, John, 151
Knox, Peter, 151
Knudsen, Fritha, 141
Knudsen, Karen, 151
Knudson, Kurt, 99, 115, 210
Kobee, Beverly Murray, 174
Koch, David Hunter, 136
Koch, Edward I., 15
Koch, Jane, 110
Koch, Patrick, 116
Kociolek, Ted, 177
Kocontes, Frank, 133
Koenig, Holly A., 169
Koenig, Jack, 62, 144
Koenig, Tommy, 81
Koflanovich, Steven, Jr., 58
Kogler, Rita Ann, 72
Kohler, Anna, 161
Kohler, Gilles, 158
Kohler, Jon, 140
Kohler, Mike, 79
Kohler, Susan, 147
Koka, Juliette, 57, 188, 210, 213
Kokol, Bob, 176
Kolber, Lynne, 76, 210
Kolinski, Joseph, 148
Kollar, Bill, 61
Kolman, Allan, 163
Kolo, Fred, 60
Koloc, Bonnie, 188, 210
Kolodner, Arnie, 59, 69
Kondoleon, Harry, 111, 116
Kondolf, George, 229
Kondrat, Michael J., 105
Konicki, Joseph, 124
Konik, Barbara, 168
Konrardy, Nancy, 81, 149
Konzal, Greg, 182
Kopache, Thomas, 63, 210
Kopelman, Charles P., 36
Kopit, Arthur, 136
Kopyc, Frank, 152, 167
Korbich, Eddie, 72
Korda, Casey, 60, 98
Korder, Howard, 98
Korf, Geoff, 137
Korhn, Aaron, 183
Korker, Ron, 134
Kornberg, Richard, 20, 45, 106, 116
Korthaze, Richard, 155
Korzen, Annie, 96, 210
Kosarin, Michael, 15
Kosek, Kenneth, 46
Kosher, Alan Ross, 132
Kostroff, Michael, 83
Koteas, Elias, 91
Kotler, Jill, 83, 210
Kotlowitz, Dan, 57, 111, 174
Kourilsky, Francoise, 76
Kourkounakis, Joanna, 96
Koustik, Art, 173
Kovaka, Michael, 94
Kovitz, Randy, 160
Kraemer, Bruce A., 80
Kraft, Arthur, 65
Kraft, Katharine E., 141
Krakowski, Jane, 111
Kralovec, Dennis, 110
Kramer, Larry, 162
Kramer, Michael, 152
Kramer, Ruth E., 58
Kramer, Terry Allen, 133
Kramer, William, 96
Krane, David, 26
Krapp's Last Tape, 172
Kraus, Andrew, 64
Krause, Marc, 66
Krause, Mark S., 132
Krausnick, Dennis, 186
Krauss, Diana, 171
Krauss, Marvin A., 50, 126
Kravat, Jerry, 15, 152
Krawford, Gary, 142
Krawitz, Patricia, 72, 73
Krebs, Eric, 62, 153
Krebs, Susan, 147
Kreider, Bill, 167
Kreinen, Rebecca, 92
Kreiss, Andrew, 95
Kremer, Dan, 185
Krempel, Jenna, 57, 109
Kreshka, Ruth, 61, 67, 108
Kress, Donna M., 150
Kressen, Sam, 167
Kressyn, Miriam, 63
Kretzu, Jon, 136
Krieger, Barbara Zinn, 119
Krieger, Henry, 126
Krielkamp, Ben, 138
Krikorion, Shari, 81
Krimmer, Wortham, 173
Kristen, Ilene, 15, 96
Kroetz, Franz Xaver, 163
Kroeze, Jan, 75
Kroh, Aaron, 183
Krohn, Charles, 139, 183
Krohn, Scott C., 80
Kroken, Daryl, 58, 150
Kronenberg, Bruce, 72
Krouse, Ian, 176
Krout, Ellen, 147
Krug, John, 52
Kruger, Karen, 63
Kruger, Kelli, 65
Krupa, Olek, 90
Ksen, Al, 62
Ktistes, Elaine, 78
Kubota, Glenn, 109
Kucharczyk, Betha A., 184
Kudan, John, 66, 210
Kuehling, Anne Marie, 99
Kuhlman, Julie, 173
Kuhn, Beth, 76
Kuhn, Bruce, 137
Kuhn, Francis X., 150, 164
Kuhn, Hans Peter, 141
Kuhn, Judy, 20, 96, 106, 210
Kuhn, Michael, 62
Kulesha, Gary, 186
Kulick, Brian, 146, 147
Kullers, John (Red), 229
Kumar, Ravinder, 107
Kumin, Fran, 12, 23, 34, 42, 47, 123, 161
Kunen, Amy, 142
Kunkle, Connie, 152
Kunz, Carol, 152
Kuramoto, Daniel, 147
Kureishi, Hanif, 70
Kuroda, Emily, 163
Kuroda, Kati, 109
Kuroemon, Onoe II, 8
Kurowski, Ron, 45, 210, 213
Kurshals, Raymond, 7
Kurth, Juliette, 50, 128, 150
Kurtz, Kenneth N., 144
Kurtz, Marcia Jean, 33, 86, 210
Kurtz, Swoosie, 43, 88, 97, 210
Kushner, Tony, 171
Kusyk, Jim, 161
Kuter, Kay E., 146, 147
Kux, William, 165, 175
Kuyk, Dirk, 179
Kuzma, Sue Ellen, 141
Kvares, Donald, 62
Kwan, Nancy, 163
Kwiat, David M., 138
Kwiat, Matthew, 59
Kyd, Thomas, 77, 90
Kyle, Michael, 146
L'Engle, Madeline, 136
L. A. Freewheeling, 81
La Belle Helene, 83
La Cage Aux Folles, 50, 128, 187
La Chunga, 73
La Mee, Maggie, 138
La Plume de Ma Tante, 187
La Verdadera Historia de Pedro Navaja, 106
LaBianca, Alex, 87, 91
LaBoit, Terry, 158
LaDuca, Phil, 79, 210, 213
LaFeber, Scott, 29
LaFlamme, Kira, 182
LaFlamme, Linda, 182
LaGrange, Eileen, 49
LaGreca, Paul, 210
LaLumia, Drinda, 114
LaManna, Raphael, 135
LaMar, Diana, 136
LaMarque, Kimberley, 141
LaPadura, Jason, 46
LaPlante, Skip, 60, 161
LaPlatney, Martin, 136, 157, 160
LaRoche, Lorenzo, 102
LaRon, Ken, 102
LaSalle, Eriq, 107, 120
LaShelle, Lance, 92
LaTouche, John, 167
LaVoie, Roger, 74, 81
Lable, Lorna, 93
Laboissonniere, Wade, 127
Laboy, Nina, 77
Lacey, Franklin, 142
Lackey, Herndon, 20, 106
Lacy, Florence, 188
Lacy, Tom, 184
Ladies and Gentlemen, Jerome Kern, 57
aLadman, Jeff, 144
Lady Day at Emerson's Bar and Grill, 119,
Lady from the Sea, The, 110
Lady in Yellow Boucle, A, 113
Lady's Not for Burning, The, 187
Laffer, Denise, 91
Lafferty, Sandra Ellis, 151
Laffey, Bruce, 62
Lagomarsino, Ron, 99, 158, 173
Lahm, Rosalie, 13
Lahti, Christine, 188, 210
Lahti, Gary, 157, 175
Laine, Cleo, 20, 21, 80, 106, 191, 193, 210
Laine, Raymond, 169
Laird, Michael, 144
Lajoie, Stephen, 110
Lakin, Gene, 78
Lally, James, 84, 98, 210
Lamb, J. Kathleen, 124
Lamb, Mary Ann, 11, 210
Lamb, Peter, 186
Lambert, Greta, 181
Lambert, Mikel, 152
Lambert, Wayne, 177
Lammel, Cynthia, 59, 105
Lamond, Andrew, 100
Lamos, Mark, 157
Lamp, Eric, 50
Lampel, Alan, 96
Lampel, Laura, 96
Lamude, Terence, 153
Lanai, Donna, 60
Lancaster, Burt, 188
Lancaster, Dorothy, 94, 210
Lancaster, Gerald, 164
Lanchester, Robert, 164
Land, Ken, 55
Landa, Walter, 80
Landau, Barry, 193
Landau, David, 76
Landau, Emily, 46
Landau, Natasha, 66
Landau, Penny M., 59, 65, 114
Landau, Vivien, 184
Landen, Elliott, 100
Lander, Marie, 80
Landes, Francine, 20, 106, 210
Landesman, Heidi, 46, 111, 146
Landfield, Timothy, 158,
Landis, Bernie, 154
Landis, Jeanette, 143
Landis, Joseph, 86
Landis, Lynn, 43, 88
Landis, Ruth, 154
Landisman, Eric, 182
Landisman, Kurt, 163
Landon, Hal, Jr., 173
Landon, Hal, Sr., 173
Landon, Sofia, 60, 101, 162, 210
Landrine, Bryan, 76
Landrum, Michael, 95
Landwehr, Hugh, 162, 172, 175
Lane, Beth, 144
Lane, Janice, 149
Lane, Nathan, 26, 106, 210
Lane, Rosalind, 176
Lane, Stewart F., 50
Lane, William, 178
Laney, George, 77
Lang, Alyson L., 93
Lang, Charles, 188
Lang, Harold, 229, 231
Lang, Morgan, 173
Lang, Perry, 91
Lang, Peter, 60
Lang, Philip J., 49, 122, 127, 229
Lang, Philip, 122
Lang, William H., 61
Langan, E. Timothy, 178
Langdon, Gregory, 105
Langdon, Sue Ann, 148
Langdon-Lloyd, Robert, 78, 157
Lange, Anne, 111, 210
Lange, Douglas A., 152
Langefeld, Shelly, 100
Langhorne, Milton, 69
Langton, Basil, 163
Lanier, Hal, 76, 140
Lanier, Jane, 40
Lanman, Victoria, 118
Lanning, Corie, 142
Lanning, Jerry, 188, 210
Lansing, Robert, 57, 210
Lansky, David, 107
Lant, John W., 80
Lantaigne, Gerry, 90
Lanzener, Sonja, 59
Lanzer, Ruth, 157
Lapidus, Jerry, 83
Lapierre, Billings, 140
Laramore, Paul, 161
Lardner, Natalie, 80
Larese, Kim, 127
Large, Norman A., 124
Largo Desolato, 108
Lariscy, Michael, 144
Larkin, Deborah J., 115
Larkin, Peter, 37
Larkin, Robert, 35, 43, 97
Larmett, Jill, 100
Laron, Ken, 102
Larrance, John C., 145
Larry, Sheldon, 146
Larsen, Liz, 64, 65, 210
Larsen, Lori, 136, 172
Larsen, Ray, 62
Larson, Barbara W., 181
Larson, Bev, 165
Larson, Brett, 142
Larson, Jill, 170
Larson, Larry, 137, 161, 168
Larson, Peter, 130
Lascelles, Kendrew, 147
Lasell, John, 163
Lashbrook, Stephen, 150
Lashuay, Brett, 165
Laskawy, Harris, 12
Lasky, Zane, 89
Lassell, John, 163
Last Judgment, 163
Laszlo, Miklos, 92
Latchaw, Paul, 229
Latham, Louise, 67
Latham, Patrick M., 96
Lattimore, Richard, 95
Laub, Mary, 148
Laub, Sandra, 93, 210
Lauck, Joe, 164
Laudicino, Dino, 210
Laughlin, Richard, 145
Laughlin, Sharon, 108, 210
Laughton, Charles, 144
Launder, Mary E., 144
Laundra, Linda, 71
Laurans, Lydia, 132
Lauren, Amy Jane, 72
Lauren, Ellen, 174
Laurence, Charles, 145
Laurence, Paula, 74, 210
Laurence, Stuart, 64
Laurenson, Diana, 37, 210
Laurents, Arthur, 50, 121, 134, 145, 161
Laurino, Adelaide, 11, 48
Lauris, Priscilla Hake, 185
Laushey, Jeane, 150
Lavery, Emmet, 229
Lavie, Raul, 13
Lavin, Linda, 188
Lavin, Richard, 159
Lavine, Audrey, 57
Lawes, George, 140
Lawhon, Travis, 161
Lawless, James, 156
Lawless, Rick, 54, 210
Lawless, Sarah, 151
Lawless, Sue, 86
Lawlor, David, 58, 59, 69
Lawrence, Barbara, 100
Lawrence, Carol, 188
Lawrence, Dale C., 140
Lawrence, Darrie, 156
Lawrence, David, 20, 122
Lawrence, Delphi, 77, 210
Lawrence, Gary, 7, 24, 57, 58, 68, 81, 96, 128
Lawrence, Jack, 64
Lawrence, Jeremy, 147, 174
Lawrence, Jerome, 142
Lawrence, Lisa, 181
Lawrence, Peter, 38
Lawrence, Piper, 14
Lawrence, Rey, 100
Lawrence, Sharon, 135
Lawrence, William A., 61, 210
Lawson, Arielle, 173
Lawson, Celeste, 152
Lawson, David, 59, 90, 114
Lawson, Douglas M., 54
Lawson, Mary, 70
Lawson, Nancy, 15
Lawson, Richard, 163
Lawson, Tom, 149
Layman, Terry, 144
Layne, Mary, 157
Layton, Michael, 145, 152
Lazarus, Frank, 176
Lazarus, Paul, 65
Le Maire, Charles, 229
Le Massena, William, 165
LeCompte, Elizabeth, 161
LeFevre, Adam, 148
LeFrak, Francine, 134
LeGallienne, Eva, 188
LeMassena, William, 165
LeNoire, Rosetta, 83
LeRoy, Zoaunne, 136
LeStrange, Philip, 153, 162
LeTang, Ellie, 83
LeTang, Henry, 83
LeVine, Marilynn, 13, 76, 78
Leach, Clare, 49, 127
Leach, Douglas, 182
Leach, James, 76, 210
Leach, Leslie Evans, 177
Leach, Wilford, 20, 106
Leachman, Cloris, 188
Leake, Sundy Leigh, 48
Leal, Pete, 176
Leaming, Chet, 54
Leaming, Greg, 82, 157
Learned, Michael, 121, 146
Leary, Champe, 145
Leask, Katherine, 156
Leatherman, Allen, 30
Leave It to Jane, 155
Leavel, Beth, 49, 127
Leaverton, Gary, 29
Leavin, Paul, 72
Lebow, Barbara, 157
Lebowsky, Stanley, 7, 48
Lecesne, James, 57
Leclercq, Arthur, 161
Lecube, Garciela, 79
Lecuru, Bruce, 183
Ledbetter, Sammy, 23
Leddy, Gerry, 31
Lederer, Suzanne, 147
Lee, Baayork, 45, 130, 152, 161
Lee, Barry, 62, 157
Lee, Carl, 229
Lee, Dana, 146
Lee, Ellen Ellis, 116
Lee, Ellen, 32, 135
Lee, Eugene, 150, 178
Lee, Irving Allen, 40, 210
Lee, Jack, 115, 130
Lee, James R., 142
Lee, Jeannie, 179
Lee, Jeff, 48
Lee, Jennifer, 210, 213
Lee, John, 136, 172
Lee, Jonathan Barlow, 146
Lee, Levi, 137, 161, 168
Lee, Liisa, 134
Lee, Liz, 140
Lee, Ming Cho, 33, 156, 180
Lee, Phil, 76, 79, 98, 119
Lee, Robert E., 142
Lee, Ronald S., 30
Lee, Sally, 142
Lee, Shyron, 75
Lee, Susan, 16, 18, 40, 69, 70, 81, 94, 127
Lee-Aranas, Mary, 109, 210
Lee-Matijevic, Patricia A., 166
Leech, Kitty, 119
Leeds, Jordan, 164
Leerhoff, Dick, 138
Leffert, Joel, 69, 210
Leffingwell, Jo, 136
Legends, 129, 146, 147
Leger, Norman M., 160
Leggett, Paula, 145
Leggio, John Vincent, 78
Legionaire, Robert, 161
Legler, Dixie, 181
Leguillou, Lisa, 172
Lehew, Stephen, 69
Lehman, Jeanne, 31, 76, 142, 210
Lehr, Wendy, 144
Lehrer, Scott, 99, 110, 111, 146
Lehrer, Tom, 173
Leibman, Ron, 188
Leifer, Judith, 169
Leigh, Carolyn, 152
Leigh, Jaime, 155
Leigh, Jennifer Jason, 146
Leigh, Mitch, 177
Leigh, Neva, 49
Leigh-Milne, Elizabeth, 186
Leigh-Smith, Andrea, 155
Leight, Warren, 15
Leighton, Bernie, 49
Leighton, Betty, 181
Leighton, Charles, 80
Leighton, John, 72, 137, 210
Leighton, Richard, 101, 164, 210
Leiner, Karen, 171
Leipzig, Adam, 163
Leitner, James L., 168
Lelyveld, Gail, 184
Lemmon, Jack, 42, 210
Lemon Sky, 116
Lemon, Ben, 95, 162, 210
Lemsky, Mitchell, 11
Lencioni, Arlene, 93, 210
Lenehan, John, 167
Lengel, Karl, 122
Lengson, Jose, 162
Lengyel, Melchior, 73
Lennart, Isobel, 93
Lennix, Harry J., 154
Lennon, John, 51
Lenox, Adriane, 74, 210
Lenthall, David, 138
Lentner, J., 175
Leo, Brian, 159
Leo, Melissa, 86, 211
Leon, Joseph, 38
Leon, Mechele, 131
Leon, Tania, 79
Leonard, Barbara, 147
Leonard, Jim, Jr., 94
Leonard, John, 143
Leonard, Linda, 164
Leonard, Robert, 88, 211
Leonard, Roger, 71
Leonard, Valerie, 101
Leonard, William P., 152
Leone, Greg, 79
Leone, Marianne, 211
Leone, Vivien, 59, 69, 77, 157, 162
Leong, David, 182
Leos, Richard, 176

Leplat, Ted, 162
Lerch, Stuart, 110
Lerian, Maggie, 171
Lerner, Alan Jay, 123, 142, 144
Leroux, Gaston, 148
Lesko, John, 49, 127
Lesko, Ruth, 170
Leslie, Bethel, 42, 211
Leslie, F., 70
Lesnick, Helen, 148
Lessane, Leroy, 109, 211
Lesser, Sally, 55, 66, 79
Lesson From Aloes, A, 162, 184, 187
Lester, Ketty, 188
Lester, Loren, 161
Lester, Todd, 124
Leu, Richard, 102
Lev, Howard P., 77
Levan, Martin, 11, 48
Leveaux, David, 70
Levels, Calvin, 97, 188, 211
Leveridge, Lynn Ann, 163
Leversee, Loretta, 188
Levin, Abby, 88, 89
Levin, Alan, 17
Levin, Irina, 152
Levine, Anna, 91, 211
Levine, David B., 144
Levine, Earl Aaron, 73
Levine, Peter A., 80
Levine, Rachel S., 62, 68
Levine, Richard, 72, 211
Levine, Ted, 123
Levis, Bill, 144
Levit, Ben, 110, 159
Levitan, Dan, 179
Levitation, 171
Levithan, Robert, 57
Leviton, Roberta, 151
Levitt, Sandy, 64
Levo, Julia, 78
Levy, Barbara R., 144
Levy, Benn W., 115
Levy, David, 158
Levy, Debbie, 22
Levy, Deena, 68
Levy, Hank, 57, 105
Levy, Jacques, 51, 66
Levy, Kate, 151
Lew, Leland, 177
Lew, Richard, 103
Lewin, Martha, 62
Lewis, Alde Jr., 37
Lewis, Arden, 158,
Lewis, Bertha, 57
Lewis, Bobo, 139, 172
Lewis, Boncellia, 174
Lewis, Bram, 137
Lewis, Carol Jean, 153
Lewis, Colleen D., 181
Lewis, Dawnn J., 58
Lewis, Edwina, 68
Lewis, Ellen, 38
Lewis, Gilbert, 102, 172, 211
Lewis, Irene, 171
Lewis, Jim, 73
Lewis, John Richard, 46
Lewis, Ken, 57
Lewis, Marcia, 111, 211
Lewis, Mark, 169
Lewis, Matthew, 174
Lewis, Mildred, 64
Lewis, Pamela, 150
Lewis, Todd, 211
Lewis, Vicki, 26, 211
Lewis-Evans, Kecia, 66
Lewisohn, Debbie, 184
Lewitin, Margot, 58, 60
Lewman, David, 159
Lewman, Lance, 170
Leyden, Leo, 161
Li, Donald, 109
Liars, 113
Liberatore, Lou, 211, 213
Libertella, Jose, 13
Libin, Claire, 14, 25, 28, 44
Libin, Paul, 14, 25, 28
Libkin, Maida, 24
Librandi, Geraldine, 72, 178
Licata, Michael, 40
Lichenstein, Mitchell, 156
Licht, David, 145
Lichtenstein, Mitchell, 111, 156
Lie of the Mind, A, 67, 187
Lieberman, Dennis, 113
Lieberman, Iris, 159
Lieberson, Will, 113
Liebgold, Leon, 64
Liebman, Steve, 158, 177
Liederman, Susan, 70
Lies My Father Told Me, 96
Life She Led, The, 177
Life and Adventures of Nicholas Nickleby, The, 187
Life and Limb, 178
Life in the Theater, A, 144
Life with Father, 170
Light Up The Sky, 96, 185
Ligon, Tom, 73, 167
Lillian, 30
Lillo, Marie, 49
Lillo, Tony, 123
Lilly, Crystal, 102
Lilly, Randy, 164
Lilly, Terry M., 15, 54, 65, 79, 133
Linardos, Stacie, 77
Lincoln, Abbey, 103
Lincoln, Michael, 160
Lind, Kirsten, 93, 211
Linden, Hal, 18, 19
Linderman, Donna, 93
Linderman, Ed, 166
Lindhart, Rachael, 171
Lindig, Jillian, 165
Lindley, Audra, 152
Lindo, Delroy, 180, 186
Lindquist, Frank, 59, 71
Lindquist, Krystov, 152
Lindquist, Valerie, 71
Lindsay, Howard, 142, 170
Lindsay, Phillip, 138
Lindsay, Priscilla, 160
Lindsay, Tedrin Blair, 68
Lindsay-Hogg, Michael, 17
Lindsey, Kathleen, 16
Lines, Sybil, 152
Link, Peter, 80
Linklater, Hamish, 186
Linklater, Kristin, 186
Linn, Bambi, 188
Linn-Baker, Mark, 61, 81
Linney, Romulus, 151, 168, 179
Linton, John, 47
Linton, Mark, 229
Linton, William, 133
Lion in Winter, The, 153
Liontis, Polly, 154
Lipman, David, 211
Lipman, Mark, 61
Lipnick, Jonathan, 72
Lippa, Louis, 168
Lippa, Nancy, 168
Lippay, MaryAnn, 156
Lippe, 69
Lipschultz, Nancy, 80
Lipscomb, Bill, 116
Lipsky, David, 79
Lipton, Michael, 160
Lisa, Luba, 188
Lisbon Traviata, The, 57
Liset, Kit, 62
Lish, Becca, 178
Litt, Sandi, 165
Litten, Jim, 45
Little Eyolf, 180
Little Footsteps, 111
Little Me, 152
Little Night Music, A, 187
Little Shop of Horrors, 55, 169, 171, 177, 187
Little Sondheim Music, A, 160
Little, Cleavon, 4, 18, 19, 57, 211
Little, David, 22, 153, 211
Little, John R., 162
Little, Robert, 164
Little, Todd, 161
Little-Roberts, Iris, 140
Littles, Avan, 61
Littman, Jonathan, 113
Litton, Rita, 152
Litwak, Jessica, 85
Liu, Frank Michael, 80
Lively-Mekka, DeLyse, 45
Living Color, 75
Livingston, 145
Lizzie Borden in the Late Afternoon, 185
Lizzul, Anthony John, 77, 211
Llosa, Mario Vargas, 73, 176
Llowell, Dy, 118, 211
Lloyd, Benjamin, 180
Lloyd, Karen, 27
Lloyd, Michael, 163
Lloyd, Sherman, 148
Lloyd, Yolanda, 149
Lo Bianco, Tony, 74
Lo Curto, Lisa, 114
LoBianco, Tony, 74, 211
LoMonaco, Thomas, 134
LoPresto, Charles, 76, 82, 106, 119
LoVullo, Stephen, 133
Loague, Katherine Marie, 90, 95
Loar, Rosemary, 127
Loatman, Richard M., 164
Lobel, Adrianne, 61, 82, 99, 111, 115, 130, 143
Lobenhofer, Lee, 78, 81
Locante, Sam, 79
Locarro, Joe, 134
Lock, Kevin, 58, 144, 167
Locke, Ennis Dexter, 179
Locker, Phillip, 165
Lockery, Patricia, 155
Lockhart, James, 135
Lockhart, June, 188
Lockman, Joel, 138
Lockner, David "Sparky", 166, 176
Lockweed, Shirley, 175
Lockwood, Carole, 64
Lockwood, Jennifer, 177
Lockwood, Vera, 63
Lockwood, W. W., Jr., 164
Locricchio, Matthew, 108, 211
Loden, Barbara, 188
Loder, John, 93, 211
Lodge, Marty, 152
Loeb, Leslie, 88, 89
Loesser, Frank, 140, 142
Loewe, Frederick, 123, 144
Loewy, Jacqi, 81
Loewy, Oscar, 127
Lofgren, Aarne, 40
Lofgren, John, 40
Loftin, Lennie, 171
Loftis, Tom, 105
Loftus, Mary Fran, 85, 120
Lohnes, Peter, 136, 175
Loigman, Mark D., 181
Lombardo, Rick, 81, 118
London Assurance, 184
London, Becky, 59
London, Chet, 121, 211
London, Chuck, 56, 88, 89
London, Howard, 178
Lonergan, Michael, 79, 135
Lonergan, Ray, 156
Lonergen, Michael, 135
Long Day's Journey Into Night, 42, 187
Long Smoldering, The, 69
Long Time Since Yesterday, 102
Long, Anni, 173
Long, Jodi, 118
Long, Kathryn, 174
Long, Richard, 98
Long, Rita M., 94, 117
Long, Ruth, 184
Long, Susan, 76, 142, 211, 213
Long, Tamara, 73
Long, William Ivey, 57, 99, 108
Longbrek, Derek, 136
Longley, Laura, 161
Longo, Teresa, 79
Lonsdale, Frederick, 122
Look Back in Anger, 187
Look Homeward Angel, 187
Loomis, Kevin C., 136
Loose Connections, 69
Loot, 36, 99, 189
Looze, Karen, 46, 142
Lopata, Linda, 169
Lopez, Michael, 211
Lopez, Priscilla, 69, 84, 211
Lopez, Ricardo T., 163
Lopez, Sal, 176
Lopez-Morillas, Julian, 182
Loprete, Elisa, 63
Loquasto, Santo, 7
Lor, Denise, 127
Lorca, Federico Garcia, 176
Lord, Chip, 60
Lord, Jack, 188
Lorendo, Cam, 71
Lorenger, Bonnie, 173
Loreto, Richard, 145
Loring, David, 167
Loring, Estelle, 188
Lormer, Jon, 229
Lortel, Lucille, 22, 62, 70, 75, 115, 193
Loschmann, John, 141
Losh, Diana, 78
Lost in the Stars, 162
Lotayef, Omar, 101, 211
Loti, Elisa, 188
Lotorto, Louis, 182
Lotz, David, 104
Loud, David, 110, 143, 167, 171, 179
Loudon, Dorothy, 24, 25, 80, 188, 192, 193, 211
Loughlin, Molly, 142
Loughlin, Patrick, 142
Loughrin, Tim, 183
Louie and Ophelia, 104
Louie, Mei-Ling, 75
Louise, Merle, 50
Louiso, Todd, 149
Louloudes, Virginia, 99
Love As We Know It, 98
Love Suicide at Schofield Barracks, The, 168
Love of Four Colonels, The, 187
Love, Edith H., 140
Love, Katie, 102
Love, Staci, 155
Love, Victor, 107, 179, 186
Love, Wil, 165, 174
Lovebirds, The, 113
Lovers & Keepers, 77
Loverso, Stefano, 99
Lovett, Marjorie, 145
Lovitt, Shifee, 64
Lovullo, Janene, 124
Low, Betty, 122
Low, Corbey Rene, 111
Lowe, Frank, 78, 145
Lowe, Frederick, 142
Lowe, Jackie, 26
Lowe, Kathleen, 37, 40
Lowell, Marguerite, 26
Lowell, Robert, 79
Loweth, Todd, 77, 90, 131
Lowey, Judy, 151
Lowman, Kristen, 173
Lowry, Jane, 165
Lowry, Malcolm, 147
LuPone, Patti, 161
LuPone, Robert, 45, 211, 213
Lubbock, Jeremy, 129
Lubeck, Chuck, 164
Lucas, Christopher, 127
Lucas, Craig, 140, 149, 173
Lucas, Harriet D., 61
Lucas, J. Frank, 127
Lucas, Jonathan, 188
Lucas, Roxie, 53, 211
Lucas, Warren "Juba", 151
Luce, William, 30, 90, 161
Lucero, Rick, 92
Luciano, Richard, 157
Luckinbill, Laurence, 153
Lucks, Marimar, 179
Ludel, William, 120
Ludlam, Charles, 65
Ludlow, Susan, 136
Ludwig, Antonia Noble, 175
Ludwig, Jon, 140
Ludwig, Karen, 86, 98, 211
Ludwig, Katie, 169
Ludwig, Kenneth, 159
Ludwig, Salem, 18, 57
Lugo, Hecmar, 176
Luhrman, Henry, 15, 54, 60, 65, 79, 133
Luigs, Jim, 137
Lukas, Victor, 121
Lukather, Suzanne, 76, 211
Luker, Rebecca, 74, 76, 142, 155
Lukins, Josh, 64
Lum, Alvin, 17
Lumbard, Dirk, 58
Lumbly, Carl, 147
Lummus, Jill, 68
Luna, Barbara, 114
Luna, Jovita, 13
Lund, John, 188
Lundeberg, Karl, 141
Lundie, Ken, 167
Lundquist, Lori, 91
Lupino, Stephen, 17
Lupton, Jennifer, 136, 175
Lupu, Michael, 156
Luschar, Karen, 123
Luse, James, 162
Lustberg, Lawrence H., 77, 90
Lustig, Alexander, 64
Lustik, Marlena, 161
Luther, 187
Lutov, Natasha, 146
Lutz, Connie, 138
Lutz, Doug, 134
Lutz, Renee, 64, 79
Luv, 175
Luzak, Dennis, 150
Lybe, Denis, 100
Lyles, Leslie, 91, 151
Lyman, Dorothy, 125
Lyman, Libby, 61
Lyman, Norton, 59
Lyman, Will, 167
Lynch, Charles, 100
Lynch, Elise, 179
Lynch, Katherine, 166
Lynch, Kevin Hugh, 175
Lynch, Kevin, 136
Lynch, Luke, 135
Lynch, Michael P., 115
Lynch, Michael S., 152
Lynch, T. Paul, 161
Lynch, Thomas, 61, 110, 111, 143
Lynd, Betty, 130, 211
Lynde, Janice, 110, 111, 211, 213
Lynes, Cynthia, 105
Lynes, Kristi, 124
Lyng, Nora Mae, 26, 118, 211
Lynley, Carol, 188
Lynn, Debra, 73
Lynne, Gillian, 48, 152
Lyon, Robin, 45
Lyons, David M., 140
Lyons, John, 110
Lyons, Paul, 153
Ma Rainey's Black Bottom,, 187
Maaske, Dee, 185
Mabry, LaDonna, 117
MacAaron, Francesca, 83
MacArthur, Charles, 121, 160
MacArthur, James, 188
MacArthur, Roy, 80
MacAteer, Thomas, 101
MacCallum, Cather, 185
MacDermot, Galt, 96
MacDermott, Laura, 42, 106, 140
MacDevitt, Brian, 167
MacDonald, Bob, 20, 45
MacDonald, David, 143
MacDonald, J. R., 110, 111
MacDonald, Janet, 186
MacDonald, Karen, 60, 141
MacDonald, Mary, 66
MacDonald, Pirie, 180
MacDonald, Stephen, 62
MacDougal, Robert, 136
MacFarland, Dorothea, 188
MacGregor-Jochim, Jeannie, 178
MacIntosh, Joan, 101, 141
MacIver, Peter, 78, 100
MacKay, John, 160
MacKenzie, Arthur, 65
MacKenzie, John C., 123
MacKenzie, Peter, 162
MacLaughlin, Don, 229
MacLean, Reid, 142
MacLeay, Lachlan, 114
MacLeod, Charles, 151
MacMillan, Gerard, 72
MacNicol, Peter, 107, 156, 188, 211
MacPherson, Greg, 69, 91, 98, 142
MacPherson, Gregory C., 82
MacPherson, Jane, 76, 90
MacPherson, Walt, 143
MacRae, Ellen, 165
MacRae, Gordon, 229, 231
MacReady, Brian, 100
MacVittie, Bruce, 91, 211
Macaulay, Lesley, 186
Macaulay, Tony, 167
Macbeth, 121, 181
Macbett, 63
Macchio, Ralph, 108, 211
Macdonald, Brian, 186
Macdonald, Janet, 186
Macdougall, Robert, 172
Mace, Cynthia, 179
Mace, Michael, 82
Maceio, Michelle, 169
Macfie, Jane, 182
Machart, Marla, 81
Machin-Smith, Helen, 175
Machray, Robert, 173, 184
Macht, Stephen, 161
Mack, Carol K., 151
Mack, Paul, 124
Mackavey, Jill, 118
Mackay, Lizbeth, 188, 211, 213
Mackenzie, Peter, 99
Mackenzie, Robb, 177
Mackenzie, Sandra, 182
Mackintosh, Cameron, 11, 48, 55, 173
Mackley, Paul, 163
Macklin, Albert, 111, 211
Macleay, Lachlan, 63, 211, 213
Macnaughton, Robert, 88, 173, 211
Macy, W. H., 97, 111, 162, 211
Madden, Corey Beth, 147
Madden, Donald, 188
Madden, John, 115
Madden, Kerry, 81
Madden, Sharon, 146, 147
Maddow, Ellen, 79
Maddox, Diana, 184
Maddrie, Leah, 184
Madeira, Marcia, 159
Madigan, Deirdre, 101
Madrid, Madrid, 78
Madrigal Opera, A, 147
Madwoman of Chaillot, The, 101, 187
Maeby, Jack, 66
Maeda, Jun, 60, 79, 161
Maeterlinck, Maurice, 113
Maffin, Neil, 161
Magdalany, Philip, 229
Magee, Rusty, 43, 59, 97
Maggart, Brandon, 188
Maggie Magalita, 79
Maggio, Michael, 166
Maggio, Tony, 163
Magic Child: An Evening With Teresa Burrell, 160
Magid, Larry, 32
Magid, Paul David, 35, 97, 136
Magie, Friedhoffer, 79
Maglich, Marko, 71
Magner, J. Anthony, 11
Magner, Tony, 124
Magnifico, Jack, 76
Magnuson, Merrilee, 130
Magradey, Jack, 48
Magrino, Jeanmarie, 92
Maguire, Kate, 186
Maguire, Michael, 31
Mahaffey, Valerie, 60, 146, 211
Maharis, George, 188
Maher, Joseph, 36, 99, 211
Mahn, Chris, 142
Mahoney, Jack, 92
Mahoney, John, 43, 97, 188, 211
Mahony-Bennett, Kathleen, 152, 179
Maidment, Steve, 98
Maier, Charlotte, 171
Maillard, Carol Lynn, 74, 211
Mailman, Carole, 57
Main, David, 174
Mainer, David, 136
Mais, Michele, 211
Majestic Kid, The, 141, 150, 185
Major, Charles L., 140
Major, Fred, 137
Makarova, Natalia, 188
Maker, Joseph, 36
Makkena, Wendy, 60, 87
Makley, Paul, 163
Mako, 147
Makover, Maxine, 76
Makover, Stanford, 76
Makowski, Rick, 174
Makuta, Billy, 65
Malague, Rose, 160
Malamud, Marc D., 60, 64, 85, 103
Malaxa, Cassandra, 114
Malcolm, Graeme, 177
Malec, Paul, 59
Maley, Peggy, 188
Malik, 103
Malkovich, John, 28, 161, 188, 211
Malleson, Miles, 152, 158
Mallow, Tom, 132
Malloy, Lisa Ann, 32
Malloy, Timothy, 60
Malm, Mia, 49
Malone, Deborah, 91
Malone, Mark, 98
Malone, Mike, 149
Maloney, Skip, 159
Maltby, Jacquey, 24
Maltby, Richard, Jr., 11, 153, 164, 174, 175, 178
Malvin, Arthur, 133
Malvin, David, 30
Mame, 142
Mamet, David, 82, 97, 127, 153, 175
Man Enough, 87
Man Who Turned Into a Stick, The, 109
Man for All Seasons, A, 184, 187
Man of La Mancha, 148, 177, 182, 187
Man's World, A, 100
Manassee, Jackie, 58, 65, 98, 148, 159, 167, 171, 177, 179
Mancuso, Dave, 174
Mandel, Frank, 76
Mandel, Pryce Arwin, 152
Mandel, Sherry, 66
Mandelbaum, Ken, 18, 31, 40, 75, 81
Mandell, Alan, 163
Mandlebaum, Ken, 76
Manfredi, John Michael, 165
Mangan, Kevin, 158,
Manger, Itsik, 86
Manis, David, 82, 94, 174, 211
Manley, Jim, 117
Manley, Sandra, 6, 22, 23, 38, 42, 47, 123
Mann, Alison, 7
Mann, Andy, 139
Mann, Emily, 33, 139, 156
Mann, Fred C., III, 40
Mann, Harry, 79
Mann, Jack, 26, 61, 134, 135
Mann, Paul, 229
Mann, Terrence V., 48
Mann, Thea, 145
Mann, Theodore, 14, 25, 28, 44
Mannell, Larry, 186
Mannen, Monique, 147
Manning, Ferd, 61
Manning, Pam, 179
Manning, Robin, 81
Manning, Ruth, 163
Manning, Susan, 65
Mannino, Susan Jones, 144
Manoff, Dinah, 188
Manos, Peter, 113
Mansdorf, Robert, 66
Mansell, Lilene, 121
Mansfield, Jayne, 188
Manson, Alan, 127
Manson, Allison Renee, 40, 211
Mantegna, Joe, 127
Mantek, Arlene, 57, 78, 96
Mantel, Michael Albert, 91, 211

Mantel, Michael S., 82, 86, 118
Mantell, Paul, 61, 77, 90, 211
Mantell, Suzy, 59
Manthey, Marisa, 142
Mantooth, Randolph, 180
Mantz, Delphine T., 32
Manzi, Warren, 180
Map of the World, A, 107
Mappin, Jefferson, 154, 186
Maquet, Auguste, 161
Mara, Susi, 99
Maraden, Frank, 107, 180
Maradudin, Peter, 147, 151, 173
Mararian, Michael, 184
Marasek, Jan, 6, 23, 38, 42, 47, 123
Marat/Sade, 169
Marathon'86:, 91
March, Barbara, 186
March, Richard, 186
Marchand, Nancy, 99
Marchesseault, Karen, 145
Marciniak, Raymond David, 131
Marciona, Anthony, 79, 212
Marcott, Miguel, 146
Marcum, Kevin, 48
Marcus, Daniel, 92, 212
Marcus, Donald, 78
Marcus, Jeffrey, 60, 212
Marcus, Peter, 142
Marcus, Steven, 139
Marcy, Helen, 72, 87, 212, 213
Marden, Anne, 178
Marder, Steve, 126
Mardirosian, Tom, 106, 108
Marek, Mary Ann, 145
Mareneck, Ellen, 65, 117
Margo, 229
Margolies, Melissa, 98
Margolin, Janet, 188
Margolis, Laura, 110, 212
Margolis, Mark, 157
Margoshes, Steven, 46
Margulies, David, 111, 212
Margulies, Shira Lynn, 119
Mariano, Patti, 111
Marich, Bob, 139
Marich, Marietta, 139
Marie, Evanne, 80
Marie, Julienne, 188
Marie, Lory, 151
Marineau, Barbara, 142
Marini, Ken, 168
Marino, Frank, 33, 123, 161
Marino, Tony, 155
Marivaux, 60
Mark VIII: xxxvi, 61
Mark, Charles C., 143
Markell, Jodie, 72
Markert, Joan, 169
Markham, Cornell, 151
Markham, Marion, 142
Markham, Monte, 148, 188
Markinson, Martin, 29
Markkanen, Douglas, 185
Markle, Lois, 78, 117, 121
Markle, Stephen, 159
Markof-Belaeff, Maria M., 161
Markovich, Terrence, 140
Marks, Christopher, 136
Marks, Jack R., 102, 212
Marks, Jonathan, 141
Marks, Kenneth L., 140, 166
Marks, Noah, 136
Marks, Penny, 59
Markus, Tom, 177
Marlatt, Richard, 165
Marlay, Andrew B., 111, 155
Marley, Donovan, 151
Marlowe, Gloria, 188
Marlowe, Theresa, 59, 69
Marmee, Doug, 152
Marmon, Harold, 61, 98
Marowitz, Charles, 63, 159, 163
Marquardt, Christopher, 138
Marquez, Benita, 176
Marquez, William, 176
Marren, Howard, 155
Marrero, Maria, 152, 175
Marrero, Ralph, 73
Marriage of Bette and Boo, The, 150, 171, 178
Marriage of Figaro, The, 14
Marriage, 180
Marriott, B. Rodney, 88
Marry Me a Little, 148, 149
Marsh, Bernard J., 37, 149
Marsh, Frazier, 137
Marsh, Saundra, 113
Marsh, Thunder, 64
Marshall, Alexander, 62
Marshall, Amelia, 37, 134, 212
Marshall, Chris, 45
Marshall, Donna Lee, 76, 212
Marshall, Dorothy L., 171
Marshall, Dylan, 136
Marshall, Edward, 79
Marshall, Gay, 45
Marshall, Kathleen, 169
Marshall, Ken, 89, 112, 118
Marshall, Larry, 37, 102, 212
Marshall, Patricia, 188
Marshall, Peter, 128
Marshall, Richard, 121
Marshall, Rob, 20, 212
Marshall, Sara, 188
Martell, Paul, 89
Martell, Ron, 165
Martello, Mary, 164
Martells, Cynthia, 164
Martens, Lora, 177
Martens, Rica, 105, 212
Martha Swope Photos, 7
Martin, Betsy M., 96
Martin, Brian, 59, 98, 136, 149, 181
Martin, Campbell, 78
Martin, Charlaine, 149
Martin, Dan J., 179
Martin, Deborah, 184
Martin, Debra Alix, 61, 74, 121
Martin, Dianna, 75
Martin, Dorothy, 52
Martin, Eduardo, 144
Martin, Elliot, 127
Martin, Ernie, 72, 75
Martin, George N., 20, 115, 212
Martin, George, 21, 178
Martin, Greg, 126
Martin, Hugh, 133
Martin, James, 139
Martin, Jane, 113
Martin, Jeff, 119
Martin, Jim, 169
Martin, John, 114
Martin, Joseph F., 151
Martin, Leila, 135
Martin, Lucy, 57
Martin, Marion, 229
Martin, Mary, 129, 146, 212
Martin, Michael X., 151
Martin, Millicent, 49, 212
Martin, Monique, 98, 103
Martin, Nan, 163, 173
Martin, Patricia, 78
Martin, Paul-James, 185
Martin, Reed C., 184
Martin, Robert, 78
Martin, Scott, 140
Martin, T. R., 171
Martin, W. T., 174
Martin, William C., 72
Martin-Beck, Steven, 185
Martinelli, Susan, 170
Martinetti, Tony, 113
Martinez, Alma, 146, 147
Martinez, Benita, 176
Martinez, Julio E., 112
Martini, Carol, 144
Martino, Ginny, 88
Martino, Mark, 53, 142, 212
Martino, Rick, 91
Martins, Peter, 11
Martinuzzi, John, 158
Martley, Lisa K., 143
Marton, Laszlo, 137
Martyn, Gregory, 140
Maruyama, Karen, 147
Marvin, Mel, 171
Marx, Margaret, 178
Maryan, Charles, 142
Marzello, Vincent, 161
Mascaro, Gary, 146, 147
Masella, Arthur, 61
Masella, Joni, 24
Mashita, Nelson, 163
Masiell, Joe, 229, 231
Masilorens, Fernando, 112
Maslon, Laurence, 90
Maso, Michael, 159
Mason, Dan, 163
Mason, Judi Ann, 104
Mason, Marshall W., 88, 89, 146, 188
Mason, Timothy, 171, 173
Mason, Tom, 145
Massee, Happy, 81
Massey, Melanie, 54
Massoth, Pat, 173
Master Class, 115
Master Harold and the Boys, 137, 170, 171, 179
Master, Arthur, 59
Masteroff, Joe, 92, 153, 155
Masterson, John, 106, 107, 108
Masterson, Kathleen, 148
Masterson, Mary Stuart, 91
Masterson, Phil, 164
Mastrantonio, Mary Elizabeth, 14, 106, 212
Mastrocola, Frank, 37
Mastrogiovanni, Vito, 84, 152
Mastrosimone, William, 141, 149, 163, 172
Matalon, Danny, 149
Matalon, Vivian, 99
Match Made in Heaven, A, 64
Mates, Olivia Laurel, 80, 212
Matesky, Jared, 142, 180
Mathers, James, 64, 177, 212
Mathews, Carmen, 170
Mathews, Deborah D., 17
Mathis, Lee, 135
Mathis, Lynn, 177, 183
Mathistad, Tim, 164
Mathwick, Nick, 161
Matlack, Deborah, 69, 83, 113
Matland, Michelle, 60, 86
Matlock, Norman, 83
Matschullat, Kay, 80
Matt, Donald, 172
Matthew, Lynne, 100
Matthews, Anderson, 71, 82, 212
Matthews, Andrew, 182
Matthews, Ann-Sara, 156
Matthews, Anne, 182
Matthews, Dakin, 141, 146, 147, 182
Matthews, Edward R. F., 59, 63, 110
Matthews, Elizabeth, 169
Matthews, Jon, 146, 186
Matthews, Julia, 182
Matthews, Nathan, 92
Matthews, Richard, 101
Matthews, Wendy, 80
Matthey, Peter, 162
Matthias, Darren, 149
Mattison, Amy, 92
Matwiow, Paul, 57
Matz, Jerry, 78, 212
Matz, Peter, 172
Mauceri, John, 11
Mauceri, Patricia, 91
Maugham, W. Somerset, 93, 101
Maulden, Dennis C., 140
Mauldin, Michael, 186
Mauldin, Randolph, 161
Maupin, Samuel, 65
Mauro, Melissa, 157
Max's Millions, 59
Maxmen, Mimi, 84, 86, 98, 118
Maxwell, James, 158
Maxwell, Jan, 110, 161
Maxwell, Roberta, 159
May, David, 64, 212, 213
May, Deborah, 147, 172, 184
May, Gary, 175
May, James, 128
May, Kyndal, 144
Maydays, 136
Mayenzet, Maria, 163
Mayer, Helen Waren, 61
Mayer, James, 58
Mayer, Jerry, 57, 111, 160, 212
Mayer, Julia, 110
Mayer, Max D., 61
Mayer, Timothy S., 130
Mayerson, Fred, 46
Mayes, Daniel, 136, 172
Mayes, Judith, 78, 212
Mayfield, Walt, 92
Mayhew, David, 15, 54, 65, 79, 162
Mayhew, Ina, 85, 103
Maynard, John, Jr., 182
Maynard, Richard, 144, 148, 166
Maynard, Ruth, 178
Mayo, J. A., 124
Mayor, 15
Mayweather, Roxanne, 147
Mazarek, Paul, 128
Mazen, Glenn, 172
Mazer, Maria, 64
Mazey, Duane, 70
Mazurek, Amy, 142
Mazurek, Colleen, 128
Mazzarese, Suzy, 127
Mazzie, Marin, 46, 212
McAllister, Sandra, 90
McAnarney, Kevin P., 8, 75
McAnuff, Des, 46
McArdle, Andrea, 188
McArthur, Sarah, 147
McAteer, Kathryn, 15, 212
McAuliffe, Jody, 147
McAvin, Andy, 123
McBride, Howard, 92
McCain, Frances Lee, 147
McCall, Kathleen, 149
McCallum, David, 167
McCallum, John, 102
McCambridge, Mercedes, 143
McCammond, James, 164
McCann, Christopher, 60, 143, 212
McCarrell, Michael, 185
McCarry, Charles E., 180
McCarthy, Andrew, 17, 212
McCarthy, Frank, 163
McCarthy, Gerry, 59, 158
McCarthy, Jeff, 121
McCarthy, Julianna, 146
McCarthy, Nobu, 163
McCarthy, Patrick, 143
McCarty, Bruce, 89
McCarty, Mary, 188
McCarty, Michael, 142, 152
McCaskill, Robert, 79
McCauley, Judith, 167
McCauley, Larry, 164
McCauley, Lawrence, 154
McCauley, Michael, 149
McCauley, Robbie, 60, 161
McClain, Marcia, 188
McClain, Saundra, 83
McClanahan, Rue, 146
McClary, William, 46
McCleary, Daniel, 66
McClelland, Jean, 73
McClelland, Kay, 133
McClenahan, Patti, 61, 100
McClendon, David, 184
McClennahan, Charles H., 60, 91, 102, 104, 116, 120, 171
McClennahan, Charles Henry, 102, 171
McClennahan, Charles, 60
McClintock, Jodie Lynne, 42, 212, 213
McCloskey, Steven, 121, 153
McCluggage, John, 156
McClure, Robert, 186
McClure, Teri, 28
McCollum, Kevin, 164
McComb, Bill, 57, 59
McCombs, Kathryn, 169
McConlough, Stephanie, 124
McConnell, Gordon, 101
McConnell, Joseph, 167
McConnell, Mark, 149
McCoo, Marilyn, 148
McCord, Lisa Merrill, 125
McCord, Patrick, 91, 155, 212
McCorkle, Pat, 18
McCorkle, Stephen, 60, 170
McCorkle, Steve, 60
McCormack, Eric, 154, 186
McCormack, John, 91
McCowan, Allen, 151
McCoy, Basia, 69, 212
McCoy, Winsome, 79
McCrane, Paul, 12, 212
McCrary, Melinda, 144
McCready, Kevin Neil, 45, 134
McCreery, Bud, 78
McCrillis, Paul, 171
McCrum, James, 169
McCue, Brian, 161
McCulloch, George, 93
McCulloh, Barbara, 121, 212
McCullough, Jack, 159
McCurdy, Steve, 87
McCurry, John R., 83
McCusker, Daniel, 171
McCutcheon, Andy, 138
McDade, Innes-Fergus, 57, 171, 179
McDaniel, Freddie, 58
McDaniel, James, 89
McDaniel, William Foster, 174, 175, 153
McDermott, James T., 146
McDermott, Keith, 78, 212
McDermott, Laura, 42
McDermott, Mark, 47
McDonagh, Philomena, 162
McDonald, Annette R., 16
McDonald, Beth, 179
McDonald, Bill, 166
McDonald, Christopher, 163
McDonald, Daniel, 146
McDonald, Elizabeth, 154, 186
McDonald, Heather, 57
McDonald, James, 166
McDonald, Liz, 68
McDonald, Peggy, 182
McDonald, Quentin H., 16
McDonald, Tanny, 100, 174, 212
McDonald-Tiknis, Sharon, 139
McDonnell, Bruce, 77
McDonnell, James, 111, 147, 186
McDonnell, Mary, 33, 61, 180, 212
McDonnell, Susan, 83
McDonnell, Terrence, 100
McDonough, Ann, 115, 162, 212
McDonough, Edwin J., 180
McDonough, Neal, 175
McDonough, Tim, 141
McDougal, Mark, 163
McDowell, Bob, 93
McDowell, Rex, 136
McDowell, W. Stuart, 59
McDuffee, Karen, 54
McEleny, Brian, 178
McElwaine, James, 119
McElwee, Theresa, 180
McEwan, Charles, 163
McFarland, Martha, 173
McFarland, Robert, 87, 212
McFerran, Patti, 183
McGarity, Patricia Greer, 177
McGarrahan, Will, 148
McGarty, Michael, 178
McGavran, Megan, 59
McGaw, Parlan, 100, 212, 213
McGhee, Susan, 164
McGillin, Howard, 20, 21, 106, 191, 192, 212
McGillis, Kelly, 161
McGinely, John C., 98, 212
McGinn, Kevin, 72
McGlinn, John, 76
McGough, Roger, 26
McGourty, Patricia, 46
McGovern, Elizabeth, 107, 188, 212
McGovern, Michael, 169
McGowan, Charles, 45
McGowan, Edward, 65
McGowan, Jack, 93
McGowan, John, 172
McGowan, Nora, 165
McGowan, Norman, 171
McGowan, Tom, 180
McGrath, Katherine, 157, 184
McGrath, Kay, 155
McGrath, Leueen, 73
McGrath, Mark, 138
McGrath, Michelle, 146
McGreevey, Annie, 62, 212
McGregor-Stewart, Kate, 111, 212
McGuin, Lori Cope, 143
McGuinness, Michael, 90
McGuire, Linda, 162
McGuire, Maeve, 96, 153, 212
McGuire, Michael, 147
McGuire, Mitchell, 98, 212
McGuire, Peter, 154
McGuire, William Biff, 172
McHale, Christopher, 12, 33
McHattie, Stephen, 180
McHugh, Christine, 161
McHugh, Elizabeth, 116
McHugh, Jimmy, 31, 133
McHugh, Kathleen M., 80
Mclernon, Dennis, 182
Mclntire, Mark, 161
Mclntyre, Dianne, 91, 116
Mclntyre, Gerry, 32
Mclntyre, Marilyn, 139
Mclntyre, Teri, 169
McKanic, Tim, 73, 80
McKaughan, Joe, 63
McKay, Gardner, 145
McKayle, Donald, 151
McKechnie, Donna, 45
McKee, Carroll, 152
McKee, Lonette, 119
McKeever, Jacqueline, 188
McKenna, Christiane, 174
McKenna, Mark, 62
McKenna, Seana, 154, 186
McKenna, Sheila, 169
McKennan, Don, 107
McKenzie, Branice Williams, 212
McKenzie, Michael, 82
McKeon, Marie, 6
McKeon, Tom, 140
McKereghan, William, 141, 185
McKernon, John, 93
McKiernan, Kathleen, 43, 97
McKinley, Philip, 167
McKinley, Sean, 168
McKinley, Tom, 57
McKinney, John, 110, 111, 143, 172
McKinnon-Miller, Camara, 82
McKnight, Ted Robin, 142
McLain, John, 66, 74, 157
McLamb-Wilcox, Sheila, 146
McLane, Derek, 63, 65, 78, 82, 157
McLarty, Heather, 173
McLarty, Ron, 161
McLaughlin, Judy, 159
McLaughlin, Lesa, 143
McLaughlin, Thom, 169
McLaughlin-Gray, Jack, 156
McLaurin, James, 83
McLellan, Amy, 131
McLeod, Neil, 186
McLerie, Allyn Ann, 188
McLernon, Dennis, 182
McLiam, John, 163
McMahon, Terri, 185
McManigal, Jay, 83
McManus, Don R., 184
McManus, Thomas, 124
McMartin, John, 188, 192
McMichael, Leon, 71
McMillan, Lisa, 128, 181
McMillan, Richard, 154, 186
McMullen, Billy, 60
McMullen, Kenneth, 83
McMullen, Randy, 183
McMurray, Sam, 158, 180, 212
McMurrer, Marie, 63
McMurrey, Sam, 81
McMurtrey, Joan, 173
McMurtry, Jonathan, 173, 184
McNair, Paul, 77, 90
McNally, Jean, 148
McNally, Kelli Ann, 124
McNally, Terrence, 57, 99
McNamara, Dermot, 148
McNamara, Pat, 12, 159, 212
McNamara, Rosemary, 105, 155, 212
McNaughton, Anne, 182
McNeeley, Gale, 172, 175
McNeely, Anna, 48
McNeil, Dan, 151
McNeil, Kate, 168
McNeill, Michael, 123
McNicholl, Brian, 81
McNickle, Jim, 214
McNitt, David, 63
McNulty, Bill, 137
McNulty, Kevin, 186
McNutt, Kim, 76
McOmber, Kori, 145
McPherson, Karen Michael, 81
McPhillips, Edward, 149
McPhillips, Tom, 32
McQueen, Armelia, 188, 214
McQueen, Jim, 139, 177
McQuiggan, John A., 54
McRee, Ruth, 136
McRobbie, Peter, 20, 214
Meacham, Paul, 90, 184, 214
Meachum, Roy, 167
Mead, Lewis, 15, 74
Mead, Winter, 110
Meade, David, 100
Meade, Julia, 160
Meader, Derek, 178
Meadow, Lynne, 99, 192
Meadows, Doris, 162
Meadows, Nancy, 123
Meadows, Robert, 229
Meaney, Colm, 163
Means, Lawr, 59
Meara, Anne, 76
Measure For Measure, 106, 183, 186
Measures, Mark, 176
Medak, Susan, 166
Medea, 109
Medford, Kay, 188
Medina, Hazel J., 149, 214, 219
Medina, Val, 7, 29, 33
Medlicott, Barbara, 183
Medoff, Mark, 141, 150, 174, 185
Mee, Charles, Jr., 78
Meeham, Donna, 169
Meehan, Joan, 95
Meehan, John, 11
Meehan, Thomas, 122
Meek, Barbara, 178
Meeker, Ralph, 188
Meeker, Roger, 159
Meeks, Donna, 176
Megginson, Courtney Michelle, 154
Meglio, Ellie, 84
Meier, Ernie, 161
Meiksins, Robert, 148
Meisle, Kathryn, 174, 177
Meisle, William, 174
Meissner, Don, 102
Meister, Brian, 71
Meister, Frederica, 97, 105
Meister, Frederikke, 214
Melanos, Jack, 87
Melchiori, Elizabetta, 139
Melde, Shari, 177
Meledandri, Wayne, 45
Melfi, Leonard, 51
Melhuse, Peder, 144
Melici, Sarah, 145
Mell, Randle, 61, 82, 108
Mellencamp, Laura, 145
Mellon, Maureen, 49
Mellor, Stephen, 66, 90, 214
Melnik, Ron, 165
Meloa, Tony, 75
Melocci, Wanda, 170
Meloche, Katherine, 55, 214
Melrose, Ronald, 64
Melville, Herman, 121
Member of the Wedding, The, 187
Memories of Riding with Joe Cool, 114
Men in White, 187
Menard, Mark, 121
Menasche, Steven, 71
Mendez, Mark, 152
Mendillo, Stephen, 171
Mendola's Rose, 151
Menhart, Laura, 127
Menhart, Sandra, 130
Menick, Jon, 163
Menke, Rick, 174
Menken, Alan, 55, 65, 169, 171, 177
Mennen, James G., 48
Mennone, Kate, 93, 98
Menson, Uriel, 100
Menteer, Craig Kenyon, 136
Menyuk, Eric D., 141

Meola, Tony, 31, 57, 121
Mercant, Marsha, 124
Mercer, Bryan, 140
Mercer, Johnny, 31
Mercer, Marian, 188
Merchant of Venice, The, 60, 131, 181, 185
Mercier, G. W., 116, 157, 160
Meredith, Jan, 214
Meredith, Michael, 140
Merediz, Olga, 70, 71, 96
Merino, Christine, 136
Merk, Ron, 51
Merkel, Una, 229, 231
Merkens, Meg, 156
Merkerson, S. Epatha, 168, 179
Merkey, Ryland, 177
Merkin, Bobby, 169
Merkin, Robby, 55, 57
Merrell, Richard, 90, 114, 214
Merriam, Eve, 167
Merrick, David, 49, 127
Merrifield, Gail, 106
Merrill, Beth, 230
Merrill, Bob, 93, 149
Merrill, Deborah, 14, 214
Merrill, Dina, 65, 101, 193, 214
Merrill, Richard, 78
Merrill, Scott, 188
Merritt, George, 46, 80, 214
Merritt, Michael, 97, 127, 154
Merritt, Theresa, 180
Merritt, Wendy, 92
Merry Wives of Windsor, The, 152, 172, 181, 183, 184
Merryman, Monica, 159
Meryll, Lisa, 92
Meseroll, Kenneth, 175
Mesney, Kathryn, 136
Mesnik, Bill, 118, 121
Mess, Suzanne, 186
Messaline, Peter, 149
Messiah, 159
Messina, Carla Lauren, 63
Mestrovic, Ivana, 121
Metcalf, Kam, 121
Metcalf, Laurie, 161, 188, 214
Metcalf, Mark, 118, 120, 214
Metcalfe, Stephen, 119
Metelits, Stan, 99
Metheny, Russell, 143, 152, 160
Metropulos, Penny, 185
Mette, Nancy, 99, 140, 162, 214
Metzger, Melanie, 152
Metzl-Pazer, Mitzi, 63
Metzler, Kerry, 65
Metzler, Lawrence, 163
Meyer, Leo, 75
Meyer, Michael, 90
Meyer, Phil, 82, 214
Meyer, Rick, 54
Meyer, Sarah E., 136
Meyer, Steve, 129
Meyer, Ursula, 136
Meyers, D. Lynn, 149
Meyers, Larry John, 93, 160
Meyers, Patrick, 150
Meyrich, Victor, 58, 144
Miami, 111
Micacchion, Al, 127, 172
Michael Lepoer Trench Photos, 11
Michael, Christine, 174
Michael, Patricia, 132
Michaelis, Lisa, 16
Michaels, Bert, 68, 214, 219
Michaels, Gregory, 146, 147
Michaels, Lisa C., 145
Michaels, Tanis, 40
Michaelson, Ron, 173
Michalski, John, 186
Micheels, Lisa, 176
Michel, Carolyn, 144
Michel, Millene, 133
Michele, Laura, 99
Michelson, Lisa, 146
Michener, Brent, 92
Michener, John, 59, 139
Michie, William, 183
Michlin, Barry, 163
Mickelsen, David, 144
Mickens, Jan, 130
Mickey, Susan, 140
Middents, Jonathan, 183
Middleton, Clark, 87, 101
Middleton, Roger, 93, 214
Middleton, Thomas, 141
Midsummer Night's Dream, A, 100, 118, 156, 179, 181, 182, 184
Mieske, Dale, 186
Mighty Gents, The, 171
Miho, 147
Mihok, Andrew, 106
Mikell, Pinkney, 110
Milani, Linda, 76
Milcos, Stacey, 179
Milder, Daniel, 136
Miles, David, 142
Miles, Julia, 84
Miles, Lou Ann, 139
Miles, Sarah, 24
Miles, Vera, 148
Milian, Donna Marie, 162
Milian, Tomas, 77
Milikin, Paul, 167
Militello, Anne E., 67, 77, 108
Millan, Bruce E., 151
Milland, Ray, 230
Millar, John, 143
Millard, Lindsay, 184
Millay Ellis, Norma, 230
Mille, Antoinette, 113
Miller, Alfred, 78
Miller, Alicia, 78
Miller, Ann, 133
Miller, Annette, 6, 214
Miller, Arthur, 153, 163, 167, 172, 175, 178, 181
Miller, Barry, 47, 188, 214
Miller, Betty, 172
Miller, Bill, 133
Miller, Bobby, 141
Miller, Branda, 60
Miller, Carlton, 183
Miller, Court, 230, 231
Miller, Craig, 26, 64, 153, 155, 156
Miller, Darleigh, 123
Miller, David, 165
Miller, Deian, 184
Miller, Eileen, 54
Miller, Gary, 62, 110
Miller, Geoffrey, 95
Miller, Gwendolyn, 49
Miller, Hariet S., 65
Miller, Jesse, 66
Miller, Joel, 82
Miller, Jonathan, 42, 141
Miller, Julie, 133
Miller, Kristine, 150
Miller, Lauren, 138
Miller, Lawrence, 57
Miller, Leslie, 186
Miller, Linda, 188
Miller, Lowry, 160
Miller, Marie, 164
Miller, Michael, 44, 158, 175, 179
Miller, Michelle, 145
Miller, Penelope Ann, 47, 214
Miller, Robert Strong, 23
Miller, Robert, 144, 147
Miller, Robin, 58, 167
Miller, Roger, 46
Miller, Sandra, 94
Miller, Scott G., 96, 164, 168, 214
Miller, Thomas J., 140
Miller, Tom, 88, 89
Miller, Wade, 167
Miller, Weiler, 65
Miller, William, 166
Miller, Wynne, 188
Miller-Shields, Megan, 164
Millholland, Bruce, 121
Milligan, John, 181
Milligan, Sarajane, 139
Milligan, Tuck, 146, 173
Millington, Marnie, 112
Millman, Devora, 153, 180
Millman, Howard J., 153
Millner, E. Frazier, 177
Mills, Amy, 177
Mills, Bill, 52
Mills, Dana, 137
Mills, Elaine, 142
Mills, Eric, 175
Mills, Georganna, 139
Mills, Juliet, 101
Millstein, Jack, 58
Milne, Kathleen, 65
Milner, Ron, 80, 149
Milton, Frank, 230
Mimbs, Michael, 121
Minahan, Greg, 124
Mineo, John, 135
Miner, Diane, 114
Miner, Jan, 70, 138, 214
Miner, Mary Michele, 146
Miner, Michael Andrew, 138
Mines, Barry, 143
Minetor, Nicholas, 153
Minkoff, Bradford, 172
Minkow, Gene, 178
Minnelli, Liza, 188
Minnigah, John, 113
Minning, Steven, 127
Minor, Michael, 160
Minor, Philip, 170, 178
Minot, Anna, 110
Minskoff, Jerome, 37, 40, 122, 132
Minsky, Greta, 93
Minteer, Maura, 170
Mintz, Terri, 63
Mirabal, Jeannette, 112, 214
Mirabal, Rafael, 112
Miracle Worker, The, 187
Miramontez, Rick, 146
Mirandolina, 118
Miratti, Tony, 214
Mirer, Jacob, 63
Mirro, Dan, 17, 33
Misani, 104
Misanthrope, The, 137, 159
Misenheimer, Linda, 158,
Miser, The, 152, 165
Miskell, Brad, 20, 106
Miskell, Kim, 176
Miss Firecracker Contest, The, 139
Miss Julie Bodiford, 171
Miss Lulu Bett, 187
Missimi, Dominic, 164
Missimi, Nancy, 164
Mister Roberts, 187
Mistero Buffo, 81, 141
Mistretta, Sal, 76, 124, 167, 214
Mitchel, Jodi, 64
Mitchell, Alan, 142
Mitchell, Alexandra, 181
Mitchell, Bill, 72
Mitchell, Bob J., 121
Mitchell, Cameron, 188
Mitchell, Chrissy, 142
Mitchell, David, 6, 17, 47, 50, 123, 146
Mitchell, Delores, 92
Mitchell, Gregory, 11, 214
Mitchell, James, 188
Mitchell, Ken, 49
Mitchell, Lizan, 76, 140
Mitchell, Mark, 53
Mitchell, Ruth, 134, 161
Mitchell, Thom, 133
Mitchell, Tricia, 142
Mitri, Paul T., 136
Mixon, Alan, 138, 175
Mixon, Christopher, 149
Mixson, Sarah S., 136
Miyares, Mia, 169
Miyazaki, Gerielani, 163
Miyori, Kim, 147
Mize, Nicolas, 178
Mizelle, Vance, 60, 214
Mizzy, Danianne, 154, 172, 180
Mlotek, Zalmen, 66
Moberly, Phyllis, 146
Moberly, Robert, 170
Moby Dick, 121
Moccia, Kevin M., 18
Mockus, Tony, 136, 161
Mode, Becky, 182
Modern Statuary, 62
Moe, Margit, 138
Moeller, Gary Dean, 122
Moersch, William, 71
Moffat, Donald, 12, 214
Moffat, John, 186
Moffett, D. W., 17
Mogi, Chikashi, 8
Mognoni, Maryanne, 62
Mohrlein, John, 154
Mohylsky, Katherine, 149
Moignard, Deborah L., 142
Moiseiwitsch, Tanya, 186
Mokae, Zakes, 22, 161, 180, 214
Moliere, Jean-Baptiste, 152, 158, 166
Molina-Tobin, Olga, 112, 214
Moline, Patricia, 80
Moll, James, 151, 185
Mollien, Roger, 188
Molloy, Bill, 6, 123
Molloy, Honour, 72
Molnar, Ferenc, 145, 162
Monaca, John, 128, 135
Monahan, Debi A., 130
Monahan, Jeff, 170
Monat, Phil, 80, 94, 96, 105, 119, 153
Moncada, Raul, 184
Monchek, Sam, 73
Mondin, Julie, 182
Monferdini, Carole, 98, 214, 219
Mong, David, 136, 172, 175
Moniak, Ted, 165
Monich, Timothy, 99, 107, 143, 162, 179
Monk, Debra, 137, 167
Monk, Isabell, 33, 161, 214
Monnot, Marguerite, 155
Monroe, Jarion King, 182
Monson, Lex, 117
Montague, Judy, 62
Montalvo, Frank, 133
Montalvo, Lina, 176
Montana, Melanie, 133
Montano, Robert, 48
Montefiore, David, 64
Montgomery, Andre H., 158
Montgomery, Elizabeth, 188
Montgomery, Gary, 179
Montgomery, John, 115
Montgomery, Kim, 160
Montgomery, Lynn, 92
Montgomery, Madge, 175
Montgomery, Rik, 77, 90
Month in the Country, A, 144
Montresor, Beni, 14, 156
Moody, Joyce, 145
Moody, Michael, 60, 99, 105
Moody, Ron, 188
Moon for the Misbegotten, A, 144
Moon, Gerald, 29
Moon, Marjorie, 61
Moon, Philip, 180
Mooney, Debra, 6, 111, 214
Mooney, Kris, 133
Mooney, Robert, 70, 80
Mooney, Sheila, 63
Moons, D. C., 165
Moor, Bill, 12, 214
Moore, A. Doyle, 161
Moore, Benjamin, 172
Moore, Bruce, 152
Moore, Catherine, 149
Moore, Charlotte, 111, 214
Moore, Christina, 149
Moore, Christopher, 32, 141
Moore, Dana, 40, 41
Moore, Daniel, 172
Moore, Donald C., 153
Moore, Elizabeth, 175
Moore, Jane, 184
Moore, Judith, 167
Moore, Kim, 52, 214
Moore, Larry, 74, 76
Moore, Leslie, 105
Moore, Maureen, 11, 80, 214
Moore, Melba, 188
Moore, Peter, 156, 165
Moore, Priscilla, 157
Moore, Richard, 105, 119, 177, 179
Moore, Steven, 76
Moore, Tom, 47, 146, 184
Mooring, Jeff, 149
Mora, Michael, 173
Morabito, Rocco, 59
Morales, Carole, 36
Morales, Mark, 124
Moran, Dan, 61
Moran, Daniel, 214
Moran, Lizzie, 49
Moran, Martin, 46
Moran, Monica, 81
Moran, Peter, 153
Moran, Robert, 141
Moran, Viki, 161
Moranz, Brad, 7, 80, 214
Morath, Kathy, 81, 214
Moray, Jill, 69
Mordecai, Benjamin, 57, 180
More Fun Than Bowling, 138
More, Julian, 155
Morean, John B., 94
Moreau, Jeanne, 135
Moreland, David, 101, 214
Moreland, Gary, 132
Moreland, Judith, 107
Moreno, Rene, 95
Moreno, Rita, 6, 214
Morfogen, George, 99, 115, 214
Morgan, Andre, 102
Morgan, Calvin, 93
Morgan, Cass, 73, 167
Morgan, Constance, 93, 214
Morgan, Dale, 164
Morgan, Edward, 179
Morgan, James, 121
Morgan, Kelly C., 182
Morgan, Lorraine, 145
Morgan, Margaret Jane, 162
Morgan, Robert, 18, 57, 159, 174, 184
Morgan, Roger, 179
Morgan, Scott, 143
Morgan, Susan, 154, 186
Morgenstern, Seymour, 60
Moriarty, Michael, 101, 135, 188, 214
Morick, Jeanine, 177
Morick, Jeanne, 166
Morin, Nicole, 163
Morin, Ricardo, 73, 77, 179
Morissey, Bob, 155
Moritz, Susan Trapnell, 136
Moriyasu, Atsushi, 109
Morka, Madeleine, 230
Morkal, Dave, 116
Morley, Carol, 146
Mornell, Ted, 113
Morning's at Seven, 187
Morocco, Mark, 175
Moroz, Barbara, 7
Morreale, Marilu, 134
Morrell, Erika, 97
Morrill, E. F., 57
Morrill, Warren, 31
Morris, Cleveland, 150
Morris, Daniel Miller, 127
Morris, Haviland, 120
Morris, Janet S., 151
Morris, Kenny, 92, 214
Morris, Kimi, 91
Morris, Marti, 164
Morris, Ruqaivah, 154
Morris, Vernon, 100
Morris, William S., 158
Morrison, Ann Leslie, 214
Morrison, Ann, 119, 188
Morrison, Malcolm, 139
Morrison, Toni, 148
Morrison, Vaughn Dwight, 168
Morriss, Bruce K., 150
Morrissette, Billy, 62
Morrissey, Tom, 63
Morrow, John, 181
Morrow, Karen, 188
Morrow, Kevyn, 126
Morrow, Rob, 17, 96
Morrow, Stephan, 60
Morse, Ben, 16, 18, 40, 69, 70, 76, 81, 94, 127
Morse, Daniel C., 142
Morse, Regan, 142
Morse, Richardson, 146
Morse, Robert, 152, 188
Morse, Robin, 86, 103, 214
Morse, Tom, 20, 33, 34, 123
Mortally Fine, 66
Mortensen, Viggo, 160
Mortimer, John, 181
Mortimer, Scott A., 93
Morton, Amy, 161
Morton, Craig, 32
Morton, Gregory, 230
Morton, Joe, 115, 149, 188, 214
Morton, Mark, 76, 140, 181
Moschen, Michael, 75
Moscou, Jacqueline, 175
Mosel, Tad, 113
Moseley, Eleanor, 81
Moseley, Robin, 59, 168
Moser, John, 81, 118, 157
Moser, Paul, 160
Moser, Stephen, 184
Moses, Burke, 120
Moses, Gilbert, 148
Mosher, Gregory, 35, 97, 127
Mosher, Mike, 142
Mosiej, James E., 51, 214
Mosiman, Marnie, 147
Moss, Gary, 155
Moss, Hughes, 14, 28
Moss, Jeffrey B., 15
Moss, Jodi, 32
Moss, Joy, 61
Moss, Spencer, 141, 179
Moss, Stephanie, 144
Moss, Sylvia, 147, 173
Moss, Thurman, 177
Mosse, Spencer, 138, 149
Mossiah, Ernest, 96
Most Happy Fella, The, 187
Mostel, Josh, 98
Mostel, Kate, 230
Motall, Lawrence, 172
Mott, Bradley, 154
Mottner, Murray, 113
Mouledoux, John, 173
Mound Builders, The, 89
Moundroukas, Tony, 149
Mourning Becomes Electra, 160
Mowry, Greg, 118
Moy, Ray, 80
Moya, Angela, 176
Moyer, Alan, 57
Moyer, Sherrill Ann, 93, 105
Moynihan, D. S., 91
Moynihan, Michael G., 177
Mozer, Elizabeth, 93
Mozzi, Leonard, 149
Mroczka, Paul, 176
Mrs. California, 147
Mrs. Warren's Profession, 115, 153
Msimang-Lew, Aurelia, 59
Much Ado About Nothing, 138, 170, 186
Mud in Your Eye, 177
Mudd, John, 113
Mueller, John, 62, 166
Mueller, Lavonne, 84, 85
Mueller, Roger, 154
Muirhead, Janice, 162
Mulberger, Chip, 7, 38
Mulcahy, John, 166
Mulcahy, Lance, 69
Mulcahy, Patrick, 175
Muldoon, Andrea Gibbs, 124
Muldoon, Mick, 62
Mulert, Carl, 110
Mulgrew, Kate, 146, 147
Mulheren, Michael, 122
Mulhern, Leonard A., 57, 70
Mulhern, Matt, 47, 120
Mulkey, Chris, 173
Mullen, Jimmy, 177
Muller, Ernst, 81
Muller, Frank, 70
Muller, Heiner, 141
Muller, Leo, 142
Mulligan, Jack, 152, 170
Mulligan, Richard, 188
Mullins, Carol, 81
Mumford, Peter B., 126
Mummenschanz, 78
Munday, Penelope, 188
Munderloh, Otts, 9, 32, 38, 40, 46, 55, 65, 106, 126, 130
Mundinger, Matthew, 115
Mundy, Meg, 188
Munger, Mary, 153
Munkelt, Suzanne, 101
Munsel, Patrice, 215
Munsell, Belinda, 113
Munte, Alex, 161
Murcell, Raymond, 96
Murcott, Derek, 179
Murder at the Vicarage, 87
Murder on the Nile, 100
Mure, Glenn, 68, 121, 215,
Murin, David, 60, 159, 170, 171
Murkoff, Erik, 91
Murmester, Leo, 46
Murphey, Mark, 141
Murphy, Alec, 142
Murphy, Brennan, 180
Murphy, Donald, 188
Murphy, Donna, 20, 106
Murphy, Gary, 59
Murphy, Greg, 166
Murphy, Harry S., 141
Murphy, James P., 176
Murphy, Janet, 77
Murphy, Joe Terrill, 177
Murphy, Kitty, 151
Murphy, M. George, 171
Murphy, M. Gregory, 171
Murphy, Maggie, 143
Murphy, Marion Z., 80
Murphy, Maura J., 149
Murphy, Michael, 98, 171
Murphy, Michaela, 186
Murphy, Rena, 230
Murphy, Rob, 147
Murphy, Robert, 170
Murphy, Rosemary, 140
Murphy-Barrosse, Maura Ann, 154
Murray, Abigail, 61, 69
Murray, Annie, 163
Murray, Brian, 23
Murray, Darlene, 110
Murray, Hannah, 106
Murray, Jane, 60, 76, 158, 215
Murray, John, 115
Murray, Johnna, 63
Murray, Margery, 144, 168
Murray, Michael, 149, 168, 177
Murray, Paul, 100
Murrell, John, 105
Murtagh, Kate, 133
Muscha, Colleen, 166
Music Man, The, 142, 187
Muskovin, Jeff, 141
Musky, Jane, 16
Musselman, David, 57, 58
Mussenden, Isis, 80, 91
Musser, Tharon, 6, 24, 45, 47, 49, 123, 126, 127, 146
Mutnick, Andrew, 178
Mutnick, Nancy, 119
Mutulation, 113
Muza, Tom, 177
Muzio, Gloria, 62, 148
Muzzy, Adam, 140
My Fair Lady, 142, 144, 187
My Fat Friend, 145
My One and Only, 130
Mycka-Stettler, Joyce, 136
Myers, Elissa, 86
Myers, Lou, 153
Myers, Maritza, 103
Myers, Michael, 159
Myers, Paulene, 215
Myler, Randal, 151
Myles, Ken, 113
Myren, Tania, 163
Myron, Diana, 58
Myrow, Fredric, 163
Mystery of Edwin Drood, The, 20, 106, 187, 191
Nabel, William, 49, 76
Naccari, Michael C., 118
Nackman, David, 123
Nadotti, Maria, 81
Naegele, Matthias, 78
Nagle, Gwendolyn, 183
Nagle, Karen, 51
Nagle, Margaret, 92, 215, 219
Nagy, Ken, 142
Nahaku, Don, 136
Nahal, Pam, 134
Nahrwold, Tom, 170
Naimo, Jennifer, 66, 215
Najeellah, Mansoor, 79
Najera, Rick, 173
Najimy, Kathy, 116, 215
Nakagawa, Jon, 36, 99, 109
Nakahara, Ron, 109, 215
Nall, Frank, 183
Nanawatai, 163
Nantz, James, 114
Nanus, Susan, 86
Napier, John, 48
Napierala, John, 173

Napolin, Elissa, 100
Narizzano, Dino, 63
Naselli, Michael, 74
Nash, Floyd T., 139
Nash, Mark, 181
Nash, Michael, 168
Nash, Richard, 156
Nash, Ron, 51, 64
Nastasi, Frank, 184
Nastasi, Marc, 72
Natale, Catherine, 96
Nathan, Fred, 11, 26, 27, 37, 39, 48, 65, 82, 83, 84, 124, 134
Nathan, Rhoda, 181
Nathanson, Lawrence, 186
National Lampoon's "Class of '86", 81
Natter, Meryl, 122
Nauffts, Geoffrey, 179
Naughton, James, 162, 188
Naumann, Michael P., 99
Navarre, Elizabeth, 68
Navarro, Tina Cantu, 180
Navigator, A Story of Micronesi, The, 136
Naymik, Jody, 161
Neal, Donald, 143
Neal, Elise, 32
Neal, Laura, 98, 100, 215
Neal, Patricia, 188, 192, 193
Neal, Renetta, 61
Neale, Nigel, 173
Nealon, Mary T., 58
Nealy, Milton Craig, 126
Near, Timothy, 156
Neary, Jack, 166
Nease, Byron, 142
Nebelthau, W. Alan, 156
Nebozenko, Jan, 17, 75, 122, 129
Neckties: A Comic Trilogy of Love-Knots, 113
Neda, Mathy, 109
Nederlander, James M., 12, 27, 40, 50, 122, 127, 132
Needham, Michael J., 152
Needles, William, 186
Neel, Debra, 63, 78
Neet, Alison Stair, 184
Neff, M. A., 71, 81, 120
Negative Balance, 163
Negron, Rick, 134
Neiden, Daniel, 96, 105, 215
Neil, Alexandra, 139
Neill, Jeffrey K., 73, 80
Neilson, Richard, 122
Nelessen, Anton, 149
Nelson, A. W., 136
Nelson, Barry, 49, 127, 215
Nelson, Bill, 96
Nelson, Bruce, 144
Nelson, Christine, 156
Nelson, Connie, 177
Nelson, Doug, 35, 59, 97, 140
Nelson, Frances, 59
Nelson, Gene, 188
Nelson, Hillary, 110
Nelson, Jennifer, 143
Nelson, Jessica, 146, 147
Nelson, Judd, 147, 148
Nelson, Judy Anne, 142
Nelson, Karen, 160
Nelson, Lois, 87, 98, 215
Nelson, Marjorie, 136
Nelson, Mark Wayne, 157
Nelson, Mark, 215
Nelson, Michael W., 140
Nelson, Murrey, 110
Nelson, Novella, 84, 179
Nelson, Randy, 35, 97, 136
Nelson, Rebecca, 81, 180
Nelson, Richard, 14, 34, 36, 42, 44, 65, 99, 106, 111
Nelson, Robert, 78, 183
Nelson, Sandra, 176
Nelson, Scott, 87
Nelson, Susie, 133
Nelson, Terry, 133
Nelson-Fleming, Gwen, 149
Nemet, Leslie C., 98
Nemetz, Lenora, 169
Nesbit, Pat, 76, 140
Nessen, Julie, 76
Nestor, George, 215
Nestroy, Johann, 136
Nettles, David, 72
Nettleton, Lois, 163
Neubauer, Nicholas, 16
Neubeck, Jack, 50
Neuberger, Jan, 215
Neudecker, Mary, 182
Neufeld, Jane, 121
Neufeld, Peter, 11, 48
Neuhaus, Robert, 154
Neuman, Katherine Elizabeth, 158
Neumann, Frederick, 12
Neumann, Krista, 15
Neuret, Edward, 179
Neusom, Daniel, 83, 215
Neustat, Betty, 79
Neuwirth, Bebe, 40, 80
Neville, John, 186
Neville-Andrews, John, 70, 152
Nevins, Kristine, 76
Newberry, Kimberly S., 151
Newborn, Phineas, III, 124
Newcomb, Don, 120, 162
Newcomb, Gary, 150
Newcomb, James, 151, 186
Newcomer, 147
Newdow, Julie, 16
Newel, Douglas, 172
Newfeld, Seth, 81
Newfield, Anthony, 62
Newhall, Anne, 87, 145
Newhouse, Miriam, 149
Newhouse, Sarah, 98
Newlin, Nick, 152
Newman, Andrew Hill, 55
Newman, Buck, Jr., 140
Newman, David, 51
Newman, Eric, 136
Newman, Harry, 88, 105
Newman, Jeff, 173
Newman, Leon, 177
Newman, Molly, 151, 159, 166
Newman, Paul, 188
Newman, Peter, 62
Newman, Phyllis, 81, 111, 215
Newman, Ronnie, 102
Newman, William, 98, 215
News, The, 16, 148
Newsome, Herbert L., III, 116
Newton, John, 96, 158, 168
Newton, Robert Boyd, 60
Next, Please!, 59
Nice and the Nasty, The, 111
Nichol, Rith, 186
Nicholas, Catherine, 37
Nicholas, Denise, 102, 215
Nicholas, Julie, 152
Nicholaw, Cassey, 145
Nichols, Mike, 38, 143
Nichols, N. Janet, 101
Nichols, Philip L., Jr., 183
Nichols, Robert, 76, 155, 215
Nicholson, James, 171
Nicholson, Patricia, 143
Nicholson, Paul, 185
Nickerson, Arnold, 76
Nickerson, Helen, 58, 59
Nicola, James C., 143
Nicolaev, Ariadne, 101
Nicoletti, John, 123, 155
Nicoll, Ron, 152
Nielsen, Kristine, 12
Nieman, Ann, 127
Niemann, Vincent, 59, 80, 121
Nieminski, Joseph, 154
Nieren, Sheryl, 107
Nieves, Maria, 13
Night of the Iguana, The, 135, 143, 187
'night, Mother, 140, 141, 143, 146, 147, 176, 187
Night We Lost Willie Nightingale, The, 113
Nightmare Abbey, 100
Nigro, Don, 94, 148
Niles, Barbara, 77
Niles, Mary Ann, 215
Nilsson, Christopher, 93, 215
Nin, Anais, 73
Nine, 187
1940's Radio Hour, The, 167
1951, 81
Nininger, Susan, 163
Nishball, Michael, 161
Nishikawa, Lane Kiyomi, 109
Nishimura, Deborah, 147
Nitchie, Vicky, 127
Nix, Catherine, 182
Nixon, Cynthia, 116, 188, 215
Nixon, James, 215
Nixon, Thomas, 163
No Exit, 187
No Mercy, 137
No One Lives on the Moon Anymore, 113
No Place to Be Somebody, 187
No, No, Nanette, 76
Noa, Jorge, 134
Noah, Dolores, 138
Noble, Eulalie, 64
Noble, Mark, 144
Noel, Craig, 184
Nogulich, Natalia, 12, 173
Noises Off, 132
Nolan, James F., 230
Nolan, Kathleen, 161, 167
Nolan, Lloyd, 230, 231
Noland, Nancy, 188
Noling, David, 63, 117
Noll, Drew C., 181
Nolte, Bill, 48, 124
Nolte, Charles, 165, 188
Nonsectarian Conversations With the Dead, 102
Noojin, Randy, 89
Noonan, John Ford, 125, 175
Noonan, John, 140
Noonan, Kerry, 163
Noone, James, 110
Noor, Kim, 124
Norberg, Catherine, 153
Norcia, Patricia, 186
Nordli, Robin, 141
Normal Heart, The, 162
Norman, Jay, 134
Norman, John, 135
Norman, Marsha, 140, 141, 143, 146, 149, 176
Norman, Monty, 155
Norman, Rende Rae, 58, 105, 215
Normand, Jacqueline A., 165
Normand, Maggie L., 162
Norment, Elizabeth, 141
Norris, Amy, 142
Norris, Bruce, 47, 215
Norris, Charles L., Jr., 113
Norris, Cheryl, 54
Norris, Mary, 142
Norris, Matthew, 182
Norris, Ruth Ann, 66, 215
North Atlantic, 161
North, Robert, 65
North, Sheree, 188
Northrop, Jessica, 48, 124
Norton, Kitty, 166
Norton, Kristin, 139
Norton, Michael, 118
Not About Heroes, 62
Not By Bed Alone, 178
Notbohm, Andrew Joel, 181
Notbohm, Bethany, 181
Noto, Lore, 52, 215
Noto, Patricia, 174
Noto, Thad, 52
Noto, Tony, 52
Nottbusch, Kaye, 166
Nourafchan, Victoria, 68
Novak, D. B., 184
Novak, Delrae, 144
Novak, Mark, 143
Novelli, Stephen, 168
November, 148
Novice, Ken, 76
Novick, Jay, 173
Novick, Kim, 116
Novy, Nita, 117
Nowak, Karen, 30
Noyes, Jeffrey, 175
Noyes, Martin, 173
Nozick, Bruce, 139
Ntinga, Themba, 59
Nuclear Follies, 105
Nugent, Anthony, 83
Nugent, James, 110
Nugit, Andrea, 80, 103
Null, Panchali, 135
Nunn, Bill, 140
Nunn, Trevor, 48
Nunnelley, Pamela Jennings, 143
Nunsense, 68
Nurphy, Sally, 164
Nusratty, Khorshied Machalle, 163
Nussbaum, Lawrence Edward, 93
Nussbaum, Mike, 91, 97, 99, 215
Nussbaum, Nel Evan, 179
Nute, Don, 215, 219
Nutu, Dan, 14, 108
Nuyen, France, 188
Nyberg, Pamela, 156
Nye, Carrie, 101, 215
Nye, Gene, 60, 61
Nygren, Carrie, 40, 135, 215
Nype, Russell, 167, 188
O'Brien, Adale, 137
O'Brien, Christopher, 74
O'Brien, Conal, 26
O'Brien, Dale, 78, 155
O'Brien, David, 111, 215, 219
O'Brien, Deborah Shippee, 167, 171
O'Brien, Denise, 164
O'Brien, Edna, 160, 173
O'Brien, Jack, 146, 184
O'Brien, Joyce, 47, 105
O'Brien, Michael Eugene, 171
O'Brien, Patrick T., 184
O'Brien, Rebecca, 81
O'Brien, Steve, 69
O'Brien, Terrence, 179
O'Brien, Toby, 100
O'Brien, Tom, 69, 100
O'Brien, Vivian, 159
O'Connell, Caitlin, 151
O'Connell, Deirdre, 66, 67
O'Connell, Patrick, 149, 170
O'Connell, Peggy, 130
O'Connor, Brian Brucker, 81
O'Connor, Grania, 147
O'Connor, J. Peter, 63
O'Connor, Kevin, 215
O'Connor, M. C., 143
O'Connor, Pamella, 140
O'Connor, Paul V., 185
O'Day, Kevin, 7
O'Dell, K. Lype, 59, 114, 139
O'Donnell, Daniel, 184
O'Donnell, Elaine, 64, 69, 81
O'Donnell, Kevin, 157
O'Donnell, Marie, 62
O'Donnell, Mark, 111
O'Donnell, Roone, 161, 166
O'Dwyer, Kyran, 182
O'Dwyer, Laurence, 177
O'Dwyer, Stephen, 139, 182
O'Flaherty, Michael, 66, 162
O'Flaherty, Ulric, 59
O'Gorman, Michael, 160
O'Grady, Dan, 50
O'Halloran, Patricia, 62
O'Halloran, Tree, 174
O'Hara, Jenny, 6, 215
O'Hara, Jill, 188
O'Hara, John Ryker, 90
O'Hara, John, 167
O'Hara, Leslie, 122
O'Hara, Paige, 142, 215
O'Hara, Patrick, 169
O'Hare, Brad, 173
O'Heaney, Caitlin, 163
O'Karma, Alexandra, 162
O'Keefe, Michael, 161, 188
O'Kelly, Aideen, 87
O'Leary, John, 100
O'Leary, William, 34
O'Malley, Brian, 77
O'Malley, Etain, 138, 149, 159
O'Malley, Judy, 154
O'Malley, Polly, 68
O'Malley, Regina, 159
O'Mara, Dan, 58
O'Meara, Evan, 117
O'Neal, Ron, 188
O'Neil, F. J., 101
O'Neil, Tricia, 188
O'Neill, Edward, 157
O'Neill, Eugene, 42, 12, 151, 160, 161
O'Neill, James, 161
O'Neill, John, 69, 76
O'Neill, Robert, 63
O'Neill, Robyn, 77
O'Neill, Steven, 110
O'Neille, Sharon, 177
O'Reilly, Allen, 140
O'Rourke, Kevin, 72, 118, 215
O'Shea, Milo, 29, 215
O'Sruitheain, Mykael, 182
O'Steen, Michael, 155
O'Steen, Michelle, 40
O'Sullivan, Anne, 91, 179, 215, 219
O'Sullivan, Barney, 172
O'Sullivan, Mary, 170, 171
O'Sullivan, Michael, 188
O'Sullivan-Moore, Emmett, 179
Oates, Joyce Carol, 163
Oberthal, Karen, 77
Obertin, Jolene, 174
Ocakte, 85
Occhiogrosso, Anne, 181
Odd Couple, The, 6
Odets, Clifford, 168, 171, 178
Odezynska, Andrea, 84
Oditz, Carol, 152
Odland, Bruce, 161, 186
Odle, Dwight Richard, 173
Odo, Chris, 179
Oei, David, 71
Oesterman, Phillip, 130
Of Mice and Men, 187
Of Thee I Sing, 187
Offenbach, Charles, 150
Offenbach, Jacques, 83
Offer, Anne Marie, 95
Officer, David, 180
Ogburn, Dennis, 104
Ogilvie, Kathy, 146
Oh! Calcutta!, 51
Ohama, Natsuko, 109, 168, 186
Ohie, Marjorie, 93, 105
Oirich, Steven, 64, 65
Ojeda, Rosita, 176
Oka, Marc C., 124
Okazaki, Alan K., 184
Okersin, Doug, 49, 127
Okhute, 102
Okun, Alexander, 118, 141
Old Maid, The, 187
Old Times, 143
Oldham, Rita G., 183
Oleniacz, Thomas S., 184
Olesen, Nanci, 138
Oleszczuk, Barbara, 122
Olich, Michael, 136, 138
Oliensis, Adam, 66, 215
Olim, Dorothy, 52, 69
Olin, Gilbert, 177
Olinka, Seth, 152
Olive, David, 77, 160
Olive, John, 158
Olivenbaum, David, 105
Oliver Oliver, 99
Oliver, LaFontaine, 143
Oliver, Michael, 122
Oliver, Robert R., 52
Oliver, Susan, 188
Oliver, Wendy, 155
Olivier, Frank, 133
Ollerman, Fred, 181
Olmos, Edward James, 188
Olon, John, 69
Olopai, Lino, 136
Olsen, Oliver C., 141
Olson, Ann, 186
Olson, James, 164, 173
Olson, Jon, 133
Olson, Marcus, 65, 215
Olster, Fredi, 141
Olympian Games, 141
Olympus on My Mind, 79
Oms, Alba, 112
On Golden Pond, 145
On the Harmfulness of Tobacco, 181
On the Razzle, 136, 156
On the 20th Century, 121
On the Verge, or The Geography of Yearning, 147, 157, 159
On Weddings and Divorces, 177
On Your Toes, 187
Once Is Never Enough, 109
Ondine, 187
One Fine Day, 117
One Flew Over the Cuckoo's Nest, 79
110 in the Shade, 159
One Man Band, 57
One Mo' Time, 149
One for the Road, 136
Onetto, Graciela, 147
Onorato, Joseph A., 79
Onouye, Mariye, 17
Onrubia, Cynthia, 11
Ontiveros, William P., 172
Ooms, Richard, 156
Opel, Nancy, 65
Opera Comique, 140, 141
Opitz, Lary, 148
Oppenheim, Ellen, 65
Options, 58
Orbach, Ron, 134
Orchard, Robert J., 141
Orchards, 82, 154, 189
Orezzoli, Hector, 13
Orgal, Yehiel, 161
Orland, Michael, 59
Orleans, Ilo, 175
Ornstein, Michael, 86
Oropeza, Luis, 151
Orphans, 139, 144, 148
Orr, Nancy Margaret, 140
Orr, Patrick, 182
Orsland, Gretchen, 136
Orson, Barbara, 178
Orth, Jeffrey E., 139
Orth, Lea, 73
Orth-Pallavicini, Nicole, 152
Ortiz, April, 124
Ortiz, Nereida, 87
Ortiz, Rico, 176
Ortlip, Michele, 148
Orton, Joe, 36, 99, 148, 176
Osborn, Leesa M., 32
Osborn, Paul, 88, 99
Osborne, Douglas, 165
Osborne, Kipp, 188
Osborne, Will, 177
Osbun, Eric, 143
Oscar Wilde: Solitaire, 80
Osgood, Kimberly, 149
Oshima, Mark, 141
Ossian, David, 99
Oster, Al, 145
Oster, Kristina, 89
Osterman, Curt, 86, 155
Osterman, Marjorie, 33
Ostermann, Curt, 58, 76, 86, 153, 157, 174
Osterwald, Bibi, 127
Ostrovsky, Alexander, 70, 170, 172
Osuna, Jess, 101, 162, 215
Otani, Jiro, 8
Otfinoski, Steven, 113
Othello, 131, 152, 180, 187
Other Places, 136
Otherwise Engaged, 187
Ott, Sharon, 143
Ottaway, James, 72
Otte, Charles, 14
Ottiwell, Frank, 141
Ottley, Rachelle, 124
Otto, Julie, 73
Otto, Victoria, 175
Ounce of Prevention, An, 64
Our Town, 187
Oure, Ursula, 182
Ousley, Robert, 123, 148
Over, Yvonne, 46
Overall, Park, 157
Overmire, Lawrence, 138
Overmyer, Eric, 105, 110, 147, 157, 159
Owen, Bobbi, 160, 170
Owen, Marianne, 111, 215
Owen, Paul, 137, 161
Owens, Carlyle B., 164
Owens, Edwin, 156
Owens, Elizabeth, 115, 215
Owens, Frank, 32
Owens, Gordon, 45
Owens, Kurt, 160
Oxenford, John, 117
Oyster, Jim, 215
Pabst, Joseph, 91
Pace, Atkin, 64, 167
Pace, Donald, 100
Pace, Georgea, 100
Pace, Michael, 55
Pacific Overtures, 187
Pacino, Al, 188
Pack of Lies, 139
Packer, Tina, 186
Packewicz, Mike, 142
Padden, Matthew, 142
Paddleford, Jim, 175
Paddock, Bruce, 66
Padilla, Elizabeth, 141
Padron, Aurelio, 135
Paffrath, Ann, 60
Pagano, Giulia, 215
Page, Evelyn, 162
Page, Geraldine, 67, 101, 188, 215
Page, Ken, 188, 215
Page, Stan, 49
Pagliotti, Douglas, 184
Painter, Walter, 155
Painting Churches, 139, 149, 159, 167, 173, 174, 179, 184
Pais, Josh, 60, 18, 215, 219
Pajama Game, The, 187
Pakledinaz, Martin, 121, 143
Pal Joey, 187
Palance, Holly, 172
Palance, Jack, 188
Palazzo, Larry, 57
Paley, Petronia, 102, 215
Palmatier, Nancy, 158
Palmer, Art Andre, 151
Palmer, Betsy, 148
Palmer, Byron, 188
Palmer, Elizabeth, 147
Palmer, Jonathan, 163, 173
Palmer, Lilli, 230, 231
Palmer, Mack, 151
Palmer, Margaret, 154, 186
Palmer, Peter, 188
Palmer, Vanessa, 71, 78
Palmieri, Joe, 149, 158
Palminteri, Chazz, 60, 216
Panaro, Hugh, 216
Panciera, Victor, 142
Paneka, Michael, 171
Pankow, John, 12
Panson, Bonnie, 6
Panzner, Linda, 63
Paoluzzi, Gianfranco, 78
Papandreas, Johniene, 72, 98, 119, 149
Papasian, Gerald, 163
Paper Promises, 60
Papoutsis, Alkis, 109, 110
Papp, Joseph, 20, 45, 59, 106, 188
Pappa, Michael, 149
Pappas, Evan, 45
Pappas, John, 146
Pappas, Theodore, 110
Papuchis, Alkis, 109
Papure, Bernie, 143
Paquet, Lucina, 154
Paradise!, 110, 111
Parady, Ron, 57, 216
Parenteau, Ilya, 170
Parham, Eric, 169
Parichy, Dennis, 56, 82, 88, 89, 146, 172, 175
Paris Bound, 162
Paris, Jeff, 157
Paris, Jerry, 230
Paris, Ronnie, 75
Parise, Tina, 127
Parisi, Julia, 63
Park, Dougald, 151
Park, R. Vincent, 16
Park, Valerie, 118
Parker, Alecia, 135
Parker, Corey, 91, 216
Parker, Dorothy, 80
Parker, Ellen, 63, 107, 216
Parker, Geoffrey, 174
Parker, James Boyd, 142
Parker, Jenifer, 144
Parker, Leonard, 180
Parker, Mary, 100
Parker, Noelle, 91
Parker, Norman, 162
Parker, Patrick, 145
Parker, Rebekka, 165
Parker, Rob, 134
Parker, Rochelle, 216
Parker, Rocky, 90
Parker, Roxann, 92, 216
Parker, Sarah Jessica, 91
Parker, Scott, 116, 119

Parker, Tina, 186
Parker, Una-Mary, 152
Parker, Wayne David, 165
Parkinson, John, 73
Parks, Charles, 163
Parks, Monica, 83
Parks, Rick, 106
Parks, Stephen Davis, 151
Parlato, Dennis, 52, 121, 149, 216
Parnell, Peter, 146
Parris, Steve, 216
Parrish, Elizabeth, 50
Parrish, Jack, 162
Parrow, Richard, 93, 216
Parry, Olivia, 182
Parsons, Charles T., 144
Parsons, Estelle, 188
Parsons, James, 158
Parsons, Jennifer, 163, 173
Parsons, Joel, 100
Partington, Rex, 145
Partington, Tony, 145
Partlan, William, 140, 180
Parva, Michael, 118
Pascal, Gabrial, 144
Pascucci, Daphne, 93
Pasekoff, Marilyn, 6, 81, 216
Paskow, Karen, 172
Pasley, William, 147
Pasqualini, Tony, 136
Passanante, Jean, 76, 81
Passeltiner, Bernie, 125
Passero, Jeffrey, 84
Passing Through, 163
Passion Cycle, The, 141
Passolt, Barbara, 83
Pasta, 178
Patch, Jerry, 140, 173
Paterson, David R., 167
Paterson, W. J., 72
Paterson, William, 140, 141
Paton, Alan, 162
Paton, Angela, 163, 173
Patria, Richard, 46
Patrick, Bonnie, 127
Patrick, Dennis, 188
Patriots, The, 187
Patten, Moultrie, 132
Patterson, Howard Jay, 35, 97
Patterson, Jackie, 80, 83
Patterson, Jamie, 48, 124
Patterson, Jay, 89, 156, 216
Patterson, Kelly, 40, 216
Patterson, Kevin, 55, 61, 66
Patterson, Michael, 165
Patterson, Neil, 165
Patterson, Rachael, 151
Patterson, Rebecca, 163
Patterson, Steve, 64
Patterson, Todd, 230, 231
Pattison, Liann, 4, 18, 57, 216
Patton, Gayle, 50, 128
Patton, Pat, 158, 185
Patton, Shirley, 185
Patton, Virginia, 111
Patton, Will, 67, 185, 216
Paul, Bobby, 153
Paul, Brian, 154, 186
Paul, David, 65
Paul, Frank, 48
Paul, Hilary, 152
Paul, Jeff, 63, 73, 80
Paul, Kent, 72, 88, 105
Paul, Linda, 78
Paul, Michael, 138
Paul, Nancy, 162
Paulsen, Jeanne, 185
Paulsen, Larry, 138, 144, 185
Paulsen, Rick, 136, 172
Paulsen, Thrim, 183
Paulson, Erica L., 64, 93
Pauly, Jennifer, 175
Paupaw, David, 57
Pavelka, Tom, 116, 162
Paxton, Vivian, 51
Payan, Ilka Tanya, 112, 216, 219
Payne, Eric, 107
Payne, Julie, 147
Payne, Tonia, 90
Payne-Rohan, Teresa, 26
Payton-Wright, Pamela, 157, 180
Peacock, Chiara, 61, 79
Peacock, Lucy, 186
Peacock, Thomas Love, 100
Peahl, Susan, 216
Peak, Danny, 150
Pearl, Jeffrey L., 104
Pearle, Gary, 111
Pearlman, Stephen, 96, 111, 216
Pearlman, Tsilke, 78
Pearls, 96
Pearson, Beatrice, 188
Pearson, Burke, 108
Pearson, David, 57, 121
Pearson, Elizabeth, 118, 216
Pearson, Scott, 216
Pearson, Sybille, 151, 178
Pearson, Ted, 186
Pearthree, Pippa, 107, 216
Peaslee, Richard, 14, 78, 169
Pechar, Thomas, 153
Peck, Alexander, 93, 216
Peck, Cecilia, 120
Peck, Gary Scott, 16
Peck, Jonathan, 102
Peck, Kenneth L., 31
Peck, Susan Rolfe, 172
Peckham, Charles S., 142
Pect, Jim, 140
Pederson, Rose, 136, 172
Peek, Brent, 59, 60
Peek, Jenny, 111
Peep into the Twentieth Century, A, 172
Pelikan, Lisa, 173
Pelinski, Stephen, 138
Pell, Amy, 7, 39
Pelleas et Melisande, 113
Pellegrino, Susan, 59, 158
Pelling, George, 173
Pelovitz, Dorothy, 184
Peltier, Meg, 95
Pen, Polly, 119
Pena, Edilio, 112
Pender, S. Chris, 123
Pender, Stephen, 230
Pendergrast, Carol, 170
Pendleton, Austin, 101, 115, 179, 121
Pendleton, Wyman, 121, 140, 179, 216
Penland, Amelia, 160
Penn & Teller, 56
Penn, Edward, 61, 96, 216
Penn, Leo, 188
Penn, Matthew, 98, 121
Pennacchini, Tom, 184
Pennel, Allison, 183
Pennell, Nicholas, 154, 186
Pennington, Gail, 216
Pennington, Russ, 69
Pennoyer, John, 186
Penrod, Rick, 166
Penrod, Shannon, 63
Pentecost, James, 50
Pepe, Neil, 182
Pepper, Pam, 167
Percassi, Don, 49
Pereira, Michael, 159
Perelman, S. J., 178
Peret, Joseph, 105
Perez, Luis, 134, 216
Perez, Mercedes, 155
Perfect Analysis Given by a Parrot, A, 82
Perfect Party, The, 111
Perkins, Anthony, 188
Perkins, David, 74
Perkins, Don, 184
Perkins, Elizabeth, 106, 216
Perkins, John, 125
Perkins, Kathy A., 163
Perkins, Lynne, 144
Perkins, Mac, 172
Perkins, Patti, 148
Perlach, Bill, 52
Perley, William, 160
Perlman, Marilyn, 166
Perloff, Carey, 115
Perloff, Richard, 131
Permutter, Alice, 117
Perr, Harvey, 161
Perrell, Pamela, 68, 74, 79
Perri, Paul, 170, 216
Perrin, Richard, 138
Perry, Bob, 142
Perry, Christy A., 177
Perry, Doug, 181
Perry, Elaine, 230
Perry, Elizabeth, 167
Perry, Ernest, Jr., 154
Perry, Jaime, 107, 216
Perry, Jeff, 28, 91, 161, 216
Perry, Karen, 107
Perry, Keith, 167, 216
Perry, Lynnette, 149
Perry, Richard James, 135
Perry, Shauneille, 85, 103
Perry, William, 26
Perryman, Stanley Wesley, 40
Perryman, Stanley, 216
Persecution and Assassination of Marat as Performed by the Inmates of the Asylum of Charenton under the Direction of the Marquis de Sade, The, 187
Personals, 65
Pesaturo, George, 216
Pescow, Donna, 148
Pestana, James, 136
Peter Pan or The Boy Who Wouldn't Grow Up, 160, 174
Peterman, Robyn, 164
Peters, Bernadette, 10, 11, 188, 192, 193, 216
Peters, Brock, 163
Peters, Janne, 112, 216
Peters, Lauri, 188
Peters, Mark, 216, 219
Peters, Michael, 126
Peters, Roger, 23, 42
Peters, Todd, 79
Petersen, David O., 181
Petersen, Erika, 90, 216
Petersen, William L., 161
Peterson, Chris, 127, 133
Peterson, David, 180
Peterson, Deirdre, 156
Peterson, Ed, 152
Peterson, Eric, 145, 167, 171, 179
Peterson, Kurt, 81, 148, 149, 216
Peterson, Lenka, 60, 72, 111, 216
Peterson, Pamela, 57, 180
Peterson, Patricia Ben, 96, 155
Peterson, Peggy, 36, 99
Peterson, Richard, 159
Peterson, Robert, 185
Peterson, Susan, 80
Petition, The, 39
Petlock, Martin, 144
Petrakis, Mark, 163
Petrarca, David, 157
Petras, Herman, 70, 80
Petrified Forest, The, 151, 163
Petroff, Greg, 77, 90
Petroni, Bill, 68
Petroski, Adam, 130
Petter, Pam, 167
Petterson, Howard Jay, 136
Pettet, Joanna, 188
Petti, Deborah, 65
Pettiford, Valarie, 37, 57
Pettiford-Wates, Tawnya, 136
Pettit, Dodie, 48
Petty, Andrea, 74, 80
Pevsner, David, 92, 216
Peyroux, Adrien, 59
Peyton, Caroline, 167
Pfeiffer, Eddie, 133
Pfister, David J., 61
Phalen, Robert, 163
Phantom of the Opera, The, 148
Phelan, Deborah, 24, 50, 80, 216
Phelan, K. Siobhan, 115
Phelan, Kate, 176
Phelan, Mark, 179
Phelps, Scott, 89
Phelps, Tracey, 93
Philadelphia Story, The, 143, 158
Philip, John Van Ness, 64
Philippi, Michael S., 161, 166
Philips, Mardi, 96
Phillips, Ayana, 102
Phillips, Barbara-Mae, 42
Phillips, Barry, 155
Phillips, Bill, 100
Phillips, Bob, 70, 74, 77, 90, 109
Phillips, Clayton, 170
Phillips, Ethan, 138
Phillips, Garrison, 110, 216
Phillips, Harvey, 181
Phillips, James David, 73
Phillips, Jayne Anne, 147
Phillips, Joseph C., 148
Phillips, Margaret, 188
Phillips, Marishka Shanice, 32
Phillips, Miriam, 76, 216, 219
Phillips, Nelson, 151
Phillips, Randy, 127
Phillips, Tim, 61
Phillipson, Adam, 79
Phippen, Mari, 93
Phippin, Jackson, 137, 147, 171
Phipps, Noel, 182
PiRoman, John, 152
Piazza, Ben, 188
Pichette, David, 136
Pickens, James, Jr., 149
Pickett, Sarah J., 175
Picnic, 146, 187
Piddock, Jim, 163
Piece of Fog, A, 62
Piedra, Julio, 96
Pielmeier, John, 17, 145, 149, 174, 177
Pierce, David, 108, 156, 216
Pierce, Jay, 50
Pierce, Katherine, 168
Pierce, Laura, 117
Pierce, Paula Kay, 62
Pierce, Victoria, 58
Pierce, Wendell, 17, 162
Pietig, Louis D., 105
Pietraszek, Rita, 166
Pietropinto, Angela, 96, 216
Pigliavento, Michele, 20, 57
Pignataro, Arthur A., 142
Pigott, Colin, 31
Pillinger, Michael, 78
Pilloud, Rod, 136, 172, 175
Pinckney, Tim, 158
Pincus, Warren, 155
Pine, Larry, 107
Pine, Margaret Rachlin, 69, 96
Pinero, Arthur Wing, 185
Pinhasik, Howard, 160
Pink, Andy, 107
Pinkins, Tonya, 64, 216
Pinkney, Scott, 98, 152
Pino, Mariangela, 82, 216, 219
Pinocchio, 140
Pinque, Erminio, 139
Pinter, Harold, 28, 136, 143, 159, 163, 181
Pintilie, Lucian, 143
Piontek, Michael, 144
Piper, Bruce, 131
Piper, Laureen Valuch, 45
Piper, Wendy, 142
Pipes, Nona, 120
Pipik, Brenda, 49
Pippin, Donald, 24, 45, 50
Pirates of Penzance, The, 186, 187
Pirillo, Vincent, 124
Pirkle, Joan, 163
Pirolo, Mark, 152
Pirovano, Mario, 81
Pistone, Charles, 16
Pitoniak, Anne, 146, 147, 174, 188, 216
Pittman, Demetra, 136
Pittman, Richard, 141
Pitts, Randy, 152
Pitts, William, 114
Pitts-Wiley, Ricardo, 178
Pizzo, Marcia, 141
Place Called Heartbreak, A, 80
Place, Dale, 76, 216, 219
Plachy, William J., 87, 92, 118
Placzek, Ron, 58
Plainsance, Sheila, 183
Plaksin, Suzie, 64
Plana, Tony, 17, 107, 216
Planet Fires, 147
Plank, Scott, 216
Plante, Carol-Ann, 14
Plante, Louis R., 146
Plass, Sara Gormley, 54
Platt, Martin L., 181
Platt, Oliver, 186
Play It Again, Sam, 87
Play's the Thing, The, 162
PlayLab, 143
Playboy of the Western World, 148
Playpen, 113
Playten, Alice, 188, 216
Playtime, 113
Pleasants, Nina, 57
Pleasants, Philip, 181
Pleasuring Ground, 151
Plenty, 187
Plienski, Stephen, 179
Plum, Sally, 92
Plumley, Jesse, 80
Plummer, Amanda, 67, 188, 216
Plummer, Chas, 73
Plummer, Christopher, 188
Plunkett, Maryann, 159
Plymale, Trip, 145
Poddubiuk, Christina, 154, 186
Poe, Edgar Allan, 147
Poe, Richard, 33, 59, 175, 217
Poets in Their Youth, 147
Poggi, Gregory, 168
Pogson, Kathryn, 107
Pohlig, Christine Orr, 153
Poindexter, Jay, 48
Poindexter, Karen, 148
Poiret, Jean, 50
Poirot, Lynn, 142
Polan, Lynn, 96
Poland, Albert, 55, 67, 70
Polen, Patricia, 182
Poli, Jessica, 101
Polk, Andrew, 123, 178
Polk, Paul, 139
Polk, Robin, 72
Pollis, Michael, 95
Pollock, Kate, 155, 55
Polner, Alex, 77, 109
Polsonetti, Chris, 100
Poltrack, Beverly, 93, 217
Pomerantz, John, 50
Pompa, Lisa, 142, 155
Pompei, Donna M., 155
Ponazecki, Joe, 91, 96, 166, 217
Ponazecki, Joe, 96
Ponzio, Laura, 169
Pool, Betsy M., 79
Poole, Jillian H., 161
Poole, Richard, 124
Poor Poet, 163
Popal, Zarmina, 163
Pope, Deborah J., 105
Pope, Nancy, 160
Pope, Stephanie, 37, 80, 217, 219
Pope, Tyree Lewis, 113
Popovics, Brian, 100
Poppe, Catherine, 151
Popper, Douglas, 71
Poppleton, L. Glenn III, 18, 40, 76, 81
Porazzi, Arturo E., 7
Porreca, Gracen, 153
Porter, Carolyn, 132
Porter, Cole, 73, 74, 139, 142, 177
Porter, Mark, 64, 68
Porter, Mary Ed, 150
Porter, Rick, 64, 92, 217
Porter, Stephen, 101
Porter, Tom, 45
Portman, Meredity, 76
Portrait of A Man, 70
Portser, Mary, 132
Posa, Joe, 162
Posener, Daniel M., 140
Posey, Trudi Anne, 73
Posner, Seth, 142
Post, James, 106
Postel, Steve, 69
Potasnik, Scott, 145
Potok, Sarah, 63
Potoker, Edward M., Dr., 80
Potter, Don, 127
Potter, Julie, 184
Pottlitzer, Joanne, 73, 176
Potts, David, 69, 88, 150, 153, 158
Poulson, Cynthia, 175
Povod, Reinaldo, 108
Powell, Addison, 57, 149, 217
Powell, Anthony, 82
Powell, Curt, 170
Powell, Jill, 140
Powell, Kobie, 162
Powell, Mary Ann, 174
Powell, Susann, 165
Powers, Ariel, 64
Powers, David, 12, 30, 60, 67
Powers, Dennis, 141, 151
Powers, Jonathan, 100
Powers, Kim, 116
Powers, Susan, 48
Pownall, David, 71, 115, 162
Poyer, Lisa M., 76
Prager, Ben, 172
Prairie Du Chien, 97
Prather, David, 163
Pratt, John, 230
Pratt, Noni, 121
Pratt, Ron, 182
Pratzon, Jim, 121
Precious Sons, 34, 190
Predovic, Dennis, 149, 217
Preece, K. K., 139
Prendergast, Shirley, 149
Prentice, Jeffrey, 186
Prescott, James O., 169
Prescripted, 113
Present Company, 113
Present Laughter, 165
Present, Judith, 61
Press, Barry, 172
Press, Richard, 85
Pressley, Brenda, 48, 80
Pressman, Lawrence, 188
Preston, Barry, 127
Preston, Don, 146
Preston, Kate, 184
Preston, Michael, 59
Preston, Tina, 146
Preston, Travis, 180
Preston, William, 184
Prestridge, Christy, 172
Previn, Ruth, 113
Pribyl, John, 136
Price, Don, 142
Price, Elaine, 148
Price, Faye, 156
Price, Gilbert, 188, 217
Price, Lonny, 84, 109, 115, 188, 217
Price, Michael P., 155
Price, Peggity, 137
Price, Roger, 188
Price, Seth, 58
Price, The, 153, 175
Prichard, Dianne M., 141
Prichette, David, 136
Pride and Prejudice, 162
Priebe, James F., 110
Priest, Dorothy, 124
Prieto, Daniel, 79
Prime Time Punch Line, 98
Primont, Marion, 144
Prince, Faith, 75, 79, 155
Principia Scriptoriae, 99, 191
Printz, Jessica, 177
Prinz, Rosemary, 168
Pritchard, Ted, 230
Pritchett, James, 101, 170
Prittie, David, 61
Pritts, Linda, 167
Pritzker, Cindy, 7
Private Lives, 141, 144, 170
Procaccino, John, 172
Proctor, Charles, 188
Proctor, Melissa, 170
Proctor, Philip, 188
Proett, Daniel, 81, 91, 104, 149, 152
Professionally Speaking, 81
Promises, 163
Proposal, The, 181
Prosser, Bertram, 162
Prostak, Edward, 57
Prouty, Laura Lee, 80
Proval, David, 162
Provenza, Rosario, 180
Pruett, Glen Allen, 165
Pruger, Joey, 182
Pruitt, Richard, 145
Pruitt, Robb, 144
Prunczik, Karen, 130
Pruneau, Phillip, 101, 217
Prutting, Stephen, 57, 86
Pryce, Jaunice, 113
Pryce, Jonathan, 188
Pryor, Deborah, 179
Pryor, John, 151
Psacharopoulos, Nikos, 162
Pucci, Maria Cristina, 33
Puente, Tito, 77
Pugh, Caroline, 143
Pugh, Richard Warren, 135, 140
Pullman, Bill, 163
Pump Boys and Dinettes, 113, 138, 167, 176
Pumpkin Carvers, The, 113
Purcell, Ann, 95
Purcell, John, 140
Purdham, David, 63, 84, 217
Purdy, Claude, 153
Purdy, Marshall B., 29, 57
Puri, Rajika, 109
Purl, Linda, 146
Purlie, 151
Purnell, Shaw, 168, 171
Pursley, David, 115, 117, 217
Puzo, Madeline, 60, 146, 147
Pygmalion, 151, 181
Pyle, Russell, 125, 163
Pyle, Stuart, 106, 107
Pyne, James F., Jr., 150
Quality Time, 167
Quarry, Michael, 89
Quartered Man, The, 163
Quartermaine's Terms, 136, 143
Quesenbery, Whitney, 62, 90
Quevli, Michael, 59
Quezada, Alba R., 144
Quiet in the Land, 89
Quigley, Erin, 161
Quillin, Mimi, 40
Quilters, 143, 159, 166
Quimby, Gerald J., 58, 139
Quimby, Priscilla, 145
Quinian, William P., 72
Quinlan, Kathleen, 188
Quinn, Aidan, 67, 91, 217
Quinn, Anthony, 135, 217
Quinn, Brian, 155
Quinn, Henry J., 63, 217, 219
Quinn, J. C., 147
Quinn, James W., 147
Quinn, John, 153
Quinn, Laura, 133
Quinn, Patrick, 74, 167, 217
Quinn, Rosemary, 79
Quinn, Thomas Anthony, 143
Quintero, Jose, 12, 161
Quinton, Everett, 65
Quiroz, Martin, 176
R., Essene, 79
Rabb, Ellis, 101
Rabboni, 58
Rabe, David, 68, 161
Raben, Lawrence, 80
Rabine, Terry, 102
Rabinowitz, Ronald A., 69
Rabins, Jay, 144
Rabold, Rex, 136, 175
Rachel's Fate, 151
Racimo, Victoria, 176
Rackleff, Owen S., 90, 217
Rader, Grant, 17
Radford, Robert, 7
Radka, William, 178
Rado, Rosemary, 49
Radomsky, Saul, 161
Radsdale, William, 47
Raether, Richard, 80
Rafael, Mark, 180
Rafalowicz, Mira, 161
Raffin, Deborah, 148
Ragan, Michael, 169
Ragland, Jim, 175
Ragney, Joe, 168
Ragsdale, William, 123
Rahman, Aishah, 91
Rahn, Karen, 164
Raider-Wexler, Victor, 170
Raiken, Lawrence, 140
Rainbow, 78
Raines, Ron, 79, 142, 217
Rainey, Ford, 173
Rainmaker, The, 156
Rainone, John, 177
Raisin in the Sun, A, 168, 187

Raisin, 187
Raiter, Frank, 160
Raitt, John, 188
Rake, Susannah, 186
Ralstin, Monte, 167
Ramage, Ed, 74
Ramage, Edmond, 77, 90
Rambo, Bubba Dean, 133
Rame, Franca, 141
Ramey, Lynn M., 185
Ramey, Nanya, 138
Ramicova, Dunya, 157, 162, 180
Ramires, Rosaura, 176
Ramirez, Octavio, 176
Ramirez, Tom, 182
Ramish, Trish, 45
Ramont, Mark, 75
Ramos, Ana, 77
Ramos, Richard Russell, 108, 115, 217
Ramos, Rudy, 163
Ramos, Santos, 128
Rampino, Lewis D., 66
Ramseur, LueCinda, 126
Ramsey, Dale, 110
Ramsey, Kevin, 58, 139
Ramsey, Marion, 32, 217
Ramsey, Robert Max, 152
Ramsey, Stanley, 153, 174, 175
Ramsey, Van Broughton, 114
Ranck, Christine, 138
Randall, Dudley, 85
Randall, Juliet, 165
Randall, Neal, 105
Randel, Melissa, 45, 217, 219
Randell, Ron, 114, 217
Randolph, Beverley, 32, 61
Randolph, James, 83
Randolph, Robert, 40
Ranii, Marti, 169
Rankin, Kenny, 25
Rankin, Steve, 137
Ransom, Kenneth, 186
Ransom, Sophia, 184
Ransom, Tim, 57, 91
Raoul, Bill, 136
Rapczynski, Kenn, 144
Rapella, Steve, 72
Raper, Lyle, 151
Raphael, Ellen, 26, 161
Raphael, Gerrianne, 63, 217
Raphael, Jay E., 149
Raphel, David, 119
Rapollo, Steve, 146
Rapp, Anthony, 34
Rasch, Karen, 144
Rasche, David, 60, 217
Rashovich, Gordana, 157, 179, 188
Rasmuson, Judy, 70, 149, 152, 156, 162
Rassel, Michael, 154
Rastall, Deborah, 142
Rat in the Skull, 147
Rataczjak, Dave, 25
Ratcliffe, Albert Helmer, 145
Rathburn, Roger, 188
Rathgeb, Laura, 110
Ratican, Eric, 163
Ratigliano, Danny, 62
Ratner, Ellen, 85, 98
Rattner, George, 103
Rauh, Joseph, 30
Rauh, Richard, 169
Rauscher, Becca, 172
Ravel, Jacqueline, 182
Ravelo, Henry, 109, 217
Ravens, Rupert, 144
Ravich, Paul, 65
Raw Youth, 110
Rawlings, Herbert L., Jr., 126
Ray, James, 110, 217, 219
Ray, Robin, 173
Ray, Stacy, 140, 158
Ray, W. Earl, 175
Raymond, Bill, 67
Raymond, Guy, 151
Raymond, John, 87
Raynor, Michael, 80
Rayppy, Gary, 156
Rayvis, Curt, 68
Raziq, Lisa, 171
Re, Tommy, 45, 72
Re-Viewing Saroyan, 162
Ready, Jonathan, 80
Reagan, Judith, 110
Real Inspector Hound, The, 175
Real Thing, The, 144, 146, 147, 166, 170, 172, 187
Reale, Willie, 63, 81
Ream, James, 139
Reams, Lee Roy, 49, 217
Reardon, Peter, 128
Reardon, Stephen, 140
Reaux, Roumel, 37, 58, 80, 149
Rebhorn, James, 91, 101, 217
Rebic, Don, 40
Rebich, Cissy, 217
Recht, Ray, 96, 170
Rechter, Yoni, 161
Rechtzeit, Jack, 63, 64
Redanty, Marisa, 72
Redcoff, Karl, 144
Reddin, Keith, 98, 107, 115, 154, 178
Reddy, Brian, 82
Redfield, Adam, 33, 188, 217, 219
Redfield, Dennis, 163
Redford, J. A. C., 173
Redford, Paul, 172
Redford, Robert, 188
Redhead, 187
Redinger, Paula, 14, 217, 219
Redmann, Jean, 73
Redmond, Barbara, 153
Redmond, Lawrence, 143
Redmond, Marge, 162
Redwood, John Henry, 61
Redwood, Lillie Marie, 61
Reed, Alexander, 99
Reed, Alyson, 74
Reed, Gavin, 140, 145
Reed, James, 63
Reed, Jay, 62
Reed, Joseph, 59, 165
Reed, Pamela, 107, 115, 217
Reed, Penelope, 164
Reed, Shanna, 147
Reed, Stella, 178
Reed, T. Michael, 48, 124
Reed, Vivian, 188
Reehling, Joyce, 140
Reeve, Christopher, 14, 217
Reeverts, Dan, 151
Reeves, Don, 162
Reeves, Philip, 184
Reeves-Phillips, Sandra, 149
Regal, David, 165
Regan, Charles, 101, 217
Regan, Sylvia, 63
Regard of Flight, The, 143
Regester, Robert, 129
Reggiardo, Carl, 173
Region, Daniel, 110, 217, 219
Regnard, Jean-Francois, 181
Rehab, Gary, 86
Reich, Sharon L., 113
Reichert, Edward, 83, 92, 162
Reichert, Whit, 145
Reid, Pamela, 59
Reidel, Leslie, 183
Reidman, Daniel, 171
Reigel-Ernst, Sandra, 181
Reilly, Nancy, 161
Reilly, Robert, 106
Reilly, William Spencer, 80
Reimer, Max, 186
Reineke, Gary, 33, 156
Reiner, Jerry, 65
Reiner, Mark, 24
Reinglas, Fred, 88, 89
Reinhardsen, David, 105, 217
Reinhardt, Shanti, 141
Reinking, Ann, 40, 41, 80, 188
Reis, Whitney, 115
Reisch, Michele, 118
Reisman, Jane, 84
Reiss, Andrew, 12
Reiss, Vicki, 115
Reissa, Eleanor, 64, 138, 217, 219
Reit, Alyssa Hess, 78
Reit, Peter, 78
Reiter, Richard, 179
Reitman, David, 124
Reitzer, Larry, 17, 27, 37, 39, 48, 124, 134
Remme, John, 74, 157, 217
Remote Conflict, 172
Remsberg, Calvin E., 124
Renaldi, Philip, 26
Rence, Mariana, 158
Rendall, Jill, 156
Renderer, Scott, 72
Rendezvous With God, A, 86
Rene, Nicky, 55
Rene, Norman, 34, 120, 149, 173
Reneau, Russell, 164
Renick, Kyle, 120
Rennagel, Marilyn, 38, 140
Renner, Daniel, 185
Rensenhouse, John, 132
Rensing, Bruce, 75
Renton, David, 154, 186
Renzaneth, Richard, 90
Repass, Mary, 176
Repole, Charles, 188, 217
Requiem for a Heavyweight, 166
Resler, Arthur, 63
Resnick, Amy, 146
Resnik, Kim, 140
Resnikoff, Robert, 86
Resseguie, Lew, 127
Restoration, 143
Reuben, Leslie, 102
Reunion, 151
Reuss, David, 32
Revson, Iris, 155
Rey, Nikko, 176
Reyes, Julian, 135
Reynolds, Blancett, 182
Reynolds, Herbert, 31
Reynolds, Sarah Bethany, 122
Reynolds, Simon, 140
Reznicek, Michael, 176
Rhames, Ving, 17, 107, 161
Rheaume, Susan, 181
Rhodes, Jennifer, 217
Rhodes, Russell, 127
Rhodes, Tran William, 63, 73
Rhodes, Walter, 153
Rhone, Trevor, 149
Rhynedance, Gwynne, 136
Rhys, William, 30
Ricardo, Michael, 49
Ricards, Telton, 102
Rice, Allyson, 164
Rice, James Goodwin, 93
Rice, Joel Key, 62
Rice, Micha, 136
Rice, Michael, 68, 143
Rice, Sarah, 140, 188, 217
Rice, Wesley, 172
Rich Full Life, A, 163
Rich Relations, 116
Rich, Beverly, 58
Rich, James, 146
Richard II, 181
Richard III, 182, 183, 184
Richard, Ellen, 115
Richards, Arleigh, 73
Richards, Beah, 188
Richards, Carol, 217
Richards, Christopher, 146
Richards, Dick, 162
Richards, Gary, 87, 96, 217, 219
Richards, Gerald, 153, 168
Richards, Jean, 63, 79, 217
Richards, Jeffrey, 16, 18, 40, 69, 70, 72, 74, 75, 76, 81, 86, 94, 127
Richards, Jess, 139, 165, 188
Richards, Lloyd, 57, 154, 172, 180
Richards, Martha Sloca, 138
Richards, Martin, 15, 50
Richards, Nancy, 70, 76
Richards, Rob G., 171
Richards, Tammy, 166
Richards, Yohance, 143
Richardson, Charles, 71
Richardson, Kathy E., 140
Richardson, Kevin, 175
Richardson, LaTanya, 102, 103, 104
Richardson, Lee, 115, 149, 217
Richardson, Lindsey, 88, 186
Richardson, Morgan, 135
Richardson, Patricia, 120, 217
Richardson, Ron, 46
Richardson, Sally, 136, 172
Richardson, Stuart, 59
Richert, Wanda, 45, 188, 217, 219
Richert, William, 131
Richter, Karol, 73
Richwine, Maria, 176
Ricketts, Jim, 60, 217
Rico, Lenette, 176
Ricossa, Maria, 154, 186
Riddell, Richard, 46, 141
Riddett, Cecelia, 153
Riddle, George, 52, 157, 166
Riddle, Kate, 77, 80, 90, 103
Riddle, Steven, 73, 83, 167
Rieder, Adrian, 177
Riedman, Kathryn, 144
Riegert, Peter, 86, 98, 217
Riehele, Richard, 33
Riehl, Mar, 165
Riehle, Richard, 33, 136, 138, 217
Riek, Les, 80
Rieser, Terry, 140
Riford, Lloyd S., III, 136
Rigby, Harry, 133
Rigdon, Kevin, 28, 97, 127, 154, 161
Riggs, Jennifer, 144
Riggsbee, Thomas, 85
Rignack, Roger, 78, 217
Riley, Eric, 129, 146
Riley, Larry, 46, 218
Rinaldi, Philip, 11, 27, 37, 39, 48, 84
Rinehart, Elaine, 65
Rinehimer, John, 16
Riner, Richard, 175
Ringham, Nancy, 218, 219
Rinklin, Ruth E., 135
Rintels, David W., 170
Rintoul, Brian, 154
Ripley, Alan, 140
Rise of David Levinsky, The, 153
Rish, Steve Roy, 72
Ritchie, Margaret, 72, 218
Ritchie, Michael F., 14, 25, 28, 44
Ritter, Erika, 186
Ritter, John, 146
Ritter, Pam, 139
Rittiman, Daryl, 174
Ritz, Jimmy, 230
Rivarola, Carlos, 13
Rivarola, Maria, 13
Rivas, Fernando, 73, 77
Rivas, Geoff, 163
Rivas, Salvador, 172
River Niger, The, 187
Rivera, Chita, 24, 218
Rivera, James, 134
Rivera, Maritza, 73
Rivera, Sonia, 20
Rivera, Voza, 80
Rivers, Fred, 92, 218
Rivers, Jimmy, 162
Rivers, Susan, 171
Rivkala's Ring, 82
Rivlin, Leora, 161
Rizzo, Alberto, 13
Roads of the Mountaintop, 149
Roark, Jonathan, 159
Robards, Jason, 12, 188, 218
Robards, Sam, 158, 161
Robare, Mary C., 26, 218
Robbins, Carrie, 17, 138
Robbins, Jana, 167
Robbins, Jerome, 134
Robbins, Kathleen M., 70
Robbins, Kerri Lee, 105
Robbins, Rex, 162
Robbins, Tom, 64, 155, 172
Robbison, J. Russell, 78
Robelen, John, 66
Roberdeau, John, 122
Robert Klein Show, The, 25
Robert, Patricia, 78
Roberts, David, 78
Roberts, Davis, 163
Roberts, Grace, 96, 218
Roberts, Jacquelyn Mari, 60
Roberts, Jeffrey, 140
Roberts, Jordan, 171
Roberts, Judith, 121, 158
Roberts, Lance, 124
Roberts, Linda, 69
Roberts, Patricia, 76
Roberts, Peter, 186
Roberts, Richard, 177
Roberts, Ruth Ann, 179
Roberts, Ruth, 123
Roberts, Sally, 172
Roberts, Tim, 152
Roberts, Tony, 218
Robertson, Alene, 164
Robertson, Barbara E., 161
Robertson, Cliff, 188
Robertson, Dario, 71
Robertson, Deborah, 51, 218
Robertson, Frances, 100
Robertson, Joel, 48
Robertson, Lanie, 119, 140
Robertson, Liz, 31
Robertson, Scott, 15, 99
Robey, Carol Ann, 142
Robie, Wendy, 175
Robillard, Robin B., 127
Robins, Barry, 230
Robins, Jay, 144
Robins, Laila, 143
Robinson, Andre, 80
Robinson, Andre, Jr., 85, 107
Robinson, Andrew, 60, 218
Robinson, Bartlett, 230
Robinson, Charles Shaw, 149
Robinson, Christine, 31
Robinson, Cleo Parker, 151
Robinson, Dean, 170
Robinson, Edward G., 62
Robinson, Hal, 61, 65, 218, 219
Robinson, Janna, 122
Robinson, JoAnne, 48
Robinson, Louise, 55
Robinson, M. Lynda, 166
Robinson, Marsha June, 184
Robinson, Martin P., 55, 169, 177
Robinson, Mary B., 116, 149
Robinson, Mary, 137
Robinson, Meghan, 59, 69
Robinson, Michael, 126
Robinson, Nell, 66
Robinson, Roger, 12, 218
Robinson, Scot, 107
Robinson, Virginia, 162
Robman, Steven, 180
Robson, Mark, 113
Robson, Penelope, 76
Robson, Robin, 70
Roby, John, 61
Rocco, Jamie, 26
Rocco, Mary, 93, 218
Rocco, Tom, 169
Roccosalva, John, 96
Roche, Tudi, 87, 172
Rock, The, 113
Rockbound, 64
Rockwell, Robert, 161
Rockwell, Stephen, 141
Rodas, Eddie, 60
Rodd, Marcia, 18, 19, 76, 218
Roderick, Connie, 14, 218
Roderick, Ray, 26
Rodgers, Carolyn, 85
Rodgers, Gaby, 188, 218
Rodgers, Richard, 80, 81, 142, 145, 167
Rodgers-Wright, Bruce, 163
Rodnunsky, Serge, 124
Rodriguez, Al, 175
Rodriguez, Diane, 163, 176
Rodriguez, Francisco, 77
Rodriguez, Jaime, 112
Rodriguez, Ricardo, 83
Rodriguez, Todd, 177
Rodriquez, Robynn, 151
Roebling, Paul, 188
Roesch, William, 184
Roffman, Rose, 93, 218
Rogak, Gina, 54
Rogel, Randy, 172
Rogers, Anne, 218
Rogers, Christopher, 74
Rogers, Dinah Anne, 146
Rogers, Elizabeth, 9
Rogers, Gil, 66, 218
Rogers, Harriet, 179
Rogers, Ken Leigh, 130
Rogers, Mark H., 166
Rogers, Michael, 153
Rogers, Patrick, 76
Rogers, Ric, 80, 107
Rogers, Robert, 26, 45
Rogers, Roxanne, 67
Rogers, Shelley, 119
Rogers, Wayne M., 6
Rogerson, Gus, 186
Roggensack, David, 24, 50, 57, 60, 61, 68, 79, 96, 101
Rogosky, Michelle, 182
Rohrbacker, Jacqueline, 145
Rohrer, Sue Ellen, 112
Rohrig, William, 139
Roland, Paul, 185
Rolfe, Lalla, 177
Rolfe, Mickey, 62
Rolfe, Penny, 62
Rolfing, Tom, 177
Rollins, Lisa, 112
Rolph, Marti, 188
Roman, Arlene, 112, 218
Roman, Kelly, 101
Romance Language, 146, 147
Romano, Annette, 136
Romano, Lisa, 57
Romano, Maria, 179
Rome, Jo Ann, 154
Romeo and Juliet, 160, 165, 175, 176, 183, 186
Romeo, Marc, 72
Rommen, Ann-Christin, 141
Ronan, Brian, 57, 75
Ronn, Susan, 175
Rood, Carol, 142
Rooks, Joel, 69
Room Service, 115
Rooney, Mickey, 133, 188
Roop, Reno, 138
Roos, Casper, 92, 130, 166, 179, 218
Root, Melina, 92, 105
Root, Stephen, 76, 140, 179
Ropes, Bradford, 127
Rosa, Dennis, 121
Rosager, Lars, 49
Rosario, Adrian, 40
Rosario, Jose Ramon, 107
Rosario, Raymond, 104
Rosario, Willie, 124
Rosato, Mary Lou, 82, 94
Rosborough, Brett C., 122
Rose Cottages, 91
Rose Tattoo, The, 187
Rose, Andrea, 133
Rose, Bob, 25
Rose, Carin, 184
Rose, Cristine, 159
Rose, George, 20, 21, 106, 122, 218
Rose, Hugh A., 132
Rose, Jack Anthony, 57, 72
Rose, Jennifer, 78
Rose, Jill, 168
Rose, Joseph, 175
Rose, Lynn, 128
Rose, Marta, 62
Rose, Norman, 57
Rose, Phillip, 151
Rose, Renee, 151
Rose, Reva, 188
Rose, Richard, 165, 166
Rose, Ruth, 81
Rosen by Any Other Name, A, 86
Rosen, Cheryl, 80
Rosen, Daniel, 133
Rosen, Louis, 82, 159
Rosen, Madelon, 29, 64, 102, 112
Rosen, Penny S., 100
Rosen, Sheldon, 113, 151
Rosenbaum, Robert A., 144
Rosenberg, D. C., 57, 96
Rosenberg, Stuart, 64
Rosenblatt, Jana, 105
Rosenblum, M. Edgar, 162
Rosencrantz and Guildenstern Are Dead, 149, 187
Rosenfeld, Moishe, 66
Rosenfield, Lois F., 7
Rosenfield, Maurice, 7
Rosenstein, Howard, 154, 186
Rosenstock, Milton, 134
Rosenstock, Susan, 138, 155
Rosensweig, Russ Lori, 12
Rosentel, Robert W., 79, 97
Rosenthal, Andrew R., 100
Rosenthal, Bernice M., 142
Rosenthal, Cindy, 184
Rosenthal, Lawrence, 116
Roshe, Deborah, 128
Roslevich, John, Jr., 171
Rosoff, Barbara, 98, 171
Rosqui, Tom, 173, 184
Ross, Anita, 69, 80
Ross, Anthony, 114
Ross, Audrey, 78
Ross, Carmella, 65
Ross, Carolyn L., 171
Ross, Cassandra, 169
Ross, Dylan, 61, 218
Ross, Elizabeth J., 179
Ross, Jaclyn, 161
Ross, Jamie, 49, 169, 218
Ross, Kathryn, 114
Ross, Philip, 144
Ross, Richard, 61
Ross, Tessa, 182
Ross, Timmie, 78
Rosse, Steve, 71
Rossen, Howard, 93
Rosser, Kip, 76
Rossetter, Kathy, 118
Rossetti, Christina, 119
Rossi, Al, 163
Rossi, Cheryl Ann, 81
Rossignol, 79
Rossomando, Teresa, 72
Rostand, Edmond, 125, 156
Roswell, Maggie, 218
Rota, Rob, 64
Rotenberg, David, 16
Roth, Ann, 6, 7, 38, 43, 47, 97, 123
Roth, Beatrice, 58
Roth, Jane, 110
Roth, Joshua, 61
Roth, Michael S., 81
Roth, Phil, 163
Roth, Wolfgang, 157
Roth-Casson, Hane, 186
Rothauser, David, 166
Rothberg, Russell, 75
Rothe, Sharon, 153
Rothhaar, Michael, 90, 218
Rothman, Carole, 116
Rothman, John, 38
Rothman, Stephen, 144, 167
Rothschild, Ami, 63
Rotondo, David, 178
Rounds, Danny, 124
Rounds, David, 188
Routh, Mark, 61
Routolo, Robert, 60, 146
Rovang, Mari, 138, 156
Rowe, Dee Etta, 145
Rowe, G. F., 179
Rowe, Greg T., 168
Rowe, Hansford, 7
Rowe, Stephen, 218
Rowe, Tonia, 158
Rowell, Jody, 175
Rowen, Jacqueline, 87
Rowse, A. L., 144
Royal Comedians, The, 137
Royal Flush, 113
Royce, Becket, 170
Roznowski, Rob, 169
Ruane, JayneRobin, 173
Rubens, Herbert, 60, 86
Rubenstein, Jay, 47
Rubeo, Ed, 93, 218
Rubin, Arthur, 40
Rubin, Brady, 146
Rubin, John Gould, 179, 180
Rubin, Judith, 113
Rubin, Julia, 64
Rubin, Margaret, 185
Rubin, Stan, 96, 218
Rubin, Steven, 64, 111, 162
Rubin, Tara Jayne, 33
Rubin, Vicki, 88
Rubins, Marjorie A., 131
Rubinstein, Carol, 179
Rubinstein, John, 188, 218
Rubio, Isabel, 93
Ruch, Roz, 170
Ruck, Alan, 47, 164
Rucker, Bo, 180, 188, 218
Rucker, Edward W., 177
Rudd, Paul, 141

Ruddy, Donn, 138
Rude, John, 106
Rudge, Michael, 169
Rudin, Stuart, 93
Rudolph, Buddy, 121, 218
Rudy, Bradley C., 186
Rue, Lisa, 142
Ruehl, Mercedes, 18, 57
Rule, Charles, 77, 218
Rum and Coke, 107
Rumbaugh, Gretchen, 172
Rumpf, Robin, 111, 116, 143
Run for Your Wife, 167
Runnels, Terry, 159
Runyon, Damon, 140
Runzo, David, 153
Ruocco, Sue, 174
Ruoti, Helena, 170
Rupert, Michael, 40, 41, 188, 192, 193, 218
Rupnik, Kevin, 76, 116, 151, 168, 171
Rupp, Debra Jo, 121
Rupp, Tom, 137
Ruscio, Elizabeth, 137, 146, 163
Rush, Deborah, 23
Rush, Jo Anna, 58, 66, 218
Rush, Sarah, 170
Russ, R. Sebastian, 77, 90
Russell, Anne, 77
Russell, Bennie, 113
Russell, Catherine, 25
Russell, Cathy, 218, 219
Russell, George, 37
Russell, Kimberly, 116
Russell, Lee, 120
Russell, Rebecca, 181
Russell, Rusty, 64
Russell, Stephen, 154, 186
Russell, Tom, 123
Russell, Willy, 145, 166
Russo, F. Wade, 162
Russo, James, 188
Russo, Larry, 186
Russom, Leon, 179
Russotto, Michael, 143
Ruta, Ken, 144
Ruth, 172
Ruth, Anita, 144
Ruth, Richard Lee, 127
Rutkowski, Mary Elizabeth, 143
Rutter, Anne, 127
Rutter, Nancy, 79
Ruyle, Deloria, 63
Ruymen, Ayn, 188
Ruzika, Donna, 173
Ruzika, Tom, 163, 173
Ryack, Rita, 54, 67, 99, 111, 130
Ryan, Catherine B., 158
Ryan, Dierdre, 90
Ryan, George, 184
Ryan, Greg, 100
Ryan, James, 91
Ryan, Jennie, 78
Ryan, Kenneth, 107
Ryan, Michael, 139
Ryan, Nancy, 185
Ryan, Robert S., 102
Ryan, Steve, 18
Ryan, Steven, 218
Ryan, Thomas, 164
Ryan, Tina, 29
Rydbert, Steven, 152
Ryder, Amy, 58
Ryder, Richard, 138, 160, 174
Ryecart, Patrick, 179
Ryland, Jack, 159
Ryoji, Takeshiba, 8
Ryskind, Morrie, 230
Ryton, Royce, 146
Sabatelli, Linda, 49
Sabath, Bernard, 44, 160
Sabellico, Richard, 58, 218, 219
Sabin, David, 71, 178
Sabino, Frank, 101
Sable, Stanley, 46
Sabo, Linda, 175
Sabovik, John, 157
Sacco, Donna, 101
Sacher, Helen, 175
Sachter, Robert L., 152
Sadanji, Ichikawa IV, 8
Saddler, Donald, 66
Sadler, Bill, 47
Saex, Robin, 98
Safety, 177
Saffer, Lisa, 141
Safford-Clark, Max, 107
Saffran, Christina, 80
Safier, Gloria, 230
Sagal, Kathy, 146
Sager, Carole Bayer, 92
Sager, Janice E., 92
Sager, Tom Gene, 7
Sahagen, Nikki, 155
Saint Joan, 159
Saint John, Cal, 72
Saint of Bleecker Street, The, 187
Saint, David, 167
Saint, Eva Marie, 188
Saint-Clair, Marie, 176
Sakon, Onoe, 8
Saks, Gene, 6, 47, 123
Saks, Mark, 69
Sakura-Hime Azuma Bunsho, 8
Sala, Ed, 114, 177
Salaks, Tina, 92, 112
Salammbo, 65
Salamone, Kathleen, 176
Salamone, Nick, 218
Salata, Gregory, 106, 218
Sale, Deborah, 169
Sale, James, 139, 158, 179
Salem, Bill, 77
Salerni, Lou, 185
Salib, Nada, 184
Salinger, Ross, 154
Salisbury, Fran, 85
Salks, Tina, 92
Sallows, Tracy, 162
Salmon, Scott, 50
Salmons, Melissa, 63
Salomon, Lisa, 59
Salovitz, David, 77
Salt, Jennifer, 188
Salter, Richard, 168
Saltz, Amy, 110, 179
Saltzman, Kenneth R., 90
Saltzman, Robert, 129
Salvatore, John, 127
Salvio, Robert, 188
Sambula, Daniel, 65
Samels, Matthew, 184
Sammler, Bronislaw, 180
Sampogna, Anne, 127
Sampson, Arden, 54, 92, 218, 219
Sampson, Julia, 83
Samuels, Steven, 65
Samuelsohn, Howard, 106
Sanchez, Esteban Fernandez, 60
Sanchez, Jaime, 188
Sand Mountain Matchmaking, 179
Sandefur, Jim, 137, 154, 171, 172
Sandel, Oran, 143
Sanders, Charles, 59, 139
Sanders, Chris, 16, 68, 76
Sanders, Fred, 65, 98, 218
Sanders, Henry G., 163
Sanders, Jane, 88, 89
Sanders, Jay O., 121, 218
Sanders, Jeff, 58
Sanders, Michael, 34, 59
Sanders, Nick, 76
Sanders, Pete, 7, 24, 50, 57, 58, 59, 60, 61, 66, 68, 69, 81, 96, 128
Sandlund, Debra, 164
Sando, Jerry, 172
Sandoe, Samuel, 183
Sandoval, Michael, 176
Sands, Diana, 188
Sandy, Gary, 167
Sandy, Lynne, 66
Sanfilippo, Michael, 128
Sanford, Beth, 59, 139
Sanford, Clark, 136
Sanford, Tim, 118
Sanker, Jeffrey, 57
Sankowich, Lee, 170
Sansonia, Michael, 81
Santacroce, Mary Nell, 138, 140
Santarelli, Gene, 59
Santee, Christopher, 125
Santell, Marie, 50, 218
Santiago, Socorro, 77, 218
Santo, Michael, 172
Santopietro, Thomas P., 12, 27
Santoriello, Alex, 83
Santos, Loida, 45
Sapp, Jim, 34, 36, 46, 49, 115
Sapp, R. LaChanze, 32
Sappington, Margo, 51
Saputo, Peter J., 83, 119, 218, 219
Saracino, Frank, 63
Sardi, Vincent, 80
Sargent, Mary, 230
Sargent, Peter, 171
Sarno, Janet, 61, 160
Saroyan, William, 101, 162
Sarp, Karen, 169
Sassone, Vinnie, 62
Sater, Steven, 69
Sato, Isao, 142
Sato, Shozo, 161
Sato, Suzanne M., 88
Saucier, John, 134
Sauer, Bernard, 64
Saunders, Anne, 151
Saunders, Fred, 113
Saunders, Kim, 73
Savage in Limbo, 61
Savage, Keith, 155
Savage, Melodee, 55, 167
Savage, Mimi, 157
Savin, Ron Lee, 179
Saviola, Camille, 218
Savitski, Cindy Jo, 161
Sawyer, Cathey Crowell, 143
Saxon, Jamie, 164
Sayers, Dorothy, 142
Sayers, Michael, 179
Sbano, James, 135
Sbarge, Raphael, 60, 119, 220, 225
Scala, David, 50
Scalera, Niki, 91, 220
Scales, Robert, 18, 57, 172
Scalise, Thomas David, 135, 220
Scally, James, 163
Scanlan, John, 171
Scanlon, Dorothy, 142
Scanlon, Maureen, 162
Scarbrough, Janeice, 120
Scardino, Don, 98, 116
Scardino, Frank, 80
Scarfe, Alan, 71, 186
Scarlata, Estala, 176
Scarpulla, Clare, 147
Schachter, David, 168
Schact, Sam, 86, 220
Schacter, Steven, 149
Schaefer, Nancy, 12, 26, 40
Schaeffer, Eric, 150
Schafer, Michael, 77
Schafroth, Ellen, 162
Schakel, Nancy, 110
Schall, Thomas, 148, 153, 159
Schanker, Larry, 154
Schanuel, Greg, 127
Scharbrough, Dan, 145
Schatz, Mari S., 78
Schauermann, Michael V., 136
Schaut, Ann Louise, 220
Schay, Danial L., 165, 166
Schear, Robert, 31
Schechter, Joel, 180
Schecter, Les, 51
Scheer, Loretta, 65
Scheerer, Bob, 188
Schein, Gideon Y., 76
Schein, Jeremy, 100
Scheine, Raynor, 180
Scheitinger, Tony, 146
Schelble, William, 14, 20, 25, 28, 44, 45
Scheldt, Coby, 175
Schenck, Ann G., 150
Schendel, James, 184
Schenk, Ernie, 61, 70
Schenk, William M., 182
Schenker, Joel W., 230
Schenkkan, Robert, 54, 175
Scherer, John, 57, 58, 167
Scherer, Marita, 160
Schermer, Phil, 136
Schermer, Shelley Henze, 136
Schertler, Nancy, 111, 143
Schiappa, John, 134
Schickle, Peter, 51
Schierholz, Peg, 110, 111
Schierhorn, Paul, 16
Schiff, Eric, 146
Schifter, Peter Mark, 101
Schimmel, Bill, 84
Schimmel, John, 167
Schirmer, Tim, 181
Schisgal, Murray, 145, 175
Schissler, Jeffrey, 83
Schlachter, Mona, 42
Schlackman, Marc, 15
Schlaht, William, 181
Schlamme, Martha, 230
Schlarth, Sharon, 89, 220, 225
Schleinig, Robert, 178
Schler, Michael S., 72, 77, 90, 131
Schlesinger, Kurt, 100
Schloss, Edwin W., 75
Schlosser, Leo, 183
Schlosser, Robert J., 146
Schmidt, Charles, 182
Schmidt, Douglas, 129, 146, 184
Schmidt, Harvey, 52, 159
Schmidt, Jack, 72, 220
Schmidt, Paul, 146
Schmidt, Robert, 183
Schmidtke, Ned, 122, 220
Schmiechen, Richard, 33
Schmiel, Bill, 171
Schmitz, Kristen A., 122
Schmutte, Peter, 145
Schnabel, Stefan, 38, 220
Schnedk, Edward, 124
Schneider, Barbara, 24, 134
Schneider, Carol, 60, 91
Schneider, Eliza, 153
Schneider, Helen, 161
Schneider, Jana, 20, 21, 106, 220
Schneider, Jeffrey, 96, 148
Schneider, Lauren Class, 65
Schneider, Pat, 113
Schneider, Susie, 98
Schnetzer, Stephen, 57, 164
Schnirman, David, 158
Schnitzler, Arthur, 105
Schoch, Carlotta, 33, 59
Schoditsch, Peggy, 163
Schoen, Walter, 144
Schoenbaum, Donald, 156
Schoenbaum, Milly, 55, 61, 66, 120
Schoenfeld, Barry, 85
Schofield, Scott, 143
Scholes, James, 170
Scholtens, Gene, 96
Scholtz, Christina, 154
Schonberg, Michal, 186
School for Scandal, The, 181
School for Wives, The, 166
Schoppert, Bill, 63
Schott, Melissa, 145
Schramm, David, 164
Schreiber, Terry, 175
Schreiner, Warner, 102, 220
Schrniman, David, 106
Schroeder, William, 149, 152, 179
Schroll, Julie, 142
Schubart, Mark, 63
Schuberg, Carol, 172
Schubert, Alan, 130
Schubert, Paul, 85
Schuenemann, E. R., 166
Schuh, Richard, 142
Schuler, Hal, 80, 92
Schull, Rebecca, 86, 162, 220
Schultz, Carol, 145
Schultz, Jacqueline, 54
Schulz, Brian, 165
Schulz, Karen, 54
Schurch, Bernie, 78
Schurr, Carl, 165
Schuster, Hilde, 148
Schutt, Debra, 186
Schwab, John, 172, 175
Schwartz, Andrea, 70
Schwartz, Becky, 144
Schwartz, Bonnie Nelson, 31
Schwartz, Clifford, 121
Schwartz, Delmore, 147
Schwartz, Gil, 98
Schwartz, Laurence, 59
Schwartz, Michael, 72, 75
Schwartz, Robert Joel, 110
Schwartz, Roni, 72
Schwartz, Stephen, 65, 169
Schwarz, Joe, 126
Schweickhardt, Kurt, 156
Schweid, Carole, 93, 220
Schwenk, Joan, 164
Schweppe, Jeanna, 127
Schwinn, Ron, 49
Schwinn, Tom, 99
Sciarro, JoLynn, 78
Scirpo, Michele, 58
Scnierholz, Peg, 23
Scofield, Pamela, 76, 94, 153
Scoles, Tony, 184
Scott, Brad, 83
Scott, Campbell, 23
Scott, Casandra, 102
Scott, Charles M., 153
Scott, Cheryl Ann, 32
Scott, Christopher, 77, 142
Scott, Clifford R., 179
Scott, Daniel D., 14
Scott, Dennis, 180
Scott, Farnham, 61
Scott, Gayton, 162, 182
Scott, George C., 44, 188, 220
Scott, Hal, 171
Scott, Harold, 149
Scott, Kimberly, 180
Scott, Mari, 109
Scott, Pamela S., 49
Scott, Pippa, 188
Scott, Robert Owens, 72
Scott, Ron, 127
Scott, Seret, 104, 220
Scott, Sharon E., 83
Scott, Susan Elizabeth, 58, 167, 220
Scott, Val, 152
Scriabin, Alexander, 161
Scripps, Sam, 80
Scrofano, Paula, 164
Scruggs, Sharon, 119
Scurria, Anne, 178
Scutieri, Jane, 169
Sea Marks, 145
Seader, Richard, 57, 76
Seagull A, 161
Seale, Douglas, 220, 225
Seale, Petie Trigg, 149
Seales, Franklyn, 163
Seamon, Edward, 88, 89, 220
Search for Signs of Intelligent Life in the Universe, The, 9, 172
Sears, Joe, 145, 153, 159, 167, 174, 184
Seascape With Sharks and Dancer, 94
Seascape, 187
Season's Greetings, 59, 160, 177, 179
Sebek, Herman W., 48
Sechrist, Linda, 167
Second Man, The, 94
Secor, Jonathan D., 158
Secrest, James, 153
Secret Dreams of Professor Isaac, The, 113
Sedgwick, Dan, 179
See Below Middle Sea, 147
Seed, Mimi, 142
Seeley, Stephanie Rae, 122
Seeman, Bernard E., 68
Seer, Richard, 188
Segal, Gury, 161
Segal, Kathrin King, 98, 220
Seger, Richard, 146, 184
Segovia, Claudio, 13
Segovia, Yolanda, 126
Seibert, John, 138
Seidel, Virginia, 81, 188, 220
Seidman, Amy, 62
Seidman, John, 114, 179, 220
Seinfeld, Barbara, 124
Seisser, Todd, 164
Seitz, John, 110
Selby, Ann, 186
Seldes, Marian, 70, 220
Self, Frank, 172
Selig, Susan, 61, 72, 91, 105
Sell, Janie, 184, 188
Sellars, Peter, 161
Sellers, Barbara, 151
Sellers, Jeff, 136
Sellon, Karen, 47
Sellon, Kim, 127
Selman-Pait, Abby, 173
Selting, Leigh, 139
Seltzer, Daniel, 188
Semel, Lisa, 162
Semeria, Yveline, 49
Semonin, David, 79
Senita, Susan, 177
Sennett, David, 90
Senske, Rebecca, 149
Serbagi, Roger, 175
Serban, Andrei, 14, 141
Serling, Rod, 166
Serpento, James, 177
Serrano, Nestor, 17, 108, 220
Serson, Paul, 101
Seruto, Nancy, 147
Sesma, Thom, 50, 220
Sessions, Cathy, 145
Seth, Roshan, 107
Seton, Mimi, 146, 147
Setrakian, Ed, 162
Settel, Ann, 75
Settler, Steve, 105
Sevec, Christine, 184
1776, 187
Sevier, Jack, 62
Sevin-Doering, Genevieve, 79
Sevra, Robert, 46
Sevy, Bruce K., 151
Sexton, Anne, 58
Sexton, Michael, 117
Sexton, Nancy Niles, 174
Sexton, Pia, 177
Seyler, Michele, 146
Seymour, Carolyn, 23
Seymour, Lynn, 182
Sh-Boom!, 83
Shabaka, 163
Shadburne, Jim, 140
Shade, Jeff, 40
Shadow Box, The, 187
Shadow and Substance, 187
Shafer, Roxanne, 113
Shaffer, Anthony, 174
Shaffer, Stephen, 60, 163, 173
Shaffer, Tracy, 163
Shaffner, Catherine, 177
Shafrir, Erez, 161
Shaheen, Dan, 80
Shahn, Judith, 136
Shairp, Mordaunt, 100
Shakar, Diane, 98
Shakar, Martin, 135
Shakes, David A., 153
Shakespeare, William, 59, 60, 63, 69, 78, 80, 90, 95, 100, 106, 110, 118, 121, 136, 138, 140, 143, 149, 152, 154, 156, 157, 160, 170, 171, 172, 173, 174, 175, 176, 179, 180, 181, 182, 184, 185, 186
Shalhoub, Tony, 6
Shalit, Willa, 57, 148
Shallat, Lee, 173
Shallo, Karen, 180
Shaman, Laurie, 181
Shamas, Laura, 151
Shamata, Michael, 154
Shame, 145
Shammai, Giora, 161
Shaner, Michael A., 146
Shange, Ntozake, 139
Shangraw, Howard, 146, 147, 173
Shanholtzer, Dale, 142
Shank, Adele Edling, 163
Shank, Theodore, 163
Shankman, Jim, 175
Shanks, Ann, 30
Shanks, Bob, 30
Shanks, Mark L., 146
Shanley, John Patrick, 61, 99
Shannon, Maureen, 143
Shannon, Peggy, 136
Shannon, Sandy, 121
Shanta, James, 47
Shaper, The, 137
Shapiro, Debbie, 78
Shapiro, Paul, 136, 175
Shapiro, Steve, 152
Shapiro, Whitey, 172
Sharaff, Irene, 134
Sharek, William, 158, 158
Sharma, Barbara, 161
Sharmat, Mary, 100
Sharp, Geoffrey, 47
Sharp, J. H., 113
Sharp, Kim, 120
Sharp, Larry, 145
Sharp, Mahlon, 145
Sharp, Michael, 80
Sharp, Penelope, 186
Shary, Linda, 64
Shatner, William, 188
Shaud, Grant, 86, 119
Shaw, Bob, 20, 46, 106, 108
Shaw, Christopher, 174
Shaw, David, 58
Shaw, Deborah, 61, 91, 119
Shaw, George Bernard, 115, 141, 144, 151, 153, 156, 157, 159, 162, 168, 177, 181
Shaw, Gillian, 121
Shaw, Glen Byam, 230
Shaw, Irwin, 96
Shaw, Lennie, 167
Shaw, Maggi, 144
Shaw, Marcie, 167
Shaw, Sheila, 163
Shaw, Steven, 81
Shaw, Vanessa, 83
Shawhan, April, 76, 171, 188, 220
Shawl, The, 97
Shawn, Allen, 106
Shawn, Michael, 58
Shawn, Wallace, 107
Shay, Michele, 73, 85, 149
Shayna Maidel, A: The Life of a Family, 157
Shayne, Tracy, 45
Shchaeffer, Viet, 168
She Loves Me, 92
She Stoops to Conquer, 170, 181, 186, 186
Shea, John V., 188
Shea, John, 192, 193
Shea, Lisa, 90
Shea, Maureen, 177
Shea, Roger, 76
Sheara, Nicola, 92, 148, 220, 225
Shearer, Andrew P., 15, 54, 65, 79
Shearman, Alan, 70, 220
Sheerin, James, 77, 90
Sheffer, Craig, 120
Sheffer, Geordie, 48
Sheffer, Isaiah, 153
Sheffer, Jonathan, 146
Sheffield, Peggy, 148
Shein, Kate, 69, 220
Sheldon, Anne, 177
Sheldon, L. A., 64
Shell, Claudia, 48
Shelley, Carole, 74, 115, 220
Shelley, Mary, 90
Shelley, Tamra, 182
Shelton, Timothy, 146, 173
Shelton, Tom, 173
Shen, Freda Foh, 33
Shenkel, Les, 69
Shepard, Duane, 80
Shepard, Eric, 192
Shepard, Harold, 76
Shepard, Jean, 100
Shepard, John, 137, 220
Shepard, Kelvin R., 140
Shepard, Sam, 51, 59, 67, 136, 144, 157, 163, 171, 173, 177
Shepard, Tina, 79
Shepherd, David, 61, 70
Shepherd, Gwendolyn, 129
Shepherd, Michael, 154, 186
Sheppard, Susan, 92, 220
Sherber, Ken, 78
Sheridan, John, 188
Sheridan, Kara, 87
Sheridan, Liz, 146
Sheridan, Peter, 163

Sheridan, Richard Brinsley, 181
Sheriff, Marina, 99
Sherin, Jeffrey, 169
Sherin, Pamela Vevers, 164
Sherlock's Last Case, 159
Sherman, Arthur, 135
Sherman, Howard, 54, 157
Sherman, Iris, 169
Sherman, Jonathan Marc, 86, 220
Sherman, Keith, 56, 115, 121, 122, 127, 135
Sherman, Loren, 65, 111, 146, 172
Sherman, Martin, 159, 175
Sherrick, David, 90
Sherrill, Brad, 140
Sherrill, Donald, 145
Sherwin, Mimi, 62, 220
Sherwood, Madeleine, 101
Sherwood, Robert E., 151, 161, 163
Sherwood, Toba, 57, 220
Shevbany, Sarvi, 163
Shevelove, Burt, 145, 162
Shibajaku, Nakamura VII, 8
Shibaraku, 8
Shick, Caryn, 147
Shield, Harvey, 64
Shield, Kathryn, 80, 117
Shields, Brooke, 76, 220
Shields, Timothy J., 164
Shilhanek, Thomas, 59, 62, 64
Shimabuku, Norris M., 109
Shimada, Shigeo, 8
Shimer, Susan, 175
Shimerman, Armin, 163
Shimizu, Sachi, 45
Shimko, Dalya, 161
Shimono, Sab, 147, 163
Shine, Stephanie, 185
Shinn, Peter H., 140
Shiomi, R. A., 109
Shire, David, 178
Shively, Debby, 145
Shoemaker's Prodigious Wife, The, 176
Shoemaker, Jeff, 66
Shofner, Susan, 66
Shokaku, Onoe II, 8
Shook, Robert, 166
Shook, Warner, 147
Shop on Main Street, The, 96
Shoroku, Onoe II, 8
Short Change, 60
Short Eyes, 187
Short, John, 46, 220
Short, Sylvia, 153, 177
Shorts '85, 137
Shortt, Paul, 149
Shoults, Lenore Nalezny, 122
Shovestull, Thom, 58, 59, 69
Show, Grant, 17
Show-Off, The, 170
Shrank, Caroline, 182
Shrike, The, 187
Shriver, Christopher J., 79, 167
Shroads, Sandi, 144
Shropshire, Anne, 149
Shropshire, Noble, 174, 220
Shrout, Rich, 162
Shue, Larry, 54, 106, 139, 167, 173, 174, 175, 177, 230
Shulman, Connie, 58, 63
Shulman, Deborah, 124
Shulman, Jonathan, 114
Shultis, Elizabeth A., 149
Shultz, Philip, 220
Shuman, David Stewart, 170
Shumate, Deborah, 179
Shurr, Carl, 165
Shushan, Elle, 17
Shuttleworth, Bill, 16, 46, 49, 69, 70, 72, 94, 127
Shvachkin, Igor, 79
Shwarz, Robin, 113
Shyre, Paul, 174
Sibley, William J., 66
Sicangco, Eduardo, 157
Siccardi, Arthur, 6, 26, 33, 47, 126, 130
Sickle, Luke, 14, 158
Sicular, Robert, 182
Siders, Irving, 126
Siebert, Ron, 144
Siefert, Lynn, 161
Siegel, David, 167
Siegel, Jason, 142
Siegenfeld, Billy, 73
Siegler, Ben, 81, 110, 146, 220
Siegmund, Nan, 68, 86, 112
Siemaszko, Nina, 154
Sienkiewicz, Carol, 63
Siering, James, 163
Sigler, Scott, 128
Signorelli, Tom, 97, 220
Silbar, Adam, 47
Silber, David, 122, 159
Silberman, Betty, 63
Silbert, Peter, 136
Siler, Patrick, 171
Silford, Dan, 169
Silk Stockings, 73
Silliman, Maureen, 173
Sills, Pawnee, 220
Silva, Donald, 69, 112, 220, 225
Silva, Marie-Louise, 16, 18, 40, 70, 76, 81, 94
Silver, Jennifer, 182
Silver, Joan Micklin, 177
Silver, Joe, 116, 220
Silver, Len, 113, 119
Silver, Matthew, 54
Silver, Phillip, 186
Silver, Ron, 38, 220
Silver, Stanley, 18, 57
Silverman, Jefrey, 58
Silverman, Jon D., 65
Silverman, Jonathan, 47, 220
Silverman, Stanley, 71, 154, 186
Silvers, Phil, 230, 231
Silverstein, Steve, 78
Silvert, Peter, 136
Silvestri, Martin, 140
Siman, Barbara, 15
Simes, Douglas, 110, 220
Simi, Pamela, 141
Simione, Donn, 7, 146
Simmons, Andy, 81
Simmons, Bonnie, 48
Simmons, Matina, 64
Simmons, Matty, 81
Simmons, Stanley, 134
Simmons, Ted, Jr., 83
Simmons, Velma, 71
Simo, Mary Lou, 87
Simon, Avivah, 79
Simon, Deborah, 177
Simon, Marcia, 114
Simon, Marion, 178
Simon, Mark, 36
Simon, Mayo, 163
Simon, Meg, 6, 12, 23, 34, 42, 47, 123, 161
Simon, Nancy, 38, 147
Simon, Neil, 6, 40, 47, 92, 123, 145, 152
Simon, Nelson, 72
Simon, Sarah, 149
Simon, Scott, 173
Simonelli, Anna, 169
Simons, Leslie A., 220
Simonson, Roald, 172
Simonson, Timothy, 107
Simonton, Robert, 72
Simotes, Tony, 146
Simpson, C. J., 97
Simpson, Eileen, 147
Simpson, Julia, 83
Simpson, Preston, 169
Simpson, Rick, 95
Simpson, Scott, 69
Simpson, Zene Olivia Latrice, 172
Sinclair, Barbara, 64
Sinclair, Eric, 188
Sinclair, Gabrielle, 78, 173
Sinclair, Madge, 163
Sing for Your Supper, 165
Singelis, James, 162
Singer, Connie, 116, 160
Singer, Larry, 179
Singer, Marla, 49, 220
Singer, Pamela, 85, 98
Singer, Stephen, 96
Singer, Steve, 75
Singh, Yvonne, 69
Singhaus, Sam, 50
Singin' in the Rain, 7, 189
Sinise, Gary, 28, 161
Sinnott, Deirdre, 125
Sipes, Ron, 182
Siravo, Joseph, 61
Siretta, Dan, 162
Sisson, Judianne, 176
Sister Mary Ignatius Explains It All for You, 160
Sister and Miss Lexie, 116, 166
Sisto, Rocco, 84, 90, 220
Sitler, Steve, 77, 80, 90
Sitomer, Joan, 66
Skaggs, Marsha, 55, 220, 225
Skala, Lilia, 96, 221
Skatula, Kathryn, 146
Skell, Aviva, 118, 221
Skelton, Thomas, 12, 30, 129, 146
Skidmore, Karen, 186
Skiles, Kevin, 165
Skill, Laura, 163
Skin of Our Teeth, The, 150, 187
Skinker, Sherry, 152
Skinner, Doug, 143
Skinner, Kate, 172
Skinner, Margo, 170, 178
Skinner, Randy, 127, 221
Skipitaris, Lukas, 114
Skipper, Linda, 60
Skipper, Mare, 182
Skiptaris, Loukas, 221
Skizlak, Kathy, 133
Skloff, Michael, 65
Skriloff, Nina, 50
Skroman, Susan, 75
Skrovan, Steve, 98, 168
Slaiman, Marjorie, 143
Slanda, Michelle, 165
Slater, Andy, 142
Slater, Christian, 80, 221
Slater, Marilee, 137
Slater, Michael, 142
Slaughter, Brenda, 81
Sleeping Beauty, 168
Sleeping Dogs, 147
Sleuth, 144, 174, 187
Slezak, Victor, 62, 101, 221
Sliwinski, Jennifer, 164
Sloan, Amanda, 182
Sloan, Gary, 159
Sloan, Larry, 154
Sloan, Lenwood, 85, 103
Sloan, Patty Gideon, 87
Sloane, Christine, 144
Sloman, John, 15, 221
Slotin, Jane, 119
Slow Fire, 147
Slowiak, James, 147
Slutsker, Peter, 7
Smadbeck, David, 140
Smaga, Jacqueline J., 162
Small Nights of Terror, 177
Small, Larry, 221
Small, Liz, 105, 157
Small, Neva, 66, 221
Small, Peg, 65, 179
Small, Robert Graham, 77, 80, 90
Small, Scott, 169
Smallwood, Alan, 80
Smart, Jean, 147
Smart, Richard, 176
Smartt, Michael V., 162
Smaw, Debbie, 184
Smeltzer, Steven, 162
Smiar, Brian, 63
Smiley, Brenda, 188
Smiley, Roger, 61
Smith, Adrienne Hampton, 175
Smith, Alice Elliott, 141
Smith, Andre, 149
Smith, Archie, 151
Smith, Barbara H., 148
Smith, Brandon, 139
Smith, Brendan, 106
Smith, Carl, 182
Smith, Dana, 180
Smith, David, 154
Smith, Derek D., 82, 120
Smith, Douglas D., 163
Smith, Dugg, 110
Smith, Elizabeth, 108, 141, 162
Smith, Ennis, 109
Smith, Ernest Allen, 142
Smith, Evelyn, 58
Smith, Felton, 68
Smith, Frances, 106, 107, 108
Smith, Frank, 136
Smith, Fred G., 101
Smith, Geddeth, 184
Smith, Glenn, 182
Smith, Grady, 152
Smith, Irene, 114
Smith, J. Scott, 93, 221
Smith, J. Thomas, 49
Smith, James, 144
Smith, Jeffrey, 162
Smith, Jennifer, 50, 111, 221, 225
Smith, Judith T., 151, 164
Smith, Justin, 230
Smith, Katherine, 149
Smith, Kelly, 151
Smith, Kendall, 166
Smith, Kendred T., 162
Smith, Kent, 232
Smith, Kevin, 175
Smith, Kiki, 186
Smith, Laurel, 93
Smith, Leland P., 163
Smith, Lindsay, 136, 172
Smith, Lindsey Margo, 157
Smith, Louise, 221
Smith, Malcolm, 160
Smith, Maryann D., 77, 87
Smith, Maxine, 139
Smith, Melissa, 173
Smith, Michael C., 68, 79
Smith, Michael J., 172
Smith, Michael O., 101, 144, 167
Smith, Muriel Burrell, 232
Smith, Oliver, 135, 171
Smith, Patrick, 173
Smith, Peter, 86
Smith, Peyton, 161
Smith, Priscilla, 108, 161
Smith, Rex, 134, 188, 221
Smith, Robin Lynn, 59
Smith, Rodney J., 151
Smith, Roger, 107
Smith, Rusty, 22, 180
Smith, Sally, 121
Smith, Sandra, 188
Smith, Sheila, 188
Smith, Tambra, 140
Smith, Tina, 93
Smith, Vicki, 144
Smith, Vincent D., 85, 103
Smith, Wynona, 57
Smith-Cameron, J., 62, 99, 175, 221
Smith-Middleman, Sylvia, 170
Smith-Niles, Jerry, 162
Smitrovich, Bill, 168
Smitty's News, 137
Smolendki, Richard, 144
Smolens, Jeanne C., 132
Smoots, Jonathan, 181
Smothers, William, 188
Smukler, Amy, 186
Smul, Jennifer, 116
Smyth, Molly, 123
Smythe, Marcus, 125
Sneed, Philip Charles, 185
Sneed, Terry, 143
Snider, Barry, 158, 158
Snipes, Wesley, 17, 33
Snitkin, Marla, 142
Snizek, David, 92
Snovell, William, 95
Snow, Dan, 131
Snow, Donna, 174, 221
Snow, Norman, 118
Snyder, Hellen, 157
Snyder, Julie, 153
Snyder, Patricia B., 152
So Long on Lonely Street, 76, 140
Sobek, Allan, 128
Sobel, Shepard, 110
Sobol, Edna, 161
Sobol, Joshua, 161
Soccadato, Nickolas, 106
Social Security, 38
Sockwell, Sally, 143
Soddu, Antonio, 116
Soeder, Fran, 96, 155
Sofronski, Bernie, 17
Sohmers, Barbara, 129, 144, 148
Sohn, Amy, 80
Sokolow, Peter, 66
Soldier's Play, A, 187
Soldiers and Sons, 119
Soldo, Sally, 177
Solinger, Laura, 182
Solis, Alba, 13
Solis, Jeffrey, 152
Solo Voyages, 60,
Solomon, Wayne, 171
Soloway, Leonard, 38
Soma, Kiyotsune, 8
Soma, Maria, 64
Some Enchanted Evenings: Songs of Rodgers and Hammerstein, The, 160
Some Things You Need to Know Before the World Ends, 137
Somers, Melodie, 43, 97, 98
Somerville, Phyllis, 61, 171
Something Unspoken, 113
Something's Afoot, 158, 166
Somewheres Better, 119
Somlyo, Roy A., 32
Somma, Maria, 29, 102, 112
Sommer, Josef, 108, 221
Sommers, Allison, 60, 75
Sommers, Avery, 151
Sondergaard, Gale, 231, 232
Sondheim, Stephen, 134, 145, 149, 161, 162, 167
Song and Dance, 10, 11
Songs of Love and Money, 90
Sonnino, Gabriel, 72
Sontag, Ellen, 93
Soon, Terry, 146
Soper, Tony, 136, 172, 175
Sophocles, 110,
Sorel, Eve, 59, 93
Sorensen, Karen, 49
Sorenson, Cheri, 175
Soriero, Jim, 134
Sorrows and Sons, 119
Sosnow, Pat, 106, 108
Soteras, Zorba, 99
Sotolongo, David, 79
Sotts, Sally, 123
Soukup, Elizabeth A., 121
Soul of a Jew, The, 161
Soule, Robert D., 178
Sound of Music, The, 142, 187
Sound of a Voice, The, 163
Sousa, Pamela, 79
South Pacific, 187
Southard, Paige, 152
Southcotte, Georgia, 144, 168
Southern Lights, 81
Southern, Daniel, 179
Souvenir, 147
Souvenirs, 151
Sowle, John, 64
Spacey, Kevin, 42, 161, 221
Spackman, Tom, 90, 221, 225
Spaisman, Zypora, 63, 221
Spalding Gray, 97
Spalla, John, 7
Spanbock, Betsy, 111
Spangler, Andy, 79, 93, 145
Spanish Tragedie, The, 77, 90
Spano, Nealla, 96, 221
Spare Seraphim, The, 61
Sparer, Kathryn C., 114, 221
Sparks, Don, 146, 163
Sparks, Rick, 48, 161
Spartz, Stacey, 142
Speaker, Dan, 146
Spear, Cary Anne, 143
Special, The, 96
Spector, Donna, 73
Speelman, Patricia Ann, 149
Speer, Alexander, 137
Speer, Marla, 92
Spellen, Suzanne, 78
Spelvin, George, 79, 146
Spelvin, Robert, 176
Spence, Jean, 54
Spencer, Amy, 7, 78
Spencer, John, 33, 91, 156
Spencer, Paul, 71
Spencer, Rebecca, 167
Spencer, Robert, 174
Spencer, Sally, 124
Spencer, Steve, 144
Spencer, Vernon, 126
Spera, Rob, 137
Speranza, Ilya, 74
Sperberg, Fritz, 76
Sperdakos, George, 173
Sperduto, Al, 62, 78
Speros, Tia, 62, 221
Spetrino, Ron, 84
Spewack, Bella, 139, 142
Spewack, Samuel, 139, 142
Spialek, Hans, 81
Spiegel, Barbara, 86, 98, 221
Spigelgass, Leonard, 232
Spina, Anthony, 125
Spindell, Ahvi, 72, 149, 221
Spindt, Carla, 185
Spiner, Anthony, 125
Spiner, Brent, 46
Spinetti, Joel, 64
Spinetti, Victor, 188
Spiritus, Lisa, 173
Spiro, Bernard, 96
Spittle, James, 165
Spitzer, Helene, 98
Spivak, Alba, 32
Spivey, Brian K., 154
Spoon River Anthology, 144
Spore, Richard, 154, 180
Sporing, Alan, 60, 112
Spray, Tom, 59
Sprecher, Ben, 70
Spring Awakening, 139
Springer, John, 193
Springston, Steve, 172
Springtime for Henry, 115
Sprinsock, Eben, 35, 97
Squadra, Carol, 65
Squibb, June, 77, 221, 225
Squires, Chris, 146
Sroka, Elliot, 79
Srubar, Jeanette, 95
St. Germain, Joan, 166
St. Germain, Mark, 64, 68, 121
St. John, Marco, 108, 218
Stach, David Alan, 174
Stack, Richard, 132
Stacklin, Andy, 67, 163
Stadlen, Lewis J., 6, 79, 188, 221
Stafford, Larry T., 181
Stafford, Richard, 124
Stafford, Ronald, 45
Stafford-Clark, Max, 107
Stage Struck, 177
Stahl, Mary Leigh, 158
Stahlhuth, Gayle, 113, 221
Stait, Brent, 154, 186
Staller, David, 78, 155
Stallings, Laurence, 78
Stallings, Lauri, 169
Stancati, Frank, 122
Stanfield, Bob, 182
Stanford, Katherine, 141
Stanley, Chuck, 78
Stanley, Donna, 177
Stanley, Dorothy, 58, 167, 221
Stanley, Florence, 99, 221
Stanley, Gordon, 121, 177, 221
Stanley, Joan, 168
Stanley, Kim, 188
Stanley, Mark W., 59
Stanton, Robert, 106, 107, 115, 170, 221, 225
Stanton, Robin, 177
Stanzione, Chris, 143
Stapleford, Tom, 150
Stapleton, Chris, 79
Stapleton, Christopher, 109
Stapleton, Maureen, 188, 192, 193
Stark, Douglas Edward, 145
Stark, Mary, 153
Stark, Suzanne, 145
Starke, Anthony, 173
Starobin, Michael, 20, 106
Starr, Lee, 58
Starr, Mike, 107, 167
Starrett, Charles, 232
Starrs, John, 154
Stasica, Victoria, 151
State of the Union, 187
Staternow, Tim, 180
Stathis, Nicholas John, 77, 90
Stattel, Robert, 90, 221
Stauder, Jim, 145
Stauffer, Michael, 181
Stauffer, Scott, 71
Staunton, Kim, 143
Stazo, Luis, 13
Steadman, Sherman F., 123
Stechschulte, Tom, 119, 146
Steckler, Michelle, 114, 182
Stedman, Joel, 162
Stehlin, Jack, 141, 221
Stein, Bob, 25
Stein, Debra, 76, 96
Stein, Douglas, 143, 146, 151, 154, 155
Stein, Jane, 96
Stein, Joseph, 135, 145
Stein, Jule, 145
Stein, Julian, 52
Stein, Liza C., 159
Stein, Lorian, 159
Stein, Mary, 170
Stein, Phil, 98
Stein, Sue Ann, 149
Steinbach, Victor, 104, 221
Steinberg, Jane, 17, 66, 68, 70, 130
Steinberg, Jeffrey, 65
Steinberg, Roy, 60, 63, 221
Steinberg, Stewart, 79
Steiner, Al, 135
Steiner, Alan, 128
Steiner, Max, 76
Steiner, Rick, 46
Steiner, Steve, 165
Steingasser, Spike, 60
Steinlein, Jean, 36
Steinmetz, Richard, 79
Steitzer, Jeff, 136
Stenborg, Helen, 88, 221
Stenborg, James, 61, 118
Stenstrom, David, 163
Stephens, David P. B., 178
Stephens, Kent, 76, 140
Stephens, Lannyl, 141
Stephens, Linda, 140
Stephens, Neal Ann, 22
Stephens, Ray, 77
Stephens, Robin, 127
Stephenson, Alphonse, 45
Stephenson, Denise, 101
Stephenson, Don, 81, 221
Stephenson, Edwin, 186
Stephenson, Erik, 102
Stephenson, Laurie, 164
Stephenson, Melissa, 102, 120
Stepney, Ronal, 168
Steppling, John, 146
Steps, 163
Sterling, Chase, 179
Sterling, James, 78
Stern, Arlene, 221
Stern, Cheryl, 153
Stern, Henry, 106
Stern, Leo, 12, 30, 60, 67
Stern, Noel, 66, 86
Sternbach, Jerry, 59
Sternberg, Jennifer, 179
Sternberg, Ruth, 178
Sterne, Gordon, 115
Sterner, Jerry, 69
Sterner, Steve, 96, 117, 221
Sternhagen, Frances, 99
Sterrett, T. O., 158, 160
Stetson, Ron, 72
Stettler, David, 136
Steuber, Michael, 49
Steuer, Gary P., 119
Stevens, Byam, 71
Stevens, Carol Leigh, 80
Stevens, Connie, 188
Stevens, Fisher, 111, 221
Stevens, Keith E., 165
Stevens, Leon B., 171
Stevens, Roger L., 39, 161
Stevens, Ron Scott, 69
Stevens, Susan, 85, 221
Stevens, Susanne, 63
Stevens, Tony, 26
Stevens, Wesley, 150
Stevensen, Scott, 188
Stevenson, Rudy, 119
Stevlingson, Edward, 145, 167
Stewart, Benjamin, 157, 173
Stewart, Billie A., 114

Stewart, Jack Bell, 66
Stewart, John, 188
Stewart, Kate, 43, 88, 97
Stewart, Larry, 126
Stewart, Maggie, 183
Stewart, Michael, 49, 127, 149
Stewart, Parry B., 144
Stewart, Paul, 232
Stewart, Thomas A., 170, 171
Stewart, William, 143
Stickler, Sam, 11
Sticks and Bones, 187
Stidfole, James, 142
Stiehm, Roberta, 48
Stiers, David Ogden, 184
Stiles, Mona, 171
Stilgoe, Richard, 48
Stiller, Amy, 81
Stiller, Ben, 43, 97
Stiller, Jamie, 92
Stiller, Jerry, 97, 221
Stillwell, Liz, 147
Stimac, Anthony J., 76
Stine, Garson, 62
Stinnette, Dorothy, 100
Stinton, Colin, 188
Stitchers and Starlight Talkers, 180
Stites, Kevin, 164, 167
Stitt, Don, 70, 80
Stives, Jeanne Anich, 164
Stock, Sara, 169
Stockdale, Muriel, 79, 119
Stocker, Robert, 149
Stockman, Edward, 145
Stockton, Rose, 110, 170
Stockwell, Sally, 171
Stoeger, Frank, 148
Stoehr, Thomas C., 128
Stoker, Bram, 160
Stoker, Sue Jane, 90, 92, 113
Stokes, Nicole, 148
Stokes, Robert S., 80
Stokes, Tony, 159
Stolarsky, Paul, 161
Stoll, Karl, 181
Stoller, Ira, 63
Stollmach, Noele, 60
Stolper, Carolyn, 110
Stone, Carl, 163
Stone, Dudley, 114
Stone, Jeremy, 140
Stone, Jessica, 153
Stone, Peter, 130
Stone, Sidney, 232
Stoneburner, Sam, 96, 158, 167
Stoneman, David, 141
Stoppard, Tom, 136, 144, 146, 149, 156, 166, 170, 172, 175
Storace, Frankie Michael, 153
Storch, Arthur, 101, 125, 152, 175
Storch, Max, 92
Storck, Philip Alan, 73
Storey, David, 64, 78, 93
Storey, Lee, 113
Stories About the Old Days, 103
Storm, Michael, 69
Storm, The, 170
Storm, William, 146, 147
Stormont, Robert, 183
Storn, William, 147
Storrs, Rob, 177
Stotter, Patricia Lee, 71
Stotts, Sally, 123
Stout, Stephen, 118, 221
Stovall, Brock-David, 184
Stover, Elizabeth, 127
Strahs, Jim, 161
Straiges, Tony, 42, 143
Straithorn, David, 67
Stram, Henry, 81
Strane, Miriam, 183
Strane, Robert, 139
Straney, Paul, 135
Strang, David S., 137
Strang, Deborah, 178
Strange Interlude, 187
Strange, Melanie, 143
Strange, Sam, 172
Strangulation, 62
Stransky, Chuck, 127
Strasberg, John, 101
Strasberg, Susan, 188
Stratford, Michael James, 78
Strathairn, David, 67, 161
Straub, John, 174
Strauss, Edward, 20, 106
Strauss, Haila, 96
Strauss, Jane, 122
Strauss, Johann, 78
Strawbridge, Stephen, 61, 84, 90, 107, 111, 116, 157, 160
Stray Dogs, 143
Streamers, 161, 187
Streep, Meryl, 188
Street Scene, 187
Streetcar Named Desire, A, 137, 171, 187
Streeter, Tim, 172
Streeter, Wendy, 143
Strempek, William, 159
Striano, Don, 61
Strickland, Bruce, 103
Strickland, Cynthia, 178
Strickland, Dan, 61
Strickland, Judith, 142
Strickland, Morgan, 157
Strickler, Dan, 153
Stricklyn, Ray, 188
Strickstein, Robert C., 125
Stride, John, 188
Strieb, Bill, 161
Strindberg, August, 118
Strobach, Benjamin, Jr., 232
Strobel, Guy, 138
Strohmeier, Robert, 81
Stroman, Guy, 66, 221
Stroman, Susan, 75
Stromsted, Vera, 62
Strong, Ken, 140
Stronger and Creditors, The, 118
Stroud, Cindy, 73
Stroud, Claude, 232
Strouse, Charles, 15, 122
Strouse, Nicholas, 86, 221
Strozier, Henry, 143
Strubbe, Darrold, 145
Struckman, Jeff, 156, 174
Struthers, Sally, 6, 221
Stuart, Cynthia, 157
Stuart, Ian, 54
Stuart, Jay, 133
Stuart, Jeremy, 60
Stuart, Mary Ellen, 11
Stuart, Roxana, 162
Stuart-Morris, Joan, 140, 141, 185
Stubblefield, Ruben, 183
Stubbs, Jim, 121, 181, 221
Stubbs, Louise, 85
Stucki, Rebecca, 136
Stuebben, Gerald, 177
Stumm, Michael, 161
Stump, Christine, 63
Stump, Howard, 105
Sturchio, Mal, 58, 88
Sturgell, James F., 140
Sturgeon, Mark, 81
Sturgis, Wesley, 64
Sturiale, Grant, 79, 138
Styne, Jule, 93
Styron, Paola, 78
Su, Haruhiko Akamat, 8
Suber, Mats, 168
Subject Was Roses, The, 187
Subject to Change, 113
Suche, Greer, 59
Sudden Memory, 73
Suddeth, J. Allen, 36, 99
Sudik, Dee Amerio, 152
Sudik, James W., 152, 167
Suenaga, Gregory P., 136
Sues, Alan, 167
Sugar Babies, 133
Sugar, Mary, 66
Sugarman, Mitchell, 175
Suggs, Harold, 139
Suitcase, 109
Sulanowski, James Stephen, 153
Sulivan, Gregg, 185
Sulka, Elaine, 131
Sullivan & Gilbert, 159
Sullivan, Daniel, 18, 57, 172
Sullivan, Frederick, Jr., 178
Sullivan, Greg, 139, 184
Sullivan, James M., 123
Sullivan, John Carver, 155, 158, 174
Sullivan, John, 93, 98, 172
Sullivan, Karl W., 161
Sullivan, Kathleen A., 128
Sullivan, Kathleen, 123
Sullivan, Kim, 221
Sullivan, Michelle, 96
Sullivan, Patricia, 77
Sullivan, Paul, 111
Sullivan, Peter Michael, 141
Sullivan, Roger, 63
Sullivan, Shan, 64
Sullivan, Susanne Leslie, 49
Sullivan, Travis, 142
Sumerall, Eric, 136
Summa, Don Anthony, 20, 106
Summerhays, Jane, 133, 158
Summers, June, 114
Summers, Terey, 173
Sunday in the Park with George, 187
Sunder, 83
Sundsten, Linnea, 123
Sunrise at Campobello, 187
Surovy, Nicolas, 188
Susa, Conrad, 146, 184
Suskin, James R., 7
Suskin, Steven, 7
Suskind, Patrick, 105
Sussel, Deborah, 141
Sussman, Anne, 184
Sussman, Bruce, 111
Sutherland, Brian, 48, 122, 165
Suttell, V. Jane, 174
Sutton, Charles S., 180
Sutton, Claudette, 60
Sutton, Dolores, 144
Sutton, Henry, 161
Sutton, Michael, 105
Sutton, William, 134
Suzuki, Pat, 188
Svenson, Jennifer, 138
Svenson, Megan, 59
Swadley, Bill, 163
Swados, Elizabeth, 146
Swagerty, Floyd, R., Jr., 86
Swagerty, Ray, 80
Swain, Iralene, 162
Swain, John R., 151
Swain, Michael, 89
Swallows, Wayne, 183
Swan, Susan P., 177
Swann, Crist, 83
Swann, Elaine, 221, 225
Swannack, Cheryl, 9
Swanson, Diane, 110
Swanson, Eric, 115, 162, 180
Swanson, Robbie, 70
Swarm, Sally Ann, 124
Swartz, Beth, 95
Swartz, Marlene, 117
Swasey, Robert, 121
Swearingen, Henriette, 159
Swedeen, Staci, 175
Sweeney Todd, 187
Sweeney, Dan, 182
Sweeney, Dana, 164
Sweeney, Kevin, 155
Sweeny-Samuelson, Emily, 172
Sweet Charity, 40, 187, 190
Sweet Will, 69
Sweet, Allyn, 176
Sweet, Arthur, 78
Sweet, Jon P., 122
Sweetshoppe Myriam, The, 113
Sweigart, Matt, 137
Swenson, Inga, 188
Swenson, Maren, 177
Swenson, Swen, 188
Swerdlow, Tommy, 163
Swerling, Jo, 140
Swetland, Dudley, 30, 182
Swetland, William, 162, 170
Swetow, Joel, 221, 225
Swetz, Theodore, 181
Swift, Allegra, 163
Swift, Allen, 12, 221
Swift, Anne, 153, 162
Swift, Cheryl, 142
Swillim, Jack, 163
Swisher, Tammy, 150
Swit, Loretta, 20, 221
Swope, Daniel Allyn, 154
Sydown, Jack, 136
Sykes, Diane, 184
Sykora, Kathleen, 161
Sylvan, Sanford, 141
Symington, Donald, 171
Symonds, Rebecca, 170
Symons, James, 183
Synge, John Millington, 148
Syzdek, Bryan, 165
Szarabajka, Keith, 99, 116, 222
Szari, Catherine, 177
Szatkowski, Robert, 171
Szentgyorgyi, Tom, 90
Szerszen, Tony, 142
Szymanski, William, 55, 222, 225
T Day Room, 141
Taber, Ben, 138
Tabor, Susan, 93, 222
Tabori, Kristoffer, 188
Tack, Diane, 143
Tackaberry, Celia, 40, 222
Tadken, Neil Alan, 184
Taeschner, Robert E., 136
Taffel, Norman, 77
Tafler, Jean, 100
Tagg, Alan, 29
Tague, Cathy, 80
Tahtinen, JoAnn, 149
Tait, Eric V., Jr., 83
Takao, Kataoka, 8
Takataro, Kataoka, 8
Takazauckas, Albert, 185
Taken in Marriage, 148, 168
Taking of Miss Janie, The, 187
Tal, Hazel, 142
Talbot, Sharon, 66
Tale of Madame Zora, The, 91
Tales From Edgar Allan Poe, 140
Tales of Tinseltown, 118
Talk to Me Like the Rain . . ., 82
Talking With, 113
Talley & Son, 88
Talley's Folly, 121, 187
Tallman, Patricia, 80
Tally, Ted, 111
Talmadge, Victor, 117, 118, 160
Talman, Ann, 43, 61, 97, 222, 225
Talyn, Olga, 96, 118, 222
Tamarkin, Nicholas, 162
Tamasaburo, Bando V, 8
Tamayose, Tremaine, 136
Tamen, Jack, 58
Tamer of Horses, 149
Taming of the Shrew, The, 59, 143
Tammi, Tom, 114
Tamosaitis, Joe, 71
Tancredi, Dorothy, 124
Tandy, Jessica, 39, 146, 222
Tango Argentino, 13
Tanner, Betsy, 99
Tanner, Jill, 139
Tanner, Marion, 232
Tanner, Tony, 81, 115, 140
Tanzman, Carol, 85
Tapley, Michaele Blake, 142
Tarantina, Brian, 17, 47, 188, 222
Tarbuck, Barbara, 147, 173, 222
Tarleton, Diane, 64, 140, 222
Tartuffe, 144
Task, Maggie, 77, 81, 222
Tassone, Ron, 169
Taste of Honey, A, 187
Tatar, Ben, 170
Tate, Kamella, 185
Tate, Marzetta, 83
Tate, Neal, 58, 83, 85, 103, 140
Tate, Robin, 78
Tatsunosuke, Onoe, 8
Tatterdemalion, 62
Tattersall, Richard, 85
Tattler, The, 168
Tatum, Marianne, 76, 150, 155, 188, 222
Tatum, Michelle E., 163
Tavares, Eric, 144
Tavern, The, 150, 178
Tavori, Doron, 161
Taylor, Amber, 136
Taylor, Andy, 175
Taylor, Bert, 58, 167
Taylor, Billie, 58
Taylor, Bryon, 171
Taylor, C. P., 138, 145, 149
Taylor, Clarence, 102
Taylor, David, 48, 124
Taylor, Drew, 92, 222, 225
Taylor, Elizabeth, 188
Taylor, Gary, 172
Taylor, Gina, 74
Taylor, Gretchen, 106
Taylor, Holland, 111, 222
Taylor, Hope, 61
Taylor, Jeanne, 165
Taylor, Jerry, 149
Taylor, Joseph L., 128
Taylor, Judy Ford, 136
Taylor, Kathy, 164, 166
Taylor, Leslie, 148, 166
Taylor, Linwood, 170
Taylor, Mark Anthony, 95
Taylor, Myra, 91, 116, 149, 222
Taylor, Noel, 163
Taylor, Peter J., 155
Taylor, Regina, 59
Taylor, Robin, 121, 222
Taylor, Ron, 55
Taylor, Stephen, 102
Taylor, Tammy, 103
Taylor, Vickie, 49
Taylor, W. Allen, 60
Taylor, Wendy E., 153
Taylor-Dunn, Corliss, 138
Taylor-Morris, Maxine, 176
Taylor-Young, Leigh, 147
Taylorr, Barb, 164
Taymor, Julie, 143
Teagarden, Geraldine, 96
Teahouse of the August Moon, The, 187
Teamer, Johnnie, 126
Tebelak, John-Michael, 169
Teich, Jessica, 146, 147
Teirstein, Alice, 110
Teitel, Carol, 14, 222
Telesco, Vincent, 158
Telford, Robert S., 146
Teller, 56
Teller, Deborah, 168
Teller, Esther, 135
Telling Time, 151
Temperley, Stephen, 179
Tempest, The, 185
Ten By Tennessee, 82
Tendulkar, Vijay, 109
Tennenbaum, Debra, 61, 69, 99
Tenney, Jon, 47
Tent Meeting, 161
terKuile, Bill, 136
Terphale, Bharatkumar, 109
Terrel, Elwin Charles, II, 70
Terrell, John Canada, 107
Terrell, Stephen, 64
Terry, Jon, 176
Terry, Karen, 158
Terry, Sonny, 232
Terry, Susan, 53, 172, 222, 225
Terry, Tony, 149
Teschner, Mark, 86
Tesler, Monica, 64
Tesreau, Krista, 79
Tessier, Claude R., 48
Testa, Mary, 59, 76, 222
Teta, Jon, 100
Teti, Tom, 167, 168
Thacker, Russ, 188
Thain, Andy, 80, 117
Thaler, Martin, 182
Thanatophobia: Fear of Death, 172
Tharp, Twyla, 7
That Championship Season, 187
Thatcher, Kristine, 166
Thayer, Alex C., 144
Theatre of the Absurd, 113
Theatresports, 172
Thelen, Jodi, 108, 111, 115, 222
Themmen, Ivana, 94
Theodore, Donna, 135, 188, 222
Theodore, Laura, 74, 222
There Shall Be No Night, 187
Theseus and the Minotaur, 136
Thesing, Jim, 167
Theus, B. J., 161
Thew, John, 116
They Dance Real Slow in Jackson, 94
They Knew What They Wanted, 187
They're Playing Our Song, 92
Thibodeau, Marc P., 11, 26, 27, 37, 39, 48, 65, 67, 82, 130
Thiel, Joan Elizabeth, 110
Thiel, Nancy, 164
Thirloway, Gregory, 147
Thirlwall, Jill, 173
Thoemke, Peter, 156
Thole, Cynthia, 7
Thoma, Carl, 81, 222
Thoma, Michael, 161
Thoman, Tony, 64
Thomann, Eric, 83
Thomas, Alexander, 80
Thomas, Bonnie, 167
Thomas, Brandon, 182
Thomas, Brenda, 175
Thomas, Brett, 174
Thomas, Donald Edmund, 114
Thomas, Dylan, 90, 175
Thomas, Eberle, 153
Thomas, Freday, 181
Thomas, G. Valmont, 136
Thomas, Isa, 144
Thomas, Ivan, 83
Thomas, Janet, 147
Thomas, Keith, 186
Thomas, Marlo, 38, 222
Thomas, Mary Ellen, 128
Thomas, Nancy, 144
Thomas, Patrice, 57, 78, 178
Thomas, Paul C., 144
Thomas, Paul, 181
Thomas, Quentin, 167
Thomas, Richard, 161
Thomas, Robert, 45
Thomas, Tim, 171
Thomas, William, Jr., 222
Thomas, Wynn P., 107
Thomasson, Peter, 140
Thompson, Adrienne, 151
Thompson, Cecile, 142
Thompson, Charlene, 177
Thompson, David, 185
Thompson, Ernest, 145
Thompson, Evan, 63, 97, 222
Thompson, Fred, 162
Thompson, Jeffery V., 32, 222, 225
Thompson, Keith, 80, 158
Thompson, Kent, 150, 179
Thompson, Lauren, 153
Thompson, M. Leslie, 68
Thompson, Mark, 169
Thompson, Peter Gregory, 144
Thompson, Sada, 186
Thompson, Tazewell, 117
Thompson, Weyman, Jr., 126
Thomsen, Richard, 119
Thomson, Ian, 132
Thomson, Paula, 186
Thomson, Tom, 50
Thor, Cameron, 163
Thoresen, Howard, 80
Thornburg, Kristin, 169
Thorne, Raymond, 155
Thorne, Tracy, 96
Thornton, Angela, 23
Thornton, Greg, 164
Thorson, Linda, 188
Three Sisters, 93, 95, 158
Throckmorton, Robert, 177
Through Line, 140
Thruman, Cherise, 154
Thuna, Leonora, 162
Thunhurst, Bill, 170
Thurston, Todd, 92, 155, 222
Tibbetts, F. Allan, 157
Tiber, Elliot, 114
Tichler, Rosemarie, 106
Tidwell, Ginger, 69
Tiefenbrunn, Mary, 98
Ties That Bind, The, 113
Tietjen, Laura, 140
Tiffany, Robert, 122
Tiffe, Angelo, 88
Tiffin, Pamela, 188
Tigani, Greg, 150
Tiger at the Gates, 187
Tighe, Andy, 173
Tighe, Kevin, 172
Tighe, Maura, 71
Tiler, Scott, 80
Tilford, Joseph P., 149
Tillinger, John, 29, 36, 57, 99, 111, 162
Tillman, Judith, 153
Tillotson, Drew, 95
Tillotson, John, 121, 125
Tillotson, Thomas, 143
Tillstrom, Burr, 231, 232
Tilton, James, 101
Time Makes Everything a Memory, 113
Time Out, 163
Time of Your Life, The, 101, 187
Time of the Cuckoo, The, 121
Times and Appetites of Toulouse-Lautrec, 84
Times Square Angel, 69
Timmers, Jack, 49
Timmons, John, 121
Timms, Rebecca, 134
Timoyko, Naanim, 13
Timpone, Glen F., 76
Tinapp, Bart, 138
Tindall, John, 157
Tine, Hal, 24
Tinsley, Jordan, 76
Tintypes, 138
Tippit, Wayne, 57, 116, 222
Tipton, Jennifer, 7, 99, 108, 141, 171, 180
Tirapelli, Teri, 106, 112
Tirelli, Jaime, 222
Tirrell, Barbara, 156
Tischler, Audrey, 83
Titus, Hiram, 156
Tkacz, Virlana, 66
Tkatch, Peter Jack, 181
To Culebra, 137
To Feed Their Hopes, 113
To Whom It May Concern, 66
Tobias, Barbara, 133
Tobin, Francis X., 181
Tobin, John, 142
Tobolowsky, Stephen, 163
Tochterman, David, 16, 115, 125, 153, 175
Today I Am a Fountain Pen, 86
Todd, Marc, 182
Toddie, William, 72
Together Again, 160
Toggenburger, Joan, 163
Tokar, Mary, 121
Tokuda, Marilyn, 163
Tolan, Kathleen, 172
Tolan, Robert W., 158
Tolaydo, Michael, 152
Toles, Bill, 107
Tolone, Zoe, 175
Tom and Viv, 171
Tomalas, Gavin, 173
Tomei, Concetta, 146, 222
Tomei, Marisa, 76, 191, 192, 222
Tomei, Paula, 173
Tomfoolery, 173
Tomlin, Caralyn, 186
Tomlin, Lily, 9, 172, 187
Tomlinson, Charles, 173
Tomlinson, Robert Michael, 222
Tomo 'n' Tomo, 115
Tomorrow's Monday, 88
Tompos, Doug, 142
Toms, Carl, 152
Tondo, Jerry, 147
Toner, Thomas, 106, 111, 159, 222
Toney, David, 91

Took, Don, 173
Toon, Tami, 146
Tooth of Crime, The, 157
Top Girls, 149
Topper, George L., 179
Torbett, David, 81
Torcellini, Jamie, 48, 124
Torch Song Trilogy, 160
Toren, Ilan, 161
Torgov, Morley, 86
Torgove, Lynn, 141
Torn, Danae, 75
Torn, Rip, 188
Toro, Puli, 112, 222
Toropov, Brandon, 98
Torren, Frank, 57, 93, 222
Tortora, Oz, 163
Tortoriello, Jerry, 59
Toscano, Loretta, 135
Toser, David, 74, 81, 170
Tost, William, 52
Toto, Karen, 127
Totten, Molly Beth, 122
Touch of the Poet, A, 151
Toulmin, Christopher, 107
Tourtillotte, Paul, 170
Tourville, Lucille, 142, 148, 149
Toussaint, Lorraine, 156
Tovar, Candace, 37, 164
Tovatt, Patrick, 161, 168
Towers, Charles, 179
Towey, John Madden, 156
Towler, Laurine, 59, 222
Townes, Robert L., 177
Townley, Jason, 92
Townley, Wyatt, 93, 222
Townsend, Eliza, 166
Townsend, Judith, 177
Townsend, Rock, 65
Townsley, Peggy, 177
Toy Factory, The, 71
Toy, Barbara, 87
Toy, Christine, 222
Toy, Patty, 147
Toys in the Attic, 187
Tracy, Bruce, 62
Tracy, John, 188
Traeger, Henry, 100
Tragedy of Julius Caesar, The, 60, 181
Tragedy of King Lear, The, 185
Trainer, David, 146
Trainor, Susan, 133
Trakker's Tel, 138
Tramel, Jay, 64, 105
Trano, Gina, 162
Trapp, Gretchen, 64
Trask, E. Z., 171
Traub, John, 146
Traveler in the Dark, 137, 147
Travers, Joseph, 80
Traverse, Martha, 123
Travesties, 187
Travis, Dianne Turley, 163
Travis, Mark W., 163
Travis, Warren, 141, 143
Trayer, Leslie, 164
Traynor, Alan, 108
Treats, 77
Treem, Douglas, 63
Trefousse, Roger, 147
Trelawny of the "Wells", 185
Trevens, Francine L., 62, 69, 113, 118
Trevor, Jeanne, 171
Triana, Patricia, 118
Tribbie, John Joseph, 114
Tribble, Darryl Eric, 126
Tribush, Nancy, 51
Trigger, Ian, 54, 140, 180, 184
Trimble, Eleanor, 111
Trinity Site, 120
Triska, Jan, 161
Trisoliere, Louie M., 128
Tritt, Don, 168
Triumph of the Spider Monkey, The, 163
Triwush, Ken, 160
Trojan Women, The, 95
Troll Palace, The, 114
Tronto, Rudy, 133
Troob, Danny, 46, 59
Troobnick, Eugene, 115, 121, 222
Troster, Gavin, 114, 150
Troth, Daniel, 72
Trott, Karen, 146
Trott, Pat, 127
Trotta, Edward, 117
Trouille, Clovis, 51
Trout, Curtis, 174
Troy, Louise, 49, 222
Troy, Mark, 113
True West, 136,
Trulock, Dianne, 30, 123
Trupin, Casey, 136
Truro, Victor, 222
Trust, Brian, 98
Truth, Daniel, 142
Truxall, Evan, 174
Tsu, Susan, 177
Tsuchigumo, 8
Tsypin, George, 141, 161, 171
Tucci, Maria, 179
Tucci, Stanley, 12, 33, 91
Tucker, Alison, 70
Tucker, Kumi, 121
Tucker, Louis, 121, 155
Tucker, Michael, 57, 70, 173
Tulin, Michael, 60
Tull, Eric, 54
Tull, Karen, 59, 222
Tull, Patrick, 90, 222
Tully, Joseph E., 6, 65
Tumbleweed, 163
Tumbo-Masabo, Zubeida, 117
Tune, Tommy, 130, 222
Tung, Allan, 109
Tunick, Jonathan, 26, 45
Tunie, Tamara, 66, 162
Tunnah, Phil A., 160
Tunstall, Tricia, 76
Tuohy, Susan, 173
Turco, Jeryl, 63
Turenne, Louis, 159
Turken, Greta, 60, 222, 225
Turmail, Dick, 69
Turman, Glynn, 104
Turner, Caroline F., 179
Turner, Craig, 170
Turner, Glenn, 130, 222
Turner, Jake, 134
Turner, Jerry, 185
Turner, Mary, 169
Turner, Patrick, 110, 222
Turner, Sandra, 133
Turner, Stephen, 61
Turner, William, 98
Turney, Wayne, 137
Turturice, Robert, 58
Turturro, John, 91, 188, 222
Turvett, Barbara, 177
Tushar, Jim, 232
Tutera, Cynthia J., 170
Tutor, Rick, 136, 175
Tutta Casa, Letto, E Chiesa (It's All Bed, Board, and Church), 141
Twelfth Night, 95, 138, 152, 154, 157, 171, 186
21A, 137
27 Wagons Full of Cotton, 113
Twice Around the Park, 144, 145
Twine, Linda, 46
Twiss, Jo, 72
Twiss, Steven D., 58
Two Can Play, 149
Two Gentlemen of Verona, 110, 187
Two Noble Kinsmen, 182
Two Orphans, The, 117
Twohill, William, 66
Twomey, Anne, 158, 188
Tyler, Edward, 152
Tyler, Edwina Lee, 60
Tyler, Jim, 24, 50
Tyler, Martin A., 177
Tyler, Robert, 119
Tyler, Royall, 110
Tylor, Edwina Lee, 161
Tynan, Kenneth, 51
Tynes, Bill, 74, 81
Tyrone, Keith, 58, 83
Tyrrel, Lyn, 175
Tyrrell, Brian, 185
Tyrrell, Tara, 64, 172
Tyson, Carl, 121
U. S. A., 174
Udall, Katherine, 135
Udell, Peter, 151
Uffner, Nancy Kay, 179
Uggams, Leslie, 24, 25, 188, 222, 225
Uguccioni, Patricia, 142
Uhler, Kathy, 118
Ukena, Paul Jr., 96, 155
Ulasinsky, Walter, 116
Ullett, Nick, 36, 99, 223
Ullman, Bill, 175
Ullman, Bob, 110
Ullman, Jeffrey, 76, 119, 170
Ullrick, Sharon, 223
Ulmer, Joan, 144, 181
Umberger, Andy, 78
Under Milk Wood, 90
Under Statements, 171
Underer, Phoebe, 135
Understanding, The, 172
Underwood, Eric, 50
Ungar, Brian, 168
Unger, Christopher, 142
Unger, Robert, 151
Union Boys, 180
Unosuke, Ichikawa III, 8
Unsoeld, Terres, 158,
Unsuitable for Adults, 173
Unvarnished Truth, The, 146
Upchurch, Reenie, 65, 140
Ups and Downs of Theophilus Maitland, The, 150
Uptown . . . It's Hot !, 32
Urbinati, Robert, 23, 27, 122
Urdang, Leslie, 61
Urdang, Terry, 176
Urla, Joe, 99, 106, 191, 192, 223
Urrutia, David, 78
Ury, Elizabeth, 185
Usdin, Robert, 110
Usher, Kevin J., 80
Ussery, Norman, 170
Utech, Greg, 165
Utley, Byron, 223
Utstein, Leslie, 79
Vaccaro, Brenda, 6, 188, 223
Vaillancourt, Tony, 165
Valdes, Ching, 109, 179, 180
Valdez, Luis, 163
Valency, Maurice, 101
Valente, Sergio, 40
Valentin, Juan, 61
Valentine, James, 123
Valentine, Peter, 16
Valentino, Eileen, 153
Valeri, Walter, 81, 141
Valk, Cindy, 34, 36, 46, 49, 56, 73, 115, 122, 127, 135
Valk, Kate, 161
Vallant, Marlies, 67
Valle, Freddy, 112
Valor, Henrietta, 156
Valvano, Michael, 99
Vampire Lesbians of Sodom and Sleeping Beauty or Coma, 59
Van Ark, Joan, 188
Van Baars, Eric, 81
Van Buskirk, Floyd, 172
Van Cleve, Edith, 232
Van Cott, Susan, 123
Van Der Meulen, Howard, 73
Van Der Veen, David, 150
Van Dyck, Jennifer, 178
Van Dyke, Dick, 188
Van Dyke, Elizabeth, 149
Van Dyke, Kimberly, 117
Van Dyke, Marcia, 188
Van Dyke, Peter, 184
Van Fossen, Diana, 138
Van Griethuysen, Ted, 175
Van Horne, Gretchen, 138
Van Hunter, William, 87, 145, 223, 225
van Itallie, Jean-Claude, 141
Van Kleeck, Annalee, 66, 85, 98
Van Lare, James, 66
Van Norden, Peter, 108, 223
Van Nostrand, Deborah, 145
Van Patten, Dick, 146
Van Pelt, Dan, 57
Van Sant, Margaret, 162
Van Slyke, Joe, 166
Van Tassel, Craig, 75
Van Tieghem, David, 75
Van Tine, Elizabeth, 184
Van Treuren, James, 7, 123
Van Zandt, Porter, 101, 121, 144
Van Zyl, Meg, 73
VanDusen, Carolyn, 65
VanNostrand, Amy, 150
Vance, Courtney B., 154
Vance, Dana, 167
Vance, Kay, 133
Vandenbroucke, Russell, 171
Vandeyacht, Jeff, 175
Vandivier, Marijane, 139
Vandivort, Terry, 177
Varela, Jay, 147
Varga, Joseph A., 117
Vargas, John, 163, 176
Varon, Rebecca, 74, 100, 145
Varon, Susan, 92, 223, 225
Vash, Bernard, 141
Vasquez, Alden, 154
Vasta, Philip, 69
Vaszary, John, 81
Vaughan-Porter, Robert, 142
Vaughn, Mark, 107
Vaughn, Maura, 93, 223
Vaux, Adrian, 161
Vaux, Lyn, 79
Vawter, Ron, 161
Vazzana, Tom, 122
Veazey, Jeff, 59, 69, 93, 223, 225
Vedder, Joanna, 84
Vedder, Williamson, 96
Veenstra, Anne, 79
Vega, Cecilia, 106
Vega, Frank, 139
Vega, Jose, 123
Vega, Millie, 112
Vega, Rosa I., 116
Vehec, Mary, 169
Velasquez, David Navarro, 73, 162
Velez, Henry, 47
Velez, Lauren, 126
Velez, Ricardo, 75
Veloudos, Spiro, 166
Venberg, Lorraine, 183
Venezia, Lisa, 107
Vennema, John C., 60, 158, 223
Vennera, Chick, 188
Vennerbeck, Eric, 92
Vennerstrom, Michael W., 151
Venom, Bill, 173
Venora, Diane, 88, 108, 223
Ventin, Steve, 72, 75
Venton, Harley, 167
Ventriss, Jeannie, 180
Ventura, Frank, 93
Ventura, Joe, 152
Venture, Richard, 107
Venus Observed, 187
Verderber, Bill, 137
Verdery, James, 136
Verdon, Gwen, 40, 188
Vereen, Ben, 188, 223
Verheyen, Mariann S., 149, 155, 159
Vernan, Ron, 174
Verow, Catherine, 184
Vetter, Jo, 136
Vickers, William, 186
Vickery, John, 146
Vickilyn, 149
Victor, James, 163
Victor, Lucia, 127, 232
Victor, Ray, 163
Victoria Station, 136
Vienna Lusthaus, 78, Jack, 146
Viertel, Jack, 147
Villa, Anna, 135
Villaire, Holly, 139
Villamor, Christen, 109
Villarreal, Edit, 180
Villella, Donna M., 96
Villenueva, Amber, 102
Vincent, Joe, 185
Vincent, Paul, 29
Vincent, Robert, 93, 160
Vining, Mary, 184
Vinovich, Stephen, 110, 111, 223
Vipond, Mathew, 61
Vipond, Neil, 101, 223
Virginia, 160, 173
Visions of Kerouac, 72
Visit, The, 187
Vitale, Carla Roetzer, 122
Vitella, Sel, 81
Vivian, John, 23
Viviano, Sal, 223
Vizen, Frank J., 154
Vlahos, Sam, 163, 176
Vlamynck, Cyrille, 80
Voet, Doug, 223
Vogel, David, 92, 223
Vogel, James Michael, 74
Vogler, Herb, 17
Vogt, Peter, 156
Vogt, Vincent, 92
Voices in the Head, 81
Voight, Jon, 188
Voigts, Richard, 87, 109, 223
Volack, Lia, 110
Volkman, Bob, 174
Vollack, Lia, 64, 110
Vollertsen, James, 122
Volz, Jim, 181
Von Bargen, Daniel, 178
von Berg, Peter, 70
von Breuning, Otto, 13
von der Heyde, Cece, 184
von Dohlen, Lenny, 91, 223
Von Kleist, Heinrich, 79
von Mayrhauser, Jennifer, 23, 33, 44, 88, 89, 125, 156, 162
von Mayrhauser, Peter, 130
von Schmid, Kathleen, 62, 63, 69, 72, 77, 91, 119
von Schoeler, Sasha, 163
Von Volz, Valerie, 94
Vool, Ruth, 38
Vorbach, Eileen, 159
Vorwald, Terrance, 148
Vos, David, 166
Vosburgh, Dick, 31, 167, 176
Waara, Scott, 26, 150, 223
Wackerman, Jorie, 136
Wackler, Rebecca, 161, 168
Waddell, Jack, 162
Waddell, Linden, 124
Wade, Janet, 176
Wade, Kevin, 120
Wade, Stephen, 143
Wade, Uel, 138, 155
Wadsworth, Don, 169
Wagener, Terri, 168
Wager, Douglas C., 143
Wager, Linda, 115
Wagg, Jim, 79
Wagner, Daniel M., 152
Wagner, Dee, 140
Wagner, Elsie C., 144
Wagner, Jane, 9, 172
Wagner, Robin, 11, 45, 49, 106, 126, 127
Wagrowski, Gregory, 163
Wahl, David, 162
Wahrer, Timothy, 156
Wainwright, Loudon, III, 125
Waite, John Thomas, 144, 167
Waite, Ralph, 173
Waites, Thomas G., 101, 117
Waitin' in the Wings, 80
Waiting for the Parade, 105
Waiwaiole, Lloyd, 62, 148
Walbye, Kay, 167
Wald, Karen, 223, 225
Wald, Shelly, 145
Waldeck, Nona, 158
Walden, Eric, 80
Walden, Larry K., 104
Walden, Russell, 84
Walden, Stanley, 51
Waldhelm, Julianne, 65, 66, 68
Waldman, Randy, 129
Waldren, Peter, 62, 223
Waldron, Michael, 155
Waldrop, Mark, 50, 223, 225
Waldrup, Stephen, 184
Waldschmidt, Hanne, 142
Wales, Whit, 170
Walken, Christopher, 97, 188, 223
Walker, Arnetia, 126
Walker, Bill, 36, 99, 160, 162, 174
Walker, Bo, 96
Walker, Bobby, 130
Walker, Chet, 40, 223
Walker, David A., 95
Walker, Don, 135
Walker, Fred, 135
Walker, Fuschia, 126
Walker, George F., 61
Walker, Jaison, 117
Walker, Janet Hayes, 121
Walker, John Haynes, 166
Walker, Kary M., 164
Walker, Kathi, 149
Walker, Kim, 62
Walker, M. Burke, 171
Walker, Margaret, 85
Walker, Paul, 108
Walker, Robert, 188
Walker, Sarah Trubey, 170
Walker, Shell, 66
Walker, Sullivan H., 149
Wall, Mary Chris, 49, 127
Wallace, Anne, 137
Wallace, Basil, 137
Wallace, Bradford, 144
Wallace, Jack, 43, 127, 154
Wallace, Maria, 90
Wallace, Marian, 144
Wallace, Marie, 68, 223
Wallace, Ronald, 62, 162
Wallach, Eli, 188
Wallas, Ted, 58
Wallen, Michelle, 173
Waller, Brad, 181
Waller, Josie, 102
Waller, Kenneth H., 155
Waller, Trina, 153
Walling, Stratton, 145
Wallnau, Carl, 60
Walls, Kurt, 172
Walsh, Gwynyth, 186
Walsh, J. T., 91, 127
Walsh, James, 18, 57, 58, 223
Walsh, Juanita, 62, 92
Walsh, Keliher, 84
Walsh, Kenneth, 38
Walsh, Martin J., 142
Walsh, Sheila, 113
Walsh, Tenney, 84, 172
Walsh, Thommie, 130, 152
Walsh, Tom, 175
Walski, James, 127
Walters, Beth, 169
Walters, Don, 99
Walters, Frederick, 148
Walters, Kelly, 223
Walters, Lisa Roxanne, 91
Walters, Marrian, 141
Walters, Valerie, 141
Walters, W. Francis, 144
Walters, William, 73, 80
Walther, Rob, 164
Waltman, Kim, 68
Walton, Bob, 167
Walton, Jim, 127
Walton, Laurie, 145, 149
Walton, Tony, 18, 38, 43, 57, 97, 130
Waltz of the Toreadors, The, 115, 187
Waltz, Lisa, 223
Walworth, Norene, 169
Walz, Chris, 175
Wanamaker, Mary, 172
Wanamaker, Zoe, 36, 99, 223
Wands, Susan, 63, 94, 223
Wann, Jim, 98, 167
Wanserski, Larisa, 152
Wanshel, Jeff, 84
Wappel, Steve, 99, 125
Ward, Bethe, 107
Ward, Billy, 16
Ward, Bryce, 128
Ward, David, 173
Ward, Doug, 61
Ward, Douglas Turner, 104, 223
Ward, Elizabeth M., 75
Ward, G. Douglas, 77, 80, 90, 131
Ward, Janis, 163
Ward, Jeanne, 114
Ward, Joanna, 121
Ward, Judy Peyton, 154, 184
Ward, Mary B., 34
Ward, Mary, 167
Ward, Marybeth, 77
Ward, Michael, 69
Ward, Peggy, 113
Ward, Susanne, 138
Ward, Tami, 177
Warda, Youssef Abu, 161
Warden, Yvonne, 116, 223
Wardlaw, Julia, 142
Warfel, William B., 22, 57, 180
Warfield, Marlene, 188
Warfield, Russell, 124
Waring, Dennis, 232
Waring, Todd, 101
Warmflash, Stuart, 83
Warner, Candace, 83
Warner, David Strong, 46
Warner, Elise, 33
Warner, Evelyn R., 142
Warner, Gary, 69
Warner, Phillip, 65
Warner, Richard, 110
Warner, Russell, 81
Warners, Robert, 232
Warnick, Clay, 150, 152
Warnock, Kathleen, 101
Warren, Harry, 49, 127
Warren, Jennifer Leigh, 46, 59, 188, 223
Warren, Joseph, 106, 108, 110, 171, 223
Warren, Leslie Ann, 188
Warren, Mary Mease, 170
Warren, Will, 182
Warren-Cooke, Barbara, 83
Warren-White, Nat, 164
Warrender, Scott, 75
Warrick, Christopher, 110
Warrilow, David, 161, 223
Wars of Attrition, 162
Warshofsky, David, 123
Warykas, James, 142
Wash, The, 147
Washington, Brynn, 121
Washington, Fran L., 151
Washington, Rhonnie, 171
Washington, Shelley, 7
Washington, Von H., 151
Wasilewski, Valeria, 58
Wasinger, Daniel J., 174
Waskow, Sara, 173
Wasley, Richard, 81
Wasman, David, 140
Wasser, Alan, 30, 129, 133, 152, 153
Wasserman, Dale, 79, 177, 182
Wassermann, Molly, 111, 223
Wasserstein, Wendy, 82, 111, 153
Wasson, Craig, 57
Wasson, David, 81
Wasted, 120
Wasula, Michael, 48
Watch Your Back, 151
Watch on the Rhine, 138, 177
Waters, Les, 107, 149, 160
Waterston, Sam, 27, 223
Watkins, Eric, 77
Watkins, James, 92, 223
Watroba, Sharon, 117
Watson, Anne Thaxter, 136, 175, 183
Watson, Douglass, 188
Watson, Janet, 46, 96, 155
Watson, Lisa L., 104
Watson, Michael Orris, 57, 174, 181
Watson, Tom, 182
Watt, Henry, 141
Watt, Kenn, 141
Watts, Dean G., 123
Watts, Gregg, 166
Watts, Holly K., 177
Way, Lillo, 79
Waye, Jared, 186
Wayne, David, 188
Weary, A. C., 159
Weathers, Danny, 45
Weathers, Patrick, 81
Weaver, Diane, 103
Weaver, Fritz, 188, 223
Weaver, Lynn, 100, 223
Weaver, Marvin E., 174
Weaver, Neal, 100
Weaver, Sylvester N., Jr., 104, 149
Weaver, William, 122

Webb, Elmon, 137
Webber, Andrew Lloyd, 11, 48
Webber, Julian, 57, 117
Webber, Mick, 73
Weber, Carl, 141
Weber, Fredricka, 188, 192, 193
Weber, Jenifer L., 175
Weber, Juliet, 71
Weber, Lawrence, 96, 223
Weber, Paul Anthony, 136
Weber, Steven, 36, 101
Webster, Albert, 111
Webster, Jeff, 161
Webster, Leigh, 124
Webster, Peter, 153, 223
Wedekind, Frank, 139
Wedge, The, 113
Wedgeworth, Ann, 67, 223
Weeks, Alan, 37, 58
Weenick, Annabelle, 145
Weidman, Jerome, 155
Weigle, Joan, 142
Weihs, Stephen, 100
Weil, Tim, 51
Weill, Kurt, 90, 162
Weill, Wendy, 72
Weinberg, Ami, 161
Weinberg, David E., 102
Weinberg-Barefield, Barbara, 151
Weindling, Craig, 137, 161
Weiner, Arn, 55
Weiner, John, 50, 223
Weingort, Karen, 116
Weingust, Don, 151
Weinstein, Charles, 141
Weinstein, Connie, 125
Weinstein, Pam, 64, 80
Weinstein, Valerie, 9
Weinstock, Jack, 142
Weintraub, Carl, 146
Weisberg, Jack, 66
Weisberg, Leslie, 84
Weisfeld, Rob, 77
Weisman, Sam, 173
Weiss, David N., 76
Weiss, Elissa, 74
Weiss, Erick, 175
Weiss, Jeff, 108, 223
Weiss, Joan, 88
Weiss, Marc B., 32, 125, 130, 134, 135
Weiss, Mitchell, 45
Weiss, Norman, 96
Weiss, Peter, 169
Weiss, Will Maitland, 90
Weissbrot, Gary, 173
Weissler, Barry, 130, 135
Weissler, Fran, 130, 135
Weissman, Cliff, 63
Weitz, Eric, 156
Weitzenhoffer, Max, 22
Weitzman, Ira, 110, 111
Welby, Donnah, 110, 223
Welby, Susan, 139
Welch, Elisabeth, 31, 75
Welch, Gregory, 144
Welch, Jane, 148
Welch, Jennie, 139
Welch, Lee, 100
Welch, Robert, 166
Weldin, Scott, 136
Weldon, Duncan C., 122
Welles, Orson, 231, 232
Wellman, Mac, 66, 81
Wells, Christopher, 105, 152, 175
Wells, Craig, 53, 223
Wells, Deanna, 121, 223
Wells, Dennis, 139, 183
Wells, Frank T., 176
Wells, Matthew, 64
Wells, Susanna, 158
Wells, Susany, 124
Wells, Tico, 64
Wells, Win, 70
Welmer, Lisa, 66
Welsh, Kenneth, 38
Welsh, Sue, 176
Welty, Eudora, 116
Welzer, Irving, 81
Wences, Senor, 133
Wendell, Susan, 79
Wendell, Victoria, 163
Wenderlick, Mark, 175
Wendkos, Gina, 85
Wendschuh, Ronald, 153, 158
Wentworth, Scott, 186
Wenzel, Lisa, 95
Werner, Dona, 165
Werner, Fred, 40
Werner, Stewart, 88, 89
Werness, Nanette, 101
Wernick, Adam, 168
Wernick, Nancy, 72
Werther, Ken, 146
Wesley, Richard, 171
West Memphis Mojo, 166
West Side Story, 134, 161
West, Caryn, 170
West, Don, 144
West, Gabrielle Suzette, 177
West, Heather, 93
West, Jane, 141
West, Jennifer, 188
West, Natalie, 166
Westenberg, Robert W., 143, 188, 223
Westenhoeffer, Suzanne, 101
Westerfer, David, 143
Westfall, John David, 68
Westfall, Ralph David, 121, 224
Westley, Meg, 186
Weston, Debora, 158
Weston, Jack, 224
Westphal, Robin, 110, 119, 224
Westry, DeForest, 92
Wetherall, Jack, 79, 156, 181
Wetter Than Water, 179
Weyenberg, Trish, 92, 224
Weyte, Stephan, 175
Whalen, Dave, 170
Whalen, Pamela, 224
Wharton, Edith, 60
What Leona Figured Out, 168
What the Butler Saw, 148
Wheeler, David, 178
Wheeler, Harold, 126
Wheeler, Hugh, 167
Wheeler, Karen, 159
Wheeler, Lois, 57
Wheeler, Saul, 173
Wheels, Helen, 101
Whelan, Cyprienne Gabel, 232
Whelan, Joseph, 184
Whelan, Susan, 76
Whelan, Tim, 186
When the Sun Slides, 151
Wherry, Robert E., Jr., 77, 90
Wherry, Toby, 98
Whigas, Anthony, 124
Whining and Dining, 63
Whipple, Patti, 100
Whitcomb, Margo, 72
White Steed, The, 187
White, Alice, 166
White, Amelia, 149, 188, 224, 225
White, Burton, 169
White, Diane, 163
White, Diz, 70, 71
White, Ellen T., 103
White, George C., 138
White, J. Steven, 151
White, Jane, 101
White, Jim, 186
White, John, 115
White, Julie, 159
White, June Daniel, 145
White, Kyle, 50
White, Laura, 116, 162, 224
White, Laurel Anne, 136
White, Linda L., 168
White, Maura, 169
White, Michael D., 60
White, Patricia, 54
White, Pauline, 69
White, Richard E. T., 182
White, Richard, 167, 224
White, Sally K., 185
White, Sandy, 73
White, Stephen Len, 58
White, Susan A., 68, 142, 143, 149, 152
White, Terri, 153, 167, 174, 175
White, Thea Ruth, 184
White, Tim, 82
Whitehead, David P., 136, 138
Whitehead, Neil, 149
Whitehead, Paxton, 172, 184
Whitehead, Robert, 30, 39, 161
Whitehill, B. T., 59, 69
Whitehurst, Scott, 117
Whitelock, Patricia A., 151
Whitemore, Hugh, 139
Whitescarver, Randall, 37, 80
Whitfield, Debra, 87, 224
Whitfield, Michael J., 154, 186
Whitford, Bradley, 59
Whitham, Sarah, 143
Whitmore, James, 152, 188
Whitney, Holly, 150
Whitney, Timothy, 158, 158
Whitson, Ben, 149
Whittington, Christan, 145
Whittington, Tom, 152
Whitton, Margaret, 107, 224
Who's Afraid of Virginia Woolf?, 187
Why Marry?, 187
Why the Lord Come to Sand Mountain, 179
Whyte, Donn, 64, 224
Wiberg, Raymond, 138
Widdoes, James, 188
Widercrantz, Jon, 76
Wido, Jude, 140
Wiedergott, Karl, 161
Wiederrecht, Carol, 121
Wiegert, Rene, 48
Wieneke, Lynne, 160
Wierney, J. Thomas, 224
Wierney, Tom, 40
Wierzel, Robert, 80, 115, 157, 170
Wieselman, Douglas, 60
Wiesner, Nickey, 64
Wiest, Dianne, 62, 188
Wieters, Donna, 142
Wiggins, Tudi, 148, 168
Wilber, Shirley, 141
Wilbur, Richard, 167, 166
Wilce, Andrew, 186
Wilcox, Clayton, 172
Wilcox, Larry, 7
Wild Duck, The, 143
Wilde, Oscar, 65, 140, 153, 174, 180
Wilder, Alan, 28, 161, 224
Wilder, Barbara, 112
Wilder, Carrie, 76
Wilder, Clinton, 232
Wilder, John-David, 93
Wilder, Susan, 119, 168
Wilding, Michael, 114, 224
Wilhelm, Kurt, 107, 110, 149, 158, 161, 172, 179, 232
Wililams, Darious Keith, 32
Wililams-Jenkins, Leslie, 32
Wilkening, Mark, 80
Wilkening, Nancy, 184
Wilkens, Claudia, 156
Wilkerson, M. P., 181
Wilkerson, Steve, 143
Wilkes, Jack, 92
Wilkinson, Steve, 59
Wilkof, Lee, 40, 224
Wilks, Talvin W., 149
Will, Lenny, 161
Willard, C. George, 16, 18, 127, 40, 69, 70, 76, 81, 94
Willeford, Martin, 150
Willems, Stephen, 161
Willen, Douglas, 92
William, David, 186
Williams & Walker, 85, 85
Williams, Adrian, 77
Williams, Allan, 126, 128
Williams, Allison, 40, 224
Williams, Amy Beth, 168
Williams, Anona, 93
Williams, Beth, 152, 164
Williams, Carol, 140
Williams, Casey, 83
Williams, Chalethia, 139
Williams, Clarence, III, 188
Williams, Clifford, 122, 129, 146
Williams, David, 160
Williams, Edward R., 136
Williams, Ellis, 157, 162
Williams, Fedye Jo, 151
Williams, Greg, 139
Williams, Jaston, 145, 153, 159, 174, 184
Williams, JoBeth, 161
Williams, John, 164
Williams, Judith W. B., 182
Williams, K. R., 16
Williams, Kathy, 142
Williams, Keith, 87, 224
Williams, Kellie, 83
Williams, Lanyard A., 153
Williams, Mara, 84
Williams, Marshall, 116
Williams, Neal, 140
Williams, Robert, 151, 162
Williams, Ron, 115
Williams, Sam, 35, 97, 136
Williams, Samm-Art, 82, 104, 175, 179
Williams, Sammy, 45
Williams, Shelley, 170
Williams, Suzi, 183
Williams, Tennessee, 82, 113, 135, 149, 162, 171, 177, 178, 179,
Williams, Treat, 162
Williams, Vanessa, 57
Williams, Vince, 144
Williams, Yolanda, 177
Williams-Vogue, Robert, 151
Williamson, Laird, 141, 151
Williamson, Laurie, 7
Willinger, David, 60, 161
Willis, Gordon, 7
Willis, Jack, 150
Willis, Richard, 93, 224, 225
Willis, Susan, 101, 224
Willison, Walter, 58, 145, 149, 188, 192, 224
Willoughby, David Alan, 140
Willoughby, Ronald, 60, 100, 224
Willrich, Rudolph, 144, 180
Willson, Meredith, 142
Wilson, August, 153, 154, 172, 180
Wilson, Ben, 161
Wilson, Bernadette, 158
Wilson, Bo, 177
Wilson, Carl, 58
Wilson, Elizabeth, 111, 224
Wilson, Gene, 49
Wilson, Helen, 70
Wilson, James, 173
Wilson, John H., 8
Wilson, K. C., 62, 71, 224
Wilson, Karen, 60
Wilson, Kathryn, 168, 186
Wilson, Lanford, 88, 89, 93, 116, 121, 139, 168
Wilson, Laurel Ann, 20, 45, 106
Wilson, Lizanne, 138
Wilson, Mark, 186
Wilson, Mary Louise, 6, 159, 224
Wilson, Michael, 166
Wilson, Pamela Ann, 45
Wilson, Peter, 31
Wilson, Robert, 141
Wilson, Tena, 55
Wilson, Trey, 60, 65, 224
Wilson, Tyrone, 162
Wilt, David, 177
Wimble, Barton, 59
Winchester, Hank, 150
Winchester, Maud, 58
Wind in the Willows, 26
Winde, Beatrice, 148, 188, 224
Windle, Erin Lynn, 142
Windy City, 167
Wines, Halo, 143
Winfield, Paul, 161
Wing, Douglas, 168
Wing, Madeline, 9
Wing, Virginia, 147
Wingate, William P., 60, 146
Winge, Stein, 163
Wingert, Sally, 138, 156
Winhorn, Fred, 117
Winkler, James R., 184
Winkler, Kevin, 26
Winkler, Mel, 148, 180
Winkler, Peter, 81
Winkler, Richard, 15, 29, 152
Winn, Cal, 184
Winn, Marie, 108
Winn-Jones, Maggie, 143
Winnicky, Paul, 118
Winnie, Richard, 146
Winograd, Judy, 140
Winscott, Cary, 183
Winslow Boy, The, 187
Winslow, Thomas, 181
Winson, Suzi, 68, 224
Winstead-Mann, Deborah, 170
Winston, Lee, 117
Winston, Michael, 184
Winter's Tale, The, 63
Winters, Gregg M., 161
Winters, Marian, 188
Winters, Michael, 151
Winters, Nancy, 58, 71, 108
Winters, Scott, 93, 224
Winters, Time, 153
Winterset, 187
Wintersteller, Lynne, 68, 155, 224
Winton, Don, 146
Wipf, Alex, 150, 162
Wise, Jim, 58
Wise, Leslie Sergeant, 98, 224
Wise, Michael, 136
Wise, Scott, 11
Wise, William, 72, 119, 224
Wiseman, Joseph, 108
Wisniski, Ron, 62, 122, 224
Withers, Lon, 186
Witherspoon, Dwight, 103
Witness for the Prosecution, 187
Witt, Howard, 147
Witten, Matthew, 113
Witter, Terrence, 152
Wittop, Freddy, 26, 129, 146
Wittstein, Ed, 52, 62
Wiz, The, 187
Wodehouse, P. G., 31, 152, 155, 162
Wojewodski, Robert, 172
Wojtasik, George, 92
Woldin, Judd, 62
Wolf, Catherine, 111, 224
Wolf, Jerry, 128
Wolf, Kelly, 91
Wolf, Michael, 146
Wolf, Peter, 78, 134
Wolf, Sheldon, 174
Wolf, Sue, 61
Wolfe, David, 130
Wolfe, George C., 110, 149
Wolff, Art, 56
Wolff, Shmuel, 161
Wolfington, Iggie, 140
Wolford, Melodie, 93, 127
Wolk, Andy, 63
Wolk, James, 57, 63, 76, 80, 91, 103, 119
Wollan, Jennifer J., 115
Wolle, Chondra, 140
Wolpe, Lenny, 15, 167, 224
Wolshonak, Derek, 64, 150
Wolsk, Eugene V., 7
Wolsky, Albert, 99
Womack, Jill Ann, 144
Woman Without a Name, A, 151
Womble, Terence, 69, 113
Women Heroes: In Praise of Exceptional Women, 85
Women and Water, 143
Women of Manhattan, 99
Wonder Years, The, 65, 158
Wonderful Town, 187
Wondisford, Diane, 71, 78
Wong, Bradd, 147
Wong, Judy Ruskin, 72
Wong, Lily-Lee, 48
Wonsek, Paul, 94
Wood, Andy, 60
Wood, Audrey, 231, 232
Wood, Durinda, 147
Wood, Frank, 70
Wood, Helen, 188
Wood, Karen, 186
Wood, Melinda, 149
Wood, Raymond, 59
Wood, Thomas Mills, 170
Wood, Virginia, 63, 73, 80
Wood, William, 164
Woodard, Alfre, 107, 224
Woodard, Charlaine, 110, 168, 224
Woodard, Jim, 138
Woodbridge, Patricia, 167, 171, 179
Woodman, William, 147
Woodruff, Barry, 133
Woodruff, Kelly, 79, 134, 224, 225
Woodruff, Robert, 60
Woods, Carol, 46
Woods, George, 173
Woods, James, 188
Woods, Richard, 161
Woods, Sean, 105, 160
Woodson, Sally, 145
Woodward, Alan, 138
Woodward, Jeffrey, 157
Woodward, Joanne, 162
Wool, Jon, 113
Woolard, David C., 98, 103, 110
Wooley-Gonzalez, Brenda, 143
Woolf, Steven, 171
Woolfolk, Charles, 149
Woolgatherer, 141
Woolley, Jim, 26, 38
Woolley, Scot, 149
Woolsey, Wysandria, 135
Woolston, George, 174
Worcell, Carol Lynn, 127
Worcell, Michael, 127
Worker's Life, The, 91
Workman, Angela, 96
World of Mirth, The, 151
Worley, JoAnne, 146
Woronicz, Henry, 141
Woronoff, Cheryl, 65
Woronov, Mary, 188
Worrell, Marilyn, 102
Worsley, Joyce, 122
Worth-Tyrrell, Caroline, 184
Worthington, Sarah, 169
Wortman, Bryna, 85
Wouk, Herman, 161
Wray, Nan, 177
Wray, Willow, 152
Wrenn-Meleck, Peter, 167
Wrestlers, 94, 95
Wright, Angela, 62
Wright, Ann, 96
Wright, Ben, 110, 111
Wright, Charles Michael, 174
Wright, David, 150
Wright, Garland, 111, 143, 151
Wright, Harland, 177
Wright, Helena-Joyce, 152
Wright, John, 47
Wright, Liz, 63
Wright, Lou Anne, 161
Wright, Mary Catherine, 171
Wright, Max, 188
Wright, Michael, 162
Wright, Nicholas, 117
Wright, R. Hamilton, 136, 172
Wright, Tom, 99, 224
Wright, Valerie, 11, 48
Wright, Victoria, 177
Wright, William, 161
Wrightson, Ann G., 60, 110, 153, 170, 175, 179
Wrinkle in Time, A, 136
Writer's Cramp, 94, 95
Wulf, Mary Kay, 152
Wulff, Roald Berton, 136
Wuthrich, Terry, 60, 61
Wyatt, Mona, 152
Wyche, Ronald, 83
Wylie, John, 106, 139, 152
Wymore, Patrice, 188
Wynkoop, Christopher, 148
Wynter, Diane, 172
Yabuku, Reuben, 151
Yaji, Shigeru, 173
Yamaguchi, Eiko, 74, 109
Yancey, Jacqueline, 57
Yancey, Kim, 58, 224, 225
Yancy, Emily, 102, 224
Yaney, Denise, 73
Yang, Daniel S. P., 183
Yarian, Stephan, 100, 127
Yarmolinsky, Avrahm, 82
Yarnell, Bruce, 188
Yashima, Momo, 147
Yasosuke, Bando V, 8
Yasutake, Patti, 163
Yates, Kathy, 142
Yavel, John, 139
Yaven, Mitchell, 106
Yawn, Gary, 177
Yeager, Barbara, 37
Yeager, Derryl, 124
Yeager, Fabian, 79, 92
Yeargan, Michael H., 23, 141, 157, 162, 180
Yeh, Ching, 76
Yehling, Vicki, 172
Yellen, Sherman, 51
Yellin, Garo, 108
Yelton, Art, 139
Yelusich, Andrew V., 151
Yenque, Teresa, 79
Yeoman, Joann, 224
Yerby, Judith, 149
Yergan, David, 148
Yes Yes No No: The Solace-of-Solstice, 171
Yeskel, Ronnie, 76
Yesutis, Joseph, 113
Yewell, Tom, 57
Yionoulis, Evan, 170
Yoakam, Stephen, 144, 161
Yockey, Denton, 139
Yoder, Jerry, 64
Yohn, Erica, 163
Yondorf, Wendy, 79
Yonek, Cathy, 169
Yonker, Donald, 61
Yorinks, Arthur, 141
York, David R., 164
York, Donald, 14
York, Lila, 78
York, Ned, 58
York, Will, 183
Yoshimura, James, 180
Yossiffon, Raquel, 63
You Can't Take It With You, 144, 187
You Never Can Tell, 141, 162, 168
You Never Know, 155
Youmans, James M., 158
Youmans, Vincent, 76, 78
Youmans, William, 46
Young Lady from Tacna, The, 176
Young, Burt, 108
Young, Dalene, 113
Young, David, 58
Young, Eban, 182
Young, Erica, 184
Young, Jerri Lee, 175
Young, Karen, 67, 224
Young, Kate, 169
Young, Keone, 147
Young, Lisa, 66
Young, Pamela, 9
Young, Phil, 162
Young, Ronald, 130
Young, Sonja, 143
Young, Thomas, 162
Young, William Allen, 60, 224
Youngberg, Donald R., 160
Younger, John, 123
Youngs, Hazel, 165
Yount, Kenneth M., 51, 66, 105
Your Own Thing, 187
Yours, Anne, 61
Yrizarry, Jim, 87
Yue, Jennie, 109
Yuk, Henry, 109
Yulin, Harris, 108, 115, 224
Yurman, Lawrence, 119
Yuter, Morris, 127
Zabriskie, Grace, 91
Zaccaro, Joyce, 146
Zacharias, Emily, 79, 224, 225
Zachary, Anne, 169
Zagier, Norman, 126
Zagnit, Stuart, 62, 150, 224
Zaguirre, Susan, 124
Zahler, Adam, 63, 78
Zahradnik, Stacy, 169
Zaki, Mark, 164
Zakowska, Donna, 73, 76, 86
Zaks, Jerry, 43, 54, 97
Zaloom, Joe, 78
Zaloom, Paul, 224
Zambo, Clay, 170
Zanarini, Tom, 28, 224
Zane Williams, 181
Zang, Edward, 108, 224

Zapata, Carmen, 176
Zapp, Pete, 91
Zappala, Jenny, 172
Zappala, Paul, 113
Zarish, Janet, 118, 137, 138
Zaslove, Arne, 136
Zatz, Asa, 112
Zea, Kristi, 141
Zehr, Robert D., 145
Zeigler, Jon Mikel, 62
Zeisler, Mark, 106, 224
Zelen, Helen, 145

Zeller, Gary, 97
Zeller, Mark, 96, 224
Zeller-Alexis, Dana, 61
Zelliot, Eleanor, 109
Zelon, Helen, 117
Zemanek, Ryan, 142
Zemon, Tom, 157
Zera, Lanie, 72
Zerbe, Anthony, 153
Zerbst, Mary, 173
Zetlin, Jack, 78
Zhukov, Katy, 116

Ziegler, Joseph, 186
Ziemba, Karen, 81, 224
Ziman, Richard, 137
Zimbalist, Galit, 115
Zimering, Bonnie, 141
Zimet, Paul, 79
Zimmer, James H. (Buddy),
   151
Zimmer, Kim, 114
Zimmerman, Andy, 150
Zimmerman, Fred, 159
Zimmermann, Tim, 92

Zinn, Howard, 72
Zinn, Larry, 74
Zinn, Randolyn, 63, 81, 224
Zinovieff, Kyril, 82
Zipin, Brian, 72
Zippel, David, 64
Zippel, Joanne L., 64
Zippi, Daniel, 141
Zipprodt, Patricia, 37, 40
Ziskie, Dan, 91
Ziskie, Kurt, 92, 224, 225
Zito, Ralph, 106

Zivot, Eric, 154, 186
Zoble, Richard, 148
Zoe Caldwell As Lillian, 161
Zoffoli, David. 166
Zollar, Jawole Willa Jo, 102, 161
Zollicoffer, Dexter, 177
Zomina, Sonia, 86
Zorba, 135
Zorich, Louis, 14, 224
Zorthian, Steve, 68
Zossimor, Dr., 64
Zubo, Catherine, 39, 90, 148

Zucker, Grover, 110
Zuckerman, Charles, 50, 126, 12⁹
Zuckerman, Nava, 161
Zuckerman, Stephen, 86, 118
Zukerman, Robert, 68, 110
Zunner, Christopher, 145
Zutz, Carl, 84
Zweibel, Alan, 91
Zweifler, Liz, 165
Zweigbaum, Steven, 7, 26
Zweigenbom, Dor, 161
Zwetsch, Jason E., 153